# Praise for Previous Editions of *A Practical Guide to Fedora*™ *and Red Hat*® *Enterprise Linux*®

"Since I'm in an educational environment, I found the content of Sobell's book to be right on target and very helpful for anyone managing Linux in the enterprise. His style of writing is very clear. He builds up to the chapter exercises, which I find to be relevant to real-world scenarios a user or admin would encounter. An IT/IS student would find this book a valuable complement to their education. The vast amount of information is extremely well balanced and Sobell manages to present the content without complicated asides and meandering prose. This is a 'must have' for anyone managing Linux systems in a networked environment or anyone running a Linux server. I would also highly recommend it to an experienced computer user who is moving to the Linux platform."

—*Mary Norbury*
*IT Director*
*Barbara Davis Center*
*University of Colorado at Denver*
*from a review posted on slashdot.org*

"I had the chance to use your UNIX books when I when was in college years ago at Cal Poly, San Luis Obispo, CA. I have to say that your books are among the best! They're quality books that teach the theoretical aspects and applications of the operating system."

—*Benton Chan*
*IS Engineer*

"The book has more than lived up to my expectations from the many reviews I read, even though it targets FC2. I have found something very rare with your book: It doesn't read like the standard technical text, it reads more like a story. It's a pleasure to read and hard to put down. Did I say that?! :-)"

—*David Hopkins*
*Business Process Architect*

"Thanks for your work and for the book you wrote. There are really few books that can help people to become more efficient administrators of different workstations. We hope (in Russia) that you will continue bringing us a new level of understanding of Linux/UNIX systems."

—*Anton Petukhov*

# PRAISE FOR OTHER BOOKS BY MARK G. SOBELL

"This book is a very useful tool for anyone who wants to 'look under the hood' so to speak, and really start putting the power of Linux to work. What I find particularly frustrating about man pages is that they never include examples. Sobell, on the other hand, outlines very clearly what the command does and then gives several common, easy-to-understand examples that make it a breeze to start shell programming on one's own. As with Sobell's other works, this is simple, straightforward, and easy to read. It's a great book and will stay on the shelf at easy arm's reach for a long time."

*—Ray Bartlett*
*Travel Writer*

"Overall I found this book to be quite excellent, and it has earned a spot on the very front of my bookshelf. It covers the real 'guts' of Linux— the command line and its utilities—and does so very well. Its strongest points are the outstanding use of examples, and the Command Reference section. Highly recommended for Linux users of all skill levels. Well done to Mark Sobell and Prentice Hall for this outstanding book!"

*—Dan Clough*
*Electronics Engineer and*
*Slackware Linux User*

"Totally unlike most Linux books, this book avoids discussing everything via GUI and jumps right into making the power of the command line your friend."

*—Bjorn Tipling*
*Software Engineer*
*ask.com*

"This book is the best distro-agnostic, foundational Linux reference I've ever seen, out of dozens of Linux-related books I've read. Finding this book was a real stroke of luck. If you want to really understand how to get things done at the command line, where the power and flexibility of free UNIX-like OSes really live, this book is among the best tools you'll find toward that end."

*—Chad Perrin*
*Writer, TechRepublic*

"I currently own one of your books, *A Practical Guide to Linux*®. I believe this book is one of the most comprehensive and, as the title says, practical guides to Linux I have ever read. I consider myself a novice and I come back to this book over and over again."

—*Albert J. Nguyen*

"Thank you for writing a book to help me get away from Windows XP and to never touch Windows Vista. The book is great; I am learning a lot of new concepts and commands. Linux is definitely getting easier to use."

—*James Moritz*

"I am so impressed by how Mark Sobell can approach a complex topic in such an understandable manner. His command examples are especially useful in providing a novice (or even an advanced) administrator with a cookbook on how to accomplish real-world tasks on Linux. He is truly an inspired technical writer!"

—*George Vish II*
*Senior Education Consultant*
*Hewlett-Packard Company*

"Overall, I think it's a great, comprehensive Ubuntu book that'll be a valuable resource for people of all technical levels."

—*John Dong*
*Ubuntu Forum Council Member*
*Backports Team Leader*

"The JumpStart sections really offer a quick way to get things up and running, allowing you to dig into the details of the book later."

—*Scott Mann*
*Aztek Networks*

"I would so love to be able to use this book to teach a class about not just Ubuntu or Linux but about computers in general. It is thorough and well written with good illustrations that explain important concepts for computer usage."

—*Nathan Eckenrode*
*New York Local Community Team*

"Ubuntu is gaining popularity at the rate alcohol did during Prohibition, and it's great to see a well-known author write a book on the latest and greatest version. Not only does it contain Ubuntu-specific information, but it also touches on general computer-related topics, which will help the average computer user to better understand what's going on in the background. Great work, Mark!"

—*Daniel R. Arfsten*
*Pro/ENGINEER Drafter/Designer*

"I read a lot of Linux technical information every day, but I'm rarely impressed by tech books. I usually prefer online information sources instead. Mark Sobell's books are a notable exception. They're clearly written, technically accurate, comprehensive, and actually enjoyable to read."

—*Matthew Miller*
*Senior Systems Analyst/Administrator*
*BU Linux Project*
*Boston University Office*
*of Information Technology*

"This is well written, clear, comprehensive information for the Linux user of any type, whether trying Ubuntu on for the first time and wanting to know a little about it, or using the book as a very good reference when doing something more complicated like setting up a server. This book's value goes well beyond its purchase price and it'll make a great addition to the Linux section of your bookshelf."

—*Linc Fessenden*
*Host of The LinuxLink TechShow*
*tllts.org*

"The author has done a very good job at clarifying such a detail-oriented operating system. I have extensive Unix and Windows experience and this text does an excellent job at bridging the gaps between Linux, Windows, and Unix. I highly recommend this book to both 'newbs' and experienced users. Great job!"

—*Mark Polczynski*
*Information Technology Consultant*

"When I first started working with Linux just a short 10 years or so ago, it was a little more difficult than now to get going. . . . Now, someone new to the community has a vast array of resources available on the web, or if they are inclined to begin with Ubuntu, they can literally find almost every single thing they will need in the single volume of Mark Sobell's *A Practical Guide to Ubuntu Linux*®.

"I'm sure this sounds a bit like hyperbole. Everything a person would need to know? Obviously not everything, but this book, weighing in at just under 1200 pages, covers so much so thoroughly that there won't be much left out. From install to admin, networking, security, shell scripting, package management, and a host of other topics, it is all there. GUI and command line tools are covered. There is not really any wasted space or fluff, just a huge amount of information. There are screen shots when appropriate but they do not take up an inordinate amount of space. This book is information-dense."

—*JR Peck*
*Editor*
*GeekBook.org*

"I have been wanting to make the jump to Linux but did not have the guts to do so—until I saw your familiarly titled *A Practical Guide to Red Hat*® *Linux*® at the bookstore. I picked up a copy and am eagerly looking forward to regaining my freedom."

—*Carmine Stoffo*
*Machine and Process Designer*
*to pharmaceutical industry*

"I am currently reading *A Practical Guide to Red Hat*® *Linux*® and am finally understanding the true power of the command line. I am new to Linux and your book is a treasure."

—*Juan Gonzalez*

"Overall, *A Practical Guide to Ubuntu Linux*® by Mark G. Sobell provides all of the information a beginner to intermediate user of Linux would need to be productive. The inclusion of the Live DVD of the Gutsy Gibbon release of Ubuntu makes it easy for the user to test-drive Linux without affecting his installed OS. I have no doubts that you will consider this book money well spent."

—*Ray Lodato*
*Slashdot contributor*
*www.slashdot.org*

# A PRACTICAL GUIDE TO FEDORA™ AND RED HAT® ENTERPRISE LINUX®

## SEVENTH EDITION

# A Practical Guide to Fedora™ and Red Hat® Enterprise Linux®

## SEVENTH EDITION

## Mark G. Sobell

PRENTICE
HALL

Upper Saddle River, NJ • Boston • Indianapolis • San Francisco
New York • Toronto • Montreal • London • Munich • Paris • Madrid
Capetown • Sydney • Tokyo • Singapore • Mexico City

For information about buying this title in bulk quantities, or for special sales opportunities (which may include electronic versions; custom cover designs; and content particular to your business, training goals, marketing focus, or branding interests), please contact our corporate sales department at corpsales@pearsoned.com or (800) 382-3419.

For government sales inquiries, please contact governmentsales@pearsoned.com.

For questions about sales outside the United States, please contact international@pearsoned.com.

Visit us on the Web: informit.com/ph

*Library of Congress Cataloging-in-Publication Data*

Sobell, Mark G.
  A practical guide to Fedora and Red Hat Enterprise Linux / Mark G. Sobell.—Seventh edition.
     pages   cm
  Includes index.
  ISBN 978-0-13-347743-6 (pbk.)
  1. Linux. 2.  Operating systems (Computers)  I. Title.
  QA76.76.O63S5945 2013
  005.4'46—dc23
                                                            2013037169

ISBN-13: 978-0-13-347743-6
ISBN-10: 0-13-347743-6

Text printed in the United States on recycled paper at Edwards Brothers Malloy in Ann Arbor, Michigan.
First printing, December 2013

*For my mother,*
*Dr. Helen L. Sobell (1918–2002)*

# Brief Contents

# JumpStarts

*JumpStarts get you off to a quick start when you need to use a client or set up a server. Once you have the client or server up and running, you can refine its configuration using the information presented in the sections following each JumpStart.*

## yum (Software Packages)

## CUPS (Printing)

## OpenSSH (Secure Communication)

## FTP (Download and Upload Files)

## Email

## NFS (Network Filesystem)

## Samba (Linux/Windows File Sharing)

## DNS (Domain Name Service)

## firewall-config (Firewall)

## Apache (HTTP)

# CONTENTS

# PART II   USING FEDORA AND RED HAT ENTERPRISE LINUX   87

## CHAPTER 4: INTRODUCTION TO FEDORA AND RED HAT ENTERPRISE LINUX   89

## CHAPTER 5: THE SHELL   141

# CHAPTER 6: THE LINUX FILESYSTEM    175

## CHAPTER 7: THE LINUX UTILITIES    215

## CHAPTER 8: NETWORKING AND THE INTERNET   279

# PART III    SYSTEM ADMINISTRATION    325

## CHAPTER 10: SYSTEM ADMINISTRATION: CORE CONCEPTS   419

## CHAPTER 12: FINDING, DOWNLOADING, AND INSTALLING SOFTWARE   531

## CHAPTER 13: PRINTING WITH CUPS    555

## CHAPTER 14: BUILDING A LINUX KERNEL    579

## CHAPTER 15: ADMINISTRATION TASKS    597

## CHAPTER 16: CONFIGURING AND MONITORING A LAN    631

## CHAPTER 17: SETTING UP VIRTUAL MACHINES LOCALLY AND IN THE CLOUD   659

## PART IV   USING CLIENTS AND SETTING UP SERVERS   683

## CHAPTER 18: OPENSSH: SECURE NETWORK COMMUNICATION   685

## CHAPTER 22: NFS: SHARING DIRECTORY HIERARCHIES    801

# CHAPTER 23: SAMBA: LINUX AND WINDOWS FILE AND PRINTER SHARING    827

# CHAPTER 24: DNS/BIND: TRACKING DOMAIN NAMES AND ADDRESSES    851

## CHAPTER 25: firewalld AND iptables: SETTING UP A FIREWALL    897

# PART V   PROGRAMMING TOOLS   979

## CHAPTER 28: THE PYTHON PROGRAMMING LANGUAGE   1081

## CHAPTER 29: THE MARIADB SQL DATABASE MANAGEMENT SYSTEM   1113

# PART VI    APPENDIXES    1137

## APPENDIX A: REGULAR EXPRESSIONS    1139

## APPENDIX B: HELP    1149

## APPENDIX C: SECURITY INCLUDING GPG    1155

## APPENDIX D: KEEPING THE SYSTEM UP-TO-DATE USING apt-get    1183

## APPENDIX E: LPI AND COMPTIA CERTIFICATION    1189

# PREFACE

**The book**  Whether you are an end user, a system administrator, or a little of both, this book explains with step-by-step examples how to get the most out of a Fedora or RHEL (Red Hat Enterprise Linux) system. In 29 chapters, this book takes you from installing a Fedora/RHEL system, through understanding its inner workings, to setting up secure servers that run on the system.

**The audience**  This book is designed for a wide range of readers. It does not require you to have programming experience, although having some experience using a general-purpose computer, such as a Windows, Macintosh, UNIX, or another Linux system is certainly helpful. This book is appropriate for:

- **Students** who are taking a class in which they use Linux

- **Home users** who want to set up and/or run Linux

- **Professionals** who use Linux at work

- **System administrators** who need an understanding of Linux and the tools that are available to them, including the bash and Python scripting languages

- **Computer science students** who are studying the Linux operating system

- **Technical executives** who want to get a grounding in Linux

**Benefits**  *A Practical Guide to Fedora™ and Red Hat® Enterprise Linux®, Seventh Edition,* gives you a broad understanding of many facets of Linux, from installing Fedora/RHEL through using and customizing it. No matter what your background, this book provides the knowledge you need to get on with your work. You will come away from this book understanding how to use Linux, and this book will remain a valuable reference for years to come.

**Features in this edition**   This edition covers many topics to help you get your work done using Fedora/RHEL.

- Full coverage of LPI's Linux Essentials certification learning goals and extensive coverage of CompTIA's Linux+ exam objectives (Appendix E; page 1189)

- Updated chapters reflecting new features in Fedora 19 and RHEL 7 (beta)

- A new chapter that covers setting up VMs (virtual machines) and working in the cloud (Chapter 17; page 659)

- A new chapter on the Python programming language (Chapter 28; page 1081)

- A new chapter covering 32 Linux utilities (Chapter 7; page 215)

- A new chapter on the MariaDB/MySQL relational database (Chapter 29; page 1113)

- New coverage of the **firewalld** service (Chapter 25; page 898)

- Tutorials on the vim and nano editors (Chapter 7; pages 262 and 270)

- Nine chapters on system administration (Part III; page 325)

- A chapter on writing programs using bash (Chapter 27; page 981)

- Coverage of the XFS filesystem (Chapter 11; page 527)

- Coverage of LDAP (Chapter 21; page 786)

- A section on the Cacti network monitoring tool (Chapter 16; page 645)

- Coverage of IPv6 (Chapter 8; page 293)

- Four indexes, making it easier to quickly find what you are looking for. These indexes locate tables (page numbers followed by the letter **t**), provide definitions (italic page numbers), and differentiate between light and comprehensive coverage (light and standard fonts).

  - The JumpStart index (page 1283) lists all JumpStart sections in this book. These sections help you set up servers and clients as quickly as possible.

  - The File Tree index (page 1285) lists, in hierarchical fashion, most files mentioned in this book. These files are also listed in the Main index.

  - The Utility index (page 1289) supplies the location of all utilities mentioned in this book. A page number in a light font indicates a brief mention of the utility, whereas the regular font indicates more substantial coverage. The Utility index also appears on the inside of the front and back covers of the print book.

  - The revised Main index (page 1295) is designed for ease of use.

Overlap   If you have read *A Practical Guide to Linux® Commands, Editors, and Shell Programming, Third Edition,* you will notice some overlap between that book and the one you are reading now. The first chapter, the chapters on the utilities and the filesystem, the appendix on regular expressions, and the Glossary are very similar in the two books, as are the three chapters on the Bourne Again Shell (bash) and the chapters on Python and MariaDB. Chapters that appear in this book but do not appear in *A Practical Guide to Linux® Commands, Editors, and Shell Programming, Third Edition,* include Chapters 2 and 3 (installation), Chapter 4 (Fedora/RHEL and the GUI), Chapter 8 (networking), all of the chapters in Part III (system administration) and Part IV (servers), and Appendix C (security).

Differences   While this book explains how to use Linux from a graphical interface and from the command line (a textual interface), *A Practical Guide to Linux® Commands, Editors, and Shell Programming, Third Edition,* works exclusively with the command line and covers Mac OS X in addition to Linux. It includes full chapters on the vim and emacs editors, as well as chapters on the gawk pattern processing language, the sed stream editor, and the rsync secure copy utility. In addition, it has a command reference section that provides extensive examples of the use of 98 of the most important Linux and Mac OS X utilities. You can use these utilities to solve problems without resorting to programming in C.

# THIS BOOK INCLUDES A FEDORA 19 (SCHRÖDINGER'S CAT) DVD

The print book includes a DVD that holds an Install Image of Fedora 19 (Schrödinger's Cat). You can use this DVD to install Fedora 19. Chapter 2 helps you get ready to install Fedora/RHEL. Chapter 3 provides step-by-step instructions for installing Fedora from this DVD as well as installing RHEL. This book guides you through learning about, using, and administrating a Fedora/RHEL system.

DVD features   The DVD includes many of the software packages supported by Fedora. You can use it to perform a graphical or textual (command-line) installation of either a graphical or a textual Fedora system. If you do not have an Internet connection, you can use the DVD as a software repository: After you have installed Fedora, you can install supported software packages from the DVD.

## FOR READERS OF DIGITAL EDITIONS

If you are reading a digital edition of this book, see "Downloading an Installation Image File and Writing to/Burning the Installation Medium" on page 46 for instructions on how to download an Install Image and create a DVD or USB flash drive that holds an that image.

# FEATURES OF THIS BOOK

This book is designed and organized so you can get the most out of it in the least amount of time. You do not have to read this book straight through in page order. Instead, once you are comfortable using Linux, you can use this book as a reference: Look up a topic of interest in the table of contents or in an index and read about it. Or think of the book as a catalog of Linux topics: Flip through the pages until a topic catches your eye. The book includes many pointers to Web sites where you can obtain additional information: Consider the Internet to be an extension of this book.

*A Practical Guide to Fedora™ and Red Hat® Enterprise Linux®, Seventh Edition,* is structured with the following features

- In this book, the term "Fedora/RHEL" refers to both **Fedora** and **Red Hat Enterprise Linux**. Features that apply to only one of these operating systems are marked as such.

- **Optional sections** enable you to read the book at different levels, returning to more difficult material when you are ready to delve into it.

- **Caution boxes** highlight procedures that can easily go wrong, giving you guidance *before* you run into trouble.

- **Tip boxes** highlight ways you can save time by doing something differently or situations when it may be useful or just interesting to have additional information.

- **Security boxes** point out places where you can make a system more secure. The **security appendix** presents a quick background in system security issues and includes a tutorial on GPG.

- Concepts are illustrated by **practical examples** throughout the book.

- Each chapter starts with a list of **chapter objectives**—a list of important tasks you should be able to perform after reading the chapter.

- **Chapter summaries** review the important points covered in each chapter.

- **Review exercises** are included at the end of each chapter for readers who want to further hone their skills. Answers to even-numbered exercises are posted at www.sobell.com.

- The **Glossary** defines more than 500 commonly encountered terms.

- The chapters covering servers include **JumpStart** sections that get you off to a quick start using clients and setting up servers. Once a server is up and running, you can test and modify its configuration, as is explained in the rest of each of these chapters.

- This book provides resources for **finding software** on the Internet. It also explains how to **download** and **install** software using yum, the Software window, and BitTorrent. It details controlling automatic updates using the Software Update Preferences window.

- This book describes in detail many important **GNU tools**, including the GNOME 3 desktop, the Nautilus File Browser, the parted and gnome-disks partition editors, the gzip compression utility, and many command-line utilities that come from the GNU Project.

- Pointers throughout the text provide help in obtaining **online documentation** from many sources, including the local system, the Fedora/RHEL Web sites, and other locations on the Internet.

- Multiple **comprehensive indexes** help you locate topics quickly and easily.

# KEY TOPICS COVERED IN THIS BOOK

This section distills and summarizes the information covered by this book. In addition, "Details" (starting on page l) describes what each chapter covers. Finally, the Table of Contents (starting on page xvii) provides more detail. This book:

Installation
- Describes how to download Fedora installation images from the Internet and write/burn the Fedora Live or Install Image to a USB flash drive or DVD.

- Helps you plan the layout of the system's hard disk. It includes a discussion of partitions, partition tables, and mount points, and assists you in using Anaconda or the gnome-disks disk utility to examine and partition the hard disk.

- Explains how to set up a dual-boot system so you can install Fedora/RHEL on a Windows system and boot either operating system.

- Discusses booting into a live Fedora session and installing Fedora from that session.

- Describes in detail how to use the new version of **Anaconda**, Fedora/RHEL's installation program, to install Fedora/RHEL from an Install Image.

- Covers testing installation media for defects, setting boot command-line parameters (boot options), and creating a RAID array.

- Describes how to set up a VM (virtual machine) and install Fedora on the VM.

- Explains how to use the Logical Volume Manager (LVM2) to set up, grow, and migrate logical volumes, which are similar in function to traditional disk partitions.

<table>
<tr><td>Working with<br>Fedora/RHEL</td><td>

- Introduces the GNOME 3 Standard and Classic desktops (GUIs), and explains how to use desktop tools, including application and context menus, the Settings window, the Nautilus File Browser, and the GNOME terminal emulator.

</td></tr>
</table>

Working with Fedora/RHEL

- Introduces the GNOME 3 Standard and Classic desktops (GUIs), and explains how to use desktop tools, including application and context menus, the Settings window, the Nautilus File Browser, and the GNOME terminal emulator.

- Covers the Bourne Again Shell (bash) in three chapters, including an entire chapter on shell programming, which includes many sample shell scripts. These chapters provide clear explanations and extensive examples of how bash works both from the command line in day-to-day work and as a programming language in which to write shell scripts.

- Explains the textual (command-line) interface and introduces more than 32 command-line utilities.

- Presents a tutorial on the vim and nano textual editors.

- Covers types of networks, network protocols (including IPv6), and network utilities.

- Explains hostnames, IP addresses, and subnets, and explores how to use host and dig to look up domain names and IP addresses on the Internet.

- Covers distributed computing and the client/server model.

- Explains how to use ACLs (Access Control Lists) to fine-tune user access permissions.

CentOS

- Describes CentOS by virtue of that operating system's compatibility with RHEL. CentOS (www.centos.org) is a free Linux distribution that has more long-term stability than Fedora but, unlike RHEL, CentOS is unsupported.

System administration

- Explains how to use the Fedora/RHEL graphical and textual (command-line) tools to configure the display, DNS, NFS, Samba, Apache, a firewall, a network interface, and more. You can also use these tools to add users and manage local and remote printers.

- Describes how to use su to work with **root** privileges (become Superuser), and the advantages and dangers of working with escalated privileges.

- Goes into detail about using sudo to allow specific users to work with **root** privileges and customizing the way sudo works by editing the **sudoers** configuration file.

- Describes how to use the following tools to download and install software to keep a system up-to-date and to install new software:

  - Based on how you set up updates in the Software Update Preferences window, the **Software Update** window appears on the desktop to let you know when software updates are available. You can download and install updates from the Software Update window.

  - The **Software** window provides an easy way to select, download, and install a wide range of software packages.

- ◆ The yum utility downloads and installs software packages from repositories on the Internet, keeping a system up-to-date and resolving dependencies as it processes the packages.

- ◆ **BitTorrent** is a good choice for distributing large amounts of data such as the Fedora/RHEL Install Image. The more people who use BitTorrent to download a file, the faster it works.

- Covers graphical system administration tools, including the many tools available from the GNOME desktop.

- Explains system operation, including the boot process, rescue (single-user) and multiuser modes, and steps to take if the system crashes.

- Details the workings of the **systemd init daemon**, which replaces both the Upstart and System V **init** daemons.

- Explains how to set up and use the **Cacti** network monitoring tool to graph system and network information over time, including installing and setting up the **LAMP** (Linux, Apache, MariaDB/MySQL, and PHP) stack.

- Provides instructions on installing, setting up, and using a **MariaDB/MySQL** relational database.

- Discusses setting up and repairing an XFS filesystem.

- Describes files, directories, and filesystems, including types of files and filesystems, **fstab** (the filesystem table), and automatically mounted filesystems, and explains how to fine-tune and check the integrity of filesystems.

- Covers backup utilities, including tar and cpio.

- Describes compression/archive utilities, including xz, gzip, bzip2, compress, and zip.

- Explains how to customize and build a Linux kernel.

Security
- Helps you manage basic system security issues using ssh (secure shell), **vsftpd** (secure FTP server), Apache (Web server), **firewalld** and iptables (firewalls), and more.

- Includes a tutorial on using GPG (GNU Privacy Guard) to provide identification, secrecy, and message integrity in email and file sharing.

- Describes how to use the graphical firewall-config utility to protect the system.

- Provides instructions on using iptables to share an Internet connection over a LAN and to build advanced firewalls.

- Presents a complete section on SELinux (Security-Enhanced Linux), including instructions for using system-config-selinux to configure SELinux.

- Describes how to set up a chroot jail to help protect a server system.

Clients and servers
- Explains how to use TCP wrappers to control who can access a server.
- Explains how to set up and use the most popular Linux servers, providing a chapter on each: Apache; Samba; OpenSSH; **sendmail**; DNS; NFS; FTP; firewall-config, **firewalld**, and iptables; and NIS/LDAP.
- Describes how to set up a CUPS printer server.
- Explains how to set up and use a MariaDB/MySQL relational database.
- Describes how to set up and use a DHCP server.

Programming
- Provides a chapter on the Python programming language and a full chapter covering shell programming using bash, including many examples.

# DETAILS

Chapter 1  **Chapter 1** presents a brief history of Linux and explains some of the features that make it a cutting-edge operating system.

Part I  Part I, "Installing Fedora and Red Hat Enterprise Linux," discusses how to install Fedora/RHEL Linux. **Chapter 2** presents an overview of the process of installing Fedora/RHEL Linux, including hardware requirements, downloading and burning or writing the installation medium, and planning the layout of the hard disk. The "Conventions Used in This Book" section on page 26 details the typefaces and terminology used in this book. **Chapter 3** is a step-by-step guide to installing Fedora and RHEL; it covers installing from an Install Image and from a live session (Fedora).

Part II  Part II, "Using Fedora and Red Hat Enterprise Linux," familiarizes you with Fedora/RHEL, covering logging in, the GUI, utilities, the filesystem, and the shell. **Chapter 4** introduces desktop features; describes configuring the system using the Settings window; explains how to use the Nautilus File Browser to manage files, run programs, and connect to FTP and HTTP servers; covers finding documentation, dealing with login problems, and using the window manager; and presents some suggestions on where to find documentation, including manuals, tutorials, software notes, and HOWTOs. The introduction to the command line includes information on terminal emulators, virtual consoles, correcting mistakes on the command line, a few basic utilities, and how to write and execute a simple shell script. **Chapter 5** introduces the Bourne Again Shell (bash) and discusses command-line arguments and options, redirecting input to and output from commands, running programs in the background, and using the shell to generate and expand filenames. **Chapter 6** discusses the Linux hierarchical filesystem, covering files, filenames, pathnames, working with directories, access permissions, and hard and symbolic links. **Chapter 7** provides in-depth coverage of 32 useful utilities, and presents tutorials on the vim and nano text editors. **Chapter 8** explains networks, network security, and the Internet, and discusses types of networks, subnets, protocols, addresses, hostnames, and various network utilities. A section covers the all-important IPv6 protocol. The section on distributed computing describes the client/server model and some of the servers you can use on a network. (Details of setting up and using clients and servers are reserved until Part IV.)

## Experienced users may want to skim Part II

**tip** If you have used a UNIX or Linux system before, you may want to skim or skip some or all of the chapters in Part II. Do *not* skip "Conventions Used in This Book" (page 26), which explains the typographic and layout conventions used in this book. Both "Getting Help" (page 113), which explains how to get help using a GUI, and "Getting Help from the Command Line" (page 128), point out both local and remote sources of Linux and Fedora/RHEL documentation.

**Part III**   Part III, "System Administration," goes into more detail about administrating the system. **Chapter 9** extends the bash coverage from Chapter 5, explaining how to redirect error output, avoid overwriting files, and work with job control, processes, startup files, important shell builtin commands, parameters, shell variables, and aliases. **Chapter 10** discusses core concepts, such as the use of su and sudo; working with **root** privileges; SELinux (Security-Enhanced Linux); system operation, including a discussion of the systemd **init** daemon; chroot jails; TCP wrappers; general information about how to set up a server; DHCP; and PAM. **Chapter 11** explains the Linux filesystem, going into detail about types of files, including special and device files; the use of fsck to verify the integrity of and repair filesystems; the use of tune2fs to change filesystem parameters; and the XFS filesystem and related utilities. **Chapter 12** explains how to keep a system up-to-date by downloading software from the Internet and installing it, including examples that use yum to perform these tasks. It also covers the RPM software packaging system and the use of the rpm utility. Finally, it explains how to use BitTorrent from the command line to download files. **Chapter 13** explains how to set up the CUPS printing system so you can print on both local and remote systems. **Chapter 14** details customizing and building a Linux kernel and includes information on GRUB 2. **Chapter 15** covers additional administration tasks, including setting up user accounts, backing up files, scheduling automated tasks, tracking disk usage, and solving general problems. **Chapter 16** explains how to set up a local area network (LAN), including both hardware (including wireless) and software configuration, and how to set up Cacti to monitor the network. **Chapter 17** describes VMs (virtual machines), how to set up and work with VMs, and how to work with VMs in the cloud.

**Part IV**   Part IV goes into detail about setting up and running servers and connecting to them using clients. Where appropriate, these chapters include JumpStart sections, which get you off to a quick start in using clients and setting up servers. The chapters in Part IV cover the following clients/servers:

- **OpenSSH**—Set up an OpenSSH server and use ssh, scp, and sftp to communicate securely over the Internet.

- **FTP**—Set up a **vsftpd** secure FTP server and use any of several FTP clients to exchange files with the server.

- **Email**—Configure **sendmail** and use Webmail, POP3, or IMAP to retrieve email; use SpamAssassin to combat spam.

- **NIS and LDAP**—Set up NIS to facilitate system administration of a LAN and LDAP to maintain databases.

- **NFS**—Share filesystems between systems on a network.

- **Samba**—Share filesystems and printers between Windows and Linux systems.

- **DNS/BIND**—Set up a domain nameserver to let other systems on the Internet know the names and IP addresses of local systems they may need to contact.

- **firewalld**, firewall-config, and iptables—Set up a firewall to protect local systems and share a single Internet connection between systems on a LAN.

- **Apache**—Set up an HTTP server that serves Web pages, which browsers can then display. This chapter includes many suggestions for increasing Apache security.

Part V  Part V covers three important programming tools that are used extensively in Fedora/RHEL system administration and general-purpose programming. **Chapter 27** continues where Chapter 9 left off, going into greater depth about shell programming using bash, with the discussion enhanced by extensive examples. **Chapter 28** introduces the flexible and friendly Python programming language, including coverage of lists and dictionaries, using libraries, defining functions, regular expressions, and list comprehensions. **Chapter 29** covers the widely used MariaDB/MySQL RDBMS (relational database management system), including installation, creating a database, adding a user, creating and modifying tables, joins, and adding data to the database.

Part VI  Part VI includes appendixes on regular expressions, helpful Web sites, system security including GPG, updating software using apt-get, and a map that indexes LPI's Linux Essentials certification learning goals and CompTIA's Linux+ exam objectives to the pages in this book that cover each topic. This part also includes an extensive Glossary with more than 500 entries plus the JumpStart index, the File Tree index, the Utility index, and the comprehensive Main index.

# SUPPLEMENTS

The author's home page (www.sobell.com) contains downloadable listings of the longer programs from this book, as well as pointers to many interesting and useful Linux sites on the World Wide Web, a list of corrections to the book, answers to even-numbered exercises, and a solicitation for corrections, comments, and suggestions.

# THANKS

First and foremost, I want to thank Mark L. Taub, Editor-in-Chief, Prentice Hall, who provided encouragement and support through the hard parts of this project. Mark is unique in my 30+ years of book writing experience: an editor who works with the tools I write about. Because Mark runs Linux on his home computer, we shared experiences as I wrote this book. Mark, your comments and direction are invaluable; this book would not exist without your help. Thank you, Mark T.

The production people at Prentice Hall are wonderful to work with: Julie Nahil, Full-Service Production Manager, worked with me day by day during production of this book providing help and keeping everything on track, while John Fuller, Managing Editor, kept the large view in focus. Thanks to Stephanie Geels, Copyeditor, and Andrea Fox, Proofreader, who made each page sparkle and found the mistakes the author left behind.

Thanks also to the folks at Prentice Hall who helped bring this book to life, especially Kim Boedigheimer, Editorial Assistant, who attended to the many details involved in publishing this book; Heather Fox, Publicist; Stephane Nakib, Marketing Manager; Dan Scherf, Media Developer; Sandra Schroeder, Design Manager; Chuti Prasertsith, Cover Designer; and everyone else who worked behind the scenes to make this book come into being.

I am also indebted to Denis Howe, Editor of *The Free On-Line Dictionary of Computing* (FOLDOC). Denis has graciously permitted me to use entries from his compilation. Be sure to visit www.foldoc.org to look at this dictionary.

A big "thank you" to the folks who read through the drafts of the book and made comments that caused me to refocus parts of the book where things were not clear or were left out altogether:

Nicklos See, Instructor, Bismarck State College; Eugene Murray, Chair, School of Information Technology, ITT Technical Institute; Doug Hughes, D. E. Shaw Research, LLC.; Carl Draper; Max Sobell; Rahul Sundaram, Fedora contributor; Tony Godfrey, TT Technical Institute, Strongsville, Ohio; Susan Lauber, Lauber System Solutions, Inc.; Sam Sobell, Student, UCLA; Ankur Sinha, Fedora project volunteer; Professor Maria Ripoll; David A. Lane, long-time Linux user and systems architect; Pete Travis, Fedora Documentation Project; Rickard Körkkö, Orc Group; Jennifer Davis, Senior Production Engineer at Yahoo; Matthew Miller, Fedora Project at Red Hat, Inc.; Jiri Popelka, Red Hat, Inc.; Thomas Woerner, Red Hat, Inc.; Ben Whaley, Co-author of the *UNIX and Linux System Administration Handbook*.

Thanks also to the following people who helped with my previous Linux books, which provided a foundation for this book:

Richard Woodbury, Site Reliability Engineer, Google, whose knowledge of IPv6 proved invaluable; Lennart Poettering, Red Hat, Inc.; George Vish II, Senior Education Consultant, Hewlett-Packard; Garth Snyder; Nathan Handler; Dick Seabrook, Professor Emeritus, Anne Arundel Community College; Chris Karr, Audacious Software; Scott McCrea, Instructor, ITT Technical Schools; John Dong, Ubuntu Developer, Forums Council Member; Andy Lester, author of *Land the Tech Job You Love: Why Skill and Luck Are Not Enough*; Scott James Remnant, Ubuntu Development Manager and Desktop Team Leader; David Chisnall, Swansea University; Scott Mann, Aztek Networks; Thomas Achtemichuk, Mansueto Ventures; Daniel R. Arfsten, Pro/Engineer

Drafter/Designer; Chris Cooper, Senior Education Consultant, Hewlett-Packard Education Services; Sameer Verma, Associate Professor of Information Systems, San Francisco State University; Valerie Chau, Palomar College and Programmers Guild; James Kratzer; Sean McAllister; Nathan Eckenrode, New York Ubuntu Local Community Team; Christer Edwards; Nicolas Merline; Michael Price; Mike Basinger, Ubuntu Community and Forums Council Member; Joe Barker, Ubuntu Forums Staff Member; James Stockford, Systemateka, Inc.; Stephanie Troeth, Book Oven; Doug Sheppard; Bryan Helvey, IT Director, OpenGeoSolutions; and Vann Scott, Baker College of Flint.

Also, thanks to Jesse Keating, Fedora Project; Carsten Pfeiffer, Software Engineer and KDE Developer; Aaron Weber, Ximian; Cristof Falk, Software Developer at CritterDesign; Steve Elgersma, Computer Science Department, Princeton University; Scott Dier, University of Minnesota; Robert Haskins, Computer Net Works; Lars Kellogg-Stedman, Harvard University; Jim A. Lola, Principal Systems Consultant, Privateer Systems; Eric S. Raymond, Cofounder, Open Source Initiative; Scott Mann; Randall Lechlitner, Independent Computer Consultant; Jason Wertz, Computer Science Instructor, Montgomery County Community College; Justin Howell, Solano Community College; Ed Sawicki, The Accelerated Learning Center; David Mercer; Jeffrey Bianchine, Advocate, Author, Journalist; John Kennedy; and Jim Dennis, Starshine Technical Services.

Thanks also to Dustin Puryear, Puryear Information Technology; Gabor Liptak, Independent Consultant; Bart Schaefer, Chief Technical Officer, iPost; Michael J. Jordan, Web Developer, Linux Online; Steven Gibson, Owner, SuperAnt.com; John Viega, Founder and Chief Scientist, Secure Software; K. Rachael Treu, Internet Security Analyst, Global Crossing; Kara Pritchard, K & S Pritchard Enterprises; Glen Wiley, Capital One Finances; Karel Baloun, Senior Software Engineer, Looksmart; Matthew Whitworth; Dameon D. Welch-Abernathy, Nokia Systems; Josh Simon, Consultant; Stan Isaacs; and Dr. Eric H. Herrin II, Vice President, Herrin Software Development.

More thanks go to consultants Lorraine Callahan and Steve Wampler; Ronald Hiller, Graburn Technology; Charles A. Plater, Wayne State University; Bob Palowoda; Tom Bialaski, Sun Microsystems; Roger Hartmuller, TIS Labs at Network Associates; Kaowen Liu; Andy Spitzer; Rik Schneider; Jesse St. Laurent; Steve Bellenot; Ray W. Hiltbrand; Jennifer Witham; Gert-Jan Hagenaars; and Casper Dik.

*A Practical Guide to Fedora™ and Red Hat® Enterprise Linux®, Seventh Edition,* is based in part on two of my previous UNIX books: *UNIX System V: A Practical Guide* and *A Practical Guide to the UNIX System.* Many people helped me with those books, and thanks here go to Pat Parseghian; Dr. Kathleen Hemenway; Brian LaRose; Byron A. Jeff, Clark Atlanta University; Charles Stross; Jeff Gitlin, Lucent Technologies; Kurt Hockenbury; Maury Bach, Intel Israel; Peter H. Salus; Rahul Dave, University of Pennsylvania; Sean Walton, Intelligent Algorithmic Solutions; Tim Segall, Computer Sciences Corporation; Behrouz Forouzan, DeAnza College; Mike Keenan, Virginia Polytechnic Institute and State University; Mike Johnson, Oregon State University; Jandelyn Plane, University of Maryland; Arnold Robbins and Sathis Menon, Georgia Institute of Technology; Cliff Shaffer, Virginia Polytechnic Institute and State University; and Steven Stepanek, California State University, Northridge, for reviewing the book.

I continue to be grateful to the many people who helped with the early editions of my UNIX books. Special thanks are due to Roger Sippl, Laura King, and Roy Harrington for introducing me to the UNIX system. My mother, Dr. Helen Sobell, provided invaluable comments on the original manuscript at several junctures. Also, thanks go to Isaac Rabinovitch, Professor Raphael Finkel, Professor Randolph Bentson, Bob Greenberg, Professor Udo Pooch, Judy Ross, Dr. Robert Veroff, Dr. Mike Denny, Joe DiMartino, Dr. John Mashey, Diane Schulz, Robert Jung, Charles Whitaker, Don Cragun, Brian Dougherty, Dr. Robert Fish, Guy Harris, Ping Liao, Gary Lindgren, Dr. Jarrett Rosenberg, Dr. Peter Smith, Bill Weber, Mike Bianchi, Scooter Morris, Clarke Echols, Oliver Grillmeyer, Dr. David Korn, Dr. Scott Weikart, and Dr. Richard Curtis.

I take responsibility for any errors and omissions in this book. If you find one or just have a comment, let me know (mgs@sobell.com) and I will fix it in the next printing. My home page (www.sobell.com) contains a list of errors. It also offers copies of the longer scripts from the book and pointers to interesting Linux pages on the Internet. You can follow me at twitter.com/marksobell.

*Mark G. Sobell*
*San Francisco, California*

# 1

# WELCOME TO LINUX

## OBJECTIVES

After reading this chapter you should be able to:

▶ Discuss the history of UNIX, Linux, and the GNU Project

▶ Explain what is meant by "free software" and list characteristics of the GNU General Public License

▶ List three characteristics that are important to you when selecting an operating system

▶ Describe the intent of the term FOSS/FLOSS; explain how it relates to free and open-source software

▶ Explain what a Linux distribution is and list three popular distributions

▶ List characteristics of Linux and reasons the Linux operating system is so popular

▶ List three factors you would consider in choosing an operating system

▶ Explain what a desktop environment is and name three desktop managers

1

An operating system is the low-level software that schedules tasks, allocates storage, and handles the interfaces to peripheral hardware, such as printers, disk drives, the screen, keyboard, and mouse. An operating system has two main parts: the *kernel* and the *system programs*. The kernel allocates machine resources—including memory, disk space, and *CPU* (page 1244) cycles—to all other programs that run on the computer. The system programs include device drivers, libraries, utility programs, shells (command interpreters), configuration scripts and files, application programs, servers, and documentation. They perform higher-level housekeeping tasks, often acting as servers in a client/server relationship. Many of the libraries, servers, and utility programs were written by the GNU Project, which is discussed shortly.

Linux kernel   The Linux *kernel* was developed by Linus Torvalds while he was an undergraduate student. He released version 0.01 in September 1991 from his home in Finland. He used the Internet to make the source code immediately available to others for free.

The new operating system came together through a lot of hard work. Programmers around the world were quick to extend the kernel and develop other tools, adding functionality to match that already found in both BSD UNIX and SVR4 (System V UNIX, release 4) as well as new functionality. The name *Linux* is a combination of *Linus* and *UNIX*.

The Linux operating system, which was developed through the cooperation of numerous people around the world, is a *product of the Internet* and is a *free* (FOSS; page 7) operating system. In other words, all the source code is free. You are free to study it, redistribute it, and modify it. As a result, the code is available free of cost—no charge for the software, source, documentation, or support (via newsgroups, mailing lists, and other Internet resources). As the GNU Free Software Definition (www.gnu.org/philosophy/free-sw.html) puts it:

Free beer   "Free software" is a matter of liberty, not price. To understand the concept, you should think of "free" as in "free speech," not as in "free beer."

# THE HISTORY OF UNIX AND GNU–LINUX

This section presents some background on the relationships between UNIX and Linux and between GNU and Linux. Visit www.levenez.com/unix for an extensive history of UNIX.

## THE HERITAGE OF LINUX: UNIX

The UNIX system was developed by researchers who needed a set of modern computing tools to help them with their projects. The system allowed a group of people working together on a project to share selected data and programs while keeping other information private.

Universities and colleges played a major role in furthering the popularity of the UNIX operating system through the "four-year effect." When the UNIX operating system became widely available in 1975, Bell Labs offered it to educational institutions at nominal cost. The schools, in turn, used it in their computer science programs, ensuring that computer science students became familiar with it. Because UNIX was such an advanced development system, the students became acclimated to a sophisticated programming environment. As these students graduated and went into industry, they expected to work in a similarly advanced environment. As more of them worked their way up the ladder in the commercial world, the UNIX operating system found its way into industry.

**LE** Berkeley UNIX (BSD)   In addition to introducing students to the UNIX operating system, the CSRG (Computer Systems Research Group) at the University of California at Berkeley made significant additions and changes to it. In fact, it made so many popular changes that one version of the system is called the BSD (Berkeley Software Distribution) of the UNIX system, or just *Berkeley UNIX*. The other major version is UNIX System V (SVR4), which descended from versions developed and maintained by AT&T and UNIX System Laboratories.

# FADE TO 1983

**LE** GNU Project   Richard Stallman (www.stallman.org) announced[1] the GNU Project for creating an operating system, both kernel and system programs, and presented the GNU Manifesto,[2] which begins as follows:

> GNU, which stands for Gnu's Not UNIX, is the name for the complete UNIX-compatible software system which I am writing so that I can give it away free to everyone who can use it.

Some years later, Stallman added a footnote to the preceding sentence when he realized that it was creating confusion:

> The wording here was careless. The intention was that nobody would have to pay for *permission* to use the GNU system. But the words don't make this clear, and people often interpret them as saying that copies of GNU should always be distributed at little or no charge. That was never the intent; later on, the manifesto mentions the possibility of companies providing the service of distribution for a profit. Subsequently I have learned to distinguish carefully between "free" in the sense of freedom and "free" in the sense of price. Free software is software that users have the freedom to distribute and change. Some users may obtain copies at no charge, while others pay to obtain copies—and if the funds help support improving the software, so much the better. The important thing is that everyone who has a copy has the freedom to cooperate with others in using it.

---

1. www.gnu.org/gnu/initial-announcement.html
2. www.gnu.org/gnu/manifesto.html

In the manifesto, after explaining a little about the project and what has been accomplished so far, Stallman continues:

> **Why I Must Write GNU**
>
> I consider that the golden rule requires that if I like a program I must share it with other people who like it. Software sellers want to divide the users and conquer them, making each user agree not to share with others. I refuse to break solidarity with other users in this way. I cannot in good conscience sign a nondisclosure agreement or a software license agreement. For years I worked within the Artificial Intelligence Lab to resist such tendencies and other inhospitalities, but eventually they had gone too far: I could not remain in an institution where such things are done for me against my will.
>
> So that I can continue to use computers without dishonor, I have decided to put together a sufficient body of free software so that I will be able to get along without any software that is not free. I have resigned from the AI Lab to deny MIT any legal excuse to prevent me from giving GNU away.

## NEXT SCENE, 1991

The GNU Project has moved well along toward its goal. Much of the GNU operating system, except for the kernel, is complete. Richard Stallman later writes:

> By the early '90s we had put together the whole system aside from the kernel (and we were also working on a kernel, the GNU Hurd,[3] which runs on top of Mach[4]). Developing this kernel has been a lot harder than we expected, and we are still working on finishing it.[5]
>
> ...[M]any believe that once Linus Torvalds finished writing the kernel, his friends looked around for other free software, and for no particular reason most everything necessary to make a UNIX-like system was already available.
>
> What they found was no accident—it was the GNU system. The available free software[6] added up to a complete system because the GNU Project had been working since 1984 to make one. The GNU Manifesto had set forth the goal of developing a free UNIX-like system, called GNU. The Initial Announcement of the GNU Project also outlines some of the original plans for the GNU system. By the time Linux was written, the [GNU] system was almost finished.[7]

---

3. www.gnu.org/software/hurd/hurd.html
4. www.gnu.org/software/hurd/gnumach.html
5. www.gnu.org/software/hurd/hurd-and-linux.html
6. See www.gnu.org/philosophy/free-sw.html
7. www.gnu.org/gnu/linux-and-gnu.html

Today the GNU "operating system" runs on top of the FreeBSD (www.freebsd.org) and NetBSD (www.netbsd.org) kernels with complete Linux binary compatibility and on top of Hurd pre-releases and Darwin (developer.apple.com/opensource) without this compatibility.

# THE CODE IS FREE

The tradition of free software dates back to the days when UNIX was released to universities at nominal cost, which contributed to its portability and success. This tradition eventually died as UNIX was commercialized and manufacturers came to regard the source code as proprietary, making it effectively unavailable. Another problem with the commercial versions of UNIX related to their complexity. As each manufacturer tuned UNIX for a specific architecture, the operating system became less portable and too unwieldy for teaching and experimentation.

MINIX  Two professors created their own stripped-down UNIX look-alikes for educational purposes: Doug Comer created XINU, and Andrew Tanenbaum created MINIX. Linus Torvalds created Linux to counteract the shortcomings in MINIX. Every time there was a choice between code simplicity and efficiency/features, Tanenbaum chose simplicity (to make it easy to teach with MINIX), which meant this system lacked many features people wanted. Linux went in the opposite direction.

*You can obtain Linux at no cost over the Internet* (page 46). You can also obtain the GNU code via the U.S. mail at a modest cost for materials and shipping. You can support the Free Software Foundation (www.fsf.org) by buying the same (GNU) code in higher-priced packages, and you can buy commercially packaged releases of Linux that include installation instructions, software, and support.

LE  GPL  Linux and GNU software are distributed under the terms of the GPL (GNU General Public License; www.gnu.org/licenses/licenses.html). The GPL says you have the right to copy, modify, and redistribute the code covered by the agreement. When you redistribute the code, however, you must also distribute the same license with the code, thereby making the code and the license inseparable. If you download source code from the Internet for an accounting program that is under the GPL and then modify that code and redistribute an executable version of the program, you must also distribute the modified source code and the GPL agreement with it. Because this arrangement is the reverse of the way a normal copyright works (it *gives* rights instead of *limiting* them), it has been termed a *copyleft*. (This paragraph is not a legal interpretation of the GPL; it is intended merely to give you an idea of how it works. Refer to the GPL itself when you want to make use of it.)

Linux software, including tools, applications, and systems software, is distributed under one of several licences. In addition to GPL 2 and GPL3, there are many more licenses available. See www.gnu.org/licenses/license-list.html#SoftwareLicenses for a partial list.

## *LE*    LINUX IS MORE THAN A KERNEL

Although technically Linux is the name of the kernel, the term *Linux* has come to mean much more. By itself, a kernel is not of much use, so the Linux kernel is typically packaged with utilities and application programs. Many of the utilities that are distributed with the Linux kernel were written as part of the FSF's GNU Project (page 3). Although the FSF prefers to refer to the combination of programs as GNU/Linux, most people simply call it Linux. As more people wanted to run Linux, groups formed that packaged the kernel and a collection of utilities from the GNU Project, BSD, and other sources, as well as application programs and servers.

*LE*  Distribution   These packages of kernel and programs are distributions of Linux and are referred to simply as *distributions* or *distros*. A distribution typically includes word processors, spreadsheets, media players, database applications, and a program to install the distribution. In addition, a distribution includes libraries and utilities from the GNU Project and graphics support from the X Window System.

All distributions are based on the same upstream code, although each might include different applications and tools. Distributions distinguish themselves in the areas of package management and installation tools, policies, community, and support.

First released in 1992, Yggdrasil was the first company to create a CD-ROM–based Linux distribution (it was also a live CD). First released in 1993, Slackware is the oldest distribution of Linux that is still being maintained. Today there are many distributions, including commercially backed distributions such as Fedora/Red Hat Enterprise Linux, Ubuntu, Mandriva, and openSUSE, and community-driven distributions such as Debian, Gentoo, and Mageia.

*LE*  Embedded and   Some companies have taken the GNU/Linux code, grown and customized it, and
mobile Linux   moved it to mobile, embedded, and consumer devices. For example, the ubiquitous Linksys WRT54G wireless router, the Cadillac XTS CUE infotainment system, and the Tivo DVR all run Linux. Linux powers many machine control, industrial automation, and medical instrumentation systems. The most widely distributed Linux release is Android, which is designed for smartphones and tablet computers. Visit linuxgizmos.com/category/devices for an up-to-date list.

## *LE*    OPEN-SOURCE SOFTWARE AND LICENSING

On January 22, 1998, Netscape announced it would make the source code for its next Web browser available for free licensing on the Internet. The month after that, Netscape staffed a project named Mozilla to coordinate the development of the Mozilla Application Suite. Netscape's decisions were business decisions. The headline on its press release said it wanted to harness the creative power of thousands of Internet developers (blog.lizardwrangler.com/2008/01/22/january-22-1998-the-beginning-of-mozilla). Netscape wanted to improve its source code by participating in an active community.

OSI   Inspired by Netscape's bold move, a group of people got together the next month and held a strategy session that created the term *open source* (opensource.org/history).

This term provided a label for Netscape's approach and contrasted with the term *free software,* which was used as a philosophical and political label rather than a pragmatic one. From that session, Eric Raymond and Bruce Perens founded OSI (Open Source Initiative; opensource.org) in late February 1998 to encourage the use of the new term.

**LE** FOSS/FLOSS  The terms FOSS (free and open-source software) and FLOSS (free/libre/open-source software; the *libre* denotes freedom) were brought into common use shortly after OSI was formed. *Free software,* the term coined and supported by the FSF (it is in the name of the organization), suggests the freedoms it gives its users (as in free speech), whereas open-source software suggests the strengths of the peer-to-peer development model. The terms FOSS and FLOSS incorporate both free software and open-source software and can be used without indicating a preference for either term.

The license and the community  The combination of a license that forces you to share software you create and improve (GPL; page 5) and a community that is comfortable sharing software and expects software to be shared, builds the best and most reliable software. Netscape had the right idea.

**LE** Making money  But how can you make money with this setup? Several companies have done quite well in this environment, notably Red Hat. Red Hat sells training, subscriptions to automated software updates, documentation, and support for FOSS. Another way of making money with FOSS is to improve or extend existing software and get paid for your time. Of course the software goes back to the community when you are done. Although it does not follow the FOSS ideals, some companies create a free version of their software and sell a version with more features (e.g., VMware).

Having fun  Two key words for Linux are "Have Fun!" These words pop up in prompts and documentation. The UNIX—now Linux—culture is steeped in humor that can be seen throughout the system. For example, less is more—GNU has replaced the UNIX paging utility named more with an improved utility named less. The utility to view PostScript documents is named ghostscript, and one of several replacements for the vi editor is named elvis. While machines with Intel processors have "Intel Inside" logos on their outside, some Linux machines sport "Linux Inside" logos. And Torvalds himself has been seen wearing a T-shirt bearing a "Linus Inside" logo.

## WHAT IS SO GOOD ABOUT LINUX?

In recent years Linux has emerged as a powerful and innovative UNIX work-alike. Its popularity has surpassed that of its UNIX predecessors. Although it mimics UNIX in many ways, the Linux operating system departs from UNIX in several significant ways: The Linux kernel is implemented independently of both BSD and System V, the continuing development of Linux is taking place through the combined efforts of many capable individuals throughout the world, and Linux puts the power of UNIX within easy reach of both business and personal computer users. Using the Internet, today's skilled programmers submit additions and improvements to open-source developers such as Linus Torvalds and the GNU Project.

Standards   In 1985, individuals from companies throughout the computer industry joined together to develop the POSIX (Portable Operating System Interface for Computer Environments) standard, which is based largely on the UNIX SVID (System V Interface Definition) and other earlier standardization efforts. These efforts were spurred by the U.S. government, which needed a standard computing environment to minimize its training and procurement costs. Released in 1988, POSIX is a group of IEEE standards that define the API (application programming interface), shell, and utility interfaces for an operating system. Although aimed at UNIX-like systems, the standards can apply to any compatible operating system. Now that these standards have gained acceptance, software developers are able to develop applications that run on all conforming versions of UNIX, Linux, and other operating systems.

Applications   A rich selection of applications is available for Linux—both free and commercial—as well as a wide variety of tools: graphical, word processing, networking, security, administration, Web server, and many others. Large software companies have recently seen the benefit in supporting Linux and now have on-staff programmers whose job it is to design and code the Linux kernel, GNU, KDE, and other software that runs on Linux. For example, IBM (www.ibm.com/linux) is a major Linux supporter. Linux conforms increasingly more closely to POSIX standards, and some distributions and parts of others meet this standard. These developments indicate that Linux is becoming mainstream and is respected as an attractive alternative to other popular operating systems.

Peripherals   Another aspect of Linux that appeals to users is the amazing range of peripherals that is supported and the speed with which support for new peripherals emerges. Linux often supports a peripheral or interface card before any company does. Unfortunately some types of peripherals—particularly proprietary graphics cards—lag in their support because the manufacturers do not release specifications or source code for drivers in a timely manner, if at all.

Software   Also important to users is the amount of software that is available—not just source code (which needs to be compiled) but also prebuilt binaries that are easy to install and ready to run. These programs include more than free software. Netscape, for example, was available for Linux from the start and included Java support before it was available from many commercial vendors. Its sibling Mozilla/Thunderbird/ Firefox is now a viable browser, mail client, and newsreader, performing many other functions as well.

Platforms   Linux is not just for Intel-based platforms (which now include Apple computers): It has been ported to and runs on the Power PC—including older Apple computers (ppclinux), Compaq's (née Digital Equipment Corporation) Alpha-based machines, MIPS-based machines, Motorola's 68K-based machines, various 32- and 64-bit systems, and IBM's S/390. Linux also runs on multiple-processor machines (*SMPs;* page 1273). It also includes an O(1) scheduler, which dramatically increases scalability on SMP systems.

Emulators   Linux supports programs, called *emulators,* that run code intended for other operating systems. By using emulators you can run some DOS, Windows, and Macintosh programs under Linux. For example, Wine (www.winehq.com) is an open-source implementation of the Windows API that runs on top of the X Window System and UNIX/Linux.

Virtual machines    A virtual machine (VM or guest) appears to the user and to the software running on it as a complete physical machine. It is, however, one of potentially many such VMs running on a single physical machine. See Chapter 17 for more information.

## LINUX IS POPULAR WITH HARDWARE COMPANIES AND DEVELOPERS

Two trends in the computer industry set the stage for the growing popularity of UNIX and Linux. First, advances in hardware technology created the need for an operating system that could take advantage of available hardware power. In the mid-1970s, minicomputers began challenging the large mainframe computers because, in many applications, minicomputers could perform the same functions less expensively. More recently, powerful 64-bit processor chips, plentiful and inexpensive memory, and lower-priced hard disk storage have allowed hardware companies to install multiuser operating systems on desktop computers.

Proprietary operating systems    Second, with the cost of hardware continually dropping, hardware manufacturers could no longer afford to develop and support proprietary operating systems. A *proprietary* operating system is one that is written and owned by the manufacturer of the hardware (for example, DEC/Compaq owns VMS). Today's manufacturers need a generic operating system they can easily adapt to their machines.

Generic operating systems    A *generic* operating system is written outside of the company manufacturing the hardware and is sold (UNIX, OS X, Windows) or given (Linux) to the manufacturer. Linux is a generic operating system because it runs on different types of hardware produced by different manufacturers. Of course, if manufacturers can pay only for development and avoid per-unit costs (which they have to pay to Microsoft for each copy of Windows they sell), they are much better off. In turn, software developers need to keep the prices of their products down; they cannot afford to create new versions of their products to run under many different proprietary operating systems. Like hardware manufacturers, software developers need a generic operating system.

Although the UNIX system once met the needs of hardware companies and researchers for a generic operating system, over time it has become more proprietary as manufacturers added support for their own specialized features and introduced new software libraries and utilities. Linux emerged to serve both needs: It is a generic operating system that takes advantage of available hardware power.

## LINUX IS PORTABLE

A *portable* operating system is one that can run on many different machines. More than 95 percent of the Linux operating system is written in the C programming language, and C is portable because it is written in a higher-level, machine-independent language. (The C compiler is written in C.)

Because Linux is portable, it can be adapted (ported) to different machines and can meet special requirements. For example, Linux is used in embedded computers, such as the ones found in cellphones, PDAs, and the cable boxes on top of many TVs. The file structure takes full advantage of large, fast hard disks. Equally important, Linux was originally designed as a multiuser operating system—it was not modified to serve several users as an afterthought. Sharing the computer's power among many users and giving them the ability to share data and programs are central features of the system.

Because it is adaptable and takes advantage of available hardware, Linux runs on many different microprocessor-based systems as well as mainframes. The popularity of the microprocessor-based hardware drives Linux; these microcomputers are getting faster all the time at about the same price point. This widespread acceptance benefits both users, who do not like having to learn a new operating system for each vendor's hardware, and system administrators, who like having a consistent software environment.

The advent of a standard operating system has given a boost to the development of the software industry. Now software manufacturers can afford to make one version of a product available on machines from different manufacturers.

## THE C PROGRAMMING LANGUAGE

Ken Thompson wrote the UNIX operating system in 1969 in PDP-7 assembly language. Assembly language is machine dependent: Programs written in assembly language work on only one machine or, at best, on one family of machines. For this reason, the original UNIX operating system could not easily be transported to run on other machines: It was not portable.

To make UNIX portable, Thompson developed the B programming language, a machine-independent language, from the BCPL language. Dennis Ritchie developed the C programming language by modifying B and, with Thompson, rewrote UNIX in C in 1973. Originally, C was touted as a "portable assembler." The revised operating system could be transported more easily to run on other machines.

That development marked the start of C. Its roots reveal some of the reasons why it is such a powerful tool. C can be used to write machine-independent programs. A programmer who designs a program to be portable can easily move it to any computer that has a C compiler. C is also designed to compile into very efficient code. With the advent of C, a programmer no longer had to resort to assembly language to produce code that would run well (that is, quickly—although an assembler will always generate more efficient code than a high-level language).

C is a good systems language. You can write a compiler or an operating system in C. It is a highly structured but not necessarily a high-level language. C allows a programmer to manipulate bits and bytes, as is necessary when writing an operating system. At the same time, it has high-level constructs that allow for efficient, modular programming.

**Figure 1-1**  A layered view of the Linux operating system

In the late 1980s, ANSI (the American National Standards Institute) defined a standard version of the C language, commonly referred to as *ANSI C* or *C89* (for the year the standard was published). Ten years later the C99 standard was published. The original version of the language is often referred to as *Kernighan & Ritchie* (or *K&R*) C, named for the authors of the book that first described the C language.

Another researcher at Bell Labs, Bjarne Stroustrup, created an object-oriented programming language named C++, which is built on the foundation of C. Because object-oriented programming is desired by many employers today, C++ is preferred over C in many environments. Another language of choice is Objective-C, which was used to write the first Web browser. The GNU Project's C compiler (gcc) supports C, C++, and Objective-C.

# OVERVIEW OF LINUX

The Linux operating system has many unique and powerful features. Like other operating systems, it is a control program for computers. But like UNIX, it is also a well-thought-out family of utility programs (Figure 1-1) and a set of tools that allow users to connect and use these utilities to build systems and applications.

## LINUX HAS A KERNEL PROGRAMMING INTERFACE

The Linux kernel—the heart of the Linux operating system—is responsible for allocating the computer's resources and scheduling user jobs so each one gets its fair share of system resources, including access to the CPU; peripheral devices, such as hard disk, DVD, and tape storage; and printers. Programs interact with the kernel through *system calls*, special functions with well-known names. A programmer can use a single system call to interact with many kinds of devices. For example, there is one **write**() system call, rather than many device-specific ones. When a program issues a **write**() request, the kernel interprets the context and passes the request to the appropriate device. This flexibility allows old utilities to work with devices that did not exist when the utilities were written. It also makes it possible to move programs to new versions of the operating system without rewriting them (provided the new version recognizes the same system calls).

## LINUX CAN SUPPORT MANY USERS

Depending on the hardware and the types of tasks the computer performs, a Linux system can support from 1 to more than 1,000 users, each concurrently running a different set of programs. The per-user cost of a computer that can be used by many people at the same time is less than that of a computer that can be used by only a single person at a time. It is less because one person cannot generally take advantage of all the resources a computer has to offer. That is, no one can keep all the printers going constantly, keep all the system memory in use, keep all the disks busy reading and writing, keep the Internet connection in use, and keep all the terminals busy at the same time. By contrast, a multiuser operating system allows many people to use all of the system resources almost simultaneously. The use of costly resources can be maximized, and the cost per user can be minimized; these are the primary objectives of a multiuser operating system.

## LINUX CAN RUN MANY TASKS

Linux is a fully protected multitasking operating system, allowing each user to run more than one job at a time. Processes can communicate with one another but remain fully protected from one another, just as the kernel remains protected from all processes. You can run several jobs in the background while giving all your attention to the job being displayed on the screen, and you can switch back and forth between jobs. If you are running the X Window System (page 16), you can run different programs in different windows on the same screen and watch all of them. This capability helps users be more productive.

## LINUX PROVIDES A SECURE HIERARCHICAL FILESYSTEM

A *file* is a collection of information, such as text for a memo or report, an accumulation of sales figures, an image, a song, or an executable program. Each file is stored under a unique identifier on a storage device, such as a hard disk. The Linux filesystem provides a structure whereby files are arranged under *directories*, which are like folders or boxes. Each directory has a name and can hold other files and directories. Directories, in turn, are arranged under other directories and so forth in a treelike organization. This structure helps users keep track of large numbers of files by grouping related files in directories. Each user has one primary directory and as many subdirectories as are required (Figure 1-2).

Standards   With the idea of making life easier for system administrators and software developers, a group got together over the Internet and developed the Linux Filesystem Standard (FSSTND), which has since evolved into the Linux Filesystem Hierarchy Standard (FHS). Before this standard was adopted, key programs were located in different places in different Linux distributions. Today you can sit down at a Linux system and expect to find a given standard program at a consistent location (page 189).

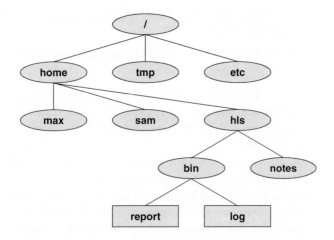

**Figure 1-2**   The Linux filesystem structure

Links   A *link* allows a given file to be accessed by means of two or more names. The alternative names can be located in the same directory as the original file or in another directory. Links can make the same file appear in several users' directories, enabling those users to share the file easily. Windows uses the term *shortcut* in place of *link* to describe this capability. Macintosh users will be more familiar with the term *alias*. Under Linux, an *alias* is different from a *link;* it is a command macro feature provided by the shell (page 392).

Security   Like most multiuser operating systems, Linux allows users to protect their data from access by other users. It also allows users to share selected data and programs with certain other users by means of a simple but effective protection scheme. This level of security is provided by file access permissions, which limit the users who can read from, write to, or execute a file. Linux also implements ACLs (Access Control Lists), which give users and administrators finer-grained control over file access permissions, and SELinux, which gives users and administrators more control over access control.

# THE SHELL: COMMAND INTERPRETER AND PROGRAMMING LANGUAGE

In a textual environment, the shell—the command interpreter—acts as an interface between you and the operating system. When you enter a command on the screen, the shell interprets the command and calls the program you want. A number of shells are available for Linux. The four most popular shells are

- The Bourne Again Shell (bash), an enhanced version of the original Bourne Shell (an original UNIX shell).

- The Debian Almquist Shell (dash; page 329), a smaller version of bash with fewer features. Many startup shell scripts call dash in place of bash to speed the boot process.

- The TC Shell (tcsh), an enhanced version of the C Shell that was developed as part of BSD UNIX.

- The Z Shell (zsh), which incorporates features from a number of shells, including the Korn Shell.

Because different users might prefer different shells, multiuser systems can have several different shells in use at any given time. The choice of shells demonstrates one of the advantages of the Linux operating system: the ability to provide a customized interface for each user.

**Shell scripts** Besides performing its function of interpreting commands from a keyboard and sending those commands to the operating system, the shell is a high-level programming language. Shell commands can be arranged in a file for later execution (Linux calls these files *shell scripts;* Windows calls them *batch files*). This flexibility allows users to perform complex operations with relative ease, often by issuing short commands, or to build with surprisingly little effort elaborate programs that perform highly complex operations.

## FILENAME GENERATION

**Wildcards and ambiguous file references** When you type commands to be processed by the shell, you can construct patterns using characters that have special meanings to the shell. These characters are called *wildcard* characters. The patterns, called *ambiguous file references,* are a kind of shorthand: Rather than typing in complete filenames, you can type patterns; the shell expands these patterns into matching filenames. An ambiguous file reference can save you the effort of typing in a long filename or a long series of similar filenames. For example, the shell might expand the pattern **mak\*tar.gz** to **make-3.80.tar.gz**. Patterns can also be useful when you know only part of a filename or cannot remember the exact spelling of a filename.

## COMPLETION

In conjunction with the Readline Library, the shell performs command, filename, pathname, and variable completion: You type a prefix and press TAB, and the shell lists the items that begin with that prefix or completes the item if the prefix specifies a unique item.

## DEVICE-INDEPENDENT INPUT AND OUTPUT

**Redirection** Devices (such as a printer or a terminal) and disk files appear as files to Linux programs. When you give a command to the Linux operating system, you can instruct it to send the output to any one of several devices or files. This diversion is called output *redirection.*

**Device independence** In a similar manner, a program's input, which normally comes from a keyboard, can be redirected so that it comes from a disk file instead. Input and output are *device independent;* that is, they can be redirected to or from any appropriate device.

As an example, the cat utility normally displays the contents of a file on the screen. When you run a cat command, you can easily cause its output to go to a disk file instead of the screen.

## Shell Functions

One of the most important features of the shell is that users can use it as a programming language. Because the shell is an interpreter, it does not compile programs written for it but rather interprets programs each time they are loaded from the disk. Loading and interpreting programs can be time-consuming.

Many shells, including the Bourne Again Shell, support shell functions that the shell holds in memory so it does not have to read them from the disk each time you execute them. The shell also keeps functions in an internal format so it does not have to spend as much time interpreting them.

## Job Control

*Job control* is a shell feature that allows users to work on several jobs at once, switching back and forth between them as desired. When you start a job, it is frequently run in the foreground so it is connected to the terminal. Using job control, you can move the job you are working with to the background and continue running it there while working on or observing another job in the foreground. If a background job then needs your attention, you can move it to the foreground so it is once again attached to the terminal. The concept of job control originated with BSD UNIX, where it appeared in the C Shell.

# X Window System

History of X    The X Window System (also called X or X11; www.x.org) was created in 1984 at MIT (the Massachusetts Institute of Technology) by researchers working on a distributed computing project and a campuswide distributed environment called Project Athena. This system was not the first windowing software to run on a UNIX system, but it was the first to become widely available and accepted. In 1985, MIT released X (version 9) to the public for use without a license. Three years later, a group of vendors formed the X Consortium to support the continued development of X, under the leadership of MIT. By 1998, the X Consortium had become part of the Open Group. In 2001, the Open Group released X version 11, release 6.6 (X11R6.6).

The X Window System was inspired by the ideas and features found in earlier proprietary window systems but is written to be portable and flexible. X is designed to run on a workstation, typically attached to a LAN. The designers built X with the network in mind. If you can communicate with a remote computer over a network, running an X application on that computer and sending the results to a local display is straightforward.

Although the X protocol has remained stable for a long time, additions to it in the form of extensions are quite common. One of the most interesting—albeit one that has not yet made its way into production—is the Media Application Server, which aims to provide the same level of network transparency for sound and video that X does for simple windowing applications.

XFree86 and X.org   Many distributions of Linux used the XFree86 X server, which inherited its license from the original MIT X server, through release 4.3. In early 2004, just before the release of XFree86 4.4, the XFree86 license was changed to one that is more restrictive and not compatible with the GPL (page 5). In the wake of this change, a number of distributions abandoned XFree86 and replaced it with an X.org X server that is based on a pre-release version of XFree86 4.4, which predates the change in the XFree86 license. Fedora/RHEL uses the X.org X server, named Xorg; it is functionally equivalent to the one distributed by XFree86 because most of the code is the same. Thus modules designed to work with one server work with the other.

Client/server   Computer networks are central to the design of X. It is possible to run an application
environment   on one computer and display the results on a screen attached to a different computer; the ease with which this can be done distinguishes X from other window systems available today. Thanks to this capability, a scientist can run and manipulate a program on a powerful supercomputer in another building or another country and view the results on a personal workstation or laptop computer. For more information refer to "Remote Computing and Local Displays" on page 460.

# GUIs: GRAPHICAL USER INTERFACES

The X Window System provides the foundation for the GUIs available with Linux. Given a terminal or workstation screen that supports X, a user can interact with the computer through multiple windows on the screen, display graphical information, or use special-purpose applications to draw pictures, monitor processes, or preview formatted output. Because X is an across-the-network protocol, it allows a user to open a window on a workstation or computer system that is remote from the CPU generating the window. Conceptually X is very simple. As a consequence, it does not provide some of the more common features found in GUIs, such as the ability to drag windows. The UNIX/Linux philosophy is one of modularity: X relies on a window manager that in turn relies on a desktop manager/environment.

Usually two layers run on top of X: a desktop manager and a window manager. A desktop manager is a picture-oriented user interface that enables you to interact with system programs by manipulating icons instead of typing the corresponding commands to a shell. Fedora/RHEL runs the GNOME desktop manager (www.gnome.org) by default, but X can also run KDE (www.kde.org) and a number of other desktop managers.

## WINDOW MANAGER

A *window manager* is a program that runs under the desktop manager and allows you to open and close windows, run programs, and set up a mouse so it has different effects depending on how and where you click it. The window manager also gives the screen its personality. Whereas Microsoft Windows allows you to change the color of key elements in a window, a window manager under X allows you to customize the overall look and feel of the screen: You can change the way a window looks and works (by giving it different borders, buttons, and scrollbars), set up virtual desktops, create menus, and more. When you are working from the command line, you can approximate a window manager by using Midnight Commander (mc).

Several popular window managers run under X and Linux. RHEL provides both Metacity (the default under GNOME 2) and kwin (the default under KDE). In addition to KDE, Fedora provides Mutter (the default under GNOME 3). *Mutter* is short for Metacity Clutter (the graphics library is named Clutter). Other window managers, such as Sawfish and WindowMaker, are also available. Chapter 4 presents information on using a window manager and other components of a GUI.

## DESKTOP ENVIRONMENTS/MANAGERS

Unlike a window manager, which has a clearly defined task, a desktop environment (manager) does many things. In general, a desktop environment, such as GNOME or KDE, provides a means of launching applications and utilities, such as a file manager, that work with a window manager.

### *LE* GNOME AND KDE

The KDE Project began in 1996, with the aim of creating a consistent, user-friendly desktop environment for free UNIX-like operating systems. KDE is based on the Qt toolkit made by Trolltech. When KDE development began, the Qt license was not compatible with the GPL (page 5). For this reason the FSF decided to support a different project, GNOME (the GNU Network Object Model Environment). Qt has since been released under the terms of the GPL, eliminating part of the rationale for GNOME's existence.

GNOME    GNOME (www.gnome.org) is the default desktop environment for Fedora/RHEL. It provides a simple, coherent user interface that is suitable for corporate use. GNOME uses GTK for drawing widgets. GTK, developed for the GNU Image Manipulation Program (gimp), is written in C, although bindings for C++ and other languages are available.

GNOME does not take much advantage of its component architecture. Instead, it continues to support the traditional UNIX philosophy of relying on many small programs, each of which is good at doing a specific task.

KDE    KDE (kde.org) is written in C++ on top of the Qt framework. KDE tries to use existing technology, if it can be reused, but creates its own if nothing else is available or if a superior solution is needed. For example, KDE implemented an HTML rendering engine long before the Mozilla project was born. Similarly, work on KOffice began a long time before StarOffice became the open-source OpenOffice.org (which is now LibreOffice). In contrast, the GNOME office applications are stand-alone programs that originated outside the GNOME Project. KDE's portability is demonstrated by the use of most of its core components, including Konqueror and KOffice, under Mac OS X.

Interoperability    Since the release of version 2, the GNOME Project has focused on simplifying the user interface, removing options where they are deemed unnecessary, and aiming for a set of default settings that the end user will not wish to change. Fedora 15 introduced

GNOME 3, which is radically different from GNOME 2, following the trend toward simpler, more graphical desktops that have more icons and fewer menus. KDE has moved in the opposite direction, emphasizing configurability.

The freedesktop.org group (freedesktop.org), whose members are drawn from the GNOME and KDE Projects, is improving interoperability and aims to produce standards that will allow the two environments to work together. One standard released by freedesktop.org allows applications to use the notification area of either the GNOME or KDE panel without being aware of which desktop environment they are running in.

### OTHER DESKTOP ENVIRONMENTS

In addition to GNOME and KDE, there are other popular desktop environments. See page 118 for information on and installation instructions for the WindowMaker, Xfce, and LXDE desktop environments.

# A LARGE COLLECTION OF USEFUL UTILITIES

Linux includes a family of several hundred utility programs, often referred to as *commands*. These utilities perform functions that are universally required by users. And each utility tends to do one thing and do it well. The sort utility, for example, puts lists (or groups of lists) in alphabetical or numerical order and can be used to sort lists by part number, last name, city, ZIP code, telephone number, age, size, cost, and so forth. The sort utility is an important programming tool that is part of the standard Linux system. Other utilities allow users to create, display, print, copy, search, and delete files as well as to edit, format, and typeset text. The man (for manual) and info utilities provide online documentation for Linux.

# INTERPROCESS COMMUNICATION

Pipelines and filters  Linux enables users to establish both pipelines and filters on the command line. A *pipeline* passes the output of one program to another program as input. A *filter* is a special kind of pipeline that processes a stream of input data to yield a stream of output data. A filter processes another program's output, altering it as a result. The filter's output then becomes input to another program.

Pipelines and filters frequently join utilities to perform a specific task. For example, you can use a pipeline to send the output of the sort utility to head (a filter that lists the first ten lines of its input); you can then use another pipeline to send the output of head to a third utility, lpr, that sends the data to a printer. Thus, in one command line, you can use three, unrelated utilities together to sort and print part of a file.

# (INTER)NETWORKING UTILITIES

Linux network support includes many utilities that enable you to access remote systems over a variety of networks. In addition to sending email to users on other systems, you can access files on disks mounted on other computers as if they were located on the local system, make your files available to other systems in a similar manner, copy files back and forth, run programs on remote systems while displaying the results on the local system, and perform many other operations across local area networks (LANs) and wide area networks (WANs), including the Internet.

Layered on top of this network access is a wide range of application programs that extend the computer's resources around the globe. You can carry on conversations with people throughout the world, gather information on a wide variety of subjects, and download new software over the Internet quickly and reliably. Chapter 8 discusses networks, the Internet, and the Linux network facilities.

## SYSTEM ADMINISTRATION

On a Linux system the system administrator is frequently the owner and only user of the system. This person has many responsibilities. The first responsibility might be to set up the system, install the software, and possibly edit configuration files. Once the system is up and running, the system administrator is responsible for downloading and installing software (including upgrading the operating system), backing up and restoring files, and managing such system facilities as printers, terminals, servers, and a local network. The system administrator is also responsible for setting up accounts for new users on a multiuser system, bringing the system up and down as needed, monitoring the system, and taking care of any problems that arise.

## SOFTWARE DEVELOPMENT

One of Linux's most impressive strengths is its rich software development environment. Linux supports compilers and interpreters for many computer languages. Besides C and C++, languages available for Linux include Ada, Fortran, Java, Lisp, Pascal, Perl, and Python. The bison utility generates parsing code that makes it easier to write programs to build compilers (tools that parse files containing structured information). The flex utility generates scanners (code that recognizes lexical patterns in text). The make utility and the GNU Configure and Build System make it easier to manage complex development projects. Source code management systems, such as CVS, simplify version control. Several debuggers, including ups and gdb, can help you track down and repair software defects. The GNU C compiler (gcc) works with the gprof profiling utility to help programmers identify potential bottlenecks in a program's performance. The C compiler includes options to perform extensive checking of C code, thereby making the code more portable and reducing debugging time.

## *LE*  CHOOSING AN OPERATING SYSTEM

If you are reading this book you are probably at least considering using/installing Linux; you know there is an alternative to Windows (Microsoft) and OS X (Macintosh) systems. This chapter details a lot of features that make Linux a great operating system. But how do you decide if Linux is for you? Following is a list of some of the factors that go into choosing an operating system.

- **Look and feel**—Can you get comfortable using the GUI? What is the learning curve?

- **Cost**—How much does the operating system cost? What is included at that cost?

- **Ease of use**—Is the GUI easy to use?

- **Bundled software**—What software comes with the operating system and what other software will you have to buy?

- **Hardware requirements**—How expensive is the hardware needed to run the operating system at a speed you will be comfortable with?

- **Bugs**—How long does it take to fix a bug, and how often are updates released?

- **Security**—How secure is the operating system? What do you need to do to make it secure enough to meet your needs? Do you need to purchase security software? Do you need to buy antivirus software?

- **Available software**—How much software is available for the operating system?

Windows, OS X, and Linux each have their strengths and weaknesses. Frequently, look and feel and ease of use depend on what you are used to. Linux allows you to customize the GUI more than OS X and much more than Windows, so you may be able to customize it so you are more comfortable working with it. If you are changing operating systems, give yourself enough time to get used to the new one. Linux does have a learning curve: It will be challenging but rewarding.

One of the biggest benefits of Linux is that you can fix it yourself; you do not have to wait for Microsoft or Apple to find and fix a bug when you run into a problem.

Linux wins the question of cost hands down: it is free software. In addition, Linux comes with a lot of bundled software, including LibreOffice, a complete Microsoft-compatible office suite, and a lot more. And you can download additional software for free. Windows comes with very little bundled software; you need to buy office software and most other software separately. Again, OS X is somewhere between.

Windows is frequently called bloated—it takes the latest and greatest hardware to run it at an acceptable speed. OS X runs only on Apple hardware, which is expensive compared with the hardware required to run Windows (PC hardware). Linux runs on PC hardware, but uses the hardware a lot more lightly than does Windows. On a nonserver system the GUI typically uses a lot of the available horsepower of a system. On older hardware you can run one of the lightweight GUIs (page 118) in place of GNOME or KDE and get good performance. Depending on what you are doing, you can get excellent performance using only the CLI on minimal hardware.

Because of community support, Linux gets excellent marks for support: bug fixes are distributed frequently and are easy to apply. Windows support has improved, but is nowhere near the level of Linux support. OS X gets mixed reviews. And viruses are almost unknown on Linux so there is less support needed.

# CHAPTER SUMMARY

The Linux operating system grew out of the UNIX heritage to become a popular alternative to traditional systems (that is, Windows) available for microcomputer (PC) hardware. UNIX users will find a familiar environment in Linux. Distributions of Linux contain the expected complement of UNIX utilities, contributed by programmers around the world, including the set of tools developed as part of the GNU Project. The Linux community is committed to the continued development of this system. Support for new microcomputer devices and features is added soon after the hardware becomes available, and the tools available on Linux continue to be refined. Given the many commercial software packages available to run on Linux platforms and the many hardware manufacturers offering Linux on their systems, it is clear that the system has evolved well beyond its origin as an undergraduate project to become an operating system of choice for academic, commercial, professional, and personal use.

Linux is packaged in distributions, each of which has an installer and a collection of software packages appropriate to the purpose of the distribution. A distribution typically includes a way to keep its software up-to-date.

Linux and much of the related software is FOSS/FLOSS (Free [Libre] Open Source Software). These terms combine the meanings of *free software* coined by the FSF (Free Software Foundation) and *open-source software*, which originated with OSI (Open Source Initiative), and can be used without indicating a preference for either.

# EXERCISES

1. What is free software? List three characteristics of free software.

2. Why is Linux popular? Why is it popular in academia?

3. What are multiuser systems? Why are they successful?

4. What is Linux? What is the Free Software Foundation/GNU? Which parts of the Linux operating system did each provide? Who else has helped build and refine this operating system?

5. In which language is Linux written? What does the language have to do with the success of Linux?

6. What is a distribution? What does it contain? Name three distributions.

7. What is the difference between the terms *free software* and *open-source software*? Who coined each term?

8. What is a utility program?

9. What is a shell? How does it work with the kernel? With the user?

10. How can you use utility programs and a shell to create your own applications?

11. Why is the Linux filesystem referred to as *hierarchical?*

12. What is the difference between a multiuser and a multitasking system?

13. Give an example of when you would want to use a multitasking system.

14. Approximately how many people wrote Linux? Why is this project unique?

15. What are the key terms of the GNU General Public License?

# PART I

## INSTALLING FEDORA AND RED HAT ENTERPRISE LINUX

# 2

# INSTALLATION OVERVIEW

## OBJECTIVES

After reading this chapter you should be able to:

▶ Choose the best distribution and version to meet your needs

▶ Download the Live or Install Image (ISO) file

▶ Burn/write the Live or Install Image to the installation medium (a DVD or USB flash drive)

▶ Use a live session to test hardware and check system requirements

▶ List considerations of disk partitioning

▶ Describe the advantages and disadvantages of software RAID and LVM partitioning schemes

Installing Linux is the process of copying operating system files from an installation medium (e.g., DVD, USB flash drive) or the network to hard disk(s) on a system and setting up configuration files so Linux runs properly on the hardware.

This chapter discusses the installation process in general: planning, partitioning the hard disk, obtaining the files for the installation, burning or writing an installation medium, and collecting information about the hardware that might be helpful for installation and administration. Chapter 3 covers the process of installing Linux.

Anaconda    Anaconda is a user-friendly tool that installs Fedora/RHEL. For standard hardware (any hardware you can install Windows on), you can typically insert an installation medium holding a Live or Install Image and boot the system. After you go through a few screens, you are done. Of course, sometimes you might want to customize the system or you might be installing on nonstandard hardware: Anaconda presents you with choices that allow you to control the installation. Refer to "Installing Fedora/RHEL" (page 59) and "Installation Tasks" (page 69) for information about installing and customizing Fedora/RHEL.

### Upgrading a Fedora System

tip    The new Anaconda installer will not upgrade a Fedora system from one release to the next. You must use FedUp (FEDora UPgrader), which works on Fedora 17 and later. Visit the Fedora Web page at fedoraproject.org/wiki/FedUp for more information.

# CONVENTIONS USED IN THIS BOOK

This book uses conventions to make its explanations shorter and clearer. The following paragraphs describe these conventions.

Text and examples    The text is set in this type, whereas examples are shown in a monospaced font (also called a *fixed-width* font):

```
$ cat practice
This is a small file I created
using a text editor.
```

Items you enter    Everything you enter at the keyboard is shown in a bold typeface. Within the text, **this bold typeface** is used; within examples and screens, **this one** is used. In the previous example, the dollar sign ($) on the first line is a prompt that Linux displays, so it is not bold; the remainder of the first line is entered by a user, so it is bold.

Utility names    Names of utilities are printed in this sans serif typeface. This book references the nano text editor and the ls utility or ls command (or just ls) but instructs you to enter ls –a on the command line. In this way the text distinguishes between utilities, which are programs, and the instructions you enter on the command line to invoke the utilities.

Filenames    Filenames appear in a bold typeface. Examples are **memo5**, **letter.1283**, and **reports**. Filenames might include uppercase and lowercase letters; however, Linux is *case sensitive* (page 1241), so **memo5**, **MEMO5**, and **Memo5** name three different files.

Character strings    Within the text, characters and character strings are marked by putting them in a bold typeface. This convention avoids the need for quotation marks or other delimiters before and after a string. An example is the following string, which is displayed by the passwd utility: **Sorry, passwords do not match.**

Keys and characters    This book uses SMALL CAPS for three kinds of items:

- Keyboard keys, such as the SPACE bar and the RETURN,[1] ESCAPE, and TAB keys.

- The characters that keys generate, such as the SPACEs generated by the SPACE bar.

- Keyboard keys that you press simultaneously with the CONTROL key, such as CONTROL-D. (Even though D is shown as an uppercase letter, you do not have to press the SHIFT key; enter CONTROL-D by holding the CONTROL key down and pressing **d**.)

Prompts and RETURNS    Most examples include the *shell prompt*—the signal that Linux is waiting for a command—as a dollar sign (**$**), a hashmark (**#**), or sometimes a percent sign (**%**). The prompt does not appear in a bold typeface in this book because you do not enter it. Do not type the prompt on the keyboard when you are experimenting with examples from this book. If you do, the examples will not work.

Examples *omit* the RETURN keystroke that you must use to execute them. An example of a command line is

```
$ nano memo.1204
```

To use this example as a model for running the nano text editor, enter the command **nano memo.1204** and press the RETURN key. (See page 270 for a nano tutorial.) This method of displaying commands makes the examples in the book correspond to what appears on the screen.

Definitions    All glossary entries marked with FOLDOC are courtesy of Denis Howe, editor of the Free Online Dictionary of Computing (foldoc.org), and are used with permission. This site is an ongoing work containing definitions, anecdotes, and trivia.

**optional**    Passages marked as optional appear in a gray box. This material is not central to the ideas presented in the chapter and often involves more challenging concepts. A good strategy when reading a chapter is to skip the optional sections and then return to them when you are comfortable with the main ideas presented in the chapter. This is an optional paragraph.

URLs (Web addresses)    Web addresses, or URLs, have an implicit **http://** prefix, unless **ftp://** or **https://** is shown. You do not normally need to specify a prefix when the prefix is **http://**, but you must use a prefix in a browser when you specify an FTP or secure HTTP site. Thus you can specify a URL in a browser exactly as it is shown in this book.

---

1. Different keyboards use different keys to move the *cursor* (page 1245) to the beginning of the next line. This book always refers to the key that ends a line as the RETURN key. The keyboard you are using might have a RET, NEWLINE, ENTER, RETURN, or some other key. Use the corresponding key on your keyboard each time this book asks you to press RETURN.

ls output   This book uses the output of **ls –l** commands as produced by including the option **––time-style=iso**. This option produces shorter lines, making the examples more readable.

Tip, caution, and security boxes   The following boxes highlight information that might be helpful while you are using or administrating a Linux system.

### This is a tip box

tip   A tip box might help you avoid repeating a common mistake or might point toward additional information.

### This box warns you about something

caution   A caution box warns you about a potential pitfall.

### This box marks a security note

security   A security box highlights a potential security issue. These notes are usually intended for system administrators, but some apply to all users.

# LPI and CompTIA Certification Icons

This book is used as the adopted text in many college classes. Because students who take these classes often seek LPI or CompTIA certification, instructors have asked for a mapping of certification objectives to the material covered in this book. This book fully covers LPI's Linux Essentials certification learning goals and provides extensive coverage of CompTIA's Linux+ exam objectives. Appendix E maps these learning goals and exam objectives to pages in this book. The following icons are used throughout the book to mark the places where learning goals and exam objectives are discussed.

*LPI*   This icon indicates coverage of a topic in the CompTIA's Linux+ exam objectives.

*LE*   This icon indicates coverage of a topic in the LPI's Linux Essentials certification learning goals.

*LE+*   This icon indicates coverage of a topic in the CompTIA's Linux+ exam objectives and a topic in the LPI's Linux Essentials certification learning goals.

# More Information

In addition to the following references, see "Getting Help from the Command Line" on page 128 and refer to Appendix B for additional resources.

Web   memtest86+: www.memtest.org
*Partition HOWTO:* tldp.org/HOWTO/Partition (dated)
Partition: www.linfo.org/partition.html
LVM Resource Page (includes many links): sourceware.org/lvm2
*LVM HOWTO:* www.tldp.org/HOWTO/LVM-HOWTO (dated)
Transmission BitTorrent client: www.transmissionbt.com
X.org release information: x.org/wiki
Distributions: distrowatch.com

Writing ISO image file to a USB flash drive (Windows and Linux): fedorahosted.org/liveusb-creator (**liveusb-creator** package) and unetbootin.sourceforge.net (**unetbootin** package)

Hardware compatibility: hardware.redhat.com

RHEL versions: www.redhat.com/products/enterprise-linux/server/compare.html

Upgrading: fedoraproject.org/wiki/FedUp

Verifying downloaded ISO image files (Linux and Windows): fedoraproject.org/en/verify

Release notes: docs.fedoraproject.org/en-US/Fedora/19/html/Release_Notes

Swap space: docs.fedoraproject.org/en-US/Fedora/13/html/Installation_Guide/s2-diskpartrecommend-x86.html

Burning a DVD or writing to a USB flash drive: docs.fedoraproject.org/en-US/Fedora/19/html/Installation_Guide/sn-making-media.html

Installing from a USB flash drive: docs.fedoraproject.org/en-US/Fedora/19/html/Installation_Guide/Making_USB_Media.html

RAID: raid.wiki.kernel.org/index.php/Linux_Raid

PXE: www.kegel.com/linux/pxe.html

Download Fedora/RHEL
Easiest download: fedoraproject.org/get-fedora

Downloads: fedoraproject.org/en/get-fedora-all

Torrents: torrent.fedoraproject.org

Fedora and EPEL Mirrors: mirrors.fedoraproject.org/publiclist

Everything: dl.fedoraproject.org/pub

RHEL extra packages: fedoraproject.org/wiki/EPEL

Spins: spins.fedoraproject.org

## LPI PLANNING THE INSTALLATION

The major decision when planning an installation is determining how to divide the hard disk into partitions or, in the case of a dual-boot system, where to put the Linux partitions. Once you have installed the system, you can decide which software packages you want to add to the base system (or whether you want to remove some). In addition to these topics, this section discusses hardware requirements.

### CONSIDERATIONS

SELinux    SELinux (Security-Enhanced Linux) improves system security by implementing mandatory access control policies in the kernel (page 472). By default, Fedora installs SELinux in Enforcing mode, which implements best practice security policies. Although you can put SELinux in Permissive or Disabled mode before or after you install the system, it is not a good idea to do so because SELinux protects the system. See page 472 for more information on SELinux. See the **noselinx** boot parameter (page 72) if you want to turn off SELinux when you install the system.

GUI    Server systems can save resources by not including a GUI. On other systems a GUI gives you the benefit of a desktop with multiple workspaces that can include many windows. Fedora/RHEL installs GNOME by default.

Software and services
As you install more software packages on a system, the number of updates and the interactions between the packages increase. More software packages make the system more vulnerable by increasing the number of ways the system can be attacked. Including additional services can also slow the system down. It is important to monitor installed software for security updates.

For a more secure production system, it is best to install and maintain the minimum number of packages required and to enable only needed services. See page 438 for information on the systemd Fedora **init** daemon, which starts and stops system services.

Disk encryption
Another security precaution is disk encryption. Encrypting the hard disk when you install Linux is easy and can prevent theft of sensitive data, especially on laptops, which are prone to theft. Typically the cost of encryption is a fraction of the cost of the damage that can be done when sensitive data is disclosed. However, it is important to remember the password you use to encrypt the disk as there is no (economical) way to recover the information on an encrypted disk without it. You can encrypt a partition during installation (see "Installation Options" on page 73). Also, Truecrypt (www.truecrypt.org) provides excellent encryption software.

# LE   REQUIREMENTS

Hardware
This chapter and Chapter 3 cover installing the operating system on 64-bit processor architectures such as AMD64 processors and Intel processors with Intel EM64T technology as well as older 32-bit Intel and compatible processor architectures (including AMD processors). Within these processor architectures, Fedora/RHEL runs on much of the available hardware. You can view a list of compatible and supported hardware at hardware.redhat.com. Although these lists pertain to RHEL, they serve as a good guide to what Fedora will run on. The Fedora release notes also provide hardware information.

Many Internet sites discuss Linux hardware; use Google to search for **linux hardware**, **fedora hardware**, or **linux** and the specific hardware you want more information on (for example, **linux sata** or **linux a8n**). In addition, many HOWTOs cover specific hardware. The *Linux Hardware Compatibility HOWTO* is also available, although it might not be up-to-date at the time you read it. Fedora/RHEL usually runs on the same systems Windows runs on, unless the system includes a very new or unusual component.

If you are installing Fedora on old or minimal hardware and want to run a GUI, consider installing LXDE (page 118), as it provides a lightweight desktop that uses system resources more efficiently than GNOME does.

CPU (processor)
At a minimum, Fedora requires an Intel Pentium Pro processor; it is optimized for i686 and newer processors. Minimum recommended processor speed for a textual system is 500–700 megahertz and for a graphical system is 1 gigahertz. Visit www.redhat.com/products/enterprise-linux/server/compare.html for information on RHEL systems.

RAM (memory)
Memory requirements are the same for 32-bit and 64-bit Fedora systems. At a minimum, a textual (command-line) system requires 512 megabytes of RAM and a graphical (desktop) system requires 1 gigabyte of RAM. In some cases you can get by with less RAM for a very minimal textual installation. Running a live session (from a Live Image) requires a minimum of 1 gigabyte of RAM. Visit www.redhat.com/rhel/compare for information on RHEL systems.

Linux makes good use of extra memory: The more memory a system has, the faster it runs. Adding memory is one of the most cost-effective ways you can speed up a Linux system that is not being slowed down by the CPU.

**Hard disk space** The amount of hard disk space a system requires depends on which edition of Fedora/RHEL you install, which packages you install, how many languages you install, and how much space you need for user data (your files). The Fedora operating system typically requires 10 gigabytes, although a minimal system can make do with much less space. User data requires additional space. Leave at least 5 percent of the disk empty for proper filesystem operation. See www.redhat.com/rhel/compare for information on RHEL systems.

**LPI  BIOS setup** Modern computers can be set up to boot from a DVD, hard disk, or USB flash drive. The BIOS determines the order in which the system tries to boot from each device. You might need to change this order: Make sure the BIOS is set up to try booting from the DVD or USB drive before it tries to boot from the hard disk. Also, if you want to run virtual machines (Chapter 17) on the system, you may need to enable virtualization in the BIOS. See page 590 for more information on the BIOS.

**LPI  CMOS** CMOS is the persistent memory that stores hardware configuration information. To change the BIOS setup, you need to edit the information stored in CMOS. When the system boots, it displays a brief message about how to enter System Setup or CMOS Setup mode. Press the key that is called for and then move the cursor to the screen and line that deal with booting the system. Generally there is a list of three or four devices that the system tries to boot from; if the first attempt fails, the system tries the second device, and so on. Manipulate the list so the DVD or USB flash drive is the first choice, save the list, and reboot. Refer to the hardware/BIOS manual for more information.

## *LE* PROCESSOR ARCHITECTURE

Installation media hold programs compiled to run on a specific processor architecture (class of processors, or CPUs). The following list describes each of the architectures Fedora/RHEL is compiled for. Visit docs.fedoraproject.org/en-US/Fedora/19/html/Installation_Guide/ch-new-users.html#sn-which-arch for a detailed list of processors in each architecture. Because Linux source code is available to everyone, a knowledgeable user can compile Fedora/RHEL to run on other processor architectures (Chapter 14).

**i386/i686 (Intel x86)** Software on Fedora/RHEL 32-bit PC installation media is compiled to run on Intel x86-compatible processors, including most machines with Intel and AMD processors, almost all machines that run Microsoft Windows, and newer Apple Macintosh machines that use Intel processors. The N200 and Z Series Atom processors are also based on this architecture. If you are not sure which type of processor a machine has, assume it has this type of processor.

**x86_64 (AMD64 and Intel EM64T)** Software on Fedora/RHEL 64-bit PC installation media is compiled to run on AMD64 processors, including the Athlon64, Opteron, and Intel 64-bit processors that incorporate EM64T technology, such as the EMT64 Xeon. The N Series Atom processors (other than the N200) are also based on this architecture.

**Mac PowerPC (ppc)** The Fedora/RHEL PPC release runs on the Apple Macintosh G3, G4, G5, PowerBook, and PPC-based Macintoshes.

### Should I install 32-bit or 64-bit Linux on a 64-bit–capable processor?

tip  The following information might help you decide whether to install 32-bit or 64-bit Linux on a 64-bit–capable processor.

- EM64T/AMD64 processors can run either version of Linux equally well.

- A 64-bit distribution allows each process to address more than 4 gigabytes of RAM. Larger address space is the biggest advantage of a 64-bit distribution. It is typically useful only for certain engineering/scientific computational work and when you are running multiple virtual machines.

- A 64-bit processor is not faster than a 32-bit processor in general; most benchmarks show more or less similar performance. In some cases the performance is better and in some cases it is worse: There is no clear performance advantage for either type of processor.

- The memory model for 64-bit Linux makes pointers twice as big as those in 32-bit Linux. This size difference translates to a more than 5 percent RAM usage increase, depending on the application. If a system is low on RAM, this overhead might make performance worse on a 64-bit system.

- ASLR (address space layout randomization) works better with the larger address space provided by a 64-bit system. ASLR can help improve system security. See en.wikipedia.org/wiki/Address_space_layout_randomization.

- Some multimedia encoders run 10–30 percent faster under 64-bit Linux.

- Some features of proprietary third-party applications are not available for 64-bit architecture.

- A 64-bit Linux system can run 32-bit applications but a 32-bit Linux system cannot run 64-bit applications.

- There is no simple way to go back and forth between 32-bit and 64-bit versions without reinstalling Linux.

- If you are not sure which version to use, install the 64-bit version.

## *LE*  INTERFACES: INSTALLER AND INSTALLED SYSTEM

When you install Fedora/RHEL, you have a choice of interfaces to use while you install it (to work with the Anaconda installer). You also have a choice of interfaces to use to work with the installed system. This section describes the two basic interfaces: textual and graphical.

Textual (TUI/CLI)  A TUI (textual user interface), also called a CLI (command-line interface) or character-based interface, displays characters and some simple graphical symbols. It is line oriented; you give it instructions using a keyboard only.

Graphical (GUI)  A GUI (graphical user interface) typically displays a desktop (such as GNOME) and windows; you give it instructions using a mouse and keyboard. You can run a textual interface within a GUI by opening a terminal emulator window (page 120). A GUI uses more computer resources (CPU time and memory) than a textual interface does.

Pseudographical   A pseudographical interface is a textual interface that takes advantage of graphical elements on a text-based display device such as a terminal. It might also use color. This interface uses text elements, including simple graphical symbols, to draw rudimentary boxes that emulate GUI windows and buttons. Frequently, pressing the TAB key moves the cursor (highlight) from one element to the next, and pressing the RETURN key selects the element the cursor is on.

Advantages   A GUI is user friendly, whereas the textual interface is compact, uses fewer system resources, and can work on a text-only terminal or over a text-only connection. Because it is more efficient, a textual interface is useful for older, slower systems and systems with minimal amounts of RAM. Server systems frequently use a textual interface because it allows the system to dedicate more resources to carrying out the job it is set up to do and fewer resources to pleasing the system administrator. Not running a GUI can also improve system security.

# FEDORA, RHEL, AND CENTOS

This book describes two products: Fedora and RHEL (Red Hat Enterprise Linux). This section briefly describes these products.

Fedora   The Fedora Project is sponsored by Red Hat and supported by the open-source community. With releases, called Fedora, coming out about every six months, this Linux distribution incorporates cutting-edge code. It is *not* a supported Red Hat product and is *not* recommended for production environments where the set of software packages and features must remain constant over a longer period of time. Fedora aims to reflect the upstream projects it incorporates, including the kernel. It is widely regarded as the most stable "free" Linux distribution. In contrast, RHEL includes many changes introduced by Fedora.

The Fedora Project distributes a new release of Fedora about every six months. Each release has both a number and a name. For example, Fedora 18 is named Spherical Cow and Fedora 19 is named Schrödinger's Cat. Previous versions were named Lovelock (15), Verne (16), and Beefy Miracle (17). See fedoraproject.org/wiki/History_of_Fedora_release_names for a description of how names are chosen.

RHEL   RHEL is typically sold through an annual subscription that includes technical support. It is more stable but less cutting edge than Fedora. RHEL provides 10 years of updates; Fedora provides 13 months.

Red Hat Enterprise Linux comes in several configurations; for more information see www.redhat.com/wapps/store/catalog.html. For more information on the various versions of RHEL, see www.redhat.com/rhel/compare.

Red Hat distributes a new major release of RHEL every few years. For information on the RHEL life cycle, see access.redhat.com/support/policy/updates/errata.

LE   CentOS   CentOS (www.centos.org) is a free, RHEL-compatible Linux distribution. It has more long-term stability than Fedora but, unlike RHEL, CentOS is unsupported. Because CentOS is RHEL compatible, this book also describes CentOS. CentOS releases generally follow RHEL releases.

# FEDORA STANDARD EDITIONS: THE LIVE, INSTALL, AND NETWORK IMAGES

Standard editions of Fedora are compiled for i386 (32-bit) and x86_64 (64-bit) architectures and are available via BitTorrent, direct download, and mirrors. To download a standard edition visit fedoraproject.org/en/get-fedora-all.

### Terminology: CD, DVD, installation medium, and installation image

tip  Fedora is available in three editions: Fedora Desktop Live Media, Fedora DVD, and Fedora Network Install CD. The DVD and CD in the names of the editions are conventional and have nothing to do with the media the edition is available on. Each of these editions is available as an installation (ISO) image file that can be written to a CD, DVD, USB flash drive, or other media of appropriate size (the *installation medium*). This book uses the term *installation image* to refer to the installation (ISO) image file as it exists on any medium. It does not refer specifically to CDs, DVDs, or USB flash drives unless it is necessary in context.

Live Image
live session

This book refers to the Fedora Desktop Live Media as a *Live Image*. A Live Image runs a *live session*: It runs Fedora without installing it on the hard disk, although you can install a basic Fedora system from a live session. Once installed, you can use an Internet connection to add more software packages to the system.

To boot from a Live Image, make sure the computer is set up to boot from a DVD or USB drive; see "BIOS setup" and "CMOS," both on page 31, for more information. Booting from a Live Image displays a GNOME desktop (or a KDE desktop if you boot from a KDE Live Image): You are running a live session. When you exit from the live session, the system returns to the state it was in before you booted from the Live Image. If the system has a Linux swap partition (most Linux systems have one; see page 40), the live session uses it to improve its performance but does not otherwise write to the hard disk. RHEL does not provide a Live Image.

Running a live session is a good way to test hardware and fix a system that will not boot from the hard disk. A live session is ideal for people who are new to Fedora or Linux and want to experiment with Fedora or different desktops but are not ready to install it on their system.

### Saving files during a live session

tip  You cannot save a file to a DVD holding a Live Image as this is a readonly medium. During a live session, even though you might appear to save a file, it will not be there after you exit from the live session. To save data from a live session, save it to a network share or a USB flash drive, or mail it to yourself. Alternately, you can boot from a Live USB flash drive with persistent storage. You can create such a USB drive using liveusb-creator (page 50). For more information see fedoraproject.org/wiki/How_to_create_and_use_Live_USB.

### An Install Image uses less memory than a Live Image

tip  Installing a Fedora system using the Install Image uses less memory (RAM) than installing a system using the Live Image. If you are having problems installing from a Live Image on an older system, try installing from an Install Image.

Install Image   This book refers to the Fedora DVD (not necessarily burned on a DVD), also called the Install Media, as an *Install Image*. Hardcopy versions of this book include an Install Image recorded on a DVD. An Install Image does not display a desktop before starting the Anaconda installer.

When you boot from an Install Image, it displays a menu that allows you to install Fedora/RHEL. You can install a graphical or textual system using a graphical or textual installer from an Install Image. An Install Image gives you more choices when you install Fedora than does a Live Image. Also, an Install Image allows you to boot a minimal textual system that you can use to rescue a previously installed system (select **Rescue a Fedora system** from the Troubleshooting menu; page 62). You can also rescue an installed system using the Network Image.

Network Image   The Network Image contains only the Anaconda installer environment. It displays the same menu as an Install Image. By default it downloads software packages from public repositories. This image is useful for creating systems that are up-to-date on the first boot and when the repository is mirrored locally and only the installation environment is required.

# FEDORA SPINS

In addition to the standard editions, Fedora releases many alternative editions called *spins* (spins.fedoraproject.org). Following is a list of some of the most popular spins. You can install a system based on a spin or you can install the spin as an afterthought. See "Installing Different Desktop Environments" on page 118 for installation instructions.

- KDE—(K Desktop Environment; kde.org) A complete, modern desktop built using the KDE Plasma Desktop; also available as a Live Image; a popular alternative to GNOME

- LXDE—(Lightweight X11 Desktop Environment; lxde.org) A speedy, energy-saving desktop environment that works well with systems with slower hardware and fewer resources such as older computers, netbooks, and mobile devices

- XFCE—(www.xfce.org) A speedy, lightweight, user-friendly desktop environment that loads and executes applications quickly, and treads lightly on system resources; also available for RHEL via the EPEL repository

- MATE—(mate-desktop.org) A fork of GNOME 2 providing an intuitive and attractive desktop using traditional metaphors

- FSL—(Fedora Security Lab) An environment in which you can work on security auditing, forensics, system rescue, and teaching security testing methodologies

## *LE+* SETTING UP THE HARD DISK

**Free space**  A hard disk must be prepared in several ways so Linux can write to and read from it. Low-level formatting is the first step in preparing a disk for use. You do not need to perform this task, as it is done at the factory where the hard disk is manufactured. The next steps in preparing a hard disk for use are to write a partition table to it and to create partitions on the disk. Finally, you need to create a filesystem on each partition. The area of a partitioned disk that is not occupied by partitions is called *free space*. A new disk has no partition table, no partitions, and no free space. Under Windows, the term *formatting* means creating a filesystem on a partition; see "Filesystems" below.

### Free space versus free space

**caution**  The preceding paragraph defines the term *free space* to be the area of a partitioned disk that is not occupied by partitions. During installation, the Anaconda installer uses *free space* to refer to unpartitioned space only. Thus, Anaconda includes an empty disk when it figures out how much "free space" is available for the installation.

**LPI** **Partitions**  A *partition*, or *slice*, is a logical section of a hard disk that has a device name, such as **/dev/sda1**, so you can refer to it separately from other sections. For normal use, you must create at least one partition on a hard disk. From a live session before you install Fedora/RHEL, you can use gnome-disks, the GNOME Disk Utility (page 78), to view, resize, and create partitions on an existing system. During installation, you can use the Anaconda graphical partition editor (page 72) to create partitions. After installation, you can use gnome-disks (page 78), parted (page 614), or fdisk to manipulate partitions. See **/dev** on page 503 for more information on device names. Visit www.linfo.org/partition.html for an excellent discussion of partitions.

**LPI** **Partition table**  A partition table holds information about the partitions on a hard disk. Before the first partition can be created on a disk, the program creating the partition must set up an empty partition table on the disk. As partitions are added, removed, and modified, information about these changes is recorded in the partition table. If you remove the partition table, you can no longer access information on the disk except by extraordinary means.

**LVM**  By default, the Anaconda installer sets up LVs (logical volumes) that function like partitions. With LVs, you can use LVM (the Logical Volume Manager; page 44) to change the sizes of volumes easily after the system is installed. Using LVM to manipulate LVs is more convenient than working with one of the tools that manipulates partitions.

**Filesystems**  Before most programs can write to a partition, a *data structure* (page 1245), called a *filesystem*, needs to be written to the partition. This data structure holds inodes (page 515) that map locations on the disk that store files to the names of the files. At the top of the data structure is a single unnamed directory. As will be explained shortly, this directory joins the system directory structure when the filesystem is mounted.

When the Anaconda installer creates a partition, it automatically writes a filesystem to the partition. You can use the mkfs (make filesystem; page 467) utility, which is similar to the Windows format utility, to manually create a filesystem on a partition. Table 11-1 on page 519 lists some common types of filesystems. Fedora/RHEL typically creates **ext4** filesystems for data; unless you have reason to use another filesystem type, use **ext4**. Windows uses FAT16, FAT32, and NTFS filesystems. OS X uses either HFS+ (Hierarchical Filesystem+) or UFS. Different types of filesystems can coexist in different partitions on a single hard disk, including Windows, OS X, and Linux filesystems.

## **LPI** PRIMARY, EXTENDED, AND LOGICAL PARTITIONS

You can divide an IDE/ATA/SATA disk into a maximum of 63 partitions and a SCSI disk into a maximum of 15 partitions. You can use each partition independently for swap devices, filesystems, databases, other resources, and even other operating systems.

Primary and extended partitions   Unfortunately, disk partitions follow the template established for DOS machines a long time ago. At most, a disk can hold four *primary partitions*. You can divide one (and only one) of these primary partitions into multiple *logical partitions;* this divided primary partition is called an *extended partition*. If you want more than four partitions on a drive—and you frequently do—you must set up an extended partition. LVM largely solves this problem by allowing you to make as many filesystems as you want within one "partition" in a much more elegant way than with extended partitions.

A typical disk is divided into three primary partitions (frequently numbered 1, 2, and 3) and one extended partition (frequently numbered 4). The three primary partitions are the sizes you want the final partitions to be. The extended partition occupies the rest of the disk. Once you establish the extended partition, you can subdivide it into additional logical partitions (numbered 5 or greater), each of which is the size you want. You cannot use the extended partition (number 4)—only the logical partitions it holds. Figure 15-3 on page 615 illustrates the disk described in this paragraph. See the *Linux Partition HOWTO* (tldp.org/HOWTO/Partition) for more information.

## THE LINUX DIRECTORY HIERARCHY

### Skip this section for a basic installation

tip  This section describes the Linux directory hierarchy so you might better understand some of the decisions you need to make when you divide the hard disk into partitions while installing Linux. You do not have to read this section to install Linux. You can use the default installation destination (page 67) to set up the disk and return to this section when and if you want to. See the beginning of Chapter 6 for a more thorough explanation of the Linux directory hierarchy.

Namespace  A *namespace* is a set of names (identifiers) in which each name is unique.

Windows versus Linux  As differentiated from a Windows machine, a Linux system presents a single namespace that holds all files, including directories, on the local system. The Linux system namespace is called the *directory hierarchy* or *directory tree*. Under Windows,

C:\ is a separate namespace from **D:\**. The directory hierarchy rooted at C:\ is separate from the directory hierarchy rooted at **D:\** and there is no path or connection between them. Under Linux, the single system namespace is rooted at **/**, which is the *root directory*. Under the root directory are top-level subdirectories such as **bin, boot, etc, home,** and **usr.**

Absolute pathnames All files on a Linux system, including directories, have a unique identifier called an *absolute pathname*. An absolute pathname traces a path through the directory hierarchy starting at the root directory and ending at the file or directory identified by the pathname. Thus the absolute pathname of the top-level directory named **home** is **/home**. For more information refer to "Absolute Pathnames" on page 181. Relative pathnames are discussed on page 182.

Slashes (/) in pathnames Within a pathname, a slash (**/**) follows (appears to the right of) the name of a directory. Thus **/home/sam** specifies that the ordinary or directory file named **sam** is located in the directory named **home**, which is a subdirectory of the root directory (**/**). The pathname **/home/sam/** (with a trailing slash) explicitly specifies **sam** is a directory file. In most instances this distinction is not important. The root directory is implied when a slash appears at the left end of a pathname or when it stands alone.

Linux filesystem namespace The Linux filesystem namespace comprises the set of absolute pathnames of all files, including directories, in the directory hierarchy of a system.

## LPI MOUNT POINTS

A filesystem on a partition holds no information about where it will be mounted in the directory hierarchy (the top-level directory of a filesystem does not have a name). When you use Anaconda to create most partitions, you specify the type of filesystem to be written to the partition and the name of a directory that Fedora/RHEL associates with the partition.

Mounting a filesystem associates the filesystem with a directory in the directory hierarchy. You can mount a filesystem on any directory in the directory hierarchy. The directory that you mount a filesystem on is called a *mount point*. The directory you specify when you use Anaconda to create a partition is the mount point for the partition. Most mount points are top-level subdirectories, with a few exceptions (such as **/usr/local**, which is frequently used as a mount point).

For example, suppose the second partition on the first hard disk has the device name **/dev/sda2**. To create an **ext4** filesystem that you want to appear as **/home** in the directory hierarchy, you must instruct Linux to mount the **/dev/sda2** partition on **/home** when the system boots. With this filesystem mounted on its normal mount point, you can access it as the **/home** directory.

### Do not create files on mount points before mounting a filesystem

caution Do not put files in a directory that is a mount point while a filesystem is not mounted on that mount point. Any files in a directory that is used as a mount point are hidden while the filesystem is mounted on that directory; you will not be able to access them. They reappear when the filesystem is unmounted.

Filesystem independence
The state of one filesystem does not affect other filesystems: One filesystem on a drive might be corrupt and unreadable, while other filesystems function normally. One filesystem might be full so you cannot write to it, whereas others have plenty of room for more data.

/etc/fstab
The file that holds the information relating partitions to mount points is **/etc/fstab** (filesystem table; page 524). The associations stored in the **fstab** file are the normal ones for the system, but you can easily override them. When you work in recovery mode, you might mount a filesystem on the **/target** directory so you can repair the filesystem. For example, if you mount on **/target** the partition holding the filesystem normally mounted on **/home**, the directory you would normally find at **/home/sam** will be located at **/target/sam**.

Naming partitions and filesystems
A partition and any filesystem it holds have no name or identification other than a device name (and a related UUID value—see page 524). Instead, the partition and the filesystem are frequently referred to by the name of the partition's normal mount point. Thus "the **/home** partition" and "the **/home** filesystem" refer to the partition that holds the filesystem normally mounted on the **/home** directory. See page 520 for more information on mounting filesystems.

## PARTITIONING A DISK

During installation, Anaconda sets up disk partitions. This section discusses how to plan partition sizes. Although this section uses the term *partition*, planning and sizing LVs (logical volumes; page 44) works the same way. For more information refer to page 72 and to the *Linux Partition HOWTO* at www.tldp.org/HOWTO/Partition.

### LPI DEFAULT PARTITIONING

It can be difficult to plan partition sizes appropriately if you are not familiar with Linux. During installation, Fedora/RHEL provides *default partitioning*. Without asking any questions, default partitioning divides the portion of the disk allotted to Fedora/RHEL into three or four partitions. One partition is a small **/boot** partition, and one is the swap partition that can be any size from 512 megabytes to 2 or more gigabytes. Another partition is designated as **/** (root) and occupies up to about 50 gigabytes. If enough disk space is available, default partitioning creates a partition designated as **/home**. This partition takes up the remainder of the disk space. The next section discusses the advantages of manual partitioning.

### GiB versus GB

tip
Historically a *gigabyte* (GB) meant either $2^{30}$ (1,073,741,824) or $10^9$ (1,000,000,000) bytes. Recently the term *gibibyte* (giga binary byte; abbreviated as GiB) has been used to mean $2^{30}$ bytes; in turn, *gigabyte* is used more frequently to mean $10^9$ bytes. Similarly, a *mebibyte* (MiB) is $2^{20}$ (1,048,576) bytes. The Fedora/RHEL partitioner still uses megabytes and gigabytes for specifying the size of partitions.

### LPI MANUAL PARTITIONING: PLANNING PARTITIONS

This section discusses additional partitions you might want to create. Consider setting up LVM (page 44) *before* you create partitions; LVM allows you to change partition sizes easily after the system is installed. By default the Anaconda installer sets up LVM. If you decide to manually partition the hard disk and set up partitions other than a root partition (**/**), a swap partition, and possibly a **/home** partition, first consider which kinds of activities will occur under each top-level subdirectory. Then decide whether it is appropriate to isolate that subdirectory by creating a filesystem in a partition and mounting it on its own mount point. Advantages of creating additional filesystems include:

- Separating data that changes frequently (e.g., **/var** and **/home**) from data that rarely changes (e.g., **/usr** and **/boot**) can reduce fragmentation on the less frequently changing filesystems, helping to maintain optimal system performance.

- Isolating filesystems (e.g., **/home**) can preserve data when you reinstall Linux.

- Additional filesystems can simplify backing up data on a system.

- If all directories are part of a single filesystem, and if a program then runs amok or the system is the target of a *DoS attack* (page 1248), the entire disk can fill up. System accounting and logging information, which might contain data that can tell you what went wrong, might be lost. On a system with multiple filesystems, such problems typically fill a single filesystem and do not affect other filesystems. Data that might help determine what went wrong will likely be preserved and the system is less likely to crash.

**LPI**   **/ (root)**   The following paragraphs discuss the advantages of making each of the major top-level subdirectories a separate, mountable filesystem. Any directories you do not create filesystems for automatically become part of the root (**/**) filesystem. For example, if you do not create a **/home** filesystem, **/home** is part of the root (**/**) filesystem.

**LPI**   **(swap)**   Linux temporarily stores programs and data on a swap partition when it does not have enough RAM to hold all the information it is processing. The swap partition is also used when a system hibernates (is suspended to disk). The size of the swap partition should be *at least* 2 gigabytes for systems with up to 4 gigabytes of RAM, 4 gigabytes for 4–16 gigabytes of RAM, and 8 gigabytes for 16–64 gigabytes of RAM. Take into account the fact that the worst-case hibernation scenario, used mostly on laptops, requires a swap size that is one and a half times the size of RAM. For example, a system with 4 gigabytes of RAM should have a 6-gigabyte swap partition if it will hibernate. Although a swap partition is not required, most systems perform better when one is present. On a system with more than one drive, having swap partitions on each drive can improve performance even further. A swap partition is not mounted, so it is not associated with a mount point. See **swap** on page 513 for more information.

**/boot**   The **/boot** partition holds the kernel and other data the system needs when it boots. This partition is typically approximately 500 megabytes, although the amount of space required depends on how many kernel images you want to keep on hand. It can be as small as 100 megabytes, although at that size it will not hold many images, and it is a good idea to keep a few older images around as the kernel gets updated.

Although you can omit the **/boot** partition, it is useful in many cases. Many administrators put an **ext2** filesystem on this partition because the data on it does not change frequently enough to justify the overhead of the **ext4** journal. Systems that use software RAID (page 42) or LVM (page 44) require a separate **/boot** partition. Some BIOSs, even on newer machines, require the **/boot** partition (or the **/** [root] partition if there is no **/boot** partition) to appear near the beginning of the disk (page 590).

### *LPI*  Where to put the /boot partition

caution   On some systems, the **/boot** partition must reside *completely below cylinder 1023* of the hard disk. An easy way to ensure compliance with this restriction is to make the **/boot** partition one of the first partitions on the disk. When a system has more than one hard disk, the **/boot** partition must also reside on a drive in the following locations:

- Multiple IDE or EIDE drives: the primary controller
- Multiple SCSI drives: ID 0 or ID 1
- Multiple IDE and SCSI drives: the primary IDE controller or SCSI ID 0

*LE+*  /var   The name **var** is short for *variable:* The data in this partition changes frequently. Because it holds the bulk of system logs, package information, and accounting data, making **/var** a separate partition is a good idea. Then, if a user runs a job that consumes all of the users' disk space, system log files in **/var/log** will not be affected. The **/var** partition can occupy from 500 megabytes to as much as several gigabytes for extremely active systems with many verbose daemons and a lot of printer and mail activity (the print queues reside in **/var/spool/cups** and incoming mail is stored in **/var/mail**). By default, Apache content (the Web pages it serves) is stored on **/var**; you might want to change the location Apache uses.

Although such a scenario is unlikely, many files or a few large files might be created under the **/var** directory. Creating a separate filesystem to hold the files in **/var** will prevent these files from overrunning the entire directory structure, bringing the system to a halt, and possibly creating a recovery problem.

/var/log   Some administrators choose to put the log directory in a separate partition to isolate system logs from other files in the **/var** directory.

*LPI*  /home   It is a common strategy to put user home directories on their own filesystem. Such a filesystem is usually mounted on **/home**. Having **/home** as a separate filesystem allows you to perform a clean installation without damaging or losing user files. Also, having a separate **/home** filesystem prevents a user from filling the directory structure with her data; at most she can fill the **/home** filesystem, which will affect other users but not bring the system down.

### Set up partitions to aid in making backups

tip   Plan partitions based on which data you want to back up and how often you want to back it up. One very large partition can be more difficult to back up than several smaller ones.

/usr/local   Both **/usr/local** and **/opt** are candidates for separation. If you plan to install a lot of
and /opt   packages, such as on an enterprise system, you might want to keep them on a separate

partition. If you install the additional software in the same partition as the users' home directories, for example, it might encroach on the users' disk space. Many sites keep all **/usr/local** or **/opt** software on one server; from there, they export the software to other systems. If you choose to create a **/usr/local** or **/opt** partition, its size should be appropriate to the software you plan to install.

Table 2-1 gives guidelines for minimum sizes for partitions. Set the sizes of other partitions, such as those for **/home, /opt,** and **/usr/local,** according to need and the size of the hard disk. If you are not sure how you will use additional disk space, you can create extra partitions using whatever names you like (for example, **/b01, /b02,** and so on). Of course, you do not have to partition the entire drive when you install Linux; you can wait until later to divide the additional space into partitions.

**Table 2-1**    **LPI**    Example minimum partition sizes[a]

| Partition | Example size |
|---|---|
| **/boot** | 200–500 megabytes |
| **/** (root) | Minimum of 2–16 gigabytes; depends on which and how many software packages you install |
| (swap) | 2–8 gigabytes (page 40) |
| **/home** | As large as necessary; depends on the number of users and the type of work they do |
| **/tmp** | Minimum of 500 megabytes |
| **/var** | Minimum of 500 megabytes—much larger if you are running a server |

a. The sizes in this table assume you create all partitions separately. For example, if you create a 2-gigabyte **/** (root) partition and do not create a **/home** partition, you might not have enough room to store all the user files.

# RAID

RAID (redundant array of inexpensive/independent disks) employs two or more hard disk drives or partitions in combination to improve fault tolerance and/or performance. Applications and utilities see these multiple drives/partitions as a single logical device. RAID, which can be implemented in hardware or software (Fedora/RHEL gives you this option), spreads data across multiple disks. Depending on which level you choose, RAID can provide data redundancy to protect data in the case of hardware failure. Although it can improve disk performance by increasing read/write speed, software RAID uses quite a bit of CPU time, which might be a consideration. True hardware RAID requires hardware designed to implement RAID and is not covered in this book (but see "Fake RAID" on the next page).

RAID can be an effective *addition* to a backup. Fedora/RHEL offers RAID software that you can install either when you install a Fedora/RHEL system or as an afterthought. The Linux kernel automatically detects RAID arrays (sets of partitions) at boot time if the partition ID is set to **0xfd** (**raid autodetect**).

## RAID does not replace backups or a good continuity plan

**caution**    The purposes of RAID are to improve performance and/or to minimize downtime in the case of a disk failure. RAID does not replace backups.

Do not use RAID as a replacement for regular backups. If the system experiences a catastrophic failure, RAID is useless. Earthquake, fire, theft, and other disasters might leave the entire system inaccessible (if the hard disks are destroyed or missing). RAID also does not take care of the simple case of replacing a file when a user deletes it by accident. In these situations, a backup on a removable medium (which has been removed) is the only way to restore a filesystem.

Do not depend on RAID as a complete business continuity plan. Whether to set up RAID, remote server colocation, regular backups, and off-site backups are all decisions to be made when considering the costs of continued business due to a catastrophic failure.

Software RAID, as implemented in the kernel, is much cheaper than hardware RAID. Not only does this approach avoid the need for specialized RAID disk controllers, but it also works with the less expensive ATA disks as well as SCSI disks.

RAID hardware disk controllers can boost performance and the drives can generally be hot-swapped (i.e., drives can be replaced while the system is up).

Fake RAID    Fedora/RHEL does not officially support motherboard-based RAID (known as *fake RAID*) but accepts it through the **dmraid** driver set. Linux software RAID is almost always better than fake RAID. Visit help.ubuntu.com/community/FakeRaidHowto for background information on fake RAID.

If the system has two or more hard disks, the Anaconda partition editor gives you the choice of implementing RAID level 0, 4, or 5, 6, or 10. Anaconda makes sure the member partitions are on different drives. That way, with all levels except 0, if one drive fails, the data will be preserved.

- **RAID level 0 (striping)**—Improves performance but offers no redundancy. The storage capacity of the RAID device is equal to that of the member partitions or disks.

- **RAID level 1 (mirroring)**—Provides simple redundancy, improving data reliability, and can improve the performance of read-intensive applications. The storage capacity of the RAID device is equal to one of the member partitions or disks.

- **RAID level 4 (disk striping with dedicated parity disk)**—Provides redundancy and improves performance (most notably, read performance). The storage capacity of the RAID device is equal to that of the member partitions or disks, minus one of the partitions or disks (assuming they are all the same size).

- **RAID level 5 (disk striping with parity)**—Provides redundancy and improves performance (most notably, read performance). The storage capacity of the RAID device is equal to that of the member partitions or disks, minus one of the partitions or disks (assuming they are all the same size).

- RAID level 6 (**disk striping with double parity**)—Improves upon level 5 RAID by protecting data when two disks fail at once. Level 6 RAID is inefficient with a small number of drives.

- RAID level 10 (**mirroring and striping**)—A combination of RAID 1 and RAID 0 (also called RAID 1+0), RAID 10 uses mirroring to improve fault tolerance and striping to improve performance. Multiple RAID 1 arrays (mirroring) are overlaid with a RAID 0 array (striping). The storage capacity of the RAID device is equal to one-half that of the member partitions or disks. You must use at least four partitions or disks.

For more information see raid.wiki.kernel.org/index.php/Linux_Raid.

## LVM: LOGICAL VOLUME MANAGER

The Logical Volume Manager (LVM2, which this book refers to as LVM) allows you to change the size of *logical volumes* (LVs, the LVM equivalent of partitions) on the fly. With LVM, if you make a mistake in setting up LVs or if your needs change, you can make LVs either smaller or larger without affecting user data. You must choose to use LVM at the time you install the system or add a hard disk; you cannot retroactively apply it to a disk full of data. LVM supports IDE and SCSI drives as well as multiple devices such as those found in RAID arrays.

LVM groups disk components (partitions, hard disks, or storage device arrays), called *physical volumes* (PVs), into a storage pool, or virtual disk, called a *volume group* (VG). See Figure 2-1. You allocate a portion of a VG to create a *logical volume* (LV).

An LV is similar in function to a traditional disk partition in that you can create a filesystem on an LV. It is much easier, however, to change and move LVs than partitions: When you run out of space on a filesystem on an LV, you can grow (expand) the LV and its filesystem into empty or new disk space, or you can move the filesystem to a larger LV. For example, you can add a hard disk to a system and incorporate it into an LV to expand the capacity of that LV. LVM's disk space manipulation is transparent to users; service is not interrupted.

LVM also eases the burden of storage migration. When you outgrow the PVs or need to upgrade them, LVM can move data to new PVs. To read more about LVM, refer to the resources listed on page 28.

## THE INSTALLATION PROCESS

The following steps outline the process of installing Fedora/RHEL from an Install Image. Installation from other installation images follows similar steps. See Chapter 3 for specifics.

1. Make sure the BIOS is set to boot from a DVD or USB flash drive (page 31). Insert the installation medium holding an Install Image in the system, and

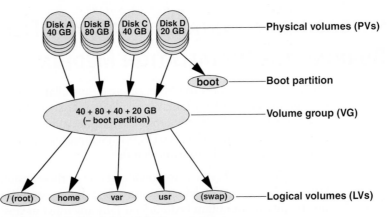

**Figure 2-1**   LVM: Logical Volume Manager

reset the computer. The computer boots and displays the Install Image Boot menu (Figure 3-4, page 61).

2. You can make a selection from the Install Image Boot menu, press the TAB key to display the boot command line (which you can modify), and begin installing Fedora/RHEL when you are ready. One of the menu items checks the installation medium. If you do nothing, Anaconda starts installing the system after 60 seconds.

3. As part of the process of bringing up a live session or installing Fedora/RHEL, Anaconda creates *RAM disks* (page 1269) that it uses in place of the hard disk used for a normal boot operation. Anaconda copies tools required for the installation or to bring up a system from a Live or Install Image to the RAM disks. The use of RAM disks allows the installation process to run through the specification and design phases without writing to the hard disk and enables you to opt out of the installation at any point before the last step of the installation. If you opt out before this point, the system is left in its original state. The RAM disks also allow a live session to leave the hard disk untouched.

4. You give Anaconda information about how you want to configure the system.

5. When Anaconda is finished collecting information, it writes the operating system files to the hard disk.

6. When you reboot the system, gnome-initial-setup asks questions that are required to set up the first user (page 68).

7. The system is ready for you to log in and use.

# DOWNLOADING AN INSTALLATION IMAGE FILE AND WRITING TO/BURNING THE INSTALLATION MEDIUM

There are several ways to obtain or create installation media (a CD, DVD, or USB flash drive). Fedora/RHEL makes available releases of Linux as CD/DVD *ISO image* files (named after the ISO 9660 standard that defines the CD/DVD filesystem). Even though they are referred to as CD/DVD ISO images, you can write these files to a USB flash drive and then boot from that drive.

This section describes how to download one of these installation images and burn a DVD or write to a USB drive. You can also purchase an installation DVD from a Web site. If you cannot obtain Fedora/RHEL by any other means, you can point a browser at fedoraproject.org/wiki/FreeMedia to display a Web page with links that enable you to request a free Fedora DVD.

## THE EASY WAY TO DOWNLOAD AN INSTALLATION IMAGE FILE

This section explains the easiest way to download an installation (ISO) image file. This technique works in most situations; it is straightforward but limited. For example, it does not allow you to use BitTorrent to download the file.

To begin, point a browser at fedoraproject.org and click **Download Now!**. The download should start shortly. If the browser gives you a choice of what to do with the file, save it to the hard disk. The browser saves the installation (ISO) image file to the hard disk. Continue reading at "Verifying an Installation (ISO) Image File" on page 49.

**You can find installation (ISO) image files for all supported architectures here**

tip   If you cannot find an installation image file that supports the type of hardware you want to install Fedora on, visit mirrors.fedoraproject.org/publiclist. For RHEL visit access.redhat.com and select **Downloads**.

## OTHER WAYS TO DOWNLOAD AN ISO IMAGE FILE

This section explains how to download an installation (DVD/ISO) image file or a release that is not downloaded automatically, and how to download a torrent that enables you to use BitTorrent to download an installation (ISO) image file. See "Download Fedora/RHEL" on page 29 for other locations you can download Fedora/RHEL from.

Browser   When you use a Web browser to download a file, the browser contacts a Web (HTTP) or FTP server and downloads the file from that server. If too many people download files from a server at the same time, the downloads become slower.

BitTorrent   BitTorrent efficiently distributes large amounts of static data, such as installation (ISO) image files. Unlike using a browser to download a file from a single server, BitTorrent

**Figure 2-2**    The mirrors.fedoraproject.org Web page

distributes the functions of a server over its clients. As each client downloads a file, it becomes a server for the parts of the file it has downloaded. To use BitTorrent, you must download a small file called a *torrent* (or have a Web browser do it for you). This file, which holds information that allows clients to communicate with one another, has a filename extension of **.torrent**. As more people use a torrent to download a file at the same time, the downloads become faster. Downloading an installation (ISO) image file using BitTorrent is covered later in this section.

Mirrors    Many sites mirror (hold copies of) the Fedora installation (ISO) image files and BitTorrent torrent files. Some mirrors use HTTP, while others use FTP; you can use a browser to download files from either type of site. FTP and HTTP sites appear slightly different.

Locate a mirror site by pointing a browser at mirrors.fedoraproject.org. Below the heading information, the page displays Public Active Mirrors. Narrow your choices by clicking a selection in the Mirror list filter at the upper-right corner of the page (Figure 2-2). For example, click **19** to list sites from which you can download Fedora 19 or click **i386** in the row that starts with 19 to list sites from which you can download the i386 version of Fedora 19.

The list on the newly displayed Web page is in country code order. For example, FR is France and US is the United States. To conserve network bandwidth, scroll to and download from a mirror site close to you. Look at the Content, Bandwidth, and Comments columns. Pick the row of an appropriate site and click the protocol you want to use in the Content column. From a browser there is little difference between the FTP and HTTP protocols, although accessing a site using FTP might be a bit faster.

**Figure 2-3**  A Fedora mirror site

When you click a protocol, the browser displays a page similar to the one shown in Figure 2-3. Follow these steps to download the installation (ISO) image file you want:

1. Click **releases**. The browser displays a list of Fedora releases. All sites have the current release. Most sites keep at least one or two older releases while others keep many older releases.

2. Click the number of the release of Fedora you want to download. The browser displays a list that includes **Fedora** and **Live**.

3. Click **Live** if you want to download a Live Image and **Fedora** if you want to download an Install Image. Make sure you have room for the file on the hard disk: An Install (DVD/ISO) Image file occupies more than 4 gigabytes.

4. Click the architecture (page 31) you want to install Fedora on: **i386** or **i686** for 32-bit systems and **x86_64** for 64-bit systems.

5. If you are downloading an Install Image, click **iso**. If you are downloading a Live Image, go to the next step.

6. Download the **CHECKSUM** file.

7. Click the name of the installation image file you want to download and choose to download (not install) the image. **Live** gives you the choice of a **Fedora-Live-Desktop-x86_64-19-1.iso**, which runs (and optionally installs) a GNOME desktop and **Fedora-Live-KDE-x86_64-19-1.iso**, which runs (and optionally installs) a KDE desktop. (The **19-1** indicates the second release of Fedora 19.) **Fedora** gives you the choice of downloading an Install Image or a Network Image (ISO image file).

*Using BitTorrent*  As mentioned earlier, you can use BitTorrent to obtain an installation (ISO) image file. BitTorrent is especially effective for downloading one of these files shortly after a new release is made available.

To download a torrent, point a browser at fedoraproject.org/en/get-fedora-all or torrent.fedoraproject.org and click the filename of the torrent. You can identify a torrent file by its filename extension of **.torrent**. A BitTorrent client should start automatically and ask where to put the downloaded file. You can also download the torrent manually. Once you have a BitTorrent client such as Transmission (www.transmissionbt.com;

installed with most Fedora/RHEL editions), you can start downloading the file from the command line (page 544) or by clicking it in a file browser such as Nautilus (page 102).

### You can download and burn/write to a DVD or USB flash drive under any operating system

tip  You can download and burn the DVD or write to a USB flash drive on any computer that is connected to the Internet, has a browser, has enough space on the hard disk to hold the image file (about 1 gigabyte for a Live Image and over 4 gigabytes for an Install Image), and can burn a DVD or write to a USB drive. You can often use **ftp** (page 716) or, on a Linux system, **Nautilus: Connect to Server** in place of a browser to download the file.

## Verifying an Installation (ISO) Image File

This section assumes you have an image file and a **CHECKSUM** file saved on the hard disk and explains how to verify the file is correct. The **CHECKSUM** file contains the *SHA2* (page 1272) sums for each of the available installation (ISO) image files. When you process a file using the sha256sum utility, sha256sum generates a number based on the file. If that number matches the corresponding number in the **CHECKSUM** file, the downloaded file is correct. With the –c option and the name of the CHECKSUM file, sha256sum checks each of the files listed in the CHECKSUM file. The following example shows the Live Desktop installation (ISO) image file is OK and the Live KDE image file is not present. The message about improperly formatted lines refers to the PGP key in the CHECKSUM file; you can ignore this message.

```
$ sha256sum -c *-CHECKSUM
Fedora-Live-Desktop-x86_64-19-1.iso: OK
sha256sum: Fedora-Live-KDE-x86_64-19-1.iso: No such file or directory
Fedora-Live-KDE-x86_64-19-1.iso: FAILED open or read
sha256sum: WARNING: 20 lines are improperly formatted
sha256sum: WARNING: 1 listed file could not be read
```

Computing an SHA2 sum for a large file can take a while. If sha256sum does not report the file is OK, you must download the file again.

### Writing to a USB flash drive might be easier

tip  Writing an installation (ISO) image file to a USB drive can be easier and more economical than burning a DVD. Also, some laptops do not have a DVD drive and so cannot boot from a DVD.

## Burning a DVD

An installation (ISO) image file is an exact image of what needs to be on the DVD. Putting that image on a DVD involves a different process than copying files to a DVD. For that reason, DVD-burning software has a special selection for burning an ISO image, which bears a label similar to **Record CD from CD Image** or **Burn CD Image**. Refer to the instructions for the software you are using for information on how to burn an ISO image file to a DVD.

### Make sure the software is set up to burn an ISO image

tip  Burning an ISO image is not the same as copying files to a DVD. Make sure the DVD-burning software is set up to burn an ISO image. If you simply copy the ISO file to a DVD, it will not work when you try to install Linux.

## LPI  WRITING TO A USB FLASH DRIVE

This section explains how to use liveusb-creator (fedorahosted.org/liveusb-creator) to write an installation (ISO) image file to a USB flash drive. Even though the name of the program includes the word *live,* you can use it to write either an Install or Live Image (ISO image file) to a USB drive. You can then boot from the USB drive to install Linux or run a live system.

### The USB flash drive must be large enough to hold the ISO file

tip  The USB drive you write to must be big enough to hold the installation (ISO) image file. An Install Image is bigger than 4 gigabytes.

Windows  Download the Windows installer (**liveusb-creator✳setup.exe**) from fedorahosted.org/liveusb-creator and run it to install liveusb-creator.

Linux  From a Fedora/RHEL system give the following command from a terminal emulator to install the program. You will need to enter the **root** password.

```
$ su -c 'yum -y install liveusb-creator'
```

Under Ubuntu, use usb-creator (**usb-creator** package), which performs the same function. See page 1184 for instructions on downloading software using apt-get.

Writing to the USB drive  The liveusb-creator utility displays the Fedora LiveUSB Creator window (Figure 2-4). Under Windows, select liveusb-creator from the main menu to open this window. Under Linux, open this window by giving the command **liveusb-creator** (or **usb-creator**) from an Enter a Command window (ALT-F2) or a terminal emulator; liveusb-creator will ask you to authenticate as **root** (provide the **root** password).

Click **Browse** to locate the installation (ISO) image file you downloaded. The program will fill in the text box labeled Target Device automatically; specify a USB drive here if you have more than one. The Persistent Storage slider sets up storage space on the USB drive for use from a live system. Click **Create Live USB**. When liveusb-creator displays **Complete!** you can close the window and remove the USB drive.

## GATHERING INFORMATION ABOUT THE SYSTEM

It is not difficult to install and bring up a Linux system. Nevertheless, the more you know about the process before you start, the easier it will be. The installation software collects information about the system and can help you make decisions during the installation process. However, the system will work better when you know how you want to partition the hard disk rather than letting the installation program create partitions without your input. There are many details, and the more details you take control of, the more pleased you are likely to be with the finished product. Finding the information this section asks for will help ensure you end up with a system you understand and know how to change when necessary. To an increasing extent, the installation software probes the hardware and figures out what it is. Newer equipment is more likely to report on itself than older equipment is.

**Figure 2-4**   The Fedora LiveUSB Creator window

### Test the installation image file and test the installation medium

tip   It is a good idea to test the installation (ISO) image file and the installation medium before you use it to install Linux. When you boot the system from the installation medium, Fedora/RHEL gives you the option of checking the image file for errors (see the tip on page 65). A bad file on an installation medium might not show up until you finish installing Fedora/RHEL and have it running. At that point, it might be difficult and time-consuming to figure out where the problem lies. Testing the file and installation medium takes a few minutes but can save you hours of trouble if something is not right. If you decide to perform one test only, test the installation medium.

It is critical to have certain pieces of information before you start. One thing Linux can never figure out is all the relevant names and IP addresses (unless you are using DHCP, in which case the addresses are set up for you).

Following is a list of items you might need information about. Gather as much information about each item as you can: manufacturer, model number, size (megabytes, gigabytes, and so forth), number of buttons, chipset (for cards), and so on. Some items, such as the network interface card and the sound card, might be built into the motherboard.

- Hard disks
- Memory; you do not need it for installation, but it is good to know
- SCSI interface card

- NIC (network interface card)

- Video interface card (including the amount of video RAM/memory)

- Sound card and compatibility with standards, such as SoundBlaster

- Mouse (PS/2, USB, AT, and number of buttons)

- Monitor (size and maximum resolution)

- IP addresses and names, unless you are using DHCP (page 491; most routers are set up as DHCP servers), in which case the IP addresses are automatically assigned to the system. Most of this information comes from the system administrator or ISP.

  - System hostname (anything you like)

  - System address

  - Network mask (netmask)

  - Gateway address (the connecting point to the network or Internet) or a phone number when you use a dial-up connection

  - Addresses for nameservers, also called DNS addresses

  - Domain name (not required)

# Chapter Summary

A Live Image can run a live Fedora session without installing Fedora on the system. You can install Fedora from a live session. Running a live session is a good way to test hardware and fix a system that will not boot from the hard disk.

When you install Fedora/RHEL, you copy operating system files from an installation medium (e.g., DVD or USB flash drive) to hard disk(s) on a system and set up configuration files so that Linux runs properly on the hardware. Operating system files are stored on installation media as an installation (ISO) image file. You can use a Web browser, FTP, or BitTorrent to download an installation (ISO) image file. It is a good idea to test the image file when it is downloaded and the installation medium before you use it to install Fedora/RHEL.

When you install Fedora/RHEL, you can let the Anaconda installer decide how to partition the hard disk (default partitioning) or you can manually specify how you want to partition it.

The Fedora Project is sponsored by Red Hat and supported by the open-source community. Fedora is a Linux release that contains cutting-edge code; it is not recommended for production environments. RHEL is more stable than Fedora.

# EXERCISES

1. Briefly, what does the process of installing an operating system such as Linux involve?

2. What is an installer? What is the name of the Fedora/RHEL installer?

3. Would you set up a GUI on a server system? Why or why not?

4. A system boots from the hard disk. To install Linux, you need it to boot from a DVD. How can you make the system boot from a DVD?

5. What is free space on a hard disk? What is a filesystem?

6. What is an ISO image? How do you burn an ISO image to a DVD?

# ADVANCED EXERCISES

7. Give two reasons why RAID cannot replace backups.

8. What are RAM disks? How are they used during installation?

9. What is SHA2? How does it work to ensure that an ISO image file you download is correct?

# 3

# STEP-BY-STEP
# INSTALLATION

## OBJECTIVES

After reading this chapter you should be able to:

▸ Run a live session and use gnome-disks to view and change disk partitioning

▸ Install Fedora from a live session

▸ Install Fedora/RHEL using an Install Image

▸ Modify system behavior using boot parameters

▸ Modify partitions during installation

▸ Select software during installation

▸ List the requirement and considerations for a dual-boot configuration

Chapter 2 covered planning the installation of Fedora/RHEL: determining the requirements; planning the layout of the hard disk; obtaining the files you need for the installation, including how to download and burn or write Install, Live, and Network Images to installation media; and collecting information about the system. This chapter focuses on installing Fedora/RHEL. Frequently the installation is quite simple, especially if you have done a good job of planning. Sometimes you might run into a problem or have a special circumstance; this chapter gives you tools to use in these cases. Read as much of this chapter as you need to; once you have installed Fedora/RHEL, continue with Chapter 4, which covers getting started using the Fedora/RHEL desktop and command line.

## THE NEW ANACONDA INSTALLER

The new Anaconda installer, introduced in Fedora 18, has been totally rewritten. The Anaconda user interface changed from a linear (wizard) model to a hub-and-spoke model. Using this model means Anaconda can perform background processing (e.g., you can still be entering information while Anaconda is installing packages) and you can skip screens that are not pertinent to your installation. See fedoraproject.org/wiki/Anaconda/NewInstaller for more information.

### Chapter 17 explains how to set up a virtual system

tip  To install Fedora/RHEL on a virtual system, you build the virtual system and then follow the instructions in this chapter for installing the operating system. See page 663 for instructions on setting up a QEMU/KVM virtual machine and page 671 for setting up a VMware virtual machine.

### Upgrading a Fedora system

tip  The new Anaconda installer will not upgrade a Fedora system from one release to the next. You must use FedUp (FEDora UPgrader), which works on Fedora 17 and later. Visit the Fedora Web page at fedoraproject.org/wiki/FedUp for more information.

## RUNNING A FEDORA LIVE SESSION

As discussed in Chapter 2, a live session is a Linux session you run on a computer without installing Linux on the computer. When you reboot after a live session, the computer is untouched. If you are running Windows, after a live session Windows boots the way it did before the live session. If you choose, you can install Fedora from a live session. RHEL does not offer a live session.

A live session gives you a chance to preview Fedora without installing it. Boot from a Live Image to begin a live session and work with Fedora as explained in Chapter 4. When you are finished, remove the installation medium and reboot the system. The system will boot as it did before you ran the live session.

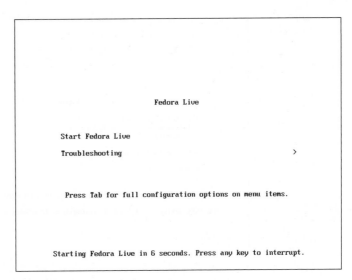

Figure 3-1   The Live Image Boot menu

Preserving files   Because a live session does not write to the hard disk (other than using a swap partition, if one is available), none of the work you save will be available once you reboot. You can use a USB flash drive, email, or another method to transfer files you want to preserve to another system. The liveusb-creator utility (page 50) can create persistent storage on a USB drive that you can write to from a live session.

## BOOTING THE SYSTEM

Before Fedora can display the desktop of a live session or install itself on a hard disk, the Linux operating system must be read into memory (booted). This process can take a few minutes on older, slower systems and systems with minimal RAM (memory).

In most cases, you can boot Fedora to run a live session that displays a desktop without doing anything after you boot from a Live Image. To begin, insert the installation medium holding a Live Image (the standard GNOME **Fedora Desktop Live Media**) into the system and turn on or reset the system. Refer to "BIOS setup" on page 31 if the system does not boot from the CD, DVD, or USB drive. Or refer to "Modifying Boot Parameters (Options)" on page 70 if Fedora does not boot or displays an error message.

A few moments after you start the system, Fedora displays a screen that says **Starting Fedora Live in 10 seconds. Press any key to interrupt.** and counts down from 10 (Figure 3-1). Next the system displays some messages and then a graphical outline of the Fedora logo that gets filled in as the system boots. The screen goes blank and then Fedora displays a Welcome to Fedora window. In this window you can click **Try Fedora** or **Install to Hard Drive**.

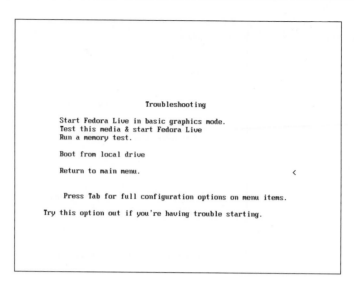

**Figure 3-2**   The Troubleshooting menu

Checking the installation medium   The first time you use an installation medium, it is a good idea to check it for defects. To do so, interrupt the automatic boot by pressing the SPACE bar while Fedora is counting down. Use the DOWN ARROW key to highlight the **Troubleshooting** line and press RETURN (the mouse will not work yet). Fedora displays the Troubleshooting menu (Figure 3-2). Use the DOWN ARROW key to highlight **Test this media & start Fedora Live**; press RETURN.

Anaconda displays a line labeled **Checking** that shows the percent of the disk it has checked as it verifies the contents of the installation medium. If the installation medium is good, the system boots.

Memory test   Selecting **Run a memory test** from the Troubleshooting menu runs memtest86+, a GPL-licensed, stand-alone memory test utility for x86-based computers. Press **C** to configure the test; press ESCAPE to exit and reboot. See www.memtest.org for more information.

## Fedora provides comprehensive installation documentation

tip   Visit docs.fedoraproject.org/en-US/Fedora/19/html/Installation_Quick_Start_Guide to display the Fedora Installation Quick Start Guide. To display the complete Fedora Installation Guide, visit docs.fedoraproject.org/en-US/Fedora/19/html/Installation_Guide.

GNOME   If you are booting from Fedora Desktop Live Media (what this book refers to as *a Live Image*), the system will run the GNOME desktop manager; Fedora automatically logs in as the user named **liveuser** and displays the Welcome to Fedora window. This window has two large buttons: **Try Fedora** and **Install to Hard Drive**. When you click **Try Fedora**, GNOME displays a window that explains how to install Fedora to the hard disk. Click **Close** and Fedora displays the GNOME desktop (Figure 3-3, page 60).

KDE   If you are booting from a Fedora KDE Live Image, the system will run the KDE desktop manager. When you boot from this disk, Fedora next displays a KDE startup screen and then the KDE desktop—there is no need to log in.

**optional   SEEING WHAT IS GOING ON**

If you are curious and want to see what Fedora is doing as it boots from a Live Image, remove **quiet**, which controls kernel messages, and **rhgb** (Red Hat graphical boot), which controls messages from the graphical installer, from the boot parameters. See Figure 3-8 on page 70; the list of parameters on the screen will be different from those in the figure. With the Fedora Live Image Boot menu displayed (Figure 3-1) and the Start Fedora Live line highlighted, press TAB to display the boot command-line parameters. Use the LEFT ARROW key to back up over—but not remove—any words to the right of **rhgb**. Press BACKSPACE or DEL to back up over and erase **rhgb** and **quiet** from the boot command line. Press RETURN. Now as Fedora boots, it displays information about what it is doing. Text scrolls on the screen, although sometimes too rapidly to read. When you boot Fedora from an Install Image and when you boot RHEL, this information is displayed by default: You do not have to change the command line.

# INSTALLING FEDORA/RHEL

You can install Fedora from a live session (preceding) or install Fedora/RHEL from an Install Image. Installing from a live session is simpler but does not give you the flexibility installing from an Install Image does. For example, you cannot select the language Anaconda uses, nor can you choose which software packages you will install when you install from a live session.

### See what is on the hard disk (and back it up) before installing Linux

caution   Unless you are certain the hard disk you are installing Fedora/RHEL on has nothing on it (it is a new disk) or you are sure the disk holds no information of value, it is a good idea to examine the contents of the disk before you start the installation. You can use the gnome-disks disk utility (page 78) from a live session for this purpose. Back up whatever is on the disk, even if it is in a partition the installation will not write to.

An Install Image holds many of the software packages Fedora/RHEL supports. You can install whichever package groups you like from an Install Image without connecting to the Internet. However, without an Internet connection, you will not be able to update the software once the system is installed.

A Live Image holds a limited set of software packages. Once you install from a Live Image, you must connect to the Internet to update the software on the system and to download and install additional packages.

To begin most installations, insert the medium holding a Live or an Install Image into the system and turn on or reset the system. For hard disk and network-based installations, you can use an Install or a Network Image.

Refer to "BIOS setup" on page 31 if the system does not boot from the installation medium.

**Figure 3-3**   The GNOME 3 Live desktop

# INSTALLING FROM A LIVE SESSION (FEDORA)

Bring up a live GNOME session as explained on page 56. GNOME will display a GNOME 3 desktop that has the word **Activities** in the upper-left corner of the screen.

### The Anaconda installer does not modify the live environment

tip   The changes you make as you install Fedora from a live session do not affect the live session. For example, when you set up networking for the system you are installing, the network connection for the live environment does not change.

From a GNOME 3 desktop, click **Activities**; GNOME displays icons along the left side of the screen and a text box with the words **Type to search** in it (Figure 3-3). Near the bottom of the icons is an icon depicting a hard drive with a green tick on top of it. Left-click this icon when you want to install Fedora. Continue reading at "Using Anaconda" on page 63.

# INSTALLING FROM AN INSTALL IMAGE

To install Fedora/RHEL from an Install Image, insert the installation medium and turn on or reset the system. After a few moments, the system displays the Fedora/RHEL Boot menu (Figure 3-4) and a message that says **Automatic boot in 60 seconds**. Refer to "BIOS setup" on page 31 if the system does not boot from the installation medium. Refer to "Modifying Boot Parameters (Options)" on page 70 if Fedora/RHEL does not boot or displays an error message.

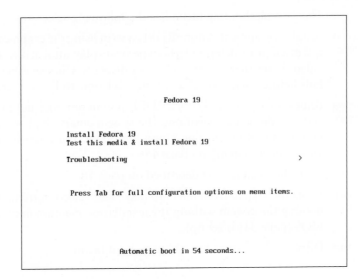

**Figure 3-4**   The Install Image Boot menu

Press the SPACE bar within 60 seconds to stop the countdown. If you do not press the SPACE bar, after 60 seconds Fedora/RHEL begins a graphical installation.

The Fedora Install Image Boot menu has the following selections:

Install Fedora   Installs a Fedora/RHEL system using the Anaconda graphical installer.

Test this media & install Fedora   Tests the installation medium and installs a Fedora/RHEL system using the Anaconda graphical installer.

Troubleshooting   Displays the Troubleshooting menu (Figure 3-5).

**Figure 3-5**   The Install Image Troubleshooting menu

The Troubleshooting menu has the following selections.

Install Fedora in basic graphics mode   Installs a graphical Fedora/RHEL system using the graphical installer. Anaconda does not attempt to determine the type of display attached to the system; it uses a basic video driver that works with most displays. Choose this selection if the installation fails before Anaconda displays the Welcome to Fedora screen (page 63).

Rescue a Fedora system   Brings up a minimal Fedora/RHEL system but does not install it. After detecting the system's disks and partitions, the system enters single-user/rescue mode and allows you to mount an existing Linux filesystem. For more information refer to "Rescue an Installed System" on page 456.

Run a memory test   Runs the memory test described on page 58.

Boot from local drive   Boots the system from the hard disk. This selection frequently has the same effect as booting the system without the installation medium in place (depending on how the BIOS [page 31] is set up).

Return to main menu   Displays the Fedora Install Image Boot menu.

# THE ANACONDA INSTALLER

Anaconda, which is written in Python and C, identifies the hardware, loads drivers, probes for the devices it will use during installation, builds the filesystems, starts the X server, and installs the Fedora/RHEL operating system. Anaconda can run in graphical interactive mode (default), limited textual mode (see the **text** on page 72), or automated mode (see "Editing a Kickstart Script" on page 83).

Exactly which screens Anaconda displays depends on whether you are installing Fedora from a live session, an Install Image, or a Network Image; whether you are installing RHEL; which paths you pick through the installation process; and which parameters you specify on the boot command line. Unless you tell it not to, Anaconda probes the video card and monitor, and starts a native X server.

While it is running, Anaconda opens the virtual consoles (page 121) shown in Table 3-1. You can display a virtual console by pressing CONTROL-ALT-F*x*, where *x* is the virtual console number and F*x* is the function key that corresponds to the virtual console number.

**Table 3-1**   Virtual console assignments during installation

| Virtual console | Install Image | Live Image |
|---|---|---|
| 1 | Installation dialog | GUI interactive installation |
| 2 | Shell | Login prompt (log in as **liveuser**) |
| 3 | Installation log | Installation log |
| 4 | Storage log | Login prompt (log in as **liveuser**) |
| 5 | Program log | Program log |

**Table 3-1**    Virtual console assignments during installation (continued)

| Virtual console | Install Image | Live Image |
|---|---|---|
| 6 | Login prompt | Login prompt (log in as **liveuser**) |
| 7 | GUI interactive installation | Nothing |

At any time during the installation, you can switch to virtual console 2 (by pressing CONTROL-ALT-F2) and give commands to see what is going on. Do not give any commands that change any part of the installation process. To switch back to the graphical installation screen, press CONTROL-ALT-F1 (Live Image) or CONTROL-ALT-F7 (Install Image).

## TESTING THE INSTALLATION MEDIUM

The first time you use an installation medium, select **Test this media & install Fedora** from the Boot menu and press RETURN to boot the system. Fedora displays a few lines before displaying a line that starts with **Checking**. This line shows the percent of the disk Anaconda has checked as it verifies the contents of the installation medium. If the installation medium is good, the system boots. If you use the same medium again, you do not have to test it: Select **Install Fedora**.

A DVD might fail the media test if the software that was used to burn the disk did not include padding. If a DVD fails the media test, try booting using the **nodma** parameter. See page 70 for information on adding parameters to the boot command line. If the DVD passes the media test when you boot the system using the **nodma** parameter, the DVD is good; reboot the system without this parameter before installing Fedora/RHEL. If you install Linux after having booted using this parameter, the kernel will be set up to always use this parameter. As a consequence, the installation and operation of the system can be slow.

## USING ANACONDA

Welcome to Fedora    Anaconda displays the Welcome to Fedora screen after it obtains enough information to start the X Window System. Scroll and click to highlight the language you want to use for installation. This language is not necessarily the same language the installed system will display. Click **Continue**. Anaconda displays the Installation Summary screen.

## THE INSTALLATION SUMMARY SCREEN

Anaconda takes a while to load the information the Installation Summary screen displays (Figure 3-6, next page). While it is loading, some items are grayed out. You must wait until Anaconda finishes loading this information and the items are no longer grayed out before you can select these items. *You might need to scroll down to display the Storage item.*

Typically an orange bar that holds an exclamation point in a triangle and the words **Please complete items marked with this icon before continuing to the next step** appears at the bottom of the window. While this bar is displayed the button labeled **Begin Installation** is grayed out to indicate it will not work. The only items you must

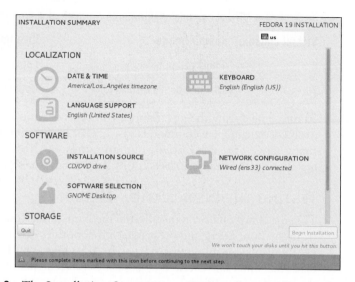

**Figure 3-6**   The Installation Summary screen (scroll to display the Storage item)

open and modify are those that display this icon. The items displayed when you are installing Fedora from a live session are a subset of those displayed when you install from an Install Image.

Click on an item to display a screen that allows you to work with that item. Click **Done** to return to the Installation Summary screen. The items that appear in the Installation Summary screen are divided into three groups: Localization, Software (not from a live installation), and Storage.

### You do not need to open most items on the Installation Summary screen

tip   Each item on the Installation Summary screen displays a note about what Anaconda has chosen for that item. You do not need to open an item if it is set properly. For example, if the Date & Time item shows **America/Los_Angeles timezone** and that is correct, you do not need to open this item. Frequently the only item you need to open is Installation Destination (page 67).

### LOCALIZATION

Date & Time   The Date & Time screen displays a world map that allows you to specify the local time zone. Click a city in the local time zone; Anaconda displays the name of the city in the spin box labeled **City**. Alternately, you can use the spin boxes labeled **Region** and **City** to specify a city.

By default, Anaconda sets up the new system to use NTP (Network Time Protocol) to keep the system clock accurate. If you do not want to use NTP, click the switch labeled Network Time to set it to **Off** and use the widgets at the bottom of the screen to set the system clock.

Keyboard   The Keyboard Layout screen allows you to specify the type of keyboard that will be attached to the installed system. The box on the left side of this screen displays available keyboard layouts. The entry at the top of the list is the default layout to be used both during installation and for the installed system. Use the buttons at the bottom of this box to add layouts and remove, move, and test the highlighted layout.

You can specify a keyboard for use during installation only, but you can specify only keyboards that are in the list on the Keyboard Layout screen. Use the small keyboard button to make this change. The button is located at the upper-right of all installation screens.

Language Support Not available with a live installation. In the Language Support screen, put ticks in the check boxes adjacent to the languages you want to install.

### SOFTWARE
Not available with a live installation.

Installation Source Typically you install Fedora from the medium you booted from. If that is the case you do not need to open the Installation Source screen. This screen allows you to

- Specify as the installation source either the medium you booted from (**Auto-detected installation media**) or a location (URL) on the network
- Choose to verify the medium you booted from
- Install updates as Anaconda installs the system
- Specify additional repositories (page 533) to use during installation.

The top part of the Installation Source screen is labeled **Which installation source would you like to use?** and has two radio buttons. By default, **Auto-detected installation media** is selected and displays the name of the device that holds and the label on the medium. Click the button labeled **Verify** to test that the image on the installation medium is good.

### Test the installation medium

caution It is possible for data to become corrupted while fetching an installation image; it is also possible for a transient error to occur while writing an image to a recordable medium. When you boot from an installation medium, the button labeled **Verify** on the Installation Source screen allows you to verify that the image on the installation medium does not contain any errors. Testing the installation medium takes a few minutes but can save you hours of aggravation if the installation fails due to a bad medium.

The second radio button in this section is labeled **On the network** and allows you to specify a Web, FTP, or NFS URL. When you select **Closest mirror** from the drop-down list, Anaconda finds the closest Fedora mirror and downloads packages from that site; after you click **Done**, Anaconda takes a moment to locate the closest mirror. If you reopen the Installation Source screen after selecting **Closest mirror**, Anaconda reverts to the installation medium and not installing updates.

By default Anaconda does not install updates while it installs Fedora/RHEL: You update the software after you install the system. Remove the tick from the check box labeled **Don't install the latest available software updates** to cause Anaconda to update software as it installs it.

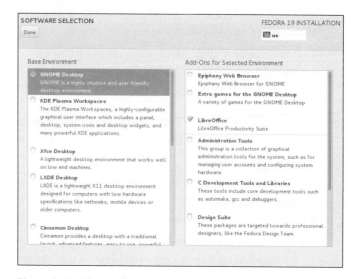

**Figure 3-7**   The Software Selection screen

The bottom portion of the screen allows you to specify additional repositories (page 542) that Anaconda can use during installation.

Network Configuration  If the local system is connected to a network that runs a DHCP server (page 491), Anaconda configures the network automatically and you do not have to open the Network Configuration screen. This screen

- Displays information about the network interface and connection Anaconda is using

- Allows you to turn off the network connection

- Allows you to (re)configure the network

- Allows you to specify a hostname for the installed system

When you click the button labeled **Configure**, Anaconda displays a window that allows you to modify the network connection.

Enter the hostname of the installed system in the text box labeled **Hostname** at the bottom of the screen.

Software Selection  The Software Selection screen (Figure 3-7) allows you to select which environmental package group and add-on package groups you want to install. An installation from a Network Image allows you to select from more package groups than does installation from an Install Image. By default, Anaconda installs the GNOME desktop and the LibreOffice productivity suite.

The left side of the Software Selection screen is labeled **Base Environment** and allows you to specify an environmental package group that specifies a desktop environment (e.g., GNOME, KDE, LXDE) or a system function (e.g., Web server, Infrastructure Server). You can make only one selection from this column. All the desktops install appropriate networking software and the Firefox Web browser. The Basic Desktop selection allows you to specify more than one desktop on the right side of the screen. The Minimal Install selection installs as few software packages as possible for a textual system (no GUI). The right side of the screen allows you to select package groups that are typically used with the base environment you selected on the left. (Fedora; RHEL selections differ slightly).

### Use a Minimal Install for older, slower hardware

tip  The last entry in the Base Environment column is Minimal Install. Select this entry for older, slower hardware. This selection installs a system that has no GUI, just a command-line (textual) interface. If the system does not have enough memory to perform a graphical installation, perform a textual installation using the **text** boot parameter (page 72) and VNC (page 72) or Kickstart (pages 71 and 83).

### You can select only package groups, not individual packages

tip  To streamline the installation process, the new Anaconda allows you to specify which package groups you want to install but not which packages. You must add or remove individual packages after the installation is complete. Visit ohjeezlinux.wordpress.com/2013/02/07/anaconda-packaging-retrospective for background information. Use Kickstart (pages 71 and 83) if you require more granular control over package selection.

#### STORAGE

Installation Destination  You might need to scroll down to display the Installation Destination selection. At a minimum, Anaconda requires you to confirm where you want to install Fedora/RHEL, although this screen gives you many more choices.

By default, with a single empty disk, Anaconda installs Fedora/RHEL on the whole disk. If the disk is not empty and there is enough free space (page 36) on the disk, Anaconda installs Fedora/RHEL in the free space.

If this default is acceptable, open the Installation Destination screen; a tick will appear over the single disk (similar to Figure 3-9 on page 73). Click **Done**; Anaconda displays the Installation Options dialog. This dialog allows you to choose whether you want to review and/or modify the default disk setup or whether you want to continue without reviewing it. The bottom of the screen has a check box that allows you to encrypt the data on the disk (page 30). For the simplest installation, do not make any change; click **Continue**.

If there is not enough free space to install Fedora/RHEL, if the computer has more than one hard disk, if you want to reclaim disk space from an exiting partition, or if you want to customize the disk partitions, see "Advanced Disk Configuration" on page 72.

## BEGIN COPYING FILES

After making the changes you want (and those that Anaconda requires) to the Installation Summary items, click the button labeled **Begin Installation**. While it is installing Fedora/RHEL, Anaconda places a Kickstart file (page 83) that corresponds to your selections in **/root/anaconda-ks.cfg**.

Installing Fedora/RHEL can take a while. The amount of time depends on the hardware you are installing the operating system on and the number of software packages you are installing.

### USER SETTINGS

While Anaconda installs Linux, it displays the User Settings screen. On this screen you must specify a password for the **root** user and set up a user.

Root Password    The Root Password screen allows you to enter a password for the **root** user (Superuser) and confirm that password by entering it a second time. See page 136 for information on selecting a secure password and page 422 for information on **root** privileges. Although you can specify a weak password, doing so is not recommended. When you specify a weak password, Anaconda tells you why it is weak on the yellow bar at the bottom of the screen. Click **Done** twice to accept a weak password or once to accept a stronger password.

User Creation    The User Creation screen allows you to add a user to the system by specifying the new user's full name, username, and password. See "Root Password," above for information on specifying a password. You can choose to make the user an administrator (see the tip named "Administrator" on page 422) and require a password for the user (see the tip on page 135 for information on why having a password is a good idea). Click the button labeled **Advanced** to work with the user's home directory, *UID* (page 1278), *group ID* (page 1252), and group membership (see **/etc/group** on page 506).

Although Anaconda allows you to skip creating a user, you will have to create one before you can log in. The exception is when you install a minimal (command-line) system on which you can log in as **root** without creating a user.

## REBOOTING THE SYSTEM

When Anaconda displays the message saying it has successfully installed Fedora/RHEL and asks you to reboot the system, click **Reboot** and remove the installation medium.

## gnome-initial-setup: SETTING UP A USER

When the system reboots, it is running Linux. The first time each user logs in, Fedora/RHEL runs gnome-initial-setup, which asks a few questions before allowing the user to continue.

Welcome    First, gnome-initial-setup displays the Welcome window. Make sure the language you want to use has a tick next to it before you click **Next**.

Input Sources    The Input Sources (also input methods) window allows you to specify characters and symbols that are not present on the keyboard attached to the system. For example, some French and Chinese characters do not appear on a en_US keyboard; you have to press combinations of keys to type these characters. These combinations of keys are input sources.

If the language that appears in this window is appropriate, click **Next**. Otherwise click the plus sign (**+**) and select additional languages. Click the small picture of a keyboard to display a keyboard on which you can test the highlighted language. When you have selected an appropriate input source, click **Next**.

Online Accounts   Clicking **Add Accounts** on the Online Accounts window opens the Add Account window. From this window you can add Google, Facebook, and other accounts to the Fedora/RHEL system. When you add an account you specify your credentials for that account. The online accounts service stores account information in GConf (a system for storing application preferences) and passwords in GNOME Keyring so you have to enter this information only once. Click **Next**.

Thank You   The Thank You window tells you that you have finished setting up the new system. Click **Start Using GNOME 3**.

The gnome-initial-setup utility displays an animated presentation that explains how to get started using GNOME. You can press ESCAPE to stop the presentation and then click the **X** at the upper-right of the GNOME Help window to close it.

## INITIALIZING DATABASES AND UPDATING THE SYSTEM

It is important to update all software on a newly installed system. You can wait for the system to prompt you or you can give the following command from a virtual terminal to update the software; you will need to supply the **root** password. See page 538 for more information on the yum **update** command. Depending on the network connection and the number of packages that need to be updated, this command can run for a long time.

```
$ su -c 'yum -y update'
```

Updating the **mandb** database ensures the whatis and apropos utilities (both on page 130) will work properly. Similarly, updating the **locate** database ensures that locate will work properly. (The locate utility indexes and allows you to search for files on the system quickly and securely.) Instead of updating these databases when you install the system, you can wait for **crond** (page 607) to update them, but be aware that whatis, apropos, and locate will not work for a while. The best way to update these databases is to manually run the cron scripts that normally run daily. Give the following commands:

```
$ su -c /etc/cron.daily/man-db.cron
$ su -c /etc/cron.daily/mlocate.cron
```

These utilities run for several minutes and might complain about not being able to find a file or two. When the system displays a prompt, the **mandb** and **locate** databases are up-to-date. Continue with Chapter 4.

## INSTALLATION TASKS

This section details some common tasks you might need to perform during or after installation. It covers modifying the boot parameters, using Anaconda to partition the disk during installation, using gnome-disks to view and modify partitions, using LVs (logical volumes) to facilitate disk partitioning, using Kickstart to automate installation, and setting up a system that will boot two or more operating systems (e.g., Windows and Linux; a dual-boot system).

```
                              Fedora 19


              Install Fedora 19
              Test this media & install Fedora 19

              Troubleshooting                                      >




  > vmlinuz initrd=initrd.img inst.stage2=hd:LABEL=Fedora\x2019\x20x86_64 quiet_
```

**Figure 3-8**   The Fedora Install Image Boot menu showing boot parameters (options)

#  MODIFYING BOOT PARAMETERS (OPTIONS)

To modify boot parameters, you must interrupt the automatic boot process by pressing the SPACE bar while the system is counting down when you first boot from a Live Image (page 57) or an Install Image (page 60). When you press the SPACE bar, Fedora displays the Fedora Live Image Boot menu (Figure 3-1, page 57) or the Fedora Install Image Boot menu (Figure 3-4, page 61). Use the ARROW keys to highlight the selection you want *before* proceeding. With the desired selection highlighted, press the TAB key to display the boot command-line parameters (Figure 3-8).

Type a SPACE before you enter any parameters. You can specify multiple parameters separated by SPACEs. Press RETURN to boot the system. For more information on boot parameters, refer to www.kernel.org/doc/Documentation/kernel-parameters.txt or use Google to search for **linux boot parameters**.

### What to do if the installation does not work

tip   On some hardware, the installation might pause for as long as ten minutes. Before experimenting with other fixes, try waiting for a while. If the installation hangs, try booting with one or more of the boot parameters described in this section.

Following are some of the parameters you can add to the boot command line. If you encounter problems with the display during installation, supply the **nofb** parameter, which turns off video memory.

Many of these parameters can be combined. For example, to install Linux on a monitor with a resolution of $1024 \times 768$, without probing for any devices, supply the following parameters.

```
resolution=1024x768 noprobe
```

noacpi    Disables ACPI (Advanced Configuration and Power Interface). This parameter is useful for systems that do not support ACPI or that have problems with their ACPI implementation. The default is to enable ACPI. Specifying **acpi=off** has the same effect.

noapic    Disables APIC (Advanced Programmable Interrupt Controller). The default is to enable APIC.

noapm    Disables APM (Advanced Power Management). The default is to enable APM. Specifying **apm=off** has the same effect.

nodma    Turns off DMA (direct memory access) for all disk controllers. This parameter might make buggy controllers (or controllers with buggy drivers) more reliable, but also cause them to perform very slowly because the connected devices have to run in PIO mode instead of DMA mode. It can facilitate testing DVDs that were not written correctly.

nofb    (**no framebuffer**) Turns off the framebuffer (video memory). This option is useful if problems arise when the graphical phase of the installation starts.

irqpoll    Changes the way the kernel handles interrupts.

ks=**URI**    Specifies the location of a Kickstart file (page 83) to use to control the installation process. The *URI* is the pathname or network location of the Kickstart file. Use this parameter with the **text** parameter (next page) to perform an installation without the use of a GUI (a textual installation).

Typically *URI* points to an NFS or Web server using one of these formats:

*ks=nfs:server:/pathname*

*ks=http://server/pathname*

where **server** is the FQDN or IP address of the server and *pathname* is the absolute pathname of the Kickstart file. For example, if Max set up an NFS server on the system at 192.168.206.1, put a Kickstart file named **ksmax2.cfg** in his home directory, and wanted to perform a textual installation, he might add the following parameters to the end of the boot command line.

```
text ks=192.168.206.1:/home/max/ksmax2.cfg
```

For a complete list of options visit the Web site at fedoraproject.org/wiki/Anaconda/ Kickstart#Chapter_6._Making_the_ Kickstart_File_Available.

nolapic    Disables local APIC. The default is to enable local APIC.

lowres    Runs the installation program at a resolution of $640 \times 480$ pixels. See also **resolution** (next page).

mem=**xxx**M    Overrides the detected memory size. Replace **xxx** with the number of megabytes of RAM in the computer.

repo=**URI**    Specifies an installation source. For example, you can use the following parameter to start installing from the specified server:

```
repo=http://dl.fedoraproject.org/pub/fedora/linux/releases/19/Fedora/x86_64/os
```

noprobe   Disables hardware probing for all devices, including NICs (network interface cards), graphics cards, and the monitor. This option forces you to select devices from a list. You must know exactly which cards or chips the system uses when you use this parameter. Use **noprobe** when probing causes the installation to hang or otherwise fail. This parameter allows you to supply arguments for each device driver you specify.

rescue   Sets up the system to rescue an installed system; see page 456 for details.

resolution=*WxH*   Specifies the resolution of the monitor you are using for a graphical installation. For example, **resolution=1024x768** specifies a monitor with a resolution of 1024 × 768 pixels.

text   Installs Linux without the use of a graphical interface. See the adjacent tip.

### A textual installation is not usually very useful

tip   A textual installation does not allow you to partition the disk or specify which packages to install and is therefore usually not very useful. If you want to install Linux without using a GUI, you can install it using a VNC connection (next) or a Kickstart file. See page 83 for information on creating a Kickstart file and page 71 for information on the **ks** boot parameter that allows you to install Linux using a Kickstart file. To perform a textual installation using a Kickstart file you must specify the **text** parameter in the Kickstart file. If you want to perform a textual installation using a VNC connection, you must specify the **text** parameter in addition to **vnc**.

vnc   Installs Linux via a VNC (virtual network computing) remote desktop session. After providing an IP address, you can control the installation remotely using a VNC client from a remote computer. You can download a free VNC client that runs on several platforms from www.realvnc.com. Use yum (page 534) to install the **tigervnc** software package to run a VNC client on a Fedora/RHEL system.

vncpassword=
*passwd*   Enables a password for a VNC connection. This option requires that you also use the **vnc** option.

noselinux   Disables SELinux (page 472) on the installed system.

## ADVANCED DISK CONFIGURATION

"Installation Destination" on page 67 covered the simplest disk configuration situation: a single hard disk with enough space to hold the new operating system. This section covers selecting disks, installation options, manual/custom partitioning, reclaiming disk space, and working with LVs. See page 36 for a discussion of the setup of the hard disk and partitions.

The Anaconda Installation Destination screen provides a graphical disk-partitioning facility that can add, delete, and modify partitions on a hard disk. This screen is available only during installation; it cannot be run on its own. You can use gnome-disks (page 78), parted (page 614), or fdisk to manipulate partitions after you install Fedora/RHEL. As explained earlier, if you want a basic set of partitions, you can allow Anaconda to partition the hard disk automatically. See page 44 for a discussion of LVM (Logical Volume Manager) including PVs, VGs, and LVs.

**INSTALLATION DESTINATION**                                               FEDORA 19 INSTALLATION

Done                                                                              us

Select the device(s) you'd like to install to. They will be left untouched until you click on the main menu's "Begin Installation" button.

**Local Standard Disks**

204.8 GB

VMware, VMware Virtual S
sda  /  204.8 GB free

*Disks left unselected here will not be touched.*

**Specialized & Network Disks**

Add a disk...

Full disk summary and bootloader...
1 disk selected; 204.8 GB capacity; 204.8 GB free

**Figure 3-9**   The Installation Destination screen showing a single, selected disk

## SELECTING DISKS

The Local Standard Disks section of the Installation Destination screen lists the disks attached to the local system. Click **Add a disk** under Specialized & Network Disks to work with other types of storage devices including *SAN* (page 1271) devices.

If the local system has one disk only, a tick will appear over that disk indicating that disk is selected and Anaconda will install the new operating system on it (Figure 3-9). If the system has two or more disks, Anaconda does not select any disks so no ticks appear. Select one or more disks for the new operating system by clicking the associated disk icons; Anaconda places a tick over the disk icon. Anaconda does not alter the disks without ticks (the disks you have not selected). Once you have selected the disks you want to use for the installation, click **Done**. Anaconda displays the Installation Options window.

## INSTALLATION OPTIONS

The Installation Options window summarizes the installation disk setup and offers options appropriate to the situation (Figure 3-10, next page). It also allows you to specify a partitioning scheme (standard partitions, LVM [page 44], or BTRFS [B-tree file system]) and encrypt the data on the disks. It always displays a button at the lower-left of the window labeled **Cancel & add more disks**. This button closes the Installation Options dialog and redisplays the Installation Destination screen.

### Here *free space* includes unpartitioned disk space

tip    The Installation Options window tells you how much free space is on the disk(s) you selected and advises you if that is not enough space to install Fedora/RHEL. This dialog uses the term "free space" to mean both free space and unpartitioned disk space (page 36).

**INSTALLATION OPTIONS**

You have **34.80 GB** of free space, which is enough to install Fedora.  What would you like to do?

○ Automatically configure my Fedora installation to the disk(s) I selected and return me to the main menu.

○ I want more space. Guide me through shrinking and/or removing partitions so I can have more space for Fedora.

○ I want to review/modify my disk partitions before continuing.

**Partition scheme:**   | LVM ⌄ |

☐ Encrypt my data. I'll set a passphrase later.

[ Cancel & add more disks ]                                        [ Continue ]

**Figure 3-10**   The Installation Options window showing several choices

When enough free space exists, the Installation Options window offers you the choice of automatically partitioning the disk(s) or having you review and modify the disk partitions. If there are partitions in use by other operating systems that Anaconda can remove or shrink, it adds the choice of guiding you through the process of reclaiming that space. Select one of these radio buttons and click **Continue**.

If there is not enough space on the disks, Anaconda tells you how much space the new operating system needs based on your selection of software packages (page 66). It also summarizes how much free space exists and how much space you can reclaim from partitions in use by other operating systems. In this case it presents two buttons: **Custom partitioning** (next) and **Reclaim space** (page 77). The first of these buttons displays the Manual Partitioning screen and the second displays the Reclaim Disk Space screen.

## LPI   MANUAL/CUSTOM PARTITIONING

The box on the left side of the Manual Partitioning screen displays information about the system you are installing (e.g., New Fedora 19 Installation) and other systems Anaconda finds on the disk (e.g., Unknown [a Windows system]; Figure 3-11). At the bottom of the box are buttons you can use to work with partitions and boxes that list the available and total space on the disk(s) you selected in the Installation Destination screen.

At the left of each system entry is a triangle you can click to expand and collapse that entry. At first the entry for the system you are installing contains only instructions for setting it up and a note on the right side of the screen that says mount points will appear here once you set them up.

**Figure 3-11**   The Manual Partitioning screen I

Automatic partition creation

To have Anaconda create partitions automatically, click **Click here to create them automatically**. Anaconda creates swap, **/boot, /** (root), and (if there is enough space) **/home** partitions and displays them in the Manual Partitioning screen so you can review and modify them (Figure 3-12).

**Figure 3-12**   The Manual Partitioning screen II

**ADD A NEW MOUNT POINT**

More customization options are available
after creating the mount point below.

Mount Point:     /var

Desired Capacity:  50 GB

Cancel    Add mount point

**Figure 3-13**    The Add a New Mount Point window

Add partition    To create a new partition on a hard disk, *the hard disk must have enough free space to accommodate the partition;* see "Reclaiming Disk Space" on the next page.

To set up a new partition and mount point (the name of the directory the partition will be mounted on; page 38), click the plus sign (**+**) button at the bottom of the box; Anaconda opens the Add a New Mount Point window (Figure 3-13). Specify the mount point and size for the new partition and click **Add mount point**. Because of block-size constraints, the final partition is not usually exactly the size you specify. Anaconda accepts a suffix of **T** for terabytes, **G** for gigabytes, and **M** for megabytes. If you leave the size blank, Anaconda makes the partition as large as possible. If the disk space you requested is not available, Anaconda allocates as much space as is available.

### Anaconda does not write to the disk until you click Begin Installation

tip    Making changes on the Manual Partitioning screen does not affect the disks immediately; you can click **Reset All** at any time to reread configuration information from the disk(s) and restore the screen so it contains the information it originally contained. Only when you click **Begin Installation** does Anaconda write to the disks.

Modify partition    To modify a mount point/partition, highlight the mount point on the left side of the screen, make changes on the right, and click **Update Settings**. Using this window, you can change the mount point or size of a partition, or format the partition as another type (e.g., **ext3**, **vfat**, **swap**, etc.). See Figure 3-12 on the previous page.

Remove partition    To remove a mount point/partition, highlight the mount point on the left side of the screen and click the minus sign (**–**) button at the bottom of the box.

Swap partition    If another system on the disk has a swap partition, Anaconda shares it with the system being installed. Otherwise it is a good idea to set up a swap partition for the system being installed. For more information on the swap partition see page 40.

Partition location    When Anaconda creates a partition on a system on which you have selected more than one disk, it decides which disk the partition will reside on. To move a partition to another disk, highlight the partition. If Anaconda can move the highlighted partition to another disk, the tool icon button at the bottom of the box will be active (not grayed out). Click this button to display the Configure Mount Point window. Click to highlight the disk you want the partition to reside on. If appropriate, you can select more than one partition by holding down the SHIFT key as you click the second and subsequent partitions.

## SETTING UP A RAID DEVICE

To set up a RAID array (page 42), click the mount point/partition you want to change to a RAID device, select RAID from the drop-down list labeled **Device Type**, and click Update Settings. Anaconda changes the partition to a RAID device. You can then select the type of RAID device you want from the drop-down list labeled **RAID Level**.

## RECLAIMING DISK SPACE

There are several situations in which you might want to reclaim disk space by shrinking or deleting a partition. Assuming you are not installing on a clean disk, any partitions on the disk that are not full are candidates for reclaiming space. A typical example occurs when you are working with a hard disk with a single partition that occupies the entire disk, such as when you are setting up a dual-boot system by adding Fedora/RHEL to a Windows system (page 84). In this case you might be able to reclaim space from the Windows partition to install Fedora/RHEL. According to the ntfsresize man page, you do not need to defragment a Windows partition before resizing. The process of resizing a partition is the same regardless of the type of partition: You can use the Reclaim Space window to resize Windows, Linux, and other types of partitions.

To reclaim disk space, click **Reclaim space** on the Installation Options window; Anaconda displays the Reclaim Disk Space window (Figure 3-14). This window displays a table listing the partitions on each of the disks you selected in the Installation Destination window (page 67). The table shows the mount point, device name, type of filesystem, amount of reclaimable space, and action to be taken for each partition. Below the table are three buttons: **Preserve, Delete,** and **Shrink to.** The default action is to preserve a partition.

**Figure 3-14**   The Reclaim Disk Space window showing the slider

As with other instructions that modify disks, Anaconda takes no action until you click **Begin Installation** in the Installation Summary screen (page 63). Highlight the partition you want to work with and click **Delete** to delete the partition or **Shrink to** to reclaim space from the partition. For Anaconda to reclaim space from (shrink) a partition, the partition must not be full of data.

When you highlight a partition and click **Shrink to**, Anaconda displays a slider below the table (Figure 3-14, previous page). The left end of the slider represents the minimum size the partition can be shrunk to and the right end the maximum (not shrunk at all). Below the slider are labels that show these sizes; above the slider is a label that moves with the slider and shows the selected size of the partition. The smaller you make the partition, the more space there is for the system you are installing. Click and drag the slider until the partition is the size you want. Repeat this procedure for each partition you want to resize or delete and then click **Reclaim space**. Anaconda will not resize the partition until you click **Begin Installation**.

### WORKING WITH LVs

When you instruct Anaconda to partition the hard disk with a default layout, it uses LVM (page 44) to set up most of the hard disk, creating LVs instead of partitions. It places **/boot** on the first partition on the drive, not under the control of LVM. LVM creates a VG (volume group) named **fedora** that occupies the rest of the disk space. Within this VG it creates two or three LVs: root (**/**, **fedora-root**), swap (**fedora-swap**), and if there is room, **/home** (**fedora-home**). The swap LV occupies up to a few gigabytes; the root LV takes up to about 50 gigabytes. If there is room for a **/home** LV, it occupies the rest of **fedora**. This section explains how to make the **/home** LV smaller so you can add an additional LV to **fedora**. If the hard drive on the machine you are working with is small and Anaconda does not create a **/home** LV, you can follow this example by making the root LV smaller instead.

To make the **/home** LV smaller and make room for additional LVs, first highlight the **/home** LV (**fedora-home**) and then change the value in the text box labeled **Desired Capacity** to a smaller value. Figure 3-15 shows the size of the **fedora-home** LV being changed to 100 gigabytes. Click **Update Settings**.

Once you decrease the size of the **fedora-home** LV, the Manual Partitioning screen shows an increase in available space. You can now add another LV to **fedora**. Click the plus sign (**+**) to display the Add a New Mount Point window (Figure 3-13, page 76). Select a value from the drop-down list labeled **Mount Point** (or enter a value) and enter a value in the text box labeled Desired Capacity. Click **Add mount point**. Anaconda adds the new mount point and partition to the left side of the screen. Click **Done** when the LVs are set up the way you want.

## gnome-disks: THE GNOME DISK UTILITY

The gnome-disks graphical disk utility can create, remove, and modify partitions and filesystems on many types of media, including internal and external hard disks, CD/DVDs, and USB flash drives. It can encrypt partitions and change passwords on already encrypted partitions.

**Figure 3-15**   The Manual Partitioning screen; changing the size of an LV

Unless you are certain the hard disk on which you are installing Fedora/RHEL has nothing on it (it is a new disk) or you are sure the disk holds no information of value, it is a good idea to examine the contents of the disk before you start the installation. The gnome-disks disk utility (**gnome-disk-utility** package) is a good tool for this job. Open the Disks window by giving the command **gnome-disks** from an Enter a Command window (ALT-F2) or a terminal emulator (page 120).

The Disks window is divided into three sections (Figure 3-16): The left side holds the Devices section, a list of CD/DVD drives, hard disks, and other devices; the

**Figure 3-16**   The Disks window

**Figure 3-17**   Browsing a partition using gnome-disks

top-right section holds information about the device that is highlighted on the left; and the bottom-right displays information about the partition highlighted in the graphical representation of the hard drive in the middle of the right side.

When you select a hard disk in the Devices section on the left, gnome-disks displays information about that disk on the right. Click one of the partitions in the graphical representation of a hard disk, and gnome-disks displays information about that partition at the bottom of the right side.

From this window you can view, create, and delete partitions. You can save time if you use gnome-disks to examine a hard disk and Anaconda to set up the partitions you install Fedora/RHEL on.

## DISPLAYING THE CONTENTS OF A FILESYSTEM

To display the contents of a filesystem, select the partition holding the filesystem as described above and click the triangle at the bottom-left of the graphical representation of the disk to mount it. Figure 3-16 on the prvious page shows a square in place of the triangle because the partition is already mounted. When you click the mount point (the link following **Contents ... mounted at**) at the bottom of the right side of the window, Nautilus displays the filesystem in a Nautilus window (Figure 3-17; more about Nautilus appears on page 102). When you have finished examining the contents of the filesystem, click the square to unmount the filesystem.

## WRITING A PARTITION TABLE

A new disk does not have a partition table (page 36) and looks similar to the disk highlighted in Figure 3-18. At the bottom-right of the Disks window, **Unknown**

**Figure 3-18**   A disk without a partition table

follows the **Contents** label and the graphical representation of the disk is marked **Unknown**. If the disk you are working with already has a partition table, skip to the next section.

To partition a hard disk, click the gears icon at the upper-right of the Disks window (not the one below the graphical image of the disk) and select **Format** from the pop-up menu: gnome-disks opens a Format Volume window. Unless you want to explicitly erase the data on the disk, accept the default of **Don't overwrite existing data** from the drop-down list labeled **Erase**. In the drop-down list labeled **Partitioning**, accept the default of **Compatible with modern systems ....** You can enter a name in the text box labeled **Name** if you like. Click **Format**; gnome-disks displays another window to confirm you want to format the disk. Click **Format** again. The gnome-disks utility takes a moment to format the disk, quickly displaying some information while it is working. When it is done, **GUID Partition Table** follows the **Partitioning** label, the graphical representation of the disk is marked **Free Space** (page 36), and **Unallocated Space** follows the **Contents** label.

If you want to create a single filesystem that occupies the entire disk drive, instead of following the instructions in the preceding paragraph, click the gears icon in the graphical representation of the disk and select Format from the drop-down menu; gnome-disks opens a Format Volume window. To create a filesystem, make a selection from the Type drop-down menu and click **Format**.

## CREATING A PARTITION AND A FILESYSTEM

Once you have created a partition table, you will be able to create a partition that holds a filesystem in the free space. Highlight the area marked Free Space and click

**Figure 3-19**   The gnome-disks Create Partition window

the plus sign at the bottom of the graphical image of the disk; gnome-disks opens a Create Partition window (Figure 3-19).

Use the slider at the top of the window or the spin box labeled **Partition Size** to specify the size of the new partition. The value in the spin box labeled **Free Space Following** changes relative to the partition size.

### Encrypt to protect data, especially on laptops

security | Encrypting partitions can prevent theft of sensitive data, especially on laptops, which are prone to theft. If you decide to encrypt a partition, remember the password: You will not get your data back without it.

Unless you want to explicitly erase the data on the disk, accept the default of **Don't overwrite existing data** from the drop-down list labeled **Erase**. In the drop-down list labeled **Type**, accept the default of **Ext4**; if you want the filesystem to be encrypted (page 30), select **LUKS + Ext4**. If you choose to encrypt the filesystem, Anaconda will ask for a passphrase. You will need this passphrase to log in on the system.

You can optionally enter a disk label in the text box labeled **Name**. This name is not the mount point for the disk. Click **Create**; gnome-disks creates the filesystem. Now the graphical representation of the disk is divided to represent the division of the hard disk, and **Contents** corresponds to the highlighted section of the graphical representation (Ext4 or Unallocated Space). If you did not use all the free space, you can create additional partitions and filesystems in the same manner.

## DELETING A PARTITION

Before deleting a partition, make sure it does not contain any data you need. To use the gnome-disks utility to delete a partition, highlight the partition you want to delete in the graphical representation of the hard disk, unmount it if necessary (click the square), and click the minus sign at the bottom of that representation. After checking with you, gnome-disks deletes the partition.

## USING SMART TO DISPLAY DISK PERFORMANCE INFORMATION

SMART (Self-Monitoring, Analysis, and Reporting Technology) monitors hard disks and attempts to predict hard disk failures. To see a SMART report for a disk on the

**Figure 3-20**   SMART data as displayed by gnome-disks

system, click the gears icon at the upper-right of the Disks window (not the one below the graphical image of the disk) and select **Smart Data & Self Tests** from the pop-up menu; gnome-disks displays a window similar to the one shown in Figure 3-20. From this window you can turn SMART on or off, start a new self test, and scroll through the information about the most recent test.

# EDITING A KICKSTART SCRIPT

Kickstart is a program that automates the installation and post-installation configuration on one or more machines. To use Kickstart, you create a script (file) that provides the information you normally provide during an installation. Anaconda then refers to this file during installation. Using Kickstart, you can automate language selection, network configuration, keyboard selection, boot loader installation, disk partitioning, and more. See the **ks** boot parameter on page 71 for instructions on how to install a system using a Kickstart script.

It is easier to modify an existing Kickstart script than to write one from scratch. A good place to start is the Kickstart script Anaconda generates when you install a system (**/root/anaconda-ks.cfg**). This script holds instructions that can duplicate the system you just installed.

Another good source of sample Kickstart scripts is the packages named **fedora-kickstarts** and **custom-kickstarts**. After you install these packages look through the files in the **/usr/share/spin-kickstarts** directory hierarchy. These files are thoroughly commented; reading the comments can help you learn how to write a Kickstart script.

Textual installation   Although a typical, interactive textual installation is no longer supported, you can perform a textual installation using a Kickstart file. A line with the word **text** or **graphical** near the beginning of the Kickstart script specifies the installation environment. Alternately you can use a VNC connection to perform a textual installation. See the tip on page 72.

system-config-
kickstart   The system-config-kickstart utility (**system-config-kickstart** package) is a graphical Kickstart script editor. Although it will create a Kickstart file, you will probably have to edit

**Figure 3-21**    The Kickstart Configurator window

the resulting file by hand. This utility displays the Kickstart Configurator window (Figure 3-21). Open this window by giving the command **system-config-kickstart** from an Enter a Command window (ALT-F2) or a terminal emulator.

Figure 3-21 shows the first window the Kickstart Configurator displays. To generate a Kickstart file (**ks.cfg** by default), go through each section of this window (the items along the left side), fill in the answers, and put ticks in the appropriate check boxes. It might be helpful to start with the Kickstart installation script that Anaconda generated when you installed the system (**/root/anaconda-ks.cfg**). Click **Help** on the menubar for instructions on completing these tasks. When you are finished, click **File⇨Save**. The Kickstart Configurator gives you a chance to review the generated script before it saves the file.

# SETTING UP A DUAL-BOOT SYSTEM

A *dual-boot* system is one that can boot one of two (or more) operating systems. This section describes how to add Fedora/RHEL to a system that can boot Windows, thereby creating a system that can boot Windows or Linux. You can use the same technique for adding Fedora/RHEL to a system that runs a different version or distribution of Linux.

Before you set up a dual-boot system, you need to find disk space for the new Fedora/RHEL system. The next section discusses several ways to create the needed space.

## CREATING FREE SPACE ON A WINDOWS SYSTEM

Typically you install Fedora/RHEL in free space on a hard disk. To add Fedora/RHEL to a Windows system, you must have enough free space on a system that already holds Windows. There are several ways to provide or create this free space. The following paragraphs discuss these options in order from easiest to most difficult.

**Add a new hard disk**—Add another hard disk to the system and install Linux on the new disk, which contains only free space. This technique is very easy and clean but requires a new hard disk.

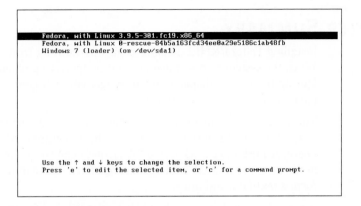

```
Fedora, with Linux 3.9.5-301.fc19.x86_64
Fedora, with Linux 0-rescue-84b5a163fcd34ee0a29e5186c1ab48fb
Windows 7 (loader) (on /dev/sda1)




          Use the ↑ and ↓ keys to change the selection.
          Press 'e' to edit the selected item, or 'c' for a command prompt.
```

**Figure 3-22**   Selecting the operating system from a dual-boot system

**Use existing free space**—If there is sufficient free space on the Windows disk, you can install Linux there. This technique is the optimal choice, but there is rarely enough free space on an installed hard disk.

**Reclaim space from a Windows partition**—Windows partitions often occupy the entire disk, which explains why reclaiming space from a Windows partition is the technique most commonly used to free up space. Windows systems typically use NTFS, FAT32, and/or FAT16 filesystems. You can reclaim space from an existing Windows partition when you install Fedora/RHEL (page 77).

**Remove a Windows partition**—If you can delete a big enough Windows partition, you can install Linux in its place. To delete a Windows partition, you must have multiple partitions under Windows and be willing to lose the data in the partition you delete. In many cases, you can save this data by moving it from the partition you will delete to another Windows partition.

Once you are sure a partition contains no useful information, you can delete it when you install Fedora/RHEL. Alternately, you can use gnome-disks from a live session to delete it (page 82). After deleting the partition, you can install Fedora/RHEL in the free space formerly occupied by the partition you deleted.

### If you install Windows after you install Linux

tip   When you install Windows as the second operating system it overwrites the existing boot loader. In this case you need to reload the boot loader. See "Reinstalling the MBR" on page 456 for instructions.

## INSTALLING FEDORA/RHEL AS THE SECOND OPERATING SYSTEM

After you have created enough free space on a Windows system, you can begin installing Fedora/RHEL in the free space you created. When you boot the updated system, you will be able to choose which operating system you want to run (Figure 3-22).

# CHAPTER SUMMARY

Installing Fedora/RHEL usually begins by booting from a Live or an Install Image. When the system boots, it displays a message saying when it will boot automatically. During the time it displays this message, you can give various commands and then have the system continue booting.

The program that installs Fedora/RHEL is named Anaconda. Anaconda calls tools that identify the hardware, build the necessary filesystems, and install the Fedora/RHEL operating system. Anaconda can run in graphical (default) interactive mode or in automated mode using Kickstart. You can use VNC or Kickstart to perform a textual installation.

Anaconda includes a graphical disk-partitioning facility that can add, delete, and modify partitions and LVs (logical volumes) on a hard disk during installation. The gnome-disks utility reports on and manipulates hard disk partitions before or after installation.

A dual-boot system can boot one of two or more operating systems, frequently Windows and Linux. The biggest task in setting up a dual-boot system, assuming you want to add Linux to a Windows system, is finding enough disk space to hold Linux.

Fedora/RHEL uses the X.org X Window System and the GNOME display manager (gdm) to provide a graphical login.

# EXERCISES

1. What is a live system? What advantages does it have over an installed system?

2. Describe the Anaconda installer.

3. Where can the installation image used by Anaconda be located?

4. Why is it important to test the installation medium? How can you do so?

5. What should you do if the graphical installer does not work?

6. When might you specify an ext2 filesystem instead of ext4?

# ADVANCED EXERCISES

7. Which utilities can you use to partition a hard disk prior to installation?

8. What do you need to do before you can install Fedora as the second operating system on a Windows machine (to create a dual-boot system)?

9. How does Anaconda set up a hard disk by default?

10. How would you turn off DMA (direct memory access) for all disk controllers when you install a new system?

# PART II

# USING FEDORA AND RED HAT ENTERPRISE LINUX

# 4

# INTRODUCTION TO FEDORA AND RED HAT ENTERPRISE LINUX

## OBJECTIVES

After reading this chapter you should be able to:

▶ Log in on the Fedora desktop

▶ Understand **root** privileges

▶ Change the desktop background

▶ Use the Nautilus File Manager to work with files

▶ Correct mistakes on a command line

▶ Explain what you can do using a window titlebar

▶ Update and install software

▶ Find documentation using man, info, and yelp

▶ Open a terminal emulator and run programs from the command line

▶ Create and run a simple shell script

One way or another you are sitting in front of a computer that is running Fedora or RHEL (Red Hat Enterprise Linux). After describing the conventions this book uses and **root** (Superuser) privileges, this chapter takes you on a tour of the system to give you some ideas about what you can do with it. The tour does not go into depth about choices, options, menus, and so on; that is left for you to experiment with and to explore in greater detail throughout later chapters of this book.

The tour covers how to log in on the system, the GNOME 3 Standard and Classic desktops, working with the desktop, the Nautilus File Manager, the Settings window, getting help, and installing software. The final part of the chapter introduces some command-line utilities and describes how to work from the command line, concluding with a section on solving problems logging in and password security.

Be sure to read the warning about the dangers of misusing the powers of **root** (Superuser) in the next section. While heeding that warning, feel free to experiment with the system: Give commands, create files, click objects, choose items from menus, follow the examples in this book, and have fun.

# CURBING YOUR POWER (SUPERUSER/root PRIVILEGES)

While you are logged in as the user named **root**, you are referred to as *Superuser* or *administrator*; you are working with **root** privileges and have extraordinary systemwide powers. Running the su or sudo utility can give you similar privileges. When working with **root** privileges, you can read from or write to almost any file on the system, execute programs that ordinary users cannot, and more. On a multiuser system you might not be able to run certain programs. Nevertheless, someone—the *system administrator*—knows the **root** password or is a member of the administrative group named **wheel**, and that person maintains the system. When you are running Linux on your own computer, you will assign a password to **root** when you install Linux. Refer to "Running Commands with **root** Privileges" on page 422 for more information.

### Do not experiment while you are working with root privileges

caution    Feel free to experiment when you are *not* working with **root** privileges. When you *are* working with **root** privileges, do only what you have to do and make sure you know exactly what you are doing. After you have completed the task at hand, revert to working as yourself. When working with **root** privileges, you can damage the system to such an extent that you will need to reinstall Linux to get it working again.

# LOGGING IN ON THE SYSTEM

When you boot a default Fedora/RHEL system, gdm (GNOME display manager) displays a Login screen (Figure 4-1) on the system console. In the middle of the screen is a list of names of users who can log in on the system. At the upper-right are icons that allow you to restart or shut down the system, adjust the volume, and display the

**Figure 4-1** The GNOME Login screen

universal access menu that allows you to change accessibility preferences (e.g., make the text larger or display a high-contrast desktop).

To log in, click your name; gdm displays the Password screen. Enter your password and press RETURN. If gdm displays an error message, try clicking your name and entering your password again. Make sure the CAPS LOCK key is not on (gdm displays a message if it is) because the routine that verifies your entry is case sensitive. See page 135 if you need help with logging in and page 112 if you want to change your password. The system takes a moment to set things up and then displays a workspace.

# THE GNOME 3 STANDARD AND CLASSIC DESKTOPS

Fedora 15 introduced GNOME 3 and the GNOME shell. GNOME 3 can run in standard mode (Standard desktop) or classic mode (Classic desktop). The GNOME 3 Standard desktop is radically different from the GNOME 2 desktop, following the trend toward simpler, more graphical desktops that have more icons and fewer menus. All versions of Fedora from 15 onward run the GNOME 3 Standard desktop by default. Figure 4-2 on page 93 and Figure 4-3 on page 94 show commonly used screens on a GNOME 3 Standard desktop. See the next section for more information.

By default, RHEL 7 runs the GNOME 3 Classic desktop, a group of GNOME Shell extensions that give GNOME 3 a GNOME 2 look and feel, including the Applications and Places menus. Figure 4-5 on page 97 shows the GNOME Classic desktop. For more information refer to "The GNOME Classic Desktop" on page 96.

This book uses the Linux textual interface (CLI) for most tasks, including setting up servers and programming in bash, SQL, and Python. Where this book describes a GUI utility, it explains how to open the utility/window by pressing ALT-F2 to display the Enter a Command window and typing the name of the utility. Alternately, you can press the SUPER (Windows) key to display the Search text box and enter the name of utility there. These techniques work from both the GNOME 3 Standard desktop (Fedora) and Classic desktop (RHEL). For more information refer to "The Search Text Box and the Enter a Command Window" on page 98.

### You can run the Classic desktop on Fedora

tip  If you like, you can install and run the Classic desktop on Fedora; see "Installing the Classic Desktop on GNOME 3" on page 95.

**optional**

gnome-tweak-tool  You can use gnome-tweak-tool (**gnome-tweak-tool** package) to change many aspects of how GNOME windows look and work. Visit wiki.gnome.org/GnomeTweakTool for more information.

# THE GNOME 3 STANDARD DESKTOP (FEDORA)

This section briefly describes how to use the GNOME 3 Standard desktop that Fedora installs by default. For more information visit wiki.gnome.org/GnomeShell/CheatSheet. The extensions.gnome.org Web site lists extensions to GNOME 3. See "The GNOME Classic Desktop" on page 96 if you are running RHEL.

When you log in on a system running GNOME 3 the workspace is empty. On the Top panel (the bar at the top of the workspace) are objects: the word **Activities**, a clock, speaker and networking icons, and your name (or Live System User). You can click one of these objects to work with it. The Top panel remains constant as the information displayed below it changes.

## THE ACTIVITIES OVERVIEW SCREEN

Click **Activities** at the top left of a workspace (or press the SUPER [Windows] key) to display the *Activities Overview* screen (Figure 4-2). This screen holds the Search text box (near the top), icons of favorite applications (on the left), and a section holding shrunken views of workspaces (on the right); each of these views contain live thumbnails of running applications. When only one workspace exists, you need to move the cursor to the right side of the screen to display this section. Shrunken views of the windows in the active workspace appear in the center of the screen. If the active workspace is empty, the center of the screen is blank.

Figure 4-2 shows an Activities Overview screen in which the active workspace holds windows that are running Firefox and Files (Nautilus; page 102). Because the shrunken Firefox window is selected (highlighted), it has an **X** in a circle at its upper-right corner. Click this **X** to close the window and terminate Firefox. Click the Firefox or Files window to close the Activities Overview screen and display the active workspace with the window you clicked in the foreground.

**Figure 4-2**  GNOME Activities Overview screen

Making a workspace active

Still looking at Figure 4-2, you can also click one of the shrunken workspaces along the right side of the screen to make that workspace active. Click the empty workspace at the bottom of the stack to open a new, empty workspace.

Running an application from the Favorites list

There are several ways to start an application. If the icon of the application you want to run is in the Favorites list, click that icon; GNOME closes the Activities Overview screen and opens in the active workspace the application whose icon you clicked.

Running an application from the Search text box (SUPER key)

You can also type the name of the (graphical) application (e.g., gnome-terminal or gnome-disks) or the name of the window the application displays (e.g., Terminal or Disks) in the Search text box, and press RETURN to open that application in the active workspace. If the Search text box is not visible, press the SUPER (Windows) key to display it.

Running an application from the Enter a Command window (ALT-F2 key)

Finally, you can press ALT-F2 to display the Enter a Command window, type the name of the application or utility you want to run, and press RETURN to run an application. You must run a textual application from a terminal emulator such as gnome-terminal (which you can start from an Enter a Command window). See page 98 for more information.

## THE APPLICATIONS OVERVIEW SCREEN

At the bottom of the list of favorite application icons on the left of the Activities Overview screen is the Show Applications icon (it holds nine small squares; see Figure 4-2).

**Figure 4-3**    The GNOME Applications Overview screen

Click this icon to display the *Applications Overview* screen (Figure 4-3). This screen displays application icons. Clicking the button labeled **Frequent** at the bottom of the screen displays only icons of applications you use frequently. Clicking **All** displays a scrollable list of application icons. Not all applications, or utilities, have icons; use the Enter a Command window (page 98) to run applications that do not have icons.

Left-click an icon to close the Applications Overview screen and open the associated application in the active workspace. Right-click an icon to display a context menu that can include Add to Favorites (if the icon is not in the list of favorites), Remove from Favorites (if it is already in the list of favorites), New Window (closes the Applications Overview screen and opens the application in a new window in the active workspace even if it is already opened), and a line that identifies an already open instance of the application (closes the Applications Overview screen and opens the application in the workspace in which it is already running).

## The Application Switcher: Changing the Input Focus

The window with the *input focus* is the one that receives keyboard characters and commands you type. In addition to using the Activities Overview screen, you can change which window has the input focus using the keyboard; this process is called *window cycling*.

When you press ALT-TAB when the desktop is displayed, GNOME displays in the center of the workspace the Application Switcher, a box that holds icons representing the programs running in the windows on the desktop. It also shifts the input focus to the window that was active just before the currently active window, making it easy to switch back and forth between two windows. When you hold ALT and press TAB multiple times, the focus moves from window to window. Holding ALT and SHIFT and repeatedly pressing TAB cycles in the other direction.

## INSTALLING THE CLASSIC DESKTOP ON GNOME 3 (FEDORA)

The following instructions explain how to install and run the Classic desktop under Fedora. RHEL 7 runs the Classic desktop by default.

1. With GNOME running the GNOME 3 Standard desktop, click the word **Activities** at the upper left of the screen. Type **terminal** and press RETURN; GNOME displays a terminal emulator.

2. With the cursor over the terminal emulator, type the following command; terminate the command using a RETURN.

```
$ su -c 'yum -y install gnome-classic-session'
Password:
...
Complete!
```

   The su utility will prompt for the **root** password. Once you enter the **root** password and press RETURN, yum will display a lot of information as it installs the **gnome-classic-session** package. When yum displays **Complete!** and the shell displays its prompt (**$**), the package is installed. For more information on using yum to install packages see page 534.

3. *From a live session only* (or if **Log Out** does not appear in the menu described in the next step), give the following additional commands from the terminal emulator. Substitute your name for **sam** in the first two commands and supply the **root** password when you are prompted.

```
$ su -c 'useradd sam'
$ su -c 'passwd sam'
Changing password for user sam.
New password:
Retype new password:
passwd: all authentication tokens updated successfully.

$ su -c 'systemctl restart gdm'
```

   After a few moments GNOME logs you in as Live System User again (or allows you to log in as yourself).

4. Log off by clicking your name or **Live System User** at the upper right of the screen, clicking **Log Out** from the menu GNOME displays, and then clicking the button labeled **Log Out** from the small window GNOME displays. (If **Log Out** does not appear in the menu, follow the previous step and then repeat this step.) After a few moments GNOME displays a Login screen (Figure 4-1, page 91).

5. Click your name (not Live System User) on the Login screen; GNOME displays the Password screen (Figure 4-4, next page). Just below the text box labeled **Password** is a small triangle followed by the word **Session**. Click the

**Figure 4-4**   The GNOME Password screen showing the Session menu

triangle to display the Session menu. Click **GNOME Classic**; GNOME moves the white dot to the entry you just clicked.

6. Type your password in the text box labeled **Password** and click **Sign In**. After a few moments GNOME displays a Classic desktop (Figure 4-5). If you followed step 3 to add a user, gnome-initial-setup will take you through setting up that user; see page 68.

Once you have selected GNOME Classic when you log in, it is your default desktop; you do not have to select it next time you log in.

# THE GNOME CLASSIC DESKTOP (RHEL AND OPTIONALLY FEDORA)

This section briefly describes how to use the GNOME Classic desktop that is installed by default on RHEL. Refer to "The GNOME 3 Standard Desktop" on page 92 if you are running Fedora. If you want to install and run a Classic desktop under Fedora refer to "Installing the Classic Desktop on GNOME 3" on the previous page.

Panels and objects  When you log in, the GNOME Classic desktop displays a workspace that includes the Top and Bottom panels (bars) that help you get your work done easily and efficiently (Figure 4-5). Each of the panels can hold several icons and words called objects.

The Applications menu  You can run an application from the Applications menu that appears at the left end of the Top panel (Figure 4-5). Click **Applications** to display the Applications menu. When you move the mouse pointer over one of the selections in this menu and leave it there for a moment (this action is called *hovering*), the menu displays a submenu. Move the cursor to and click one of the items in the submenu to select and run it.

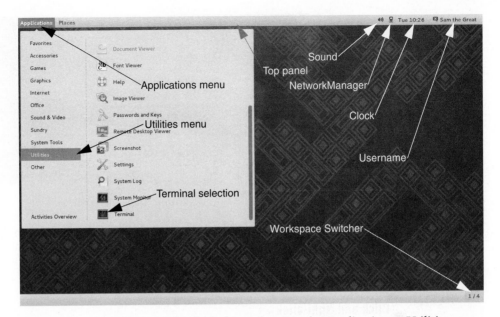

**Figure 4-5**    The GNOME Classic desktop showing the **Applications⇨Utilities** menu

The Places menu    The Places menu has no submenus; click an entry in this menu to select it. The Places menu on the GNOME Classic desktop is the same as Places in the Nautilus File Browser Sidebar; see page 103 for more information.

# WORKING WITH THE DESKTOP

This section discusses several ways you can work with the desktop. It applies to both the GNOME 3 Standard and Classic desktops.

## TERMINOLOGY

In addition to this section, see the Glossary, which defines data entry *widgets* (page 1281) such as the *combo box* (page 1243), *drop-down list* (page 1248), *list box* (page 1258), and *text box* (page 1277).

Workspace    A *workspace* is a screen that holds windows of one or more applications. The Activities Overview screen (page 92) and the Application Switcher (page 94) enable you to display any of the running applications and its workspace.

Active workspace    The *active workspace* is the workspace that displays the windows you can work with immediately. Only one workspace can be active at a time.

Desktop    The *desktop*, which is not displayed all at once, is the collection of all workspaces.

**Figure 4-6**   The Enter a Command window

Panel   Panels are bars that can appear on the desktop and hold objects. The Top panel appears at the top of the screen and the Bottom panel, if it is present, appears at the bottom of the screen.

Object   An *object* is a word, icon, or menu that you can select by clicking.

### Click and right-click

tip   This book uses the term **click** when you need to click the *left* mouse button. It uses the term **right-click** when you need to click the *right* mouse button. See page 110 for instructions on adapting the mouse for left-handed use.

## THE SEARCH TEXT BOX AND THE ENTER A COMMAND WINDOW

You can start a graphical application (open a window) by pressing the SUPER (Windows) key to display the Search text box (Figure 4-2, page 93) or by pressing ALT-F2 to display the Enter a Command window (Figure 4-6) and typing the name of the application. Try typing **firefox** and pressing RETURN to start Firefox. The new window opens on the active workspace.

### You must run a textual application (utility) from a terminal emulator

tip   A textual application or utility requires a textual environment such as a terminal emulator to run. The Search text box and Enter a Command window do not provide a textual environment and so cannot run a textual application. However, you can run **gnome-terminal**, a graphical application that provides a textual environment using either of these methods. You can then run the textual application from the terminal emulator that **gnome-terminal** displays.

## APPLICATION MENUS

Many applications have an Application menu that allows you to set preferences and get help with the application. While the application is active (has the focus), click the object (the name of the window) for the application on the Top panel; GNOME

**Figure 4-7** The Software (gpk-application) Application menu

opens the Application menu for the application. Figure 4-7 shows the Application menu for the Software (gpk-application) application. See "Updating, Installing, and Removing Software Packages" on page 116 for more information on this application.

# CONTEXT MENUS

A *context menu* has choices that apply specifically to the window or object you click. The choices differ from window to window and from object to object. Some windows do not have context menus. Frequently a right-click displays a context menu.

### Right-click to display a context menu

tip  Right-click an object to display its context menu. Each object displays its own context menu, although similar objects have similar context menus. Most context menus have either a Preferences or Properties selection.

**Figure 4-8**   A typical window

# WINDOWS

Window    In a workspace, a *window* is a region that runs, or is controlled by, a particular program.

Titlebar    A *titlebar* (Figure 4-8) appears at the top of most windows and controls the window it is attached to. You can double-click the titlebar to maximize and restore a window. Some windows can be restored only by pressing SUPER-DOWN ARROW (SUPER is the Windows key) or by dragging down from an empty spot on the Top panel. Clicking the close button (X) closes the window and usually terminates the program running in it. To reposition the window, left-click the titlebar and drag the window to the desired location.

Window Operations menu    The Window Operations menu contains operations you can perform on any window. Right-click the titlebar to display this menu. This menu allows you to minimize, maximize, resize, or close a window; move the window within the workspace; move a window to another workspace; keep the window on top of or below other windows; and cause the window to always be visible on the displayed workspace. It also shows the keyboard shortcuts for some of these actions. SUPER refers to the Windows key (e.g., **Super+Up** means hold the Windows key down and press the UP ARROW key).

Menubar    The *menubar* (Figure 4-8) holds icons you can use to work with the window contents.

Toolbar    A *toolbar* (Figure 4-8) usually appears near the top of a window and contains icons, text, applets, menus, and more. Many kinds of toolbars exist. The titlebar is not a toolbar.

Resizing a window    To resize a window, position the mouse pointer over an edge of the window; the pointer turns into an arrow pointing to a line. When the pointer is an arrow pointing to a line, you can click and drag the side of a window. When you position the mouse pointer over a corner of the window, you can resize both the height and the width of the window simultaneously. Some windows are not resizeable and some windows do not allow you to resize them from all four sides.

Moving a window    To move a window, click and drag the titlebar. Dragging a window to the top of the screen maximizes the window.

## Cutting and Pasting Objects Using the Clipboard

There are two similar ways to cut/copy and paste objects and text both within and between windows. In the first method, you use the clipboard, technically called the *copy buffer*, to copy or move objects or text. To do so, you explicitly copy an object or text to the buffer and then paste it somewhere else. Applications that follow the user interface guidelines use CONTROL-X to cut, CONTROL-C to copy, and CONTROL-V to paste. Application context menus frequently provide these options.

You might not be familiar with the second method to copy and paste text—using the *selection* or *primary* buffer, which always contains the text you most recently selected (highlighted). You cannot use this method to copy objects. Clicking the middle mouse button (click the scroll wheel on a mouse that has one) pastes the contents of the selection buffer at the location of the mouse pointer. If you are using a two-button mouse, click both buttons at the same time to simulate clicking the middle button.

With both of these techniques, start by highlighting an object or text to select it. You can drag a box around multiple objects to select them or drag the mouse pointer over text to select it. Double-click to select a word or triple-click to select a line or a paragraph.

Next, to use the clipboard, explicitly copy (CONTROL-C) or cut (CONTROL-X) the objects or text. If you want to use the selection buffer, skip this step.

To paste the selected objects or text, position the mouse pointer where you want to put it and then either press CONTROL-V (clipboard method) or press the middle mouse button (selection buffer method).

### Use SHIFT-CONTROL-C and SHIFT-CONTROL-V within a terminal emulator

tip    The CONTROL-C, CONTROL-X, and CONTROL-V characters do not work in a terminal emulator window because the shell running in the window intercepts them before the terminal emulator can receive them. However, you can use SHIFT-CONTROL-C and SHIFT-CONTROL-V in place of CONTROL-C and CONTROL-V, respectively. There is no keyboard shortcut for CONTROL-X. You can also use the selection buffer in this environment or use copy/paste from the **Edit** selection on the menubar or from the context (right-click) menu.

When using the clipboard, you can give as many commands as you like between the CONTROL-C or CONTROL-X and CONTROL-V, as long as you do not press CONTROL-C or CONTROL-X again. When using the selection buffer, you can give other commands after selecting text and before pasting it, as long as you do not select (highlight) other text.

## LOGGING OFF

Log off by clicking your name or **Live System User** at the upper-right corner of the screen, click **Log Out** from the menu GNOME displays, and then click the button labeled **Log Out** from the small window GNOME displays. Select **Power Off** to shut down or restart the system, among other options. Alternately, you can give the command **gnome-session-quit** from an Enter a Command window (ALT-F2) or a terminal emulator.

# USING THE NAUTILUS FILE MANAGER

Nautilus (the Files program) is the simple, powerful GNOME file manager. You can use it to create, open, view, move, and copy files and folders as well as to execute applications and scripts.

Terms: folder and directory — Nautilus displays the File Browser window, which displays the contents of a folder. The terms *folder* and *directory* are synonymous; "folder" is frequently used in graphical contexts, whereas "directory" might be used in textual or command-line contexts. This book uses these terms interchangeably.

Term: File Browser — This book sometimes uses the terms *File Browser window* and *File Browser* when referring to the Nautilus File Browser window.

Opening Nautilus — Give the command **nautilus** from an Enter a Command window (ALT-F2) or a terminal emulator to open a Nautilus File Browser window that shows the files in your home directory (Figure 4-9). From a GNOME 3 desktop you can type **nautilus** or **files** in the Search text box in the Activities Overview screen (page 92). Alternately, you can click the filing cabinet icon in the Applications Overview screen (page 93). From a Classic desktop you can select Home from the Places menu.

## THE NAUTILUS FILE BROWSER WINDOW

The right side of a File Browser window shows the View pane that holds file objects; the left side shows the Sidebar that holds the Places, Devices, and Network lists.

Application menu — With a File Browser window active, click **Files** on the Top panel to display the Files Application menu. This menu allows you to set preferences for, open a location bar in, and close the File Browser window.

View pane — The View pane displays file icons or a list of filenames. Select the view you prefer by clicking the dots or lines button near the right end of the toolbar.

Sidebar — The Sidebar allows you to work with Nautilus in different ways. Close or display the Sidebar by pressing F9. To change the horizontal size of the Sidebar, drag the handle (Figure 4-9) on its right side. See "The Sidebar" on the next page for more information.

Toolbar — The left end of the toolbar allows you to display different directories in the View pane. Select **Application menu**⇨**Enter Location** to open a location bar in which you

**Figure 4-9**    A Nautilus File Browser window

can enter a pathname. The right end of the toolbar holds icons that allow you to
search for files, control the type of display Nautilus presents in the View pane, and
display view options and location options.

## THE SIDEBAR

The Places section of the Sidebar holds objects that you click to change what Nautilus
displays in the View pane. The Home, Documents, and Downloads objects display
your directories with corresponding names. The Computer object displays the local
filesystem. The Browse Network object displays systems and files on the local network. The Connect to Server object opens a window that allows you to enter a URL
to connect to an SSH, FTP, or other type of server.

Trash    Selecting **Move to Trash** from an object's context (right-click) menu moves the object
to the **Trash** directory. Because files in the trash take up space on the hard disk (just
as all files do), it is a good idea to remove them periodically. To display the **Trash**
directory, double-click the Trash icon in the Sidebar.

Emptying the trash    Select **Empty Trash** from the Trash icon context (right-click) menu to permanently
remove all files from the trash. (This selection is grayed out if there are no files in the
trash.) Alternately, you can right-click an object in the Trash File Browser window
and select **Delete** to remove only that object (file), or you can select **Restore** to move
the file back to its original location. You can drag and drop files to and from the trash
just as you can with any folder.

Deleting files    You can delete files without first sending them to the trash. Add **Delete** to the context
menu by selecting Preferences from the Files Application menu, then selecting the
Behavior tab, and putting a tick in the check box labeled **Include a Delete command
that bypasses Trash.**

### Nautilus can open a terminal emulator

**tip**   When you install the **nautilus-open-terminal** package (see page 534 for instructions) and log out and log back in, Nautilus presents an Open in Terminal selection in context menus where appropriate. For example, with this package installed, when you right-click a directory object and select **Open in Terminal**, Nautilus opens a terminal emulator with that directory as the working directory (page 143).

## OPENING FILES

By default, you double-click a file object in the View pane to open it; alternately, you can right-click the object and select **Open** from the drop-down list. When you open a file, GNOME figures out the appropriate tool to use by determining the file's *MIME* (page 1261) type. GNOME associates each filename extension with a MIME type and each MIME type with a program. Initially GNOME uses the filename extension to try to determine a file's MIME type. If it does not recognize the filename extension, it examines the file's *magic number* (page 1259).

For example, when you open a file with a filename extension of **ps**, GNOME calls the Evince document viewer, which displays the PostScript file in a readable format. When you open a text file, GNOME uses **gedit** to display and allow you to edit the file. When you open a directory, GNOME displays its contents in a File Browser window. When you open an executable file such as Firefox, GNOME runs the executable file. When GNOME uses the wrong tool to open a file, the tool generally issues an error message. See "Open With" on page 106 for information on how to use a tool other than the default tool to open a file.

From within a File Browser window, you can open a folder in a new tab. To do so, middle-click the folder or right-click the folder and select **Open in New Tab** from the drop-down list; Nautilus displays a new tab named for the folder you clicked. Click the tab to display contents of the directory.

## SELECTING OBJECTS

Within a File Browser window, select an object by clicking it once; GNOME highlights the object. Select additional objects by holding down the CONTROL key while you click each object. To select a group of adjacent objects, highlight the first object and then, while holding down the SHIFT key, click the last object; GNOME highlights all objects between the two objects you clicked. Alternately, you can use the mouse pointer to drag a box around a group of objects.

## THE OBJECT PROPERTIES WINDOW

The Object Properties window displays information about a file, such as its owner, permissions, size, location, MIME type, ways to work with it, and so on. This window is titled *filename* **Properties**, where *filename* is the name of the file you clicked to open the window. To display this window, right-click an object and select **Properties** from the

**Figure 4-10**   The Object Properties window, Permissions tab

drop-down list. The Properties window initially displays some basic information. Click the tabs at the top of the window to display additional information. Different sets of tabs appear for different types of files. You can modify the settings in this window only if you have permission to do so. This section describes the three tabs most commonly found in Object Properties windows.

Basic   The Basic tab displays information about the file, including its *MIME* (page 1261) type, and enables you to select a custom icon for the file and change its name. To change the name of the file, replace the name in the text box labeled **Name**. If the filename is not listed in a text box, you do not have permission to change it. An easy way to change the icon is to open a File Browser window at **/usr/share/icons** (give the command **nautilus /usr/share/icons** in an Enter a Command window [ALT-F2]). Work your way down through the directories until you find an icon you like (**gnome/24x24** has some interesting icons), and then drag and drop it on the icon to the left of **Name** in the Basic tab.

Permissions   The Permissions tab (Figure 4-10) allows the owner of a file to change the file's permissions (page 191) and to change the group (see **/etc/group** on page 506) the file is associated with to any group the owner is associated with.Nautilus grays out items you are not allowed to change.

**Figure 4-11**   The Object Properties window, Open With tab, and the context menu, Open With submenu for the same file

Using the drop-down lists, you can give the owner (called *user* elsewhere; see the tip about chmod on page 194), group, and others read, read-only, or write permission for a file. Alternately, you can prohibit the group and others from accessing the file by specifying permissions as **None**. Put a tick in the check box labeled **Execute** to give all users permission to execute the file. This tab does not give you the fine-grained control over assigning permissions that chmod (page 193) does.

Permissions for a directory work as explained on page 197. Owner, group, and others can be allowed to list files in a directory, access (read and—with the proper permissions—execute) files, or create and delete files. Group and others permissions can also be set to **None**. Click **Change Permissions for Enclosed Files** to change the permissions of all files in a directory.

Open With   When you ask Nautilus to open a file that is not executable (by double-clicking its icon or right-clicking and selecting the first **Open with** selection), Nautilus determines which application or utility it will use to open the file. Nautilus uses several techniques to determine the *MIME* (page 1261) type of a file and selects the default application based on that determination.

The Open With tab (Figure 4-11) enables you to change which applications Nautilus can use to open the file and other files of the same MIME type (typically files with the same filename extension). Scroll the list of applications, highlight one, and click the **Add** button to add to the list of applications. Right-click an application and select **Forget association** to remove an application from the list. You cannot remove the default application.

**Figure 4-12**   The Settings window

When you add an application, Nautilus adds that application to the Open With list but does not change the default application it uses to open that type of file. Highlight the application and click **Set as default** to cause that application to become the default application Nautilus uses to open this type of file.

When a file has more than one application in the Open With tab, the context menu displays an Open With submenu (Figure 4-11).

# THE SETTINGS WINDOW

The Settings window (Figure 4-12) enables you to customize your account so it better meets your needs. Click your name or **Live System User** at the upper right of the desktop and then click **Settings** to display this window. Alternately, you can open this window by giving the command **gnome-control-center** from an Enter a Command window (ALT-F2) or a terminal emulator. This section discusses the items in this window. Click an item to display its corresponding window.

### You might need to click Unlock before you can change settings

tip    In the upper right of some windows there is an unlocked lock icon with the word **Unlock** next to it. See Figure 4-16 on page 111 for an example. When you click this icon, GNOME displays an Authentication Required dialog box. If you are an administrative user, the dialog box will request your password. If not, it will request the password of Administrator, which is the **root** password.

The Settings window has the following items:

- **Background**—Sets the desktop background. For more information refer to "Desktop Background" on page 109.

- **Notifications**—Specifies which applications display notifications and how much information each includes in pop-ups.

- **Online Accounts**—Adds credentials for Google, Facebook, and other accounts to be stored securely by the system.

- **Privacy**—Controls automatic screen lock, how you appear on the desktop and network, recent usage and history, and how often trash and temporary files are purged.

- **Region & Language**—Specifies language, format, and input sources.

- **Search**—Specifies which applications are consulted when you use the Search text box in the Activities Overview screen (page 92).

- **Bluetooth**—Controls Bluetooth adapters.

- **Color**—Specifies a color profile for a monitor.

- **Displays**—Configures display (monitor) resolution. Refer to "Displays," next page.

- **Keyboard**—Controls whether and how keys repeat, cursor blinking, and keyboard shortcuts.

- **Mouse & Touchpad**—Switches between right- and left-handed mouse, and controls double-click and pointer speed. For more information refer to "Mouse & Touchpad" on page 110.

- **Network**—Displays the Settings window that controls network connections and operation. See page 638 for information on connecting to a Wi-Fi network and page 639 for general information on this window.

- **Power**—Controls when GNOME blanks the screen and how long the system must be idle before it is suspended.

- **Printers**—Adds, removes, and configures printers. See Chapter 13.

- **Sound**—Controls sound volume, balance, profile, and effects. On systems with more than one sound device, choose which device to use.

- **Wacom Tablet**—Sets up a tablet.

- **Date & Time**—Turns NTP (Network Time Protocol; sets/maintains the system clock automatically) on and off, sets the system date, time, and time zone, and causes GNOME to display a 12- or 24-hour clock. For more information refer to "Date & Time" on page 110.

- **Details**—Displays hardware and software information, specifies default applications, and tells the system what to do when it detects removable media.

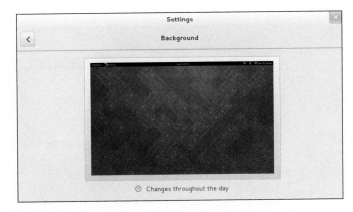

**Figure 4-13**   The Background window

- **Sharing**—Turns remote access via ssh (Chapter 18) on and off, and specifies which content you share.

- **Universal Access**—Changes settings to help you use the desktop more easily. Tabs allow you to control seeing, hearing, typing, and mouse (pointing and clicking) features.

- **Users**—Adds, removes, and sets up users. For more information refer to "Users: Changing Your Account Type and Password (GUI)" on page 112.

# DESKTOP BACKGROUND

The Background window (Figure 4-13) enables you to change the desktop background. To display this window, click **Background** in the Settings window (Figure 4-12, page 107) or right-click anywhere on an empty space on the desktop and select **Change Background**. Initially this window displays a picture of the current desktop background. Click that picture to display the Select Background window.

Three buttons labeled **Wallpapers**, **Pictures**, and **Colors** appear at the top of the Select Background Window. Click one of these buttons, click to highlight a desktop background from those displayed, and click **Select** to change the desktop background to the highlighted one. The Background window reappears; click **X** to close the window or click the back arrow to return to the Settings window.

Several utilities and applications allow you to select a picture to use as the desktop background. For example, when you select **Set as Wallpaper** from an picture's context (right-click) menu in a Nautilus File Browser window, GNOME sets that picture as the desktop background.

# LPI  DISPLAYS

Most of the time the monitor attached to the system just works: Fedora/RHEL probes the monitor and autoconfigures X.org to work properly. This section explains how to configure the display in case you need to. The Displays window

**Figure 4-14**   The Displays window

(Figure 4-14) configures the monitor. Check the specifications for the monitor and select the appropriate resolution value from the drop-down list. With multiple monitors, this window allows you to drag monitors to change their relative positions. Click **Apply** confirm the changes you have made.

## MOUSE & TOUCHPAD

The Mouse & Touchpad window (Figure 4-15) enables you to change the characteristics of the mouse (and touchpad if there is one). To display this window, click **Mouse & Touchpad** in the Settings window (Figure 4-12, page 107).

Left-handed mouse    To change the orientation of the mouse buttons for use by a left-handed person, click the radio button labeled **Left**. If you change the setup of the mouse buttons, remember to reinterpret the descriptions in this book accordingly. That is, when this book asks you to click the left button or does not specify a button to click, click the right button, and vice versa. See page 463 for instructions on remapping mouse buttons from the command line.

Double-click    Use the slider labeled **Double-click** to change the speed with which you must double-
timeout    click a mouse button to have the system recognize your action as a double-click rather than as two single clicks. You can control the mouse pointer speed using the slider labeled **Pointer speed**. Click **Test Your Settings** to experiment with the mouse settings. Click **X** to close the window or click the back arrow to return to the Settings window.

## DATE & TIME

The Date & Time window (Figure 4-16) allows you to specify a date format (a 12- or 24-hour clock), specify a time zone (region), and turn NTP (Network Time Protocol)

**Figure 4-15**   The Mouse & Touchpad window

on or off. To display this window, click **Date & Time** in the Settings window (Figure 4-12, page 107) or click the time at the top of the screen and select **Date & Time Settings.** You must unlock this window to make changes other than changing the date format; see the tip on page 107.

Turning NTP on causes the system to set and maintain its clock from network time servers. When NTP is off, you can use this window to set the system clock manually. To specify a time zone, click a city in the local time zone; GNOME displays the name of the city in the spin box labeled **City.** Alternately, you can use the spin boxes labeled **Region** and **City** to specify a city. Click **X** to close the window or click the back arrow to return to the Settings window.

**Figure 4-16**   The Date & Time window

**Figure 4-17**   The Users window

## LE+   USERS: CHANGING YOUR ACCOUNT TYPE AND PASSWORD (GUI)

See "Password Security" on page 136 for help selecting a more secure password for your account. See page 137 for instructions on changing your password from the command line.

The Users window (Figure 4-17) allows you to add and remove users and change the characteristics of a user, including changing the user's password and making the user an administrator (page 422). To display this window, click **Users** in the Settings window (Figure 4-12, page 107). You must unlock this window to make changes other than changing your own password or language; see the tip on page 107.

To change your password click the text box labeled **Password**; GNOME displays a new window. The first item you must enter in this window is your current (old) password. The system verifies this password to ensure that an unauthorized user is not trying to alter your password. There are also text boxes where you enter and verify the new password. When you have entered a strong enough password the same way two times the system allows you to click **Change**. When you successfully change your password, you change the way you log in. If you forget your password, a user running with **root** privileges can change it and tell you the new password. Click **X** to close the window or click the back arrow to return to the Settings window.

**Figure 4-18** The GNOME Help window

## GETTING HELP

Linux provides help in many forms and formats. This section describes how to get help while using a GUI. See page 128 for resources that are available from the command line.

### THE GNOME HELP WINDOW

The GNOME Help window (Figure 4-18) is displayed by yelp (projects.gnome.org/yelp) and provides information on using Linux in a graphical environment. Open this window by giving the command **yelp** from a Search text box (SUPER), an Enter a Command window (ALT-F2), or a terminal emulator.

Click a topic in this window to display information on that topic. You can also enter text to search for in the text box at the top of the window and then press RETURN. In addition, most Application menus (page 98) provide a Help selection.

### USING THE INTERNET TO GET HELP

The Internet provides many helpful sites related to Linux. Aside from sites that offer various forms of documentation, you can enter an error message from a program you are having a problem with in a search engine such as Google (www.google.com). The

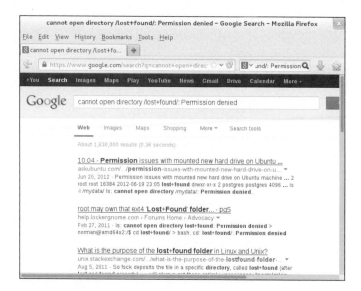

**Figure 4-19** Google reporting on an error message

search will likely yield a post concerning your problem and suggestions about how to solve it. See Figure 4-19.

Fedora/Red Hat Web sites
The Red Hat and Fedora Web sites are rich sources of information. The following list identifies locations that may be of interest:

- Fedora documentation is available at docs.fedoraproject.org.

- A list of all methods of getting help using Fedora is available at fedoraproject.org/wiki/Communicating_and_getting_help.

- A useful site that answers questions is ask.fedoraproject.org.

- Manuals and other documentation for RHEL are available at access.redhat.com/site/documentation and access.redhat.com.

- Various types of support documents and support are available at www.redhat.com/support (requires free registration).

- You can query the Red Hat Knowledgebase at access.redhat.com/site (requires free registration).

- The home pages for Fedora (fedoraproject.org) and RHEL (www.redhat.com) have a wealth of information.

- Fedora/RHEL support forums are online discussions about any issues people want to raise. One forum is dedicated to new users; others to Apache, the X Window System, and so on. Visit www.redhat.com/mailman/listinfo and admin.fedoraproject.org/mailman/listinfo to browse the lists.

- The Fedora/RHEL bugs database is available at bugzilla.redhat.com. Anyone can search the database. To submit new bugs or append to existing bugs, you need to sign up for a free account.

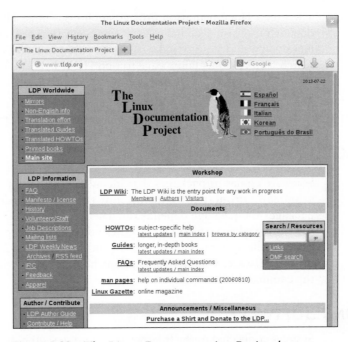

**Figure 4-20**   The Linux Documentation Project home page

- You can find community-sourced solutions to common problems at fedorasolved.org.

- Fedora Magazine is available at fedoramagazine.org.

- RHEL hardware help is available from the Red Hat hardware catalog at hardware.redhat.com. The hardware that Fedora supports is mostly a superset of that supported by RHEL.

GNU  GNU manuals are available at www.gnu.org/manual. In addition, you can visit the GNU home page (www.gnu.org) to obtain other documentation and GNU resources. Many of the GNU pages and resources are available in a variety of languages.

The Linux Documentation Project  The Linux Documentation Project (www.tldp.org; Figure 4-20), which has been around for almost as long as Linux, houses a complete collection of guides, HOWTOs, FAQs, man pages, and Linux magazines. The home page is available in English, Portuguese (Brazilian), Spanish, Italian, Korean, and French. It is easy to use and supports local text searches. This site also provides a complete set of links you can use to find almost anything you want related to Linux (click **Links** in the Search box or go to www.tldp.org/links). The links page includes sections on general information, events, getting started, user groups, mailing lists, and newsgroups, with each section containing many subsections.

HOWTOs  A HOWTO document explains in detail how to do something related to Linux—from setting up a specialized piece of hardware to performing a system administration task to setting up specific networking software. Mini-HOWTOs offer shorter explanations.

The Linux Documentation Project site houses most HOWTO and mini-HOWTO documents. Use a Web browser to visit www.tldp.org, click **HOWTOs,** and pick the index you want to use to find a HOWTO or mini-HOWTO. You can also use the LDP search feature on its home page to find HOWTOs and other documents.

# UPDATING, INSTALLING, AND REMOVING SOFTWARE PACKAGES

Software comes in packages that include all necessary files, instructions so a program can automatically install and remove the software, and a list of other packages the package depends on. There are many ways to search for and install software packages. GNOME notifies you each time updates are available for software on the system. The Software window (Figure 4-22) provides an easy way to install software. Chapter 12 explains how to work with software packages from the command line.

## UPDATING SOFTWARE

Systems connected to the Internet are set up to search daily for software updates and notify you when updates are available. GNOME displays the message **Important software updates are available** in a pop-up notification window and places a notification indicator (an envelope icon) toward the right end of the Top panel when updates are available. Clicking **Install updates** in this window opens the Software Update window (Figure 4-21). You can open this window manually by selecting the Software Update icon from the GNOME 3 desktop Applications Overview screen (page 93) or by giving the command **gpk-update-viewer** from an Enter a Command window (ALT-F2) or a terminal emulator.

Software Update window
When the Software Update window opens, it displays the message **Checking for updates;** after it finishes checking it displays the number of available updates. If no updates are available, it displays **All software is up to date.**

If updates are available, click **Install Updates.** As it downloads and installs the software packages, the Software Update window displays messages and a progress bar. If the updates require you to reboot the system or log off, the Software Update window prompts you to do so.

Software Update Preferences window
You can control how often the system checks for updates and which sources it checks from the Software Update Preferences window. Open this window by giving the command **gpk-prefs** from an Enter a Command window (ALT-F2) or a terminal emulator.

## ADDING AND REMOVING SOFTWARE

The Software window (Figure 4-22) allows you to add and remove applications from the system. Open this window by giving the command **gpk-application** from an Enter

**Figure 4-21**    The Software Update window

a Command window (ALT-F2) or a terminal emulator. Maximizing this window might make it easier to use. See page 534 for instructions on adding and removing software on the command line.

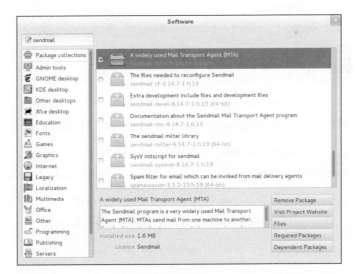

**Figure 4-22**    The Software window

Enter the name or part of the name of an application in the text box at the upper-left corner of the window and press RETURN to search for that application. The Software window displays a list of matching software packages in the frame on the right side of the window. Alternately, you can select one of the entries from the list on the left side of the window to display a list of related packages.

Scroll through the packages displayed in the frame on the right side of the window. When you click/highlight an application, the window displays a summary of the application in the frame at the lower-right corner of the window. Put a tick in the check box next to each application you want to install. Remove ticks from applications you want to remove. Click **Apply Changes** to implement the changes you have marked. If a package you want to install depends on other packages that are not installed, gpk-application will ask for permission to install the dependent packages. Because you need to work with **root** privileges to install and remove software, the utility might ask for the **root** password. When it is finished, the utility might ask if you want to run the new application. Close the Software window when you are finished.

# Installing Different Desktop Environments

If you are installing a new Fedora system you can download a spin to install a system with a desktop environment other than GNOME. See page 35 for a list of popular spins. On a system that is already set up, you can use yum to download and install the packages necessary to run a different desktop. When more than one desktop is installed on a system, the Password screen displays the Sessions menu (Figure 4-4, page 96) so you can choose which desktop you want to run. The following commands, which must be run from a terminal emulator and prompt for the **root** password, install package groups that include all necessary packages for each desktop.

Xfce  The following command installs the Xfce desktop:

```
$ su -c 'yum -y group install xfce-desktop'
```

LXDE  The following command installs the LXDE desktop:

```
$ su -c 'yum -y group install lxde-desktop'
```

MATE  The following command installs the MATE desktop:

```
$ su -c 'yum -y group install mate-desktop'
```

Security  The following command installs FSL (the Fedora Security Lab):

```
$ su -c 'yum -y group install "Security Lab"'
```

KDE  The following command installs the KDE desktop:

```
$ su -c 'yum -y group install kde-desktop'
```

# LE    WORKING FROM THE COMMAND LINE

Before the introduction of the GUI, UNIX and then Linux provided only a textual (command-line) interface (CLI). Today, a textual interface is available when you log in from a terminal, a terminal emulator, or a textual virtual console, or when you use ssh to log in on a system.

*Advantages of the textual interface*    Although the concept might seem antiquated, the textual interface has a place in modern computing. In some cases an administrator might use a command-line tool either because a graphical equivalent does not exist or because the graphical tool is not as powerful, flexible, or refined as the textual one. For example, chmod (page 193) provides finer granularity than its GUI counterpart (File Browser Object Properties window, Permissions tab; page 105). On a server system, a graphical interface might not even be installed. The first reason for this omission is that a GUI consumes a lot of system resources; on a server, those resources are better dedicated to the main task of the server. Additionally, security considerations mandate that a server system run as few tasks as possible because each additional task provides an additional attack vector.

You can also write scripts using the textual interface. Using scripts, you can easily reproduce tasks on multiple systems, enabling you to scale the tasks to larger environments. When you are the administrator of only a single system, using a GUI is often the easiest way to configure the system. When you act as administrator for many systems, all of which need the same configuration installed or updated, a script can make the task go more quickly. Writing a script using command-line tools is frequently easy, whereas the same task can be difficult to impossible using graphical tools.

*Pseudographical interface*    Before the introduction of GUIs, resourceful programmers created textual interfaces that included graphical elements such as boxes, borders outlining rudimentary windows, highlights, and, more recently, color. These textual interfaces, called pseudographical interfaces, bridge the gap between textual and graphical interfaces. The Midnight Commander file management utility (mc; midnight-commander.org) is a good example of a utility with a well-designed pseudographical interface.

*Command-line (bash) coverage*    This section introduces the Linux CLI. Chapter 5 is the first of three chapters dedicated to the Bourne Again Shell (bash). Chapter 7 describes some of the more important utilities you can use from the command line. Chapter 9 covers advanced bash concepts. Chapter 27 describes shell programming using bash. Most of the examples in Parts III and IV of this book use the CLI, adding examples of graphical tools where available.

## RUNNING COMMANDS FROM THE COMMAND LINE

This section describes three ways to work from the command line: using a terminal emulator, using a virtual console, and logging in remotely. If the local system does not

**Figure 4-23** A Terminal (emulator) window

support a graphical interface, you have no choice: You must work from the command line—skip to "Logging Out" on page 121.

## USING A TERMINAL EMULATOR/SHELL

A *terminal emulator* is a window that presents a CLI (command-line interface); it functions as a textual (character-based) terminal and is displayed in a graphical environment. To open the GNOME terminal emulator named Terminal (gnome-terminal; Figure 4-23), give the command **gnome-terminal** from an Enter a Command window (ALT-F2) or a terminal emulator. Because you are already logged in and are creating a subshell in a desktop environment, you do not need to log in again.

Terminal displays your username, the name of the system you are working on, and the name of the directory you are working in (the working directory) on the titlebar. Figure 4-23 shows **sam** working on the system named **guava**. He is working in his home directory (page 143), which the shell refers to using a tilde (~; page 182).

You can run character-based (textual) programs that would normally run on a terminal or from the console in a terminal emulator window. You can also start graphical programs, such as gnome-calculator, from this window. A graphical program opens its own window.

To open an additional terminal session within the same Terminal window, right-click the window and select **Open Tab** from the context menu. A row of tabs appears below the menubar as gnome-terminal opens another terminal session on top of the existing one. Add as many terminal sessions as you like; click the tabs to switch between sessions.

### GNOME Terminal (emulator) shortcuts

tip While using GNOME Terminal, CONTROL-SHIFT-N opens a new window and CONTROL-SHIFT-T opens a new tab. New windows and tabs open to the working directory. In addition, you can use CONTROL-PAGE UP and CONTROL-PAGE DOWN to switch between tabs; ALT-*x* switches to tab number *x*.

A session you add from the context menu uses the same profile as the session you open it from. When you use the menubar to open a session, GNOME gives you a choice of profiles if more than one is available. You can add a profile by selecting **Terminal menubar: File⇨New Profile** and specifying a name for the new profile.

## LE  USING A VIRTUAL CONSOLE

When running Linux on a personal computer, you will frequently work with the display and keyboard attached to the computer. Using this physical console, you can access as many as 63 *virtual consoles* (also called *virtual terminals*). Some are set up to allow logins; others act as graphical displays. To switch between virtual consoles, hold the CONTROL and ALT keys down and press the function key that corresponds to the console you want to view. For example, CONTROL-ALT-F5 displays the fifth virtual console.

By default, five or six virtual consoles are active and have textual login sessions running. When you want to use both textual and graphical interfaces, you can set up a textual session on one virtual console and a graphical session on another. By default, a graphical session runs on virtual console number 1.

## LOGGING IN REMOTELY: TERMINAL EMULATION, ssh, AND DIAL-UP CONNECTIONS

When you are not using a console, terminal, or other device connected directly to the Linux system you are logging in on, you are probably connected using terminal emulation software on another system. Running on the local system, this software connects to the remote Linux system via a network (Ethernet, asynchronous phone line, PPP, or other type) and allows you to log in.

When you log in via a dial-up line, the connection is straightforward: You instruct the local emulator program to contact the remote Linux system, it dials the phone, and the remote system displays a login prompt. When you log in via a directly connected network, you use either ssh (secure; page 685) or telnet (not secure; page 303) to connect to the remote system. The ssh program has been implemented on many operating systems, not just Linux. Many user interfaces to ssh include a terminal emulator. From an Apple, Windows, or UNIX machine, open the program that runs ssh and give it the name or IP address of the system you want to log in on.

## LOGGING OUT

To log out from a character-based interface, press CONTROL-D in response to the shell prompt. This action sends the shell an EOF (end of file) signal. Alternately, you can give the command **exit**. Logging out from a shell does not end a graphical session; it just exits from the shell you are working with. For example, exiting from the shell that GNOME Terminal provides closes the Terminal window.

# THE SHELL

Once you open a terminal emulator window, you are communicating with the command interpreter called the *shell*. The shell plays an important part in much of your command-line communication with Linux. When you enter a command at the keyboard in response to the shell prompt on the screen, the shell interprets the command and initiates the appropriate action—for example, executing a program; calling a compiler, a Linux utility, or another standard program; or displaying an error message indicating you entered a command incorrectly. When you are working on a GUI, you bypass the shell and execute a program by clicking an object or a name. Refer to Chapter 5 for more information on the shell.

Special characters When you are working on the command line, several characters, including *, ?, |, [, and ], have special meanings. Avoid using these characters until you have read "Special Characters" on page 142.

### Make sure **TERM** is set correctly

tip No matter how you connect, make sure the **TERM** variable is set to the type of terminal your emulator is emulating. For more information refer to "Specifying a Terminal" on page 1153.

## WHICH SHELL ARE YOU RUNNING?

This book discusses the Bourne Again Shell (bash). You are probably running bash, but you might be running another shell such as the TC Shell (tcsh) or the Z Shell (zsh). When you give the command **echo $0** and press RETURN in response to a shell prompt (usually $ or %), the shell displays the name of the shell you are working with. This command works because the shell expands $0 to the name of the program you are running (page 1022). This command might display output like this:

```
$ echo $0
-bash
```

or like this:

```
$ echo $0
/bin/bash
```

Either way, this output shows you are running bash. If you are running a different shell, the shell will display appropriate output; if you want to run bash, give the command **bash**. To permanently change the shell you run when you log in, see the tip on page 329. You may need to install bash (the **bash** package) as explained on page 534.

## CORRECTING MISTAKES

This section explains how to correct typographical and other errors you might make on the command line. Because the shell and most other utilities do not interpret the command line or other text you enter until you press RETURN, you can readily correct a typing mistake before you press RETURN.

You can correct such mistakes in several ways: Erase one character at a time, back up a word at a time, or back up to the beginning of the line in one step. After you press RETURN, it is too late to correct a mistake: At that point, you must either wait for the command to run to completion or abort execution of the program (next page).

### ERASING A CHARACTER

While entering characters from the keyboard, you can back up and erase a mistake by pressing the *erase key* once for each character you want to delete. The erase key backs over as many characters as you wish. It does not, in general, back up past the beginning of the line.

The default erase key is BACKSPACE. If this key does not work, try pressing DEL or CONTROL-H. If these keys do not work, give the following stty[1] command to set the erase and line kill (see "Deleting a Line") keys to their default values:

```
$ stty ek
```

Alternately, you can give the next command to reset most terminal parameters to a sane value. If the RETURN key does not move the cursor to the next line, press CONTROL-J instead.

```
$ stty sane
```

### DELETING A WORD

You can delete a word you entered by pressing CONTROL-W. A *word* is any sequence of characters that does not contain a SPACE or TAB. When you press CONTROL-W, the cursor moves left to the beginning of the current word (as you are entering a word) or the previous word (when you have just entered a SPACE or TAB), removing the word.

## CONTROL-Z suspends a program

tip    Although it is not a way of correcting a mistake, you might press the suspend key (typically CONTROL-Z) by mistake and wonder what happened. If you see a message containing the word **Stopped**, you have just stopped your job using job control (page 164). If you give the command **fg** to continue your job in the foreground, you return to where you were before you pressed the suspend key. For more information refer to "bg: Sends a Job to the Background" on page 348.

### DELETING A LINE

Any time before you press RETURN, you can delete the line you are entering by pressing the *(line) kill key*. When you press this key, the cursor moves to the left, erasing characters as it goes, back to the beginning of the line. The default line kill key is CONTROL-U. If this key does not work, try CONTROL-X. If these keys do not work, give the stty command described under "Erasing a Character."

### *LPI*  ABORTING EXECUTION

Sometimes you might want to terminate a running program. For example, you might want to stop a program that is performing a lengthy task such as displaying the contents of a file that is several hundred pages long or copying a large file that is not the one you meant to copy.

---

1. The command stty is an abbreviation for *set teletypewriter*, the first terminal UNIX ran on. Today stty is commonly thought of as meaning *set terminal*.

To terminate a program that you are running from the command line, press the *interrupt key* (CONTROL-C or sometimes DELETE or DEL). When you press this key, the Linux kernel sends a TERM (termination) signal to the program you are running and to the shell. Exactly what effect this signal has depends on the program. Some programs stop execution immediately, some ignore the signal, and some take other actions. When the shell receives a TERM signal, it displays a prompt and waits for another command.

If these methods do not terminate the program, try sending the program a QUIT signal (CONTROL-\). If all else fails, try pressing the suspend key (typically CONTROL-Z), giving a **jobs** command to verify the number of the job running the program, and using kill to abort the job. The job number is the number within the brackets at the left end of the line displayed by **jobs** ([1]). In the next example, the **kill** command (pages 164 and 465) uses **–TERM** to send a TERM signal to the job specified by the job number, which is preceded by a percent sign (**%1**). You can omit **–TERM** from the command, because kill sends a TERM signal by default. Table 27-5 on page 1047 lists some signals.

### Use the KILL signal as a last resort

caution  When the termination signal does not work, use the KILL signal (specify **–KILL** in place of **–TERM** in the example). A running program cannot ignore a KILL signal; it is sure to abort the program.

Because a program receiving a KILL signal has no chance to clean up its open files before being terminated, using KILL can corrupt application data. Use the KILL signal as a last resort. Before using KILL, give a termination (TERM) or quit (QUIT) signal ten seconds to take effect.

The following example demonstrates the use of the suspend key and the jobs and kill commands.

```
$ bigjob
^Z
[1]+  Stopped                 bigjob
$ jobs
[1]+  Stopped                 bigjob
$ kill -TERM %1
[1]+  Killed                  bigjob
```

The **kill** command returns a prompt; you might need to press RETURN again to see the confirmation message. For more information refer to "Running a Command in the Background" on page 163.

## REPEATING/EDITING COMMAND LINES

To repeat a previous command, press the UP ARROW key. Each time you press this key, the shell displays an earlier command line. Press the DOWN ARROW key to browse through the command lines in the other direction. To execute the displayed command line, press RETURN.

The RIGHT ARROW and LEFT ARROW keys move the cursor back and forth along the displayed command line. At any point along the command line, you can add characters by typing them. Use the erase key (page 123) to remove characters from the command line. Press

RETURN to execute the modified command (it does not matter where the cursor is on the command line).

You can also repeat the previous command using **!!**. This technique is useful if you forgot to use su (page 425) to prefix a command. In this case, if you type **su −c "!!"**, the shell will run the previous command with **root** privileges. Or, if the local system is set up to use sudo (page 428), you can type **sudo !!** and the shell will run the previous command with **root** privileges.

The command **^old^new^** reruns the previous command, substituting the first occurrence of the string **old** with **new**. Also, on a command line, the shell replaces the characters **!$** with the last token (word) on the previous command line. The following example shows the user correcting the filename **meno** to **memo** using **^n^m^** and then printing the file named **memo** by giving the command **lpr !$**. The shell replaces **!$** with **memo**, the last token on the previous command line.

```
$ cat meno
cat: meno: No such file or directory
$ ^n^m^
cat memo
This is the memo file.
$ lpr !$
lpr memo
```

For information about more complex command-line editing, see page 378.

# Running Basic Command-Line Utilities

This section describes a few basic command-line utilities. You can experiment with these utilities from a terminal, a terminal emulator within a GUI (page 120), or a virtual console (page 121). See Chapter 7 for more complete coverage of these and other utilities.

## ls: Lists the Names of Files

Using the editor of your choice, create a small file named **practice**. (See the tutorials on the vim [page 262] and nano [page 270] editors.) After exiting from the editor, you can use the ls (list; page 221) utility to display a list of filenames. Following, ls lists the name of the **practice** file. (On the system you are using it might also list some files the system or a program created.)

```
$ ls
practice
```

By default, ls lists the names of most of the files in the working directory (the directory you are working in). You can list the names of specified files by providing their names as arguments on the command line. Put a SPACE between the name of the utility and any arguments.

```
$ ls practice
practice
```

### Arguments

tip    An argument specifies something, such as a filename, the command acts on. An argument typically appears following the name of the utility you are calling and a SPACE. For more information refer to "Arguments" on page 145.

You can list more information about a file by using the –l option to ls. Options must also be preceded by a SPACE.

```
$ ls -l practice
-rw-r--r--. 1 sam pubs 52 07-24 14:09 practice
```

From left to right, the –l option causes ls to display file access permissions (page 191), links (page 203), owner and group names, size in bytes, modification date and time, and name.

### Options

tip    An option modifies the way a utility works. Options typically precede arguments and are usually specified as one or more letters that are preceded by one or two hyphens. An option generally appears following the name of the utility you are calling and a SPACE. For more information refer to "Options" on page 145.

## cat: COPIES A TEXT FILE TO THE SCREEN

A convenient way to display the contents of a text file on the screen is by giving the command **cat** with an argument of the name of the file. The following example shows the cat utility (page 216) displaying the contents of **practice**. Whereas ls displays the *name* of a file, cat displays the *contents* of a file.

```
$ cat practice
This is a small file I created
using a text editor.
```

## cp: COPIES A FILE

The cp (copy; page 224) utility makes a copy of a file. This utility can copy any file, including text and executable program (binary) files. You can use cp to make a backup copy of a file or a copy to experiment with.

```
$ cp practice practice.copy
$ ls
practice practice.copy
```

The preceding example copies the file named **practice** to **practice.copy**. The period is part of the filename—just another character. The ls command shows two files in the working directory, **practice** and **practice.copy**.

## rm: DELETES A FILE

The rm (remove; page 222) utility deletes a file. The following example shows rm deleting the file named **practice**. After rm deletes **practice**, ls and cat show that **practice** no longer exists. Use rm carefully.

```
$ rm practice
$ ls practice
ls: cannot access practice: No such file or directory
$ cat practice
cat: practice: No such file or directory
```

### echo: COPIES ITS ARGUMENTS TO THE SCREEN

The echo utility (page 219) copies its arguments to the screen. The following example shows two echo commands.

```
$ echo Hi
Hi
$ echo My name is Sam.
My name is Sam.
```

This book makes extensive use of echo to demonstrate how the shell works.

### date: DISPLAYS THE TIME AND DATE

The date utility (page 218) displays the current date and time:

```
$ date
Thu Apr  3 10:14:41 PDT 2014
```

### touch: CREATES AN EMPTY FILE

The touch utility (page 243) creates an empty (zero-length) file with the name that you specify as an argument. Following, touch creates **myfile** and ls shows that the file is zero bytes long.

```
$ touch myfile
$ ls -l myfile
-rw-r--r--. 1 sam pubs 0 07-24 14:12 myfile
```

## *LE* WRITING AND EXECUTING A BASIC SHELL SCRIPT

A shell script, called a batch file under Windows, is a program written using shell commands and utilities. This section explains how to write a basic shell script. See "Writing and Executing a Shell Script" on page 336 for more information on creating and executing shell scripts. Before you can run a shell script you must put commands in a file (the script) and tell Linux that the file is executable. You can use an editor to create the file or you can give the following command, which uses redirection to create the file. See page 154 for information on using cat and redirection to create a file.

```
$ cat > myprog
echo This is my shell script
date
who
CONTROL-D
```

This shell script, named **myprog**, holds three commands (utilities): echo, date, and who. After you type each of the lines and a final RETURN, press CONTROL-D to tell the shell you have finished writing to the file; the shell displays a prompt.

```
                                     sam@guava:~
File  Edit  View  Search  Terminal  Help
MAN(1)                          Manual pager utils                          MAN(1)

NAME
       man - an interface to the on-line reference manuals

SYNOPSIS
       man  [-C  file]  [-d] [-D] [--warnings[=warnings]] [-R encoding] [-L
       locale] [-m system[,...]] [-M path] [-S list] [-e extension] [-i|-I]
       [--regex|--wildcard]  [--names-only]  [-a]  [-u] [--no-subpages] [-P
       pager] [-r prompt] [-7] [-E encoding] [--no-hyphenation]  [--no-jus-
       tification]  [-p string]  [-t] [-T[device]] [-H[browser]] [-X[dpi]]
       [-Z] [[section] page ...] ...
       man -k [apropos options] regexp ...
       man -K [-w|-W] [-S list] [-i|-I] [--regex] [section] term ...
       man -f [whatis options] page ...
       man -l [-C file] [-d] [-D] [--warnings[=warnings]] [-R encoding] [-L
       locale]  [-P  pager] [-r prompt] [-7] [-E encoding] [-p string] [-t]
       [-T[device]] [-H[browser]] [-X[dpi]] [-Z] file ...
       man -w|-W [-C file] [-d] [-D] page ...
       man -c [-C file] [-d] [-D] page ...
       man [-?V]

DESCRIPTION
       man is the system's manual pager. Each page argument given to man is
       normally  the  name  of  a program, utility or function. The manual
       page associated with each of these arguments is then found and  dis-
Manual page man(1) line 1 (press h for help or q to quit)
```

**Figure 4-24**  The man utility displaying information about itself

Next you need to tell Linux that **myprog** is an executable file. Following, the chmod utility (page 193) makes **myprog** readable and executable.

```
$ chmod a+rx myprog
```

Finally, you can execute the **myprog** script. Because of the way the shell looks for files, you must precede the name of the program with a period and a slash (**./**). See the discussion of absolute and relative pathnames on page 149 for details. Following, the shell runs the three utilities in **myprog** and displays their output.

```
$ ./myprog
This is my shell script
Mon Jul 22 17:15:50 PDT 2013
sam        pts/0          2013-07-21 13:17 (:0)
```

# Getting Help from the Command Line

Distributions of Linux typically do not come with hardcopy reference manuals. However, its online documentation has always been one of Linux's strengths. The man (or manual) and info pages have been available via the man and info utilities since early releases of the operating system. Not surprisingly, with the ongoing growth of Linux and the Internet, the sources of documentation have expanded as well. This section discusses some of the places you can look for information on Linux while you are working from the command line. If you are working in a graphical environment see "Getting Help" on page 113. See also Appendix B.

## LE+ man: Displays the System Manual

The man (manual) utility displays (man) pages from the system documentation. This documentation is helpful when you know which utility you want to use but have forgotten exactly how to use it. You can also refer to the man pages to get more information about specific topics or to determine which features are available with Linux. Because the descriptions in the system documentation are often terse, they are most helpful if you already understand the basic functions of a utility. You can search for topics covered by man pages using the apropos utility (next page).

To find out more about a utility, give the command **man**, with the name of the utility as an argument. Figure 4-24 shows man displaying information about itself; the user entered **man man** on the command line. Within a man page you can search for a term by typing a slash followed by the term and a RETURN. For example, to search for the term **function** in a man page, type **/function**RETURN; man will highlight all occurrences of the string **function** and move the cursor to the next one.

less (pager)   The man utility sends its output through a *pager*—usually less (page 220), which displays one screen of information at a time. When you display a manual page using man, less displays a prompt [e.g., **Manual page man(1) line 1 ...**] at the bottom of the screen after it displays each screen of text and waits for you to take one of the following actions:

- Press the SPACE bar to display another screen of text.

- Press PAGE UP, PAGE DOWN, UP ARROW, or DOWN ARROW to navigate through the text.

- Press **h** (help) to display a list of less commands.

- Press **q** (quit) to quit man and less and cause the shell to display a prompt.

Manual sections   Based on the FHS (Filesystem Hierarchy Standard; page 189), the Linux system manual and the man pages are divided into ten sections, where each section describes related tools:

1. User Commands
2. System Calls
3. Subroutines
4. Devices
5. File Formats
6. Games
7. Miscellaneous
8. System Administration
9. Kernel
10. New

This layout closely mimics the way the set of UNIX manuals has always been divided. Unless you specify a manual section, man displays the earliest occurrence in the manual of the word you specify as an argument. Most users find the information they need in Sections 1, 6, and 7; programmers and system administrators frequently need to consult the other sections.

In some cases the manual contains entries for different tools with the same name. For example, the following command displays the man page for the crontab utility from Section 1 of the system manual:

```
$ man crontab
```

To see the man page for the **crontab** file from Section 5, enter this command:

```
$ man 5 crontab
```

The preceding command instructs man to look only in Section 5 for the man page. In documentation you might see this man page referred to as **crontab(5)**. Use the **–a** option to view all man pages for a given subject (press **q**RETURN to display each subsequent man page). For example, give the command **man –a crontab** to view all man pages for **crontab**.

## LE apropos: SEARCHES FOR A KEYWORD

When you do not know the name of the utility required to carry out a particular task, you can use apropos with a keyword as an argument to search for it. This utility searches for the keyword in the short description line of all man pages and displays those lines that contain a match. The man utility, when called with the **–k** (keyword) option, provides the same output as apropos.

The database apropos uses, named **mandb** or **makewhatis**, is not available when a system is first installed but is built automatically by **cron** or **crond** (see page 607 for a discussion of **cron/crond** and page 69 for instructions on manually building this database).

The following example shows the output of apropos when you call it with the **who** keyword. The output includes the name of each utility, the section of the manual that contains it, and the short description from the man page. This list includes the utility you need (who) and identifies other, related tools you might find useful.

```
$ apropos who
at.allow (5)         - determine who can submit jobs via at or batch
at.deny (5)          - determine who can submit jobs via at or batch
jwhois (1)           - client for the whois service
w (1)                - Show who is logged on and what they are doing.
who (1)              - show who is logged on
who (1p)             - display who is on the system
whoami (1)           - print effective userid
whois (1)            - client for the whois service
whois.jwhois (1)     - client for the whois service
```

whatis   The whatis utility is similar to apropos but finds only complete word matches for the name of the utility:

```
$ whatis who
who (1)              - show who is logged on
who (1p)             - display who is on the system
```

**Figure 4-25**    The initial screen displayed by the command **info coreutils**

## info: DISPLAYS INFORMATION ABOUT UTILITIES

The textual info utility (www.gnu.org/software/texinfo/manual/info) is a menu-based hypertext system developed by the GNU Project (page 3) and distributed with Linux. It includes a tutorial on itself (give the command **info info**) and documentation on many Linux shells, utilities, and programs developed by the GNU Project. Figure 4-25 shows the screen that info displays when you give the command **info coreutils** (the **coreutils** software package holds the Linux core utilities).

### man and info display different information

tip    The info utility displays more complete and up-to-date information on GNU utilities than does man. When a man page displays abbreviated information on a utility that is covered by info, the man page refers to info. The man utility frequently displays the only information available on non-GNU utilities. When info displays information on non-GNU utilities, it is frequently a copy of the man page.

Because the information on this screen is drawn from an editable file, your display might differ from the screens shown in this section. You can press any of the following keys while the initial info screen is displayed:

- **h** or **?** to list info commands
- SPACE to page through the display
- **m** followed by the name of the menu you want to display or followed by a SPACE to display a list of menus
- **q** or CONTROL-C to quit

```
                          sam@guava:~                              [x]
 File  Edit  View  Search  Terminal  Help
* env invocation::              Run a command in a modified environment
* nice invocation::             Run a command with modified niceness
* nohup invocation::            Run a command immune to hangups
* stdbuf invocation::           Run a command with modified I/O buffering
* timeout invocation::          Run a command with a time limit

Process control

* kill invocation::             Sending a signal to processes.

Delaying

* sleep invocation::            Delay for a specified time

Numeric operations

* factor invocation::           Print prime factors
* seq invocation::              Print numeric sequences

File permissions

* Mode Structure::              Structure of file mode bits
* Symbolic Modes::              Mnemonic representation of file mode bits
* Numeric Modes::               File mode bits as octal numbers
* Directory Setuid and Setgid:: Set-user-ID and set-group-ID on directories
--zz-Info: (coreutils.info.gz)Top, 348 lines --84%--------------------------
```

**Figure 4-26**    The screen displayed by the command **info coreutils** after you type **/sleep**RETURN twice

The notation info uses to describe keyboard keys is the same notation emacs uses and might not be familiar to you. For example, the notation **C-h** is the same as CONTROL-H. Similarly, **M-x** means hold down the META or ALT key and press **x**. On some systems you need to press ESCAPE and then **x** to duplicate the function of META-X.

After giving the command **info coreutils**, press the SPACE bar a few times to page through the display. Type **/sleep**RETURN to search for the string **sleep**. When you type **/**, info moves the cursor to the bottom line of the window and displays **Regexp search** [*string*]:, where *string* is the last string you searched for. Press RETURN to search for *string* or enter the string you want to search for. Typing **sleep** displays **sleep** on that line, and pressing RETURN displays the next occurrence of **sleep** in the info text.

### You might find pinfo **easier to use than** info

tip    The pinfo utility is similar to info but is more intuitive if you are not familiar with emacs editor commands. This utility runs in a textual environment, as does info. When it is available, pinfo uses color to make its interface easier to use. If pinfo is not installed on the system, install the **pinfo** package as explained on page 534. Run pinfo from a terminal emulator.

Now type **/**RETURN (or **/sleep**RETURN) to search for the next occurrence of **sleep** as shown in Figure 4-26. The asterisk at the left end of the line indicates that this entry is a menu item. Following the asterisk is the name of the menu item and a description of the item.

Each menu item is a link to the info page that describes the item. To jump to that page, search for or use the ARROW keys to move the cursor to the line containing the menu item and press RETURN. With the cursor positioned as it is in Figure 4-26, press RETURN to display information on **sleep**. Alternately, you can type the name of the menu item in a menu command to view the information: To display information

```
                              sam@guava:~                        [x]
  File  Edit  View  Search  Terminal  Help
  File: coreutils.info,  Node: sleep invocation,  Up: Delaying

  25.1 'sleep': Delay for a specified time
  ========================================

  'sleep' pauses for an amount of time specified by the sum of the values
  of the command line arguments.  Synopsis:

       sleep NUMBER[smhd]...

     Each argument is a number followed by an optional unit; the default
  is seconds.  The units are:

  's'
       seconds
  'm'
       minutes
  'h'
       hours
  'd'
       days

     Historical implementations of 'sleep' have required that NUMBER be an
  integer, and only accepted a single argument without a suffix.  However,
  GNU 'sleep' accepts arbitrary floating point numbers.  *Note Floating
  --zz-Info: (coreutils.info.gz)sleep invocation, 38 lines --Top----------
```

**Figure 4-27**   The info page on the sleep utility

on sleep, for example, give the command **m sleep**, followed by RETURN. When you type **m** (for *menu*), info moves the cursor to the bottom line of the window (as it did when you typed **/**) and displays **Menu item:**. Typing **sleep** displays **sleep** on that line, and pressing RETURN displays information about the menu item you specified.

Figure 4-27 shows the *top node* of information on sleep. A node groups a set of information you can page through by pressing the SPACE bar. To display the next node, press **n**. Press **p** to display the previous node.

As you read through this book and learn about new utilities, you can use man or info to find out more about those utilities. If the local system can print PostScript documents, you can print a manual page by using the man utility with the **–t** option. For example, **man –t cat | lpr** prints information about the cat utility. You can also use a Web browser to display documentation and then print the desired information from the browser.

## THE ––help OPTION

Another tool you can use on the command line is the **––help** option. Most GNU utilities provide a **––help** option that displays information about the utility. A non-GNU utility might use a **–h** or **–help** option to display information about itself.

```
$ cat --help
Usage: cat [OPTION] [FILE]...
Concatenate FILE(s), or standard input, to standard output.

  -A, --show-all           equivalent to -vET
  -b, --number-nonblank    number nonempty output lines, overrides -n
  -e                       equivalent to -vE
  -E, --show-ends          display $ at end of each line
...
```

If the information that **--help** displays runs off the screen, send the output through the less pager (page 129) using a pipeline (a vertical bar; page 158):

```
$ ls --help | less
```

## THE bash help COMMAND

The bash **help** command displays information about bash (the Bourne Again Shell) commands, control structures, and other features. From the bash prompt, give the command **help** followed by the keyword you are interested in. Following are some examples.

```
$ help help
help: help [-dms] [pattern ...]
    Display information about builtin commands.

    Displays brief summaries of builtin commands.  If PATTERN is
    specified, gives detailed help on all commands matching PATTERN,
    otherwise the list of help topics is printed.
...

$ help echo
echo: echo [-neE] [arg ...]
    Write arguments to the standard output.

    Display the ARGs on the standard output followed by a newline.

    Options:
      -n          do not append a newline
...

$ help while
while: while COMMANDS; do COMMANDS; done
    Execute commands as long as a test succeeds.
...
```

## LE /usr/share/doc

The **/usr/share/doc** directory often contains more detailed and different information about a utility than either man or info provides. Frequently this information is meant for people who will be compiling and modifying the utility, not just using it. These directories hold thousands of files, each containing information on a separate topic. As the following example shows, the names of most directories in **/usr/share/doc** end in version numbers:

```
$ ls /usr/share/doc
abattis-cantarell-fonts-0.0.12   iwl1000-firmware-39.31.5.1   ncftp-3.2.5
abrt-2.1.5                       iwl100-firmware-39.31.5.1    ncurses-5.9
abrt-dbus-2.1.5                  iwl105-firmware-18.168.6.1   ncurses-base-5.9
accountsservice-0.6.34           iwl135-firmware-18.168.6.1   neon-0.29.6
acl-2.2.51                       iwl2000-firmware-18.168.6.1  netcf-libs-0.2.3
aic94xx-firmware-30              iwl2030-firmware-18.168.6.1  net-snmp-libs-5.7.2
```

```
aisleriot-3.8.0              iwl3945-firmware-15.32.2.9    nettle-2.6
alsa-firmware-1.0.27         iwl4965-firmware-228.61.2.24  net-tools-2.0
...
```

Most of these directories hold a **README** file, which is a good place to start reading about the utility or file the directory describes. Use an asterisk (∗; page 166) in place of the version number to make it easier to type the filename. The following **README** file for bzip2 (page 245) explains how to compile the source code.

```
$ less /usr/share/doc/bzip2∗/README
This is the README for bzip2/libzip2.
This version is fully compatible with the previous public releases.
...
Complete documentation is available in Postscript form (manual.ps),
PDF (manual.pdf) or html (manual.html).  A plain-text version of the
manual page is available as bzip2.txt.

HOW TO BUILD -- UNIX

Type 'make'.  This builds the library libbz2.a and then the programs
bzip2 and bzip2recover.  Six self-tests are run.  If the self-tests
complete ok, carry on to installation:

To install in /usr/local/bin, /usr/local/lib, /usr/local/man and
/usr/local/include, type

    make install
...
```

# More About Logging In and Passwords

Refer to "Logging In on the System" on page 90 for information about logging in. This section covers solutions to common login problems, choosing a password and password security, and changing your password from the command line.

### Always use a password

*security*  Unless you are the only user of a system, the system is not connected to any other systems or the Internet, and you are the only one with physical access to the system, it is poor practice to maintain a user account without a password.

# What to Do If You Cannot Log In

If you enter either your username or your password incorrectly, the system displays an error message after you enter *both* your username *and* your password. This message indicates that you have entered either the username or the password incorrectly or that they are not valid. It does not differentiate between an unacceptable username and an unacceptable password—a strategy meant to discourage unauthorized people from guessing names and passwords to gain access to the system.

Following are some common reasons why logins fail:

- **The username and password are case sensitive.** Make sure the CAPS LOCK key is off and enter your username and password exactly as specified or as you set them up.

- **You are not logging in on the right machine.** The login/password combination might not be valid if you are trying to log in on the wrong machine. On a larger, networked system, you might have to specify the machine you want to connect to before you can log in.

- **Your username is not valid.** The login/password combination might not be valid if you have not been set up as a user.

- **A filesystem is full.** When a filesystem critical to the login process is full, it might appear as though you have logged in successfully, but after a moment the login prompt reappears. In this situation you must boot the system in rescue/recovery mode and delete some files.

- **The account is disabled.** On some systems, the **root** account is disabled by default. An administrator might disable other accounts. Often the **root** account is not allowed to log in over a network: In this case, log in as yourself and then gain **root** privileges using su/sudo.

## 🄻🄴 Password Security

This section contains a practical discussion of password security; see page 625 for a more technical discussion.

If someone else assigned you a password, it is a good idea to give yourself a new one. For security reasons, passwords you enter are not displayed by any utility.

### Protect your password

security   Do not allow someone to find out your password: *Do not* put your password in a file that is not encrypted, allow someone to watch you type your password, or give your password to someone you do not know (a system administrator never needs to know your password). You can always write your password down and keep it in a safe, private place.

### Choose a password that is difficult to guess

security   Do not use phone numbers, names of pets or kids, birthdays, words from a dictionary (not even a foreign language), and so forth. Do not use permutations of these items or a l33t-speak variation of a word: Modern dictionary crackers try these permutations.

### Include nonalphanumeric characters in your password

security   Automated password cracking tools first try using alphabetic and numeric characters when they try to guess your password. Including at least one character such as @ or # in a password increases the amount of time it takes for one of these tools to crack your password.

### Differentiate between important and less important passwords

security  It is a good idea to differentiate between important and less important passwords. For example, Web site passwords for blogs or download access are not very important; it is acceptable to use the same password for these types of sites. However, your login, mail server, and bank account Web site passwords are critical: Never use these passwords for an unimportant Web site and use a different password for each of these accounts.

### Use a password vault

security  You might want to use a program such as revelation (**revelation** package) and its command-line counterpart relevation (**relevation** package) or keepassx (**keepassx** package) that generates and stores passwords. A password vault makes it easier to maintain different, complex passwords for several important sites. Visit revelation.olasagasti.info or keepass.info for more information.

Secure passwords  To be relatively secure, a password should contain a combination of numbers, upper-case and lowercase letters, and nonalphanumeric characters. It should also meet the following criteria:

- Must be at least eight characters long (or longer if the system administrator sets it up that way). Eight or ten characters is a good compromise between being easy to remember and being secure.

- Should not be a word in a dictionary of any language, no matter how seemingly obscure.

- Should not be the name of a person, place, pet, or other thing that might be discovered easily.

- Should contain at least two letters and one nonalphanumeric character.

- Should not be your username, the reverse of your username, or your username shifted by one or more characters.

Only the first item is mandatory. Avoid using control characters (such as CONTROL-H) because they might have a special meaning to the system, making it impossible for you to log in. If you are changing your password, the new password should differ from the old one by at least three characters. Changing the case of a character does not make it count as a different character.

### pwgen **helps you pick a password**

security  The pwgen utility (**pwgen** package) generates a list of almost random passwords. With a little imagination, you can pronounce, and therefore remember, some of these passwords.

## *LE+*  passwd: CHANGING YOUR PASSWORD (CLI)

See the previous section for help selecting a secure password. See page 112 if you want to change your password using a GUI. Use the passwd utility to change your password from the command line. The first item passwd asks for is your current (old) password. This password is verified to ensure that an unauthorized user is not trying to alter your password. Then the system requests a new password.

```
$ passwd
Changing password for user sam.
Changing password for sam.
(current) UNIX password:
New password:
Retype new password:
passwd: all authentication tokens updated successfully.
```

After you enter your new password, the system asks you to retype it to make sure you did not make a mistake when you entered it the first time. If the new password is the same both times you enter it, passwd changes your password. If the passwords differ, it means that you made an error in one of them, and passwd displays this error message:

```
Sorry, passwords do not match
```

If your password is not long enough, passwd displays a messages similar to the following:

```
BAD PASSWORD: The password is shorter than 8 characters
```

When it is too simple, passwd displays this message:

```
BAD PASSWORD: The password fails the dictionary check - it is too
simplistic/systematic
```

After several failures, passwd displays an error message and exits, allowing the shell to display its prompt. At this point you need to run passwd again.

Working with **root** privileges you can assign a new password to any user on the system without knowing the user's old password. As an administrator you can use this technique when a user forgets his password. The following command requests the **root** password before requesting a new password for Sam.

```
$ su -c "passwd sam"
Password:
Changing password for user sam.
New password:
...
```

# Chapter Summary

As with many operating systems, your access to a Linux system is authorized when you log in. To do so, you click your username on the Login screen and enter your password on the Password screen. You can change your password at any time while you are logged in. Choose a password that is difficult to guess and that conforms to the criteria imposed by the utility that changes the password.

The system administrator is responsible for maintaining the system. On a single-user system, you are the system administrator. On a small, multiuser system, you or another user might act as the system administrator, or this job might be shared. On a large, multiuser system or a network of systems, there is frequently a full-time system administrator.

When extra (**root**) privileges are required to perform certain system tasks, a system administrator uses su (or sudo) or logs in as the user named **root** to obtain these privileges. An administrator working with **root** privileges is sometimes referred to as Superuser.

Do not work with **root** privileges as a matter of course. When you have to do something that requires **root** privileges, work with **root** privileges for only as long as absolutely necessary; revert to working as yourself as soon as possible.

Understanding the desktop and its components is essential to getting the most out of the GUI. A terminal emulator allows you to use the Linux CLI from a graphical environment. You can use a terminal emulator to launch both textual and graphical programs.

The GNOME environment provides users with a variety of interests and experience levels—the casual user, the office worker, the power user, and the programmer/system designer—with a space to work in and a set of tools to work with. GNOME also provides off-the-shelf productivity and many ways to customize its look, feel, and response. Nautilus is GNOME's simple, yet powerful file manager. It can create, open, display, move, and copy files and directories as well as execute programs and scripts.

The man utility provides online documentation for system utilities. This utility is helpful both to new Linux users and to experienced users, who must often delve into system documentation for information on the finer points of a utility's behavior. The info utility also helps the beginner and the expert alike. It provides a tutorial on its use and documentation on many Linux utilities.

The textual interface (CLI) continues to have a place in modern computing. For example, sometimes a graphical tool does not exist or might not be as powerful, flexible, or refined as its textual counterpart. Security concerns on a server system mandate that the system run as few tasks as possible. Because each additional task can make a server more vulnerable to attack, frequently these systems do not have GUIs installed.

# EXERCISES

1. The system displays the following message when you attempt to log in with an incorrect username *or* an incorrect password:

   ```
   Login incorrect
   ```

   a. This message does not indicate whether your username, your password, or both are invalid. Why does it not reveal this information?

   b. Why does the system wait for a couple of seconds to respond after you supply an incorrect username or password?

2. Give three examples of poor password choices. What is wrong with each?

3. Is **fido** an acceptable password? Give several reasons why or why not.

4. What is a context menu? How does a context menu differ from other menus?

5. What is a workspace? What is the relationship between a workspace and the desktop?

6. How would you swap the effects of the right and left buttons on a mouse? What is the double-click speed? How would you change it?

7. What is an Application menu? What does it allow you to do?

8. What is Nautilus? What does it allow you to do?

9. Describe three ways to

   a. Change the size of a window.

   b. Delete a window.

10. What are the functions of a Window Operations menu? How do you display this menu?

11. How would you set the system time manually?

12. When you are working on the command line, how do you erase (back up over) a character? How do you delete the line you are typing? How do you terminate a program?

# ADVANCED EXERCISES

13. While working on the command line you get an error that includes the words **missing destination file operand**. What would be a good way to get help figuring out what the problem is?

14. How does the mouse pointer change when you move it to the edge of a window? What happens when you left-click and drag the mouse pointer when it looks like this? Repeat this experiment with the mouse pointer at the corner of a window.

15. What is the Session menu? When and where does it appear? How do you use it?

16. What happens when you run nano from the Enter a Command window? Where does the output go?

17. The example on page 130 shows that the man pages for **crontab** appear in Sections 1 and 5 of the system manual. Explain how you can use man to determine which sections of the system manual contain a manual page with a given name.

18. How many man pages are in the Devices subsection of the system manual? (*Hint:* Devices is a subsection of Special Files.)

# 5

# THE SHELL

## OBJECTIVES

After reading this chapter you should be able to:

▶ List special characters and methods of preventing the shell from interpreting these characters

▶ Describe a simple command

▶ Understand command-line syntax and run commands that include options and arguments

▶ Explain how the shell interprets the command line

▶ Redirect output of a command to a file, overwriting the file or appending to it

▶ Redirect input for a command so it comes from a file

▶ Connect commands using a pipeline

▶ Run commands in the background

▶ Use special characters as wildcards to generate filenames

▶ Explain the difference between a stand-alone utility and a shell builtin

The introduction to the command line on page 119 described some of the advantages of using the command line over a GUI, how to use a terminal emulator, how to correct mistakes on the command line, and how to run some command-line utilities. This chapter takes a close look at the shell and explains how to use some of its features. It discusses command-line syntax and describes how the shell processes a command line and initiates execution of a program. This chapter also explains how to redirect input to and output from a command, construct pipelines and filters on the command line, and run a command in the background. The final section covers filename expansion and explains how you can use this feature in your everyday work.

The exact wording of the shell output differs from shell to shell: What the shell you are using displays might differ slightly from what appears in this book. Refer to Chapter 9 for more information on bash (the default shell under Fedora/ RHEL) and to Chapter 27 for information on writing and executing bash shell scripts.

# SPECIAL CHARACTERS

*Special characters,* which have a special meaning to the shell, are discussed in "Filename Generation/Pathname Expansion" on page 165. These characters are mentioned here so you can avoid accidentally using them as regular characters until you understand how the shell interprets them. Avoid using any of the following characters in a filename (even though emacs and some other programs do) because they make the file harder to reference on the command line:

      & ; | * ? ' " ` [ ] ( ) $ < > { } # / \ ! ~

Whitespace   Although not considered special characters, RETURN, SPACE, and TAB have special meanings to the shell. RETURN usually ends a command line and initiates execution of a command. The SPACE and TAB characters separate tokens (elements) on the command line and are collectively known as *whitespace* or *blanks.*

Quoting special characters   If you need to use a character that has a special meaning to the shell as a regular character, you can *quote* (or *escape*) it. When you quote a special character, you prevent the shell from giving it special meaning. The shell treats a quoted special character as a regular character. However, a slash (/) is always a separator in a pathname, even when you quote it.

Backslash   To quote a character, precede it with a backslash (\). When two or more special characters appear together, you must precede each with a backslash (e.g., you would enter ** as \*\*). You can quote a backslash just as you would quote any other special character—by preceding it with a backslash (\\).

Single quotation marks   Another way of quoting special characters is to enclose them between single quotation marks: '**'. You can quote many special and regular characters between a pair of single quotation marks: '**This is a special character: >**'. The regular characters are interpreted as usual, and the shell also interprets the special characters as regular characters.

The only way to quote the erase character (CONTROL-H), the line kill character (CONTROL-U), and other control characters (try CONTROL-M) is by preceding each with a CONTROL-V. Single quotation marks and backslashes do not work. Try the following:

```
$ echo 'xxxxxxCONTROL-U'
$ echo xxxxxxCONTROL-V CONTROL-U
```

**optional**   Although you cannot see the CONTROL-U displayed by the second of the preceding pair of commands, it is there. The following command sends the output of echo (page 219) through a pipeline (page 158) to od (octal display; see the od man page) to display CONTROL-U as octal 25 (025):

```
$ echo xxxxxxCONTROL-V CONTROL-U | od -c
0000000   x   x   x   x   x   x 025  \n
0000010
```

The **\n** is the NEWLINE character that echo sends at the end of its output.

# ORDINARY FILES AND DIRECTORY FILES

*Ordinary files,* or simply *files,* are files that can hold documents, pictures, programs, and other kinds of data. *Directory files,* also referred to as *directories* or *folders,* can hold ordinary files and other directory files. For more information refer to "Ordinary Files and Directory Files" on page 177.

## THE WORKING DIRECTORY

**LPI**  pwd   While you are logged in on a character-based interface to a Linux system, you are always associated with a directory. The directory you are associated with is called the *working directory* or *current directory*. Sometimes this association is referred to in a physical sense: "You are *in* (or *working in*) the **zach** directory." The pwd (print working directory) builtin displays the pathname of the working directory.

```
login: max
Password:
Last login: Wed Oct 20 11:14:21 from 172.16.192.150
$ pwd
/home/max
```

## YOUR HOME DIRECTORY

When you first log in on a Linux system or start a terminal emulator window, the working directory is your *home directory*. To display the pathname of your home directory, use pwd just after you log in.

## LE   THE COMMAND LINE

Command   This book uses the term *command* to refer to both the characters you type on the command line and the program that action invokes.

Command line   A *command line* comprises a simple command (below), a pipeline (page 158), or a list (page 162).

## A SIMPLE COMMAND

The shell executes a program when you enter a command in response to its prompt. For example, when you give an ls command, the shell executes the utility program named ls. You can cause the shell to execute other types of programs—such as shell scripts, application programs, and programs you have written—in the same way. The line that contains the command, including any arguments, is called a *simple command*. The following sections discuss simple commands; see page 147 for a more technical and complete description of a simple command.

## SYNTAX

Command-line syntax dictates the ordering and separation of the elements on a command line. When you press the RETURN key after entering a command, the shell scans the command line for proper syntax. The syntax for a simple command is

> *command [arg1] [arg2] ... [argn]* RETURN

*Whitespace* (any combination of SPACEs and/or TABs) must separate elements on the command line. The **command** is the name of the command, **arg1** through **argn** are arguments, and RETURN is the keystroke that terminates the command line. The brackets in the command-line syntax indicate that the arguments they enclose are optional. Not all commands require arguments: Some commands do not allow arguments; other commands allow a variable number of arguments; and still others require a specific number of arguments. Options, a special kind of argument, are usually preceded by one or two hyphens (–).

### COMMAND NAME

Usage message   Some useful Linux command lines consist of only the name of the command without any arguments. For example, ls by itself lists the contents of the working directory. Commands that require arguments typically give a short error message, called a *usage message,* when you use them without arguments, with incorrect arguments, or with the wrong number of arguments.

For example, the mkdir (make directory) utility requires an argument that specifies the name of the directory you want it to create. Without this argument, it displays a usage message (*operand* is another term for "argument"):

```
$ mkdir
mkdir: missing operand
Try 'mkdir --help' for more information.
```

## *LE* ARGUMENTS

Token   On the command line each sequence of nonblank characters is called a *token* or *word*. An *argument* is a token that a command acts on (e.g., a filename, a string of characters, a number). For example, the argument to a vim or emacs command is the name of the file you want to edit.

The following command line uses cp to copy the file named **temp** to **tempcopy**:

```
$ cp temp tempcopy
```

Arguments are numbered starting with the command itself, which is argument zero. In this example, **cp** is argument zero, **temp** is argument one, and **tempcopy** is argument two. The cp utility requires at least two arguments on the command line. Argument one is the name of an existing file. In this case, argument two is the name of the file that cp is creating or overwriting. Here the arguments are not optional; both arguments must be present for the command to work. When you do not supply the right number or kind of arguments, cp displays a usage message. Try typing **cp** and then pressing RETURN.

## *LE* OPTIONS

An *option* is an argument that modifies the effects of a command. These arguments are called options because they are usually optional. You can frequently specify more than one option, modifying the command in several ways. Options are specific to and interpreted by the program that the command line calls, not the shell.

By convention, options are separate arguments that follow the name of the command and usually precede other arguments, such as filenames. Many utilities require options to be prefixed with a single hyphen. However, this requirement is specific to the utility and not the shell. GNU long (multicharacter) program options are frequently prefixed with two hyphens. For example, **--help** generates a (sometimes extensive) usage message.

The first of the following commands shows the output of an ls command without any options. By default, ls lists the contents of the working directory in alphabetical order, vertically sorted in columns. Next the **–r** (reverse order; because this is a GNU utility, you can also specify **--reverse**) option causes the ls utility to display the list of files in reverse alphabetical order, still sorted in columns. The **–x** option causes ls to display the list of files in horizontally sorted rows.

```
$ ls
hold    mark    names   oldstuff  temp  zach
house   max     office  personal  test
$ ls -r
zach  temp       oldstuff  names  mark   hold
test  personal   office    max    house
$ ls -x
hold     house     mark   max   names  office
oldstuff personal  temp   test  zach
```

Combining options When you need to use several options, you can usually group multiple single-letter options into one argument that starts with a single hyphen; do not put SPACEs between the options. You cannot combine options that are preceded by two hyphens in this way. Specific rules for combining options depend on the program you are running. The next example shows both the –r and –x options with the ls utility. Together these options generate a list of filenames in horizontally sorted rows in reverse alphabetical order.

```
$ ls -rx
zach    test   temp   personal   oldstuff   office
names   max    mark   house      hold
```

Most utilities allow you to list options in any order; thus ls –xr produces the same results as ls –rx. The command ls –x –r also generates the same list.

## The ––help option

tip Many utilities display a (sometimes extensive) help message when you call them with an argument of ––**help**. All utilities developed by the GNU Project (page 3) accept this option. Following is the help message displayed by the bzip2 compression utility (page 245).

```
$ bzip2 --help
bzip2, a block-sorting file compressor.   Version 1.0.6, 6-Sept-2010.

   usage: bunzip2 [flags and input files in any order]

   -h --help           print this message
   -d --decompress     force decompression
   -z --compress       force compression
   -k --keep           keep (don't delete) input files
   -f --force          overwrite existing output files
...
   If invoked as 'bzip2', default action is to compress.
              as 'bunzip2',  default action is to decompress.
              as 'bzcat', default action is to decompress to stdout.
...
```

Option arguments Some utilities have options that require arguments. These arguments are not optional. For example, the gcc utility (C compiler) has a –o (output) option that must be followed by the name you want to give the executable file that gcc generates. Typically an argument to an option is separated from its option letter by a SPACE:

```
$ gcc -o prog prog.c
```

Some utilities sometimes require an equal sign between an option and its argument. For example, you can specify the width of output from diff in two ways:

```
$ diff -W 60 filea fileb
```

*or*

```
$ diff --width=60 filea fileb
```

Arguments that start with a hyphen Another convention allows utilities to work with arguments, such as filenames, that start with a hyphen. If a file named –l is in the working directory, the following command is ambiguous:

```
$ ls -l
```

This command could be a request to display a long listing of all files in the working directory (–l option) or a request for a listing of the file named –l. The ls utility interprets it as the former. Avoid creating a file whose name begins with a hyphen. If you do create such a file, many utilities follow the convention that a –– argument (two consecutive hyphens) indicates the end of the options (and the beginning of the arguments). To disambiguate the preceding command, you can type

```
$ ls -- -l
```

Using two consecutive hyphens to indicate the end of the options is a convention, not a hard-and-fast rule, and a number of utilities do not follow it (e.g., find). Following this convention makes it easier for users to work with a program you write.

### Displaying readable file sizes: the –h option

tip  Most utilities that report on file sizes specify the size of a file in bytes. Bytes work well when you are dealing with smaller files, but the numbers can be difficult to read when you are working with file sizes that are measured in gigabytes or terabytes. Use the **–h** (or **––human-readable**) option to display file sizes in kilobytes, megabytes, gigabytes, and terabytes. Experiment with the **df –h** (disk free) and **ls –lh** commands.

For utilities that do not follow this convention, there are other ways to specify a filename that begins with a hyphen. You can use a period to refer to the working directory and a slash to indicate the following filename refers to a file in the working directory:

```
$ ls ./-l
```

You can also specify the absolute pathname of the file:

```
$ ls /home/max/-l
```

### optional
## SIMPLE COMMANDS

This section expands on the discussion of command-line syntax that starts on page 144.

A simple command comprises zero or more variable assignments followed by a command line. It is terminated by a control operator (e.g., &, ;, |, NEWLINE; page 341). A simple command has the following syntax:

*[name=value ...] command-line*

The shell assigns a *value* to each *name* and places it in the environment (page 1032) of the program that *command-line* calls so it is available to the called program and its children as a variable. The shell evaluates the *name=value* pairs from left to right, so if *name* appears more than once in this list, the rightmost *value* takes precedence.

The *command-line* might include redirection operators such as > and < (page 153). The exit status (page 1029) of a simple command is its return value.

Placing a variable in the environment of a child

The following commands demonstrate how you can assign a value to a name (variable) and place that name in the environment of a child program; the variable is not available to the interactive shell you are running (the parent program). The script named echo_ee displays the value of the variable named ee. The first call to echo_ee shows ee is not set in the child shell running the script. When the call to echo_ee is preceded by assigning a value to ee, the script displays the value of ee in the child shell. The final command shows ee has not been set in the interactive shell.

```
$ cat echo_ee
echo "The value of the ee variable is: $ee"

$ ./echo_ee
The value of the ee variable is:
$ ee=88 ./echo_ee
The value of the ee variable is: 88
$ echo $ee

$
```

## PROCESSING THE COMMAND LINE

As you enter a command line, the tty device driver (part of the Linux kernel) examines each character to see whether it must take immediate action. When you press CONTROL-H (to erase a character) or CONTROL-U (to kill a line), the device driver immediately adjusts the command line as required; the shell never sees the character(s) you erased or the line you killed. Often a similar adjustment occurs when you press CONTROL-W (to erase a word). When the character you entered does not require immediate action, the device driver stores the character in a buffer and waits for additional characters. When you press RETURN, the device driver passes the command line to the shell for processing.

Parsing the command line

When the shell processes a command line, it looks at the line as a whole and *parses* (breaks) it into its component parts (Figure 5-1). Next the shell looks for the name of the command. Usually the name of the command is the first item on the command line after the prompt (argument zero). The shell takes the first characters on the command line up to the first blank (TAB or SPACE) and then looks for a command with that name. The command name (the first token) can be specified on the command line either as a simple filename or as a pathname. For example, you can call the ls command in either of the following ways:

```
$ ls
```

*or*

```
$ /bin/ls
```

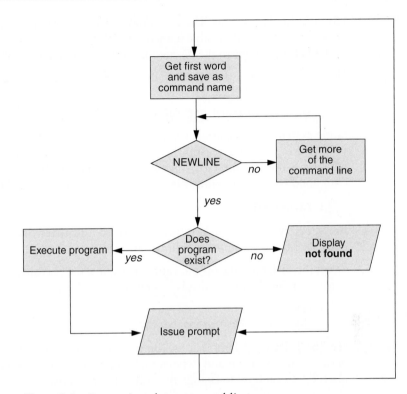

**Figure 5-1** Processing the command line

**optional** The shell does not require the name of the program to appear first on the command line. Thus you can structure a command line as follows:

```
$ >bb <aa cat
```

This command runs **cat** with standard input coming from the file named **aa** and standard output going to the file named **bb**. When the shell recognizes the redirect symbols (page 153), it processes them and their arguments before finding the name of the program that the command line is calling. This is a properly structured—albeit rarely encountered and possibly confusing—command line.

**LPI** Absolute versus relative pathnames From the command line, there are three ways you can specify the name of a file you want the shell to execute: as an absolute pathname (starts with a slash [/]; page 181), as a relative pathname (includes a slash but does not start with a slash; page 182), or as a simple filename (no slash). When you specify the name of a file for the shell to execute in either of the first two ways (the pathname includes a slash), the shell looks in the specified directory for a file with the specified name that you have permission to execute. When you specify a simple filename (no slash), the shell searches through a list of directories for a filename that matches the specified name and for which you have execute permission. The shell does not look through all directories but only the ones specified by the variable named **PATH**. Refer to page 359 for more information on **PATH**. Also refer to the discussion of the which and whereis utilities on page 255.

When it cannot find the file, bash displays the following message:

```
$ abc
bash: abc: command not found...
```

Some systems are set up to suggest where you might be able to find the program you tried to run. One reason the shell might not be able to find the executable file is that it is not in a directory listed in the **PATH** variable. Under bash the following command temporarily adds the working directory (.) to **PATH**:

```
$ PATH=$PATH:.
```

For security reasons, it is poor practice to add the working directory to **PATH** permanently; see the following tip and the one on page 360.

When the shell finds the file but cannot execute it (i.e., because you do not have execute permission for the file), it displays a message similar to

```
$ def
bash: ./def: Permission denied
```

See "ls –l: Displays Permissions" on page 191 for information on displaying access permissions for a file and "chmod: Changes Access Permissions" on page 193 for instructions on how to change file access permissions.

### Try giving a command as ./command

tip   You can always execute an executable file in the working directory by prepending ./ to the name of the file. Because ./**filename** is a relative pathname, the shell does not consult **PATH** when looking for **filename**. For example, if **myprog** is an executable file in the working directory, you can execute it using the following command (regardless of how **PATH** is set):

```
$ ./myprog
```

## EXECUTING A COMMAND

LE   Process   If it finds an executable file with the name specified on the command line, the shell starts a new process. A *process* is the execution of a command by Linux (page 373). The shell makes each command-line argument, including options and the name of the command, available to the called program. While the command is executing, the shell waits for the process to finish. At this point the shell is in an inactive state named *sleep*. When the program finishes execution, it passes its exit status (page 1029) to the shell. The shell then returns to an active state (wakes up), issues a prompt, and waits for another command.

The shell does not process arguments   Because the shell does not process command-line arguments but merely passes them to the called program, the shell has no way of knowing whether a particular option or other argument is valid for a given program. Any error or usage messages about options or arguments come from the program itself. Some utilities ignore bad options.

**Figure 5-2**   The command does not know where standard input comes from or where standard output and standard error go

## EDITING THE COMMAND LINE

You can repeat and edit previous commands and edit the current command line. See pages 124 and 378 for more information.

# STANDARD INPUT AND STANDARD OUTPUT

*Standard output* is a place to which a program can send information (e.g., text). The program never "knows" where the information it sends to standard output is going (Figure 5-2). The information can go to a printer, an ordinary file, or the screen. The following sections show that by default the shell directs standard output from a command to the screen[1] and describe how you can cause the shell to redirect this output to another file.

*Standard input* is a place a program gets information from; by default, the shell directs standard input from the keyboard. As with standard output the program never "knows" where the information comes from. The following sections explain how to redirect standard input to a command so it comes from an ordinary file instead of from the keyboard.

In addition to standard input and standard output, a running program has a place to send error messages: *standard error*. By default, the shell directs standard error to the screen. Refer to page 333 for more information on redirecting standard error.

**optional**   By convention, a process expects that the program that called it (frequently the shell) has set up standard input, standard output, and standard error so the process can use them immediately. The called process does not *have* to know which files or devices are connected to standard input, standard output, or standard error.

However, a process *can* query the kernel to get information about the device that standard input, standard output, or standard error is connected to. For example, the ls utility displays output in multiple columns when the output goes to the screen, but generates a single column of output when the output is redirected to a file or another

---

1. This book uses the term *screen* to refer to a screen, terminal emulator window, or workstation—in other words, to the device that the shell displays its prompt and messages on.

program. The ls utility uses the **isatty()** system call to determine whether output is going to the screen (a tty). In addition, ls can use another system call to determine the width of the screen it is sending output to; with this information it can modify its output to fit the screen. Compare the output of ls by itself and when you send it through a pipeline to less. See page 1020 for information on how you can determine whether standard input and standard output of shell scripts is going to/coming from the terminal.

## THE SCREEN AS A FILE

*LPI*    Device file    Chapter 6 discusses ordinary files, directory files, and hard and soft links. Linux has an additional type of file: a *device file*. A device file resides in the file structure, usually in the **/dev** directory, and represents a peripheral device, such as a terminal, printer, or disk drive.

The device name the who utility displays following a username is the filename of the terminal that user is working on. For example, when who displays the device name **pts/4**, the pathname of the terminal is **/dev/pts/4**. When you work with multiple windows, each window has its own device name. You can also use the tty utility to display the name of the device that you give the command from. Although you would not normally have occasion to do so, you can read from and write to this file as though it were a text file. Reading from the device file that represents the terminal you are using reads what you enter on the keyboard; writing to it displays what you write on the screen.

## THE KEYBOARD AND SCREEN AS STANDARD INPUT AND STANDARD OUTPUT

After you log in, the shell directs standard output of commands you enter to the device file that represents the terminal (Figure 5-3). Directing output in this manner causes it to appear on the screen. The shell also directs standard input to come from the same file, so commands receive as input anything you type on the keyboard.

*LPI*    cat    The cat utility provides a good example of the way the keyboard and screen function as standard input and standard output, respectively. When you run cat, it copies a file to standard output. Because the shell directs standard output to the screen, cat displays the file on the screen.

Up to this point cat has taken its input from the filename (argument) you specify on the command line. When you do not give cat an argument (i.e., when you give the command cat followed immediately by RETURN), cat takes its input from standard input. Thus, when called without an argument, cat copies standard input to standard output, one line at a time.

To see how cat works, type **cat** and press RETURN in response to the shell prompt. Nothing happens. Enter a line of text and press RETURN. The same line appears just under the one

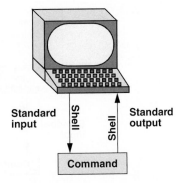

**Figure 5-3**   By default, standard input comes from the keyboard, and standard output goes to the screen

you entered. The cat utility is working. Because the shell associates cat's standard input with the keyboard and cat's standard output with the screen, when you type a line of text cat copies the text from standard input (the keyboard) to standard output (the screen). The next example shows this exchange.

```
$ cat
This is a line of text.
This is a line of text.
Cat keeps copying lines of text
Cat keeps copying lines of text
until you press CONTROL-D at the beginning
until you press CONTROL-D at the beginning
of a line.
of a line.
CONTROL-D
$
```

CONTROL-D signals EOF  The cat utility keeps copying text until you enter CONTROL-D on a line by itself. Pressing CONTROL-D causes the tty device driver to send an EOF (end of file) signal to cat. This signal indicates to cat that it has reached the end of standard input and there is no more text for it to copy. The cat utility then finishes execution and returns control to the shell, which displays a prompt.

## LE+  REDIRECTION

The term *redirection* encompasses the various ways you can cause the shell to alter where standard input of a command comes from and where standard output goes to. By default, the shell associates standard input and standard output of a command with the keyboard and the screen. You can cause the shell to redirect standard input or standard output of any command by associating the input or output with a command or file other than the device file representing the keyboard or the screen. This section demonstrates how to redirect input/output from/to text files and utilities.

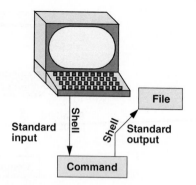

**Figure 5-4**   Redirecting standard output

## *LPI* REDIRECTING STANDARD OUTPUT

The *redirect output symbol* (>) instructs the shell to redirect the output of a command to the specified file instead of to the screen (Figure 5-4). The syntax of a command line that redirects output is

> *command [arguments] > filename*

where **command** is any executable program (e.g., an application program or a utility), **arguments** are optional arguments, and **filename** is the name of the ordinary file the shell redirects the output to.

Using cat to create a file
The next example uses cat to demonstrate output redirection. This example contrasts with the example on page 153, where standard input *and* standard output are associated with the keyboard and screen. The input in the following example comes from the keyboard. The redirect output symbol on the command line causes the shell to associate cat's standard output with the **sample.txt** file specified following this symbol.

```
$ cat > sample.txt
This text is being entered at the keyboard and
cat is copying it to a file.
Press CONTROL-D to indicate the
end of file.
CONTROL-D
$
```

### Redirecting output can destroy a file I

caution   Use caution when you redirect output to a file. If the file exists, the shell will overwrite it and destroy its contents. For more information see the tip "Redirecting output can destroy a file II" on page 156.

After giving the command and typing the text shown in the previous example, the **sample.txt** file contains the text you entered. You can use cat with an argument of **sample.txt** to display this file. The next section shows another way to use cat to display the file.

The previous example shows that redirecting standard output from cat is a handy way to create a file without using an editor. The drawback is that once you enter a line and press RETURN, you cannot edit the text until after you finish creating the file. While you are entering a line, the erase and kill keys work to delete text on that line. This procedure is useful for creating short, simple files.

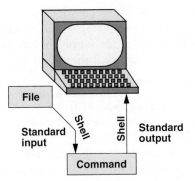

**Figure 5-5**  Redirecting standard input

The next example shows how to run cat and use the redirect output symbol to *catenate* (join one after the other—the derivation of the name of the cat utility) several files into one larger file. The first three commands display the contents of three files: **stationery**, **tape**, and **pens**. The next command shows cat with three filenames as arguments. When you call it with more than one filename, cat copies the files, one at a time, to standard output. This command redirects standard output to the file named **supply_orders**. The final cat command shows that **supply_orders** contains the contents of the three original files.

```
$ cat stationery
2,000 sheets letterhead ordered:    October 7
$ cat tape
1 box masking tape ordered:         October 14
5 boxes filament tape ordered:      October 28
$ cat pens
12 doz. black pens ordered:         October 4

$ cat stationery tape pens > supply_orders

$ cat supply_orders
2,000 sheets letterhead ordered:    October 7
1 box masking tape ordered:         October 14
5 boxes filament tape ordered:      October 28
12 doz. black pens ordered:         October 4
```

## *LPI* REDIRECTING STANDARD INPUT

Just as you can redirect standard output, so you can redirect standard input. The *redirect input symbol* (<) instructs the shell to redirect a command's input to come from the specified file instead of from the keyboard (Figure 5-5). The syntax of a command line that redirects input is

    *command [arguments] < filename*

where ***command*** is any executable program (such as an application program or a utility), ***arguments*** are optional arguments, and ***filename*** is the name of the ordinary file the shell redirects the input from.

The next example shows cat with its input redirected from the **supply_orders** file created in the previous example and standard output going to the screen. This setup causes cat to display the **supply_orders** file on the screen. The system automatically supplies an EOF signal at the end of an ordinary file.

```
$ cat < supply_orders
2,000 sheets letterhead ordered:    October 7
1 box masking tape ordered:         October 14
5 boxes filament tape ordered:      October 28
12 doz. black pens ordered:         October 4
```

**Utilities that take input from a file or standard input**  Giving a cat command with input redirected from a file yields the same result as giving a cat command with the filename as an argument. The cat utility is a member of a class of utilities that function in this manner. Other members of this class of utilities include lpr, sort, grep, and Perl. These utilities first examine the command line that called them. If the command line includes a filename as an argument, the utility takes its input from the specified file. If no filename argument is present, the utility takes its input from standard input. It is the utility or program—not the shell or operating system—that functions in this manner.

### Redirecting output can destroy a file II

**caution**  Depending on which shell you are using and how the environment is set up, a command such as the following can yield undesired results:

```
$ cat orange pear > orange
cat: orange: input file is output file
```

Although cat displays an error message, the shell destroys the contents of the existing **orange** file. The new **orange** file will have the same contents as **pear** because the first action the shell takes when it sees the redirection symbol (>) is to remove the contents of the original **orange** file. If you want to catenate two files into one, use cat to put the two files into a temporary file and then use mv to rename the temporary file:

```
$ cat orange pear > temp
$ mv temp orange
```

What happens in the next example can be even worse. The user giving the command wants to search through files **a**, **b**, and **c** for the word **apple** and redirect the output from grep (page 232) to the file **a.output**. Unfortunately the user enters the filename as **a output**, omitting the period and inserting a SPACE in its place:

```
$ grep apple a b c > a output
grep: output: No such file or directory
```

The shell obediently removes the contents of **a** and then calls grep. The error message could take a moment to appear, giving you a sense that the command is running correctly. Even after you see the error message, it might take a while to realize that you have destroyed the contents of **a**.

## noclobber: PREVENTS OVERWRITING FILES

The shell provides the **noclobber** feature, which prevents you from overwriting a file using redirection. Enable this feature by setting **noclobber** using the command **set –o noclobber**. The same command with **+o** unsets **noclobber**. With **noclobber** set, if you redirect output to an existing file, the shell displays an error message and does not execute the command. The following example creates a file using touch, sets **noclobber,** attempts to redirect the output from echo to the newly created file, unsets **noclobber,** and performs the same redirection:

```
$ touch tmp
$ set -o noclobber
$ echo "hi there" > tmp
-bash: tmp: cannot overwrite existing file
$ set +o noclobber
$ echo "hi there" > tmp
```

You can override **noclobber** by putting a pipeline symbol after the redirect symbol (>|). In the following example, the user creates a file by redirecting the output of date. Next the user sets the **noclobber** variable and redirects output to the same file again. The shell displays an error message. Then the user places a pipeline symbol after the redirect symbol, and the shell allows the user to overwrite the file.

```
$ date > tmp2
$ set -o noclobber
$ date > tmp2
-bash: tmp2: cannot overwrite existing file
$ date >| tmp2
```

## APPENDING STANDARD OUTPUT TO A FILE

### Do not trust **noclobber**

Appending output is simpler than the two-step procedure described in the preceding caution box but you must be careful to include both greater than signs. If you accidentally use only one greater than sign and the **noclobber** feature is not set, the shell will overwrite the **orange** file. Even if you have the **noclobber** feature turned on, it is a good idea to keep backup copies of the files you are manipulating in case you make a mistake.

Although it protects you from overwriting a file using redirection, **noclobber** does not stop you from overwriting a file using cp or mv. These utilities include the **–i** (interactive) option that helps protect you from this type of mistake by verifying your intentions when you try to overwrite a file. For more information see the tip "cp can destroy a file" on page 224.

The *append output symbol* (>>) causes the shell to add new information to the end of a file, leaving existing information intact. This symbol provides a convenient way of catenating two files into one. The following commands demonstrate the action of the append output symbol. The second command accomplishes the catenation described in the preceding caution box:

```
$ cat orange
this is orange
$ cat pear >> orange
$ cat orange
this is orange
this is pear
```

The first command displays the contents of the **orange** file. The second command appends the contents of the **pear** file to the **orange** file. The final command displays the result.

The next example shows how to create a file that contains the date and time (the output from date), followed by a list of who is logged in (the output from who). The first command in the example redirects the output from date to the file named **whoson**. Then cat displays the file. The next command appends the output from who to the **whoson** file. Finally cat displays the file containing the output of both utilities.

```
$ date > whoson
$ cat whoson
Wed Mar 27 14:31:18 PST 2013
$ who >> whoson
$ cat whoson
Wed Mar 27 14:31:18 PST 2013
sam        tty1         2013-03-27 05:00(:0)
max        pts/4        2013-03-27 12:23(:0.0)
max        pts/5        2013-03-27 12:33(:0.0)
zach       pts/7        2013-03-26 08:45 (172.16.192.1)
```

## /dev/null: MAKING DATA DISAPPEAR

The **/dev/null** device is a *data sink*, commonly referred to as a *bit bucket*. You can redirect output you do not want to keep or see to **/dev/null**, and the output will disappear without a trace:

```
$ echo "hi there" > /dev/null
$
```

Reading from **/dev/null** yields a null string. The following command truncates the file named **messages** to zero length while preserving the ownership and permissions of the file:

```
$ ls -lh messages
-rw-rw-r--. 1 sam pubs 125K 03-16 14:30 messages
$ cat /dev/null > messages
$ ls -lh messages
-rw-rw-r--. 1 sam pubs 0 03-16 14:32 messages
```

See also page 503.

## *LE+*    PIPELINES

A *pipeline* consists of one or more commands separated by a pipeline symbol (|). The shell connects standard output (and optionally standard error) of the command preceding the pipeline symbol to standard input of the command following the pipeline symbol. A pipeline has the same effect as redirecting standard output of one command to a file and then using that file as standard input to another command. A pipeline does away with separate commands and the intermediate file. The syntax of a pipeline is

*command_a [arguments]* | *command_b [arguments]*

The preceding command line uses a pipeline to effect the same result as the following three commands:

*command_a [arguments] > temp*
*command_b [arguments] < temp*
*rm temp*

In the preceding sequence of commands, the first line redirects standard output from *command_a* to an intermediate file named ***temp***. The second line redirects standard input for *command_b* to come from ***temp***. The final line deletes ***temp***. The pipeline syntax is not only easier to type but also is more efficient because it does not create a temporary file.

**optional**    More precisely, a bash pipeline comprises one or more simple commands (page 147) separated by a | or |& control operator. A pipeline has the following syntax:

*[time] [!] command1 [| | |& command2 ... ]*

where *time* is an optional utility that summarizes the system resources used by the pipeline, *!* logically negates the exit status returned by the pipeline, and the *commands* are simple commands (page 147) separated by | or |&. The | control operator sends standard output of *command1* to standard input of *command2*. The |& control operator is short for 2>&1 | (see "Sending errors through a pipeline" on page 335) and sends standard output and standard error of *command1* to standard input of *command2*. The exit status of a pipeline is the exit status of the last simple command unless **pipefail** (page 403) is set, in which case the exit status is the rightmost simple command that failed (returned a nonzero exit status) or zero if all simple commands completed successfully.

## EXAMPLES OF PIPELINES

*LPI*   tr   You can include in a pipeline any utility that accepts input either from a file specified on the command line or from standard input. You can also include utilities that accept input only from standard input. For example, the tr (translate) utility takes its input from standard input only. In its simplest usage tr has the following syntax:

*tr string1 string2*

The tr utility accepts input from standard input and looks for characters that match one of the characters in ***string1***. Upon finding a match, it translates the matched character in ***string1*** to the corresponding character in ***string2***. That is, the first character in ***string1*** translates into the first character in ***string2***, and so forth. The tr utility sends its output to standard output. In both of the following tr commands, tr displays the contents of the **abstract** file with the letters **a**, **b**, and **c** translated into **A**, **B**, and **C**, respectively:

```
$ cat abstract
I took a cab today!

$ cat abstract | tr abc ABC
I took A CAB todAy!
$ tr abc ABC < abstract
I took A CAB todAy!
```

The tr utility does not change the contents of the original file; it cannot change the original file because it does not "know" the source of its input.

lpr   The lpr (line printer) utility accepts input from either a file or standard input. When you type the name of a file following lpr on the command line, it places that file in the print queue. When you do not specify a filename on the command line, lpr takes input from standard input. This feature enables you to use a pipeline to redirect input to lpr. The first set of the following commands shows how you can use ls and lpr with an intermediate file (**temp**) to send a list of the files in the working directory to the printer. If the **temp** file exists, the first command overwrites its contents. The second set of commands uses a pipeline to send the same list (with the exception of **temp**) to the printer.

```
$ ls > temp
$ lpr temp
$ rm temp
```

*or*

```
$ ls | lpr
```

sort   The commands in next example redirect the output from the who utility to **temp** and then display this file in sorted order. The sort utility (page 239) takes its input from the file specified on the command line or, when a file is not specified, from standard input; it sends its output to standard output. The sort command line takes its input from standard input, which is redirected (<) to come from **temp**. The output sort sends to the screen lists the users in sorted (alphabetical) order. Because sort can take its input from standard input or from a file named on the command line, omitting the < symbol from the command line yields the same result.

```
$ who > temp
$ sort < temp
max          pts/4        2013-03-24 12:23
max          pts/5        2013-03-24 12:33
sam          tty1         2013-03-24 05:00
zach         pts/7        2013-03-23 08:45
$ rm temp
```

The next example achieves the same result without creating the **temp** file. Using a pipeline, the shell redirects the output from who to the input of sort. The sort utility takes input from standard input because no filename follows it on the command line.

```
$ who | sort
max          pts/4        2013-03-24 12:23
max          pts/5        2013-03-24 12:33
sam          tty1         2013-03-24 05:00
zach         pts/7        2013-03-23 08:45
```

grep   When many people are using the system and you want information about only one of them, you can send the output from who to grep (page 232) using a pipeline. The grep utility displays the line containing the string you specify—**sam** in the following example:

```
$ who | grep sam
sam       tty1         2013-03-24 05:00
```

less and more   Another way of handling output that is too long to fit on the screen, such as a list of files in a crowded directory, is to use a pipeline to send the output through less or more (both on page 220).

```
$ ls | less
```

The less utility displays text one screen at a time. To view another screen of text, press the SPACE bar. To view one more line, press RETURN. Press **h** for help and **q** to quit.

**optional**   The pipeline symbol (|) implies continuation. Thus the following command line

```
$ who | grep 'sam'
sam       tty1         2013-03-24 05:00
```

is the same as these command lines

```
$ who |
> grep 'sam'
sam       tty1         2013-03-24 05:00
```

When the shell parses a line that ends with a pipeline symbol, it requires more input before it can execute the command line. In an interactive environment, it issues a secondary prompt (>; page 362) as shown above. Within a shell script, it processes the next line as a continuation of the line that ends with the pipeline symbol. See page 1063 for information about control operators and implicit command-line continuation.

## _LPI_ FILTERS

A *filter* is a command that processes an input stream of data to produce an output stream of data. A command line that includes a filter uses a pipeline symbol to connect standard output of one command to standard input of the filter. Another pipeline symbol connects standard output of the filter to standard input of another command. Not all utilities can be used as filters.

In the following example, sort is a filter, taking standard input from standard output of who and using a pipeline symbol to redirect standard output to standard input of lpr. This command line sends the sorted output of who to the printer:

```
$ who | sort | lpr
```

The preceding example demonstrates the power of the shell combined with the versatility of Linux utilities. The three utilities who, sort, and lpr were not designed to work with one another, but they all use standard input and standard output in the conventional way. By using the shell to handle input and output, you can piece standard utilities together on the command line to achieve the results you want.

*LPI*   tee   The tee utility copies its standard input both to a file and to standard output. This utility is aptly named: It takes a single stream of input and sends the output in two directions. The next example sends the output of who via a pipeline to standard input of tee. The tee utility saves a copy of standard input in a file named **who.out** and also sends a copy to standard output. Standard output of tee goes via a pipeline to standard input of grep, which displays only those lines containing the string **sam**. Use tee with the **–a** (append) option to cause it to append to a file instead of overwriting it.

```
$ who | tee who.out | grep sam
sam        tty1         2013-03-24 05:00
$ cat who.out
sam        tty1         2013-03-24 05:00
max        pts/4        2013-03-24 12:23
max        pts/5        2013-03-24 12:33
zach       pts/7        2013 -03-23 08:45
```

**optional**

*LE+*   # Lists

A *list* is one or more pipelines (including simple commands), each separated from the next by one of the following control operators: **;**, **&**, **&&**, or **||**. The **&&** and **||** control operators have equal precedence; they are followed by **;** and **&**, which have equal precedence. The **;** control operator is covered on page 341 and **&** on page 342. See page 1063 for information about control operators and implicit command-line continuation.

An AND list has the following syntax:

*pipeline1* **&&** *pipeline2*

where *pipeline2* is executed if and only if *pipeline1* returns a *true* (zero) exit status. In the following example, the first command in the list fails (and displays an error message) so the shell does not execute the second command (**cd /newdir**; because it is not executed, it does not display an error message):

```
$ mkdir /newdir && cd /newdir
mkdir: cannot create directory '/newdir': Permission denied
```

The exit status of AND and OR lists is the exit status of the last command in the list that is executed. The exit status of the preceding list is *false* because mkdir was the last command executed and it failed.

An OR list has the following syntax:

*pipeline1* **||** *pipeline2*

where *pipeline2* is executed if and only if *pipeline1* returns a *false* (nonzero) exit status. In the next example, the first command (ping tests the connection to a remote machine and sends standard output and standard error to **/dev/null**) in the list fails so the shell executes the second command (it displays a message). If the first command had completed successfully, the shell would not have executed the second command (and would not have displayed the message). The list returns an exit status of *true*.

```
$ ping -c1 station &>/dev/null || echo "station is down"
station is down
```

For more information refer to "&& and || Boolean Control Operators" on page 343.

# *LPI*  RUNNING A COMMAND IN THE BACKGROUND

*LPI* Foreground    All commands up to this point have been run in the foreground. When you run a command in the *foreground*, the shell waits for it to finish before displaying another prompt and allowing you to continue. When you run a command in the *background*, you do not have to wait for the command to finish before running another command.

Jobs    A *job* is another name for a process running a pipeline (which can be a simple command). You can have only one foreground job in a window or on a screen, but you can have many background jobs. By running more than one job at a time, you are using one of Linux's features: multitasking. Running a command in the background can be useful when the command will run for a long time and does not need supervision. It leaves the screen free so you can use it for other work. Alternately, when you are using a GUI, you can open another window to run another job.

Job number,    To run a command in the background, type an ampersand (&; a control operator)
PID number    just before the RETURN that ends the command line. The shell assigns a small number to the job and displays this *job number* between brackets. Following the job number, the shell displays the *process identification (PID) number*—a larger number assigned by the operating system. Each of these numbers identifies the command running in the background. The shell then displays another prompt, and you can enter another command. When the background job finishes, the shell displays a message giving both the job number and the command line used to run the command.

The following example runs in the background; it is a pipeline that sends the output of ls to lpr, which sends it to the printer.

```
$ ls -l | lpr &
[1] 22092
$
```

The [1] following the command line indicates that the shell has assigned job number 1 to this job. The **22092** is the PID number of the first command in the job. When this background job completes execution, you see the message

```
[1]+ Done          ls -l | lpr
```

(In place of **ls –l**, the shell might display something similar to **ls ––color=auto –l**. This difference is due to the fact that ls is aliased [page 392] to **ls ––color=auto**.)

## *LPI*   Moving a Job from the Foreground to the Background

CONTROL-Z
and bg

You can suspend a foreground job (stop it from running) by pressing the suspend key, usually CONTROL-Z. The shell then stops the process and disconnects standard input from the keyboard. It does, however, still send standard output and standard error to the screen. You can put a suspended job in the background and restart it by using the bg command followed by the job number. You do not need to specify the job number when there is only one suspended job.

Redirect the output of a job you run in the background to keep it from interfering with whatever you are working on in the foreground (on the screen). Refer to "Control Operators: Separate and Group Commands" on page 341 for more detail about background tasks.

fg

Only the foreground job can take input from the keyboard. To connect the keyboard to a program running in the background, you must bring the program to the foreground. To do so, type **fg** without any arguments when only one job is in the background. When more than one job is in the background, type **fg**, or a percent sign (**%**), followed by the number of the job you want to bring to the foreground. The shell displays the command you used to start the job (**promptme** in the following example), and you can enter input the program requires to continue.

```
$ fg 1
promptme
```

## *LPI*   kill: Aborting a Background Job

The interrupt key (usually CONTROL-C) cannot abort a background process because the keyboard is not attached to the job; you must use kill (page 465) for this purpose. Follow **kill** on the command line with either the PID number of the process you want to abort or a percent sign (**%**) followed by the job number.

Determining the
PID of a process
using ps

If you forget a PID number, you can use the ps (process status) utility (page 374) to display it. The following example runs a find command in the background, uses ps to display the PID number of the process, and aborts the job using kill:

```
$ find / -name memo55 > mem.out &
[1] 18228
$ ps | grep find
18228 pts/10    00:00:01 find
$ kill 18228
[1]+  Terminated              find / -name memo55 > mem.out
$
```

*LPI* Determining
the number of a job
using jobs

If you forget a job number, you can use the jobs command to display a list of jobs that includes job numbers. The next example is similar to the previous one except it uses the job number instead of the PID number to identify the job to be killed. Sometimes the message saying the job is terminated does not appear until you press RETURN after the RETURN that executes the kill command.

```
$ find / -name memo55 > mem.out &
[1] 18236

$ bigjob &
[2] 18237

$ jobs
[1]-  Running                    find / -name memo55 > mem.out &
[2]+  Running                    bigjob &
$ kill %1
$ RETURN
[1]-  Terminated                 find / -name memo55 > mem.out
$
```

## *LE+* FILENAME GENERATION/PATHNAME EXPANSION

Wildcards, globbing    When you specify an abbreviated filename that contains *special characters*, also called *metacharacters*, the shell can generate filenames that match the names of existing files. These special characters are also referred to as *wildcards* because they act much as the jokers do in a deck of cards. When one of these characters appears in an argument on the command line, the shell expands that argument in sorted order into a list of filenames and passes the list to the program called by the command line. Filenames that contain these special characters are called *ambiguous file references* because they do not refer to one specific file. The process the shell performs on these filenames is called *pathname expansion* or *globbing*.

Ambiguous file references can quickly refer to a group of files with similar names, saving the effort of typing the names individually. They can also help find a file whose name you do not remember in its entirety. If no filename matches the ambiguous file reference, the shell generally passes the unexpanded reference—special characters and all—to the command. See "Brace Expansion" on page 405 for a technique that generates strings that do not necessarily match filenames.

## THE ? SPECIAL CHARACTER

The question mark (?) is a special character that causes the shell to generate filenames. It matches any single character in the name of an existing file. The following command uses this special character in an argument to the lpr utility:

```
$ lpr memo?
```

The shell expands the **memo?** argument and generates a list of files in the working directory that have names composed of **memo** followed by any single character. The shell then passes this list to lpr. The lpr utility never "knows" the shell generated the filenames it was called with. If no filename matches the ambiguous file reference, the shell passes the string itself (**memo?**) to lpr or, if it is set up to do so, passes a null string (see **nullglob** on page 402).

The following example uses ls first to display the names of all files in the working directory and then to display the filenames that **memo?** matches:

```
$ ls
mem    memo12   memo9   memomax     newmemo5
memo   memo5    memoa   memos

$ ls memo?
memo5   memo9   memoa   memos
```

The **memo?** ambiguous file reference does not match **mem, memo, memo12, memomax,** or **newmemo5.** You can also use a question mark in the middle of an ambiguous file reference:

```
$ ls
7may4report   may4report       mayqreport   may_report
may14report   may4report.79    mayreport    may.report

$ ls may?report
may4report   mayqreport   may_report   may.report
```

echo    You can use echo and ls to practice generating filenames. The echo builtin displays the arguments the shell passes to it:

```
$ echo may?report
may4report mayqreport may_report may.report
```

The shell first expands the ambiguous file reference into a list of files in the working directory that match the string **may?report.** It then passes this list to echo, as though you had entered the list of filenames as arguments to echo. The echo utility displays the list of filenames.

A question mark does not match a leading period (one that indicates a hidden filename; page 180). When you want to match filenames that begin with a period, you must explicitly include the period in the ambiguous file reference.

## THE * SPECIAL CHARACTER

The asterisk (*) performs a function similar to that of the question mark but matches any number of characters, *including zero characters*, in a filename. The following example first shows all files in the working directory and then shows commands that display all the filenames that begin with the string **memo,** end with the string **mo,** and contain the string **alx:**

```
$ ls
amemo   memalx   memo.0612   memoalx.0620   memorandum   sallymemo
mem     memo     memoa       memoalx.keep   memosally    user.memo

$ echo memo*
memo memo.0612 memoa memoalx.0620 memoalx.keep memorandum memosally

$ echo *mo
amemo memo sallymemo user.memo

$ echo *alx*
memalx memoalx.0620 memoalx.keep
```

The ambiguous file reference **memo** does not match **amemo, mem, sallymemo,** or **user.memo.** Like the question mark, an asterisk does *not* match a leading period in a filename.

The **–a** option causes ls to display hidden filenames (page 180). The command **echo** * does not display **.** (the working directory), **..** (the parent of the working directory), **.aaa,** or **.profile.** In contrast, the command **echo .** * displays only those four names:

```
$ ls
aaa  memo.0612  memo.sally  report  sally.0612  saturday  thurs

$ ls -a
.    aaa   memo.0612   .profile  sally.0612  thurs
..   .aaa  memo.sally  report    saturday

$ echo *
aaa memo.0612 memo.sally report sally.0612 saturday thurs

$ echo .*
. .. .aaa .profile
```

In the following example, **.p** * does not match **memo.0612, private, reminder,** or **report.** The **ls .** * command causes ls to list **.private** and **.profile** in addition to the contents of the **.** directory (the working directory) and the **..** directory (the parent of the working directory). When called with the same argument, echo displays the names of files (including directories) in the working directory that begin with a dot (.) but not the contents of directories.

```
$ ls -a
. ..  memo.0612  private  .private  .profile  reminder  report

$ echo .p*
.private .profile

$ ls .*
.private .profile
.:
memo.0612  private   reminder   report
..:
...

$ echo .*
. .. .private .profile
```

You can plan to take advantage of ambiguous file references when you establish conventions for naming files. For example, when you end the names of all text files with **.txt,** you can reference that group of files with *** .txt.** The next command uses this convention to send all text files in the working directory to the printer. The ampersand causes lpr to run in the background.

```
$ lpr *.txt &
```

### The shell expands ambiguous file references

tip *The shell does the expansion* when it processes an ambiguous file reference, not the program that the shell runs. In the examples in this section, *the utilities* (ls, cat, echo, lpr) *never see the ambiguous file references.* The shell expands the ambiguous file references and passes a list of ordinary filenames to the utility. In the previous examples, echo demonstrates this fact because it simply displays its arguments; it never displays the ambiguous file reference.

# THE [ ] SPECIAL CHARACTERS

A pair of brackets surrounding one or more characters causes the shell to match filenames containing the individual characters within the brackets. Whereas **memo?** matches **memo** followed by any character, **memo[17a]** is more restrictive: It matches only **memo1**, **memo7**, and **memoa**. The brackets define a *character class* that includes all the characters within the brackets. (GNU calls this a *character list*; a *GNU character class* is something different.) The shell expands an argument that includes a character-class definition by substituting each member of the character class, *one at a time*, in place of the brackets and their contents. The shell then passes the list of matching filenames to the program it is calling.

Each character-class definition can replace only a single character within a filename. The brackets and their contents are like a question mark that substitutes only the members of the character class.

The first of the following commands lists the names of all files in the working directory that begin with **a**, **e**, **i**, **o**, or **u**. The second command displays the contents of the files named **page2.txt**, **page4.txt**, **page6.txt**, and **page8.txt**.

```
$ echo [aeiou]*
. . .

$ less page[2468].txt
. . .
```

A hyphen within brackets defines a range of characters within a character-class definition. For example, [6–9] represents [6789], [a–z] represents all lowercase letters in English, and [a–zA–Z] represents all letters, both uppercase and lowercase, in English.

The following command lines show three ways to print the files named **part0**, **part1**, **part2**, **part3**, and **part5**. Each of these command lines causes the shell to call lpr with five filenames:

```
$ lpr part0 part1 part2 part3 part5

$ lpr part[01235]

$ lpr part[0-35]
```

The first command line explicitly specifies the five filenames. The second and third command lines use ambiguous file references, incorporating character-class definitions. The shell expands the argument on the second command line to include all files that have names beginning with **part** and ending with any of the characters in the character class. The character class is explicitly defined as 0, 1, 2, 3, and 5. The third command line also uses a character-class definition but defines the character class to be all characters in the range 0–3 plus 5.

The following command line prints 39 files, **part0** through **part38**:

```
$ lpr part[0-9] part[12][0-9] part3[0-8]
```

The first of the following commands lists the files in the working directory whose names start with **a** through **m**. The second lists files whose names end with **x**, **y**, or **z**.

```
$ echo [a-m]*
...

$ echo *[x-z]
...
```

**optional**  When an exclamation point (!) or a caret (^) immediately follows the opening bracket ([) that starts a character-class definition, the character class matches any character *not* between the brackets. Thus [^tsq]* matches any filename that does *not* begin with **t**, **s**, or **q**.

The following examples show that *[^ab] matches filenames that do not end with the letter **a** or **b** and that [^b-d]* matches filenames that do not begin with **b**, **c**, or **d**.

```
$ ls
aa  ab  ac  ad  ba  bb  bc  bd  cc  dd

$ ls *[^ab]
ac  ad  bc  bd  cc  dd

$ ls [^b-d]*
aa  ab  ac  ad
```

You can cause a character class to match a hyphen (–) or a closing bracket (]) by placing it immediately before the final (closing) bracket.

The next example demonstrates that the **ls** utility cannot interpret ambiguous file references. First **ls** is called with an argument of **?old**. The shell expands **?old** into a matching filename, **hold**, and passes that name to **ls**. The second command is the same as the first, except the **?** is quoted (by preceding it with a backslash [\]; refer to "Special Characters" on page 142). Because the **?** is quoted, the shell does not recognize it as a special character and passes it to **ls**. The **ls** utility generates an error message saying that it cannot find a file named **?old** (because there is no file named **?old**).

```
$ ls ?old
hold

$ ls \?old
ls: ?old: No such file or directory
```

Like most utilities and programs, **ls** cannot interpret ambiguous file references; that work is left to the shell.

# BUILTINS

A *builtin* is a utility (also called a *command*) that is built into a shell. Each of the shells has its own set of builtins. When it runs a builtin, the shell does not fork a new process. Consequently builtins run more quickly and can affect the environment of the current shell. Because builtins are used in the same way as utilities, you will not typically be aware of whether a utility is built into the shell or is a stand-alone utility.

For example, echo is a shell builtin. It is also a stand-alone utility. The shell always executes a shell builtin before trying to find a command or utility with the same name. See page 1040 for an in-depth discussion of builtin commands and page 1055 for a list of bash builtins.

Listing bash builtins   To display a list of bash builtins, give the command **info bash shell builtin**. To display a page with information on each builtin, move the cursor to the **Bash Builtins** line and press RETURN. Alternately, you can view the **builtins** man page.

Getting help with bash builtins   You can use the bash **help** command to display information about bash builtins. See page 134 for more information.

# CHAPTER SUMMARY

The shell is the Linux command interpreter. It scans the command line for proper syntax, picking out the command name and arguments. The name of the command is argument zero. The first argument is argument one, the second is argument two, and so on. Many programs use options to modify the effects of a command. Most Linux utilities identify an option by its leading one or two hyphens.

When you give it a command, the shell tries to find an executable program with the same name as the command. When it does, the shell executes the program. When it does not, the shell tells you it cannot find or execute the program. If the command is a simple filename, the shell searches the directories listed in the **PATH** variable to locate the command.

When it executes a command, the shell assigns one file or device to the command's standard input and another file to its standard output. By default, the shell causes a command's standard input to come from the keyboard and its standard output to go to the screen. You can instruct the shell to redirect a command's standard input from or standard output to any file or device. You can also connect standard output of one command to standard input of another command to form a pipeline. A filter is a command that reads its standard input from standard output of one command and writes its standard output to standard input of another command.

When a command runs in the foreground, the shell waits for the command to finish before it displays a prompt and allows you to continue. When you put an ampersand (&) at the end of a command line, the shell executes the command in the background and displays another prompt immediately. Run slow commands in the background when you want to enter other commands at the shell prompt. The jobs builtin displays a list of suspended jobs and jobs running in the background and includes the job number of each.

The shell interprets special characters on a command line to generate filenames. A reference that uses special characters (wildcards) to abbreviate a list of one or more filenames is called an ambiguous file reference. A question mark represents any single character, and an asterisk represents zero or more characters. A single character might also be represented by a character class: a list of characters within brackets.

A builtin is a utility that is built into a shell. Each shell has its own set of builtins. When it runs a builtin, the shell does not fork a new process. Consequently builtins run more quickly and can affect the environment of the current shell.

## UTILITIES AND BUILTINS INTRODUCED IN THIS CHAPTER

Table 5-1 lists the utilities introduced in this chapter.

**Table 5-1**   New utilities

| Utility | Function |
| --- | --- |
| tr | Maps one string of characters to another (page 159) |
| tee | Sends standard input to both a file and standard output (page 162) |
| bg | Moves a process to the background (page 164) |
| fg | Moves a process to the foreground (page 164) |
| jobs | Displays a list of suspended jobs and jobs running in the background (page 164) |

# EXERCISES

1. What does the shell ordinarily do while a command is executing? What should you do if you do not want to wait for a command to finish before running another command?

2. Using sort as a filter, rewrite the following sequence of commands:

   ```
   $ sort list > temp
   $ lpr temp
   $ rm temp
   ```

3. What is a PID number? Why are these numbers useful when you run processes in the background? Which utility displays the PID numbers of the commands you are running?

4. Assume the following files are in the working directory:

```
$ ls
intro      notesb     ref2     section1   section3   section4b
notesa     ref1       ref3     section2   section4a  sentrev
```

Give commands for each of the following, using wildcards to express filenames with as few characters as possible.

a. List all files that begin with **section**.

b. List the **section1**, **section2**, and **section3** files only.

c. List the **intro** file only.

d. List the **section1**, **section3**, **ref1**, and **ref3** files.

5. Refer to the info or man pages to determine which command will

a. Display the number of lines in its standard input that contain the *word* **a** or **A**.

b. Display only the names of the files in the working directory that contain the pattern **$(**.

c. List the files in the working directory in reverse alphabetical order.

d. Send a list of files in the working directory to the printer, sorted by size.

6. Give a command to

a. Redirect standard output from a **sort** command to a file named **phone_list**. Assume the input file is named **numbers**.

b. Translate all occurrences of the characters [ and { to the character (, and all occurrences of the characters ] and } to the character ), in the file **permdemos.c**. (*Hint:* Refer to the tr man page.)

c. Create a file named **book** that contains the contents of two other files: **part1** and **part2**.

7. The lpr and sort utilities accept input either from a file named on the command line or from standard input.

a. Name two other utilities that function in a similar manner.

b. Name a utility that accepts its input only from standard input.

8. Give an example of a command that uses grep

a. With both input and output redirected.

b. With only input redirected.

c. With only output redirected.

d. Within a pipeline.

In which of the preceding cases is grep used as a filter?

9. Explain the following error message. Which filenames would a subsequent ls command display?

```
$ ls
abc   abd   abe   abf   abg   abh
$ rm abc ab*
rm: cannot remove 'abc': No such file or directory
```

# ADVANCED EXERCISES

10. When you use the redirect output symbol (>) on a command line, the shell creates the output file immediately, before the command is executed. Demonstrate that this is true.

11. In experimenting with variables, Max accidentally deletes his **PATH** variable. He decides he does not need the **PATH** variable. Discuss some of the problems he could soon encounter and explain the reasons for these problems. How could he *easily* return **PATH** to its original value?

12. Assume permissions on a file allow you to write to the file but not to delete it.

   a. Give a command to empty the file without invoking an editor.

   b. Explain how you might have permission to modify a file that you cannot delete.

13. If you accidentally create a filename that contains a nonprinting character, such as a CONTROL character, how can you remove the file?

14. Why does the **noclobber** variable *not* protect you from overwriting an existing file with cp or mv?

15. Why do command names and filenames usually not have embedded SPACEs? How would you create a filename containing a SPACE? How would you remove it? (This is a thought exercise, not recommended practice. If you want to experiment, create a file and work in a directory that contains only your experimental file.)

16. Create a file named **answer** and give the following command:

```
$ > answers.0102 < answer cat
```

Explain what the command does and why. What is a more conventional way of expressing this command?

# 6

# THE LINUX FILESYSTEM

## OBJECTIVES

After reading this chapter you should be able to:

▶ Define hierarchical filesystem, ordinary files, directory files, home directory, working directory, and parent directory

▶ List best practices for filenames

▶ Determine the name of the working directory

▶ Explain the difference between absolute and relative pathnames

▶ Create and remove directories

▶ List files in a directory, remove files from a directory, and copy and move files between directories

▶ List and describe the uses of standard Linux directories and files

▶ View and interpret file and directory ownership and permissions

▶ Modify file and directory permissions

▶ Expand access control using ACLs

▶ Describe the uses, differences, and methods of creating hard links and symbolic links

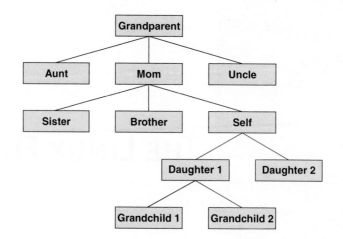

**Figure 6-1**   A family tree

A *filesystem* is a set of *data structures* (page 1245) that usually resides on part of a disk and that holds directories of files. Filesystems store user and system data that are the basis of users' work on the system and the system's existence. This chapter discusses the organization and terminology of the Linux filesystem, defines ordinary and directory files, and explains the rules for naming them. It also shows how to create and delete directories, move through the filesystem, and use absolute and relative pathnames to access files in various directories. It includes a discussion of important files and directories as well as file access permissions and ACLs (Access Control Lists), which allow you to share selected files with specified users. It concludes with a discussion of hard and symbolic links, which can make a single file appear in more than one directory.

In addition to reading this chapter, you can refer to the df info page and to the fsck, mkfs, and tune2fs man pages for more information on filesystems. For information on additional important Linux files, see "Important Files and Directories" on page 502.

# THE HIERARCHICAL FILESYSTEM

Family tree   A *hierarchical* (page 1253) structure frequently takes the shape of a pyramid. One example of this type of structure is found by tracing a family's lineage: A couple has a child, who might in turn have several children, each of whom might have more children. This hierarchical structure is called a *family tree* (Figure 6-1).

Directory tree   Like the family tree it resembles, the Linux filesystem is called a *tree*. It consists of a set of connected files. This structure allows you to organize files so you can easily find any particular one. On a standard Linux system, each user starts with one directory, to

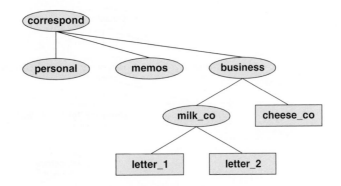

**Figure 6-2**   A secretary's directories

which the user can add subdirectories to any desired level. By creating multiple levels of subdirectories, a user can expand the structure as needed.

Subdirectories  Typically each subdirectory is dedicated to a single subject, such as a person, project, or event. The subject dictates whether a subdirectory should be subdivided further. For example, Figure 6-2 shows a secretary's subdirectory named **correspond**. This directory contains three subdirectories: **business, memos,** and **personal**. The **business** directory contains files that store each letter the secretary types. If you expect many letters to go to one client, as is the case with **milk_co**, you can dedicate a subdirectory to that client.

One major strength of the Linux filesystem is its ability to adapt to users' needs. You can take advantage of this strength by strategically organizing your files so they are most convenient and useful for you.

## *LE*   ORDINARY FILES AND DIRECTORY FILES

Like a family tree, the tree representing the filesystem is usually pictured upside down with its *root* at the top. Figures 6-2 and 6-3 (next page) show that the tree "grows" downward from the root with paths connecting the root to each of the other files. At the end of each path is either an ordinary file or a directory file. Special files, which can also appear at the ends of paths, are described on page 515. *Ordinary files,* or simply *files,* appear at the ends of paths that cannot support other paths. *Directory files,* also referred to as *directories* or *folders,* are the points that other paths can branch off from. (Figures 6-2 and 6-3 show some empty directories.) When you refer to the tree, *up* is toward the root and *down* is away from the root. Directories directly connected by a path are called *parents* (closer to the root) and *children* (farther from the root). A *pathname* is a series of names that trace a path along branches from one file to another. See page 181 for more information about pathnames.

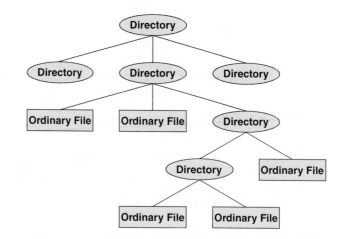

**Figure 6-3**   Directories and ordinary files

# FILENAMES

Every file has a *filename*. The maximum length of a filename varies with the type of filesystem; Linux supports several types of filesystems. Although most of today's filesystems allow files with names up to 255 characters long, some filesystems restrict filenames to fewer characters. Although you can use almost any character in a filename, you will avoid confusion if you choose characters from the following list:

- Uppercase letters (A–Z)
- Lowercase letters (a–z)
- Numbers (0–9)
- Underscore (_)
- Period (.)
- Comma (,)

Like the children of one parent, no two files in the same directory can have the same name. (Parents give their children different names because it makes good sense, but Linux requires it.) Files in different directories, like the children of different parents, can have the same name.

The filenames you choose should mean something. Too often a directory is filled with important files with such unhelpful names as **hold1**, **wombat**, and **junk**, not to mention **foo** and **foobar**. Such names are poor choices because they do not help you recall what you stored in a file. The following filenames conform to the suggested syntax *and* convey information about the contents of the file:

- **correspond**
- **january**

- davis
- reports
- 2001
- acct_payable

Filename length When you share your files with users on other systems, you might need to make long filenames differ within the first few characters. Systems running DOS or older versions of Windows have an 8-character filename body length limit and a 3-character filename extension length limit. Some UNIX systems have a 14-character limit, and older Macintosh systems have a 31-character limit. If you keep filenames short, they are easy to type; later you can add extensions to them without exceeding the shorter limits imposed by some filesystems. The disadvantage of short filenames is that they are typically less descriptive than long filenames. See "stat: Displays Information About a File or Filesystem" on page 468 for a way to determine the maximum length of a filename on the local system.

Long filenames enable you to assign descriptive names to files. To help you select among files without typing entire filenames, shells support filename completion. For more information about this feature, see the "Filename completion" tip on page 224.

**LE** Case sensitivity You can use uppercase and/or lowercase letters within filenames. Linux is case sensitive, so files named **JANUARY**, **January**, and **january** represent three distinct files.

### Do not use SPACEs within filenames

caution Although Linux allows you to use SPACEs within filenames, it is a poor idea. Because a SPACE is a special character, you must quote it on a command line. Quoting a character on a command line can be difficult for a novice user and cumbersome for an experienced user. Use periods or underscores instead of SPACES: **joe.05.04.26**, **new_stuff**.

If you are working with a filename that includes a SPACE, such as a file from another operating system, you must quote the SPACE on the command line by preceding it with a backslash or by placing quotation marks on either side of the filename. The two following commands send the file named **my file** to the printer.

```
$ lpr my\ file
$ lpr "my file"
```

## FILENAME EXTENSIONS

A *filename extension* is the part of the filename that follows an embedded period. In the filenames listed in Table 6-1 on the next page, filename extensions help describe the contents of the file. Some programs, such as the C programming language compiler, default to specific filename extensions; in most cases, however, filename extensions are optional. Use extensions freely to make filenames easy to understand. If you like, you can use several periods within the same filename—for example, **notes.4.10.54** or **files.tar.gz**.

**Table 6-1**    Filename extensions

| Filename with extension | Meaning of extension |
| --- | --- |
| **compute.c** | A C programming language source file |
| **compute.o** | The object code file for **compute.c** |
| **compute** | The executable file for **compute.c** |
| **memo.0410.txt** | A text file |
| **memo.pdf** | A PDF file; view with xpdf or kpdf under a GUI |
| **memo.ps** | A PostScript file; view with ghostscript or kpdf under a GUI |
| **memo.Z** | A file compressed with compress (page 249); use uncompress or gunzip (page 248) to decompress |
| **memo.gz** | A file compressed with gzip (page 245); view with zcat or decompress with gunzip (both on page 248) |
| **memo.tgz** or **memo.tar.gz** | A tar (page 249) archive of files compressed with gzip (page 245) |
| **memo.bz2** | A file compressed with bzip2 (page 245); view with bzcat or decompress with bunzip2 (both on page 245) |
| **memo.html** | A file meant to be viewed using a Web browser, such as Firefox |
| **photo.gif**, **photo.jpg**, **photo.jpeg**, **photo.bmp**, **photo.tif**, or **photo.tiff** | A file containing graphical information, such as a picture |

## *LE* HIDDEN FILENAMES

A filename that begins with a period is called a *hidden filename* (or a *hidden file* or sometimes an *invisible file*) because ls does not normally display it. The command ls –a displays *all* filenames, even hidden ones. Names of startup files (next) usually begin with a period so that they are hidden and do not clutter a directory listing. Two special hidden entries—single and double periods (. and ..)—appear in every directory (page 186).

## STARTUP FILES

*Startup files*, which appear in your home directory (page 143), give the shell and other programs information about you and your preferences. Frequently one of these files tells the shell what kind of terminal you are using (page 1153) and executes the stty (set terminal) utility to establish the erase (page 123) and line kill (page 123) keys.

Either you or the system administrator can put a shell startup file containing shell commands in your home directory. The shell executes the commands in this file each time you log in. Because the startup files have hidden filenames (filenames that begin with a period; above), you must use the ls –a command to see whether one is in your home directory. A GUI has many startup files. Usually you do not need to work with

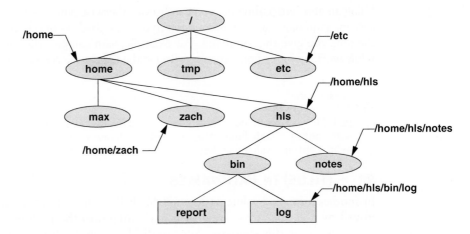

**Figure 6-4** Absolute pathnames

these files directly but can control startup sequences using icons on the desktop. See page 329 for more information about startup files.

# PATHNAMES

Every file has a *pathname*, which is a trail from a directory through part of the directory hierarchy to an ordinary file or a directory. Within a pathname, a slash (/) following (to the right of) a filename indicates that the file is a directory file. The file following (to the right of) the slash can be an ordinary file or a directory file. The simplest pathname is a simple filename, which points to a file in the working directory (page 143). This section discusses absolute and relative pathnames and explains how to use each.

## *LE* ABSOLUTE PATHNAMES

*LPI* / (root)  The root directory of the filesystem hierarchy does not have a name; it is referred to as the *root directory* and is represented by a slash (/) standing alone or at the left end of a pathname.

An *absolute pathname* starts with a slash (/), which represents the root directory. The slash is followed by the name of a file located in the root directory. An absolute pathname can continue, tracing a path through all intermediate directories, to the file identified by the pathname. String all the filenames in the path together, following each directory with a slash (/). This string of filenames is called an absolute pathname because it locates a file absolutely by tracing a path from the root directory to the file. Typically the absolute pathname of a directory does not include the trailing slash, although that format can be used to emphasize that the pathname specifies a directory (e.g., **/home/zach/**). The part of a pathname following the final slash is called a *simple filename, filename,* or *basename.* Figure 6-4 shows the absolute pathnames of directories and ordinary files in part of a filesystem hierarchy.

Using an absolute pathname, you can list or otherwise work with any file on the local system, assuming you have permission to do so, regardless of the working directory at the time you give the command. For example, Sam can give the following command while working in his home directory to list the files in the **/etc/ssh** directory:

```
$ pwd
/home/sam
$ ls /etc/ssh
moduli          ssh_host_dsa_key        ssh_host_key.pub
ssh_config      ssh_host_dsa_key.pub    ssh_host_rsa_key
sshd_config     ssh_host_key            ssh_host_rsa_key.pub
```

### LE  ~ (TILDE) IN PATHNAMES

In another form of absolute pathname, the shell expands the characters ~/ (a tilde followed by a slash) at the start of a pathname into the pathname of your home directory. Using this shortcut, you can display your **.bashrc** startup file (page 331) with the following command no matter which directory is the working directory:

```
$ less ~/.bashrc
```

A tilde quickly references paths that start with your or someone else's home directory. The shell expands a tilde followed by a username at the beginning of a pathname into the pathname of that user's home directory. For example, assuming he has permission to do so, Max can examine Sam's **.bashrc** file with the following command:

```
$ less ~sam/.bashrc
```

Refer to "Tilde Expansion" on page 407 for more information.

## LE  RELATIVE PATHNAMES

A *relative pathname* traces a path from the working directory to a file. The pathname is *relative* to the working directory. Any pathname that does not begin with the root directory (represented by **/**) or a tilde (**~**) is a relative pathname. Like absolute pathnames, relative pathnames can trace a path through many directories. The simplest relative pathname is a simple filename, which identifies a file in the working directory. The examples in the next sections use absolute and relative pathnames.

### SIGNIFICANCE OF THE WORKING DIRECTORY

To access any file in the working directory, you need only a simple filename. To access a file in another directory, you *must* use a pathname. Typing a long pathname is tedious and increases the chance of making a mistake. This possibility is less likely under a GUI, where you click filenames or icons. You can choose a working directory for any particular task to reduce the need for long pathnames. Your choice of a working directory does not allow you to do anything you could not do otherwise—it just makes some operations easier.

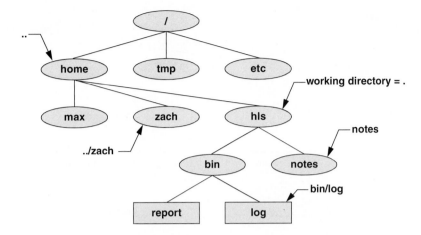

**Figure 6-5**   Relative pathnames

### When using a relative pathname, know which directory is the working directory

**caution**   The location of the file you are accessing with a relative pathname is dependent on (is relative to) the working directory. Always make sure you know which directory is the working directory before you use a relative pathname. Use **pwd** to verify the directory. If you are creating a file using **vim** and you are not where you think you are in the file hierarchy, the new file will end up in an unexpected location.

It does not matter which directory is the working directory when you use an absolute pathname. Thus, the following command always edits a file named **goals** in your home directory:

```
$ vim ~/goals
```

Refer to Figure 6-5 as you read this paragraph. Files that are children of the working directory can be referenced by simple filenames. Grandchildren of the working directory can be referenced by short relative pathnames: two filenames separated by a slash. When you manipulate files in a large directory structure, using short relative pathnames can save you time and aggravation. If you choose a working directory that contains the files used most often for a particular task, you need use fewer long, cumbersome pathnames.

# WORKING WITH DIRECTORIES

This section discusses how to create directories (mkdir), switch between directories (cd), remove directories (rmdir), use pathnames to make your work easier, and move and copy files and directories between directories. It concludes with brief descriptions of important standard directories and files in the Linux filesystem.

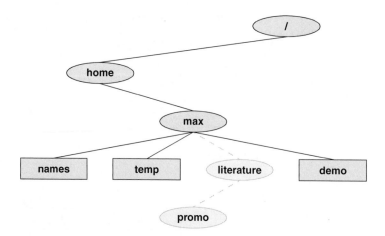

**Figure 6-6**   The file structure developed in the examples

## LPI   mkdir: CREATES A DIRECTORY

The mkdir utility creates a directory. The *argument* (page 1237) to mkdir is the pathname of the new directory. The following examples develop the directory structure shown in Figure 6-6. In the figure, the directories that are added appear in a lighter shade than the others and are connected by dashes.

Following, pwd shows that Max is working in his home directory (**/home/max**), and ls shows the names of the files in his home directory: **demo**, **names**, and **temp**.

```
$ pwd
/home/max
$ ls
demo   names   temp
$ mkdir literature
```

Using mkdir, Max creates a directory named **literature** as a child of his home directory. He uses a relative pathname (a simple filename) because he wants the **literature** directory to be a child of the working directory. Max could have used an absolute pathname to create the same directory: **mkdir /home/max/literature**, **mkdir ~max/literature**, or **mkdir ~/literature**.

The following ls commands verify the presence of the new directory. The **–F** option to ls displays a slash after the name of each directory and an asterisk after each executable file (shell script, utility, or application). When you call it with an argument that is the name of a directory, ls lists the contents of that directory. The final ls displays nothing because there are no files in the **literature** directory.

```
$ ls
demo   literature   names   temp
$ ls -F
demo   literature/   names   temp
$ ls literature
$
```

The following commands show two ways for Max to create the **promo** directory as a child of the newly created **literature** directory. The first way checks that **/home/max** is the working directory and uses a relative pathname:

```
$ pwd
/home/max
$ mkdir literature/promo
```

The second way uses an absolute pathname:

```
$ mkdir /home/max/literature/promo
```

Use the –p (parents) option to mkdir to create both the **literature** and **promo** directories with one command:

```
$ pwd
/home/max
$ ls
demo   names   temp
$ mkdir -p literature/promo
```

*or*

```
$ mkdir -p /home/max/literature/promo
```

## *LE*   cd: CHANGES TO ANOTHER WORKING DIRECTORY

The cd (change directory) utility makes another directory the working directory; it does not *change* the contents of the working directory. The following examples show two ways to make the **/home/max/literature** directory the working directory, as verified by pwd. First Max uses cd with an absolute pathname to make **literature** his working directory—it does not matter which is the working directory when you give a command with an absolute pathname. A pwd command confirms the change Max made.

```
$ cd /home/max/literature
$ pwd
/home/max/literature
```

When used without an argument, cd makes your home directory the working directory, as it was when you logged in. The following cd command does not have an argument, so it makes Max's home directory the working directory. Finally, knowing that he is working in his home directory, Max uses a simple filename to make the **literature** directory his working directory (**cd literature**) and confirms the change using pwd.

```
$ cd
$ pwd
/home/max
$ cd literature
$ pwd
/home/max/literature
```

## *LE*   THE . AND .. DIRECTORY ENTRIES

The mkdir utility automatically puts two entries in each directory it creates: a single period (.) and a double period (..). The . is synonymous with the pathname of the working directory and can be used in its place; the .. is synonymous with the pathname of the parent of the working directory. These entries are hidden because their filenames begin with a period.

With the **literature** directory as the working directory, the following example uses .. three times: first to list the contents of the parent directory (**/home/max**), second to copy the **memoA** file to the parent directory, and third to list the contents of the parent directory again.

```
$ pwd
/home/max/literature
$ ls ..
demo   literature   names   temp
$ cp memoA ..
$ ls ..
demo   literature   memoA   names   temp
```

After using cd to make **promo** (a subdirectory of **literature**) his working directory, Max can use a relative pathname to call vim to edit a file in his home directory.

```
$ cd promo
$ vim ../../names
```

You can use an absolute or relative pathname or a simple filename virtually anywhere a utility or program requires a filename or pathname. This usage holds true for ls, vim, mkdir, rm, and most other Linux utilities.

### The working directory versus your home directory

tip   The working directory is not the same as your home directory. Your home directory remains the same for the duration of your session and usually from session to session. Immediately after you log in, you are always working in the same directory: your home directory.

Unlike your home directory, the working directory can change as often as you like. You have no set working directory, which explains why some people refer to it as the *current directory.* When you log in and until you change directories using cd, your home directory is the working directory. If you were to change directories to Sam's home directory, then Sam's home directory would be the working directory.

## *LPI*   rmdir: DELETES A DIRECTORY

The rmdir (remove directory) utility deletes a directory. You cannot delete the working directory or a directory that contains files other than the . and .. entries. If you need to delete a directory that has files in it, first use rm to delete the files and then delete the directory. You do not have to (nor can you) delete the . and .. entries; rmdir removes them automatically. The following command deletes the **promo** directory:

```
$ rmdir /home/max/literature/promo
```

The rm utility has a **−r** option (**rm −r** *filename*) that recursively deletes files, including directories, within a directory and also deletes the directory itself.

### Use rm −r carefully, if at all

**caution**   Although **rm −r** is a handy command, you must use it carefully. Do not use it with an ambiguous file reference such as ✳. It is frighteningly easy to wipe out your entire home directory with a single short command.

## USING PATHNAMES

touch   Use a text editor to create a file named **letter** if you want to experiment with the examples that follow. Alternately you can use touch to create an empty file:

```
$ cd
$ pwd
/home/max
$ touch letter
```

With **/home/max** as the working directory, the following example uses cp with a relative pathname to copy the file **letter** to the **/home/max/literature/promo** directory. (You will need to create **promo** again if you deleted it earlier.) The copy of the file has the simple filename **letter.0210**:

```
$ cp letter literature/promo/letter.0210
```

If Max does not change to another directory, he can use vim as shown to edit the copy of the file he just made:

```
$ vim literature/promo/letter.0210
```

If Max does not want to use a long pathname to specify the file, he can use cd to make **promo** the working directory before using vim:

```
$ cd literature/promo
$ pwd
/home/max/literature/promo
$ vim letter.0210
```

To make the parent of the working directory (named **/home/max/literature**) the new working directory, Max can give the following command, which takes advantage of the **..** directory entry:

```
$ cd ..
$ pwd
/home/max/literature
```

## *LE+*   mv, cp: MOVE OR COPY FILES

Chapter 7 discusses the use of mv to rename files. However, mv works even more generally: You can use this utility to move files from one directory to another (change the pathname of a file) as well as to change a simple filename. When used to move one or more files to a new directory, the mv command has this syntax:

*mv existing-file-list directory*

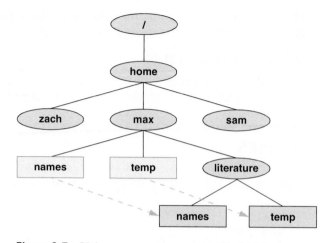

**Figure 6-7**   Using mv to move **names** and **temp**

If the working directory is **/home/max,** Max can use the following command to move the files **names** and **temp** from the working directory to the **literature** directory:

```
$ mv names temp literature
```

This command changes the absolute pathnames of the **names** and **temp** files from **/home/max/names** and **/home/max/temp** to **/home/max/literature/names** and **/home/max/literature/temp,** respectively (Figure 6-7). Like most Linux commands, mv accepts either absolute or relative pathnames.

As you work with Linux and create more files, you will need to create new directories using mkdir to keep the files organized. The mv utility is a useful tool for moving files from one directory to another as you extend your directory hierarchy.

The cp utility works in the same way mv does, except that it makes copies of the *existing-file-list* in the specified *directory.*

## LE+   mv: Moves a Directory

Just as it moves ordinary files from one directory to another, so mv can move directories. The syntax is similar except you specify one or more directories, not ordinary files, to move:

*mv existing-directory-list new-directory*

If *new-directory* does not exist, the *existing-directory-list* must contain just one directory name, which mv changes to *new-directory* (mv renames the directory). Although you can rename directories using mv, you cannot copy their contents with cp unless you use the **–r** (recursive) option. Refer to the tar and cpio man pages for other ways to copy and move directories.

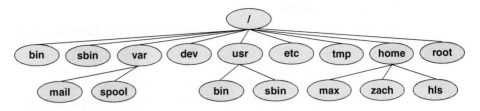

**Figure 6-8** A typical FHS-based Linux filesystem structure

## LE+ IMPORTANT STANDARD DIRECTORIES AND FILES

Originally files on a Linux system were not located in standard places within the directory hierarchy. The scattered files made it difficult to document and maintain a Linux system and just about impossible for someone to release a software package that would compile and run on all Linux systems. The first standard for the Linux filesystem, the FSSTND (Linux Filesystem Standard), was released early in 1994. In early 1995 work was started on a broader standard covering many UNIX-like systems: FHS (Linux Filesystem Hierarchy Standard; proton.pathname.com/fhs). More recently FHS has been incorporated in LSB (Linux Standard Base; www.linuxfoundation.org/collaborate/workgroups/lsb), a workgroup of FSG (Free Standards Group). Finally, FSG combined with OSDL (Open Source Development Labs) to form the Linux Foundation (www.linuxfoundation.org). Figure 6-8 shows the locations of some important directories and files as specified by FHS. The significance of many of these directories will become clear as you continue reading.

The following list describes the directories shown in Figure 6-8, some of the directories specified by FHS, and some other directories. Fedora/RHEL, however, does not use all the directories specified by FHS. Be aware that you cannot always determine the function of a directory by its name. For example, although **/opt** stores add-on software, **/etc/opt** stores configuration files for the software in **/opt**. See also "Important Files and Directories" on page 502.

**/bin /usr/bin**
**/sbin /usr/sbin**    Recently, the files in **/bin** and **/sbin** were moved to **/usr/bin** and **/usr/sbin**, respectively, and **/bin** and **/sbin** were set up as symbolic links (page 206) to those directories:

```
$ ls -ld /bin /usr/bin /sbin /usr/sbin
lrwxrwxrwx. 1 root root     7 07-16 18:37 /bin -> usr/bin
lrwxrwxrwx. 1 root root     8 07-16 18:37 /sbin -> usr/sbin
dr-xr-xr-x. 2 root root 53248 07-27 15:36 /usr/bin
dr-xr-xr-x. 2 root root 20480 07-27 15:36 /usr/sbin
```

See fedoraproject.org/wiki/Features/UsrMove for more information.

**LPI /**    **Root** The root directory, present in all Linux filesystem structures, is the ancestor of all files in the filesystem. It does not have a name and is represented by a slash (**/**) standing alone or at the left end of a pathname.

**/bin**   A link to **/usr/bin**.

**/boot**   **Static files of the boot loader** Contains all of the files needed to boot the system.

**LPI**  **/dev**   **Device files** Contains all files that represent peripheral devices, such as disk drives, terminals, and printers. Previously this directory was filled with all possible devices. The udev utility (page 516) provides a dynamic device directory that enables **/dev** to contain only devices that are present on the system. See also **/dev** on page 503.

**LE**  **/etc**   **Machine–local system configuration files** Holds administrative, configuration, and other system files.

**/etc/opt**   **Configuration files for add-on software packages kept in /opt**

**/etc/X11**   **Machine–local configuration files for the X Window System**

**LPI**  **/home**   **User home directories** Each user's home directory is typically one of many sub-directories of the **/home** directory. As an example, assuming that users' directories are under **/home**, the absolute pathname of Zach's home directory is **/home/zach**. On some systems the users' directories might not be found under **/home** but instead might be spread among other directories such as **/inhouse** and **/clients**.

**LE**  **/lib**   A link to **/usr/lib**.

**LE**  **/lib64**   A link to **/usr/lib64**.

**/lib/modules**   **Loadable kernel modules**

**/mnt**   **Mount point for temporarily mounting filesystems**

**/opt**   **Add-on (optional) software packages**

**LPI**  **/proc**   **Kernel and process information virtual filesystem**

**/root**   **Home directory for the root account**

**/run**   **Runtime (volatile) data** A tmpfs filesystem (mounted, but stored in RAM) that holds startup files previously hidden in **/dev** and other directories. For more information see lists.fedoraproject.org/pipermail/devel/2011-March/150031.html.

**/sbin**   A link to **/usr/sbin**.

**LPI**  **/sys**   **Device pseudofilesystem** See udev on page 516 for more information.

**LE**  **/tmp**   **Temporary files**

**/usr**   **Installed system** Includes subdirectories that contain information used by the system. Files in subdirectories do not change often and can be shared by several systems.

**LE**  **/usr/bin**   **Most user commands** Contains the standard Linux utility programs.

**LE**  **/usr/sbin**   **Essential system binaries** Utilities used for system administration.

**/usr/games**   **Games and educational programs**

**/usr/include**   **Header files included by C programs**

**LE**  **/usr/lib**   **Shared libraries** (32-bit)

*LE*    /usr/lib64    Shared libraries (64-bit)

/usr/local    **Local hierarchy** Holds locally important files and directories that are added to the system. Subdirectories can include **bin, games, include, lib, sbin, share,** and **src.**

/usr/sbin    **Nonvital system administration binaries** See **/sbin.**

/usr/share    **Architecture-independent data** Subdirectories can include **dict, doc, games, info, locale, man, misc, terminfo,** and **zoneinfo.**

/usr/share/doc    Documentation

/usr/share/info    GNU info system's primary directory

/usr/share/man    Online manuals

/usr/src    Source code

*LE+*    /var    **Variable data** Files with contents that vary as the system runs are kept in sub-directories under **/var.** The most common examples are temporary files, system log files, spooled files, and user mailbox files. Subdirectories can include **cache, lib, lock, log, mail, opt, run, spool, tmp,** and **yp.**

*LE*    /var/log    **Log files** Contains **lastlog** (a record of the last login by each user), **messages** (system messages from **syslogd**), and **wtmp** (a record of all logins/logouts), among other log files.

/var/spool    **Spooled application data** Contains **anacron, at, cron, lpd, mail, mqueue, samba,** and other directories. The file **/var/mail** is typically a link to **/var/spool/mail.**

## *LE*  ACCESS PERMISSIONS

In addition to the controls imposed by SELinux (page 472), Fedora/RHEL supports two methods of controlling who can access a file and how they can access it: traditional Linux access permissions and ACLs (Access Control Lists). This section describes traditional Linux access permissions. See page 198 for a discussion of ACLs, which provide finer-grained control of access permissions than do traditional access permissions.

Three types of users can access a file: the owner of the file (*owner*), a member of a group that the file is associated with (*group*; see page 506 for more information on groups), and everyone else (*other*). A user can attempt to access an ordinary file in three ways: by trying to *read from, write to,* or *execute* it.

## *LE+*  ls –l: DISPLAYS PERMISSIONS

When you call ls with the –l option and the name of one or more ordinary files, ls displays a line of information about the file(s). See "ls output" on page 28 for information about the format of the display this book uses. The following example

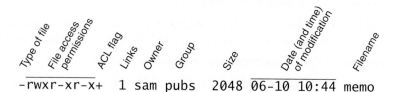

**Figure 6-9**   The columns displayed by the **ls –l** command

displays information for two files. The file **letter.0210** contains the text of a letter, and **check_spell** contains a shell script, a program written in a high-level shell programming language:

```
$ ls -l check_spell letter.0210
-rwxr-xr-x. 1 sam pubs  766 03-21 14:02 check_spell
-rw-r--r--. 1 sam pubs 6193 02-10 14:22 letter.0210
```

From left to right, the lines that an **ls –l** command displays contain the following information (refer to Figure 6-9):

- The type of file (first character)
- The file's access permissions (the next nine characters)
- The ACL flag (present if the file has an ACL, page 198)
- The number of links to the file (page 203)
- The name of the owner of the file (usually the person who created the file)
- The name of the group the file is associated with
- The size of the file in characters (bytes)
- The date and time the file was created or last modified
- The name of the file

The type of file (first column) for **letter.0210** is a hyphen (–) because it is an ordinary file (directory files have a **d** in this column).

The next three characters specify the access permissions for the *owner* of the file: **r** indicates read permission, **w** indicates write permission, and **x** indicates execute permission. A – in a column indicates that the owner does *not* have the permission that could have appeared in that position.

In a similar manner the next three characters represent permissions for the *group,* and the final three characters represent permissions for *other* (everyone else). In the preceding example, the owner of **letter.0210** can read from and write to the file, whereas the group and others can only read from the file, and no one is allowed to execute it. Although execute permission can be allowed for any file, it does not make sense to assign execute permission to a file that contains a document such as a letter. The **check_spell** file is an executable shell script, so execute permission is appropriate for it. (The owner, group, and others have execute permission.)

## *LE+*   chmod: CHANGES FILE ACCESS PERMISSIONS

The Linux file access permission scheme lets you give other users access to the files you want to share while keeping your private files confidential. You can allow other users to read from *and* write to a file (handy if you are one of several people working on a joint project). You can allow others only to read from a file (perhaps a project specification you are proposing). Or you can allow others only to write to a file (similar to an inbox or mailbox, where you want others to be able to send you mail but do not want them to read your mail). Similarly you can protect entire directories from being scanned (covered shortly).

### A user with **root** privileges can access any file on the system

security   There is an exception to the access permissions described in this section. Anyone who can gain **root** privileges has full access to *all* files, regardless of the file's owner or access permissions. Of course, if the file is encrypted, read access does not mean the person reading the file can understand what is in the file.

The owner of a file controls which users have permission to access the file and how those users can access it. When you own a file, you can use the chmod (change mode) utility to change access permissions for that file. You can specify symbolic (relative) or numeric (absolute) arguments to chmod.

## SYMBOLIC ARGUMENTS TO chmod

The following example, which uses symbolic arguments to chmod, adds (**+**) read and write permissions (**rw**) for all (**a**) users:

```
$ ls -l letter.0210
-rw-r-----. 1 sam pubs 6193 02-10 14:22 letter.0210
$ chmod a+rw letter.0210
$ ls -l letter.0210
-rw-rw-rw-. 1 sam pubs 6193 02-10 14:22 letter.0210
```

### You must have read permission to execute a shell script

tip   Because a shell needs to read a shell script (a text file containing shell commands) before it can execute the commands within that script, you must have read permission for the file containing the script to execute it. You also need execute permission to execute a shell script directly from the command line. In contrast, binary (program) files do not need to be read; they are executed directly. You need only execute permission to run a binary program.

Using symbolic arguments with chmod modifies existing permissions; the change a given argument makes depends on (is relative to) the existing permissions. In the next example, chmod removes (**–**) read (**r**) and execute (**x**) permissions for other (**o**) users. The owner and group permissions are not affected.

```
$ ls -l check_spell
-rwxr-xr-x. 1 sam pubs 766 03-21 14:02 check_spell
$ chmod o-rx check_spell
$ ls -l check_spell
-rwxr-x---. 1 sam pubs 766 03-21 14:02 check_spell
```

In addition to **a** (all) and **o** (other), you can use **g** (group) and **u** (user, although *user* refers to the *owner* of the file who might or might not be the user of the file at any given time) in the argument to chmod. For example, **chmod a+x** adds execute permission for all users (other, group, and owner), and **chmod go–rwx** removes all permissions for all but the owner of the file.

### chmod: **o** for other, **u** for owner

When using chmod, many people assume that the **o** stands for *owner;* it does not. The **o** stands for *other,* whereas **u** stands for *owner* (*user*). The acronym UGO (user-group-other) might help you remember how permissions are named.

## NUMERIC ARGUMENTS TO chmod

You can also use numeric arguments to specify permissions with chmod. In place of the letters and symbols specifying permissions used in the previous examples, numeric arguments comprise three octal digits. (A fourth, leading digit controls setuid and setgid permissions and is discussed next.) The first digit specifies permissions for the owner, the second for the group, and the third for other users. A **1** gives the specified user(s) execute permission, a **2** gives write permission, and a **4** gives read permission. Construct the digit representing the permissions for the owner, group, or others by ORing (adding) the appropriate values as shown in the following examples. Using numeric arguments sets file permissions absolutely; it does not modify existing permissions as symbolic arguments do.

In the following example, chmod changes permissions so only the owner of the file can read from and write to the file, regardless of how permissions were previously set. The **6** in the first position gives the owner read (**4**) and write (**2**) permissions. The 0s remove all permissions for the group and other users.

```
$ chmod 600 letter.0210
$ ls -l letter.0210
-rw-------. 1 sam pubs 6193 02-10 14:22 letter.0210
```

Next, 7 (4 + 2 + 1) gives the owner read, write, and execute permissions. The 5 (4 + 1) gives the group and other users read and execute permissions:

```
$ chmod 755 check_spell
$ ls -l check_spell
-rwxr-xr-x. 1 sam pubs 766 03-21 14:02 check_spell
```

Refer to Table 6-2 for more examples of numeric permissions.

**Table 6-2**   Examples of numeric permission specifications

| Mode | Meaning |
| --- | --- |
| 777 | Owner, group, and others can read, write, and execute file |
| 755 | Owner can read, write, and execute file; group and others can read and execute file |

Table 6-2    Examples of numeric permission specifications (continued)

| Mode | Meaning |
|------|---------|
| 711 | Owner can read, write, and execute file; group and others can execute file |
| 644 | Owner can read and write file; group and others can read file |
| 640 | Owner can read and write file, group can read file, and others cannot access file |

Refer to page 337 for more information on using chmod to make a file executable and refer to the chmod man page for more information on absolute arguments and chmod in general. Refer to page 506 for more information on groups.

## LE+    chown: CHANGES FILE OWNERSHIP

The chown utility changes the owner of one or more files specified as arguments. Only a user working with **root** privileges can change the ownership of a file. In the following example, a user working with **root** privileges changes the owner of the **memo** file from Sam to Max, displaying the name of the owner before and after the change.

```
$ ls -l memo
-rw-rw-r--. 1 sam pubs 3933 04-30 17:26 memo
$ su -c 'chown max memo'
Password:
$ ls -l memo
-rw-rw-r--. 1 max pubs 3933 04-30 17:26 memo
```

The **–R** (**--recursive**) option allows you to specify a directory as an argument; it changes the ownership of all files in the specified directory hierarchy. The **–v** (**--verbose**) option displays a message for each file chown processes, saying whether its owner was retained or changed.

## LE+    chgrp: CHANGES FILE GROUP ASSOCIATION

The chgrp utility changes the group associated with of one or more files specified as arguments. Only the owner of a file or a user working with **root** privileges can change the group associated with a file. In the following example, Max, who owns the file named **memo**, changes the group associated with **memo** from **pubs** to **max**, displaying the name of the group before and after the change.

```
$ ls -l memo
-rw-rw-r--. 1 max pubs 3933 04-30 17:26 memo
$ chgrp max memo
$ ls -l memo
-rw-rw-r--. 1 max max 3933 04-30 17:26 memo
```

The **–R** (**--recursive**) option allows you to specify a directory as an argument; it changes the group associated with of all files in the specified directory hierarchy. The **–v** (**--verbose**) option displays a message for each file chgrp processes, saying whether its group was retained or changed.

## *LE+* SETUID AND SETGID PERMISSIONS

When you execute a file that has setuid (set user ID) permission, the process executing the file takes on the privileges of the file's owner. For example, if you run a setuid program that removes all files in a directory, you can remove files in any of the file owner's directories, even if you do not normally have permission to do so. In a similar manner, setgid (set group ID) permission gives the process executing the file the privileges of the group the file is associated with.

### Minimize use of setuid and setgid programs owned by root

security
Executable files that are setuid and owned by **root** have **root** privileges when they run, even if they are not run by **root**. This type of program is very powerful because it can do anything that **root** can do (and that the program is designed to do). Similarly executable files that are setgid and belong to the group **root** have extensive privileges.

Because of the power they hold and their potential for destruction, it is wise to avoid indiscriminately creating and using setuid programs owned by **root** and setgid programs belonging to the group **root**. Because of their inherent dangers, many sites minimize the use of these programs on their systems. One necessary setuid program is passwd. See page 425 for a tip on setuid files owned by **root** and page 458 for a command that lists setuid files on the local system.

Because of this danger, Fedora/RHEL has removed most setuid files. For more information see fedoraproject.org/wiki/Features/RemoveSETUID.

The following example shows a user working with **root** privileges and using symbolic arguments to chmod to give one program setuid privileges and another program setgid privileges. The ls –l output (page 191) shows setuid permission by displaying an **s** in the owner's executable position and setgid permission by displaying an **s** in the group's executable position:

```
# ls -l myprog*
-rwxr-xr-x. 1 root pubs 362804 03-21 15:38 myprog1
-rwxr-xr-x. 1 root pubs 189960 03-21 15:38 myprog2

# chmod u+s myprog1
# chmod g+s myprog2

# ls -l myprog*
-rwsr-xr-x. 1 root pubs 362804 03-21 15:38 myprog1
-rwxr-sr-x. 1 root pubs 189960 03-21 15:38 myprog2
```

LE Sticky bit
The next example uses numeric arguments to chmod to make the same changes. When you use four digits to specify permissions, setting the first digit to **1** sets the *sticky bit* (page 1275), setting it to **2** specifies setgid permissions, and setting it to **4** specifies setuid permissions:

```
# ls -l myprog*
-rwxr-xr-x. 1 root pubs 362804 03-21 15:38 myprog1
-rwxr-xr-x. 1 root pubs 189960 03-21 15:38 myprog2

# chmod 4755 myprog1
# chmod 2755 myprog2
```

```
# ls -l myprog*
-rwsr-xr-x. 1 root pubs 362804 03-21 15:38 myprog1
-rwxr-sr-x. 1 root pubs 189960 03-21 15:38 myprog2
```

### Do not write setuid shell scripts

**security**  Never give shell scripts setuid permission. Several techniques for subverting them are well known.

# DIRECTORY ACCESS PERMISSIONS

Access permissions have slightly different meanings when they are applied to directories. Although the three types of users can read from or write to a directory, the directory cannot be executed. Execute permission is redefined for a directory: It means that you can cd into the directory and/or examine files that you have permission to read from in the directory. It has nothing to do with executing a file.

When you have only execute permission for a directory, you can use ls to list a file in the directory if you know its name. You cannot use ls to list the entire contents of the directory. In the following exchange, Zach first verifies that he is logged in as himself. He then checks the permissions on Max's **info** directory. You can view the access permissions associated with a directory by running ls with the **–d** (directory) and **–l** (long) options:

```
$ who am i
zach      pts/7   Aug 21 10:02
$ ls -ld /home/max/info
drwx-----x. 2 max pubs 4096 08-21 09:31 /home/max/info
$ ls -l /home/max/info
ls: /home/max/info: Permission denied
```

The **d** at the left end of the line that ls displays indicates **/home/max/info** is a directory. Max has read, write, and execute permissions; members of the pubs group have no access permissions; and other users have execute permission only, indicated by the **x** at the right end of the permissions. Because Zach does not have read permission for the directory, the ls –l command returns an error.

When Zach specifies the names of the files he wants information about, he is not reading new directory information but rather searching for specific information, which he is allowed to do with execute access to the directory. He has read permission for **notes** so he has no problem using cat to display the file. He cannot display **financial** because he does not have read permission for it:

```
$ ls -l /home/max/info/financial /home/max/info/notes
-rw-------. 1 max pubs 34 08-21 09:31 /home/max/info/financial
-rw-r--r--. 1 max pubs 30 08-21 09:32 /home/max/info/notes
$ cat /home/max/info/notes
This is the file named notes.
$ cat /home/max/info/financial
cat: /home/max/info/financial: Permission denied
```

Next Max gives others read access to his **info** directory:

```
$ chmod o+r /home/max/info
```

When Zach checks his access permissions on **info**, he finds he has both read and execute access to the directory. Now **ls –l** displays the contents of the **info** directory, but he still cannot read **financial**. (This restriction is an issue of file permissions, not directory permissions.) Finally, Zach tries to create a file named **newfile** using touch. If Max were to give him write permission to the **info** directory, Zach would be able to create new files in it:

```
$ ls -ld /home/max/info
drwx---r-x. 2 max pubs 4096 08-21 09:31 /home/max/info
$ ls -l /home/max/info
total 8
-rw-------. 1 max pubs 34 08-21 09:31 financial
-rw-r--r--. 1 max pubs 30 08-21 09:32 notes
$ cat /home/max/info/financial
cat: financial: Permission denied
$ touch /home/max/info/newfile
touch: cannot touch '/home/max/info/newfile': Permission denied
```

# ACLs: ACCESS CONTROL LISTS

ACLs (Access Control Lists) provide finer-grained control over which users can access specific directories and files than do traditional Linux permissions (page 191). Using ACLs you can specify the ways in which each of several users can access a directory or file. Because ACLs can reduce performance, do not enable them on filesystems that hold system files, where the traditional Linux permissions are sufficient. Also, be careful when moving, copying, or archiving files: Not all utilities preserve ACLs. In addition, you cannot copy ACLs to filesystems that do not support ACLs.

An ACL comprises a set of rules. A rule specifies how a specific user or group can access the file that the ACL is associated with. There are two kinds of rules: *access rules* and *default rules*. (The documentation refers to *access ACLs* and *default ACLs*, even though there is only one type of ACL: There is one type of list [ACL] and there are two types of rules that an ACL can contain.)

An access rule specifies access information for a single file or directory. A default ACL pertains to a directory only; it specifies default access information (an ACL) for any file in the directory that is not given an explicit ACL.

### Most utilities do not preserve ACLs

caution    When used with the **–p** (preserve) or **–a** (archive) option, cp preserves ACLs when it copies files. The mv utility also preserves ACLs. When you use cp with the **–p** or **–a** option and it is not able to copy ACLs, and in the case where mv is unable to preserve ACLs, the utility performs the operation and issues an error message:

```
$ mv report /tmp
mv: preserving permissions for '/tmp/report': Operation not supported
```

Other utilities, such as tar, cpio, and dump, do not support ACLs. You can use cp with the **–a** option to copy directory hierarchies, including ACLs.

You can never copy ACLs to a filesystem that does not support ACLs or to a filesystem that does not have ACL support turned on.

# Enabling ACLs

The **acl** package must be installed before you can use ACLs. Fedora/RHEL officially supports ACLs on **ext2**, **ext3**, and **ext4** filesystems only, although informal support for ACLs is available on other filesystems. To use ACLs on an **ext2/ext3/ext4** filesystem, you must mount the device with the **acl** option (**no_acl** is the default). For example, if you want to mount the device represented by **/home** so that you can use ACLs on files in **/home**, you can add **acl** to its options list in **/etc/fstab**:

```
$ grep home /etc/fstab
LABEL=/home              /home          ext4    defaults,acl        1 2
```

**remount** option   After changing **fstab**, you need to remount **/home** before you can use ACLs. If no one else is using the system, you can unmount it and mount it again (working with **root** privileges) as long as the working directory is not in the **/home** hierarchy. Alternately you can use the **remount** option to mount to remount **/home** while the device is in use:

```
# mount -v -o remount /home
/dev/sda3 on /home type ext4 (rw,acl)
```

See page 524 for information on **fstab** and page 520 for information on mount.

# Working with Access Rules

The setfacl utility modifies a file's ACL and getfacl displays a file's ACL. When you use getfacl to obtain information about a file that does not have an ACL, it displays some of the same information as an **ls –l** command, albeit in a different format:

```
$ ls -l report
-rw-r--r--. 1 max pubs 9537 01-12 23:17 report

$ getfacl report
# file: report
# owner: max
# group: pubs
user::rw-
group::r--
other::r--
```

The first three lines of the getfacl output compose the header; they specify the name of the file, the owner of the file, and the group the file is associated with. For more information refer to "ls –l: Displays Permissions" on page 191. The **--omit-header** (or just **--omit**) option causes getfacl not to display the header:

```
$ getfacl --omit-header report
user::rw-
group::r--
other::r--
```

In the line that starts with **user**, the two colons (::) with no name between them indicate that the line specifies the permissions for the owner of the file. Similarly, the two colons in the **group** line indicate that the line specifies permissions for the group the file is associated with. The two colons following **other** are there for consistency: No name can be associated with **other**.

The setfacl --**modify** (or –**m**) option adds or modifies one or more rules in a file's ACL using the following format:

*setfacl --modify **ugo:name:permissions file-list***

where ***ugo*** can be either **u**, **g**, or **o** to indicate that the command sets file permissions for a user, a group, or all other users, respectively; ***name*** is the name of the user or group that permissions are being set for; ***permissions*** is the permissions in either symbolic or absolute format; and ***file-list*** is the list of files the permissions are to be applied to. You must omit ***name*** when you specify permissions for other users (**o**). Symbolic permissions use letters to represent file permissions (**rwx**, **r–x**, and so on), whereas absolute permissions use an octal number. While chmod uses three sets of permissions or three octal numbers (one each for the owner, group, and other users), setfacl uses a single set of permissions or a single octal number to represent the permissions being granted to the user or group represented by ***ugo*** and ***name***. See the discussion of chmod on page 193 for more information about symbolic and absolute representations of file permissions.

For example, both of the following commands add a rule to the ACL for the **report** file that gives Sam read and write permission to that file:

```
$ setfacl --modify u:sam:rw- report
```

*or*

```
$ setfacl --modify u:sam:6 report

$ getfacl report
# file: report
# owner: max
# group: pubs
user::rw-
user:sam:rw-
group::r--
mask::rw-
other::r--
```

The line containing **user:sam:rw–** shows that the user named **sam** has read and write access (**rw–**) to the file. See page 191 for an explanation of how to read access permissions. See the following optional section for a description of the line that starts with **mask**.

When a file has an ACL, ls –**l** displays a plus sign (**+**) following the permissions, even if the ACL is empty:

```
$ ls -l report
-rw-rw-r--+ 1 max pubs 9537 01-12 23:17 report
```

**optional    EFFECTIVE RIGHTS MASK**

The line in the output of getfacl that starts with **mask** specifies the *effective rights mask*. This mask limits the effective permissions granted to ACL groups and users. It does not affect the owner of the file or the group the file is associated with. In other words, it does not affect traditional Linux permissions. However, because setfacl always sets the effective rights mask to the least restrictive ACL permissions for the file, the mask has no effect unless you set it explicitly after you set up an ACL for the file. You can set the mask by specifying **mask** in place of *ugo* and by not specifying a *name* in a setfacl command.

The following example sets the effective rights mask to **read** for the **report** file:

```
$ setfacl -m mask::r-- report
```

The **mask** line in the following getfacl output shows the effective rights mask set to read (**r--**). The line that displays Sam's file access permissions shows them still set to read and write. However, the comment at the right end of the line shows that his effective permission is read.

```
$ getfacl report
# file: report
# owner: max
# group: pubs
user::rw-
user:sam:rw-                          #effective:r--
group::r--
mask::r--
other::r--
```

As the next example shows, setfacl can modify ACL rules and can set more than one ACL rule at a time:

```
$ setfacl -m u:sam:r--,u:zach:rw- report

$ getfacl --omit-header report
user::rw-
user:sam:r--
user:zach:rw-
group::r--
mask::rw-
other::r--
```

The **–x** option removes ACL rules for a user or a group. It has no effect on permissions for the owner of the file or the group that the file is associated with. The next example shows setfacl removing the rule that gives Sam permission to access the file:

```
$ setfacl -x u:sam report

$ getfacl --omit-header report
user::rw-
user:zach:rw-
group::r--
mask::rw-
other::r--
```

You must not specify *permissions* when you use the **–x** option. Instead, specify only the *ugo* and *name*. The **–b** option, followed by a filename only, removes all ACL rules and the ACL itself from the file or directory you specify.

Both setfacl and getfacl have many options. Use the **––help** option to display brief lists of options or refer to the man pages for details.

# SETTING DEFAULT RULES FOR A DIRECTORY

The following example shows that the **dir** directory initially has no ACL. The setfacl command uses the –**d** (default) option to add two default rules to the ACL for **dir**. These rules apply to all files in the **dir** directory that do not have explicit ACLs. The rules give members of the **pubs** group read and execute permissions and give members of the **adm** group read, write, and execute permissions.

```
$ ls -ld dir
drwx------. 2 max pubs 4096 02-12 23:15 dir
$ getfacl dir
# file: dir
# owner: max
# group: pubs
user::rwx
group::---
other::---

$ setfacl -d -m g:pubs:r-x,g:adm:rwx dir
```

The following ls command shows that the **dir** directory now has an ACL, as indicated by the **+** to the right of the permissions. Each of the default rules that getfacl displays starts with **default:**. The first two default rules and the last default rule specify the permissions for the owner of the file, the group that the file is associated with, and all other users. These three rules specify the traditional Linux permissions and take precedence over other ACL rules. The third and fourth rules specify the permissions for the **pubs** and **adm** groups. Next is the default effective rights mask.

```
$ ls -ld dir
drwx------+ 2 max pubs 4096 02-12 23:15 dir
$ getfacl dir
# file: dir
# owner: max
# group: pubs
user::rwx
group::---
other::---
default:user::rwx
default:group::---
default:group:pubs:r-x
default:group:adm:rwx
default:mask::rwx
default:other::---
```

Remember that the default rules pertain to files held in the directory that are not assigned ACLs explicitly. You can also specify access rules for the directory itself.

When you create a file within a directory that has default rules in its ACL, the effective rights mask for that file is created based on the file's permissions. In some cases the mask can override default ACL rules.

In the next example, touch creates a file named **new** in the **dir** directory. The ls command shows this file has an ACL. Based on the value of umask (page 469), both the owner and the group that the file is associated with have read and write permissions for the file. The effective rights mask is set to read and write so that the effective permission for **pubs** is read and the effective permissions for **adm** are read and write. Neither group has execute permission.

```
$ cd dir
$ touch new
$ ls -l new
-rw-rw----+ 1 max pubs 0 02-13 00:39 new
$ getfacl --omit new
user::rw-
group::---
group:pubs:r-x                         #effective:r--
group:adm:rwx                          #effective:rw-
mask::rw-
other::---
```

If you change the file's traditional permissions to read, write, and execute for the owner and the group, the effective rights mask changes to read, write, and execute, and the groups specified by the default rules gain execute access to the file.

```
$ chmod 770 new
$ ls -l new
-rwxrwx---+ 1 max pubs 0 02-13 00:39 new
$ getfacl --omit new
user::rwx
group::---
group:pubs:r-x
group:adm:rwx
mask::rwx
other::---
```

# LINKS

A *link* is a pointer to a file. Each time you create a file using vim, touch, cp, or some other means, you are putting a pointer in a directory. This pointer associates a filename with a place on the disk. When you specify a filename in a command, you are indirectly pointing to the place on the disk that holds the information you want.

Sharing files can be useful when two or more people are working on the same project and need to share some information. You can make it easy for other users to access one of your files by creating additional links to the file.

To share a file with another user, first give the user permission to read from and write to the file (page 193). You might also have to change the access permissions of the parent directory of the file to give the user read, write, or execute permission (page 197). When the permissions are appropriately set, the user can create a link to the file so each of you can access the file from your separate directory hierarchies.

A link can also be useful to a single user with a large directory hierarchy. You can create links to cross-classify files in your directory hierarchy, using different classifications for

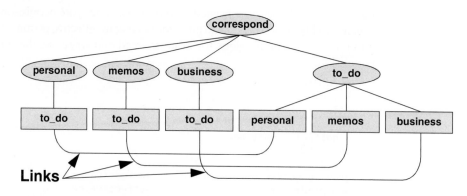

**Figure 6-10**   Using links to cross-classify files

different tasks. For example, if you have the file layout depicted in Figure 6-2 on page 177, a file named **to_do** might appear in each subdirectory of the **correspond** directory—that is, in **personal**, **memos**, and **business**. If you find it difficult to keep track of everything you need to do, you can create a separate directory named **to_do** in the **correspond** directory. You can then link each subdirectory's to-do list into that directory. For example, you could link the file named **to_do** in the **memos** directory to a file named **memos** in the **to_do** directory. This set of links is shown in Figure 6-10.

Although it might sound complicated, this technique keeps all your to-do lists conveniently in one place. The appropriate list is easily accessible in the task-related directory when you are busy composing letters, writing memos, or handling personal business.

### About the discussion of hard links

tip   Two kinds of links exist: hard links and symbolic (soft) links. Hard links are older and becoming outdated. The section on hard links is marked as optional; you can skip it, although it discusses inodes and gives you insight into the structure of the filesystem.

### optional

## *LE*  HARD LINKS

A hard link to a file appears as another file. If the file appears in the same directory as the linked-to file, the links must have different filenames because two files in the same directory cannot have the same name. You can create a hard link to a file only from within the filesystem that holds the file.

### *LPI*  ln: CREATES A HARD LINK

The **ln** (link) utility (without the **–s** or **––symbolic** option) creates a hard link to an existing file using the following syntax:

*ln existing-file new-link*

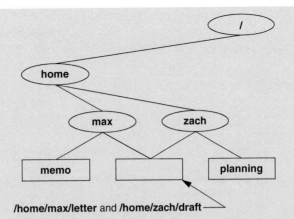

**/home/max/letter** and **/home/zach/draft** ➞

**Figure 6-11**    Two links to the same file: **/home/max/letter** and **/home/zach/draft**

The next command shows Zach making the link shown in Figure 6-11 by creating a new link named **/home/max/letter** to an existing file named **draft** in Zach's home directory:

```
$ pwd
/home/zach
$ ln draft /home/max/letter
```

The new link appears in the **/home/max** directory with the filename **letter**. In practice, Max might need to change directory permissions so Zach will be able to create the link. Even though **/home/max/letter** appears in Max's directory, Zach is the owner of the file because he created it.

The ln utility creates an additional pointer to an existing file, but it does *not* make another copy of the file. Because there is only one file, the file status information—such as access permissions, owner, and the time the file was last modified—is the same for all links; only the filenames differ. When Zach modifies **/home/zach/draft**, for example, Max sees the changes in **/home/max/letter**.

## *LPI* cp VERSUS ln

The following commands verify that ln does not make an additional copy of a file. Create a file, use ln to make an additional link to the file, change the contents of the file through one link, and verify the change through the other link:

```
$ cat file_a
This is file A.
$ ln file_a file_b
$ cat file_b
This is file A.
$ vim file_b
...
$ cat file_b
This is file B after the change.
$ cat file_a
This is file B after the change.
```

If you try the same experiment using cp instead of ln and change a *copy* of the file, the difference between the two utilities will become clearer. After you change a *copy* of a file, the two files are different:

```
$ cat file_c
This is file C.
$ cp file_c file_d
$ cat file_d
This is file C.
$ vim file_d
...
$ cat file_d
This is file D after the change.
$ cat file_c
This is file C.
```

*LPI*  **ls and link counts**    You can use ls with the –l option, followed by the names of the files you want to compare, to confirm that the status information is the same for two links to the same file and is different for files that are not linked. In the following example, the **2** in the links field (just to the left of **max**) shows there are two links to **file_a** and **file_b** (from the previous example):

```
$ ls -l file_a file_b file_c file_d
-rw-r--r--. 2 max pubs 33 05-24 10:52 file_a
-rw-r--r--. 2 max pubs 33 05-24 10:52 file_b
-rw-r--r--. 1 max pubs 16 05-24 10:55 file_c
-rw-r--r--. 1 max pubs 33 05-24 10:57 file_d
```

Although it is easy to guess which files are linked to one another in this example, ls does not explicitly tell you.

*LPI*  **ls and inodes**    Use ls with the –i option to determine without a doubt which files are linked. The –i option lists the *inode* (page 1254) number for each file. An inode is the control structure for a file. If the two filenames have the same inode number, they share the same control structure and are links to the same file. Conversely, when two filenames have different inode numbers, they are different files. The following example shows that **file_a** and **file_b** have the same inode number and that **file_c** and **file_d** have different inode numbers:

```
$ ls -i file_a file_b file_c file_d
3534 file_a  3534 file_b  5800 file_c  7328 file_d
```

All links to a file are of equal value: The operating system cannot distinguish the order in which multiple links were created. When a file has two links, you can remove either one and still access the file through the remaining link. You can remove the link used to create the file, for example, and as long as one link remains, still access the file through that link.

## *LE*  SYMBOLIC LINKS

In addition to hard links, Linux supports *symbolic links*, also called *soft links* or *symlinks*. A hard link is a pointer to a file (the directory entry points to the inode), whereas a symbolic link is an *indirect* pointer to a file (the directory entry contains the pathname of the pointed-to file—a pointer to the hard link to the file).

**Advantages of symbolic links** Symbolic links were developed because of the limitations inherent in hard links. You cannot create a hard link to a directory, but you can create a symbolic link to a directory.

In many cases the Linux file hierarchy encompasses several filesystems. Because each filesystem keeps separate control information (i.e., separate inode tables or filesystem structures) for the files it holds, it is not possible to create hard links between files in different filesystems. A symbolic link can point to any file, regardless of where it is located in the file structure, but a hard link to a file must be in the same filesystem as the other hard link(s) to the file. When you create links only among files in your home directory, you will not notice this limitation.

A major advantage of a symbolic link is that it can point to a nonexistent file. This ability is useful if you need a link to a file that is periodically removed and re-created. A hard link keeps pointing to a "removed" file, which the link keeps alive even after a new file is created. In contrast, a symbolic link always points to the newly created file and does not interfere when you delete the old file. For example, a symbolic link could point to a file that gets checked in and out under a source code control system, a **.o** file that is re-created by the C compiler each time you run make, or a log file that is repeatedly archived.

Although they are more general than hard links, symbolic links have some disadvantages. Whereas all hard links to a file have equal status, symbolic links do not have the same status as hard links. When a file has multiple hard links, it is analogous to a person having multiple full legal names, as many married women do. In contrast, symbolic links are analogous to nicknames. Anyone can have one or more nicknames, but these nicknames have a lesser status than legal names. The following sections describe some of the peculiarities of symbolic links.

## *LPI* ln: CREATES SYMBOLIC LINKS

The ln utility with the **--symbolic** (or **-s**) option creates a symbolic link. The following example creates a symbolic link **/tmp/s3** to the file **sum** in Max's home directory. When you use an ls –l command to look at the symbolic link, ls displays the name of the link and the name of the file it points to. The first character of the listing is l (for link).

```
$ ln --symbolic /home/max/sum /tmp/s3
$ ls -l /home/max/sum /tmp/s3
-rw-rw-r--. 1 max pubs 38 06-12 09:51 /home/max/sum
lrwxrwxrwx. 1 max pubs 14 06-12 09:52 /tmp/s3 -> /home/max/sum
$ cat /tmp/s3
This is sum.
```

The sizes and times of the last modifications of the two files are different. Unlike a hard link, a symbolic link to a file does not have the same status information as the file itself.

You can also use ln to create a symbolic link to a directory. When you use the −−symbolic option, ln works as expected whether the file you are creating a link to is an ordinary file or a directory.

### Use absolute pathnames with symbolic links

**caution** Symbolic links are literal and are not aware of directories. A link that points to a relative pathname, which includes simple filenames, assumes the relative pathname is relative to the directory that the link was created *in* (not the directory the link was created *from*). In the following example, the link points to the file named **sum** in the **/tmp** directory. Because no such file exists, cat gives an error message:

```
$ pwd
/home/max
$ ln --symbolic sum /tmp/s4
$ ls -l sum /tmp/s4
lrwxrwxrwx. 1 max pubs 3 06-12 10:13 /tmp/s4 -> sum
-rw-rw-r--. 1 max pubs 38 06-12 09:51 sum
$ cat /tmp/s4
cat: /tmp/s4: No such file or directory
```

**optional** ### cd AND SYMBOLIC LINKS

When you use a symbolic link as an argument to cd to change directories, the results can be confusing, particularly if you did not realize that you were using a symbolic link.

If you use cd to change to a directory that is represented by a symbolic link, the pwd shell builtin (page 170) lists the name of the symbolic link. The pwd utility (**/bin/pwd**) lists the name of the linked-to directory, not the link, regardless of how you got there.

```
$ ln -s /home/max/grades /tmp/grades.old
$ pwd
/home/max
$ cd /tmp/grades.old
$ pwd
/tmp/grades.old
$ /bin/pwd
/home/max/grades
```

When you change directories back to the parent, you end up in the directory holding the symbolic link:

```
$ cd ..
$ pwd
/tmp
$ /bin/pwd
/tmp
```

**LE+** ## rm: REMOVES A LINK

When you create a file, there is one hard link to it. You can then delete the file or, using Linux terminology, remove the link with the rm utility. When you remove the last hard link to a file, you can no longer access the information stored there, and the operating system releases the space the file occupied on the disk for use by other files. This space is released even if symbolic links to the file remain. When there is more than one hard link to a file, you can remove a hard link and still access the file from any remaining link. Unlike DOS and Windows, Linux does not provide an easy way to undelete a file once you have removed it. A skilled hacker, however, can sometimes piece the file together with time and effort.

When you remove all hard links to a file, you will not be able to access the file through a symbolic link. In the following example, cat reports that the file **total** does not exist because it is a symbolic link to a file that has been removed:

```
$ ls -l sum
-rw-r--r--. 1 max pubs 981 05-24 11:05 sum
$ ln -s sum total
$ rm sum
$ cat total
cat: total: No such file or directory
$ ls -l total
lrwxrwxrwx. 1 max pubs 6 05-24 11:09 total -> sum
```

When you remove a file, be sure to remove all symbolic links to it. Remove a symbolic link in the same way you remove other files:

```
$ rm total
```

# CHAPTER SUMMARY

Linux has a hierarchical, or treelike, file structure that makes it possible to organize files so you can find them quickly and easily. The file structure contains directory files and ordinary files. Directories contain other files, including other directories; ordinary files generally contain text, programs, or images. The ancestor of all files is the root directory and is represented by / standing alone or at the left end of a pathname.

Most Linux filesystems support 255-character filenames. Nonetheless, it is a good idea to keep filenames simple and intuitive. Filename extensions can help make filenames more meaningful.

When you are logged in, you are always associated with a working directory. Your home directory is the working directory from the time you log in until you use cd to change directories.

An absolute pathname starts with the root directory and contains all the filenames that trace a path to a given file. The pathname starts with a slash, representing the root directory, and contains additional slashes following each of the directories in the path, except for the last directory in the case of a path that points to a directory file.

A relative pathname is similar to an absolute pathname but traces the path starting from the working directory. A simple filename is the last element of a pathname and is a form of a relative pathname; it represents a file in the working directory.

A Linux filesystem contains many important directories, including **/usr/bin**, which stores most of the Linux utilities, and **/dev**, which stores device files, many of which represent physical pieces of hardware. An important standard file is **/etc/passwd**; it contains information about users, such as a user's ID and full name.

Among the attributes associated with each file are access permissions. They determine who can access the file and how the file may be accessed. Three groups of users can potentially access the file: the owner, the members of a group, and all other users. An ordinary file can be accessed in three ways: read, write, and execute. The ls utility with the –l option displays these permissions. For directories, execute access is redefined to mean that the directory can be searched.

The owner of a file or a user working with **root** privileges can use the chmod utility to change the access permissions of a file. This utility specifies read, write, and execute permissions for the file's owner, the group, and all other users on the system.

ACLs (Access Control Lists) provide finer-grained control over which users can access specific directories and files than do traditional Linux permissions. Using ACLs you can specify the ways in which each of several users can access a directory or file. Few utilities preserve ACLs when working with files.

An ordinary file stores user data, such as textual information, programs, or images. A directory is a standard-format disk file that stores information, including names, about ordinary files and other directory files. An inode is a data structure, stored on disk, that defines a file's existence and is identified by an inode number. A directory relates each of the filenames it stores to an inode.

A link is a pointer to a file. You can have several links to a file so you can share the file with other users or have the file appear in more than one directory. Because only one copy of a file with multiple links exists, changing the file through any one link causes the changes to appear in all the links. Hard links cannot link directories or span filesystems, whereas symbolic links can.

Table 6-3 summarizes the utilities introduced in this chapter.

**Table 6-3**    Utilities introduced in Chapter 6

| Utility | Function |
| --- | --- |
| cd | Associates you with another working directory (page 185) |
| chmod | Changes access permissions on a file (page 193) |
| getfacl | Displays a file's ACL (page 199) |
| ln | Makes a link to an existing file (page 204) |
| mkdir | Creates a directory (page 184) |
| pwd | Displays the pathname of the working directory (page 143) |
| rmdir | Deletes a directory (page 186) |
| setfacl | Modifies a file's ACL (page 199) |

# EXERCISES

1. Is each of the following an absolute pathname, a relative pathname, or a simple filename?

   a. **milk_co**

   b. **correspond/business/milk_co**

   c. **/home/max**

   d. **/home/max/literature/promo**

   e. **..**

   f. **letter.0210**

2. List the commands you can use to perform these operations:

   a. Make your home directory the working directory

   b. Identify the working directory

3. If the working directory is **/home/max** with a subdirectory named **literature**, give three sets of commands you can use to create a subdirectory named **classics** under **literature**. Also give several sets of commands you can use to remove the **classics** directory and its contents.

4. The df utility displays all mounted filesystems along with information about each. Use the df utility with the **–h** (human-readable) option to answer the following questions.

   a. How many filesystems are mounted on your Linux system?

   b. Which filesystem stores your home directory?

   c. Assuming your answer to exercise 4a is two or more, attempt to create a hard link to a file on another filesystem. What error message do you get? What happens when you attempt to create a symbolic link to the file instead?

5. Suppose you have a file that is linked to a file owned by another user. How can you ensure that changes to the file are no longer shared?

6. You should have read permission for the **/etc/passwd** file. To answer the following questions, use cat or less to display **/etc/passwd**. Look at the fields of information in **/etc/passwd** for the users on the local system.

   a. Which character is used to separate fields in **/etc/passwd**?

   b. How many fields are used to describe each user?

   c. How many users are on the local system?

   d. How many different login shells are in use on your system? (*Hint:* Look at the last field.)

e. The second field of **/etc/passwd** stores user passwords in encoded form. If the password field contains an **x**, your system uses shadow passwords and stores the encoded passwords elsewhere. Does your system use shadow passwords?

7. If **/home/zach/draft** and **/home/max/letter** are links to the same file and the following sequence of events occurs, what will be the date in the opening of the letter?

   a. Max gives the command **vim letter.**

   b. Zach gives the command **vim draft.**

   c. Zach changes the date in the opening of the letter to January 31, writes the file, and exits from vim.

   d. Max changes the date to February 1, writes the file, and exits from vim.

8. Suppose a user belongs to a group that has all permissions on a file named **jobs_list,** but the user, as the owner of the file, has no permissions. Describe which operations, if any, the user/owner can perform on **jobs_list.** Which command can the user/owner give that will grant the user/owner all permissions on the file?

9. Does the root directory have any subdirectories you cannot search as an ordinary user? Does the root directory have any subdirectories you cannot read as a regular user? Explain.

10. Assume you are given the directory structure shown in Figure 6-2 on page 177 and the following directory permissions:

```
d--x--x---   3 zach pubs 512 2010-03-10 15:16 business
drwxr-xr-x   2 zach pubs 512 2010-03-10 15:16 business/milk_co
```

For each category of permissions—owner, group, and other—what happens when you run each of the following commands? Assume the working directory is the parent of **correspond** and that the file **cheese_co** is readable by everyone.

   a. **cd correspond/business/milk_co**

   b. **ls –l correspond/business**

   c. **cat correspond/business/cheese_co**

# ADVANCED EXERCISES

11. What is an inode? What happens to the inode when you move a file within a filesystem?

12. What does the **..** entry in a directory point to? What does this entry point to in the root (**/**) directory?

13. How can you create a file named –i? Which techniques do not work, and why do they not work? How can you remove the file named –i?

14. Suppose the working directory contains a single file named **andor**. What error message do you get when you run the following command line?

    ```
    $ mv andor and\/or
    ```

    Under what circumstances is it possible to run the command without producing an error?

15. The **ls –i** command displays a filename preceded by the inode number of the file (page 206). Write a command to output inode/filename pairs for the files in the working directory, sorted by inode number. (*Hint:* Use a pipeline.)

16. Do you think the system administrator has access to a program that can decode user passwords? Why or why not? (See exercise 6.)

17. Is it possible to distinguish a file from a hard link to a file? That is, given a filename, can you tell whether it was created using an **ln** command? Explain.

18. Explain the error messages displayed in the following sequence of commands:

    ```
    $ ls -l
    total 1
    drwxrwxr-x. 2 max pubs 1024 03-02 17:57 dirtmp
    $ ls dirtmp
    $ rmdir dirtmp
    rmdir: dirtmp: Directory not empty
    $ rm dirtmp/*
    rm: No match.
    ```

# 7

# THE LINUX UTILITIES

## OBJECTIVES

After reading this chapter you should be able to:

▸ Use basic utilities to list files and display text files

▸ Copy, move, and remove files

▸ Display the beginning or end of a file

▸ Search, sort, print, categorize, and compare text files

▸ Compress, decompress, and archive files

▸ Count the number of letters, words, and lines in a file

▸ Locate utilities on the system

▸ Change the modification time of a file

▸ Display information about users and the system

▸ Record a session in a file

▸ Edit text files

When Linus Torvalds introduced Linux and for a long time thereafter, Linux did not have a GUI (graphical user interface): It ran on character-based terminals only, using a CLI (command-line interface), also referred to as a textual interface. All the tools ran from a command line. Today the Linux GUI is important, but many people—especially system administrators—run many command-line utilities. Command-line utilities are often faster, more powerful, or more complete than their GUI counterparts. Sometimes there is no GUI counterpart to a textual utility; some people just prefer the hands-on feeling of the command line. This chapter describes a number of frequently used utilities and concludes with tutorials on the vim and nano text editors. See "Working from the Command Line" on page 119 for an introduction to the command line.

When you work with a CLI, you are working with a shell (Chapters 5, 9, and 27). When you are working on the command line it is important to quote special characters as explained on page 142.

### More utilities are covered throughout the book

tip    This chapter introduces a few important utilities that are good to know as you start using Linux. More utilities are covered throughout the book. See the inside of the front and back covers for a complete list.

# BASIC UTILITIES

One of the advantages of Linux is that it comes with thousands of utilities that perform myriad functions. You will use utilities whenever you work with Linux, whether you use them directly by name from the command line or indirectly from a graphical menu or icon. The following sections discuss some of the most basic and important utilities that are available from a CLI. Some of the more important utilities are also available from a GUI; others are available only from a GUI.

### Run these utilities from a command line

tip    This chapter describes command-line, or textual, utilities. You can experiment with these utilities from a terminal, a terminal emulator within a GUI (page 120), or a virtual console (page 121).

## LPI    cat: JOINS AND DISPLAYS FILES

The cat utility joins and copies files to standard output. The name of the cat utility is derived from *catenate*, which means to join together, one after the other. You can also use cat to display virtual system files in the **/proc** directory hierarchy as explained on page 512.

### ARGUMENTS
The arguments are the pathnames of one or more files that cat processes. You can use cat to display the contents of one or more text files on the screen. More precisely, cat copies the files to standard output, which by default is attached to the screen.

```
$ cat practice
This is a small file that I created
using:  a text editor!

End.
```

If you do not specify an argument or if you specify a hyphen (–) in place of a filename, cat reads from standard input. The following example shows cat working without an argument; the < symbol causes the shell to redirect standard input to cat to come from **practice**. The shell passes no arguments to cat.

```
$ cat < practice
This is a small file that I created
using:  a text editor!

End.
```

You can use cat to create short, simple files. See "The Keyboard and Screen as Standard Input and Standard Output" on page 152 and "Redirection" on page 153 for more examples of redirecting the standard input and standard output of cat.

### OPTIONS

Number  The –**n** (––**number**) option numbers all lines as they are written to standard output while the –**b** (––**number-nonblank**) numbers only non-blank lines.

```
$ cat -n practice
     1  This is a small file that I created
     2  using:  a text editor!
     3
     4  End.
```

Tabs  The –**T** (––**show-tabs**) option displays TABs as ^I.

```
$ cat -T practice
This is a small file that I created
using:^Ia text editor!

End.
```

You can combine options like this

```
$ cat -bT practice
```

Or, using long options, like this

```
$ cat --number-nonblank --show-tabs practice
```

Nonprinting  The –**v** (––**show-nonprinting**) option displays CONTROL characters using the caret notation (e.g., ^M means CONTROL-M) and displays characters that have the high bit set (META characters) using the **M**- notation (e.g., **M-M** means META-M). This option does not convert TABs and LINEFEEDs. Use –**T** (––**show-tabs**) if you want to display TABs as ^I. LINEFEEDs cannot be displayed as anything but themselves; otherwise, the line could be too long.

### RELATED UTILITIES

tac The tac (cat spelled backwards) utility works the same way as cat works except it reverses the order of the lines in each file.

rev The rev (reverse) utility works the same way as cat works except it reverses the order of the characters in each line.

## *LPI* date: DISPLAYS THE SYSTEM TIME AND DATE

Without any arguments, the date utility displays the date and time known to the local system. If you set up a locale database (page 368), date uses that database to substitute in its output terms appropriate to the locale for your account. Use timedatectl (page 613) to set the system clock.

```
$ date
Mon Aug 19 14:39:55 PDT 2013
```

### The hardware clock and the system clock

tip The hardware clock is the time kept in the BIOS (page 31). This clock is battery powered and keeps time even when the computer is off. The system clock runs only while the system is running and is what Linux uses when it needs to know the time. On some systems the system clock is adjusted periodically by NTP (Network Time Protocol; page 315) so it stays accurate.

### ARGUMENTS

The following example formats and specifies the contents of the output of date. See the date man page for a complete list of format sequences.

```
$ date +"%A %B %d"
Monday August 19
```

### OPTIONS

Date The **–d** *datestring* (**––date**=*datestring*) option displays the date specified by *datestring*, not the date known to the system. According to the date man page, "the *datestring* is a mostly free-format date string" such as **2pm next thursday**. See **DATE STRING** in the date man page for details about the syntax of *datestring*. This option does not change the system clock.

UTC The **–u** (**––utc** *or* **––universal**) option displays or sets the time and date using UTC (Universal Coordinated Time; page 1279). UTC is also called GMT (Greenwich Mean Time).

```
$ date -u
Mon Aug 19 21:40:19 UTC 2013
```

### RELATED UTILITIES

timedtectl The timedtectl utility, which is part of systemd (page 438), displays more information about the system clock. You can also use it to set the system clock. See page 613.

cal The cal utility displays a calendar for the month and year you specify. Without any arguments it displays a calendar for the current month.

**LE+** ## echo: DISPLAYS ARGUMENTS

The echo utility copies its arguments, followed by a NEWLINE, to standard output. The Bourne Again Shell has an echo builtin that works similarly to the echo utility.

The echo builtin/utility is a good tool for learning about the shell and other Linux utilities. Some examples on page 166 use echo to illustrate how special characters, such as the asterisk, work. Throughout Chapters 5, 9, and 27, echo helps explain how shell variables work and how you can send messages from shell scripts to the screen. You can even use echo to create a short file by redirecting its output:

```
$ echo "This is a short file." > short
$ cat short
This is a short file.
```

### ARGUMENTS

The arguments can include quoted strings, ambiguous file references, and shell variables. The shell recognizes and expands unquoted special characters in arguments.

The following example shows echo copying its arguments to standard output. The second command includes an unquoted asterisk (*; page 166) that the shell expands into a list of files in the working directory before passing that list as arguments to echo; echo copies this list to standard output.

```
$ echo This is a sentence.
This is a sentence.
$ echo star: *
star: memo memo.0714 practice
$ ls
memo   memo.0714   practice
```

### OPTION

NEWLINE   The **−n** option suppresses the NEWLINE that normally terminates the output of echo. This option is useful in shell scripts when you want to prompt a user and have the response appear on the same line as the prompt. See page 1041 for an example of a shell script that uses this feature.

**LPI** ## hostname: DISPLAYS THE SYSTEM NAME

The hostname utility displays the name of the system you are working on. Use this utility if you are not sure that you are logged in on the correct machine. See also **/etc/hostname** on page 507.

```
$ hostname
guava
```

### OPTION

The following option works with hostname.

FQDN   The **−f** (**−−fqdn**) option displays the *FQDN* (page 1250) of the local system.

### RELATED UTILITY

hostnamectl   The hostnamectl utility, which is part of systemd (page 438), displays more information about the local system. You can also use it to change the hostname.

# *LE*   less **Is** more: **DISPLAY A TEXT FILE ONE SCREEN AT A TIME**

You can use the less or more utilities, called *pagers*, to view a long text file one screen at a time. Each of these utilities pauses after displaying a screen of text. You can then press the SPACE bar to display the next screen of text.

Although less and more are very similar, they have subtle differences. The less utility, for example, allows you to move backward while viewing a file in some situations where more does not. Whereas more must read an entire file before displaying anything, less does not have to and so starts more quickly than more when displaying a large file. At the end of the file less displays an **END** message and waits for you to press q before returning you to the shell. In contrast, more returns you directly to the shell. While using both utilities you can press **h** to display a Help screen that lists commands you can use while paging through a file. Give the command **less /etc/services** to experiment with paging through a file.

## ARGUMENTS

Both less and more take the names of files you want to view as arguments. If you do not specify an argument or if you specify a hyphen (–; less only) in place of a filename, less and more read from standard input.

## OPTIONS

The following options work with less.

Clear screen    The –c (**--clear-screen**) option paints each new screen from the top down; by default less scrolls the display.

EOF    The –e (**--quit-at-eof**) option causes less to exit when it reaches the second EOF (when you press SPACE while less is displaying **END** at the end of a file) so you do not need to type **q** to quit.

Truncate    The –S (**--chop-long-lines**) option truncates lines wider than the screen. By default less wraps long lines.

No initialization    The –X (**--no-init**) option prevents less from sending terminal initialization and deinitialization strings to the terminal. By default, less clears the screen when it finishes; this option causes the last page of what you were viewing to remain on the screen.

**optional**    You can set the **LESS** environment variable (page 1032) in your ~/.bash_profile file (page 330) to set options for less each time you call it and when it is called from another program such as man. For example, the following line in the .bash_profile file in your home directory will cause less to always run with the –X option.

```
export LESS='-X'
```

## RELATED UTILITY

most    The most utility (part of the **most** package; see page 534 for installation instructions) is newer and more capable than less and more. See the most man page for details.

# *LPI* ls: DISPLAYS INFORMATION ABOUT FILES

The ls utility displays information about one or more files. It lists the information alphabetically by filename unless you use an option to change the order.

When you do not provide an argument, ls displays the names of the visible files (those with filenames that do not begin with a period; page 180) in the working directory.

## ARGUMENTS

The arguments are one or more pathnames of any ordinary, directory, or device files. The shell expands ambiguous file references (page 165) in the arguments.

When you specify an ordinary file as an argument, ls displays information about that one file. When the argument is a directory, ls displays the contents of the directory. It displays the name of the directory only when needed to avoid ambiguity, such as when the listing includes more than one directory.

```
$ ls memos.zach/130715.1
memos.zach/130715.1

$ ls memos.zach
130712.1   130714.2   130714.3   130715.1

$ ls memos.*
memos.max:
130619.1   130621.2   130622.1

memos.sam:
130811.2   130811.3   130812.1

memos.zach:
130712.1   130714.2   130714.3   130715.1
```

## *LE* OPTIONS

Options determine the type of information ls displays, and the manner and order in which it displays the information. When you do not use an option, ls displays a short list that contains just the names of files, in alphabetical order. See page 145 for examples of how options affect ls output.

All    The **–a** (**––all**) option includes hidden filenames (those filenames that begin with a period; page 180) in the listing. Without this option ls does not list information about files with hidden filenames unless you specify the name of a hidden file as an argument. The * ambiguous file reference does not match a leading period in a filename, so you must use this option or explicitly specify a filename (ambiguous or not) that begins with a period to display information about files with hidden filenames.

*LE* Directory    The **–d** (**––directory**) option displays directories without displaying their contents.

```
$ ls -ld /
dr-xr-xr-x. 27 root root 4096 07-16 18:37 /
```

This option is useful when you want to find out, for example, the name of the user who owns a directory in a large directory such as /etc. Instead of scrolling through the output of **ls −l** /etc looking for a directory, you can give the command **ls −ld** /etc/*filename* (e.g., **ls −ld** /etc/cron.d).

Human readable   The **−h** (**−−human-readable**) option, when specified with the **−l** option, displays sizes in K (kilobyte), M (megabyte), and G (gigabyte) blocks, as appropriate. This option works with the **−l** and **−s** options only. It displays powers of 1,024. Use **−−si** to display powers of 1,000.

```
$ ls -lh /usr/bin
...
-rwxr-xr-x. 1 root root     105K 05-08 00:45 tac
-rwxr-xr-x. 1 root root      68K 05-08 00:45 tail
-rwxr-xr-x. 1 root root      24K 08-01 01:08 tailf
-rwxr-xr-x. 1 root root      29K 05-02 08:55 talk
-rwxr-xr-x. 1 root root     340K 06-04 08:23 tar
...
```

Long   The **−l** (lowercase "el"; **−−format=long**) option lists more information about each file. See page 191 for an explanation of this output. If standard output for a directory listing is sent to the screen, this option displays the number of blocks used by all files in the listing on a line before the listing.

*LE*   Recursive   The **−R** (**−−recursive**) option recursively lists directory hierarchies.

Reverse   The **−r** (**−−reverse**) option displays the list of filenames in reverse sorted order.

*LE*   Size   The **−s** (**−−size**) option displays the number of 1,024-byte blocks allocated to the file. The size precedes the filename. With the **−l** option, this option displays the size in column 1 and shifts other items one column to the right. If standard output for a directory listing is sent to the screen, this option displays the number of blocks used by all files in the listing on a line before the listing. You can include the **−h** option to make the file sizes easier to read. The following example recursively lists the **memos** directory hierarchy in reverse size order.

```
$ ls -lRrs memos
memos:
4 drwxrwxr-x. 2 sam sam 4096 04-29 14:11 memos.zach
4 drwxrwxr-x. 2 sam sam 4096 04-29 14:32 memos.sam
4 drwxrwxr-x. 2 sam sam 4096 04-30 14:15 memos.max

memos/memos.zach:
4 -rw-rw-r--. 1 sam sam 4064 04-29 14:11 130715.1
4 -rw-rw-r--. 1 sam sam 3933 04-29 14:11 130714.3
4 -rw-rw-r--. 1 sam sam 3317 04-29 14:11 130714.2
...
```

# *LE+*   rm: REMOVES A FILE (DELETES A LINK)

The rm utility removes hard and/or symbolic links to one or more files. Frequently this action results in the file being deleted. See page 203 for information on links.

## ARGUMENTS

The arguments are the pathnames of the files whose links rm will remove. Removing the only (last) hard link to a file deletes the file (page 208). Removing a symbolic link deletes the symbolic link only.

### Be careful when you use rm with ambiguous file references

caution   Because this utility enables you to remove a large number of files with a single command, use rm cautiously, especially when you are working with ambiguous file references. *Never use* rm *with ambiguous file references while you are working with* **root** *privileges.* If you have any doubts about the effect of an rm command with an ambiguous file reference, first use **echo** with the same file reference and evaluate the list of files the reference generates. Alternately, you can use the rm **–i** (**––interactive**) option.

## OPTIONS

Force   The **–f** (**––force**) option, without asking for your consent, removes files for which you do not have write access permission. This option suppresses informative messages if a file does not exist.

Interactive   The **–i** (**––interactive**) option prompts you before removing each file. If you use **–r** (**––recursive**) with this option, rm also prompts you before examining each directory.

```
$ rm -ri memos
rm: descend into directory 'memos'? y
rm: descend into directory 'memos/memos.max'? y
rm: remove regular file 'memos/memos.max/130621.2'? y
rm: remove regular file 'memos/memos.max/130619.1'? n
...
```

You can create an alias (page 392) for **rm –i** and put it in a startup file (page 180) so rm always runs in interactive mode. The **–i** option is set up by default for the **root** user under Fedora/RHEL.

Recursive   The **–r** (**––recursive**) option deletes the contents of the specified directory, including all its subdirectories, and the directory itself. Use this option with caution; do not use it with wildcards (\* and ?).

Verbose   The **–v** (**––verbose**) option displays the name of each file as it is removed.

## RELATED UTILITIES

shred   The shred utility overwrites a file to hide its contents and make it very difficult to recover the data that was stored in it. The **–u** (**––remove**) option causes shred to delete the file after overwriting it. The following command overwrites the file named **myfile** three times and then deletes it.

```
$ shred -u myfile
```

testdisk   The testdisk utility (**testdisk** package) scans, repairs, and sometimes can recover disk partitions. In some cases can undelete files. See the testdisk man page for details.

# WORKING WITH FILES

This section describes utilities that copy, move, print, search through, display, sort, compare, and identify files.

### Filename completion

tip   After you enter one or more letters of a filename (as an argument) on a command line, press TAB, and the shell will complete as much of the filename as it can. When only one filename starts with the characters you entered, the shell completes the filename and places a SPACE after it. You can keep typing or you can press RETURN to execute the command at this point. When the characters you entered do not uniquely identify a filename, the shell completes what it can and waits for more input. If pressing TAB does not change the display, press TAB again to display a list of possible completions. For more information refer to "Pathname Completion" on page 389.

## *LE+*   cp: COPIES FILES

The cp utility copies one or more files. Use scp (page 695) or rsync (page 696) to copy files from one system to another (or to make local copies). See page 237 for a description of the related mv (move) utility.

### ARGUMENTS

With two arguments that are pathnames, neither of which specifies a directory, cp copies the file named by the first argument to the file named by the second argument.

```
$ cp memo memo.cp
```

With two or more arguments that are pathnames, the last of which is an existing directory, cp copies the files named by all but the last argument to the directory named by the last argument.

```
$ cp memo1 memo2 memo4 memo.dir
```

### cp can destroy a file

caution   If the destination file exists *before* you give a cp command, cp overwrites it. Because cp overwrites (and destroys the contents of) an existing destination file without warning, you must take care not to cause cp to overwrite a file that you need. The cp –i (interactive) option prompts you before it overwrites a file.

The following example assumes the file named **orange.2** exists before you give the cp command. The user answers **y** to overwrite the file.

```
$ cp -i orange orange.2
cp: overwrite 'orange.2'? y
```

### OPTIONS

Archive   The –a (––archive) option attempts to preserve the owner, group, permissions, access date, and modification date of source file(s) while copying a directory recursively.

Backup   The –b (––backup) option makes a backup copy of a file that would be removed or overwritten by cp. The backup copy has the same name as the destination file with a tilde (~) appended to it. When you use both **–b** and **–f**, cp makes a backup copy when you try to copy a file over itself. For more backup options, search for **Backup options** in the **coreutils** info page.

Force  The **–f** (**––force**) option causes cp to try to remove the destination file (when it exists but cannot be opened for writing) before copying the source file. This option is useful when the user copying a file does not have write permission to an existing file but does have write permission to the directory containing the file. Use this option with **–b** to back up a destination file before removing or overwriting it.

Interactive  The **–i** (**––interactive**) option prompts you whenever cp would overwrite a file. If you respond with a string that starts with **y** or **Y**, cp copies the file. If you enter anything else, cp does not copy the file.

```
$ cp -i * ../memos.helen
cp: overwrite '../memos.helen/130619.1'? y
cp: overwrite '../memos.helen/130622.1'? n
```

Preserve  The **–p** (**––preserve**[**=***attr*]) option creates a destination file with the same owner, group, permissions, access date, modification date, and ACLs as the source file. The **–p** option does not take an argument.

Without *attr*, **––preserve** works as described above. The *attr* is a comma-separated list that can include **mode** (permissions), **ownership** (owner and group), **timestamps** (access and modification dates), **links** (hard links), and **all** (all attributes).

Recursive  The **–R** *or* **–r** (**––recursive**) option recursively copies directory hierarchies including ordinary files. The last argument must be the name of a directory.

Verbose  The **–v** (**––verbose**) option displays the name of each file as cp copies it.

```
$ cp -rv memos memos.bak
'memos' -> 'memos.bak'
'memos/memos.max' -> 'memos.bak/memos.max'
'memos/memos.max/130619.1' -> 'memos.bak/memos.max/130619.1'
'memos/memos.max/130622.1' -> 'memos.bak/memos.max/130622.1'
'memos/memos.sam' -> 'memos.bak/memos.sam'
'memos/memos.sam/130811.3' -> 'memos.bak/memos.sam/130811.3'
'memos/memos.sam/130811.2' -> 'memos.bak/memos.sam/130811.2'
...
```

## *LE+*  cut: Selects Characters or Fields from Input Lines

The cut utility selects characters or fields from lines of input and writes them to standard output. Character and field numbering start with 1. Although limited in functionality, cut is easy to learn and use and is a good choice when columns and fields can be specified without using pattern matching.

### Arguments

Arguments to cut are pathnames of ordinary files. If you do not specify an argument or if you specify a hyphen (–) in place of a pathname, cut reads from standard input.

## Options

Characters   The **−c** *clist* (**−−characters=***clist*) option selects the characters given by the column numbers in *clist*. The value of *clist* is one or more comma-separated column numbers or column ranges. A range is specified by two column numbers separated by a hyphen. A range of *−n* means columns **1** through *n*; *n−* means columns *n* through the end of the line.

The following example displays the permissions of the files in the working directory. The **−c2-10** option selects characters 2 through 10 from each input line.

```
$ ls -l | cut -c2-10
otal 2944
rwxr-xr-x
rw-rw-r--
rw-rw-r--
rw-rw-r--
rw-rw-r--
```

Input delimiter   The **−d** *dchar* (**−−delimiter=***dchar*) option specifies *dchar* as the input field delimiter. This option also specifies *dchar* as the output field delimiter unless you use the **−−output-delimiter** option. The default delimiter is a TAB character. Quote *dchar* as necessary to protect it from shell expansion.

Fields   The **−f** *flist* (**−−fields=***flist*) option selects the fields specified by *flist*. The value of *flist* is one or more comma-separated field numbers or field ranges. A range is specified by two field numbers separated by a hyphen. A range of *−n* means fields **1** through *n*; *n−* means fields *n* through the last field. The field delimiter is a TAB character unless you use the **−d** option to change it.

The following example displays a list of full names as stored in the fifth field (**−f5**) of the /etc/passwd file. The **−d** option specifies that the colon character is the field delimiter.

```
$ cut -d: -f5 /etc/passwd
Sam the Great
Sam the Great
Zach Brill
Max Wild
...
```

The next command outputs the size and name of each file in the working directory. The **−f** option selects the fifth and ninth fields from the input lines. The **−d** option tells cut to use SPACEs, not TABs, as delimiters. The tr utility (page 258) with the **−s** option changes sequences of two or more SPACE characters to a single SPACE; otherwise, cut counts the extra SPACE characters as separate fields.

```
$ ls -l | tr -s ' ' ' ' | cut -f5,9 -d' '

259 countout
9453 headers
1474828 memo
1474828 memos_save
```

```
7134 tmp1
4770 tmp2
13580 typescript
```

Output delimiter   The **––output-delimiter=***ochar* option specifies *ochar* as the output field delimiter. By default, the output field delimiter is the same as the input field delimiter (the TAB character unless you change it using **–d**). Quote *ochar* as necessary to protect it from shell expansion.

# diff: DISPLAYS THE DIFFERENCES BETWEEN TWO TEXT FILES

The diff (difference) utility displays line-by-line differences between two text files. By default diff displays the differences as instructions that you can use to edit one of the files to make it the same as the other.

The sdiff utility is similar to diff but its output might be easier to read; its output is the same as that of the diff **–y** (**––side-by-side**) option. Use the diff3 utility to compare three files and cmp to compare nontext (binary) files.

## ARGUMENTS

The diff utility commonly takes the pathnames of two ordinary files it is to compare as arguments.

When you call diff without any options, it produces a series of lines containing Add (**a**), Delete (**d**), and Change (**c**) instructions. Each of these lines is followed by the lines from the file you need to add to, delete from, or change, respectively, to make the files the same. A less than symbol (**<**) precedes lines from *file1*. A greater than symbol (**>**) precedes lines from *file2*. The diff output appears in the format shown in Table 7-1. A pair of line numbers separated by a comma represents a range of lines; a single line number represents a single line.

**Table 7-1**   diff output

| Instruction | Meaning (to change file1 to file2) |
|---|---|
| `line1 a line2,line3`<br>`> lines from file2` | Append *line2* through *line3* from **file2** after *line1* in **file1** |
| `line1,line2 d line3`<br>`< lines from file1` | Delete *line1* through *line2* from **file1** |
| `line1,line2 c line3,line4`<br>`< lines from file1`<br>`---`<br>`> lines from file 2` | Change *line1* through *line2* in **file1** to *line3* through *line4* from **file2** |

The diff utility assumes you will convert the file named by the first argument to the file named by the second argument. The line numbers to the left of each of the **a**, **c**, or **d** instructions always pertain to the first file; the line numbers to the right of the instructions apply to the second file. To display instructions to convert the files in the opposite order, reverse the arguments.

## OPTIONS

Ignore blank lines    The **–B** (**––ignore-blank-lines**) option ignores differences that involve only blank lines. See also "Ignore whitespace at end of lines" (following) and "Ignore whitespace" (next page).

Ignore whitespace at end of lines    The **–b** (**––ignore-space-change**) option ignores whitespace (SPACEs and TABs) at the ends of lines and considers other strings of whitespace (such as multiple SPACEs or TABs to be equal. See also "Ignore blank lines" (preceding) and "Ignore whitespace" (next page).

Context    The **–C** *[lines]* (**––context[=lines]**) option displays the sections of the two files that differ, including *lines* lines (the default is 3) around each line that differs to show the context. Each line in the first file that is missing from the second file is preceded by a hyphen (**–**); each extra line in the second file is preceded by a plus sign (**+**); and lines that have different versions in the two files are preceded by an exclamation point (**!**). When lines that differ are within *lines* lines of each other, they are grouped together in the output.

Ignore case    The **–i** (**––ignore-case**) option ignores differences in case when comparing files.

Unified    The **–U** *lines or* **–u** (**––unified[=lines]**) option uses the easier-to-read unified output format. The *lines* argument is the number of lines of context; the default is three. The **–u** option does not take an argument and provides three lines of context.

This option first displays two lines that indicate which of the files you are comparing will be denoted by a plus sign (**+**) and which by a minus sign (**–**). In the following example, a minus sign indicates the **colors.1** file; a plus sign indicates the **colors.2** file.

```
$ diff -u colors.1 colors.2
--- colors.1    2014-04-05 10:12:12.322528610 -0700
+++ colors.2    2014-04-05 10:12:18.420531033 -0700
@@ -1,6 +1,5 @@
 red
+blue
 green
 yellow
-pink
-purple
 orange
```

The **diff –u** command breaks long, multiline text into *hunks*. Each hunk is preceded by a line starting and ending with two at signs (**@@**). This hunk identifier indicates the starting line number and the number of lines from each file for this hunk. In the example, the hunk covers the section of the **colors.1** file (indicated by a minus sign) from the first line through the sixth line. The **+1,5** indicates the hunk covers **colors.2** from the first line through the fifth line.

Following these header lines, **diff –u** displays each line of text with a leading minus sign, a leading plus sign, or a SPACE. A leading minus sign indicates the line occurs only in the file denoted by the minus sign. A leading plus sign indicates the line occurs only in the file denoted by the plus sign. A line that begins with a SPACE (neither a plus sign nor a minus sign) occurs in both files in the same location.

Ignore whitespace  The **–w** (whitespace; **--ignore-all-space**) option ignores whitespace when comparing lines. See also "Ignore blank lines" (previous page) and "Ignore whitespace at end of lines" (previous page).

## *LPI*  file: DISPLAYS THE CLASSIFICATION OF A FILE

The file utility classifies files according to their contents. You can use the file utility to learn about the contents of any file on a Linux system without having to open and examine the file yourself.

### ARGUMENTS

The arguments are the pathnames of one or more files that file classifies. You can specify any kind of file, including ordinary, directory, and special files.

In the following example, file reports that **letter_e.bz2** contains data that was compressed using the bzip2 utility (page 245):

```
$ file letter_e.bz2
letter_e.bz2: bzip2 compressed data, block size = 900k
```

Next file reports on two more files:

```
$ file memo zach.png
memo:     ASCII text
zach.png: PNG image data, 3840 x 1200, 8-bit/color RGB, non-interlaced
```

### OPTIONS

Mime  The **–i** (**--mime**) option displays *MIME* (page 1261) type strings.

```
$ file -i letter_e.bz2 memo zach.png
letter_e.bz2: application/x-bzip2; charset=binary
memo:         text/plain; charset=us-ascii
zach.png:     image/png; charset=binary
```

Zip  The **–z** (**--uncompress**) option attempts to classify files within a compressed file.

```
$ file -z letter_e.bz2
letter_e.bz2: ASCII text (bzip2 compressed data, block size = 900k)
```

## *LE+*  find: FINDS FILES BASED ON CRITERIA

The find utility selects files that meet search criteria and acts on action criteria.

### ARGUMENTS

The argument(s) specify the directory hierarchies that find searches. Without an argument, find searches the working directory hierarchy.

Expression  The find utility does not take options per se, but rather uses an expression made up of one or more criteria (next page) to specify files. The find utility tests each of the files in each of the specified directory hierarchies to see whether the file meets the criteria described by the expression. The absence of an expression implies **–print**. Thus, find without an argument or expression displays files in the working directory hierarchy.

```
$ find
.
./memos.max
./memos.max/130619.1
./memos.max/130622.1
./memos.sam
./memos.sam/130811.3
```

A SPACE separating two criteria is a Boolean AND operator: The file must meet *both* criteria to be selected. (You can also explicitly specify **–and** or **–a**). A **–or** or **–o** separating the criteria is a Boolean OR operator: The file must meet one or the other (or both) of the criteria to be selected. You can negate a criterion by preceding it with an exclamation point (**!**) or **–not**. The find utility evaluates criteria from left to right unless you group them using parentheses.

Within the expression you must quote special characters so the shell does not expand them but rather passes them to find. Special characters that are frequently used with find include parentheses, brackets, question marks, and asterisks.

Each element within the expression is a separate argument. You must separate arguments from each other using SPACEs. A SPACE must appear on both sides of each parenthesis, exclamation point, criterion, or other element.

### SEARCH CRITERIA

You can use the following criteria within the expression. As used in this section, $\pm n$ is a decimal integer that can be expressed as **+n** (more than $n$), **–n** (fewer than $n$), or **n** (exactly $n$). Action criteria are described on the next page. See the find man page for a complete list of criteria.

Access time The file being evaluated meets the **–atime** $\pm n$ (access time) criterion if it was last accessed $\pm n$ days ago. The following command lists files in the working directory hierarchy that were last accessed more than ten days ago. The period representing the working directory is optional but makes the command more readable.

```
$ find . -atime +10
```

Links The file being evaluated meets the **–links** $\pm n$ criterion if it has $\pm n$ links.

Modification time The file being evaluated meets the **–mtime** $\pm n$ (modify time) criterion if it was last modified $\pm n$ days ago.

Filename The file being evaluated meets the **–name** *filename* criterion if the pattern *filename* matches its name. The *filename* can include wildcard characters (*, ?, and []) but these characters must be quoted. The following command lists files in the **/etc** directory that have a filename extension of **.xml**.

```
$ find /etc -name "*.xml"
```

Size The file being evaluated meets the **–size ±n[c|k|M|G]** criterion if it is the size specified by **±n**, measured in 512-byte blocks. Follow **n** with the letter **c** to measure files in characters, **k** to measure files in kilobytes, **M** to measure files in megabytes, or **G** to measure files in gigabytes. The following command finds files in the **/etc** directory that have a filename extension of **xml** and are bigger than 100 kilobytes. It then uses the **–exec** action criterion (below) to display information about each of these files using an **ls –lh** command. Error messages are redirected to **/dev/null** so they are not displayed (page 158).

```
$ find /etc -name "*.xml" -size +100k -exec ls -lh {} \; 2> /dev/null
```

Type The file being evaluated meets the **–type** *filetype* criterion if its file type is specified by *filetype*. Select a *filetype* from the following list:

| | |
|---|---|
| b | Block special file |
| c | Character special file |
| d | Directory file |
| f | Ordinary file |
| l | Symbolic link |
| p | FIFO (named pipe) |
| s | Socket |

The following command lists the directories in the **/etc** directory hierarchy.

```
$ find /etc -type d
```

Username The file being evaluated meets the **–user** *name* criterion if it belongs to the user with the username *name*. You can use a numeric user ID in place of *name*. The following example lists files in Max's home directory hierarchy that are not (**!**) owned by **max**.

```
$ find ~max ! -user max
```

You can use the **–nouser** and **–nogroup** criteria for finding files whose numeric user ID and group ID, respectively, do not exist on the system.

## ACTION CRITERIA

Print The file being evaluated always meets the **–print** action criterion. When evaluation of the expression reaches this criterion, find displays the pathname of the file it is evaluating. If **–print** is the only criterion in the expression, find displays the names of all files in the directory hierarchy specified on the command line. If this criterion appears with other criteria, find displays the name only if the preceding criteria are met. The following example finds files in the working directory hierarchy that are named **core** and were modified more than 30 days ago. It displays the names of these files and removes them.

```
$ find . -name core -mtime +30 -print -exec rm {} \;
```

Execute The file being evaluated meets the **–exec** *command* **\;** action criterion if the *command* returns a 0 (zero [*true*]) exit status. You must terminate the *command* with a quoted semicolon (**\;**) . The find utility replaces a pair of braces (**{}**) within the *command* with the name of the file being evaluated. You can use the **–exec** action criterion at the end of a group of other criteria to execute the ***command*** if the preceding criteria are met. See the section on xargs on page 260 for a more efficient way of doing what this option does. The following command finds files in the working directory hierarchy that were last accessed more than ten days ago and lists each file using an ls –l command. See page 458 for another example of the –exec criterion.

```
$ find . -atime +10 -exec ls -l {} \;
```

Filesystem The file being evaluated always meets the **–xdev** action criterion. It prevents find from searching directories in filesystems other than the one specified on the command line. Also **–mount**.

## grep: SEARCHES FOR A PATTERN IN FILES

The grep[1] utility searches one or more text files for a pattern, which can be a simple string or another form of a regular expression. The grep utility takes various actions, specified by options, each time it finds a line that contains a match for the pattern. This utility takes its input either from files specified on the command line or from standard input.

### ARGUMENTS

The first argument on a grep command line is the pattern grep is to search for. The pattern is a regular expression, as defined in Appendix A. You must quote regular expressions that contain special characters, SPACEs, or TABs. An easy way to quote these characters is to enclose the entire expression within single quotation marks.

The pattern is followed by a list of the pathnames of text files grep is to search through. With the –r option, this list can contain directories; grep searches the files in the specified directory hierarchies.

Without any options grep sends lines that contain a match for ***pattern*** to standard output. The following command displays all lines from the **memo1** file that contain the string **Sam** (with an uppercase S).

```
$ grep Sam memo1
Dear Samuel --
I hope this finds you and Sammy Jr. well and
```

When you specify more than one file on the command line, grep precedes each line it displays with the name of the file it came from, followed by a colon. The next command displays all lines from all files in the working directory that contain the string **sam**. The second command uses \< in the regular expression to force the match to the beginning of a word. The last command uses a caret (^) in a regular expression to anchor the string to the beginning of the line: It lists all lines that begin with the string **sam**. See Appendix A for information on regular expressions.

---

1. Originally the name grep was a play on an ed—an original UNIX editor, available on Fedora/RHEL—command: **g/re/p**. In this command **g** stands for global, **re** is a regular expression delimited by slashes, and **p** means print.

```
$ grep sam *
memo1:This is a letter to sam:
memo1:not eating too much samak.
memo2:subsample by the end of the day.
memo5:sam, what is going on?

$ grep '\<sam' *
memo1:This is a letter to sam:
memo1:not eating too much samak.
memo5:sam, what is going on?

$ grep '^sam' *
memo5:sam, what is going on?
```

## OPTIONS

Count    The **–c** (**––count**) option displays only the number of lines that contain a match in each file. The following example lists all files in the working directory, each followed by the number of times the regular expression (a simple string in this example) occurs in each file.

```
$ grep -c sam *
memo1:2
memo2:1
memo3:0
memo4:0
memo5:1
```

Color    The **––color** option causes grep to display the match in color on a terminal.

**_LPI_** Extended regular expression    The **–E** (**––extended-regexp**) option causes grep to accept extended regular expressions (page 1145). The following example uses an extended regular expression to display in color lines that contain a match for either **vmx** or **svm** in the **/proc/cpuinfo** virtual file, indicating whether the system supports hardware virtualization.

```
$ grep --color -E 'vmx|svm' /proc/cpuinfo
```

See page 664 for a slightly different version of this command. Calling grep with the **–E** option is the same as calling egrep.

Ignore case    The **–i** (**––ignore-case**) option causes lowercase letters in the pattern to match uppercase letters in the file, and vice versa. This example lists all lines that contain the string **sam** with any combination of upper- and lowercase letters.

```
$ grep -i sam *
memo1:This is a letter to sam:
memo1:Dear Samuel --
memo1:I hope this finds you and Sammy Jr. well and
memo1:not eating too much samak.
memo2:subsample by the end of the day.
memo3:How is Sam doing?
memo5:sam, what is going on?
```

List filenames  The **–l** (lowercase "el"; **––files-with-matches**) option displays only the name of each file that contains one or more matches. A filename is displayed only once, even if the file contains more than one match.

```
$ grep -li sam *
memo1
memo2
memo3
memo5
```

Quiet  The **–q** (**––quiet** *or* **––silent**) option does not write anything to standard output, it only sets the exit code. The following grep command returns an exit code of 0 (true) as displayed by the **$?** special parameter (page 1029). This exit code indicates that grep found the string **sam** in the **memo5** file.

```
$ grep -q sam memo5
$ echo $?
0
```

Recursive  The **–r** *or* **–R** (**––recursive**) option recursively descends directories specified in the list of files to be searched and processes files within these directories.

Invert match  The **–v** (**––invert-match**) option causes lines *not* containing a match to satisfy the search. When you use this option by itself, grep displays all lines that do *not* contain a match for the pattern. The following example lists all lines that do not contain the string **sam** (regardless of case).

```
$ grep -vi Sam *
memo1:
memo1:
memo1:Good day.
memo2:This is a letter to Max
memo2:
memo2:Hi Max --
memo2:
memo2:How are you?
memo2:I hope you are able to get me a
memo3:Better I hope!
memo4:Only Max here, no one else.
memo5:I have not seen you in days!
```

Match word  **–w** (**––word-regexp**) With this option, the pattern must match a whole word. This option is helpful if you are searching for a specific word that might also appear as a substring of another word in the file. The following examples show grep searching for a word, first using the **–w** option and then using a regular expression.

```
$ grep -w sam *
memo1:This is a letter to sam:
memo5:sam, what is going on?
```

```
$ grep '\<sam\>' *
memo1:This is a letter to sam:
memo5:sam, what is going on?
```

## **LE+** head: **DISPLAYS THE BEGINNING OF A FILE**

The head utility displays the beginning of a file. This utility takes its input either from one or more files specified on the command line or from standard input. See page 241 for a description of the related tail utility.

### ARGUMENTS

The arguments are the pathnames of the text files that head displays. When you specify more than one file, head displays the filename before displaying the first few lines of each file. When you do not specify a file, head takes its input from standard input.

Without any options, head displays the first ten lines of a file. For example, if the file named **months** lists the 12 months of the year in calendar order, one to a line, then head displays **January** through **October**.

```
$ head months
January
February
March
April
May
June
July
August
September
October
```

### OPTIONS

Bytes    The **–c** *n* (**––bytes=***n*) option displays the first *n* bytes (characters) of a file.

```
$ head -c 60 /etc/passwd
root:x:0:0:root:/root:/bin/bash
bin:x:1:1:bin:/bin:/sbin/nol
```

Lines    The **–n** *n* (**––lines=***n*) option displays the first *n* lines of a file. You can use **–***n* to specify *n* lines without using the **––lines** or **–n** option. If you specify a negative value for *n*, head displays all but the last *n* lines of the file.

```
$ head -2 /etc/passwd
root:x:0:0:root:/root:/bin/bash
bin:x:1:1:bin:/bin:/sbin/nologin
```

# lpr: **SENDS FILES TO PRINTERS**

The lpr (line printer) utility places one or more files in a print queue for printing. Linux provides print queues so only one job is printed on a given printer at a time. A queue allows several people or jobs to send output simultaneously to a single printer with the expected results. This utility can work with local and remote printers. Refer to Chapter 13 for information on setting up a printer and defining the default printer.

The lpr utility takes input either from files specified on the command line or from standard input; it adds these files to the print queue as print jobs. The utility assigns a unique identification number to each print job.

## ARGUMENTS

The arguments are the pathnames of one or more files that lpr prints. Often these files are text files, but many systems are configured so lpr can accept and properly print a variety of file types, including PostScript and PDF files. Without arguments, lpr accepts input from standard input. The following command prints the file named **report**:

```
$ lpr report
```

Because this command does not specify a printer, the output goes to the default printer, which is *the* printer when you have only one printer. You can send more than one file to the printer with a single command. The following command prints three files on the default printer:

```
$ lpr 05.txt 108.txt 12.txt
```

## OPTIONS

Some of the following options depend on which type of file is being printed as well as on how the system is configured for printing.

No header   The **–h** (**no header**) option suppresses printing of the header (burst) page. This page is useful for identifying the owner of the output in a multiuser setup, but it is a waste of paper when this identification is not needed.

No filter   The **–l** (lowercase "el") option specifies that lpr should not preprocess (filter) the file being printed. Use this option when the file is already formatted for the printer.

Printer   The **–P** *printer* option routes a print job to the queue for the printer named *printer*. If you do not use this option, print jobs are routed to the default printer for the local system. The acceptable values for *printer* are stored in the **/etc/printcap** file and can be displayed using an **lpstat –t** command. These values vary from system to system. The following command prints **report** on the printer named **mailroom**:

```
$ lpr -P mailroom report
```

The next example uses a pipeline to send the output of ls to the printer named **deskjet**:

```
$ ls | lpr -Pdeskjet
```

## Setting your personal default printer

tip   If you normally use a printer other than the system default printer, you can set up lpr to use another printer as your personal default by assigning the name of this printer to the environment variable **PRINTER**. For example, if you use bash, you can add the following line to **~/.bash_profile** to set your default printer to the printer named **ps**:

```
export PRINTER=ps
```

Remove   The **–r** (**remove**) option deletes the files being printed after calling lpr.

Copies The *–# n* option prints *n* copies of each file. Depending on which shell you are using, you might need to escape the # by preceding it with a backslash to keep the shell from interpreting it as a special character. The following command prints two copies of **memo** on the printer named **laser**.

```
$ lpr -Plaser -#2 memo
```

### RELATED UTILITIES

lpq The lpq utility displays information about jobs in a print queue. When called without arguments, lpq lists all print jobs queued for the default printer. Use the *–P printer* option with lpq to look at other print queues—even those for printers connected to remote systems. With the *–l* (lowercase "el") option, lpq displays more information about each job. If you specify a username as an argument, lpq displays only the print jobs belonging to that user.

The next example shows a number of print jobs queued for the default printer. Max owns all the jobs, and the first one is being printed (it is active). Jobs 635 and 639 were created by sending input to lpr's standard input; job 638 was created by giving **ncut.icn** as an argument to the lpr command. The last column gives the size of each print job.

```
$ lpq
deskjet is ready and printing
Rank    Owner    Job  Files                        Total Size
active  max      635  (stdin)                      38128 bytes
1st     max      638  ncut.icn                      3587 bytes
2nd     max      639  (stdin)                       3960 bytes
```

lprm One item displayed by lpq is the job number for each print job in the queue. To remove a job from the print queue, give the job number as an argument to lprm.

Unless you are working with **root** privileges, you can remove only your own jobs. Even a user working with **root** privileges might not be able to remove a job from a queue for a remote printer. Without an argument, lprm removes the active printer job (i.e., the job that is now printing) from the queue, if you own that job. The next command removes job 638 from the default print queue:

```
$ lprm 638
```

## *LE+* mv: RENAMES OR MOVES A FILE

The mv (move) utility, which renames or moves one or more files, has three forms. The first renames a single file with a new filename that you supply. The second renames one or more files so that they appear in a specified directory. The third renames a directory. The mv utility physically moves (copies and deletes) the original file if it is not possible to rename it (that is, if you move the file from one filesystem to another). See page 224 for a description of the related cp (copy) utility.

### mv **can destroy a file**

caution Just as cp can destroy a file, so can mv. Also like cp, mv has a *–i* (interactive) option. See the caution box on page 224.

## ARGUMENTS

The first form of mv takes two arguments: the pathname of the ordinary file you want to rename and/or move and the new pathname of the file. The first of the following commands renames **memo** in the working directory to **memo.copy**. The second command moves **memo** from the working directory to the **copies** directory and renames it **memo.130808**.

```
$ mv memo memo.copy
```

```
$ mv memo copies/memo.130808
```

The second form of mv takes two or more arguments; all but the last are the pathnames of ordinary files you want to move and the last specifies the new parent directory for the files. The files you move will have the same simple filenames as each of the original files but new absolute pathnames. The following command moves **memo1**, **memo2**, and **memo3** from the working directory and **memoX** from the **/tmp** directory to the (existing) **memo.copy** subdirectory of the working directory.

```
$ mv memo1 memo2 memo3 /tmp/memoX memo.copy
```

The third form of mv takes two arguments: the pathname of an existing directory that you want to move and/or rename, and the new pathname for the directory, which does not exist. (If the directory exists, the command is the second form of mv and moves the file to the directory without changing the file's name.) The first of the following commands renames the **memo.copy** directory in the working directory **memo.old**. The second moves the **feb** subdirectory of **memos** to the directory named **archive** and renames it **1302**.

```
$ mv memo.copy memo.old
```

```
$ mv memos/feb archive/1302
```

## OPTIONS

Force       The **–f** (**––force**) option causes mv *not* to prompt you if a move would overwrite an existing file that you do not have write permission for. You must have write permission for the directory holding the existing file.

Interactive   The **–i** (**––interactive**) option prompts for confirmation if mv would overwrite a file. If your response begins with a y or Y, mv overwrites the file; otherwise, mv does not move the file. The following example copies all files named **memo** followed by a single character to the **memo.copy** directory, prompting you if it would overwrite a file.

```
$ mv -i memo? memo.copy
mv: overwrite 'memo.copy/memo3'? y
```

If mv would not overwrite a file, it does not prompt even with this option.

Verbose     The **–v** (**––verbose**) option lists files as they are moved.

```
$ mv -v memo? memo.copy
'memo1' -> 'memo.copy/memo1'
'memo2' -> 'memo.copy/memo2'
```

```
'memo3' -> 'memo.copy/memo3'
'memo4' -> 'memo.copy/memo4'
'memo5' -> 'memo.copy/memo5'
```

## LE+   sort: Sorts and/or Merges Files

The sort utility sorts and/or merges one or more text files. It orders the output using the collating sequence specified by the **LC_COLLATE** locale variable (page 368). This section explains how to use sort to order a file by lines. See the sort man page for information on sorting on fields.

Without the **–o** option, sort sends its output to standard output. This utility sorts and merges files unless you use the **–m** (merge only) or **–c** (check only) option.

### Arguments

The arguments are the pathnames of one or more ordinary files that contain the text to be sorted. Without arguments, sort takes its input from standard input. The following example shows sort processing a file named **days** that holds the days of the week, one per line, in calendar order. The sort utility outputs the contents of the file in alphabetical order.

```
$ sort days
Friday
Monday
Saturday
Sunday
Thursday
Tuesday
Wednesday
```

The next example merges and sorts the **days** and **months** files.

```
$ sort days months
April
August
December
February
Friday
...
```

### Options

Check   The **–c** (**––check**) option checks whether the file is properly sorted. The sort utility does not display anything if everything is in order. It displays a message if the file is not in sorted order and returns an exit status of 1. The following example shows that the fourth line of **days**, which contains **Thursday**, is the first line of the file that is not in alphabetical order.

```
$ sort -c days
sort: days:4: disorder: Thursday
```

Dictionary   The **–d** (**––dictionary-order**) option ignores all characters that are not alphanumeric characters or blanks. For example, sort does not consider punctuation with this option. The **LC_CTYPE** locale variable (page 368) affects the outcome when you specify this option.

Ignore case (fold)  The **–f** (**––ignore-case**) option considers all lowercase letters to be uppercase letters.

Ignore nonprinting  The **–i** (**––ignore-nonprinting**) option ignores nonprinting characters. This option is overridden by the **–d** option. The **LC_CTYPE** locale variable (page 368) affects the outcome when you specify this option.

Merge  The **–m** (**––merge**) option assumes that each of the multiple input files is in sorted order and merges them without verifying they are sorted.

Numeric  The **–n** (**––numeric-sort**) option orders in arithmetic sequence, it does not order lines in the machine collating sequence. With this option, minus signs and decimal points take on their arithmetic meaning. The following example shows the difference between sorting a numeric file without using the **–n** option and with it.

```
$ sort num
09.0
10.5
 1.24
-5
9

$ sort -n num
-5
 1.24
09.0
9
10.5
```

Output  The **–o** *filename* (**––output=***filename*) option sends output to *filename* instead of standard output; *filename* can be the same as one of the names of the files that sort is sorting. The following command sends the output to the **days.sort** file.

```
$ sort -o days.sort days
```

Reverse  The **–r** (**––reverse**) option reverses the sense of the sort (e.g., **z** precedes **a**). The following examples order **days** in reverse alphabetic order and **num** in reverse arithmetic order.

```
$ sort -r days
Wednesday
Tuesday
Thursday
Sunday
Saturday
Monday
Friday

$ sort -rn num
10.5
9
09.0
 1.24
-5
```

Unique  The **–u** (**––unique**) option outputs repeated lines only once. When you use this option with **–c**, sort displays a message if the same line appears more than once in the input file, even if the file is in sorted order. The following example sorts (and merges) two copies of **days**. Without any options, the first command displays two copies of each day in alphabetic order. The second command uses the **–u** option and displays one copy of each day.

```
$ sort days days | head -5
Friday
Friday
Monday
Monday
Saturday

$ sort -u days days | head -5
Friday
Monday
Saturday
Sunday
Thursday
```

The next example works with the **fol** file, which holds the names of three months, each listed twice. One of each pair begins with an uppercase letter, the other with a lowercase letter. With just the **–u** option, the first command displays all six lines. The second command adds the **–f** option, which causes sort to consider upper- and lowercase letters to be equivalent. Now the **–u** option considers each pair of months to be equivalent and sort displays only one of each pair of months.

```
$ sort -u fol
april
April
february
February
january
January

$ sort -uf fol
April
February
January
```

## *LE+*  tail: DISPLAYS THE LAST PART OF A FILE

The tail utility displays the last part, or end, of a file. See page 235 for a description of the related head utility.

### ARGUMENTS

The arguments are the pathnames of the files that tail displays. When you specify more than one file, tail displays the filename of each file before displaying lines from that file. If you do not specify an argument or if you specify a hyphen (–) instead of a filename, tail reads from standard input. By default tail displays the last ten lines of its input. The following example shows tail displaying the last ten lines of the **months** file.

```
$ tail months
March
April
May
June
July
August
September
October
November
December
```

### OPTIONS

Bytes   The −c *[+]n* (−−**bytes=***[+]n*) option counts by bytes (characters) instead of lines. The *n* argument is an integer that specifies the number of bytes. The following example displays the last 16 bytes, including 2 NEWLINEs, of the **months** file.

```
$ tail -c 16 months
vember
December
```

If you put a plus sign (**+**) in front of *n,* tail counts from the start of the file instead of the end. The tail utility still *displays characters through the end* of the file, even though it *starts counting* from the beginning. This example shows that **tail −c +16** causes tail to display from the 16th character through the end of the file.

```
$ tail -c +16 months
y
March
April
...
```

Follow   The −f (−−**follow**) option causes tail to enter an endless loop after copying the last line of the file, waiting for and copying additional lines from the file as the file grows. If you specify multiple files in the arguments with this option, tail includes a new header each time it displays output from a different file so you know which file is being added to. This option is useful for tracking the progress of a process that is running in the background and sending its output to a file. The tail utility continues to wait indefinitely, so you must use the interrupt key to terminate it.

Lines   The −n *[+]n* (−−**lines=***[+]n*) option counts by lines (the default). The *n* argument is an integer that specifies the number of lines. Although it is not documented, you can use ±*n* to specify a number of lines without using this option. The next example displays the last five lines of the **months** file.

```
$ tail -5 months
August
September
October
November
December
```

If you put a plus sign (+) in front of *n*, tail counts from the start of the file instead of the end. The tail utility still *displays lines through the end* of the file, even though it *starts counting* from the beginning. Thus **tail –n +5** causes tail to display from the fifth line through the last line of the file.

## *LE+* touch: CHANGES FILE MODIFICATION AND ACCESS TIMES

The touch utility changes the modification and access times of a file to the system time or a time you specify. You can also use touch to create a file.

### ARGUMENTS

The arguments are the pathnames of the files that touch creates or updates. Without options, touch changes the access and modification times to the system time. When you do not specify the **–c** (**––no-create**) option, touch creates files if they do not exist.

The following example shows that **f1** exists in the working directory with a modification date of July 24, 2014, and that **f2** does not exist. The date utility shows the system time. When touch is given these two filenames as arguments, it updates the modification time of **f1** and creates **f2**. Use the ls **–lu** options to display access times.

```
$ ls -l
-rwxr-xr-x. 1 max pubs 898028 2014-07-24   f1

$ date
Wed May   8 15:20:36 PDT 2013
$ touch f1 f2
$ ls -l
-rwxr-xr-x. 1 max pubs 898028 05-08 15:20 f1
-rw-r--r--. 1 max pubs      0 05-08 15:20 f2
```

### OPTIONS

No create    The **–c** (**––no-create**) option does not create files, it only modifies times on existing files.

Date    The **–d** *datestring* (**––date=***datestring*) option changes times using the date specified by *datestring*. Most familiar formats are permitted for *datestring*. Components of the date and time not included in *datestring* are assumed to be the current date and time. This option may not be used with **–t**. This example changes the date on **f1** to May 15, 2020.

```
$ touch -d 'may 15 2020' f1
$ ls -l f1
-rw-rw-r--. 1 max max 978160 2020-05-15 f1
```

Time    The **–t** [[*cc*]*yy*]*nnddhhmm*[.*ss*] option changes times to the date specified by the argument. The *nn* argument is the number of the month (01–12), *dd* is the day of the month (01–31), *hh* is the hour based on a 24-hour clock (00–23), and *mm* is the minutes (00–59). You must specify at least these fields. You can specify the number of seconds past the start of the minute using .*ss*.

The optional *cc* specifies the first two digits of the year (the value of the century minus 1), and *yy* specifies the last two digits of the year. When you do not specify a year, touch assumes the current year. When you do not specify *cc*, touch assumes 20 for *yy* in the range 0–68 and 19 for *yy* in the range 69–99. This option may not be used with **–d**.

The following example creates a file with a modification and access time of August (08) 2 (02) at 2:30 PM (**1420**). The command assumes the year known to the system and zero seconds.

```
$ touch -t 08021420 xx
$ ls -l xx
-rw-r--r--. 1 sam pubs 0 08-02 14:20 xx
```

## *LE+*   wc: DISPLAYS THE NUMBER OF LINES, WORDS, AND BYTES IN FILES

The wc (word count) utility displays the number of lines, words, and bytes in one or more files. When you specify more than one filename on the command line, wc displays totals for each file as well as combined totals for all files.

### ARGUMENTS

The arguments are the pathnames of one or more files that wc analyzes. The columns wc displays show the number of lines, words, and bytes, in that order. (A *word* is a sequence of characters bounded by SPACEs, TABs, NEWLINEs, or a combination of these characters.) Without any arguments, wc takes its input from standard input. The following commands show wc analyzing the **days** and **months** files. When you redirect its input, wc does not display the name of the file.

```
$ wc days months
   7    7  57 days
  12   12  86 months
  19   19 143 total

$ cat days months | wc
      19      19     143
```

### OPTIONS

Lines   The **–l** (lowercase "el"; **––lines**) option displays only the number of lines (i.e., NEWLINE characters) in the input. The following example shows that there are seven lines in the **days** file.

```
$ wc -l days
7 days
```

Bytes   The **–m** (**––chars**) option displays only the number of bytes in the input. The next example shows that there are 57 bytes, including NEWLINEs, in the **days** file.

```
$ wc -m days
57 days
```

Words   The **–w** (**––words**) option displays only the number of words in the input. The final example shows that there are seven words (each line holds one word) in the **days** file.

```
$ wc -w days
7 days
```

# *LE* COMPRESSING AND ARCHIVING FILES

Large files use more disk space and take longer to transfer over a network than smaller files. To reduce these factors you can compress a file without losing any of the information it holds (*lossless* data compression). Similarly, a single archive of several files packed into a larger file is easier to manipulate, upload, download, and email than multiple files. You might frequently download compressed, archived files from the Internet. The utilities described in this section compress and decompress files and pack and unpack archives.

### dtrx: **extracts and decompresses files intelligently**

tip The dtrx utility (Do the Right Extraction; **dtrx** package) extracts and decompresses many types of files intelligently. It decompresses xz, bzip2, and gzip files and it extracts and decompresses compressed **tar** archives. This utility (it is a Python script) determines which utility was used to compress a file and calls that utility to decompress it.

The dtrx utility will

- Not overwrite a file, but will instead rename the decompressed/extracted file and tell you what it named it

- Extract an archive into a new directory so the extracted files do not clutter and mingle with those in the working directory; see the tips on page 251

- Perform recursive extraction: it will extract archives from within archives

- Set the permissions of extracted files to sane values

The dtrx utility does not have a **man** page. For more information use the **--help** option or visit brettcsmith.org/2007/dtrx.

# *LE+* xz, bzip2, AND gzip: COMPRESS AND DECOMPRESS FILES

This section discusses three compression utilities: xz, bzip2, and gzip (GNU zip). Because these utilities work similarly and take many of the same options, this one section covers all three utilities. Because xz is the newest and most effective tool, all examples in this section use xz. Differences between the utilities are noted.

### xz, bzip2, **and** gzip

tip The bzip2 utility is block based, provides good compression, and is CPU intensive. The older alternative, gzip, is stream based and does not compress as well as bzip2. However, gzip can compress on-the-fly (e.g., while downloading a file) whereas bzip2 cannot begin compression until it has read a complete block. Also, bzip2 is a Linux utility whereas gzip is a cross-platform utility that is recognized natively by Windows, Linux, and other *nix systems. The xz utility is newer than bzip2 and gzip and can do a better job of compressing files than either.

The xz, bzip2, and gzip utilities compress a file by analyzing it and recoding it more efficiently. The new version of the file looks completely different from the original file. In fact, because the new file contains many nonprinting characters, you cannot view it directly. These utilities work particularly well on files that contain a lot of repeated information, such as text and image data, although most image data is already in a compressed format. The xz utility can yield a smaller compressed file than bzip2 and bzip2 can yield a smaller compressed file than gzip.

Normally these utilities do not overwrite a file; you must use ––**force** to overwrite a file during compression or decompression.

### gzip **versus** zip

tip    Do not confuse gzip and gunzip with the zip and unzip utilities. The zip and unzip utilities pack and unpack an archive that might contain several files compressed into a single file. That compressed file is typically imported from or exported to a Windows system.

In contrast, when given multiple filenames as arguments, gzip compresses each file individually and gunzip decompresses individual files. It does not create an archive.

The zip and unzip utilities are compatible with WinZip, a Windows program that compresses and archives files.

### ARGUMENTS

The arguments are the pathnames of one or more ordinary files (no directories except when you call gzip with the **–r** option) that are to be compressed or decompressed. Without arguments, or if the special option **–** is present, these utilities read from standard input. By default, when these utilities compress a file, they create a new, compressed version of the file with a filename extension of **.xz** (xz), **.bz2** (bzip2), or **.gz** (gzip) and delete the original file. They reverse the process when they decompress a file. In the following example, xz compresses the **myprog** file, reducing its size, deleting the original file, and creating a new file named **myprog.xz**.

```
$ ls -l
-rwxr-xr-x. 1 sam sam 982296 06-07 13:50 myprog

$ xz myprog
$ ls -l
-rwxr-xr-x. 1 sam sam 387536 06-07 13:50 myprog.xz
```

### OPTIONS

Standard output    The **–c** (––**stdout**) option writes the results of compression or decompression to standard output. This option implies the **–k** option.

Decompress    The **–d** (––**decompress**) option decompresses a file that was compressed using xz. This option with xz is equivalent to the unxz utility (unxz is a link to xz). With bzip2 it is equivalent to bunzip2, and with gzip it is equivalent to gunzip.

```
$ xz -d myprog.xz
$ ls -l
-rwxr-xr-x. 1 sam sam 982296 06-07 13:50 myprog
```

Quality    The **–***n* option sets the compression level when compressing a file. Under xz, the *n* is a digit from 0 to 9; under bzip2 and gzip it is from 1 to 9. Level 0 or 1 compression yields the largest file but runs quickly and uses the least memory. Level 9 compression yields the smallest file but runs slowly and uses the most memory. The default level is 6. The next example shows that with xz the –9 option yields about a 9 percent smaller compressed file than does –0. This option has more impact on file size and speed with xz than with bzip2 or gzip.

```
$ xz -0 myprog
$ ls -l
-rwxr-xr-x. 1 sam sam 423704 06-07 13:50 myprog.xz

$ unxz myprog.xz
$ xz -9 myprog
$ ls -l
-rwxr-xr-x. 1 sam sam 387536 06-07 13:50 myprog.xz
```

**optional** The time utility displays execution times for the command you specify as its argument. The line labeled **real** reports the elapsed clock time, **user** is the time the execution spent in *userspace* (page 1279), and **sys** is the time it spent in *kernelspace* (page 1257). The following example shows that it took about one-tenth of a second of clock time to compress **myprog** using level 0 compression and about seven-tenths of a second using level 9. The difference in the system time is even more dramatic.

```
$ time xz -0 myprog
real    0m0.115s
user    0m0.043s
sys     0m0.071s

$ unxz myprog.xz
$ time xz -9 myprog
real    0m0.705s
user    0m0.078s
sys     0m0.599s
```

Force The –f (––force) option forces compression even if a file already exists, is a symbolic link to a regular file, or has multiple hard links. The following example shows that, by default, xz will not compress a file that has a hard link (page 204). With the –f option, xz compresses the file, creating a new, compressed file and deleting the old, linked file.

```
$ ls -l
-rwxr-xr-x. 2 sam sam 982296 06-07 13:50 myprog
-rwxr-xr-x. 2 sam sam 982296 06-07 13:50 myprog.lnk

$ xz myprog
xz: myprog: Input file has more than one hard link, skipping

$ xz -f myprog
$ ls -l
-rwxr-xr-x. 1 sam sam 982296 06-07 13:50 myprog.lnk
-rwxr-xr-x. 1 sam sam 387536 06-07 13:50 myprog.xz
```

Keep    The –k (––keep) option does not delete input files after compressing or decompressing them. The following command uses the –k option so that after compressing **myprog**, the original file remains along with the compressed version.

```
$ xz -k myprog
$ ls -l
-rwxr-xr-x. 1 sam sam 982296 06-07 13:50 myprog
-rwxr-xr-x. 1 sam sam 387536 06-07 13:50 myprog.xz
```

### Keep the original file by using the –k option

tip    The xz, bzip2, and gzip utilities and their counterparts, unxz, bunzip2, and gunzip, remove the original file when they compress or decompress a file. Use the –k (keep) option to keep the original file.

Recursive    The –r (––recursive) option recursively descends directories listed in the arguments and compresses or decompresses each file within these directories. This option does not create an archive; see the tip on page 246. Works with gzip only.

Verbose    The –v (––verbose) option displays the name of the file, the percent of compression completed, the sizes of the compressed and original files, and the compression ratio. The output of the following xz command shows that the compressed file is almost 40 percent smaller than the original file.

```
$ xz -v myprog
myprog (1/1)
  100 %        378.5 KiB / 959.3 KiB = 0.395
```

### Related Utilities

xzcat bzcat zcat    The xzcat, bzcat, and zcat utilities display files that have been compressed using xz, bzip2, and gzip, respectively. The equivalent of cat for compressed files, these utilities decompress the compressed data and display the decompressed data. Like cat, they do not change the source file. The following command decompresses and displays **memo.xz** on the fly.

```
$ xzcat memo.xz
```

After xzcat is run, the content of **memo.xz** is unchanged; the file is still stored on the disk in compressed form.

xzless bzless    Use xzless/bzless/zless in place of xzcat/bzcat/zcat when you decompress and view a
zless    large text file. These utilities send the decompressed output through a pipeline to less so you can view it one screen at a time.

xzgrep bzgrep    Use xzgrep/bzgrep/zgrep to search for a pattern in a compressed file without changing
zgrep    the file. Because these utilities invoke grep, they accept the same arguments as grep.

LPI    unxz bunzip2    The unxz/bunzip2/gunzip utilities restore a compressed file just as running xz/bzip2/gzip
gunzip    with the –d option does:

```
$ unxz myprog.xz
$ ls -l
-rwxr-xr-x. 1 sam sam 982296 06-07 13:50 myprog
```

compress The compress utility compresses files, albeit not as well as gzip. This utility marks a file it has compressed by adding a **.Z** filename extension to its name.

**LE** unzip The unzip utility restores a file that has been compressed using zip.

**LE** zip The zip utility compresses and archives files; the **–r** option processes files in a directory hierarchy. This utility marks a file it has compressed by adding a **.zip** filename extension to its name. The zip and unzip utilities are compatible with WinZip, a Windows program that compresses and archives files. Give the command **zip** without any arguments or see the zip man page for more information including a list of options.

```
$ zip -r allmemos memos
  adding: memos/ (stored 0%)
  adding: memos/typescript (deflated 33%)
  adding: memos/memos.sam/ (stored 0%)
  adding: memos/memos.sam/130811.2 (deflated 77%)
  adding: memos/memos.sam/130811.3 (deflated 73%)
```

# **LPI** tar: STORES OR EXTRACTS FILES TO/FROM AN ARCHIVE FILE

The tar (tape archive) utility, also discussed on page 603, creates, adds to, lists, and retrieves files from an archive file. Its name is short for *tape archive,* as its original function was to create and read archive and backup tapes. Today it is used to create a single file (called a *tar file, archive,* or *tarball*) from multiple files or directory hierarchies and to extract files from a tar file. See page 603 for more information and examples that use tar to back up files; see page 605 for information on cpio, a similar utility.

You can use xz, bzip2, gzip, or compress to compress tar files, making them easier to store and handle. Many files you download from the Internet will already be in one of these formats.

Files that have been processed by tar and compressed by xz frequently have a filename extension of **.txz**. Those processed by tar and compressed by bzip2 use **.tar.bz2** or **.tbz**, those processed by tar and gzip use **.tar.gz** or **.tgz**, and files processed by tar and compress use **.tar.Z** as the filename extension.

## ARGUMENTS
The arguments are pathnames of the files that tar archives or extracts. If you do not specify an argument, tar reads from standard input or writes to standard output.

## OPTIONS
You must use one and only one of the following options to indicate which action you want tar to take. You can alter the action of the option by following it with one or more modifiers (page 251).[2]

---

2. Although the original UNIX tar did not use a leading hyphen to indicate an option on the command line, the GNU/Linux version accepts hyphens but works as well without them. This book precedes tar options with a hyphen for consistency with most other utilities.

Create    The **–c** (**––create**) option creates an archive. This option stores the files named as arguments in a new archive. If the archive already exists, tar destroys it before creating the new archive. If an argument is a directory, tar copies the directory hierarchy into the archive. Without the **––file** modifier, tar writes the archive to standard output.

In the following example, the first ls shows the sizes of the files **g**, **b**, and **d**. Next tar uses the **–c** (create) option along with the **–v** (verbose; page 252) and **–f** (write to or read from a file; next page) modifiers to create an archive named **all.tar** from these files. Each line of output displays the name of the file tar is appending to the archive it is creating.

The tar utility adds overhead when it creates an archive. The next command shows that the archive file **all.tar** occupies more than 9,700 bytes, whereas the sum of the sizes of the three files is about 6,000 bytes. This overhead is more appreciable on smaller files, such as the ones in this example:

```
$ ls -l g b d
-rw-r--r--. 1 zach other 1178 08-20 14:16 b
-rw-r--r--. 1 zach zach  3783 08-20 14:17 d
-rw-r--r--. 1 zach zach  1302 08-20 14:16 g

$ tar -cvf all.tar g b d
g
b
d

$ ls -l all.tar
-rw-r--r--. 1 zach zach 9728 08-20 14:17 all.tar
```

TOC    Without arguments, the **–t** (**––list**) option produces a table of contents listing all files in an archive. With arguments, it displays the name of each file in the arguments each time it occurs in the archive. You can use this option with the **–v** option to display detailed information about files in an archive. The next example calls tar with the **–t** and **–v** options to display a table of contents for the archive created in the previous example.

```
$ tar -tvf all.tar
-rw-r--r-- zach /zach    1302 2013-08-20 14:16 g
-rw-r--r-- zach /other   1178 2013-08-20 14:16 b
-rw-r--r-- zach /zach    3783 2013-08-20 14:17 d
```

**LE**  Extract    The **–x** (**––extract**) option extracts files listed in the arguments from the archive and writes them to the disk, overwriting existing files with the same names. Without arguments, this option extracts all files from the archive. If the arguments include a directory, tar extracts the directory hierarchy. The tar utility attempts to keep the owner, modification time, and access privileges the same as those of the original file. If tar reads the same file more than once, the last version read will appear on the disk when tar is finished.

## tar: the –x option can overwrite files

caution    The **–x** option to tar overwrites a file that has the same filename as a file you are extracting. Follow the suggestion in the following caution box to avoid overwriting files.

### tar: the –x option might extract a lot of files

caution  Some tar archives contain many files. To list the files in the archive without unpacking them, run tar with the **–tf** options followed by the name of the tar file. In some cases you might want to create a new directory (mkdir [page 184]), cd to that directory, and expand the tar file from there (i.e., **tar –xf ../filename**). That way the unpacked files will not mingle with existing files, and no confusion will occur. This strategy also makes it easier to delete the extracted files. Depending on how they were created, some tar files automatically create a new directory and put the files into it; the **–t** option shows where tar will place the files you extract. See also the tip on dtrx (page 245).

The next example extracts a single file from a tar archive file. The **–x** option tells tar to extract files and the **–f** modifier takes an argument of the name of the archive file. The **–v** option causes tar to list the files as it extracts each one. The argument to tar, **b**, tells tar the name of the file to extract from the archive file.

```
$ tar -xvf all.tar b
-rw-r--r-- zach /other    1178 2013-08-20 14:16 b
```

Omit the argument (**b**) to extract all files from the archive file.

### MODIFIERS

Preserve ACLs  The **––acls** modifier preserves ACL permissions (page 198).

Filename  The **–f** *filename* (**––file** *filename*) modifier uses *filename* as the name of the file the archive is created in or extracted from. The *filename* can be the name of an ordinary file or a device (e.g., a DVD or USB flash drive). You can use a hyphen (–) instead of *filename* to refer to standard input when creating an archive and standard output when extracting files from an archive.

xz  The **–J** (**––xz**) modifier uses xz (page 245) to compress/decompress files when creating an archive and extracting files from an archive. This modifier is optional when you decompress files because tar recognizes a compressed file and decompresses it automatically.

The first command in the following example uses the **–c** option to create an archive, the **–J** modifier to use xz to compress the files going into the archive, the **–f** modifier with an argument of **mfiles.txz** to specify the name of the archive file, and an asterisk, which the shell expands into a list of all files in the working directory, to specify the names of the files that tar is to archive. The second command extracts (**–x** option) the files from the archive named **mfiles.tbz** (**–f mfiles.tbz**) specifying the **–v** (verbose) modifier two times to create a long listing of the extracted files and the optional **–J** (xz) modifier to decompress the files as tar extracts them. It extracts the files named by the arguments.

```
$ tar -cJf mfiles.txz *

$ tar -xvvJf mfiles.txz mkdir more
-rwxr-xr-x max/pubs    128899 2013-05-06 13:23 mkdir
-rwxr-xr-x max/pubs     36176 2013-05-06 13:22 more
```

bzip2   The **–j** (**––bzip2**) modifier uses bzip2 (page 245) to compress/decompress files when creating an archive and extracting files from an archive. This modifier is optional when you decompress files because tar recognizes a compressed file and decompresses it automatically.

Verbose   The **–v** (**––verbose**) modifier lists each file as tar reads or writes it. When combined with the **–t** option, **–v** causes tar to display a more detailed listing of the files in the archive, showing their ownership, permissions, size, and other information. Similarly, two **–v** options cause tar to display a more detailed listing while extracting files.

Interactive   The **–w** (**––interactive**) modifier asks you for confirmation before reading or writing each file. Respond with a string that begins with **Y** or **y** if you want tar to take the action. Any other response causes tar not to take the action.

```
$ tar -xwf mfiles.tbz
extract 'mkdir'?y
extract 'mknod'?n
...
```

gzip   The **–z** (**––gzip** *or* **––gunzip**) modifier uses gzip when creating an archive and gunzip when extracting files from an archive. This modifier also works to extract files from archives that have been compressed using the compress utility. This modifier is optional when you decompress files because tar recognizes a compressed file and decompresses it automatically.

The following two commands are equivalent ways of creating a compressed archive of the files in the **/home** directory hierarchy on the device mounted at **/dev/sde1**:

```
$ tar -zcf /dev/sde1 /home
$ tar -cf - /home | gzip > /dev/sde1
```

# DISPLAYING USER AND SYSTEM INFORMATION

This section covers utilities that provide information about who is using the system, what those users are doing, and how the system is running. In addition to the utilities covered in this section, see

- df—displays a list of the directory hierarchies available on the system, along with the amount of disk space, free and used, on each (page 804)
- dmesg—displays kernel messages (page 595)
- du—displays disk usage information (page 523)
- lsblk—lists block device information (page 635)
- lshw—lists hardware information (page 636)
- lspci—lists PCI device information (page 635)
- lsusb—lists USB bus and USB device information (page 636)

- top—lists processes using the most resources (page 612)
- uname—displays information about the system (page 470)

**LE+**

# free: DISPLAYS MEMORY USAGE INFORMATION

The free utility displays the amount of physical (RAM) and *swap space* (page 1276) memory in the local system. It displays columns for total, used, and free memory as well as for kernel buffers. The column labeled **shared** is obsolete.

### OPTIONS

Human   The **–h** option displays memory in easy-to-read units.

Total   The **–t** option adds a line labeled **Total** to the end of the output.

In the following example, the **–h** option causes free to display memory sizes in human readable format (gigabytes in this case) and the **–t** option displays a total line.

```
$ free -mth
                total        used        free      shared     buffers      cached
Mem:             988M        781M        207M          0B         25M        279M
-/+ buffers/cache:           476M        512M
Swap:            2.0G          0B        2.0G
Total:           3.0G        781M        2.2G
```

One of the ways Linux takes advantage of free memory is to allocate memory it is not otherwise using to *buffers* (page 1240) and *cache* (page 1241). Thus the value on the **Mem** line in the **free** column will be small and is not representative of the total available memory when the kernel is working properly. As the kernel needs more memory, it reallocates memory it had allocated to buffers and cache.

The **–/+ buffers/cache** line gives values assuming memory used for buffers and cache is free memory. The value in the **used** column on this line assumes buffers and cache (25M + 279M = 304M on the **Mem** line) are freed; thus the value in the **used** column is 476M (~781M – 304M) while the value in the **free** column value increases to 512M (~207M + 304M). Unlike the value in the **free** column on the **Mem** line, as the value in the **free** column on the **–/+ buffers/cache** line approaches zero, the system is truly running out of memory.

The **Swap** line displays the total, used, and free amounts of swap space.

**LPI**

# uptime: DISPLAYS SYSTEM LOAD AND DURATION INFORMATION

The uptime utility displays a single line that includes the time of day, the period of time the computer has been running (in days, hours, and minutes), the number of users logged in, and the load average (how busy the system is). The three load average numbers represent the number of jobs waiting to run, averaged over the past 1, 5, and 15 minutes.

```
$ uptime
 09:49:14 up 2 days, 23:13,   3 users,  load average: 0.00, 0.01, 0.05
```

## LE   w: LISTS USERS ON THE SYSTEM

The first line the w utility displays is the same as the output of uptime (previous page). Following that line, w displays a list of the users who are logged in.

The first column in the following example shows that Max, Zach, and Sam are logged in (Max is logged in twice). The second column shows the name of the device file each user's terminal, workstation, or terminal emulator is connected to. The third column shows the system that a remote user is logged in from. The fourth column shows the time each user logged in. The fifth column indicates how long each user has been idle (how much time has elapsed since the user pressed a key on the keyboard). The next two columns identify how much computer processor time each user has used during this login session and on the task that user is running. The last column shows the command each user is running.

```
$ w
 17:47:35 up 1 day,  8:10,  6 users,  load average: 0.34, 0.23, 0.26
 USER     TTY     FROM            LOGIN@   IDLE   JCPU   PCPU WHAT
 sam      tty4    -               17:18  29:14m  0.20s  0.00s vi memo
 max      tty2    -               16:42   0.00s  0.20s  0.07s w
 zach     tty1    -               16:39   1:07    0.05s  0.00s run_bdgt
 max      pts/4   guava           17:27   3:10m  0.24s  0.24s -bash
```

## LE   who: LISTS USERS ON THE SYSTEM

The who utility displays information about the local system. Without options it displays a list of users who are logged in. In the following example, the first column who displays shows that Sam, Max, and Zach are logged in. (Max is logged in from two locations.) The second column shows the name of the device that each user's terminal, workstation, or terminal emulator is connected to. The third column shows the date and time the user logged in. An optional fourth column shows (in parentheses) the name of the system a remote user logged in from.

```
$ who
 sam      tty4        2013-07-25 17:18
 max      tty2        2013-07-25 16:42
 zach     tty1        2013-07-25 16:39
 max      pts/4       2013-07-25 17:27 (guava)
```

### ARGUMENTS

Boot   The **–b** option displays the time the system was last booted.

```
$ who -b
         system boot  2013-04-30 17:48
```

Run level   The **–r** option displays the system runlevel (page 449) and the time the system entered that runlevel.

```
$ who -r
         run-level 5  2013-04-30 17:51
```

Me   The **–m** option displays the standard information for the user issuing the command.

```
$ who -m
 max      pts/4       2013-07-25 17:27 (guava)
```

In place of **–m** you can supply any two arguments; **am i** or **mom likes** are classic.

```
$ who am i
max       pts/4         2013-07-25 17:27 (guava)
```

**RELATED UTILITIES**

whoami  While the who utility (e.g., **who am i**) displays the real UID of a user, whoami displays the effective UID of a user. For more information refer to "Real UID Versus Effective UID" on page 425.

# MISCELLANEOUS UTILITIES

This section covers which and whereis (determine the location of a utility), locate (searches for a file), script (records a shell session), tr (replaces specified characters), unix2dos (converts Linux files to Windows format), dos2unix (converts Windows files to Linux format), and xargs (converts standard input to command lines).

## which AND whereis: LOCATE A UTILITY

When you give Linux a command, the shell searches a list of directories for a program with that name. This list of directories is called a *search path*. For information on how to change the search path, refer to "PATH: Where the Shell Looks for Programs" on page 359. If you do not change the search path, the shell searches only a standard set of directories and then stops searching. However, other directories on the system might also contain useful utilities.

*LE+* which  The which utility locates utilities by displaying the full pathname of the file for the utility. The local system might include several utilities that have the same name. When you type the name of a utility, the shell searches for the utility in your search path and runs the first one it finds. You can find out which copy of the utility the shell will run by using which. In the following example, which reports the location of the tar utility:

```
$ which tar
/usr/bin/tar
```

The which utility can be helpful when a utility is working in unexpected ways. By running which, you might discover that you are running a nonstandard version of a tool or a different one from the one you expected. ("Important Standard Directories and Files" on page 189 provides a list of standard locations for executable files.) For example, if tar is not working properly and you find that you are running **/usr/local/bin/tar** instead of **/bin/tar**, you might suspect the local version is broken.

*LE+* whereis  The whereis utility searches for files related to a utility by looking in standard locations instead of using your search path. For example, you can find the locations for files related to tar:

```
$ whereis tar
tar: /usr/bin/tar /usr/share/man/man1/tar.1.gz /usr/share/man/man5/tar.5.gz
```

In this example whereis finds three references to tar: the tar utility file and two (compressed) tar man pages.

### which **versus** whereis

tip   Given the name of a utility, which looks through the directories in your *search path* (page 359) in order and locates the utility. If your search path includes more than one utility with the specified name, which displays the name of only the first one (the one you would run).

The whereis utility looks through a list of *standard directories* and works independently of your search path. Use whereis to locate a binary (executable) file, any manual pages, and source code for a program you specify; whereis displays all the files it finds.

### which, whereis, **and builtin commands**

caution   Both the which and whereis utilities report only the names for utilities as they exist on the disk; they do not report shell builtins (utilities that are built into a shell; page 170). When you use whereis to try to find where the echo command (which exists as both a utility program and a shell builtin) is kept, it displays the following information:

```
$ whereis echo
echo: /usr/bin/echo /usr/share/man/man1/echo.1.gz
/usr/share/man/man1p/echo.1p.gz
```

The whereis utility does not display the echo builtin. Even the which utility reports the wrong information:

```
$ which echo
/usr/bin/echo
```

Under bash you can use the type builtin (page 1041) to determine whether a command is a builtin:

```
$ type echo
echo is a shell builtin
```

## **LE+**  locate: SEARCHES FOR A FILE

The locate utility (**locate** package) searches for files on the local system.

```
$ locate logrotate
/etc/logrotate.conf
/etc/logrotate.d
/etc/cron.daily/logrotate
/etc/logrotate.d/chrony
/etc/logrotate.d/cups
...
```

*LPI*   updatedb   Before you can use locate, the updatedb utility must build or update the locate database. Typically the database is updated once a day by a cron script (page 607).

### locate **does not return real-time results the way** find **does**

tip   Because locate relies on the locate database, which is typically updated once a day, results may not be accurate. The locate utility will display the names of files that have been deleted since the database was last updated. Similarly, it will not display the names of files that have been created since the last update. For accurate, real-time results, search for filenames using find (page 229).

The locate utility searches for the string you provide as its argument anywhere in the absolute pathname of a file. Thus, the command **locate sam** returns the names of all files that have the string **sam** anywhere in their absolute pathname, including all files in the hierarchy of a directory named **sample**. Use find if you want a more refined search. The command **find / –name "sam"** returns only files named **sam** and **find / –name "✳sam✳"** returns only files that have the string **sam** in their simple filename.

By default locate searches for simple strings; use the **–r** option to cause it to search for regular expressions.

# script: RECORDS A SHELL SESSION

The script utility records part of a login session, including your input and the system's responses. This utility is useful only from character-based devices, such as a terminal or a terminal emulator. It does capture a session with vim; however, because vim uses control characters to position the cursor and display different typefaces, such as bold, the output will be difficult to read and might not be useful. When you cat a file that has captured a vim session, the session quickly passes before your eyes.

By default script captures the session in a file named **typescript**, overwriting a file with the same name. Following is a session being recorded by script:

```
$ script
Script started, file is typescript
$ ls -l /bin | head -5
-rwxr-xr-x. 1 root root      123 02-07 17:32 alsaunmute
-rwxr-xr-x. 1 root root    25948 02-08 03:46 arch
lrwxrwxrwx. 1 root root        4 02-25 16:52 awk -> gawk
-rwxr-xr-x. 1 root root    25088 02-08 03:46 basename
$ exit
exit
Script done, file is typescript
```

Use the exit command to terminate a script session. You can then view the file you created using cat, less, more, or an editor. Following is the file created by the preceding script command:

```
$ cat typescript
Script started on Tue 08 Apr 2014 10:16:36 AM PDT
$ ls -l /bin | head -5
-rwxr-xr-x. 1 root root      123 02-07 17:32 alsaunmute
-rwxr-xr-x. 1 root root    25948 02-08 03:46 arch
lrwxrwxrwx. 1 root root        4 02-25 16:52 awk -> gawk
-rwxr-xr-x. 1 root root    25088 02-08 03:46 basename
$ exit
exit

Script done on Tue 08 Apr 2014 10:16:50 AM PDT
```

If you will be editing the file, you can use dos2unix (page 260) to eliminate from the **typescript** file the **^M** (carriage return) characters that appear at the ends of the lines. Refer to the script man page for more information.

### ARGUMENTS

The argument is the pathname of the file that script writes to. If you do not specify an argument, script writes to **typescript**, overwriting this file if it exists.

### OPTIONS

Append  The **–a** (**––append**) option appends to the output file. Without this option script overwrites an existing file.

Command  The **–c** *cmd* (**––command** *cmd*) option runs *cmd* instead of an interactive shell. Useful when a program produces different output when standard output is not connected to the screen. For example, the ls utility displays its output in a column when it is redirected and in rows when it is not.

```
$ ls
memos.max   memos.sam   memos.zach   old

$ ls | cat
memos.max
memos.sam
memos.zach
old
```

The **–c** option enables you to capture the output of ls without redirecting its output.

```
$ script -c ls
Script started, file is typescript
memos.max   memos.sam   memos.zach   old   typescript
Script done, file is typescript
```

## *LPI*  tr: REPLACES SPECIFIED CHARACTERS

The tr utility reads standard input and, for each input character, maps it to an alternate character, deletes the character, or leaves the character unchanged. This utility reads from standard input and writes to standard output.

### ARGUMENTS

The tr utility is typically used with two arguments, *string1* and *string2*. The position of each character in the two strings is important: Each time tr finds a character from *string1* in its input, it replaces that character with the corresponding character from *string2*.

When *string1* is longer than *string2*, the initial portion of *string1* (equal in length to *string2*) is used in the translation. When *string1* is shorter than *string2*, tr repeats the last character of *string1* to extend *string1* to the length of *string2*. In this case tr departs from the POSIX standard, which does not define a result.

You can use a hyphen to represent a range of characters in *string1* or *string2*. The two command lines in the following example produce the same result:

```
$ echo abcdef | tr  'abcdef' 'xyzabc'
xyzabc
$ echo abcdef | tr  'a-f'  'x-za-c'
xyzabc
```

The next example demonstrates a popular method for disguising text, often called ROT13 (rotate 13) because it replaces the first letter of the alphabet with the thirteenth, the second with the fourteenth, and so forth. The first line ends with a pipeline symbol that implicitly continues the line (see the optional section on page 161) and causes bash to start the next line with a secondary prompt (page 362).

```
$ echo The punchline of the joke is ... |
> tr 'A-M N-Z a-m n-z' 'N-Z A-M n-z a-m'
Gur chapuyvar bs gur wbxr vf ...
```

To make the text intelligible again, reverse the order of the arguments to tr:

```
$ echo Gur chapuyvar bs gur wbxr vf ... |
> tr 'N-Z A-M n-z a-m' 'A-M N-Z a-m n-z'
The punchline of the joke is ...
```

### OPTIONS

Complement  The **–c** (**––complement**) option complements *string1*, causing tr to match all characters *except* those in *string1*.

Delete  The **–d** (**––delete**) option deletes characters that match those specified in *string1*. If you use this option with the **–s** (**––squeeze-repeats**) option, you must specify both *string1* and *string2*.

```
$ echo If you can read this, you can spot the missing vowels! |
> tr --delete 'aeiou'
If y cn rd ths, y cn spt th mssng vwls!
```

Help  The **––help** option summarizes how to use tr, including the special symbols you can use in *string1* and *string2*.

Squeeze  The **–s** (**––squeeze-repeats**) option replaces multiple sequential occurrences of a character in *string1* with a single occurrence of the character when you call tr with only one string argument. If you use both *string1* and *string2*, the tr utility first translates the characters in *string1* to those in *string2;* it then replaces multiple sequential occurrences of a character in *string2* with a single occurrence of the character.

If you use the **–d** (**––delete**) and **–s** (**––squeeze-repeats**) options at the same time, tr first deletes the characters in *string1* and then replaces multiple sequential occurrences of a character in *string2* with a single occurrence of the character.

In the following example, tr replaces characters and reduces pairs of identical characters to single characters:

```
$ echo tennessee | tr -s 'tnse' 'srne'
serene
```

The next example replaces each sequence of nonalphabetic characters (the complement of all the alphabetic characters as specified by the character ranges **A-Za-z**) in the file **draft1** with a single NEWLINE character. The output is a list of words, one per line.

```
$ tr -c -s 'A-Za-z' '\n' < draft1
```

# unix2dos: Converts Linux Files to Windows and Macintosh Format

unix2dos, unix2mac  If you want to share a text file you created on a Linux system with someone on a Windows or Macintosh OS X system, you need to convert the file for the person on the other system to read it easily. The unix2dos utility converts a Linux text file so it can be read on a Windows machine; use unix2mac to convert a Linux file so it can be read on a Macintosh system. These utilities are part of the **dos2unix** software package. Enter the following command to convert a Linux-format file named **memo.txt** to a Windows-format file (use unix2mac to convert to a Macintosh-format file):

```
$ unix2dos memo.txt
```

You can now email the file as an attachment to someone on a Windows or an OS X system. This utility overwrites the original file.

dos2unix, mac2unix  The dos2unix utility converts Windows-format files so they can be read on a Linux system (use mac2unix to convert from Macintosh format):

```
$ dos2unix memo.txt
```

tr  You can also use tr (translate; page 258) to change a Widows or an OS X text file into a Linux text file. In the following example, the **–d** (delete) option causes tr to remove RETURNs (represented by **\r**) as it makes a copy of the file:

```
$ cat memo | tr -d '\r' > memo.txt
```

The greater than (>) symbol (page 154) redirects the standard output of tr to the file named **memo.txt**. Converting a file the other way without using unix2dos is not as easy.

# LE+    xargs: Converts Standard Input to Command Lines

The xargs utility is a convenient, efficient way to convert standard output of one command into arguments for another command. The format of an xargs command line is

*xargs [options] [command]*

The xargs utility reads arguments to *command* from standard input, interpreting each whitespace-delimited string as a separate argument. It then constructs a command line from *command* and a series of arguments. When the maximum command-line length would be exceeded by adding another argument, xargs runs the command line it has built. If there is more input, xargs repeats the process of building a command line and running it. This process continues until all input has been read.

## Arguments

The *command* argument is the command line you want xargs to use as a base for the command it constructs. Without an argument, *command* defaults to echo. The xargs utility appends to *command* the arguments it receives from standard input. If any arguments need to precede the arguments from standard input, you must include them as part of *command*.

The xargs utility is often used as an efficient alternative to the –exec option of find (page 231). If you call find with the –exec option to run a command, it runs the command once for each file it processes. Each execution of the command creates a new process, which can drain system resources when you are processing many files. By accumulating as many arguments as possible, xargs can greatly reduce the number of processes needed.

To locate and remove all files with names ending in .o from the working directory and its subdirectories, you can use the find –exec option:

```
$ find . -name \*.o -exec rm --force {} \;
```

This approach calls the rm utility once for each .o file that find locates. Each invocation of rm requires a new process. If a lot of .o files exist, the system must spend a significant amount of time creating, starting, and then cleaning up these processes. You can reduce the number of processes by allowing xargs to accumulate as many filenames as possible before calling rm:

```
$ find . -name \*.o -print | xargs rm --force
```

In the next example, the content of all *.txt files located by find is searched for lines containing the word **login**. The names of all files that contain **login** are displayed by grep.

```
$ find . -name \*.txt -print | xargs grep -w -l login
```

## Options

Replace    The –I [*marker*] option allows you to place arguments from standard input anywhere within *command*. All occurrences of *marker* in *command* are replaced by the arguments generated from standard input of xargs. The –l option is ignored when you use this option.

The next example shows how to use the –I option to cause xargs to embed standard input within *command* instead of appending it to *command*. This option causes xargs to execute *command* each time a NEWLINE character is encountered in standard input.

```
$ cat names
Tom,
Dick,
and Harry

$ xargs echo "Hello," < names
Hello, Tom, Dick, and Harry

$ xargs -I xxx echo "Hello xxx. Join me for lunch?" < names
Hello Tom,. Join me for lunch?
Hello Dick,. Join me for lunch?
Hello and Harry. Join me for lunch?
```

Max lines   The **–l** *[num]* (lowercase "el"; **––max-lines***[=num]*) option executes *command* once for every *num* lines of input. When you include this option and do not specify *num*, xargs sets *num* to 1.

Max arguments   The **–n** *num* (**––max-args=***num*) option executes *command* once for every *num* arguments in the input line. The next example uses the same input file as the previous examples and includes the **–n** and **–l** options:

```
$ xargs -n 1 echo "Hi there" < names
Hi there Tom,
Hi there Dick,
Hi there and
Hi there Harry

$ xargs -l 2 echo "Hi there" < names
Hi there Tom, Dick,
Hi there and Harry
```

Max processes   The **–P** *num* (**––max-procs=***num*) option allows xargs to run up to *num* instances of *command* simultaneously. (The default is 1, which runs *commands* sequentially.) This option might improve the throughput if xargs is running on a multiprocessor system.

Interactive   The **–p** (**––interactive**) option prompts prior to each execution of *command*.

Empty   The **–r** (**––no-run-if-empty**) option causes xargs not to execute *command* if standard input is empty. Ordinarily xargs executes *command* at least once, even if standard input includes only blanks (SPACEs and TABs).

# EDITING FILES

This section presents tutorials on two editors: vim and nano. The nano editor is less powerful than vim but takes less time to learn and is powerful enough for writing simple programs and notes.

## LE+  TUTORIAL: USING vim TO CREATE AND EDIT A FILE

This section explains how to start vim, enter text, move the cursor, correct text, save the file to the disk, and exit from vim. The tutorial discusses three of the modes of operation of vim and explains how to switch from one mode to another.

vimtutor   In addition to working with this tutorial, you might want to try vim's instructional program, vimtutor. Enter its name as a command to run it.

Specifying a terminal   Because vim takes advantage of features that are specific to various kinds of terminals, you must tell it what type of terminal or terminal emulator you are using. On many systems, and usually when you work on a terminal emulator, your terminal type is set automatically. If you need to specify your terminal type explicitly, refer to "Specifying a Terminal" on page 1024.

**Figure 7-1** Starting vim

### vimtutor **and** vim **help files are not installed by default**

tip  To run vimtutor and to get help as described on page 266, you must install the **vim-enhanced** package. See page 534 for instructions on installing software.

## STARTING vim

Start vim with the following command to create and edit a file named **practice** (use **vi** in place of **vim** if you have not installed the **vim-enhanced** package):

```
$ vim practice
```

When you press RETURN, the command line disappears, and the screen looks similar to the one shown in Figure 7-1.

### vim **is not installed by default: use** vi

tip  The full version of the vim editor is not installed by default. Instead, a small version of **vim**, named **vi**, is installed. You can either replace each **vim** command in this section with **vi**, or you can install the full vim editor by installing the **vim-enhanced** package and then using the **vim** command as shown in this section. See page 534 for instructions on installing software.

The tildes (~) at the left of the screen indicate the file is empty. They disappear as you add lines of text to the file. If the screen looks like a distorted version of the one shown in Figure 7-1, the terminal type is probably not set correctly (see "Problem," next).

The **practice** file is new so it contains no text. The vim editor displays a message similar to the one shown in Figure 7-1 on the status (bottom) line of the terminal to indicate you are creating and editing a new file. When you edit an existing file, vim

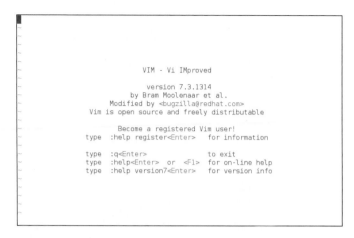

**Figure 7-2**    Starting vim without a filename

displays the first few lines of the file and gives status information about the file on the status line.

Problem    If you start vim with a terminal type that is not in the **terminfo** database, vim displays an error message and waits for you to press RETURN or sets the terminal type to **ansi**, which works on many terminals.

Emergency exit    To reset the terminal type, press ESCAPE and then give the following command to exit from vim and display the shell prompt:

> **:q!**

When you enter the colon (:), vim moves the cursor to the bottom line of the screen. The characters **q!** tell vim to quit without saving your work. (You will not ordinarily exit from vim this way because you typically want to save your work.) You must press RETURN after you give this command. When the shell displays its prompt, refer to "Specifying a Terminal" on page 1024 and start vim again.

If you start vim without a filename, it displays information about itself (Figure 7-2).

## _LPI_  COMMAND AND INPUT MODES

Two of vim's modes of operation are *Command mode* (also called *Normal mode*) and *Input mode* (Figure 7-3). While vim is in Command mode, you can give vim commands. For example, you can delete text or exit from vim. You can also command vim to enter Input mode. In Input mode, vim accepts anything you enter as text and displays it on the screen. Press ESCAPE to return vim to Command mode. By default the vim editor keeps you informed about which mode it is in: It displays **INSERT** at the lower-left corner of the screen while it is in Insert mode.

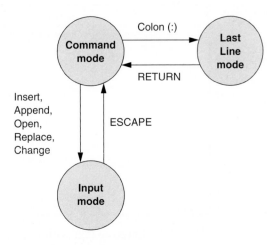

**Figure 7-3** Modes in vim

The following command causes vim to display line numbers next to the text you are editing:

```
:set number RETURN
```

Last Line mode   The colon (:) in the preceding command puts vim into another mode, *Last Line mode*. While in this mode, vim keeps the cursor on the bottom line of the screen. When you finish entering the command by pressing RETURN, vim restores the cursor to its place in the text. Give the command **:set nonumber** RETURN to turn off line numbering.

vim is case sensitive   When you give vim a command, remember that the editor is case sensitive. In other words, vim interprets the same letter as two different commands, depending on whether you enter an uppercase or lowercase character. Beware of the CAPS LOCK (SHIFTLOCK) key. If you set this key to enter uppercase text while you are in Input mode and then exit to Command mode, vim interprets your commands as uppercase letters. It can be confusing when this happens because vim does not appear to be executing the commands you are entering.

## _LPI_ ENTERING TEXT

i/a (Input mode)   When you start vim, you must put it in Input mode before you can enter text. To put vim in Input mode, press the **i** (insert before cursor) key or the **a** (append after cursor) key.

If you are not sure whether vim is in Input mode, press the ESCAPE key; vim returns to Command mode if it is in Input mode or beeps, flashes, or does nothing if it is already in Command mode. You can put vim back in Input mode by pressing the **i** or **a** key again.

```
If you are not sure whether vim is in Input mode, press the ESCAPE
key; vim returns to Command mode if it was in Input mode or beeps,
flashes, or does nothing if it is already in Command mode. You can
put vim back in Input mode by pressing the i or a key again.█
~
~
~
~
~
~
~
~
~
~
~
~
~
~
~
~
~
~
-- INSERT --
```

**Figure 7-4**   Entering text with vim

While vim is in Input mode, you can enter text by typing on the keyboard. If the text does not appear on the screen as you type, vim is not in Input mode.

To continue with this tutorial, enter the sample paragraph shown in Figure 7-4, pressing the RETURN key at the end of each line. If you do not press RETURN before the cursor reaches the right side of the screen or window, vim wraps the text so that it appears to start a new line. Physical lines will not correspond to programmatic (logical) lines in this situation, so editing will be more difficult. While you are using vim, you can correct typing mistakes. If you notice a mistake on the line you are entering, you can correct it before you continue (page 267). You can correct other mistakes later. When you finish entering the paragraph, press ESCAPE to return vim to Command mode.

## GETTING HELP

You must have the **vim-runtime** package installed to use vim's help system; see page 534.

To get help while you are using vim, enter the command **:help** [*feature*] followed by RETURN. The editor must be in Command mode when you enter this command. The colon moves the cursor to the last line of the screen. If you type **:help**, vim displays an introduction to vim Help (Figure 7-5). Each dark band near the bottom of the screen names the file that is displayed above it. (Each area of the screen that displays a file, such as the two areas shown in Figure 7-5, is a vim "window.") The **help.txt** file occupies most of the screen (the upper window) in Figure 7-5. The file that is being edited (**practice**) occupies a few lines in the lower portion of the screen (the lower window).

Read through the introduction to Help by scrolling the text as you read. Press **j** or the DOWN ARROW key to move the cursor down one line at a time; press CONTROL-D or CONTROL-U to scroll the cursor down or up half a window at a time. Give the command **:q** to close the Help window.

```
help.txt         For Vim version 7.4.  Last change: 2012 Dec 06

                       VIM - main help file
                                                                    k
        Move around:  Use the cursor keys, or "h" to go left,     h   l
                      "j" to go down, "k" to go up, "l" to go right.  j
Close this window:  Use ":q<Enter>".
  Get out of Vim:  Use ":qa!<Enter>" (careful, all changes are lost!).

Jump to a subject:  Position the cursor on a tag (e.g. bars) and hit CTRL-].
    With the mouse:  ":set mouse=a" to enable the mouse (in xterm or GUI).
                      Double-click the left mouse button on a tag, e.g. bars.
        Jump back:  Type CTRL-T or CTRL-O (repeat to go further back).

Get specific help:  It is possible to go directly to whatever you want help
                      on, by giving an argument to the :help command.
                      It is possible to further specify the context:
                                                        help-context
                        WHAT              PREPEND   EXAMPLE
                      Normal mode command (nothing)  :help x
help.txt [Help][RO]                                    1,1            Top
put vim back in Input mode by pressing the i or a key again.

practice                                               4,60           Bot
"help.txt" [readonly] 221L, 8249C
```

**Figure 7-5**  The main vim Help screen

You can display information about the insert commands by giving the command **:help insert** while vim is in Command mode (Figure 7-6).

## A FEW vim COMMANDS

This section describes a few useful vim commands.

### CORRECTING TEXT AS YOU INSERT IT

The keys that back up and correct a shell command line serve the same functions when vim is in Input mode. These keys include the erase, line kill, and word kill keys (usually CONTROL-H, CONTROL-U, and CONTROL-W, respectively). Although vim might not remove deleted text from the screen as you back up over it using one of these keys, the editor does remove it when you type over the text or press RETURN.

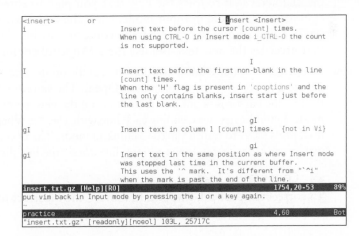

```
<insert>         or                        i Insert <Insert>
i                           Insert text before the cursor [count] times.
                            When using CTRL-O in Insert mode i_CTRL-O the count
                            is not supported.

                                                I
I                           Insert text before the first non-blank in the line
                            [count] times.
                            When the 'H' flag is present in 'cpoptions' and the
                            line only contains blanks, insert start just before
                            the last blank.

                                               gI
gI                          Insert text in column 1 [count] times.  {not in Vi}

                                               gi
gi                          Insert text in the same position as where Insert mode
                            was stopped last time in the current buffer.
                            This uses the '^ mark.  It's different from "`^i"
                            when the mark is past the end of the line.
insert.txt.gz [Help][RO]                           1754,20-53       89%
put vim back in Input mode by pressing the i or a key again.

practice                                               4,60          Bot
"insert.txt.gz" [readonly][noeol] 103L, 25717C
```

**Figure 7-6**  Help with insert commands

### *LPI* Moving the Cursor

You need to be able to move the cursor on the screen so you can delete, insert, and correct text. While vim is in Command mode, the RETURN key, the SPACE bar, and the ARROW keys move the cursor. If you prefer to keep your hand closer to the center of the keyboard, if your terminal does not have ARROW keys, or if the emulator you are using does not support them, you can use the **h**, **j**, **k**, and **l** (lowercase "el") keys to move the cursor left, down, up, and right, respectively.

### *LPI* Deleting Text

**x** (Delete character)
**dw** (Delete word)
**dd** (Delete line)

You can delete a single character by moving the cursor until it is over the character you want to delete and then giving the command **x**. You can delete a word by positioning the cursor on the first letter of the word and then giving the command **dw** (Delete word). You can delete a line of text by moving the cursor until it is anywhere on the line and then giving the command **dd**.

### Undoing Mistakes

**u** (Undo)

If you delete a character, line, or word by mistake or give any command you want to reverse, give the command **u** (Undo) immediately after the command you want to undo. The vim editor will restore the text to the way it was before you gave the last command. If you give the **u** command again, vim will undo the command you gave before the one it just undid. You can use this technique to back up over many of your actions. With the **compatible** parameter (page 269) set, however, vim can undo only the most recent change.

**:redo** (Redo)

If you undo a command you did not mean to undo, give a Redo command: CONTROL-R or **:redo** (followed by a RETURN). The vim editor will redo the undone command. As with the Undo command, you can give the Redo command many times in a row.

### *LPI* Entering Additional Text

**i** (Insert)
**a** (Append)

When you want to insert new text within existing text, move the cursor so it is on the character that follows the new text you plan to enter. Then give the **i** (Insert) command to put vim in Input mode, enter the new text, and press ESCAPE to return vim to Command mode. Alternately, you can position the cursor on the character that precedes the new text and use the **a** (Append) command.

**o/O** (Open)

To enter one or more lines, position the cursor on the line above where you want the new text to go. Give the command **o** (Open). The vim editor opens a blank line below the line the cursor was on; puts the cursor on the new, empty line; and goes into Input mode. Enter the new text, ending each line with a RETURN. When you are finished entering text, press ESCAPE to return vim to Command mode. The **O** command works in the same way **o** works, except it opens a blank line *above* the line the cursor is on.

### *LPI* Correcting Text

To correct text, use **dd**, **dw**, or **x** to remove the incorrect text. Then use **i**, **a**, **o**, or **O** to insert the correct text.

For example, to change the word **pressing** to **hitting** in Figure 7-4 on page 266, you might use the ARROW keys to move the cursor until it is on top of the **p** in **pressing**. Then give the command **dw** to delete the word **pressing**. Put vim in Input mode by giving an **i** command, enter the word **hitting** followed by a SPACE, and press ESCAPE. The word is changed, and vim is in Command mode, waiting for another command. A short-hand for the two commands **dw** followed by the **i** command is **cw** (Change word). The command **cw** puts vim into Input mode.

### Page breaks for the printer

tip   CONTROL-L tells the printer to skip to the top of the next page. You can enter this character anywhere in a document by pressing CONTROL-L while you are in Input mode. If **^L** does not appear, press CONTROL-V before CONTROL-L.

## *LPI* ENDING THE EDITING SESSION

While you are editing, vim keeps the edited text in an area named the *Work buffer.* When you finish editing, you must write out the contents of the Work buffer to a disk file so the edited text is saved and available when you next want it.

Make sure vim is in Command mode and use the **ZZ** command (you must use upper-case **Z**s) to write the newly entered text to the disk and end the editing session. After you give the **ZZ** command, vim returns control to the shell. You can exit with **:q!** if you do not want to save your work.

### Do not confuse ZZ with CONTROL-Z

caution   When you exit from vim with **ZZ**, make sure that you type **ZZ** and not CONTROL-Z (typically the suspend key). When you press CONTROL-Z, vim disappears from your screen, almost as though you had exited from it. In fact, **vim** will continue running in the background with your work unsaved. Refer to "Job Control" on page 294. If you try to start editing the same file with a new **vim** command, vim displays a message about a swap file.

## THE compatible PARAMETER

The **compatible** parameter makes vim more compatible with vi. By default this parameter is not set. To get started with vim, you can ignore this parameter.

Setting the **compatible** parameter changes many aspects of how vim works. For example, when the **compatible** parameter is set, the Undo command (page 268) can undo only the most recent change; in contrast, with the **compatible** parameter unset, you can call Undo repeatedly to undo many changes. To obtain more details on the **compatible** parameter, give the command **:help compatible** RETURN. To display a complete list of vim's differences from the original vi, use **:help vi-diff** RETURN. See page 266 for a discussion of the **help** command.

## *LE* TUTORIAL: USING nano TO CREATE AND EDIT A FILE

The nano text editor (www.nano-editor.org) is a user-friendly, pseudographical text editor, written by Chris Allegretta. It is based on the pico text editor that was distributed with the now defunct Pine mail client (www.washington.edu/pine) developed at the University of Washington. Although not as comprehensive as vim (page 262) and emacs (www.gnu.org/software/emacs), nano has a much gentler learning curve and is adequate for writing and maintaining system files, shell scripts, and Python programs. The nano editor is distributed with Fedora and RHEL as the **nano** package.

### nano **might not be available on a rescue system**

tip   The nano editor might not be available when you try to rescue a system (page 450). It is a good idea to know how to perform basic editing using vim for those occasions.

Specifying a   Because nano takes advantage of features that are specific to various kinds of terminals,
terminal   you must tell it what type of terminal or terminal emulator you are using. On many systems, and usually when you work on a terminal emulator, the terminal type is set automatically. If you need to specify a terminal type explicitly, refer to "Specifying a Terminal" on page 1024.

### STARTING nano

Start nano using the following command to (create and) edit a file named **practice**:

```
$ nano practice
```

When you press RETURN, the command line disappears, and the screen looks similar to the one shown in Figure 7-7.

If nano displays an **Error opening terminal** message, see Specifying a terminal, above.

### THE nano SCREEN

The top line of the screen has three fields and is called the Title bar (Figure 7-7). The left field displays the name (**nano**) and version of the program you are running. The center field displays the name of the file you are editing; if you do not specify a file-name when you start nano, the words **New Buffer** appear in place of the filename. The right field displays the word **Modified** if the buffer (what nano displays on the screen) differs from what is in the file you are editing. When you save the file, nano removes **Modified** from the screen because the buffer and the file contain the same information.

The third line from the bottom of the screen is the Status bar. This line displays status, informational, and error messages. It also displays prompts and your

```
GNU nano 2.3.1                    File: practice








                              [ New File ]
^G Get Help  ^O WriteOut   ^R Read File ^Y Prev Page ^K Cut Text  ^C Cur Pos
^X Exit      ^J Justify    ^W Where Is  ^V Next Page ^U UnCut Text^T To Spell
```

**Figure 7-7**  Starting nano

response to prompts, such as the characters you enter in response to a prompt for a search string.

The bottom two lines hold the Shortcut list. This list displays the most frequently used commands in a given context along with the keys you need to press to execute each command. Figure 7-7 shows that you can press CONTROL-G to display nano help information (^G Get Help), CONTROL-O to write out the modified buffer (the changes you have made; ^O WriteOut), CONTROL-X to exit from nano (nano will prompt you to write out the buffer if you have modified it; ^X Exit), etc.

## ENTERING TEXT AND EXITING FROM nano

Wrapping lines By default, nano does not wrap long lines: It just keeps going, placing a dollar sign at the beginning (and end) of the part of the line that appears on the screen to show that some text is not displayed. If you want to break a long line into shorter lines so you can see all the text at one time on the screen, press CONTROL-J (justify). Alternately, you can cause nano to wrap lines as you type them by calling nano with the –r *cols* (––fill=*cols*) option. Set *cols* to the desired width of the text or, more frequently, to a negative value that specifies the width of the right margin. Using **nano –r –8** (or **––fill=–8**) works well.

Entering text To create a new file, start typing. To edit text you have entered, use the ARROW keys to move the cursor, type text to enter new text, and use the keys you use to correct mistakes on the command line (page 122) to remove text from the screen. The nano editor keeps the text you are working on in a buffer until you tell it to write the buffer to disk or to exit.

Exiting from nano When you are finished creating or modifying a document and want to write the buffer to disk and exit from nano, press CONTROL-X (Exit). If you have modified the

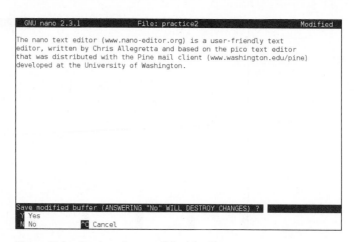

**Figure 7-8**    Saving the modified buffer

buffer since the last time you wrote it out, nano asks whether you want to save the modified buffer; type **y** to save it (Figure 7-8). The nano editor then confirms the name of the file you are writing the buffer to by prompting with **Filename to Write:** *filename* (Figure 7-9). Press RETURN to write to that filename or enter a different filename before you press RETURN. The nano editor terminates execution and returns control to the shell.

Saving the buffer    While you are editing a document, you can use CONTROL-O (WriteOut) to save the buffer without exiting from nano; nano confirms the name of the file you want to write to.

## THE nano COMMAND KEYS

Get Help (CONTROL-G)    Press CONTROL-G (Get Help) to view more nano commands including commands that move the cursor and delete text. In the help text some keys are preceded by a caret (^) and some by an M-.

```
  GNU nano 2.3.1              File: practice2                    Modified

The nano text editor (www.nano-editor.org) is a user-friendly text
editor, written by Chris Allegretta and based on the pico text editor
that was distributed with the Pine mail client (www.washington.edu/pine)
developed at the University of Washington.















File Name to Write: practice2
^G Get Help          M-D DOS Format      M-A Append       M-B Backup File
^C Cancel            M-M Mac Format      M-P Prepend
```

**Figure 7-9**    Confirming the name of the file you are writing to

The control key    To enter a command specified by a caret followed by a key, press the CONTROL key and the specified key at the same time (e.g., CONTROL-W for Where, which searches for text or moves the cursor). Alternately, you can press the ESCAPE key twice and then press the specified key.

The META key    To enter a command specified by M- followed by a key, press the META or ALT key and the specified key at the same time (e.g., ALT-\ to move the cursor to the first line of the file). Alternately, you can press the ESCAPE key one time and then press the specified key.

# Chapter Summary

The utilities introduced in this chapter are a powerful subset of the many utilities available on Linux. Because you will use them frequently and because they are integral to the following chapters, it is important that you become comfortable using them. The utilities listed in Table 7-2 manipulate, display, locate, compare, and print files.

**Table 7-2**    File utilities

| Utility | Function |
| --- | --- |
| cat | Joins and displays files (page 216) |
| cp | Copies files (page 224) |
| cut | Selects characters or fields from input lines (page 225) |
| diff | Displays the differences between two text files (page 227) |
| dos2unix | Converts Windows files to Linux format (page 260) |
| file | Displays the classification of a file (page 229) |
| find | Finds files based on criteria (page 229) |
| grep | Searches for a pattern in files (page 232) |
| head | Displays the beginning of a file (page 235) |
| less | Displays a text file one screen at a time (page 220) |
| lpq | Displays a list of jobs in the print queue (page 237) |
| lpr | Sends files to the printer (page 235) |
| lprm | Removes a job from the print queue (page 237) |
| ls | Displays information about files (page 221) |
| mac2unix | Converts Macintosh files to Linux format (page 260) |
| more | Displays a text file one screen at a time (page 220) |
| mv | Renames or moves a file (page 237) |

**Table 7-2**   File utilities (continued)

| Utility | Function |
|---------|----------|
| rm | Removes a file (page 222) |
| sort | Sorts and/or merges files (page 239) |
| tail | Displays the last part of a file (page 241) |
| touch | Changes file modification and access times (page 243) |
| tr | Replaces specified characters (page 258) |
| unix2dos | Converts Linux files to Windows and Macintosh format (page 260) |
| unix2mac | Converts Linux files to Macintosh format (page 260) |
| wc | Displays the number of lines, words, and bytes in files (page 244) |

To reduce the amount of disk space a file occupies, you can compress it. Compression works especially well on files that contain patterns, as do most text files, but it reduces the size of almost all files. The inverse of bzip2—bunzip2—restores a file to its original, decompressed form. The bzip2 utility is the most efficient of these. An archive is a file, frequently compressed, that contains a group of files. The tar utility packs and unpacks archives. The filename extensions **.tar.bz2**, **.tar.gz**, and **.tgz** identify compressed tar archive files and are often seen on software packages obtained over the Internet. Table 7-3 lists utilities that compress, decompress, and archive files.

**Table 7-3**   (De)compression and archive utilities

| Utility | Function |
|---------|----------|
| bunzip2 | Decompresses a file compressed using bzip2 (page 248) |
| bzcat | Displays a file compressed using bzip2 (page 248) |
| bzip2 | Compresses or decompresses files (page 245) |
| compress | Compresses a file (page 249) |
| dtrx | Extracts and decompresses files intelligently (page 245) |
| gunzip | Decompresses a file compressed using gzip or compress (page 248) |
| gzip | Compresses or decompresses files (page 245) |
| tar | Stores or retrieves files to/from an archive file (page 249) |
| unzip | Unpacks zip archives (page 249) |
| zcat | Displays a file compressed using gzip (page 248) |
| zip | Constructs zip archives (page 249) |

Table 7-4 lists utilities that display information about the local system and users.

Table 7-4   User and system information utilities

| Utility | Function |
| --- | --- |
| date | Displays or sets the system time and date (page 218) |
| free | Displays memory usage information (page 253) |
| hostname | Displays the system name (page 219) |
| uptime | Displays system load and duration information (page 253) |
| w | Lists users on the system (page 254) |
| who | Lists users on the system (page 254) |

Table 7-5 lists miscellaneous utilities.

Table 7-5   Miscellaneous utilities

| Utility | Function |
| --- | --- |
| echo | Displays arguments (page 219) |
| locate | Searches for a file (page 256) |
| nano | Edits a text file (page 270) |
| script | Records a shell session (page 257) |
| vi/vim | Edits a text file (page 262) |
| whereis | Locates a utility (page 255) |
| which | Locates a utility (page 255) |
| xargs | Converts standard input to command lines (page 260) |

# EXERCISES

1. Which commands can you use to determine who is logged in on a specific terminal? Which command shows you which terminal you are giving the command from?

2. Give a command that displays a long listing of the files in **/bin** in reverse chronological order. Give the command again but this time display the output one screen at a time.

3. What happens when you give the following commands if the file named **done** already exists?

```
$ cp to_do done
$ mv to_do done
```

4. List the first 20 lines in **/etc/services** that describe TCP ports.

5. How can you find the phone number for **Ace Electronics** in a file named **phone** that contains a list of names and phone numbers? Which command can you use to display the entire file in alphabetical order? How can you display the file without any adjacent duplicate lines? How can you display the file without any duplicate lines?

6. What happens when you use diff to compare two binary files that are not identical? (You can use gzip to create the binary files.) Explain why the diff output for binary files is different from the diff output for ASCII files.

7. What is the result of giving the which utility the name of a command that resides in a directory that is *not* in your search path?

8. Are any of the utilities discussed in this chapter located in more than one directory on the local system? If so, which ones?

9. Experiment by calling the file utility with the names of files in **/usr/bin**. How many different types of files are there?

10. Which command can you use to look at the first few lines of a file named **status.report**? Which command can you use to look at the end of the file?

# ADVANCED EXERCISES

11. Display only the names of the last ten services listed in **/etc/services**. (*Hint:* the services are listed in the first column.)

12. Display a long listing of the files in the **/etc/pam.d** directory hierarchy that are links.

13. Display a count of the number of words in the **/etc/passwd** file.

14. Display the **/etc/passwd** file, replacing all colons (**:**) with TABs. Display the **/etc/services** file, substituting one SPACE for each occurrence of multiple SPACEs.

15. Change the modification time of **/bin/bash** to the system time. What happens? Why? Copy **/bin/bash** to the working directory, display its modification time, and then change its modification time to the system time. Display the modification time of your copy of bash and the system time. Change its modification time to January 5, 2018 at 2:34 PM and display its modification time.

16. Copy **/bin/bash** to the working directory and make two copies so you have three identical files: **bash1**, **bash2**, and **bash3**. Compress **bash1** using gzip and **bash2** using bzip2. Do not change **bash3**. Which utility does the best job of compressing the file? Which does the worst? How big is **bash2.bz2** compared to **bash3**?

17. Re-create the **colors.1** and **colors.2** files used in the example on page 228. Test your files by running **diff –u** on them. Does diff display the same results as in the figure?

18. Try giving these two commands:

```
$ echo cat
$ cat echo
```

Explain the differences between the output of each command.

19. Repeat exercise 5 using the file **phone.gz**, a compressed version of the list of names and phone numbers. Consider more than one approach to answer each question and explain how you made your choices.

20. Find or create files that

   a. gzip compresses by more than 80 percent.

   b. gzip compresses by less than 10 percent.

   c. Get larger when compressed with gzip.

   d. Use **ls –l** to determine the sizes of the files in question. Can you characterize the files in a, b, and c?

# 8

# NETWORKING AND THE INTERNET

## OBJECTIVES

After reading this chapter you should be able to:

▶ Discuss a variety of network types

▶ Define several network protocols

▶ List the software and hardware components of
   networks

▶ Explain the features and advantages of IPv6

▶ List several network utilities

▶ Explain how ping works

▶ Use dig to determine the nameserver for a Web site

▶ Describe distributed computing

▶ Explain the role of the World Wide Web

# *LE*  INTRODUCTION TO NETWORKING

The communications facilities linking computers are continually improving, allowing faster and more economical connections. The earliest computers were unconnected stand-alone systems. To transfer information from one system to another, you had to store it in some form (usually magnetic tape, paper tape, or punch cards—called IBM or Hollerith cards), carry it to a compatible system, and read it back in. A notable advance occurred when computers began to exchange data over serial lines, although the transfer rate was slow (hundreds of bits per second). People quickly invented new ways to take advantage of this computing power, such as email, news retrieval, and bulletin board services. With the speed and ubiquity of today's networks, a piece of email can cross the country or even travel halfway around the world in a fraction of a second.

Today it would be difficult to find a computer facility that does not include a LAN to link its systems. Linux systems are typically attached to an *Ethernet* (page 1249) network. Wireless networks are also prevalent. Large computer facilities usually maintain several networks, often of different types, and almost certainly have connections to larger networks (companywide or campuswide and beyond).

*LE*  Internet   The Internet is a loosely administered network of networks (an *internetwork*) that links computers on diverse LANs around the globe. An internet (small *i*) is a generic network of networks that might share some parts in common with the public Internet. It is the Internet that makes it possible to send an email message to a colleague thousands of miles away and receive a reply within minutes. A related term, *intranet,* refers to the networking infrastructure within a company or other institution. Intranets are usually private; access to them from external networks might be limited and carefully controlled, typically using firewalls (page 288).

Network services   Over the past decade many network services have emerged and become standardized. On Linux and UNIX systems, special processes called *daemons* (page 1245) support such services by exchanging specialized messages with other systems over the network. Several software systems have been created to allow computers to share filesystems with one another, making it appear as though remote files are stored on local disks. Sharing remote filesystems allows users to share information without knowing where the files physically reside, without making unnecessary copies, and without learning a new set of utilities to manipulate them. Because the files appear to be stored locally, you can use standard utilities (e.g., cat, vim, lpr, mv, or their graphical counterparts) to work with them.

Many tools take advantage of networks for more than sharing files. These tools have varied tasks, from executing programs remotely to communicating between computers, programs, and people. The ssh (secure shell, page 685) utility is the standard tool for remote command execution and remote computer access. Years ago it replaced insecure tools such as rsh, telnet, and rlogin. The ssh utility encompasses the features of these tools and includes builtin security features for safe and private access across public networks. Some devices do not implement ssh, but not many.

Previously, users communicated using command-line tools such as talk, write, and IRC (Internet Relay Chat). These tools are still around, particularly IRC, but their use has waned in preference to Facebook, Twitter, Google Talk, Skype, and older IM (Instant Messaging) tools like MSN, AIM, ICQ, and Yahoo Messenger. Many people use the Empathy IM client for Linux. Jabber is popular in private company networks.

Intranet An *intranet* is a network that connects computing resources at a school, company, or other organization but, unlike the Internet, typically restricts access to internal users. An intranet is usually composed of one or more local area networks (LANs) but could be fairly large for a regional, national, or worldwide company. An intranet can provide database, email, and Web page access to a limited group of people, regardless of their geographic location.

The ability of an intranet to connect dissimilar machines is one of its strengths. Think of all the machines you can find on the Internet: Macintosh systems, PCs running different versions of Windows, machines running UNIX and Linux, and so on. Each of these machines can communicate via the IP protocol suite (page 290). The intranet defines the communication boundaries and security trust zones that enable this communication.

Another key difference between the Internet and an intranet is that the Internet transmits only one protocol suite natively: IP. In contrast, an intranet can be set up to use a number of protocols, such as IP, AppleTalk, or other protocols developed by vendors over the years. Although these protocols cannot be transmitted directly over the Internet, you can set up gateway boxes at remote sites that tunnel or encapsulate these protocols into IP packets and then use the Internet to pass them. In practice, most of the older protocols have been rewritten to use IP as a transport. Even storage protocols and networks like SCSI and Fibre Channel have IP implementations now (iSCSI, FCoE).

You can use an *extranet* (also called a *partner net*) or a VPN (virtual private network) to improve security. These terms describe ways to connect remote sites securely to a local site, typically by using the public Internet as a carrier and employing encryption as a means of protecting data in transit. A typical use of an extranet is to link research institutions for collaboration or to link a parts supplier and a manufacturer to obtain direct inventory access.

Following are some terms you might want to become familiar with before you read the rest of this chapter:

| | | |
|---|---|---|
| *ASP* (page 1237) | *hub* (page 1254) | *packet* (page 1265) |
| *bridge* (page 1240) | *internet* (page 1255) | *router* (page 1271) |
| *extranet* (page 1249) | *Internet* (page 1255) | *sneakernet* (page 1273) |
| *firewall* (page 1250) | *intranet* (page 1255) | *switch* (page 1276) |
| *gateway* (page 1251) | *ISP* (page 1256) | *VPN* (page 1280) |

# TYPES OF NETWORKS AND HOW THEY WORK

Computers communicate over IP networks using unique addresses assigned by system software. An IP *packet* includes the address of the destination computer and the sender's return address. Networks can consist of many distinct *topologies,* or arrangements of computers and networking equipment. The most common topologies are broadcast, point-to-point, and switched. Ethernet is the most common topology used in LANs (local area networks, discussed shortly). Ethernet speeds range from 10 megabits per second to 100 gigabits per second (not formally accepted as of this writing). Other types of LANs include Myrinet, Infiniband, and Quadrics, but they are used mostly in high-performance computing.

Speed is critical to the proper functioning of the Internet. Newer specifications (cat 6 and cat 7) are being adopted for 10000BaseT (10 gigabits per second; also called 10GE) and faster networking. Specialized cables are required for higher speeds. SFP+ and QSFP are in common use. Many of the networks that form the backbone of the Internet run at speeds of 38 gigabits per second (OC768) to accommodate the ever-increasing demand for network services. Table 8-1 lists some of the specifications in use today.

**Table 8-1**   Network specifications

| Specification | Speed |
| --- | --- |
| DS0 | 64 kilobits per second |
| ISDN | Two DS0 lines plus signaling (16 kilobits per second) or 128 kilobits per second |
| T-1 | 1.544 megabits per second (24 DS0 lines) |
| T-3 | 43.232 megabits per second (28 T-1s) |
| OC3 | 155 megabits per second (100 T-1s) |
| OC12 | 622 megabits per second (4 OC3s) |
| OC48 | 2.5 gigabits per second (4 OC12s) |
| OC192 | 9.6 gigabits per second (4 OC48s) |
| OC768 | 38.4 gigabits per second (4 OC192s) |

## BROADCAST NETWORKS

On a *broadcast network,* any of the many systems attached to the network cable can send a message at any time; each system examines the destination address in each message and responds only to messages addressed to it. A problem occurs on a broadcast network when multiple systems send data at the same time, resulting in a collision of the messages on the cable. When messages collide, they can become garbled. The sending system notices the garbled message and resends it after waiting a short but random amount of time. Waiting a random amount of time helps prevent those same systems from resending the data at the same moment and experiencing yet another collision. The extra traffic that results from collisions can strain the network; if the collision rate gets too high, retransmissions might result in more collisions. Ultimately the network might become unusable.

A special *broadcast* (page 1240) packet in a network requires all machines to inspect the packet. Certain protocols take advantage of this feature: The ARP protocol, which is used for IP addresses to MAC (Ethernet) addresses resolution, the PXE network boot protocol, DHCP, and some service discovery protocols all use broadcast packets.

## POINT-TO-POINT NETWORKS

A point-to-point link does not seem like much of a network because only two endpoints are involved. However, most connections to WANs (wide area networks) go through point-to-point links, using wire cable, radio, or satellite links. The advantage of a point-to-point link is its simplicity: Because only two systems are involved, the traffic on the link is limited and well understood. A disadvantage is that each system can typically be equipped for only a small number of such links; it is impractical and costly to establish point-to-point links that connect each computer to all the rest. For example two hosts require one link, three hosts require three links, four hosts require six links, and five hosts require ten links to connect a point-to-point network. The number of required links increases more quickly as you add more hosts. Point-to-point links often use serial links and specialized interfaces.

The most common types of point-to-point links are the ones used to connect to the Internet. When you use DSL[1] (digital subscriber line), you are using a point-to-point link to connect to the Internet. Serial lines, such as T-1, T-3, ATM links, FIOS, and ISDN, are all point-to-point. Although it might seem like a point-to-point link, a cable modem is based on broadcast technology and in that way is similar to Ethernet.

## SWITCHED NETWORKS

With the introduction of switched networks, pure broadcast networks became a thing of the past. A switched network runs in full duplex mode, allowing machines and network equipment to send and receive data at the same time. Support for full duplex is built-in and required in gigabit networks and above, on 100-megabit networks it is optional, and on 10-megabit networks it is rare.

A *switch* is a device that establishes a virtual path between source and destination hosts in such a way that each path appears to be a point-to-point link, much like an old-fashioned telephone switchboard. Instead of the operator using a plug to connect

---

1. The term *DSL* incorporates the xDSL suite of technologies, which includes ADSL, IDSL, HDSL, SDSL, and XDSL.

your local line to an outgoing line, the switch inspects each packet to determine its destination and directs the packet appropriately.

The switch creates and tears down virtual paths as hosts seek to communicate with each other. Each host thinks it has a direct point-to-point path to the host it is talking to. Contrast this approach with a broadcast network, where each host also sees traffic bound for other hosts. The advantage of a switched network over a pure point-to-point network is that each host requires only one connection: the connection to the switch. Using pure point-to-point connections, each host must have a connection to every other host. Scalability is provided by further linking switches.

To achieve this reduction in traffic, Ethernet switches learn which hosts are on which ports. When traffic comes in destined for a host, the switch looks up which port that host is connected to in its CAM[2] and sends the packet out that port. When a switch has not yet heard from a host matching the destination, or if the packet is a special broadcast packet, the packet is flooded out on all ports just like a packet in a broadcast network. A switched Ethernet network is a technological enhancement over a broadcast network.

# LAN: LOCAL AREA NETWORK

Local area networks (LANs) are confined to a relatively small area—a single computer facility, building, or campus. Today most LANs run over copper. Fiberoptic (glass or plastic) cable, wireless (Wi-Fi), and sometimes infrared (similar to most television remote control devices) are also common infrastructure.

If its destination address is not on the local network, a packet must be passed on to another network by a router (page 287). A router might be a general-purpose computer or a special-purpose device attached to multiple networks to act as a gateway among them.

Switching terminology — You might see references to a *layer-2 switch*, *layer-3 switch*, or *layer-4 switch*. These terms refer to the IP networking model (page 290). A layer-2 switch is what the preceding discussion of switched networks describes. A layer-3 switch is equivalent to a router; it combines features of layer-2 switching and routing. A single layer-3 switch can connect multiple independent LANs. Layer-4 switches inspect higher-level packets to make decisions. Most Web load balancers are layer-4 switches. They can route traffic to many devices to spread the load on the network.

## ETHERNET

A Linux system connected to a LAN usually connects to a network using Ethernet. A typical Ethernet connection can support data transfer rates from 10 megabits per second to 100 gigabits per second. Transfer rates of 10 megabits per second, 100 megabits per second, and 1 gigabit per second use the same, older technology. However, 10, 40, and 100 gigabit per second transfer rates require newer technology and

---

2. A memory table used to *dereference* (page 1246) Ethernet addresses.

specialized cables. Ten gigabit per second Ethernet can be compatible with 1 gigabit per second Ethernet by using physical media adapters. Because of the need for extremely tight tolerances, 40 and 100 gigabit per second Ethernet are not backward compatible. The technology required for these higher-speed transfer rates requires very precisely defined physical interfaces. The hardware is quite expensive and common only in the network infrastructure realm and HPC (high performance computing) environments, connecting multiple switches using high-speed links.

Cables  As mentioned earlier, a modern Ethernet network transfers data using copper or fiber-optic cable or wireless transmitters and receivers. Originally, each computer was attached to a thick coaxial cable (called *thicknet*) at tap points spaced at six-foot intervals along the cable. The thick cable was awkward to deal with, so other solutions, including a thinner coaxial cable called *thinnet*, or 10Base2,[3] were developed.

Today most Ethernet connections are either wireless or made over UTP (unshielded twisted pair). There are a number of UTP standards, each referred to by a category and a number. Some examples are Category 5 [cat 5], Category 5e [cat 5e], and Category 6 [cat 6]. These categories specify how far the cable can carry a signal. The higher the number, the tighter the tolerances and the more expensive the cable, but the farther it can reliably carry a signal. These standards specify the physical connectors at the ends of the cables, how tightly the wires in the cable are twisted, and various other parameters. The terms 10BaseT, 100BaseT, and 1000BaseT refer to Ethernet over cat-3/4/5/5e/6/7 cables. STP (shielded twisted pair) is not very common.

Segment  A network *segment* is a part of a network in which all systems communicate using the same physical layer (layer 1) of the IP and OSI models (page 291). It is of arbitrary size and can be a part of a WAN, MAN, or another network.

Duplex  In *half-duplex* mode, packets travel in one direction at a time over the cable. In *full-duplex* mode, packets travel in both directions.

Hub  A *hub* (sometimes called a *concentrator*) is a device that connects systems so they are all part of one network segment and share the network bandwidth. Hubs work at the physical layer of the IP and OSI models (layer 1, page 291). All packets are sent to all hosts (flooded). For the most part, hubs have been replaced by switches.

Switch  A *switch* connects network segments. A switch inspects each data packet; it learns which devices are connected to which of its ports. The switch sends each packet only to the device it is intended for. Because a switch sends packets only to their destination devices, it can conserve network bandwidth and perform better than a hub. Some switches have buffers that hold and queue packets.

Switches work at layers 2 and higher of the IP and OSI models (page 290). A layer-2 switch works at the data link layer, and a layer-3 switch works at the IP layer and routes packets. Layer-4 switches work at the transport and application layers and are the basis for load balancers and application proxies.

---

3. Versions of Ethernet are classified as **XBaseY**, where **X** is the data rate in megabits per second, **Base** means baseband (as opposed to radio frequency), and **Y** is the category of cabling.

All modern Ethernet switches have enough bandwidth to communicate simultaneously, in full-duplex mode, with all connected devices. A nonswitched (hub-based) broadcast network can run in only half-duplex mode. Full-duplex Ethernet further improves efficiency by eliminating collisions. Each host on a full-duplex switched network can transmit and receive simultaneously at the speed of the network (e.g., 100 megabits per second) for an effective bandwidth between hosts of twice the speed of the network (e.g., 200 megabits per second), depending on the capacity of the switch.

Bridge   A network *bridge* connects multiple network segments at the data link layer (IP layer 2) of the OSI model. A bridge is similar to a repeater or network hub, devices that connect network segments at the physical layer; however, a bridge works by forwarding traffic from one network segment to another only if the destination device specified in the packet is known to be on the remote segment. A bridge does not forward traffic between LAN hosts on the same side of the bridge.

In Ethernet networks, the term *bridge* formally means a device that behaves according to the IEEE 802.1D standard. Marketing literature frequently refers to this type of device as a network switch.

Router   A *router* connects networks at layer 3 of the IP and OSI models (page 291). For example, a router can connect a LAN to a WAN (such as the Internet) or it can connect two LANs. A router determines which path packets should take to travel to a different network and forwards the packets. Routers work at the network layer of the IP and OSI models (layer 3). "Internetworking Through Gateways and Routers" on the next page covers routers in more depth.

VLAN   A VLAN (virtual local area network or virtual LAN) is a logical entity defined in software. It defines a group of hosts that share the same broadcast domain (layer 2). That is, when a host sends out a broadcast packet, such as an ARP packet, it will arrive at all other hosts in the same VLAN. All modern, managed switches, those that have a command line or Web interface, have VLAN capability. A VLAN allows an administrator to group hosts into IP ranges (LANs). VLANs commonly group hosts by department, organization, or security needs. Hosts in the same VLAN communicate with each other using layer 2, and hosts in different VLANs communicate using layer 3. The primary difference between a LAN and a VLAN is that in a LAN (a nonmanaged switch), all hosts are in the same broadcast domain, whereas in a VLAN, there can be multiple broadcast domains on a single switch.

Broadcast domains and IP protocol layer 2 segments are effectively the same thing. However, layer 2 can be confused with hosts (network addresses) being in the same IP network. Consider the classic concentrator, a device that sends out all packets on all ports all the time. These ports might include separate networks. For example, some hosts might be in network 10.0.1.0, and others might be in network 192.168.1.0. Ethernet broadcast packets do not know the difference between the networks; these packets go to all hosts regardless of IP address. This setup is sometimes referred to as a *collision domain*. VLANs enable you to place the hosts in the IP network 10.0.1.0 into one VLAN and the hosts in 192.168.1.0 into another, so the networks do not share each other's broadcasts. VLANs also enable you to connect hosts that share the same function across a corporate network.

## WIRELESS

Wireless networks are becoming increasingly common. They are found in offices, homes, and public places, such as universities, coffee shops, and airports. Wireless access points provide functionality similar to an Ethernet hub. They allow multiple users to interact via a common radio frequency spectrum. A wireless, point-to-point connection allows you to wander about your home or office with a laptop, using an antenna to link to a LAN or to the Internet via an in-house base station. Linux includes drivers for many wireless devices. A wireless access point, or base station, connects a wireless network to a wired network so that no special protocol is required for a wireless connection. Refer to the *Linux Wireless LAN HOWTO* at www.hpl.hp.com/personal/Jean_Tourrilhes/Linux.

# WAN: WIDE AREA NETWORK

A WAN (wide area network) covers a large geographic area. In contrast, the technologies (such as Ethernet) used for LANs were designed to work over limited distances and for a certain number of host connections. A WAN might span long distances over dedicated data lines (leased from a telephone company) or radio or satellite links. Such networks are often used to connect LANs and typically support much lower bandwidth than LANs because of the expense of the connection. Major Internet service providers rely on WANs to connect to their customers within a country and around the globe.

MAN   Some networks do not fit into either the LAN or the WAN designation. A *metropolitan area network* (MAN) is a network that is contained in a smaller geographic area, such as a city. Like WANs, MANs are typically used to interconnect LANs.

# INTERNETWORKING THROUGH GATEWAYS AND ROUTERS

Gateway   A LAN connects to a WAN through a *gateway*, a generic term for a computer or a special device with multiple network connections that passes data from one network to another. A gateway connects a LAN to other LANs, VLANs, or to a WAN. Data that crosses the country from one Ethernet to another over a WAN, for example, is repackaged from the Ethernet format to a different format that can be processed by the communications equipment that makes up the WAN backbone. When it reaches the end of its journey over the WAN, the data is converted by another gateway to a format appropriate for the receiving network. For the most part, these details are of concern only to the network administrators; the end user does not need to know anything about how the data transfer takes place.

Router   The modern, canonical reference to a gateway is to the default gateway, which is the *router* that connects a LAN or VLAN to other networks. Routers play an important role in internetworking. Just as you might study a map to plan your route when you need to drive to an unfamiliar place, so a computer needs to know how to deliver a message to a system attached to a distant network by passing through intermediary systems and networks along the way. Although you might envision using a giant network road map to choose the route that your data should follow, a static map of computer routes is usually a poor choice for a large network. Computers and networks along the route you choose might be overloaded or down and not provide a detour for your message.

Routers instead communicate dynamically, keeping each other informed about which routes are open for use. To extend the analogy, this situation is like heading out on a car trip without consulting a map to find a route to your destination; instead you head for a nearby gas station and ask directions. Throughout the journey you continue to stop at one gas station after another, getting directions at each to find the next one. Although it would take a while to make the stops, the owner of each gas station would advise you of bad traffic, closed roads, alternative routes, and shortcuts.

The stops made by the data are much quicker than those you would make in your car, but each message leaves each router on a path chosen based on the most current information. Think of this system as a GPS (global positioning system) setup that automatically gets updates at each intersection and tells you where to go next, based on traffic and highway conditions.

Figure 8-1 shows an example of how LANs might be set up at three sites interconnected by a WAN (the Internet). In this type of network diagram, Ethernet LANs are drawn as straight lines, with devices attached at right angles; WANs are represented as clouds, indicating the details have been left out; and wireless connections are drawn as zigzag lines with breaks, indicating the connection might be intermittent.

In Figure 8-1, a gateway or a router relays messages between each LAN and the Internet. The figure shows the three routers in the Internet that are closest to each site. Site A has a server, a workstation, a network computer, and a PC sharing a single Ethernet LAN. Site B has an Ethernet LAN that serves a printer and four Linux workstations. A firewall permits only certain traffic to pass between the Internet router and the site's local router. Site C has three LANs linked by a single router, perhaps to reduce the traffic load that would result if the LANs were combined or to keep workgroups or locations on separate networks. Site C also includes a wireless access point that enables wireless communication with nearby computers.

## Firewall

A firewall in a car separates the engine compartment from the passenger compartment, protecting the driver and passengers from engine fires, noise, and fumes. In much the same way, computer firewalls separate computers from malicious and unwanted users.

A *firewall* prevents certain types of traffic from entering or leaving a network. For example, a firewall might prevent traffic from your IP address from leaving the network and prevent anyone except users from selected domains from using FTP

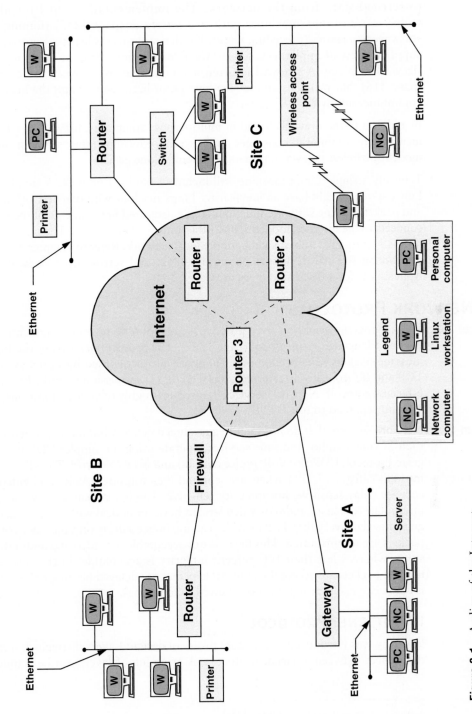

**Figure 8-1**    A slice of the Internet

to retrieve data from the network. The implementations of firewalls vary widely—from Linux machines with two *interfaces* (page 1255) running custom software to a router (preceding section) with simple access lists to esoteric, vendor-supplied firewall appliances. Most larger installations have at least one kind of firewall in place. A firewall is often accompanied by a proxy server/gateway (page 316) that provides an intermediate point between you and the host you are communicating with.

In addition to the firewalls found in multipurpose computers, firewalls are becoming increasingly common in consumer appliances. For example, they are built into cable modems, wireless gateways, routers, and stand-alone devices.

Typically a single Linux machine will include a minimal firewall. A small group of Linux systems might have an inexpensive Linux machine with two network interfaces and packet-filtering software functioning as a dedicated firewall. One of the interfaces connects to the Internet, modems, and other outside data sources. The other connects, normally through a hub or switch, to the local network. Refer to Chapter 25 for information on **firewalld**, firewall-config, iptables, and setting up a firewall and to Appendix C for a discussion of security.

## *LPI*  NETWORK PROTOCOLS

*LPI*  TCP   To exchange information over a network, computers must communicate using a common language, or *protocol* (page 1267). The protocol determines the format of message packets. The predominant network protocols used by Linux systems are TCP and IP,[4] collectively referred to as TCP/IP (Transmission Control Protocol and Internet Protocol). Network services that require highly reliable connections, such as ssh and scp, tend to use TCP/IP.

*LPI*  UDP   Network services that do not require guaranteed delivery but require timely delivery, such as video, audio, and time services, operate using the simpler UDP (User Datagram Protocol; UDP/IP). VoIP (voice over IP) and NTP (Network Time Protocol) fall into this category. UDP packets are sent and then forgotten. Voice and video protocols are delay sensitive, not integrity sensitive. The human ear and eye accept and interpolate loss in an audio or video stream but cannot deal with variable delay. The guaranteed delivery that TCP provides can introduce a delay on a busy network when packets are retransmitted. This delay is not acceptable for video and audio transmissions, whereas less than 100 percent integrity is acceptable. In the case of NTP, missing packets are acceptable, but packets that are delayed because of TCP retransmission can result in significantly skewed time settings.

### IP: INTERNET PROTOCOL

Layering was introduced to facilitate protocol design: Layers distinguish functional differences between adjacent protocols. A grouping of layers can be standardized

---

4. All references to IP imply *IPv4* (page 1256).

into a protocol model. IP has a model that distinguishes protocol layers and that differs from the ISO seven-layer protocol model (also called the OSI model) often illustrated in networking textbooks. Specifically IP uses the following simplified five-layer model:

1. The first layer of the IP protocol, called the *physical layer,* describes the physical medium (e.g., copper, fiber, wireless) and the data encoding used to transmit signals on that medium (e.g., pulses of light, electrical waves, or radio waves).

2. The second layer, called the *data link layer,* covers media access by network devices and describes how to put data into packets, transmit the data, and check it for errors. Ethernet is found at this layer, as is *802.11* (page 1236) wireless.

3. The third layer, called the *network layer,* frequently uses IP and addresses and routes packets. It allows data to traverse the networks.

4. The fourth layer, called the *transport layer,* is where TCP and UDP exist. This layer provides a means for applications to communicate with each other. Functions commonly performed by the transport layer include guaranteed delivery, delivery of packets in the order of their transmission, flow control, error detection, and error correction. The transport layer is responsible for dividing data streams into packets. In addition, this layer performs port addressing, which allows it to distinguish among different services using the same transport protocol. Port addressing keeps the data from multiple applications using the same protocol (for example, TCP) separate.

5. Anything above the transport layer is the domain of the application and is part of the *fifth layer.* Unlike the ISO model, the Internet model does not distinguish among application, presentation, and session layers. All the upper-layer characteristics, such as character encoding, encryption, and GUIs, are part of the application. Applications choose the transport characteristics they require as well as the corresponding transport layer protocol with which to send and receive data.

## LPI TCP: Transmission Control Protocol

TCP is most frequently run on top of IP in a combination referred to as TCP/IP. This protocol provides error recovery and guaranteed delivery in packet transmission order; it also works with multiple ports so that it can handle more than one application. TCP is a *connection-oriented protocol* (page 1244), also known as a *stream-based* protocol. Once established, a TCP connection looks like a stream of data, not individual IP packets. The connection is assumed to remain up and be uniquely addressable. Every piece of information you write to the connection always goes to the same destination and arrives in the order it was sent. Because TCP is connection oriented and establishes a *virtual circuit* between two systems, this protocol is not suitable for one-to-many transmissions (see the discussion of UDP, following). TCP has builtin mechanisms for dealing with congestion (or flow) control over busy networks and throttles back (slows the speed of data flow) when it has to retransmit dropped packets. TCP can also deal with acknowledgments, wide area links, high-delay links, and other situations.

### LPI  UDP: USER DATAGRAM PROTOCOL

UDP runs at layer 4 of the IP stack, just as TCP does, but is much simpler. Like TCP, UDP works with multiple ports and multiple applications. It has checksums for error detection but does not automatically retransmit *datagrams* (page 1246) that fail the checksum test. UDP is a datagram-oriented protocol: Each datagram must carry its own address and port information. Each router along the way examines each datagram to determine the destination, one hop at a time. You can broadcast or multicast UDP datagrams to many destinations at the same time by using special addresses.

### PPP: POINT-TO-POINT PROTOCOL

PPP provides serial line point-to-point connections that support IP. It compresses data to make the most of the limited bandwidth available on these connections. PPP acts as a point-to-point layer 2/3 transport that many other types of protocols can ride on. Today it is used mostly in devices such as cable modems. Previously, it was used as a transport for TCP and UDP on dial-up modems that connected a computer to the Internet.

## LE+  IPv4

Under IPv4, the network address of a machine is an IP address that is represented as one number broken into four *octets*[5] separated by periods (for example, 192.168.184.5). Domain names and IP addresses are assigned through a highly distributed system coordinated by ICANN (Internet Corporation for Assigned Names and Numbers—www.icann.org) via many registrars (see www.internic.net). ICANN is funded by the various domain name registries and registrars and by IP address registries, which supply globally unique identifiers for hosts and services on the Internet. Although you might not deal with any of these agencies directly, your Internet service provider most assuredly does.

How a company uses IP addresses is determined by the system or network administrator. For example, the two leftmost sets of numbers in an IP address might represent a large network (campuswide or companywide); the third set, a subnetwork (perhaps a department or a single floor in a building); and the rightmost number, an individual computer. The operating system uses the address in a different, lower-level form, converting it to its binary equivalent, a series of 1s and 0s. Refer to "Private address space" on page 637 for information about addresses you can use on a LAN without registering them.

---

5. Using binary notation, an eight-bit byte can represent the range of 0–255, thus the term octet.

## *LE+*  IPv6

### Getting started with IPv6

tip   Even if the ISP you do business with does not provide IPv6 service, it is still easy and free to participate on the IPv6 Internet by using a tunnel broker. For more information on tunnel brokers see en.wikipedia.org/wiki/List_of_IPv6_tunnel_brokers. Setting up a small home or lab network through a tunnel broker is an excellent way to gain experience with IPv6 and experiment with its configurations and capabilities. Most tunnel brokers offer instructions on how to get various platforms working with their service.

IPv6 (Internet Protocol version 6)[6] is the next generation of the Internet Protocol. Since the introduction of IPv4 (Internet Protocol version 4) in 1980, the Internet has undergone explosive growth that has caused its needs to exceed the capabilities of IPv4. A proliferation of Internet connected devices, including cellular telephones, tablet computers, electronic book readers, and advanced televisions and set-top boxes, all of which need an IP address in order to communicate on the Internet, has fueled that growth. IPv4 uses a 32-bit address space, which is no longer sufficient to give a unique IP address to every device on the Internet. The lack of IPv4 address space has been mitigated by the use of *NAT* (page 1262) and by other techniques, but each of these techniques comes with limitations and overhead.

IPv6 uses a 128-bit address space, which ensures that all devices can have unique IP addresses without resorting to such mitigations, and provides enormous room to grow as the Internet continues to expand. While the enormous address space in IPv6 is its most compelling feature in light of the shortage of IPv4 addresses, IPv6 has many other desirable features:

- IPv6 enables stateless address autoconfiguration. With IPv4, DHCP (page 491) is usually used to automate network configuration. With IPv6, autoconfiguration makes it possible for hosts to configure their IP addresses automatically and autonomously without the need for a central service like DHCP.

- In IPv6, *multicast* (page 1262 and next) is mandatory and fundamental to its operation.

- IPv6 provides a simplified packet header that reduces router complexity by improving routing efficiency and cuts router cost by eliminating the need for much hardware acceleration.

- IPv6 reserves 20 bits in the header for advanced services, such as resource reservation protocols, better backbone routing, and improved traffic engineering.

---

6. IPv5 referred to an experimental real-time stream protocol named ST—thus the jump from IPv4 to IPv6.

IPv6 can coexist with IPv4. Even though the protocols are very similar in many ways, the network considers them to be different protocols, so one will not interfere with the other. Also, most operating systems support IPv4 and IPv6 simultaneously by using a dual-stack configuration. This configuration is likely to be common for a long time because it allows IPv6-enabled hosts to reach legacy IPv4-only hosts easily.

## MULTICAST PACKETS

IPv6 does not use *broadcast* (page 1240) packets and therefore does not have a *broadcast address* (page 1240) that corresponds to the IPv4 broadcast address. IPv6 mandates the implementation and use of *multicast* (page 1262).

Multicast improves the efficiency of the network by reducing the amount of traffic that each host must process: The system network interface does not ordinarily pass to the host multicast traffic it is not registered to receive.

For example, when a host wants to discover a DHCPv6 server, it sends a packet to the "all DHCPv6 servers" well-known link-local multicast address (ff05::1:3). This packet is processed only by hosts running DHCPv6. Under IPv4 the host must send a broadcast packet to discover the DHCP server. This packet is processed by every host on the network.

Many tools, such as ssh, work with IPv6 and IPv4 without difficulty. Some tools have special versions that work with IPv6 (e.g., ping6, traceroute6, and ip6tables).

## ADDRESSES

Because they are much longer, IPv6 addresses are quite different from IPv4 addresses. For brevity and clarity, IPv6 addresses are usually expressed as eight sets of four hexadecimal digits, each set separated from the next by a colon. As an example, consider the IPv6 address 2001:4860:800a:0000:0000:0000:0000:0067.

To shorten the address and allow it to remain unambiguous, you can replace any number of adjacent sets of four zeros and the colons that enclose them with two colons. After making this replacement, you can represent the example address as 2001:4860:800a::0067. With this replacement, you (or a computer) can easily expand the shortened address by adding enough sets of four zeros to fill out the eight sets in the address. You cannot make this replacement more than once in an address. If you did, when you tried to expand the address you would not know how many sets of zeros to replace each double colon with.

As an additional way of shortening an address, you can eliminate any leading zeros in any set of four digits. Using this technique, you can write the example address as 2001:4860:800a::67, which is much more manageable than the original address. You can also use CIDR notation (page 300): The example host might be in an allocation such as 2001:4860:800a::/48.

In IPv6, the network prefix is always 64 bits, and the host part is always the remaining 64 bits. In other words, all networks are the same size. If an organization were given the network allocation 2001:4860:800a::/48, it would have 16 bits of network address space to use, each network being of the form 2001:4860:800a:*xxxx*::/64, where *xxxx* is any one of the 65,536 possible numbers in 16 bits. Because of the immense size of the IPv6 address space, this allocation is considered small, although even very large organizations would fit well within it.

## AUTOCONFIGURATION

A constant host address length of 64 bits allows for stateless address autoconfiguration. Using a multicast ICMPv6 packet, the router sends periodic advertisements to all hosts on the network, telling them of its ability to route for a given network prefix. At the same time, it gives hosts permission to assign themselves addresses using that prefix.

A host that hears this advertisement can construct a host address in a deterministic way by incorporating the hardware address of the network adapter (i.e., the MAC address [page 296]). Without resorting to the use of a stateful service (e.g., DHCP) to maintain a list of assigned addresses, this construction guarantees that no other host on the network will have the same address. After constructing a host address, the host finalizes the configuration by adding a default route to the router from which the advertisement came. Alternately, when a host interface initially comes up, it can solicit router information by sending a request to all routers instead of waiting for the periodic advertisement, speeding up the process. Once it has assigned itself an address, the host expects to hear periodic advertisements from the router. If it does not hear these advertisements, the host will eventually expire its knowledge of this autoconfigured route and address.

## LINK-LOCAL ADDRESSES

A *link-local* IP address can be used to communicate only with other systems on the network; a router will not forward a packet that has a link-local address. This address is autoconfigured in a manner similar to that explained in the preceding section, except the network prefix is always fe80::/64, marking it as a link-local address.

This setup contrasts with how IPv4 DHCP works: Because an IPv4 host does not have an address when it initially communicates with a DHCP server, a *hack* is needed to use a fake address for the host. Such hacks are not necessary in IPv6 because of auto-configured link-local addresses. For example, when a host solicits router information, it uses a link-local address to do so.

Multihoming   The IPv6 specification requires *multihoming* (allowing a single network interface to have multiple addresses). Multihoming allows the link-local address to persist after a global-scope address has been assigned to a system, allowing continued access to the host via the link-local address.

Interface-local   The IPv6 loopback address is ::1 and is considered *interface-local*.

Well-known link-local addresses   Certain link-local addresses are not autoconfigured. These addresses are well-known and are registered with IANA. For a list of these addresses visit IANA at www.iana.org/assignments/ipv6-multicast-addresses/ipv6-multicast-addresses.xml.

Servers subscribe to these addresses as needed, allowing them to receive requests. For example, a DHCPv6 server will subscribe to ff05::1:3 so it receives configuration requests from hosts.

DHCPv6    DHCPv6 is a completely new implementation of DHCP (page 491) that covers IPv6. Although autoconfiguration works for most situations, network administrators who wish to have more control over their networks might choose to use DHCPv6. It enables an administrator to specify certain host addresses that can persist even if the host or network interface has to be replaced. (Autoconfigured addresses depend on the interface hardware address [NIC]).

It also allows configuration of other operational parameters, such as local DNS resolver address(es), which are not well supported with autoconfiguration. This feature is important on networks that run IPv6 only.

DHCPv6 also introduces the notion of a stateless mode, which is a way to enjoy the simplicity of autoconfiguration using router advertisements while also allowing the administrator to manage static configuration elements (e.g., DNS resolver addresses) using a very simple DHCP configuration that is easily made fault tolerant.

DNS    DNS works like in IPv4, except instead of having A records to associate names with addresses, there are AAAA records (sometimes called quad-A records; page 858). Just as a DNS name can have multiple A records, it can have multiple AAAA records and/or a combination of both. DNS does not place any restriction on which record type will be delivered based on which protocol was used by the requestor; DNS returns the record type(s) requested. This setup enables the DNS server to provide AAAA records for services that are available over IPv6, even when DNS itself has not been made available over IPv6.

Fragmentation    Under IPv6, if a router receives a packet larger than the network can support (the MTU, or maximum transmission unit), it sends a "fragmentation needed" ICMP packet back to the originator. Instead of the router bearing the burden of fragmenting the packet in-transit, the router depends on the originator to keep the packets down to a manageable size. Because the intervening routers do not have to concern themselves with fragmenting packets, they are able to work more efficiently and with less specialized hardware.

# HOST ADDRESS

MAC address    Each *NIC* (page 1263) on a system connected to a network has a unique identifier[7] called a *MAC address* (page 1259), sometimes referred to as an *Ethernet address*. A system attached to more than one network has multiple interfaces—one for each network. Such a system might have one MAC address for the system, or it might have one MAC address for each interface. Both setups work as long as a given MAC address is unique on a given LAN or VLAN.

---

7. In fact, each identifier might not be unique. Vendors have been known to reuse MAC addresses for physical devices shipped to different regions. In practice, you are unlikely to run into duplicate addresses. The only requirement is that a MAC address must be unique on a given LAN or VLAN segment.

Each system on a network also has a one or more unique IP addresses. At IP layer 3 (the network layer), systems communicate using IP addresses. However, at IP layer 2 (the data link layer), they communicate using MAC addresses.

**ARP** For hosts to talk to each other over a network, a map between IP addresses and MAC addresses must exist. ARP (Address Resolution Protocol) is a method for finding a host's MAC (Ethernet) address from its IP address. Each host builds an ARP cache that holds a map that translates IP addresses into MAC addresses. The arp utility works with this cache; use the –a option to display the cache:

```
$ arp -a
plum (192.168.206.181) at 00:0c:29:86:bf:35 [ether] on ens33
...
```

The preceding output shows the IP and Ethernet addresses of all hosts the local host is aware of. The example maps the IP address of **plum** (192.168.206.181) to the MAC address of the NIC on **plum** (00:0c:29:86:bf:35).

Each packet of information transmitted over a LAN has a destination MAC address. The NIC on each host on the network checks each packet to see if the destination address matches its MAC address. If it matches, the NIC passes the packet to the kernel for processing; if it does not match, and the packet does not have the special FF:FF:FF:FF:FF:FF destination address, the NIC silently drops the packet. All NICs examine all packets that have the special FF:FF:FF:FF:FF:FF destination address.

When the local system has a packet to send to another system, but knows only the remote system's IP address and not its MAC address, it sends an ARP broadcast packet to the special FF:FF:FF:FF:FF:FF destination address. That packet specifies the IP address the local system is trying to contact and requests the system with that IP address respond with its MAC address. When the host with the IP address the packet specifies examines the packet, it responds with its MAC address directly to the host that sent the packet. Once the systems have each other's IP addresses mapped to their MAC addresses in their ARP caches, they can communicate directly using this information. For more detail, refer to a book such as *Internetworking with TCP/IP*, Volume 1, 6th edition, by Douglas E. Comer, Prentice Hall (May 2013).

When the local system needs to send a packet to a host on another network, it sends the packet to the router (default gateway) on the local network. The local system knows the IP address of the router and uses ARP to determine its MAC address. The router and all hosts use the same process to determine the MAC address of hosts they need to send packets to. Then they can communicate directly with each of these hosts.

Each host and router keeps an ARP cache. Entries in the cache expire in about five minutes, balancing the currency of the address resolution table and the frequency of ARP requests.

## STATIC VERSUS DYNAMIC IP ADDRESSES

A static IP address is one that always remains the same. A server (e.g., mail, Web) usually has a static address so clients can find the server machine on the network. See pages 494 and 641 for information on configuring a static IP address.

A dynamic IP address is one that is allocated (leased) to a client and that has a defined expiration time. Typically the client renews the lease before it expires, at which time the server provides a new lease on the same IP address. A dynamic IP address can change each time a system connects to the network but frequently remains the same. End-user systems usually work well with dynamic addresses. During a given login session, these systems can function as a client (e.g., Web browser) because they maintain a constant IP address. When you log out and log in again, it does not matter that a system has a different IP address because, acting as a client, it establishes a new connection with a server. The advantage of dynamic addressing is that it allows inactive addresses to be reused, reducing the total number of IP addresses needed. Dynamic addressing is particularly popular on wireless access points.

## optional   SUBNETS

IP addresses are divided into two parts, the *network address*, also called the *subnet* (subnetwork address), and the *host address*, or *node address*. The network address specifies a set of computers that can communicate without sending packets through a router. The host address specifies an individual computer. IP is an internetwork protocol and was originally intended to connect networks together.

When sending a packet, a computer examines the network portion of the destination IP address. If the network address matches that of the sending computer's network, the computer can send the packet to the destination computer directly. If it does not match, the computer must send the packet to the router. The portion of the IP address used to identify the network is given by the subnet mask (next).

Terminology: subnet mask, network mask,
Although the term *subnet mask* is in common use, the preferred term is *network mask* or simply *mask*. This book uses the term subnet mask to make a clear distinction between the network prefix and the subnet prefix. Otherwise it uses the term network mask.

*LPI*   Subnet mask
A *subnet mask* (or *network mask*) is a bit mask that identifies which parts of an IP address correspond to the network address and the subnet portion of the address. This mask has 1s in positions corresponding to the network and subnet numbers and 0s in the host number positions. When you perform a bitwise AND on an IP address and a subnet mask, the resulting address contains everything except the host address (hostid) portion. There are several ways to represent a subnet mask: A network could have a subnet mask of 255.255.255.0 (decimal), FFFFFF00 (*hexadecimal* [page 1253]), or /24 (the number of bits used for the subnet mask).

A subnet mask of /24 has 8 bits for hosts (32-24). However, the last address in the range is reserved as a broadcast address, and the first address in the range is the network address. The second address is typically reserved for the router, although some setups use the broadcast address − 1 for this purpose. Thus there are $2^8 - 3 = 253$ IP addresses.

As another example, when you divide the address 192.25.4.0 into eight subnets, you get a subnet mask of 255.255.255.224, FFFFFFE0, or /27 (27 1s). The eight resultant networks are 192.25.4.0, 192.25.4.32, 192.25.4.64, 192.25.4.96, 192.25.4.128, 192.25.4.160, 192.25.4.192, and 192.25.4.224. You can use a Web-based subnet mask calculator to calculate subnet masks (search for **network calculator** on the Web). To use this type of calculator to determine the preceding subnet mask, start with an IP network address of 192.25.4.0.

Table 8-2 shows some of the computations for the IP address 131.204.027.027. Each address is shown in decimal, hexadecimal, and binary form. Binary is the easiest to work with for bitwise (binary) computations. The first three lines show the IP address. The next three lines show the *subnet mask* in three bases. Next the IP address and the subnet mask are ANDed together bitwise to yield the *subnet number* (page 1275), which is shown in three bases. The last three lines show the *broadcast address* (page 1240), which is computed by taking the subnet number and turning the hostid bits into 1s. The subnet number identifies the local network. The subnet number and the subnet mask determine what range the IP address of the machine must be in. They are also used by routers to segment traffic; see *network segment* (page 1263). A broadcast on this network goes to all hosts in the range 131.204.27.1 through 131.204.27.254 but will be acted on only by hosts that have a use for it. For more information refer to "Specifying a Subnet" on page 483.

Table 8-2    Computations for IP address 131.204.027.027

| | ---------------Class B----------- | | netid | hostid | |
|---|---|---|---|---|---|
| | 131 | .204 | .027 | .027 | decimal |
| IP address | 83 | CC | 1B | 1B | hexadecimal |
| | 1000 0011 | 1100 1100 | 0001 1011 | 0001 1011 | binary |
| | 255 | .255 | .255 | .000 | decimal |
| Subnet mask | FF | FF | FF | 00 | hexadecimal |
| | 1111 1111 | 1111 1111 | 1111 1111 | 0000 0000 | binary |
| IP address bitwise AND | 1000 0011 | 1100 1100 | 0001 1011 | 0001 1011 | |
| Subnet mask | 1111 1111 | 1111 1111 | 1111 1111 | 0000 0000 | binary |
| = Subnet number | 1000 0011 | 1100 1100 | 0001 1011 | 0000 0000 | |
| | 131 | .204 | .027 | .000 | decimal |
| Subnet number | 83 | CC | 1B | 00 | hexadecimal |
| | 1000 0011 | 1100 1100 | 0001 1011 | 0000 0000 | binary |
| | 131 | .204 | .27 | .255 | decimal |
| Broadcast address | 83 | CC | 1B | FF | hexadecimal |
| (set host bits to 1) | 1000 0011 | 1100 1100 | 0001 1011 | 1111 1111 | binary |

# CIDR: Classless Inter-Domain Routing

CIDR (pronounced "cider") allows groups of addresses to be assigned to an organization or ISP and then further subdivided and parceled out. In addition, it helps prevent routing tables on Internet backbone providers from becoming too large to manage by consolidating arbitrary network ranges along bit boundaries.

IPv6 (page 293) is the solution to IPv4 address exhaustion. The trend is to reclaim older, large address blocks, if possible, and recycle them into groups of smaller address blocks. Larger blocks are allocated to ISPs, which in turn subdivide these blocks and allocate them to their customers. When you request an address block, your ISP usually gives you as many addresses as you need—and no more. The ISP aggregates one or more contiguous smaller blocks to satisfy your request. This aggregation is CIDR. Without CIDR, the Internet as we know it would not function.

For example, you might be allocated the 192.168.5.0/22 IP address block, which can support $2^{10}$ hosts ($32 - 22 = 10$). Your ISP would set its routers so packets going to an address in that block would be sent to your network. Internally, your own routers might further subdivide this block of 1,024 potential hosts into four networks. Four networks require an additional two bits of addressing ($2^2 = 4$). You could therefore set up your router to support four networks with this allocation: 192.168.5.0/24, 192.168.6.0/24, 192.168.7.0/24, and 192.168.8.0/24. Each of these networks could then have 254 hosts. CIDR lets you arbitrarily divide networks and subnetworks into increasingly smaller blocks along the way. Each router has enough memory to keep track of the addresses it needs to direct and aggregates the rest.

This scheme uses memory and address space efficiently. For example, you could take 192.168.8.0/24 and further divide it into 16 networks with 14 hosts each. The 16 networks require four more bits ($2^4 = 16$), so you would have 192.168.8.0/28, 192.168.8.16/28, 192.168.8.32/28, and so on, up through the last subnet of 192.168.8.240/16, which would have the hosts 192.168.8.241 through 192.168.8.254.

## LPI  HOSTNAMES

People generally find it easier to work with names than with numbers, so Linux provides several ways to associate hostnames with IP addresses. The oldest method is to consult a list of names and addresses stored in the **/etc/hosts** file:

```
$ cat /etc/hosts
127.0.0.1       localhost
130.128.52.1    gw-example.example.com    gw-example
130.128.52.2    bravo.example.com         bravo
130.128.52.3    hurrah.example.com        hurrah
130.128.52.4    kudos.example.com         kudos
```

**localhost =** The address 127.0.0.1 is reserved for the special hostname **localhost**, which serves as
**127.0.0.1** a hook for the system's networking software to operate on the local machine without going onto a physical network. The names of the other systems are shown in two forms: in a *fully qualified domain name* (FQDN) format that is unique on the Internet and as a nickname that is locally unique. Use of these names is a convention; the system does not check the contents of the **hosts** file.

NIS  As more hosts joined networks, storing these name-to-address mappings in a text file proved to be inefficient and inconvenient. The **hosts** file grew bigger and became impossible to keep up-to-date. To solve this problem Linux supports NIS (Network Information Service; Chapter 21), which was developed for use on Sun computers. NIS stores information in a database, making it easier to find a specific address, but it is useful only for host information within a single administrative domain. Hosts outside the domain cannot access the information. Also, by default NIS is not secure and is difficult to secure.

DNS  The solution to this dilemma is DNS (Domain Name Service; Chapter 24). DNS effectively addresses the efficiency and update issues by arranging the entire network *namespace* (page 1262) as a hierarchy. Each domain in the DNS manages its own namespace (addressing and name resolution), and each domain can easily query for any host or IP address by following the tree up or down the namespace until it finds the appropriate domain. By providing a hierarchical naming structure, DNS distributes name administration across the entire Internet.

# Communicate over a Network

Many commands that you can use to communicate with other users on a single computer system have been extended to work over a network. Examples of extended utilities include electronic mail programs, information-gathering utilities, and communications utilities (e.g., Empathy). These utilities are examples of the UNIX philosophy: Instead of creating a new, special-purpose tool, modify an existing one.

Many utilities understand a convention for the format of network addresses: **user@host** (spoken as "user at host"). When you use an @ sign in an argument to one of these utilities, the utility interprets the text that follows as the name of a remote host. When you omit the @ sign, a utility assumes you are requesting information from or corresponding with someone on the local system.

If you frequently use more than one system over a network, you might find it difficult to keep track of which system you are interacting with at any particular moment. If you set your prompt to include the hostname of the current system, it will always be clear which system you are using. To identify the computer you are using, run hostname or give the command **uname –n**:

```
$ hostname
kudos
```

See page 361 for information on how you can change the prompt.

# Mailing List Servers

A mailing list server (listserv[8]) allows you to create and manage an email list. An electronic mailing list provides a means for people interested in a particular topic to

---

8. Although the term *listserv* is sometimes used generically to include many different list server programs, it is a specific product and a registered trademark of L-soft International, Inc.: LISTSERV (for more information visit www.lsoft.com).

participate in an electronic discussion. One of the most powerful features of most list servers is their ability to archive email postings to the list, create an archive index, and allow users to retrieve postings from the archive based on keywords or discussion threads. Typically you can subscribe and unsubscribe from the list with or without human intervention. The owner of the list can restrict who can subscribe, unsubscribe, and post messages to the list. See page 762 for instructions on configuring the Mailman list server. Other popular list servers include LISTSERV (www.lsoft.com), phplist (www.phplist.com), Lyris (www.lyris.com), and Majordomo (www.greatcircle.com/majordomo). Fedora/RHEL maintains mailing lists and list archives for those mailing lists at www.redhat.com/mailman/listinfo. Use Google to search on **linux mailing list** to find other lists.

# NETWORK UTILITIES

To realize the full benefits of a networked environment, it made sense to extend certain tools, some of which have already been described. The advent of networks also created a need for new utilities to control and monitor them, spurring the development of new tools that took advantage of network speed and connectivity. This section describes concepts and utilities for systems attached to a network.

# TRUSTED HOSTS

Although they are deprecated in favor of ssh (next), some commands, such as rcp and rsh, work only if the remote system trusts the local computer (that is, if the remote system knows the local computer and believes that it is not pretending to be another system). The **/etc/hosts.equiv** file lists trusted systems. For reasons of security, the **root** account does not rely on this file to identify trusted privileged users from other systems.

Host-based trust is largely obsolete. Because there are many ways to circumvent trusted host security, including subverting DNS systems and *IP spoofing* (page 1256), authentication based on IP address is insecure.

In a small homogeneous network it might be tempting to use these tools, and it might suffice. However, because ssh is easy to set up, provides privacy and authentication, and does not slow down modern CPUs appreciably, it is a good idea to use it instead of the older tools.

### Do not share your login account

security    It is poor practice to use a ~/.rhosts file to allow another user to log in as you from a remote system without knowing your password. Do not compromise the security of your files or the entire system by sharing your login account. Use ssh and scp instead of rsh and rcp.

# OpenSSH Tools

The OpenSSH project provides a set of tools that replace rcp, rsh, and others with secure equivalents. These tools are installed by default in Fedora/RHEL and can be used as drop-in replacements for their insecure counterparts. The OpenSSH tool suite is covered in detail in Chapter 18.

## *LPI*   telnet: Logs In on a Remote System

You can use the TELNET protocol to interact with a remote computer. The telnet utility (**telnet** package), a user interface to this protocol, is older than ssh and is not secure. Nevertheless, it might work where ssh (page 693) is not available (there is more non-UNIX support for TELNET access than for ssh access). In addition, some legacy devices, such as terminal servers, facilities infrastructure, and network devices, still do not support ssh. The following example shows Sam using telnet to log in on a remote system that is running the **in.telnetd** daemon (**telnet-server** package):

```
[sam@guava ~]$ telnet plum
Trying 192.168.206.181...
Connected to plum.
Escape character is '^]'.
Fedora release 19 (Schrödinger's Cat)
Kernel 3.10.3-300.fc19.x86_64 on an x86_64 (2)
plum login: sam
Password:
Last login: Tue Mar  8 13:20:14 from 192.168.206.180
...
[sam@plum ~]$ logout
Connection closed by foreign host.
[sam@guava ~]$
```

telnet versus ssh   When you connect to a remote UNIX or Linux system, telnet presents a textual **login:** prompt. Because telnet is designed to work with non-UNIX and non-Linux systems, it does not assume your remote username is the same as your local username (ssh does make this assumption). In some cases, telnet requires no login credentials.

### telnet is not secure

security   Whenever you enter sensitive information, such as your password, while you are using telnet, it is transmitted in cleartext and can be read by someone who is eavesdropping on the session.

In addition, telnet allows you to configure special parameters, such as how RETURNS or interrupts are processed (ssh does not give you this option). When using telnet between UNIX and/or Linux systems, you rarely need to change any parameters.

When you do not specify the name of a remote host on the command line, telnet runs in an interactive mode. The following example is equivalent to the previous telnet example:

```
[sam@guava ~]$ telnet
telnet> open plum
Trying 192.168.206.181...
Connected to plum.
Escape character is '^]'.
...
```

Before connecting to a remote system, telnet tells you what the *escape character* is; in most cases, it is ^] (where ^ represents the CONTROL key). When you press CONTROL-], you escape to telnet's interactive mode. Continuing the preceding example:

```
[sam@guava ~]$ CONTROL-]
telnet> ?
Commands may be abbreviated.   Commands are:

close              close current connection
logout             forcibly logout remote user and close the connection
display            display operating parameters
mode               try to enter line or character mode ('mode ?' for more)
...
telnet> close
Connection closed.
[sam@guava ~]$
```

When you enter a question mark in response to the **telnet>** prompt, telnet lists its commands. The **close** command ends the current telnet session, returning you to the local system. To get out of telnet's interactive mode and resume communication with the remote system, press RETURN in response to a prompt.

## USING telnet TO CONNECT TO OTHER PORTS

By default telnet connects to port 23, which is used for remote logins. However, you can use telnet to connect to other services by specifying a port number. In addition to standard services, many of the special remote services available on the Internet use unallocated port numbers. Unlike the port numbers for standard protocols, these port numbers can be picked arbitrarily by the administrator of the service.

Although telnet is no longer commonly employed to log in on remote systems, it is still used extensively as a debugging tool by allowing you to communicate directly with a TCP server. Some standard protocols are simple enough that an experienced user can debug problems by connecting to a remote service directly using telnet. If you are having a problem with a network server, a good first step is to try to connect to it using telnet.

If you use telnet to connect to port 25 on a host, you can interact with SMTP. In addition, port 110 connects to the POP protocol, port 80 connects with a WWW server, and port 143 connects to IMAP. All these protocols are ASCII protocols and are documented in *RFCs* (page 1270). You can read the RFCs or search the Web for examples on how to use them interactively.

In the following example, a system administrator who is debugging a problem with email delivery uses telnet to connect to the SMTP port (port 25) on the server at **example.com** to see why it is bouncing mail from the **spammer.com** domain. The first line of output indicates which IP address telnet is trying to connect to. After telnet displays the **Connected to smtpsrv.example.com** message, the user emulates an SMTP dialog, following the standard SMTP protocol. The first line, which starts with **helo**, begins the session and identifies the local system. After the SMTP server identifies itself, the user enters a line that identifies the mail sender as **user@spammer.com**. The SMTP server's response explains why the message is bouncing, so the user ends the session with **quit**.

```
$ telnet smtpsrv 25
Trying 192.168.1.1...
Connected to smtpsrv.example.com.
Escape character is '^]'.
helo example.com
220 smtpsrv.example.com ESMTP Sendmail 8.13.1/8.13.1; Wed, 4 May 2011 00:13:43 -0500 (CDT)
250 smtpsrv.example.com Hello desktop.example.com [192.168.1.97], pleased to meet you
mail from:user@spammer.com
571 5.0.0 Domain banned for spamming
quit
221 2.0.0 smtpsrv.example.com closing connection
```

The telnet utility allows you to use any protocol you want, as long as you know it well enough to type commands manually.

## ftp: TRANSFERS FILES OVER A NETWORK

FTP (File Transfer Protocol) is a method of downloading files from and uploading files to a remote system using TCP/IP over a network. Most Web browsers can download files from FTP servers. Some vendors use anonymous FTP (page 719) to accept uploaded debugging sessions or to allow clients to download firmware. FTP is not a secure protocol; use it only for downloading public information from a public server. See page 714 for more information on FTP security. Use one of the OpenSSH tools described in Chapter 18 for secure communication. Chapter 19 covers FTP clients and servers.

## **LE+**  ping: TESTS A NETWORK CONNECTION

The ping[9] and ping6 utilities (referred to in this section as ping; read the story of ping at http://ftp.arl.mil/~mike/ping.html) send an ECHO_REQUEST packet to a remote computer. This packet causes the remote system to send back a reply. This exchange is a quick way to verify that a remote system is available and to check how well the network is operating, such as how fast it is or whether it is dropping data packets. The ping utility uses the ICMP (Internet Control Message Protocol) protocol. Without any options, ping tests the connection once per second until you abort execution using CONTROL-C. With the –c option ping tests the connection the number of times specified by the number that follows the option.

```
$ ping -c 4 www.slashdot.org
PING www.slashdot.org (216.34.181.48) 56(84) bytes of data.
64 bytes from star.slashdot.org (216.34.181.48): icmp_seq=1 ttl=238 time=70.2 ms
64 bytes from star.slashdot.org (216.34.181.48): icmp_seq=2 ttl=238 time=72.6 ms
64 bytes from star.slashdot.org (216.34.181.48): icmp_seq=3 ttl=238 time=57.5 ms
64 bytes from star.slashdot.org (216.34.181.48): icmp_seq=4 ttl=238 time=71.2 ms

--- www.slashdot.org ping statistics ---
4 packets transmitted, 4 received, 0% packet loss, time 3024ms
rtt min/avg/max/mdev = 57.553/67.899/72.605/6.039 ms
```

---

9. The name ping mimics the sound of a sonar burst used by submarines to identify and communicate with each other. The word ping also expands to packet internet groper.

This example shows that a connection to **www.slashdot.org** is answered by **star.slashdot.org** (**www.slashdot.org** is an alias for **star.slashdot.org**) and that that system is up and available over the network.

By default ping sends packets containing 64 bytes (56 data bytes and 8 bytes of protocol header information). In the preceding example, four packets were sent to the system **star.slashdot.org** as specified by the **–c** option. The four-part number in parentheses on each line is the remote system's IP address. A packet sequence number (named **icmp_seq**) is also given. If a packet is dropped, a gap occurs in the number sequence. The round-trip time is listed last; it represents the time (in milliseconds) that elapsed from when the packet was sent from the local system to the remote system until the reply from the remote system was received by the local system. This time is affected by the distance between the two systems, network traffic, and the load on both computers. Before it terminates, ping summarizes the results, indicating how many packets were sent and received as well as the minimum, average, maximum, and mean deviation round-trip times it measured. Use ping6 to test IPv6 networks.

### When ping cannot connect

tip   If it is unable to contact the remote system, ping continues trying until you interrupt it by pressing CONTROL-C. A system might not answer for any of several reasons: The remote computer might be down, the network interface or some part of the network between the systems might be broken, a software failure might have occurred, or the remote machine might be set up (for reasons of security) not to return pings (try pinging www.microsoft.com or www.ibm.com).

## LE+  traceroute: TRACES A ROUTE OVER THE INTERNET

The traceroute and traceroute6 utilities (referred to in this section as traceroute; **traceroute** package) trace the route that an IP packet follows, including all intermediary points traversed (called *network hops*), to its destination (the argument to traceroute—a remote system). They display a numbered list of hostnames, if available, and IP addresses, together with the round-trip time it took for a packet to reach each router along the way and for the local system to receive a response. You can put this information to good use when you are trying to identify the location of a network bottleneck.

The traceroute utility has no concept of the path from one host to the next; instead, it simply sends UDP packets with increasing *TTL* (time to live) values. TTL is an IP header field that indicates how many more hops the packet should be allowed to make before being discarded or returned. Each router along the way inspects the TTL and decrements it by 1. When the TTL reaches 0 the router that has the packet sends back an ICMP TIME EXCEEDED to the local system, where traceroute records the IP address of the router that sent it back. The result is a list of hosts that the packet traveled through to get to its destination.

The traceroute utility can help solve routing configuration problems and locate routing path failures. When you cannot reach a host, use traceroute to discover which path the packet follows, how far it gets, and what the delay is.

The example on the next page shows the output of traceroute when it follows a route from a local computer to **www.linux.org**. The first line indicates the IP address of the target, the maximum number of hops that will be traced, and the size of the packets that will be used. Each numbered line contains the name and IP address of the intermediate destination, followed by the time it takes a packet to make a trip to that destination and back again. The traceroute utility sends three packets to each destination; thus three times appear on each line. Line 1 shows the statistics when a packet is sent to the local gateway (less than 3 milliseconds). Lines 4–6 show the packet bouncing around Mountain View (California) before it goes to San Jose. Between hops 13 and 14 the packet travels across the United States (San Francisco to somewhere in the East). By hop 18 the packet has found **www.linux.org**. The traceroute utility displays asterisks when it does not receive a response. Each asterisk indicates that traceroute has waited three seconds. Use traceroute6 to test IPv6 networks.

```
$ traceroute www.linux.org
traceroute to www.linux.org (198.182.196.56), 30 hops max, 38 byte packets
 1  gw.localco.com. (204.94.139.65)  2.904 ms  2.425 ms  2.783 ms
 2  covad-gw2.meer.net (209.157.140.1)  19.727 ms  23.287 ms  24.783 ms
 3  gw-mv1.meer.net (140.174.164.1)  18.795 ms  24.973 ms  19.207 ms
 4  d1-4-2.a02.mtvwca01.us.ra.verio.net (206.184.210.241)  59.091 ms d1-10-0-0-200.a03.
      mtvwca01.us.ra.verio.net (206.86.28.5)  54.948 ms  39.485 ms
 5  fa-11-0-0.a01.mtvwca01.us.ra.verio.net (206.184.188.1)  40.182 ms  44.405 ms 49.362 ms
 6  p1-1-0-0.a09.mtvwca01.us.ra.verio.net (205.149.170.66)  78.688 ms  66.266 ms 28.003 ms
 7  p1-12-0-0.a01.snjsca01.us.ra.verio.net (209.157.181.166) 32.424 ms 94.337 ms 54.946 ms
 8  f4-1-0.sjc0.verio.net (129.250.31.81)  38.952 ms  63.111 ms  49.083 ms
 9  sjc0.nuq0.verio.net (129.250.3.98)  45.031 ms  43.496 ms  44.925 ms
10  mae-west1.US.CRL.NET (198.32.136.10)  48.525 ms  66.296 ms  38.996 ms
11  t3-ames.3.sfo.us.crl.net (165.113.0.249)  138.808 ms  78.579 ms  68.699 ms
12  E0-CRL-SFO-02-E0X0.US.CRL.NET (165.113.55.2)  43.023 ms  51.910 ms  42.967 ms
13  sfo2-vva1.ATM.us.crl.net (165.113.0.254)  135.551 ms  154.606 ms  178.632 ms
14  mae-east-02.ix.ai.net (192.41.177.202)  158.351 ms  201.811 ms  204.560 ms
15  oc12-3-0-0.mae-east.ix.ai.net (205.134.161.2)  202.851 ms  155.667 ms  219.116 ms
16  border-ai.invlogic.com (205.134.175.254)  214.622 ms  *  190.423 ms
17  router.invlogic.com (198.182.196.1)  224.378 ms  235.427 ms  228.856 ms
18  www.linux.org (198.182.196.56)  207.964 ms  178.683 ms  179.483 ms
```

Some firewalls block UDP/traceroute. If traceroute fails, try using the **–T** (sends TCP SYN packets) or **–I** (sends ICMP ECHO packets) option. Another useful tool is mtr (**mtr** package), which provides traceroute functionality plus information about dropped packets. The mtr utility is useful for debugging packet loss along a multi-hop network path.

## *LE+* host AND dig: QUERY INTERNET NAMESERVERS

Given a name, the host utility looks up an IP address, or vice versa. The following example shows how to use host to look up the domain name of a machine, given an IP address:

```
$ host  64.13.141.6
6.141.13.64.in-addr.arpa domain name pointer ns.meer.net.
```

You can also use host to determine the IP address of a domain name:

```
$ host ns.meer.net
ns.meer.net has address 64.13.141.6
```

The dig (domain information groper) utility queries DNS servers and individual machines for information about a domain. A powerful utility, dig has many features you might never use. It is more complex than host. Chapter 24 on DNS has many examples of the use of host and dig.

# whois: LOOKS UP INFORMATION ABOUT AN INTERNET SITE

The whois utility (**whois** package) queries a **whois** server for information about an Internet site. This utility returns site contact and InterNIC or other registry information that can help you track down the person who is responsible for a site: Perhaps that person is sending you or your company spam. Many sites on the Internet are easier to use and faster than whois. Use a browser and search engine to search on **whois** or go to www.networksolutions.com/whois or apps.db.ripe.net/search to get started.

When you do not specify a **whois** server, whois defaults to **whois.internic.net**. Use the **–h** option to whois to specify a different **whois** server. See the whois info page for more options and setup information.

To obtain information on a domain name, specify the complete domain name, as in the following example:

```
$ whois sobell.com
   Domain Name: SOBELL.COM
   Registrar: GODADDY.COM, INC.
   Whois Server: whois.godaddy.com
   Referral URL: http://registrar.godaddy.com
   Name Server: NS1.HUNGERHOST.COM
...
Registrant:
   Sobell Associates Inc
   660 Market Street
   Fifth Floor
   San Francisco, California 94104
   United States

   Registered through: GoDaddy.com, Inc. (http://www.godaddy.com)
   Domain Name: SOBELL.COM
      Created on: 07-Apr-95
      Expires on: 08-Apr-13
      Last Updated on: 01-Mar-10

   Administrative Contact:
      Sobell, Mark  sobell@meer.net
      Sobell Associates Inc
      660 Market Street
      Fifth Floor
      SAN FRANCISCO, California 94104
      United States
      18888446337      Fax -- 18888446337

   Technical Contact:
      W., Tim  hostmaster@meer.net
      meer.net
      po box 390804
```

```
         Mountain View, California 94039
         United States
         18888446337      Fax -- 18888446337

    Domain servers in listed order:
       NS1.HUNGERHOST.COM
       NS2.HUNGERHOST.COM
```

Several top-level registries serve various regions of the world. You are most likely to use the following ones:

| | |
|---|---|
| North American registry | **whois.arin.net** |
| European registry | **www.ripe.net** |
| Asia-Pacific registry | **www.apnic.net** |
| U.S. military | **whois.nic.mil** |
| U.S. government | **www.nic.gov** |

# DISTRIBUTED COMPUTING

When many similar systems are part of a network, it is often desirable to share common files and utilities among them. For example, a system administrator might choose to keep a copy of the system documentation on one computer's disk and to make those files available to remote systems. In this case, the system administrator configures the files so users who need to access the online documentation are not aware that the files are stored on a remote system. This type of setup, which is an example of *distributed computing*, not only conserves disk space but also allows you to update one central copy of the documentation rather than tracking down and updating copies scattered throughout the network on many different systems.

Figure 8-2 illustrates a *fileserver* that stores the system manual pages and users' home directories. With this arrangement, a user's files are always available to that user no matter which system the user logs in on. Each system's disk might contain a directory to hold temporary files as well as a copy of the operating system. Chapter 22 contains instructions for setting up NFS clients and servers in networked configurations.

## THE CLIENT/SERVER MODEL

Mainframe model  The client/server model was not the first computational model. First came the mainframe, which follows a one-machine-does-it-all model. That is, all the intelligence

**Figure 8-2**  A fileserver

resides in one system, including the data and the program that manipulates and reports on the data. Users connect to a mainframe using terminals.

**File-sharing model**    With the introduction of PCs, file-sharing networks became available. In this scheme data is downloaded from a shared location to a user's PC, where a program then manipulates the data. The file-sharing model ran into problems as networks expanded and more users needed access to the data.

**Client/server model**    In the client/server model, a client uses a protocol, such as HTTP or SCP, to request services, and a server provides the services the client requests. Rather than providing data files as the file-sharing model does, the server in a client/server relationship is a database that provides only those pieces of information the client needs or requests.

The client/server model dominates UNIX and Linux system networking and underlies most of the network services described in this book. FTP, NFS, DNS, email, and HTTP (the Web browsing protocol) all rely on the client/server model. Some servers, such as Web servers and browser clients, are designed to interact with specific utilities. Other servers, such as those supporting DNS, communicate with one another, in addition to answering queries from a variety of clients. Clients and servers can reside on the same or different systems running the same or different operating systems. The systems can be proximate or thousands of miles apart. A system that is a server to one system can turn around and act as a client to another. A server can reside on a single system or, as is the case with DNS, be distributed among thousands of geographically separated systems running many different operating systems.

**Peer-to-peer model**    The peer-to-peer (PTP) model, in which either program can initiate a transaction, stands in contrast to the client/server model. PTP protocols are common on small networks. For example, Microsoft's Network Neighborhood and Apple's Bonjour both rely on broadcast-based PTP protocols for browsing and automatic configuration. The Zeroconf multicast DNS protocol is a PTP alternative DNS for small networks. The highest-profile PTP networks are those used for file sharing, such as Kazaa and GNUtella. Many of these networks are not pure PTP topologies. Pure PTP networks do not scale well, so networks such as BitTorrent employ a hybrid approach.

## DNS: DOMAIN NAME SERVICE

DNS is a distributed service: Nameservers on thousands of machines around the world cooperate to keep the DNS database up-to-date. The database itself, which maps hundreds of thousands of alphanumeric hostnames to numeric IP addresses, does not exist in one place. That is, no system has a complete copy of the database. Instead, each system that runs DNS knows which hosts are local to that site and understands how to contact other nameservers to learn about other, nonlocal hosts.

Like the Linux filesystem, DNS is organized hierarchically. Each country has an ISO (International Organization for Standardization) country code designation as its domain name. (For example, **AU** represents Australia, **IL** is Israel, and **JP** is Japan; see country-code.org for a complete list.) Although the United States is represented in the same way (**US**) and uses the standard two-letter Postal Service state abbreviations to identify the next level of the domain, only governments and a few organizations use these codes. Schools in the **US** domain are represented by a third- (and sometimes second-) level domain: **k12**. For example, the domain name for Myschool in New York state could be www.myschool.k12.ny.us.

**Figure 8-3** U.S. top-level domains

Following is a list of the seven original top-level domains. These domains are used extensively within the United States and, to a lesser degree, by users in other countries:

| | |
|---|---|
| COM | Commercial enterprises |
| EDU | Educational institutions |
| GOV | Nonmilitary government agencies |
| INT | International organizations recognized by treaty |
| MIL | Military government agencies |
| NET | Networking organizations |
| ORG | Other (often nonprofit) organizations |

Recently, the following additional top-level domains have been approved for use. Visit en.wikipedia.org/wiki/List_of_Internet_top-level_domains for a complete, current list.

| | |
|---|---|
| AERO | Air-transport industry |
| BIZ | Business |
| COOP | Cooperatives |
| INFO | Unrestricted use |
| MUSEUM | Museums |
| NAME | Name registries |

FQDN  Like Internet addresses, domain names were once assigned by the Network Information Center (NIC); now they are assigned by several companies. A system's full name, referred to as its *fully qualified domain name* (FQDN), is unambiguous in the way that a simple hostname cannot be. The system **okeeffe.berkeley.edu** at the University of California at Berkeley (Figure 8-3) is not the same as one named **okeeffe.moma.org**, which might represent a host at the Museum of Modern Art. The domain name not only tells you something about where the system is located but also adds enough diversity to the namespace to avoid confusion when different sites choose similar names for their systems.

Unlike the filesystem hierarchy, the top-level domain name appears last (reading from left to right). Also, domain names are not case sensitive, so the names **okeeffe.berkeley.edu**, **okeeffe.Berkeley.edu**, and **okeeffe.Berkeley.EDU** refer to the same computer. Once a domain has been assigned, the local site is free to extend the hierarchy to meet local needs.

With DNS, email addressed to **user@example.com** can be delivered to the computer named **example.com** that handles the corporate mail and knows how to forward messages to user mailboxes on individual machines. As the company grows, its site administrator might decide to create organizational or geographical subdomains. The name **delta.ca.example.com** might refer to a system that supports California offices, for example, while **alpha.co.example.com** is dedicated to Colorado. Functional subdomains are another choice, with **delta.sales.example.com** and **alpha.dev.example.com** representing the sales and development divisions, respectively.

BIND    On Linux systems, the most common interface to the DNS is BIND (Berkeley Internet Name Domain). BIND follows the client/server model. On any given local network, one or more systems might be running a nameserver, supporting all the local hosts as clients. When it wants to send a message to another host, a system queries the nearest nameserver to learn the remote host's IP address. The client, called a *resolver,* might be a process running on the same computer as the nameserver, or it might pass the request over the network to reach a server. To reduce network traffic and facilitate name lookups, the local nameserver maintains some knowledge of distant hosts. If the local server must contact a remote server to pick up an address, when the answer comes back, the local server adds that address to its internal table and reuses it for a while. The nameserver deletes the nonlocal information before it can become outdated. Refer to "TTL" on page 1278.

The system's translation of symbolic hostnames into IP addresses is transparent to most users; only the system administrator of a networked system needs to be concerned with the details of name resolution. Systems that use DNS for name resolution are generally capable of communicating with the greatest number of hosts—more than would be practical to maintain in a **/etc/hosts** file or private NIS database. Chapter 24 covers setting up and running a DNS server.

Three common sources are referenced for hostname resolution: NIS, DNS, and system files (such as **/etc/hosts**). Linux does not ask you to choose among these sources; rather, the **nsswitch.conf** file (page 495) allows you to choose any of these sources, in any combination, and in any order.

# *LPI*  PORTS

Ports are logical channels on a network interface and are numbered from 1 to 65,535. Each network connection is uniquely identified by the IP address and port number of each endpoint.

In a system that has many network connections open simultaneously, the use of ports keeps *packets* (page 1265) flowing to and from the appropriate programs. A program that needs to receive data *binds* to a port and then uses that port for communication.

Privileged ports    Services are associated with specific ports, generally with numbers less than 1024. These ports are called *privileged* (or *reserved*) *ports.* For security reasons, only a process running with **root** privileges can bind to a privileged port. A service run on a privileged port provides assurance that the service is being provided by someone with authority over the system, with the exception that any user on Windows 98 and earlier Windows systems can bind to any port. Commonly used ports include 22 (SSH), 23 (TELNET), 80 (HTTP), 111 (Sun RPC), and 201–208 (AppleTalk).

**Privileged ports do not provide absolute security**

security    Any user who can gain **root** privileges can easily start a service on any port. Thus, it is necessary to treat privileged ports as a necessary but not sufficient component in a security policy and to be aware of which other systems are on the local network.

# NIS: NETWORK INFORMATION SERVICE

NIS (Network Information Service) simplifies the maintenance of frequently used administrative files by keeping them in a central database and having clients contact the database server to retrieve information from the database. Just as DNS addresses the problem of keeping multiple copies of **hosts** files up-to-date, NIS deals with the issue of keeping system-independent configuration files (such as **/etc/passwd**) current. Although NIS has been functionally replaced by LDAP, LDAP is harder to configure, and so NIS is still in common use. Refer to Chapter 21 for coverage of NIS and LDAP.

# NFS: NETWORK FILESYSTEM

The NFS (Network Filesystem) protocol allows a server to share selected local directory hierarchies with client systems on a heterogeneous network. Files on the remote fileserver appear as if they are present on the local system. Chapter 22 covers NFS.

optional

_LPI_   # NETWORK SERVICES

Linux Internet services are provided by daemons that run continuously or by a daemon that is started automatically by the systemd init daemon (page 438) when a service request comes in. The **/etc/services** file lists network services (for example, **telnet, ftp,** and **ssh**) and their associated numbers. Any service that uses TCP/IP or UDP/IP has an entry in this file. IANA (Internet Assigned Numbers Authority) maintains a database of all permanent, registered services. The **/etc/services** file usually lists a small, commonly used subset of services.

Most executable daemon files are stored in **/usr/sbin**. By convention the names of many daemons end with the letter **d** to distinguish them from utilities (one common daemon whose name does not end in **d** is **sendmail**). The prefix **in.** or **rpc.** is often used for daemon names. Give the command **ls /usr/sbin/\*d** to see a list of many of the daemon programs on the local system. Refer to "Configuring Daemons (Services)" on page 445 for information about starting and stopping these daemons.

To see how a daemon works, consider what happens when you run ssh. The local system contacts the ssh daemon (**sshd**) on the remote system to establish a connection. The two systems negotiate the connection according to a fixed protocol. Each system identifies itself to the other, and they then take turns asking each other specific questions and waiting for valid replies. Each network service follows its own protocol.

# COMMON DAEMONS

In addition to the daemons that support the utilities described in this chapter, many other daemons support system-level services that you will not typically interact with. Table 8-3 lists some of these daemons.

Table 8-3   Common daemons

| Daemon | Used for or by | Function |
|--------|----------------|----------|
| **acpid** | Advanced configuration and power interface | Flexible daemon for delivering ACPI events. Replaces **apmd**. |
| **anacron** | anacrontab | Used for periodic execution of tasks. This daemon looks in the **/etc/anacrontab** file. When a task comes up for execution, **anacron** executes it as the user who owns the file that describes the task. See page 607. |
| **apmd** | Advanced power management | Reports and takes action on specified changes in system power, including shutdowns. Useful with machines, such as laptops, that run on batteries. |
| **atd** | at | Executes a command once at a specific time and date. See **crond** for periodic execution of a command. See page 611. |
| **automount** | Automatic mounting | Automatically mounts filesystems when they are accessed. Automatic mounting is a way of demand-mounting remote directories without having to hard-configure them into **/etc/fstab**. See page 821. |
| **crond** | cron | Used for periodic execution of tasks. This daemon looks in the **/var/spool/cron** directory for files with filenames that correspond to usernames. It also looks at the **/etc/crontab** file and at files in the **/etc/cron.d** directory. When a task comes up for execution, **crond** executes it as the user who owns the file that describes the task. See page 607. |
| **cupsd** | Printing daemon | Configures local and remote printers and handles printing jobs. See Chapter 13 for more information. |

**Table 8-3** Common daemons (continued)

| Daemon | Used for or by | Function |
|---|---|---|
| **dhcpd**, **dhcpd6** | DHCP | Assigns Internet address, network mask, default gateway, DNS, and other information to hosts. This protocol answers DHCP requests and, optionally, BOOTP requests. Refer to "DHCP: Configures Network Interfaces" on page 491. |
| **exim4** | Mail programs | The **exim4** daemon came from the University of Cambridge. The **exim4** daemon listens on port 25 for incoming mail connections and then calls a local delivery agent, such as **/bin/mail**. Mail user agents (MUAs), such as KMail and Thunderbird, typically use **exim4** to deliver mail messages. See also **sendmail**. |
| **ftpd** | FTP | Handles FTP requests. Refer to "ftp: Transfers Files over a Network" on page 305. See also **vsftpd** (page 713). |
| **gpm** | General-purpose mouse or GNU paste manager | Allows you to use a mouse to cut and paste text on console applications. |
| **hald** | Hardware Abstraction Layer (HAL) daemon | Collects and maintains system hardware information in real time. Part of the **hal** package. |
| **httpd** | HTTP | The Web server daemon (Apache; page 931). |
| **in.fingerd** | finger | Handles requests for user information from the finger utility. |
| **munged** | Authentication daemon | Allows processes running on different machines to authenticate each other. Part of the **munge** package. |
| **mysqld** | The MariaDB/MySQL daemon | Supports queries on a MariaDB/MySQL database. It is the M in LAMP (Linux, Apache, MariaDB/MySQL, PHP/Perl/Python). See Chapter 29. |
| **named** | DNS | Supports DNS. See page 851. |
| **nfsd, statd, lockd, mountd, rquotad** | NFS | These five daemons operate together to handle NFSv3 (page 801) operations. The **nfsd** daemon handles file and directory requests. The **statd** and **lockd** daemons implement network file and record locking. The **mountd** daemon converts filesystem name requests from the mount utility into NFS handles and checks access permissions. If disk quotas are enabled, **rquotad** handles those. |
| **ntpd** | NTP | Synchronizes time on network computers. For more information visit www.ntp.org. |

**Table 8-3**   Common daemons (continued)

| Daemon | Used for or by | Function |
|---|---|---|
| radvd | IPv6 | IPv6 Router ADVertisement Daemon. Provides autoconfiguration on the network if the local system is being used as a router. |
| rpcbind | RPC | Maps incoming requests for RPC service numbers to TCP or UDP port numbers on the local system. Refer to "RPC Network Services" on page 317. |
| rsyslogd | System log | Transcribes important system events and stores them in files and/or forwards them to users or another host running the **rsyslogd** daemon. See page 620. |
| sendmail | Mail programs | The **sendmail** daemon came from Berkeley UNIX and has been available for a long time. The de facto mail transfer program on the Internet, the **sendmail** daemon always listens on port 25 for incoming mail connections and then calls a local delivery agent, such as **/bin/mail**. Mail user agents (MUAs), such as KMail and Thunderbird, typically use **sendmail** to deliver mail messages. See also **exim4**. See page 739. |
| smartd | SMART Disk Monitoring Daemon | Monitors the Self-Monitoring, Analysis and Reporting Technology (SMART) system built into many hard drives. SMART tests drive reliability, predicts failure, and performs other self tests. Part of the **smartmontools** package. See page 82. |
| smbd, nmbd | Samba | Allow Windows PCs to share files and printers with UNIX and Linux computers. See page 827. |
| sshd | ssh, scp | Enables secure logins between remote systems (page 700). |
| talkd | talk | Allows you to have a conversation with another user on the same or a remote machine. The **talkd** daemon handles the connections between the machines. The **talk** utility on each system contacts the **talkd** daemon on the other system for a bidirectional conversation. |
| telnetd | TELNET | One of the original Internet remote access protocols. |
| tftpd | TFTP | Used to boot a system or get information from a network. Examples include network computers, routers, and some printers. |
| timed | Time server | On a LAN synchronizes time with other computers that are also running **timed**. |

# Proxy Servers

A *proxy* is a network service that is authorized to act for a system while not being part of that system. A proxy server or proxy gateway provides proxy services; it is a transparent intermediary that relays communications back and forth between an application (e.g., a browser) and a server that usually resides outside of a LAN and frequently on the Internet. When more than one process uses the proxy gateway/server, the proxy must keep track of which processes are connecting to which hosts/servers so that it can route the return messages to the proper process. The most commonly encountered proxies are email and Web proxies.

A proxy server/gateway insulates the local computer from all other computers or from specified domains by using at least two IP addresses: one to communicate with the local computer and one to communicate with a server. The proxy server/gateway examines and changes the header information on all packets it handles so it can encode, route, and decode them properly. The difference between a proxy gateway and a proxy server is that the proxy server usually includes *cache* (page 1241) to store frequently used Web pages so the next request for that page is available locally and quickly; a proxy gateway typically does not use cache. The terms "proxy server" and "proxy gateway" are frequently used interchangeably.

Proxy servers/gateways are available for such common Internet services as HTTP, HTTPS, FTP, SMTP, and SNMP. When an HTTP proxy sends queries from local systems, it presents a single organizationwide IP address (the external IP address of the proxy server/gateway) to all servers. It funnels all user requests to the appropriate servers and keeps track of them. When the responses come back, the HTTP proxy fans them out to the appropriate applications using each machine's unique IP address, thereby protecting local addresses from remote/specified servers.

Proxy servers/gateways are generally just one part of an overall firewall strategy to prevent intruders from stealing information or damaging an internal network. Other functions, which can be either combined with or kept separate from the proxy server/gateway, include packet filtering, which blocks traffic based on origin and type, and user activity reporting, which helps management learn how the Internet is being used.

# RPC NETWORK SERVICES

Much of the client/server interaction over a network is implemented using the RPC (Remote Procedure Call) protocol, which is implemented as a set of library calls that make network access transparent to the client and server. RPC specifies and interprets messages but does not concern itself with transport protocols; it runs on top of TCP/IP and UDP/IP. Services that use RPC include NFS and NIS. RPC was developed by Sun as ONC RPC (Open Network Computing Remote Procedure Calls) and differs from Microsoft RPC.

**rpcbind**  In the client/server model, a client contacts a server on a specific port (page 312) to avoid any mixup between services, clients, and servers. RPC has two possible ways of registering a port. The first works in the manner of a traditional daemon: The server binds to the port it wants to bind to but then registers with the RPC portmapper daemon (**rpcbind**) on the server. As an example, NFS uses this mechanism to always bind to port 2049. The client's port is irrelevant most of the time, so it picks a random port.

More commonly, to avoid maintaining a long list of port numbers and to enable new clients/servers to start up without registering a port number with a central registry, when a server that uses RPC starts, it looks in **/etc/rpc** for the service number and then registers itself with **rpcbind** as just described. The **rpcbind** daemon assigns the server a TCP or UDP port number, and the server binds to that port. RPC servers typically use service numbers (**/etc/rpc**) that were defined by Sun, but the TCP or UDP port number it uses is random. When a client wants to connect to an RPC server, it first asks **rpcbind** on the server, which listens on port 111, for the name of the service it is interested in (e.g., **mountd**). If that service is registered, **rpcbind** returns the TCP or UDP port number of the server to the client. The client then contacts the RPC server daemon directly to finish the transaction.

Files   The **/etc/rpc** file (page 510) maps RPC service names to RPC numbers. The **/etc/services** file (page 511) maps system service names to TCP or UDP ports.

RPC client/server communication   The sequence of events for communication between an RPC client and server is as follows:

1. The client system needs to talk to a server application running on a remote system. The client system knows which system the server application is running on but not which port it is using. The client system looks for the service name in **/etc/rpc** to determine the service number.

2. The client system contacts **rpcbind** on port 111 of the remote system with the service number to ask which UDP or TCP port the server on the remote system is listening on.

3. The **rpcbind** daemon on the remote system checks which server applications have registered with it. If the service number the client system asked for is registered, the **rpcbind** daemon on the remote system returns the UDP or TCP port assigned to that server application.

4. The RPC libraries on the client system encode procedure calls and send them to the server application on the remote system on the specified port. (The client system issues a "read record from a file" request.)

5. The server application running on the remote system receives the call, sends it through the RPC libraries to decode it, and generates results. (The filesystem receives the "read record from file" request.)

6. The server application passes the results back through the RPC libraries, which encode the results, and then sends the encoded results to the client using the client's registered port. (The read record is returned to the calling program.)

7. The client system receives the results, passes them through the RPC libraries for decoding, and presents the decoded results to the user or application that requested them.

If the **rpcbind** daemon stops, you must restart all RPC servers on the local system.

# WWW: WORLD WIDE WEB

The World Wide Web (WWW, W3, or the Web) provides a unified, interconnected interface to the vast amount of information stored on computers around the world. The idea that spawned the World Wide Web came from the mind of Tim Berners-Lee (www.w3.org/People/Berners-Lee) of the European Particle Physics Laboratory (CERN) in response to a need to improve communications throughout the high-energy physics community. The first-generation solution consisted of a notebook program named Enquire, short for *Enquire Within Upon Everything* (the name of a book from Berners-Lee's childhood), which he created in 1980 on a NeXT computer and which supported links between named nodes. Not until 1989 was the concept proposed as a global hypertext project to be known as the World Wide Web. In 1990, Berners-Lee wrote a proposal for a hypertext project, which eventually produced HTML (Hypertext Markup Language), the common language of the Web. The World Wide Web program became available on the Internet in the summer of 1991. By designing the tools to work with existing protocols, such as FTP and gopher, the researchers who created the Web produced a system that is generally useful for many types of information and across many types of hardware and operating systems.

The WWW is another example of the client/server paradigm. You use a WWW client application, or *browser,* to retrieve and display information stored on a server that might be located anywhere on the local network or the Internet. WWW clients can interact with many types of servers. For example, you can use a WWW client to contact a remote FTP server and display the list of files it offers for anonymous FTP download. Most commonly you use a WWW client to contact a WWW server, which offers support for the special features of the World Wide Web that are described in the remainder of this chapter.

The power of the Web derives from its use of *hypertext,* a way to navigate through information by following cross-references (called *links*) from one piece of information to another. To use the Web effectively, you need to run interactive network applications. The first GUI for browsing the Web was a tool named Mosaic, which was released in February 1993. Designed at the National Center for Supercomputer Applications at the University of Illinois, its introduction sparked a dramatic increase in the number of users of the World Wide Web. Marc Andreessen, who participated in the Mosaic project at the University of Illinois, later cofounded Netscape Communications with the founder of Silicon Graphics, Jim Clark. The pair created Netscape Navigator, a Web client program that was designed to perform better and support more features than the Mosaic browser. Netscape Navigator enjoyed immense success and was a popular choice for exploring the World Wide Web. Important for Linux users is the fact that from its inception Netscape has provided versions of its tools that run on Linux.

# BROWSERS

Mozilla (www.mozilla.org) is the open-source counterpart to Netscape and was first released in March 1998, based on Netscape 4 code. Since then, Mozilla has been under continuous development by employees of Netscape (now a division of AOL), Red Hat, and other companies and by contributors from the community. Firefox is the Web browser component of Mozilla. KDE offers Konqueror, an all-purpose file manager and Web browser. Other browsers include Safari (www.apple.com/safari), Chrome (www.google.com/chrome), Epiphany (projects.gnome.org/epiphany) and Opera (www.opera.com). Although each Web browser is unique, all of them allow you to move about the Internet, viewing HTML documents, watching videos, and retrieving files. If you do not use the X Window System, try a text browser, such as lynx or links. The lynx browser works well with Braille terminals.

# SEARCH ENGINES

*Search engine* is a name that applies to a group of hardware and software tools that help you search for World Wide Web sites that contain specific information. A search engine relies on a database of information collected by a *Web crawler,* a program that regularly looks through the millions of pages that make up the World Wide Web. A search engine must also have a way of collating the information the Web crawler collects so you can access it quickly, easily, and in a manner that makes it most useful to you. This part of the search engine, called an *index*, allows you to search for a word, a group of words, or a concept; it returns the URLs of Web pages that pertain to what you are searching for. Many different types of search engines are available on the Internet, each with its own set of strengths and weaknesses.

# URL: UNIFORM RESOURCE LOCATOR

Consider the URL (Uniform Resource Locator) www.w3.org/Consortium/siteindex. The first component in the URL indicates the type of resource, in this case **http** (HTTP—Hypertext Transfer Protocol). Other valid resource names, such as **https** (HTTPS—secure HTTP) and **ftp** (FTP—File Transfer Protocol), represent information available on the Web using other protocols. Next come a colon and double slash (**://**). Frequently the **http://** string is omitted from a URL in print, as you seldom need to enter it to reach the URL. The next element is the full name of the host that acts as the server for the information (**www.w3.org/**). The rest of the URL consists of a relative pathname to the file that contains the information (**Consortium/siteindex**). If you enter a URL in the location bar of a Web browser, the Web server returns the page, frequently an *HTML* (page 1254) file, pointed to by this URL.

By convention many sites identify their WWW servers by prefixing a host or domain name with **www**. For example, you can reach the Web server at the New Jersey Institute of Technology at www.njit.edu. When you use a browser to explore the World Wide Web, you might never need to enter a URL. However, as more information is published in hypertext form, you cannot help but find URLs everywhere—not just online in email messages and blogs, but also in newspapers, in advertisements, and on product labels.

URI   Whereas a URL indicates the location of a resource and a method of retrieving it (e.g., a network address and protocol), a URI (Uniform Resource Identifier) simply indicates something about the resource (e.g., an ISBN number). All URLs are URIs, but not all URIs are URLs. The terms are frequently used interchangeably because very few URIs that are not URLs are in common use.

# CHAPTER SUMMARY

A Linux system attached to a network is probably communicating on an Ethernet network, which might in turn be linked to other local area networks (LANs) and wide area networks (WANs). Communication between LANs and WANs requires the use of gateways and routers. Gateways translate the local data into a format suitable for the WAN, and routers make decisions about the optimal routing of the data along the way. The most widely used network, by far, is the Internet.

Basic networking tools allow Linux users to log in and run commands on remote systems (ssh, telnet, rsync) and copy files quickly from one system to another (scp, ftp/sftp). Other features, such as the Network Filesystem (NFS), were created to extend the basic UNIX model and to simplify information sharing.

Concern is growing about our ability to protect the security and privacy of machines connected to networks and of data transmitted over networks. Toward this end, many tools and protocols have been created: ssh, scp, HTTPS, IPv6, firewall hardware and software, VPN, and so on. Many of these tools take advantage of newer, more impenetrable encryption techniques. In addition, some weaker concepts (such as that of trusted hosts) and some tools (such as finger and rwho) have been deprecated in the name of security.

Computer networks offer two major advantages over other ways of connecting computers: They enable systems to communicate at high speeds, and they require few physical interconnections (typically one per system). The Internet Protocol (IP), the universal language of the Internet, has made it possible for dissimilar computer systems around the world to readily communicate with one another. Technological advances continue to improve the performance of computer systems and the networks that link them.

The rapid increase of network communication speeds in recent years has encouraged the development of many new applications and services. The World Wide Web provides access to vast information stores on the Internet and makes extensive use of hypertext links to promote efficient searching through related documents. It adheres to the client/server model that is so pervasive in networking. Typically the WWW client is local to a site or is made available through an Internet service provider. WWW servers are responsible for providing the information requested by their many clients.

Mozilla/Firefox is a WWW client program that has enormous popular appeal. Firefox and other browsers use a GUI to give you access to text, picture, and audio information: Making extensive use of these hypermedia simplifies access to and enhances the presentation of information.

# EXERCISES

1. Describe the similarities and differences between these utilities:

   a. scp and ftp

   b. ssh and telnet

2. Describe two ways to find out who is logged in on some of the other machines attached to your network.

3. Explain the client/server model. Give three examples of services on Linux systems that take advantage of this model.

4. A software implementation of chess was developed by GNU and is available for free. How can you use the Internet to find and download this program?

5. What is the difference between the World Wide Web and the Internet?

6. If you have access to the World Wide Web, answer the following questions.

   a. Which browser do you use?

   b. What is the URL of the author of this book's home page? How many links does it have?

   c. Does your browser allow you to create bookmarks? If so, how do you create a bookmark? How can you delete one?

7. Give one advantage and two disadvantages of using a wireless network.

8. What is the fully abbreviated form of the IPv6 address 2620:0100:e000:0000:0000:0000:0000:8001?

9. IPv6 supports 128-bit addresses. What is the size of the host part of the address? How many hosts would that address space theoretically support on one LAN?

# ADVANCED EXERCISES

10. Suppose the link between routers 1 and 2 is down in the Internet shown in Figure 8-1 on page 289. What happens if someone at site C sends a message to a user on a workstation attached to the Ethernet cable at site A? What happens if the router at site A is down? What does this tell you about designing network configurations?

11. If you have a class B IPv4 network and want to divide it into subnets, each with 126 hosts, which subnet mask should you use? How many networks

will be available? What are the four addresses (broadcast and network number) for the network starting at 131.204.18?

12. Suppose you have 300 hosts and want to have no more than 50 hosts per subnet. What size of address block should you request from your ISP? How many /24 addresses would you need? How many subnets would you have left over from your allocation?

    d. a. On the local system, find two daemons running that are not listed in this chapter and explain what purpose they serve.

    b. Review which services/daemons are automatically started on your system and consider which you might turn off. Are there any services/daemons in the list in Table 8-3 on page 314 you would consider adding?

13. Determine if IPv6 is enabled on the local system by finding the link-local address of a network interface.

14. Use ssh to connect to a remote system on the local LAN using the remote system's autoconfigured link-local IPv6 address. (*Hint:* To specify the network interface to use for link-local addresses, append **%IFNAME** to the end of the address, where **IFNAME** is the local operating system's name for the interface.

# PART III
## SYSTEM ADMINISTRATION

# THE BOURNE AGAIN SHELL (bash)

## OBJECTIVES

After reading this chapter you should be able to:

▶ Describe the purpose and history of bash

▶ List the startup files bash runs

▶ Use three different methods to run a shell script

▶ Understand the purpose of the **PATH** variable

▶ Manage multiple processes using job control

▶ Redirect error messages to a file

▶ Use control operators to separate and group commands

▶ Create variables and display the values of variables and parameters

▶ List and describe common variables found on the system

▶ Reference, repeat, and modify previous commands using history

▶ Use control characters to edit the command line

▶ Create, display, and remove aliases and functions

▶ Customize the bash environment using the set and shopt builtins

▶ List the order of command-line expansion

This chapter picks up where Chapter 5 left off. Chapter 27 expands on this chapter, exploring control flow commands and more advanced aspects of programming the Bourne Again Shell. The bash home page is at www.gnu.org/software/bash. The bash info page is a complete Bourne Again Shell reference.

The Bourne Again Shell is a command interpreter and high-level programming language. As a command interpreter, it processes commands you enter on the command line in response to a prompt. When you use the shell as a programming language, it processes commands stored in files called *shell scripts*. Like other languages, shells have variables and control flow commands (e.g., **for** loops and **if** statements).

When you use a shell as a command interpreter, you can customize the environment you work in. You can make the prompt display the name of the working directory, create a function or an alias for cp that keeps it from overwriting certain kinds of files, take advantage of keyword variables to change aspects of how the shell works, and so on. You can also write shell scripts that do your bidding—anything from a one-line script that stores a long, complex command to a longer script that runs a set of reports, prints them, and mails you a reminder when the job is done. More complex shell scripts are themselves programs; they do not just run other programs. Chapter 27 has some examples of these types of scripts.

Most system shell scripts are written to run under bash (or dash; next page). If you will ever work in single-user mode—when you boot the system or perform system maintenance, administration, or repair work, for example—it is a good idea to become familiar with this shell.

This chapter expands on the interactive features of the shell described in Chapter 5, explains how to create and run simple shell scripts, discusses job control, talks about locale, introduces the basic aspects of shell programming, talks about history and aliases, and describes command-line expansion. Chapter 27 presents some more challenging shell programming problems.

# BACKGROUND

bash Shell   The Bourne Again Shell is based on the Bourne Shell (an early UNIX shell; this book refers to it as the *original Bourne Shell* to avoid confusion), which was written by Steve Bourne of AT&T's Bell Laboratories. Over the years the original Bourne Shell has been expanded, but it remains the basic shell provided with many commercial versions of UNIX.

**LE**   sh Shell   Because of its long and successful history, the original Bourne Shell has been used to write many of the shell scripts that help manage UNIX systems. Some of these scripts appear in Linux as Bourne Again Shell scripts. Although the Bourne Again Shell includes many extensions and features not found in the original Bourne Shell, bash maintains compatibility with the original Bourne Shell so you can run Bourne Shell scripts under bash. On UNIX systems the original Bourne Shell is named sh. On Fedora/RHEL systems sh is a symbolic link to bash, ensuring that scripts that require the presence of the Bourne Shell still run. When called as sh, bash does its best to emulate the original Bourne Shell.

**dash Shell** The bash executable file is almost 900 kilobytes, has many features, and is well suited as a user login shell. The dash (Debian Almquist) shell is about 100 kilobytes, offers Bourne Shell compatibility for shell scripts (noninteractive use), and because of its size, can load and execute shell scripts much more quickly than bash.

**Korn Shell** The Korn Shell (ksh), written by David Korn, ran on System V UNIX. This shell extended many features of the original Bourne Shell and added many new features. Some features of the Bourne Again Shell, such as command aliases and command-line editing, are based on similar features from the Korn Shell.

**POSIX** The POSIX (Portable Operating System Interface) family of related standards is being developed by PASC (IEEE's Portable Application Standards Committee; www.pasc.org/plato). A comprehensive FAQ on POSIX, including many links, appears at www.opengroup.org/austin/papers/posix_faq.html.

POSIX standard 1003.2 describes shell functionality. The Bourne Again Shell provides the features that match the requirements of this standard. Efforts are under way to make the Bourne Again Shell fully comply with the POSIX standard. In the meantime, if you invoke bash with the **--posix** option, the behavior of the Bourne Again Shell will closely match the POSIX requirements.

### chsh: changes your login shell

**tip** The person who sets up your account determines which shell you use when you first log in on the system or when you open a terminal emulator window in a GUI environment. Under Fedora/RHEL, bash is the default shell. You can run any shell you like after you are logged in. Enter the name of the shell you want to use (bash, tcsh, or another shell) and press RETURN; the next prompt will be that of the new shell. Give an **exit** command to return to the previous shell. Because shells you call in this manner are nested (one runs on top of the other), you will be able to log out only from your original shell. When you have nested several shells, keep giving **exit** commands until you reach your original shell. You will then be able to log out.

The chsh utility changes your login shell more permanently. First give the command **chsh**. In response to the prompts, enter your password and the absolute pathname of the shell you want to use (**/bin/bash**, **/bin/tcsh**, or the pathname of another shell). When you change your login shell in this manner using a terminal emulator (page 120) under a GUI, subsequent terminal emulator windows might not reflect the change until you log out of the system and log back in. See page 464 for an example of how to use chsh.

## LPI STARTUP FILES

When a shell starts, it runs startup files to initialize itself. Which files the shell runs depends on whether it is a login shell, an interactive shell that is not a login shell (give the command **bash** to run one of these shells), or a noninteractive shell (one used to execute a shell script). You must have read access to a startup file to execute the commands in it. Fedora/RHEL puts appropriate commands in some of these files. This section covers bash startup files.

# LOGIN SHELLS

A *login shell* is the first shell that displays a prompt when you log in on a system from the system console or a virtual console (page 121), remotely using ssh or another program (page 121), or by another means. When you are running a GUI and open a terminal emulator such as gnome-terminal (page 120), you are not logging in on the system (you do not provide your username and password), so the shell the emulator displays is (usually) not a login shell; it is an interactive nonlogin shell (below). Login shells are, by their nature, interactive. See "bash versus –bash" on page 1023 for a way to tell which type of shell you are running.

This section describes the startup files that are executed by login shells and shells that you start with the bash --login option.

**LPI /etc/profile** The shell first executes the commands in **/etc/profile**, establishing systemwide default characteristics for users running bash. In addition to executing the commands it holds, **profile** executes the commands within each of the files with a **.sh** filename extension in the **/etc/profile.d** directory. This setup allows a user working with **root** privileges to modify the commands **profile** runs without changing the **profile** file itself. Because **profile** can be replaced when the system is updated, making changes to files in the **profile.d** directory ensures the changes will remain when the system is updated.

### Set environment variables for all users in /etc/profile or in a �֍ .sh file in /etc/profile.d

**tip** Setting and exporting a variable in **/etc/profile** or in a file with a **.sh** filename extension in the **/etc/profile.d** directory makes that variable available to every user's login shell. Variables that are exported (placed in the environment) are also available to all interactive and noninteractive subshells of the login shell.

**LPI .bash_profile,** Next the shell looks for **~/.bash_profile**, **~/.bash_login**, or **~/.profile** (**~/** is shorthand
**.bash_login,** for your home directory), in that order, executing the commands in the first of these
**and .profile** files it finds. You can put commands in one of these files to override the defaults set in **/etc/profile**.

By default, Fedora/RHEL sets up new accounts with **~/.bash_profile** and **~/.bashrc** files. The default **~/.bash_profile** file calls **~/.bashrc**, which calls **/etc/bashrc**.

**LPI .bash_logout** When you log out, bash executes commands in the **~/.bash_logout** file. This file often holds commands that clean up after a session, such as those that remove temporary files.

# INTERACTIVE NONLOGIN SHELLS

The commands in the preceding startup files are not executed by interactive, nonlogin shells. However, these shells inherit from the login shell variables that are declared and exported in these startup files.

*LPI*  .bashrc   An interactive nonlogin shell executes commands in the ~/.bashrc file. The default ~/.bashrc file calls /etc/bashrc.

/etc/bashrc   Although not called by bash directly, the Fedora/RHEL ~/.bashrc file calls /etc/bashrc.

## Noninteractive Shells

The commands in the previously described startup files are not executed by noninteractive shells, such as those that run shell scripts. However, if these shells are forked by a login shell, they inherit variables that are declared and exported in these startup files. Specifically, crontab files (page 607) do not inherit variables from startup files.

BASH_ENV   Noninteractive shells look for the environment variable **BASH_ENV** (or **ENV** if the shell is called as sh) and execute commands in the file named by this variable.

## Setting Up Startup Files

Although many startup files and types of shells exist, usually all you need are the .bash_profile and .bashrc files in your home directory. Commands similar to the following in .bash_profile run commands from .bashrc for login shells (when .bashrc exists). With this setup, the commands in .bashrc are executed by login and nonlogin shells.

```
if [ -f ~/.bashrc ]; then . ~/.bashrc; fi
```

The [ –f ~/.bashrc ] tests whether the file named .bashrc in your home directory exists. See pages 983 and 986 for more information on test and its synonym [ ]. See page 332 for information on the . (dot) builtin.

### *LE*   Set PATH in .bash_profile

tip   Because commands in .**bashrc** might be executed many times, and because subshells inherit environment (exported) variables, it is a good idea to put commands that add to existing variables in the .**bash_profile** file. For example, the following command adds the **bin** subdirectory of the **home** directory to **PATH** (page 359) and should go in .**bash_profile**:

```
PATH=$PATH:$HOME/bin
```

When you put this command in .**bash_profile** and not in .**bashrc**, the string is added to the **PATH** variable only once, when you log in.

Modifying a variable in .**bash_profile** causes changes you make in an interactive session to propagate to subshells. In contrast, modifying a variable in .**bashrc** overrides changes inherited from a parent shell.

Sample .bash_profile and .bashrc files appear on the next page. Some commands used in these files are not covered until later in this chapter. In any startup file, you must place in the environment (export) those variables and functions that you want to be available to child processes. For more information refer to "Environment, Environment Variables, and Inheritance" on page 1032.

```
$ cat ~/.bash_profile
if [ -f ~/.bashrc ]; then
    . ~/.bashrc                        # Read local startup file if it exists
fi
PATH=$PATH:/usr/local/bin              # Add /usr/local/bin to PATH
export PS1='[\h \W \!]\$ '             # Set prompt
```

The first command in the preceding **.bash_profile** file executes the commands in the user's **.bashrc** file if it exists. The next command adds to the **PATH** variable (page 359). Typically **PATH** is set and exported in **/etc/profile**, so it does not need to be exported in a user's startup file. The final command sets and exports **PS1** (page 361), which controls the user's prompt.

The first command in the **.bashrc** file shown below executes the commands in the **/etc/bashrc** file if it exists. Next the file sets **noclobber** (page 156), unsets **MAILCHECK** (page 361), exports **LANG** (page 366) and **VIMINIT** (for vim initialization), and defines several aliases. The final command defines a function (page 396) that swaps the names of two files.

```
$ cat ~/.bashrc
if [ -f /etc/bashrc ]; then
    source /etc/bashrc                 # read global startup file if it exists
fi

set -o noclobber                       # prevent overwriting files
unset MAILCHECK                        # turn off "you have new mail" notice
export LANG=C                          # set LANG variable
export VIMINIT='set ai aw'             # set vim options
alias df='df -h'                       # set up aliases
alias rm='rm -i'                       # always do interactive rm's
alias lt='ls -ltrh | tail'
alias h='history | tail'
alias ch='chmod 755 '

function switch() {                     # a function to exchange
    local tmp=$$switch                 # the names of two files
    mv "$1" $tmp
    mv "$2" "$1"
    mv $tmp "$2"
}
```

# *LPI* . (DOT) OR source: RUNS A STARTUP FILE IN THE CURRENT SHELL

After you edit a startup file such as **.bashrc**, you do not have to log out and log in again to put the changes into effect. Instead, you can run the startup file using the **.** (dot) or **source** builtin (they are the same command). As with other commands, the **.** must be followed by a SPACE on the command line. Using **.** or **source** is similar to running a shell script, except these commands run the script as part of the current process. Consequently, when you use **.** or **source** to run a script, changes you make to variables from within the script affect the shell you run the script from. If you ran a startup file as a regular shell script and did not use the . or source builtin, the variables created in the startup file would remain in effect only in the subshell running the script—not in the shell you ran the script from. You can use the . or source command to run any shell script—not just a startup file—but undesirable side effects (such as changes in the values of shell variables you rely on) might occur. For more information refer to "Environment, Environment Variables, and Inheritance" on page 1032.

In the following example, **.bashrc** sets several variables and sets **PS1**, the bash prompt, to the name of the host. The . builtin puts the new values into effect.

```
$ cat ~/.bashrc
export TERM=xterm               # set the terminal type
export PS1="$(hostname -f): "   # set the prompt string
export CDPATH=:$HOME            # add HOME to CDPATH string
stty kill '^u'                  # set kill line to control-u

$ . ~/.bashrc
guava:
```

# COMMANDS THAT ARE SYMBOLS

The Bourne Again Shell uses the symbols (, ), [, ], and $ in a variety of ways. To minimize confusion, Table 9-1 lists the most common use of each of these symbols and the page on which it is discussed.

**Table 9-1**    Builtin commands that are symbols

| Symbol | Command |
|--------|---------|
| ( ) | Subshell (page 344) |
| $( ) | Command substitution (page 410) |
| (( )) | Arithmetic evaluation; a synonym for let (use when the enclosed value contains an equal sign; page 1056) |
| $(( )) | Arithmetic expansion (not for use with an enclosed equal sign; page 408) |
| [ ] | The test command (pages 983 and 986) |
| [[ ]] | Conditional expression; similar to [ ] but adds string comparisons (page 1057) |

## *LPI*   REDIRECTING STANDARD ERROR

Chapter 5 covered the concept of standard output and explained how to redirect standard output of a command. In addition to standard output, commands can send output to *standard error*. A command might send error messages to standard error to keep them from getting mixed up with the information it sends to standard output.

Just as it does with standard output, by default the shell directs standard error to the screen. Unless you redirect one or the other, you might not know the difference between the output a command sends to standard output and the output it sends to standard error. One difference is that the system buffers standard output but does not buffer standard error. This section describes the syntax used by bash to redirect standard error and to distinguish between standard output and standard error.

File descriptors    A *file descriptor* is the place a program sends its output to and gets its input from. When you execute a program, the shell opens three file descriptors for the program: 0 (standard input), 1 (standard output), and 2 (standard error). The redirect output symbol (> [page 154]) is shorthand for 1>, which tells the shell to redirect standard output. Similarly < (page 155) is short for 0<, which redirects standard input. The symbols 2> redirect standard error. For more information refer to "File Descriptors" on page 1016.

The following examples demonstrate how to redirect standard output and standard error to different files and to the same file. When you run the cat utility with the name of a file that does not exist and the name of a file that does exist, cat sends an error message to standard error and copies the file that does exist to standard output. Unless you redirect them, both messages appear on the screen.

```
$ cat y
This is y.
$ cat x
cat: x: No such file or directory

$ cat x y
cat: x: No such file or directory
This is y.
```

When you redirect standard output of a command, output sent to standard error is not affected and still appears on the screen.

```
$ cat x y > hold
cat: x: No such file or directory
$ cat hold
This is y.
```

Similarly, when you send standard output through a pipeline, standard error is not affected. The following example sends standard output of cat through a pipeline to tr, which in this example converts lowercase characters to uppercase. (See the tr info page for more information.) The text that cat sends to standard error is not translated because it goes directly to the screen rather than through the pipeline.

```
$ cat x y | tr "[a-z]" "[A-Z]"
cat: x: No such file or directory
THIS IS Y.
```

The following example redirects standard output and standard error to different files. The shell redirects standard output (file descriptor 1) to the filename following 1>.

You can specify **>** in place of **1>**. The shell redirects standard error (file descriptor 2) to the filename following **2>**.

```
$ cat x y 1> hold1 2> hold2
$ cat hold1
This is y.
$ cat hold2
cat: x: No such file or directory
```

*Combining standard output and standard error* In the next example, the **&>** token redirects standard output and standard error to a single file:

```
$ cat x y &> hold
$ cat hold
cat: x: No such file or directory
This is y.
```

*Duplicating a file descriptor* In the next example, first **1>** redirects standard output to **hold**, and then **2>&1** declares file descriptor 2 to be a duplicate of file descriptor 1. As a result, both standard output and standard error are redirected to **hold**.

```
$ cat x y 1> hold 2>&1
$ cat hold
cat: x: No such file or directory
This is y.
```

In this case, **1> hold** precedes **2>&1**. If they had appeared in the opposite order, standard error would have been made a duplicate of standard output before standard output was redirected to **hold**. Only standard output would have been redirected to **hold** in that case.

*Sending errors through a pipeline* The next example declares file descriptor 2 to be a duplicate of file descriptor 1 and sends the output for file descriptor 1 (as well as file descriptor 2) through a pipeline to the tr command.

```
$ cat x y 2>&1 | tr "[a-z]" "[A-Z]"
CAT: X: NO SUCH FILE OR DIRECTORY
THIS IS Y.
```

The token **|&** is shorthand for **2>&1 |**:

```
$ cat x y |& tr "[a-z]" "[A-Z]"
CAT: X: NO SUCH FILE OR DIRECTORY
THIS IS Y.
```

*Sending errors to standard error* You can use **1>&2** (or simply **>&2**; the **1** is not required) to redirect standard output of a command to standard error. Shell scripts use this technique to send the output of echo to standard error. In the following script, standard output of the first echo is redirected to standard error:

```
$ cat message_demo
echo This is an error message. 1>&2
echo This is not an error message.
```

If you redirect standard output of **message_demo**, error messages such as the one produced by the first echo appear on the screen because you have not redirected standard error. Because standard output of a shell script is frequently redirected to a file, you can use this technique to display on the screen any error messages generated by the script. The **lnks** script (page 991) uses this technique. You can use the exec builtin to create additional file descriptors and to redirect standard input, standard output, and standard error of a shell script from within the script (page 1046).

The Bourne Again Shell supports the redirection operators shown in Table 9-2.

**Table 9-2**   Redirection operators

| Operator | Meaning |
|----------|---------|
| < *filename* | Redirects standard input from *filename*. |
| > *filename* | Redirects standard output to *filename* unless *filename* exists and **noclobber** (page 156) is set. If **noclobber** is not set, this redirection creates *filename* if it does not exist and overwrites it if it does exist. |
| >! *filename* | Redirects standard output to *filename*, even if the file exists and **noclobber** (page 156) is set. |
| >> *filename* | Redirects and appends standard output to *filename;* creates *filename* if it does not exist. |
| &> *filename* | Redirects standard output and standard error to *filename*. |
| <&*m* | Duplicates standard input from file descriptor *m* (page 1017). |
| [n]>&*m* | Duplicates standard output or file descriptor *n* if specified from file descriptor *m* (page 1017). |
| [n]<&– | Closes standard input or file descriptor *n* if specified (page 1017). |
| [n]>&– | Closes standard output or file descriptor *n* if specified. |

# WRITING AND EXECUTING A SHELL SCRIPT

A *shell script* is a file that holds commands the shell can execute. The commands in a shell script can be any commands you can enter in response to a shell prompt. For example, a command in a shell script might run a utility, a compiled program, or another shell script. Like the commands you give on the command line, a command in a shell script can use ambiguous file references and can have its input or output redirected from or to a file or sent through a pipeline. You can also use pipelines and redirection with the input and output of the script itself.

In addition to the commands you would ordinarily use on the command line, *control flow* commands (also called *control structures*) find most of their use in shell scripts. This group of commands enables you to alter the order of execution of commands in a script in the same way you would alter the order of execution of statements using a structured programming language. Refer to "Control Structures" on page 982 for specifics.

```
$ ls -l whoson
-rw-rw-r--. 1 max pubs 40 05-24 11:30 whoson

$ chmod u+x whoson
$ ls -l whoson
-rwxrw-r--. 1 max pubs 40 05-24 11:30 whoson

$ ./whoson
Sat May 25 11:40:49 PDT 2013
Users Currently Logged In
zach     pts/7     2013-05-23 18:17
hls      pts/1     2013-05-24 09:59
sam      pts/12    2013-05-24 06:29 (guava)
max      pts/4     2013-05-24 09:08
```

**Figure 9-1**   Using chmod to make a shell script executable

The shell interprets and executes the commands in a shell script, one after another. Thus a shell script enables you to simply and quickly initiate a complex series of tasks or a repetitive procedure.

## chmod: MAKES A FILE EXECUTABLE

*LE+*

To execute a shell script by giving its name as a command, you must have permission to read and execute the file that contains the script (refer to "Access Permissions" on page 191). Read permission enables you to read the file that holds the script. Execute permission tells the system that the owner, group, and/or public has permission to execute the file; it implies the content of the file is executable.

When you create a shell script using an editor, the file does not typically have its execute permission set. The following example shows a file named **whoson** that contains a shell script:

```
$ cat whoson
date
echo "Users Currently Logged In"
who
$ ./whoson
bash: ./whoson: Permission denied
```

You cannot execute **whoson** by giving its name as a command because you do not have execute permission for the file. The system does not recognize **whoson** as an executable file and issues the error message **Permission denied** when you try to execute it. (See the tip on the next page if the shell issues a **command not found** error message.) When you give the filename as an argument to bash (**bash whoson**), bash assumes the argument is a shell script and executes it. In this case **bash** is executable, and **whoson** is an argument that bash executes, so you do not need execute permission to **whoson**. You must have read permission.

The chmod utility changes the access privileges associated with a file. Figure 9-1 shows ls with the –l option displaying the access privileges of **whoson** before and after chmod gives execute permission to the file's owner.

The first ls displays a hyphen (–) as the fourth character, indicating the owner does not have permission to execute the file. Next chmod gives the owner execute permission: **u+x** causes chmod to add (**+**) execute permission (**x**) for the owner (**u**). (The **u** stands for *user*, although it means the owner of the file.) The second argument is the name of the file. The second ls shows an **x** in the fourth position, indicating the owner has execute permission.

### Command not found?

tip   If you give the name of a shell script as a command without including the leading ./, the shell typically displays the following error message:

```
$ whoson
bash: whoson: command not found
```

This message indicates the shell is not set up to search for executable files in the working directory. Enter this command instead:

```
$ ./whoson
```

The ./ tells the shell explicitly to look for an executable file in the working directory. Although not recommended for security reasons, you can change the **PATH** variable so the shell searches the working directory automatically; see **PATH** on page 359.

If other users will execute the file, you must also change group and/or public access permissions for the file. Any user must have execute access to use the file's name as a command. If the file is a shell script, the user trying to execute the file must have read access to the file as well. You do not need read access to execute a binary executable (compiled program).

The final command in Figure 9-1 (prevous page) shows the shell executing the file when its name is given as a command. For more information refer to "Access Permissions" on page 191 as well as the discussions of ls (page 191) and chmod (page 193).

## *LPI* #! SPECIFIES A SHELL

You can put a special sequence of characters on the first line of a shell script to tell the operating system which shell (or other program) should execute the file and which options you want to include. Because the operating system checks the initial characters of a program before attempting to execute it using **exec**, these characters save the system from making an unsuccessful attempt. If #! (sometimes said out loud as *hashbang* or *shebang*) are the first two characters of a script, the system interprets the characters that follow as the absolute pathname of the program that is to execute the script. This pathname can point to any program, not just a shell, and can be useful if you have a script you want to run with a shell other than the shell you are running the script from. The following example specifies that bash should run the script:

```
$ cat bash_script
#!/bin/bash
echo "This is a Bourne Again Shell script."
```

## The bash −e and −u options can make your programs less fractious

tip  The bash **−e** (errexit) option causes bash to exit when a simple command (e.g., not a control structure) fails. The bash **−u** (nounset) option causes bash to display a message and exit when it tries to expand an unset variable. See Table 9-13 on page 401 for details. It is easy to turn these options on in the **#!** line of a bash script:

```
#!/bin/bash -eu
```

These options can prevent disaster when you mistype lines like this in a script:

```
MYDIR=/tmp/$$
cd $MYDIr; rm -rf .
```

During development, you can also specify the **−x** option in the **#!** line to turn on debugging (page 994).

The next example runs under Perl and can be run directly from the shell without explicitly calling Perl on the command line:

```
$ cat ./perl_script.pl
#!/usr/bin/perl -w
print "This is a Perl script.\n";

$ ./perl_script.pl
This is a Perl script.
```

The next example shows a script that should be executed by tcsh (**tcsh** package):

```
$ cat tcsh_script
#!/bin/tcsh
echo "This is a tcsh script."
set person = zach
echo "person is $person"
```

Because of the **#!** line, the operating system ensures that tcsh executes the script no matter which shell you run it from.

You can use **ps −f** within a shell script to display the name of the program that is executing the script. The three lines that ps displays in the following example show the process running the parent bash shell, the process running the tcsh script, and the process running the ps command:

```
$ cat tcsh_script2
#!/bin/tcsh
ps -f

$ ./tcsh_script2
UID         PID  PPID  C STIME TTY        TIME CMD
max        3031  3030  0 Nov16 pts/4   00:00:00 -bash
max        9358  3031  0 21:13 pts/4   00:00:00 /bin/tcsh ./tcsh_script2
max        9375  9358  0 21:13 pts/4   00:00:00 ps -f
```

If you do not follow #! with the name of an executable program, the shell reports it cannot find the program you asked it to run. You can optionally follow #! with SPACEs before the name of the program. If you omit the #! line and try to run, for example, a tcsh script from bash, the script will run under bash and might generate error messages or not run properly.

# # BEGINS A COMMENT

Comments make shell scripts and all code easier to read and maintain by you and others. If a hashmark (#) in the first character position of the first line of a script is not immediately followed by an exclamation point (!) or if a hashmark occurs in any other location in a script, the shell interprets it as the beginning of a comment. The shell then ignores everything between the hashmark and the end of the line (the next NEWLINE character).

# EXECUTING A SHELL SCRIPT

**fork** and **exec**
system calls
As discussed earlier, you can execute commands in a shell script file that you do not have execute permission for by using a bash command to **exec** a shell that runs the script directly. In the following example, bash creates a new shell that takes its input from the file named **whoson**:

```
$ bash whoson
```

Because the bash command expects to read a file containing commands, you do not need execute permission for **whoson**. (You do need read permission.) Even though bash reads and executes the commands in **whoson**, standard input, standard output, and standard error remain directed from/to the terminal. Alternately, you can supply commands to bash using standard input:

```
$ bash < whoson
```

Although you can use bash to execute a shell script, these techniques cause the script to run more slowly than if you give yourself execute permission and directly invoke the script. Users typically prefer to make the file executable and run the script by typing its name on the command line. It is also easier to type the name, and this practice is consistent with the way other kinds of programs are invoked (so you do not need to know whether you are running a shell script or an executable file). However, if bash is not your interactive shell or if you want to see how the script runs with different shells, you might want to run a script as an argument to **bash** or **tcsh**.

### sh does not call the original Bourne Shell

caution   The original Bourne Shell was invoked with the command **sh**. Although you can call bash with an **sh** command, it is not the original Bourne Shell. The **sh** command (**/bin/sh**) is a symbolic link to **/bin/bash**, so it is simply another name for the **bash** command. When you call bash using the command **sh**, bash tries to mimic the behavior of the original Bourne Shell as closely as possible—but it does not always succeed.

# CONTROL OPERATORS: SEPARATE AND GROUP COMMANDS

Whether you give the shell commands interactively or write a shell script, you must separate commands from one another. This section reviews the ways to separate commands that were covered in Chapter 5 and introduces a few new ones.

The tokens that separate, terminate, and group commands are called *control operators*. Each of the control operators implies line continuation as explained on page 1063. Following is a list of the control operators and the page each is discussed on.

- ; Command separator (below)
- NEWLINE Command initiator (below)
- & Background task (next page)
- | Pipeline (next page)
- |& Standard error pipeline (page 335)
- () Groups commands (page 344)
- || Boolean OR (page 343)
- && Boolean AND (page 343)
- ;; Case terminator (page 1006)

## *LE*   ; AND NEWLINE SEPARATE COMMANDS

The NEWLINE character is a unique control operator because it initiates execution of the command preceding it. You have seen this behavior throughout this book each time you press the RETURN key at the end of a command line.

The semicolon (;) is a control operator that *does not* initiate execution of a command and *does not* change any aspect of how the command functions. You can execute a series of commands sequentially by entering them on a single command line and separating each from the next using a semicolon (;). You initiate execution of the sequence of commands by pressing RETURN:

```
$ x ; y ; z
```

If **x**, **y**, and **z** are commands, the preceding command line yields the same results as the next three commands. The difference is that in the next example the shell issues a prompt after each of the commands finishes executing, whereas the preceding command line causes the shell to issue a prompt only after **z** is complete:

```
$ x
$ y
$ z
```

**Whitespace**    Although the whitespace (SPACES and/or TABS) around the semicolons in the previous example makes the command line easier to read, it is not necessary. None of the control operators needs to be surrounded by whitespace.

# | AND & SEPARATE COMMANDS AND DO SOMETHING ELSE

The pipeline symbol (|) and the background task symbol (&) are also control operators. They *do not* start execution of a command but *do* change some aspect of how the command functions. The pipeline symbol alters the source of standard input or the destination of standard output. The background task symbol causes the shell to execute the task in the background and display a prompt immediately so you can continue working on other tasks.

Each of the following command lines initiates a pipeline (page 158) comprising three simple commands:

```
$ x | y | z
$ ls -l | grep tmp | less
```

In the first pipeline, the shell redirects standard output of **x** to standard input of **y** and redirects **y**'s standard output to **z**'s standard input. Because it runs the entire pipeline in the foreground, the shell does not display a prompt until task **z** runs to completion: **z** does not finish until **y** finishes, and **y** does not finish until **x** finishes. In the second pipeline, **x** is an **ls –l** command, **y** is **grep tmp**, and **z** is the pager **less**. The shell displays a long (wide) listing of the files in the working directory that contain the string **tmp**, sent via a pipeline through **less**.

The next command line executes a list (page 162) running the simple commands **d** and **e** in the background and the simple command **f** in the foreground:

```
$ d & e & f
[1] 14271
[2] 14272
```

The shell displays the job number between brackets and the PID number for each process running in the background. It displays a prompt as soon as **f** finishes, which might be before **d** or **e** finishes.

Before displaying a prompt for a new command, the shell checks whether any background jobs have completed. For each completed job, the shell displays its job number, the word **Done**, and the command line that invoked the job; the shell then displays a prompt. When the job numbers are listed, the number of the last job started is followed by a **+** character, and the job number of the previous job is followed by a **–** character. Other job numbers are followed by a SPACE character. After running the last command, the shell displays the following lines before issuing a prompt:

```
[1]-  Done                    d
[2]+  Done                    e
```

The next command line executes a list that runs three commands as background jobs. The shell displays a shell prompt immediately:

```
$ d & e & f &
[1] 14290
[2] 14291
[3] 14292
```

The next example uses a pipeline symbol to send the output from one command to the next command and an ampersand (&) to run the entire pipeline in the background. Again the shell displays the prompt immediately. The shell commands that are part of a pipeline form a single job. That is, the shell treats a pipeline as a single job, no matter how many commands are connected using pipeline (|) symbols or how complex they are. The Bourne Again Shell reports only one process in the background (although there are three):

```
$ d | e | f &
[1] 14295
```

## *LE*    && AND || BOOLEAN CONTROL OPERATORS

The && (AND) and || (OR) Boolean operators are called *short-circuiting* control operators. If the result of using one of these operators can be decided by looking only at the left operand, the right operand is not evaluated. The result of a Boolean operation is either 0 (*true*) or 1 (*false*).

**&&**   The && operator causes the shell to test the exit status of the command preceding it. If the command succeeds, bash executes the next command; otherwise, it skips the next command. You can use this construct to execute commands conditionally.

```
$ mkdir bkup && cp -r src bkup
```

This compound command creates the directory **bkup**. If mkdir succeeds, the content of directory **src** is copied recursively to **bkup**.

**||**   The || control operator also causes bash to test the exit status of the first command but has the opposite effect: The remaining command(s) are executed only if the first command failed (that is, exited with nonzero status).

```
$ mkdir bkup || echo "mkdir of bkup failed" >> /tmp/log
```

The exit status of a command list is the exit status of the last command in the list. You can group lists with parentheses. For example, you could combine the previous two examples as

```
$ (mkdir bkup && cp -r src bkup) || echo "mkdir failed" >> /tmp/log
```

In the absence of parentheses, && and || have equal precedence and are grouped from left to right. The following examples use the true and false utilities. These utilities do nothing and return *true* (0) and *false* (1) exit statuses, respectively:

```
$ false; echo $?
1
```

The $? variable holds the exit status of the preceding command (page 1029). The next two commands yield an exit status of 1 (*false*):

```
$ true || false && false
$ echo $?
1
$ (true || false) && false
$ echo $?
1
```

Similarly the next two commands yield an exit status of 0 (*true*):

```
$ false && false || true
$ echo $?
0
$ (false && false) || true
$ echo $?
0
```

See "Lists" on page 162 for more examples.

**optional**

# ( ) GROUPS COMMANDS

You can use the parentheses control operator to group commands. When you use this technique, the shell creates a copy of itself, called a *subshell,* for each group. It treats each group of commands as a list and creates a new process to execute each command (refer to "Process Structure" on page 373 for more information on creating subshells). Each subshell has its own environment, meaning it has its own set of variables whose values can differ from those in other subshells.

The following command line executes commands **a** and **b** sequentially in the background while executing **c** in the background. The shell displays a prompt immediately.

```
$ (a ; b) & c &
[1] 15520
[2] 15521
```

The preceding example differs from the earlier example **d & e & f &** in that tasks **a** and **b** are initiated sequentially, not concurrently.

Similarly the following command line executes **a** and **b** sequentially in the background and, at the same time, executes **c** and **d** sequentially in the background. The subshell running **a** and **b** and the subshell running **c** and **d** run concurrently. The shell displays a prompt immediately.

```
$ (a ; b) & (c ; d) &
[1] 15528
[2] 15529
```

The next script copies one directory to another. The second pair of parentheses creates a subshell to run the commands following the pipeline symbol. Because of these parentheses, the output of the first tar command is available for the second tar command, despite the intervening cd command. Without the parentheses, the output of the first tar command would be sent to cd and lost because cd does not process standard input. The shell variables **$1** and **$2** hold the first and second command-line arguments (page 1023), respectively. The first pair of parentheses, which creates a subshell to run the first two commands, allows users to call **cpdir** with relative pathnames. Without them, the first cd command would change the working directory of the script (and consequently the working directory of the second cd command). With them, only the working directory of the subshell is changed.

```
$ cat cpdir
(cd $1 ; tar -cf - . ) | (cd $2 ; tar -xvf - )
$ ./cpdir /home/max/sources /home/max/memo/biblio
```

The **cpdir** command line copies the files and directories in the **/home/max/sources** directory to the directory named **/home/max/memo/biblio**. Running this shell script is the same as using **cp** with the **–r** option. Refer to the **cp** man page for more information.

# \ CONTINUES A COMMAND

Although it is not a control operator, you can use a backslash (\) character in the middle of commands. When you enter a long command line and the cursor reaches the right side of the screen, you can use a backslash to continue the command on the next line. The backslash quotes, or escapes, the NEWLINE character that follows it so the shell does not treat the NEWLINE as a control operator. Enclosing a backslash within single quotation marks or preceding it with another backslash turns off the power of a backslash to quote special characters such as NEWLINE. Enclosing a backslash within double quotation marks has no effect on the power of the backslash.

Although you can break a line in the middle of a word (token), it is typically simpler, and makes code easier to read, if you break a line immediately before or after whitespace.

**optional**   You can enter a RETURN in the middle of a quoted string on a command line without using a backslash. The NEWLINE (RETURN) you enter will then be part of the string:

```
$ echo "Please enter the three values
> required to complete the transaction."
Please enter the three values
required to complete the transaction.
```

In the three examples in this section, the shell does not interpret RETURN as a control operator because it occurs within a quoted string. The greater than sign (**>**) is a secondary prompt (**PS2**; page 362) indicating the shell is waiting for you to continue the unfinished command. In the next example, the first RETURN is quoted (escaped) so the shell treats it as a separator and does not interpret it literally.

```
$ echo "Please enter the three values \
> required to complete the transaction."
Please enter the three values required to complete the transaction.
```

Single quotation marks cause the shell to interpret a backslash literally:

```
$ echo 'Please enter the three values \
> required to complete the transaction.'
Please enter the three values \
required to complete the transaction.
```

# JOB CONTROL

As explained on page 163, a *job* is another name for a process running a pipeline (which can be a simple command). You run one or more jobs whenever you give the shell a command. For example, if you type **date** on the command line and press RETURN, you have run a job. You can also create several jobs on a single command line by entering several simple commands separated by control operators (& in the following example):

```
$ find . -print | sort | lpr & grep -l max /tmp/* > maxfiles &
[1] 18839
[2] 18876
```

The portion of the command line up to the first & is one job—a pipeline comprising three simple commands connected by pipeline symbols: find, sort, and lpr. The second job is a pipeline that is a simple command (grep). The & characters following each pipeline put each job in the background, so bash does not wait for them to complete before displaying a prompt.

Using job control you can move jobs from the foreground to the background, and vice versa; temporarily stop jobs; and list jobs that are running in the background or stopped.

## *LPI* jobs: LISTS JOBS

The jobs builtin lists all background jobs. In the following example, the sleep command runs in the background and creates a background job that the jobs builtin reports on:

```
$ sleep 60 &
[1] 7809
$ jobs
[1] + Running                    sleep 60 &
```

## *LPI*   fg: BRINGS A JOB TO THE FOREGROUND

The shell assigns a job number to each job you run in the background. For each job run in the background, the shell lists the job number and PID number immediately, just before it issues a prompt:

```
$ gnome-calculator &
[1] 1246
$ date &
[2] 1247
$ Sat Dec 7 11:44:40 PST 2013
[2]+ Done          date
$ find /usr -name ace -print > findout &
[2] 1269
$ jobs
[1]- Running          gnome-calculator &
[2]+ Running          find /usr -name ace -print > findout &
```

The shell discards job numbers when a job is finished and reuses discarded job numbers. When you start or put a job in the background, the shell assigns a job number that is one more than the highest job number in use.

In the preceding example, the jobs command lists the first job, gnome-calculator, as job 1. The date command does not appear in the jobs list because it finished before jobs was run. Because the date command was completed before find was run, the find command became job 2.

To move a background job to the foreground, use the fg builtin followed by the job number. Alternately, you can give a percent sign (%) followed by the job number as a command. Either of the following commands moves job 2 to the foreground. When you move a job to the foreground, the shell displays the command it is now executing in the foreground.

```
$ fg 2
find /usr -name ace -print > findout
```

*or*

```
$ %2
find /usr -name ace -print > findout
```

You can also refer to a job by following the percent sign with a string that uniquely identifies the beginning of the command line used to start the job. Instead of the preceding command, you could have used either **fg %find** or **fg %f** because both uniquely identify job 2. If you follow the percent sign with a question mark and a string, the string can match any part of the command line. In the preceding example, **fg %?ace** would also bring job 2 to the foreground.

Often the job you wish to bring to the foreground is the only job running in the background or is the job that jobs lists with a plus (+). In these cases, calling fg without an argument brings the job to the foreground.

## SUSPENDING A JOB

Pressing the suspend key (usually CONTROL-Z) immediately suspends (temporarily stops) the job in the foreground and displays a message that includes the word **Stopped**.

```
CONTROL-Z
[2]+  Stopped                          find /usr -name ace -print > findout
```

For more information refer to "Moving a Job from the Foreground to the Background" on page 164.

## *LPI*   bg: SENDS A JOB TO THE BACKGROUND

To move the foreground job to the background, you must first suspend the job (above). You can then use the bg builtin to resume execution of the job in the background.

```
$ bg
[2]+ find /usr -name ace -print > findout &
```

If a background job attempts to read from the terminal, the shell stops the job and displays a message saying the job has been stopped. You must then move the job to the foreground so it can read from the terminal.

```
$ (sleep 5; cat > mytext) &
[1] 1343
$ date
Sat Dec  7 11:58:20 PST 2013
[1]+ Stopped                     ( sleep 5; cat >mytext )
$ fg
( sleep 5; cat >mytext )
Remember to let the cat out!
CONTROL-D
$
```

In the preceding example, the shell displays the job number and PID number of the background job as soon as it starts, followed by a prompt. Demonstrating that you can give a command at this point, the user gives the command date, and its output appears on the screen. The shell waits until just before it issues a prompt (after date has finished) to notify you that job 1 is stopped. When you give an **fg** command, the shell puts the job in the foreground, and you can enter the data the command is waiting for. In this case the input needs to be terminated using CONTROL-D, which sends an EOF (end of file) signal to cat. The shell then displays another prompt.

The shell keeps you informed about changes in the status of a job, notifying you when a background job starts, completes, or stops, perhaps because it is waiting for input from the terminal. The shell also lets you know when a foreground job is

**Figure 9-2**   The directory structure used in the examples

suspended. Because notices about a job being run in the background can disrupt your work, the shell delays displaying these notices until just before it displays a prompt. You can set **notify** (page 402) to cause the shell to display these notices without delay.

If you try to exit from a nonlogin shell while jobs are stopped, the shell issues a warning and does not allow you to exit. If you then use jobs to review the list of jobs or you immediately try to exit from the shell again, the shell allows you to exit. If **huponexit** (page 402) is not set (it is not set by default), stopped jobs remain stopped and background jobs keep running in the background. If it is set, the shell terminates these jobs.

# MANIPULATING THE DIRECTORY STACK

The Bourne Again Shell allows you to store a list of directories you are working with, enabling you to move easily among them. This list is referred to as a *stack*. It is analogous to a stack of dinner plates: You typically add plates to and remove plates from the top of the stack, so this type of stack is named a LIFO (last in, first out) stack.

## dirs: DISPLAYS THE STACK

The dirs builtin displays the contents of the directory stack. If you call dirs when the directory stack is empty, it displays the name of the working directory:

```
$ dirs
~/literature
```

The dirs builtin uses a tilde (~) to represent the name of a user's home directory. The examples in the next several sections assume you are referring to the directory structure shown in Figure 9-2.

**Figure 9-3**    Creating a directory stack

## pushd: PUSHES A DIRECTORY ON THE STACK

When you supply the pushd (push directory) builtin with one argument, it pushes the directory specified by the argument on the stack, changes directories to the specified directory, and displays the stack. The following example is illustrated in Figure 9-3:

```
$ pushd ../demo
~/demo ~/literature
$ pwd
/home/sam/demo
$ pushd ../names
~/names ~/demo ~/literature
$ pwd
/home/sam/names
```

When you call pushd without an argument, it swaps the top two directories on the stack, makes the new top directory (which was the second directory) the new working directory, and displays the stack (Figure 9-4).

```
$ pushd
~/demo ~/names ~/literature
$ pwd
/home/sam/demo
```

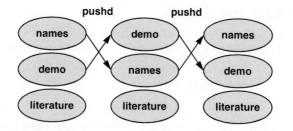

**Figure 9-4**    Using pushd to change working directories

**Figure 9-5**   Using popd to remove a directory from the stack

Using pushd in this way, you can easily move back and forth between two directories. You can also use **cd –** to change to the previous directory, whether or not you have explicitly created a directory stack. To access another directory in the stack, call pushd with a numeric argument preceded by a plus sign. The directories in the stack are numbered starting with the top directory, which is number 0. The following pushd command continues with the previous example, changing the working directory to **literature** and moving **literature** to the top of the stack:

```
$ pushd +2
~/literature ~/demo ~/names
$ pwd
/home/sam/literature
```

## popd: **POPS A DIRECTORY OFF THE STACK**

To remove a directory from the stack, use the popd (pop directory) builtin. As the following example and Figure 9-5 show, without an argument, popd removes the top directory from the stack and changes the working directory to the new top directory:

```
$ dirs
~/literature ~/demo ~/names
$ popd
~/demo ~/names
$ pwd
/home/sam/demo
```

To remove a directory other than the top one from the stack, use popd with a numeric argument preceded by a plus sign. The following example removes directory number 1, **demo**. Removing a directory other than directory number 0 does not change the working directory.

```
$ dirs
~/literature ~/demo ~/names
$ popd +1
~/literature ~/names
```

## LE+    PARAMETERS AND VARIABLES

**Shell parameter**  Within a shell, a *shell parameter* is associated with a value you or a shell script can access. This section introduces the following kinds of shell parameters: user-created variables, keyword variables, positional parameters, and special parameters.

**Variables**  Parameters whose names consist of letters, digits, and underscores are referred to as *variables*. A variable name must start with a letter or underscore, not with a number. Thus **A76**, **MY_CAT**, and **___X___** are valid variable names, whereas **69TH_STREET** (starts with a digit) and **MY-NAME** (contains a hyphen) are not.

**User-created variables**  Variables that you name and assign values to are *user-created variables*. You can change the values of user-created variables at any time, or you can make them *readonly* so that their values cannot be changed.

**Shell variables and environment variables**  By default, a variable is available only in the shell it was created in (i.e., local); this type of variable is called a *shell variable*. You can use export to make a variable available in shells spawned from the shell it was created in (i.e., global); this type of variable is called an *environment variable*. One naming convention is to use mixed-case or lowercase letters for shell variables and only uppercase letters for environment variables. Refer to "Variables" on page 1031 for more information on shell variables and environment variables.

To declare and initialize a variable in bash, use the following syntax:

*VARIABLE=value*

There can be no whitespace on either side of the equal sign (=). An example follows:

```
$ myvar=abc
```

**Declaring and initializing a variable for a script**  The Bourne Again Shell permits you to put variable assignments at the beginning of a command line. This type of assignment places variables in the environment of the command shell—that is, the variable is accessible only from the program (and the children of the program) the command runs. It is not available from the shell running the command. The **my_script** shell script displays the value of **TEMPDIR**. The following command runs **my_script** with **TEMPDIR** set to **/home/sam/temp**. The echo builtin shows that the interactive shell has no value for **TEMPDIR** after running **my_script**. If **TEMPDIR** had been set in the interactive shell, running **my_script** in this manner would have had no effect on its value.

```
$ cat my_script
echo $TEMPDIR
$ TEMPDIR=/home/sam/temp ./my_script
/home/sam/temp
$ echo $TEMPDIR

$
```

*LPI* Keyword variables *Keyword variables* have special meaning to the shell and usually have short, mnemonic names. When you start a shell (by logging in, for example), the shell inherits several keyword variables from the environment. Among these variables are **HOME**, which identifies your home directory, and **PATH**, which determines which directories the shell searches and in which order to locate commands you give the shell. The shell creates and initializes (with default values) other keyword variables when you start it. Still other variables do not exist until you set them.

You can change the values of most keyword shell variables. It is usually not necessary to change the values of keyword variables initialized in the **/etc/profile** or **/etc/csh.cshrc** systemwide startup files. If you need to change the value of a bash keyword variable, do so in one of your startup files (page 329). Just as you can make user-created variables environment variables, so you can make keyword variables environment variables—a task usually done automatically in startup files. You can also make a keyword variable readonly. See page 358 for a discussion of keyword variables.

Positional and special parameters The names of positional and special parameters do not resemble variable names. Most of these parameters have one-character names (for example, **1**, **?**, and **#**) and are referenced (as are all variables) by preceding the name with a dollar sign (**$1**, **$?**, and **$#**). The values of these parameters reflect different aspects of your ongoing interaction with the shell.

Whenever you run a command, each argument on the command line becomes the value of a *positional parameter* (page 1022). Positional parameters enable you to access command-line arguments, a capability you will often require when you write shell scripts. The set builtin (page 1024) enables you to assign values to positional parameters.

Other frequently needed shell script values, such as the name of the last command executed, the number of positional parameters, and the status of the most recently executed command, are available as *special parameters* (page 1027). You cannot assign values to special parameters.

## USER-CREATED VARIABLES

The first line in the following example declares the variable named **person** and initializes it with the value **max**:

```
$ person=max
$ echo person
person
$ echo $person
max
```

Parameter substitution Because the echo builtin copies its arguments to standard output, you can use it to display the values of variables. The second line of the preceding example shows that **person** does not represent **max**. Instead, the string **person** is echoed as **person**. The shell substitutes the value of a variable only when you precede the name of the variable with a dollar sign (**$**). Thus the command echo **$person** displays the value of the variable

**person**; it does not display **$person** because the shell does not pass **$person** to echo as an argument. Because of the leading **$**, the shell recognizes that **$person** is the name of a variable, *substitutes* the value of the variable, and passes that value to echo. The echo builtin displays the value of the variable (not its name), never "knowing" you called it with the name of a variable.

**LE**  Quoting the **$**    You can prevent the shell from substituting the value of a variable by quoting the leading **$**. Double quotation marks do not prevent the substitution; single quotation marks or a backslash (\) do.

```
$ echo $person
max
$ echo "$person"
max
$ echo '$person'
$person
$ echo \$person
$person
```

SPACES    Because they do not prevent variable substitution but do turn off the special meanings of most other characters, double quotation marks are useful when you assign values to variables and when you use those values. To assign a value that contains SPACEs or TABs to a variable, use double quotation marks around the value. Although double quotation marks are not required in all cases, using them is a good habit.

```
$ person="max and zach"
$ echo $person
max and zach
$ person=max and zach
bash: and: command not found
```

When you reference a variable whose value contains TABs or multiple adjacent SPACEs, you must use quotation marks to preserve the spacing. If you do not quote the variable, the shell collapses each string of blank characters into a single SPACE before passing the variable to the utility:

```
$ person="max    and    zach"
$ echo $person
max and zach
$ echo "$person"
max    and    zach
```

Pathname expansion in assignments    When you execute a command with a variable as an argument, the shell replaces the name of the variable with the value of the variable and passes that value to the program being executed. If the value of the variable contains a special character, such as * or ?, the shell *might* expand that variable.

The first line in the following sequence of commands assigns the string **max*** to the variable **memo**. All shells interpret special characters as special when you reference a variable that contains an unquoted special character. In the following example, the shell expands the value of the **memo** variable because it is not quoted:

```
$ memo=max*
$ ls
max.report
max.summary
$ echo $memo
max.report max.summary
```

Above, the shell expands the **$memo** variable to **max\***, expands **max\*** to **max.report** and **max.summary**, and passes these two values to echo. In the next example, the Bourne Again Shell *does not expand the string* because bash does not perform pathname expansion (page 165) when it assigns a value to a variable.

```
$ echo "$memo"
max*
```

All shells process a command line in a specific order. Within this order bash expands variables before it interprets commands. In the preceding echo command line, the double quotation marks quote the asterisk (\*) in the expanded value of **$memo** and prevent bash from performing pathname expansion on the expanded **memo** variable before passing its value to the echo command.

**optional**

Braces around variables

The *$VARIABLE* syntax is a special case of the more general syntax *${VARIABLE}*, in which the variable name is enclosed by ${}. The braces insulate the variable name from adjacent characters. Braces are necessary when catenating a variable value with a string:

```
$ PREF=counter
$ WAY=$PREFclockwise
$ FAKE=$PREFfeit
$ echo $WAY $FAKE

$
```

The preceding example does not work as expected. Only a blank line is output because although **PREFclockwise** and **PREFfeit** are valid variable names, they are not initialized. By default bash evaluates an unset variable as an empty (null) string and displays this value. To achieve the intent of these statements, refer to the **PREF** variable using braces:

```
$ PREF=counter
$ WAY=${PREF}clockwise
$ FAKE=${PREF}feit
$ echo $WAY $FAKE
counterclockwise counterfeit
```

The Bourne Again Shell refers to command-line arguments using the positional parameters **$1**, **$2**, **$3**, and so forth up to **$9**. You must use braces to refer to arguments past the ninth argument: **${10}**. The name of the command is held in **$0** (page 1022).

### *LPI* unset: REMOVES A VARIABLE

Unless you remove a variable, it exists as long as the shell in which it was created exists. To remove the *value* of a variable but not the variable itself, assign a null value to the variable. In the following example, set (page 1024) displays a list of all variables and their values; grep extracts the line that shows the value of person.

```
$ echo $person
zach
$ person=
$ echo $person

$ set | grep person
person=
```

You can remove a variable using the unset builtin. The following command removes the variable **person**:

```
$ unset person
$ echo $person

$ set | grep person
$
```

## VARIABLE ATTRIBUTES

This section discusses attributes and explains how to assign attributes to variables.

### readonly: MAKES THE VALUE OF A VARIABLE PERMANENT

You can use the readonly builtin to ensure the value of a variable cannot be changed. The next example declares the variable **person** to be readonly. You must assign a value to a variable *before* you declare it to be readonly; you cannot change its value after the declaration. When you attempt to change the value of or unset a readonly variable, the shell displays an error message:

```
$ person=zach
$ echo $person
zach
$ readonly person
$ person=helen
bash: person: readonly variable
$ unset person
bash: unset: person: cannot unset: readonly variable
```

If you use the readonly builtin without an argument, it displays a list of all readonly shell variables. This list includes keyword variables that are automatically set as readonly as well as keyword or user-created variables that you have declared as readonly. See the next page for an example (**readonly** and **declare –r** produce the same output).

## _LPI_ declare: LISTS AND ASSIGNS ATTRIBUTES TO VARIABLES

The declare builtin lists and sets attributes and values for shell variables. The typeset builtin (another name for declare) performs the same function but is deprecated. Table 9-3 lists five of these attributes.

**Table 9-3**  Variable attributes (declare)

| Attribute | Meaning |
|-----------|---------|
| −a | Declares a variable as an array (page 1038) |
| −f | Declares a variable to be a function name (page 396) |
| −i | Declares a variable to be of type integer (page 358) |
| −r | Makes a variable readonly; also readonly (previous page) |
| −x | Makes a variable an environment variable; also export (page 1032) |

The following commands declare several variables and set some attributes. The first line declares **person1** and initializes it to **max**. This command has the same effect with or without the word **declare**.

```
$ declare person1=max
$ declare -r person2=zach
$ declare -rx person3=helen
$ declare -x person4
```

_LPI_ readonly and export  The readonly and export builtins are synonyms for the commands **declare −r** and **declare −x**, respectively. You can declare a variable without initializing it, as the preceding declaration of the variable **person4** illustrates. This declaration makes **person4** an environment variable so it is available to all subshells. Until **person4** is initialized, it has a null value.

You can list the options to declare separately in any order. The following is equivalent to the preceding declaration of **person3**:

```
$ declare -x -r person3=helen
```

Use the + character in place of − when you want to remove an attribute from a variable. You cannot remove the readonly attribute. After the following command is given, the variable **person3** is no longer exported, but it is still readonly:

```
$ declare +x person3
```

See page 1032 for more information on exporting variables.

Listing variable attributes  Without any arguments or options, declare lists all shell variables. The same list is output when you run set (page 1025) without any arguments.

If you call declare with options but no variable names, the command lists all shell variables that have the specified attributes set. For example, the command **declare −r** displays a list of all readonly variables. This list is the same as that produced by the

**readonly** command without any arguments. After the declarations in the preceding example have been given, the results are as follows:

```
$ declare -r
declare -r BASHOPTS="checkwinsize:cmdhist:expand_aliases: ... "
declare -ir BASHPID
declare -ar BASH_VERSINFO='([0]="4" [1]="2" [2]="24" [3]="1" ... '
declare -ir EUID="500"
declare -ir PPID="1936"
declare -r SHELLOPTS="braceexpand:emacs:hashall:histexpand: ... "
declare -ir UID="500"
declare -r person2="zach"
declare -rx person3="helen"
```

The first seven entries are keyword variables that are automatically declared as readonly. Some of these variables are stored as integers (**–i**). The **–a** option indicates that **BASH_VERSINFO** is an array variable; the value of each element of the array is listed to the right of an equal sign.

Integer    By default, the values of variables are stored as strings. When you perform arithmetic on a string variable, the shell converts the variable into a number, manipulates it, and then converts it back to a string. A variable with the integer attribute is stored as an integer. Assign the integer attribute as follows:

```
$ declare -i COUNT
```

You can use declare to display integer variables:

```
$ declare -i
declare -ir BASHPID
declare -i COUNT
declare -ir EUID="1000"
declare -i HISTCMD
declare -i LINENO
declare -i MAILCHECK="60"
declare -i OPTIND="1"
...
```

## LPI  KEYWORD VARIABLES

Keyword variables are either inherited or declared and initialized by the shell when it starts. You can assign values to these variables from the command line or from a startup file. Typically these variables are environment variables (exported) so they are available to subshells you start as well as your login shell.

### HOME: YOUR HOME DIRECTORY

By default, your home directory is the working directory when you log in. Your home directory is established when your account is set up; its name is stored in the **/etc/passwd** file.

```
$ grep sam /etc/passwd
sam:x:500:500:Sam the Great:/home/sam:/bin/bash
```

When you log in, the shell inherits the pathname of your home directory and assigns it to the environment variable **HOME**. When you give a **cd** command without an argument, **cd** makes the directory whose name is stored in **HOME** the working directory:

```
$ pwd
/home/max/laptop
$ echo $HOME
/home/max
$ cd
$ pwd
/home/max
```

This example shows the value of the **HOME** variable and the effect of the **cd** builtin. After you execute **cd** without an argument, the pathname of the working directory is the same as the value of **HOME**: your home directory.

**LE** Tilde (~)    The shell uses the value of **HOME** to expand pathnames that use the shorthand tilde (~) notation (page 182) to denote a user's home directory. The following example uses echo to display the value of this shortcut and then uses ls to list the files in Max's **laptop** directory, which is a subdirectory of his home directory.

```
$ echo ~
/home/max
$ ls ~/laptop
tester        count        lineup
```

## **LE** PATH: WHERE THE SHELL LOOKS FOR PROGRAMS

When you give the shell an absolute or relative pathname as a command, it looks in the specified directory for an executable file with the specified filename. If the file with the pathname you specified does not exist, the shell reports **No such file or directory**. If the file exists as specified but you do not have execute permission for it, or in the case of a shell script you do not have read and execute permission for it, the shell reports **Permission denied**.

When you give a simple filename as a command, the shell searches through certain directories (your search path) for the program you want to execute. It looks in several directories for a file that has the same name as the command and that you have execute permission for (a compiled program) or read and execute permission for (a shell script). The **PATH** variable controls this search.

The default value of **PATH** is determined when bash is compiled. It is not set in a startup file, although it might be modified there. Normally the default specifies that the shell search several system directories used to hold common commands. These system directories include **/usr/bin** and **/usr/sbin** and other directories appropriate to the local system. When you give a command, if the shell does not find the executable—and, in the case of a shell script, readable—file named by the command in any of the directories listed in **PATH**, the shell generates one of the aforementioned error messages.

Working directory    The **PATH** variable specifies the directories in the order the shell should search them. Each directory must be separated from the next by a colon. The following command sets **PATH** so a search for an executable file starts with the **/usr/local/bin** directory. If it does not find the file in this directory, the shell looks next in **/usr/bin**. If the search fails in those directories, the shell looks in the **~/bin** directory, a subdirectory of the user's home directory. Finally the shell looks in the working directory. Exporting **PATH** makes sure it is an environment variable so it is available to subshells, although it is typically exported when it is declared so exporting it again is not necessary:

```
$ export PATH=/usr/local/bin:/usr/bin:~/bin:
```

A null value in the string indicates the working directory. In the preceding example, a null value (nothing between the colon and the end of the line) appears as the last element of the string. The working directory is represented by a leading colon (not recommended; see the following security tip), a trailing colon (as in the example), or two colons next to each other anywhere in the string. You can also represent the working directory explicitly using a period (.).

Because Linux stores many executable files in directories named **bin** (*binary*), users typically put their executable files in their own **~/bin** directories. If you put your own **bin** directory toward the end of **PATH**, as in the preceding example, the shell looks there for any commands it cannot find in directories listed earlier in **PATH**.

If you want to add directories to **PATH**, you can reference the old value of the **PATH** variable in setting **PATH** to a new value (but see the following security tip). The following command adds **/usr/local/bin** to the beginning of the current **PATH** and the **bin** directory in the user's home directory (**~/bin**) to the end:

```
$ PATH=/usr/local/bin:$PATH:~/bin
```

Set **PATH** in **~/.bash_profile**; see the tip on page 331.

### PATH and security

security    Do not put the working directory first in **PATH** when security is a concern. If you are working as **root**, you should *never* put the working directory first in **PATH**. It is common for **root**'s **PATH** to omit the working directory entirely. You can always execute a file in the working directory by prepending **./** to the name: **./myprog**.

Putting the working directory first in **PATH** can create a security hole. Most people type **ls** as the first command when entering a directory. If the owner of a directory places an executable file named **ls** in the directory, and the working directory appears first in a user's **PATH**, the user giving an **ls** command from the directory executes the **ls** program in the working directory instead of the system **ls** utility, possibly with undesirable results.

## MAIL: WHERE YOUR MAIL IS KEPT

The **MAIL** variable usually contains the pathname of the file that holds your mail (your *mailbox*, usually **/var/mail/***name*, where *name* is your username). However, you can use **MAIL** to watch any file (including a directory): Set **MAIL** to the name of the file you want to watch.

If **MAIL** is set and **MAILPATH** (below) is not set, the shell informs you when the file specified by **MAIL** is modified (such as when mail arrives). In a graphical environment you can unset **MAIL** so the shell does not display mail reminders in a terminal emulator window (assuming you are using a graphical mail program).

The **MAILPATH** variable contains a list of filenames separated by colons. If this variable is set, the shell informs you when any one of the files is modified (for example, when mail arrives). You can follow any of the filenames in the list with a question mark (**?**) and a message. The message replaces the **you have mail** message when you receive mail while you are logged in.

The **MAILCHECK** variable specifies how often, in seconds, the shell checks the directories specified by **MAIL** or **MAILPATH**. The default is 60 seconds. If you set this variable to zero, the shell checks before it issues each prompt.

## PS1: USER PROMPT (PRIMARY)

The default Bourne Again Shell prompt is a dollar sign (**$**). When you run bash with **root** privileges, bash typically displays a hashmark (**#**) prompt. The **PS1** variable holds the prompt string the shell uses to let you know it is waiting for a command. When you change the value of **PS1**, you change the appearance of your prompt.

You can customize the prompt displayed by **PS1**. For example, the assignment

```
$ PS1="[\u@\h \W \!]$ "
```

displays the following prompt:

*[user@host directory event]$*

where *user* is the username, *host* is the hostname up to the first period, *directory* is the basename of the working directory, and *event* is the event number (page 377) of the current command.

If you are working on more than one system, it can be helpful to incorporate the system name into your prompt. The first example that follows changes the prompt to the name of the local host, a SPACE, and a dollar sign (or, if the user is running with **root** privileges, a hashmark), followed by a SPACE. A SPACE at the end of the prompt makes commands you enter following the prompt easier to read. The second example changes the prompt to the time followed by the name of the user. The third example changes the prompt to the one used in this book (a hashmark for a user running with **root** privileges and a dollar sign otherwise):

```
$ PS1='\h \$ '
guava $

$ PS1='\@ \u $ '
09:44 PM max $

$ PS1='\$ '
$
```

Table 9-4 describes some of the symbols you can use in **PS1**. For a complete list of special characters you can use in the prompt strings, open the bash man page and search for the third occurrence of **PROMPTING** (enter the command **/PROMPTING** followed by a RETURN and then press **n** two times).

**Table 9-4**   **PS1** symbols

| Symbol | Display in prompt |
|--------|-------------------|
| \$ | # if the user is running with **root** privileges; otherwise, **$** |
| \w | Pathname of the working directory |
| \W | Basename of the working directory |
| \! | Current event (history) number (page 381) |
| \d | Date in Weekday Month Date format |
| \h | Machine hostname, without the domain |
| \H | Full machine hostname, including the domain |
| \u | Username of the current user |
| \@ | Current time of day in 12-hour, AM/PM format |
| \T | Current time of day in 12-hour HH:MM:SS format |
| \A | Current time of day in 24-hour HH:MM format |
| \t | Current time of day in 24-hour HH:MM:SS format |

## PS2: USER PROMPT (SECONDARY)

The **PS2** variable holds the secondary prompt. On the first line of the next example, an unclosed quoted string follows echo. The shell assumes the command is not finished and on the second line displays the default secondary prompt (>). This prompt indicates the shell is waiting for the user to continue the command line. The shell waits until it receives the quotation mark that closes the string and then executes the command:

```
$ echo "demonstration of prompt string
> 2"
demonstration of prompt string
2
```

The next command changes the secondary prompt to **Input =>** followed by a SPACE. On the line with who, a pipeline symbol (|) implies the command line is continued (page 1063) and causes bash to display the new secondary prompt. The command **grep sam** (followed by a RETURN) completes the command; grep displays its output.

```
$ PS2="Input => "
$ who |
Input => grep sam
sam       tty1          2012-05-01 10:37 (:0)
```

## PS3: MENU PROMPT

The **PS3** variable holds the menu prompt for the **select** control structure (page 1013).

## PS4: DEBUGGING PROMPT

The **PS4** variable holds the bash debugging symbol (page 995).

## IFS: SEPARATES INPUT FIELDS (WORD SPLITTING)

The **IFS** (Internal Field Separator) shell variable specifies the characters you can use to separate arguments on a command line. It has the default value of SPACE-TAB-NEWLINE. Regardless of the value of **IFS**, you can always use one or more SPACE or TAB characters to separate arguments on the command line, provided these characters are not quoted or escaped. When you assign character values to **IFS**, these characters can also separate fields—but only if they undergo expansion. This type of interpretation of the command line is called *word splitting* and is discussed on page 411.

### Be careful when changing IFS

caution    Changing **IFS** has a variety of side effects, so work cautiously. You might find it useful to save the value of **IFS** before changing it. You can then easily restore the original value if a change yields unexpected results. Alternately, you can fork a new shell using a **bash** command before experimenting with **IFS**; if you run into trouble, you can **exit** back to the old shell, where **IFS** is working properly.

The following example demonstrates how setting **IFS** can affect the interpretation of a command line:

```
$ a=w:x:y:z

$ cat $a
cat: w:x:y:z: No such file or directory
$ IFS=":"

$ cat $a
cat: w: No such file or directory
cat: x: No such file or directory
cat: y: No such file or directory
cat: z: No such file or directory
```

The first time cat is called, the shell expands the variable a, interpreting the string **w:x:y:z** as a single word to be used as the argument to cat. The cat utility cannot find a file named **w:x:y:z** and reports an error for that filename. After **IFS** is set to a colon (:), the shell expands the variable **a** into four words, each of which is an argument to **cat**. Now **cat** reports errors for four files: **w**, **x**, **y**, and **z**. Word splitting based on the colon (:) takes place only *after* the variable **a** is expanded.

The shell splits all *expanded* words on a command line according to the separating characters found in **IFS**. When there is no expansion, there is no splitting. Consider the following commands:

```
$ IFS="p"
$ export VAR
```

Although **IFS** is set to **p**, the **p** on the **export** command line is not expanded, so the word **export** is not split.

The following example uses variable expansion in an attempt to produce an **export** command:

```
$ IFS="p"
$ aa=export
$ echo $aa
ex ort
```

This time expansion occurs, so the **p** in the token **export** is interpreted as a separator (as the **echo** command shows). Next, when you try to use the value of the **aa** variable to export the **VAR** variable, the shell parses the **$aa VAR** command line as **ex ort VAR**. The effect is that the command line starts the **ex** editor with two filenames: **ort** and **VAR**.

```
$ $aa VAR
2 files to edit
"ort" [New File]
Entering Ex mode.  Type "visual" to go to Normal mode.
:q
E173: 1 more file to edit
:q
$
```

If **IFS** is unset, **bash** uses its default value (SPACE-TAB-NEWLINE). If **IFS** is null, **bash** does not split words.

### Multiple separator characters

tip   Although the shell treats sequences of multiple SPACE or TAB characters as a single separator, it treats *each occurrence* of another field-separator character as a separator.

## CDPATH: BROADENS THE SCOPE OF cd

The **CDPATH** variable allows you to use a simple filename as an argument to the **cd** builtin to change the working directory to a directory other than a child of the working directory. If you typically work in several directories, this variable can speed things up and save you the tedium of using **cd** with longer pathnames to switch among them.

When **CDPATH** is not set and you specify a simple filename as an argument to cd, cd searches the working directory for a subdirectory with the same name as the argument. If the subdirectory does not exist, cd displays an error message. When **CDPATH** is set, cd searches for an appropriately named subdirectory in the directories in the **CDPATH** list. If it finds one, that directory becomes the working directory. With **CDPATH** set, you can use cd and a simple filename to change the working directory to a child of any of the directories listed in **CDPATH**.

The **CDPATH** variable takes on the value of a colon-separated list of directory pathnames (similar to the **PATH** variable). It is usually set in the ~/**.bash_profile** startup file with a command line such as the following:

```
export CDPATH=$HOME:$HOME/literature
```

This command causes cd to search your home directory, the **literature** directory, and then the working directory when you give a cd command. If you do not include the working directory in **CDPATH**, cd searches the working directory if the search of all the other directories in **CDPATH** fails. If you want cd to search the working directory first, include a colon (**:**) as the first entry in **CDPATH**:

```
export CDPATH=:$HOME:$HOME/literature
```

If the argument to the cd builtin is anything other than a simple filename (i.e., if the argument contains a slash [**/**]), the shell does not consult **CDPATH**.

## KEYWORD VARIABLES: A SUMMARY

Table 9-5 lists the bash keyword variables.

**Table 9-5**    bash keyword variables

| Variable | Value |
|---|---|
| **BASH_ENV** | The pathname of the startup file for noninteractive shells (page 331) |
| **CDPATH** | The cd search path (page 364) |
| **COLUMNS** | The width of the display used by **select** (page 1012) |
| **HISTFILE** | The pathname of the file that holds the history list (default: ~/**.bash_history**; page 377) |
| **HISTFILESIZE** | The maximum number of entries saved in **HISTFILE** (default: 1000; page 377) |
| **HISTSIZE** | The maximum number of entries saved in the history list (default: 1,000; page 377) |
| **HOME** | The pathname of the user's home directory (page 358); used as the default argument for cd and in tilde expansion (page 182) |
| **IFS** | Internal Field Separator (page 363); used for word splitting (page 411) |
| **INPUTRC** | The pathname of the Readline startup file (default: ~/**.inputrc**; page 390) |

Table 9-5    bash keyword variables (continued)

| Variable | Value |
|---|---|
| LANG | The locale category when that category is not specifically set using one of the LC_ variables (page 368) |
| LC_ | A group of variables that specify locale categories including **LC_ALL**, **LC_COLLATE**, **LC_CTYPE**, **LC_MESSAGES**, and **LC_NUMERIC**; use the locale builtin (page 369) to display a more complete list including values |
| LINES | The height of the display used by **select** (page 1012) |
| MAIL | The pathname of the file that holds a user's mail (page 360) |
| MAILCHECK | How often, in seconds, bash checks for mail (default: 60; page 360) |
| MAILPATH | A colon-separated list of file pathnames that bash checks for mail in (page 360) |
| OLDPWD | The pathname of the previous working directory |
| PATH | A colon-separated list of directory pathnames that bash looks for commands in (page 359) |
| PROMPT_COMMAND | A command that bash executes just before it displays the primary prompt |
| PS1 | Prompt String 1; the primary prompt (page 361) |
| PS2 | Prompt String 2; the secondary prompt (page 362) |
| PS3 | The prompt issued by **select** (page 1012) |
| PS4 | The bash debugging symbol (page 995) |
| PWD | The pathname of the working directory |
| REPLY | Holds the line that read accepts (page 1042); also used by **select** (page 1012) |

# SPECIAL CHARACTERS

Table 9-6 lists most of the characters that are special to the bash shell.

Table 9-6    Shell special characters

| Character | Use |
|---|---|
| NEWLINE | A control operator that initiates execution of a command (page 341) |
| ; | A control operator that separates commands (page 341) |
| ( ) | A control operator that groups commands (page 344) for execution by a subshell; these characters are also used to identify a function (page 396) |

**Table 9-6** Shell special characters (continued)

| Character | Use |
|---|---|
| (( )) | Evaluates an arithmetic expression (pages 408 and 1056) |
| & | A control operator that executes a command in the background (pages 163 and 342) |
| \| | A control operator that sends standard output of the preceding command to standard input of the following command (pipeline; page 342) |
| \|& | A control operator that sends standard output and standard error of the preceding command to standard input of the following command (page 335) |
| > | Redirects standard output (page 154) |
| >> | Appends standard output (page 157) |
| < | Redirects standard input (page 155) |
| << | Here document (page 1014) |
| * | Matches any string of zero or more characters in an ambiguous file reference (page 166) |
| ? | Matches any single character in an ambiguous file reference (page 165) |
| \ | Quotes the following character (page 142) |
| ' | Quotes a string, preventing all substitution (page 142) |
| " | Quotes a string, allowing only variable and command substitution (pages 142 and 354) |
| ` ... ` | Performs command substitution [deprecated, see **$()**] |
| [ ] | Character class in an ambiguous file reference (page 168) |
| $ | References a variable (page 352) |
| . (dot builtin) | Executes a command in the current shell (page 332) |
| # | Begins a comment (page 340) |
| { } | Surrounds the contents of a function (page 396) |
| : (null builtin) | Returns *true* (page 1049) |
| **&&** (Boolean AND) | A control operator that executes the command on the right only if the command on the left succeeds (returns a zero exit status; page 343) |
| \|\| (Boolean OR) | A control operator that executes the command on the right only if the command on the left fails (returns a nonzero exit status; page 343) |
| ! (Boolean NOT) | Reverses the exit status of a command |
| **$()** | Performs command substitution (preferred form; page 410) |

# *LPI* Locale

In conversational English, a *locale* is a place or location. When working with Linux, a locale specifies the way locale-aware programs display certain kinds of data such as times and dates, money and other numeric values, telephone numbers, and measurements. It can also specify collating sequence and printer paper size.

Localization and internationalization

Localization and internationalization go hand in hand: Internationalization is the process of making software portable to multiple locales while localization is the process of adapting software so that it meets the language, cultural, and other requirements of a specific locale. Linux is well internationalized so you can easily specify a locale for a given system or user. Linux uses variables to specify a locale.

i18n  The term i18n is an abbreviation of the word *internationalization:* the letter *i* followed by 18 letters (*nternationalizatio*) followed by the letter *n*.

l10n  The term l10n is an abbreviation of the word *localization:* the letter *l* followed by 10 letters (*ocalizatio*) followed by the letter *n*.

# *LPI* LC_: Locale Variables

The bash man page lists the following locale variables; other programs use additional locale variables. See the locale man pages (sections 1, 5, and 7) or use the locale **--help** option for more information.

- **LANG**—Specifies the locale category for categories not specified by an **LC_** variable (except see **LC_ALL**). Many setups use only this locale variable and do not specify any of the **LC_** variables.

- **LC_ALL**—Overrides the value of **LANG** and all other **LC_** variables.

- **LC_COLLATE**—Specifies the collating sequence for the sort utility and for sorting the results of pathname expansion (page 354).

- **LC_CTYPE**—Specifies how characters are interpreted and how character classes within pathname expansion and pattern matching behave. Also affects the sort utility when you specify the **–d** (**--dictionary-order**) or **–i** (**--ignore-nonprinting**) options.

- **LC_MESSAGES**—Specifies how affirmative and negative answers appear and the language messages are displayed in.

- **LC_NUMERIC**—Specifies how numbers are formatted (e.g., are thousands separated by a comma or a period?).

You can set one or more of the **LC_** variables to a value using the following syntax:

*xx_YY.CHARSET*

where *xx* is the ISO-639 language code (e.g., **en** = English, **fr** = French, **zu** = Zulu), *YY* is the ISO-3166 country code (e.g., **FR** = France, **GF** = French Guiana, **PF** = French Polynesia), and *CHARSET* is the name of the character set (e.g., **UTF-8** [page 1279], **ASCII** [page 1237], **ISO-8859-1** [Western Europe]; also called the *character map* or *charmap*). On some systems you can specify *CHARSET* using lowercase letters. For example, **en_GB.UTF-8** can specify English as written in Great Britain, **en_US.UTF-8** can specify English as written in the United States, and **fr_FR.UTF-8** can specify French as written in France.

### Internationalized C programs call setlocale()

tip    Internationalized C programs call **setlocale**(). Other languages have analogous facilities. Shell scripts are typically internationalized to the degree that the routines they call are. Without a call to **setlocale**(), the **hello, world** program will always display **hello, world**, regardless of how you set **LANG**.

### The C locale

tip    Setting the locale to C forces a program to process and display strings as the program was written (i.e., without translating input or output), which frequently means the program works in English. Many system scripts set **LANG** to **C** so they run in a known environment. Some text processing utilities run slightly faster when you set **LANG** to **C**. Setting **LANG** to **C** before you run sort can help ensure you get the results you expect.

If you want to make sure your shell script will work properly, put the following line near the top of the file:

```
export LANG=C
```

Following is an example of a difference that setting **LANG** can cause. It shows that having **LANG** set to different values can cause commands to behave differently, especially with regard to sorting.

```
$ echo $LANG
en_US.UTF-8
$ ls
m666  Makefile   merry
$ ls [1-n]*
m666  Makefile   merry
$ export LANG=C
$ ls
Makefile  m666   merry
$ ls [1-n]*
m666  merry
```

## *LPI*    locale: DISPLAYS LOCALE INFORMATION

The locale utility displays information about the current and available locales. Without options, locale displays the value of the locale variables. In the following example, only the **LANG** variable is set, although you cannot determine this fact from the output. Unless explicitly set, each of the **LC_** variables derives its value from **LANG**.

```
$ locale
LANG=en_US.UTF-8
LC_CTYPE="en_US.UTF-8"
LC_NUMERIC="en_US.UTF-8"
LC_TIME="en_US.UTF-8"
LC_COLLATE="en_US.UTF-8"
LC_MONETARY="en_US.UTF-8"
LC_MESSAGES="en_US.UTF-8"
LC_PAPER="en_US.UTF-8"
LC_NAME="en_US.UTF-8"
LC_ADDRESS="en_US.UTF-8"
LC_TELEPHONE="en_US.UTF-8"
LC_MEASUREMENT="en_US.UTF-8"
LC_IDENTIFICATION="en_US.UTF-8"
LC_ALL=
```

Typically you will want all locale variables to have the same value. However, in some cases you might want to change the value of one or more locale variables. For example, if you are using paper size A4 but working in English, you could change the value of **LC_PAPER** to **nl_NL.utf8**.

The **–a** (all) option causes locale to display the names of available locales; **–v** (verbose) displays more complete information.

```
$ locale -av
locale: aa_DJ                 archive: /usr/lib/locale/locale-archive
-------------------------------------------------------------------
     title | Afar language locale for Djibouti (CaduLaaqo Dialects).
    source | Ge'ez Frontier Foundation
   address | 7802 Solomon Seal Dr., Springfield, VA 22152, USA
     email | locales@geez.org
  language | aa
 territory | DJ
  revision | 0.20
      date | 2003-07-05
   codeset | ISO-8859-1
...
```

The **–m** (maps) option causes locale to display the names of available character maps. Locale definition files are kept in the **/usr/share/i18n/locales** directory.

Following are some examples of how some **LC_** variables change displayed values. Each of these command lines sets an **LC_** variable and places it in the environment of the utility it calls. The **+%x** format causes date to display the locale's date representation.

```
$ LC_TIME=en_GB.UTF-8 date +%x
24/01/12
$ LC_TIME=en_US.UTF-8 date +%x
01/24/2012

$ ls xx
ls: impossible d'accéder à xx: Aucun fichier ou dossier de ce type
$ LC_MESSAGES=en_US.UTF-8 ls xx
ls: cannot access xx: No such file or directory
```

## SETTING THE LOCALE

You might have to install a language package for a locale before you can specify a locale. Put locale variable assignments in **~/.profile** or **~/.bash_profile** to affect both GUI and bash command-line logins for a single user. Remember to export the variables. The following line in one of these files will set all **LC_** variables for the given user to French as spoken in France:

```
export LANG=fr_FR.UTF-8
```

To change the locale for all users, put locale variable assignments (previous page) in **/etc/profile.d/zlang.sh** (you will need to create this file; the filename was chosen to be executed after **lang.sh**) to affect both GUI and command-line logins for all users.

# LPI TIME

UTC On networks with systems in different time zones it can be helpful to set all systems to the *UTC* (page 1279) time zone. Among other benefits, doing so can make it easier for an administrator to compare logged events on different systems over time. Each user account can be set to the local time for that user.

Time zone The time zone for a user is specified by an environment variable or, if one is not set, by the time zone for the system.

TZ The **TZ** variable gives a program access to information about the local time zone. This variable is typically set in a startup file (page 329) and placed in the environment (page 1032) so called programs have access to it. It has two syntaxes.

The first syntax of the **TZ** variable is

*nam±val[nam2]*

where ***nam*** is a string comprising three or more letters that typically name the time zone (e.g., PST; its value is not significant) and ***±val*** is the offset of the time zone from UTC, with positive values indicating the local time zone is west of the prime meridian and negative values indicating the local time zone is east of the prime meridian. If the ***nam2*** is present, it indicates the time zone observes daylight savings time; it is the name of the daylight savings time zone (e.g., PDT).

In the following example, date is called twice, once without setting the **TZ** variable and then with the **TZ** variable set in the environment in which date is called:

```
$ date
Thu May  3 10:08:06 PDT 2012
$ TZ=EST+5EDT date
Thu May  3 13:08:08 EDT 2012
```

The second syntax of the **TZ** variable is

*continent/country*

where ***continent*** is the name of the continent or ocean and ***country*** is the name of the country that includes the desired time zone. This syntax points to a file in the **/usr/share/zoneinfo** hierarchy (next page). See tzselect (next page) if you need help determining these values.

In the next example, date is called twice, once without setting the **TZ** variable and then with the **TZ** variable set in the environment in which date is called:

```
$ date
Thu May  3 10:09:27 PDT 2012
$ TZ=America/New_York date
Thu May  3 13:09:28 EDT 2012
```

See www.gnu.org/software/libc/manual/html_node/TZ-Variable.html for extensive documentation on the **TZ** variable.

*LPI*   tzconfig   The tzconfig utility was available under Debian/Ubuntu and is now deprecated; use **dpkg-reconfigure tzdata** in its place.

*LPI*   tzselect   The tzselect utility can help you determine the name of a time zone by asking you first to name the continent or ocean and then the country the time zone is in. If necessary, it asks for a time zone region (e.g., Pacific Time). This utility does not change system settings but rather displays a line telling you the name of the time zone. In the following example, the time zone is named **Europe/Paris**. Newer releases keep time zone information in **/usr/share/zoneinfo** (below). Specifications such as **Europe/Paris** refer to the file in that directory (**/usr/share/zoneinfo/Europe/Paris**).

```
$ tzselect
Please identify a location so that time zone rules can be set correctly.
Please select a continent or ocean.
 1) Africa
...
 8) Europe
 9) Indian Ocean
10) Pacific Ocean
11) none - I want to specify the time zone using the Posix TZ format.
#? 8
Please select a country.
 1) Aaland Islands     18) Greece            35) Norway
...
15) France             32) Monaco            49) Vatican City
16) Germany            33) Montenegro
17) Gibraltar          34) Netherlands
#? 15
...
Here is that TZ value again, this time on standard output so that you
can use the /usr/bin/tzselect command in shell scripts:
Europe/Paris
```

*LPI*   /etc/timezone   Under some distributions, including Debian/Ubuntu/Mint, the **/etc/timezone** file holds the name of the local time zone.

```
$ cat /etc/timezone
America/Los_Angeles
```

*LPI*
**/usr/share/zoneinfo**   The **/usr/share/zoneinfo** directory hierarchy holds time zone data files. Some time zones are held in regular files in the **zoneinfo** directory (e.g., Japan and GB) while others are held in subdirectories (e.g., Azores and Pacific). The following example shows a small part of the **/usr/share/zoneinfo** directory hierarchy and illustrates how file (page 229) reports on a time zone file.

```
$ find /usr/share/zoneinfo
/usr/share/zoneinfo
/usr/share/zoneinfo/Atlantic
/usr/share/zoneinfo/Atlantic/Azores
/usr/share/zoneinfo/Atlantic/Madeira
/usr/share/zoneinfo/Atlantic/Jan_Mayen
...
/usr/share/zoneinfo/Japan
/usr/share/zoneinfo/GB
```

```
/usr/share/zoneinfo/US
/usr/share/zoneinfo/US/Pacific
/usr/share/zoneinfo/US/Arizona
/usr/share/zoneinfo/US/Michigan
...

$ file /usr/share/zoneinfo/Atlantic/Azores
/usr/share/zoneinfo/Atlantic/Azores: timezone data, version 2, 12 gmt
time flags, 12 std time flags, no leap seconds, 220 transition times, 12
abbreviation chars
```

**LPI** /etc/localtime  Some Linux distributions use a link at **/etc/localtime** to a file in **/usr/share/zoneinfo** to specify the local time zone. Others copy the file from the **zoneinfo** directory to **localtime**. Following is an example of setting up this link; to create this link you must work with **root** privileges.

```
# date
Tue Jan 24 13:55:00 PST 2012
# cd /etc
# ln -sf /usr/share/zoneinfo/Europe/Paris localtime
# date
Tue Jan 24 22:55:38 CET 2012
```

On some of these systems, the **/etc/systemconfig/clock** file sets the **ZONE** variable to the name of the time zone:

```
$ cat /etc/sysconfig/clock
# The time zone of the system is defined by the contents of /etc/localtime.
# This file is only for evaluation by system-config-date, do not rely on its
# contents elsewhere.
ZONE="Europe/Paris"
```

# **LE** PROCESSES

A *process* is the execution of a command by the Linux kernel. The shell that starts when you log in is a process, like any other. When you specify the name of a utility as a command, you initiate a process. When you run a shell script, another shell process is started, and additional processes are created for each command in the script. Depending on how you invoke the shell script, the script is run either by the current shell or, more typically, by a subshell (child) of the current shell. Running a shell builtin, such as cd, does not start a new process.

## PROCESS STRUCTURE

fork() system call  Like the file structure, the process structure is hierarchical, with parents, children, and a *root*. A parent process *forks* (or *spawns*) a child process, which in turn can fork other processes. The term *fork* indicates that, as with a fork in the road, one process turns into two. Initially the two forks are identical except that one is identified as the parent and one as the child. The operating system routine, or *system call,* that creates a new process is named **fork()**.

*LPI*  init daemon   A Linux system begins execution by starting the **init** daemon, a single process called a *spontaneous process*, with PID number 1. This process holds the same position in the process structure as the root directory does in the file structure: It is the ancestor of all processes the system and users work with. When a command-line system is in multiuser mode, init runs getty or mingetty processes, which display **login:** prompts on terminals and virtual consoles. When a user responds to the prompt and presses RETURN, getty or mingetty passes control to a utility named login, which checks the user-name and password combination. After the user logs in, the login process becomes the user's shell process.

When you enter the name of a program on the command line, the shell **fork**s a new process, creating a duplicate of the shell process (a subshell). The new process attempts to **exec** (execute) the program. Like **fork**(), **exec**() is a system call. If the program is a binary executable, such as a compiled C program, **exec**() succeeds, and the system overlays the newly created subshell with the executable program. If the command is a shell script, **exec**() fails. When **exec** fails, the program is assumed to be a shell script, and the subshell runs the commands in the script. Unlike a login shell, which expects input from the command line, the subshell takes its input from a file—namely, the shell script.

## *LE+* PROCESS IDENTIFICATION

PID numbers   Linux assigns a unique PID (process identification) number at the inception of each process. As long as a process exists, it keeps the same PID number. During one session the same process is always executing the login shell (page 330). When you fork a new process—for example, when you use an editor—the PID number of the new (child) process is different from that of its parent process. When you return to the login shell, it is still being executed by the same process and has the same PID number as when you logged in.

*LPI*  ps   The following example shows that the process running the shell forked (is the parent of) the process running ps. When you call it with the –f option, ps displays a full list-ing of information about each process. The line of the ps display with **bash** in the **CMD** column refers to the process running the shell. The column headed by **PID** iden-tifies the PID number. The column headed by **PPID** identifies the PID number of the *parent* of the process. From the PID and PPID columns you can see that the process running the shell (PID 21341) is the parent of the processes running sleep (PID 22789) and ps (PID 22790).

```
$ sleep 10 &
[1] 22789
$ ps -f
UID        PID  PPID  C STIME TTY         TIME CMD
max      21341 21340  0 10:42 pts/16  00:00:00 bash
max      22789 21341  0 17:30 pts/16  00:00:00 sleep 10
max      22790 21341  0 17:30 pts/16  00:00:00 ps -f
```

Refer to the ps man page for more information on ps and the columns it displays when you specify the –f option. A second pair of **sleep** and **ps –f** commands shows that the shell is still being run by the same process but that it forked another process to run sleep:

```
$ sleep 10 &
[1] 22791
$ ps -f
UID         PID  PPID C STIME TTY         TIME CMD
max       21341 21340 0 10:42 pts/16   00:00:00 bash
max       22791 21341 0 17:31 pts/16   00:00:00 sleep 10
max       22792 21341 0 17:31 pts/16   00:00:00 ps -f
```

You can also use pstree (or **ps --forest**, with or without the **–e** option) to see the parent–child relationship of processes. The next example shows the **–p** option to pstree, which causes it to display PID numbers:

```
$ pstree -p
systemd(1)-+-NetworkManager(655)---{NetworkManager}(702)
           |-abrtd(657)---abrt-dump-oops(696)
           |-accounts-daemon(1204)---{accounts-daemo}(1206)
           |-agetty(979)
  ...
           |-login(984)---bash(2071)-+-pstree(2095)
           |                         `-sleep(2094)
  ...
```

The preceding output is abbreviated. The first line shows the PID 1 (**systemd init**) and a few of the processes it is running. The line that starts with **–login** shows a textual user running sleep in the background and pstree in the foreground. The tree for a user running a GUI is much more complex. Refer to "$$: PID Number" on page 1028 for a description of how to instruct the shell to report on PID numbers.

# EXECUTING A COMMAND

**fork() and sleep()**     When you give the shell a command, it usually forks [spawns using the **fork()** system call] a child process to execute the command. While the child process is executing the command, the parent process (running the shell) *sleeps* [implemented as the **sleep()** system call]. While a process is sleeping, it does not use any computer time; it remains inactive, waiting to wake up. When the child process finishes executing the command, it tells its parent of its success or failure via its exit status and then dies. The parent process (which is running the shell) wakes up and prompts for another command.

**LPI** Background process     When you run a process in the background by ending a command with the ampersand control operator (**&**), the shell forks a child process without going to sleep and without waiting for the child process to run to completion. The parent process, which is executing the shell, reports the job number and PID number of the child process and prompts for another command. The child process runs in the background, independent of its parent.

Builtins     Although the shell forks a process to run most commands, some commands are built into the shell (e.g., cd, alias, jobs, pwd). The shell does not fork a process to run builtins. For more information refer to "Builtins" on page 170.

Variables   Within a given process, such as a login shell or subshell, you can declare, initialize, read, and change variables. Some variables, called shell variables, are local to a process. Other variables, called environment variables, are available to child processes. For more information refer to "Variables" on page 1031.

Hash table   The first time you specify a command as a simple filename (and not a relative or absolute pathname), bash looks in the directories specified by the **PATH** (page 359) variable to find that file. When it finds the file, bash records the absolute pathname of the file in its *hash table*. When you give the command again, bash finds it in its hash table, saving the time needed to search through the directories in **PATH**. The shell deletes the hash table when you log out and starts a new hash table when you start a session.

When you call the hash builtin without any arguments, it displays the hash table. When you first log in, the hash table is empty:

```
$ hash
hash: hash table empty
$ who am i
sam      pts/2         2013-03-09 14:24 (plum)
$ hash
hits    command
   1    /usr/bin/who
```

The hash –r option causes bash to empty the hash table, as though you had just logged in.

```
$ hash -r
$ hash
hash: hash table empty
```

Having bash empty its hash table is useful when you move a program to a different directory in **PATH** and bash cannot find the program in its new location, or when you have two programs with the same name and bash is calling the wrong one. Refer to the bash info page for more information on the hash builtin.

# LE+    HISTORY

The history mechanism, a feature adapted from the C Shell, maintains a list of recently issued command lines, called *events,* that provides a quick way to reexecute any events in the list. This mechanism also enables you to edit and then execute previous commands and to reuse arguments from them. You can use the history list to replicate complicated commands and arguments that you used previously and to enter a series of commands that differ from one another in minor ways. The history list also serves as a record of what you have done. It can prove helpful when you have made a mistake and are not sure what you did or when you want to keep a record of a procedure that involved a series of commands.

### history **can help track down mistakes**

tip When you have made a mistake on a command line (not an error within a script or program) and are not sure what you did wrong, look at the history list to review your recent commands. Sometimes this list can help you figure out what went wrong and how to fix things.

The history builtin displays the history list. If it does not, read the next section, which describes the variables you might need to set.

# VARIABLES THAT CONTROL HISTORY

The value of the **HISTSIZE** variable determines the number of events preserved in the history list during a session. A value in the range of 100 to 1,000 is normal.

When you exit from the shell, the most recently executed commands are saved in the file whose name is stored in the **HISTFILE** variable (default is **~/.bash_history**). The next time you start the shell, this file initializes the history list. The value of the **HISTFILESIZE** variable determines the number of lines of history saved in **HISTFILE** (see Table 9-7).

**Table 9-7**  History variables

| Variable | Default | Function |
|---|---|---|
| **HISTSIZE** | 1,000 events | Maximum number of events saved during a session |
| **HISTFILE** | **~/.bash_history** | Location of the history file |
| **HISTFILESIZE** | 1,000  events | Maximum number of events saved between sessions |

Event number  The Bourne Again Shell assigns a sequential *event number* to each command line. You can display this event number as part of the bash prompt by including \! in **PS1** (page 361). Examples in this section show numbered prompts when they help to illustrate the behavior of a command.

Enter the following command manually to establish a history list of the 100 most recent events; place it in **~/.bash_profile** to affect future sessions:

```
$ HISTSIZE=100
```

The following command causes bash to save the 100 most recent events across login sessions:

```
$ HISTFILESIZE=100
```

After you set **HISTFILESIZE**, you can log out and log in again, and the 100 most recent events from the previous login session will appear in your history list.

Enter the command **history** to display the events in the history list. This list is ordered with the oldest events at the top. The following history list includes a command to modify the bash prompt so it displays the history event number. The last event in the history list is the **history** command that displayed the list.

```
32 $ history | tail
   23   PS1="\! bash$ "
   24   ls -l
   25   cat temp
   26   rm temp
   27   vim memo
   28   lpr memo
   29   vim memo
   30   lpr memo
   31   rm memo
   32   history | tail
```

As you run commands and your history list becomes longer, it might run off the top of the screen when you use the history builtin. Send the output of history through a pipeline to less to browse through it or give the command **history 10** or **history | tail** to look at the ten most recent commands.

### Handy history aliases

tip Creating the following aliases makes working with history easier. The first allows you to give the command **h** to display the ten most recent events. The second alias causes the command **hg** *string* to display all events in the history list that contain *string*. Put these aliases in your ~/.**bashrc** file to make them available each time you log in. See page 392 for more information on aliases.

```
$ alias 'h=history | tail'
$ alias 'hg=history | grep'
```

# REEXECUTING AND EDITING COMMANDS

You can reexecute any event in the history list. Not having to reenter long command lines allows you to reexecute events more easily, quickly, and accurately than you could if you had to retype the command line in its entirety. You can recall, modify, and reexecute previously executed events in three ways: You can use the fc builtin (next), the exclamation point commands (page 381), or the Readline Library, which uses a one-line vi- or emacs-like editor to edit and execute events (page 386).

### Which method to use?

tip If you are more familiar with vi or emacs and less familiar with the C or TC Shell, use fc or the Readline Library. If you are more familiar with the C or TC Shell, use the exclamation point commands. If it is a toss-up, try the Readline Library; it will benefit you in other areas of Linux more than learning the exclamation point commands will.

## fc: DISPLAYS, EDITS, AND REEXECUTES COMMANDS

The fc (fix command) builtin enables you to display the history list and to edit and reexecute previous commands. It provides many of the same capabilities as the command-line editors.

## VIEWING THE HISTORY LIST

When you call fc with the –l option, it displays commands from the history list. Without any arguments, **fc –l** lists the 16 most recent commands in a list that includes event numbers, with the oldest appearing first:

```
$ fc -l
1024     cd
1025     view calendar
1026     vim letter.adams01
1027     aspell -c letter.adams01
1028     vim letter.adams01
1029     lpr letter.adams01
1030     cd ../memos
1031     ls
1032     rm *0405
1033     fc -l
1034     cd
1035     whereis aspell
1036     man aspell
1037     cd /usr/share/doc/*aspell*
1038     pwd
1039     ls
1040     ls man-html
```

The fc builtin can take zero, one, or two arguments with the –l option. The arguments specify the part of the history list to be displayed:

*fc –l [first [last]]*

The fc builtin lists commands beginning with the most recent event that matches *first*. The argument can be an event number, the first few characters of the command line, or a negative number, which specifies the *n*th previous command. Without *last,* fc displays events through the most recent. If you include *last,* fc displays commands from the most recent event that matches *first* through the most recent event that matches *last.*

The next command displays the history list from event 1030 through event 1035:

```
$ fc -l 1030 1035
1030     cd ../memos
1031     ls
1032     rm *0405
1033     fc -l
1034     cd
1035     whereis aspell
```

The command on the next page lists the most recent event that begins with **view** through the most recent command line that begins with **whereis**.

```
$ fc -l view whereis
1025     view calendar
1026     vim letter.adams01
1027     aspell -c letter.adams01
1028     vim letter.adams01
1029     lpr letter.adams01
1030     cd ../memos
1031     ls
1032     rm *0405
1033     fc -l
1034     cd
1035     whereis aspell
```

To list a single command from the history list, use the same identifier for the first and second arguments. The following command lists event 1027:

```
$ fc -l 1027 1027
1027     aspell -c letter.adams01
```

### EDITING AND REEXECUTING PREVIOUS COMMANDS

You can use fc to edit and reexecute previous commands.

*fc [–e editor] [first [last]]*

When you call fc with the –e option followed by the name of an editor, fc calls the editor with event(s) in the Work buffer. By default, fc invokes the vi(m) editor. Without *first* and *last*, it defaults to the most recent command. The next example invokes the vim editor to edit the most recent command. When you exit from the editor, the shell executes the command.

```
$ fc -e vi
```

The fc builtin uses the stand-alone vim editor. If you set the **EDITOR** variable, you do not need to use the –e option to specify an editor on the command line. Because the value of **EDITOR** has been changed to **/usr/bin/emacs** and fc has no arguments, the following command edits the most recent command using the emacs editor (emacs package):

```
$ export EDITOR=/usr/bin/emacs
$ fc
```

### Clean up the fc buffer

caution   When you execute an fc command, the shell executes whatever you leave in the editor buffer, possibly with unwanted results. If you decide you do not want to execute a command, delete everything from the buffer before you exit from the editor.

If you call it with a single argument, fc invokes the editor on the specified command. The following example starts the editor with event 1029 in the Work buffer:

```
$ fc 1029
```

As described earlier, you can identify commands either by using numbers or by specifying the first few characters of the command name. The following example calls the editor to work on events from the most recent event that begins with the letters **vim** through event 1030:

```
$ fc vim 1030
```

### REEXECUTING COMMANDS WITHOUT CALLING THE EDITOR

You can also reexecute previous commands without using an editor. If you call fc with the –s option, it skips the editing phase and reexecutes the command. The following example reexecutes event 1029:

```
$ fc -s 1029
lpr letter.adams01
```

The next example reexecutes the previous command:

```
$ fc -s
```

When you reexecute a command, you can tell fc to substitute one string for another. The next example substitutes the string **john** for the string **adams** in event 1029 and executes the modified event:

```
$ fc -s adams=john 1029
lpr letter.john01
```

## USING AN EXCLAMATION POINT (!) TO REFERENCE EVENTS

The C Shell history mechanism uses an exclamation point to reference events. This technique, which is available under bash, is frequently more cumbersome to use than fc but nevertheless has some useful features. For example, the !! command reexecutes the previous event, and the shell replaces the !$ token with the last word from the previous command line.

You can reference an event by using its absolute event number, its relative event number, or the text it contains. All references to events, called event designators, begin with an exclamation point (!). One or more characters follow the exclamation point to specify an event.

You can put history events anywhere on a command line. To escape an exclamation point so the shell interprets it literally instead of as the start of a history event, precede it with a backslash (\) or enclose it within single quotation marks.

### EVENT DESIGNATORS

An event designator specifies a command in the history list. Table 9-8 (next page) lists event designators.

**Table 9-8**   Event designators

| Designator | Meaning |
|---|---|
| ! | Starts a history event unless followed immediately by SPACE, NEWLINE, =, or (. |
| !! | The previous command. |
| !*n* | Command number *n* in the history list. |
| !–*n* | The *n*th preceding command. |
| !*string* | The most recent command line that started with *string*. |
| !?*string*[?] | The most recent command that contained *string*. The last ? is optional. |
| !# | The current command (as you have it typed so far). |
| !{*event*} | The *event* is an event designator. The braces isolate *event* from the surrounding text. For example, !{–3}3 is the third most recently executed command followed by a **3**. |

**!! reexecutes the previous event**  You can reexecute the previous event by giving a !! command. In the following example, event 45 reexecutes event 44:

```
44 $ ls -l text
-rw-rw-r--. 1 max pubs 45 04-30 14:53 text
45 $ !!
ls -l text
-rw-rw-r--. 1 max pubs 45 04-30 14:53 text
```

The !! command works whether or not your prompt displays an event number. As this example shows, when you use the history mechanism to reexecute an event, the shell displays the command it is reexecuting.

**!*n* event number**  A number following an exclamation point refers to an event. If that event is in the history list, the shell executes it. Otherwise, the shell displays an error message. A negative number following an exclamation point references an event relative to the current event. For example, the command !–3 refers to the third preceding event. After you issue a command, the relative event number of a given event changes (event –3 becomes event –4). Both of the following commands reexecute event 44:

```
51 $ !44
ls -l text
-rw-rw-r--. 1 max pubs 45 04-30 14:53 text
52 $ !-8
ls -l text
-rw-rw-r--. 1 max pubs 45 04-30 14:53 text
```

**!*string* event text**  When a string of text follows an exclamation point, the shell searches for and executes the most recent event that *began* with that string. If you enclose the string within question marks, the shell executes the most recent event that *contained* that string. The final question mark is optional if a RETURN would immediately follow it.

```
68 $ history 10
   59  ls -l text*
   60  tail text5
   61  cat text1 text5 > letter
   62  vim letter
   63  cat letter
   64  cat memo
   65  lpr memo
   66  pine zach
   67  ls -l
   68  history
69 $ !1
ls -l
...
70 $ !lpr
lpr memo
71 $ !?letter?
cat letter
...
```

**optional  WORD DESIGNATORS**

A *word designator* specifies a word (token) or series of words from an event (a command line). Table 9-9 lists word designators. The words on a command line are numbered starting with 0 (the first word, usually the command), continuing with 1 (the first word following the command), and ending with *n* (the last word on the command line).

**Table 9-9**   Word designators

| Designator | Meaning |
|---|---|
| *n* | The *n*th word. Word 0 is normally the command name. |
| ^ | The first word (after the command name). |
| $ | The last word. |
| *m–n* | All words from word number *m* through word number *n*; *m* defaults to 0 if you omit it (0–*n*). |
| *n*∗ | All words from word number *n* through the last word. |
| ∗ | All words except the command name. The same as **1**∗. |
| % | The word matched by the most recent *?string?* search. |

To specify a particular word from a previous event, follow the event designator (such as **!14**) with a colon and the number of the word in the previous event. For example, **!14:3** specifies the third word following the command from event 14. You can specify the first word following the command (word number 1) using a caret (^) and the last word using a dollar sign ($). You can specify a range of words by separating two word designators with a hyphen.

```
72 $ echo apple grape orange pear
apple grape orange pear
73 $ echo !72:2
echo grape
grape
74 $ echo !72:^
echo apple
apple
75 $ !72:0 !72:$
echo pear
pear
76 $ echo !72:2-4
echo grape orange pear
grape orange pear
77 $ !72:0-$
echo apple grape orange pear
apple grape orange pear
```

As the next example shows, **!$** refers to the last word of the previous event. You can use this shorthand to edit, for example, a file you just displayed using cat:

```
$ cat report.718
...
$ vim !$
vim report.718
...
```

If an event contains a single command, the word numbers correspond to the argument numbers. If an event contains more than one command, this correspondence does not hold for commands after the first. In the next example, event 78 contains two commands separated by a semicolon so the shell executes them sequentially; the semicolon is word number 5.

```
78 $ !72 ; echo helen zach barbara
echo apple grape orange pear ; echo helen zach barbara
apple grape orange pear
helen zach barbara
79 $ echo !78:7
echo helen
helen
80 $ echo !78:4-7
echo pear ; echo helen
pear
helen
```

## MODIFIERS

On occasion you might want to change an aspect of an event you are reexecuting. Perhaps you entered a complex command line with a typo or incorrect pathname or you want to specify a different argument. You can modify an event or a word of an event by putting one or more modifiers after the word designator or after the event designator if there is no word designator. Each modifier must be preceded by a colon (:).

Substitute modifier   The following example shows the *substitute modifier* correcting a typo in the previous event:

```
$ car /home/zach/memo.0507 /home/max/letter.0507
bash: car: command not found
$ !!:s/car/cat
cat /home/zach/memo.0507 /home/max/letter.0507
...
```

The substitute modifier has the following syntax:

[*g*]*s*/*old*/*new*/

where *old* is the original string (not a regular expression) and *new* is the string that replaces *old*. The substitute modifier substitutes the first occurrence of *old* with *new*. Placing a **g** before the **s** causes a global substitution, replacing all occurrences of *old*. Although **/** is the delimiter in the examples, you can use any character that is not in either *old* or *new*. The final delimiter is optional if a RETURN would immediately follow it. As with the vim Substitute command, the history mechanism replaces an ampersand (**&**) in *new* with *old*. The shell replaces a null old string (*s*//*new*/) with the previous old string or the string within a command you searched for using ?*string*?.

Quick substitution An abbreviated form of the substitute modifier is *quick substitution*. Use it to reexecute the most recent event while changing some of the event text. The quick substitution character is the caret (**^**). For example, the command

```
$ ^old^new^
```

produces the same results as

```
$ !!:s/old/new/
```

Thus substituting **cat** for **car** in the previous event could have been entered as

```
$ ^car^cat
cat /home/zach/memo.0507 /home/max/letter.0507
...
```

You can omit the final caret if it would be followed immediately by a RETURN. As with other command-line substitutions, the shell displays the command line as it appears after the substitution.

Other modifiers Modifiers (other than the substitute modifier) perform simple edits on the part of the event that has been selected by the event designator and the optional word designators. You can use multiple modifiers, each preceded by a colon (:).

The following series of commands uses ls to list the name of a file, repeats the command without executing it (**p** modifier), and repeats the last command, removing the last part of the pathname (**h** modifier) again without executing it:

```
$ ls /etc/ssh/ssh_config
/etc/ssh/ssh_config
$ !!:p
ls /etc/ssh/ssh_config
$ !!:h:p
ls /etc/ssh
```

Table 9-10 lists event modifiers other than the substitute modifier.

**Table 9-10**   Event modifiers

| Modifier | | Function |
|---|---|---|
| **e** | (extension) | Removes all but the filename extension |
| **h** | (head) | Removes the last part of a pathname |
| **p** | (print) | Displays the command but does not execute it |
| **q** | (quote) | Quotes the substitution to prevent further substitutions on it |
| **r** | (root) | Removes the filename extension |
| **t** | (tail) | Removes all elements of a pathname except the last |
| **x** | | Like **q** but quotes each word in the substitution individually |

# THE READLINE LIBRARY

Command-line editing under the Bourne Again Shell is implemented through the *Readline Library,* which is available to any application written in C. Any application that uses the Readline Library supports line editing that is consistent with that provided by bash. Programs that use the Readline Library, including bash, read ~/.inputrc (page 390) for key binding information and configuration settings. The ––noediting command-line option turns off command-line editing in bash.

vi mode   You can choose one of two editing modes when using the Readline Library in bash: emacs or vi(m). Both modes provide many of the commands available in the stand-alone versions of the emacs and vim editors. You can also use the ARROW keys to move around. Up and down movements move you backward and forward through the history list. In addition, Readline provides several types of interactive word completion (page 388). The default mode is emacs; you can switch to vi mode using the following command:

```
$ set -o vi
```

emacs mode   The next command switches back to emacs mode:

```
$ set -o emacs
```

## vi EDITING MODE

Before you start, make sure the shell is in vi mode.

When you enter bash commands while in vi editing mode, you are in Input mode (page 264). As you enter a command, if you discover an error before you press RETURN, you can press ESCAPE to switch to vim Command mode. This setup is different from the stand-alone vim editor's initial mode. While in Command mode you can use many vim commands to edit the command line. It is as though you were using vim to edit a copy of the history file with a screen that has room for only one command. When you use the **k** command or the UP ARROW to move up a line, you access the previous command. If you then use the **j** command or the DOWN ARROW to move down a line, you return to the original command. To use the **k** and **j** keys to move between commands, you must be in Command mode; you can use the ARROW keys in both Command and Input modes.

### The command-line vim editor starts in Input mode

tip The stand-alone vim editor starts in Command mode, whereas the command-line vim editor starts in Input mode. If commands display characters and do not work properly, you are in Input mode. Press ESCAPE and enter the command again.

In addition to cursor-positioning commands, you can use the search-backward (**?**) command followed by a search string to look *back* through the history list for the most recent command containing a string. If you have moved back in the history list, use a forward slash (**/**) to search *forward* toward the most recent command. Unlike the search strings in the stand-alone vim editor, these search strings cannot contain regular expressions. You can, however, start the search string with a caret (**^**) to force the shell to locate commands that start with the search string. As in vim, pressing **n** after a successful search looks for the next occurrence of the same string.

You can also use event numbers to access events in the history list. While you are in Command mode (press ESCAPE), enter the event number followed by a **G** to go to the command with that event number.

When you use **/**, **?**, or **G** to move to a command line, you are in Command mode, not Input mode: You can edit the command or press RETURN to execute it.

When the command you want to edit is displayed, you can modify the command line using vim Command mode editing commands such as **x** (delete character), **r** (replace character), **~** (change case), and **.** (repeat last change). To switch to Input mode, use an Insert (**i**, **I**), Append (**a**, **A**), Replace (**R**), or Change (**c**, **C**) command. You do not have to return to Command mode to execute a command; simply press RETURN, even if the cursor is in the middle of the command line. For more information refer to the vim tutorial on page 262.

## emacs EDITING MODE

Unlike the vim editor, emacs is modeless. You need not switch between Command mode and Input mode because most emacs commands are control characters, allowing emacs to distinguish between input and commands. Like vim, the emacs command-line editor provides commands for moving the cursor on the command line and through the command history list and for modifying part or all of a command. However, in a few cases, the emacs command-line editor commands differ from those used in the stand-alone emacs editor.

In emacs you perform cursor movement by using both CONTROL and ESCAPE commands. To move the cursor one character backward on the command line, press CONTROL-B. Press

CONTROL-F to move one character forward. As in vim, you can precede these movements with counts. To use a count you must first press ESCAPE; otherwise, the numbers you type will appear on the command line.

Like vim, emacs provides word and line movement commands. To move backward or forward one word on the command line, press ESCAPE b or ESCAPE f, respectively. To move several words using a count, press ESCAPE followed by the number and the appropriate escape sequence. To move to the beginning of the line, press CONTROL-A; to move to the end of the line, press CONTROL-E; and to move to the next instance of the character *c*, press CONTROL-X CONTROL-F followed by *c*.

You can add text to the command line by moving the cursor to the position you want to enter text and typing. To delete text, move the cursor just to the right of the characters you want to delete and press the erase key (page 123) once for each character you want to delete.

### CONTROL-D can terminate your screen session

caution    If you want to delete the character directly under the cursor, press CONTROL-D. If you enter CONTROL-D at the beginning of the line, it might terminate your shell session.

If you want to delete the entire command line, press the line kill key (page 123). You can press this key while the cursor is anywhere in the command line. Use CONTROL-K to delete from the cursor to the end of the line.

## READLINE COMPLETION COMMANDS

You can use the TAB key to complete words you are entering on the command line. This facility, called *completion*, works in both vi and emacs editing modes. Several types of completion are possible, and which one you use depends on which part of a command line you are typing when you press TAB.

### COMMAND COMPLETION

If you are typing the name of a command, pressing TAB initiates *command completion*, in which bash looks for a command whose name starts with the part of the word you have typed. If no command starts with the characters you entered, bash beeps. If there is one such command, bash completes the command name. If there is more than one choice, bash does nothing in vi mode and beeps in emacs mode. Pressing TAB a second time causes bash to display a list of commands whose names start with the prefix you typed and allows you to continue typing the command name.

In the following example, the user types **bz** and presses TAB. The shell beeps (the user is in emacs mode) to indicate that several commands start with the letters **bz**. The user enters another TAB to cause the shell to display a list of commands that start with **bz** followed by the command line as the user has entered it so far:

```
$ bz ⇨ TAB (beep) ⇨ TAB
bzcat          bzdiff        bzip2         bzless
bzcmp          bzgrep        bzip2recover  bzmore
$ bz█
```

Next the user types **c** and presses TAB twice. The shell displays the two commands that start with **bzc**. The user types **a** followed by TAB. At this point the shell completes the command because only one command starts with **bzca**.

```
$ bzc ⇨ TAB (beep) ⇨ TAB
bzcat  bzcmp
$ bzca ⇨ TAB ⇨ t ■
```

## PATHNAME COMPLETION

*Pathname completion*, which also uses TABs, allows you to type a portion of a pathname and have bash supply the rest. If the portion of the pathname you have typed is sufficient to determine a unique pathname, bash displays that pathname. If more than one pathname would match it, bash completes the pathname up to the point where there are choices so that you can type more.

When you are entering a pathname, including a simple filename, and press TAB, the shell beeps (if the shell is in emacs mode—in vi mode there is no beep). It then extends the command line as far as it can.

```
$ cat films/dar ⇨ TAB (beep) cat films/dark_■
```

In the **films** directory every file that starts with **dar** has **k_** as the next characters, so bash cannot extend the line further without making a choice among files. The shell leaves the cursor just past the _ character. At this point you can continue typing the pathname or press TAB twice. In the latter case bash beeps, displays the choices, redisplays the command line, and again leaves the cursor just after the _ character.

```
$ cat films/dark_ ⇨ TAB (beep) ⇨ TAB
dark_passage  dark_victory
$ cat films/dark_■
```

When you add enough information to distinguish between the two possible files and press TAB, bash displays the unique pathname. If you enter **p** followed by TAB after the _ character, the shell completes the command line:

```
$ cat films/dark_p ⇨ TAB ⇨ assage
```

Because there is no further ambiguity, the shell appends a SPACE so you can either finish typing the command line or press RETURN to execute the command. If the complete pathname is that of a directory, bash appends a slash (**/**) in place of a SPACE.

## VARIABLE COMPLETION

When you are typing a variable name, pressing TAB results in *variable completion*, wherein bash attempts to complete the name of the variable. In case of an ambiguity, pressing TAB twice displays a list of choices:

```
$ echo $HO ⇨ TAB (beep) ⇨ TAB
$HOME        $HOSTNAME  $HOSTTYPE
$ echo $HOM ⇨ TAB ⇨ E
```

### Pressing RETURN executes the command

caution  Pressing RETURN causes the shell to execute the command regardless of where the cursor is on the command line.

## .inputrc: CONFIGURING THE READLINE LIBRARY

The Bourne Again Shell and other programs that use the Readline Library read the file specified by the **INPUTRC** environment variable to obtain initialization information. If **INPUTRC** is not set, these programs read the **~/.inputrc** file. They ignore lines of **.inputrc** that are blank or that start with a hashmark (#).

### VARIABLES

You can set variables in **.inputrc** to control the behavior of the Readline Library using the following syntax:

> set *variable value*

Table 9-11 lists some variables and values you can use. See "Readline Variables" in the bash man or info page for a complete list.

**Table 9-11**   Readline variables

| Variable | Effect |
| --- | --- |
| editing-mode | Set to **vi** to start Readline in vi mode. Set to **emacs** to start Readline in emacs mode (the default). Similar to the **set –o vi** and **set –o emacs** shell commands (page 386). |
| horizontal-scroll-mode | Set to **on** to cause long lines to extend off the right edge of the display area. Moving the cursor to the right when it is at the right edge of the display area shifts the line to the left so you can see more of the line. Shift the line back by moving the cursor back past the left edge. The default value is **off**, which causes long lines to wrap onto multiple lines of the display. |
| mark-directories | Set to **off** to cause Readline not to place a slash (/) at the end of directory names it completes. The default value is **on**. |
| mark-modified-lines | Set to **on** to cause Readline to precede modified history lines with an asterisk. The default value is **off**. |

### KEY BINDINGS

You can map keystroke sequences to Readline commands, changing or extending the default bindings. Like the emacs editor, the Readline Library includes many commands that are not bound to a keystroke sequence. To use an unbound command, you must map it using one of the following forms:

> *keyname*: *command_name*
> "*keystroke_sequence*": *command_name*

In the first form, you spell out the name for a single key. For example, CONTROL-U would be written as **control-u**. This form is useful for binding commands to single keys.

In the second form, you specify a string that describes a sequence of keys that will be bound to the command. You can use the emacs-style backslash escape sequences to represent the special keys CONTROL (\C), META (\M), and ESCAPE (\e). Specify a backslash by escaping it with another backslash: \\. Similarly a double or single quotation mark can be escaped with a backslash: \" or \'.

The **kill-whole-line** command, available in emacs mode only, deletes the current line. Put the following command in **.inputrc** to bind the **kill-whole-line** command (which is unbound by default) to the keystroke sequence CONTROL-R:

```
control-r: kill-whole-line
```

bind  Give the command **bind –P** to display a list of all Readline commands. If a command is bound to a key sequence, that sequence is shown. Commands you can use in vi mode start with **vi**. For example, **vi-next-word** and **vi-prev-word** move the cursor to the beginning of the next and previous words, respectively. Commands that do not begin with **vi** are generally available in emacs mode.

Use **bind –q** to determine which key sequence is bound to a command:

```
$ bind -q kill-whole-line
kill-whole-line can be invoked via "\C-r".
```

You can also bind text by enclosing it within double quotation marks (emacs mode only):

```
"QQ": "The Linux Operating System"
```

This command causes bash to insert the string **The Linux Operating System** when you type **QQ** on the command line.

### CONDITIONAL CONSTRUCTS

You can conditionally select parts of the **.inputrc** file using the **$if** directive. The syntax of the conditional construct is

> *$if test[=value]*
> > ***commands***
> *[$else*
> > ***commands]***
> *$endif*

where *test* is **mode**, **term**, or a program name such as **bash**. If *test* equals *value* (or if *test* is *true* when *value* is not specified), this structure executes the first set of ***commands***. If *test* does not equal *value* (or if *test* is *false* when *value* is not specified), it executes the second set of ***commands*** if they are present or exits from the structure if they are not present.

The power of the **$if** directive lies in the three types of tests it can perform.

1. You can test to see which mode is currently set.

   ```
   $if mode=vi
   ```

   The preceding test is *true* if the current Readline mode is **vi** and *false* otherwise. You can test for **vi** or **emacs**.

2. You can test the type of terminal.

```
$if term=xterm
```

The preceding test is *true* if the **TERM** variable is set to **xterm**. You can test for any value of **TERM**.

3. You can test the application name.

```
$if bash
```

The preceding test is *true* when you are running **bash** and not another program that uses the Readline Library. You can test for any application name.

These tests can customize the Readline Library based on the current mode, the type of terminal, and the application you are using. They give you a great deal of power and flexibility when you are using the Readline Library with **bash** and other programs.

The following commands in **.inputrc** cause CONTROL-Y to move the cursor to the beginning of the next word regardless of whether **bash** is in **vi** or **emacs** mode:

```
$ cat ~/.inputrc
set editing-mode vi
$if mode=vi
        "\C-y": vi-next-word
    $else
        "\C-y": forward-word
$endif
```

Because **bash** reads the preceding conditional construct when it is started, you must set the editing mode in **.inputrc**. Changing modes interactively using **set** will not change the binding of CONTROL-Y.

For more information on the Readline Library, open the **bash** man page and give the command **/^READLINE**, which searches for the word **READLINE** at the beginning of a line.

### If Readline commands do not work, log out and log in again

tip    The Bourne Again Shell reads **~/.inputrc** when you log in. After you make changes to this file, you must log out and log in again before the changes will take effect.

## LPI  ALIASES

An *alias* is a (usually short) name that the shell translates into another (usually longer) name or command. Aliases allow you to define new commands by substituting a string for the first token of a simple command. They are typically placed in the **~/.bashrc** or **~/.bash_aliases** startup file so that they are available to interactive subshells.

The syntax of the alias builtin is

*alias [name[=value]]*

No SPACEs are permitted around the equal sign. If *value* contains SPACEs or TABs, you must enclose *value* within quotation marks. An alias does not accept an argument from the command line in *value*. Use a function (page 396) when you need to use an argument.

An alias does not replace itself, which avoids the possibility of infinite recursion in handling an alias such as the following:

```
$ alias ls='ls -F'
```

You can nest aliases. Aliases are disabled for noninteractive shells (that is, shell scripts). Use the unalias builtin to remove an alias. When you give an alias builtin command without any arguments, the shell displays a list of all defined aliases:

```
$ alias
alias ll='ls -l'
alias l='ls -ltr'
alias ls='ls -F'
alias zap='rm -i'
```

To view the alias for a particular name, enter the command **alias** followed by the name of the alias. Fedora/RHEL defines some aliases. Enter an **alias** command to see which aliases are in effect. You can delete the aliases you do not want from the appropriate startup file.

## SINGLE VERSUS DOUBLE QUOTATION MARKS IN ALIASES

The choice of single or double quotation marks is significant in the alias syntax when the alias includes variables. If you enclose *value* within double quotation marks, any variables that appear in *value* are expanded when the alias is created. If you enclose *value* within single quotation marks, variables are not expanded until the alias is used. The following example illustrates the difference.

The **PWD** keyword variable holds the pathname of the working directory. Max creates two aliases while he is working in his home directory. Because he uses double quotation marks when he creates the **dirA** alias, the shell substitutes the value of the working directory when he creates this alias. The **alias dirA** command displays the **dirA** alias and shows that the substitution has already taken place:

```
$ echo $PWD
/home/max
$ alias dirA="echo Working directory is $PWD"
$ alias dirA
alias dirA='echo Working directory is /home/max'
```

When Max creates the **dirB** alias, he uses single quotation marks, which prevent the shell from expanding the **$PWD** variable. The **alias dirB** command shows that the **dirB** alias still holds the unexpanded **$PWD** variable:

```
$ alias dirB='echo Working directory is $PWD'
$ alias dirB
alias dirB='echo Working directory is $PWD'
```

After creating the **dirA** and **dirB** aliases, Max uses cd to make **cars** his working directory and gives each of the aliases as a command. The alias he created using double quotation marks displays the name of the directory he created the alias in as the working directory (which is wrong). In contrast, the **dirB** alias displays the proper name of the working directory:

```
$ cd cars
$ dirA
Working directory is /home/max
$ dirB
Working directory is /home/max/cars
```

### How to prevent the shell from invoking an alias

tip  The shell checks only simple, unquoted commands to see if they are aliases. Commands given as relative or absolute pathnames and quoted commands are not checked. When you want to give a command that has an alias but do not want to use the alias, precede the command with a backslash, specify the command's absolute pathname, or give the command as *./command*.

## EXAMPLES OF ALIASES

The following alias allows you to type **r** to repeat the previous command or **r abc** to repeat the last command line that began with **abc**:

```
$ alias r='fc -s'
```

If you use the command **ls –ltr** frequently, you can create an alias that substitutes **ls –ltr** when you give the command **l**:

```
$ alias l='ls -ltr'
$ l
-rw-r-----.  1 max pubs   3089 02-11 16:24 XTerm.ad
-rw-r--r--.  1 max pubs  30015 03-01 14:24 flute.ps
-rw-r--r--.  1 max pubs    641 04-01 08:12 fixtax.icn
-rw-r--r--.  1 max pubs    484 04-09 08:14 maptax.icn
drwxrwxr-x.  2 max pubs   1024 08-09 17:41 Tiger
drwxrwxr-x.  2 max pubs   1024 09-10 11:32 testdir
-rwxr-xr-x.  1 max pubs    485 09-21 08:03 floor
drwxrwxr-x.  2 max pubs   1024 09-27 20:19 Test_Emacs
```

Another common use of aliases is to protect yourself from mistakes. The following example substitutes the interactive version of the rm utility when you enter the command **zap**:

```
$ alias zap='rm -i'
$ zap f*
rm: remove 'fixtax.icn'? n
rm: remove 'flute.ps'? n
rm: remove 'floor'? n
```

The **–i** option causes rm to ask you to verify each file that would be deleted, thereby helping you avoid deleting the wrong file. You can also alias rm with the **rm –i** command: **alias rm='rm –i'**.

The aliases in the next example cause the shell to substitute **ls –l** each time you give an **ll** command and **ls –F** each time you use **ls**. The **–F** option causes **ls** to print a slash (/) at the end of directory names and an asterisk (*) at the end of the names of executable files.

```
$ alias ls='ls -F'
$ alias ll='ls -l'
$ ll
drwxrwxr-x. 2 max pubs  1024 09-27 20:19 Test_Emacs/
drwxrwxr-x. 2 max pubs  1024 08-09 17:41 Tiger/
-rw-r-----. 1 max pubs  3089 02-11 16:24 XTerm.ad
-rw-r--r--. 1 max pubs   641 04-01 08:12 fixtax.icn
-rw-r--r--. 1 max pubs 30015 03-01 14:24 flute.ps
-rwxr-xr-x. 1 max pubs   485 09-21 08:03 floor*
-rw-r--r--. 1 max pubs   484 04-09 08:14 maptax.icn
drwxrwxr-x. 2 max pubs  1024 09-10 11:32 testdir/
```

In this example, the string that replaces the alias **ll** (**ls –l**) itself contains an alias (**ls**). When it replaces an alias with its value, the shell looks at the first word of the replacement string to see whether it is an alias. In the preceding example, the replacement string contains the alias **ls**, so a second substitution occurs to produce the final command **ls –F –l**. (To avoid a *recursive plunge*, the **ls** in the replacement text, although an alias, is not expanded a second time.)

When given a list of aliases without the **=**_value_ or _value_ field, the alias builtin displays the value of each defined alias. The alias builtin reports an error if an alias has not been defined:

```
$ alias ll l ls zap wx
alias ll='ls -l'
alias l='ls -ltr'
alias ls='ls -F'
alias zap='rm -i'
bash: alias: wx: not found
```

You can avoid alias substitution by preceding the aliased command with a backslash (**\**):

```
$ \ls
Test_Emacs XTerm.ad  flute.ps  maptax.icn
Tiger      fixtax.icn floor     testdir
```

Because the replacement of an alias name with the alias value does not change the rest of the command line, any arguments are still received by the command that is executed:

```
$ ll f*
-rw-r--r--. 1 max pubs   641 04-01 08:12 fixtax.icn
-rw-r--r--. 1 max pubs 30015 03-01 14:24 flute.ps
-rwxr-xr-x. 1 max pubs   485 09-21 08:03 floor*
```

You can remove an alias using the unalias builtin. When the **zap** alias is removed, it is no longer displayed by the alias builtin, and its subsequent use results in an error message:

```
$ unalias zap
$ alias
alias ll='ls -l'
alias l='ls -ltr'
alias ls='ls -F'
$ zap maptax.icn
bash: zap: command not found
```

# LPI  FUNCTIONS

A shell function is similar to a shell script in that it stores a series of commands for execution at a later time. However, because the shell stores a function in the computer's main memory (RAM) instead of in a file on the disk, the shell can access it more quickly than the shell can access a script. The shell also preprocesses (parses) a function so it starts more quickly than a script. Finally the shell executes a shell function in the same shell that called it. If you define too many functions, the overhead of starting a subshell (as when you run a script) can become unacceptable.

You can declare a shell function in the **~/.bash_profile** startup file, in the script that uses it, or directly from the command line. You can remove functions using the **unset** builtin. The shell does not retain functions after you log out.

### Removing variables and functions that have the same name

tip   If you have a shell variable and a function that have the same name, using **unset** removes the shell variable. If you then use **unset** again with the same name, it removes the function.

The syntax that declares a shell function is

> *[function] **function-name** () {*
>     ***commands***
> *}*

where the word *function* is optional (and is frequently omitted; it is not portable), *function-name* is the name you use to call the function, and *commands* comprise the list of commands the function executes when you call it. The *commands* can be anything you would include in a shell script, including calls to other functions.

The opening brace ({) can appear on the line following the function name. Aliases and variables are expanded when a function is read, not when it is executed. You can use the **break** statement (page 1005) within a function to terminate its execution.

You can declare a function on a single line. Because the closing brace must appear as a separate command, you must place a semicolon before the closing brace when you use this syntax:

```
$ say_hi() { echo "hi" ; }
$ say_hi
hi
```

Shell functions are useful as a shorthand as well as to define special commands. The following function starts a process named **process** in the background, with the output normally displayed by **process** being saved in **.process.out**.

```
start_process() {
process > .process.out 2>&1 &
}
```

The next example creates a simple function that displays the date, a header, and a list of the people who are logged in on the system. This function runs the same commands as the **whoson** script described on page 337. In this example the function is being entered from the keyboard. The greater than (**>**) signs are secondary shell prompts (**PS2**); do not enter them.

```
$ function whoson () {
>    date
>    echo "Users Currently Logged On"
>    who
> }

$ whoson
Fri Aug 9 15:44:58 PDT 2013
Users Currently Logged On
hls        console      2013-08-08 08:59   (:0)
max        pts/4        2013-08-08 09:33   (0.0)
zach       pts/7        2013-08-08 09:23   (guava)
```

**Function local variables**  You can use the local builtin only within a function. This builtin causes its arguments to be local to the function it is called from and its children. Without local, variables declared in a function are available to the shell that called the function (functions are run in the shell they are called from). The following function demonstrates the use of local.

```
$ demo () {
> x=4
> local y=8
> echo "demo: $x $y"
> }
$ demo
demo: 4 8
$ echo $x
4
$ echo $y

$
```

The **demo** function, which is entered from the keyboard, declares two variables, **x** and **y**, and displays their values. The variable **x** is declared with a normal assignment statement while **y** is declared using local. After running the function, the shell that called the function has access to **x** but knows nothing of **y**. See page 1040 for another example of function local variables.

**Export a function**  An **export –f** command places the named function in the environment so it is available to child processes.

**Functions in startup files**  If you want the **whoson** function to be available without having to enter it each time you log in, put its definition in **~/.bash_profile**. Then run **.bash_profile**, using the **.** (dot) command to put the changes into effect immediately:

```
$ cat ~/.bash_profile
export TERM=vt100
stty kill '^u'
whoson () {
    date
    echo "Users Currently Logged On"
    who
}

$ . ~/.bash_profile
```

You can specify arguments when you call a function. Within the function these arguments are available as positional parameters (page 1022). The following example shows the **arg1** function entered from the keyboard:

```
$ arg1 ( ) { echo "$1" ; }
$ arg1 first_arg
first_arg
```

See the function **switch** () on page 332 for another example of a function.

**optional**   The following function allows you to place variables in the environment (export them) using tcsh syntax. The env utility lists all environment variables and their values and verifies that **setenv** worked correctly:

```
$ cat .bash_profile
...
# setenv - keep tcsh users happy
setenv() {
    if [ $# -eq 2 ]
        then
            eval $1=$2
            export $1
        else
            echo "Usage: setenv NAME VALUE" 1>&2
    fi
}
$ . ~/.bash_profile
$ setenv TCL_LIBRARY /usr/local/lib/tcl
$ env | grep TCL_LIBRARY
TCL_LIBRARY=/usr/local/lib/tcl
```

eval   The **$#** special parameter (page 1027) takes on the value of the number of command-line arguments. This function uses the eval builtin to force bash to scan the command **$1=$2** *twice*. Because **$1=$2** begins with a dollar sign ($), the shell treats the entire string as a single token—a command. With variable substitution performed, the command name becomes **TCL_LIBRARY=/usr/local/lib/tcl**, which results in an error. With eval, a second scanning splits the string into the three desired tokens, and the correct assignment occurs. See page 1051 for more information on eval.

# CONTROLLING bash: FEATURES AND OPTIONS

This section explains how to control bash features and options using command-line options and the set and shopt builtins. The shell sets flags to indicate which options are set (on) and expands $- to a list of flags that are set; see page 1030 for more information.

# bash COMMAND-LINE OPTIONS

You can specify short and long command-line options. Short options consist of a hyphen followed by a letter; long options have two hyphens followed by multiple characters. Long options must appear before short options on a command line that calls bash. Table 9-12 lists some commonly used command-line options.

**Table 9-12**   bash command-line options

| Option | Explanation | Syntax |
|--------|-------------|--------|
| Help | Displays a usage message. | **--help** |
| No edit | Prevents users from using the Readline Library (page 386) to edit command lines in an interactive shell. | **--noediting** |
| No profile | Prevents reading these startup files (page 329): **/etc/profile**, **~/.bash_profile**, **~/.bash_login**, and **~/.profile**. | **--noprofile** |
| No rc | Prevents reading the **~/.bashrc** startup file (page 331). This option is on by default if the shell is called as **sh**. | **--norc** |
| POSIX | Runs **bash** in POSIX mode. | **--posix** |
| Version | Displays **bash** version information and exits. | **--version** |
| Login | Causes **bash** to run as though it were a login shell. | **-l** (lowercase "el") |
| shopt | Runs a shell with the *opt* shopt option (next page). A **-O** (uppercase "O") sets the option; **+O** unsets it. | [±]**O** [*opt*] |
| End of options | On the command line, signals the end of options. Subsequent tokens are treated as arguments even if they begin with a hyphen (**-**). | **--** |

# SHELL FEATURES

You can control the behavior of the Bourne Again Shell by turning features on and off. Different methods turn different features on and off: The set builtin controls one group of features, and the shopt builtin controls another group. You can also control many features from the command line you use to call bash.

### Features, options, variables, attributes?

tip   To avoid confusing terminology, this book refers to the various shell behaviors that you can control as *features*. The bash info page refers to them as "options" and "values of variables controlling optional shell behavior." In some places you might see them referred to as *attributes*.

### *LPI* set ±o: Turns Shell Features On and Off

The set builtin, when used with the –o or +o option, enables, disables, and lists certain bash features. For example, the following command turns on the **noclobber** feature (page 156):

```
$ set -o noclobber
```

You can turn this feature off (the default) by giving this command:

```
$ set +o noclobber
```

The command **set –o** without an option lists each of the features controlled by set, followed by its state (on or off). The command **set +o** without an option lists the same features in a form you can use as input to the shell. Table 9-13 lists bash features. This table does not list the –i option because you cannot set it. The shell sets this option when it is invoked as an interactive shell. See page 1024 for a discussion of other uses of set.

## shopt: Turns Shell Features On and Off

The shopt (shell option) builtin enables, disables, and lists certain bash features that control the behavior of the shell. For example, the following command causes bash to include filenames that begin with a period (.) when it expands ambiguous file references (the –s stands for *set*):

```
$ shopt -s dotglob
```

You can turn this feature off (the default) by giving the following command (the –u stands for *unset*):

```
$ shopt -u dotglob
```

The shell displays how a feature is set if you give the name of the feature as the only argument to shopt:

```
$ shopt dotglob
dotglob         off
```

Without any options or arguments, shopt lists the features it controls and their states. The command **shopt –s** without an argument lists the features controlled by shopt that are set or on. The command **shopt –u** lists the features that are unset or off. Table 9-13 lists bash features.

### Setting set ±o features using shopt

tip    You can use shopt to set/unset features that are otherwise controlled by **set ±o**. Use the regular shopt syntax using **–s** or **–u** and include the **–o** option. For example, the following command turns on the **noclobber** feature:

```
$ shopt -o -s noclobber
```

**Table 9-13**  bash features

| Feature | Description | Syntax | Alternate syntax |
|---|---|---|---|
| allexport | Automatically places in the environment (exports) all variables and functions you create or modify after giving this command (default is off). | set −o allexport | set −a |
| braceexpand | Causes bash to perform brace expansion (default is on; page 405). | set −o braceexpand | set −B |
| cdspell | Corrects minor spelling errors in directory names used as arguments to cd (default is off). | shopt −s cdspell | |
| cmdhist | Saves all lines of a multiline command in the same history entry, adding semicolons as needed (default is on). | shopt −s cmdhist | |
| dotglob | Causes shell special characters (wildcards; page 165) in an ambiguous file reference to match a leading period in a filename. By default, special characters do not match a leading period: You must always specify the filenames . and .. explicitly because no pattern ever matches them (default is off). | shopt −s dotglob | |
| emacs | Specifies emacs editing mode for command-line editing (default is on; page 387). | set −o emacs | |
| errexit | Causes bash to exit when a pipeline (page 158), which can be a simple command (page 147; not a control structure), fails (default is off). | set −o errexit | set −e |
| execfail | Causes a shell script to continue running when it cannot find the file that is given as an argument to exec. By default, a script terminates when exec cannot find the file that is given as its argument (default is off). | shopt −s execfail | |
| expand_aliases | Causes aliases (page 392) to be expanded (default is on for interactive shells and off for noninteractive shells). | shopt −s expand_aliases | |
| hashall | Causes bash to remember where commands it has found using **PATH** (page 359) are located (default is on). | set −o hashall | set −h |

**Table 9-13**   bash features (continued)

| Feature | Description | Syntax | Alternate syntax |
|---------|-------------|--------|------------------|
| **histappend** | Causes bash to append the history list to the file named by **HISTFILE** (page 377) when the shell exits (default is off [bash overwrites this file]). | **shopt –s histappend** | |
| **histexpand** | Turns on the history mechanism (which uses exclamation points by default; page 381). Turn this feature off to turn off history expansion (default is on). | **set –o histexpand** | **set –H** |
| **history** | Enables command history (default is on; page 376). | **set –o history** | |
| **huponexit** | Specifies that bash send a SIGHUP signal to all jobs when an interactive login shell exits (default is off). | **shopt –s huponexit** | |
| **ignoreeof** | Specifies that bash must receive ten EOF characters before it exits. Useful on noisy dial-up lines (default is off). | **set –o ignoreeof** | |
| **monitor** | Enables job control (default is on; page 346). | **set –o monitor** | **set –m** |
| **nocaseglob** | Causes ambiguous file references (page 165) to match filenames without regard to case (default is off). | **shopt –s nocaseglob** | |
| **noclobber** | Helps prevent overwriting files (default is off; page 156). | **set –o noclobber** | **set –C** |
| **noglob** | Disables pathname expansion (default is off; page 165). | **set –o noglob** | **set –f** |
| **notify** | With job control (page 346) enabled, reports the termination status of background jobs immediately (default is off: bash displays the status just before the next prompt). | **set –o notify** | **set –b** |
| **nounset** | Displays an error when the shell tries to expand an unset variable; bash exits from a script but not from an interactive shell (default is off: bash substitutes a null value for an unset variable). | **set –o nounset** | **set –u** |
| **nullglob** | Causes bash to substitute a null string for ambiguous file references (page 165) that do not match a filename (default is off: bash passes these file references as is). | **shopt –s nullglob** | |

**Table 9-13**   bash features (continued)

| Feature | Description | Syntax | Alternate syntax |
|---------|-------------|--------|------------------|
| pipefail | Sets the exit status of a pipeline to the exit status of the last (rightmost) simple command that failed (returned a nonzero exit status) in the pipeline; if no command failed, exit status is set to zero (default is off: bash sets the exit status of a pipeline to the exit status of the final command in the pipeline). | **set −o pipefail** | |
| posix | Runs bash in POSIX mode (default is off). | **set −o posix** | |
| verbose | Displays each command line after bash reads it but before bash expands it (default is off). See also **xtrace**. | **set −o verbose** | **set −v** |
| vi | Specifies vi editing mode for command-line editing (default is off; page 386). | **set −o vi** | |
| xpg_echo | Causes the echo builtin to expand backslash escape sequences without the need for the **−e** option (default is off; page 1009). | **shopt −s xpg_echo** | |
| xtrace | Turns on shell debugging: Displays the value of **PS4** (page 363) followed by each input line after the shell reads and expands it (default is off; see page 994 for a discussion). See also **verbose**. | **set −o xtrace** | **set −x** |

# PROCESSING THE COMMAND LINE

Whether you are working interactively or running a shell script, bash needs to read a command line before it can start processing it—bash always reads at least one line before processing a command. Some bash builtins, such as **if** and **case**, as well as functions and quoted strings, span multiple lines. When bash recognizes a command that covers more than one line, it reads the entire command before processing it. In interactive sessions, bash prompts with the secondary prompt (**PS2, >** by default; page 362) as you type each line of a multiline command until it recognizes the end of the command:

```
$ ps -ef |
> grep emacs
zach     26880 24579  1 14:42 pts/10   00:00:00 emacs notes
zach     26890 24579  0 14:42 pts/10   00:00:00 grep emacs

$ function hello () {
> echo hello there
> }
$
```

For more information refer to "Implicit Command-Line Continuation" on page 1063. After reading a command line, bash applies history expansion and alias substitution to the command line.

# HISTORY EXPANSION

"Reexecuting and Editing Commands" on page 378 discusses the commands you can give to modify and reexecute command lines from the history list. History expansion is the process bash uses to turn a history command into an executable command line. For example, when you enter the command !!, history expansion changes that command line so it is the same as the previous one. History expansion is turned on by default for interactive shells; **set +o histexpand** turns it off. History expansion does not apply to noninteractive shells (shell scripts).

# **LPI**   ALIAS SUBSTITUTION

Aliases (page 392) substitute a string for the first word of a simple command. By default, alias substitution is turned on for interactive shells and off for noninteractive shells; **shopt –u expand_aliases** turns it off.

# PARSING AND SCANNING THE COMMAND LINE

After processing history commands and aliases, bash does not execute the command immediately. One of the first things the shell does is to *parse* (isolate strings of characters in) the command line into tokens (words). After separating tokens and before executing the command, the shell scans the tokens and performs *command-line expansion*.

# COMMAND-LINE EXPANSION

Both interactive and noninteractive shells transform the command line using *command-line expansion* before passing the command line to the program being called. You can use a shell without knowing much about command-line expansion, but you can use what a shell has to offer to a better advantage with an understanding of this topic. This section covers Bourne Again Shell command-line expansion.

The Bourne Again Shell scans each token for the various types of expansion and substitution in the following order. Most of these processes expand a word into a single word. Only brace expansion, word splitting, and pathname expansion can change the number of words in a command (except for the expansion of the variable "$@"—see page 1026).

1. Brace expansion (next page)

2. Tilde expansion (page 407)

3. Parameter and variable expansion (page 408)

4. Arithmetic expansion (page 408)

5. Command substitution (page 410)

6. Word splitting (page 411)

7. Pathname expansion (page 412)

8. Process substitution (page 413)

9. Quote removal (page 413)

## ORDER OF EXPANSION

The order in which bash carries out these steps affects the interpretation of commands. For example, if you set a variable to a value that looks like the instruction for output redirection and then enter a command that uses the variable's value to perform redirection, you might expect bash to redirect the output.

```
$ SENDIT="> /tmp/saveit"
$ echo xxx $SENDIT
xxx > /tmp/saveit
$ cat /tmp/saveit
cat: /tmp/saveit: No such file or directory
```

In fact, the shell does *not* redirect the output—it recognizes input and output redirection before it evaluates variables. When it executes the command line, the shell checks for redirection and, finding none, evaluates the **SENDIT** variable. After replacing the variable with **> /tmp/saveit**, bash passes the arguments to echo, which dutifully copies its arguments to standard output. No **/tmp/saveit** file is created.

### Quotation marks can alter expansion

tip Double and single quotation marks cause the shell to behave differently when performing expansions. Double quotation marks permit parameter and variable expansion but suppress other types of expansion. Single quotation marks suppress all types of expansion.

## BRACE EXPANSION

*Brace expansion,* which originated in the C Shell, provides a convenient way to specify a series of strings or numbers. Although brace expansion is frequently used to specify filenames, the mechanism can be used to generate arbitrary strings; the shell does not attempt to match the brace notation with the names of existing files. Brace expansion is turned on in interactive and noninteractive shells by default; you can turn it off using **set +o braceexpand**. The shell also uses braces to isolate variable names (page 355).

The following example illustrates how brace expansion works. The ls command does not display any output because there are no files in the working directory. The echo builtin displays the strings the shell generates using brace expansion.

```
$ ls
$ echo chap_{one,two,three}.txt
chap_one.txt chap_two.txt chap_three.txt
```

The shell expands the comma-separated strings inside the braces on the command line into a SPACE-separated list of strings. Each string from the list is prepended with the string **chap_**, called the *preamble,* and appended with the string **.txt**, called the *postscript*. Both the preamble and the postscript are optional. The left-to-right order of the strings within the braces is preserved in the expansion. For the shell to treat the left and right braces specially and for brace expansion to occur, at least one comma must be inside the braces and no unquoted whitespace can appear inside the braces. You can nest brace expansions.

Brace expansion *can* match filenames. This feature is useful when there is a long preamble or postscript. The following example copies four files—main.c, f1.c, f2.c, and **tmp.c**—located in the **/usr/local/src/C** directory to the working directory:

```
$ cp /usr/local/src/C/{main,f1,f2,tmp}.c .
```

You can also use brace expansion to create directories with related names:

```
$ ls -F
file1  file2  file3
$ mkdir vrs{A,B,C,D,E}
$ ls -F
file1  file2  file3  vrsA/  vrsB/  vrsC/  vrsD/  vrsE/
```

The **–F** option causes ls to display a slash (/) after a directory and an asterisk (*) after an executable file. If you tried to use an ambiguous file reference instead of braces to specify the directories, the result would be different (and not what you wanted):

```
$ rmdir vrs*
$ mkdir vrs[A-E]
$ ls -F
file1  file2  file3  vrs[A-E]/
```

An ambiguous file reference matches the names of existing files. In the preceding example, because it found no filenames matching **vrs[A–E]**, bash passed the ambiguous file reference to mkdir, which created a directory with that name. Brackets in ambiguous file references are discussed on page 168.

**Sequence expression**    Under newer versions of bash, brace expansion can include a sequence expression to generate a sequence of characters. It can generate a sequential series of numbers or letters using the following syntax:

*{n1..n2[..incr]}*

where *n1* and *n2* are numbers or single letters and *incr* is a number. This syntax works on bash version 4.0+; give the command **echo $BASH_VERSION** to see which version you are using. When you specify invalid arguments, bash copies the arguments to standard output. Following are some examples:

```
$ echo {4..8}
4 5 6 7 8
$ echo {8..16..2}
8 10 12 14 16
$ echo {a..m..3}
a d g j m
$ echo {a..m..b}
{a..m..b}
$ echo {2..m}
{2..m}
```

See page 1051 for a way to use variables to specify the values used by a sequence expression. Page 996 shows an example in which a sequence expression is used to specify step values in a **for...in** loop.

*LPI*  seq   Older versions of bash do not support sequence expressions. Although you can use the seq utility to perform a similar function, seq does not work with letters and displays an error when given invalid arguments. The seq utility uses the following syntax:

> *seq n1 [incr] n2*

The –s option causes seq to use the specified character to separate its output. Following are some examples:

```
$ seq 4 8
4
5
6
7
8

$ seq -s\  8 2 16
8 10 12 14 16

$ seq a d
seq: invalid floating point argument: a
Try 'seq --help' for more information.
```

## *LE*  TILDE EXPANSION

Chapter 6 introduced a shorthand notation to specify your home directory or the home directory of another user. This section provides a more detailed explanation of *tilde expansion.*

The tilde (~) is a special character when it appears at the start of a token on a command line. When it sees a tilde in this position, bash looks at the following string of characters—up to the first slash (/) or to the end of the word if there is no slash—as a possible username. If this possible username is null (that is, if the tilde appears as a word by itself or if it is immediately followed by a slash), the shell substitutes the value of the **HOME** variable for the tilde. The following example demonstrates this expansion, where the last command copies the file named **letter** from Max's home directory to the working directory:

```
$ echo $HOME
/home/max
$ echo ~
/home/max
$ echo ~/letter
/home/max/letter
$ cp ~/letter .
```

If the string of characters following the tilde forms a valid username, the shell substitutes the path of the home directory associated with that username for the tilde and name. If the string is not null and not a valid username, the shell does not make any substitution:

```
$ echo ~zach
/home/zach
$ echo ~root
/root
$ echo ~xx
~xx
```

Tildes are also used in directory stack manipulation (page 349). In addition, **~+** is a synonym for **PWD** (the name of the working directory), and **~–** is a synonym for **OLDPWD** (the name of the previous working directory).

## PARAMETER AND VARIABLE EXPANSION

On a command line, a dollar sign (**$**) that is not followed by an open parenthesis introduces parameter or variable expansion. *Parameters* include both command-line, or positional, parameters (page 1022) and special parameters (page 1027). *Variables* include both user-created variables (page 353) and keyword variables (page 358). The bash man and info pages do not make this distinction.

The shell does not expand parameters and variables that are enclosed within single quotation marks and those in which the leading dollar sign is escaped (i.e., preceded with a backslash). The shell does expand parameters and variables enclosed within double quotation marks.

## ARITHMETIC EXPANSION

The shell performs *arithmetic expansion* by evaluating an arithmetic expression and replacing it with the result. Under bash the syntax for arithmetic expansion is

> *$((expression))*

The shell evaluates *expression* and replaces *$((expression))* with the result. This syntax is similar to the syntax used for command substitution [*$(...)*] and performs a parallel function. You can use *$((expression))* as an argument to a command or in place of any numeric value on a command line.

The rules for forming *expression* are the same as those found in the C programming language; all standard C arithmetic operators are available (see Table 27-8 on page 1059). Arithmetic in bash is done using integers. Unless you use variables of type integer (page 358) or actual integers, however, the shell must convert string-valued variables to integers for the purpose of the arithmetic evaluation.

You do not need to precede variable names within *expression* with a dollar sign (**$**). In the following example, after read (page 1041) assigns the user's response to **age**, an arithmetic expression determines how many years are left until age 100:

```
$ cat age_check
#!/bin/bash
read -p "How old are you? " age
echo "Wow, in $((100-age)) years, you'll be 100!"
```

```
$ ./age_check
How old are you? 55
Wow, in 45 years, you'll be 100!
```

You do not need to enclose the *expression* within quotation marks because bash does not perform pathname expansion until later. This feature makes it easier for you to use an asterisk (*) for multiplication, as the following example shows:

```
$ echo There are $((60*60*24*365)) seconds in a non-leap year.
There are 31536000 seconds in a non-leap year.
```

The next example uses wc, cut, arithmetic expansion, and command substitution (page 410) to estimate the number of pages required to print the contents of the file **letter.txt**. The output of the wc (word count) utility used with the –l option is the number of lines in the file, in columns (character positions) 1 through 4, followed by a SPACE and the name of the file (the first command following). The cut utility with the –c1–4 option extracts the first four columns.

```
$ wc -l letter.txt
351 letter.txt
$ wc -l letter.txt | cut -c1-4
351
```

The dollar sign and single parenthesis instruct the shell to perform command substitution; the dollar sign and double parentheses indicate arithmetic expansion:

```
$ echo $(( $(wc -l letter.txt | cut -c1-4)/66 + 1))
6
```

The preceding example sets up a pipeline that sends standard output from wc to standard input of cut. Because of command substitution, the output of both commands replaces the commands between the $( and the matching ) on the command line. Arithmetic expansion then divides this number by 66, the number of lines on a page. A 1 is added because integer division discards remainders.

### Fewer dollar signs ($)

tip  When you specify variables within $(( and )), the dollar signs that precede individual variable references are optional. This format also allows you to include whitespace around operators, making expressions easier to read.

```
$ x=23 y=37
$ echo $(( 2 * $x + 3 * $y ))
157
$ echo $(( 2 * x + 3 * y ))
157
```

Another way to get the same result without using cut is to redirect the input to wc instead of having wc get its input from a file you name on the command line. When you redirect its input, wc does not display the name of the file:

```
$ wc -l < letter.txt
    351
```

It is common practice to assign the result of arithmetic expansion to a variable:

```
$ numpages=$(( $(wc -l < letter.txt)/66 + 1))
```

**let builtin**    The let builtin evaluates arithmetic expressions just as the $(( )) syntax does. The following command is equivalent to the preceding one:

```
$ let "numpages=$(wc -l < letter.txt)/66 + 1"
```

The double quotation marks keep the SPACEs (both those you can see and those that result from the command substitution) from separating the expression into separate arguments to let. The value of the last expression determines the exit status of let. If the value of the last expression is 0, the exit status of let is 1; otherwise, the exit status is 0.

You can supply let with multiple arguments on a single command line:

```
$ let a=5+3 b=7+2
$ echo $a $b
8 9
```

When you refer to variables when doing arithmetic expansion with let or $(( )), the shell does not require a variable name to begin with a dollar sign ($). Nevertheless, it is a good practice to do so for consistency, because in most places you must precede a variable name with a dollar sign.

## **LE+**  COMMAND SUBSTITUTION

*Command substitution* replaces a command with the output of that command. The preferred syntax for command substitution under bash is

$(command)

Under bash you can also use the following, older syntax:

` command `

The shell executes *command* within a subshell and replaces *command*, along with the surrounding punctuation, with standard output of *command*. Standard error of *command* is not affected.

In the following example, the shell executes pwd and substitutes the output of the command for the command and surrounding punctuation. Then the shell passes the output of the command, which is now an argument, to echo, which displays it.

```
$ echo $(pwd)
/home/max
```

The next script assigns the output of the pwd builtin to the variable **where** and displays a message containing the value of this variable:

```
$ cat where
where=$(pwd)
echo "You are using the $where directory."
```

```
$ ./where
You are using the /home/zach directory.
```

Although it illustrates how to assign the output of a command to a variable, this example is not realistic. You can more directly display the output of pwd without using a variable:

```
$ cat where2
echo "You are using the $(pwd) directory."
$ ./where2
You are using the /home/zach directory.
```

The following command uses find to locate files with the name **README** in the directory tree rooted at the working directory. This list of files is standard output of find and becomes the list of arguments to ls.

```
$ ls -l $(find . -name README -print)
```

The next command line shows the older `command` syntax:

```
$ ls -l `find . -name README -print`
```

One advantage of the newer syntax is that it avoids the rather arcane rules for token handling, quotation mark handling, and escaped back ticks within the old syntax. Another advantage of the new syntax is that it can be nested, unlike the old syntax. For example, you can produce a long listing of all **README** files whose size exceeds the size of **./README** using the following command:

```
$ ls -l $(find . -name README -size +$(echo $(cat ./README | wc -c)c ) -print )
```

Try giving this command after giving a **set –x** command (page 994) to see how bash expands it. If there is no **README** file, the command displays the output of **ls –l**.

For additional scripts that use command substitution, see pages 991, 1010, and 1050.

### $(( versus $(

tip The symbols **$((** constitute a single token. They introduce an arithmetic expression, not a command substitution. Thus, if you want to use a parenthesized subshell (page 344) within **$( )**, you must put a SPACE between the **$(** and the following **(**.

## WORD SPLITTING

The results of parameter and variable expansion, command substitution, and arithmetic expansion are candidates for word splitting. Using each character of **IFS** (page 363) as a possible delimiter, bash splits these candidates into words or tokens. If **IFS** is unset, bash uses its default value (SPACE-TAB-NEWLINE). If **IFS** is null, bash does not split words.

## LE+  PATHNAME EXPANSION

*Pathname expansion* (page 165), also called *filename generation* or *globbing,* is the process of interpreting ambiguous file references and substituting the appropriate list of filenames. Unless **noglob** (page 402) is set, the shell performs this function when it encounters an ambiguous file reference—a token containing any of the unquoted characters *, ?, [, or ]. If bash cannot locate any files that match the specified pattern, the token with the ambiguous file reference remains unchanged. The shell does not delete the token or replace it with a null string but rather passes it to the program as is (except see **nullglob** on page 402).

In the first echo command in the following example, the shell expands the ambiguous file reference **tmp\*** and passes three tokens (**tmp1, tmp2,** and **tmp3**) to echo. The echo builtin displays the three filenames it was passed by the shell. After rm removes the three **tmp\*** files, the shell finds no filenames that match **tmp\*** when it tries to expand it. It then passes the unexpanded string to the echo builtin, which displays the string it was passed.

```
$ ls
tmp1 tmp2 tmp3
$ echo tmp*
tmp1 tmp2 tmp3
$ rm tmp*
$ echo tmp*
tmp*
```

A period that either starts a pathname or follows a slash (/) in a pathname must be matched explicitly unless you have set **dotglob** (page 401). The option **nocaseglob** (page 402) causes ambiguous file references to match filenames without regard to case.

**LE   Quotation marks**  Putting double quotation marks around an argument causes the shell to suppress pathname and all other kinds of expansion except parameter and variable expansion. Putting single quotation marks around an argument suppresses all types of expansion. The second echo command in the following example shows the variable **$max** between double quotation marks, which allow variable expansion. As a result the shell expands the variable to its value: **sonar.** This expansion does not occur in the third echo command, which uses single quotation marks. Because neither single nor double quotation marks allow pathname expansion, the last two commands display the unexpanded argument **tmp\*** .

```
$ echo tmp* $max
tmp1 tmp2 tmp3 sonar
$ echo "tmp* $max"
tmp* sonar
$ echo 'tmp* $max'
tmp* $max
```

The shell distinguishes between the value of a variable and a reference to the variable and does not expand ambiguous file references if they occur in the value of a variable. As a consequence you can assign to a variable a value that includes special characters, such as an asterisk (*).

**Levels of expansion**  In the next example, the working directory has three files whose names begin with letter. When you assign the value **letter\*** to the variable **var**, the shell does not expand the ambiguous file reference because it occurs in the value of a variable (in the assignment statement for the variable). No quotation marks surround the string **letter\***; context alone prevents the expansion. After the assignment the set builtin (with the help of grep) shows the value of **var** to be **letter\***.

```
$ ls letter*
letter1  letter2  letter3
$ var=letter*
$ set | grep var
var='letter*'
$ echo '$var'
$var
$ echo "$var"
letter*
$ echo $var
letter1 letter2 letter3
```

The three **echo** commands demonstrate three levels of expansion. When **$var** is quoted with single quotation marks, the shell performs no expansion and passes the character string **$var** to echo, which displays it. With double quotation marks, the shell performs variable expansion only and substitutes the value of the **var** variable for its name, preceded by a dollar sign. No pathname expansion is performed on this command because double quotation marks suppress it. In the final command, the shell, without the limitations of quotation marks, performs variable substitution and then pathname expansion before passing the arguments to echo.

## PROCESS SUBSTITUTION

The Bourne Again Shell can replace filename arguments with processes. An argument with the syntax <*(command)* causes *command* to be executed and the output to be written to a named pipe (FIFO). The shell replaces that argument with the name of the pipe. If that argument is then used as the name of an input file during processing, the output of *command* is read. Similarly an argument with the syntax >*(command)* is replaced by the name of a pipe that *command* reads as standard input.

The following example uses sort (page 239) with the **–m** (merge, which works correctly only if the input files are already sorted) option to combine two word lists into a single list. Each word list is generated by a pipeline that extracts words matching a pattern from a file and sorts the words in that list.

```
$ sort -m -f <(grep "[^A-Z]..$" memo1 | sort) <(grep ".*aba.*" memo2 |sort)
```

## QUOTE REMOVAL

After bash finishes with the preceding list, it performs *quote removal*. This process removes from the command line single quotation marks, double quotation marks, and backslashes that are not a result of an expansion.

# Chapter Summary

The shell is both a command interpreter and a programming language. As a command interpreter, it executes commands you enter in response to its prompt. As a programming language, it executes commands from files called shell scripts. When you start a shell, it typically runs one or more startup files.

Running a shell script

When the file holding a shell script is in the working directory, there are three basic ways to execute the shell script from the command line.

1. Type the simple filename of the file that holds the script.

2. Type an absolute or relative pathname, including the simple filename preceded by ./.

3. Type **bash** followed by the name of the file.

Technique 1 requires the working directory to be in the **PATH** variable. Techniques 1 and 2 require you to have execute and read permission for the file holding the script. Technique 3 requires you to have read permission for the file holding the script.

Job control

A job is another name for a process running a pipeline (which can be a simple command). You can bring a job running in the background into the foreground using the fg builtin. You can put a foreground job into the background using the bg builtin, provided you first suspend the job by pressing the suspend key (typically CONTROL-Z). Use the jobs builtin to display the list of jobs that are running in the background or are suspended.

Variables

The shell allows you to define variables. You can declare and initialize a variable by assigning a value to it; you can remove a variable declaration using unset. *Shell variables* are local to the process they are defined in. Environment variables are global and are placed in the environment using the export builtin so they are available to child processes. Variables you declare are called *user-created* variables. The shell defines *keyword* variables. Within a shell script you can work with the *positional* (command-line) parameters the script was called with.

Locale

Locale specifies the way locale-aware programs display certain kinds of data, such as times and dates, money and other numeric values, telephone numbers, and measurements. It can also specify collating sequence and printer paper size.

Process

Each process is the execution of a single command and has a unique identification (PID) number. When you give the shell a command, it forks a new (child) process to execute the command (unless the command is built into the shell). While the child process is running, the shell is in a state called sleep. By ending a command line with an ampersand (&), you can run a child process in the background and bypass the sleep state so the shell prompt returns immediately after you press RETURN. Each command in a shell script forks a separate process, each of which might in turn fork other processes. When a process terminates, it returns its exit status to its parent process. An exit status of zero signifies success; a nonzero value signifies failure.

History    The history mechanism maintains a list of recently issued command lines called *events,* which provides a way to reexecute previous commands quickly. There are several ways to work with the history list; one of the easiest is to use a command-line editor.

Command-line editors    When using an interactive Bourne Again Shell, you can edit a command line and commands from the history list, using either of the Bourne Again Shell's command-line editors (vim or emacs). When you use the vim command-line editor, you start in Input mode, unlike with the stand-alone version of vim. You can switch between Command and Input modes. The emacs editor is modeless and distinguishes commands from editor input by recognizing control characters as commands.

Aliases    An alias is a name the shell translates into another name or command. Aliases allow you to define new commands by substituting a string for the first token of a simple command.

Functions    A shell function is a series of commands that, unlike a shell script, is parsed prior to being stored in memory. As a consequence shell functions run faster than shell scripts. Shell scripts are parsed at runtime and are stored on disk. A function can be defined on the command line or within a shell script. If you want the function definition to remain in effect across login sessions, you can define it in a startup file. Like functions in many programming languages, a shell function is called by giving its name followed by any arguments.

Shell features    There are several ways to customize the shell's behavior. You can use options on the command line when you call bash. You can also use the bash set and shopt builtins to turn features on and off.

Command-line expansion    When it processes a command line, the Bourne Again Shell replaces some words with expanded text. Most types of command-line expansion are invoked by the appearance of a special character within a word (for example, the leading dollar sign that denotes a variable). Table 9-6 on page 366 lists these special characters. The expansions take place in a specific order. Following the history and alias expansions, the common expansions are parameter and variable expansion, command substitution, and pathname expansion. Surrounding a word with double quotation marks suppresses all types of expansion except parameter and variable expansion. Single quotation marks suppress all types of expansion, as does quoting (escaping) a special character by preceding it with a backslash.

# EXERCISES

1. Explain the following unexpected result:

```
$ whereis date
date: /bin/date ...
$ echo $PATH
.:/usr/local/bin:/usr/bin:/bin
$ cat > date
echo "This is my own version of date."
$ ./date
Tue May 21 11:45:49 PDT 2013
```

2. What are two ways you can execute a shell script when you do not have execute permission for the file containing the script? Can you execute a shell script if you do not have read permission for the file containing the script?

3. What is the purpose of the **PATH** variable?

    a. Set the **PATH** variable and place it in the environment so it causes the shell to search the following directories in order:

    - /usr/local/bin

    - /usr/bin

    - /bin

    - /usr/kerberos/bin

    - The **bin** directory in your home directory

    - The working directory

    b. If there is an executable file named **doit** in **/usr/bin** and another file with the same name in your **~/bin** directory, which one will be executed?

    c. If your **PATH** variable is not set to search the working directory, how can you execute a program located there?

    d. Which command can you use to add the directory **/usr/games** to the end of the list of directories in **PATH**?

4. Assume you have made the following assignment:

    ```
    $ person=zach
    ```

    Give the output of each of the following commands.

    a. echo $person

    b. echo '$person'

    c. echo "$person"

5. The following shell script adds entries to a file named **journal-file** in your home directory. This script helps you keep track of phone conversations and meetings.

    ```
    $ cat journal
    # journal: add journal entries to the file
    # $HOME/journal-file

    file=$HOME/journal-file
    date >> $file
    echo -n "Enter name of person or group: "
    read name
    echo "$name" >> $file
    echo >> $file
    cat >> $file
    echo "---------------------------------------------------------" >>
    $file
    echo >> $file
    ```

a. What do you have to do to the script to be able to execute it?

b. Why does the script use the read builtin the first time it accepts input from the terminal and the cat utility the second time?

6. Assume the **/home/zach/grants/biblios** and **/home/zach/biblios** directories exist. Specify Zach's working directory after he executes each sequence of commands. Explain what happens in each case.

a.
```
$ pwd
/home/zach/grants
$ CDPATH=$(pwd)
$ cd
$ cd biblios
```

b.
```
$ pwd
/home/zach/grants
$ CDPATH=$(pwd)
$ cd $HOME/biblios
```

7. Name two ways you can identify the PID number of the login shell.

8. Enter the following command:

```
$ sleep 30 | cat /etc/services
```

Is there any output from sleep? Where does cat get its input from? What has to happen before the shell will display a prompt?

# ADVANCED EXERCISES

9. Write a sequence of commands or a script that demonstrates variable expansion occurs before pathname expansion.

10. Write a shell script that outputs the name of the shell executing it.

11. Explain the behavior of the following shell script:

```
$ cat quote_demo
twoliner="This is line 1.
This is line 2."
echo "$twoliner"
echo $twoliner
```

a. How many arguments does each echo command see in this script? Explain.

b. Redefine the **IFS** shell variable so the output of the second echo is the same as the first.

12. Add the exit status of the previous command to your prompt so it behaves similarly to the following:

```
$ [0] ls xxx
ls: xxx: No such file or directory
$ [1]
```

13. The dirname utility treats its argument as a pathname and writes to standard output the path prefix—that is, everything up to but not including the last component:

    ```
    $ dirname a/b/c/d
    a/b/c
    ```

    If you give **dirname** a simple filename (no **/** characters) as an argument, **dirname** writes a **.** to standard output:

    ```
    $ dirname simple
    .
    ```

    Implement dirname as a bash function. Make sure it behaves sensibly when given such arguments as **/**.

14. Implement the basename utility, which writes the last component of its pathname argument to standard output, as a bash function. For example, given the pathname **a/b/c/d**, basename writes **d** to standard output:

    ```
    $ basename a/b/c/d
    d
    ```

15. The Linux basename utility has an optional second argument. If you give the command **basename** *path suffix*, basename removes the *suffix* and the prefix from *path*:

    ```
    $ basename src/shellfiles/prog.bash .bash
    prog
    $ basename src/shellfiles/prog.bash .c
    prog.bash
    ```

    Add this feature to the function you wrote for exercise 14.

# 10

# SYSTEM ADMINISTRATION: CORE CONCEPTS

## OBJECTIVES

After reading this chapter you should be able to:

▶ Explain the need for and the responsibility of a privileged user (**root**)

▶ Gain **root** privileges using su and sudo

▶ Describe the startup sequence using systemd

▶ Manage which services start at boot time

▶ List four characteristics of a well-maintained system

▶ Start and stop services on a running system

▶ Boot into single-user mode for system maintenance

▶ Shut down a running system

▶ Secure a system by applying updates, monitoring logs, and controlling access to files using SELinux, setuid permission, and PAM

▶ Use system administration tools to monitor and maintain the system

▶ List common steps for installing, configuring, and securing a server

▶ Configure a system using a static IP address or using DHCP

The job of a system administrator is to keep one or more systems in a useful and convenient state for users. On a Linux system, the administrator and user might both be you, with you and the computer being separated by only a few feet. Alternately, the system administrator might be halfway around the world, supporting a network of systems, with you being one of thousands of users. Or a system administrator can be one person who works part-time taking care of a system and perhaps is also a user of the system. In some cases several administrators might work together full-time to keep many systems running.

A well-maintained system:

- Runs quickly enough so users do not get frustrated waiting for the system to respond or complete a task

- Has enough storage to accommodate the reasonable needs of users

- Provides a working environment appropriate to each user's abilities and requirements

- Is secure from malicious and accidental acts altering its performance or compromising the security of the data it holds and exchanges with other systems

- Is backed up regularly, with recently backed-up files readily available to users

- Has recent copies of the software that users need to get their jobs done

- Is easier to administer than a poorly maintained system

In addition, a system administrator should be available to help users with all types of system-related problems—from logging in to obtaining and installing software updates to tracking down and fixing obscure network issues.

Part III of this book breaks system administration into nine chapters.

- Chapter 9 covers bash (Bourne Again Shell) to a depth that you can use it interactively to administer a system and begin to understand complex administration shell scripts.

- Chapter 10 covers the core concepts of system administration, including working with **root** (Superuser) privileges, system operation, configuration tools and other useful utilities, general information about setting up and securing a server (including a section on DHCP), and PAM.

- Chapter 11 covers files, directories, and filesystems from an administrator's point of view.

- Chapter 12 covers installing software on the system, including the use of yum, BitTorrent, and curl.

- Chapter 13 discusses how to set up local and remote printers that use the CUPS printing system.

- Chapter 14 explains how to rebuild the Linux kernel and work with GRUB, the Linux boot loader.

- Chapter 15 covers additional system administrator tasks and tools, including setting up users and groups, backing up files, scheduling tasks, printing system reports, and general problem solving.

- Chapter 16 goes into detail about how to set up a LAN, including setting up and configuring network hardware and configuring software.

- Chapter 17 describes how to set up virtual machines locally (gnome-boxes, KVM/QEMU, and VMware) and in the cloud (AWS).

Because Linux is readily configurable and runs on a wide variety of platforms, this chapter cannot discuss every system configuration or every action you might have to take as a system administrator. Instead, this chapter seeks to familiarize you with the concepts you need to understand and the tools you will use to maintain a Linux system. Where it is not possible to go into depth about a subject, the chapter provides references to other sources.

This chapter assumes you are familiar with the following terms:

| | | |
|---|---|---|
| *block device* (page 1239) | *filesystem* (page 1250) | *root filesystem* (page 1271) |
| *daemon* (page 1245) | *fork* (page 1250) | *runlevel* (page 1271) |
| *device* (page 1246) | *kernel* (page 1257) | *signal* (page 1273) |
| *device filename* (page 1247) | *login shell* (page 1259) | *spawn* (page 1274) |
| *disk partition* (page 1247) | *mount* (page 1261) | *system console* (page 1276) |
| *environment* (page 1249) | *process* (page 1267) | *X server* (page 1281) |

### If there is a problem, check the log files

tip   If something on the system is not working as expected, check the log files in **/var/log**. This directory holds many files and subdirectories. If you cannot connect to a server, also check the log files on the server.

### If something does not work, see if the problem is caused by SELinux

tip   If a server or other system software does not work properly, especially if it displays a permissions-related error message, the problem might lie with SELinux. To see whether SELinux is the cause of the problem, put SELinux in permissive mode and run the software again. If the problem goes away, you need to modify the SELinux policy. Remember to turn SELinux back on. See the tip on page 473 and refer to "Setting the Targeted Policy using system-config-selinux" on page 475.

### If you cannot access a remote system, check the firewall

tip   If a server does not appear to work or you cannot access a remote system, make sure the firewall is not the problem. On a non-production system, use **systemctl** to turn the firewall off (page 900) and see if the problem goes away. Then turn the firewall back on and open only the necessary port using **firewall-cmd** (page 906).

# RUNNING COMMANDS WITH root PRIVILEGES

Some commands can damage the filesystem or crash the operating system. Other commands can invade users' privacy or make the system less secure. To keep a Linux system up and running as well as secure, most systems are configured not to permit ordinary users to execute some commands and access certain files. Linux provides several ways for a trusted user to execute these commands and access these files. A user running with these privileges is sometimes referred to as an *administrator, privileged user,* or *Superuser.*

## Administrator

security  During installation (page 68) and whenever you add or modify a user (pages 112 and 598), you have the opportunity to specify that user as an *administrator.* Two characteristics give an administrator special privileges. First, an administrator is a member of the **wheel** group (page 429) and as such can use **sudo** to authenticate using her password; she does not need to know the **root** password. Second, **polkit** (www.freedesktop.org/wiki/Software/polkit) is set up so that an administrator can do some kinds of administrative work on the desktop (e.g., updating software and adding a printer) without needing to enter a password.

# THE SPECIAL POWERS OF A PRIVILEGED USER

root privileges  A user running with **root** privileges has the following powers—and more.

- Some commands, such as those that add new users, partition hard drives, and change system configuration, can be executed only by a user working with **root** privileges. Such a user can configure tools, such as **sudo**, to give specific users permission to perform tasks that are normally reserved for a user running with **root** privileges.

- Read, write, and execute file access and directory access permissions do not affect a user with **root** privileges. A user with **root** privileges can read from, write to, and execute all files, as well as examine and work in all directories.

  Exceptions to these privileges exist. For example, SELinux mandatory access can be configured to limit **root** access to a file. Also, a user working with **root** privileges cannot make sense of an encrypted file without possessing the key.

- Some restrictions and safeguards that are built into some commands do not apply to a user with **root** privileges. For example, a user with **root** privileges can change any user's password without knowing the old password.

## Console security

security  Linux is not secure from a person who has physical access to the computer. Additional security measures, such as setting boot loader and BIOS passwords, can help secure the computer. However, if someone has physical access to the hardware, as system console users typically do, it is very difficult to secure a system from that user.

**# prompt**  When you are running with **root** privileges in a command-line environment, by convention the shell displays a special prompt to remind you of your status. By default, this prompt is (or ends with) a hashmark (#).

### Least privilege

**caution**  When you are working on any computer system, but especially when you are working as the system administrator (working with **root** privileges), perform any task while using the least privilege possible. When you can perform a task logged in as an ordinary user, do so. When you must run a command with **root** privileges, do as much as you can as an ordinary user, log in or use su or sudo so you have **root** privileges, complete the part of the task that has to be done with **root** privileges, and revert to being an ordinary user as soon as you can. Because you are more likely to make a mistake when you are rushing, this concept becomes even more important when you have less time to apply it.

## **LE**   GAINING root PRIVILEGES

Classically a user gained **root** privileges by logging in as the user named **root** or by giving an su (substitute user) command and providing the **root** password. More recently the use of sudo has taken over this classic technique of gaining **root** privileges. With sudo, the user logs in as herself, gives an **sudo** command, and provides her own password (not the **root** password) to gain **root** privileges. "Advantages of sudo" on page 428 discusses some of the advantages of sudo.

**Graphical environment**  When an ordinary user executes a privileged command in a graphical environment, the system prompts for the **root** password or the user's password, depending on how the system is set up.

Some distributions lock the **root** account by not assigning a **root** password. On these systems, you cannot gain **root** privileges using a technique that requires you to supply the **root** password unless you unlock the **root** account as explained on page 438. Fedora/RHEL assigns a **root** password when the system is installed, so you can use these techniques from the start.

### There is a **root** account, but no **root** password

**tip**  As installed, some systems (not Fedora/RHEL) lock the **root** account by not providing a **root** password. This setup prevents anyone from logging in to the **root** account (except when you bring the system up in single-user mode [page 450]). There is, however, a **root** account (a user with the username **root**—look at the first line in **/etc/passwd**). This account/user owns files (give the command **ls –l /usr/bin**) and runs processes (give the command **ps –ef** and look at the left column of the output). The **root** account is critical to the functioning of a Linux system.

When properly set up, the sudo utility enables you to run a command as though it had been run by a user logged in as **root**. This book uses the phrase **working (or run) with root privileges** to emphasize that, although you might not be logged in as **root**, when you use su or sudo you have the powers of the **root** user.

The following list describes some of the ways you can gain or grant **root** privileges. Some of these techniques depend on you supplying the password for the **root** account. Again, if the **root** account is locked, you cannot use these techniques unless you unlock the **root** account (set up a **root** password), as explained on page 438. Other techniques depend on the **sudoers** file being set up to allow you to gain **root** privileges (page 433). If this file is not set up in this manner, you cannot use these techniques.

- When you bring the system up in single-user/rescue mode (page 450), you log in as the user named **root**.

- You can give an su (substitute user) command while you are logged in as yourself. When you then provide the **root** password, you will be running with **root** privileges. See page 425.

- The sudo utility allows specified users to run selected commands with **root** privileges while they are logged in as themselves. You can set up sudo to allow certain users to perform specific tasks that require **root** privileges without granting these users systemwide **root** privileges. See page 428.

- Once the system is up and running in multiuser mode (page 452), you can log in as **root**. When you then supply the **root** password, you will be running with **root** privileges.

- Some programs ask for a password (either your password or the **root** password, depending on the command and the configuration of the system) when they start or when you ask them to perform certain tasks. When you provide a password, the program runs with **root** privileges. You stop running as a privileged user when you quit using the program. This setup keeps you from remaining logged in with **root** privileges when you do not need or intend to be.

**LE+**   Setuid file
- Any user can create a *setuid* (set user ID) file. Setuid programs run on behalf of the owner of the file and have all the access privileges the owner has. While you are working with **root** privileges, you can change the permissions of a file owned by **root** to setuid. When an ordinary user executes a file that is owned by **root** and has setuid permissions, the program has *effective root privileges*. In other words, the program can do anything a program running with **root** privileges can do that the program normally does. The user's privileges do not change. When the program finishes running, all user privileges are as they were before the program started. Setuid programs owned by **root** are both extremely powerful and extremely dangerous to system security, which is why a system contains very few of them. Examples of setuid programs that are owned by **root** include passwd, at, and crontab. For more information refer to "Setuid and Setgid Permissions" on page 196 and "Real UID Versus Effective UID" (next).

Logging in   The **/etc/securetty** file controls which terminals (ttys) a user can log in on as **root**.

Using the **/etc/security/access.conf** file, PAM controls the who, when, and how of logging in. Initially this file contains only comments. See page 476, the comments in the file, and the **access.conf** man page for details.

### root-owned setuid programs are extremely dangerous

security   Because **root**-owned setuid programs allow someone who does not know the **root** password and cannot use sudo to gain **root** privileges, they are tempting targets for a malicious user. Also, programming errors that make normal programs crash can become **root** exploits in setuid programs. A system should have as few of these programs as possible. You can disable setuid programs at the filesystem level by mounting a filesystem with the **nosuid** option (page 522). You can also use SELinux (page 472) to disable setuid programs. See page 458 for a find command that lists all setuid files on the local system. Future releases of Fedora/RHEL will remove most setuid files; see fedoraproject.org/wiki/Features/RemoveSETUID.

### Do not allow root access over the Internet

security   Prohibiting a user from logging in as **root** over a network is the default policy of Fedora/RHEL. The **/etc/securetty** file must contain the names of all devices you want a user to be able to log in on as **root**.

You can, however, log in as **root** over a network using ssh (page 685). As shipped by Fedora/RHEL, PAM configuration for ssh does not call the modules that use the **securetty** or **access.conf** configuration files. Also, in **/etc/ssh/sshd_config**, Fedora/RHEL sets **PermitRootLogin** to **yes** (it is set by default) to permit **root** to log in using ssh (page 705). For a more secure system, change **PermitRootLogin** to **no**.

## *LE* REAL UID VERSUS EFFECTIVE UID

UID and username   A UID (user ID) is the number the system associates with a username. UID 0 is typically associated with the username **root**. To speed things up, the kernel keeps track of a user by UID, not username. Most utilities display the associated username in place of a UID.

The kernel associates two UIDs with each process: a *real UID* and an *effective UID*. The third column of the **/etc/passwd** file (or NIS/LDAP) specifies your real UID. When you log in, your real UID is associated with the process running the login shell. Because you have done nothing to change it, the effective UID associated with the process running the login shell is the same as the real UID associated with that process.

process privilege   The kernel determines which privileges a process has based on that process' effective UID. For example, when a process asks to open a file or execute a program, the kernel looks at the effective UID of the process to determine whether it is allowed to do so. When a user runs a setuid program (page 196), the program runs with the UID of the owner of the program, not the user running the program.

terminology: root privileges   When this book uses the phrase **run with root privileges** or **gain root privileges**, it means run with an effective UID of 0 (**root**).

## *LE+* USING su TO GAIN root PRIVILEGES

When you install Fedora/RHEL, you assign a password to the **root** account. Thus you can use su to gain **root** privileges without any further setup.

The su (substitute user) utility can spawn a shell or execute a program with the identity and privileges (effective UID) of a specified user, including **root**:

- Follow **su** on the command line with the name of a user; if you are working with **root** privileges or if you know the user's password, the newly spawned shell will take on the identity (effective UID) of that user.

- When you give an su command without an argument, su defaults to spawning a shell with **root** privileges (you have to supply the **root** password). That shell runs with an effective UID of 0 (**root**).

## SPAWNING A root SHELL

When you give an su command to work with **root** privileges, su spawns a new shell, which displays the # prompt. That shell runs with an effective UID of 0 (**root**). You can return to your normal status (and your former shell and prompt) by terminating this shell: Press CONTROL-D or give an **exit** command.

**LE** who, whoami   The who utility, when called with the arguments **am i**, displays the real UID (translated to a username) of the process that called it. The whoami utility displays the effective UID (translated to a username) of the process that called it. As the following example shows, the su utility (the same is true for sudo) changes the effective UID of the process it spawns but leaves the real UID unchanged.

```
$ who am i
sam        pts/2           2013-06-12 13:43 (192.168.206.1)
$ whoami
sam
$ su
Password:
# who am i
sam        pts/2           2013-06-12 13:43 (192.168.206.1)
# whoami
root
```

**LE**   id   Giving an su command without any arguments changes your effective user and group IDs but makes minimal changes to the environment. For example, **PATH** has the same value as it did before you gave the su command. The id utility displays the effective UID and GID of the process that called it as well as the groups the process is associated with. In the following example, the information that starts with **context** pertains to SELinux:

```
$ pwd
/home/sam
$ echo $PATH
/usr/local/bin:/usr/bin:/usr/local/sbin:/usr/sbin:/home/sam/.local/bin:/home/sam/bin
$ id
uid=1000(sam) gid=1400(pubs) groups=1400(pubs),10(wheel) context=unconfined_u: ...
$ su
Password:
# pwd
/home/sam
# echo $PATH
/usr/local/bin:/usr/bin:/usr/local/sbin:/usr/sbin:/home/sam/.local/bin:/home/sam/bin
```

```
# id
uid=0(root) gid=0(root) groups=0(root) context=unconfined_u: ...
# exit
exit
$
```

When you give the command **su –** (you can use **–l** or **––login** in place of the hyphen), su provides a **root** login shell: It is as though you logged in as **root**. Not only do the shell's effective user and group IDs match those of **root**, but the environment is the same as when you log in as **root**. The login shell executes the appropriate startup files (page 329) before displaying a prompt, and the working directory is set to what it would be if you had logged in as **root** (**/root**). PATH is also set as though you had logged in as **root**. However, as who shows, the real UID of the new process is not changed from that of the parent process.

```
$ su -
Password:
# pwd
/root
# echo $PATH
/usr/local/sbin:/usr/local/bin:/sbin:/bin:/usr/sbin:/usr/bin:/root/bin
# who am i
sam        pts/2           2013-06-12 13:43 (192.168.206.1)
```

## EXECUTING A SINGLE COMMAND

You can use su with the **–c** option to run a command with **root** privileges, returning to the original shell when the command finishes executing. In the following example, Sam tries to display the **/etc/shadow** file while working as himself, a nonprivileged user. The cat utility displays an error message. When he uses su to run cat to display the file, su prompts him for a password, he responds with the **root** password, and the command succeeds. The quotation marks are necessary because **su –c** takes the command it is to execute as a single argument.

```
$ cat /etc/shadow
cat: /etc/shadow: Permission denied

$ su -c 'cat /etc/shadow'
Password:
root:$6$il96HvSfmvep.m2F$2RI1LZ ... fYc3wYZFQ/:15861:0:99999:7:::
bin:*:15839:0:99999:7:::
daemon:*:15839:0:99999:7:::
adm:*:15839:0:99999:7:::
...
```

The next example first shows that Sam is not permitted to kill (page 465) a process. With the use of **su –c** and the **root** password, however, Sam is working with **root** privileges and is permitted to kill the process.

```
$ kill -15 4982
-bash: kill: (4982) - Operation not permitted
$ su -c "kill -15 4982"
Password:
$
```

The final example combines the – and –c options to show how to run a single command with **root** privileges in the **root** environment:

```
$ su -c pwd
Password:
/home/sam
$ su - -c pwd
Password:
/root
```

### Root privileges, PATH, and security

security   The fewer directories you keep in **PATH** when you are working with **root** privileges, the less likely you will be to execute an untrusted program while working with **root** privileges. If possible, keep only the default directories, along with **/usr/bin** and **/usr/sbin**, in **root**'s **PATH**. *Never include the working directory in PATH (as . or : : anywhere in PATH, or : as the last element of PATH)*. For more information refer to "PATH: Where the Shell Looks for Programs" on page 359.

## *LE+*   USING sudo TO GAIN root PRIVILEGES

If sudo (www.sudo.ws) is not set up so you can use it, and a **root** password exists and you know what it is, see "Administrator and the **wheel** group" on the next page for instructions on setting up sudo so you can use it to gain **root** privileges.

### ADVANTAGES OF sudo

Using sudo rather than the **root** account for system administration offers many advantages.

- When you run sudo, it requests *your* password—not the **root** password—so you have to remember only one password.

- The sudo utility logs all commands it executes. This log can be useful for retracing your steps for system auditing and if you make a mistake.

- The sudo utility logs the username of a user who issues an sudo command. On systems with more than one administrator, this log tells you which users have issued sudo commands. Without sudo, you would not know which user issued a command while working with **root** privileges.

- The sudo utility allows implementation of a finer-grained security policy than does the use of su and the **root** account. Using sudo, you can enable specific users to execute specific commands—something you cannot do with the classic **root** account setup.

- Using sudo makes it harder for a malicious user to gain access to a system. When there is an unlocked **root** account, a malicious user knows the username of the account she wants to crack before she starts. When the **root** account is locked, the user has to determine the username *and* the password to break into a system.

- Managing **root** passwords over many systems is challenging. Remembering each system's password is difficult without writing them down (and storing them in a safe), and then retrieving a password is time-consuming. Keeping track of which users know which **root** passwords is impossible. Using sudo, even for full **root**-shell access, makes the tasks of gaining **root** privileges on a large number of systems and tracking who can gain **root** privileges on each system much easier.

## SECURITY OF sudo

Some users question whether sudo is less secure than su. Because both rely on passwords, they share the same strengths and weaknesses. If the password is compromised, the system is compromised. However, if the password of a user who is allowed by sudo to do one task is compromised, the entire system might not be at risk. Thus, *if used properly*, the finer granularity of sudo's permissions structure *can* make it a more secure tool than su. Also, when sudo is used to invoke a single command, it is less likely that a user will be tempted to keep working with **root** privileges than if the user opens a **root** shell using su.

Using sudo might not always be the best, most secure way to set up a system. On a system used by a single user, there is not much difference between using sudo and carefully using su and a **root** password. In contrast, on a system with several users, and especially on a network of systems with central administration, sudo can be set up to be more secure than su.

## USING sudo

Administrator and the **wheel** group
When you add or modify a user, you can specify that the user is an administrator by making the user a member of the **wheel** group. When you specify an account type of Administrator in the Users window (Figure 4-17, page 112), the user becomes a member of the **wheel** group. Based on the following line in the **/etc/sudoers** file, members of the **wheel** group can use sudo to gain **root** privileges:

```
%wheel  ALL=(ALL)        ALL
```

To make a user a member of the **wheel** group, working with **root** privileges, run usermod with the –a and –G **wheel** options to add the user to the **wheel** group. Substitute a username for **sam** in the following example.

```
# usermod -a -G wheel sam
# grep wheel /etc/group
wheel:x:10:root,sam
```

The grep command shows Sam as a member of the **wheel** group. See **/etc/group** on page 506 for more information on groups.

Timestamp
By default, sudo asks for *your* password (not the **root** password) the first time you run it. At that time, sudo sets your *timestamp*. After you supply a password, sudo will not prompt you again for a password for five minutes (by default), based on your timestamp.

### EXECUTING A SINGLE COMMAND

In the following example, Sam tries to set the system clock while working as himself, a nonprivileged user. The date utility displays an error message followed by the expanded version of the date Sam entered. When he uses sudo to run date to set the system clock, sudo prompts him for his password, and the command succeeds.

```
$ date 12121500
date: cannot set date: Operation not permitted
Thu Dec 12 15:00:00 PST 2013
```

```
$ sudo date 12121500
[sudo] password for sam:
Thu Dec 12 15:00:00 PST 2013
```

Next Sam uses sudo to unmount a filesystem. Because he gives this command within five minutes of the previous sudo command, he does not need to supply a password:

```
$ sudo umount /music
$
```

Now Sam uses the **–l** option to check which commands sudo will allow him to run. Because the **sudoers** file is set up as explained in "Administrator and the **wheel** group," on the previous page, he is allowed to run any command as any user.

```
$ sudo -l
...
User sam may run the following commands on this host:
    (ALL) ALL
```

## Granting **root** privileges to edit a file

tip   With the **–e** option, or when called as sudoedit, sudo edits with **root** privileges the file named by its argument. By default sudo uses the vi editor; see page 432 for instructions on how to specify a different editor.

Any user who can run commands with **root** privileges can use the **–e** option. To give other users permission to edit any file using **root** privileges, specify in the **sudoers** file that that user can execute the command **sudoedit**. For more information refer to "User Privilege Specifications" on page 433.

Calling an editor in this manner runs the editor in the user's environment, maintaining the concept of least privilege. The sudo utility first copies the file to be edited to a temporary file that is owned by the user. If the file does not exist, sudo creates a new file that is owned by the user. Once the user has finished editing the file, sudo copies it back in place of the original file (maintaining the original permissions).

### SPAWNING A root SHELL

When you have several commands you need to run with **root** privileges, it might be easier to spawn a **root** shell, give the commands without having to type **sudo** in front of each one, and exit from the shell. This technique defeats some of the safeguards built into sudo, so use it carefully and remember to return to a non**root** shell as soon as possible. See the caution on least privilege on page 423. Use the sudo –i option (page 432) to spawn a **root** shell:

```
$ pwd
/home/sam
$ sudo -i
# id
uid=0(root) gid=0(root) groups=0(root),1(bin),2(daemon),3(sys) ...
# pwd
/root
# exit
logout
$
```

In this example, sudo spawns a **root** shell, which displays a # prompt to remind Sam that he is running with **root** privileges. The id utility displays the effective UID of the user running the shell. The exit command (you can also use CONTROL-D) terminates the **root** shell, returning Sam to his normal status and his former shell and prompt.

sudo's environment   The pwd builtin in the preceding example shows one aspect of the modified environment created by the –i option. This option spawns a **root** login shell (a shell with the same environment as a user logging in as **root** would have) and executes **root's** startup files (page 329). Before issuing the **sudo –i** command, the pwd builtin shows **/home/sam** as Sam's working directory; after the command, it shows **/root**, **root's** home directory, as the working directory. Use the –s option (page 432) to spawn a **root** shell without modifying the environment. When you call sudo without an option, it runs the command you specify in an unmodified environment. To demonstrate this feature, the following example calls sudo without an option to run pwd. The working directory of a command run in this manner does not change.

```
$ pwd
/home/sam
$ sudo pwd
/home/sam
```

Redirecting output   The following command fails because although the shell that sudo spawns executes ls with **root** privileges, the nonprivileged shell that the user is running redirects the output. The user's shell does not have permission to write to **/root**.

```
$ sudo ls > /root/ls.sam
-bash: /root/ls.sam: Permission denied
```

There are several ways around this problem. The easiest is to pass the whole command line to a shell running under sudo:

```
$ sudo bash -c "ls > /root/ls.sam"
```

The bash –c option spawns a shell that executes the string following the option and then terminates. The sudo utility runs the spawned shell with **root** privileges. You must quote the string to prevent the nonprivileged shell from interpreting special characters. You can also spawn a **root** shell using **sudo –i**, execute the command, and exit from the privileged shell. (See the preceding section.)

**optional**  Another way to deal with the issue of redirecting output of a command run by sudo is to use tee (page 162):

```
$ ls | sudo tee /root/ls.sam
...
```

This command line sends standard output of ls through sudo to tee, which copies its standard input to the file named by its argument and to standard output. If you do not want to display the output, you can have the nonprivileged shell redirect the output to /dev/null (page 503). The next example uses this technique to do away with the displayed output and uses the **–a** option to tee to append to the file instead of overwriting it:

```
$ ls | sudo tee -a /root/ls.sam > /dev/null
```

## OPTIONS

You can use command-line options to control how sudo runs a command. Following is the syntax of an sudo command line:

*sudo [options] [command]*

where *options* is one or more options and *command* is the command you want to execute. Without the **–u** option, sudo runs *command* with **root** privileges. Some of the more common *options* follow; see the sudo man page for a complete list.

**–b**  (**background**) Runs *command* in the background.

**–e**  (**edit**) With this option, *command* is a filename and not a command. This option causes sudo to edit the file named *command* with **root** privileges using the editor named by the **SUDO_EDITOR, VISUAL,** or **EDITOR** environment variable. Default is the vi editor. Alternately, you can use the sudoedit utility without any options. Using this technique, the editor does not run with **root** privileges. See the tip on page 430.

**–i**  (**initial login environment**) Spawns the shell that is specified for **root** (or another user specified by **–u**) in /etc/passwd, running **root**'s (or the other user's) startup files, with some exceptions (e.g., **TERM** is not changed). Does not take a *command*. See "Spawning a **root** Shell" on page 426 for an example.

**–k**  (**kill**) Resets the timestamp (page 429) of the user running the command, which means the user must enter her password the next time she runs sudo.

**–L**  (**list defaults**) Lists the parameters that you can set on a Defaults line (page 436) in the **sudoers** file. Does not take a *command*.

**–l**  (**list commands**) Lists the commands the user who is running sudo is allowed to run on the local system. Does not take a *command*.

**–s**  (**shell**) Spawns a new **root** (or another user specified by **–u**) shell as specified in the /etc/passwd file. Similar to **–i** but does not change the environment. Does not take a *command*.

**–u** *user*  Runs *command* with the privileges of *user*. Without this option, sudo runs *command* with **root** privileges.

## *LPI* sudoers: CONFIGURING sudo

As installed, sudo is not as secure and robust as it can be if you configure it carefully. The sudo configuration file is **/etc/sudoers**. You can edit this file to give specific users the ability to run only certain commands with **root** privileges as opposed to any commands. You can also limit these users to running commands only with certain options or arguments. Or you can set up sudo so a specific user cannot use a specific option or argument when running a command with **root** privileges.

The best way to edit **sudoers** is to use visudo by giving the command: **su -c visudo** or **sudo visudo**. The visudo utility locks, edits, and checks the grammar of the **sudoers** file. By default, visudo calls the vi editor. You can set the **SUDO_EDITOR, VISUAL,** or **EDITOR** environment variable to cause visudo to call a different editor. The following command causes visudo to use the nano editor (page 270):

```
$ export EDITOR=$(which nano)
```

Replace **nano** with the textual editor of your choice. Put this command in a startup file (page 329) to set this variable each time you log in.

### Always use visudo to edit the sudoers file

caution   A syntax error in the **sudoers** file can prevent you from using sudo to gain **root** privileges. If you edit this file directly (without using visudo), you will not know that you introduced a syntax error until you find that you cannot use sudo. The visudo utility checks the syntax of **sudoers** before it allows you to exit. If it finds an error, it gives you the choice of fixing the error, exiting without saving the changes to the file, or saving the changes and exiting. The last choice is usually a poor one, so visudo marks it with **(DANGER!)**.

In the **sudoers** file, comments, which start with a hashmark (#), can appear anywhere on a line. In addition to comments, this file holds three types of entries: user privilege specifications, aliases, and defaults. Each of these entries occupies a line. You can continue a line by terminating it with a backslash (\).

### USER PRIVILEGE SPECIFICATIONS

The format of a line that specifies user privileges is as follows (the whitespace around the equal sign is optional). In each case,

> *user_list host_list = [(runas_list)] command_list*

- The *user_list* specifies the user(s) this specification line applies to. This list can contain usernames, groups (prefixed with %), and user aliases (next section). You can use the builtin alias ALL to cause the line to apply to all users.

- The *host_list* specifies the host(s) this specification line applies to. This list can contain one or more hostnames, IP addresses, or host aliases (next section). You can use the builtin alias ALL to cause the line to apply to all systems that refer to this **sudoers** file.

- The *runas_list* specifies the user(s) the commands in the *command_list* can be run as when sudo is called with the **–u** option (page 432). This list can contain usernames, groups (prefixed with **%**), and runas aliases (next section). It must be enclosed within parentheses. Without *runas_list*, sudo assumes **root**. You can use the builtin alias ALL to cause the line to apply to all usernames and groups.

- The *command_list* specifies the utilities this specification line applies to. This comma-separated list can contain names of utilities, names of directories holding utilities, and command aliases (next section). All names must be absolute pathnames; directory names must end with a slash (*/*). Precede a command with an exclamation point (**!**) to exclude that command. You can use the builtin alias ALL to cause the line to apply to all commands.

  Including the string **sudoedit** in the *command_list* gives users in the *user_list* permission to edit files using **root** privileges. See the tip on page 430 for more information.

If you follow a command in the *command_list* with two adjacent double quotation marks (**" "**), the user will not be able to specify any command-line arguments, including options to that command. Alternately, you can specify arguments, including wildcards, to limit the arguments a user is allowed to specify with that command.

**Examples**   The following user privilege specification allows Sam to use sudo to mount and unmount filesystems (run mount and umount with **root** privileges) on all systems (as specified by **ALL**) that refer to the **sudoers** file containing this specification:

```
sam     ALL=(root) /bin/mount, /bin/umount
```

The (**root**) *runas_list* is optional. If you omit it, sudo allows the user to run the commands in the *command_list* with **root** privileges. In the following example, Sam takes advantage of these permissions. He cannot run umount directly; instead, he must call sudo to run it.

```
$ whoami
sam
$ umount /music
umount: only root can unmount /dev/sdb7 from /music
$ sudo umount /music
[sudo] password for sam:
$
```

If you replace the line in **sudoers** described above with the following line, Sam is not allowed to unmount **/p03**, although he can still unmount any other filesystem and can mount any filesystem:

```
sam     ALL=(root) /bin/mount, /bin/umount, !/bin/umount /p03
```

The result of the preceding line in **sudoers** is shown next. The sudo utility does not prompt for a password because Sam has entered his password within the last five minutes.

```
$ sudo umount /p03
Sorry, user sam is not allowed to execute '/bin/umount /p03' as root on localhost.
```

The following line limits Sam to mounting and unmounting filesystems mounted on **/p01, /p02, /p03,** and **/p04:**

```
sam     ALL= /bin/mount /p0[1-4], /bin/umount /p0[1-4]
```

The following commands show the result:

```
$ sudo umount /music
Sorry, user sam is not allowed to execute '/bin/umount /music' as root on localhost.
$ sudo umount /p03
$
```

**Administrator: using the wheel group**   As explained under "Administrator and the **wheel** group" on page 429, the following lines in **sudoers** allow users who are members of the **wheel** group (administrators) to use sudo to gain **root** privileges:

```
## Allows people in group wheel to run all commands
%wheel  ALL=(ALL)       ALL
```

This user privilege specification applies to all systems (as indicated by the **ALL** to the left of the equal sign). As the comment indicates, this line allows members of the **wheel** group (specified by preceding the name of the group with a percent sign: **%wheel**) to run any command (the rightmost **ALL**) as any user (the **ALL** within parentheses). When you call it without the **–u** option, the sudo utility runs the command you specify with **root** privileges, which is what sudo is used for most of the time.

If you modified the preceding line in **sudoers** as follows, it would allow members of the **wheel** group to run any command as any user with one exception: They would not be allowed to run passwd to change the **root** password (although they could gain **root** privileges and edit it manually).

```
%wheel ALL=(ALL) ALL, !/usr/bin/passwd root
```

**optional**   In the **%wheel ALL=(ALL) ALL** line in **/etc/sudoers,** if you replaced **(ALL)** with **(root)** or if you omitted **(ALL),** you would still be able to run any command with **root** privileges. You would not, however, be able to use the **–u** option to run a command as another user. Typically, when you can have **root** privileges, this limitation is not an issue. Working as a user other than **root** allows you to use the least privilege possible to accomplish a task, which is a good idea.

For example, if you are in the **wheel** group, the default entry in the **sudoers** file allows you to give the following command to create and edit a file in Sam's home directory. Because you are working as Sam, he will own the file and be able to read from and write to it.

```
$ sudo -u sam vi ~sam/reminder
$ ls -l ~sam/reminder
-rw-r--r--. 1 sam pubs 15 03-09 15:29 /home/sam/reminder
```

### ALIASES

An alias enables you to rename and/or group users, hosts, or commands. Following is the format of an alias definition:

*alias_type alias_name = alias_list*

where *alias_type* is the type of alias (**User_Alias, Runas_Alias, Host_Alias, Cmnd_Alias**), *alias_name* is the name of the alias (by convention all uppercase), and *alias_list* is a comma-separated list of one or more elements that make up the alias. Preceding an element of an alias with an exclamation point (**!**) negates it.

**User_Alias**    The *alias_list* for a user alias is the same as the *user_list* for a user privilege specification (previous section). The following lines from a **sudoers** file define three user aliases: OFFICE, ADMIN, and ADMIN2. The *alias_list* that defines the first alias includes the usernames **zach, sam,** and **sls**; the second includes two usernames and members of the **admin** group; and the third includes all members of the **admin** group except Sam.

```
User_Alias      OFFICE = zach, sam, sls
User_Alias      ADMIN = max, zach, %admin
User_Alias      ADMIN2 = %admin, !sam
```

**Runas_Alias**    The *alias_list* for a runas alias is the same as the *runas_list* for a user privilege specification (previous section). The following SM runas alias includes the usernames **sam** and **sls**:

```
Runas_Alias     SM = sam, sls
```

**Host_Alias**    Host aliases are meaningful only when the **sudoers** file is referenced by sudo running on more than one system. The *alias_list* for a host alias is the same as the *host_list* for a user privilege specification (previous section). The following line defines the LCL alias to include the systems named **guava** and **plum**:

```
Host_Alias      LCL = guava, plum
```

If you want to use fully qualified hostnames (**hosta.example.com** instead of just **hosta**) in this list, you must set the **fqdn** flag (next section). However, doing so might slow the performance of sudo.

**Cmnd_Alias**    The *alias_list* for a command alias is the same as the *command_list* for a user privilege specification (previous section). The following command alias includes three files and by including a directory (denoted by its trailing **/**), incorporates all the files in that directory:

```
Cmnd_Alias      BASIC = /bin/cat, /usr/bin/vi, /bin/df, /usr/local/safe/
```

### DEFAULTS (OPTIONS)

You can change configuration options from their default values by using the **Defaults** keyword. Most values in this list are flags that are implicitly Boolean (can either be on or off) or strings. You turn on a flag by naming it on a Defaults line, and you turn it off by preceding it with a **!**. The following line in the **sudoers** file turns off the **lecture** and **fqdn** flags and turns on **tty_tickets**:

```
Defaults        !lecture,tty_tickets,!fqdn
```

This section lists some common flags; see the **sudoers** man page for a complete list.

**env_reset** Causes sudo to reset the environment variables to contain the **LOGNAME, SHELL, USER, USERNAME, MAIL,** and **SUDO_\*** variables only. Default is **on**. See the **sudoers** man page for more information.

**fqdn** (**fully qualified domain name**) Performs DNS lookups on *FQDNs* (page 1250) in the **sudoers** file. When this flag is set, you can use FQDNs in the **sudoers** file, but doing so might negatively affect sudo's performance, especially if DNS is not working. When this flag is set, you must use the local host's official DNS name, not an alias. If hostname returns an FQDN, you do not need to set this flag. Default is **on**.

**insults** Displays mild, humorous insults when a user enters a wrong password. Default is **off**. See also **passwd_tries**.

**lecture=***freq* Controls when sudo displays a reminder message before the password prompt. Possible values of *freq* are **never, once,** and **always**. Specifying **!lecture** is the same as specifying a *freq* of **never**. Default is **once**.

**mail_always** Sends email to the **mailto** user each time a user runs sudo. Default is **off**.

**mail_badpass** Sends email to the **mailto** user when a user enters an incorrect password while running sudo. Default is **off**.

**mail_no_host** Sends email to the **mailto** user when a user whose username is in the **sudoers** file but who does not have permission to run commands on the local host runs sudo. Default is **off**.

**mail_no_perms** Sends email to the **mailto** user when a user whose username is in the **sudoers** file but who does not have permission to run the requested command runs sudo. Default is **off**.

**mail_no_user** Sends email to the **mailto** user when a user whose username is not in the **sudoers** file runs sudo. Default is **on**.

**mailsub=***subj* (**mail subject**) Changes the default email subject for warning and error messages from the default **✱✱✱ SECURITY information for %h ✱✱✱** to *subj*. The sudo utility expands **%h** within *subj* to the local system's hostname. Place *subj* between quotation marks if it contains shell special characters.

**mailto=***eadd* Sends sudo warning and error messages to *eadd* (an email address; default is **root**). Place *eadd* between quotation marks if it contains shell special characters.

**passwd_timeout=***mins*
The *mins* is the number of minutes before a sudo password prompt times out. A value of 0 (zero) indicates the password does not time out. Default is **5**.

**passwd_tries=***num*
The *num* is the number of times the user can enter an incorrect password in response to the sudo password prompt before sudo quits. Default is **3**. See also **insults** and **lecture**.

rootpw   Causes sudo to accept only the **root** password in response to its prompt. Because sudo issues the same prompt whether it is asking for your password or the **root** password, turning this flag on might confuse users. Default is **off**, causing sudo to accept the password of the user running sudo.

shell_noargs   Causes sudo, when called without any arguments, to spawn a **root** shell without changing the environment. Default is **off**. This option causes the same behavior as the sudo –s option.

timestamp_timeout=*mins*

The *mins* is the number of minutes that the sudo timestamp (page 429) is valid. Set *mins* to **–1** to cause the timestamp to be valid forever; set to **0** (zero) to cause sudo to always prompt for a password. Default is **5**.

tty_tickets   Causes sudo to authenticate users on a per-tty basis, not a per-user basis. Default is **on**.

umask=*val*   The *val* is the umask (page 469) that sudo uses to run the command that the user specifies. Set *val* to **0777** to preserve the user's umask value. Default is **0022**.

## LOCKING THE root ACCOUNT (REMOVING THE root PASSWORD)

If you decide you want to lock the **root** account, give the command **su –c 'passwd –l root'**. This command renders the encrypted password in **/etc/shadow** invalid by prepending two exclamation points (**!!**) to it. You can unlock the account again by removing the exclamation points or by giving the command shown in the following example.

Unlocking the **root** account   If you decide you want to unlock the **root** account after locking it, give the following command. This command assumes you can use sudo to gain **root** privileges and unlocks the **root** account by assigning a password to it:

```
$ sudo passwd root
[sudo] password for sam:
Changing password for user root.
New password:
Retype new password:
passwd: all authentication tokens updated successfully.
```

## LPI THE systemd init DAEMON

The **init** daemon is the system and service manager for Linux. As explained on page 374, it is the first true process Linux starts when it boots and, as such, has a PID of 1 and is the ancestor of all processes. The **init** daemon has been around since the early days of UNIX, and many people have worked to improve it. The first Linux **init** daemon was based on the UNIX System V **init** daemon and is referred to as SysVinit (System V **init** daemon).

Because SysVinit does not deal well with modern hardware, including hotplug (page 516) devices, USB hard and flash drives, and network-mounted filesystems,

Fedora 15 replaced it with the systemd **init** daemon, which is described in this section. Several other replacements for SysVinit are also available. Ubuntu uses Upstart (upstart.ubuntu.com), Solaris uses SMF (Service Management Facility), and MacOS uses **launchd**.

The name *systemd* comprises *system,* which systemd manages, followed by *d.* Under UNIX/Linux, daemon names frequently end in **d**: systemd is the system daemon. At boot time, systemd renames itself **init**, so you will not see a process named systemd. However, **init** is simply a link to systemd:

```
$ ls -l /sbin/init
lrwxrwxrwx. 1 root root 22 05-28 12:17 /sbin/init -> ../lib/systemd/systemd
```

The name is also a play on words with *System D,* a reference to the French débrouillard (to untangle) or démerder. System D is a manner of responding to challenges that requires fast thinking, adapting, and improvising.

The systemd **init** daemon is a drop-in replacement for SysVinit; most of the administration tools that worked with SysVinit and Upstart work with systemd. Although systemd is relatively new, most of the user interfaces pertinent to administrators will remain stable (www.freedesktop.org/wiki/Software/systemd/InterfaceStabilityPromise).

## MORE INFORMATION

Local   Use apropos to list man pages that pertain to systemd (**apropos systemd**). Some of the most interesting of these are **systemd**, systemctl, **systemd.unit**, and **systemd.special**.

Web   systemd home page: www.freedesktop.org/wiki/Software/systemd
Fedora systemd home page: fedoraproject.org/wiki/Systemd
SysVinit to systemd conversion notes:
    fedoraproject.org/wiki/SysVinit_to_Systemd_Cheatsheet
Blog about systemd by its creator, Lennart Poettering:
    0pointer.de/blog/projects/systemd.html
systemd compatibility with SysV:
    www.freedesktop.org/wiki/Software/systemd/Incompatibilities
systemd stability promise:
    www.freedesktop.org/wiki/Software/systemd/InterfaceStabilityPromise
cgroups (control groups): www.kernel.org/doc/Documentation/cgroups/cgroups.txt

## SERVICE UNITS AND TARGET UNITS

The systemd **init** daemon is based on the concept of units, each of which has a name and type. Typically information about a unit is stored in a file that has the same name as the unit (e.g., **dbus.service**). The types of units are service, socket, device, mount, automount, target, snapshot, timer, swap, and path. This section discusses service and target units, which are critical to controlling daemons and runlevel under systemd.

Service unit
A service unit refers to a daemon (service) that systemd controls, including those controlled natively by systemd and those controlled by systemd via SysVinit init scripts. The systemd **init** daemon controls almost all services natively.

Target unit
A target unit groups other units. Of concern in this section are targets that control the system runlevel. By default, Fedora activates **graphical.target**, which brings the system to a runlevel that equates to what was formerly called runlevel 5 (multiuser graphical mode). Activating **multi-user.target** brings the system to what was formerly called runlevel 3 (multiuser textual mode). Table 10-1 on page 449 lists all predefined target units (runlevels).

Terminology: server, service, daemon
A *daemon*, such as **atd** or **cupsd**, provides a *service* that runs on a *server*. The daemon itself is also sometimes referred to as a *server*. These three terms can be used interchangeably.

# RUNLEVELS

The systemd **init** daemon does not support runlevels the way SysVinit did. It supports *target units*, which parallel runlevels but are different. To ease the transition, this book continues to use the term *runlevel* to refer to target units. One difference between SysVinit runlevels and systemd target units is that the former can be changed only when the system changes runlevels whereas the latter can be activated by any of a large group of triggers. Another difference is that a systemd-based system can activate more than one target unit at a time, allowing the system to be in more than one "runlevel" at a time. For example, **graphical.target** pulls in **multi-user.target** so they are both active at the same time.

### systemd runlevels differ from SysVinit runlevels

tip
For consistency and clarity during the transition from SysVinit to systemd, this book refers to systemd *target units* as *runlevels*. Target units are not true runlevels, but they perform a function similar to the function performed by SysVinit runlevels.

A systemd-based system can activate more than one target unit at a time, allowing the system to be in more than one "runlevel" at a time. A system running SysVinit can be in only one runlevel at a time.

# WANTS AND REQUIRES

Under systemd, the terms *wants* and *requires* specify units that are to be activated when the unit that wants or requires the other unit is activated. A unit that *requires* another unit will not start if the other unit is not available. Wants is similar to requires, except a unit that *wants* another unit will not fail if the wanted unit is not available.

## DISPLAYING PROPERTIES

The following systemctl **show** command displays the Requires properties of the **graphical.target** unit. It shows that **graphical.target** requires **multi-user.target**:

```
$ systemctl show --property "Requires" graphical.target
Requires=multi-user.target
```

This relationship causes systemd not to start **graphical.target** if **multi-user.target** is not available. It means **graphical.target** requires units that **multi-user.target** requires and wants units that **multi-user.target** wants. Because of this relationship, **multi-user.target** (runlevel) is active at the same time **graphical.target** (runlevel) is active.

You can also use the systemctl **show** command to display the Wants properties of a target:

```
$ systemctl show --property "Wants" multi-user.target
Wants=vmtoolsd.service abrt-xorg.service rpcbind.service ...
lines 1-1/1 (END) q
```

The list is long. Although systemctl passes the output through a pager, it runs off the right edge of the screen. When the command displays (**END**), press **q** to return to the shell prompt. Sending the output through the fmt text formatter with a line-length specification of 10 displays the list one service per line:

```
$ systemctl show --property "Wants" multi-user.target | fmt -10
Wants=vmtoolsd.service
abrt-xorg.service
rpcbind.service
remote-fs.target
sm-client.service
sssd.service
...
```

To see whether a target wants a specific service, send the output of the previous command through grep:

```
$ systemctl show --property "Wants" multi-user.target | fmt -10 | grep atd
Wants=atd.service
```

The output shows that **multi-user.target** wants the **atd.service** service. Because **graphical.target** requires **multi-user.target** and **multi-user.target** wants **atd.service**, systemd will start **atd.service** when the system enters the runlevel defined by **graphical.target**.

# /etc/systemd/system HIERARCHY: CONTROLS SERVICES AND THE PERSISTENT RUNLEVEL

The services wanted by a runlevel target appear in directories named \*.wants under the **/etc/systemd/system** directory:

```
$ ls -ld /etc/systemd/system/*.wants
...
drwxr-xr-x. 2 root root 4096 06-04 19:29 /etc/systemd/system/graphical.target.wants
drwxr-xr-x. 2 root root 4096 06-05 19:44 /etc/systemd/system/multi-user.target.wants
...
```

The following command lists the runlevel targets that want **atd.service**:

```
$ ls /etc/systemd/system/*.wants/atd.service
/etc/systemd/system/multi-user.target.wants/atd.service
```

As explained in the previous section, you can also display this information using the systemctl **show** command.

The directory hierarchy with its root at **/etc/systemd/system** controls the persistent runlevel of the system. That is, this directory hierarchy specifies which daemons will be started when the system boots or otherwise changes runlevel or when the daemon is activated for another reason.

All service unit files are kept in the **/lib/systemd/system** directory. All plain files in the **/etc/systemd/system** hierarchy are links to files in the **/usr/lib/systemd/system** or **/lib/systemd/system** hierarchy. For example, **atd.service** shown in the preceding example is a link to the appropriate service unit file in **/usr/lib/systemd/system**:

```
$ ls -l /etc/systemd/system/multi-user.target.wants/atd.service
lrwxrwxrwx. 1 root root 35 07-02 12:56 /etc/systemd/system/multi-user.target.wants/atd.service ->
/usr/lib/systemd/system/atd.service
```

The service unit file provides systemd with information it needs to start the service and specifies the system runlevel target that wants the service:

```
$ cat /lib/systemd/system/atd.service
[Unit]
Description=Job spooling tools
After=syslog.target systemd-user-sessions.service

[Service]
EnvironmentFile=/etc/sysconfig/atd
ExecStart=/usr/sbin/atd -f $OPTS

[Install]
WantedBy=multi-user.target
```

When you instruct systemd to start a service when the system boots (make the service persistent), it places a link to the service file in the directory specified by WantedBy in the service file. Continuing with the example, systemd places a link to **atd.service** in the **multi-user.target.wants** directory as shown previously. When you instruct systemd to not start a service when the system boots, it removes the link. "Setting the Persistent State of a Daemon" on page 445 explains how to use systemctl to make these changes.

The persistent (default) runlevel is also controlled by a link:

```
$ ls -l /etc/systemd/system/default.target
lrwxrwxrwx. 1 root root 36 06-04 19:34 /etc/systemd/system/default.target ->
/lib/systemd/system/graphical.target
```

See "Setting the Persistent Runlevel" on page 444 for more information.

# Custom Service Files

As explained in the previous section, files in the **/etc/systemd/system** directory hierarchy are symbolic links to files in the **/lib/systemd/system** directory hierarchy. The systemd **init** daemon treats files in the **/etc/systemd/system** directory hierarchy and files in the **/lib/systemd/system** directory hierarchy the same way, with files in **/etc/systemd/system** overriding files with the same name in **/lib/systemd/system**. An important difference between these directory hierarchies is that **/lib/systemd/system** is managed by yum/RPM while **/etc/systemd/system** is managed by the system administrator.

Put custom service files in the **/etc/systemd/system** hierarchy. If you want to modify a service file, copy it from the **/lib/systemd/system** hierarchy to the **/etc/systemd/system** hierarchy and edit the copy. The custom file in the **/etc/systemd/system** hierarchy will not be overwritten by yum/RPM and will take precedence over a file with the same name in the **/lib/systemd/system** hierarchy.

## DETERMINING WHETHER systemd RUNS A DAEMON NATIVELY

To ease migration from SysVinit to systemd and to provide compatibility with software intended for other distributions, systemd can control daemons via SysVinit scripts (page 448). You can use the systemctl **status** command to determine whether systemd is controlling a daemon natively or via a SysVinit script. Following, systemctl displays the status of **cups** and **network**:

```
$ systemctl status cups.service
cups.service - CUPS Printing Service
   Loaded: loaded (/usr/lib/systemd/system/cups.service; enabled)
   Active: active (running) since Wed 2013-06-05 17:29:38 PDT; 2h 30min ago

$ systemctl status network.service
network.service - LSB: Bring up/down networking
   Loaded: loaded (/etc/rc.d/init.d/network)
   Active: inactive (dead)
```

The systemctl utility does not require a period and unit type (**.service** in the preceding example) following a unit name (**cups** and **network** in the preceding example). The lines that start with **Loaded** name the file controlling each daemon (service). The **cups** daemon is controlled by **/usr/lib/systemd/system/cups.service**. The location of the file (the **/usr/lib/systemd** hierarchy) and its filename extension (**.service**) indicate systemd is running the daemon natively. The **network** daemon is controlled by **/etc/rc.d/init.d/network**. The location of the file (the **init.d** directory) and the lack of a filename extension indicate systemd is running the daemon via a SysVinit script. See fedoraproject.org/wiki/User:Johannbg/QA/Systemd/compatability for a list of services that have been ported to systemd (and are run natively by systemd).

*LPI* service   Although it is deprecated, you can use service to display information similar to that displayed by systemctl **status**. However, service does not accept a period and unit type.

```
$ service cups status
Redirecting to /bin/systemctl status  cups.service
cups.service - CUPS Printing Service
   Loaded: loaded (/usr/lib/systemd/system/cups.service; enabled)
   Active: active (running) since Wed 2013-06-05 17:29:38 PDT; 2h 30min ago
...

$ service network status
Configured devices:
lo Wired_connection_1 ens33
Currently active devices:
lo ens33
```

# Setting and Changing Runlevels

The runlevel specifies which daemons are running and which interfaces are available on a system. See "Runlevels" on page 440 and Table 10-1 on page 449 for more information. This section describes how to set the persistent (default) runlevel (the runlevel the system boots to) and how to change the current runlevel.

## *LPI* Setting the Persistent Runlevel

Under systemd no true runlevels exist; see "Runlevels" on page 449. For example, the default runlevel under Fedora is **graphical.target** and has an alternative name of **runlevel5.target**. Under SysVinit this runlevel is referred to as runlevel 5 (multiuser graphical mode). The **/etc/systemd/system/default.target** file is a link to the file that specifies the target the system will boot to by default:

```
$ ls -l /etc/systemd/system/default.target
lrwxrwxrwx. 1 root root 36 06-04 19:34 /etc/systemd/system/default.target ->
/lib/systemd/system/graphical.target
```

The following command shows **runlevel5.target** is a link to **graphical.target**:

```
$ ls -l /lib/systemd/system/runlevel5.target
lrwxrwxrwx. 1 root root 16 06-04 20:02 /lib/systemd/system/runlevel5.target ->
graphical.target
```

The **multi-user.target** file (and the link to it, **runlevel3.target**) causes the system to boot to the multiuser runlevel (multiuser textual mode; SysVinit runlevel 3). The following command replaces the link shown in the previous example and will cause the system enter multiuser textual mode each time it is booted. This command does not change the current runlevel. (Newer versions of systemd use the command **systemctl set-default** *target*, where *target* is replaced with the new runlevel target, in place of the following ln command.)

```
# ln -sf /lib/systemd/system/multi-user.target /etc/systemd/system/default.target
```

The ln –s (symbolic) option creates a symbolic link, and the –f (force) option overwrites any existing file.

The systemctl **list-units** command with the **--type=target** option lists all active target units. Before rebooting the system, this command shows that both **graphical.target** and **multi-user.target** are active.

```
$ systemctl list-units --type=target | egrep 'multi-user|graphical'
graphical.target    loaded active active Graphical Interface
multi-user.target   loaded active active Multi-User System
```

After giving the ln command and rebooting the system, **graphical.target** is no longer active but **multi-user.target** is:

```
$ systemctl list-units --type=target | egrep 'multi-user|graphical'
multi-user.target   loaded active active Multi-User System
```

See page 452 for instructions on how to boot to a specific runlevel using target units.

## *LPI* CHANGING THE CURRENT RUNLEVEL

The systemctl **isolate** command changes the current runlevel of the system. The following command changes the runlevel to multiuser graphical mode (**graphical.target**). When the system is rebooted, it will return to the default runlevel as specified by the link at **/etc/systemd/system/default.target**.

```
# systemctl isolate graphical.target
```

After a moment systemctl shows that, again, both **graphical.target** and **multi-user.target** are active:

```
$ systemctl list-units --type=target | egrep 'multi-user|graphical'
graphical.target    loaded active active Graphical Interface
multi-user.target   loaded active active Multi-User System
```

The preceding examples were run from an ssh login. If you give these commands from a terminal emulator running on the console, the system will log you out each time it changes runlevels.

# *LPI* CONFIGURING DAEMONS (SERVICES)

Two states are important when you consider a daemon: its current state and its persistent state (the state it will be in after the system is booted). Possible states are running and stopped. When you install a package that includes a daemon, the daemon is stopped and is not set up to start when the system is booted.

chkconfig and service | The systemctl utility controls the current and persistent states of daemons that run natively under systemd. The service and chkconfig utilities originally controlled daemons that run under SysVinit and were upgraded to control daemons that run under Upstart. Now these utilities have been retrofitted to control daemons that run under systemd, which they do by calling systemctl. You can still use service to control the current state of a daemon and chkconfig to control the persistent state of a daemon.

The next sections describe the systemctl commands that control daemons.

### SETTING THE PERSISTENT STATE OF A DAEMON

The systemctl **disable** command causes a daemon not to start when the system is booted. This command has no effect on the current state of the daemon. You do not need to specify the **.service** part of the service name.

```
# systemctl disable atd.service
rm '/etc/systemd/system/multi-user.target.wants/atd.service'
```

The preceding command removes the link that causes systemd to start **atd** when the system enters multi-user runlevel and, by inheritance, graphical runlevel. See "**/etc/systemd/system** Hierarchy: Controls Services and the Persistent Runlevel" on page 441 for a discussion of these links.

The following commands each verify that the **atd** daemon will not start when the system boots. The first command shows no links in the **\*.wants** directories for atd.service. The second uses the systemctl **is-enabled** command, which returns **disabled**.

```
$ ls /etc/systemd/system/*.wants/atd.service
ls: cannot access /etc/systemd/system/*.wants/add.service: No such file or directory
```

```
$ systemctl is-enabled atd.service
disabled
```

The systemctl **enable** command causes a daemon to start when the system is booted. This command has no effect on the current state of the daemon. The following command creates the link that causes systemd to start **atd** when the system enters multiuser textual mode and, by inheritance, multiuser graphical mode.

```
# systemctl enable atd.service
ln -s '/usr/lib/systemd/system/atd.service' '/etc/systemd/system/multi-user.target.wants/atd.service'
```

As in the preceding example, the next two commands check whether the daemon will start when the system is booted.

```
$ ls /etc/systemd/system/*.wants/atd.service
/etc/systemd/system/multi-user.target.wants/atd.service
```

```
$ systemctl is-enabled atd.service
enabled
```

## CHANGING THE CURRENT STATE OF A DAEMON

The systemctl **stop** command immediately stops a daemon from running. This command has no effect on whether the daemon starts when the system is booted. The following command works on the **atd** daemon, which is run natively by systemd. It will also work on a daemon systemd controls via a SysVinit script. You do not need to specify the .service part of the service name.

```
# systemctl stop atd.service
```

The preceding command stops the **atd** daemon and displays no output. The following commands each verify that the **atd** daemon is not running.

```
$ systemctl status atd.service
atd.service - Job spooling tools
   Loaded: loaded (/usr/lib/systemd/system/atd.service; enabled)
   Active: inactive (dead) since Wed 2013-07-24 18:03:18 PDT; 53s ago
 Main PID: 404 (code=exited, status=0/SUCCESS)
   CGroup: name=systemd:/system/atd.service

Jul 24 18:03:18 guava.example.com systemd[1]: Stopping Job spooling tools...
Jul 24 18:03:18 guava.example.com systemd[1]: Stopped Job spooling tools.
```

```
$ systemctl is-active atd.service
inactive
```

The systemctl **status** command shows an **Active** status of **inactive (dead)**. The systemctl **is-active** command displays a status of **inactive**. You can also use **ps –ef | grep atd** to determine whether the daemon is running.

**Figure 10-1**   The Service Configuration window

The systemctl **start** command immediately starts a daemon running. This command has no effect on whether the daemon starts when the system is booted.

```
# systemctl start atd.service
```

The next two commands each show the daemon is running.

```
$ systemctl status atd.service
atd.service - Job spooling tools
   Loaded: loaded (/usr/lib/systemd/system/atd.service; enabled)
   Active: active (running) since Wed 2013-07-24 18:06:55 PDT; 41s ago
 Main PID: 2010 (atd)
   CGroup: name=systemd:/system/atd.service
           |+2010 /usr/sbin/atd -f

Jul 24 18:06:55 guava.example.com systemd[1]: Started Job spooling tools.


$ systemctl is-active atd.service
active
```

### *LPI*   system-config-services: CONFIGURES SERVICES

The system-config-services utility (**system-config-services** package) displays the Service Configuration window (Figure 10-1). Open this window by giving the command **system-config-services** from an Enter a Command window (ALT-F2) or a terminal emulator. This utility uses a GUI to provide the functionality of the systemctl **start** and **stop** commands (see "Changing the Current State of a Daemon" on page 446) as well as the **enable** and **disable** commands (see "Setting the Persistent State of a Daemon" on page 445). It turns system services on and off immediately, and it controls which services are started when the system boots.

The left side of the Service Configuration window displays a scrollable list of services (daemons). Scroll to and highlight the service you want to work with; the right side of the window displays a description of the service. Click the buttons on the toolbar to start (triangle), stop (square), enable (plugged in plug), or disable (unplugged plug) the highlighted service. The Start and Stop buttons turn the service on or off immediately; the Enable and Disable buttons specify whether the service will run the next time the system boots.

**optional**

## *LPI*   SYSVINIT (rc) SCRIPTS: START AND STOP SYSTEM SERVICES

rc scripts   The SysVinit daemon is driven by init (initialization) scripts. These scripts, also called rc (run command) scripts, are shell scripts located in the **/etc/rc.d/init.d** directory. A symbolic link at **/etc/init.d** points to **/etc/rc.d/init.d**. The scripts are run via symbolic links in the **/etc/rc.d/rc*n*.d** directories, where *n* is the runlevel the system is entering.

### Most of the files in the /etc/rc.d/rc*n*.d and /etc/rc.d/init.d directories are gone

tip   Under systemd, Linux uses targets with the names of runlevels to aid migration and provide compatibility with software for other distributions (see Table 10-1). Most of the files in the **/etc/rc.d/rc*n*.d** and **/etc/rc.d/init.d** directories have gone away; they have been replaced by systemd service files.

The **/etc/rc.d/rc*n*.d** directories contain scripts whose names begin with **K** and scripts whose names begin with **S**. When entering a new runlevel, each **K** (kill) script is executed with an argument of **stop,** and then each **S** (start) script is executed with an argument of **start.** Each of the **K** files is run in numerical order. The S files are run in similar fashion. This arrangement allows the person who sets up these files to control which services are stopped and which are started, and in what order, whenever the system enters a given runlevel. Using scripts with **start** and **stop** arguments promotes flexibility because it allows one script to both start and kill a process, depending on which argument it is called with.

You can use systemctl (page 445) or system-config-services (previous page) to run SysVinit scripts.

## SYSTEM OPERATION

This section covers the basics of how the system functions and can help you make intelligent decisions as a system administrator. It is a guide to bringing a system up and keeping it running day to day.

# RUNLEVELS

As described on page 440, systemd has done away with traditional runlevels although vestiges remain. Table 10-1 lists the runlevels (target units) as they exist under systemd.

**Table 10-1** Runlevels (target units)

| SysVinit runlevel | systemd runlevel (target unit) | Name/function |
|---|---|---|
| 0 | **runlevel0.target**, **poweroff.target** | Shuts down the system |
| 1 | **runlevel1.target**, **rescue.target** | Brings the system to single-user/rescue mode |
| 2, 3, 4 | **runlevel2.target**, **runlevel3.target**, **runlevel4.target**, **multi-user.target** | Brings the system to multiuser textual mode |
| 5 | **runlevel5.target**, **graphical.target** | Brings the system to multiuser graphical mode |
| 6 | **runlevel6.target**, **reboot.target** | Reboots the system |
| | **emergency.target** | Emergency shell |

Default (persistent) runlevel — By default, systems boot to multiuser graphical mode (**graphical.target**). See "Setting the Persistent Runlevel" on page 444 for instructions on how to change this default.

runlevel — The runlevel utility (runlevel man page) displays the previous and current runlevels. This utility is a transitional tool; it provides compatibility with SysVinit. In the following example, the **N** indicates the system does not know which was the previous runlevel, and the **5** indicates the system is in multiuser graphical mode.

```
$ runlevel
N 5
```

who — The who utility with the **–r** option also displays the current runlevel:

```
$ who -r
         run-level 5  2013-07-21 14:41
```

**LPI** telinit — The telinit utility (telinit man page) allows a user working with **root** privileges to bring the system down, reboot the system, or change between runlevels. The telinit utility is a transitional tool; it provides compatibility with SysVinit and calls systemctl. The format of a telinit command is

*telinit **runlevel***

where ***runlevel*** is one of the runlevels described in Table 10-1.

## _LPI_  BOOTING THE SYSTEM

_Booting_ a system is the process of reading the Linux _kernel_ (page 1257) into system memory and starting it running. Refer to "GRUB: The Linux Boot Loader" on page 590 for more information on the initial steps of bringing a system up.

### List the kernel boot messages

**tip**    To save a list of kernel boot messages, run dmesg immediately after booting the system and logging in:

```
$ dmesg > dmesg.boot
```

This command saves the kernel messages in a file named **dmesg.boot**. This list can be educational; it can also be useful when you are having a problem with the boot process. For more information see page 595.

_LPI_  **systemd init daemon**    As the last step of the boot procedure, Linux starts the systemd **init** daemon (page 438) as PID number 1. This daemon is the first genuine process to run after booting and is the parent of all system processes.

Reinstalling the MBR    If the MBR (master boot record) is overwritten, the system will not boot; you might need to regenerate and rewrite the MBR as explained on page 456.

# SINGLE-USER MODE

When the system is in single-user mode, only the system console is enabled. You can run programs from the console in single-user mode just as you would from any terminal in multiuser mode with two differences: You cannot run graphical programs (because you are working in textual mode) and few of the system daemons are running.

With the system in single-user/rescue mode, you can perform system maintenance that requires filesystems to be unmounted or that requires just a quiet system—no one except you using it, so no user programs interfere with disk maintenance and backup programs. The classical UNIX term for this state is _quiescent_. You can often boot to single-user mode when the system will not boot normally, allowing you to change or replace configuration files, check and repair partitions using fsck (page 525), rewrite boot information (page 456), and more.

## _LPI_  BOOTING THE SYSTEM TO SINGLE-USER/RESCUE MODE

This section explains how to bring a system up to single-user/rescue mode by booting from the hard disk and giving GRUB the appropriate instructions.

Displaying the GRUB menu    The first step in bringing a system up in single-user mode from the hard disk is to display the GRUB menu (Figure 10-2). Boot the system normally (turn on the power or reboot the system). The GRUB menu will be hidden or displayed. Either way, if you hold down the SHIFT key as the system is booting, GRUB displays its menu and stops booting the system. As the system is initially configured, you must press a key as the system starts to boot or, after a few seconds, it will boot normally.

Selecting single-user/rescue mode    Unless you have modified the GRUB setup (page 591), the GRUB menu starts with a few lines similar to the following:

```
Fedora (3.9.9-301.fc19.x86_64) 19 (Schrödinger's Cat)
Fedora, with Linux 3.9.5-301.fc19.x86_64
Fedora, with Linux 0-rescue-40b9b79ed60f47c5b31224f23b76e2e0
```

Typically the first line is highlighted.

### Single-user/rescue mode versus rescuing an installed system

tip When you bring a system up in single-user/rescue mode, it boots from the hard disk and displays a bash prompt. This section explains how to bring a system up in single-user/rescue mode.

When you bring a system up to rescue an installed system, you boot from an Install or Network Image and select **Rescue installed system** from the Troubleshooting menu as explained on page 456.

Editing the GRUB menu With the GRUB menu displayed, follow these instructions to bring the system up in single-user/rescue mode:

1. Highlight the kernel you want to boot—GRUB highlights the default kernel when it displays its menu.

2. Press **e** to edit to the GRUB boot command line for the highlighted kernel.

3. Use the DOWN ARROW key to move the cursor as far down as it will go and then use the UP ARROW key to move it up two lines. The cursor will be at the beginning of the kernel line (the line that begins with eight SPACEs followed by the word **linux**). This line is long and wraps several times.

4. Use the RIGHT ARROW key to move the cursor until it is just past the first argument following **linux**; it will be just before the word **root=**. Enter SPACE **single** SPACE and press CONTROL-X to boot the system using the modified kernel line. After a few moments, the system displays

   ```
   Give root password for maintenance
   (or type Control-D to continue):
   ```

5. Enter the **root** password; Linux displays a shell **root** prompt (#).

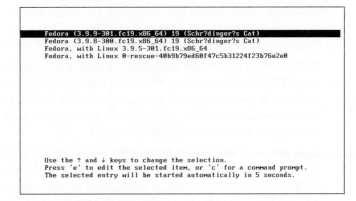

**Figure 10-2**   The GRUB menu

Booting to a target unit — The system is running in **rescue.target** (single-user) mode and you are logged in as **root**. In place of **single** in step number 4 on the previous page, you can specify one of the target units from Table 10-1 on page 449 (e.g., **systemd.unit=rescue.target** also boots the system to rescue mode).

## LPI   GOING TO GRAPHICAL MULTIUSER MODE

Graphical multiuser mode (the old runlevel 5) is the default state for a system. In this mode all appropriate filesystems are mounted, and users can log in from all connected terminals, dial-up lines, and network connections. All support services and daemons are enabled and running. When the system is in multiuser mode, it displays a graphical login screen on the console.

If you booted to single-user mode to fix something, give a **reboot** command, which reboots the system starting with the BIOS. If the system entered single-user mode automatically to allow you to repair the filesystem, give an **exit** command that causes the system to continue booting: systemd brings the system to the default runlevel—usually multiuser graphical mode. Alternately, you can give the following command while working with **root** privileges to bring the system to multiuser graphical mode, even if that is not the default mode:

```
# systemctl isolate graphical.target
```

## LOGGING IN

Textual login: **init**, agetty, and login — With a textual login, the system uses systemd, agetty, and login to allow a user to log in; login uses PAM modules (page 476) to authenticate a user. When you enter your username, agetty establishes the characteristics of the terminal. It then overlays itself with a login process and passes to the login process whatever you entered in response to the **login:** prompt. One authentication technique uses PAM: The login process consults the **/etc/passwd** file to see whether any username there matches the username you entered. Next, PAM examines the **/etc/shadow** file to see whether a password is associated with the username. If it is, login prompts you for a password; if not, it continues without requiring a password. When your username requires a password, login verifies the password you enter by checking the **/etc/shadow** file again. If either your username or your password is not correct, login displays **Login incorrect**, pauses, and prompts you to log in again.

By default, all passwords in the **/etc/shadow** file are hashed using the 512-bit *SHA2* (page 1272) hash function. When you log in, the login process hashes the password you type at the prompt and compares it to the hashed password in **/etc/shadow**. If the two passwords match, you are authenticated. See page 136 for more information on selecting a secure password.

With NIS or LDAP, login compares the username and password with the information in the appropriate naming service instead of (or in addition to) the **passwd** and **shadow** files. If the system is configured to use both methods (**/etc/passwd** and NIS/LDAP), it checks the **/etc/nsswitch.conf** file (page 495) to see in which order it should consult them.

**LPI** Graphical login   By default, with a graphical login the systemd daemon spawns gdm (GNOME display manager) on the first free virtual terminal, providing features similar to those offered by agetty and login. The gdm utility starts an X server and presents a login window. The gdm display manager then uses PAM to authenticate the user and runs the scripts in the **/etc/gdm/PreSession** directory. These scripts launch the user's session.

PAM   PAM (page 476)—the Pluggable Authentication Module facility—gives you greater control over user logins than the **/etc/passwd** and **/etc/shadow** files do. Using PAM, you can specify multiple levels of authentication, mutually exclusive authentication methods, or parallel methods, each of which is by itself sufficient to grant access to the system. For example, you can have different authentication methods for console logins and for ssh logins. Similarly, you can require modem users to authenticate themselves using two or more methods (such as a smartcard or badge reader and a password). PAM modules also provide security technology vendors with a convenient way to interface their hardware or software products with a system.

Initializing the session   When both the username and the password are correct, login or the scripts in **PreSession** consult the appropriate services to initialize the user and group IDs, establish the user's home directory, and determine which shell or desktop manager the user works with.

The login utility and **PreSession** scripts assign values to variables and look in the **/etc/group** file (page 506) to identify the groups the user belongs to. When login has finished its work, it overlays itself with the login shell, which inherits the variables set by login. In a graphical environment, the **PreSession** scripts start the desktop manager.

During a textual login, the login shell assigns values to additional shell variables and executes the commands in the system startup files **/etc/profile** and **/etc/bashrc**. Some systems have other system startup files as well. Although the actions performed by these scripts are system dependent, they typically display the contents of the **/etc/motd** (message of the day) and **/etc/issue** files, let you know if you have email, and set umask (page 469), the file-creation mask.

Along with executing the system startup commands, the shell executes the commands from the personal startup files in the user's home directory. These scripts are described on page 329. Because the shell executes personal startup files *after* the system startup files, a sophisticated user can override any variables or conventions that were established by the system. A new user, by contrast, can remain uninvolved in these matters.

# LOGGING OUT

With a shell prompt displayed in a textual environment, you can either execute a program or exit from the shell. If you exit from the shell, the process running the shell dies, and the parent process wakes up. When the shell is a child of another shell, the parent shell wakes up and displays a prompt. Exiting from a login shell causes the operating system to send systemd a signal that one of its children has died. Upon receiving this signal, systemd takes appropriate action. In the case of a process controlling a line for a terminal, systemd calls the appropriate tty service, which then respawns agetty so another user can log in. When you exit from a GUI, the GNOME display manager, gdm, displays a Login screen.

# *LPI* BRINGING THE SYSTEM DOWN

Textual    The **reboot, halt,** and **poweroff** systemctl commands perform the tasks needed to bring the system down safely. These utilities can restart the system (**reboot**), prepare the system to be turned off (**halt**), and, on most hardware, power down the system (**poweroff**).

From the console, any user can run these commands without authentication as long as no other user is logged in on the system. From a remote login, any user can run these commands but must first authenticate with an administrator's (page 422) password; systemctl uses sudo to authenticate. A user running with **root** privileges can always run these commands without further authentication. The following example shows Sam, working as himself remotely and providing his password, shutting down the system.

```
$ systemctl poweroff
==== AUTHENTICATING FOR org.freedesktop.login1.power-off ===
Authentication is required for powering off the system.
Multiple identities can be used for authentication:
 1.  Sam the Great (sam)
 2.  Max Wild (max)
Choose identity to authenticate as (1-2): 1
Password:
==== AUTHENTICATION COMPLETE ===
```

The legacy reboot, shutdown, halt, and poweroff utilities call systemctl.

Graphical    Bring the system down by clicking your name or **Live System User** at the upper-right corner of the screen, clicking **Power Off** from the menu GNOME displays, and then clicking the button labeled **Power Off** from the small window GNOME displays.

## CONTROL-ALT-DEL: REBOOTS THE SYSTEM

In a textual environment, pressing the CONTROL-ALT-DEL keys simultaneously (also referred to as the *three-finger salute* or the *Vulcan death grip*) on the console causes systemctl to reboot the system. In a graphical environment, the X Window System traps this key set and GNOME displays the Power Off dialog box.

## *LPI* GOING TO SINGLE-USER MODE

The following steps describe a method of manually bringing the system down to single-user mode. In some cases it might be easier to simply reboot the system and bring it up in single-user mode; see page 450. Before starting, make sure you give other users enough warning before switching to single-user mode; otherwise, they might lose the data they are working on. Because going from multiuser to single-user mode can affect other users, you must work with **root** privileges to perform these tasks.

1. Give the command **touch /etc/nologin** to prevent users from logging on as you bring the system down. See the **nologin** man page for more information.

2. Use wall (see the wall man page) to warn everyone who is using the system to log out.

3. If you are sharing files via NFS, use **exportfs –ua** to disable network access to the shared filesystems. (Use **exportfs** without an argument to see which filesystems are being shared.)

4. Confirm no critical processes are running in the background (e.g., an unattended compile).

5. Give the command **systemctl isolate rescue.target** (page 445) to bring the system down to single-user mode. After a few moments, the system displays

```
Give root password for maintenance
(or type Control-D to continue):
```

When you type the root password, bash displays the **root** prompt (#). The system does not run most services in rescue mode. The systemctl or runlevel utilities can confirm the current runlevel.

6. Use **umount –a** to unmount all mounted devices that are not in use. Use **mount** without an argument to make sure no devices other than root (**/**) are mounted before continuing. Alternately, you can perform maintenance tasks that do not require devices to be unmounted.

## TURNING THE POWER OFF

Once the system is in single-user mode, give the command **systemctl poweroff** to bring the system down. If the system does not power off by itself, turn the power off when prompted to do so or when the system starts rebooting.

# CRASH

A *crash* occurs when the system stops suddenly or fails unexpectedly. A crash might result from software or hardware problems or from a loss of power. As a running system loses power, it might behave in erratic or unpredictable ways. In a fraction of a second, some components are supplied with enough voltage; others are not. Buffers are not flushed, corrupt data might be written to hard disks, and so on. IDE and SATA drives do not behave as predictably as SCSI drives under these circumstances. After a crash, you must bring the operating system up carefully to minimize possible damage to the filesystems. On many occasions, little or no damage will have occurred.

## REPAIRING A FILESYSTEM

Although the filesystems are checked automatically during the boot process if needed, you will have to check them manually if a problem cannot be repaired automatically. By default, when fsck cannot repair a filesystem automatically at boot time, Linux enters single-user mode so you can run fsck manually. If necessary, you can explicitly boot the system to single-user mode (page 450). *Do not* mount any devices other than root, which Linux mounts automatically.

With the system in single-user mode, give a **mount** command to make sure none of the local filesystems you want to check are mounted. Then run fsck (page 525) on these filesystems, repairing them as needed. Make note of any ordinary files or directories that you repair (and can identify), and inform their owners that these files might not be complete or correct. Look in the **lost+found** directory (page 502) *in each filesystem* for missing files. After successfully running fsck, if the system entered single-user mode automatically, type **exit** to exit from the single-user shell and resume booting the system; otherwise, give a **reboot** command.

### Back up a badly damaged filesystem *before* running fsck on it

caution    When a filesystem is badly broken, fsck sometimes makes the situation worse while trying to repair it. In these cases, it might be possible to recover *more* data by copying the readable data from the broken filesystem before attempting to repair it. When a damaged filesystem holds important data, use dd (dd man page) to make a full binary backup *of an unmounted filesystem before* attempting to repair it using fsck.

If files are not correct or are missing altogether, you might have to re-create them from a backup copy of the filesystem. For more information refer to "Backing Up Files" on page 602.

### *LPI*    REINSTALLING THE MBR

To reinstall the MBR, as is necessary when it gets overwritten by a Windows installation, boot the system from an Install or Network Image and select **Troubleshooting⇨ Rescue a Fedora system**. Then mount the system image as described in "Rescue an Installed System" below and run grub2-mkconfig (page 593) to regenerate the **grub.cfg** file and grub2-install (page 594) to install it on the appropriate device:

```
# chroot /mnt/sysimage
# grub2-mkconfig -o /boot/grub2/grub.cfg
# grub2-install /dev/sda
```

Exit from the rescue shell and reboot the system.

### WHEN THE SYSTEM DOES NOT BOOT

When a system will not boot from the hard disk, boot the system to rescue an installed system (next) or single-user/rescue mode (page 450). If the system comes up, run fsck (page 525) on the root filesystem on the hard disk and try booting from the hard disk again. If the system still does not boot, you might have to regenerate the **grub.cfg** file and reinstall the master boot record (previous).

## RESCUE AN INSTALLED SYSTEM

When you rescue an installed system you can fix a system that does not boot normally: You can change or replace configuration files, check and repair partitions using fsck (page 525), rewrite boot information, and more. To rescue an installed system, boot the system from an Install or Network Image and select **Troubleshooting** from the Install

**Figure 10-3** The Rescue screen

Image Boot menu (Figure 3-4, page 61) and **Rescue a Fedora system** from the Troubleshooting menu (Figure 3-5, page 61). When the system comes up it displays the pseudographical Rescue screen (Figure 10-3).

This screen gives you the choice between having the system look for and mount an existing Linux installation, and simply displaying a shell prompt. Because it is not a true graphical screen, the mouse does not work on the Rescue screen. Use TAB to move the highlight between buttons and SPACE to select the highlighted button.

Select **Continue** or **Read-Only** to have the system search for an existing system; select **Skip** to not have it search. If you have the system search and it finds an existing system, **Continue** then mounts the system in read-write mode; **Read-Only** mounts it read-only. If the mount is successful, the next two screens tell you that the existing system was mounted under **/mnt/sysimage**. Select **OK** two times. The next screen allows you to start a shell, run a diagnostic, or reboot. Use the ARROW keys to highlight **Start shell** and press RETURN.

With the existing installation mounted, once the system displays a shell prompt (similar to **bash-4.2#**), you can give the command **chroot /mnt/sysimage** to access the existing installation as it would be if you had booted normally, with the existing installation's root directory available as **/** (root). See page 487 for more information on chroot. At this point you can reinstall the MBR if necessary (prevous page). If you choose not to mount the existing installation, you are running a rescue system with standard tools mounted in standard locations (**/usr/bin, /usr/sbin**, and so on). You can fix or mount partitions from the local installation. When you exit from the rescue shell, you can reboot the system. Remove the installation medium if you want to boot from the hard drive.

# AVOIDING A TROJAN HORSE

A *Trojan horse* is a program, usually embedded in or masquerading as another program. The program does something destructive and/or disruptive to a system while appearing to be benign. Because of the way it is disguised, a user typically runs it without realizing what he is doing. As an example, you could store the following script in an executable file named mkfs:

```
while true
    do
        echo 'Good Morning Mr. Jones. How are you? Ha Ha Ha.' > /dev/console
    done
```

If you are working with **root** privileges when you run this command, it will continuously write a message to the console. If the programmer were malicious, it could do worse. The only thing missing in this plot is access permissions.

A malicious user could implement this Trojan horse by changing **root**'s **PATH** variable to include a publicly writable directory at the start of the **PATH** string. (The catch is that you need to be able to write to **/etc/profile** or **/root/.bash_profile**—where the **PATH** variable is set for **root**—and only a user working with **root** privileges can do that.) Then you would need to put the bogus mkfs program file in that directory. Because the fraudulent version appears in a directory mentioned earlier than the real one in **PATH**, the shell would run it rather than the real version. Thus, the next time a user working with **root** privileges tries to run mkfs, the fraudulent version would run.

Trojan horses that lie in wait for and take advantage of the misspellings most people make are among the most insidious types. For example, you might type **sl** instead of **ls**. Because you do not regularly execute a utility named **sl** and you might not remember typing the command **sl**, it is more difficult to track down this type of Trojan horse than one that takes the name of a more familiar utility.

A good way to help prevent the execution of a Trojan horse is to make sure your **PATH** variable does not contain a single colon (:) at the beginning or end of the **PATH** string or a period (.) or double colon (::) anywhere in the **PATH** string. This precaution helps ensure that you will not execute a file in the working directory by accident.

To check for a possible Trojan horse, examine the filesystem periodically for files with setuid (page 196) permission. The following command lists these files:

*LPI*  Listing setuid
files
```
# find / - perm /4000 -exec ls -lh {} \; 2> /dev/null
...
-rwsr-xr-x. 1 root root 53K Jun 11 11:48 /usr/bin/crontab
-rwsr-xr-x. 1 root root 32K Jun 13 02:48 /usr/bin/su
-rwsr-xr-x. 1 root root 23K May 29 07:52 /usr/bin/pkexec
-rwsr-xr-x. 1 root root 28K Jun 21 17:51 /usr/bin/passwd
-rws--x--x. 1 root root 24K Jun 13 02:48 /usr/bin/chsh
---s--x--x. 1 root root 124K Feb 28 04:55 /usr/bin/sudo
-rwsr-xr-x. 1 root root 44K Jun 13 02:48 /usr/bin/mount
-rwsr-xr-x. 1 root root 37K Mar 19 12:59 /usr/bin/newgrp
-rwsr-xr-x. 1 root root 77K Mar 19 12:59 /usr/bin/gpasswd
...
```

This command uses find (page 229) to locate all files that have their setuid bit set (mode 4000). The slash preceding the mode causes find to report on any file that has this bit set, regardless of how the other bits are set. The output sent to standard error is redirected to **/dev/null** so it does not clutter the screen.

**LPI** Listing setgid files  You can display all files with setgid permission (page 196) by substituting 2000 for 4000 in the preceding command.

Run software only from sources you trust  Another way a Trojan horse can enter a system is via a tainted **~/.bashrc** (page 502) file. A bogus sudo command or alias in this file can capture a user's password, which might then be used to gain **root** privileges. Because a user has write permission to this file, any program the user executes can easily modify it. The best way to prevent this type of Trojan horse from entering a system is to run software only from sources you trust.

You can set up a program, such as AIDE (Advanced Intrusion Detection Environment; **aide** package), that will take a snapshot of the system and periodically check files for changes. For more information see aide.sourceforge.net.

# **LPI** X WINDOW SYSTEM

When you start an X Window System (graphical) session, you set up a *client/server environment*. One process, called the *X server*, displays a desktop and windows under X. Each application program and utility that makes a request of the X server is a *client* of that server. Examples of X clients include xterm, Compiz, gnome-calculator, and such general applications as word processing and spreadsheet programs. A typical request from a client is to display an image or open a window.

### **The roles of X client and server might be counterintuitive**

tip  The terms *client* and *server*, when referring to X, have the opposite meanings of how you might think of them intuitively: The server runs the mouse, keyboard, and display; the application program is the client.

This disparity becomes even more apparent when you run an application program on a remote system. You might think of the system running the program as the server and the system providing the display as the client, but in fact it is the other way around. With X, the system providing the display is the server, and the system running the program is the client.

Events  The server also monitors keyboard and mouse actions (*events*) and passes them to the appropriate client. For example, when you click the border of a window, the server sends this event to the window manager (client). Characters you type into a terminal emulation window are sent to that terminal emulator (client). The client takes appropriate action when it receives an event—for example, making a window active or displaying the typed characters on the server.

Separating the physical control of the display (the server) from the processes needing access to the display (the client) makes it possible to run the server on one computer and the client on another computer. Most of the time, this book discusses running the X server and client applications on a single system. "Remote Computing and Local Displays" on the next page describes using X in a distributed environment.

**optional**   You can run xev (X event) by giving the command **xev** from a terminal emulator window and then watch the information flow from the client to the server and back again. This utility opens the Event Tester window, which has a box in it. The X server sends the client (xev) events each time anything happens, such as moving the mouse pointer, clicking a mouse button, moving the mouse pointer into the box, typing, or resizing the window. The xev utility displays information about each event in the window you opened it from. You can use xev as an educational tool: Start it and see how much information is processed each time you move the mouse. Close the Event Tester window to exit from xev.

This section provides basic information about starting and configuring X from the command line. For more information see the Xserver man page and the man pages listed at the bottom of the Xserver man page.

## STARTING X FROM A CHARACTER-BASED DISPLAY

Once you have logged in on a virtual console (page 121), you can start an X Window System server by using startx. See "Setting the Persistent Runlevel" on page 444 for instructions on setting Fedora to boot to single-user/rescue mode (specify a target of **rescue.target**) where it displays a textual interface. When you run startx, the X server displays an X screen, using the first available virtual console. The following command causes startx to run in the background so you can switch back to this virtual console and give additional commands:

```
$ startx &
```

## REMOTE COMPUTING AND LOCAL DISPLAYS

Typically the X server and the X client run on the same machine. To identify a remote X server (display) an X client (application) is to use, you can either set a global shell variable or use a command-line option. Before you can connect to a remote X server, you must make these changes on the server:

1. Turn off the Xorg **–nolisten tcp** option (next).

2. Run xhost to give the client permission to connect to the X server (next page).

3. Open TCP port 6000 (page 906).

Unless you have a reason to leave these features off, turn them back on when you finish with the examples in this section—leaving them off weakens system security. These tasks must be performed on the X server because the features protect the server. You do not have to prepare the client. The examples in this section assume the server is named **plum** and the client is named **guava**.

### *LPI*   THE Xorg –nolisten tcp OPTION

As Fedora/RHEL is installed, the X server starts with the **–nolisten tcp** option, which protects the X server by preventing TCP connections to the X server. To connect to a remote X server, you must turn this option off on the server. To turn it off, while working with **root** privileges edit the file named **/etc/gdm/custom.conf** and add the following line just below [**security**]:

```
max@plum:~$ cat /etc/gdm/custom.conf
[security]
DisallowTCP=false
```

To effect this change, restart the X server and gdm (GNOME display manager) by giving the following command while working with **root** privileges.

```
# systemctl restart gdm.service
```

Use the command **ps –ef | grep Xorg** to display the options the X server is running with. See library.gnome.org/admin/gdm/3.0/configuration.html.en#daemonconfig for more information.

### Security and the Xorg –nolisten tcp option

security    In a production environment, if you need to place an X server and the clients on different systems, it is best to forward (tunnel) X over ssh. This setup provides a secure, encrypted connection. The method described in this section is useful on local, secure networks and for understanding how X works. See "Forwarding X11" on page 707 for information on setting up ssh so it forwards X.

### LPI xhost GRANTS ACCESS TO A DISPLAY

As installed, xhost protects each user's X server. A user who wants to grant access to his X server needs to run xhost. Assume Max is logged in on the system named **plum** and wants to allow a user on **guava** to use his display (X server). Max runs this command:

```
max@plum:~$ xhost +guava
guava being added to access control list
max@plum:~$ xhost
access control enabled, only authorized clients can connect
INET:guava
...
```

Without any arguments, xhost describes its state. In the preceding example, **INET** indicates an IPv4 connection. If Max wants to allow all systems to access his display, he can give the following command:

```
$ xhost +
access control disabled, clients can connect from any host
```

### Security and xhost

security    Giving a remote system access to your display using xhost means any user on the remote system can watch everything you type in a terminal emulation window, including passwords. For this reason, some software packages, such as the Tcl/Tk development system (www.tcl.tk), restrict their own capabilities when xhost permits remote access to the X server. If you are concerned about security or want to take full advantage of systems such as Tcl/Tk, use a safer means of granting remote access to your X session. See the xauth man page for information about a more secure replacement for xhost.

If you frequently work with other users via a network, you might find it convenient to add an xhost line to your **.bash_profile** file (page 330)—but see the tip on the previous page regarding security and xhost. Be selective in granting access to your X display using xhost; if another system has access to your display, you might find your work frequently interrupted.

### LPI THE DISPLAY VARIABLE

The most common method of identifying a display is to use the **DISPLAY** shell environment variable to hold the X server ID string. This locally unique identification string holds the screen number of a display:

```
$ echo $DISPLAY
:0
```

The format of the complete (globally unique) ID string for a display is

*[hostname]:display-number[.screen-number]*

where *hostname* is the name of the system running the X server, *display-number* is the number of the logical (physical) display (0 unless multiple monitors or graphical terminals are attached to the system, or if you are running X over ssh), and *screen-number* is the logical number of the (virtual) terminal (0 unless you are running multiple instances of X). When you are working with a single physical screen, you can shorten the identification string. For example, you can use **plum:0.0** or **plum:0** to identify the only physical display on the system named **plum**. When the X server and the X clients are running on the same system, you can shorten this identification string even further to **:0.0** or **:0**. An ssh connection shows **DISPLAY** as **localhost:10.0**. You might have to connect using **ssh –X** to see this value. See "X11 forwarding" on page 687 for information on setting up ssh so it forwards X.

### When you change the value of DISPLAY

**tip**   When you change the value of the **DISPLAY** variable, all X programs send their output to the new display named by **DISPLAY**.

If **DISPLAY** is empty or not set, the screen you are working from is not running X. An application (the X client) uses the value of the **DISPLAY** variable to determine which display, keyboard, and mouse (collectively, the X server) to use. One way to run an X application, such as gnome-calculator, on the local system but have it use the X display on a remote system is to change the value of the **DISPLAY** variable on the client system so it identifies the remote X server.

```
sam@guava:~$ export DISPLAY=plum:0.0
sam@guava:~$ gnome-calculator &
```

The preceding example shows Sam running gnome-calculator with the default X server running on the system named **plum**. After setting the **DISPLAY** variable to the ID of the **plum** server, all X programs (clients) Sam starts use **plum** as their server (i.e., output appears on **plum**'s display and input comes from **plum**'s keyboard and mouse).

Try running xterm in place of gnome-calculator and see which keyboard it accepts input from. If this example generates an error, refer to the two preceding sections, which explain how to set up the server to allow a remote system to connect to it.

### THE ––display OPTION

For a single command, you can usually specify the X server on the command line:

```
sam@guava:~$ gnome-calculator --display plum:0.0
```

Many X programs accept the **––display** option. Those that do not accept this option send their output to the display specified by the **DISPLAY** variable.

## STOPPING THE X SERVER

How you terminate a window manager depends on which window manager is running and how it is configured. If X stops responding, switch to a virtual terminal, log in from another terminal or a remote system, or use ssh to access the system. Then kill (page 465) the process running Xorg.

## REMAPPING MOUSE BUTTONS (CLI)

Throughout this book, each description of a mouse click refers to the button by its position (left, middle, or right, with left implied when no button is specified) because the position of a mouse button is more intuitive than an arbitrary name or number. X numbers buttons starting at the left and continuing with the mouse wheel. The buttons on a three-button mouse are numbered 1 (left), 2 (middle), and 3 (right). A mouse wheel, if present, is numbered 4 (rolling it up) and 5 (rolling it down). Clicking the wheel is equivalent to clicking the middle mouse button. The buttons on a two-button mouse are 1 (left) and 2 (right).

If you are right-handed, you can conveniently press the left mouse button with your index finger; X programs take advantage of this fact by relying on button 1 for the most common operations. If you are left-handed, your index finger rests most conveniently on button 2 or 3 (the right button on a two- or three-button mouse).

"Left-handed mouse" on page 110 describes how to use a GUI to change a mouse between right-handed and left-handed, causing X to swap the functions of the left and right buttons. You can also change how X interprets the mouse buttons using xmodmap. If you are left-handed and using a three-button mouse with a wheel, the following command causes X to interpret the right button as button 1 and the left button as button 3:

```
$ xmodmap -e 'pointer = 3 2 1 4 5'
Warning: Only changing the first 5 of 24 buttons.
```

The warning says that xmodmap is not changing the settings of the last 19 buttons, which is fine. Omit the 4 and 5 if the mouse does not have a wheel. The following command works for a two-button mouse without a wheel:

```
$ xmodmap -e 'pointer = 2 1'
```

Use the xmodmap **–pp** option to display all the buttons X has defined for the mouse and how those buttons are mapped. After making the changes described above for the mouse with a wheel, xmodmap shows the following mapping.

```
$ xmodmap -pp
There are 24 pointer buttons defined.

    Physical        Button
    Button          Code
       1               3
       2               2
       3               1
       4               4
       5               5
       6               6
       7               7
  ...
```

Changing the order of the first three buttons is critical to making the mouse suitable for a left-handed user. When you remap the mouse buttons, remember to reinterpret the descriptions in this book accordingly. When this book asks you to click the left button or does not specify which button to click, use the right button, and vice versa.

# SYSTEM ADMINISTRATION TOOLS

This section describes a few of the textual (command-line) tools that can help you be an efficient and thorough system administrator. Some are simply mentioned here and are described in detail elsewhere in the book. It also presents a list of graphical administration tools available under Fedora/RHEL. You can learn more about these tools by reading the appropriate man or info pages.

## TEXTUAL ADMINISTRATION UTILITIES

### blkid: DISPLAYS BLOCK DEVICE INFORMATION

The blkid utility, which must be run with **root** privileges, displays the label, UUID value, and filesystem type for block devices:

```
# blkid
/dev/sda1: UUID="c07cf9ea-df3c-42a6-8bca-38dbc154a52c" TYPE="ext4"
/dev/sda2: UUID="KyxKaK-k5W1-uljD-sbxD-2X75-M67C-fkkpn1" TYPE="LVM2_member"
/dev/mapper/fedora-swap: UUID="ca3835a5-5789-4aa0-a114-1a1783606d87" TYPE="swap"
/dev/mapper/fedora-root: UUID="10f4196d-b561-4830-a603-8eb98e5704c0" TYPE="ext4"
/dev/mapper/fedora-home: UUID="5d5391fe-252a-4a06-a117-aadc81994057" TYPE="ext4"
```

### chsh: CHANGES THE LOGIN SHELL FOR A USER

The chsh utility changes the login shell for a user. When you call chsh without an argument, you change your login shell. When an ordinary user changes his login shell with chsh, he must specify an installed shell that is listed in the file **/etc/shells**, exactly as it is listed there; chsh rejects other entries. When working with **root** privileges, you can change any user's shell to any value by calling chsh with the username as an argument. The **chsh ––list-shells** command displays the list of available shells. In the following example, a user working with **root** privileges changes Sam's shell to tcsh:

```
# chsh sam
Changing shell for sam.
New shell [/bin/bash]: /bin/tcsh
Shell changed.
```

See page 329 for more information.

## clear: CLEARS THE SCREEN

The clear utility clears the screen. You can also use CONTROL-L from bash to clear the screen. The value of the environment variable **TERM** (page 1153) determines how to clear the screen.

## dmesg: DISPLAYS SYSTEM MESSAGES

The dmesg utility displays recent system log messages (the kernel ring buffer; page 595).

## e2label: WORKS WITH VOLUME LABELS

The e2label utility displays or creates a volume label on an **ext2**, **ext3**, or **ext4** filesystem. You must run this utility with **root** privileges. An e2label command has the following format:

> e2label *device* [*newlabel*]

where ***device*** is the name of the device (e.g., **/dev/hda2**, **/dev/sdb1**, **/dev/sr0**) you want to work with. When you include the optional ***newlabel*** parameter, e2label changes the label on ***device*** to ***newlabel***. Without this parameter, e2label displays the label. You can also create a volume label using the **–L** option of tune2fs (page 526). See also blkid on the previous page.

## *LPI*  kill: SENDS A SIGNAL TO A PROCESS

The kill builtin sends a signal to a process. This signal might or might not terminate (kill) the process, depending on which signal it is and how the process is designed. Refer to "trap: Catches a Signal" on page 1047 for a discussion of the various signals and their interaction with a process. Running kill is definitely not the first method to try when a process needs to be aborted. See also killall (page 467) and pkill (page 468).

Usually a user can kill a process by working in another window or by logging in on another terminal. Sometimes, however, you might have to work with **root** privileges to kill a process for a user. To kill a process, you need to know its PID. The ps utility can provide this information once you determine the name of the program the user is running and/or the username of the user. The top utility (page 612) can also be helpful in finding and killing a runaway process (use the top **k** command).

## kill: **Use the kill signal (–KILL or –9) as a method of last resort**

caution    When you do need to use kill, send the termination signal (**kill –TERM** or **kill –15**) first. Only if the termination signal does not work should you attempt to use the kill signal (**kill –KILL** or **kill –9**).

Because of its inherent dangers, using a kill signal is a method of last resort, especially when you are working with **root** privileges. One kill command issued while working with **root** privileges can bring the system down without warning. The kill signal can also cause the target program to corrupt its configuration or state.

**LE+**  ps    In the following example, Sam complains that gnome-calculator is stuck and that he cannot do anything from the gnome-calculator window—not even close it. A more experienced user could open another window and kill the process, but in this case you kill it for Sam. You use ps to produce a long list of all processes and a pipeline to send standard output of ls to grep to find which one is running gnome-calculator:

```
$ ps -ef | grep gnome-calculator
sam       3730  2424  0 14:07 ?         00:00:00 gnome-calculator
sam       3766  3568  0 14:14 pts/3     00:00:00 grep gnome-calculator
```

If several people are running gnome-calculator, look in the left column to find the correct username so you can kill the correct process.

pgrep    You can also use the pgrep utility to list all processes owned by Sam with the string **calc** in the name of the program the process is running:

```
$ pgrep -u sam -l calc
3730 gnome-calculato
```

Now that you know Sam's process running gnome-calculator has a PID of 3730, you can use kill to terminate it. The safest way to do so is to log in as Sam (perhaps you could allow him to log in for you or su to sam [**su sam**] if you are logged in as **root**) and give any of the following commands (all of which send a termination signal to process 3730):

```
$ kill 3730
```

*or*

```
$ kill -15 3730
```

*or*

```
$ kill -TERM 3730
```

Only if this command fails should you send the kill signal:

```
$ kill -KILL 3730
```

The –KILL option instructs kill to send a **SIGKILL** signal, which the process cannot ignore. Although you can give the same command while you are working with **root** privileges, a typing mistake in this situation can have much more far-reaching consequences than if you make the same mistake while you are working as a nonprivileged user. A nonprivileged user can kill only her own processes, whereas a user with **root** privileges can kill any process, including system processes.

As a compromise between speed and safety, you can combine the su or sudo and kill utilities by using the su –c or the sudo –u option. The following command runs the kill command with the identity of Sam (Sam's privileges):

```
# su sam -c "kill -TERM 3730"
```

*or*

```
$ sudo -u sam kill -TERM 3730
```

See also killall (next) and pkill (next page).

### **LPI** killall: KILLS A COMMAND

The killall utility is similar to kill (previous) but uses a command name instead of a PID number. Give the following command to kill all your processes that are running gnome-calculator or vi:

```
$ killall gnome-calculator vi
```

Running this command while working with **root** privileges kills all processes running gnome-calculator or vi. See also kill (page 465) and pkill (next page).

### lshw: DISPLAYS HARDWARE INFORMATION

The lshw utility (**lshw** package) lists system hardware. This utility provides complete information only when run with **root** privileges. Use the **–short** option to display a brief listing. See page 636 for more information.

### **LPI** mkfs: CREATES A FILESYSTEM

The mkfs utility creates a new filesystem on a device, destroying all data on the device as it does so. This utility is a front end for many utilities, each of which builds a different type of filesystem. By default, mkfs builds an **ext2** filesystem and works on a hard disk partition. Although it can take many options and arguments, you can use mkfs simply as

```
# mkfs device
```

where *device* is the name of the device (e.g., **/dev/hda2**, **/dev/sdb1**, **/dev/sr0**) you want to make a filesystem on. Use the **–t** option to specify a type of filesystem. For example, the following command creates an **ext4** filesystem on **/dev/sda2**:

```
# mkfs -t ext4 /dev/sda2
```

### pidof: DISPLAYS PID NUMBERS OF COMMANDS

The pidof utility displays the PID number of each process running the command you specify:

```
$ pidof httpd
567 566 565 564 563 562 561 560 553
```

If it is difficult to find the right process, try using top. Refer to the man pages for these utilities for more information, including lists of options.

## ping: SENDS A PACKET TO A REMOTE SYSTEM

The ping utility sends packets to a remote system. This utility determines whether you can reach a remote system through the network and tells you how long it takes to exchange messages with the remote system. Refer to "ping: Tests a Network Connection" on page 305.

## _LPI_   pkill: KILLS A COMMAND

The pkill utility, which has a syntax similar to pgrep, kills a process based on the command line that initiated the process. The next command sends a termination signal to all processes owned by username **sam** that have the string **calc** in the command line that started the process.

```
$ pkill -u sam calc
```

Caution dictates that you give the same command using pgrep (page 466) in place of pkill before attempting to kill a process.

## reset (LINK TO tset): RESETS A TERMINAL

The reset utility, which is a link to tset, resets terminal characteristics. The value of the **TERM** environment variable (page 1153) determines how the screen will be reset. The screen is cleared, the kill and interrupt characters are set to their default values, and character echo is turned on. When given from a graphical terminal emulator, this command also changes the size of the window to its default. The reset utility is useful for restoring the screen to a sane state after it has been corrupted, such as after attempting to cat a binary file. In this sense, it is similar to an **stty sane** command.

## setserial: WORKS WITH A SERIAL PORT

The setserial utility (**setserial** package) gets and sets serial port information. When run with **root** privileges, this utility can configure a serial port. It does not configure the hardware. The following command sets the input address of **/dev/ttyS0** to 0x100, the interrupt (IRQ) to 5, and the baud rate to 115,000 baud:

```
# setserial /dev/ttyS0 port 0x100 irq 5 spd_vhi
```

You can also use setserial to check the configuration of a serial port:

```
# setserial /dev/ttyS0
/dev/ttyS0, UART: 16550A, Port: 0x0100, IRQ: 5, Flags: spd_vhi
```

Normally the system calls setserial as it is booting if a serial port needs custom configuration.

## stat: DISPLAYS INFORMATION ABOUT A FILE OR FILESYSTEM

The stat utility displays information about a file or filesystem. Giving the **–f** (filesystem) option followed by the mount point for a filesystem displays information about the filesystem, including the maximum number of characters allowed in a filename (**Namelen** in the following example). See the stat man page for more information.

```
$ stat -f /dev/sda
  File: "/dev/sda"
    ID: 0           Namelen: 255       Type: tmpfs
Block size: 4096          Fundamental block size: 4096
Blocks: Total: 127271     Free: 127207     Available: 127207
Inodes: Total: 127271     Free: 126600
```

## LPI umask: SPECIFIES THE FILE PERMISSION MASK

The umask shell builtin specifies the mask the system uses to set up access permissions when it creates a file. A umask command has the following format:

*umask [mask]*

where **mask** is a three- or four-digit octal number or a symbolic value such as you would use with chmod (page 193). A **mask** that you specify using octal numbers specifies the permissions that are *not* allowed; the digits correspond to the permissions for the owner of the file, members of the group the file is associated with, and everyone else. Because **mask** specifies the permissions that are *not* allowed, the system uses binary arithmetic to subtract each of the three digits from 7 when you create a file. If the file is an ordinary file (and not a directory file), the system then removes execute permissions from the file. The result is three or four octal numbers that specify the access permissions for the file (the numbers you would use with chmod).

You must use binary or octal arithmetic when performing permissions calculations. To calculate file permissions given a umask value, subtract the umask value from octal 777. For example, assume a umask value of 003:

|      |                                         |
|------|-----------------------------------------|
| 777  | starting permissions for calculation    |
| −003 | subtract umask value                    |
| 774  | resulting permissions for a directory   |
| 111  | remove execute permissions              |
| 664  | resulting permissions for an ordinary file |

To calculate permissions for a directory, umask subtracts the umask value from 777: In the example where umask has a value of 003, octal 7 minus octal 0 equals octal 7 (for two positions). Octal 7 minus octal 3 equals octal 4. Or using binary arithmetic, 111 − 011 = 100. The result is that the system gives permissions of 774 (**rwxrwxr--**) to a directory.

To calculate permissions for an ordinary file, the system changes the execute bit (001 binary) to 0 for each position. If the execute bit is not set, the system does not change the execute bit. In the example, removing the execute bit from octal 7 yields octal 6 (removing 001 from 111 yields 110; two positions). Octal 4 remains octal 4 because the execute bit is not set (the 001 bit is not set in 100, so it remains 100). The result is that the system gives permissions of 664 (**rw-rw-r--**) to an ordinary file.

The following commands set the file-creation mask and display the mask and its effect when you create a file and a directory. The mask of 022, when subtracted from 777, gives permissions of 755 (**rwxr–xr–x**) for a directory. For an ordinary file, the system subtracts execute permissions from 755 yielding permissions of 644 (**rw–r––r––**).

```
$ umask 022
$ umask
0022
$ touch afile
$ mkdir adirectory
$ ls -ld afile adirectory
drwxr-xr-x. 2 sam pubs 4096 07-25 14:39 adirectory/
-rw-r--r--. 1 sam pubs    0 07-25 14:39 afile
```

A *mask* that you specify using symbolic values specifies the permissions that *are* allowed. The next example sets the same mask using symbolic values. The **–S** option displays the mask symbolically:

```
$ umask u=rwx,g=rx,o=rx
$ umask
0022
$ umask -S
u=rwx,g=rx,o=rx
```

## LPI uname: DISPLAYS SYSTEM INFORMATION

The uname utility displays information about the system. Without arguments, it displays the name of the operating system (**Linux**). The **–r** (release) option displays the kernel release (e.g., 3.10.3-300.fc19.x86_64). The **–a** (all) option displays the operating system name, hostname, kernel release, release date of the operating system, and type of hardware you are using:

```
$ uname -a
Linux guava.example.com 3.9.9-302.fc19.x86_64 #1 SMP Sat Jul 6 13:41:07 UTC 2013 x86_64
x86_64 x86_64 GNU/Linux
```

# GRAPHICAL CONFIGURATION TOOLS

The Fedora/RHEL graphical configuration tools bring up graphical displays when called from a GUI; some display a textual interface when called from a command line in a non-GUI environment. In general, these tools, which are listed in Table 10-2, are simple to use and require little explanation beyond what the tool presents. Some have Help selections on their toolbars. Most do not have man pages, but some have a useful **––help** option. Many of the older tools have been replaced by the gnome-control-center (the Settings window; page 107).

**Table 10-2**    Graphical configuration tools

| Tool | Function |
| --- | --- |
| authconfig[-tui] | The authconfig-tui utility displays the pseudographical Authentication Configuration window. The User Information column allows you to configure user accounts to cache information and use LDAP, NIS, IPAv2, or Winbind support. The Authentication column allows you to specify how the system authenticates users, depending on how you configure user accounts. For a purely textual (scriptable) interface use authconfig. |
| firewall-config | Displays the Firewall Configuration window (page 900). |
| system-config-bind | Displays the BIND Configuration GUI window (**system-config-bind** package; page 867). |
| system-config-httpd | Displays the HTTP Server Configuration window (**system-config-httpd** package). |
| system-config-kickstart | Displays the Kickstart Configurator window, which allows you to create a Kickstart script (**system-config-kickstart** package; page 83). |
| system-config-nfs | Displays the NFS Server Configuration window (**system-config-nfs** package; page 812). |
| system-config-printer | Displays the Print Settings window, which allows you to set up printers and edit printer configurations (page 558). |
| system-config-rootpassword | Displays the Root Password window, which allows you to change the **root** password. Working with **root** privileges, you can also use passwd (page 137) from a command line to change the **root** password (**system-config-rootpassword** package). |
| system-config-samba | Displays the Samba Server Configuration window, which can help you configure Samba (**system-config-samba** package; page 837). |
| system-config-selinux | Displays the SELinux Administration window, which controls SELinux (**policycoreutils-gui** package; page 475). |
| system-config-services | Displays the Service Configuration window, which allows you to specify which daemons (services) run at each runlevel (**system-config-services** package; page 447). |

**Table 10-2**   Graphical configuration tools (continued)

| Tool | Function |
|------|----------|
| system-config-users | Displays the User Manager window, which allows you to work with users and groups (page 598). |
| system-switch-mail | Displays the system-switch-mail pseudographical window, which allows you to choose between the **sendmail** (page 739) and Postfix (page 742) MTAs when both packages are installed on the system (**system-switch-mail** package). |

# SELINUX

Traditional Linux security, called DAC (Discretionary Access Control), is based on users and groups. ACLs (page 198) implement DAC and can achieve fine-grained control over which users and processes can access files and how they can access them. Fine-grained access control is particularly important on servers, which often hold programs that require **root** privileges to run. The problem is that under DAC, the owner of a file has control over the permissions to the file, which is not always ideal.

SELinux (Security-Enhanced Linux), developed by the NSA (U.S. National Security Agency), implements MAC (Mandatory Access Control) in the Linux kernel. MAC, which is under the control of the system administrator, enforces security policies that limit what a user or program can do. It defines a security policy that controls some or all objects, such as files, devices, sockets, and ports, and some or all subjects, such as processes. Using SELinux, you can grant a process only those permissions it needs to be functional, following the principle of least privilege (page 423). Users are assigned roles that determine the primary function of the user. SELinux roles are conceptually similar to groups, except under SELinux, a user must actively switch between permitted roles. MAC is an important tool for limiting security threats that come from user errors, software flaws, and malicious users. The kernel checks MAC rules after it checks DAC rules; either can deny access.

### DAC versus MAC: who has the final say?

tip   Both DAC (Discretionary Access Control) and MAC (Mandatory Access Control) are effective at controlling access. The difference is that DAC is under the control of the user who owns a file and is therefore more easily subverted than is MAC, which is under the control of the system administrator. The kernel checks MAC rules after it checks DAC rules; either can deny access.

Modes   SELinux can be in one of three modes (states):

- **Enforcing/Active**—The default state, wherein SELinux security policy is enforced. A user or program can do only that which is permitted by the security policy.

- **Permissive/Warn**—The diagnostic state, wherein SELinux sends warning messages to a log but does not enforce the security policy. You can use the log to build a security policy that matches your requirements.

- **Disabled**—SELinux does not enforce a security policy nor does it issue warnings because no policy is loaded.

Running SELinux in permissive or enforcing state is estimated to degrade system performance between 0 and 7 percent, depending on tuning and usage. If you are unsure whether to use SELinux, selecting permissive state allows you to change to disabled or enforcing state easily at a later date.

Policies SELinux implements one of the following policies:

- **Targeted**—Applies SELinux MAC controls only to certain (targeted) processes (default).

- **MLS**—Multilevel Security protection for servers.

- **Minimum**—Protects virtual machines only.

This section discusses the targeted policy. With this policy, daemons and system processes that do not have a specified policy are controlled by traditional Linux DACs.

### Is SELinux causing a problem?

tip If a server or other system software does not work when you set it up, improper SELinux configuration may be the cause of the problem. Many services include instructions for secure use with SELinux (e.g., **smb.conf**) or have a man page in the **selinux-policy-devel** package (e.g., after you install the package, give the command **man 8 httpd_selinux**). You can also check **/var/log/audit/audit.log** if you suspect the SELinux policy needs to be adjusted.

## MORE INFORMATION

Web NSA: www.nsa.gov/research/selinux/docs.shtml
Fedora SELinux Wiki: fedoraproject.org/wiki/SELinux
SELinux Project: selinuxproject.org
SELinux HOWTO: wiki.centos.org/HowTos/SELinux
Warning about disabling SELinux: stopdisablingselinux.com
Fedora SELinux mailing list: admin.fedoraproject.org/mailman/listinfo/selinux

### Turning off SELinux

tip There are two ways to disable SELinux. You can either modify the **/etc/selinux/config** file so it includes the line **SELINUX=disabled** and reboot the system, or you can use **system-config-selinux** (as explained on page 475). However, see stopdisablingselinux.com.

If there is a chance you will want to enable SELinux in the future, putting SELinux in permissive mode is a better choice than disabling it. This strategy allows you to turn on SELinux more quickly when you decide to use it.

## config: The SELinux Configuration File

The /etc/selinux/config file, which has a link at /etc/sysconfig/selinux, controls the state of SELinux on the local system. Although you can modify this file, it might be more straightforward to work with system-config-selinux (next page). In the following example, the policy is set to targeted, but that setting is of no consequence because SELinux is disabled:

```
$ cat /etc/selinux/config
# This file controls the state of SELinux on the system.
# SELINUX= can take one of these three values:
#     enforcing - SELinux security policy is enforced.
#     permissive - SELinux prints warnings instead of enforcing.
#     disabled - No SELinux policy is loaded.
SELINUX=disabled
# SELINUXTYPE= can take one of these two values:
#     targeted - Targeted processes are protected,
#     minimum - Modification of targeted policy. Only selected processes are protected.
#     mls - Multi Level Security protection.
SELINUXTYPE=targeted
```

To put SELinux in enforcing mode, change the line containing the **SELINUX** assignment to **SELINUX=enforcing**. Similarly, you can change the policy by setting **SELINUXTYPE**. The change takes effect when the system reboots.

### If you will use SELinux in the future

tip   If you will use SELinux in the future but not now, turn it on when you install Linux and run it in permissive state with the policy set to the policy you will eventually use. Permissive state writes the required extended information to inodes, but it does not stop you from doing anything on the system.

If you turn on SELinux after it has been disabled, when you reboot the system SELinux has to add extended attributes to the files in the filesystem. This process can take a long time on a large filesystem. If you are never going to use SELinux, disable it.

## getenforce, setenforce, AND sestatus: Work with SELinux

The getenforce and setenforce utilities report on and temporarily set the SELinux state. The sestatus utility displays a summary of SELinux on the local system:

```
# getenforce
Enforcing

# setenforce permissive

# sestatus
SELinux status:               enabled
SELinuxfs mount:              /sys/fs/selinux
SELinux root directory:       /etc/selinux
Loaded policy name:           targeted
Current mode:                 permissive
```

```
Mode from config file:          permissive
Policy MLS status:              enabled
Policy deny_unknown status:     allowed
Max kernel policy version:      28
```

## SETTING THE TARGETED POLICY USING system-config-selinux

The system-config-selinux utility (**policycoreutils-gui** package) displays the SELinux Administration window (Figure 10-4), which controls SELinux. Open this window by giving the command **system-config-selinux** from an Enter a Command window (ALT-F2) or a terminal emulator.

With **Status** highlighted on the left side of the SELinux Administration window, choose Enforcing (default), Permissive, or Disabled from the drop-down list labeled **System Default Enforcing Mode**. The mode you choose becomes effective next time the system boots. You can use the drop-down list labeled **Current Enforcing Mode** to change between Enforcing and Permissive modes immediately. When you change the mode using this list, the system resumes the default mode when you reboot it.

To modify the SELinux policy, highlight **Boolean** on the left side of the SELinux Administration window and scroll through the list of modules. For example, the SpamAssassin (page 753) module has two policies: **Allow spamd to read/write user home directories** and **Allow user spamassassin clients to use the network.**

The first of these policies has a tick in the check box in the column labeled **Active** (on the left), so SELinux allows the SpamAssassin daemon (**spamd**) to read from and write to the home directories of users. The second of these policies does not have a tick in the check box in the column labeled **Active**, so SELinux does *not* allow user SpamAssassin clients to use the network. Add or remove ticks in these check boxes to turn on or off these policies.

**Figure 10-4**   The SELinux Administration window

To find Booleans that pertain to NFS, type **nfs** in the text box labeled **Filter** and press RETURN. The SELinux Administration window displays all Booleans with the string **nfs** in their descriptions. The modules with ticks in the column labeled **Active** are in use.

The last item on the left side of the SELinux Administration window, **Process Domain**, allows you put a single module into permissive mode as needed. This selection avoids putting the entire system into permissive mode when just one or two modules are not working properly with the system in enforcing mode.

# PAM

PAM (Linux-PAM or Linux Pluggable Authentication Modules) allows a system administrator to determine how applications use *authentication* (page 1238) to verify the identity of a user. PAM provides shared libraries of modules (located in **/lib64/security** or **/lib/security**) that, when called by an application, authenticate a user. The configuration files kept in the **/etc/pam.d** directory determine the method of authentication and contain a list (i.e., stack) of calls to the modules. PAM might also use other files, such as **/etc/passwd**, when necessary. The term "Pluggable" in PAM's name refers to the ease with which you can add and remove modules from an authentication stack.

The configuration files stored in **/etc/pam.d** describe the authentication procedure for each application. These files usually have names that are the same as or similar to the names of the applications that they authenticate for. For example, authentication for the login utility is configured in **/etc/pam.d/login**. The name of the file is the name of the PAM service that the file configures. Occasionally one file might serve two programs. PAM accepts only lowercase letters in the names of files in the **/etc/pam.d** directory.

Authentication stack   The files in **/etc/pam.d** list the set of modules to be used for each application to perform each task. Each such set of the modules is called an *authentication stack* or simply a *stack*. PAM calls the modules one at a time in order, going from the top of the stack (the first module listed in the configuration file) to the bottom. Each module reports success or failure back to PAM. When all stacks of modules (with some exceptions) within a configuration file have been called, the PAM library reports success or failure back to the application.

Instead of building the authentication code into each application, PAM provides shared libraries that keep the authentication code separate from the application code. The techniques of authenticating users stay the same from application to application. In this way PAM enables a system administrator to change the authentication mechanism for a given application without modifying the application.

PAM provides authentication for a variety of system-entry services (such as login, ftp, su, and sudo). You can take advantage of its ability to stack authentication modules to integrate system-entry services with different authentication mechanisms, such as RSA, DCE, Kerberos, and smartcards.

From login to using su or sudo to shutting the system down, whenever you are asked for a password (or not asked for a password because the system trusts you are who you say you are), PAM makes it possible for the system administrator to configure the authentication process. It also makes the configuration process essentially the same for all applications that use PAM for authentication.

### Do not create /etc/pam.conf

caution You might have encountered PAM on other systems where all configuration is arranged in a single file (**/etc/pam.conf**). This file does not exist on Fedora/RHEL systems. Instead, the **/etc/pam.d** directory contains individual configuration files, one per application that uses PAM. This setup makes it easy to install and uninstall applications that use PAM because you do not have to modify the **/etc/pam.conf** file each time. If you create a **/etc/pam.conf** file on a system that does not use this file, the PAM configuration might become confused. Do not use PAM documentation from a different system. Also, the **requisite** control flag is not available on some systems that support PAM.

Error messages PAM warns you about errors it encounters, logging them to **/var/log/messages** or **/var/log/secure**. Review these files if you are trying to figure out why a changed PAM file is not working properly. To prevent a malicious user from seeing information about PAM, PAM sends error messages to a file rather than to the screen.

## MORE INFORMATION

Local *Linux-PAM System Administrators' Guide:*
 /usr/share/doc/pam-1.1.6/html/Linux-PAM_SAG.html
 pam man page
 PAM modules: **apropos pam_** lists man pages describing PAM modules

Web Description: www.netbsd.org/docs/guide/en/chap-pam.html

HOWTO *User Authentication HOWTO*

## CONFIGURATION FILES, MODULE TYPES, AND CONTROL FLAGS

Login module Following is an example of a PAM configuration file. Comment lines begin with a hashmark (#).

```
$ cat /etc/pam.d/login
#%PAM-1.0
auth [user_unknown=ignore success=ok ignore=ignore default=bad] pam_securetty.so
auth       substack     system-auth
auth       include      postlogin
account    required     pam_nologin.so
account    include      system-auth
password   include      system-auth
# pam_selinux.so close should be the first session rule
session    required     pam_selinux.so close
session    required     pam_loginuid.so
session    optional     pam_console.so
# pam_selinux.so open should only be followed by sessions to be executed in the user context
session    required     pam_selinux.so open
session    required     pam_namespace.so
session    optional     pam_keyinit.so force revoke
session    include      system-auth
session    include      postlogin
-session   optional     pam_ck_connector.so
```

The first line is a special comment; it will become significant only if another PAM format is released. Do not use #% other than in the first line of the preceding example.

The rest of the lines tell PAM to do something as part of the authentication process. The first word on each line is a module type indicator: **account, auth, password,** or **session** (Table 10-3). The second is a control flag (Table 10-4) that indicates the action PAM should take if authentication fails. The rest of the line contains the name of a PAM module (located in **/lib64/security** or **/lib/security**) and any arguments for that module. The PAM library itself uses the **/etc/pam.d** files to determine which modules to delegate work to. Lines that have a control flag of **include** include the file named in the third field.

**Table 10-3**   Module type indicators

| Module type | Description | Controls |
| --- | --- | --- |
| **account** | Account management | Determining whether an already authenticated user is allowed to use the service she is trying to use. (That is, has the account expired? Is the user allowed to use this service at this time of day?) |
| **auth** | Authentication | Proving that the user is authorized to use the service; uses passwords or another mechanism. |
| **password** | Password modification | Updating authentication mechanisms such as user passwords. |
| **session** | Session management | Setting things up when the service is started (as when a user logs in) and breaking them down when the service is terminated (as when a user logs out). |

You can use one of the control flag keywords listed in Table 10-4 to set the control flags.

**Table 10-4**   Control flag keywords

| Keyword | Flag function |
| --- | --- |
| **required** | Success is required for authentication to succeed. Control and a failure result are returned after all modules in the stack have been executed. The technique of delaying the report to the calling program until all modules have been executed might keep attackers from knowing precisely what caused their authentication attempts to fail and tell them less about the system, making it more difficult for them to break in. |
| **requisite** | Success is required for authentication to succeed. Further module processing is aborted, and control is returned immediately after a module fails. This technique might expose information about the system to an attacker. However, if it prevents a user from giving a password over an insecure connection, it might keep information out of the hands of an attacker. |

**Table 10-4**  Control flag keywords (continued)

| Keyword | Flag function |
| --- | --- |
| **sufficient** | Success indicates this module type has succeeded; no subsequent **required** modules of this type are executed. Failure is not fatal to the stack of this module type. This technique is generally used when one form of authentication or another is good enough: If one fails, PAM tries the other. For example, when you use su to escalate privileges, **/etc/pam.d/su** first uses **pam_rootok** to check whether you are running with a UID of zero (**root** privileges). Because **su** calls **pam_rootok** with a control flag of **sufficient**, if you are running with a UID of zero, the **pam_rootok** module reports success, and PAM immediately reports success to the su utility that called it. If you are not running with **root** privileges, PAM starts the authentication again and asks for a password. If this second authentication succeeds, PAM ignores the fact that the **pam_rootok** module reported failure. If both modules fail, PAM reports failure to the su utility that called it. |
| **optional** | Result is generally ignored. An optional module is relevant only when it is the sole module on the stack for a particular service. |

PAM uses each of the module types as requested by the application. That is, the application asks PAM separately to authenticate, check account status, manage sessions, and change the password. PAM uses one or more modules from the **/lib64/security** or **/lib/security** directory to accomplish each of these tasks.

## EXAMPLE

Part of the login service's authentication stack follows:

```
$ cat /etc/pam.d/login
auth [user_unknown=ignore success=ok ignore=ignore default=bad] pam_securetty.so
auth       include        system-auth
account    required       pam_nologin.so
...
```

The login utility first asks for a username and then calls PAM to run this stack to authenticate the user. Refer to Table 10-3 and Table 10-4.

1. PAM first calls **pam_securetty** (secure tty; **pam_securetty** man page) as an auth (authentication) module to make sure the **root** user logs in only from an allowed terminal. This module looks at the **/etc/securetty** file for a list of terminals that the user named **root** is allowed to log in from. Thus PAM implements the longtime UNIX practice of not allowing **root** to use telnet to log in on the system (telnet uses login for authentication). This technique is not used but could be added to the **sshd**, **vsftpd**, and other PAM configuration files.

   Within the brackets ([]) in the control flag field are *value=action* pairs. When the module returns *value*, PAM evaluates *action*. In the example, when the module returns **user_unknown**, the result of running the module is ignored, and when the module returns success, the user is allowed to continue authentication. See the **pam_securetty** man page for details.

The **pam_securetty** module is *required* to succeed if the authentication stack is to succeed. The **pam_securetty** module reports failure only if someone is trying to log in as **root** from an unauthorized terminal. Otherwise (if the username being authenticated is not **root** or if the username is **root** and the login attempt is being made from a secure terminal), the **pam_securetty** module reports success.

Success and failure within PAM are opaque concepts that apply only to PAM. They do not equate to "true" and "false" as used elsewhere in the operating system.

2. Next, PAM includes the **/etc/pam.d/system-auth** file (**system-auth** man page). This file provides a common interface with which to call PAM.

3. The **pam_nologin** module (**pam_nologin** man page) makes sure that if the **/etc/nologin** file exists, only the **root** user is allowed to log in. (That is, the **pam_nologin** module reports success only if **/etc/nologin** does not exist or if the **root** user is logging in.) Thus, when a shutdown has been scheduled to occur in the near future, the system keeps users from logging in, only to have the system shut down moments later.

The **account** module type works like the **auth** module type but is called after the user has been authenticated; it acts as an additional security check or requirement that must be met for a user to gain access to the system. For example, **account** modules might enforce a policy that a user can log in only during business hours or check whether a password has expired.

The **session** module type sets up and tears down the session (perhaps mounting and unmounting the user's home directory). One common **session** module is the **pam_console** module, which sets the system up especially for users who log in at the physical console, rather than remotely. A local user is able to access the flash and DVD drives, the sound card, and sometimes other devices as defined by the system administrator.

The **password** module type is a bit unusual: All modules in the stack are called once and told to get all information they need to store the password to persistent memory, such as a disk, but not actually to store it. If it determines that it cannot or should not store the password, a module reports failure. If all **password** modules in the stack report success, they are called a second time and told to store to persistent memory the password they obtained on the first pass. The **password** module is responsible for updating the authentication information (i.e., changing the user's password).

Any one module can act as more than one module type; many modules can act as all four module types. For example, **pam_unix** can be called as an **auth** module to check a username and password against the **passwd** and **shadow** files, as an **account** module to check password expiration, as a **password** module to update a password (i.e., if login prompts with **your password has expired, enter a new password**), or as a **session** module to record login and logout timestamps for **wtmp** (for use with the last utility).

## MODIFYING THE PAM CONFIGURATION

### Do not lock yourself out of the system

caution   Editing PAM configuration files correctly requires careful attention. It is easy to lock yourself out of the system with a mistake. To avoid this problem, keep backup copies of the PAM configuration files you edit, test every change thoroughly, and make sure you can still log in after the change is installed. Keep a **root** shell open (use **su** or **sudo –i**) until you have finished testing. If a change fails and you cannot log in, use the **root** shell to replace the newly edited files with the backup copies.

Some UNIX systems require that a user be a member of the **wheel** group to use the su command. Although Fedora/RHEL is not configured this way by default, PAM allows you to change this behavior by editing the **/etc/pam.d/su** file:

```
$ cat /etc/pam.d/su
...
# Uncomment the following line to implicitly trust users in the "wheel" group.
#auth           sufficient      pam_wheel.so trust use_uid
# Uncomment the following line to require a user to be in the "wheel" group.
#auth           required        pam_wheel.so use_uid
...
```

The lines of the **su** module contain comments that include the lines necessary to permit only users who are in the **wheel** group to use su (required) and to permit members of the **wheel** group to run su without supplying a password (sufficient). Uncomment one of these lines when you want the system to follow one of these rules.

# SETTING UP A SERVER

This section discusses issues you might need to address when setting up a server: how to write configuration files; how to specify hosts and subnets; how to use **rpcbind**, rpcinfo, and TCP wrappers (**hosts.allow** and **hosts.deny**); and how to set up a chroot jail. Chapters 13 and 18–26 cover setting up specific servers; Chapter 16 discusses setting up a LAN.

## STANDARD RULES IN CONFIGURATION FILES

Most configuration files, which are typically named *.conf, rely on the following conventions:

- Blank lines are ignored.
- A # anywhere on a line starts a comment that continues to the end of the line. Comments are ignored.

- When a name contains a SPACE, you must quote the SPACE by preceding it with a backslash (\) or by enclosing the entire name within single or double quotation marks.

- To make long lines easier to read and edit, you can break them into several shorter lines. To break a line, insert a backslash (\) immediately followed by a NEWLINE (press RETURN in a text editor). When you insert the NEWLINE before or after a SPACE, you can indent the following line to make it easier to read. Do not break lines in this manner while editing on a Windows machine, as the NEWLINEs might not be properly escaped (Windows uses a RETURN-LINEFEED combination to end lines).

Configuration files that do not follow these conventions are noted in the text.

## SPECIFYING CLIENTS

Table 10-5 shows some common ways to specify a host or a subnet. In most cases you can specify multiple hosts or subnets by separating their specifications with SPACEs.

**Table 10-5**   Specifying a client

| Client name pattern | Matches |
| --- | --- |
| n.n.n.n | One IP address. |
| name | One hostname, either local or remote. |
| Name that starts with . | Matches a hostname that ends with the specified string. For example, **.example.com** matches the systems named **kudos.example.com** and **speedy.example.com**, among others. |
| IP address that ends with . | Matches a host address that starts with the specified numbers. For example, **192.168.0.** matches **192.168.0.0–192.168.0.255**. If you omit the trailing period, this format does not work. |
| n.n.n.n/m.m.m.m *or* n.n.n.n/mm | An IP address and network mask specifying a subnet. |
| Starts with / | An absolute pathname of a file containing one or more names or addresses as specified in this table. |
| **Wildcard** | **Matches** |
| * *and* ? | Matches one (**?**) or more (**\***) characters in a simple hostname or IP address. These wildcards do not match periods in a domain name. |
| ALL | Always matches. |
| LOCAL | Matches any hostname that does not contain a period. |

**Table 10-5** Specifying a client (continued)

| Operator | Matches |
|----------|---------|
| EXCEPT | Matches anything in the preceding list that is not in the following list. For example, **a b c d EXCEPT c** matches **a**, **b**, and **d**. Thus you could use **192.168. EXCEPT 192.168.0.1** to match all IP addresses that start with **192.168.** except **192.168.0.1**. |

Examples  Each of the following examples specifies one or more systems:

| | |
|---|---|
| 10.10. | Matches all systems with IP addresses that start with 10.10. |
| .redhat.com | Matches all named hosts on the Red Hat network |
| localhost | Matches the local system |
| 127.0.0.1 | The loopback address; always resolves to **localhost** |
| 192.168.*.1 | Could match all routers on a network of /24 subnets (next) |

## SPECIFYING A SUBNET

When you set up a server, you frequently need to specify which clients are allowed to connect to it. Sometimes it is convenient to specify a range of IP addresses, called a subnet. The discussion on page 298 explains what a subnet is and how to use a network mask to specify a subnet. Usually you can specify a subnet as

   *n.n.n.n/m.m.m.m*

*or*

   *n.n.n.n/maskbits*

where *n.n.n.n* is the base IP address and the subnet is represented by *m.m.m.m* (the network mask) or *maskbits* (the number of bits used for the network mask). For example, **192.168.0.1/255.255.255.0** represents the same subnet as **192.168.0.1/24**. In binary, decimal **255.255.255.0** is represented by 24 ones followed by 8 zeros. The **/24** is shorthand for a network mask with 24 ones. Each line in Table 10-6 presents two notations for the same subnet, followed by the range of IP addresses the subnet includes.

**Table 10-6** Different ways to represent a subnet

| Bits | Mask | Range |
|------|------|-------|
| 10.0.0.0/8 | 10.0.0.0/255.0.0.0 | 10.0.0.0–10.255.255.255 |
| 172.16.0.0/12 | 172.16.0.0/255.240.0.0 | 172.16.0.0–172.16.255.255 |
| 192.168.0.0/16 | 192.168.0.0/255.255.0.0 | 192.168.0.0–192.168.255.255 |

# rpcinfo: DISPLAYS INFORMATION ABOUT rpcbind

The rpcinfo utility (**rpcbind** package) displays information about programs registered with **rpcbind** and makes RPC calls to programs to see whether they are alive. For more information on **rpcbind**, refer to "RPC Network Services" on page 317. The rpcinfo utility takes the following options and arguments:

Syntax  *rpcinfo –p [host]*
*rpcinfo [–n port] [–u | –t] host program [version]*
*rpcinfo –b | –d program version*

–b  (**broadcast**) Makes an RPC broadcast to *version* of *program* and lists hosts that respond.

–d  (**delete**) Removes local RPC registration for *version* of *program*. Available to a user running with **root** privileges only.

–n  (**port number**) With –t or –u, uses the port numbered *port* instead of the port number specified by **rpcbind**.

–p  (**probe**) Lists all RPC programs registered, with **rpcbind** on *host* or on the local system when you do not specify *host*.

–t  (**TCP**) Makes a TCP RPC call to *version* (if specified) of *program* on *host* and reports whether it receives a response.

–u  (**UDP**) Makes a UDP RPC call to *version* (if specified) of *program* on *host* and reports whether it receives a response.

Examples  The following command displays the RPC programs registered with the **rpcbind** daemon on the system named **plum**. If you get a **No route to host** error make sure the firewall on the remote system allows inbound traffic on TCP port 111.

```
$ rpcinfo -p plum
   program vers proto   port  service
    100000   4   tcp    111  portmapper
    100000   3   tcp    111  portmapper
...

    100021   1   udp  44202  nlockmgr
    100021   3   udp  44202  nlockmgr
...

    100003   2   tcp   2049  nfs
    100003   3   tcp   2049  nfs
...
```

Use the –u option to display a list of versions of a daemon, such as **nfs**, registered on a remote system (**plum**):

```
$ rpcinfo -u plum nfs
program 100003 version 2 ready and waiting
program 100003 version 3 ready and waiting
program 100003 version 4 ready and waiting
```

Specify **localhost** to display a list of versions of a daemon registered on the local system:

```
$ rpcinfo -u localhost ypbind
program 100007 version 1 ready and waiting
program 100007 version 2 ready and waiting
```

Locking down rpcbind

Because the **rpcbind** daemon holds information about which servers are running on the local system and which port each server is running on, only trusted systems should have access to this information. One way to ensure only selected systems have access to **rpcbind** is to lock it down in the **/etc/hosts.allow** and **/etc/hosts.deny** files (below). Put the following line in **hosts.deny** to prevent all systems from using **rpcbind** on the local (server) system:

```
rpcbind: ALL
```

Alternately you can block TCP port 111 using firewall-cmd (page 906). Test this setup from a remote system by giving the following command:

```
$ rpcinfo -p hostname
rpcinfo: can't contact portmapper: RPC: Authentication error; ...
```

Replace *hostname* with the name of the remote system that you changed the **hosts.deny** file on. The change is usually immediate; in most cases you do not need to restart **rpcbind**.

Next add the following line to the **hosts.allow** file on the server system:

```
rpcbind: host-IP
```

where *host-IP* is the IP address of the trusted, remote system that you gave the preceding rpcinfo command from. Use only IP addresses with **rpcbind** in **hosts.allow**; do not use system names that **rpcbind** could get stuck trying to resolve. If you give the same command, rpcinfo should display a list of the servers that RPC knows about, including **rpcbind**. See page 776 for more examples.

### Set the clocks

security

The **rpcbind** daemon relies on the client and the server clocks being synchronized. A simple *DoS attack* (page 1248) can be initiated by setting the server clock to the wrong time.

# SECURING A SERVER

Two ways you can secure a server are by using TCP wrappers and by setting up a chroot jail. This section describes both techniques. Alternately, you can use firewall-cmd (page 906) to secure a system. A firewall covers protocols such as **httpd** that are not protected by **libwrap**, which is required for TCP wrappers.

## LPI TCP WRAPPERS: SECURE A SERVER (hosts.allow AND hosts.deny)

Follow these guidelines when you open a local system to access from remote systems:

- Open the local system only to systems you want to allow to access it.

- Allow each remote system to access only the data you want it to access.

- Allow each remote system to access data only in the appropriate manner (readonly, read/write, write only).

**LPI** ldd & libwrap  As part of the client/server model, TCP wrappers, which can be used for any daemon that is linked against **libwrap**, relies on the **/etc/hosts.allow** and **/etc/hosts.deny** files as the basis of a simple access control list. This access control language defines rules that selectively allow clients to access server daemons on a local system based on the client's address and the daemon the client tries to access. The output of ldd shows that one of the shared library dependencies of **sshd** is **libwrap**:

```
$ ldd /usr/sbin/sshd | grep libwrap
        libwrap.so.0 => /lib64/libwrap.so.0 (0x00007fe99c955000)
```

**LPI** hosts.allow  Each line in the **hosts.allow** and **hosts.deny** files has the following format:
and hosts.deny

*daemon_list : client_list [: command]*

where *daemon_list* is a comma-separated list of one or more server daemons (e.g., **rpcbind**, **vsftpd**, **sshd**), *client_list* is a comma-separated list of one or more clients (see Table 10-5 on page 482), and the optional *command* is the command that is executed when a client from *client_list* tries to access a server daemon from *daemon_list*.

When a client requests a connection to a server, the **hosts.allow** and **hosts.deny** files on the server system are consulted in the following order until a match is found:

1. If the daemon/client pair matches a line in **hosts.allow**, access is granted.

2. If the daemon/client pair matches a line in **hosts.deny**, access is denied.

3. If there is no match in **hosts.allow** or **hosts.deny**, access is granted.

The first match determines whether the client is allowed to access the server. When either **hosts.allow** or **hosts.deny** does not exist, it is as though that file were empty. Although not recommended, you can allow access to all daemons for all clients by removing both files.

Examples  For a more secure system, put the following line in **hosts.deny** to block all access:

```
$ cat /etc/hosts.deny
...
ALL : ALL : echo '%c tried to connect to %d and was blocked' >> /var/log/tcpwrappers.log
```

This line prevents any client from connecting to any service, unless specifically permitted to do so in **hosts.allow**. When this rule is matched, it adds a line to the file named **/var/log/tcpwrappers.log**. The **%c** expands to client information, and the **%d** expands to the name of the daemon the client attempted to connect to.

With the preceding **hosts.deny** file in place, you can include lines in **hosts.allow** that explicitly allow access to certain services and systems. For example, the following **hosts.allow** file allows any client to connect to the OpenSSH daemon (ssh, scp, sftp) but allows telnet connections only from the same network as the local system and users on the 192.168. subnet:

```
$ cat /etc/hosts.allow
sshd: ALL
in.telnet: LOCAL
in.telnet: 192.168.* 127.0.0.1
...
```

The first line allows connection from any system (ALL) to **sshd**. The second line allows connection from any system in the same domain as the server (LOCAL). The third line matches any system whose IP address starts with **192.168.** as well as the local system.

## SETTING UP A chroot JAIL

On early UNIX systems, the root directory was a fixed point in the filesystem. On modern UNIX variants, including Linux, you can define the root directory on a per-process basis. The chroot utility allows you to run a process with a root directory other than **/**.

The root directory appears at the top of the directory hierarchy and has no parent. Thus a process cannot access files above the root directory because none exist. If, for example, you run a program (process) and specify its root directory as **/home/sam/jail**, the program would have no concept of any files in **/home/sam** or above: **jail** is the program's root directory and is labeled **/** (not **jail**).

By creating an artificial root directory, frequently called a (chroot) jail, you prevent a program from accessing, executing, or modifying—possibly maliciously—files outside the directory hierarchy starting at its root. You must set up a chroot jail properly to increase security: If you do not set up the chroot jail correctly, you can make it easier for a malicious user to gain access to a system than if there were no chroot jail.

### USING chroot

Creating a chroot jail is simple: Working with **root** privileges, give the command **/usr/sbin/chroot** *directory*. The *directory* becomes the root directory, and the process attempts to run the default shell. Working with **root** privileges, the following command sets up a chroot jail in the (existing) **/home/sam/jail** directory running bash (**/usr/bin/bash**):

```
# /usr/sbin/chroot /home/sam/jail /usr/bin/bash
/usr/sbin/chroot: failed to run command '/usr/bin/bash': No such file or directory
```

This example sets up a chroot jail, but when the system attempts to run the bash shell, the operation fails. Once the jail is set up, the directory that was named **jail** takes on the name of the root directory, **/**. As a consequence, chroot cannot find the file identified by the pathname **/usr/bin/bash**. In this situation the chroot jail works correctly but is not useful.

Getting a chroot jail to work the way you want is more complicated. To have the preceding example run bash in a chroot jail, create a **usr/bin** directory in **jail** (**/home/sam/jail/usr/bin**) and copy **/usr/bin/bash** to this directory. Because the bash binary is dynamically linked to shared libraries, you need to copy these libraries into **jail** as well. The libraries go in **lib64** (64-bit system) or **lib** (32-bit system).

**LPI**   ldd   The next example creates the necessary directories, copies **bash**, uses ldd to display the shared library dependencies of bash, and copies the necessary libraries to **lib64**. The **linux-vdso.so.1** file is a DSO (dynamically shared object) provided by the kernel to speed system calls; you do not need to copy it.

```
$ pwd
/home/sam/jail
$ mkdir -p usr/bin lib64
$ cp /usr/bin/bash usr/bin
$ ldd usr/bin/bash
    linux-vdso.so.1 =>   (0x00007fffe3f26000)
    libtinfo.so.5 => /lib64/libtinfo.so.5 (0x00007fdb3b7f1000)
    libdl.so.2 => /lib64/libdl.so.2 (0x00007fdb3b5ed000)
    libc.so.6 => /lib64/libc.so.6 (0x00007fdb3b22c000)
    /lib64/ld-linux-x86-64.so.2 (0x00007fdb3ba2d000)
```

**$ cp /lib64/{libtinfo.so.5,libdl.so.2,libc.so.6,ld-linux-x86-64.so.2} lib64**

Now start the chroot jail again. Although all the setup can be done by an ordinary user, you must work with **root** privileges to run chroot:

```
$ su
Password:
# /usr/sbin/chroot /home/sam/jail /usr/bin/bash
bash-4.2# pwd
/
bash-4.2# ls
bash: ls: command not found
bash-4.2#
```

This time chroot finds and starts bash, which displays its default prompt (**bash-4.2#**). The pwd command works because it is a shell builtin (page 170). However, bash cannot find the ls utility because it is not in the chroot jail. You can copy **/bin/ls** and its libraries into the jail if you want users in the jail to be able to use ls. An **exit** command allows you to escape from the jail.

To set up a useful chroot jail, first determine which utilities the users of the chroot jail need. Then copy the appropriate binaries and their libraries into the jail. Alternately, you can build static copies of the binaries and put them in the jail without installing separate libraries. (The statically linked binaries are considerably larger than their dynamic counterparts. The size of the base system with bash and the core utilities exceeds 50 megabytes.) You can find the source code for most common utilities in the **bash** and **coreutils** SRPM (source rpm) packages.

The chroot utility fails unless you run it with **root** privileges. The result of running chroot with **root** privileges is a **root** shell (a shell with **root** privileges) running inside a chroot jail. Because a user with **root** privileges can break out of a chroot jail, it is imperative that you run a program in the chroot jail with reduced privileges (i.e., privileges other than those of **root**).

There are several ways to reduce the privileges of a user. For example, you can put su or sudo in the jail and then start a shell or a daemon inside the jail, using one of these programs to reduce the privileges of the user working in the jail. A command such as the following starts a shell with reduced privileges inside the jail:

> **# /usr/sbin/chroot** *jailpath* **/usr/bin/su** *user* **-c /usr/bin/bash**

where *jailpath* is the pathname of the jail directory, and *user* is the username under whose privileges the shell runs. The problem with this scenario is that sudo and su, as compiled for Fedora/RHEL, call PAM. To run one of these utilities you need to put all of PAM, including its libraries and configuration files, in the jail, along with sudo (or su) and the **/etc/passwd** file. Alternately, you can recompile su or sudo. The source code calls PAM, however, so you would need to modify the source so it does not call PAM. Either one of these techniques is time consuming and introduces complexities that can lead to an unsecure jail.

The following C program[1] runs a program with reduced privileges in a chroot jail. Because this program obtains the UID and GID of the user you specify on the command line before calling **chroot()**, you do not need to put **/etc/passwd** in the jail. The program reduces the privileges of the specified program to those of the specified user. This program is presented as a simple solution to the preceding issues so you can experiment with a chroot jail and better understand how it works.

```
$ cat uchroot.c
/* See svn.gna.org/viewcvs/etoile/trunk/Etoile/LiveCD/uchroot.c for terms of use. */

#include <stdio.h>
#include <stdlib.h>
#include <pwd.h>

int main(int argc, char * argv[])
{
        if(argc < 4)
        {
                printf("Usage: %s {username} {directory} {program} [arguments]\n", argv[0]);
                return 1;
        }
        /* Parse arguments */
        struct passwd * pass = getpwnam(argv[1]);
        if(pass == NULL)
        {
                printf("Unknown user %s\n", argv[1]);
                return 2;
        }
        /* Set the required UID */
        chdir(argv[2]);
        if(chroot(argv[2])
                ||
                setgid(pass->pw_gid)
                ||
                setuid(pass->pw_uid))
        {
                printf("%s must be run as root.  Current uid=%d, euid=%d\n",
                                argv[0],
                                (int)getuid(),
                                (int)geteuid()
                                );
                return 3;
        }
        return execv(argv[3], argv + 3);
}
```

---

1. Thanks to David Chisnall and the Étoilé Project (etoileos.com) for the **uchroot.c** program.

The first of the following commands compiles **uchroot.c** using **cc** (**gcc** package), creating an executable file named uchroot. Subsequent commands move uchroot to **/usr/local/bin** and give it appropriate ownership.

```
$ cc -o uchroot uchroot.c
$ su
password:
# mv uchroot /usr/local/bin
# chown root:root /usr/local/bin/uchroot
# exit
$ ls -l /usr/local/bin/uchroot
-rwxr-xr-x. 1 root root 8924 07-26 14:24 /usr/local/bin/uchroot
```

Using the setup from earlier in this section, give the following command to run a shell with the privileges of the user **sam** inside a chroot jail:

```
# /usr/local/bin/uchroot sam /home/sam/jail /usr/bin/bash
```

### Keeping multiple chroot jails

tip   If you plan to deploy multiple chroot jails, it is a good idea to keep a clean copy of the **bin** and **lib** directories somewhere other than in one of the active jails.

### RUNNING A SERVICE IN A chroot JAIL

Running a shell inside a jail has limited usefulness. In reality, you are more likely to want to run a specific service inside the jail. To run a service inside a jail, make sure all files needed by that service are inside the jail. Using uchroot, the format of a command to start a service in a chroot jail is

```
# /usr/local/bin/uchroot user jailpath daemonname
```

where *jailpath* is the pathname of the jail directory, *user* is the username that runs the daemon, and *daemonname* is the pathname (inside the jail) of the daemon that provides the service.

Some servers are already set up to take advantage of chroot jails. For example, you can set up DNS so that **named** runs in a jail (page 883), and the **vsftpd** FTP server can automatically start chroot jails for clients (page 729).

### SECURITY CONSIDERATIONS

Some services need to be run by a user or process with **root** privileges but release their **root** privileges once started (Apache, Procmail, and **vsftpd** are examples). If you are running such a service, you do not need to use uchroot or put su or sudo inside the jail.

A process run with **root** privileges can potentially escape from a chroot jail. For this reason, you should reduce privileges before starting a program running inside the jail. Also, be careful about which setuid (page 196) binaries you allow inside a jail—a security hole in one of them could compromise the security of the jail. In addition, make sure the user cannot access executable files that he uploads to the jail.

# *LE* DHCP: CONFIGURES NETWORK INTERFACES

Instead of storing network configuration information in local files on each system, DHCP (Dynamic Host Configuration Protocol) enables client systems to retrieve the necessary network configuration information from a DHCP server each time they connect to the network. A DHCP server assigns IP addresses from a pool of addresses to clients as needed. Assigned addresses are typically temporary but need not be.

This technique has several advantages over storing network configuration information in local files:

- A new user can set up an Internet connection without having to deal with IP addresses, netmasks, DNS addresses, and other technical details. An experienced user can set up a connection more quickly.

- DHCP facilitates assignment and management of IP addresses and related network information by centralizing the process on a server. A system administrator can configure new systems, including laptops that connect to the network from different locations, to use DHCP; DHCP then assigns IP addresses only when each system connects to the network. The pool of IP addresses is managed as a group on the DHCP server.

- DHCP facilitates the use of IP addresses by more than one system, reducing the total number of IP addresses needed. This conservation of addresses is important because the Internet has run out of IPv4 addresses. Although a particular IP address can be used by only one system at a time, many end-user systems require addresses only occasionally, when they connect to the Internet. By reusing IP addresses, DHCP has lengthened the life of the IPv4 protocol.

DHCP is particularly useful for an administrator who is responsible for maintaining a large number of systems because new systems no longer need to be set up with unique configuration information.

## How DHCP Works

Using dhclient, the client contacts the server daemon, **dhcpd**, to obtain the IP address, netmask, broadcast address, nameserver address, and other networking parameters. In turn, the server provides a *lease* on the IP address to the client. The client can request the specific terms of the lease, including its duration; the server can limit these terms. While connected to the network, a client typically requests extensions of its lease as necessary so its IP address remains the same. This lease might expire once the client is disconnected from the network, with the server giving the client a new IP address when it requests a new lease. You can also set up a DHCP server to provide static IP addresses for specific clients (refer to "Static Versus Dynamic IP Addresses" on page 298).

When you start Fedora/RHEL, the system runs a DHCP client, connects to a DHCP server if it can find one, and configures its network interface.

# DHCP CLIENT

A DHCP client requests network configuration parameters from the DHCP server and uses those parameters to configure its network interface.

## PREREQUISITES

Make sure the following package is installed:

- dhclient

## dhclient: THE DHCP CLIENT

When a DHCP client system connects to the network, dhclient requests a lease from the DHCP server and configures the client's network interface(s). Once a DHCP client has requested and established a lease, it stores the lease information in a file named **dhclient-\*-*interface*.lease**, which resides in the **/var/lib/NetworkManager** directory. The *interface* is the name of the interface the client uses, such as **eth0**. The system uses this information to reestablish a lease when either the server or the client needs to reboot. The DHCP client configuration file, **/etc/dhcp/dhclient.conf**, is required only for custom configurations. The **/usr/share/doc/dhclient\*** directory holds a well-commented **dhclient.conf** file.

The following **dhclient.conf** file specifies a single interface, **ens33**:

```
$ cat /etc/dhcp/dhclient.conf
interface "ens33"
{
send dhcp-client-identifier 1:xx:xx:xx:xx:xx:xx;
send dhcp-lease-time 86400;
}
```

In the preceding file, the 1 in the **dhcp-client-identifier** specifies an Ethernet network and **xx:xx:xx:xx:xx:xx** is the *MAC address* (page 1259) of the device controlling that interface. See page 494 for instructions on how to determine the MAC address of a device. The **dhcp-lease-time** is the duration, in seconds, of the lease on the IP address. While the client is connected to the network, dhclient automatically renews the lease each time half of the lease time is up. A lease time of 86,400 seconds (one day) is a reasonable choice for a workstation.

# DHCP SERVER

A DHCP server maintains a list of IP addresses and other configuration parameters. Clients request network configuration parameters from the server. The DHCP server does not ship with a working configuration. See the **/usr/share/doc/dhcp\*/\*example** files for sample **dhcpd.conf** files that include a lot of documentation.

## PREREQUISITES

Install the following package:

- dhcp

Enable and start
**dhcpd**

Run systemctl to cause the **dhcpd** service (**dhcpd** daemon) to start each time the system enters multiuser mode and then start the **dhcpd** service. Use the systemctl **status** command to make sure the service is running.

```
# systemctl enable dhcpd.service
# systemctl start dhcpd.service
```

After modifying **dhcpd** configuration files, give the second command again, replacing **start** with **restart** to cause **dhcpd** to reread those files.

## dhcpd: THE DHCP DAEMON

A simple DHCP server (**dhcpd**) allows you to add clients to a network without maintaining a list of assigned IP addresses. A simple network, such as a home-based LAN sharing an Internet connection, can use DHCP to assign a dynamic IP address to almost all nodes. The exceptions are servers and routers, which must be at known network locations if clients are to find them. If servers and routers are configured without DHCP, you can specify a simple DHCP server configuration in **/etc/dhcp/dhcpd.conf**:

```
$ cat /etc/dhcp/dhcpd.conf
default-lease-time 600;
max-lease-time 86400;

option subnet-mask 255.255.255.0;
option broadcast-address 192.168.1.255;
option routers 192.168.1.1;
option domain-name-servers 192.168.1.1;
option domain-name "example.com";

subnet 192.168.1.0 netmask 255.255.255.0 {
    range 192.168.1.2 192.168.1.200;
}
```

By default, **dhcpd** serves requests on all nonbroadcast network interfaces.

The preceding configuration file specifies a LAN where both the router and the DNS server are located on **192.168.1.1**. The **default-lease-time** specifies the number of seconds the dynamic IP lease will remain valid if the client does not specify a duration. The **max-lease-time** is the maximum time allowed for a lease.

The information in the **option** lines is sent to each client when it connects. The names following the word **option** specify what the following argument represents. For example, the **option broadcast-address** line specifies the broadcast address of the network. The **routers** and **domain-name-servers** options can be followed by multiple values separated by commas.

The **subnet** section includes a **range** line that specifies the range of IP addresses the DHCP server can assign. In the case of multiple subnets, you can define options, such as **subnet-mask**, inside the **subnet** section. Options defined outside all **subnet** sections are global and apply to all subnets.

The preceding configuration file assigns addresses in the range from 192.168.1.2 to 192.168.1.200. The DHCP server starts at the bottom of this range and attempts to assign a new IP address to each new client. Once the DHCP server reaches the top of the range, it starts reassigning IP addresses that have been used in the past but are not currently in use. If you have fewer systems than IP addresses, the IP address of each system should remain fairly constant. Two systems cannot use the same IP address at the same time.

Once you have configured a DHCP server, restart it using systemctl (previous page). When the server is running, clients configured to obtain an IP address from the server using DHCP should be able to do so. See the **/usr/share/doc/dhcp\*/\*example** files for sample **dhcpd.conf** files.

## STATIC IP ADDRESSES

As mentioned earlier, routers and servers typically require static IP addresses. Although you can manually configure IP addresses for these systems, it might be more convenient to have the DHCP server provide them with static IP addresses. See page 641 if you want to configure a system to use a static IP address without using DHCP.

When a system that requires a specific static IP address connects to the network and contacts the DHCP server, the server needs a way to identify the system so it can assign the proper IP address to that system. The DHCP server uses the *MAC address* (page 1259) of the system's NIC (network interface card) as an identifier. When you set up the server, you must know the MAC address of each system that requires a static IP address.

Determining a MAC address
The ip utility displays the MAC addresses of the Ethernet cards in a system. In the following example, the MAC address is the colon-separated series of hexadecimal number pairs following **link/ether**:

```
$ ip link show ens33
2: ens33: <BROADCAST,MULTICAST,UP,LOWER_UP> mtu 1500 qdisc pfifo_fast state UP mode DEFAULT qlen 1000
    link/ether 00:0c:29:13:f4:35 brd ff:ff:ff:ff:ff:ff
```

Run ip on each system that requires a static IP address. Once you have determined the MAC addresses of these systems, you can add a **host** section to the **/etc/dhcp/dhcpd.conf** file for each one, instructing the DHCP server to assign a specific address to that system. The following **host** section assigns the address **192.168.1.1** to the system with the MAC address of **BA:DF:00:DF:C0:FF**:

```
$ cat /etc/dhcp/dhcpd.conf
...
host router {
    hardware ethernet BA:DF:00:DF:C0:FF;
    fixed-address 192.168.1.1;
    option host-name router;
}
```

The name following **host** is used internally by **dhcpd**. The name specified after **option host-name** is passed to the client and can be a hostname or an FQDN. After making changes to **dhcpd.conf**, restart **dhcpd** using systemctl (previous page).

# *LPI*  nsswitch.conf: WHICH SERVICE TO LOOK AT FIRST

Once NIS and DNS were introduced, finding user and system information was no longer a simple matter of searching a local file. When once you looked in **/etc/passwd** to get user information and in **/etc/hosts** to find system address information, now you can use several methods to obtain this type of information. The **/etc/nsswitch.conf** (name service switch configuration) file specifies which methods to use and the order in which to use them when looking for a certain type of information. You can also specify which action the system should take based on whether a method succeeds or fails.

Syntax    Each line in **nsswitch.conf** specifies how to search for a piece of information, such as a user's password. A line in **nsswitch.conf** has the following syntax:

> *info:*    *method [[action]] [method [[action]]...]*

where *info* is the type of information the line describes, *method* is the method used to find the information, and *action* is the response to the return status of the preceding *method*. The action is enclosed within square brackets.

When called upon to supply information that **nsswitch.conf** describes, the system examines the line with the appropriate *info* field. It uses the methods specified on this line, starting with the method on the left. By default, when it finds the desired information, the system stops searching. Without an *action* specification, when a method fails to return a result, the system tries the next action. It is possible for the search to end without finding the requested information.

## INFORMATION

The **nsswitch.conf** file commonly controls searches for usernames, passwords, host IP addresses, and group information. The following list describes most of the types of information (*info* in the syntax given earlier) that **nsswitch.conf** controls searches for:

| | |
|---|---|
| **automount** | Automount (**/etc/auto.master** and **/etc/auto.misc**; page 821) |
| **bootparam** | Diskless and other booting options (**bootparam** man page) |
| **ethers** | MAC address (page 1259) |
| **group** | Groups of users (**/etc/group**; page 506) |
| **hosts** | System information (**/etc/hosts**; page 507) |
| **networks** | Network information (**/etc/networks**) |
| **passwd** | User information (**/etc/passwd**; page 508) |
| **protocols** | Protocol information (**/etc/protocols**; page 510) |
| **publickey** | Used for NFS running in secure mode |
| **rpc** | RPC names and numbers (**/etc/rpc**; page 510) |
| **services** | Services information (**/etc/services**; page 511) |
| **shadow** | Shadow password information (**/etc/shadow**; page 511) |

# METHODS

Following is a list of the methods that **nsswitch.conf** uses to search for information (*method* in the syntax shown on the previous page). For each type of information, you can specify one or more of the following methods:[2]

| | |
|---|---|
| compat | ± syntax in **passwd**, **group**, and **shadow** files (next page) |
| dns | Queries the DNS (**hosts** queries only) |
| files | Searches local files such as **/etc/passwd** and **/etc/hosts** |
| ldap | Queries an LDAP server (page 786) |
| nis | Searches the NIS database; **yp** is an alias for **nis** |

# SEARCH ORDER

The information provided by two or more methods might overlap: For example, both **files** and **nis** might provide password information for the same user. With overlapping information, you need to consider which method you want to be authoritative (take precedence) and then place that method at the left of the list of methods.

The default **nsswitch.conf** file lists methods without actions, assuming no overlap (which is normal). In this case, the order is not critical: When one method fails, the system goes to the next one and all that is lost is a little time. Order becomes critical when you use actions between methods or when overlapping entries differ.

The first of the following lines from **nsswitch.conf** causes the system to search for password information in **/etc/passwd** and if that fails, to use NIS to find the information. If the user you are looking for is listed in both places, the information in the local file is used and is considered authoritative. The second line uses NIS to find an IP address given a hostname; if that fails, it searches **/etc/hosts**; if that fails, it checks with DNS to find the information.

```
passwd          files nis
hosts           nis files dns
```

# ACTION ITEMS

Each method can optionally be followed by an action item that specifies what to do if the method succeeds or fails. An action item has the following format:

*[[!]STATUS=action]*

where the opening and closing square brackets are part of the format and do not indicate that the contents are optional; *STATUS* (uppercase by convention) is the status being tested for; and *action* is the action to be taken if *STATUS* matches the status returned by the preceding method. The leading exclamation point (!) is optional and negates the status.

---

2. Other, less commonly used methods also exist. See the default **/etc/nsswitch.conf** file and the **nsswitch.conf** man page for more information. Although NIS+ belongs in this list, it is not implemented as a Linux server and is not discussed in this book.

*STATUS*  *STATUS* might have any of the following values:

NOTFOUND—The method worked, but the value being searched for was not found. The default action is **continue**.

SUCCESS—The method worked, and the value being searched for was found; no error was returned. The default action is **return**.

TRYAGAIN—The method failed because it was temporarily unavailable. For example, a file might be locked or a server overloaded. The default action is **continue**.

UNAVAIL—The method failed because it is permanently unavailable. For example, the required file might not be accessible or the required server might be down. The default action is **continue**.

*action*  There are two possible values for *action:*

return—Returns to the calling routine with or without a value.

continue—Continues with the next method. Any returned value is overwritten by a value found by a subsequent method.

Example  The following line from **nsswitch.conf** causes the system first to use DNS to search for the IP address of a given host. The action item following the DNS method tests whether the status returned by the method is not (**!**) UNAVAIL.

```
hosts        dns [!UNAVAIL=return] files
```

The system takes the action associated with the *STATUS* (**return**) if the DNS method does not return UNAVAIL (**!UNAVAIL**)—that is, if DNS returns SUCCESS, NOTFOUND, or TRYAGAIN. As a consequence, the following method (**files**) is used only when the DNS server is unavailable. If the DNS server is *not un*available (read the two negatives as "is available"), the search returns the domain name or reports that the domain name was not found. The search uses the **files** method (checks the local **/etc/hosts** file) only if the server is not available.

# compat METHOD: ± IN passwd, group, AND shadow FILES

You can put special codes in the **/etc/passwd**, **/etc/group**, and **/etc/shadow** files that cause the system, when you specify the **compat** method in **nsswitch.conf**, to combine and modify entries in the local files and the NIS maps. That is, a plus sign (**+**) at the beginning of a line in one of these files adds NIS information; a minus sign (**–**) removes information.

For example, to use these codes in the **passwd** file, specify **passwd: compat** in the **nsswitch.conf** file. The system then goes through the **passwd** file in order, adding or removing the appropriate NIS entries when it reaches each line that starts with a **+** or **–**.

Although you can put a plus sign at the end of the **passwd** file, specify **passwd: compat** in **nsswitch.conf** to search the local **passwd** file, and then go through the NIS map, it is more efficient to put **passwd: file nis** in **nsswitch.conf** and not modify the **passwd** file.

# Getting Help

Fedora/RHEL comes with extensive documentation (pages 113 and 128). Fedora maintains a page that points to many useful support documents at docs.fedoraproject.org; fedoraproject.org/en/get-help has links to ask.fedoraproject.org, email lists, and IRC chatrooms; Red Hat maintains a similar page at access.redhat.com and keeps documentation at access.redhat.com/docs. Although some sections of these Red Hat sites require an account to access, anyone can get an account for free. You can also find help on the Linux SIG site (formerly SAGE; www.usenix.org/lisa). The Internet is another rich source of information on managing a Linux system; refer to Appendix B (page 1149) and to the author's home page (www.sobell.com) for pointers to useful sites.

You need not act as a Fedora/RHEL system administrator in isolation; a large community of Fedora/RHEL experts is willing to assist you in getting the most out of a Linux system. Of course, you will get better help if you have already tried to solve a problem yourself by reading the available documentation. If you are unable to solve a problem by consulting the documentation, a well-thought-out question posed to the appropriate newsgroup (such as **comp.os.linux.misc**) or mailing list can often generate useful information. Be sure to describe the problem accurately and identify the system carefully. Include information about the version of Fedora/RHEL running on the system and any software packages and hardware you think relate to the problem. The newsgroup **comp.os.linux.answers** contains postings of solutions to common problems and periodic postings of the most up-to-date versions of FAQs and HOWTO documents. See www.catb.org/~esr/faqs/smart-questions.html for a helpful paper by Eric S. Raymond and Rick Moen titled "How to Ask Questions the Smart Way."

# Chapter Summary

A system administrator is someone who keeps the system in a useful and convenient state for its users. Much of the work you do as the system administrator will require you to work with **root** privileges. A user with these privileges (sometimes referred to as Superuser) has extensive systemwide powers that normal users do not have. A user with **root** privileges can read from and write to almost any file and can execute programs that ordinary users are not permitted to execute.

The system administrator controls system operation, including configuring the system; booting up; running systemctl to set up services; working in single-user, multiuser, and rescue modes; bringing the system down; and handling system crashes. Fedora/RHEL provides both graphical and textual configuration tools.

When you bring the system up in single-user mode, only the system console is functional. While working in single-user mode, you can back up files and use fsck to check the integrity of filesystems before you mount them. The systemctl utility can bring the system to its default multiuser state. With the system running in multiuser mode, you can still perform many administration tasks, such as adding users and printers.

When you install a Fedora/RHEL system, you specify a password for the **root** account. You use this password to gain **root** privileges, either by logging in as the user named **root** or by using su and providing the **root** password. Alternately, you can configure sudo, which grants **root** privileges based on your password. A system that does not have a **root** password and that relies on sudo to escalate permissions can be more secure than one with a **root** password.

The systemd **init** daemon, which replaces the traditional System V **init** daemon (SysVinit), is event based: It can start and stop services upon receiving information that something on the system has changed (an *event*). Events include adding devices to and removing them from the system as well as bringing the system up and shutting it down. The systemctl utility works with systemd and can turn services on and off and alter their persistent state (i.e., whether they come up when the system boots).

You can use TCP wrappers to control who can use which system services by editing the **hosts.allow** and **hosts.deny** files in the **/etc** directory. Setting up a chroot jail limits the portion of the filesystem a user sees, so it can help control the damage a malicious user can do.

You can set up a DHCP server so you do not have to configure each system on a network manually. DHCP can provide both static and dynamic IP addresses. Whether a system uses NIS, DNS, local files, or a combination (and in which order) as a source of information is determined by **/etc/nsswitch.conf**. Linux-PAM enables you to maintain fine-grained control over who can access the system, how they can access it, and what they can do.

# EXERCISES

1. How does single-user mode differ from multiuser mode?

2. How would you communicate each of the following messages?

   a. The system is coming down tomorrow at 6:00 in the evening for periodic maintenance.

   b. The system is coming down in five minutes.

   c. Zach's jobs are slowing the system down drastically, and he should postpone them.

   d. Zach's wife just had a baby girl.

3. What do the letters of the su command stand for? (*Hint:* It is not Superuser.) What can you do using su besides give yourself **root** privileges? How would you log in as Zach if you did not know his password but knew the **root** password? How would you establish the same environment that Zach has when he first logs in?

4. How would you allow a user to execute a specific, privileged command without giving the user the **root** password or permission to use sudo to run any command with **root** privileges?

5. How do you kill process 1648? How do you kill all processes running kmail? In which instances do you need to work with **root** privileges?

6. How can you disable SELinux?

7. Develop a strategy for coming up with a password that an intruder would not be likely to guess but that you will be able to remember.

# ADVANCED EXERCISES

8. Give the command:

   ```
   $ /usr/sbin/fuser -uv /
   ```

   What does the output list? Why is it so long? Give the same command while working with **root** privileges (or ask the system administrator to do so and email you the results). How does this list differ from the first? Why is it different?

9. When it puts files in a **lost+found** directory, fsck has lost the directory information for the files and thus has lost the names of the files. Each file is given a new name, which is the same as the inode number for the file:

   ```
   $ ls -l lost+found
   -rw-r--r-- 1 max pubs 110 06-10 10:55 51262
   ```

   How can you identify these files and restore them?

10. Take a look at **/usr/bin/lesspipe.sh**. Explain its purpose and describe six ways it works.

11. Why are **root**-owned setuid shell scripts inherently unsafe?

12. When a user logs in, you would like the system to first check the local **/etc/passwd** file for a username and then check NIS. How do you implement this strategy?

13. Some older kernels contain a vulnerability that allows a local user to gain **root** privileges. Explain how this kind of vulnerability negates the value of a chroot jail.

# 11

# FILES, DIRECTORIES, AND FILESYSTEMS

## OBJECTIVES

After reading this chapter you should be able to:

▸ List four important directories and describe their uses

▸ List common system startup configuration files and describe their uses

▸ List typical network configuration files and describe their uses

▸ List common login configuration files and describe their uses

▸ List a few device filenames and describe their uses

▸ Define the seven types of files found on the system

▸ Describe several filesystem types found on a Linux system

▸ View, check, tune, mount, and unmount local filesystems

Filesystems hold directories of files. These structures store user data and system data that are the basis of users' work on the system and the system's existence. This chapter discusses important files and directories, various types of files and ways to work with them, and the use and maintenance of filesystems.

# Important Files and Directories

This section details the files most commonly used to administer the system. For a more general list of files, refer to "Important Standard Directories and Files" on page 189.

**lost+found**  Holds preallocated disk blocks of directories that fsck uses to store pointers to unlinked files (files that have lost their directory [and therefore filename] information). Having these blocks available ensures that fsck does not have to allocate data blocks during recovery, a process that could further damage a corrupted filesystem. See page 525 for more information on fsck. However, fsck will allocate blocks if they do not exist.

Each **ext2**, **ext3**, and **ext4** filesystem contains a **lost+found** directory in the filesystem's root directory. If, for example, a filesystem is mounted at **/home**, there will be a **/home/lost+found** directory. There is always a **/lost+found** directory. These directories are normally created by mkfs when it writes an **ext2/ext3/ext4** filesystem to a partition. Although rarely necessary, you can create a **lost+found** directory manually using mklost+found.

**LPI**
**~/.bash_profile**  Contains an individual user's *login shell* (page 1259) initialization script. The shell executes the commands in this file in the same environment as the shell each time a user logs in. (For information about executing a shell script in this manner, refer to the discussion of the . [dot] command on page 332.) The file must be located in a user's home directory. It is not run from terminal emulator windows because you do not log in in those windows.

The default Fedora/RHEL **.bash_profile** file executes the commands in **~/.bashrc**.

You can use **.bash_profile** to specify the editor you want to use, run stty to establish the terminal characteristics, set up aliases, and perform other housekeeping functions when a user logs in.

A simple **.bash_profile** file that sets **EDITOR** to vi and CONTROL-H as the erase key follows:

```
$ cat .bash_profile
export EDITOR=$(which vi)
stty erase '^h'
```

Using command substitution and **which vi** sets **EDITOR** to the absolute pathname of the vi editor. For more information refer to "Startup Files" on page 329.

**LPI**
**~/.bashrc**  Contains an individual user's interactive, nonlogin shell initialization script. The shell executes the commands in this file in the same environment as the (new) shell each

time a user creates a new interactive shell, including when a user opens a terminal emulator window. (For information about executing a shell script in this manner, refer to the discussion of the . [dot] command on page 332.) The **.bashrc** script differs from **.bash_profile** in that it is executed each time a new shell is spawned, not just when a user logs in. The default Fedora/RHEL **.bash_profile** file executes the commands in ~/**.bashrc** so that these commands are executed when a user logs in. For more information refer to "Startup Files" on page 329.

**LPI**  /dev    Contains files representing pseudodevices and physical devices that might be attached to the system. The **/dev/sda** device was traditionally the first SCSI disk; now it is the first drive, including IDE, SATA, and USB drives. Other similar drives are named **/dev/sdb**, **/dev/sdc**, etc.

These names, such as **/dev/sda**, represent the order of the devices on the bus the devices are connected to, not the devices themselves. For example, if you swap the data cables on the disks referred to as **/dev/sda** and **/dev/sdb**, the drive's designations will change. Similarly, if you remove the device referred to as **/dev/sda**, the device that was referred to as **/dev/sdb** will now be referred to as **/dev/sda**. See **/dev/disk/by-uuid** (below) for a way to refer to specific devices and not to their order on the bus.

/dev/disk/by-path

Holds symbolic links to local devices. The names of the devices in this directory identify the devices. Each entry points to the device in **/dev** that it refers to (**sr0** is the CD/DVD drive).

```
$ ls -l /dev/disk/by-path
lrwxrwxrwx. 1 root root  9 06-05 17:29 pci-0000:00:10.0-scsi-0:0:0:0 -> ../../sda
lrwxrwxrwx. 1 root root 10 06-05 17:29 pci-0000:00:10.0-scsi-0:0:0:0-part1 -> ../../sda1
lrwxrwxrwx. 1 root root 10 06-05 17:29 pci-0000:00:10.0-scsi-0:0:0:0-part2 -> ../../sda2
```

/dev/disk/by-uuid

Holds symbolic links to local devices. The names of the devices in this directory consist of the *UUID* (page 1280) numbers of the devices. Each entry points to the device in **/dev** that it refers to. See page 524 for more information. The **dm** in the partition names stands for *device mapper*, which is used by LVM (page 44).

```
$ ls -l /dev/disk/by-uuid
lrwxrwxrwx. 1 root root 10 06-05 17:29 24908841-6308-4304-a52f-c1a76c69bd57 -> ../../sda1
lrwxrwxrwx. 1 root root 10 06-05 17:29 2d9ea1c9-bfbb-4302-b715-1b258c946c55 -> ../../dm-1
lrwxrwxrwx. 1 root root 10 06-05 17:29 cfd3669e-b888-4691-bf54-e229c16eba06 -> ../../dm-0
```

/dev/null   Also called a *bit bucket*. Output sent to this file disappears. The **/dev/null** file is a device file. Input you redirect to come from this file appears as null values, creating an empty file. You can create an empty file named **nothing** by giving one of the following commands:

```
$ cat /dev/null > nothing
$ cp /dev/null nothing
```

*or*, without explicitly using **/dev/null**,

```
$ > nothing
```

The last command redirects the output of a null command to the file with the same result as the previous commands. You can use any of these commands to truncate an existing file to zero length without changing its permissions. You can also use **/dev/null** to get rid of output you do not want:

```
$ grep portable * 2> /dev/null
```

This command displays all lines in all files in the working directory that contain the string **portable**. Any output to standard error (page 333), such as a permission or directory error, is discarded, while output to standard output appears on the screen. See also page 158.

**/dev/pts**  A hook into the Linux kernel. This pseudofilesystem is part of the pseudoterminal support. Pseudoterminals are used by remote login programs, such as ssh and telnet, as well as xterm and other graphical terminal emulators. The following sequence of commands demonstrates that Sam is logged in on **/dev/pts/1**. After using tty to verify the pseudoterminal he is logged in on and using ls to show that this pseudoterminal exists, Sam redirects the output of an echo command to **/dev/pts/1**, whereupon the output appears on his screen:

```
$ tty
/dev/pts/1
$ ls /dev/pts
0  1  2  ptmx
$ echo Hi there > /dev/pts/1
Hi there
```

**/dev/random**
**and**
**/dev/urandom**  Interfaces to the kernel's random number generator. You can use either file with dd to create a file filled with pseudorandom bytes. However, if there is not enough entropy, urandom can generate potentially inferior results (although for most purposes the difference is irrelevant). Following is an example:

```
$ dd if=/dev/urandom of=randfile bs=1 count=100
100+0 records in
100+0 records out
100 bytes (100 B) copied, 0.000884387 seconds, 113 kB/s
```

The preceding command reads from **/dev/urandom** and writes to the file named **randfile**. The block size is 1, and the count is 100; thus **randfile** is 100 bytes long. For bytes that are more random, you can read from **/dev/random**. See the **urandom** and **random** man pages for more information.

## Using **random** can cause the system to hang

**tip**  Reading from **/dev/random** can cause the system to hang for a long time if there is not enough entropy. This problem is common on virtual systems. You can create entropy and free the system by moving the mouse, typing on the keyboard, or copying files. Alternately, you can read from **/dev/urandom**.

**optional**

Wiping a file  You can use a similar technique to wipe data from a file before deleting it, making it almost impossible to recover data from the deleted file. You might want to wipe a file for security reasons.

In the following example, ls shows the size of the file named **secret**. Using a block size of 1 and a count corresponding to the number of bytes in **secret**, dd wipes the file. The **conv=notrunc** argument ensures that dd writes over the data in the file and not another (erroneous) place on the disk.

```
$ ls -l secret
-rw-r--r--. 1 sam pubs 5733 01-27 13:12 secret
$ dd if=/dev/urandom of=secret bs=1 count=5733 conv=notrunc
5733+0 records in
5733+0 records out
5733 bytes (5.7 kB) copied, 0.0358146 seconds, 160 kB/s
$ rm secret
```

For added security, run sync to flush the disk buffers after running dd and repeat the two commands several times before deleting the file. Alternately you can use shred (page 223) to wipe a file. See wipe.sourceforge.net for more information about wiping files.

/dev/shm  Implements shared memory, which provides an efficient way for processes to share information.

/dev/zero  Input you take from this file contains an infinite string of zeros (numerical zeros, not ASCII zeros). You can fill a file (e.g., a swap file; page 513) or overwrite a file with zeros with a command such as the following:

```
$ dd if=/dev/zero of=zeros bs=1024 count=10
10+0 records in
10+0 records out
10240 bytes (10 kB) copied, 0.000160263 seconds, 63.9 MB/s

$ od -c zeros
0000000  \0  \0  \0  \0  \0  \0  \0  \0  \0  \0  \0  \0  \0  \0  \0  \0
*
0024000
```

The od utility shows the contents of the new file.

If you try to fill a file with zeros using **/dev/null**, you fill the partition in which you are working:

```
$ cp /dev/zero bigzero
cp: error writing 'bigzero': No space left on device
cp: failed to extend 'bigzero': No space left on device
$ rm bigzero
```

**_LE_**   **/etc**   Holds machine–local system configuration files.

**/etc/aliases**   Used by the mail delivery system to hold **aliases** for users. Edit this file to suit local needs. For more information refer to **/etc/aliases** on page 746.

**/etc/alternatives**   Holds symbolic links so you can call a utility by a name other than that of the file that holds the utility. For example, when you give the command **cancel**, the shell calls **cancel.cups** using the following links:

```
$ ls -l /usr/bin/cancel
lrwxrwxrwx. 1 root root 30 06-04 19:31 /usr/bin/cancel -> /etc/alternatives/print-cancel
$ ls -l /etc/alternatives/print-cancel
lrwxrwxrwx. 1 root root 20 06-04 19:31 /etc/alternatives/print-cancel -> /usr/bin/cancel.cups
```

The **alternatives** directory also allows a utility to appear in more than one directory and can ease an administrator's learning curve by providing familiar commands to do similar tasks (e.g., mailq can call sendmail or postfix commands depending on which server is being used).

In addition, this directory allows you to call one utility by several names. Although the **alternatives** directory does not allow developers to do anything they could not do without it, it provides an orderly way to keep and update these links. Use whereis (page 255) to find all links to a utility.

**_LPI_**   **/etc/at.allow, /etc/at.deny, /etc/cron.allow, and /etc/cron.deny**
By default, users can use the at and crontab utilities. The **at.allow** and **cron.allow** files list the users who are allowed to use at and crontab, respectively. The **at.deny** and **cron.deny** files specify users who are not permitted to use the corresponding utilities. As Fedora/RHEL is configured, an empty **at.deny** file and the absence of an **at.allow** file allows anyone to use at; the absence of **cron.allow** and an empty **cron.deny** file allows anyone to use crontab. To prevent anyone except a user running with **root** privileges from using at, remove the **at.deny** file. To prevent anyone except a user running with **root** privileges from using crontab, create a **cron.allow** file with the single entry **root**. For more information on crontab, refer to "Scheduling Tasks" on page 607.

**/etc/default**   A directory that holds files that set default values for system services and utilities such as NFS and useradd. Look at the files in this directory for more information.

**/etc/fstab**   **filesystem (mount) table**—Contains a list of mountable devices as specified by the system administrator. See page 524 for more information.

**_LE+_**   **/etc/group**   Groups allow users to share files or programs without giving all system users access to those files or programs. This scheme is useful when several users are working with files that are not public. The **/etc/group** file associates one or more usernames with each group (GID [group ID number]). Members of the group named **wheel** are administrators and can use sudo to gain **root** privileges; see "Administrator and the **wheel** group" on page 429 for a finer-grained way to control file access.

Each entry in the **/etc/group** file has four colon-separated fields that describe one group:

> *group-name:password:group-ID:login-name-list*

The *group-name* is the name of the group. The *password* is an optional hashed (page 1252) password. This field frequently contains an **x**, indicating that group passwords are not used. The *group-ID* is a number, with 1–499 reserved for system accounts. The *login-name-list* is a comma-separated list of users who belong to the group. If an entry is too long to fit on one line, end the line with a backslash (\), which quotes the following RETURN, and continue the entry on the next line. A sample entry from a **group** file follows. The group is named **pubs**, has no password, and has a group ID of 1103:

```
pubs:x:1103:max,sam,zach,mark
```

You can use the groups utility to display the groups to which a user belongs:

```
$ groups sam
sam : sam pubs
```

Each user has a primary group, which is the group that user is assigned to in the **/etc/passwd** file. By default, Fedora/RHEL has user private groups: Each user's primary group has the same name as the user. In addition, a user can belong to other groups, depending on which *login-name-list*s the user appears on in the **/etc/group** file. In effect, you simultaneously belong both to your primary group and to any groups you are assigned to in **/etc/group**. When you attempt to access a file you do not own, Linux checks whether you are a member of the group that has access to the file. If you are, you are subject to the group access permissions for the file. If you are not a member of the group that has access to the file and you do not own the file, you are subject to the public access permissions for the file.

When you create a file, Linux assigns it to your primary group. Refer to page 600 for information on using system-config-users to work with groups.

**LPI**   /etc/hostname

Holds the name of the system. Use hostnamectl (page 219) to change the hostname of a system. See page 300 for more information on hostnames.

**LPI**   /etc/hosts   Stores the names, IP addresses, and optionally aliases of other systems. Typically, this file holds the hostname and IP address of the local system. It also holds a special entry for **localhost**. This entry supports the *loopback service*, which allows the local system to talk to itself (e.g., for RPC services). The IP address of the loopback service is always 127.0.0.1 (IPv4) or ::1 (IPv6), while 127.0.1.1 names the local system. See page 300 for more information. Following is a simple **/etc/hosts** file:

```
$ cat /etc/hosts
127.0.0.1     localhost localhost.localdomain localhost4 localhost4.localdomain4
::1           localhost localhost.localdomain localhost6 localhost6.localdomain6
127.0.1.1     tiny
192.168.0.9   jam
192.168.0.10  plum
192.168.0.12  dog
...
```

If you are not using NIS or DNS to look up hostnames (called *hostname resolution*), you must include in **/etc/hosts** all systems that the local system should be able to contact by hostname. (A system can always contact another system by using the IP address of the system.) The **hosts** entry in the **/etc/nsswitch.conf** file (page 495) controls the order in which hostname resolution services are checked.

/etc/hosts.allow   As part of the client/server model, TCP wrappers use these files for access control.
/etc/hosts.deny   See page 485 for more information.

/etc/init.d   A symbolic link to **/etc/rc.d/init.d** (page 448).

**LPI**   /etc/inittab   **initialization table**—A system running systemd ignores this file.

/etc/motd   Contains the message of the day, which can be displayed each time someone logs in using a textual login. This file typically contains site policy and legal information. Keep this file short because users tend to see the message many times.

/etc/mtab   A symbolic link to the kernel mount table at **/proc/self/mounts**. When you call mount without any arguments, it consults this file and displays a list of mounted devices. Each time you (or systemd) call mount or umount, these utilities make the necessary changes to **mtab**. Although this is an ASCII text file, you should not edit it. See also **/etc/fstab**.

/etc/nsswitch.conf
   Specifies whether a system uses NIS, DNS, local files, or a combination as the source of certain information and in which order it consults these services (page 495).

/etc/pam.d   Files in this directory specify the authentication methods used by PAM (page 476) applications.

**LE+**   /etc/passwd   Describes users to the system. Do not edit this file directly; instead, use one of the utilities discussed in "Configuring User and Group Accounts" on page 598. Each line in **passwd** has seven colon-separated fields that describe one user:

   *login-name:password:user-ID:group-ID:info:directory:program*

The *login-name* is the user's username—the name you enter in response to the **login:** prompt or on a GUI login screen. The value of the *password* is the character **x**. The **/etc/shadow** file (page 511) stores the real password, which is hashed (page 1252). For security reasons, every account should have a password. By convention, disabled accounts have an asterisk (**✳**) in this field.

The *user-ID* is a number, with 0 indicating the **root** account and 1–999 being reserved for system accounts. The *group-ID* identifies the user's primary group. It is a number, with 0–999 being reserved for system accounts; see **/etc/group** (page 506). You can change these values and set maximum values in **/etc/login.defs**.

The *info* is information that various programs, such as accounting and email programs, use to identify the user further. Normally it contains at least the first and last names of the user. It is referred to as the *GECOS* (page 1251) field.

The *directory* is the absolute pathname of the user's home directory. The *program* is the program that runs once the user logs in to a textual session. If *program* is not present, a value of **/bin/bash** is assumed. You can put **/bin/tcsh** here to log in using the TC Shell or **/bin/zsh** to log in using the Z Shell, assuming the shell you specify is installed. The chsh utility (page 464) changes this value.

The *program* is usually a shell, but it can be any program. The following line in the **passwd** file creates a "user" whose only purpose is to execute the who utility:

```
who:x:1000:1000:execute who:/usr:/usr/bin/who
```

Logging in with **who** as a username causes the system to log you in, execute the who utility, and log you out. The output of who flashes by quickly because the new login prompt clears the screen immediately after who finishes running. This entry in the **passwd** file does not provide a shell, so you cannot stay logged in after who finishes executing.

This technique is useful for providing special accounts that might do only one thing. The **ftp** account, for example, enables anonymous FTP (page 713) access to an FTP server. Because no one logs in on this account, the shell is set to **/bin/false** (which returns a false exit status) or to **/sbin/nologin** (which does not permit a nonprivileged user to log in). When you put a message in **/etc/nologin.txt**, nologin displays that message (except it has the same problem as the output of who—it is removed so quickly it is hard to see).

### Do not replace a login shell with a shell script

security   Do not use shell scripts as replacements for shells in **/etc/passwd**. A user might be able to interrupt a shell script, giving him full shell access when you did not intend to do so. When installing a dummy shell, use a compiled program, not a shell script.

/etc/printcap   The printer capability database for LPD/LPR (page 556). It is not used with CUPS (Chapter 13), the Fedora/RHEL default printing system. This file describes system printers and is derived from 4.3BSD UNIX.

LPI   /etc/profile   Contain systemwide interactive shell initialization scripts for environment and
and   startup programs. When you log in, the shell immediately executes the commands in
/etc/profile.d   **/etc/profile**. This script executes all the commands in all the files in the **/etc/profile.d** directory (next) that have a filename extension of **.sh**. Both **profile** and the files in **profile.d** are executed in the same environment as the shell. (For information on executing a shell script in this manner, refer to the discussion of the **.** [dot] command on page 332.) As the comments at the beginning of **profile** say, if you want to make a systemwide change to users' environments, place a script with a filename extension of **.sh** in **profile.d**. Do not modify **profile** because it might be replaced when the system is updated; a file you create in **profile.d** will not be replaced.

The system administrator can create a file with a filename extension of **.sh** in **profile.d** to establish systemwide environment parameters that individual users can override in their **~/.bash_profile** (page 502) files. For example, this file can set shell variables, execute utilities, set up aliases, and take care of other housekeeping tasks. Following is an example of a file in **/etc/profile.d** that displays the message of the day (the **/etc/motd** file), sets the file-creation mask (umask; page 469), and sets the interrupt character to CONTROL-C:

```
# cat /etc/profile.d/simple.sh
cat /etc/motd
umask 022
stty intr '^c'
```

See the **/etc/profile** file and the files in **/etc/profile.d** on the local system for more complex examples.

**/etc/protocols**   Provides protocol numbers, aliases, and brief definitions for DARPA Internet TCP/IP protocols. Do not modify this file.

**/etc/rc.d**   Holds SysVinit initialization scripts and links. See page 448 for more information.

**LE+**   **/etc/resolv.conf**

The resolver (page 854) configuration file; provides access to DNS. This file is built by NetworkManager (page 637) if it is running.

The following example shows the **resolv.conf** file for the **example.com** domain. A **resolv.conf** file usually contains at least two lines—a search line (optional) and a nameserver line:

```
$ cat /etc/resolv.conf
search example.com
nameserver 10.0.0.50
nameserver 10.0.0.51
```

The **search** keyword might be followed by a maximum of six domain names. The first domain is interpreted as the host's local domain. These names are appended one at a time to all DNS queries, shortening the time needed to query local hosts. The domains are searched in order in the process of resolving hostnames that are not fully qualified. See *FQDN* on page 1250.

When you put **search example.com** in **resolv.conf**, any reference to a host within the **example.com** domain or a subdomain (such as **marketing.example.com**) can use the abbreviated form of the host. For example, instead of issuing the command **ping speedy.marketing.example.com**, you can use **ping speedy.marketing**; however, a trailing period causes DNS to assume the name is complete so it appends no suffix. The following line in **resolv.conf** causes the **marketing** subdomain to be searched first, followed by **sales**, and finally the entire **example.com** domain:

```
search marketing.example.com sales.example.com example.com
```

It is a good idea to put the most frequently used domain names first to try to outguess possible conflicts. If both **speedy.marketing.example.com** and **speedy.example.com** exist, for example, the order of the search determines which one is selected when you invoke DNS. Do not overuse this feature: The longer the search path, the more network DNS requests generated, and the slower the response. Three or four names are typically sufficient.

Up to a maximum of three **nameserver** lines indicate which systems the local system queries to resolve hostnames to IP addresses, and vice versa. These machines are consulted in the order they appear, with a timeout between queries. The first timeout is a few seconds; each subsequent timeout is twice as long as the previous one. The preceding file causes this system to query 10.0.0.50, followed by 10.0.0.51 when the first system does not answer within a few seconds. The **resolv.conf** file might be automatically updated when a PPP (Point-to-Point Protocol) or DHCP (Dynamic Host Configuration Protocol) controlled interface is activated.

**/etc/rpc**   Maps RPC services to RPC numbers. The three columns in this file show the name of the server for the RPC program, the RPC program number, and any aliases.

**LPI** **/etc/services** Lists system services. The three columns in this file show the informal name of the service, the port number/protocol the service uses most frequently, and any aliases for the service. This file does not specify which services are running on the local system, nor does it map services to port numbers. The **services** file is used internally to map port numbers to services for display purposes; editing this file does not change which ports and protocols the local system uses.

**LE+** **/etc/shadow** Contains *SHA2* (page 1272) or *MD5* (page 1260) hashed user passwords, depending on system configuration. Each entry occupies one line composed of nine fields, separated by colons:

*login-name:password:last-mod:min:max:warn:inactive:expire:flag*

The *login-name* is the user's username—the name that the user enters in response to the **login:** prompt or on a GUI login screen. The *password* is a hashed password that passwd puts in this file. New accounts that are not set up with a password are given a value of !, !!, or * in this field to prevent the user from logging in until you assign a password to that user (page 600).

The *last-mod* field indicates when the password was last modified. The *min* is the minimum number of days that must elapse before the password can be changed; the *max* is the maximum number of days before the password must be changed. The *warn* field specifies how much advance warning (in days) will be given to the user before the password expires. The account will be closed if the number of days between login sessions exceeds the number of days specified in the *inactive* field. The account will also be closed as of the date in the *expire* field. The last field in an entry, *flag*, is reserved for future use. You can use the Password Info tab in system-config-users (page 600) or chage to modify these fields.

The **shadow** password file must be owned by **root** and must not be publicly readable or writable. Setting ownership and permissions in this way makes it more difficult for someone to break into the system by identifying accounts without passwords or by using specialized programs that try to match hashed passwords.

A number of conventions exist for creating special **shadow** entries. An entry of *LK* or NP in the *password* field indicates *locked* or *no password*, respectively. *No password* is different from an empty password; no password implies that this is an administrative account that no one ever logs in on directly. Occasionally programs will run with the privileges of this account for system maintenance functions. These accounts are set up under the principle of least privilege (page 423).

Entries in the **shadow** file must appear in the same order as in the **passwd** file. There must be exactly one **shadow** entry for each **passwd** entry.

**/etc/sysconfig** A directory containing a hierarchy of system configuration files. For more information refer to the **/usr/share/doc/initscripts*/sysconfig.txt** file.

**LPI** **/etc/sysconfig/network** Describes the network setup for the local system.

**LPI**    **/proc**  Provides a window into the Linux kernel. Through the **/proc** pseudofilesystem you can obtain information on any process running on the system, including its current state, memory usage, CPU usage, terminal association, parent, and group. You can extract information directly from the files in **/proc**. An example follows:

```
$ sleep 1000 &
[1] 3104
$ cd /proc/3104
$ ls -l
dr-xr-xr-x. 2 sam pubs 0 04-09 14:00 attr
-r-------- 1 sam pubs 0 04-09 14:00 auxv
-r--r--r-- 1 sam pubs 0 04-09 14:00 cgroup
--w------- 1 sam pubs 0 04-09 14:00 clear_refs
-r--r--r-- 1 sam pubs 0 04-09 14:00 cmdline
-rw-r--r-- 1 sam pubs 0 04-09 14:00 coredump_filter
-r--r--r-- 1 sam pubs 0 04-09 14:00 cpuset
lrwxrwxrwx 1 sam pubs 0 04-09 14:00 cwd -> /home/sam
-r-------- 1 sam pubs 0 04-09 14:00 environ
lrwxrwxrwx 1 sam pubs 0 04-09 14:00 exe -> /bin/sleep
dr-x------ 2 sam pubs 0 04-09 14:00 fd
...
$ cat status
Name:   sleep
State:  S (sleeping)
Tgid:   3104
Pid:    3104
PPid:   1503
TracerPid:      0
Uid:    1000    1000    1000    1000
Gid:    1000    1000    1000    1000
FDSize: 256
Groups: 4 20 24 46 105 119 122 1000
VmPeak:     3232 kB
VmSize:     3232 kB
VmLck:         0 kB
...
```

In this example, bash creates a background process (PID 3104) for sleep. Next the user changes directories to the directory in **/proc** that has the same name as the PID of the background process (**cd /proc/3104**). This directory holds information about the process it is named for—the sleep process in the example. The **ls –l** command shows that some entries in this directory are links (**cwd** is a link to the directory the process was started from, and **exe** is a link to the executable file that this process is running) and some appear to be ordinary files. All appear to be empty. However, when you use cat to display one of these pseudofiles (**status** in the example), cat displays output. Obviously it is not an ordinary file.

You can also obtain information about the local system by examining pseudofiles in **/proc**. The following examples display information about the CPU and RAM (memory).

```
$ cat /proc/cpuinfo
processor       : 0
vendor_id       : GenuineIntel
cpu family      : 6
model           : 23
```

```
model name       : Intel(R) Core(TM)2 Quad CPU    Q9650  @ 3.00GHz
stepping         : 10
microcode        : 0xa0b
...

$ cat /proc/meminfo
MemTotal:        1012484 kB
MemFree:          221216 kB
Buffers:           14176 kB
Cached:           267940 kB
SwapCached:         2124 kB
Active:           215912 kB
Inactive:         412792 kB
```

**LPI** swap    Swap space is used by the virtual memory subsystem of the kernel. When it runs low on real memory (RAM), the kernel writes memory pages from RAM to the swap space. Which pages are written and when they are written are controlled by finely tuned algorithms in the Linux kernel. When needed by running programs, the kernel brings these pages back into RAM—a technique called *paging* (page 1265). When a system is running very short on memory, an entire process might be paged out to disk.

Running an application that requires a large amount of virtual memory might result in the need for additional swap space. Swap space can be added and deleted from the system dynamically: If you run out of swap space, you can use mkswap to create a swap file and swapon to enable it. Normally the kernel uses a disk partition as swap space, but it can also use a file for this purpose. However, a disk partition provides much better performance than a file.

If you are creating a file as swap space, first use df to ensure the partition you are creating it in has adequate space for the file. The following commands first use dd and **/dev/zero** (page 505) to create an empty file (do not use cp because you might create a file with holes, which might not work) in the working directory. Next mkswap takes as an argument the name of the file created in the first step to set up the swap space. For security reasons, change the file so it cannot be read from or written to by anyone except a user with **root** privileges. Use swapon with the same argument to turn the swap file on; then use **swapon –s** to confirm the swap space is available. The final two commands turn off the swap file and remove it:

```
# dd if=/dev/zero of=swapfile bs=1024 count=65536
65536+0 records in
65536+0 records out
67108864 bytes (67 MB) copied, 0.40442 s, 166 MB/s
# mkswap swapfile
Setting up swapspace version 1, size = 65532 KiB
no label, UUID=49ec7f5b-1391-4b24-bd0a-a07e55752666
# chmod 600 swapfile
# swapon swapfile
# swapon -s
Filename                      Type          Size     Used    Priority
/dev/dm-1                     partition     2031612  0       -1
/swapfile                     file          65532    0       -2
# swapoff swapfile
# rm swapfile
rm: remove regular file 'swapfile'? y
```

**LPI** /sys     A pseudofilesystem that was added in the Linux 2.6 kernel to make it easy for programs running in kernelspace, such as device drivers, to exchange information with programs running in userspace. See page 516 for more information.

/usr/libexec     Holds binary files that are not executed directly by a user.

/usr/share/magic     Most files begin with a unique identifier called a *magic number*. This file is a text database listing all known magic numbers on the system. When you use the file utility, it consults **/usr/share/magic** to determine the type of a file. Occasionally you might acquire a new tool that creates a new type of file that is unrecognized by the file utility. In this situation you need to update the **/usr/share/magic** file; refer to the **magic** man page for details. See also "magic number" on page 1259.

**LE** /var/log     Holds system log files, many of which are generated by **syslogd** (page 620). You can use a text display program such as less, tail, or cat, or the graphical program gnome-system-log (**gnome-system-log** package) to view the files in this directory. To run gnome-system-log, enter **gnome-system-log** from a terminal emulator or in an Enter a Command window (ALT-F2).

**LPI** /var/log/messages
                 Contains messages from daemons, the Linux kernel, and security programs. For example, you will find **filesystem full** warning messages, error messages from system daemons (e.g., NFS, **ntpd**, printer daemons), SCSI and IDE disk error messages, and more in **messages**. Check **/var/log/messages** periodically to keep informed about important system events. Much of the information displayed on the system console is also sent to **messages**. If the system experiences a problem and you cannot access the console, check this file for messages about the problem. See page 620 for information on **syslogd**, which generates many of these messages.

/var/log/secure     Holds messages from security-related programs such as su and the **sshd** daemon.

# FILE TYPES

Linux supports many types of files. This section discusses the following types of files:

- Ordinary files, directories, links, and inodes (next)
- **LE** Symbolic links (page 515)
- Device special files (page 515)
- FIFO special files (named pipes) (page 516)
- Sockets (page 517)
- Block and character devices (page 518)
- Raw devices (page 518)

## ORDINARY FILES, DIRECTORIES, LINKS, AND INODES

Ordinary and     An *ordinary* file stores user data, such as textual information, programs, or images,
directory files   such as a **jpeg** or **tiff** file. A *directory* is a standard-format disk file that stores information, including names, about ordinary files and other directory files.

Inodes   An *inode* is a *data structure* (page 1245), stored on disk, that defines a file's existence and is identified by an inode number. Use ls with the **–i** option to display the inode number of a file. An inode contains critical information about a file, such as the UID of the owner, where it is physically located on the disk, access mode, and how many hard links point to it. In addition, SELinux (page 472) stores extended information about files in inodes. Directory files, not inodes, hold filename information. This setup allows an inode to be associated with more than one filename and to be pointed to from more than one directory.

When you move (mv) a file, including a directory file, within a filesystem, you change the filename portion of the directory entry associated with the inode that describes the file. You do not create a new inode. If you move a file to another filesystem, mv first creates a new inode on the destination filesystem and then deletes the original inode. You can also use mv to move a directory recursively from one filesystem to another. In this case mv copies the directory and all the files in it and deletes the original directory and its contents.

Hard links   When you make an additional hard link (ln; page 204) to a file, you add a directory entry that points to the inode that describes the file. You do not create a new inode. It is not possible to create a hard link to a directory.

When you remove (rm) a file, you delete the directory entry that describes the file. When you remove the last hard link to a file, the operating system puts all blocks the inode pointed to back in the *free list* (the list of blocks that are available for use on the disk) and frees the inode to be used again.

The . and .. directory entries   Every directory contains at least two entries (. and ..). The . entry is a link to the directory itself. The .. entry is a link to the parent directory. In the case of the root directory, there is no parent; the .. entry is a link to the root directory itself.

**LE** Symbolic links   Because each filesystem has a separate set of inodes, you can create hard links to a file only from within the filesystem that holds that file. To get around this limitation, Linux provides symbolic links, which are files that point to other files. Files that are linked by a symbolic link do not share an inode. As a consequence, you can create a symbolic link to a file from any filesystem. You can also create a symbolic link to a directory, device, or other special file. For more information refer to "Symbolic Links" on page 206.

# DEVICE SPECIAL FILES

*Device special files* (also called *device files* and *special files*) represent Linux kernel routines that provide access to an operating system feature. FIFO (first in, first out) special files allow unrelated programs to exchange information. Sockets allow unrelated processes on the same or different systems to exchange information. One type of socket, the UNIX domain socket, is a special file. Symbolic links are another type of special file.

**LE+** Device files   *Device files* include both block and character special files and represent device drivers that allow the system to communicate with peripheral devices, such as terminals, printers, and hard disks. By convention, device files appear in the **/dev** directory and its subdirectories. Each device file represents a device; hence, the system reads from and writes to the file to read from and write to the device it represents. The following example shows part of a listing for the **/dev** directory:

```
$ ls -l /dev
crw-rw----. 1 root video   10, 175 01-25 12:17 agpgart
crw-------. 1 root root     10, 235 01-25 12:17 autofs
drwxr-xr-x. 2 root root         640 01-25 04:17 block
drwxr-xr-x. 2 root root          80 01-25 04:17 bsg
drwxr-xr-x. 3 root root          60 01-25 04:17 bus
lrwxrwxrwx. 1 root root           3 01-25 04:17 cdrom -> sr0
drwxr-xr-x. 2 root root        2760 01-25 12:17 char
crw-------. 1 root root      5,   1 01-25 12:17 console
lrwxrwxrwx. 1 root root          11 01-25 04:17 core -> /proc/kcore
...
brw-rw----. 1 root disk      8,   0 01-25 04:17 sda
brw-rw----. 1 root disk      8,   1 01-25 12:17 sda1
brw-rw----. 1 root disk      8,   2 01-25 04:17 sda2
...
```

The first character of each line is always **–**, **b**, **c**, **d**, **l**, or **p**, representing the file type—ordinary (plain), block, character, directory, symbolic link, or named pipe (next), respectively. The next nine characters identify the permissions for the file, followed by the number of hard links and the names of the owner and the group. Where the number of bytes in a file would appear for an ordinary or directory file, a device file shows *major* and *minor device numbers* (page 517) separated by a comma. The rest of the line is the same as for any other **ls –l** listing (page 191).

**LPI**  udev   The udev utility manages device naming dynamically. It replaces **devfs** and moves the device-naming functionality from the kernel to userspace. Because devices are added to and removed from a system infrequently, the performance penalty associated with this change is minimal. The benefit of the move is that a bug in udev cannot compromise or crash the kernel.

**LPI**  /sys   The udev utility is part of the hotplug system (next). When a device is added to or removed from the system, the kernel creates a device name in the **/sys** pseudofilesystem and notifies hotplug of the event, which is received by udev. The udev utility then creates the device file, usually in the **/dev** directory, or removes the device file from the system. The udev utility can also rename network interfaces. See the page at www.kernel.org/pub/linux/utils/kernel/hotplug/udev.html for more information.

**LPI**  Hotplug   The hotplug system allows you to plug a device into a running system and use it immediately. Although hotplug was available in the Linux 2.4 kernel, the 2.6 kernel integrates hotplug with the unified device driver model framework (the *driver model core*) so any bus can report an event when a device is added to or removed from the system. User software can be notified of the event so it can take appropriate action. See linux-hotplug.sourceforge.net for more information.

## FIFO SPECIAL FILE (NAMED PIPE)

A *FIFO special* file, also called a *named pipe*, represents a pipe: You read from and write to the file to read from and write to the pipe. The term *FIFO* stands for *first in, first out*—the way any pipe works. In other words, the first information you put in one end is the first information that comes out the other end. When you use a pipeline on a command line to send the output of a program to the printer, the printer outputs the information in the same order that the program produced it and sent it to the pipeline.

Unless you are writing sophisticated programs, you will not be working with FIFO special files. However, programs use named pipes for interprocess communication. You can create a pipe using mkfifo:

```
$ mkfifo AA
$ ls -l AA
prw-rw-r--. 1 sam pubs 0 01-27 17:55 AA
```

The **p** at the left end of the output indicates the file is a pipe.

Both UNIX and Linux systems have included pipes for many generations. Without named pipes, only processes that were children of the same ancestor could use pipes to exchange information. Using named pipes, *any* two processes on a single system can exchange information. When one program writes to a FIFO special file, another program can read from the same file. The programs do not have to run at the same time or be aware of each other's activity. The operating system handles all buffering and information storage. This type of communication is termed *asynchronous* (*async*) because the programs on the opposite ends of the pipe do not have to be synchronized.

## SOCKETS

Like FIFO special files, UNIX/Linux domain *sockets* allow asynchronous processes that are not children of the same ancestor to exchange information. These sockets are the central mechanism of the interprocess communication that forms the basis of the networking facility. They differ from TCP/IP sockets, which are not represented in the filesystem. When you use networking utilities, pairs of cooperating sockets manage the communication between the processes on the local system and the remote system. Sockets form the basis of such utilities as ssh and scp.

## MAJOR AND MINOR DEVICE NUMBERS

A *major device number* points to a driver in the kernel that works with a class of hardware devices: terminal, printer, tape drive, hard disk, and so on. In the listing of the **/dev** directory on page 516, all the hard disk partitions have a major device number of 8.

A *minor device number* identifies a particular piece of hardware within a class. Although all hard disk partitions are grouped together by their major device number, each has a different minor device number (**sda1** is 1, **sda2** is 2, and so on). This setup allows one piece of software (the device driver) to service all similar hardware yet still be able to distinguish among different physical units.

## LE BLOCK AND CHARACTER DEVICES

This section describes typical device drivers. Because device drivers can be changed to suit a particular purpose, the descriptions in this section do not pertain to every system.

Block device   A *block device* is an I/O (input/output) device that has the following characteristics:

- Able to perform random access reads
- Has a specific block size
- Handles only single blocks of data at a time
- Accepts only transactions that involve whole blocks of data
- Able to have a filesystem mounted on it
- Has the Linux kernel buffer its input and output
- Appears to the operating system as a series of blocks numbered from 0 through $n - 1$, where $n$ is the number of blocks on the device

Block devices commonly found on a Linux system include hard disks, USB flash drives, CDs, and DVDs.

Character device   A *character device* is any device that is not a block device. Examples of character devices include printers, terminals, tape drives, and modems.

The device driver for a character device determines how a program reads from and writes to that device. For example, the device driver for a terminal allows a program to read the information you type on the terminal in two ways. First, a program can read single characters from a terminal in *raw* mode—that is, without the driver interpreting characters. (This mode has nothing to do with the raw device described next.) Alternately, a program can read one line at a time. When a program reads one line at a time, the driver handles the erase and kill characters so the program never sees typing mistakes that have been corrected. In this case, the program reads everything from the beginning of a line to the RETURN that ends a line; the number of characters in a line can vary.

## RAW DEVICES

Device driver programs for block devices usually have two entry points so they can be used in two ways: as block devices or as character devices. The character device form of a block device is called a *raw device*. A raw device is characterized by

- Direct I/O (no buffering through the Linux kernel).
- One-to-one correspondence between system calls and hardware requests.
- Device-dependent restrictions on I/O.

fsck   An example of a utility that uses a raw device is fsck. It is more efficient for fsck to operate on the disk as a raw device rather than being restricted by the fixed size of blocks in the block device interface. Because it has full knowledge of the underlying filesystem structure, fsck can operate on the raw device using the largest possible units. When a filesystem is mounted, processes normally access the disk through the block device interface, which explains why it is important to allow fsck to modify only unmounted filesystems. On a mounted filesystem, there is the danger that while fsck is rearranging the underlying structure through the raw device, another process could change a disk block using the block device, resulting in a corrupted filesystem.

# FILESYSTEMS

Table 11-1 lists some types of filesystems available under Linux.

**Table 11-1**    Filesystems

| Filesystem | Features |
| --- | --- |
| adfs | Advanced Disc Filing System. Used on Acorn computers. The word *Advanced* differentiated this filesystem from its predecessor DFS, which did not support advanced features such as hierarchical filesystems. |
| affs | Amiga Fast Filesystem (FFS). |
| autofs | Automounting filesystem (page 821). |
| cifs | Common Internet Filesystem (page 1242). Formerly the Samba Filesystem (**smbfs**). |
| coda | CODA distributed filesystem (developed at Carnegie Mellon). |
| devpts | A pseudofilesystem for pseudoterminals (page 504). |
| *LPI* ext2 | A standard filesystem for Fedora/RHEL systems, usually with the **ext4** extension. |
| *LPI* ext3 | A journaling (page 1256) extension to the **ext2** filesystem. It greatly improves recovery time from crashes (it takes a lot less time to run fsck), promoting increased availability. As with any filesystem, a journaling filesystem can lose data during a system crash or hardware failure. |
| ext4 | An extension to the **ext3** filesystem. It is backward compatible with **ext2/ext3** filesystems and provides improved performance over **ext3** the filesystem. |
| GFS | Global Filesystem. GFS is a journaling, clustering filesystem. It enables a cluster of Linux servers to share a common storage pool. |
| hfs | Hierarchical Filesystem. Used by older Macintosh systems. Newer Macintosh systems use **hfs+**. |
| hpfs | High-Performance Filesystem. The native filesystem for IBM's OS/2. |
| jffs2 | Journaling Flash Filesystem (**jffs**). A filesystem for flash memory. |
| iso9660 | The standard filesystem for CDs and DVDs. |
| minix | Very similar to Linux. The filesystem of a small operating system that was written for educational purposes by Andrew S. Tanenbaum (www.minix3.org). |

**Table 11-1**  Filesystems (continued)

| Filesystem | Features |
|---|---|
| msdos | Filesystem used by DOS and subsequent Microsoft operating systems. Do not use **msdos** for mounting Windows filesystems; it does not read VFAT attributes. |
| ncpfs | Novell NetWare NCP Protocol Filesystem. Used to mount remote filesystems under NetWare. |
| nfs | Network Filesystem. Developed by Sun Microsystems, this protocol allows a computer to access remote files over a network as if the files were local (page 801). |
| ntfs | NT Filesystem. The native filesystem of Windows NT. See www.linux-ntfs.org. |
| *LPI* proc | An interface to several Linux kernel *data structures* (page 1245) that behaves like a filesystem (page 512). |
| qnx4 | QNX 4 operating system filesystem. |
| reiserfs | A journaling (page 1256) filesystem based on balanced-tree algorithms. See **ext4** for more on journaling filesystems. |
| romfs | A dumb, readonly filesystem used mainly for *RAM disks* (page 1269) during installation. |
| smbfs | Samba Filesystem (deprecated). See **cifs**. |
| sysv | System V UNIX filesystem. |
| ufs | Default filesystem under Sun's Solaris operating system and other UNIXs. |
| umsdos | A full-feature UNIX-like filesystem that runs on top of a DOS FAT filesystem. |
| vfat | Developed by Microsoft, a standard that allows long filenames on FAT partitions. |
| VxFS | Veritas Extended Filesystem. The first commercial journaling (page 1256) filesystem, popular under HP-UX and Solaris. |
| XFS | SGI's journaling filesystem (ported from Irix; page 527). |

## *LPI*  mount: MOUNTS A FILESYSTEM

The mount utility connects directory hierarchies—typically filesystems—to the Linux directory hierarchy. These directory hierarchies can be on remote and local disks, CDs, DVDs, and USB flash drives. Linux can also mount *virtual filesystems* that have been built inside ordinary files, filesystems built for other operating systems, and the special **/proc** filesystem (page 512), which maps Linux kernel information to a pseudodirectory. This section covers mounting local filesystems; refer to page 801 for information on using NFS to mount remote directory hierarchies. See **/dev** on page 503 for information on device names.

**LPI** Mount point  The *mount point* for the filesystem/directory hierarchy that you are mounting is a directory in the local filesystem. This directory must exist before you can mount a filesystem; its contents disappear as long as a filesystem is mounted on it and reappear when you unmount the filesystem. See page 38 for a discussion of mount points.

Without any arguments, mount lists the mounted filesystems, showing the physical device holding each filesystem, the mount point, the type of filesystem, and any options set when each filesystem was mounted. The mount utility gets this information from the **/etc/mtab** file (page 508), which is a link to **/proc/self/mounts**. On a system running systemd page 438, mount lists so many virtual filesystems it can be difficult to find the physical filesystems. Instead you can use findmnt with the **–t** (**––types**) option to display one type of filesystem such as **ext4**:

```
$ findmnt -t ext4
TARGET    SOURCE                FSTYPE OPTIONS
/         /dev/mapper/fedora-root ext4   rw,relatime,seclabel,data=ordered
|--/boot /dev/sda1              ext4   rw,relatime,seclabel,data=ordered
```

The first entry in the preceding example shows an LV mounted by the LVM (page 44) device mapper on **/** (root). As explained on page 40, the **/boot** partition cannot reside on an LV; it is mounted on **/dev/sda1**.

## Do not mount anything on root (/)

caution  Always mount network directory hierarchies and removable devices at least one level below the root level of the filesystem. The root filesystem is mounted on /; you cannot mount two filesystems in the same place. If you were to try to mount something on /, all files, directories, and filesystems that were under the root directory would no longer be available, and the system would crash.

optional  An easy way to know when a filesystem is not mounted is to create a file named **NOTMOUNTED** in the directory that is the mount point. That way, ls shows **NOTMOUNTED** when the filesystem is not mounted, making it clear the filesystem is not mounted. When the filesystem is mounted, the **NOTMOUNTED** file is hidden and ls does not display its name.

Give the following touch command (you will probably need to work with **root** privileges) to create a file named **NOTMOUNTED** in the **/p02** directory. You must give the command while the filesystem that gets mounted on **/p02** is not mounted. Otherwise the file appears when the filesystem is mounted. The subsequent commands show ls displaying **NOTMOUNTED** while the filesystem is not mounted and displaying the files on the mounted filesystem.

```
$ su -c 'touch /p02/NOTMOUNTED'
$ ls /p02
NOTMOUNTED
$ su -c 'mount /p02'
$ ls /p02
memo1
...
```

When you add a line for a filesystem to the **/etc/fstab** file (page 506), you can mount that filesystem by giving the associated mount point or device name as the argument to mount. For example, the following command mounts a backup volume at **/backup**:

```
$ mount /backup
```

This command works because **/etc/fstab** contains the additional information needed to mount the file. A nonprivileged user is able to mount the file because of the **user** option.

```
/dev/sda7       /backup     ext4 user,noauto,rw 0 0
```

On the local system, the mount point and device name will differ from those in this example. You can specify a filesystem type of **auto** (in place of **ext4**) to cause the system to probe the filesystem to determine its type. You can also manually mount filesystems that do not appear in **/etc/fstab**. For example, you can mount a CD-ROM, filesystem type *ISO9660* (page 1256), at **/media/cd** using the following command:

```
# mount -t iso9660 /dev/cdrom /media/cd
```

## LPI  MOUNT OPTIONS

The mount utility takes many options, which you can specify either on the command line or in the **/etc/fstab** file (page 524). For a complete list of mount options for local filesystems, see the mount man page; for remote directory hierarchies, see page 807 and the nfs man page.

The system mounts most filesystems specified in **fstab** when it boots. You can specify the **noauto** option to cause Linux not to mount a filesystem automatically.

### Mount removable devices with the nosuid option

security  Always mount removable devices with the **nosuid** option so a malicious user cannot, for example, put a setuid copy of bash on a disk and have a shell with **root** privileges. By default, Fedora/RHEL uses the **nosuid** option when mounting removable media. See page 806 for more information.

Unless you specify the **user, users,** or **owner** option, only a user running with **root** privileges can mount and unmount a filesystem. The **user** option allows any user to mount the filesystem, but the filesystem can be unmounted only by the user who mounted it; the **users** option allows any user to mount and unmount the filesystem. These options are frequently specified for CD, DVD, and USB flash drives. The **owner** option, which is used only under special circumstances, is similar to the **user** option except that the user mounting the device must own the device.

Three options can help ensure the security of the system when you allow nonprivileged users to mount filesystems. The **noexec** option prevents a user from running an executable file on the mounted filesystem, **nosuid** forces mounted setuid and setgid executable files to run with regular permissions (no effective user or group ID change) on the mounted filesystem (page 806), and **nodev** prevents the system from recognizing a device special file on the mounted filesystem (page 806). The **user** and **users** option imply all three of these options; **owner** implies **nosuid** and **nodev**.

## *LPI*  umount: UNMOUNTS A FILESYSTEM

The umount utility unmounts a filesystem as long as it does not contain any files or directories that are in use (open). For example, a logged-in user's working directory cannot be on the filesystem you want to unmount. The next command unmounts the CD mounted earlier:

```
$ umount /media/cdrom
```

Unmount a USB flash drive or a remote (NFS) directory hierarchy the same way you would unmount a partition of a hard drive.

The umount utility consults **/etc/fstab** to get the necessary information and then unmounts the appropriate filesystem from its server. When a process has a file open on the filesystem you are trying to unmount, umount displays a message similar to the following:

```
umount: /home: device is busy
```

### When you cannot unmount a device because it is in use

tip  When a process has a file open on a device you need to unmount, use fuser to determine which process has the file open and to kill it. For example, when you want to unmount a CD, give the command **fuser –ki /media/cdrom** (substitute the mount point for the diskette on the local system for **/media/cdrom**). After checking with you, this command kills the process(es) using the CD. You can also use lsof (page 624) to find open files.

Use the **–a** option to umount to unmount all mounted filesystems that are not in use. You can never unmount the filesystem mounted at **/**. You can combine **–a** with the **–t** option to unmount filesystems of a given type (e.g., **ext4** or **nfs**). For example, the following command unmounts all mounted **nfs** directory hierarchies that are not in use:

```
# umount -at nfs
```

## *LPI*  du: DISPLAYS DISK USAGE INFORMATION

The du (disk usage) utility displays estimates of file space usage. It is commonly called with the **–h** (**--human-readable**) option which causes du to display file sizes in kilobytes, megabytes, and gigabytes instead of blocks and with the **–s** (**--summarize**) option which causes du to display a total for each of its directory arguments instead of displaying the size of each file in the directory. The first of the following examples shows du listing the sizes of each file in the **/etc** directory (without the **–s** option); the second uses the **–s** option to cause du to list the size of the **/etc** directory itself. When run without **root** privileges, the examples display an error message for each file the user is not permitted to read.

```
# du -h /etc | head -4
76K     /etc/logrotate.d
12K     /etc/highlight
4.0K    /etc/terminfo
8.0K    /etc/wpa_supplicant

# du -sh /etc
37M     /etc
```

## *LPI* fstab: KEEPS TRACK OF FILESYSTEMS

The system administrator maintains the **/etc/fstab** file, which lists local and remote directory hierarchies, most of which the system mounts automatically when it boots. The **fstab** file has six columns; a hyphen is a placeholder for a column that has no value:

1. **Name**—The name, label, or UUID number of a local block device (page 518) or a pointer to a remote directory hierarchy. When you install the system, Fedora/RHEL uses UUID numbers for fixed devices (but not for LVs). Using UUID numbers in **fstab** during installation circumvents the need for consistent device naming. Because udev (page 516) manages device naming dynamically, the installer might not be aware, for example, that the first disk is not named **/dev/hda1** but rather **/dev/sda1**, but it always knows the UUID number of a device. Using UUID numbers to identify devices also keeps partitions and mount points correctly correlated when you remove or exchange devices. When run with **root** privileges, blkid (page 464) displays device UUID numbers. See **/dev/disk/by-uuid** (page 503) for more information on UUID numbers. You can use the volume label of a local filesystem by using the form **LABEL=xx,** where *xx* is the volume label. For information on labeling devices, refer to e2label on page 465.

   A remote directory hierarchy appears as *hostname:pathname*, where *hostname* is the name of the remote system that houses the filesystem, and *pathname* is the absolute pathname (on the remote system) of the directory that is to be mounted.

2. **Mount point**—The name of the directory file that the filesystem/directory hierarchy is to be mounted on. If it does not already exist, create this directory using mkdir. See pages 38 and 521.

3. **Type**—The type of filesystem/directory hierarchy that is to be mounted. Local filesystems are generally of type **ext2**, **ext4**, or **iso9660**, and remote directory hierarchies are of type **nfs** or **cifs**. Table 11-1 on page 519 lists filesystem types.

4. **Mount options**—A comma-separated list of mount options, such as whether the filesystem is mounted for reading and writing (**rw**, the default) or readonly (**ro**). See pages 522 and 807 and refer to the mount and nfs man pages for lists of options.

5. **Dump**—Previously used by dump to determine when to back up the filesystem.

6. **Fsck**—Specifies the order in which fsck checks filesystems. Root (**/**) should have a **1** in this column. Filesystems that are mounted to a directory just below the root directory should have a **2**. Filesystems that are mounted on another mounted filesystem (other than root) should have a **3**. For example,

if **local** is a separate filesystem from **/usr** and is mounted on **/usr** (as **/usr/local**), then **local** should have a **3**. Filesystems and directory hierarchies that do not need to be checked (for example, remotely mounted directory hierarchies and CDs/DVDs) should have a **0**.

The following example shows a typical **fstab** file:

```
# cat /etc/fstab
...
/dev/mapper/fedora-root                          /      ext4    defaults 1 1
UUID=24908841-6308-4304-a52f-c1a76c69bd57   /boot ext4    defaults 1 2
/dev/mapper/fedora-swap swap                        swap    defaults 0 0
```

See page 520 for information about mount and the types of devices it mounts.

## LPI  fsck: CHECKS FILESYSTEM INTEGRITY

The fsck (filesystem check) utility verifies the integrity of many types of filesystems and, if possible, repairs problems it finds. Use xfs_repair (page 528) to repair XFS filesystems. Because many filesystem repairs can destroy data, particularly on non*journaling filesystems* (page 1256), such as **ext2**, by default fsck asks you for confirmation before making each repair.

### Do not run fsck on a mounted filesystem

caution   Do not run fsck on a mounted filesystem. When you attempt to check a mounted filesystem, fsck warns you and asks whether you want to continue. Reply **no**. You can run fsck with the **–N** option on a mounted filesystem because it will not write to the filesystem; as a result, no harm can come from running it. See page 518 for more information.

When fsck repairs a damaged filesystem, it might find unlinked files: files that have lost their directory information. These files have no filenames. The fsck utility gives these files their inode numbers as names and stores them in the **lost+found** directory (page 502) in the filesystem that holds the file. You can use file (page 229) to determine the type of these files and less to view readable files. Because ls –l displays the name of the owner of these files, you can return them to their owners.

The following command checks all unmounted filesystems that are marked to be checked in **/etc/fstab** (page 524) except for the root filesystem:

```
# fsck -AR
```

The **–A** option causes fsck to check filesystems listed in **fstab**. When used with the **–A** option, the **–R** option causes fsck not to check the root filesystem. You can check a specific filesystem with a command similar to one of the following:

```
# fsck /home
```

*or*

```
# fsck /dev/sda1
```

## *LPI*   tune2fs: CHANGES FILESYSTEM PARAMETERS

The tune2fs utility displays and modifies filesystem parameters on **ext2**, **ext3**, and **ext4** filesystems. This utility can also set up journaling on an **ext2** filesystem, turning it into an **ext3** filesystem. With the introduction of increasingly reliable hardware and software, systems tend to be rebooted less frequently, so it is important to check filesystems regularly. By default, fsck is run on each partition while the system is brought up, before the partition is mounted. (The checks scheduled by tune2fs are separate and scheduled differently from the checks that are done following a system crash or hard disk error [see the previous section].)

Depending on the flags, fsck might do nothing more than display a message saying the filesystem is clean. The larger the partition, the more time it takes to check it, assuming a nonjournaling filesystem. These checks are often unnecessary. The tune2fs utility helps you to find a happy medium between checking filesystems each time you reboot the system and never checking them. It does so by scheduling when fsck checks a filesystem (these checks occur only when the system is booted).[1] You can use two scheduling patterns: time elapsed since the last check and number of mounts since the last check. The following command causes fsck to check **/dev/sda1** after it has been mounted 8 times or after 15 days have elapsed since its last check, whichever happens first:

```
# tune2fs -c 8 -i 15 /dev/sda1
tune2fs 1.42.7 (21-Jan-2013)
Setting maximal mount count to 8
Setting interval between checks to 1296000 seconds
```

A maximum mount count of −1 or 0 causes fsck and the kernel to ignore the mount count information. The next tune2fs command is similar but works on a different partition (an LV) and sets the current mount count to 4. When you do not specify a current mount count, it is set to zero:

```
# tune2fs -c 8 -i 15 -C 4 /dev/mapper/fedora-root
tune2fs 1.42.7 (21-Jan-2013)
Setting maximal mount count to 8
Setting current mount count to 4
Setting interval between checks to 1296000 seconds
```

The **–l** option lists a variety of information about the partition. You can combine this option with others.

```
# tune2fs -l /dev/mapper/fedora-root
tune2fs 1.42.7 (21-Jan-2013)
Filesystem volume name:    <none>
Last mounted on:           /
Filesystem UUID:           2d9ea1c9-bfbb-4302-b715-1b258c946c55
Filesystem magic number:   0xEF53
Filesystem revision #:     1 (dynamic)
Filesystem features:       has_journal ext_attr resize_inode dir_index
```

---

1. For systems whose purpose in life is to run continuously, this kind of scheduling does not work. You must develop a schedule that is not based on system reboots but rather on a clock. Each filesystem must be unmounted periodically, checked with fsck (preceding section), and then remounted.

```
filetype needs_recovery extent flex_bg sparse_super large_file huge_file
uninit_bg dir_nlink extra_isize
Filesystem flags:         signed_directory_hash
Default mount options:    user_xattr acl
Filesystem state:         clean
Errors behavior:          Continue
Filesystem OS type:       Linux
Inode count:              2457600
Block count:              9824256
...
Last mount time:          Wed Jun  5 17:29:12 2013
Last write time:          Mon Jun 10 19:00:09 2013
Mount count:              4
Maximum mount count:      8
Last checked:             Tue Jun  4 19:27:35 2013
Check interval:           1296000 (2 weeks, 1 day)
...
```

Set the filesystem parameters on the local system so they are appropriate to the way you use it. When using the mount count to control when fsck checks filesystems, use the –C option to stagger the checks to ensure all checks do not occur at the same time. Always make sure new and upgraded filesystems have checks scheduled as you desire.

**LPI ext2 to ext3** To change an **ext2** filesystem to an **ext3** filesystem, you must put a *journal* (page 1256) on the filesystem, and the kernel must support **ext3** filesystems. Use the –j option to set up a journal on an unmounted filesystem:

```
# tune2fs -j /dev/sda1
tune2fs 1.42.7 (21-Jan-2013)
Creating journal inode: done
This filesystem will be automatically checked every 8 mounts or
15 days, whichever comes first.  Use tune2fs -c or -i to override.
```

Before you can use **fstab** (page 506) to mount the changed filesystem, you must modify its entry in the **fstab** file to reflect its new type. To do so, change the third column to **ext3**.

**LPI ext3 to ext2** The following command changes an unmounted or readonly **ext3** filesystem to an **ext2** filesystem:

```
# tune2fs -O ^has_journal /dev/sda1
tune2fs 1.42.7 (21-Jan-2013)
```

Speeding lookups The **dir_index** option, which is turned off by default, adds a balanced-tree binary hash lookup method for directories. This feature improves scalability of directories with large numbers of files, although it means that the hash needs to be updated each time a directory changes. Turn on using **tune2fs –O dir_index** and reboot to create the hash.

Refer to the tune2fs man page for more details.

# THE XFS FILESYSTEM

XFS (xfs.org) is a high-performance, journaling, 64-bit filesystem created by Silicon Graphics, Inc. It supports filesystems as large as 64 *exabytes* (page 1249), containing files up to 8 exabytes in size, and directory structures with tens of millions of entries. XFS is the default filesystem under RHEL 7 (beta) and is available under Fedora.

Following is a list of XFS filesystem features:

- Defragmentation with filesystems mounted and active

- Expansion (growing the filesystem) with filesystems mounted and active

- Backup and restore facilities specific to XFS

- Improved filesystem performance, especially when reading and writing large files, provided by B+ trees that contain metadata that describe extents

- Parallel (simultaneous) I/O provided by allocation groups, allowing multiple application threads to perform I/O simultaneously, enhancing filesystem throughput on multiprocessor systems; throughput is even better when the filesystem spans multiple devices

- Metadata consistency and quick crash recovery ensured by metadata journaling

- Reduced fragmentation and reduced CPU usage provided by delayed allocation (allocate-on-flush) that causes the kernel to batch disk writes

- Multiple name/value pairs per file provided by extended attributes (xattr)

- Quota journaling speeds crash recovery

- Quotas for directory hierarchies provided by project quotas

mkfs.xfs   To create an XFS partition on a clean disk, first use parted (page 614) or gnome-disks (page 78) to create a partition (you may have to label the disk first), and then use mkfs.xfs to create a filesystem on the partition. The mkfs.xfs utility has many options; see the mkfs.xfs man page for details.

```
# mkfs.xfs /dev/sdb1
meta-data=/dev/sdb1              isize=256    agcount=4, agsize=6103424 blks
         =                       sectsz=512   attr=2, projid32bit=0
data     =                       bsize=4096   blocks=24413696, imaxpct=25
         =                       sunit=0      swidth=0 blks
naming   =version 2              bsize=4096   ascii-ci=0
log      =internal log           bsize=4096   blocks=11920, version=2
         =                       sectsz=512   sunit=0 blks, lazy-count=1
realtime =none                   extsz=4096   blocks=0, rtextents=0
```

Once you have created an XFS filesystem, you can put an entry for it in **fstab** (page 524) and mount it (page 520) as you would any other type of filesystem. The following command mounts the XFS filesystem created above on the mount point named **/myxfs**.

```
# mount /dev/sdb1 /myxfs
```

xfs_repair   XFS has its own set of tools for working with XFS filesystems. Give the command **apropos xfs** to display a list of XFS utilities. The fsck (fsck.xfs) utility does nothing when run against an XFS filesystem; use xfs_repair in its place. A filesystem must not be mounted when you use xfs_repair to check or repair it. Run xfs_repair with the **–n** (no change) option to verify the integrity of a filesystem; run xfs_repair without an option to repair a filesystem. The following message explains that you must mount the XFS filesystem to play the changes stored in the log before you repair it. After mounting the filesystem, unmount it and run xfs_repair to repair the filesystem.

```
# xfs_repair /dev/sdb1
Phase 1 - find and verify superblock...
Phase 2 - using internal log
- zero log...
ERROR: The filesystem has valuable metadata changes in a log which needs to
be replayed.  Mount the filesystem to replay the log, and unmount it before
re-running xfs_repair.  If you are unable to mount the filesystem, then use
the -L option to destroy the log and attempt a repair.
Note that destroying the log may cause corruption -- please attempt a mount
of the filesystem before doing this.

# mount /dev/sdb1 /myxfs
# umount /dev/sdb1
# xfs_check /dev/sdb1

# xfs_repair /dev/sdb1
Phase 1 - find and verify superblock...
Phase 2 - using internal log
         - zero log...
         - scan filesystem freespace and inode maps...
         - found root inode chunk
Phase 3 - for each AG...
         - scan and clear agi unlinked lists...
         - process known inodes and perform inode discovery...
         - agno = 0
         - agno = 1
         - agno = 2
         - agno = 3
         - process newly discovered inodes...
Phase 4 - check for duplicate blocks...
         - setting up duplicate extent list...
         - check for inodes claiming duplicate blocks...
         - agno = 0
         - agno = 1
         - agno = 2
         - agno = 3
Phase 5 - rebuild AG headers and trees...
         - reset superblock...
Phase 6 - check inode connectivity...
         - resetting contents of realtime bitmap and summary inodes
         - traversing filesystem ...
         - traversal finished ...
         - moving disconnected inodes to lost+found ...
Phase 7 - verify and correct link counts...
done
```

xfs_fsr   The xfs_fsr (filesystem reorganizer) utility improves the organization of a file on a *mounted* XFS filesystem. Give the command xfs_fsr followed by the name of the file you want to reorganize.

# CHAPTER SUMMARY

Filesystems hold directories of files. These structures store user data and system data that are the basis of users' work on the system and the system's existence. Linux supports many types of files, including ordinary files, directories, links, and special files. Special files provide access to operating system features. The kernel uses major and minor device numbers to identify classes of devices and specific devices within each class. Character and block devices represent I/O devices such as hard disks and printers. Inodes, which are identified by inode numbers, are stored on disk and define a file's existence.

When the system comes up, the **/etc/fstab** file controls which filesystems are mounted and how they are mounted (readonly, read-write, and so on). After a system crash, filesystems are automatically verified and repaired if necessary by fsck. You can use tune2fs to force the system to cause fsck to verify a filesystem periodically when the system boots.

# EXERCISES

1. What is the function of the **/etc/hosts** file? Which services can you use in place of or to supplement the **hosts** file?

2. What does the **/etc/resolv.conf** file do? What do the **nameserver** lines in this file do?

3. What is an inode? What happens to the inode when you move a file within a filesystem?

4. What does the **..** entry in a directory point to? What does this entry point to in the root (**/**) directory?

5. What is a device file? Where are device files located?

6. What is a FIFO? What does FIFO stand for? What is another name for a FIFO? How does a FIFO work?

# ADVANCED EXERCISES

7. Write a line for the **/etc/fstab** file that mounts the **/dev/sdb1 ext4** filesystem on **/extra** with the following characteristics: The filesystem will not be mounted automatically when the system boots, and anyone can mount and unmount the filesystem.

8. Without using rm, how can you delete a file? (*Hint:* How do you rename a file?)

9. After burning an ISO image file named **image.iso** to a CD on **/dev/hdc**, how can you can verify the copy from the command line?

10. Why should **/var** reside on a separate partition from **/usr**?

11. Create a FIFO. Using the shell, demonstrate that two users can use this FIFO to communicate asynchronously.

12. How would you mount an ISO image so you could copy files from it without burning it to a CD?

# 12

# FINDING, DOWNLOADING, AND INSTALLING SOFTWARE

## OBJECTIVES

After reading this chapter you should be able to:

▶ Explain the purpose of a software package, a package management system, and a software repository

▶ List the uses and benefits of yum

▶ Use yum to list installed and available packages

▶ Use yum to search for packages containing specific applications or utilities

▶ Use yum to install and remove a software package

▶ Use yum to update all software packages on the local system.

▶ Download large files with BitTorrent

▶ Use rpm to display information about a package and install software

▶ List common steps for installing non-RPM software from source

531

# INTRODUCTION

Linux is based on millions of lines of code and includes thousands of programs. Each of these programs is updated periodically, and most depend on other programs or files to run. The source code for each program must be compiled for each processor architecture and each release of each Linux distribution. With the first releases of Linux, these tasks were done by hand. Over time, this process has been automated. This chapter explains how you can make your life easier by taking advantage of the facilities Fedora/RHEL provides for finding, installing, updating, and removing software.

**LE** Software package
A *software package,* or simply *package,* is the collection of scripts, programs, files, and directories required to install and run an application, utility, server, or system software. A package also includes a list of other packages the package depends on (*dependencies*). Using software packages makes it easier to install, update, and uninstall software. A package contains either executable files or source code files. Executable files are precompiled for a specific processor architecture and operating system, whereas source files need to be compiled but will run on a wide range of machines and operating systems.

**LE** PMS
A *PMS,* or *package management system,* is a set of utilities that allow you to install, upgrade, remove, and search software packages easily and in a consistent manner. It is based on a local database that holds information about each installed package, including its dependencies and version information.

One of the biggest advantages of a PMS is how easy it makes it to uninstall a package. If you compile from source, a **make install** command typically installs the files, but there is frequently no **make uninstall** command. A PMS keeps track of all the files that belong to a package. These files might be distributed among many directories throughout a system. This tracking allows you to remove all files belonging to a package with a single command. A PMS also enables you to query packages, a great troubleshooting tool that does not come with manual installation. When you manually install a package, you must obtain the source code (again, and in some cases the same version as you installed) to learn which files are a part of the package, what was done during installation, and how to remove the software.

**LE** Software package formats
Software packages come in different formats. Fedora/RHEL and SUSE use RPM (RPM Package Manager; page 546). Ubuntu and Debian use **dpkg** (Debian package), which was the first Linux packaging system to incorporate dependency information. Other formats include the GNU Configure and Build System (page 550), and compressed tar. Formats such as compressed tar, which were popular before the introduction of RPM, are used less often today because they require more work on the part of the installer (you) and do not provide the dependency and compatibility checking RPM offers.

**LPI  yum**  Early releases of Red Hat Linux did not include a tool for managing updates. Although RPM could install or upgrade individual software packages, it was up to the user to locate a package and any packages it was dependent on. When Terra Soft produced its Red Hat–based Linux distribution for the PowerPC, the company created the Yellow Dog Updater to fill this gap. This program has since been ported to other architectures and distributions. The result, named Yellow Dog Updater, Modified (yum; yum.baseurl.org), is included with Fedora/RHEL. This chapter covers many yum commands and features.

**PackageKit**  PackageKit (www.packagekit.org) is a front end for several PMSs, providing a uniform interface. Fedora, Kubuntu, and SUSE use PackageKit. The **gnome-packagekit** package holds graphical tools designed for the GNOME desktop; each of these tools is named **gpk∗**.

**Graphical interfaces**  This chapter describes yum, which provides a textual interface. The yumex utility (yum extender; **yumex** package), which this book does not cover, provides a graphical interface to **yum**. The gpk-application utility, part of PackageKit (previous), also provides a way to work with software packages graphically.

**Kernel source code**  Chapter 14 discusses downloading, configuring, compiling, and installing kernel source code. See page 582 for an example of downloading kernel source code using yumdownloader.

**LE  Repositories**  The yum utility downloads package headers and packages from servers, called *repositories,* that can reside on the Internet, a DVD, or the local network. See page 542 for more information. If you need to distribute locally built packages to a group of systems, you might want to consider setting up a local repository.

**Keeping software up-to-date**  Of the many reasons to keep software up-to-date, one of the most important is security. Although you often hear about software-based security breaches after the fact, you rarely hear about the fixes that were available but never installed before the breach occurred. Timely installation of software updates is critical to system security. Linux open-source software is the ideal environment to find and fix bugs and make repaired software available quickly. When you keep a system and application software up-to-date, you keep abreast of bug fixes, new features, support for new hardware, speed enhancements, and more.

As shipped, Fedora/RHEL checks for updates daily, automatically installs security updates, and advises you when other updates are available. Use the Software Update Preferences window (page 116) to change these options.

**Bug tracking**  Fedora/RHEL uses Bugzilla (bugzilla.redhat.com), which belongs to a class of programs formally known as *defect tracking systems,* to track bugs. You can use Bugzilla to read about existing bugs and to report new ones. See page 552 for information on how Fedora/RHEL handles errata.

# *LPI* JUMPSTART: INSTALLING AND REMOVING SOFTWARE PACKAGES USING yum

This section explains how to use yum to install packages on and remove packages from the local system. The yum utility provides a textual interface; see "Graphical interfaces" on page 533 if you want to use a GUI.

## Work with **root** privileges when you install and remove packages

tip Because installing and removing packages involves writing to directories that only a user working with **root** privileges can write to, you must work with **root** privileges when you install and remove packages.

If you do not know the name of the package you want to install, see page 536. If you want yum to download a package that is not supported by Fedora/RHEL, you must add to the **/etc/yum.repos.d** directory (page 542) a file that specifies the repository that holds the package.

Before using yum to install a package, work with **root** privileges to give the command **yum update** (page 538) to update the local RPM installation database. By default, the system updates this database daily. Even so, it is a good idea to give this command periodically until you are sure the script is updating the database properly.

yum **install**    The following example calls yum to install the tcsh shell, which is part of the **tcsh** package. After yum determines what it needs to do, it asks for confirmation. Reply **y** if you want to continue or **n** to quit.

```
# yum install tcsh
Loaded plugins: langpacks, refresh-packagekit
Resolving Dependencies
--> Running transaction check
---> Package tcsh.x86_64 0:6.18.01-2.fc19 will be installed
--> Finished Dependency Resolution
Dependencies Resolved

================================================================================
 Package       Arch          Version            Repository            Size
================================================================================
Installing:
 tcsh          x86_64        6.18.01-2.fc19     updates-testing       336 k

Transaction Summary
================================================================================
Install  1 Package

Total download size: 336 k
Installed size: 658 k
Is this ok [y/d/N]: y
Downloading packages:
tcsh-6.18.01-2.fc19.x86_64.rpm                        | 336 kB   00:00
Running transaction check
Running transaction test
Transaction test succeeded
Running transaction
  Installing : tcsh-6.18.01-2.fc19.x86_64                              1/1
  Verifying  : tcsh-6.18.01-2.fc19.x86_64                              1/1

Installed:
  tcsh.x86_64 0:6.18.01-2.fc19

Complete!
```

## Installing a package group

tip Installing a package group installs a group of related packages. For example, the command **yum group install virtualization** installs the group of software packages needed to run virtualization programs. See page 540 for more information on groups.

**Automatically installs dependencies** The next command installs the **ypbind** (NIS) package. Because this package depends on another package that is not installed (**yp-tools**), yum lists the package under **Installing for dependencies** and installs it automatically. The yum utility asks for confirmation before installing the packages.

```
# yum install ypbind
Loaded plugins: langpacks, refresh-packagekit
Resolving Dependencies
--> Running transaction check
---> Package ypbind.x86_64 3:1.37.1-3.fc19 will be installed
--> Processing Dependency: yp-tools for package: 3:ypbind-1.37.1-3.fc19.x86_64
--> Running transaction check
---> Package yp-tools.x86_64 0:2.14-1.fc19 will be installed
--> Finished Dependency Resolution

Dependencies Resolved

===============================================================================
 Package            Arch          Version              Repository       Size
===============================================================================
Installing:
 ypbind             x86_64        3:1.37.1-3.fc19       fedora          62 k
Installing for dependencies:
 yp-tools           x86_64        2.14-1.fc19           fedora          79 k

Transaction Summary
===============================================================================
Install  1 Package (+1 Dependent package)

Total download size: 141 k
Installed size: 299 k
Is this ok [y/d/N]: y
...
```

**yum remove** You can also use yum to remove packages, using a similar syntax. The following example removes the **tcsh** package:

```
# yum remove tcsh
Loaded plugins: langpacks, refresh-packagekit
Resolving Dependencies
--> Running transaction check
---> Package tcsh.x86_64 0:6.18.01-2.fc19 will be erased
--> Finished Dependency Resolution

Dependencies Resolved

===============================================================================
 Package          Arch         Version             Repository          Size
===============================================================================
Removing:
 tcsh             x86_64       6.18.01-2.fc19       @updates-testing    658 k

Transaction Summary
===============================================================================
Remove  1 Package

Installed size: 658 k
Is this ok [y/N]: y
Downloading packages:
Running transaction check
```

```
Running transaction test
Transaction test succeeded
Running transaction
  Erasing    : tcsh-6.18.01-2.fc19.x86_64                              1/1
  Verifying  : tcsh-6.18.01-2.fc19.x86_64                              1/1

Removed:
  tcsh.x86_64 0:6.18.01-2.fc19

Complete!
```

**Automatically removes dependencies**

When yum removes a package, it also removes packages that are dependent on the package it is removing. The following example removes **ypbind** and its dependency, **yp-tools**.

```
# yum remove ypbind
Loaded plugins: langpacks, refresh-packagekit
Resolving Dependencies
--> Running transaction check
---> Package ypbind.x86_64 3:1.37.1-3.fc19 will be erased
--> Processing Dependency: ypbind for package: yp-tools-2.14-1.fc19.x86_64
--> Running transaction check
---> Package yp-tools.x86_64 0:2.14-1.fc19 will be erased
--> Finished Dependency Resolution

Dependencies Resolved

================================================================================
 Package          Arch         Version              Repository        Size
================================================================================
Removing:
 ypbind           x86_64       3:1.37.1-3.fc19      @fedora           98 k
Removing for dependencies:
 yp-tools         x86_64       2.14-1.fc19          @fedora           201 k

Transaction Summary
================================================================================
Remove  1 Package (+1 Dependent package)

Installed size: 299 k
Is this ok [y/N]: y
...
```

# FINDING THE PACKAGE THAT HOLDS AN APPLICATION OR FILE YOU NEED

You might know the name of an application, utility, or file you need but not know the name of the package that holds the file. This section describes several ways you can locate the package.

### Finding a package with a name that sounds like...

**tip**   The yum **search** command (next page) searches package names, descriptions, and summaries. The yum **list** command (next page) searches package names only.

**Fedora package database**

Visit admin.fedoraproject.org/pkgdb. After entering the string you are searching for in the text box labeled **Search**, click **APPLICATIONS** or **PACKAGES** to display software packages with the string you entered in their names or descriptions.

**gpk-application**  You can use gpk-application to search for packages by filename, program or application name, or package name. When you find the package you want, this program will install it.

**yum whatprovides**  You can also use yum to search repositories for a package that contains a specified file. For example, suppose you are compiling a program and get the following error message:

```
xv.h:174:22: error: X11/Xlib.h: No such file or directory
```

Following, the yum **whatprovides** (or just **provides**) command displays a list of packages that contain the file named **Xlib.h** in the **X11** directory:

```
$ yum whatprovides "*X11/Xlib.h"
Loaded plugins: langpacks, refresh-packagekit
...
libX11-devel-1.5.99.902-1.fc19.i686 : Development files for libX11
Repo        : fedora
Matched from:
Filename    : /usr/include/X11/Xlib.h
...
```

The most likely candidate is the entry shown in the preceding example, which is the most generic. You can install this package using the following command:

```
# yum install libX11-devel
```

**yum search**  The yum **search** command searches for a string in the package description, summary, and name fields. The following example searches for packages that have the string **vim** in these fields:

```
$ yum search vim
Loaded plugins: langpacks, refresh-packagekit
updates-testing/19/x86_64/pkgtags                      | 301 kB     00:00
============================== N/S matched: vim ==============================
apvlv.x86_64 : PDF viewer which behaves like Vim
drupal6-media_vimeo.noarch : Vimeo Video Module for Drupal6
eclipse-vrapper.noarch : Vim-like editing in Eclipse
...
vim-X11.x86_64 : The VIM version of the vi editor for the X Window System
vim-clustershell.noarch : VIM files for ClusterShell
vim-command-t.x86_64 : An extremely fast, intuitive mechanism for opening files
             : in VIM
vim-common.x86_64 : The common files needed by any version of the VIM editor
vim-enhanced.x86_64 : A version of the VIM editor which includes recent
             : enhancements
...
```

**yum list**  The yum **list** command searches for a package name field that matches a string. Specify **list available** without an argument to list all packages that can be installed from the yum repositories. The following example searches for packages whose name fields match the string **\*emacs\***:

```
$ yum list '*emacs*'
Loaded plugins: langpacks, presto, refresh-packagekit
Available Packages
clips-emacs.noarch              6.30.0-0.3.20090722svn.fc15      fedora
coq-emacs.i686                  8.2p11-1.fc12                    fedora
crm114-emacs.i686               0-2.14.20100106.fc15            fedora
cvc3-emacs.noarch               2.2-3.fc15                       fedora
cvc3-emacs-el.noarch            2.2-3.fc15                       fedora
cvc3-xemacs.noarch              2.2-3.fc15                       fedora
cvc3-xemacs-el.noarch           2.2-3.fc15                       fedora
emacs.i686                      1:23.2-17.fc15                   fedora
...
```

## *LPI*   yum: KEEPS THE SYSTEM UP-TO-DATE

This section continues to describe yum. It covers updating installed packages, yum commands and groups, downloading RPM package files, configuring yum, and adding a repository specification. Refer to yum.baseurl.org for more information.

### Do not upgrade to a new release using yum

caution   Using yum to upgrade a system from one release to another can be problematic and is not recommended. Visit fedoraproject.org/wiki/YumUpgradeFaq for more information.

## *LPI*   UPDATING PACKAGES

In the following example, yum determines that two packages need to be updated and checks dependencies. By default, Fedora/RHEL notifies you when packages need to be updated. The yum **update** command, without additional parameters, updates all installed packages. It downloads package headers for installed packages, determines which packages need to be updated, prompts you to continue, and downloads and installs the updated packages.

```
# yum update
Loaded plugins: langpacks, refresh-packagekit
Resolving Dependencies
--> Running transaction check
---> Package gnome-terminal.x86_64 0:3.8.2-1.fc19 will be updated
---> Package gnome-terminal.x86_64 0:3.8.3-1.fc19 will be an update
---> Package libpcap.x86_64 14:1.3.0-4.fc19 will be updated
---> Package libpcap.x86_64 14:1.4.0-1.fc19 will be an update
--> Finished Dependency Resolution

Dependencies Resolved

================================================================================
 Package            Arch        Version              Repository          Size
================================================================================
Updating:
 gnome-terminal     x86_64      3.8.3-1.fc19         updates-testing     936 k
 libpcap            x86_64      14:1.4.0-1.fc19      updates-testing     131 k

Transaction Summary
================================================================================
Upgrade  2 Packages

Total download size: 1.0 M
Is this ok [y/d/N]: y
Downloading packages:
Delta RPMs reduced 1.0 M of updates to 223 k (79% saved)
(1/2): gnome-terminal-3.8.2-1.fc19_3.8.3-1.fc19.x86_64.drp | 177 kB   00:00
(2/2): libpcap-1.3.0-4.fc19_1.4.0-1.fc19.x86_64.drpm       |  45 kB   00:00
Finishing delta rebuilds of 2 package(s) (1.0 M)
--------------------------------------------------------------------------------
Total                                       183 kB/s | 223 kB     00:01
Running transaction check
Running transaction test
Transaction test succeeded
Running transaction
  Updating   : gnome-terminal-3.8.3-1.fc19.x86_64                         1/4
  Updating   : 14:libpcap-1.4.0-1.fc19.x86_64                             2/4
  Cleanup    : gnome-terminal-3.8.2-1.fc19.x86_64                         3/4
  Cleanup    : 14:libpcap-1.3.0-4.fc19.x86_64                             4/4
```

```
        Verifying   : 14:libpcap-1.4.0-1.fc19.x86_64                          1/4
        Verifying   : gnome-terminal-3.8.3-1.fc19.x86_64                      2/4
        Verifying   : gnome-terminal-3.8.2-1.fc19.x86_64                      3/4
        Verifying   : 14:libpcap-1.3.0-4.fc19.x86_64                          4/4

    Updated:
        gnome-terminal.x86_64 0:3.8.3-1.fc19        libpcap.x86_64 14:1.4.0-1.fc19

    Complete!
```

You can update specific packages by specifying the names of the packages on the command line following the word **update**. The yum **check-update** command (next) lists packages that can be updated.

# yum COMMANDS

This section describes a few commonly used yum commands. The yum man page contains a complete list.

**check**  Reports on problems in the local RPM database.

**check-update**  Lists packages that are installed on the local system and have updates available in the yum repositories.

**clean all**  Removes header files that yum uses for resolving dependencies. Also removes cached packages. However, because yum removes packages after they have been installed, typically no cached packages exist (see **keepcache** on page 541).

**clean metadata**  Removes the files yum uses to determine remote package availability. Using this command forces yum to download all metadata the next time you run it.

**group list**  Lists yum groups (next).

**group info** *group*
Lists information about the yum group named *group* (next).

**group install** *group*
Installs the packages in the yum group named *group* (next).

**info** *word*  Displays information about packages in the yum repositories named *word*. Specify *word* as "∗*word*∗" to search for *word* anywhere in the package name.

**list** *word*  Lists packages in the yum repositories whose name is *word*. Specify *word* as "∗*word*∗" to search for *word* anywhere in the package name. See page 537 for an example.

**list available**  Lists all packages that can be installed from the yum repositories. Use a pipeline and grep to search for packages (e.g., **yum list available | grep samba**).

**provides**  Same as **whatprovides**.

**search** *word*  Lists packages in the yum repositories that have *word* in their descriptions, summaries, or names. See page 537 for an example.

**whatprovides** *word*
Searches repositories and displays a list of packages that provides a feature or file that matches *word*. Specify *word* as "∗*word*∗" to search for *word* anywhere in a feature or filename. See page 537 for an example.

# yum Package Groups

In addition to working with single packages, yum can work with groups of packages. The next example shows how to display a list of installed and available package groups:

```
$ yum group list
Loaded plugins: langpacks, refresh-packagekit
There is no installed groups file.
Available environment groups:
    GNOME Desktop
    KDE Plasma Workspaces
    Xfce Desktop
...
Available Groups:
    3D Printing
    Administration Tools
    Authoring and Publishing
    Books and Guides
...
    Window Managers
Done
```

The command **yum group info** followed by the name of a package group displays information about the package group, including a description and a list of mandatory, default, and optional packages. A plus sign (**+**) before a package name indicates that the package will be installed with the package group; the absence of a plus sign indicates that you must install the package manually. The next example displays information about the Administration Tools package group. You must quote package group names that include SPACEs.

```
$ yum group info "Administration Tools"
Loaded plugins: langpacks, refresh-packagekit
There is no installed groups file.

Group: Administration Tools
 Group-Id: admin-tools
 Description: This group is a collection of graphical administration tools for the
system, such as for managing user accounts and configuring system hardware.
 Default Packages:
    +authconfig-gtk
     gnome-disk-utility
     gnome-packagekit
     setroubleshoot
    +system-config-date
...
 Optional Packages:
    +apper
    +cacti
    +dbench
...
```

To install a package group, give the command **yum group install** followed by the name of the package group.

## LPI  Downloading RPM Package Files with yumdownloader

The yumdownloader utility (**yum-utils** package) locates and downloads—but does not install—RPM files. Because it does not install software, you do not need to work with **root** privileges to run it; you need only permission to write to the working directory.

The following example downloads the **samba** RPM file to the working directory:

```
$ yumdownloader samba
$ yumdownloader samba
Loaded plugins: langpacks, refresh-packagekit
samba-4.0.6-3.fc19.x86_64.rpm                          | 523 kB   00:00
```

Downloading source files You can use yumdownloader with the **--source** option to download RPM source package files. The yumdownloader utility automatically enables the necessary source repositories. See page 582 for an example that downloads in the working directory the RPM file for the latest version of the kernel source code for the release installed on the local system. Without the **--source** option, yumdownloader would have downloaded an executable RPM file. See page 549 for information on installing this type of file.

## *LPI* yum.conf: CONFIGURES yum

You do not need to configure yum: As installed, it is ready to use. This section describes the yum configuration files for users who want to modify them. The primary configuration file, **/etc/yum.conf**, holds global settings. As distributed with Fedora/RHEL, files in the **/etc/yum.repos.d** directory define repositories. Following is the default **yum.conf** file:

```
$ cat /etc/yum.conf
[main]
cachedir=/var/cache/yum/$basearch/$releasever
keepcache=0
debuglevel=2
logfile=/var/log/yum.log
exactarch=1
obsoletes=1
gpgcheck=1
plugins=1
installonly_limit=3
...
# PUT YOUR REPOS HERE OR IN separate files named file.repo
# in /etc/yum.repos.d
```

The section labeled [**main**] defines global configuration options. The **cachedir** specifies the directory where yum stores downloaded packages, although with **keepcache** set to 0, yum does not store these packages after installing them. The amount of information logged is specified by **debuglevel**, with a value of 10 producing the most information. The **logfile** specifies where yum keeps its log.

Setting **exactarch** to **1** causes yum to update packages only with packages of the same architecture, thereby preventing an i686 package from replacing an i386 package, for example. You can use **retries** to specify the number of times yum will try to retrieve a file before returning an error (the default is 6). Set this parameter to 0 to cause yum to continue trying forever.

Setting **obsoletes** to **1** causes yum to replace obsolete packages when updating packages; it has no effect when you install packages. When **gpgcheck** is set to **1**, yum checks the GPG (page 1160) signatures on packages it installs. This check verifies the authenticity of the packages. Setting **plugins** to **1** enables yum plugins, which extend yum functionality. The **metadata_expire** parameter specifies the number of seconds (or minutes if the value is followed by **m**) that yum uses the metadata (about packages it downloads from the repository) before it downloads the information again. This parameter defaults to 90 minutes.

Although the balance of the yum configuration information, which specifies the yum repositories, can appear in the **yum.conf** file, Fedora/RHEL puts this information in **/etc/yum.repos.d**.

**optional**  Some packages should only be installed; they should not be updated. The parameter **installonlypkgs** in **/etc/yum.conf** identifies these packages. Packages related to the kernel default to **installonlypkgs**: Typically you do not want to update a kernel; you want to install a new one and keep the old one around in case you need it. The **installonly_limit** parameter specifies the number of versions of **installonlypkgs** packages that yum keeps. See the **yum.conf** man page for more information.

## yum REPOSITORIES

As noted in **/etc/yum.conf**, Fedora/RHEL stores information about each repository in a separate file in the **/etc/yum.repos.d** directory:

```
$ ls /etc/yum.repos.d
fedora.repo  fedora-updates.repo  fedora-updates-testing.repo
```

A parameter set in one of these files overrides the same parameter set in the [**main**] section (in **yum.conf**). Each of these files contains a header, such as [**fedora**], which provides a unique name for the repository. The name of the file is generally similar to the repository name, with the addition of a **fedora-** prefix and a **.repo** filename extension. Commonly used repositories include **fedora** (held in the **fedora.repo** file), which contains the packages present on the installation medium (stable packages); **updates** (held in the **fedora-updates.repo** file), which contains updated versions of the stable packages; and **updates-testing** (held in the **fedora-updates-testing.repo** file), which contains updates that are not ready for release. This last repository is not enabled; do not enable it unless you are testing unstable packages. Never enable the **updates-testing** repository on a production system.

**optional**  Each **\*.repo** file includes specifications for several related repositories, which are usually disabled. For example, the **fedora.repo** file holds [**fedora-debuginfo**] and [**fedora-source**] in addition to [**fedora**]. You cannot download source files using yum. Instead, use yumdownloader (page 540) for this task.

The next example shows part of the **fedora.repo** file that specifies the parameters for the **fedora** repository:

```
$ cat /etc/yum.repos.d/fedora.repo
[fedora]
name=Fedora $releasever - $basearch
failovermethod=priority
#baseurl=http://download.fedoraproject.org/pub/fedora/linux/releases/$releasever/Everything/$basearch/os/
mirrorlist=https://mirrors.fedoraproject.org/metalink?repo=fedora-$releasever&arch=$basearch
enabled=1
#metadata_expire=7d
gpgcheck=1
gpgkey=file:///etc/pki/rpm-gpg/RPM-GPG-KEY-fedora-$basearch
...
```

Repository specification files    Each repository specification file contains the name of the repository enclosed in brackets ([]), a **name**, a **failovermethod**, a **baseurl**, and a **mirrorlist**. The **name** provides an informal name for the repository that yum displays. The **failovermethod** determines the order in which yum contacts an initial mirror site and additional mirror sites if the first one fails; **priority** selects the sites in the order in which they appear, while **roundrobin** selects sites randomly. The **baseurl** indicates the location of the main repository; it is commented out by default. The **mirrorlist** specifies the URL of a file that holds a list of **baseurl**s, or mirrors of the main repository. Only **baseurl** or **mirrorlist** can be enabled at one time. These definitions use two variables: yum sets **$basearch** to the architecture of the system (e.g., i686) and $releasever to the version of the release (e.g., **15** for Fedora 15).

The repository described by the file is enabled (yum will use it) if **enabled** is set to **1** and is disabled if **enabled** is set to **0**. The **metadata_expire** specifies how long yum considers metadata valid: After this amount of time, yum downloads fresh metadata. Default is six hours. As described earlier, **gpgcheck** determines whether yum checks GPG signatures on files it downloads. The **gpgkey** specifies the location of the GPG key. Refer to the **yum.conf** man page for more options.

Adding a repository    There are many repositories of software packages. For more information and a list of repositories, visit fedoraproject.org/wiki/Third_party_repositories. You can also search the Internet for **fedora repositories**. One of the most interesting of these sites is repos.fedorapeople.org. These sites provide repository specification files for their repositories. Add a repository to the local system by placing a repository specification file in the **/etc/yum.repos.d** directory but see the following security tip.

### Use repositories you trust

security    Be selective in which repositories you add to a system: When you add a repository, you are trusting the person who runs the repository not to put malicious software in packages you download. In addition, packages that are not supported by Fedora/RHEL can conflict with other packages and/or cause upgrades to fail.

# BitTorrent

The easiest way to download a BitTorrent file is to click the torrent file object in a Web browser or in the Nautilus File Browser; this action opens a GUI running a transmission BitTorrent client. This section describes how BitTorrent works and explains how to download a BitTorrent file from the command line.

The BitTorrent protocol implements a hybrid client/server and *P2P* (page 1265) file transfer mechanism. BitTorrent efficiently distributes large amounts of static data, such as the Fedora/RHEL installation ISO images. It can replace protocols such as anonymous FTP, where client authentication is not required. Each BitTorrent client that downloads a file provides additional bandwidth for uploading the file, thereby reducing the load on the initial source. In general, BitTorrent downloads proceed faster than FTP downloads. Unlike protocols such as FTP, BitTorrent groups multiple files into a single package: a BitTorrent file.

Tracker, peer, seed, and swarm  BitTorrent, like other P2P systems, does not use a dedicated server. Instead, the functions of a server are performed by the tracker, peers, and seeds. The *tracker* is a server that allows clients to communicate with each other. Each client—called a *peer* when it has downloaded part of the BitTorrent file and a *seed* after it has downloaded the entire BitTorrent file—acts as an additional source for the BitTorrent file. Peers and seeds are collectively called a *swarm*. As with a P2P network, a member of a swarm uploads to other clients the sections of the BitTorrent file it has already downloaded. There is nothing special about a seed: It can be removed at any time after the torrent is available for download from other seeds.

The torrent  The first step in downloading a BitTorrent file is to locate or acquire the *torrent*, a file with the filename extension of **.torrent**. A torrent contains pertinent information (metadata) about the BitTorrent file to be downloaded, such as its size and the location of the tracker. You can obtain a torrent by accessing its URI, or you can acquire it via the Web, an email attachment, or other means. The BitTorrent client can then connect to the tracker to learn the locations of other members of the swarm it can download the BitTorrent file from.

Manners  After you have downloaded a BitTorrent file (the local system has become a seed), it is good manners to allow the local BitTorrent client to continue to run so peers (clients that have not downloaded the entire BitTorrent file) can upload *at least* as much information as you have downloaded.

## PREREQUISITES

Use yum (page 534) to install the **transmission-cli** package. Put the following lines in the **/etc/sysctl.conf** file and reboot the system. Without these lines transmission-cli will work more slowly and display messages suggesting you add the lines to **sysctl.conf**.

```
$ cat /etc/sysctl.conf
net.core.rmem_max = 4194304
net.core.wmem_max = 1048576
```

## transmission-cli: DOWNLOADING A BITTORRENT FILE

The following example shows transmission-cli (www.transmissionbt.com) downloading a Fedora DVD ISO image. (Visit torrent.fedoraproject.org for a list of Fedora torrents you can download.) Depending on the speed of the Internet connection and the number of seeds, downloading a large BitTorrent file can take from hours to days. A torrent can download one or more files; the torrent specifies the filename(s) for the downloaded file(s) and, in the case of a multifile torrent, a directory to hold the files. The torrent in the example saves the BitTorrent files in the **Fedora-19-x86_64-DVD** directory in the working directory.

With a torrent in the working directory, enter a command such as the following, substituting the name of the torrent you want to use for the Fedora torrent:

```
$ transmission-cli Fedora-19-x86_64-DVD.torrent
[15:20:29.914] Transmission 2.77 (14031) started
[15:20:29.915] RPC Server: Adding address to whitelist: 127.0.0.1
[15:20:29.916] DHT: Generating new id
[15:20:30.021] Saved "/home/sam/.config/transmission/torrents/Fedora-19-x86_64-
DVD.687077ec95f03111.torrent"
[15:20:30.021] Fedora-19-x86_64-DVD: Queued for verification
[15:20:30.022] Fedora-19-x86_64-DVD: Verifying torrent
[15:20:30.248] Port Forwarding (NAT-PMP): initnatpmp succeeded (0)
[15:20:30.248] Port Forwarding (NAT-PMP): sendpublicaddressrequest succeeded (2) Progress: 0.0%, dl
from 0 of 0 peers (0 kB/s), ul to 0 (0 kB/s) [None]
[15:20:38.258] Port Forwarding: State changed from "Not forwarded" to "Starting"
Progress: 0.0%, dl from 0 of 14 peers (0 kB/s), ul to 0 (0 kB/s) [None]
[15:20:49.001] Fedora-19-x86_64-DVD: Starting IPv4 DHT announce (poor, 9 nodes)
Progress: 1.1%, dl from 27 of 36 peers (2.45 MB/s), ul to 1 (123 kB/s) [0.03]
[15:21:23.157] DHT: Attempting bootstrap from dht.transmissionbt.com
[15:22:38.250] Port Forwarding: State changed from "Starting" to "???"
Progress: 14.1%, dl from 28 of 35 peers (2.10 MB/s), ul to 2 (40 kB/s) [0.02]
```

The transmission-cli utility displays messages about what it is doing. The lines that begin with **Progress** show how much of the BitTorrent file transmission-cli has downloaded, the number of peers and the total download speed, and the number of clients it is uploading to and that speed.

You can abort the download by pressing CONTROL-C. The download will automatically resume from where it left off when you download the same torrent to the same location again.

### Make sure you have enough room to download the torrent

caution   Some torrents are huge. Make sure the partition you are working in has enough room to hold the BitTorrent file you are downloading.

See the transmission-cli man page for a list of options. One of the most useful options is **–u** (**––uplimit**), which limits how much bandwidth in kilobytes per second the swarm can use while downloading the torrent *from the local system* (upstream bandwidth). Use **–U** (**––no-uplimit**) to place no limit on the bandwidth the swarm can use. The following command prevents BitTorrent from using more than 100 kilobytes per second of upstream bandwidth:

```
$ transmission-cli -u 100 Fedora-xxxx.torrent
```

BitTorrent usually allows higher download rates for members of the swarm that upload more data, so it is to your advantage to increase this value if you have spare bandwidth. You need to leave enough free upstream bandwidth for the acknowledgment packets from your download to get through or the download will be very slow.

The name of the file or directory BitTorrent saves a file or files in is specified by the torrent. You can specify a different file or directory name by using the **––save_as** option. The transmission-show utility displays the name the BitTorrent file will be saved as, the size of the file, the name of the torrent (**metainfo file**), and other information:

```
$ transmission-show Fedora-19-x86_64-DVD.torrent
Name: Fedora-19-x86_64-DVD
File: Fedora-19-x86_64-DVD.torrent

GENERAL

  Name: Fedora-19-x86_64-DVD
  Hash: 687077ec95f03111a0f7326e42ba518bb7161c29
  Created by:
  Created on: Mon May 27 20:08:14 2013
  Piece Count: 17113
  Piece Size: 256.0 KiB
  Total Size: 4.49 GB
  Privacy: Public torrent

TRACKERS

  Tier #1
  http://torrent.fedoraproject.org:6969/announce

FILES

  Fedora-19-x86_64-DVD/Fedora-19-x86_64-CHECKSUM (1.14 kB)
  Fedora-19-x86_64-DVD/Fedora-19-x86_64-DVD.iso (4.49 GB)
```

# *LPI*　RPM: The RPM Package Manager

RPM (RPM Package Manager; www.rpm.org) works only with software packages built for processing by RPM; it can download, install, uninstall, upgrade, query, and verify RPM packages. The files that hold these packages have a filename extension of **.rpm**. RPM uses the local RPM installation database to track the locations where software packages are installed, the versions of the installed packages, and the dependencies between the packages. RPM uses the Berkeley Database (Berkeley DB or BDB) and stores the database files in **/var/lib/rpm**. RPM forms the basis for yum: yum finds packages, downloads them from repositories, and then calls RPM to install/upgrade/remove the packages.

Source RPM packages are frequently found in a directory named **SRPMS** (source RPMs), whereas binary RPM packages usually reside in **Packages**. When you download binary packages, make sure they are relevant to the local operating system (both distribution and release—for example, Fedora 15).[1] They should also be compiled for the appropriate processor architecture:

Processor
architectures

- **i386** covers all Intel- and most AMD-based systems; the N and Z Series Atom processors are also based on this architecture.

- **i586** covers Pentium-class or higher processors.

---

1. Many RPM packages run on releases and even distributions other than the ones they were compiled for. However, installing packages intended for other distributions can create problems.

- **i686** refers to Pentium II or better and includes MMX extensions.

- **S390x** is for IBM System/390.

- **ia64** is for the Intel 64-bit Itanium (not compatible with x86_64)

- **alpha** is for the DEC/Compaq Alpha chip.

- **ppc** and **ppc64** denotes the Power PC 32- and 64-bit processors.

- **x86_64** is for Intel and AMD 64-bit processors (not Itanium); the 230 and 330 Series Atom processors are also based on this architecture.

- **sparc** covers the Sun Sparc processor.

**noarch** The name of the rpm file contains almost all the necessary information. Packages marked **noarch** ("no architecture") contain resources, such as images or scripts, that are run by an interpreter. You can install and run **noarch** packages on any architecture.

**yumdownloader** See page 540 for instructions on using yumdownloader to download RPM package files.

## *LPI* QUERYING PACKAGES AND FILES

The following rpm command displays a list of one-line summaries of all packages installed on the system:

```
$ rpm -qa
samba-common-4.0.9-1.fc19.x86_64
mythes-1.2.3-4.fc19.x86_64
gnome-themes-standard-3.8.4-1.fc19.x86_64
xorg-x11-drv-openchrome-0.3.3-1.fc19.x86_64
caribou-0.4.11-1.fc19.x86_64
gnome-shell-3.8.4-2.fc19.x86_64
gstreamer-plugins-good-0.10.31-9.fc19.x86_64
libnl-1.1-17.fc19.x86_64
gnome-shell-extension-window-list-3.8.4-1.fc19.noarch
...
```

The **–q** option queries the package database; the **–a** option specifies all packages. Without **–a**, **–q** takes the name of a package as an argument and displays information about that package only. For instance, **rpm –q ypserv** tells you whether the **ypserv** package is installed and, if so, which version is installed. Use the **–ql** options to list the files in a package.

```
$ rpm -q ypserv
package ypserv is not installed

$ rpm -ql logrotate
/etc/cron.daily/logrotate
/etc/logrotate.conf
/etc/logrotate.d
/usr/sbin/logrotate
/usr/share/doc/logrotate-3.8.4
/usr/share/doc/logrotate-3.8.4/CHANGES
/usr/share/doc/logrotate-3.8.4/COPYING
/usr/share/man/man5/logrotate.conf.5.gz
/usr/share/man/man8/logrotate.8.gz
/var/lib/logrotate.status
```

With the **–qi** options, rpm displays information about a package:

```
$ rpm -qi logrotate
Name         : logrotate
Version      : 3.8.4
Release      : 1.fc19
Architecture: x86_64
Install Date: Tue 04 Jun 2013 07:29:46 PM PDT
Group        : System Environment/Base
Size         : 97523
License      : GPL+
Signature    : RSA/SHA256, Tue 30 Apr 2013 08:32:12 AM PDT, Key ID 07477e65fb4b18e6
Source RPM   : logrotate-3.8.4-1.fc19.src.rpm
Build Date   : Tue 30 Apr 2013 02:16:03 AM PDT
Build Host   : buildvm-07.phx2.fedoraproject.org
Relocations  : (not relocatable)
Packager     : Fedora Project
Vendor       : Fedora Project
URL          : https://fedorahosted.org/logrotate/
Summary      : Rotates, compresses, removes and mails system log files
Description :
The logrotate utility is designed to simplify the administration of
log files on a system which generates a lot of log files.  Logrotate
allows for the automatic rotation compression, removal and mailing of
log files.  Logrotate can be set to handle a log file daily, weekly,
monthly or when the log file gets to a certain size.  Normally,
logrotate runs as a daily cron job.

Install the logrotate package if you need a utility to deal with the
log files on your system.
```

You can use the **–qf** options to determine which package a file belongs to; it works with installed packages only. Use the yum **whatprovides** command (page 537) to search repositories for the same information. The following command shows that more is part of the **util-linux** package:

```
$ rpm -qf /bin/more
util-linux-2.23.1-2.fc19.x86_64
```

Include the **–p** option with other options to query an uninstalled RPM package file:

```
$ $ ls ypser**
ypserv-2.31-2.fc19.x86_64.rpm

$ rpm -qip ypserv-2.31-2.fc19.x86_64.rpm
Name         : ypserv
Version      : 2.31
Release      : 2.fc19
...
```

## LPI  INSTALLING, UPGRADING, AND REMOVING PACKAGES

Although it is frequently easier to use yum or gpk-application, you can use rpm to download, install, upgrade, or remove a package. Run rpm with **root** privileges; although you can run rpm as a nonprivileged user, you will not have permission to write to the necessary directories during an install or uninstall, and the procedure will fail. During a query, you do not need to work with **root** privileges, so you can and should work as a nonprivileged user. Give the **–U** (upgrade) option, followed by the name of the file that contains the RPM version of the package you want to install. The **–U** option upgrades existing packages and installs new packages (as though you had used the **–i** option). For kernels, use **–i** (not **–U**) to leave the old kernel intact when you install a new kernel. Add the **–v** (verbose) option to display more information about what is happening and the **–h** (or **––hash**) option to display hash marks as the package is unpacked and installed.

Installing a package · For example, the following command installs the **samba** package on the local system:

```
# ls samba**
samba-4.0.6-3.fc19.x86_64.rpm

# rpm -Uvh samba-4.0.6-3.fc19.x86_64.rpm
Preparing...                       ################################ [100%]
Updating / installing...
   1:samba-2:4.0.6-3.fc19          ################################ [100%]
```

When you install a package, the rpm file must be in the working directory, or you must use a pathname that points to the rpm file. If you specify an FTP or HTTP URL, rpm will download the package before installing it (but it will not download or install dependencies):

```
# rpm -Uvh http://dl.fedoraproject.org/pub/fedora/linux/updates/18/x86_64/bind-9.9.3-4.P2.fc18.x86_64.rpm
```

Removing a package · The following command removes the **samba** package. You can give the command from any directory:

```
# rpm -e samba
error: Failed dependencies:
        samba is needed by (installed) system-config-samba-1.2.100-1.fc19.noarch
```

When you run this command, rpm reports that another package, **system-config-samba**, is dependent on the **samba** package. To remove the **samba** package, you have two choices: You can ignore the dependency by including the rpm **––nodeps** option or you can remove the dependent package and then remove the **samba** package.

```
# rpm -e system-config-samba
# rpm -e samba
```

If you remove the samba package without removing the package that is dependent on it, the utilities within the dependent package will not work. In the preceding example, the system-config-samba utility will not work.

When you use rpm to remove a package, rpm queries the package database to find the information it needs to uninstall the package and removes links, unloads device drivers, and stops daemons as necessary. Refer to the rpm man page for more rpm options.

# INSTALLING A LINUX KERNEL BINARY

The following steps install a Linux kernel binary from an RPM package. If you simply want to install the latest kernel for the local system, give the command **yum install kernel** instead. Refer to Chapter 14 when you want to configure and rebuild a kernel from source files, rather than installing a new, prebuilt kernel binary.

1. Run rpm with the **–i** option to install the new kernel. Do not use the **–U** option: You are installing a new kernel that has a different name than the old kernel; you are not upgrading the existing kernel.

2. Make sure the new kernel works before you remove the old kernel. To verify the new kernel works, reboot the system using the new kernel. You might

want to wait a while before removing the old kernel to make sure that no problems arise with the new one.

3. When you are satisfied with the new kernel, remove the old kernel using rpm with the –e option; you must specify the kernel version number. If necessary, you can manually remove an old kernel by removing files whose names contain the release number from **/boot** or **/** (root). Remove information about the old kernel from **grub.conf** (page 590). Removing the kernel manually is not recommended because it is too easy to miss a file and because it does not remove the kernel from the RPM database.

# INSTALLING NON-rpm SOFTWARE

Most software that is not in RPM format comes with detailed instructions on how to configure, build (if necessary), and install it. Some binary distributions (those containing prebuilt executables that run on Fedora/RHEL) require you to unpack the software from the root directory (i.e., you must cd to **/** before unpacking it).

## THE /opt AND /usr/local DIRECTORIES

Some newer application packages include scripts that install themselves automatically into a directory hierarchy under **/opt**, with files in a **/opt** subdirectory that is named after the package and executables in **/opt/bin** or **/opt/*package*/bin**.

Other software packages allow you to choose where you unpack them. Because many different people develop software for Linux, there is no consistent method for installing it. As you acquire software, install it on the local system in as consistent and predictable a manner as possible. The standard Linux file structure has a directory hierarchy under **/usr/local** for binaries (**/usr/local/bin**), manual pages (**/usr/local/man**), and so forth. Because many GNU build tools search the **/usr/local** hierarchy by default and could find the wrong version of a utility if you install developer tools there, putting these tools in **/opt** is a good idea.

To prevent confusion later and to avoid overwriting or losing the software when you install standard software upgrades, avoid installing nonstandard software in standard system directories (such as **/usr/bin**). On a multiuser system, make sure users know where to find the local software and advise them whenever you install, change, or remove local tools.

## GNU CONFIGURE AND BUILD SYSTEM

The GNU Configure and Build System makes it easy to build a program that is distributed as source code (see www.gnu.org/software/autoconf). This process requires a shell, make (**make** package), and gcc (the GNU C compiler; **gcc** package). You do not need to work with **root** privileges except to install the program.

The following example assumes you have downloaded the GNU **which** program (ftp.gnu.org/pub/gnu/which; page 255) to the working directory. First unpack and decompress the file and **cd** to the new directory:

```
$ tar -xvzf which-2.20.tar.gz
which-2.20/
which-2.20/EXAMPLES
which-2.20/posixstat.h
...
which-2.20/configure.ac
which-2.20/COPYING

$ cd which-2.20
```

After reading the **README** and **INSTALL** files and installing the **gcc** package, run the **configure** script, which gathers information about the local system and generates the **Makefile** file:

```
$ ./configure
checking for a BSD-compatible install... /usr/bin/install -c
checking whether build environment is sane... yes
checking for a thread-safe mkdir -p... /bin/mkdir -p
checking for gawk... gawk
checking whether make sets $(MAKE)... yes
checking whether to enable maintainer-specific portions of Makefiles... no
...
config.status: creating Makefile
config.status: creating maintMakefile
config.status: creating tilde/Makefile
config.status: creating config.h
config.status: executing depfiles commands
```

Refer to the **configure** info page, specifically the **--prefix** option, which causes the install phase to place the software in a directory other than **/usr/local**. For package-specific options enter the command **configure --help**. Next, run make:

```
$ make
make  all-recursive
make[1]: Entering directory `/home/sam/which-2.20'
Making all in tilde
make[2]: Entering directory `/home/sam/which-2.20/tilde'
source='tilde.c' object='tilde.o' libtool=no \
        DEPDIR=.deps depmode=pch /bin/bash ../depcomp \
        gcc -DHAVE_CONFIG_H -I. -I..     -g -O2 -c tilde.c
source='shell.c' object='shell.o' libtool=no \
        DEPDIR=.deps depmode=pch /bin/bash ../depcomp \
        gcc -DHAVE_CONFIG_H -I. -I..     -g -O2 -c shell.c
rm -f libtilde.a
ar cru libtilde.a tilde.o shell.o
...
source='which.c' object='which.o' libtool=no \
        DEPDIR=.deps depmode=pch /bin/bash ./depcomp \
        gcc -DHAVE_CONFIG_H -I.      -g -O2 -c which.c
gcc  -g -O2    -o which getopt.o getopt1.o bash.o which.o ./tilde/libtilde.a
make[2]: Leaving directory `/home/sam/which-2.20'
make[1]: Leaving directory `/home/sam/which-2.20'

$ ls which
which
```

After make finishes, the which executable is in the working directory. Some packages place the executable in a subdirectory. If you want to install it, give the following command while running with **root** privileges. By default this command installs which in **/usr/local/bin** so it is known to be the local version of which.

```
$ su -c "make install"
Password:
make  install-recursive
make[1]: Entering directory `/home/sam/which-2.20'
Making install in tilde
make[2]: Entering directory `/home/sam/which-2.20/tilde'
make[3]: Entering directory `/home/sam/which-2.20/tilde'
...
```

You can complete the entire task with the following command line:

```
$ su -c "./configure && make && make install"
```

The Boolean AND operator (&&) allows the execution of a subsequent command only if the previous step returned a successful exit status.

# Keeping Software Up-to-Date

See page 533 for a discussion of why it is important to keep software up-to-date.

# Bugs

A *bug* is an unwanted and unintended program property, especially one that causes the program to malfunction (definition courtesy of foldoc.org). Bugs have been around forever, in many types of systems, machinery, thinking, and so on. All sophisticated software contains bugs. Bugs in system software or application packages can cause the system to crash or programs not to run correctly. Security holes (a type of bug) can compromise the security of the system, allowing malicious users to read and write files, send mail to your contacts in your name, or destroy all data on the system, rendering the system useless.

Even if the engineers fixed all the bugs, there would still be feature requests as long as anyone used the software. Bugs, feature requests, and security holes are here to stay. Thus they must be properly tracked if developers are to fix the most dangerous/important bugs first, users are to research and report bugs in a logical manner, and administrators are to apply the developers' fixes quickly and easily.

Bug tracking   Early on, Netscape used an internal bug-tracking system named BugSplat. Later, after Netscape created Mozilla (mozilla.org) as an open-source browser project, the Mozilla team decided that it needed its own bug-tracking system. Netscape's IS department wrote a very short-lived version of Bugzilla. Terry Weissman, who had been maintaining BugSplat, then wrote a new open-source version of Bugzilla in Tcl, rewriting it in Perl a couple of months later.

Bugzilla belongs to a class of programs formally known as *defect-tracking systems*, of which Bugzilla is preeminent. Almost all Linux developers use this tool to track problems and enhancement requests for their software. Fedora/RHEL uses Bugzilla to track bugs and bug fixes for its Linux distributions. To use Bugzilla, visit bugzilla.redhat.com.

## ERRATA

As the Linux community, including Red Hat and the Fedora Project, finds and fixes operating system and software package bugs, including security holes, Red Hat and the Fedora Project generate RPM files (page 546) that contain the code that fixes the problems. When you upgrade a system software package, rpm renames modified configuration files with a **.rpmsave** extension. You must manually merge the changes you made to the original files into the new files. The easiest way to learn about, obtain, and install updates is to use yum.

The Fedora Announce List (admin.fedoraproject.org/mailman/listinfo/announce) holds information about Fedora updates. Under Fedora/RHEL, **packagekitd** via gpk-update-icon notifies you when updates are available.

# curl: DOWNLOADS FILES NONINTERACTIVELY

The curl utility is a noninteractive, command-line utility that retrieves files from the Web using HTTP, HTTPS, or FTP. In the following example, curl downloads the Fedora Project home page, named **index.html**, to a file in the working directory with the same name.

```
$ curl http://fedoraproject.org/index.html > index.html
  % Total    % Received % Xferd  Average Speed   Time    Time     Time  Current
                                 Dload  Upload   Total   Spent    Left  Speed
100 23076  100 23076    0     0  71837      0 --:--:-- --:--:-- --:--:-- 72112
```

The curl ––**continue** (–**c**) option with an argument of – automatically continues an interrupted download. For example, if you decide to stop a download so you can run it in the background, you can continue it from where it left off with this option.

# CHAPTER SUMMARY

As a system administrator, you need to keep applications and system software current. Of the many reasons to keep the software on a system up-to-date, one of the most important is system security.

A PMS (package management system) is a set of utilities that allow you to install, upgrade, remove, and search software packages easily and in a consistent manner. It is based on a local database that holds information about each installed package, including its dependencies and version information. The development of the RPM PMS has made the process of adding and removing the software packages quite easy. You can use yum, a front end to RPM, to install and upgrade software packages. The yum utility is installed by default and is easy to configure and use.

In addition, you can use the rpm utility to install, uninstall, upgrade, query, and verify RPM packages. For packages distributed as source code, the GNU Configure and Build System makes it easy to build executable files.

BitTorrent is a handy tool for downloading large static data files such as the Fedora installation ISO images. BitTorrent can replace protocols such as anonymous FTP, where client authentication is not required.

# EXERCISES

1. Which command installs the **samba** package? Which installs the **Web Server** package group?

2. Which command would you give to update all installed packages using yum?

3. Why would you build a package from its source code when a (binary) rpm file is available?

4. Suggest two advantages that rpm files have over source distributions.

# ADVANCED EXERCISES

5. When you compile a package yourself, rather than from an rpm file, which directory hierarchy should you put it in?

6. What are some steps you should take before performing an upgrade on a mission-critical server? When should you use **rpm –i** instead of **rpm –U**?

# 13

# PRINTING WITH CUPS

## OBJECTIVES

After reading this chapter you should be able to:

▸ Explain the purpose of a printing subsystem

▸ Describe the capabilities of CUPS

▸ Define IPP and explain its role with CUPS

▸ Use system-config-printer to install and manage local and remote printers

▸ Use the CUPS Web interface to install and manage local and remote printers

▸ Share local printers

▸ Print from a Windows system to a Linux printer

▸ Print from a Linux system to a Windows printer

▸ Use command-line tools to submit, list, and cancel print jobs

▸ Limit printing using quotas

A *printing system* handles the tasks involved in getting a print job from an application (or the command line) through the appropriate *filters* (page 1250) and into a queue for a suitable printer and then getting it printed. When a printer fails, the printing system can redirect jobs to other, similar printers.

# INTRODUCTION

LPD and LPR   Originally, UNIX had two printing systems: the BSD LPD (Line Printer Daemon) and the System V LPR (Line Printer system). Linux adopted these systems at first, and both UNIX and Linux have seen modifications to and replacements for these systems. Today CUPS is the default printing system under Linux.

CUPS   CUPS (Common UNIX Printing System) is a cross-platform print server built around IPP (next). CUPS provides many printer drivers and can print different types of files, including PostScript. Because it is built on IPP and written to be portable, CUPS runs under many operating systems, including Linux and Windows. Other UNIX variants, including Mac OS X, use CUPS; recent versions of Windows include the ability to print to IPP printers. Thus CUPS is an ideal solution for printing in a heterogeneous environment. CUPS provides System V and BSD command-line interfaces and, in addition to IPP, supports LPD/LPR, HTTP, SMB, and JetDirect (socket) protocols, among others.

If the printer you are configuring is on an older Linux system or another UNIX-like operating system that does not run CUPS, the system probably runs LPD/LPR. Most devices that connect printers directly to a network support LPR/LPD; some support IPP.

IPP   The IPP project (Internet Printing Protocol; www.pwg.org/ipp) began in 1996, when Novell and several other companies designed a protocol for printing over the Internet. IPP enables users to

- Determine the capabilities of a printer.
- Submit jobs to a printer.
- Determine the status of a printer.
- Determine the status of a print job.
- Cancel a print job.

IPP is an HTTP-based client/server protocol in which the server side can be a print server or a network-capable stand-alone printer.

Network printers   Printers connected directly to a network are functionally equivalent to printers connected to a system running a print server: They listen on the same ports as systems running print servers, and they queue jobs.

Printers and queues   On a modern computing system, when you "send a job to the printer," you add the job to the list of jobs waiting their turn to be printed on a printer. This list is called a *print queue* or simply a *queue*. The phrase *configuring* (or *setting up*) *a printer* is often used to mean *configuring a (print) queue*. This chapter uses these phrases interchangeably.

Configuration tools   This chapter explores two tools you can use to configure a print queue: system-config-printer (page 558) and the CUPS Web interface (page 565), with an emphasis on the former.

Using the CUPS Web interface is very similar to using system-config-printer; thus much of the discussion of system-config-printer applies to the CUPS Web interface. However, system-config-printer is a native application written in Python, not a Web interface.

# PREREQUISITES

Make sure the following packages are installed (most are installed with the base Fedora/RHEL system):

- **cups**
- **system-config-printer** (optional)
- **cups-pdf** (optional; sets up a virtual PDF printer)

The CUPS Web interface requires an X server and a Web browser. Although it is a poor solution, a text Web browser such as elinks (**elinks** package) will work, too.

Enable and start **cups**  Run systemctl to cause the **cups** service (**cupsd** daemon) to start each time the system enters multiuser mode and then start the **cups** service. Use the systemctl **status** command to make sure the service is running.

```
# systemctl enable cups.service
# systemctl start cups.service
```

After modifying **cups** configuration files, give the second command again, replacing **start** with **restart** to cause **cups** to reread those files.

# MORE INFORMATION

Local  CUPS Documentation: With the CUPS Web interface up (page 567), point a local browser at localhost:631/help

Web  Information on printers and printing under Linux, including forums and articles: www.linuxfoundation.org/collaborate/workgroups/openprinting
A support database with details about many printers, including notes and driver information: www.openprinting.org/printers
CUPS home page: www.cups.org
IPP information: www.pwg.org/ipp

HOWTO  The *SMB HOWTO* has a section titled "Sharing a Windows Printer with Linux Machines."

# NOTES

SELinux  When SELinux is set to use a targeted policy, CUPS is protected by SELinux. You can disable this protection if necessary. For more information refer to "Setting the Targeted Policy using system-config-selinux" on page 475.

Firewall  A CUPS server normally uses TCP port 631 and UDP port 631 for an IPP connection and TCP port 80 for an LPR/LPD connection. If the server accepts print jobs from remote systems and is running a firewall or is behind a firewall, you need to open one or both of these ports. Give the following commands to open the ports each time the

**Figure 13-1**   The Print Settings window

system boots (permanently) and on the running system; see page 906 for information on firewall-cmd.

```
# firewall-cmd --add-port=631/tcp
# firewall-cmd --permanent --add-port=631/tcp
# firewall-cmd --add-port=631/udp
# firewall-cmd --permanent --add-port=631/udp
# firewall-cmd --add-port=80/tcp
# firewall-cmd --permanent --add-port=80/tcp
```

PDF printer  You can set up a virtual PDF printer by installing the **cups-pdf** package, or you can set up this printer manually.

# LPI  THE SYSTEM CONFIGURES A LOCAL PRINTER AUTOMATICALLY

In most cases, when you connect a printer to the local system and turn it on, the system displays a message as it install drivers. When the drivers are installed, the printer is ready for use. Two graphical tools allow you to add and modify printers as well as work with print jobs. You can use Printers from the Settings window (page 107) for most work with printers and system-config-printer (next) for more complex printer-related tasks. Use one of these tools to verify that the printer is installed, send a test page to the printer, and change the configuration of the printer.

# LPI  JUMPSTART I: CONFIGURING A PRINTER USING system-config-printer

The Print Settings window (Figure 13-1) enables you to add, remove, and configure local and remote printers. Open this window by giving the command **system-config-printer** from an Enter a Command window (ALT-F2) or a terminal emulator. This JumpStart

**Figure 13-2**    The Printer Properties window

explains how to modify the configuration of an existing printer. See page 560 for instructions on how to set up a new printer.

Default printer    Highlight a printer in the Print Settings window and select **menubar: Printer⇨Set as Default** from the window menu to specify the highlighted printer as the default printer. If just one printer appears in the Print Settings window, it is the default printer; you do not have to set it up as such. The tick on the printer in Figure 13-1 indicates the default printer.

Server Settings    Select **menubar: Server⇨Settings** from the Print Settings window to display the Server Settings window. The top two check boxes in this window specify whether the local system publishes printers it shares (so remote systems can find the printers) and whether it allows printing from the Internet. If you elect to share printers, system-config-printer asks whether you want to adjust the firewall to allow incoming IPP connections. When you click **Adjust Firewall**, system-config-printer opens TCP port 631 and UDP port 631. You control whether a specific printer is shared from the Policies selection of the Printer Properties window (next).

## CONFIGURATION TABS

Double-click a printer in the Print Settings window or highlight a printer and select **menubar: Printer⇨Properties** to display the Printer Properties window (Figure 13-2) for that printer.

This section describes the six tabs found in the frame at the left side of the Printer Properties window. These tabs allow you to configure the printer you chose in the Print Settings window.

Settings    Figure 13-2 shows the Settings tab for a Brother printer. The text boxes labeled **Description** and **Location** hold information that can help users identify the printer. The system does not use this information; change it as you like. For example, it might be helpful to put the physical location of the printer, such as **Sam's Office**, in the text box labeled **Location**. The text boxes labeled **Device URI** and **Make and Model** specify the location of the printer on the computer or network and type of the printer.

Policies  The Policies tab enables you to control printer state, sharing, and banners. Under the word **State** are check boxes labeled **Enabled, Accepting jobs,** and **Shared.** Table 13-1 describes the effects of putting ticks in the first two check boxes. Putting a tick in the check box labeled **Shared** shares the printer with other systems if the local system publishes shared printers (see "Server Settings"). The Policies tab also controls whether the printer prints banners before and after jobs and what CUPS does when the printer reports an error.

**Table 13-1**   Printer status

|  | Enabled | Disabled |
|---|---|---|
| **Accepting jobs** | Accepts new jobs into the queue. | Accepts new jobs into the queue. |
|  | Prints jobs from the queue. | Does not print jobs from the queue until the printer is enabled. |
| **Rejecting jobs** | Rejects new jobs. | Rejects new jobs. |
|  | Prints jobs from the queue. | Does not print jobs from the queue until the printer is enabled. |

Access Control  The Access Control tab enables you to set the policy for printer access. By default, anyone can use the printer. To restrict access, you can create a blacklist of users who *are not* allowed to use it. Alternately, you can prohibit anyone from using the printer and then create a whitelist of users who *are* allowed to use it.

Printer Options  The Printer Options tab controls image quality, paper size and source (tray), and other generic printer options.

Job Options  The Job Options tab controls the number of copies, orientation (portrait or landscape), scaling, margins, and more. Options specified by an application sending a job to the printer override options you set in this tab. Scroll down to see all options.

Ink/Toner Levels  The Ink/Toner Levels tab reports on ink/toner (marker) levels and displays status messages.

# *LPI*  JumpStart II: Setting Up a Local or Remote Printer

This section describes how to set up three types of printers for local use: a printer attached to the local system, a printer hosted by another system, and a printer that resides on the local network (a network printer). For instructions on how to use the CUPS Web interface to perform the same tasks, see page 565.

To add a printer to the local system, click **Add** on the toolbar in the Print Settings window (Figure 13-1, page 558). The system-config-printer utility looks for printers

**Figure 13-3**   The New Printer window, Select Device screen I

attached to the system or the local network. It then asks whether you want to adjust the firewall so the local system can detect printers on the network and, when you click **Adjust Firewall**, displays the Select Device screen of the New Printer window (Figure 13-3).

To configure a printer, highlight the printer in the frame labeled **Select Device**. The system-config-printer utility displays a description of the printer you highlighted. Click the triangle to the left of Network Printer to display network printers.

### Avoid repeated requests for authentication

tip    When you run system-config-printer as a nonprivileged user it repeatedly asks you to authenticate yourself. To avoid that annoyance, run system-config-printer from a terminal emulator command line while working with **root** privileges by using the following command. You will need to supply the **root** password one time.

```
$ su -c system-config-printer
```

Specifying a URI    The easiest way to locate a remote printer that is not listed is to select **Find Network Printer** under **Network Printer** in the frame labeled **Select Device**. Then enter in the text box labeled **Host** the name of the host the printer is attached to (the server) or, for a network printer, the name of the printer. You can specify an IP address instead of a hostname. Click **Find**. If it finds a printer, system-config-printer displays the name of the printer under **Network Printer** and a description of the printer on the right side

**Figure 13-4** The New Printer window, Select Device screen II

of the window (Figure 13-4). For IPP printers, system-config-printer displays a *URI* (page 1279), which is the printer's location on the network; see page 568 for more information. The system-config-printer utility might offer you a choice of connection types; a CUPS printer is a better choice.

If the printer is not listed, select one of the first few entries (for a local printer) or one of the selections under Network Printer (for a remote printer) from the frame labeled **Select Device**; system-config-printer displays appropriate text boxes on the right side of the window. All selections under Network Printer require you to specify a host and a queue or port number to locate the printer on the network.

To specify the queue for an LPD/LPR printer, use the form *printer-name*; for an IPP printer, use the form **ipp://***hostname***/printers/***printer-name*; for an HP JetDirect–compatible network printer, specify the *printer-name* and Port number. Replace *hostname* with the name of the host the printer is attached to (the server) and *printer-name* with the name of the printer on the server.

If you are unsure of the name of a printer, give the command **lpstat –p** on the server to display the names of all printers on that system. After selecting or specifying a printer, click the button labeled **Verify** (if present) to make sure the printer is accessible and then click **Forward**. The system-config-printer utility searches for the printer driver.

Next the utility might ask you which printer options you want to install. Specify the options and click **Forward**.

If system-config-printer displays the Choose Driver screen of the New Printer window (there are two Choose Driver screens, the first is shown in Figure 13-5), you can specify a printer make (a manufacturer such as Brother). Typically system-config-printer selects the make automatically. Alternately, you can specify a PPD file (page 568) or search for a driver to download. Click **Forward**.

**Figure 13-5**   Selecting a printer make/manufacturer

The next screen (the second Choose Driver screen; Figure 13-6), which system-config-printer might not display, allows you to specify the model of the printer and select which driver you want to use (if more than one is available). A selection is usually highlighted automatically.

**Figure 13-6**   Selecting a printer model and driver

**Figure 13-7** Specifying the name of the printer

The system-config-printer utility might display a screen showing installable (printer-specific) options. Generally you do not need to make changes to this screen. Click **Forward**.

### If a printer is not listed...

tip    If the printer you are configuring is not listed, you can select **Generic** (at the top of the list in the first Choose Driver screen) as the make of the printer and choose a type of generic printer from the list box labeled **Models** in the second Choose Driver screen. Choose **PostScript** from the list of drivers if the printer is PostScript-capable. Alternately, you can specify a PostScript printer such as the Apple Laser-Writer 12/640ps. (Select Apple from the first Choose Driver screen and 12/640ps from the second Choose Driver screen.) In both cases, select a PostScript driver from the list box labeled **Drivers**.

If the printer is not PostScript-capable, check whether the printer supports PCL; if it does, select another, similar PCL printer. If it does not support PCL, select **Generic** (at the top of the list in the first Choose Driver screen) and then choose **text-only** from the second Choose Driver screen; you will not be able to print graphics, but you should be able to print text.

Or you can check whether the printer can emulate another printer (i.e., if it has an *emulation mode*). If it can, check whether the manufacturer and model of the printer it can emulate are listed and set it up that way.

If all else fails, determine which listed printer is most similar to the one you are configuring and specify that printer. You can also try configuring the printer using the CUPS Web interface (page 565), which offers a different choice of models.

On the next screen (Describe Printer; Figure 13-7), you must specify a name for the printer; specifying the description and location is optional. The name of the printer must start with a letter and cannot contain SPACEs. If you use only one printer, the name you choose is not important. If you use two or more printers, the name should

**Figure 13-8**  The CUPS Home page

help users distinguish between them. CUPS uses the printer name as the name of the print queue on the local system. Click **Apply**.

At this point, the system-config-printer utility closes the New Printer window, asks whether you want to print a test page, and displays the new printer in the Print Settings window. If you have more than one print queue and want to set up the new print queue to be the default, highlight the printer and select **menubar: Printer⇨Set As Default**. You then have the option of setting the printer as the system-wide default or your personal default printer.

LPI # Working with the CUPS Web Interface

The CUPS Web interface allows you to do the same things as system-config-printer (pages 558 and 560). Because the two interfaces are functionally similar, this section does not go into as much detail as the section on system-config-printer. This section describes how to configure/reconfigure for local use a printer attached to the local system, a printer hosted by another system, or a printer that resides on the local network (a network printer).

Username and password
At some point the CUPS Web interface asks for a username and password. Supply **root** and the **root** password.

Display the CUPS Web interface by pointing a Web browser at **localhost:631** on the system on which you are configuring the printer (Figure 13-8).

## Remote administration

security
When you provide a username and password to the CUPS Web interface, they are transmitted in cleartext over HTTP. The lack of encryption is a security issue when you are administrating printers over an unsecure network.

**Figure 13-9**   A CUPS printer page

Clicking the **Administration** tab at the top of the page displays the Administration page. On this page click **Add Printer** (under the word **Printers**) to display the first Add Printer page. This page is functionally equivalent to the Select Device screen of the New Printer window displayed by system-config-printer (Figure 13-3, page 561).

Clicking the Printers tab at the top of the page displays a page that lists the configured printers. Clicking the name of the printer in the column labeled **Queue Name** displays a page that allows you to work with that printer and queue (Figure 13-9).

On the Printer page, select **Print Test Page** from the **Maintenance** drop-down list to test the printer. If you want to make this printer the default printer, select **Set As Server Default** from the **Administration** drop-down list.

# _LPI_   CONFIGURING PRINTERS

You can use the CUPS Web interface, the CUPS command-line interface, or the system-config-printer utility to manage printers and queues.

## MODIFYING A PRINTER

"JumpStart II: Setting Up a Local or Remote Printer" (page 560) explains how to configure a printer using system-config-printer. "Working with the CUPS Web Interface" (page 565) discusses how to configure a printer using the CUPS Web interface.

This section explains how to use either of these tools to modify a printer that is already configured. In both cases, modifying a printer takes you through the same steps as setting up a printer, except the fields are filled in so you only need to modify the ones that need to be changed.

Using system-config-printer   Open the Print Settings window, select the printer whose configuration you want to modify, and proceed as explained on page 558. Reconfiguring an existing printer follows the same steps as installing a new printer.

Using the CUPS Web interface   Open the CUPS Web interface as explained on page 565. To modify a printer, click the Printers tab at the top of the page and then click the name of the printer you want to modify. The CUPS Web interface displays two drop-down lists near the top of the page: **Administration** and **Maintenance** (Figure 13-9). These lists allow you to work with the selected printer. The **Administration** drop-down list allows you to modify the printer; this selection takes you through the same steps as when you set up a new printer. From this list you can also delete and set default options for the printer as well as set the printer as the default printer and specify which users are allowed to use the printer. From the **Maintenance** drop-down list, you can print a test page and pause the printer. You can also reject, move, and cancel all jobs. In addition to these tasks, you might be able to reprint jobs.

# THE CUPS WEB INTERFACE

To connect to the CUPS Web interface (page 565), point a Web browser running on the local system at **localhost:631**. You must supply the username **root** and the **root** password to change a printer configuration using the CUPS Web interface.

This section describes two tasks: modifying jobs and setting up printer classes. You can also perform these tasks from the command line using lpadmin (page 569) or from system-config-printer (page 558) by selecting **menu bar: Printer⇨View Print Queue** or **menu bar: Printer⇨Create class**, respectively.

## JOBS

Click the Jobs tab near the top of the page to display the Jobs page, which lists jobs in the print queues. From this page you can cancel print jobs and move them to other queues. Click **Show Completed Jobs** to display a list of recently completed jobs. In some cases, you can reprint completed jobs from this page. You can perform the same tasks from the Printer page.

## CLASSES

CUPS allows you to organize similar printers into a group called a *class*. To clients, a class of printers appears as a single printer. For each class, you must specify a name; optionally, you can specify a location and description. A printer can belong to more than one class. CUPS prints jobs sent to a class on the first available printer in the class. For example, you might be able to divide your print jobs into black-and-white jobs and color jobs. If more than one printer can fulfill each of these roles, you can allow users to select a printer manually, or you can define two printer classes (black-and-white and color) and have users send their jobs to a certain class of printers. Place printers that are members of the same class physically close to each other so users can easily find their output.

### Plan for the future

tip   If you expect to add printers to the network, you might want to configure classes containing the existing printers when you set up the network. You can then add printers later without having to change printer configurations on client systems.

To define a class, first click the Administration tab at the top of the page and then click **Add Class**. At a minimum, you must enter a name for the class. You might also enter a description and location. The **Members** list displays the names of all CUPS printers and classes. Highlight the printers you want to be members of the class you are defining; hold SHIFT and click another printer to highlight more than one printer. To define a class that includes printers that are not adjacent in the list, define the class to have a single printer and then modify the class after you create it to add other printers. To modify existing classes, click **Manage Classes** in the Administration tab.

# CUPS ON THE COMMAND LINE

In addition to using system-config-printer and the CUPS Web interface, you can control CUPS and manage print queues from the command line. This section describes the utilities that enable you to manage printers and print queues and establish printing quotas.

## lpinfo: DISPLAYS AVAILABLE DRIVERS

PPD files   The lpinfo utility provides information about the printer drivers and interfaces available to CUPS. The **–m** option displays the list of available PostScript Printer Definition (PPD) files/drivers.

```
$ lpinfo -m | head
foomatic:Alps-MD-1000-md2k.ppd Alps MD-1000 Foomatic/md2k
foomatic:Alps-MD-1000-ppmtomd.ppd Alps MD-1000 Foomatic/ppmtomd
foomatic:Alps-MD-1300-md1xMono.ppd Alps MD-1300 Foomatic/md1xMono
foomatic:Alps-MD-1300-md2k.ppd Alps MD-1300 Foomatic/md2k
foomatic:Alps-MD-1300-ppmtomd.ppd Alps MD-1300 Foomatic/ppmtomd
foomatic:Alps-MD-1500-md1xMono.ppd Alps MD-1500 Foomatic/md1xMono
foomatic:Alps-MD-1500-md2k.ppd Alps MD-1500 Foomatic/md2k
foomatic:Alps-MD-1500-ppmtomd.ppd Alps MD-1500 Foomatic/ppmtomd
foomatic:Alps-MD-2000-md2k.ppd Alps MD-2000 Foomatic/md2k
foomatic:Alps-MD-2000-ppmtomd.ppd Alps MD-2000 Foomatic/ppmtomd
```

URIs   CUPS uses URIs (page 561) to identify printer ports by type and location, just as a browser identifies documents by protocol and location. A parallel port has a URI with the format **parallel:/dev/lp0**; a remote LPD printer uses the format **lpd://192.168.0.101**, and a USB printer uses the format **usb://Brother/HL-2140%20series**. When run with **root** privileges, lpinfo with the **–v** option displays a list of available connections:

```
# lpinfo -v
network ipps
network ipp
network socket
network https
network http
network lpd
network beh
direct parallel:/dev/lp0
serial serial:/dev/ttyS0?baud=115200
serial serial:/dev/ttyS1?baud=115200
direct hp
network smb
direct hpfax
direct usb://Brother/HL-2140%20series?serial=L7J157453
```

The –v option to lpinfo does not display every possible network address for the socket, HTTP, IPP, LPD, and SMB protocols because there are more than 4 billion of these addresses in the IPv4 address space.

## lpadmin: CONFIGURES PRINTERS

You can use the lpadmin utility to add and remove printers from the system, modify printer configurations, and manage printer classes. This utility has three major options: –d (set the default printer), –x (remove a printer), and –p (add or modify a printer). The first two options are simple; examples follow the next subsection. Each of these three options takes the name of a printer as an argument. The name of the printer must start with a letter and cannot contain SPACES.

### ADDING OR MODIFYING A PRINTER

Add a printer or modify an existing printer by giving a command in the following format:

# *lpadmin –p printer-name options*

where *printer-name* is the name of the printer and *options* is a combination of options from the following list:

**–c** *class*  Adds the printer to the class *class*, creating the class if necessary.

**–D** *info*  The *info* is a string that describes the printer for the benefit of users; it has no meaning to the system. Enclose *info* within quotation marks if it contains SPACES.

**–E**  Enables the printer, instructing CUPS to accept jobs into its print queue.

**–L** *loc*  The *loc* is a string that indicates the physical location of the printer (e.g., office, building, floor). It has no meaning to the system. Enclose *loc* within quotation marks if it contains SPACES.

**–m** *model*  The *model* is the name of the PPD file (page 568) that describes the printer. Use **lpinfo –m** to display a list of installed PPD files. If you have a manufacturer-provided PPD file, copy it to **/usr/share/cups/model**. Use the –P option to specify the pathname of the file. Specifying **–m postscript.ppd.gz**, for example, is the same as specifying **–P /usr/share/cups/model/postscript.ppd.gz**.

**–P** *file*   The *file* is the absolute pathname of the PPD file (page 568) that describes the printer. Use **lpinfo –m** to display a list of installed PPD files. If you have a manufacturer-provided PPD file, copy it to **/usr/share/cups/model**. See **–m** for an alternate way to specify a PPD file.

**–r** *class*   Removes the printer from the class *class*. This option removes the class if, after removing the printer, the class would be empty.

**–v** *URI*   The *URI* is the device to which the printer is attached. Use **lpinfo –v** to list possible devices.

### LPI   EXAMPLE lpadmin COMMANDS

At a minimum, you need to provide a device and a model when you add a printer to the system. The following command adds a Brother HL-2140 printer to the system and enables it for use. This printer is connected locally to a USB port and is named **HL2140**.

```
# lpadmin -p HL2140 -E -v usb://Brother/HL-2140%20series -m Brother-HL-2140-hpijs-pcl5e.ppd
```

The printer information generated by the preceding command is stored in the **/etc/cups/printers.conf** file:

```
# cat /etc/cups/printers.conf
# Printer configuration file for CUPS v1.6.3
# Written by cupsd on 2013-07-30 20:07
# DO NOT EDIT THIS FILE WHEN CUPSD IS RUNNING
<DefaultPrinter HL-2140-series>
Info Brother HL-2140 series
Location guava
MakeModel Brother HL-2140 Foomatic/hpijs-pcl5e (recommended)
DeviceURI usb://Brother/HL-2140%20series
State Idle
StateTime 1302648023
Type 8433684
Product (HL-2140 series)
Filter application/vnd.cups-raw 0 -
Filter application/vnd.cups-postscript 100 foomatic-rip
Filter application/vnd.cups-pdf 0 foomatic-rip
Filter application/vnd.cups-command 0 commandtops
Accepting Yes
Shared Yes
JobSheets none none
QuotaPeriod 0
PageLimit 0
KLimit 0
OpPolicy default
ErrorPolicy stop-printer
</Printer>
```

The **lpadmin** command decompresses and copies the printer driver information from the **/usr/share/cups/model/stcolor.ppd.gz** file to **/etc/cups/ppd**. The resulting file is given the printer's name: **/etc/cups/ppd/HL-2140-series.ppd**.

You can modify a printer configuration with lpadmin using the same options that you used to add it. When you specify the name of an existing printer, lpadmin modifies the printer rather than creating a new one.

The next command configures an HP LaserJet–compatible printer with a JetDirect interface that is connected directly to the LAN at 192.168.1.103 and names this printer HPLJ. Specifying **socket** in the protocol part of the URI instructs CUPS to use the JetDirect protocol, a proprietary protocol developed by HP for printers connected directly to a network.

```
# lpadmin -p HPLJ -E -v socket://192.168.1.103 -m laserjet.ppd.gz
```

The lpstat utility with the **–d** option displays the name of the default printer:

```
# lpstat -d
system default destination: MainPrinter
```

CUPS automatically makes the first printer you define the default printer. The following command makes HPLJ the default printer:

```
#lpstat -d HPLJ
```

The following command removes the configuration for the HL2140 printer:

```
#lpstat -x HL2140
```

## PRINTING QUOTAS

CUPS provides rudimentary printing quotas. You can define two forms of quotas: page count and file size. File size quotas are almost meaningless because a small PostScript file can take a long time to interpret and can require a lot more ink to print than a large one. Page quotas are more useful, although their implementation is flawed. To determine the number of pages in a document, CUPS examines the PostScript input. If a job is submitted in the printer's native language, such as PCL, CUPS bypasses this accounting mechanism. Also, if mpage is used to create a PostScript file with multiple pages printed on each sheet, CUPS counts each page in the original document, rather than each sheet of paper it prints on.

Use **job-quota-period** and either **job-page-limit** or **job-k-limit** to establish a quota for each user on a given printer. The **job-quota-period** option specifies the number of seconds that the quota remains valid. The following command establishes a quota of 20 pages per day per user for the printer named HPLJ:

```
#lpadmin -p HPLJ -o job-quota-period=86400 -o job-page-limit=20
```

The **job-k-limit** option works similarly but defines a file size limit in kilobytes. The limit is the total number of kilobytes that each user can print during the quota period. After a user has exceeded her quota, she will not be allowed to print until the next quota period.

## LPI MANAGING PRINT QUEUES

When a printer is operating normally, it accepts jobs into its print queue and prints those jobs in the order in which they are received. You can give the command **cupsreject** followed by the name of a printer to cause a printer to not accept jobs into its print queue; enter the command **cupsaccept** to re-enable it. You can also use system-config-printer to control the print queue; refer to "Settings" on page 559. Two factors determine how a printer handles a job: if the printer is accepting jobs and if it is enabled. Table 13-1 on page 560 describes what happens with the various combinations of the two factors.

The utilities that change these factors are cupsdisable, cupsenable, cupsreject, and cupsaccept. Each utility takes the name of a printer as an argument. The following commands first disable and then enable the printer named HPLJ:

```
# cupsdisable HPLJ
# cupsenable HPLJ
```

The next commands cause HPLJ to reject and then accept jobs:

```
# cupsreject HPLJ
# cupsaccept HPLJ
```

# LPI SHARING CUPS PRINTERS

This section describes how to use textual tools to share local printers. Alternately, you can use system-config-printer (page 558) to share printers: Display the Server Settings window by selecting **menubar: Server⇨Settings** and put a tick in the check box labeled **Publish shared printers connected to this system.** Using this technique allows you to choose whether to share each printer.

IPP facilitates remote printing. The Listen directive in the CUPS configuration file, **/etc/cups/cupsd.conf**, specifies which IP address and port or which domain socket path CUPS binds to and accepts requests on. The Listen directive has the following format:

*Listen **IP:port** | path*

where **IP** is the IP address that CUPS accepts connections on, **port** is the port number that CUPS listens on for connections on **IP**, and **path** is the pathname of the domain socket CUPS uses to communicate with printers. CUPS typically uses port 631 and by default binds to **localhost**. Thus it accepts connections from the loopback service of the local system only. CUPS uses **/var/run/cups/cups.sock**, a local domain socket, to communicate with local printers. It can also use a Port directive to specify the port number it listens to for HTTP requests.

```
$ grep -i listen /etc/cups/cupsd.conf
# Only listen for connections from the local machine.
Listen localhost:631
Listen /var/run/cups/cups.sock
```

To allow other systems to connect to the CUPS server on the local system, you must instruct CUPS to bind to an IP address that the other systems can reach. First remove or comment out the **Listen localhost:631** directive; leave the other Listen directive in place:

```
# Listen localhost:631
Listen /var/run/cups/cups.sock
```

In place of the commented-out Listen directive, use an access control list to permit only selected machines to connect to local printers. An access control list is defined inside a <Location> container (see page 948 for the Apache equivalent). The following example allows only the system at IP address 192.168.1.101 and the local system to print to the specified printer.

```
<Location />
Order Allow,Deny
# Allow access from the local system and 192.168.1.101
Allow from localhost
Allow from 192.168.1.101
# Uncomment the following to permit access from all local interfaces
# Allow @LOCAL
</Location>
```

The **@LOCAL** macro is internal to CUPS and specifies the local system. This macro accepts communication from any address that resolves to the local system. Specify **Allow @LOCAL** to share the printer with all local interfaces.

When you change **cupsd.conf**, you must restart the **cupsd** daemon (page 557).

The **Order Allow,Deny** directive denies print requests by default and allows requests from specified addresses. An Order Deny,Allow directive would allow access by default and denies access only to clients specified in Deny from directives. You can use domain names, including wildcards, and IP ranges with either wildcards or netmasks in Allow from and Deny from directives. These directives work the same way they do in Apache. For more information refer to "Order" on page 961.

With the Order Deny,Allow directive, **Deny from** specifies the only IP addresses CUPS does not accept connections from. When you use the Order Allow,Deny directive, **Allow from** specifies the only IP addresses CUPS accepts connections from.

After you restart **cupsd**, remote systems can print on the local system's printers using the IP address and port number specified by the Listen directive. If the server is running a firewall, you need to allow remote systems to connect through it on port 631; see page 557. You might also need to modify the SELinux policy (page 475) depending on the system setup.

# TRADITIONAL UNIX PRINTING

*LPI*

Before the advent of GUIs and *WYSIWYG* (page 1281) word processors, UNIX users would create documents using an editor such as vi and a typesetting markup language such as TeX or nroff/troff, convert the resulting files to PostScript using an interpreter, and send the PostScript files to the printer using lpr (BSD) or lp (System V). Linux implements both BSD and System V command-line printing utilities for compatibility. However, these utilities are now wrappers around the equivalent functionality in

CUPS rather than core components of the printing system. The corresponding utilities are functionally equivalent; use whichever you prefer (Table 13-2).

**Table 13-2**   *LPI*   BSD and System V command-line print utilities

| BSD/SysV | Purpose |
|----------|---------|
| lpr/lp | Sends job(s) to the printer |
| lpq/lpstat | Displays the status of the print queue |
| lprm/cancel | Removes job(s) from the print queue |

From the command line, you can print a text, PostScript, or PDF file using lp:

```
$ lp memo.txt
request id is MainPrinter-25 (1 file(s))
```

The preceding command adds **memo.txt** to the print queue of the default printer and assigns it job number 25. When this printer is available, it prints the file. You can specify a printer using the **–d** option:

```
$ lp -d HL2140 graph.ps
request id is HL2140-26 (1 file(s))
```

The lpr **–P** option is equivalent to the lp **–d** option.

Without arguments, lp and lpr send their standard input to the printer:

```
$ cat memo2.txt | lp
request id is MainPrinter-27 (1 file(s))
```

The lpq and lpstat commands display information about the print queue:

```
$ lpstat
MainPrinter-25          zach                13312   Sun Feb 23 18:28:38 2014
HL2140-26               zach                75776   Sun Feb 23 18:28:48 2014
MainPrinter-27          zach                 8192   Sun Feb 23 18:28:57 2014
```

Use cancel or lprm to remove jobs from the print queue. By default, only the owner of a print job or a user working with **root** privileges can remove a job.

```
$ cancel 27
$ lpstat
MainPrinter-25          zach                13312   Sun Feb 23 18:28:38 2014
HL2140-26               zach                75776   Sun Feb 23 18:28:48 2014
```

While working with **root** privileges, give the command **cancel –a** or **lprm –** to remove all jobs from the print queues.

# PRINTING FROM WINDOWS

This section explains how to use printers on Linux CUPS servers from Windows machines. CUPS is easier to manage and can be made more secure than using Samba to print from Windows.

# PRINTING USING CUPS

Modern versions of Windows (2000 and later) support IPP and as a result can communicate directly with CUPS. To use this feature, you must have CUPS configured on the Linux print server to allow remote IPP printing; you also need to create a new printer on the Windows system that points to the IP address of the Linux print server.

First set up the **/etc/cups/cupsd.conf** file to allow network printing from a client, as explained in "Sharing CUPS Printers" on page 572. Setting up CUPS to allow printing from a Windows machine is exactly the same as setting it up to allow printing from a Linux client system. If necessary, open the firewall as explained on page 557.

Windows XP   From Windows XP, go to **Control Panel⇨Printers and Faxes** and click **Add Printer**. Click **Next** in the introductory window and select **A network printer or a printer attached to another computer**. Click **Next**. Select **Connect to a printer on the Internet or on a home or office network**. Continue following the next paragraph at "Enter URL."

Windows 7   From Windows 7, go to **Control Panel⇨Devices and Printers** and click **Add a printer**. Click **Add a network, wireless, or Bluetooth printer**. Assuming Windows does not find the printer, click **The printer that I want isn't listed**. Click the radio button labeled **Select a shared printer by name**.

Enter URL   Enter the following information in the text box (under Windows XP it is labeled **URL**):

*http://hostname:631/printers/printer-name*

where *hostname* is the name or IP address of the Linux CUPS server system and *printer-name* is the name of the printer on that system. For example, for the printer named **dog88** on the system named **dog** at IP address 192.168.0.12, you could enter **http://dog:631/printers/dog88** or **http://192.168.0.12:631/printers/dog88**. If you use a hostname, it must be defined in the **hosts** file on the Windows machine. Click **Next**. Windows requests that you specify the manufacturer and model of the printer or provide a driver for the printer. If you supply a printer driver, use the Windows version of the driver.

After Windows copies some files, the printer appears in the Printers and Faxes/Devices and Printers window. Under Windows 7 you need to click through two more screens. Right-click the printer and select **Set as Default Printer** to make it the default printer. You can specify comments, a location, and other attributes of the printer by right-clicking the printer and selecting **Properties** or **Printer Properties**.

# PRINTING USING SAMBA

This section assumes that Samba (page 827) is installed and working on the Linux system that controls the printer you want to use from Windows. Samba must be set up so that the Windows user who will be printing is mapped to a Linux user (including mapping the Windows **guest** user to the Linux user **nobody**). Make sure these users have Samba passwords. Refer to "Samba Users, User Maps, and Passwords" on page 829.

Windows supports printer sharing via SMB, which allows a printer to be shared transparently between Windows systems using the same mechanism as file sharing.

Samba allows Windows users to use printers connected to Linux systems just as they would use any other shared printers. Because all Linux printers traditionally appear to be PostScript printers, the Linux print server appears to share a PostScript printer. Windows does not include a generic PostScript printer driver. Instead, Windows users must select a printer driver for a PostScript printer. The Apple LaserWriter 12/640ps driver is a good choice.

When you use rpm to install Samba, it creates a directory named **/var/spool/samba** that is owned by the **root** account and that anyone can read from and write to. The sticky bit (page 1275) is set for this directory, allowing a Windows user who starts a print job as a Linux user to be able to delete that job, but denying users the ability to delete the print jobs of other users. Make sure this directory is in place and has the proper ownership and permissions:

```
$ ls -ld /var/spool/samba
drwxrwxrwt. 2 root root 4096 02-03 15:23 /var/spool/samba
```

Uncomment following two lines in the [**global**] section of the **/etc/samba/smb.conf** file.

```
[global]
...
printing = cups
printcap name = cups
```

The printer's share is listed in the [**printers**] section in **smb.conf**. In the following example, the **path** is the path Samba uses as a spool directory and is not a normal share path. The settings allow anyone, including **guest**, to use the printer. The [**printers**] section in the default **smb.conf** file has the following entries, which are appropriate for most setups:

```
[printers]
        comment = All Printers
        path = /var/spool/samba
        browseable = no
        guest ok = no
        writable = no
        printable = yes
```

Ideally each user who plans to print should have an account. Otherwise, when multiple users share the same account (e.g., the **nobody** account), they can delete one another's print jobs.

# PRINTING TO WINDOWS

CUPS views a printer on a Windows machine exactly the same way it views any other printer. The only difference is the URI you need to specify when connecting it. To configure a printer connected to a Windows machine, click the **Administration** tab in the CUPS Web interface and select **Add Printer**, just as you would for a local printer.

When you are asked to select the device, choose **Windows Printer via SAMBA**. Enter the URI of the printer in the following format:

    *smb://windows_system/printer_name*

where ***windows_system*** can be an IP address or a hostname. After you have added the printer, you can use it as you would any other printer.

Alternately, you can use system-config-printer (page 558) to set up a Windows printer. When you choose to install a Windows printer, you can specify a URL as described previously, or you can click **Browse**. By default, this setup prompts the user if authentication is required; you can choose **Set authentication details now** if you prefer.

# CHAPTER SUMMARY

A printing system such as CUPS sets up printers. It also moves print jobs from an application or the command line through the appropriate filters and into a queue for a suitable printer and then prints those jobs.

CUPS is a cross-platform print server built around IPP (Internet Printing Protocol). It handles setting up and sending jobs through print queues. The easiest way to configure printers is using Printers from the Settings window or the Print Settings window (system-config-printer). You can also configure CUPS using the Web interface, which you can access by pointing a Web browser at **localhost:631** on the system the printer is connected to. From the Web interface, you can configure print queues and modify print jobs in the queues.

You can use the traditional UNIX commands from a command line to send jobs to a printer (lpr/lp), display a print queue (lpq/lpstat), and remove jobs from a print queue (lprm/cancel). In addition, CUPS provides the lpinfo and lpadmin utilities, which allow you to configure printers from the command line.

CUPS and Samba enable you to print on a Linux printer from a Windows machine and vice versa.

# EXERCISES

1. Which commands can you use from the command line to send a file to the default printer?

2. Which command would you give to cancel all print jobs on the system?

3. Which commands list your outstanding print jobs?

4. What is the purpose of sharing a Linux printer using Samba?

5. Name three printing protocols that CUPS supports. Which is the CUPS native protocol?

# ADVANCED EXERCISES

6. Which command lists the installed printer drivers available to CUPS?

7. How would you send a text file to a printer connected to the first parallel port without using a print queue? Why is doing so a bad idea?

8. Assume you have a USB printer with a manufacturer-supplied PostScript printer definition file named **newprinter.ppd**. Which command would you use to add this printer to the system on the first USB port with the name USBPrinter?

9. How would you define a quota that allows each user to print up to 50 pages per week to the printer named LaserJet?

10. Define a set of access control rules for a <Location> container inside **/etc/cups/cupsd.conf** that would allow anyone to print to all printers as long as they were either on the local system or in the **mydomain.com** domain.

# 14

# BUILDING A LINUX KERNEL

## OBJECTIVES

After reading this chapter you should be able to:

▶ Download, install, and prep the kernel source code

▶ Choose kernel compile options

▶ Configure the system to use the newly compiled kernel

▶ Explain the purpose of the GRUB boot loader

▶ Modify the boot loader configuration

▶ Troubleshoot kernel messages using dmesg

After you have installed a system, you might want to reconfigure and build a new Linux kernel. Fedora/RHEL comes with a prebuilt kernel that simplifies the installation process. However, this kernel might not be properly configured for all system features. By configuring and building a new kernel, you can create one that is customized for a system and its unique needs. A customized kernel is typically smaller than a generic one. However, compiling and maintaining a custom kernel takes a lot of time and work.

Sometimes you do not need to build a new kernel. Instead, you can dynamically change many aspects of the installed kernel. Two ways to make these changes are by using boot command-line parameters (page 70) or by modifying **/etc/sysctl.conf**, which sysctl (next) reads when the system boots.

You can add the same parameters you use on the boot command line to **/boot/grub2/grub.cfg** or to its symbolic link, **/etc/grub2.cfg**. For example, **acpi=off** prevents **acpid** (the advanced configuration and power interface daemon) from starting. See page 70 for more information.

sysctl   The sysctl utility can modify kernel parameters while the system is running. This utility takes advantage of the facilities of **/proc/sys**, which defines the parameters that sysctl can modify.

The command **sysctl –a** displays a complete list of sysctl parameters. An example of displaying and changing the **domainname** kernel parameter follows. The double quotation marks are not required in this example, but you must quote any characters that would otherwise be interpreted by the shell. You must work with **root** privileges when you change a parameter.

```
$ sysctl kernel.domainname
kernel.domainname = (none)
$ su -c 'sysctl -w kernel.domainname="example.com"'
kernel.domainname = example.com
$ sysctl kernel.domainname
kernel.domainname = example.com
```

### Have the installation medium handy when you build a new kernel

caution   When you build a new Linux kernel to install a new version or to change the configuration of the existing version, make sure you have the installation medium handy. This disk allows you to reboot the system, even when you have destroyed the system software completely. Having this medium available can mean the difference between momentary panic and a full-scale nervous breakdown. Refer to "Rescue an Installed System" on page 456 for more information.

### Secure Boot

tip   On newer machines, Secure Boot might keep a custom kernel from booting. On these machines you need to disable Secure Boot or set up your own keys and sign the kernel with them. For more information visit both fedoraproject.org/wiki/Secureboot#Questions_and_Answers and jwboyer.livejournal.com/46149.html.

Before you can start building a new kernel, you must download, install, and prep the source code. You also need to build a configuration file that describes the new kernel you want to build. This chapter describes the steps involved in completing these tasks.

# DOWNLOADING, INSTALLING, AND PREPPING THE KERNEL SOURCE CODE

This section describes how to download kernel source code on the local system. If you want to download code that has not been customized (patched) by Fedora/RHEL, visit kernel.org/pub. This section also covers prepping and installing the kernel source code. See "Configuring and Compiling the Linux Kernel" on page 584 for information on how to proceed after you have downloaded, installed, and prepped the kernel source code.

## PREREQUISITES

Install the following packages:

- **rpmdevtools**
- **yum-utils** (installed with the default system)
- **ncurses-devel** (used to configure the kernel using **make menuconfig**)
- **libglade2-devel** (used to configure the kernel using **make gconfig**)

### Compiling a kernel takes a lot of disk space

tip    Make sure you have enough disk space before you compile a kernel. When you compile a default kernel, it occupies approximately 3.5 gigabytes. This disk space must be available on the filesystem in which you compile the kernel.

## MORE INFORMATION

Local    The kernel package includes the latest documentation, some of which might not be available in other documents. You might wish to review the **README** files included within the source code directories and the relevant files in the **Documentation** subdirectory.

Howto    Detailed, somewhat dated, generic guide to installing and configuring the Linux kernel: *Linux Kernel-HOWTO*

Web    Kernel source code: kernel.org
Secure Boot: fedoraproject.org/wiki/Secureboot#Questions_and_Answers and jwboyer.livejournal.com/46149.html
All builds of all packages for multiple architectures plus source code: koji.fedoraproject.org

# DOWNLOADING THE SOURCE CODE

rpmdev-setuptree   After you download the required packages (previous section), run rpmdev-setuptree. This utility sets up an SRPM build environment comprising an **rpmbuild** directory hierarchy in your home directory:

```
$ rpmdev-setuptree
$ ls rpmbuild
BUILD  RPMS  SOURCES  SPECS  SRPMS
```

After you compile the kernel, the five directories rpmdev-setuptree creates will hold files as follows: **BUILD** holds the results of compiling the kernel, **RPMS** holds compiled RPM files, **SOURCES** holds source and patch files, **SPECS** holds the kernel specification file, and **SRPMS** holds source RPM files, if any.

### Do not work with **root** privileges

caution   You do not need to—nor should you—work with **root** privileges for any portion of configuring or building the kernel except for installing software packages and installing the kernel (the last step). The kernel **README** file says, "Don't take the name of **root** in vain."

The sections on building, customizing, and installing the kernel use **su –c** when it is necessary to work with root privileges. This practice helps keep you from working with **root** privileges when you do not mean to. It also provides a better record for you to review in the shell history (page 376) should something go wrong. For more information on **su –c**, refer to "Executing a Single Command" on page 427.

**LPI**
yumdownloader   The easiest way to download the updated kernel source code for the most recently released version of the kernel is to use yumdownloader. Work in and download the kernel source code RPM file to your home directory:

```
$ cd
$ yumdownloader --source kernel
Loaded plugins: langpacks, refresh-packagekit
Enabling updates-source repository
Enabling fedora-source repository
...
kernel-3.9.8-300.fc19.src.rpm                          | 69 MB   00:27
```

### About the examples in this section

tip   The examples in this section show Sam, whose home directory is **/home/sam** (**~sam**), working with the kernel named **kernel-3.9.8-300.fc19**. When you build a kernel, you will probably work in your home directory, and the name of the kernel you work with will differ from the name of Sam's kernel. Make the necessary substitutions as you follow the examples.

# INSTALLING THE SOURCE CODE

yum-builddep   With the kernel source code RPM package file in your home directory, run yum-builddep to download and install the packages needed to build the source code package (dependencies). Because you are installing packages, you must work with **root** privileges. Replace **sam** and **3.9.8-300.fc19** in the following example with your username and the name of the kernel you are using to specify the location of the RPM file on the system.

```
$ su -c 'yum-builddep ~sam/kernel-3.9.8-300.fc19.src.rpm'
Password:
Loaded plugins: langpacks, refresh-packagekit
Getting requirements for kernel-3.9.8-300.fc19.src
...
Install  15 Packages (+37 Dependent packages)

Total download size: 36 M
Installed size: 108 M
Is this ok [y/d/N]: y
...
Complete!
```

Finally, working from your home directory as a nonprivileged user, use rpm to install the kernel source code in the **rpmbuild** directory hierarchy in your home directory:

```
$ rpm -Uvh kernel-3.9.8-300.fc19.src.rpm
   1:kernel                      warning: user mockbuild does not exist - using root
warning: group mockbuild does not exist - using root
warning: user mockbuild does not exist - using root
...
   1:kernel-3.9.8-300.fc19        ############################### [100%]
```

You can ignore errors, such as those shown above, about groups and users that do not exist.

## PREPPING THE SOURCE CODE

The final step before you can work with the source code is to prep it. Prepping unpacks compressed files and applies patches. The following rpmbuild command uses the **–bp** option to prep the source code:

```
$ cd /home/sam/rpmbuild/SPECS
$ rpmbuild -bp --target $(arch) kernel.spec
Building target platforms: x86_64
Building for target x86_64
Executing(%prep): /bin/sh -e /var/tmp/rpm-tmp.qVGqoc
+ umask 022
+ cd /home/sam/rpmbuild/BUILD
...
```

If rpmbuild cannot find a package it needs to prep the code, it displays a message such as the following:

```
error: Failed build dependencies:
        elfutils-libelf-devel is needed by kernel-3.9.8-300.fc19.x86_64
        zlib-devel is needed by kernel-3.9.8-300.fc19.x86_64
        binutils-devel is needed by kernel-3.9.8-300.fc19.x86_64
```

In this case, install the needed packages (you might have to install different packages than those in the example):

```
$ su -c 'yum install elfutils-libelf-devel zlib-devel binutils-devel'
```

After you install the packages, give the preceding rpmbuild command again. With the kernel source code installed and prepped on the local system, you can configure, compile, and install it.

# CONFIGURING AND COMPILING THE LINUX KERNEL

This section describes how to configure and compile the kernel.

### Where are the kernel source code and the kernel specification file?

tip After installing and prepping the source code as described in the previous section, Sam's source code is in **/home/sam/rpmbuild/BUILD/kernel-3.9.fc19/linux-3.9.8-300.fc19.x86_64/**, and his kernel specification file is in **/home/sam/rpmbuild/SPECS**. Your source code will be in a similarly named directory (**~/rpmbuild/BUILD/kernel**∗**/linux**∗) and your kernel specification file will be in the directory named **~/rpmbuild/SPECS**.

Most of the work in this section is done in the directory in which the source code is located (**linux**∗). Labeling and installing the kernel is done in the **SPECS** directory.

## LABELING THE KERNEL

To prevent overwriting existing kernel files and to identify various compilations of the kernel, you can change the **buildid** variable in the **kernel.spec** file. This variable is initially set to **.local**. Whatever value you assign to this variable is placed at the end of the kernel name and release number to identify the kernel. You can make note of patches applied to the kernel in this string to help people track down problems later. Use cd to change directories to **~/rpmbuild/SPECS**, edit **kernel.spec**, and change **local** in the line

```
# % define buildid .local
```

to a value that identifies the kernel you are building. You must also remove the leading hash mark (#), the SPACE following the hash mark, and the SPACE between % and **define**:

```
%define buildid .sam1307021000
```

## .config: CONFIGURES THE KERNEL

Before you can compile the code and create a Linux kernel, you must decide on and specify which features you want the kernel to support. You can configure the kernel to support most features in one of two ways: by building the feature into the kernel or by specifying the feature as a loadable kernel module (page 589), which is loaded into the kernel only as needed. In deciding which method to use, you must weigh the size of the kernel against the time it takes to load a module. Make the kernel as small as possible while minimizing how often modules have to be loaded.

The **.config** file in the **~/rpmbuild/BUILD/kernel**∗**/linux**∗ directory controls which features the new kernel will support and how it will support them. The next section provides instructions for replacing an existing custom kernel. "Customizing a Kernel" on page 586 explains how to create a default version of the **.config** file if it does not exist and how to edit the file if it does exist.

## REPLACING A CUSTOM KERNEL

If you have already configured a custom kernel, you might want to replace it with a similarly configured, newer kernel. Each kernel potentially has new configuration options, however—which explains why it is poor practice to use an old **.config** file for compiling a new kernel. This section explains how to upgrade an existing **.config** file so it includes options that are new to the new kernel and maintains the existing configuration for the old options.

Work in the **~/rpmbuild/BUILD/kernel*/linux*** directory. The system keeps a copy of the configuration file for the kernel the local system is running in **/boot**. The following command copies this file to **.config** in the working directory:

```
$ pwd
/home/sam/rpmbuild/BUILD/kernel-3.9.fc19/linux-3.9.8-300.fc19.x86_64
$ cp /boot/config-$(uname -r) .config
```

In this command, the shell executes **uname –r** and uses command substitution (page 410) to replace **$(uname –r)** with the output of the command, which is the name of the release of the kernel running on the local system.

Next give the command **make oldconfig** to patch the **.config** file with options from the new kernel that are not present in the old kernel. This command displays each kernel option that is the same in the new and old kernels and automatically sets the state of the option in the new kernel the same way it was set in the old kernel. It stops when it finds an option that appears in the new kernel but not in the old kernel. It then displays a prompt, which is similar to **[N/y/?]** (**NEW**), showing possible responses and indicating that this option is new. The prompt shows the default response as an uppercase letter; you can type this letter (uppercase or lowercase) and press RETURN, or just press RETURN to select this response. In the example, the Tickless System option is new, and the default response is **Y** for *yes, include the option in the new kernel*. To select a nondefault response (**n** means *no, do not include the option,* and **m** means *include the option as a module*), you must type the letter and press RETURN. Enter **?** followed by RETURN to display more information about the option.

```
$ make oldconfig
scripts/kconfig/conf --oldconfig Kconfig
*
* Linux Kernel Configuration
*
*
* Code maturity level options
*
Prompt for development and/or incomplete code/drivers (EXPERIMENTAL) [Y/n/?] y
*
* General setup
*
Local version - append to kernel release (LOCALVERSION) []
Automatically append version information to version string (LOCALVERSION_AUTO) [N/y/?] n
...
```

```
*
* Processor type and features
*
Tickless System (Dynamic Ticks) (NO_HZ) [Y/n/?] (NEW) ? ?
This option enables a tickless system: timer interrupts will
only trigger on an as-needed basis both when the system is
busy and when the system is idle.

Tickless System (Dynamic Ticks) (NO_HZ) [Y/n/?] (NEW) ? RETURN
High Resolution Timer Support (HIGH_RES_TIMERS) [Y/n/?] y
Symmetric multi-processing support (SMP) [Y/n/?] y
Subarchitecture Type
> 1. PC-compatible (X86_PC)
  2. AMD Elan (X86_ELAN)
...
#
# configuration written to .config
#
```

# CUSTOMIZING A KERNEL

The **~/rpmbuild/BUILD/kernel\*/linux\*** directory and the **configs** subdirectory provide sample configuration files for various processors, multiple processors, and configurations. You might want to look at these files before you get started or use one of them as your starting point. To use one of these files, copy it to **.config**.

You can use one of three standard commands to build the **.config** file that configures a Linux kernel:

```
$ make config
$ make menuconfig
$ make gconfig
```

See "Prerequisites" on page 581 for a list of packages required to run all but the first of these commands.

If a **.config** file does not exist in the working directory, each of these commands except the first sets up a **.config** file that matches the kernel the local system is running and then allows you to modify that configuration. The commands can set up this **.config** file only if the configuration file for the locally running kernel is at **/boot/config-$(uname –r)**. See the preceding section if you want to build a new kernel with a configuration similar to that of an existing kernel.

The **make config** command is the simplest of the three commands, uses a textual interface, and does not require additional software. It is, however, the most unforgiving and hardest to use of the configuration interfaces. The **make menuconfig** command uses a pseudographical interface and also displays a textual interface. The **make gconfig** command uses GTK+ (www.gtk.org) and displays a graphical interface.

Each command asks the same questions and produces the same result, given the same responses. The first and second commands work in character-based environments;

**Figure 14-1**   The Linux Kernel Configuration window, split view

the third command works in graphical environments. For many administrators working with a GUI, the third method is the easiest to use.

The **make gconfig** command displays the Linux Kernel Configuration window, which you can view in three configurations: single, split, or full view. Choose a view by clicking one of the three icons to the right of the save icon on the toolbar. Figure 14-1 shows the split view. In this view, the left frame shows the options and the top-right view lists the features for each option. The bottom-right view describes the highlighted option or feature. Figure 14-2 shows the full view.

At the far right of all views are four columns labeled **N, M, Y,** and **Value**. An **N** appears in the **N** column if the feature on that line is not being used. An **M** in the **M** column means the feature is included as a module. A **Y** in the **Y** column means the feature is compiled in the kernel. An underscore in any of these columns means that the value that would appear in that column is valid for the feature (e.g., an underscore in the column labeled **M** means that that feature can be included as a module, although it is not included as a module). The Value column holds the value of the feature (**N, M,** or **Y**).

**Figure 14-2**   The Linux Kernel Configuration window, full view

In any view, you can double-click the check boxes and radio buttons next to the features to select or deselect that feature. An empty check box/radio button indicates that the feature is disabled, a tick indicates that it is to be compiled in the kernel, and a minus sign means that it is to be compiled as a module. With a choice highlighted, you can also press **M** for module, **N** for not included, and **Y** for compiled into the kernel. Select **menubar: Options⇨Show All Options** to display all options and features.

Go through the options and mark the features as you would like them to be configured in the new kernel. At any time during the configuration process, you can store the currently defined configuration to a file, load a configuration from a file, or exit with or without saving your changes. The selections to do so are available in **menubar: File**. When you are done, select **menubar: File⇨Save** and close the window.

## Cleaning the Source Tree

After generating a **.config** file, but before compiling or recompiling the kernel, purge the source tree of all potentially stale **\*.o** files using the following command:

```
$ make clean
  CLEAN    arch/x86/boot/compressed
  CLEAN    arch/x86/boot
  CLEAN    arch/x86/kernel/acpi/realmode
  CLEAN    arch/x86/kernel/cpu
...
  CLEAN    Documentation/watchdog/src
  CLEAN    .tmp_versions
...
```

This command ensures that make correctly applies any numbering scheme you use when you compile the kernel.

## Copying the Configuration File

Before compiling the kernel, you must copy the **.config** file you want to use to the directory you will compile the kernel in. This file must have a name that corresponds to the kernel in use on the local system (e.g., **config-i686-generic**):

```
$ cp .config ~/rpmbuild/SOURCES/config-$(arch)-generic
```

## Compiling a Kernel Image File and Loadable Modules

The next command compiles the kernel and modules. Compiling the kernel takes upwards of several hours, depending on the power of the system you are using.

```
$ pwd
/home/sam/rpmbuild/SPECS
$ rpmbuild -bb --target $(arch) kernel.spec
Building target platforms: x86_64
Building for target x86_64
Executing(%prep): /bin/sh -e /var/tmp/rpm-tmp.0TbzHg
+ umask 022
+ cd /home/sam/rpmbuild/BUILD
...
Wrote: /home/sam/rpmbuild/RPMS/x86_64/kernel-debug-modules-extra-3.9.8-
300.sam1307021000.fc19.x86_64.rpm
Wrote: /home/sam/rpmbuild/RPMS/x86_64/kernel-debug-debuginfo-3.9.8-300.sam1307021000.fc19.x86_64.rpm
```

```
Executing(%clean): /bin/sh -e /var/tmp/rpm-tmp.zcobng
+ umask 022
+ cd /home/sam/rpmbuild/BUILD
+ cd kernel-3.9.fc19
+ rm -rf /home/sam/rpmbuild/BUILDROOT/kernel-3.9.8-300.sam1307021000.fc19.x86_64
+ exit 0
```

# USING LOADABLE KERNEL MODULES

A *loadable kernel module* (page 1258) (sometimes called a *module* or *loadable module*) is an object file—part of the kernel—that is linked into the kernel at runtime. Modules can be inserted into and removed from a running kernel at almost any time (except when a module is being used). This ability gives the kernel the flexibility to be as small as possible at any given time. Modules are a good way to code some kernel features, including drivers that are not used continually (such as a tape driver). Module filenames end in **.ko** and are stored in subdirectories in **/lib/modules**. Under Fedora/RHEL, kernel modules are compiled along with the kernel as explained in the preceding section.

Table 14-1 lists some of the tools available to help you work with modules. Refer to the corresponding man pages for options and more information.

Table 14-1    Tools for working with modules

| Tool/utility | Function |
|---|---|
| depmod | Works with dependencies for modules. |
| insmod | Loads modules in a running kernel. |
| *LPI* lsmod | Lists information about all loaded modules. |
| modinfo | Lists information about a module. |
| *LPI* modprobe | Loads, unloads, and reports on modules. When it loads a module, it also loads dependencies. |
| rmmod | Unloads modules from a running kernel. |

# INSTALLING THE KERNEL, MODULES, AND ASSOCIATED FILES

The next step, which you must execute with **root** privileges, is to copy the compiled kernel, modules, and associated files to the appropriate directories—usually **/boot** and a subdirectory of **/lib/modules**. When you have a partition mounted at **/boot**, the files are kept in the root of this partition (**/boot**). Because you have created an RPM package, installing these files is quite easy. The following command installs the new kernel files from the **rpmbuild** directory hierarchy in Sam's home directory into the proper directories:

```
$ su -c 'rpm -ivh /home/sam/rpmbuild/RPMS/x86_64/kernel-3.9.8-300.sam1307021000.fc19.x86_64.rpm'
Preparing...                          ############################### [100%]
Updating / installing...
   1:kernel-3.9.8-300.sam1307021000.fc############################### [100%]
```

Installing the kernel in this manner updates the **grub.cfg** (page 593) GRUB configuration file to include the new kernel.

Reboot  Reboot the system by clicking your name at the upper-right corner of the screen and selecting **Shut Down** and then selecting **Restart**. If you are working at the console, press CONTROL-ALT-DEL. You can also give a **reboot** command from the console, a character-based terminal, or a terminal emulator. When the system is rebooted, you can use uname to verify the new kernel is loaded:

```
$ uname -r
3.9.8-300.sam1307021000.fc19.x86_64
```

## *LPI* GRUB: THE LINUX BOOT LOADER

*LPI* MBR  A boot loader is a very small program that the *bootstrap* (page 1240) process uses as it brings a computer from an off or reset state to a fully functional state. The boot loader frequently resides on the starting sectors of a hard disk called the MBR (master boot record).

GPT  In place of MBR you can set up GPT (GUID Partition Table) on a new system; changing an installed system from MBR to GPT is a destructive process. GPT has several advantages over MBR including the ability to work with disks larger than two terabytes. Linux and newer versions of Windows support GPT and it is the default for RHEV-H (Red Hat Enterprise Virtualization Hypervisor) machines. You must use parted (page 614) and not fdisk to manage partitions under GPT. For more information visit wiki.archlinux.org/index.php/GUID_Partition_Table.

*LPI* BIOS  The *BIOS* (page 1239), which is stored in an *EEPROM* (page 1248) on the system's motherboard, gains control of a system when you turn on or reset the computer. After testing the hardware, the BIOS transfers control to the MBR, which usually passes control to the partition boot record. This transfer of control starts the boot loader, which is responsible for locating the operating system kernel (kept in the / or **/boot** directory), loading that kernel into memory, and starting it running. If you use a **/boot** directory, which might be mounted on a separate partition, this directory or partition must be present for the system to boot Linux. Refer to "Booting the System" on page 450 for more information on what happens from this point forward.

*LPI* LBA addressing mode and the **/boot** partition  All newer hard disks support LBA (logical block addressing) mode. LBA permits the **/boot** directory to appear anywhere on the hard disk. For LBA to work, it must be supported by the hard disk, the BIOS, and the operating system (GRUB in the case of Linux). Although GRUB supports LBA mode, some BIOSes do not. For this reason, it is a good idea to place the **/boot** directory in its own partition located near the beginning of the hard disk. With this setup, the root (/) filesystem can be anywhere on any hard drive that Linux can access regardless of LBA support. In some instances, without a separate **/boot** partition, the system might boot at first but then fail as you update the kernel and the kernel files move further from the beginning of the disk.

LVM  Systems that use LVM require a separate boot partition that is not an LV. For more information on LVM see page 44.

GRUB 2  Fedora 16 and RHEL 7 introduced GRUB 2 (Grand Unified Boot loader 2), which this book refers to simply as GRUB. This book refers to the first release as GRUB legacy. GRUB 2 is a complete rewrite of GRUB legacy; few of the configuration files are the same.

A product of the GNU Project, the GRUB loader conforms to the *multiboot specification* (page 1261), which allows it to load many free operating systems directly as well as to *chain load* (page 1241) proprietary operating systems. The GRUB loader can recognize various types of filesystems and kernel executable formats, allowing it to load an arbitrary operating system. When you boot the system, GRUB can display a menu of choices that is generated by the **/boot/grub2/grub.cfg** file (page 593). At this point you can modify a menu selection, choose which operating system or kernel to boot, or do nothing and allow GRUB to boot the default system.

When you install GRUB at the time you install Linux, the installation program configures GRUB automatically. See the **grub2** info page and www.gnu.org/software/grub for more information on GRUB.

## LPI  CONFIGURING GRUB

As mentioned earlier, GRUB 2 uses a different set of files than GRUB legacy. You control most of the frequently changed aspects of GRUB by editing the **/etc/default/grub** file (next) and running grub2-mkconfig, which generates the **/boot/grub2/grub.cfg** file (page 593). You can edit files in the **/etc/grub.d** directory (page 592) to perform advanced configuration of the GRUB menu. The **grub.cfg** file is comparable to the GRUB legacy **/boot/grub/menu.lst** file, but it is a poor idea to edit the **grub.cfg** file because it is generated by grub2-mkconfig and is usually overwritten by that utility.

### /etc/default/grub: THE PRIMARY GRUB CONFIGURATION FILE

Changing the values of variables in the **/etc/default/grub** file allows you to modify many aspects of how the system boots and how GRUB displays its menu (Figure 10-2, page 451). In most cases, you can force GRUB to display its menu by holding down the SHIFT key as the system boots (page 450).

The effects of some of the variables you can set in the **/etc/default/grub** file depend on whether GRUB finds one or more than one bootable operating systems on the machine. Some variables do not need to be set. Toward this end, GRUB does not evaluate a line that begins with a hashmark (#; these lines are comments). Remove or add a hashmark to cause GRUB to evaluate or not evaluate an assignment, respectively.

The **/etc/default/grub** file is shown following.

```
$ cat /etc/default/grub
GRUB_TIMEOUT=5
GRUB_DISTRIBUTOR="$(sed 's, release .*$,,g' /etc/system-release)"
GRUB_DEFAULT=saved
GRUB_DISABLE_SUBMENU=true
GRUB_TERMINAL_OUTPUT="console"
GRUB_CMDLINE_LINUX="rd.lvm.lv=fedora/swap rd.md=0 rd.dm=0
vconsole.keymap=us $([ -x /usr/sbin/rhcrashkernel-param ] &&
/usr/sbin/rhcrashkernel-param || :) rd.luks=0
vconsole.font=latarcyrheb-sun16 rd.lvm.lv=fedora/root rhgb quiet"
GRUB_DISABLE_RECOVERY="true"
```

You can assign values to the following variables:

**GRUB_TIMEOUT=*num***

The *num* specifies the number of seconds GRUB waits before booting the system. Set *num* to –1 to cause GRUB to wait until the user selects a menu item. Setting *num* to 0 causes the SHIFT key to lose its effect: The user will not be able to display the GRUB menu before the system boots.

**GRUB_DISTRIBUTOR=*string***

The *string* specifies the name of the distribution as displayed by GRUB. The *string* as supplied with Fedora is executable and is replaced with its output because it is enclosed within **$(...)** (command substitution; page 410):

```
$(sed 's, release .*$,,g' /etc/system-release)
```

The sed command truncates everything following **Fedora** from the **system-release** file.

**GRUB_DEFAULT=*num* | saved**

The *num* specifies the ordinal number of the default menu entry. The default menu entry is the one GRUB boots if you do not select a different entry as GRUB boots the system. Menu entries are numbered starting with 0, so setting this variable to 0 specifies the first menu entry. Setting **GRUB_DEFAULT** to **saved** causes GRUB to boot the most recently booted menu entry.

**GRUB_DISABLE_SUBMENU=true | false**

When set to **true**, causes grub2-mkconfig not to generate submenu entries for the GRUB menu. Setting it to **false** causes submenu entries to be generated.

**GRUB_TERMINAL_OUTPUT="console"**

Specifies the terminal output device such as **console** or **serial**.

**GRUB_CMDLINE_LINUX=*string***

GRUB appends *string* to the **linux** boot line that GRUB passes to the kernel when booting in both normal *and* single-user/rescue modes (page 450). As supplied with Fedora, the *string* is long, supplying Fedora the information it needs to boot. For more information refer to "Seeing What Is Going on" on page 59. You can also add boot command-line parameters to *string*; see page 451 for instructions on editing the GRUB menu. Separate each word from the next with a SPACE and, if *string* includes SPACES, enclose *string* within double quotation marks.

**GRUB_DISABLE_RECOVERY=true | false**

When set to **true**, causes grub2-mkconfig not to generate recovery entries for the GRUB menu. Setting it to **false** causes recovery entries to be generated.

## /etc/grub.d/✲: GRUB Configuration Templates

The files in the **/etc/grub.d** directory determine many aspects of the GRUB menu. The grub2-mkconfig utility (next) processes these files in numerical order. See the **README** file in this directory for more information.

You can add files to this directory and modify the existing files, but it is not usually necessary to do so. Each of these files must be executable in order for grub2-mkconfig to process it.

As installed, the **/etc/grub.d** directory holds the following files:

00_header  Runs the initial GRUB setup and provides the header information that appears at the beginning of the **grub.cfg** file.

10_linux  Creates a menu entry for each kernel specified by a file named **/boot/vmlinu[xz]–\***
or **/vmlinu[xz]–\***. If **GRUB_DISABLE_RECOVERY** is set to **false** or commented out, this file also creates a recovery menu entry for each of these kernels.

20_linux_xen  Configures the Xen kernel, which has a different **initrd** configuration from the Linux kernel.

20_ppc_terminfo  Configures a terminal for a PPC system.

30_os-prober  Creates menus for Linux and other operating systems located on partitions other than **/** and **/boot**.

40_custom  Accepts manual custom menu entries.

41_custom  Accepts automated custom menu entries.

# grub2-mkconfig: GENERATES THE grub.cfg FILE

The grub2-mkconfig utility is a shell script that generates output based on the contents of the **/etc/default/grub** file (page 591) and the files in the **/etc/grub.d** directory (previous page). By default grub2-mkconfig sends its output to standard output. Typically this utility is run with the **–o** option sending the output to **/boot/grub2/grub.cfg**. A sample run of grub2-mkconfig is shown here:

```
# grub2-mkconfig -o /boot/grub2/grub.cfg
Generating grub.cfg ...
Found linux image: /boot/vmlinuz-3.10.3-300.fc19.x86_64
Found initrd image: /boot/initramfs-3.10.3-300.fc19.x86_64.img
Found linux image: /boot/vmlinuz-3.9.9-302.fc19.x86_64
Found initrd image: /boot/initramfs-3.9.9-302.fc19.x86_64.img
Found linux image: /boot/vmlinuz-0-rescue-40b9b79ed60f47c5b31224f23b76e2e0
Found initrd image: /boot/initramfs-0-rescue-40b9b79ed60f47c5b31224f23b76e2e0.img
done
```

By default, grub2-mkconfig searches for Linux and other operating system kernel files and creates a menu entry (boot specification) in its output file for each kernel it finds. It also adds an **initrd** (initial RAM disk) line to **grub.cfg** for each file in **/boot** whose name starts with the string **initramfs–** and whose version number matches one of the kernel files it found. For example, if grub2-mkconfig finds the kernel file named **vmlinuz-3.10.3-300.fc19.x86_64** in **/boot** and then finds **initramfs-3.10.3-300.fc19.x86_64.img**, it creates an **initrd** line for that RAM disk image file.

Listing installed kernel packages  Each time grub2-mkconfig runs, it searches for kernel files. If a kernel file is no longer present, it will no longer include a menu entry for that kernel. Similarly, if a new kernel file is present, it will include a menu entry for that kernel. You can remove a kernel's menu entry by removing the kernel package, which removes the kernel files, and rerunning grub2-mkconfig.

The command **uname –r** displays the name of the kernel the system is running. The following commands display the name of the kernel the system is running and list the installed kernel packages. See page 547 for more information about using rpm to query packages.

```
$ uname -r
3.10.3-300.fc19.x86_64

$ rpm -qa | grep kernel-3
kernel-3.9.9-301.fc19.x86_64
kernel-3.10.3-300.fc19.x86_64
kernel-3.9.9-302.fc19.x86_64
```

yum removes a kernel    The easiest way to remove a kernel package is to use the yum **remove** command. Substitute the name of the kernel package you want to remove for the one in the following example. The following command removes the first kernel package listed by the previous rpm command:

```
# yum -y remove kernel-3.9.9-301.fc19.x86_64
Loaded plugins: langpacks, refresh-packagekit
Resolving Dependencies
--> Running transaction check
---> Package kernel.x86_64 0:3.9.9-301.fc19 will be erased
...
Running transaction
  Erasing     : kernel-modules-extra-3.9.9-301.fc19.x86_64      1/2
  Erasing     : kernel-3.9.9-301.fc19.x86_64                    2/2
  Verifying   : kernel-modules-extra-3.9.9-301.fc19.x86_64      1/2
  Verifying   : kernel-3.9.9-301.fc19.x86_64                    2/2

Removed:
  kernel.x86_64 0:3.9.9-301.fc19

Dependency Removed:
  kernel-modules-extra.x86_64 0:3.9.9-301.fc19

Complete!
```

It is good practice to keep at least one known-good kernel in addition to the one the system is running. See page 535 for more information on the yum **remove** command.

## LPI   grub2-install: INSTALLS THE MBR AND GRUB FILES

The grub2-install utility installs the MBR (page 590) and the files GRUB needs to boot the system. This utility takes a single argument—the name of the device that is to hold the MBR. You can specify the device name as a GRUB device name (e.g., **hd0**) or a device filename (e.g., **/dev/sda**). The following example shows grub2-install installing files in the default location (**/boot/grub**) and the MBR on device **/dev/sda**:

```
# grub2-install /dev/sda
Installation finished. No error reported.
```

See page 456 for instructions on how to reinstall the MBR.

## *LPI*   dmesg: DISPLAYS KERNEL MESSAGES

The dmesg utility displays the kernel-ring buffer, where the kernel stores messages. When the system boots, the kernel fills this buffer with messages related to hardware and module initialization. Messages in the kernel-ring buffer are often useful for diagnosing system problems.

When you run dmesg, it displays a lot of information. It is frequently easier to use a pipeline to send the output of dmesg through grep to find what you are looking for. For example, if you find that your hard disks are performing poorly, you can use dmesg to check whether they are running in DMA mode:

```
$ dmesg | grep DMA
...
[    0.859219] ata1: PATA max UDMA/33 cmd 0x1f0 ctl 0x3f6 bmdma 0x10c0 irq 14
[    0.859220] ata2: PATA max UDMA/33 cmd 0x170 ctl 0x376 bmdma 0x10c8 irq 15
...
```

The preceding lines tell you which mode each ATA device is operating in. If you are having problems with the Ethernet connection, search the dmesg buffer for **eth**:

```
$ dmesg | grep eth
[    5.509495] e1000 0000:02:01.0 eth0: (PCI:66MHz:32-bit) 00:0c:29:13:f4:35
[    5.509500] e1000 0000:02:01.0 eth0: Intel(R) PRO/1000 Network Connection
[    6.086764] systemd-udevd[314]: renamed network interface eth0 to ens33
```

If everything is working properly, dmesg displays the hardware configuration information for each network interface.

The **–H** (**––human**) option causes dmesg to send its output through a pager, display relative times in the left column, and display important messages in color. This option is useful when you want to scan dmesg output.

# CHAPTER SUMMARY

You can build a Linux kernel from the source code. Sometimes you do not need to build a kernel; instead, you can change many aspects of the kernel by using boot options in **/etc/grub.cfg**. You can dynamically change options by modifying **/etc/sysctl.conf**.

Before you can build a Linux kernel, you must download the kernel source files to the local system. After you have downloaded the source files, you need to install and prep the source code, configure and compile the kernel and the loadable modules, and install the kernel and loadable modules.

The GRUB boot loader is a small program that controls the process of bringing the system up. You must configure the boot loader so that it recognizes the new kernel.

The dmesg utility displays the kernel-ring buffer, where the kernel stores messages. You can use this utility to help diagnose boot-time problems.

# EXERCISES

1. What is the purpose of the kernel?

2. How would you display a list of all loaded modules in the current kernel?

3. Which command would you give to upgrade the kernel from an rpm file, and how is this different from upgrading other packages?

4. How would you display information from the kernel about the hard disk on the first SATA channel?

5. The **acpi=off** kernel argument prevents **acpid** from starting. How would you use this argument?

6. What is a boot loader?

# ADVANCED EXERCISES

7. How would you label the kernel before compiling it? Why would you want to label the kernel?

8. You have just installed an Adaptec SCSI card. How can you find out whether it has been recognized and which entry in **/dev** represents it?

9. When you install an experimental kernel for testing purposes, how do you instruct GRUB not to load it by default?

10. How would you obtain a list of all network-related kernel parameters?

# 15

# ADMINISTRATION TASKS

## OBJECTIVES

After reading this chapter you should be able to:

▶ Add and manage user accounts using
system-config-users

▶ Add and manage user accounts from the command line

▶ Back up files using tar and cpio

▶ Schedule tasks to be run in the future using **crond**,
anacron, and at

▶ Monitor the system using various tools including
vmstat and top

▶ Monitor and manage log files

▶ Manage disk partitions using parted

▶ Communicate with users

The system administrator has many responsibilities. This chapter discusses tasks not covered in Chapter 10, including configuring user and group accounts, backing up files, scheduling tasks, general problem solving, and using the system log daemon, **rsyslogd**.

# CONFIGURING USER AND GROUP ACCOUNTS

More than a username is required for a user to be able to log in on and use a system: A user must have the necessary files, directories, permissions, and usually a password to log in. At a minimum a user must have an entry in the **/etc/passwd** and **/etc/shadow** files and a home directory. The Settings⇨Users window (page 112) allows you to configure basic aspects of a user account. This section describes several additional ways you can work with user accounts. Refer to Chapter 21 if you want to run NIS to manage the **passwd** database.

### Administrators and the **wheel** group

tip    A member of the **wheel** group, called an administrator, is able to use her password to authenticate using sudo and does not need to know or use the **root** password for most administration tasks. Refer to "Administrator and the **wheel** group" on page 429 for more information.

## *LPI*    system-config-users: MANAGES USER ACCOUNTS

The system-config-users utility (**system-config-users** package) displays the User Manager window and enables you to add, delete, and modify system users and groups. Open this window by giving the command **system-config-users** from an Enter a Command window (ALT-F2) or a terminal emulator. This window has two tabs: Users and Groups, where each tab displays information appropriate to its name. Figure 15-1 shows the Users tab.

### By default, system-config-users does not display system users and groups

tip    By default, system-config-users does not display users with UIDs less than 1000 and groups with GIDs less than 1000. To display these users and groups, click **menubar: Edit⇨Preferences** and remove the tick from the check box labeled **Hide system users and groups**.

Authentication    Because you can use system-config-users to make changes to the system that affect other users, this utility asks you to authenticate yourself.

Search filter    The Search filter, located just below the toolbar, selects users or groups whose names match the string you enter in the text box labeled **Search filter**. The string can include wildcards. The string matches the beginning of a name. For example, **\*nob** matches **nobody** and **nfsnobody**, whereas **nob** matches only **nobody**. After you enter the string, click **Apply filter** or press RETURN. If you have only a few users, you will not need to use the Search filter.

**Figure 15-1**   The User Manager window, Users tab

## ADDING A USER

To add a user to the system, click the button on the toolbar labeled **Add User**. The User Manager window displays the Add New User window, which gathers much of the same information as the User Data tab of the User Properties window (Figure 15-2). Enter the information for the new user and click **OK**. After you create a user, you can modify information related to that user.

**Figure 15-2**   The User Properties window, User Data tab

### LPI   Modifying a User

To modify a user, highlight the user in the User Manager window and click **Properties** on the toolbar; the utility displays the User Properties window (Figure 15-2), which has four tabs. The User Data tab holds basic user information such as name and password. The Account Info tab allows you to specify an expiration date for the account and to lock the account so the user cannot log in locally. The Password Info tab allows you to turn on password expiration and specify various related parameters. In the Groups tab, you can specify which groups the user is a member of. Click **OK** when you are done making changes in this window.

### LPI   Working with Groups

Click the **Groups** tab in the User Manager window to work with groups. To create a group, click **Add Group** on the toolbar and specify the name of the group. To change the name of a group or to add or remove users from a group, highlight the group and click **Properties** on the toolbar. Click the appropriate tab, make the changes you want, and click **OK**. See page 506 for more information on groups. Refer to "Administrator and the **wheel** group" on page 429 for information about how being a member of the **wheel** group allows a user to use sudo to authenticate using his password (not the **root** password).

Help   To obtain assistance, click **Help** on the toolbar.

When you are done working with users and groups, close the window.

## LPI   Managing User Accounts from the Command Line

In addition to using the graphical User Manager window to manage user accounts, you can use the command-line tools described in this section.

### LE+   useradd: Adds a User Account

The useradd utility adds a user account to the system. By default, useradd assigns the next highest unused user ID to a new account and specifies bash as the user's login shell. The following example adds entries to the **/etc/passwd** and **/etc/shadow** files, creates the user's home directory (in **/home**), specifies the user's group ID as 1105, and puts the user's full name in the comment field in **passwd**. The group ID you specify must exist in **/etc/group** or the command will fail. Use groupadd (next page) to add a group.

```
# useradd -g 1105 -c "Max W." max
```

LPI  /etc/skel   The useradd utility puts a !! in the password field of the **shadow** file (page 511) to prevent the user from logging in until you use passwd to assign a password to that user (page 137). Based on the **/etc/login.defs** and **/etc/default/useradd** files, useradd creates a home directory for the new user. When doing so, it copies the contents of **/etc/skel** to that directory. For more information on adding user information, see the useradd man page.

### LE+   userdel: Removes a User Account

The userdel utility deletes a user account. If appropriate, back up the files belonging to the user before deleting them. The following command removes Max's account. The **–r** (**––remove**) option causes the command to remove his home directory hierarchy:

```
# userdel --remove max
```

See the userdel man page for more information.

## LE+ usermod: MODIFIES A USER ACCOUNT

To turn off a user's account temporarily, you can use usermod to change the expiration date for the account. Because it specifies that his account expired in the past (December 31, 2010), the following command prevents Max from logging in:

```
# usermod -e "12/31/10" max
```

LPI chage You can also use chage to view and modify account expiry information. The –l (––list) option displays information about password expiration, and –E (––expiredate) changes the date an account expires. The following command has the same effect as the preceding one:

```
# chage -E "12/31/10" max
```

See the usermod and chage man pages for more information.

## LE+ groupadd: ADDS A GROUP

Just as useradd adds a new user to the system, so groupadd adds a new group by adding an entry to **/etc/group** (page 506). The following example creates a group named **pubs** with a group ID of 1024:

```
# groupadd -g 1024 pubs
```

Unless you use the –g option to assign a group ID, the system picks the next available sequential number greater than 1000. The –o option allows the group ID to be nonunique, which allows you to assign multiple names to a group ID.

## LE+ groupdel AND groupmod: REMOVE AND MODIFY A GROUP

The analogue of userdel for groups is groupdel, which takes a group name as an argument. You can also use groupmod to change the name or group ID of a group, as in the following examples:

```
# groupmod -g 1025 pubs
# groupmod -n manuals pubs
```

The first example changes the group ID number of the previously created **pubs** group. The second example renames the **pubs** group to **manuals**.

### Changing group ID numbers

caution The groupmod utility does not change group numbers in **/etc/passwd** when you renumber a group. Instead, you must edit **/etc/passwd** and change the entries manually. If you change the number of a group, files that are associated with the group will no longer be associated with the group. Rather, they might be associated with no group or with another group with the old group ID number.

# Backing Up Files

One of the most neglected tasks of system administration is making backup copies of files on a regular basis. The backup copies are vital in three instances: when the system malfunctions and files are lost, when a catastrophic disaster (fire, earthquake, and so on) occurs, and when a user or the system administrator deletes or corrupts a file by accident. Even when you set up RAID (page 42), you still need to back up files. Although RAID can provide fault tolerance (helpful in the event of disk failure), it does not help when a catastrophic disaster occurs or when a file is corrupted or removed accidentally. It is a good idea to have a written backup policy and to keep copies of backups offsite (in another building, at home, or at a different facility or campus) in a fireproof vault or safe.

The time to start thinking about backups is when you partition the disk. Refer to "Partitioning a Disk" on page 39. Make sure the capacity of the backup device and your partition sizes are comparable. Although you can back up a partition onto multiple volumes, it is easier not to—and it is much easier to restore data from a single volume.

You must back up filesystems regularly. Backup files are usually kept on magnetic tape, an external hard disk, or other removable media. Alternately, you can keep backup files on a remote system. How often and which files you back up depend on the system and your needs. Use this criterion when determining a backup schedule: If the system crashes, how much work are you willing to lose? Ideally you would back up all files on the system every few minutes so you would never lose more than a few minutes of work.

Of course, there is a tradeoff: How often are you willing to back up the files? The backup procedure typically slows the system for users, takes a certain amount of your time, and requires that you have and store the media holding the backup. Avoid backing up an active filesystem; the results might be inconsistent, and restoring from the backup might be impossible. This requirement is a function of the backup program and the filesystem you are backing up.

Another question is when to run the backup. Unless you plan to kick users off and bring the system down to single-user mode (not a user-friendly practice), you will want to perform this task when the machine is at its quietest. Depending on the use of the system, sometime in the middle of the night can work well. Then the backup is least likely to affect users, and the files are not likely to change as they are being read for backup.

A *full* backup makes copies of all files, regardless of when they were created or accessed. An *incremental* backup makes copies of those files that have been created or modified since the last (usually full) backup.

The more people using the system, the more often you should back up the filesystems. One popular schedule is to perform an incremental backup one or two times a day and a full backup one or two times a week.

# CHOOSING A BACKUP MEDIUM

If the local system is connected to a network, you can write backups to a drive on another system. This technique is often used with networked computers to avoid the cost of having a backup drive on each computer in the network and to simplify management of backing up many computers in a network. Although tapes are still used for backups, hard disks are being used more frequently. Backing up to a hard disk on a remote system is cost-effective, reliable, and practical. Because hard disks hold terabytes of data, using them simplifies the task of backing up the system, making it more likely that you will take care of this important task regularly. Other options for holding backups are writable CD/DVDs and USB flash drives. These devices, although not as cost-effective or able to store as much information as hard disk or tape systems, offer the benefit of convenience.

# BACKUP UTILITIES

A number of utilities are available to help you back up a system, and most work with any media. Most Linux backup utilities are based on one of the archive programs—tar or cpio—and augment these basic programs with bookkeeping support for managing backups conveniently.

You can use any of the tar, cpio, or dump/restore utilities to construct full or partial backups of a system. Each utility constructs a large file that contains, or archives, other files. In addition to file contents, an archive includes header information for each file it holds. This header information can be used when extracting files from the archive to restore file permissions and modification dates. An archive file can be saved to disk, written to tape, or shipped across the network while it is being created.

In addition to helping you back up the system, these programs offer a convenient way to bundle files for distribution to other sites. The tar program is often used for this purpose, and some software packages available on the Internet are bundled as tar archive files.

amanda  The amanda (Advanced Maryland Automatic Network Disk Archiver) utility (www.amanda.org), which is one of the more popular backup systems, uses dump or tar and takes advantage of Samba to back up Windows systems. The amanda utility backs up a LAN of heterogeneous hosts to a hard disk or tape. Relevant software packages are **amanda-client** and **amanda-server**.

### **LE+** tar: ARCHIVES FILES

The tar (tape archive) utility—see page 249 for an introduction—writes files to and retrieves files from an archive; it can compress this archive to conserve space. If you do not specify an archive device, tar writes to standard output and reads from standard input. With the –f (––**file**) option, tar uses the argument to –f as the name of the archive device. You can use this option to refer to a device on another system on the network. Although tar has many options, you need only a few in most situations. The following command displays a complete list of options:

```
$ tar --help | less
```

Most options for tar can be given either in a short form (a single letter) or as a descriptive word. Descriptive-word options are preceded by two hyphens, as in **--help**. Single-letter options can be combined into a single command-line argument and need not be preceded by a hyphen (for consistency with other utilities, it is good practice to use the hyphen anyway).

Although the following two commands look quite different, they specify the same tar options in the same order. The first version combines single-letter options into a single command-line argument; the second version uses descriptive words for the same options:

```
# tar -ztvf /dev/st0
# tar --gzip --list --verbose --file /dev/st0
```

Both commands tell tar to generate a (**v, verbose**) table of contents (**t, list**) from the tape on **/dev/st0** (**f, file**), using gzip (**z, gzip**) to decompress the files.

Unlike the original UNIX tar utility, when you specify an absolute pathname when you archive a file, the GNU version strips the leading **/** from the file pathname. Also, when it extracts files from a compressed archive, it decompresses them automatically. The first of the following commands shows tar compressing (**j** causes tar to compress using bzip2; page 245) and archiving some files from the **/etc** directory; it displays a message telling you it is stripping the leading **/s**. The second command extracts the files to the working directory. Because tar strips the leading **/** from each pathname, the files are not restored to their original locations in the root directory (**/**). The third command shows the extracted files in the working directory.

```
$ tar -cvjf etc.gtk /etc/gtk*
tar: Removing leading '/' from member names
/etc/gtk-2.0/
/etc/gtk-2.0/x86_64-redhat-linux-gnu/
/etc/gtk-2.0/x86_64-redhat-linux-gnu/gtk.immodules
/etc/gtk-2.0/gtkrc
/etc/gtk-3.0/
/etc/gtk-3.0/settings.ini

$ tar -xvf etc.gtk
etc/gtk-2.0/
etc/gtk-2.0/x86_64-redhat-linux-gnu/
etc/gtk-2.0/x86_64-redhat-linux-gnu/gtk.immodules
etc/gtk-2.0/gtkrc
etc/gtk-3.0/
etc/gtk-3.0/settings.ini

$ ls etc
gtk-2.0   gtk-3.0
```

You can use the **–C** option to cause tar to extract files to a directory other than the working directory. The argument to this option specifies the directory tar extracts the files to.

The options in Table 15-1 tell the tar program what to do. You must include exactly one of these options in a tar command. The **–c**, **–t**, and **–x** options are used most frequently.

**Table 15-1** tar options

| Option | Effect |
|---|---|
| --append (-r) | Appends files to an archive |
| --catenate (-A) | Adds one or more archives to the end of an existing archive |
| --create (-c) | Creates a new archive |
| --delete | Deletes files in an archive (not on tapes) |
| --diff (-d) | Compares files in an archive with disk files |
| --extract (-x) | Extracts files from an archive |
| --help | Displays a help list of tar options |
| --list (-t) | Lists the files in an archive |
| --update (-u) | Like the -r option, but the file is not appended if a newer version is already in the archive |

## *LPI* cpio: ARCHIVES FILES

The cpio (copy in/out) program is similar to tar but can read and write archive files in various formats, including the one used by tar. Normally cpio reads the names of the files to add to the archive from standard input and produces the archive file as standard output. When extracting files from an archive, it reads the archive as standard input.

While tar takes the name of a directory as an argument and traverses the directory hierarchy recursively to archive the directory, cpio must be presented with each filename it is to archive. For example, the following commands each back up the **/bin** directory:

```
$ tar cf bin.tar.bak /bin
$ find /bin -print | cpio -o > bin.cpio.bak
```

In the second command, find (page 229) sends a list of files in the **/bin** directory hierarchy to standard output; cpio reads this list from standard input and creates an archive of these files.

Another difference between these two utilities is that cpio does not strip the leading **/** from each pathname when it creates an archive. Restoring the cpio archive created in the preceding example will attempt to overwrite the files in **/bin**; it fails because the files in **/bin** are the same age as the files in the archive. Even if the files in the archive were newer, it would fail because the user does not have permission to overwrite the files in **/bin**.

As with tar, some options can be given in both a short, single-letter form and a more descriptive word form. However, unlike with tar, the syntax of the two forms in cpio differs when the option must be followed by additional information. In the short form, you must include a SPACE between the option and the additional information; with the word form, you must separate the two with an equal sign and no SPACEs.

Running cpio with the ––**help** option displays a complete list of options. See the next section for more examples of cpio.

# PERFORMING A SIMPLE BACKUP

When you prepare to make a major change to a system, such as replacing a disk drive, upgrading to a new release, or updating the Linux kernel, it is a good idea to archive some or all of the files so you can restore any that become damaged if something goes wrong. For this type of backup, tar or cpio works well. For example, if you have a SCSI tape drive as device **/dev/st0** (or it could be a hard disk at **/dev/sda**) that is capable of holding all the files on a single tape, you can use the following commands to construct a backup tape of the entire filesystem:

```
# cd /
# tar -cf /dev/st0 .
```

All the commands in this section start by using cd to change to the root directory so you are sure to back up the entire filesystem. The tar command then creates an archive (**c**) on the device **/dev/st0** (**f**). To compress the archive, replace the preceding tar command with the following command, which uses **j** to call bzip2:

```
# tar -cjf /dev/st0 .
```

You can back up a system with a combination of find and cpio. The following commands create an output file and set the I/O block size to 5120 bytes (the default is 512 bytes):

```
# cd /
# find . -depth | cpio -oB > /dev/st0
```

The next command restores the files in the **/home** directory from the preceding backup. The options extract files from an archive (**–i**) in verbose mode (**–v**), keeping the modification times (**–m**), and creating directories (**–d**) as needed. The asterisk is escaped (preceded by a backslash) so the shell does not expand it but rather passes it to cpio.

```
# cd /
# cpio -ivmd /home/\* < /dev/st0
```

Although all the archive programs work well for simple backups, utilities such as amanda (page 603) provide more sophisticated backup and restore systems. For example, to determine whether a file is in an archive, you must read the entire archive. If the archive is split across several tapes, this process is particularly tiresome. More sophisticated utilities, including amanda, assist you in several ways, including keeping a table of contents of the files in a backup.

dump, restore    The dump utility (**dump** package) first appeared in UNIX version 6. It backs up either an entire **ext2**, **ext3**, or **ext4** filesystem or only those files that have changed since a recent dump. The restore utility can then restore an entire filesystem, a directory hierarchy, or an individual file. Although it is available, not many people use this utility. Refer to dump.sourceforge.net and the dump and restore man pages for more information.

### Exclude some directories from a backup

tip In practice, you will likely want to exclude some directories from the backup process. For example, not backing up **/tmp** or **/var/tmp** (or its link, **/usr/tmp**) can save room in the archive. Also, do not back up the files in **proc**. Because the **/proc** pseudofilesystem is not a true disk filesystem but rather a way for the Linux kernel to provide information about the operating system and system memory, you need not back up **/proc**; you cannot restore it later. Similarly, you do not need to back up filesystems that are mounted from disks on other systems on the network. Do not back up FIFOs; the results are unpredictable.

# Scheduling Tasks

It is a good practice to schedule certain routine tasks to run automatically. For example, you might want to remove old core files once a week, summarize accounting data daily, and rotate system log files monthly.

### crond **stops for no one; try** anacron

tip The **crond** daemon assumes the system is always running. A similar utility, anacron, does not make that assumption and is well suited to portable and home computers that are frequently turned off. The anacron utility takes its instructions from the **/etc/anacrontab** file unless you specify otherwise. It is enabled by default and is set up to catch any missed **cron.daily**, **cron.weekly**, and **cron.monthly run-parts** commands as described in the following sections. Refer to the anacron and anacrontab man pages for more information.

## *LPI* crond **AND** anacron: Schedule Routine Tasks

The **crond** daemon (service) executes scheduled commands periodically. This daemon can execute commands at specific times on systems that are always running. The anacron utility executes scheduled commands when it is called. It works well on laptops and other systems that are not on all the time. The 0anacron script (page 609), which calls anacron, will not run commands when a system is running on batteries (i.e., not on AC).

SELinux When SELinux is set to use a targeted policy, it protects the **crond** daemon. You can disable this protection if necessary. For more information refer to "Setting the Targeted Policy with system-config-selinux" on page 475.

### *LPI* Crontab Files

The **crond** daemon reads the commands it is to execute from crontab files. System crontab files are kept in the **/etc/cron.d** directory and in **/etc/crontab**. Users can use the crontab utility to set up personal crontab files in **/var/spool/cron**. (The term *crontab* has three meanings: It refers to a text file in a specific format [a crontab file; crontab(5) man page], it is the name of a utility [crontab; crontab(1) man page], and it is the name of a file [**/etc/crontab**].)

By default, Fedora/RHEL is set up with no restrictions on which users can have **crond** run commands in their personal crontab files. See **cron.allow** and **cron.deny** on page 506 for ways of restricting this access.

System crontab files    Crontab files specify how often **crond** is to run a command. Within these files, comments begin with a hashmark (#). Crontab files frequently include assignments to several environment variables: The **SHELL** and **PATH** environment variables are described on page 359; **MAILTO** determines which user receives output (via email) from jobs run by the file.

A line describing a job in a system crontab file, such as **/etc/crontab**, has the following format:

> *minute hour day-of-month month day-of-week user command*

The first five fields indicate when **crond** will execute the *command*. The *minute* is the number of minutes after the start of the hour, the *hour* is the hour of the day based on a 24-hour clock, the *day-of-month* is a number from 1 to 31, and the *day-of-week* is a number from 0 to 7, with 0 and 7 indicating Sunday. An asterisk (\*) substitutes for any value in a field. The *user* is the username or user ID of the user that the *command* will run as. Specify *command* as an absolute pathname to ensure **crond** executes the correct *command*.

Following are some examples:

```
20 1 * * *    root    /usr/local/bin/checkit
25 9 17 * *   root    /usr/local/bin/monthly.check
40 23 * * 7   root    /usr/local/bin/sunday.check
10/* * * * *  root    /usr/local/bin/tenmin.check
```

All four lines run their commands with **root** privileges. The first line runs **checkit** every day at 1:20 AM. The second line runs **monthly.check** at 9:25 AM on day 17 of every month. The third line runs **sunday.check** at 11:40 PM every Sunday. The fourth line uses the step syntax to run **tenmin.check** every ten minutes; the **10/\*** is equivalent to **0,10,20,30,40,50**. Enter the command **man 5 crontab** to obtain more information on crontab files.

**LPI** User crontab files    A user crontab file has the same format as a system crontab file except it does not include the *user* field because it always runs as the user who is running it. Users can work with their own crontab files by giving the command **crontab** followed by **–l** to list the file, **–r** to remove the file, or **–e** to edit the file. The **–e** option uses the vi editor by default; if you prefer, export (page 1032) and set the **VISUAL** or **EDITOR** environment variable to the textual editor of your choice. See the crontab man page for more information.

**LPI** /etc/crontab    The **crond** daemon looks for crontab files at **/etc/crontab** and in the **/etc/cron.d** directory. Following is the default **/etc/crontab** file, which does not run any jobs:

```
$ cat /etc/crontab
SHELL=/bin/bash
PATH=/sbin:/bin:/usr/sbin:/usr/bin
MAILTO=root

# For details see man 4 crontabs

# Example of job definition:
# .---------------- minute (0 - 59)
# |  .------------- hour (0 - 23)
# |  |  .---------- day of month (1 - 31)
# |  |  |  .------- month (1 - 12) OR jan,feb,mar,apr ...
# |  |  |  |  .---- day of week (0 - 6) (Sunday=0 or 7) OR sun,mon,tue,wed,thu,fri,sat
# |  |  |  |  |
# *  *  *  *  * user-name  command to be executed
```

**/etc/cron.d/0hourly**  Following is the default **/etc/cron.d/0hourly** crontab file:

```
$ cat /etc/cron.d/0hourly
# Run the hourly jobs
SHELL=/bin/bash
PATH=/sbin:/bin:/usr/sbin:/usr/bin
MAILTO=root
01 * * * * root run-parts /etc/cron.hourly
```

**run-parts**  After setting some variables, this script executes run-parts with **root** privileges. The
**01 * * * *** at the beginning of the line causes **crond** to run the job one minute past
the start of every hour. The run-parts utility runs the executable files in the directory
named by its argument (**/etc/cron.hourly**). Output from the execution of these files
is sent to the user named by **MAILTO** (**root**).

**/etc/cron.hourly/**  Following is the default **/etc/cron.hourly/0anacron** shell script:
**0anacron**

```
$ cat /etc/cron.hourly/0anacron
#!/bin/bash
# Check whether 0anacron was run today already
if test -r /var/spool/anacron/cron.daily; then
    day=`cat /var/spool/anacron/cron.daily`
fi
if [ `date +%Y%m%d` = "$day" ]; then
    exit 0;
fi

# Do not run jobs when on battery power
if test -x /usr/bin/on_ac_power; then
    /usr/bin/on_ac_power &> /dev/null
    if test $? -eq 1; then
    exit 0
    fi
fi
/usr/sbin/anacron -s
```

The anacron utility keeps track of the last time it ran each of its jobs so when it is
called, it can tell which jobs need to be run. The **/var/spool/anacron/cron.daily** file
holds the date anacron last ran the job with the jobID of **cron.daily**. The **0anacron**

script first tests to see if today's date is the same as the one held by the **cron.daily** file. If it is, anacron has already run today, so the script exits. Next the script tests to see if the system is running on AC power. If it is not, the script exits. Thus, if the **cron.daily** job has not been run today and if the system is running on AC power, the script executes anacron. The **–s** option causes anacron to run its jobs serially (not all at once).

**/etc/anacrontab**   When anacron is run, it reads the commands it is to execute from the **/etc/anacrontab** file. This file is where the files in the **/etc/cron.daily**, **/etc/cron.weekly**, and **/etc/cron.monthly** directories get executed on a system running anacron. The **anacrontab** file specifies how often anacron is to run one or more jobs, but has a different syntax from a crontab file. Within the **anacrontab** file, comments begin with a hashmark (#). Several variables that establish the environment a job runs in can appear within the **anacrontab** file: The **SHELL** and **PATH** environment variables are described on page 359; **MAILTO** determines which user receives output (via email) from jobs; **RANDOM_DELAY** delays the start of jobs by a random number of minutes up to the value of this variable; and **START_HOURS_RANGE** specifies the hours during which anacron can start a job.

A job entry in the **anacrontab** file has the following format:

*period delay jobID command*

where the *period* is the frequency in days (how often) that anacron executes the *command*, the *delay* is the number of minutes after anacron starts that it executes the *command*, and the *jobID* is the name of the file in **/var/spool/anacron** that anacron uses to keep track of when it last executed the *command*.

Following is the default **anacrontab** file. Based on the value of the variable named **START_HOURS_RANGE**, anacron can start jobs in this file between 3 AM and 10 PM (3–22).

```
$ cat /etc/anacrontab
# /etc/anacrontab: configuration file for anacron

# See anacron(8) and anacrontab(5) for details.

SHELL=/bin/sh
PATH=/sbin:/bin:/usr/sbin:/usr/bin
MAILTO=root
# the maximal random delay added to the base delay of the jobs
RANDOM_DELAY=45
# the jobs will be started during the following hours only
START_HOURS_RANGE=3-22

#period in days   delay in minutes   job-identifier   command
1       5        cron.daily              nice run-parts /etc/cron.daily
7       25       cron.weekly             nice run-parts /etc/cron.weekly
@monthly 45      cron.monthly            nice run-parts /etc/cron.monthly
```

The line that begins with **1** specifies the job with the jobID of **cron.daily**. This job is run once a day with a delay of 5 minutes. It runs nice, which executes run-parts (page 609) with a low priority; the job passes run-parts an argument of **/etc/cron.daily**. Similarly, the next line runs **cron.weekly** every seven days with a delay of 25 minutes. Because a month does not have a fixed number of days, the last line uses the **@monthly** macro to run **cron.monthly** once a month with a delay of 45 minutes.

As explained earlier, the **crond** daemon runs the shell scripts in the **/etc/cron.hourly** directory.

## *LPI*  at: RUNS OCCASIONAL TASKS

Like the **crond** daemon, at runs a job sometime in the future. Unlike **crond**, at runs a job only once. For instance, you can schedule an at job that will reboot the system at 3:00 AM (when all users are probably logged off):

```
# at 3am
at> systemctl reboot
at> <EOT>
job 3 at Wed Jul 31 03:00:00 2013
```

It is also possible to run an at job from within an at job. For instance, an at job might check for new patches every 18 days—something that would be more difficult with **crond**. See the at man page for more information.

By default, Fedora/RHEL is not set up with restrictions that prevent users from running at. See **at.allow** and **at.deny** on page 506 for more information.

# SYSTEM REPORTS

Many utilities report on one thing or another. The who, finger, ls, ps, and other utilities, for example, generate simple end-user reports. In some cases, these reports can help with system administration. This section describes utilities that generate more in-depth reports that can provide greater assistance with system administration tasks. Linux has many other report utilities, including sar (system activity report), iostat (input/output and CPU statistics), and mpstat (processor statistics), all part of the **sysstat** package; netstat (network report; **net-tools** package); and nfsstat (NFS statistics; **nfs-utils** package).

## vmstat: REPORTS VIRTUAL MEMORY STATISTICS

The vmstat utility (virtual memory statistics; **procps-ng** package) generates virtual memory information along with (limited) disk and CPU activity data. The following example shows virtual memory statistics at three-second intervals for seven iterations (from the arguments 3 7). The first line covers the time since the system was booted; each subsequent line covers the period since the previous line.

```
$ vmstat 3 7
procs -----------memory---------- ---swap-- -----io---- --system-- ----cpu----
 r  b   swpd   free   buff  cache   si   so    bi    bo   in    cs us sy id wa
 0  2      0 684328  33924 219916    0    0   430   105 1052   134  2  4 86  8
 0  2      0 654632  34160 248840    0    0  4897  7683 1142   237  0  5  0 95
 0  3      0 623528  34224 279080    0    0  5056  8237 1094   178  0  4  0 95
 0  2      0 603176  34576 298936    0    0  3416   141 1161   255  0  4  0 96
 0  2      0 575912  34792 325616    0    0  4516  7267 1147   231  0  4  0 96
 1  2      0 549032  35164 351464    0    0  4429    77 1120   210  0  4  0 96
 0  2      0 523432  35448 376376    0    0  4173  6577 1135   234  0  4  0 95
```

The following list explains the column heads displayed by vmstat:

- **procs**   Process information
  - ◆ **r**        Number of waiting, runnable processes
  - ◆ **b**        Number of blocked processes (in uninterruptable sleep)
- **memory**   Memory information (in kilobytes)
  - ◆ **swpd**   Used virtual memory
  - ◆ **free**    Idle memory
  - ◆ **buff**    Memory used as buffers
  - ◆ **cache**   Memory used as cache
- **swap**   System paging activity (in kilobytes per second)
  - ◆ **si**        Memory swapped in from disk
  - ◆ **so**       Memory swapped out to disk
- **io**   System I/O activity (in blocks per second)
  - ◆ **bi**        Blocks received from a block device
  - ◆ **bo**       Blocks sent to a block device
- **system**   (Values are per second)
  - ◆ **in**        Interrupts (including the clock)
  - ◆ **cs**       Context switches
- **cpu**   Percentage of total CPU time spent in each of these states
  - ◆ **us**       User (nonkernel)
  - ◆ **sy**       System (kernel)
  - ◆ **id**        Idle
  - ◆ **wa**      Waiting for I/O
  - ◆ **st**        Stolen from a virtual machine (only on virtual machines)

## *LE+*   top: LISTS PROCESSES USING THE MOST RESOURCES

The top utility is a useful supplement to ps. At its simplest, top displays system information followed by the most CPU-intensive processes. The top utility updates itself periodically; type **q** to quit. Although you can use command-line options, the interactive commands are often more helpful. Refer to Table 15-2 and to the top man page for more information.

```
$ top
top - 17:58:53 up 3 days,  4:20,  1 user,  load average: 2.16, 1.61, 0.83
Tasks: 167 total,   5 running, 162 sleeping,   0 stopped,   0 zombie
Cpu(s):  1.5%us,  0.5%sy,  1.3%ni, 96.0%id,  0.2%wa,  0.6%hi,  0.0%si,  0.0%st
Mem:   2076092k total,  1990652k used,    85440k free,    18416k buffers
Swap:  7815580k total,    34908k used,  7780672k free,  1330008k cached
```

```
   PID USER       PR  NI  VIRT  RES  SHR S %CPU %MEM    TIME+  COMMAND
 31323 zach       25   0  9020 6960  396 R   63  0.3  0:17.58 bzip2
 31327 zach       18   0  2092  596  492 R   57  0.0  0:00.92 cp
 31311 root       15   0     0    0    0 S   16  0.0  0:00.38 pdflush
  6870 zach       27  12  331m 190m  37m R    2  9.4 198:42.98 firefox-bin
 31303 root       15   0     0    0    0 S    2  0.0  0:00.42 pdflush
     1 root       15   0  2912 1808  488 S    0  0.1  0:01.55 systemd
...
```

The htop utility (**htop** package) is similar to top but it is pseudographical. Using htop, you can scroll vertically and horizontally, allowing you to view all processes and full command lines.

Table 15-2    top: interactive commands

| Command | Function |
| --- | --- |
| **h** or **?** | Displays a Help screen. |
| **k** | (**kill**) Prompts for a PID number and type of signal and sends the process that signal. Defaults to signal 15 (SIGTERM); specify 9 (SIGKILL) only when 15 does not work. |
| **F** | Displays a page that allows you to specify a sort field. |
| **f** | Displays a page that allows you to specify which fields top displays. |
| **o** | Displays a page that allows you to specify the order of the displayed fields. |
| **q** | Quits top. |
| **s** | Prompts for time between updates in seconds. Use 0 (zero) for continuous updates; such updates can slow the system by consuming a lot of resources. |
| SPACE | Updates the display immediately. |
| **u** | Prompts for username and displays only processes owned by that user. |
| **W** | Writes a startup file named **~/.toprc** so that the next time you start top, it uses the same parameters it is currently using. |

# MAINTAINING THE SYSTEM

This section discusses several tools and concepts that are important to a system administrator. It covers setting the system clock, using parted to work with partitions on a hard disk, how to avoid creating problems, and how to solve system problems.

## *LPI* timedatectl: REPORTS ON AND SETS THE SYSTEM CLOCK

The timedatectl utility, which is part of systemd (page 438), displays more information about the system clock than does date (page 218). You can also use it to set the system clock. Following, timedatectl sets the system clock and displays information about the system clock, time zone, NTP, and DST.

```
# timedatectl set-time "2014-02-14 18:17:16"

# timedatectl
      Local time: Fri 2014-02-14 18:17:21 PST
  Universal time: Sat 2014-02-15 02:17:21 UTC
        RTC time: Sat 2014-02-15 02:17:21
        Timezone: America/Los_Angeles (PST, -0800)
     NTP enabled: n/a
NTP synchronized: no
 RTC in local TZ: no
      DST active: no
 Last DST change: DST ended at
                  Sun 2013-11-03 01:59:59 PDT
                  Sun 2013-11-03 01:00:00 PST
 Next DST change: DST begins (the clock jumps one hour forward) at
                  Sun 2014-03-09 01:59:59 PST
                  Sun 2014-03-09 03:00:00 PDT
```

# *LPI* parted: REPORTS ON AND PARTITIONS A HARD DISK

The parted (partition editor) utility reports on and manipulates hard disk partitions from the command line. The gnome-disks utility (page 78) allows you to perform the same tasks using a GUI. Following, the parted **print** command displays information about the partitions on the **/dev/sda** drive:

```
# parted /dev/sda print
Model: ATA Hitachi HDS12345 (scsi)
Disk /dev/sda: 165GB
Sector size (logical/physical): 512B/512B
Partition Table: msdos
Disk Flags:

Number  Start   End     Size    Type      File system   Flags
1       32kB    1045MB  1045MB  primary   ext4          boot
2       1045MB  12GB    10GB    primary   ext4
3       12GB    22GB    10GB    primary   ext4
4       22GB    165GB   143GB   extended
5       22GB    23GB    1045MB  logical   linux-swap(v1)
6       23GB    41GB    18GB    logical   ext4
7       41GB    82GB    41GB    logical   ext4
```

Figure 15-3 graphically depicts the partitions shown in this example. The first few lines that parted displays present the model name, device name, device capacity, and the type of partition table on the device. Following that information, the **print** command displays the these columns:

- **Number**—The minor device number (page 517) of the device holding the partition. This number is the same as the last number in the device name. In the example, **5** corresponds to **/dev/sda5**.

- **Start**—The location on the disk where the partition starts. The parted utility specifies a location on the disk as the distance (in bytes) from the start of the disk. Thus partition 3 starts 12 gigabytes from the start of the disk.

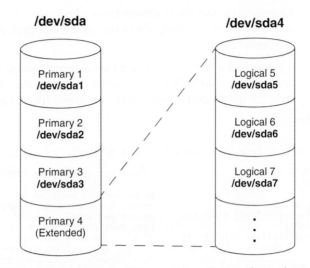

**Figure 15-3**   The primary and extended partitions from the example

- **End**—The location on the disk where the partition stops. Although parted shows partition 2 ending 12 gigabytes from the start of the disk and partition 3 starting at the same location, parted takes care that the partitions do not overlap at this single byte.

- **Size**—The size of the partition in kilobytes (kB), megabytes (MB), or gigabytes (GB).

- **Type**—The partition type: primary, extended, or logical. See Figure 15-3 and page 37 for information on partitions.

- **File system**—The filesystem type: ext2, ext3, ext4, fat32, linux-swap, and so on. See Table 11-1 on page 519 for a list of filesystem types.

- **Flags**—The flags that are turned on for the partition, including **boot**, **raid**, and **lvm**. In the example, partition 1 is bootable.

In the preceding example, partition 4 defines an extended partition that includes 143 gigabytes of the 165-gigabyte disk (Figure 15-3). You cannot make changes to an extended partition without affecting all logical partitions within it.

### parted **can destroy everything**

caution   Be as careful with **parted** as you would be with a utility that formats a hard disk. Changes you make with **parted** can easily result in the loss of large amounts of data. If you are using **parted** and have any question about what you are doing, quit with a **q** command before making any changes. When you enter a command, **parted** immediately makes the change you requested.

In addition to reporting on the layout and size of a hard disk, you can use parted interactively to modify the disk layout. Be *extremely* careful when using parted in this manner and always back up the system before starting to work with this utility.

Changing the partition information (the *partition table*) on a disk can destroy the information on the disk. Read the parted info page before you attempt to modify a partition table.

To partition a disk, give the command **parted** followed by the name of the device you want to work with. In the following example, after starting parted, the user enters a **help** (or just **h**) command, which displays a list of parted commands:

```
# parted /dev/sda
GNU Parted 3.1
Using /dev/sda
Welcome to GNU Parted! Type 'help' to view a list of commands.
(parted) help
  align-check TYPE N                       check partition N for TYPE(min|opt)
        alignment
  help [COMMAND]                           print general help, or help on COMMAND
  mklabel,mktable LABEL-TYPE               create a new disklabel (partition table)
  mkpart PART-TYPE [FS-TYPE] START END     make a partition
  name NUMBER NAME                         name partition NUMBER as NAME
  print [devices|free|list,all|NUMBER]     display the partition table, available
        devices, free space, all found partitions, or a particular partition
  quit                                     exit program
  rescue START END                         rescue a lost partition near START and END
  rm NUMBER                                delete partition NUMBER
  select DEVICE                            choose the device to edit
  disk_set FLAG STATE                      change the FLAG on selected device
  disk_toggle [FLAG]                       toggle the state of FLAG on selected device
  set NUMBER FLAG STATE                    change the FLAG on partition NUMBER
  toggle [NUMBER [FLAG]]                   toggle the state of FLAG on partition NUMBER
  unit UNIT                                set the default unit to UNIT
  version                                  display the version number and copyright information ...
(parted)
```

Follow the command **help** with the name of a parted command to display more information about that command. When you enter a **print** (or just **p**) command, parted displays current partition information, just as a **print** command on the command line does.

The parted utility will not allow you to set up overlapping partitions (except for logical partitions overlapping their containing extended partition). Similarly, it will not allow you to create a partition that starts at the very beginning of the disk (cylinder 0). Both of these situations can cause loss of data.

Following are guidelines to remember when defining a partition table for a disk. For more information refer to "Partitioning a Disk" on page 39.

- Do not delete or modify the partition that defines the extended partition unless you are willing to lose all data on all the logical partitions within the extended partition.

- If you put **/boot** on a separate partition, it is a good idea to put it at the beginning of the drive (partition 1) so there is no issue of Linux having to boot from a partition located too far into the drive. When you can afford the disk space, it is desirable to put each major filesystem on a separate partition. Many people choose to combine **/** (root), **/var**, and **/usr** into a single partition, which generally results in less wasted space but can on rare occasions cause problems. For more information refer to "Manual Partitioning: Planning Partitions" on page 39.

- Although parted can create some types of filesystems, it is typically easiest to use parted to create partitions and then use mkfs and mkswap to create filesystems on the partitions.

The following sequence of commands defines a 50-gigabyte, bootable, Linux partition as partition 1 on a clean disk:

```
# parted /dev/sdb
GNU Parted 3.1
Using /dev/sdb
Welcome to GNU Parted! Type 'help' to view a list of commands.
(parted) mkpart                              (create new partition)
Partition type?  primary/extended? primary   (select primary partition)
File system type?  [ext2]? ext4              (set up an ext4 filesystem)
Start? 1                                     (start at the beginning of the disk)
End? 50g                                     (specify a 50-gigabyte partition)
(parted) help set                            (use help to check the syntax of the set command)
  set NUMBER FLAG STATE                      change the FLAG on partition NUMBER

        NUMBER is the partition number used by Linux.  On MS-DOS disk labels, the
        primary partitions number from 1 to 4, logical partitions from 5 onwards.
        FLAG is one of: boot, root, swap, hidden, raid, lvm, lba, hp-service, palo, prep,
        msftres, bios_grub, atvrecv, diag, legacy_boot
        STATE is one of: on, off
(parted) set 1 boot on                       (turn on the boot flag on partition 1)
(parted) print                               (verify that the partition is correct)
Model: VMware, VMware Virtual S (scsi)
Disk /dev/sdb: 215GB
Sector size (logical/physical): 512B/512B
Partition Table: msdos
Disk Flags:

Number  Start    End     Size    Type     File system  Flags
 1      1049kB   50.0GB  50.0GB  primary               boot

(parted) quit
Information: You may need to update /etc/fstab.
```

When you specify a size within parted, you can use a suffix of **k** (kilobytes), **m** (megabytes), or **g** (gigabytes). After creating a partition, enter a **print** command to see where the partition ends. Perform this task before defining the next contiguous partition so you do not waste space. After setting up all the partitions, exit from parted using a **quit** command.

Next make a filesystem (mkfs, page 467) on each partition that is to hold a filesystem (not swap). Make all partitions, except swap, of type **ext4**, unless you have a reason to do otherwise. Use mkswap (page 513) to set up a swap area on a partition. You can use e2label (page 465) to label a partition.

# logrotate: MANAGES LOG FILES

Rather than deleting or truncating log files, you might want to keep these files for a while in case you need to refer to them. The logrotate utility manages system log (and other) files automatically by *rotating* (page 1271), compressing, mailing, and removing each file as you specify. The logrotate utility is controlled by the **/etc/logrotate.conf** file, which sets default values and can optionally specify files to be rotated. Typically **logrotate.conf** has an **include** statement that points to utility-specific specification files in **/etc/logrotate.d**. Following is the default **logrotate.conf** file:

```
$ cat /etc/logrotate.conf
# see "man logrotate" for details
# rotate log files weekly
weekly

# keep 4 weeks worth of backlogs
rotate 4

# create new (empty) log files after rotating old ones
create

# use date as a suffix of the rotated file
dateext

# uncomment this if you want your log files compressed
#compress

# RPM packages drop log rotation information into this directory
include /etc/logrotate.d

# no packages own wtmp and btmp -- we'll rotate them here
/var/log/wtmp {
    monthly
    create 0664 root utmp
        minsize 1M
    rotate 1
}

/var/log/btmp {
    missingok
    monthly
    create 0600 root utmp
    rotate 1
}

# system-specific logs may be also be configured here.
```

The **logrotate.conf** file sets default values for common parameters. Whenever logrotate reads another value for one of these parameters, it resets the default value. You have a choice of rotating files **daily, weekly,** or **monthly.** The number following the **rotate** keyword specifies the number of rotated log files you want to keep. The **create** keyword causes logrotate to create a new log file with the same name and attributes as the newly rotated log file. The **dateext** keyword causes logrotate to use the date as a filename extension. The **compress** keyword (commented out in the default file) causes log files to be compressed using gzip. The **include** keyword specifies the standard **/etc/logrotate.d** directory for program-specific logrotate specification files. When you install a program using rpm (page 548) or an rpm-based utility such as yum (Chapter 12), rpm puts the logrotate specification file in this directory.

The last sets of instructions in **logrotate.conf** take care of the **/var/log/wtmp** and **/var/log/btmp** log files (**wtmp** holds login records and **btmp** holds records of failed [bad] login attempts); you can view these files using **who**). The keyword **missingok** overrides the implicit default value of **nomissingok** *for this file only*. This keyword causes logrotate to continue without issuing an error message if the log file is missing. The keyword **monthly** overrides the default value of **weekly** *for this file only*. The **create** keyword is followed by the arguments establishing the permissions, owner, and group for the new file. Finally **rotate** establishes that one rotated log file should be kept.

The **/etc/logrotate.d/httpd** file is an example of a utility-specific logrotate specification file:

```
$ cat /etc/logrotate.d/httpd
/var/log/httpd/*log {
    missingok
    notifempty
    sharedscripts
    delaycompress
    postrotate
        /bin/systemctl reload httpd.service > /dev/null 2>/dev/null || true
    endscript
}
```

This file, which is installed by the **httpd** package install script and incorporated in **/etc/logrotate.d** because of the **include** statement in **logrotate.conf**, works with each of the files in **/var/log/httpd** that has a filename ending in **log** (**\*log**). The **notifempty** keyword causes logrotate not to rotate the log file if it is empty, overriding the default action of rotating empty log files. The **sharedscripts** keyword causes logrotate to execute the command(s) in the **prerotate** and **postrotate** sections one time only—not one time for each log that is rotated. The **delaycompress** keyword causes logrotate to delay compression for one cycle. Although it does not appear in this example, the **copytruncate** keyword causes logrotate to truncate the original log file immediately after it copies it. This keyword is useful for programs that cannot be instructed to close and reopen their log files because they might continue writing to the original file even after it has been moved. The logrotate utility executes the commands between **prerotate** and **endscript** before the rotation begins. Similarly, commands between **postrotate** and **endscript** are executed after the rotation is complete.

The logrotate utility works with a variety of keywords, many of which take arguments and have side effects. Refer to the logrotate man page for details.

# *LE+* rsyslogd: LOGS SYSTEM MESSAGES

Traditionally, UNIX programs sent log messages to standard error. If a more permanent log was required, the output was redirected to a file. Because of the limitations of this approach, 4.3BSD introduced the system log daemon (**rsyslogd**; www.rsyslog.com) now used by Linux. This daemon listens for log messages and stores them in the **/var/log** hierarchy. In addition to providing logging facilities, **rsyslogd** allows a single machine to serve as a log repository for a network and allows arbitrary programs to process specific log messages.

*LPI* **rsyslog.conf**  The **/etc/rsyslog.conf** file stores configuration information for **rsyslogd**. Each line in this file contains one or more *selectors* and an *action* separated by whitespace. The selectors define the origin and type of the messages; the action specifies how **rsyslogd** processes the message. Sample lines from **rsyslog.conf** follow (a **#** begins a comment):

```
# Log all kernel messages to the console.
kern.*                                    /dev/console
# Log all the mail messages in one place.
mail.*                                    -/var/log/maillog
# Log cron stuff
cron.*                                    /var/log/cron
# Everybody gets emergency messages
*.emerg                                   :omusrmsg:*
# Save boot messages also to boot.log
local7.*                                  /var/log/boot.log
```

*LPI* Selectors  A selector is split into two parts, a *facility* and a *priority,* which are separated by a period. The facility indicates the origin of the message. For example, **kern** messages come from the kernel, and **mail** messages come from the mail subsystem. Following is a list of facility names used by **rsyslogd** and the systems that generate these messages:

*LPI* Facilities

| | |
|---|---|
| **auth** | Authorization and security systems including login |
| **authpriv** | Same as **auth,** but should be logged to a secure location |
| **cron** | **crond** |
| **daemon** | System and network daemons without their own categories |
| **kern** | Kernel |
| **lpr** | Printing subsystem |
| **mail** | Mail subsystem |
| **news** | Network news subsystem |
| **user** | Default facility; all user programs use this facility |
| **uucp** | The UNIX-to-UNIX copy protocol subsystem |
| **local0** to **local7** | Reserved for local use |

The priority indicates the severity of the message. The following list of the priority names and the conditions they represent appears in ascending priority order:

*LPI* Priorities

| | |
|---|---|
| **debug** | Debugging information |
| **info** | Information that does not require intervention |
| **notice** | Conditions that might require intervention |

| warning | Warnings |
| err | Errors |
| crit | Critical conditions such as hardware failure |
| alert | Conditions that require immediate attention |
| emerg | Emergency conditions |

A selector consisting of a single facility and priority, such as **kern.info**, causes the corresponding action to be applied to every message from that facility with that priority *or higher* (more urgent). Use **.=** to specify a single priority; for example, **kern.=info** applies the action to kernel messages of **info** priority. An exclamation point specifies that a priority is not matched. Thus **kern.!info** matches kernel messages with a priority lower than **info**, and **kern.!=info** matches kernel messages with a priority other than **info**.

A line with multiple selectors, separated by semicolons, applies the action if any of the selectors is matched. Each of the selectors on a line with multiple selectors constrains the match, with subsequent selectors frequently tightening the constraints. For example, the selectors **mail.info;mail.!err** match mail subsystem messages with **debug**, **info**, **notice**, or **warning** priorities.

You can replace either part of the selector with an asterisk to match anything. The keyword **none** in either part of the selector indicates no match is possible. The selector **\*.crit;kern.none** matches all critical or higher-priority messages, except those from the kernel.

**Actions**    The action specifies how **rsyslogd** processes a message that matches the selector. The simplest actions are ordinary files, which are specified by their absolute pathnames; **rsyslogd** appends messages to these files. Specify **/dev/console** to send messages to the system console. If you want a hardcopy record of messages, specify a device file that represents a dedicated printer. Precede a filename with a hyphen (–) to keep **rsyslogd** from writing each message to the file as it is generated (syncing). Doing so might improve performance, but you might lose data if the system crashes after the message is generated but before it gets written to a file.

You can write important messages to users' terminals by specifying one or more usernames separated by commas. Very important messages can be written to every logged-in terminal by using an asterisk.

To forward messages to **rsyslogd** on a remote system, specify the name or IP address of the system preceded by **@** (sends messages to UDP port 514) or **@@** (sends messages to TCP port 514). It is a good idea to forward critical messages from the kernel to another system because these messages often precede a system crash and might not be saved to the local disk. The following line from **rsyslog.conf** sends critical kernel messages to **plum**:

```
kern.crit       @plum
```

On the remote system edit **/etc/rsyslog.conf** and one or both sets of the following lines depending on whether you want to use UDP or TCP. Do not remove the hash marks from the comments. After editing this file restart the **rsyslogd** daemon using **rsyslog.service**.

```
# Provides UDP syslog reception
#$ModLoad imudp
#$UDPServerRun 514

# Provides TCP syslog reception
#$ModLoad imtcp
#$InputTCPServerRun 514
```

# SOLVING PROBLEMS

As the system administrator, it is your responsibility to keep the system secure and running smoothly. When a user is having a problem, it usually falls to the administrator to help the user get back on track. This section suggests ways to keep users happy and the system functioning at peak performance.

## HELPING WHEN A USER CANNOT LOG IN

When a user has trouble logging in on the system, the source might be a user error or a problem with the system software or hardware. The following steps can help determine where the problem is:

*LPI*

- Check the log files in **/var/log**. The **/var/log/messages** file accumulates system errors, messages from daemon processes, and other important information. It might indicate the cause or more symptoms of a problem. Also check the system console. Occasionally messages about system problems that are not written to **/var/log/messages** (for instance, a full disk) are displayed on the system console.

- Determine whether only that one user or only that one user's terminal/workstation has a problem or if the problem is more widespread.

- Check that the user's CAPS LOCK key is not on.

- Make sure the user's home directory exists and corresponds to that user's entry in the **/etc/passwd** file. Verify that the user owns her home directory and startup files and that they are readable (and, in the case of the user's home directory, executable). Confirm that the entry for the user's login shell in the **/etc/passwd** file is accurate and the shell exists as specified.

- Change the user's password if there is a chance that he has forgotten it.

- Check the user's startup files (**.profile**, **.login**, **.bashrc**, and so on). The user might have edited one of these files and introduced a syntax error that prevents login.

- Check the terminal or monitor data cable from where it plugs into the terminal to where it plugs into the computer (or as far as you can follow it). Try turning the terminal or monitor off and then turning it back on.

- When the problem appears to be widespread, check whether you can log in from the system console. Make sure the system is not in single-user mode. If you cannot log in, the system might have crashed; reboot it and perform any necessary recovery steps (the system usually does quite a bit automatically).

- Use df to check for full filesystems. If the /tmp filesystem or the user's home directory is full, login sometimes fails in unexpected ways. In some cases you might be able to log in to a textual environment but not a graphical one. When applications that start when the user logs in cannot create temporary files or cannot update files in the user's home directory, the login process itself might terminate.

- If the user is logging in over a network connection

  - Restart the service the user is trying to use (e.g., ssh). See "Changing the Current State of a Daemon" on page 446.

  - Make sure the system clocks on the two systems are synchronized. Clocks set to different times can cause login failures when using encrypted login methods such as HTTPS, ssh, LDAP, and especially kerberos.

  - Make sure DNS is working properly. Some network services are particular about name resolution including reverse lookups (i.e., slow connections via ssh can be caused by a name resolution problem).

## SPEEDING UP THE SYSTEM

When the system is running slowly for no apparent reason, perhaps a process did not exit when a user logged out. Symptoms of this problem include poor response time and a system load, as shown by w or uptime, greater than 1.0. Running top (page 612) is an excellent way to find rogue processes quickly. Use ps –ef to list all processes. One thing to look for in ps –ef output is a large number in the TIME column. For example, if a Firefox process has a TIME field greater than 100.0, this process has likely run amok. However, if the user is doing a lot of Java work and has not logged out for a long time, this value might be normal. Look at the STIME field to see when the process was started. If the process has been running for longer than the user has been logged in, it is a good candidate to be killed.

When a user gets stuck and leaves her terminal unattended without notifying anyone, it is convenient to kill (page 465) all processes owned by that user. If the user is running a GUI on the console, kill the process that started the desktop environment or the window manager itself. Processes to look for include **gnome-session, startkde,** or another process name that ends in **wm**. Usually the window manager is either the first or last thing to be run, and exiting from the window manager logs the user out. If killing the window manager does not work, try killing the X server process. This process is typically listed as **/usr/bin/Xorg**. If that fails, you can kill all processes owned by a user by giving the command **kill –15 –1** or, equivalently, **kill –TERM –1** *while you are logged in as that user.* Using **–1** (one) in place of the process ID tells kill to send the signal to all processes that are owned by that user. For example, working as **root** you could enter the following command:

```
# su zach -c 'kill -TERM -1'
```

If this does not kill all processes (sometimes TERM does not kill a process), you can use the KILL signal (**–9**). The following line will definitely kill all processes owned by Zach and will not be friendly about it:

```
# su zach -c 'kill -KILL -1'
```

If you do not include **su zach –c**, this command brings the system down.

## *LPI* lsof: FINDS OPEN FILES

The lsof (list open files) utility displays the names of open files. Its options display only certain processes, only certain file descriptors of a process, or only certain network connections (network connections use file descriptors just as normal files do and lsof can show these as well). After you have identified a suspect process using **ps –ef**, enter the following command:

```
# lsof -s -p pid
```

Replace *pid* with the process ID of the suspect process; lsof displays a list of file descriptors that process *pid* has open. The **–s** option displays the sizes of all open files, and the **–p** option allows you to specify the PID number of the process of interest (lsof does not work if you combine these options). This size information is helpful in determining whether the process has a very large file open. If it does, contact the owner of the process or, if necessary, kill the process. The **–r***n* option redisplays the output of lsof every *n* seconds.

## KEEPING A MACHINE LOG

A machine log that includes the information shown in Table 15-3 can help you find and fix system problems. It it useful to note the time and date of each entry in the log. Avoid the temptation to keep the log *only* on the computer—it will be most useful to you when the system is down. Also keep email that details user problems. One strategy is to save this mail to a separate file or folder as you read it. Another approach is to set up a mail alias that users can send mail to when they have problems. This alias can then forward mail to you and also store a copy in an archive file. Following is an example of an entry in the **/etc/aliases** file (page 746) that sets up this type of alias:

```
trouble: admin,/var/spool/mail/admin.archive
```

Email sent to the **trouble** alias will be forwarded to the **admin** user as well as stored in the file **/var/spool/mail/admin.archive**.

Table 15-3   Machine log

| Entry | Function |
| --- | --- |
| Hardware modifications | Keep track of the system hardware configuration: which devices hold which partitions, the model of the new NIC you added, and so on. |
| System software modifications | Keep track of the options used when building Linux. Print such files as **/usr/src/linux/.config** (Linux kernel configuration). The file hierarchy under **/etc/sysconfig** and **/etc/default** contain valuable information about the network configuration, among other things. |
| Hardware malfunctions | Keep as accurate a list as possible of any problems with the system. Make note of any error messages or numbers the system displays on the system console and identify what users were doing when the problem occurred. |
| User complaints | Make a list of all reasonable complaints made by knowledgeable users (for example, "Machine is abnormally slow"). |

## KEEPING THE SYSTEM SECURE

No system with dial-in lines or public access to terminals is absolutely secure. Nevertheless, you can make a system as secure as possible by changing the passwords of the **root** password frequently and by choosing passwords that are difficult to guess. Do not tell anyone who does not *absolutely* need to know the **root** password. You can also encourage system users to choose difficult passwords and to change them periodically.

**LE**   Passwords   This section contains a technical discussion of passwords; see "Password Security" on page 136 for a more practical discussion.

By default, passwords on Fedora/RHEL use *MD5* (page 1260) hashing, which makes them more difficult to crack than passwords encrypted with DES (page 1159). Of course, it makes little difference how well encrypted your password is if you make it easy for someone to find out or guess what the password is. The system-config-authentication utility allows you to specify a local password hashing algorithm: Select the Advanced Options tab and make a selection from the drop-down box labeled **Password Hashing Algorithm**.

A password that is difficult to guess is one that someone else would not be likely to think you would have chosen. Do not use words from the dictionary (spelled forward or backward); names of relatives, pets, or friends; or words from a foreign language. A good strategy is to choose a couple of short words, include some punctuation (for example, put a ^ between them), mix the case, and replace some of the letters in the words with numbers. If it were not printed in this book, an example of a good password would be **C&yGram5** (candygrams). Ideally you would use a random combination of ASCII characters, but that would be difficult to remember.

You can use one of several password-cracking programs to find users who have chosen poor passwords. These programs work by repeatedly hashing words from dictionaries, phrases, names, and other sources. If the hashed password matches the output of the program, then the program has found the password of the user. Two programs that crack passwords are crack (**crack** package) and john (John the Ripper; www.openwall.com/john; **john** package). These and many other programs and security tips are available from CERT (www.cert.org), which was originally called the Computer Emergency Response Team.

It takes a lot of computational power to crack a good password. Password-cracking programs generally start by looking at the character set comprising uppercase and lowercase letters and numbers. When you add symbols, they have to do more work to crack a password. Also, the longer the password, the more computational power it takes to crack. Make your password long enough so it will be harder to crack and short enough so you can remember it; 8–20 characters is usually a good length. Include a few symbols such as #, @, and %. If it takes too long to crack your password, the person or machine doing the dirty work might move on to easier accounts.

**LE+**   Setuid files   Make sure no one except a user with **root** privileges can write to files containing programs that are owned by **root** and run in setuid mode (for example, passwd, su, and sudo; page 196). Also make sure users do not transfer programs that run in setuid mode and are owned by **root** onto the system by means of mounting tapes or disks. These programs can be used to circumvent system security. One technique that prevents users from having setuid files is to use the **nosuid** flag to mount, which you can set in the flags section in the **fstab** file. Refer to "Mount Options" on page 522.

BIOS   The BIOS in many machines gives you some degree of protection from an unauthorized person who tries to modify the BIOS or reboot the system. When you set up the BIOS, look for a section named **Security**. You can probably add a BIOS password. If you depend on the BIOS password, lock the computer case—it is usually a simple matter to reset the BIOS password by using a jumper on the motherboard.

## **LE**   LOG FILES AND MAIL FOR root

Users frequently email **root** and **postmaster** to communicate with the system administrator. If you do not forward **root**'s mail to yourself (/etc/aliases on page 746), remember to check **root**'s mail periodically. You will not receive reminders about mail that arrives for **root** when you use su to perform system administration tasks. However, you can use the command **su –c 'mail –u root'** to look at **root**'s mail.

Review the system log files regularly for evidence of problems. Some important files are **/var/log/messages**, where the operating system and some applications record errors; **/var/log/secure**, which holds messages pertaining to system security; **/var/log/maillog**, which contains errors from the mail system; and **/var/log/cron**, which contains messages from **crond**.

The logwatch utility (**logwatch** package) is a report writer that is written in Perl and sends email reports about log files. Installing the **logwatch** package creates the **/etc/cron.daily/0logwatch** file that runs this script daily and emails its output to **root**. Refer to the logwatch man page and to the script itself for more information.

## MONITORING DISK USAGE

Sooner or later you will probably start to run out of disk space. Do not fill up a partition; Linux can write to files significantly faster if at least 5 to 30 percent of the space in a partition remains free. Using more than the maximum optimal disk space in a partition can degrade system performance.

Fragmentation    As a filesystem becomes full, it can become fragmented. This is similar to the DOS concept of fragmentation but is not nearly as pronounced and is typically rare on modern Linux filesystems; by design Linux filesystems are resistant to fragmentation. If you keep filesystems from running near full capacity, you might never need to worry about fragmentation. If there is no space on a filesystem, you cannot write to it at all.

To check for filesystem fragmentation, unmount the filesystem and run fsck (page 525) on it; use the –f option on **ext2**, **ext3**, and **ext4** filesystems. The output of fsck includes a percent fragmentation figure for the filesystem. You can defragment a filesystem by backing it up; using mkfs (page 467) to make a clean, empty image; and then restoring the filesystem. Which utility you use to perform the backup and restore—dump/restore, tar, cpio, or a third-party backup program—is not important.

Reports    Linux provides several programs that report on who is using how much disk space on which filesystems. Refer to the du, quota, and df man pages and the **–size** option in the find utility man page. In addition to these utilities, you can use the disk quota system (page 629) to manage disk space.

Four strategies to increase the amount of free space on a filesystem are to compress files, delete files, grow LVM-based filesystems, and condense directories. This section contains some ideas on ways to maintain a filesystem so it does not become overloaded.

Files that grow quickly    Some files, such as log files and temporary files, inevitably grow over time. Core dump files, for example, take up substantial space and are rarely needed. Also, users occasionally run programs that accidentally generate huge files. As the system administrator, you must review these files periodically so they do not get out of hand.

If a filesystem is running out of space quickly (that is, over a period of an hour rather than weeks or months), first figure out why it is running out of space. Use a **ps –ef** command to determine if a user has created a runaway process that is creating a huge file. When evaluating the output of ps, look for a process that has consumed a large amount of CPU time. If such a process is running and creating a large file, the file will continue to grow as you free up space. If you remove the huge file, the space it occupied will not be freed until the process terminates, so you need to kill the process. Try to contact the user running the process and ask him to kill it. If you cannot contact the user, use **root** privileges to kill the process yourself. Refer to kill on page 465 for more information.

*LPI*    You can also truncate a large log file rather than remove it, although you can better deal with this recurring situation using logrotate (page 618). For example, if the

/var/log/messages file has become very large because a system daemon is misconfigured, you can use **/dev/null** to truncate it:

```
# cp /dev/null /var/log/messages
```

*or*

```
# cat /dev/null > /var/log/messages
```

*or,* without spawning a new process,

```
# : > /var/log/messages
```

If you remove **/var/log/messages**, you have to restart the **rsyslogd** daemon. If you do not restart **rsyslogd**, the space on the filesystem will not be released.

When no single process is consuming the disk space but capacity has instead been used up gradually, locate unneeded files and delete them. You can archive these files by using **cpio**, **dump**, or **tar** before you delete them. You can safely remove most files named **core** that have not been accessed for several days. The following command line performs this function without removing necessary files named **core** (such as **/dev/core**):

```
# find / -type f -name core | xargs file | grep 'B core file' | sed 's/:ELF.*//g' | xargs rm -f
```

The find command lists all ordinary files named **core** and sends its output to xargs (page 260), which runs file on each of the files in the list. The file utility displays a string that includes **B core file** for files created as the result of a core dump. These files need to be removed. The grep command filters out from file any lines that do not contain this string. Finally sed removes everything following the colon so that all that is left on the line is the pathname of the **core** file; xargs then removes the file.

To free up more disk space, look through the **/tmp** and **/var/tmp** directories for old temporary files and remove them. Keep track of disk usage in **/var/mail**, **/var/spool**, and **/var/log**.

## REMOVING UNUSED SPACE FROM DIRECTORIES

A directory that contains too many filenames is inefficient. The point at which a directory on an **ext2**, **ext3**, or **ext4** filesystem becomes inefficient varies, depending partly on the length of the filenames it contains. Best practice is to keep directories relatively small. Having fewer than several hundred files (or directories) in a directory is generally a good idea, and having more than several thousand is generally a bad idea. Additionally, Linux uses a caching mechanism for frequently accessed files that speeds the process of locating an inode from a filename. This caching mechanism works only on filenames of up to 30 characters in length, so avoid giving frequently accessed files extremely long filenames.

When a directory becomes too large, you can usually break it into several smaller directories by moving its contents to those new directories. Make sure you remove the original directory after you have moved its contents.

Because Linux directories do not shrink automatically, removing a file from a directory does not shrink the directory, even though it frees up space on the disk. To remove unused space and make a directory smaller, you must copy or move all the files to a new directory *and* remove the original directory.

The following procedure removes unused directory space. First remove all unneeded files from the large directory. Then create a new, empty directory. Next move or copy all remaining files from the old large directory to the new empty directory. Remember to copy hidden files. Finally delete the old directory and rename the new directory.

```
# mkdir /home/max/new
# mv /home/max/large/* /home/max/large/.[A-z]* /home/max/new
# rmdir /home/max/large
# mv /home/max/new /home/max/large
```

**optional** *LPI* **DISK QUOTA SYSTEM**

The disk quota system (**quota** package) limits the disk space and number of files owned by individual users. You can choose to limit each user's disk space, the number of files each user can own, or both. Each resource that is limited has a lower limit and an upper limit. The user can exceed the lower limit, or *quota*, although a warning is given each time the user logs in when he is above the quota. After a certain number of warnings (one warning per day; the number of days is set by the system administrator), the system behaves as if the user had reached the upper limit. When the upper limit is reached or the user has received the specified number of warnings, the user will not be allowed to create any more files or use any more disk space. The user's only recourse at that point is to remove files.

*LPI* quota and repquota — Users can review their usage and limits with the quota utility. A user running with **root** privileges can use repquota to display quota information on multiple users. You can turn on quotas only if the filesystem is mounted with the **usrquota** and/or **grpquota** options (**ext3** and **ext4** filesystems).

*LPI* edquota and quotaon — First you must decide which filesystems to limit and how to allocate space among users. Typically only filesystems that contain users' home directories, such as **/home**, are limited. Use the edquota utility to set the quotas and then use quotaon to start the quota system. You will probably want to put a quotaon command in a startup file so the quota system will be enabled when you bring up the system (page 448). Unmounting a filesystem automatically disables the quota system for that filesystem.

# CHAPTER SUMMARY

The system-config-users utility adds new users and groups to the system and modifies existing users' accounts. You can also use the equivalent command-line tools (useradd, usermod, userdel, chage, groupadd, and groupmod) to work with user accounts.

Backing up files on the system is a critical but often-overlooked part of system administration. Linux includes the tar, cpio, dump, and restore utilities to back up and restore files. You can also use more sophisticated packages such as amanda and various commercial products.

The system scheduling daemon, **crond**, periodically executes scheduled tasks. You can schedule tasks using crontab, anacrontab, and at.

System reports present information on the health of the system. Two useful tools that generate these reports are vmstat, which details virtual memory, I/O, and CPU usage, and top, which reports on how the system is performing from moment to moment and can help you figure out what might be slowing it down.

Another aspect of system administration is solving problems. Linux includes several tools that can help track down system problems. One of the most important of these tools is **rsyslogd**, the system log daemon. Using **/etc/rsyslog.conf**, you can control which error messages appear on the console or a user's terminal, which are sent to a remote system, and which go to one of several log files.

# EXERCISES

1. How would you list all the processes running vi?

2. How would you use kill to log Max off the system?

3. From the command line, how would you create a user named John Doe who has the username **jd** and who belongs to group 65535?

4. Which problem does logrotate solve? Which is the primary configuration file for logrotate?

5. Give a command that creates a gzip compressed tar backup of the **/usr** filesystem on **/dev/sdg**. Which command would you use to make the same backup using bzip2? Using cpio?

# ADVANCED EXERCISES

6. If the system is less responsive than normal, what is a good first step in figuring out where the problem is?

7. A process stores its PID number in a file named **process.pid**. Write a command line that terminates this process.

8. Working with **root** privileges, you are planning to delete some files but want to make sure that the wildcard expression you use is correct. Suggest two ways you could make sure you delete the correct files.

# 16

# CONFIGURING AND MONITORING A LAN

## OBJECTIVES

After reading this chapter you should be able to:

▶ List and describe the uses of each hardware component of wired and wireless LANs

▶ Determine which network interface card is installed in the local Linux system

▶ List the software settings required to communicate on a network

▶ Use NetworkManager to configure the system to use static network settings

▶ List several types of network services and their uses

▶ Monitor devices on the network using Cacti

Networks allow computers to communicate and share resources. A LAN (local area network; page 284) connects computers at one site, such as an office, a home, or library, and can allow the connected computers to share an Internet connection, files, and a printer. Smart homes make extensive use of networks. Of course, one of the most important reasons to set up a LAN is to allow systems to communicate while users enjoy multiplayer games.

This chapter covers the two aspects of configuring a LAN: setting up the hardware and configuring the software. It is not necessarily organized in the order you will perform the tasks involved in setting up a particular LAN. Instead, read the chapter through, figure out how you will set up your LAN, and then read the parts of the chapter in the order appropriate to your setup. The final section discusses how to monitor devices on a network using Cacti.

# MORE INFORMATION

Web   Router operating systems: www.smoothwall.org, www.pfsense.com, m0n0.ch/wall
NetworkManager: projects.gnome.org/NetworkManager
Wireless NIC drivers: wireless.kernel.org/en/users/Drivers
PCI vendors, devices, and ID numbers: pciids.sourceforge.net/pci.ids and
    www.pcidatabase.com/reports.php?type=tab-delimeted.
NdisWrapper: sourceforge.net/projects/ndiswrapper
Cacti: cacti.net, cacti.net/additional_scripts.php
Cacti manual: cacti.net/downloads/docs/html
Cacti forums: forums.cacti.net
Cacti plugins and extensions: cacti.net/additional_scripts.php
RRDtool: oss.oetiker.ch/rrdtool
SNMP: www.net-snmp.org
Hardware compatibility list: hardware.redhat.com
Time zone list: php.net/date.timezone

HOWTOs   *Linux Wireless LAN HOWTO:* www.hpl.hp.com/personal/Jean_Tourrilhes/Linux
*Wireless HOWTO*
*Linux Hardware Compatibility HOWTO*

# SETTING UP THE HARDWARE

Each system, or *node,* on a LAN must have a NIC (network interface card), and each system must connect to a central switch (or hub if it is an older setup). If the LAN is connected to another network, such as the Internet, it must also have a router.

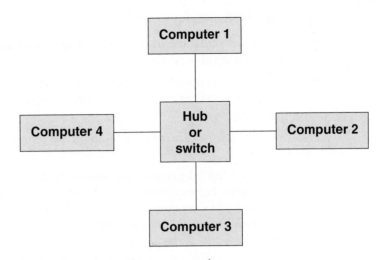

**Figure 16-1**  A simple star network

## CONNECTING THE COMPUTERS

Computers are connected to a network using cables (wired; page 285) or radio waves (wireless or Wi-Fi, page 287). The cables can connect to a variety of devices, some of which are described in this section. See "LAN: Local Area Network" on page 284 for an explanation of cables and definitions of *hub, switch,* and *router.*

In the simple star network shown in Figure 16-1, four computers are connected to a single hub or switch. Assume computers 1 and 2 are communicating at the same time as computers 3 and 4. With a hub (page 285), each conversation is limited to a maximum of half the network bandwidth. With a switch (page 285), each conversation can theoretically use the full network bandwidth.

WAP (wireless access point)   A WAP (wireless access point) connects a wireless network to a wired one. Typically a WAP acts as a transparent bridge, forwarding packets between the two networks as if they were one. If you connect multiple WAPs in different locations to the same wired network, wireless clients can roam transparently between the WAPs.

Wireless networks do not require a hub or switch, although a WAP can optionally fill the role of a switch. In a wireless network, the bandwidth is shared among all nodes within range of one another; the maximum speed is limited by the slowest node.

## ROUTERS

A router (page 287) connects a LAN to another network, such as the Internet. A router can perform additional functions, the most common of which is allowing several systems to share a single Internet connection and IP address (NAT; page 910). With NAT, the packets from all systems on the LAN appear to come from a single IP address; the router passes return packets to the correct system. A router can also provide firewall services.

You have several choices for routers:

- A simple hardware router is relatively cheap and does most of the things required by a small network.

- You can set up a Fedora/RHEL system as a router. The Linux kernel can use **firewalld** (page 898) or iptables (page 908) to implement a firewall to help protect a system.

- The DSL or cable modem supplied by an ISP is a router and can also function as a firewall.

- You can use a special-purpose distribution/operating system tailored for use as a router. For example, Smoothwall (www.smoothwall.org), pfSense (www.pfsense.com), Shorewall (shorewall.net), redWall (www.redwall-firewall.com), and m0n0wall (m0n0.ch/wall) provide browser-based configurations in the style of a hardware router.

# NIC: NETWORK INTERFACE CARD

The NIC for a system can be built into the motherboard or it can be a separate Ethernet card (wired or wireless).

Supported NICs    Linux supports most wired and many wireless Ethernet NICs. For a list of drivers for wireless NICs, visit wireless.kernel.org/en/users/Drivers.

Unsupported wireless NICs    If a wireless network card is not supported under Linux directly, you might be able to get it to work with NdisWrapper (sourceforge.net/projects/ndiswrapper), which uses Win32 drivers. NdisWrapper is a kernel module that provides a subset of the Windows network driver API. No Fedora/RHEL package contains this program.

Wireless bridge    An alternative to a wireless NIC is a wireless bridge. A wireless bridge forwards packets between wired and wireless interfaces, eliminating the need for wireless drivers. This simple device has an Ethernet port that plugs into a NIC and an 802.11 (wireless) controller. Although carrying a bridge around is usually not feasible for mobile users, a wireless bridge is an easy way to migrate a desktop computer to a wireless configuration.

Ad hoc and infrastructure modes    Wireless networks operate in either ad hoc or infrastructure mode. In ad hoc mode, individual nodes in the network communicate directly with one another. In infrastructure mode, nodes communicate via a WAP (previous page). Infrastructure mode is generally more reliable if the wireless LAN must communicate with a wired LAN.

If you do not want to use a WAP, it might be possible to set up a wireless bridge so it acts as a WAP. Consult the NIC/driver documentation for more information.

# TOOLS

This section describes four tools you can use to examine system hardware.

## LPI  lspci: LISTS PCI INFORMATION

PCI (Peripheral Component Interconnect) devices include network, sound, video, and TV tuner cards; modems; USB ports; and disk controllers. For information about PCI vendors, devices, and ID numbers visit pciids.sourceforge.net/pci.ids and www.pcidatabase.com/reports.php?type=tab-delimeted. The lspci utility (**pciutils** package) lists PCI device information:

```
$ lspci
00:00.0 Host bridge: Intel Corporation 440BX/ZX/DX - 82443BX/ZX/DX Host bridge (rev 01)
00:01.0 PCI bridge: Intel Corporation 440BX/ZX/DX - 82443BX/ZX/DX AGP bridge (rev 01)
00:07.0 ISA bridge: Intel Corporation 82371AB/EB/MB PIIX4 ISA (rev 08)
00:07.1 IDE interface: Intel Corporation 82371AB/EB/MB PIIX4 IDE (rev 01)
00:07.3 Bridge: Intel Corporation 82371AB/EB/MB PIIX4 ACPI (rev 08)
00:07.7 System peripheral: VMware Virtual Machine Communication Interface (rev 10)
00:0f.0 VGA compatible controller: VMware SVGA II Adapter
00:10.0 SCSI controller: LSI Logic / Symbios Logic 53c1030 PCI-X Fusion-MPT Dual Ultra320 SCSI (rev 01)
00:11.0 PCI bridge: VMware PCI bridge (rev 02)
...
02:00.0 USB controller: VMware USB1.1 UHCI Controller
02:01.0 Ethernet controller: Intel Corporation 82545EM Gigabit Ethernet Controller (Copper) (rev 01)
02:02.0 Multimedia audio controller: Ensoniq ES1371 [AudioPCI-97] (rev 02)
02:03.0 USB controller: VMware USB2 EHCI Controller
```

With the **–v** option, lspci is more verbose. You can use the **–vv** or **–vvv** option to display even more information.

```
$ lspci -v | head -14
00:00.0 Host bridge: Intel Corporation 440BX/ZX/DX - 82443BX/ZX/DX Host bridge (rev 01)
        Subsystem: VMware Virtual Machine Chipset
        Flags: bus master, medium devsel, latency 0
        Kernel driver in use: agpgart-intel

00:01.0 PCI bridge: Intel Corporation 440BX/ZX/DX - 82443BX/ZX/DX AGP bridge (rev 01) (prog-if 00
[Normal decode])
        Flags: bus master, 66MHz, medium devsel, latency 0
        Bus: primary=00, secondary=01, subordinate=01, sec-latency=64

00:07.0 ISA bridge: Intel Corporation 82371AB/EB/MB PIIX4 ISA (rev 08)
        Subsystem: VMware Virtual Machine Chipset
        Flags: bus master, medium devsel, latency 0

00:07.1 IDE interface: Intel Corp 82371AB/EB/MB PIIX4 IDE (rev 01) (prog-if 8a [Master SecP PriP])
```

## LPI  lsblk: LISTS BLOCK DEVICE INFORMATION

The lsblk utility (**util-linux** package) lists block devices in a tree format that shows which filesystems are mounted on each device.

```
$ lsblk
NAME            MAJ:MIN RM    SIZE RO TYPE MOUNTPOINT
sda                 8:0  0    200G  0 disk
+-sda1              8:1  0    500M  0 part /boot
+-sda2              8:2  0  199.5G  0 part
  +-fedora-swap 253:0  0      2G  0 lvm  [SWAP]
  +-fedora-root 253:1  0     50G  0 lvm  /
  +-fedora-home 253:2  0  147.5G  0 lvm  /home
sr0                11:0  1   1024M  0 rom
```

## LPI lshw: LISTS HARDWARE INFORMATION

The lshw utility (**lshw** package) lists information about the hardware configuration of the local system. Run this utility with **root** privileges to display a more detailed report. The **–short** option displays a brief report.

```
# lshw -short
H/W path            Device      Class       Description
========================================================
                                system      VMware Virtual Platform ()
/0                              bus         440BX Desktop Reference Platform
/0/0                            memory      87KiB BIOS
/0/4                            processor   Intel(R) Core(TM)2 Quad CPU    Q9650   @ 3.00GHz
/0/4/54                         memory      16KiB L1 cache
/0/4/55                         memory      6MiB L2 cache
/0/5                            processor   CPU
...
/0/100                          bridge      440BX/ZX/DX - 82443BX/ZX/DX Host bridge
/0/100/1                        bridge      440BX/ZX/DX - 82443BX/ZX/DX AGP bridge
/0/100/7                        bridge      82371AB/EB/MB PIIX4 ISA
/0/100/7.1                      storage     82371AB/EB/MB PIIX4 IDE
/0/100/7.3                      bridge      82371AB/EB/MB PIIX4 ACPI
/0/100/7.7                      generic     Virtual Machine Communication Interface
/0/100/f                        display     SVGA II Adapter
/0/100/10           scsi2       storage     53c1030 PCI-X Fusion-MPT Dual Ultra320 SCSI
/0/100/10/0.0.0     /dev/sda    disk        214GB SCSI Disk
/0/100/10/0.0.0/1   /dev/sda1   volume      500MiB EXT4 volume
/0/100/10/0.0.0/2   /dev/sda2   volume      199GiB Linux LVM Physical Volume partition
/0/100/11                       bridge      PCI bridge
/0/100/11/0                     bus         USB1.1 UHCI Controller
/0/100/11/1         ens33       network     82545EM Gigabit Ethernet Controller (Copper)
/0/100/11/2                     multimedia  ES1371 [AudioPCI-97]
/0/100/11/3                     bus         USB2 EHCI Controller
...
```

## LPI lsusb: LISTS USB DEVICES

The lsusb utility (**usbutils** package) displays information about USBs and USB devices. Use the **–v** (**--verbose**) option to display additional information.

```
$ lsusb
Bus 002 Device 002: ID 0e0f:0003 VMware, Inc. Virtual Mouse
Bus 002 Device 003: ID 0e0f:0002 VMware, Inc. Virtual USB Hub
Bus 001 Device 001: ID 1d6b:0002 Linux Foundation 2.0 root hub
Bus 002 Device 001: ID 1d6b:0001 Linux Foundation 1.1 root hub
Bus 002 Device 004: ID 04f9:0033 Brother Industries, Ltd
```

# LPI CONFIGURING THE SYSTEMS

After the hardware is in place, each system must be configured so it knows about the NIC that connects it to the network. Normally the system detects and configures new hardware automatically when you install Fedora/RHEL or the first time you boot it after you install a NIC. You can use NetworkManager (next page) to augment the information Fedora/RHEL collects or to set up things differently: For a server, you might want to assign a static IP address to the NIC and not use DHCP (page 641).

System information   In addition to information about the NIC, each system needs to be configured with:

- The system's *IP address* (page 1256)
- The netmask (network mask or subnet mask) for the system's address (page 483)
- The IP address of the router or gateway (page 633)
- The IP addresses of the nameservers (DNS addresses—specify two or three for more reliable network connections) unless you specify IP addresses in the **/etc/hosts** file (page 507)
- The system's hostname (set when you install Linux or run hostnamectl [page 219])

If a DHCP server (page 491) distributes network configuration information to systems on the LAN, you do not need to specify the preceding information on each system. Instead, you just specify that the system is using DHCP to obtain this information (which Fedora/RHEL does by default). You must specify this information when you set up the DHCP server.

*LPI* Private address space   When you set up a LAN, the IP addresses of the systems on the LAN are generally not made public on the Internet. Special IP addresses, which are part of the *private address space* defined by *IANA* (page 1254), are reserved for private use and are appropriate to use on a LAN (Table 16-1). Unless you have been assigned IP addresses for the systems on the LAN, choose addresses from the private address space.

Table 16-1   Private IP ranges (defined in RFC 1918)

| Range of IP addresses | From IP address | To IP address |
|---|---|---|
| 10.0.0.0/8 | 10.0.0.1 | 10.255.255.254 |
| 172.16.0.0/12 | 172.16.0.1 | 172.31.255.254 |
| 192.168.0.0/16 | 192.168.0.1 | 192.168.255.254 |

## *LPI* NETWORKMANAGER: CONFIGURES NETWORK CONNECTIONS

By default, the **NetworkManager** daemon (projects.gnome.org/NetworkManager) configures and manages the network. When it detects a new wired or wireless connection, NetworkManager starts the appropriate interface. For a wireless connection, it prompts for and stores keys and passwords. It also detects new hardware—for example, when you plug a USB wireless adapter into the system.

**Figure 16-2**   The NetworkManager applet on the Top panel

NetworkManager applet    The NetworkManager applet appears toward the right end of the Top panel. It appears as an outline of a monitor when the system is using a wired connection and as a series of radiating curves when the system is using a wireless connection (Figure 16-2). Exactly what appears when you click the NetworkManager applet depends on the system hardware and the items you have previously set up.

## THE NETWORKMANAGER APPLET MENU

Right- or left-click the NetworkManager applet to display the NetworkManager applet menu that allows you to turn on/off wired networking and, if available,

**Figure 16-3**   The NetworkManager applet menu

**Figure 16-4**  The Network window showing a Wired NIC

wireless networking (Wi-Fi). With wireless networking turned on, this menu also displays a list of available wireless networks (Figure 16-3). Click the switch adjacent to **Wired** or **Wi-Fi** to enable or disable the respective service.

With wireless networking turned on, click the name of a wireless network (under the word **Wi-Fi**) to connect to that network. The NetworkManager applet shows activity while it connects to the new network. It then prompts for a password if one is required and displays the wireless applet (Figure 16-2). Normally NetworkManager uses DHCP (page 491) to set up the network automatically so you do not have to open the Network window.

## THE NETWORK WINDOW

Selecting **Network Settings** from the NetworkManager menu displays the Network window (Figure 16-4), which allows you to modify the configuration of wired and wireless NICs. Alternately, you can open this window from the Settings window (page 107) or by giving the command **gnome-control-center network** from an Enter a Command window (ALT-F2) or a terminal emulator.

The frame on the left side of the Network window holds a list of the available types of networks. The list matches the list in the NetworkManager menu and can include Wired and Wi-Fi. When you click the plus sign (**+**) at the bottom of the this list, the Network window gives you the choice of which type of NIC you want to add (VPN, bond, bridge, or VLAN). However, this step is not normally necessary because NetworkManager configures NICs automatically. See "Identity" on the next page for a method of naming multiple NICs of the same type. Click the minus sign (**–**) to remove a NIC (if NetworkManager permits you to do so).

**Figure 16-5**   The Wired window, Details screen

See page 643 if you want to modify the connection of a wireless NIC. To modify the configuration of a wired NIC, highlight the description of the connection you want to modify (Wired) and click the gear at the lower-right of the window; NetworkManager displays a window named for the type of connection (i.e., Wired; Figure 16-5).

## THE WIRED/WI-FI WINDOW

The Wired window (Figure 16-5) holds a list of screens in the frame on the left. Click an item in the list to display the corresponding screen. The Wi-Fi window (Figure 16-8, page 643) holds the same list. You can change most of the items in these screens. The list includes

- **Details**—Lists connection information including IP, MAC, and DNS addresses. You cannot make changes in this screen.

- **Security**—For a wired connection, displays and allows you to turn on/off and modify 802.1x PNAC (port-based Network Access Control). For a Wi-Fi connection, displays the type of security (e.g., WEP, WPA) and password.

- **Identity**—Displays the name, MAC address, and other information that identifies the connection. If multiple NICs of the same type exist, this screen allows you to assign a different name to each one.

- **IPv4**—Displays IPv4 connection information including DHCP, network addresses, DNS addresses, and routes.

- **IPv6**—Displays IPv6 connection information including network addresses, DNS addresses, and routes.

- **Reset**—Allows you to reset or forget the connection.

**Figure 16-6**   The Wired window, IPv4 screen

The next sections describe how to use this window to set up a NIC with a static IP address and how to set up a W-Fi NIC. When you are finished making changes in these screens, click **Apply**.

### CONFIGURING A STATIC IP ADDRESS FOR A WIRED NIC

By default, DHCP (page 491) assigns a *dynamic IP address* to a NIC, so the IP address might not stay the same over time. To make the server easy for clients to find on the Internet, it must have the same IP address all the time (a *static IP address*). See page 298 for information on static IP addresses and page 494 if you want to set up a static IP address using DHCP.

This section describes how to configure a static IPv4 address that does not use DHCP. You can perform the same task by editing the appropriate configuration file in **/etc/sysconfig/network-scripts** (e.g., **ifcfg-ens33**); see the sample file on the next page.

First, select **Wired** in the Network window. If there is more than one connection highlight the one you want to configure and click the gear at the lower-right. NetworkManager displays the Details screen of the Wired window (Figure 16-5).

IPv4   If you are setting up an IPv4 address, select **IPv4** (Figure 16-6); for an IPv6 address, select **IPv6**. Make sure the switch at the upper-right (across from IPv4) is set to ON. Select **Manual** from the drop-down list just below the switch. Enter the IP address of the NIC, the netmask, and the IP address of the gateway (router) for the connection you are setting up.

Set the switch across from DNS to OFF if you want to configure DNS manually. Enter the IP address of the DNS server in the text box labeled **Server**. Click the plus sign (**+**) just below the text box to add additional DNS servers. Click the trash can at the right of a text box to remove an entry. These actions set the values of IPADDR0, PREFIX0, GATEWAY0, and DNS1 in **/etc/sysconfig/network-scripts/ifcfg**∗

**Figure 16-7**   The Network window showing a Wi-Fi NIC

(below). With no entries in the Routes section, NetworkManager sets up default routes (DEFROUTE=yes). A tick in the check box labeled **Use this connection only for resources on its network** limits connections to the local network.

Identity   The Identity screen has two important check boxes. A tick in the check box labeled **Connect automatically** causes the system to bring up the connection when it boots and sets ONBOOT=yes in **ifcfg***. Without a tick you must bring up the connection manually.

A tick in the check box labeled **Make available to other users** causes the connection to be available to all users and to be up even when the user who set up the connection is not logged in. Without a tick, the connection is up only when the user who set up the connection is logged in. Typically you want a tick in this check box.

Activating changes   When you are finished, click **Apply** to update the configuration files. Turn the interface off and then on again to make the changes active.

Next is the **ifcfg***️ file that results from running NetworkManager and following the preceding instructions. For more information about this type of file, see **/usr/share/doc/initscripts-***/sysconfig.txt**.

```
$ cat /etc/sysconfig/network-scripts/ifcfg-Wired_connection_1
HWADDR=00:0C:29:13:F4:35
TYPE=Ethernet
BOOTPROTO=none
IPADDR0=192.168.206.180
PREFIX0=24
GATEWAY0=192.168.206.2
DNS1=192.168.206.2
DEFROUTE=yes
IPV4_FAILURE_FATAL=no
IPV6INIT=no
NAME="Wired connection 1"
UUID=d4511286-79bb-4e53-9cfc-6cfbf54ff475
ONBOOT=yes
```

**Figure 16-8**    The Wi-Fi Secuity screen

nmcli    You can use the nmcli utility to control NetworkManager from the command line. See the nmcli man page for more information.

system-config-network    The system-config-network utility (**system-config-network** package) presents a simple, pseudographical window you can use to configure a device or DNS from the command line.

### Wireless Settings

It is usually easier to configure a wireless connection using the NetworkManager applet menu (Figure 16-3, page 638) than using the Settings window. To use the Settings window, click **Wi-Fi** on the left side of the Network window (Figure 16-7); NetworkManager displays a list of wireless networks on the right. Click the gear in the line with name of the network you want to set up; if there is no gear, click the name of the network.

If you click the name of the network, NetworkManager might ask for a password. You do not need to enter a password at this time to set up the connection: Even if you click Cancel in the authentication window, NetworkManager will add a gear to the name of the network. Click the gear.

Setting up a wireless connection is similar to setting up a wired connection (page 641) except for the Security screen (Figure 16-8). In this screen select the type of security you want to use from the drop-down list labeled **Security** and enter the connection password in the text box labeled **Password**. Click **Apply**. See "Activating changes" on page 642.

# Setting Up Servers

Setting up local clients and servers can make a LAN both easier to use and more useful. The following list briefly describes some clients and servers, and it references the pages that describe each in detail.

Firewall  Although not a server, a firewall is an important part of a LAN. See Chapter 25 for more information.

LDAP  LDAP is a database server that can hold names and addresses, authentication information, and other types of data. It can provide a uniform login regardless of which system you log in on. See page 786 for more information.

NIS  The NIS authentication server is covered on page 779 and the client on page 773. NIS is often combined with home directories that are mounted using NFS. Although still popular, NIS is at the end of its life: If you are setting up a new system, choose LDAP over NIS.

NFS  NFS allows you to share directory hierarchies. Sharing directories using NFS requires that the server export the directory hierarchy (page 814) and that clients mount the directory hierarchy (page 806).

Using NFS, you can store all home directories on one system and mount them from other systems as needed. This configuration works well with LDAP login authentication. With this setup, it can be convenient to create a world-writable directory—for example, **/home/shared**—that users can use to exchange files. If you set the sticky bit (page 1275) on this directory (**chmod 1777 /home/shared**), users can delete only files they created. If you do not set the sticky bit, any user can delete any file.

OpenSSH  OpenSSH tools include **ssh** (logs in on a remote system; page 693) and **scp** (copies files to and from a remote system; page 695). You can also set up automatic logins using OpenSSH: If you set up a shared home directory using NFS, each user's **~/.ssh** directory (page 688) is the same on each system; a user who sets up a personal authentication key (page 700) will be able to use OpenSSH tools between systems without entering a password. See page 700 for information on how to set up an OpenSSH server. You can use the **ssh** and **scp** clients as installed—you do not have to set them up.

DNS cache  Setting up a local DNS cache can reduce the traffic between the LAN and the Internet and can improve response times. For more information refer to "JumpStart I: Setting Up a DNS Cache" on page 866.

DHCP  DHCP enables a client system to retrieve network configuration information from a server each time it connects to a network. See page 491 for more information.

Samba  Samba allows Linux systems to participate in a Windows network, sharing directories and printers, and accessing those directories and printers shared by Windows systems. Samba includes a special share for accessing users' home directories. For more information on the [**homes**] share see page 840.

You can also use Samba to set up a shared directory similar to the one described under "NFS." To share a Linux directory with Windows computers, the value of **Workgroup** in **/etc/samba/smb.conf** must be the same as that of the Windows workgroup (frequently MSHOME or WORKGROUP by default). Place the following code in **smb.conf** (page 841):

```
[public]
    comment = Public file space
    path = /home/shared
    read only = no
    public = yes
    browseable = yes
```

By default, SELinux will not allow you to share your home directory. Use system-config-selinux (page 475) to activate the **samba_enable_home_dirs** Boolean if you want to allow sharing. Any Windows or Mac user can access this share, which can be used to exchange files between users and among Linux, Mac, and Windows systems.

# INTRODUCTION TO CACTI

Cacti (cacti.net) is a network monitoring tool that graphs system and network information over time (*time-series data*) and provides a comprehensive Web interface for browsing and examining the ongoing performance of the devices on a network.

For example, Cacti can monitor the network traffic passing through the network ports on local servers and the switch and router ports on the local network. Cacti graphs provide information on traffic levels on the various parts of the network. When the network is slow, for example, you can refer to the historical graphs and see if anything out of the ordinary has occurred. In addition to network traffic levels, Cacti can collect data on CPU usage, disk space usage, page views on a Web server, and almost any other data points available on the local network.

Cacti collects baseline (typical) data over time. You can use that information to gain insight into the ongoing behavior of a system and network, and to help resolve problems. The information can even predict what might happen in the future (e.g., when a disk is likely to become full).

Cacti periodically polls devices on a network for the data it needs, and stores the data in RRD files for use with RRDtool (round-robin database tool; oss.oetiker.ch/rrdtool). The Cacti Web interface allows you to browse a list of devices and graphs and see visual representations of device activity over time.

Cacti builds on the lessons learned from tools such as MRTG (oss.oetiker.ch/mrtg; page 975) and Cricket (sourceforge.net/projects/cricket). Each of these tools has the following characteristics:

- Periodically polls tracked devices for data. The tool most commonly used to collect this data is SNMP (Simple Network Management Protocol; www.net-snmp.org).

- Stores the data in an RRD file.

- Has a Web interface that allows you to examine graphs generated from the stored data. These graphs typically display daily, weekly, monthly, and yearly information.

Cacti's configuration is performed through its Web interface, whereas MRTG and Cricket are configured by editing text files.

RRD files and RRDtool are the key to much of Cacti's functionality. The Cacti Web site describes Cacti as "the complete RRDtool-based graphing solution." RRD files store time-series data efficiently and, through the use of aggregation functions, make it easy to keep a lot of detail for recent time periods but progressively less detail as the data in the files ages. RRDtool easily generates both simple and complex graphs from RRD files.

Extending Cacti   Many extensions and plugins are available for Cacti. Once you are familiar with the basic use and operation of Cacti, visit cacti.net/additional_scripts.php for a partial list of these additions. Also visit the documentation and the user forums at the same site to obtain more information about Cacti and to learn how you can add functionality and support for different devices and data sources.

# CONFIGURING SNMP

To monitor data sources on a system, you must install and run the SNMP daemon on that system as explained under "Setting Up a Data Source" on page 652. Displaying the automatically generated default graphs based on the local system is a good way to check that Cacti is working. To do so you must install and run the SNMP daemon on the local system. However, see the tip on page 647.

# SETTING UP LAMP

Cacti is a LAMP (Linux, Apache, MariaDB/MySQL, PHP) application; you must install and configure these applications before you can configure Cacti. This section explains how to set up the software on the system running Cacti.

## NOTES

See page 1114 for an explanation of why MySQL is now MariaDB.

When you set up LAMP, you use the MariaDB/MySQL databases named **mysql** and **cacti**. Fedora/RHEL sets up the **mysql** database when you install the MySQL/MariaDB server. You set up and populate the **cacti** database as explained under "Configuring MariaDB" on the next page.

The following database users must be set up. Each of these accounts should have a password:

- A user named **root** for the database named **mysql**. This user must be named **root**. The MariaDB installation script sets up this user.

- A user named **cactiuser** for the database named **mysql**. You can change this username, but as installed, Cacti is set up to use **cactiuser**.

- A Cacti administrative user for the database named **cacti**. As set up when you install Cacti, this user has the name **admin** and the password **admin**. You can set up additional Cacti user accounts.

As of this writing, Fedora/RHEL has Cacti 0.8.8a-8 in its repositories. Do not be misled by the pre-1.0 version number: Cacti is stable and in use on many systems.

## PREREQUISITES

Install the following packages:

- **cacti**

- **mariadb** (page 1118)

- **mariadb-server** (page 1118)

- **php** (installed with **cacti**)

- **httpd** (Apache; page 931; installed with **cacti**)

- **rrdtool** (installed with **cacti**)

- **net-snmp** (optional; needed only to monitor the local system)

- **net-snmp-utils** (optional)

Firewall    If you want to work with Cacti from a browser on a system other than the one running Cacti, and the system running Cacti is running a firewall or is behind a firewall, you need to open TCP port 80 on the system running Cacti. Give the following commands to open the port each time the system boots (permanently) and on the running system; see page 906 for information on firewall-cmd.

```
# firewall-cmd --add-port=80/tcp
# firewall-cmd --permanent --add-port=80/tcp
```

SELinux    When SELinux is set to use a targeted policy, **httpd** on the system running Cacti is protected by SELinux. For more information refer to "Setting the Targeted Policy with system-config-selinux" on page 475.

## Configuring MariaDB

Install MariaDB and run systemctl to enable and start the **mysqld** daemon as explained under "Installing a MariaDB Server and Client" on page 1118. Be sure to assign a password to the MariaDB user named **root** by using either or mysqladmin or mysql_secure_installation. For more help, see "Setting Up MariaDB" on page 1119.

### Cacti does not create the default graphs automatically

tip    A good way to make sure Cacti is working is by the presence of the automatically generated default graphs that are based on the device named **localhost** (the loopback network device). As of version 0.8.8a-8, a change in one of the Cacti installation files causes Cacti not to populate these graphs nor any graphs based on **localhost**. For a description of the change see the Web page at svn.cacti.net/viewvc/cacti/branches/0.8.8/install/index.php?r1=6952&r2=6953.

Make the following change *before the first time you start Cacti* if you want Cacti to populate the automatically generated default graphs and any graphs you create based on **localhost**. This change is not necessary if you are interested only in graphs based on devices you set up, including devices on the local system. For more information on setting up a device that Cacti will monitor, see "Adding a Device" on page 653.

The change involves adding a line to the file named **/usr/share/cacti/install/index.php**. As of Cacti version 0.8.8a-8, line 358 of this file is as follows (do not change this line):

```
db_execute("delete from version");
```

Add the following line just above the preceding one (both lines are indented using one TAB character):

```
repopulate_poller_cache();
```

Save the file and exit from the editor; continue with the installation and setup.

Create the **cacti** database

Next, issue the following commands to create a database named **cacti**, create a **mysql** database user named **cactiuser**, grant that user the necessary privileges, and assign a password to that user. Replace *cactipassword* in the following example with your choice of a password. Although the FLUSH PRIVILEGES statement is not required, it is good practice to include it.

```
# mysql -p
Enter password:
Welcome to the MariaDB monitor.  Commands end with ; or \g.
Your MariaDB connection id is 11
...
MariaDB [(none)]> CREATE DATABASE cacti;
Query OK, 1 row affected (0.00 sec)

MariaDB [(none)]> GRANT ALL ON cacti.*
    -> TO cactiuser@localhost
    -> IDENTIFIED BY 'cactipassword';
Query OK, 0 rows affected (0.00 sec)

MariaDB [(none)]> FLUSH PRIVILEGES;
Query OK, 0 rows affected (0.00 sec)

MariaDB [(none)]> EXIT
Bye
```

Set up and populate the **cacti** database

Give the following command to set up and populate the database named **cacti**. When MariaDB prompts for a password, provide the password for the MariaDB user named **root** (not the MariaDB user named **cactiuser**).

```
# mysql -p cacti < /usr/share/doc/cacti*/cacti.sql
Enter password:
```

Edit **db.php**

Most of the information in the **/etc/cacti/db.php** file is correct as installed. Edit this file to change the value assigned to **$database_password** from **cactiuser** to the same value you used for *cactipassword* when you created the **cacti** database (the password for the MariaDB user named **cactiuser**). Do not change the value assigned to **$database_username**.

```
$database_type = "mysql";
$database_default = "cacti";
$database_hostname = "localhost";
$database_username = "cactiuser";
$database_password = "cactiuser";
$database_port = "3306";
$database_ssl = false;
```

## CONFIGURING APACHE

Apache is installed when you install Cacti. Modify the **httpd.conf** file as explained on page 936; if you do not make this modification, Apache will display errors when it starts but will work anyway. Use systemctl to enable and start the **httpd** daemon (page 935). Cacti supplies the content.

Set the time zone

The **/etc/php.ini** file initializes many things including the time zone for Cacti. As installed, this file includes a commented-out example of how to set the time zone causing Cacti to use UTC by default. With this setup, Cacti might not appear to work at first because the times on the graphs will be wrong. Visit php.net/date.timezone, look up the name of the local time zone, and edit the time zone line in **php.ini** to include that name. If you are on the West Coast of the United States the time zone is America/Los_Angeles and the line will look like this:

```
date.timezone = America/Los_Angeles
```

Make sure to remove the semicolon from the beginning of the line. Reload the **httpd** daemon (page 935).

### Cacti initializes the time zone to UTC

tip   With the time zone set to UTC, the times on the Cacti graphs will be wrong in most parts of the world. This error can lead an administrator to thinking Cacti is not working because no data is displayed for the current time. To avoid this problem set the time zone as explained in the preceding section.

Apache accessibility   The **/etc/httpd/conf.d/cacti.conf** file controls the location and accessibility of Cacti on the Apache server. By default, Cacti is available as **127.0.0.1/cacti** (based on the Alias statement), and only a user on **127.0.0.1** (and not **localhost**) can access Cacti.

No change is required to follow the example in this section. Modify the <Directory> container near the top of **cacti.conf** to allow access from other systems. The following change allows access from **127.0.0.1** and the remote system at **192.168.206.181** (assuming the host system is running **httpd** version 2.4):

```
<Directory /usr/share/cacti/>
        <IfModule mod_authz_core.c>
                # httpd 2.4
                Require host localhost
                Require ip 192.168.206.181
        </IfModule>
...
</Directory>
```

Reload the **httpd** daemon (page 935). See "Alias" (page 953), "<Directory>" (page 945), and "Require" (page 961) for more information.

## ENABLING THE CACTI POLLER

Enable the Cacti poller by removing the hash mark from the left end of the line in the **/etc/cron.d/cacti** crontab file. The **\*/5** entry in this file causes **crond** to execute the script every five minutes. For more information refer to "Crontab Files" on page 607.

```
$ cat /etc/cron.d/cacti
*/5 * * * * cacti /usr/bin/php /usr/share/cacti/poller.php > /dev/null 2>&1
```

## CONFIGURING CACTI

After starting or restarting Apache, point a Web browser on the system running Cacti at **127.0.0.1/cacti**; Apache redirects the browser to the Cacti installation page at **127.0.0.1/cacti/install** and displays the first Cacti Installation Guide screen. Click **Next**.

**Figure 16-9**   The second Cacti Installation Guide screen

Confirm the information on the second Cacti Installation Guide screen (Figure 16-9) and click **Next**.

The next screen displays several pathnames and information about which versions of Net-SNMP and RRDtool are installed. Review this information and click **Finish**.

Next Cacti displays the User Login screen. Log in with the username **admin** and the password **admin**. Cacti then forces you to change the password for the **cacti** database user named **admin**. After you change the password, Cacti displays the main Console screen (Figure 16-10). The name of the screen appears just below the Console tab at the upper-left of the screen.

**Figure 16-10**   The Cacti main Console screen

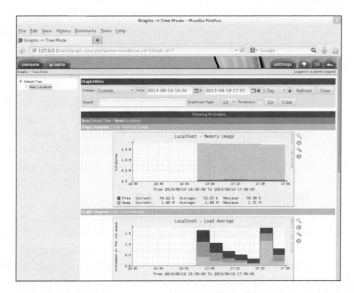

**Figure 16-11**   Default graphs for **localhost**

# BASIC CACTI ADMINISTRATION

By default, Cacti collects data from **localhost** (the system it is installed on). After a few poller cycles have passed (approximately 15 minutes after you added the **crond** job for Cacti and started the **snmpd** daemon), Cacti will display this information. You must install **snmpd** on the local system and follow the instructions in the tip on page 647 if you want to monitor the local system.

### You must install **snmpd** on the local system to monitor the local system

tip   You must install, configure, enable, and start **snmpd** on the local system, just as you would on a remote system, if you want to monitor the local system. For more information refer to "Setting Up a Data Source" on the next page. Also see the tip on page 647.

From the main Console screen, click **View your new graphs** or click the Graphs tab at the top of the screen. At the left of the screen, click the triangle to the left of the words **Default tree**; Cacti displays **Host: Localhost** below these words. Click **Host: Localhost**; Cacti displays the default graphs in tree mode for **localhost** (Figure 16-11).

Cacti creates graphs for the following data sources: memory usage, load average, logged-in users, and number of processes. When you click one of the graphs, Cacti displays a page with four graphs for the data source you clicked: daily, weekly, monthly, and yearly. These graphs will mostly be blank until Cacti collects sufficient data to fill them.

To store the data it collects and to display graphs, Cacti uses RRDtool. Cacti graphs show more detail over short time spans and less detail (averaged, or otherwise aggregated) over longer time spans.

To zoom in on a graph, click the magnifying glass icon on the right side of a graph; Cacti displays a single graph, and the mouse pointer changes to a cross hairs. Drag the cross hairs horizontally over the part of the graph that represents the time period you are interested in. In response, Cacti regenerates the graph for that time period.

You can control the graphs using the tabs along the upper-right of the screen. The Settings tab allows you to set your preferences for displaying graphs; the Tree View tab displays a hierarchy of graphs, allowing you to select the devices or graphs you are interested in; the List View tab displays a list of all available graphs; and the Preview tab displays small previews of all available graphs. In addition, each of these tabs provides a filter at the top of the screen that allows you to display a subset of graphs.

### THE CACTI CONSOLE TAB

Clicking the Console tab displays the main Console screen (Figure 16-10, page 650) from which you can manage Cacti. The main Console screen has a menu on the left side and shows the pathname of the screen it is displaying just below the Console tab. At the upper-right of the screen is the name of the user (**admin**) and a button labeled **Logout**.

## SETTING UP A DATA SOURCE

You can set up any device that runs SNMP as a data source that Cacti can monitor and report on. This section explains how to set up the local system or a remote system on the local network as a data source and how to set up Cacti to monitor that source.

### PREREQUISITES

Install the following packages on the system that Cacti will monitor. You must install and configure these packages on the local system if you want to monitor the local system; they are not installed with the **cacti** package.

- **net-snmp**
- **net-snmp-utils** (optional)

Firewall   The **snmpd** daemon, which runs on systems monitored by Cacti, uses UDP port 161. If the monitored system is running a firewall or is behind a firewall, you need to open this port. Give the following commands to open the port each time the system boots (permanently) and on the running system; see page 906 for information on firewall-cmd.

```
# firewall-cmd --add-port=161/udp
# firewall-cmd --permanent --add-port=161/udp
```

SELinux   When SELinux is set to use a targeted policy, **snmpd** on the systems being monitored is protected by SELinux. For more information refer to "Setting the Targeted Policy with system-config-selinux" on page 475.

snmpd.conf   The **/etc/snmp/snmpd.conf** file controls the **snmpd** daemon. Save the installed **snmpd.conf** file so you can refer to it later. Set up the following **snmpd.conf** file, which sets the SNMP community to **public** and allows queries from **localhost** and **192.168.206.180** (the system running Cacti; replace this address with that of the local Cacti server):

```
$ cat /etc/snmp/snmpd.conf
rocommunity public localhost
rocommunity public 192.168.206.180
```

**Figure 16-12** Adding a new device

/etc/default/snmpd Under Ubuntu and other Debian-based systems, the **/etc/default/snmpd** file controls various aspects of the **snmpd** daemon. (Fedora/RHEL systems do not use this file.) For example, this file specifies which address(es) **snmpd** listens for queries on. You must edit the following line, which specifies the options **snmpd** is run with, if you want **snmpd** to listen for queries from a remote system:

```
$ cat /etc/default/snmpd
...
SNMPDOPTS='-Lsd -Lf /dev/null -u snmp -g snmp -I -smux -p /var/run/snmpd.pid 127.0.0.1'
...
```

Change the **127.0.0.1** to the IP address of the local system, as this is the address the system running Cacti will query the local system on. If you do not make this change, the local system will not respond to **snmpd** queries from a remote system.

Enable and start Run systemctl to cause the **snmpd** service (**snmpd** daemon) to start each time the sys-
snmpd tem enters multiuser mode and then start the **snmpd** service. Use the systemctl **status** command to make sure the service is running.

```
# systemctl enable snmpd.service
# systemctl start snmpd.service
```

## ADDING A DEVICE

In the Web browser connected to Cacti, click the **Console** tab and select **Configuration⇒ Settings** and then click the **General** tab and select **Version 1** from the drop-down list labeled **SNMP Version** (not **SNMP Utility Version**). By default, SNMP runs with community set to **public**; do not change this setting unless you have reason to do so. Click **Save**.

Next select **Management⇒Devices** and click the word **Add** (it is small) at the upper-right of the screen. Alternately, you can select **Create⇒New Graphs** and then click **Create New Host**. Cacti displays a screen that allows you to specify a new device (Figure 16-12).

**Figure 16-13**    Information about the new device

If you have set the SNMP Version as just explained (i.e., Version 1), the SNMP settings will appear as shown in Figure 16-12 (previous page). Fill in the text box labeled **Description** with an appropriate description of the system to be monitored. Enter the IP address or fully qualified domain name in the text box labeled **Hostname**. Select an appropriate item from the drop-down list labeled **Host Template**. The example uses **Generic SNMP-enabled Host**. Alternately, you can use **Local Linux Machine**. Make sure **Downed Device Detection** is set to **SNMP Uptime** and **SNMP Version** is set to **Version 1**. Click **Create**.

Cacti uses SNMP to collect information from the device. If all goes well, it will report **Save Successful** and display the information about the new system near the top of the screen (Figure 16-13).

Creating a graph    Click **Create Graphs for this Host**. Cacti displays the Create New Graph page, which holds a drop-down list labeled **Create**. Select a type of graph to create from the drop-down list (e.g., **Unix—Load Average**) and click **Create**. Cacti displays a message at the top of the screen that tells you which graphs it created (Figure 16-14). In some cases Cacti prompts for a Legend Color; accept the default and click **Create**. Repeat for each graph you want to create.

Adding a node to the graph tree    Select **Management⇨Graph Trees** and click **Add** to add a node to the graph tree. Enter a name for the new node (e.g., **Servers**) and click **Create**.

Now click **Add** (on the right) to add a Tree Item, select **Host** from the drop-down list labeled **Tree Item Type**, select the host you just added (Cacti might add **Host** for you), and click **Create**.

Wait    Take a break for 10 or 15 minutes to allow Cacti to poll the new device a few times.

**Figure 16-14**    A list of queries and data sources for the new device

Displaying the graph    Click the **Graphs** tab. The name for the new node appears in the device tree on the left side of the screen. When you click the triangle that appears to the left of the node name, Cacti expands the tree and displays the node you just added. Click the node name to display the graphs for that device (Figure 16-15).

You can now browse through the graphs that are being generated, choose time periods you are interested in, and learn more about the behavior of the devices and networks.

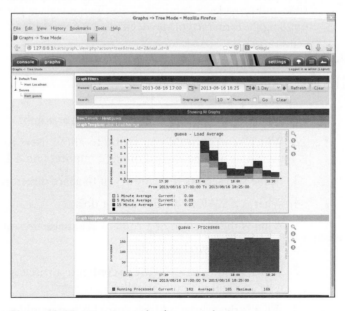

**Figure 16-15**    Cacti graphs for new devices

# CHAPTER SUMMARY

A LAN (local area network) connects computers at one site and can allow the connected computers to share an Internet connection, files, and a printer. Each system, or node, on a LAN must have a NIC (network interface card). NICs can be connected to the network via cables (wired) or radio waves (wireless or Wi-Fi).

An Ethernet-based LAN has a connection between each computer and a central hub or switch. A WAP (wireless access point) connects a wireless network to a wired one. If the LAN you are setting up is connected to another network, such as the Internet, the LAN requires a router. Some routers can perform several additional functions, the most common of which is NAT—allowing several systems to share a single Internet connection and IP address.

Each system on a LAN must have a wired or wireless NIC that can be built into the motherboard or can be a separate Ethernet card.

Several tools are useful when you are setting up a LAN. In particular, the Network-Manager applet menu and the Network window enable you to configure NICs.

You can configure the systems on the LAN to use LDAP as a login server so you do not have to set up accounts on each system. You can use NFS, which allows you to mount remote directory hierarchies, to set up a universal home directory. Samba is an important part of many LANs: It allows Linux systems to participate in a Windows network, sharing directories and printers and accessing those directories and printers shared by Windows systems.

Cacti is a network monitoring tool that graphs system and network information over time and provides a comprehensive Web interface for browsing and examining the ongoing performance of the devices on a network.

# EXERCISES

1. What advantage does a switch have over a hub?
2. Which server would you set up to allow users to log in with the same username and password on all computers on a LAN?
3. Name two servers that allow you to share directories between systems.
4. What is a WAP, and what does it do?
5. What is the function of a router? What else do some routers do?
6. What does a wireless bridge do?
7. Which window can you use to configure a wireless NIC (rather than having it be configured automatically)?
8. What is the private address space? When would you use a private address?

# ADVANCED EXERCISES

9. If you set a system's network mask to 255.255.255.0, how many computers can you put on the network without using a router?

10. Which file stores information about which DNS servers the system uses?

11. What is LAMP? What is a LAMP application?

12. What is Cacti? How does it communicate the information it provides?

# 17

# SETTING UP VIRTUAL MACHINES LOCALLY AND IN THE CLOUD

## OBJECTIVES

After reading this chapter you should be able to:

▸ List three advantages of using a VM (virtual machine) over a physical machine

▸ Talk about the different VM solutions

▸ Use gnome-boxes to instantiate a VM

▸ Install KVM and instantiate a VM

▸ Install VMware Player and instantiate a VM

▸ Set up and log in on a system in the cloud using AWS

The *cloud* is a colloquial term that refers to a public or private system that provides access to hardware and/or software computing resources via a network. A *virtual machine* is a software/hardware emulation of a physical computer. By its nature, the cloud relies on virtual machines. This chapter covers both of these topics.

# VMs (VIRTUAL MACHINES)

A VM (virtual machine; also *guest* or *domain*) appears to the user and to the software running on it as a complete physical machine. It is, however, one of potentially many such VMs running on a single physical machine (the *host* or *node*). Just as a multitasking operating system allows you to run many programs on a single physical system, a hypervisor allows you to run many operating systems (VMs) on a single physical system.

The software that provides the virtualization is called a *hypervisor*. Each VM can run a different operating system from the other VMs. For example, on a single host you could have VMs running Windows 8, Ubuntu 13.10, Ubuntu 14.04, and Fedora 19. Some hypervisors can emulate architectures other than the local architecture. On these systems you can run operating systems under different architectures (e.g., i386, ia64, ppc64).

VMs provide many advantages over single, physical machines:

- **Isolation**—Each VM is isolated from the other VMs running on the same host: If one VM crashes or is compromised, the others are not affected.

- **Security**—When a single system running several servers is compromised, all servers are compromised. If each server is running on its own VM, only the compromised server is affected; other servers remain secure.

- **Power consumption**—Using VMs, a single powerful machine can replace many less powerful machines, thereby cutting power consumption.

- **Development and support**—Multiple VMs, each running a different version of an operating system and/or different operating system, can facilitate development and support of software designed to run in many environments. With this organization you can easily test a product in different environments before releasing it. Similarly, when a user submits a bug, you can reproduce the bug in the same environment it occurred in.

- **Servers**—In some cases, different servers require different versions of system libraries. In this instance, you can run each server on its own VM, all on a single physical machine.

- **Testing**—Using VMs, you can experiment with cutting-edge releases of operating systems and applications without concern for the base (stable) system, all on a single physical machine.

- **Networks**—You can set up and test networks of systems on a single physical machine.

- **Sandboxes**—A VM presents a *sandbox*—an area (system) you can work in without regard for the results of your work or for the need to clean up.

- **Snapshots**—You can take a *snapshot* of a VM and return the VM to the state it was in when you took the snapshot simply by reloading the VM from the snapshot.

- **Forensics**—An investigator can load data, take a snapshot, and repeatedly manipulate and examine the data, always able to return to the original data.

- **Migration and duplication**—You can migrate and copy VMs to other hosts quickly and easily.

- **Dynamic resource allocation**—You can easily change the resources a VM has access to, allowing you to dynamically alter resource allocation of several VMs on a single host.

When setting up a host to run VMs, keep in mind that each VM requires the same resources as a physical machine. Multiple VMs running on a single host require, at a minimum, the sum of the resources required by each of the VMs.

- **Network I/O**—Make sure the network I/O from all the VMs you are setting up on a host will not overload the network connection of the host.

- **Disk I/O**—Make sure the disk I/O from all the VMs you are setting up on a host will not overload the I/O capabilities of the local disks, *SAN* (page 1271), or *NAS* (page 1262).

- **RAM**—Allocate enough RAM so your VMs do not have to *swap* (page 1276), the same as you would for a physical system.

There are some situations in which virtualization does not give you an advantage. VMs do not give a physical machine more resources but they do allow you to make better use of existing resources. Following are cases in which virtualization might not be a good idea.

- Some software does not run well or at all under a VM.

- Some software is not supported when it is run under a VM.

- A server that uses most of a machine's resources and is suffering from performance issues is not a good candidate for virtualization. The virtualized server will still use most of the system's resources. It will only make things worse if you run additional VMs on the same host.

- Heavily used databases and Web servers can cause and suffer from resource contention and might not be good candidates for virtualization.

- VMs do not keep time accurately; they tend to suffer more from drift than physical systems. Systems that require accurate timekeeping, such as VoIP systems, might not be good candidates for virtualization.

- Graphics-intensive applications, especially those that make use of 3D graphics, might not work well when virtualized.

## IMPLEMENTATIONS

**libvirt**  Many VM platforms, including QEMU, KVM, Xen, and VMware, can take advantage of on the **libvirt**[1] library and management tool that provides a consistent interface to create, monitor, and control VMs. While **libvirt** is not usually required, it can make the job of an administrator easier.

**Xen**  Xen (www.cl.cam.ac.uk/research/srg/netos/xen, xenproject.org, and wiki.xen.org/wiki/Fedora_Host_Installation), which was created at the University of Cambridge and is now being developed in the open-source community, is an open-source hypervisor. Xen introduces minimal performance overhead compared with running each of the operating systems natively.

**VMware**  VMware, Inc. (www.vmware.com) offers VMware Player, a free, downloadable, proprietary product you can install and run as an application under Fedora/RHEL. See page 671. VMware also offers ESXi, a hypervisor that runs directly on a machine (bare metal) without the need for an underlying operating system.

**KVM**  KVM (the Kernel-based Virtual Machine; www.linux-kvm.org) is an open-source hypervisor that runs as part of the Linux kernel. See page 663.

**QEMU**  QEMU (Quick EMUlator; wiki.QEMU.org), written by Fabrice Bellard, is an open-source hypervisor that runs as a user application with no CPU requirements. It can run code written for a different CPU than that of the host machine. See page 663.

**GNOME Boxes**  The gnome-boxes utility (live.gnome.org/Boxes) is a simple although powerful GUI front end to **libvirt** that is designed to be run by end users. See the next section.

**VirtualBox**  VirtualBox (www.virtualbox.org) is a VM developed by innotek GmbH, which was purchased by Sun Microsystems (now Oracle). It has been open source since version 4.

**virt-manager**  The virt-manager utility is a GUI front end to **libvirt** that manages VMs. It typically manages QEMU/KVM VMs, although it can manage many different types of VMs. See page 665.

## gnome-boxes

The gnome-boxes utility, also called GNOME Boxes (live.gnome.org/Boxes), can connect to a VM or a remote system. It has a deceptively simple interface and can automatically detect VMs and perform an unattended installation of a VM running any one of several different operating systems. It is not as powerful as virt-manager (page 665), which is designed for use by a system administrator, but it is very easy to use and convenient if you want to test a system quickly or if you do not want to get involved in the details of setting up a VM. Both gnome-boxes and virt-manager use the **libvirt** library and QEMU. You might need to enable hardware virtualization

---

1. Visit libvirt.org and access.redhat.com/site/documentation/en-US/Red_Hat_Enterprise_Linux/6/html/Virtualization_Getting_Started_Guide/sec_libvirt-libvirt-tools.html.

**Figure 17-1**   The gnome-boxes Create a Box window

in the BIOS before gnome-boxes will work; see "CPU" on the next page for more information.

ISO image file   Download an ISO image file of the operating system you want to install on the VM. See page 46 for instructions on downloading a Fedora ISO image file.

Give the following command from a terminal emulator to set up a VM running Fedora 19 from an ISO image file; gnome-boxes will display the Create a Box window shown in Figure 17-1.

```
$ gnome-boxes Fedora-19-x86_64-DVD.iso
```

For the simplest installation, leave the switch labeled **Express Install** set to ON, enter a password, and click **Continue**. The gnome-boxes utility displays a summary of the VM it will create. When you click **Create**, gnome-boxes begins to install Fedora. The gnome-boxes window shows the same things the console display shows when you install the operating system on a physical machine. Follow the instructions on page 59 to install the operating system.

You can also start gnome-boxes by giving the command **gnome-boxes** from an Enter a Command window (ALT-F2) or a terminal emulator. When you set the switch labeled **Express Install** to OFF or when you click **Customize** on the second Create a Box window, gnome-boxes allows you to customize the VM.

# QEMU/KVM

QEMU (Quick EMUlator) is a flexible hypervisor that runs in *userspace* (page 1279). Because QEMU can emulate processors in software, you can use it to host guest operating systems running on a variety of processors. The KVM

(Kernel-based Virtual Machine) kernel module allows a program running in user-space (e.g., QEMU) to take advantage of hardware virtualization features of processors including Intel, AMD, PPC, and ARM. See "CPU" below. When the host and guest architectures are the same, QEMU uses the KVM to provide hardware acceleration for VMs, allowing them to run more quickly and use fewer host resources.

# PREREQUISITES

Host resources    A VM takes up about as much hard disk space and RAM as a native system; see "Requirements" on page 30 for information about how much space to allocate for a Fedora/RHEL system. Because a VM takes its resources from the host system, these resources must be available for each VM running simultaneously on a host. When it is not running, a VM does not use RAM or CPU resources but does occupy space on the hard disk.

CPU    QEMU/KVM can take advantage of the CPU virtualization extensions (hardware virtualization) available on most CPUs manufactured in the last few years. **You might need to enable hardware virtualization in the BIOS (page 31) before you can use these extensions.** Although QEMU/KVM does not require the host to have these extensions, a host without them will use software virtualization and run more slowly than a host with them. Run the following command on the host to see whether the CPU has these extensions. If the command does not produce any output, the CPU does not support hardware virtualization or hardware virtualization has not been enabled in the BIOS.

```
$ egrep '^flags.*(vmx|svm)' /proc/cpuinfo
flags    : fpu vme de pse tsc msr pae mce cx8 apic sep mtrr pge mca cmov
pat pse36 clflush dts acpi mmx fxsr sse sse2 ss ht tm pbe syscall nx lm
constant_tsc arch_perfmon pebs bts rep_good nopl aperfmperf pni dtes64
monitor ds_cpl vmx smx est tm2 ssse3 cx16 xtpr pdcm sse4_1 xsave lahf_lm
dtherm tpr_shadow vnmi flexpriority
...
```

Packages    QEMU/KVM is contained in many packages. When installing a new system, select a Base Environment of Infrastructure Server and an Add On of Virtualization from the Software Selection screen (Figure 3-7, page 66). On an existing system, use the following command to install the **virtualization** group of software packages:

```
# yum -y group install virtualization
```

Enable and start **libvirtd**    Run systemctl to cause the **libvirt-guests** service (**libvirtd** daemon) to start each time the system enters multiuser mode and then start the **libvirt-guests** service. Use the systemctl **status** command to make sure the service is running.

```
# systemctl enable libvirt-guests.service
# systemctl start libvirt-guests.service
```

**Figure 17-2**   Virtual Machine Manager window

KVM kernel modules
The following command verifies that the KVM kernel modules are loaded:

```
$ lsmod | grep kvm
kvm_intel              137762  6
kvm                    439197  1 kvm_intel
```

If the preceding command does not list **kvm_intel** or **kvm_amd**, KVM is not configured properly. The system may not support hardware virtualization; see "CPU" (previous page).

Network
By default, **libvirt** creates a private network that VMs can use. This network uses a 192.168.x.x subnet. The host network cannot reach this subnet directly. However, the VMs can use the host as a gateway and connect to the network via that gateway. To allow VMs to be reached from outside this private network, you can use iptables DNAT rules to forward ports or you can set up a bridged network. For more information refer to "Connecting Several Servers to a Single Internet Connection" on page 928 and visit wiki.libvirt.org/page/Networking.

ISO image file
Download an ISO image file of the operating system you want to install on the VM. See page 46 for instructions on downloading a Fedora ISO image file.

## virt-manager: INSTALLING FEDORA ON QEMU/KV

The virt-manager[2] utility displays the Virtual Machine Manager window. Open this window by giving the command **virt-manager** from an Enter a Command window (ALT-F2) or a terminal emulator. A message about searching for a hypervisor will appear and then a dialog box will request authentication. Figure 17-2 shows two VMs running on the local system. When you first run virt-manager, this window will show no VMs, only **localhost (QEMU)**.

---

2. Visit access.redhat.com/site/documentation/en-US/Red_Hat_Enterprise_Linux/6/html/
Virtualization_Tuning_and_Optimization_Guide/
chap-Virtualization_Tuning_Optimization_Guide-Virt_Manager.html.

**Figure 17-3**   The New VM window, Step 1 of 5

To install a new VM, click the icon at the far left of the toolbar (the terminal with an arrow and a yellow star on it); virt-manager opens Step 1 of 5 of the New VM window (Figure 17-3).

This window allows you to specify the name of the VM and the location of the installation medium for the guest operating system. First, enter the name you want to assign to the VM in the text box labeled **Name**. Then, in the lower portion of the window, click a radio button to specify the source of the operating system you will install on the VM. This example uses a Fedora ISO image file. The other radio buttons allow you to perform a network installation or a network boot (PXE). You can also import an existing disk image. Click **Forward**.

### Duplicating a VM

tip   You can copy the image file of a VM that is shut down and, in Step 1 of 5, import that file as an existing disk image to create another, identical VM.

In the Step 2 of 5 window (Figure 17-4), click the radio button labeled **Use CDROM or DVD** and select a device from the drop-down list to specify one of these media. Because the example in this section uses an ISO image file, Figure 17-4 shows the radio button labeled **Use ISO image** selected. Enter the absolute pathname of the ISO image file in the text box below this radio button or click **Browse** to open the Locate ISO Media Volume window. To select a file on the local system, click **Browse Local** at the lower-left of the window, select the appropriate directory, highlight the ISO image file, and click **Open**. At the bottom of the Step 2 of 5 window are two drop-down lists that allow you to specify an operating system type (OS type) and version; virt-manager might select the version automatically. After specifying these items click **Forward**.

**Figure 17-4** The New VM window, Step 2 of 5

The next window, Step 3 of 5, has two spin boxes that allow you to specify how much memory (RAM) the VM will use and, if the host has multiple CPUs or a multicore processor, how many CPUs the VM will run on. After specifying these items click **Forward**.

The Step 4 of 5 window (Figure 17-5, next page) allows you to specify storage (disk space) for the VM. A VM that runs a live system does not need any storage. To specify storage make sure there is a tick in the check box labeled **Enable storage for this virtual machine.** By default, virt-manager allocates eight gigabytes of storage, which is enough for a system to experiment with. See page 31 for information on estimating hard disk storage needs. You can cause virt-manager to allocate space on the disk immediately or as needed (see the following tip). To specify a file on the local system that the VM will use for storage, click the radio button labeled **Select managed or other existing storage.** Then enter the absolute pathname of a new (nonexistent) ordinary file in the text box below this label either by entering the pathname in the text box or by clicking **Browse** and specifying the file in the resulting window. Click **Forward**.

### Allocate disk space all at once or as needed?

tip You can cause virt-manager to allocate space on the disk immediately or as needed. Allocating it immediately takes more time in the setup phase but makes the installation phase go more quickly. If you allocate storage as needed, you can run into problems if the local system runs out of disk space. On the other hand, allocating storage as needed allows you to specify a maximum amount of storage but use only what the VM needs.

The Step 5 of 5 window summarizes the selections you have made. Putting a tick in the check box labeled **Customize configuration before install** causes virt-manager

**Figure 17-5**  The New VM window, Step 4 of 5

to open the Details window before starting to install the operating system. You can also display this window after the operating system is installed. See page 670. The Advanced options section allows you to specify a network other than the default, specify a MAC address (page 296), and specify the type and architecture of the VM; virt-manager fills in these fields with appropriate values. You can specify an architecture other than that of the host. If the summary information looks accurate, click **Finish**.

### Speed things up and lose portability

tip  The Processor tab of the Details window has a plus sign (**+**) labeled **Configuration**. Click the plus sign to display a button labeled **Copy host CPU configuration**. Copying the host CPU configuration can improve performance by 20–30 percent but means you cannot migrate the VM to a host with a different CPU.

The virt-manager utility displays the Creating Virtual Machine window as it allocates disk storage and retrieves the installation image. If you chose to allocate all storage immediately and you are using a lot of storage, this step might take a while to complete.

When the VM starts booting from the ISO image file, virt-manager displays the Console window. This window is the console for the VM; it shows the same things the console display shows when you began installing the operating system on a physical machine. If the virt-manager window does not display the entire VM screen select

**Figure 17-6**   The top of the Console window

**main menu: View⇨Resize to VM** from the Console window; virt-manger will enlarge the window. Follow the instructions on page 59 to install the operating system.

### The Console window does not define the VM

tip You can close and open the Console window for a VM as you please without affecting the state of the VM. For example, if you close the Console window while you are installing Fedora, the installation proceeds as it would if you left the window open. When you open the Console window again, it will show the installation continuing (or waiting for input) as though you had never closed the window. The Virtual Machine Manager window works the same way: Closing it has no effect on the states of the VMs. However, you must shut down or save (suspend) VMs before shutting down the host.

## THE CONSOLE WINDOW

To display the Console window for a VM from the Virtual Machine Manager window (Figure 17-2, page 665), double-click the VM icon (the picture of a monitor with a tri-angle/arrow in it) to the left of the name of the VM whose console you want to display. Alternately, you can use the virt-viewer command-line tool to display a Console window: Give the command **virt-viewer** followed by the name of the VM. Figure 17-6 shows the top of a Console window.

The name of the Console window is the name of the VM followed by **Virtual Machine**. Selections on **main menu: Virtual Machine** drop-down menu allow you to control the state of the machine. Some of the same selections are available by right-clicking the VM icon in the Virtual Machine Manager window. Useful selections on this menu are

- **Run**—Boots the VM if it is off
- **Restore**—Restores a suspended VM
- **Shut Down/Force Off**—Powers off the VM; not a graceful shutdown, data might be lost
- **Shut Down/Save**—Suspends the VM to disk

Selections on the **main menu: View** drop-down menu allow you to display the Console or Details window, expand the Console window to fill the screen, resize the VM (useful when the window is bigger or smaller than the VM), and toggle the display of the toolbar.

**Figure 17-7** The Details window

## THE DETAILS WINDOW

Display the Details window for a VM by selecting **main menu: View⇨Details** from the Console window. Figure 17-7 shows the Overview tab of a Details window.

The Details window displays information about a VM. You can change some of the information with the VM running; to change other information (e.g., the name of the VM) the VM must be shut down. The Overview tab allows you to change the name and enter a description of the VM. The Processor and Memory tabs allow you to change the number of processors and the amount of RAM allocated to the VM, respectively. To speed up the VM, see the tip on page 668. The Performance tab displays graphs of VM performance.

# virsh: WORK WITH VMS ON THE COMMAND LINE

The virsh utility is a powerful tool for working with QEMU/KVM VMs from the command line. It has an extensive set of commands that allow you to create, manipulate, and display VMs. You can run it interactively or from the shell command line. The following command lists all the virsh commands by groups:

```
$ virsh help | less
Grouped commands:

  Domain Management (help keyword 'domain'):
      attach-device                      attach device from an XML file
      attach-disk                        attach disk device
  ...
```

The preceding command lists the group of Domain Management commands first. The string **help keyword 'domain'** indicates you can display a complete list of this group of commands by giving the command **virsh help domain**. The next command lists all the virsh command groups:

```
$ virsh help | grep keyword
Domain Management (help keyword 'domain'):
Domain Monitoring (help keyword 'monitor'):
Host and Hypervisor (help keyword 'host'):
Interface (help keyword 'interface'):
Network Filter (help keyword 'filter'):
Networking (help keyword 'network'):
Node Device (help keyword 'nodedev'):
Secret (help keyword 'secret'):
Snapshot (help keyword 'snapshot'):
Storage Pool (help keyword 'pool'):
Storage Volume (help keyword 'volume'):
Virsh itself (help keyword 'virsh'):
```

The following command lists the VM created earlier in this section. You must run this command with **root** privileges because the VM was instantiated using **root** privileges.

```
$ su -c 'virsh list'
Password:
 Id    Name                           State
----------------------------------------------------
 2     pomelo                         running
```

You can run virsh interactively by giving the command **virsh** (or **su –c virsh**). See the virsh man page or use the virsh help facilities for more information.

# VMWARE PLAYER: INSTALLING FEDORA ON VMWARE

VMware Player, which must be run on a GUI, is available for no cost for noncommercial applications. To download this application, visit www.vmware.com/products/player, scroll down to the section labeled "Free for Personal Use," and click the highlighted word **Download**. Alternately, you can visit www.vmware.com/go/downloadplayer. Next, click the button labeled **Download** adjacent to the version you want to install. Generally you will install the version that corresponds to the operating system running on the host: Linux 32 bit, Linux 64 bit, or Windows. The Windows version works on both 32- and 64-bit versions of Windows. If you are given a choice, save the file.

Linux    Verify the file you downloaded is correct by comparing two *SHA1* (page 1272) values. Give the command **sha1sum VMware-Player**✲**bundle** to display the first SHA1 value. The second SHA1 value is on the VMware Web page, following **SHA1SUM** when you click **Show Details** below the name of the version of vmplayer you just downloaded. The two values must be identical.

The next section explains how to install VMware Player on a Linux system. See page 673 if you are installing it on a Windows system.

# INSTALLING VMWARE PLAYER ON A LINUX SYSTEM

You might need to enable hardware virtualization in the BIOS before VMware Player will work; see "CPU" on page 664 for more information. The file you downloaded, **VMware-Player**✱**bundle**, is a shell script that installs VMware Player. After giving yourself execute permission to the file, run this script with **root** privileges; ignore any error messages.

```
$ chmod 755 VMware-Player✱bundle

$ su -c ./VMware-Player✱bundle
Password:
Extracting VMware Installer...done.
```

After a moment VMware displays a window holding a license agreement; click the radio button labeled **I accept ...** and click **Next** (you have to accept the license agreement twice). VMware displays several screens of questions; accept the default answers by clicking **Next** on each screen. Do not enter information on the screen that asks for a license key. Click the button labeled **Install** when it appears; VMware installs Player. When the installer displays **Installation was successful**, VMware Player is installed, but not ready to run. Click **Close**.

## DOWNLOADING AND INSTALLING UTILITIES FOR COMPILING THE KERNEL MODULES

When you start vmplayer for the first time, and each time you install a new kernel, it compiles and loads some kernel modules. To do so, vmplayer requires kernel header files and utilities (e.g., gcc). Before running vmplayer, give the following command to download and install the files and utilities vmplayer requires to compile and load the kernel modules. You need to repeat this step each time you install a new kernel.

```
$ su -c 'yum -y install gcc binutils kernel-headers kernel-devel'
```

## VMWARE TOOLS

The **open-vm-tools** package, installed by default, obviates the need for installing VMware Tools (page 676). Before running vmplayer, give the following command to make sure this package is installed on the local system.

```
$ su -c 'yum -y install open-vm-tools'
```

## RUNNING VMWARE PLAYER

Now vmplayer is ready to build the kernel modules. Working as yourself (not a privileged user), give the command **vmplayer**; vmplayer displays the VMware Kernel Module Updater window while it is compiling and installing the kernel modules.

If necessary, accept the end-user license agreement. If you are given a chance to update the *Player* software, do so at your discretion. However, vmplayer might display a Software Updates window that has a button labeled **Get More Information**; this window links to a page on which you can *purchase* VMware Workstation. You do not need to purchase anything to run vmplayer. Player displays the VMware Player window, Welcome To VMware Player screen (Figure 17-8). Continue at "Installing Fedora on VMware Player."

**Figure 17-8**   VMware Player window, Welcome To VMware Player screen

# INSTALLING VMWARE PLAYER ON A WINDOWS SYSTEM

Once you have downloaded VMware Player, open Explorer and display the Downloads directory. Double-click the **VMware-player∗.exe** file. Click **Yes** if you are asked whether you want to allow the program to make changes to the computer; Windows loads the VMware Player installation wizard. Click **Next** repeatedly until the button labeled **Continue** appears. Click **Continue** to start the installation. When the wizard displays **Setup Wizard Complete**, click **Finish**. If you are given a chance to update the software (Player), do so at your discretion.

Double-click the VMware Player icon on the desktop to start Player. Accept the license agreement; VMware Player displays the VMware Player window, Welcome To VMware Player screen (Figure 17-8).

# INSTALLING FEDORA ON VMWARE PLAYER

Once you have installed VMware Player on either a Linux or Windows system, you can install an operating system on Player. This section explains how to install Fedora. You can install another operating system in a similar manner.

First, download the ISO image file for the version of Fedora you want to install. If the host is running a 64-bit operating system you can install either a 32- or 64-bit version of Fedora. If it is running a 32-bit operating system you can install only a 32-bit version. See page 46 for instructions on locating and downloading a Fedora ISO image file. You do not need to burn an installation image; you will install the operating system from the image file.

## CREATING A VM

This section uses the 32-bit live version of Fedora that has a filename of **Fedora-Live-Desktop-i686-19-1.iso**.

**Figure 17-9**  New Virtual Machine Wizard window,
Virtual Machine Name screen

On the left side of the VMware Player window is a tab labeled **Home**. Additional tabs will appear for each VM you create. With multiple VMs, you can click these tabs to switch between VMs.

Click **Create a New Virtual Machine**. On the first New Virtual Machine Wizard screen, click the radio button labeled **I will install the operating system later** and click **Next**. *This step is critical.* On the second screen, click the radio button with the label appropriate to the operating system you are installing. To follow this example, click the radio button labeled **Linux**. The drop-down list labeled **Version** allows you to specify a distribution and number of bits. Select **Fedora** (implies 32-bit) or **Fedora 64-bit** depending on which version of Fedora you are installing. Click **Next**.

The third screen (Figure 17-9) allows you to specify the name of the VM and the location of the directory that holds the VM files. By default the name is the name of the distribution (Fedora) and the location is a directory that has the same name as the VM. Under Linux, this directory is a subdirectory of **vmware** which is a subdirectory of your home directory. Under Windows this directory is a subdirectory of **Documents/Virtual Machines**, which is a subdirectory of your home directory. In Figure 17-9, the name of the VM has been changed to **F19a**; Player has changed the default location to **/home/sam/vmware/F19a**. Click **Next**.

The next screen allows you to specify a *maximum* disk size. By default, Player does not allocate disk space on the host when you create the VM, but rather allocates disk space as needed. See the tip on page 667. The 20-gigabyte default is good for a system to experiment with. Unless you have reason to do otherwise, accept the default of splitting the virtual disk into multiple files. Click **Next**.

**Figure 17-10**   Virtual Machine Settings window,
Hardware tab, CD/DVD selection

On the next screen you can customize the hardware or you can wait until the following screen to do so. Click **Finish**. If the next screen holds information about installing the guest operating system and VMware Tools, click **Close**.

Player displays the VMware Player window again, this time with a tab for the VM you just created under the tab labeled **Home** on the left. In the example the tab is labeled **F19a**; click that tab to select the VM. On the right side of this window is a picture of the state of the VM; because it has not been started, the picture is blank. The two buttons on the bottom of the right side are labeled **Play virtual machine** and **Edit virtual machine settings**.

## INSTALLING THE OPERATING SYSTEM

You have created a VM without an operating system. The next step is to install Fedora (or another operating system) on the VM. To do so you must tell the VM which medium to boot from. It is as though you had a new physical computer: You have to put the installation medium (e.g., DVD or flash drive) with Fedora on it in the system before you boot the system.

Click **Edit virtual machine settings**; Player displays the Hardware tab of the Virtual Machine Settings window. On the left side, click **CD/DVD(IDE)**; Player displays information about the virtual DVD drive on the right side of the window. Click the radio button labeled **Use ISO image** and then the button labeled **Browse**. Highlight the ISO image file (**Fedora-Live-Desktop-i686-19-1.iso** in the example) and click the button labeled **Open**. The window should look similar to the one shown in Figure 17-10. Click **OK** or **Save**; Player redisplays the VMware Player window.

In the VMware Player window, click **Play virtual machine**. Player will boot the operating system you selected. Run the live system or install Fedora as explained in Chapter 3. Player might display a window asking whether you want to download and install VMware Tools. It is not necessary to install VMware Tools under Linux; see the next section. Under Windows, wait to install VMware Tools until after you have installed the full operating system as explained in the next section.

## VMware Tools

VMware Tools is software that resides on the VM and improves its performance, functionality, and the ease with which it can be managed. For example, VMware Tools can improve graphics and mouse performance. It enables the VM and host to share folders, drag and drop, synchronize time, as well as copy and paste.

Linux    The Linux **open-vm-tools** package holds an open-source implementation of VMware Tools. Because VMware has merged the functionality of VMware Tools into the kernel and **open-vm-tools**, you do not need to install VMware Tools on a Linux system when **open-vm-tools** is installed.

Windows    With the guest operating system installed on the VM, select *from the VMware menu* **Player: Manage⇨Install VMware Tools**. Alternately, the VMware Player window might display a button labeled **Install Tools**; clicking this button performs the same function as making the menu selection. If you are prompted to download VMware Tools, do so.

Once the software is downloaded and ready to install, Windows asks whether you want to allow VMware to make changes to the computer; click **Yes**. You might need to supply the **root** password *for the VM* in order to install VMware Tools. Also, you might need to unmount the virtual DVD from the virtual DVD drive before you can install VMware Tools. If you are prompted with **Disconnect anyway and override the lock?** click **Yes**. When the Software Updates window displays **All updates finished**, click **Close**. VMware Tools is installed.

# Cloud Computing

Cloud computing is the result of evolution and the combination of virtualization, networking, and powerful hardware. Cloud computing allows users to reap the benefits of these tools without knowing how to use each individually, needing only a lightweight system to access the cloud.

The cloud as a service    As an alternative to setting up the hardware and software to run a cloud, you can purchase a cloud computing platform as a service. Buying the service means the provider takes care of the infrastructure, software, and management (including scaling), and it is faster to set up and (frequently) cheaper to build than setting up and running your own cloud server.

OpenShift    OpenShift (www.openshift.com) is a cloud computing platform as a service from Red Hat. The open-source software that runs the service is named OpenShift Origin. OpenShift maintains the service and scales as needed.

AWS  AWS (Amazon Web Services) is a popular cloud computing platform as a service from Amazon. See the next section.

Eucalyptus  Eucalyptus (www.eucalyptus.com) produces open-source software for building cloud computing platforms. Because of its AWS compatibility, you can develop on Eucalyptus and migrate to AWS.

OpenStack  OpenStack (www.openstack.org) is a community-based collaboration of developers that produces open-source software for building cloud computing platforms.

# AWS: SETTING UP A VIRTUAL SYSTEM IN THE CLOUD

This section explains how to start a virtual Linux system in the cloud using Amazon EC2 (Amazon Elastic Compute Cloud; aws.amazon.com/ec2). Although there are several open-source cloud platforms, this book covers AWS because it is very popular, easy to set up and use, inexpensive, and readily available.

The AWS system is complex and has many facets. This section briefly explains how to set up a very basic system. It does not go into detail about different services AWS offers and other types of systems you can set up. It is intended to get you started using AWS.

Because AWS allows you to create many virtual systems, each of these systems is referred to as an *instance*. You will be able to use ssh to connect to the instance you set up (Linux; Windows users use RDP). Amazon typically charges for the use of each instance and for storage, but offers a year of free (minimal) use to get users familiar with AWS.

## Using AWS costs money

caution  When you set up an AWS account as explained in this section, you must provide a credit card number. Amazon typically charges for the time you run an instance of a virtual machine and it charges for storage even when the virtual machine is not running.

## GETTING STARTED

To get started, visit aws.amazon.com/console. The AWS account username and password are different from your Amazon shopping account. Create a new account and log in or log in to an existing account. Select AWS Management Console; AWS displays the Amazon Web Services page.

Under Compute & Networking click **EC2 Virtual Servers in the Cloud**. To create an instance (a new VM in the cloud), click the button labeled **Launch Instance**. Amazon displays the Create a New Instance window. You can launch many different kinds of virtual systems from this window. This example creates a RHEL 6.4 64-bit system.

## Fedora quick-launch images

tip  Fedora provides quick-launch images you can use in place of those supplied by AWS. You can use these images to build a VM in the AWS cloud. Visit cloud.fedoraproject.org for more information.

**Figure 17-11** The Launch with the Classic Wizard window

## LAUNCHING AN INSTANCE

Click the radio button labeled **Classic Wizard** at the left side of the page; AWS displays the Launch with the Classic Wizard window on the right (Figure 17-11). Click within this window to open the Request Instances Wizard window. Scroll through the list of operating systems. Click the radio button labeled **32 bit** or **64 bit** for the system you want. This example launces a 64-bit RHEL system. Click **Select** adjacent to the type of system you want to launch.

When you click **Select**, AWS displays the Instance Details screen (this screen has many pages). You can accept the defaults (click **Continue**) on all the screens until you get to the screen that has a radio button labeled **Create a new Key Pair**. The key pair is used to encrypt the connection to the machine you set up; see "Public Key (Asymmetric) Encryption" on page 1157 for more information. Enter the name you want to use for the key pair in the text box labeled **Enter a name for your key pair** and click **Create & Download your Key Pair**. This example uses the name **ec2.key**. Save the key pair in the directory you will be working in. Amazon appends the filename extension **.pem** to the name you specified. After downloading the ✱**.pem** file, you must change its permissions so no one can write to it and only the owner (you) can read it. If the key pair is named **ec2.key.pem**, the following command changes its permissions appropriately.

```
$ chmod 400 ec2.key.pem
```

The next screen allows you to define a security group. By default AWS sets up a security group named **quick-start-1** that has only port 22 open so you can log in to the machine using ssh. You do not need to change anything on this page; click **Continue**.

The final screen, named Review, displays information about the machine you are about to launch; click **Launch**.

## MANAGING AN INSTANCE

After you click **Launch**, Amazon displays a message saying that your instances are now launching. Click **View your instances in the Instances page**; Amazon displays the

**Figure 17-12**   The Instances page showing the Actions drop-down menu

Instances page (Figure 17-12). This page lists all the instances that you have created (and not terminated).

On the Instances page, put tick in the check box at left end of the instance you just launched (near the top of the page). The column labeled **State** tells you when the instance is running. Allow the mouse pointer to hover over the word **empty** in the column labeled **Name** and click the resulting pencil. Enter the name you want to assign to the system in the pop-up text box and click **Save**. This example uses the name **sam4**.

Click the **Actions** button at the top of the page to display a drop-down menu of items that allow you to control the instance (Figure 17-12). The items on that menu include

- **Connect**—Displays a window explaining how to connect to the instance you created, including the ssh command line you can use to connect to the instance.

- **Terminate**—Terminates the instance; you lose all information stored on the instance.

- **Reboot**—Reboots the instance.

- **Stop**—Shuts down the instance; the storage remains intact.

- **Start**—Boots the instance.

The lower portion of the page displays information about the instance. Make sure the tab labeled **Description** in the lower portion of the page is selected. When the instance is running, important information in the lower portion of the page includes

- **Key Pair Name**—The name of the key pair that allows you to log in on this instance.

- **Public DNS**—The URL of the instance; this URL allows you to connect to the instance (you might have to scroll down to see this entry).

- **Security Groups**—The firewall rules for the instance; click **view rules**; port 22 (ssh) should be open so you can connect to the instance.

## CONNECTING TO AN INSTANCE

Using the information in the bottom portion of the Instances page, you can construct an ssh command that will connect to the instance. In this example the filename of the key pair file is **ec2.key.pem** (it is in the working directory) and the Public DNS is **ec2-54-244-133-141.us-west-2.compute.amazonaws.com**. The default name of the user whose account you will connect to is **ec2-user**. The following command uses this information to connect to the instance; your information will be different. The **−i** option specifies the file that holds the private key for public key authentication.

```
$ ssh -i ec2.key.pem ec2-user@ec2-54-244-133-141.us-west-2.compute.amazonaws.com
The authenticity of host 'ec2-54-244-133-141.us-west-2.compute.amazonaws.com
(54.244.133.141)' can't be established.
RSA key fingerprint is ef:73:ff:49:1c:dc:72:f9:8e:44:33:a4:ca:d5:16:96.
Are you sure you want to continue connecting (yes/no)? yes
Warning: Permanently added 'ec2-54-244-133-141.us-west-
2.compute.amazonaws.com,54.244.133.141' (RSA) to the list of known hosts.
[ec2-user@ip-10-250-71-103 ~]$
```

The first time you connect to an instance and each time you restart an instance, ssh asks you to verify you are connecting to the right system (page 691).

### AWS provides a new URL each time you start an instance

**tip**  Each time you stop and restart an instance, AWS provides the instance with a new URL so you must use a slightly different command to connect to the instance. The Instance page (Figure 17-12) displays the URL of the instance on the line labeled **Public DNS**.

### Leaving an instance running or stopped costs money

**caution**  In any state except terminated, AWS charges you for an instance. When the instance is running you are charged for the instance and the volume (storage) it uses. When the instance is stopped, you pay for the volume only. When you terminate the instance AWS normally deletes the volume so you pay nothing. Terminate an instance using the Actions drop-down list and make sure the volume has been deleted.

## GAINING root PRIVILEGES

The default RHEL system is set up without a **root** password—you must use sudo to gain **root** privileges. The **/etc/sudoers** file enables the **ec2-user** to execute any command without providing a password. See "Executing a Single Command" (page 430) and "Spawning a **root** Shell" (page 430) for more information. See page 600 for information on adding users.

## TERMINATING AN INSTANCE

On the Instances page (Figure 17-12, page 679), click **Actions** and select **Terminate** to delete the instance you created. AWS asks you to confirm; click **Yes, Terminate**. Click **EC2 Dashboard** at the top of the left column; AWS displays the EC2 Dashboard. It may take a few minutes for the instance to terminate. When it does, this page should show **0 Running Instances** and **0 Volumes**.

# CHAPTER SUMMARY

A VM (virtual machine) appears to the user and to the software running on it as a complete physical machine. It is, however, one of potentially many such VMs running on a single physical machine (the host). Each VM is called a guest. The software that provides the virtualization is called a hypervisor.

Advantages VMs have over physical machines include isolation, security, lower power consumption, dynamic resource allocation, and easy migration and duplication. There are many implementations of VMs. This chapter discusses GNOME Boxes, KVM, QEMU, and VMware. The **libvirt** library and management tool provides a consistent interface to QEMU, KVM, and VMware.

GNOME Boxes has an easy-to-use interface and does not involve the user in details. It is not as powerful as virt-manager, which is designed for system administrators. Both of these tools are based on QEMU and can take advantage of **libvirt**. QEMU is a flexible hypervisor that runs in userspace and can emulate processors in software. KVM is a kernel module that allows a program running in userspace to take advantage of hardware virtualization. The virsh utility runs from the command line and allows you to create, manipulate, and display VMs. VMware Player is a proprietary VM that is available at no cost for noncommercial applications.

Cloud computing is the result of evolution and the combination of virtualization, networking, and powerful hardware. Cloud computing puts powerful VMs at remote locations; a user needs only a lightweight system to access the VMs over a network.

As an alternative to setting up the hardware and software to run a cloud, you can purchase a cloud computing platform as a service. Buying the service means the provider takes care of the infrastructure, software, and management, and it is faster to set up and (frequently) cheaper to build than setting up and running your own cloud server. Eucalyptus and OpenStack are popular open-source packages for building cloud computing platforms. OpenShift (Red Hat) and AWS (Amazon) provide cloud computing platforms as services.

# EXERCISES

1. Does a VM require fewer resources than a physical machine?
2. What is KVM?
3. What is QEMU?
4. What is **libvirt**?
5. List three advantages VMs have over physical machines.

# ADVANCED EXERCISES

6. What is the purpose of VMware Tools? Do you need to install VMware Tools when running **vmplayer** on a Linux system? Why or why not?
7. Is hardware virtualization supported on the local system?
8. What is the **virt-manager** utility?
9. What happens when you close the **virt-manager** console window of a running VM? What happens if you reboot the host system without first shutting down a VM?

# PART IV

## USING CLIENTS AND SETTING UP SERVERS

# 18

# OpenSSH: Secure Network Communication

## Objectives

After reading this chapter you should be able to:

▶ Explain the need for encrypted services

▶ Log in on a remote OpenSSH server system using ssh

▶ Copy files and directories to and from a remote system securely

▶ Set up an OpenSSH server

▶ Configure OpenSSH server options

▶ Set up a client/server so you do not need to use a password to log in using ssh or scp

▶ Enable trusted X11 tunneling between the client and the OpenSSH server

▶ Remove a known host record from the **~/.ssh/known_hosts** file

▶ Enable trusted X11 forwarding

▶ List the uses of ssh tunneling (port forwarding)

OpenSSH is a suite of secure network connectivity tools that replaces telnet/**telnetd**, rcp, rsh/**rshd**, rlogin/**rlogind**, and ftp/**ftpd**. Unlike the tools they replace, OpenSSH tools encrypt all traffic, including passwords. In this way they can thwart malicious users who attempt to eavesdrop, hijack connections, and steal passwords.

This chapter covers the following OpenSSH tools:

- scp—Copies files to and from a remote system
- sftp—Copies files to and from a remote system (a secure replacement for ftp)
- ssh—Runs a command on or logs in on a remote system
- **sshd**—The OpenSSH daemon (runs on the server)
- ssh-keygen—Creates, manages, and converts RSA or DSA host/user authentication keys

# INTRODUCTION TO OPENSSH

Using public key encryption (page 1157), OpenSSH provides two levels of authentication: server and client/user. First the client verifies it is connected to the correct server. Then OpenSSH encrypts communication between the systems. When a secure, encrypted connection has been established, OpenSSH makes sure the user is authorized to log in on or copy files to and from the server. After verifying the system and user, OpenSSH allows different services to be passed through the connection. These services include interactive shell sessions (ssh), remote command execution (ssh), file copying (scp), FTP services (sftp), X11 client/server connections, and TCP/IP port tunneling.

SSH1 versus SSH2   SSH protocol version 2 (SSH2) is a complete rewrite of SSH protocol version 1 (SSH1) that offers improved security, performance, and portability. The two protocols are not compatible. Because SSH1 is being rapidly supplanted by SSH2 and because SSH1 is vulnerable to a man-in-the-middle attack (page 1160), this chapter does not discuss SSH1. Because version 2 is floating-point intensive, version 1 does have a place on systems without FPUs (floating-point units or accelerators), such as old 486SX systems. As installed, the OpenSSH tools supplied with Fedora/RHEL support both protocols; you need run only one server to communicate with systems using either protocol.

ssh   The ssh utility allows you to log in on a remote system over a network. You might choose to use a remote system to access a special-purpose application or to take advantage of a device that is available only on that system, or you might use a remote system because you know it is faster or less busy than the local system. While traveling, many businesspeople use ssh on a laptop to log in on a system at company headquarters. From a GUI you can use several systems simultaneously by logging in on each one from a different terminal emulator window.

X11 forwarding   When you turn on trusted X11 forwarding on an ssh client, it is a simple matter to run a graphical program over an ssh connection to a server that has X11 forwarding enabled: Run ssh from a terminal emulator running on an X11 server and give an X11 command such as **gnome-calculator**; the graphical output appears on the local display. For more information refer to "Forwarding X11" on page 707.

# **LPI** How OpenSSH Works

When OpenSSH starts, it first establishes an encrypted connection and then authenticates the user. When these two tasks are complete, OpenSSH allows the two systems to send information back and forth.

keys   OpenSSH uses a *host key* pair and a *session key* to negotiate an encrypted session. The host key pair is a set of public/private keys that is established the first time the server system runs **sshd** (page 700). The session key is a symmetric key that the server and client share. For more information on keys see "Encryption" on page 1156.

The first time an OpenSSH client connects with an OpenSSH server, OpenSSH asks you to verify the client is connected to the correct server (see "First-time authentication" on page 691). This verification helps prevent a man-in-the-middle attack (page 1160). After verification, the client makes a copy of the server's public host key. On subsequent connections, the client compares the key provided by the server with the original key it stored. Although this test is not foolproof, the next one is quite secure.

The client then generates a random key, which it encrypts with both the server's public host key and the session key. The client sends this encrypted key to the server. The server, in turn, uses its private keys to decrypt the encrypted key. This process creates the session key, a key that is known only to the client and the server and is used to encrypt the rest of the session.

# Files

OpenSSH clients and servers rely on many files. Global files are kept in **/etc/ssh** and user files in **~/.ssh**. In this section, the first word in the description of each file indicates whether the client or the server uses the file.

### rhost authentication is a security risk

security   Although OpenSSH can get authentication information from **/etc/hosts.equiv**, **/etc/shosts.equiv**, **~/.rhosts**, and **~/.shosts**, this chapter does not cover the use of these files because they present security risks. The default settings in the **/etc/ssh/sshd_config** configuration file prevent their use.

## /etc/ssh: Global Files

Global files listed in this section appear in the **/etc/ssh** directory. They affect all users, but a user can override them with files in her **~/.ssh** directory.

**moduli**   **client and server**   Contains key exchange information that OpenSSH uses to establish a secure connection. Do not modify this file.

**ssh_config**   **client**   The global OpenSSH configuration file (page 698). Entries here can be overridden by entries in a user's **~/.ssh/config** file.

**sshd_config**   **server**   The configuration file for **sshd** (page 704).

**LPI**   ssh_host_dsa_key,
ssh_host_dsa_key.pub

**server**   SSH protocol version 2 DSA host keys. Both files should be owned by **root**. The **ssh_host_dsa_key.pub** public file should be readable by anyone but writable only by its owner (644 permissions). The **ssh_host_dsa_key** private file should not be readable or writable by anyone except its owner (600 permissions).

ssh_host_key,
ssh_host_key.pub

**server**   SSH protocol version 1 host keys. Both files should be owned by **root**. The **ssh_host_key.pub** public file should be readable by anyone but writable only by its owner (644 permissions). The **ssh_host_key** private file should not be readable or writable by anyone except its owner (600 permissions).

**LPI**   ssh_host_rsa_key,
ssh_host_rsa_key.pub

**server**   SSH protocol version 2 RSA host keys. Both files should be owned by **root**. The **ssh_host_rsa_key.pub** public file should be readable by anyone but writable only by its owner (644 permissions). The **ssh_host_rsa_key** private file should not be readable or writable by anyone except its owner (600 permissions).

ssh_known_hosts

**client**   Contains public RSA (by default) keys of hosts that users on the local system can connect to. This file contains information similar to that found in **~/.ssh/known_hosts** but is set up by the administrator and is available to all users. This file should be owned by **root** and should be readable by anyone but writable only by its owner (644 permissions).

## ~/.ssh: USER FILES

OpenSSH creates the **~/.ssh** directory and the **known_hosts** file therein automatically when a user connects to a remote system.

**LPI**   authorized_keys

**server**   Enables a user to log in on or copy files to and from another system without supplying a user login password (page 700). However, the user might need to supply a passphrase, depending on how the key was set up. No one except the owner should be able to write to this file.

**config**   **client**   A user's private OpenSSH configuration file (page 698). Entries here override those in **/etc/ssh/ssh_config**.

**environment**   **server**   Contains assignment statements that define environment variables on a server when a user logs in using **ssh**.

**LPI**  id_dsa  **client**  User authentication DSA keys generated by ssh-keygen (page 701). Both
id_dsa.pub  files should be owned by the user in whose home directory they appear. The
**id_dsa.pub** public file should be readable by anyone but writable only by its owner
(644 permissions). The **id_dsa** private file should not be readable or writable by
anyone except its owner (600 permissions).

**LPI**  id_rsa  **client**  User authentication RSA keys generated by ssh-keygen (page 701). Both
id_rsa.pub  files should be owned by the user in whose home directory they appear. The
**id_rsa.pub** public file should be readable by anyone but writable only by its owner
(644 permissions). The **id_rsa** private file should not be readable or writable by anyone except its owner (600 permissions).

known_hosts  **client**  Contains public RSA keys (by default) of hosts the user has connected to.
OpenSSH automatically adds entries each time the user connects to a new server
(page 690). Refer to "HostKeyAlgorithms" (page 699) for information on using
DSA keys. If **HashKnownHosts** (page 699) is set to **yes**, the hostnames and addresses
in this file are hashed to improve security.

## MORE INFORMATION

Local  man pages: ssh, scp, sftp, ssh-keygen, ssh_config, sshd, sshd_config

Web  OpenSSH home page: www.openssh.com
Search on **ssh** to find various HOWTOs and other documents: tldp.org

Books  *Implementing SSH: Strategies for Optimizing the Secure Shell* by Dwivedi; John
Wiley & Sons (October 2003)
*SSH, The Secure Shell: The Definitive Guide* by Barrett, Silverman, & Byrnes;
O'Reilly Media (May 2005)

# **LPI**   RUNNING THE ssh, scp, AND sftp OpenSSH Clients

This section covers setting up and using the ssh, scp, and sftp clients.

## PREREQUISITES

Install the following package (both are installed by default):

- openssh
- openssh-clients

OpenSSH clients do not run a daemon so there is no service to set up.

## JUMPSTART I: USING ssh AND scp TO CONNECT TO AN OpenSSH SERVER

The ssh and scp clients do not require setup beyond installing the requisite packages,
although you can create and edit files that facilitate their use. To run a secure shell on or

securely copy a file to or from a remote system, the following criteria must be met: The remote system must be running the OpenSSH daemon (**sshd**), you must have an account on the remote system, and the server must positively identify itself to the client.

ssh   The following example shows Zach using ssh to log in on the remote host named **plum**, running who, and finally giving an **exit** command to return to the shell on the local system. The who utility displays the hostname of the system Zach logged in from.

```
[zach@guava ~]$ ssh zach@plum
zach@plum's password:
Last login: Wed Jun 12 16:34:10 2013 from guava
[zach@plum ~]$ who am i
zach     pts/1          2013-06-12 16:38 (guava)
[zach@plum ~]$ exit
logout
Connection to plum closed.
[zach@guava ~]$
```

You can omit *user@* (**zach@** in the preceding example) from the command line if you want to log in as yourself and you have the same username on both systems. The first time you connect to a remote OpenSSH server, ssh or scp asks you to confirm that you are connected to the right system. Refer to "First-time authentication" on page 691.

scp   The following example uses scp to copy **ty1** from the working directory on the local system to Zach's home directory on **plum**:

```
$ scp ty1 zach@plum:
zach@plum's password:
ty1                                      100%   97KB  96.8KB/s   00:00
```

Remember to follow the system name with a colon (**:**). If you omit the colon, scp copies the file locally; in the example you would end up with a copy of **ty1** named **zach@plum**.

# CONFIGURING OPENSSH CLIENTS

This section describes how to set up OpenSSH on the client side.

## RECOMMENDED SETTINGS

X11 forwarding   The configuration files provided by Fedora/RHEL establish a mostly secure system that might or might not meet your needs. One OpenSSH parameter you might want to change is ForwardX11Trusted, which is set to **yes** in the **/etc/ssh/ssh_config** configuration file (page 698). To increase security, and in some cases reduce usability, set ForwardX11Trusted to **no**. See page 707 for more information on X11 forwarding.

## SERVER AUTHENTICATION/KNOWN HOSTS

Two files list the hosts the local system has connected to and positively identified: **~/.ssh/known_hosts** (user) and **/etc/ssh/ssh_known_hosts** (global). No one except the owner (**root** in the case of the second file) should be able to write to either of these files. No one except the owner should have any access to a **~/.ssh** directory.

First-time authentication    When you connect to an OpenSSH server for the first time, the OpenSSH client prompts you to confirm that you are connected to the right system. This behavior is controlled by **StrictHostKeyChecking** (page 699). This check can help prevent a man-in-the-middle attack (page 1160):

```
The authenticity of host 'plum (192.168.206.181)' can't be established.
RSA key fingerprint is d1:9d:1b:5b:97:5c:80:e9:4b:41:9a:b7:bc:1a:ea:a1.
Are you sure you want to continue connecting (yes/no)? yes
Warning: Permanently added 'plum,192.168.206.181' (RSA) to the list of
known hosts.
```

Before you respond to the preceding query, make sure you are logging in on the correct system and not on an imposter. If you are not sure, a telephone call to someone who logs in on that system locally can help verify that you are on the intended system. When you answer **yes** (you must spell it out), the client appends the server's public host key (the single line in the **/etc/ssh/ssh_host_rsa_key.pub** or **/etc/ssh/ssh_host_dsa_key.pub** file on the server) to the user's **~/.ssh/known_hosts** file on the local system, creating the **~/.ssh** directory if necessary. So that it can keep track of which line in **known_hosts** applies to which server, OpenSSH prepends the name of the server and the server's IP address to the line.

When you subsequently use OpenSSH to connect to that server, the client verifies it is connected to the correct server by comparing this key to the one supplied by the server.

known_hosts    The **~/.ssh/known_hosts** file uses one or two very long lines to identify each host it keeps track of. Each line starts with the hostname and IP address of the system the line corresponds to, followed by the type of encryption being used and the server's public host key. When **HashKnownHosts** (page 699) is set to **yes** (the default is **no**), OpenSSH hashes the system name and address to improve security. Because **HashKnownHosts** hashes the hostname and IP address separately, OpenSSH puts two lines in **known_hosts** for each host. The following line (it is one logical line that wraps on to several physical lines) from **known_hosts** is used to connect to **plum** at 192.168.206.181 using *RSA* (page 1271) encryption:

```
$ cat ~/.ssh/known_hosts
plum,192.168.206.181 ssh-rsa AAAAB3NzaC1yc2EAAAADAQABAAAABAQDbhLRVTfI
v9gy7oP+5T3HjZmrKt2q6ydyKmLlHNUjZFXM4hCdkJlpTfJ4wy260UAZBWvrBLP6N9k
...
```

You can use **ssh-keygen** with the **–R** option followed by the hostname to remove an entry, even a hashed one. Alternately, you can use a text editor to remove an entry. The **–F** option to **ssh-keygen** displays a line in a **known_hosts** file that corresponds to a specified system, even if the entry is hashed:

```
$ ssh-keygen -F plum
# Host plum found: line 1 type RSA
plum ssh-rsa AAAAB3NzaC1yc2EAAAADAQABAAAABAQDbhLRVTfIv9gy7oP+5T3HjZmr
Kt2q6ydyKmLlHNUjZFXM4hCdkJlpTfJ4wy260UAZBWvrBLP6N9kYA+KRG1FyuwROUwXQ
...
```

OpenSSH automatically stores keys from servers it has connected to in user-private files (**~/.ssh/known_hosts**). These files work only for the user whose directory they appear in. Working with **root** privileges and using a text editor, you can copy nonhashed lines from a user's private list of known hosts to the public list in **/etc/ssh/ssh_known_hosts** to make a server known globally on the local system.

The following example shows how Sam puts the hashed entry from his **known_hosts** file into the global **ssh_known_hosts** file. First, working as himself, Sam sends the output of ssh-keygen through tail to strip off the **Host plum found** line and redirects the output to a file named **tmp_known_hosts** in his home directory. Next, working with **root** privileges, Sam appends the contents of the file he just created to **/etc/ssh/ssh_known_hosts**. This command creates this file if it does not exist. Finally, Sam returns to working as himself and removes the temporary file he created.

```
$ ssh-keygen -F plum | tail -1 > ~sam/tmp_known_hosts
$ su
Password:
# cat ~sam/tmp_known_hosts >> /etc/ssh/ssh_known_hosts
# exit
exit
$ rm ~/tmp_known_hosts
```

If, after a remote system's public key is stored in one of the known-hosts files, the remote system supplies a different fingerprint when the systems connect, OpenSSH displays the following message and does not complete the connection:

```
@@@@@@@@@@@@@@@@@@@@@@@@@@@@@@@@@@@@@@@@@@@@@@@@@@@@@@@@@@@
@    WARNING: REMOTE HOST IDENTIFICATION HAS CHANGED!     @
@@@@@@@@@@@@@@@@@@@@@@@@@@@@@@@@@@@@@@@@@@@@@@@@@@@@@@@@@@@
IT IS POSSIBLE THAT SOMEONE IS DOING SOMETHING NASTY!
Someone could be eavesdropping on you right now (man-in-the-middle attack)!
It is also possible that the RSA host key has just been changed.
The fingerprint for the RSA key sent by the remote host is
f1:6f:ea:87:bb:1b:df:cd:e3:45:24:60:d3:25:b1:0a.
Please contact your system administrator.
Add correct host key in /home/sam/.ssh/known_hosts to get rid of this message.
Offending key in /home/sam/.ssh/known_hosts:1
RSA host key for plum has changed and you have requested strict checking.
Host key verification failed.
```

If you see this message, you might be the subject of a man-in-the-middle attack. More likely, however, something on the remote system has changed, causing it to supply a new fingerprint. Check with the remote system's administrator. If all is well, remove the offending key from the specified file (the third line from the bottom in the preceding message points to the line you need to remove) and try connecting again. You can use ssh-keygen with the **–R** option followed by the name of a host to remove a hashed entry. You will be subject to first-time authentication (page 691) again as OpenSSH verifies you are connecting to the correct system. Follow the same steps as when you initially connected to the remote host.

## LE+ ssh: Logs in or Executes Commands on a Remote System

The format of an ssh command line is

*ssh [options] [user@]host [command]*

where *host*, the name of the OpenSSH server (the remote system) you want to connect to, is the only required argument. The *host* can be a local system name, the *FQDN* (page 1250) of a system on the Internet, or an IP address.

With the command **ssh** *host*, you log in on the remote system *host* with the same username you are using on the local system. The remote system displays a shell prompt, and you can run commands on *host*. Enter the command **exit** to close the connection to *host* and return to the local system's prompt. Include *user@* when you want to log in with a username other than the one you are using on the local system. Depending on how the server is set up, you might need to supply the password you use on the remote system.

When you include *command*, ssh logs in on *host*, executes *command*, closes the connection to *host*, and returns control to the local system. The remote system never displays a shell prompt.

Opening a remote shell
In the following example, Sam, who is logged in on **guava**, uses ssh to log in on **plum**, gives a **uname** command that shows the name and type of the system, and uses **exit** to close the connection to **plum** and return to the local system's prompt:

```
[sam@guava ~]$ ssh plum
sam@plum's password:
Last login: Wed Jun 12 16:55:47 2013 from guava
[sam@plum ~]$ uname -nm
plum x86_64
[sam@plum ~]$ exit
logout
Connection to plum closed.
[sam@guava ~]$
```

Running commands remotely
The following example uses ls to display a listing of the files in the **memos** directory on the remote system **plum**. The example assumes the user running the command (Sam) has a login on **plum** and that the **memos** directory is in Sam's home directory on **plum**:

```
$ ssh plum ls memos
sam@plum's password:
memo.0921
memo.draft
$
```

When you run ssh, standard output of the command run on the remote system is passed to the local shell as though the command had been run on the local system. As with all shell commands, you must quote special characters you do not want the local shell to interpret.

In the next example, standard output of the ls command, which is run on the remote system, is sent to **ls.out** on the local system.

```
$ ssh plum ls memos > ls.out
sam@plum's password:
$ cat ls.out
memo.0921
memo.draft
```

In the preceding ssh command the redirect symbol (>) is not quoted, so it is interpreted by the local shell and creates the **ls.out** file on the local system.

The next command is similar, but the redirect symbol is quoted, so the local shell does not interpret it but passes it to the remote shell. The first command creates the **ls.out2** file on the remote system, and the second command displays the file.

```
$ ssh plum 'ls memos > ls.out2'
sam@plum's password:
$ ssh plum cat ls.out2
sam@plum's password:
memo.0921
memo.draft
```

For the next example, assume the working directory on the local system holds a file named **memo.new**. You cannot remember whether this file contains certain changes or whether you made these changes to the file named **memo.draft** in the **memos** directory on **plum**. You could copy **memo.draft** to the local system and run diff (page 227) on the two files, but then you would have three similar copies of the file spread across two systems. If you are not careful about removing the old copies when you are done, you might just become confused again in a few days. Instead of copying the file, you can use ssh. This example shows that only the date line differs between the two files:

```
$ ssh plum cat memos/memo.draft | diff memo.new -
sam@plum's password:
1c1
< Wed Jun 14 12:22:14 PDT 2013
---
> Wed Jun 12 17:05:51 PDT 2013
```

In the preceding example, the output of the cat command on **plum** is sent through a pipeline on the local system to diff (running on the local system), which compares the local file **memos.new** to standard input (–). The following command line has the same effect but causes diff to run on the remote system:

```
$ cat memo.new | ssh plum diff - memos/memo.draft
sam@plum's password:
1c1
< Wed Jun 14 12:22:14 PDT 2013
---
> Wed Jun 12 17:05:51 PDT 2013
```

Standard output from diff on the remote system is sent to the local shell, which displays it on the screen (because it is not redirected).

## OPTIONS

This section describes some of the options you can use with ssh.

−C    (**compression**) Enables compression (page 710). In the commercial version of ssh, −C disables compression and **+C** enables compression.

−f    (**not foreground**) Sends ssh to the background after asking for a password and before executing the *command.* Useful when you want to run the *command* in the background but must supply a password. Implies −n.

−i *filename*    (**identity**) Instructs ssh to read the private key from *filename* instead of ~/.ssh/id_dsa or ~/.ssh/id_rsa for automatic login (page 700). See page 680 for an example.

−L    Forwards a port on the local system to a remote system. For more information refer to "Tunneling/Port Forwarding" on page 707.

−l *user*    (**login**) Attempts to log in as *user.*

−n    (**null**) Redirects standard input to ssh to come from /dev/null. Required when running ssh in the background (−f option).

−o *option*    (**option**) Specifies *option* in the format used in configuration files (page 698).

−p    (**port**) Specifies the port on the remote host that the connection is made to. Using the **host** declaration (page 699) in the configuration file, you can specify a different port for each system you connect to.

−R    Forwards a port on the remote system to the local client. For more information refer to "Tunneling/Port Forwarding" on page 707.

−t    (**tty**) Allocates a pseudo-tty (terminal) to the ssh process on the remote system. Without this option, when you run a command on a remote system, ssh does not allocate a tty (terminal) to the process. Instead, it attaches standard input and standard output of the remote process to the ssh session—which is normally, but not always, what you want. This option forces ssh to allocate a tty on the remote system so programs that require a tty will work.

−v    (**verbose**) Displays debugging messages about the connection and transfer. Useful if things are not going as expected. Repeat this option up to a total of three times to increase verbosity.

−X    (**X11**) Turns on nontrusted X11 forwarding. This option is not necessary if you turn on nontrusted X11 forwarding in the configuration file. For more information refer to "Forwarding X11" on page 707.

−x    (**X11**) Turns off X11 forwarding.

−Y    (**X11trusted**) Turns on trusted X11 forwarding. This option is not necessary if you turn on trusted X11 forwarding in the configuration file. For more information refer to "Forwarding X11" on page 707.

# scp: COPIES FILES TO AND FROM A REMOTE SYSTEM

The scp (secure copy) utility copies an ordinary or directory file from one system to another over a network; both systems can be remote. This utility uses ssh to transfer files and employs the same authentication mechanism as ssh; thus it provides the same security as ssh. The scp utility asks for a password when one is required. The format of an scp command is

*scp [[user@]from-host:]source-file [[user@]to-host:][destination-file]*

where *from-host* is the name of the system you are copying files from and *to-host* is the system you are copying to. The *from-host* and *to-host* arguments can be local system names, *FQDNs* (page 1250) of systems on the Internet, or IP addresses. When you do not specify a host, scp assumes the local system. The *user* on either system defaults to the user on the local system who is giving the command; you can specify a different user with *user@*.

The *source-file* is the file you are copying, and the *destination-file* is the resulting copy. Make sure you have read permission for the file you are copying and write permission for the directory you are copying it into. You can specify plain or directory files as relative or absolute pathnames. (A relative pathname is relative to the specified directory or to the implicit user's home directory.) When the *source-file* is a directory, you must use the **–r** option to copy its contents. When the *destination-file* is a directory, each of the source files maintains its simple filename. When the *destination-file* is missing, scp assumes the user's home directory.

Suppose Sam has an alternate username, **sls**, on **plum**. In the following example, Sam uses scp to copy **memo.txt** from the home directory of his **sls** account on **plum** to the **allmemos** directory in the working directory on the local system. If **allmemos** were not the name of a directory, **memo.txt** would be copied to a file named **allmemos** in the working directory.

```
[sam@guava ~]$ scp sls@plum:memo.txt allmemos
sls@plum's password:
memo.txt                                        100%    12KB   12.3KB/s    00:00
```

As the transfer progresses, the percentage and number of bytes transferred increase, and the time remaining decreases.

### rsync **is much more versatile than** scp

tip   The rsync utility is more configurable than scp and uses OpenSSH security by default. It has many options; the most commonly used are **–a** and **–v**. The **–a** option causes rsync to copy ordinary files and directories, preserving the ownership, group, permissions, and modification times associated with the files. It usually does no harm to specify the **–a** option and frequently helps. The **–v** option causes rsync to list files as it copies them. For example, Sam could have given the preceding command as

```
$ rsync -av sls@plum:memo.txt allmemos
sls@plum's password:
receiving incremental file list
memo.txt

sent 30 bytes  received 87495 bytes  19450.00 bytes/sec
total size is 87395  speedup is 1.00
```

The rsync utility is also smarter than scp. If the source and destination files exist, rsync copies only the parts of the source file that are different from the destination file. This feature can save a lot of time when copying large files with few changes, such as when making backups. The number following **speedup** in the output indicates how much rsync's algorithm has speeded up the process of copying a file.

In the next example, Sam, while working from **guava**, copies the same file as in the previous example to the directory named **old** in his home directory on **speedy**. For this example to work, Sam must be able to use ssh to log in on **speedy** from **plum** without using a password. For more information refer to "Authorized Keys: Automatic Login" on page 700.

```
[sam@guava ~]$ scp sls@plum:memo.txt speedy:old
sls@plum's password:
```

### OPTIONS

This section describes some of the options you can use with scp.

–C    (**compression**) Enables compression (page 710).

–o *option*    (**option**) Specifies *option* in the format used in configuration files (discussed shortly).

–P *port*    (**port**) Connects to port *port* on the remote host. This option is uppercase for scp and in lowercase for ssh.

–p    (**preserve**) Preserves the modification and access times as well as the modes of the original file.

–q    (**quiet**) Does not display the progress information as scp copies a file.

–r    (**recursive**) Recursively copies a directory hierarchy (follows symbolic links).

–v    (**verbose**) Displays debugging messages about the connection and transfer. Useful if things are not going as expected.

# sftp: A SECURE FTP CLIENT

As part of OpenSSH, Fedora/RHEL provides sftp, a secure alternative to ftp (page 713). Functionally the same as ftp, sftp maps ftp commands to OpenSSH commands. You can replace ftp with sftp when you are logging in on a server that is running the OpenSSH daemon, **sshd**. When you are connected to a system with sftp, enter the command **?** to display a list of commands. For secure communication, use sftp or scp to perform all file transfers requiring authentication. Refer to the sftp man page for more information.

lftp    Fedora/RHEL also offers lftp, which is more sophisticated than sftp and supports sftp. The lftp utility provides a shell-like command syntax that has many features, including support for tab completion and the ability to run jobs in the background. Place the following **.lftprc** file in your home directory to ensure lftp uses OpenSSH to connect to a server.

```
$ cat ~/.lftprc
set default-protocol sftp
```

You can also use **/etc/lftp.conf** to configure lftp; see the lftp man page for more information.

# ~/.ssh/config AND /etc/ssh/ssh_config CONFIGURATION FILES

It is rarely necessary to modify OpenSSH client configuration files. For a given user there might be two configuration files: **~/.ssh/config** (user) and **/etc/ssh/ssh_config** (global). These files are read in this order and, for a given parameter, the first one found is the one OpenSSH uses. A user can override a global parameter setting by setting the same parameter in her user configuration file. Parameters given on the **ssh** or **scp** command line take precedence over parameters set in either of these files.

For security, a user's **~/.ssh/config** file should be owned by the user in whose home directory it appears and should not be writable by anyone except the owner. This file is typically set to mode 600 as there is no reason for anyone except its owner to be able to read it.

Lines in the configuration files contain declarations. Each of these declarations starts with a keyword that is not case sensitive. Some keywords must be followed by whitespace and one or more case-sensitive arguments. You can use the **Host** keyword to cause declarations to apply to a specific system. A Host declaration applies to all the lines between it and the next Host declaration.

Following are some of the keywords and arguments you can specify:

**CheckHostIP yes | no**

Identifies a remote system using the IP address in addition to a hostname from the **known_hosts** file when set to **yes**. Set it to **no** to use a hostname only. Setting CheckHostIP to **yes** can improve system security. Default is **yes**.

**ForwardX11 yes | no**

When set to **yes**, automatically forwards X11 connections over a secure channel in nontrusted mode and sets the **DISPLAY** shell variable. Fedora/RHEL allows this keyword to default to **no** so X11 forwarding is *not* initially enabled. If ForwardX11Trusted is also set to **yes**, the connections are made in trusted mode. Alternately, you can use **–X** on the command line to redirect X11 connections in nontrusted mode. For X11 forwarding to work, you must also set X11Forwarding to **yes** in the **/etc/sshd_config** file on the server (page 706). For more information refer to "Forwarding X11" on page 707.

**ForwardX11Trusted yes | no**

Works in conjunction with ForwardX11, which must be set to **yes** for this keyword to have any effect. When this keyword is set to **yes** (as it is under Fedora/RHEL) and ForwardX11 is set to **yes**, this keyword gives remote X11 clients full access to the original (server) X11 display. Alternately, you can use **–Y** on the command line to redirect X11 connections in trusted mode. For X11 forwarding to work, X11Forwarding must also be set to **yes** in the **/etc/sshd_config** file on the server (page 706). Default value is **no**, but Fedora/RHEL sets this keyword to **yes**. For more information refer to "Forwarding X11" on page 707.

**HashKnownHosts**

> Causes OpenSSH to hash hostnames and addresses in the ~/.ssh/known_hosts file when set to **yes**. When set to **no**, the hostnames and addresses are written in cleartext. Default is **no**. See page 691 for more information on the **known_hosts** file.

**Host** *hostnames*

> Specifies that the following declarations, until the next Host declaration, apply only to hosts that *hostnames* matches. The *hostnames* is a whitespace-separated list that can include ? and * wildcards. A single * specifies all hosts. Without this keyword, all declarations apply to all hosts.

**HostbasedAuthentication yes | no**

> Tries **rhosts** authentication when set to **yes**. For a more secure system, set to **no**. Default is **no**.

**HostKeyAlgorithms** *algorithms*

> The *algorithms* is a comma-separated list of algorithms the client uses in order of preference. Choose *algorithms* from **ssh-rsa** or **ssh-dss**. Default is **ssh-rsa,ssh-dss**.

**Port** *num*    Causes OpenSSH to connect to the remote system on port *num*. Default is 22.

**StrictHostKeyChecking yes | no | ask**

> Determines whether and how OpenSSH adds host keys to a user's **known_hosts** file. Set this option to **ask** to ask whether to add a host key when connecting to a new system, set it to **no** to add a host key automatically, and set it to **yes** to require host keys to be added manually. The **yes** and **ask** arguments cause OpenSSH to refuse to connect to a system whose host key has changed. For a more secure system, set to **yes** or **ask**. Default is **ask**.

**TCPKeepAlive yes | no**

> Periodically checks whether a connection is alive when set to **yes**. Checking causes the ssh or scp connection to be dropped when the server crashes or the connection dies for another reason, even if it is only temporary. This option tests the connection at the transport (TCP) layer (page 291). Setting this parameter to **no** causes the client not to check whether the connection is alive. Default is **yes**.
>
> This declaration uses the TCP **keepalive** option, which is not encrypted and is susceptible to *IP spoofing* (page 1256). Refer to **ClientAliveInterval** on page 704 for a server-based nonspoofable alternative.

**User** *name*    Specifies a username to use when logging in on a system. You can specify a system with the Host declaration. This option means you do not have to enter a username on the command line when you are using a username that differs from your username on the local system.

**VisualHostKey yes | no**

> Displays an ASCII art representation of the key of the remote system in addition to displaying the hexadecimal representation of the key when set to **yes**. When set to **no**, this declaration displays the hexadecimal key only. For more information refer to "Randomart" on page 702. Default is **no**.

# SETTING UP AN OPENSSH SERVER (sshd)

This section describes how to set up an OpenSSH server.

## PREREQUISITES

Install the following packages (both are installed by default):

- openssh
- openssh-server

Check **sshd** is running    A new Fedora/RHEL system boots with **sshd** installed and running. Use the systemctl **status** command to make sure the service is running.

```
# systemctl status sshd.service
```

After modifying **sshd** configuration files, give the second command again, replacing **status** with **restart** to cause **sshd** to reread those files.

When the system is booted just after it is installed, the **sshd** daemon is started and automatically creates host key files (page 687) in **/etc/ssh**. OpenSSH uses the files it creates to identify the server.

## NOTES

Firewall    An OpenSSH server normally uses TCP port 22. Under Fedora/RHEL, this port is open when the system is installed. If the OpenSSH server system is running a firewall, this port must be open.

SELinux    When SELinux is set to use a targeted policy, **sshd** is protected by SELinux. You can disable this protection if necessary. For more information refer to "Setting the Targeted Policy with system-config-selinux" on page 475.

## JUMPSTART II: STARTING AN OPENSSH SERVER

By default, the **sshd** server is installed and running when you first boot a Fedora/RHEL system (page 700). You can look in **/var/log/secure** and **/var/log/messages** or give the command **systemctl status httpd** to make sure everything is working properly.

### RECOMMENDED SETTINGS

The configuration files provided by Fedora/RHEL establish a mostly secure system that might or might not meet your needs. The Fedora/RHEL **/etc/ssh/sshd_config** file turns on X11 forwarding (page 707). It is important to set PermitRootLogin (page 705) to **no**, which prevents a known-name, privileged account from being exposed to the outside world with only password protection.

## LPI   AUTHORIZED KEYS: AUTOMATIC LOGIN

You can configure OpenSSH so you do not have to enter a password each time you connect to a server (remote system). To set up this feature, you need to generate a personal authentication key on the client (local system), place the public part of the key on the server, and keep the private part of the key on the client. When you connect to the server, it issues a challenge based on the public part of the key. OpenSSH then uses the private part of the key to respond to this challenge. If the client provides the appropriate response, the server logs you in.

The first step in setting up an automatic login is to generate your personal authentication keys. First check whether these authentication keys already exist on the local system (client) by looking in **~/.ssh** for either **id_dsa** and **id_dsa.pub** or **id_rsa** and **id_rsa.pub**. If one of these pairs of files is present, skip the next step (do not create a new key).

**LPI** ssh-keygen   On the client, the ssh-keygen utility creates the public and private parts of an RSA key. The key's randomart image is a visual representation of the public key; see page 702.

```
$ ssh-keygen -t rsa
Generating public/private rsa key pair.
Enter file in which to save the key (/home/sam/.ssh/id_rsa):
Enter passphrase (empty for no passphrase):
Enter same passphrase again:
Your identification has been saved in /home/sam/.ssh/id_rsa.
Your public key has been saved in /home/sam/.ssh/id_rsa.pub.
The key fingerprint is:
23:8f:99:2e:43:36:93:ed:c6:38:fe:4d:04:61:27:28 sam@guava
The key's randomart image is:
+--[ RSA 2048]----+
|       .+ .       |
|   E .. +         |
|    .  .          |
|        .         |
|     o. S         |
|    * .B .        |
|   o *+ o         |
|    =.+o          |
|    ..*o .        |
+-----------------+
```

Replace **rsa** with **dsa** to generate DSA keys. In this example, the user pressed RETURN in response to each query. You have the option of specifying a passphrase (10–30 characters is a good length) to encrypt the private part of the key. There is no way to recover a lost passphrase. See the security tip on page 703 for more information about the passphrase.

**LPI** id_rsa and   The ssh-keygen utility generates two keys: a private key or identification in **~/.ssh/id_rsa**
id_rsa.pub   and a public key in **~/.ssh/id_rsa.pub**. No one except the owner should be able to write to either of these files, and only the owner should be able to read from the private key file.

You can display the local server's RSA key fingerprint using ssh-keygen:

```
$ ssh-keygen -lf /etc/ssh/ssh_host_rsa_key.pub
2048 d1:9d:1b:5b:97:5c:80:e9:4b:41:9a:b7:bc:1a:ea:a1 /etc/ssh/ssh_host_rsa_key.pub (RSA)
```

Or you can display the fingerprint of the public key you just created:

```
$ ssh-keygen -lf ~/.ssh/id_rsa.pub
2048 23:8f:99:2e:43:36:93:ed:c6:38:fe:4d:04:61:27:28 /home/sam/.ssh/id_rsa.pub sam@plum (RSA)
```

ssh-copy-id To log in on or copy files to and from another system without supplying a password, you must copy the **~/.ssh/id_rsa.pub** from the client (local system) to a file named **~/.ssh/authorized_keys** on the server (remote system). The ssh-copy-id utility creates the **~/.ssh** directory on the server if necessary, copies **id_rsa.pub**, and makes sure permissions are correct. The following example shows Sam setting up automatic login on the system named **plum**:

```
$ ssh-copy-id sam@plum
sam@plum's password:
...
Number of key(s) added: 1

Now try logging into the machine, with:   "ssh 'sam@plum'"
and check to make sure that only the key(s) you wanted were added.

$ ssh sam@plum
$
```

Sam must supply his password to copy the file to **plum**. After running ssh-copy-id, Sam can log in on **plum** without providing a password. To make the server even more secure, disable password authentication (see the adjacent tip).

### Use a personal authentication key instead of a password

security Using a personal authentication key is more secure than using a password. When you turn off password authentication, brute force authentication attacks become very unlikely.

Disable password authentication by setting **PasswordAuthentication** to **no** in **/etc/ssh/sshd_config** (remove the # from the beginning of the **PasswordAuthentication** line and change the **yes** to **no**; page 705).

Randomart The *randomart* image of a system is an experimental OpenSSH ASCII visualization of the system's host key. This image is displayed by OpenSSH utilities, including ssh, scp, and ssh-keygen. Its display is controlled by the **VisualHostKey** keyword in the **ssh_config** file (page 699). With this keyword set to **yes**, OpenSSH displays a system's randomart image when you connect:

```
$ ssh plum
Host key fingerprint is 0b:90:12:02:97:fb:93:6e:d4:14:f8:e0:ac:f3:26:36
+--[ RSA 2048]----+
|+ o. .           |
| o..o..          |
|  .+oo .         |
|  ..o.o          |
|   o +. S        |
|  o = .. .       |
|   = .  .        |
|   E =           |
|   . =           |
+-----------------+

sam@plum's password:
...
```

The randomart image renders a system's host key in a visual format that can be easier to recall than a host key fingerprint (see the preceding example). Making it easier for a user to detect a change in the fingerprint can mean that a user will be aware when he is connecting to a system other than the one he intended to connect to.

**_LPI_** ## ssh-agent: HOLDS YOUR PRIVATE KEYS

### Personal key encryption, passphrase, and ssh-agent

**security**  The private part of your personal authentication key is kept in a file that only you can read. When you set up automatic login on a remote system, any user who has access to your account on the local system also has access to your account on the remote system because that user can read the private part of your personal key. Thus, if a malicious user compromises your account or the **root** account on the local system, that user then has access to your account on the remote system.

Encrypting the private part of your personal key protects the key and, therefore, restricts access to the remote system should someone compromise your local account. However, if you encrypt your personal key, you must supply the passphrase you used to encrypt the key each time you use the key, negating the benefit of not having to type a password when logging in on the remote system.

You can use ssh-agent to remember the private part of your personal key for the duration of a session; you supply your passphrase once, at the beginning of the session.

### Storing private keys on a removable medium

**security**  You can store the private keys on a removable medium, such as a USB flash drive, and use your **~/.ssh** directory as the mount point for the filesystem stored on this drive. You might want to encrypt these keys with a passphrase in case you lose the flash drive.

When you use ssh-keygen to generate a public/private key pair, you have the option of specifying a passphrase. If you specify a passphrase, you must supply that passphrase each time you use the key. The result is, when you set up a key pair to avoid specifying your password when you log in on a remote system using ssh, you end up supplying the passphrase instead.

The ssh-agent utility allows you to use a passphrase with your personal key while entering the key one time, at the beginning of each session. When you log out, ssh-agent forgets the key. Because Fedora/RHEL is set up with ssh-agent enabled for X sessions, it is very easy to use in a graphical environment. It is also easy to set up in a textual environment.

If you are running a textual session (not within a terminal emulator window), you must give the following command to enable ssh-agent. If you are running a graphical session, skip this step (ssh-agent is set up in the files in **/etc/X11/xinit/xinitrc**).

```
$ eval $(ssh-agent -s)
Agent pid 9882
```

**_LPI_**  ssh-add  Once ssh-agent is enabled, use ssh-add to specify the passphrase for a key pair:

```
$ ssh-add ~/.ssh/id_rsa
Enter passphrase for /home/sam/.ssh/id_rsa:
Identity added: /home/sam/.ssh/id_rsa (/home/sam/.ssh/id_rsa)
```

If you omit the argument to ssh-add, it adds a passphrase for each of the **~/.ssh/id_rsa**, **~/.ssh/id_dsa**, and **~/.ssh/identity** files that exist.

With this setup, you can use ssh to work on a remote system without supplying a login password and by supplying your passphrase one time per session.

## COMMAND-LINE OPTIONS

Command-line options override declarations in the configuration files. Following are descriptions of some of the more useful **sshd** options.

–D   (**noDetach**) Keeps **sshd** in the foreground. Useful for debugging; implied by **–d**.

–d   (**debug**) Sets debug mode so that **sshd** sends debugging messages to the system log and the server stays in the foreground (implies **–D**). You can specify this option a maximum of three times to increase the verbosity of the output. See also **–e**. (The ssh client uses **–v** for debugging; page 695.)

–e   (**error**) Sends output to standard error, not to the system log. Useful with **–d**.

–f *file*   Specifies *file* as the configuration file instead of **/etc/ssh/sshd_config**.

–t   (**test**) Checks the configuration file syntax and the sanity of the key files.

## /etc/ssh/sshd_config CONFIGURATION FILE

Lines in the **/etc/ssh/sshd_config** configuration file contain declarations. Each of these declarations starts with a keyword that is not case sensitive. Some keywords must be followed by whitespace and one or more case-sensitive arguments. You must reload the **sshd** server before these changes will take effect.

**AllowUsers** *userlist*

The *userlist* is a SPACE-separated list of usernames that specifies which users are allowed to log in using **sshd**. This list can include * and ? wildcards. You can specify a user as *user* or *user@host*. If you use the second format, make sure you specify the host as returned by hostname. Without this declaration, any user who can log in locally can log in using an OpenSSH client. Does not work with numeric user IDs.

**ClientAliveCountMax** *n*

The *n* specifies the number of client-alive messages that can be sent without receiving a response before **sshd** disconnects from the client. See **ClientAliveInterval**. Default is 3.

**ClientAliveInterval** *n*

Sends a message through the encrypted channel after *n* seconds of not receiving a message from the client. See **ClientAliveCountMax**. The default is 0, meaning that no messages are sent.

This declaration passes messages over the encrypted channel (application layer; page 291) and is not susceptible to *IP spoofing* (page 1256). It differs from **TCPKeepAlive**, which uses the TCP **keepalive** option (transport layer; page 291) and is susceptible to IP spoofing.

**DenyUsers** *userlist*

The *userlist* is a SPACE-separated list of usernames that specifies users who are not allowed to log in using **sshd**. This list can include ❊ and ? wildcards. You can specify a user as *user* or *user@host*. If you use the second format, make sure you specify the host as returned by hostname. Does not work with numeric user IDs.

**ForceCommand** *command*

Executes *command*, ignoring commands specified by the client and commands in the optional **~/.ssh/ssh/rc** file.

**HostbasedAuthentication yes | no**

Tries **rhosts** and **/etc/hosts.equiv** authentication when set to **yes**. For a more secure system, set this declaration to **no**. Default is **no**.

**IgnoreRhosts yes | no**

Ignores **.rhosts** and **.shosts** files for authentication. Does not affect the use of **/etc/hosts.equiv** and **/etc/ssh/shosts.equiv** files for authentication. For a more secure system, set this declaration to **yes**. Default is **yes**.

**LoginGraceTime** *n*

Waits *n* seconds for a user to log in on the server before disconnecting. A value of 0 means there is no time limit. Default is 120 seconds.

**LogLevel** *val*   Specifies how detailed the log messages are. Choose *val* from QUIET, FATAL, ERROR, INFO, and VERBOSE. Default is INFO.

**PasswordAuthentication yes | no**

Permits a user to use a password for authentication. For a more secure system, set up automatic login (page 700) and set this declaration to **no**. Default is **yes**.

**PermitEmptyPasswords yes | no**

Permits a user to log in on an account that has an empty password. Default is **no**.

**PermitRootLogin yes | without-password | forced-commands-only | no**

Permits **root** to log in using an OpenSSH client. Default is **yes**.

Setting this declaration to **yes** allows a user to log in as a privileged user by suppling the **root** password. This setup allows the **root** password to be sent over the network, although it is encrypted, so it is not a big security risk. It also requires all users connecting as a privileged user to know the **root** password.

Setting this declaration to **no** does not allow **root** to authenticate directly; privilege must come from sudo or su after a user has logged in. Given the number of brute-force attacks on a typical system connected to the Internet, this is a good choice.

Setting this declaration to **without-password** means the only way for a user to authenticate as **root** is by using an authorized key (page 700). This choice eliminates the need for a group of people to know the **root** password. However, one user must be able to run with **root** privileges so new keys can be added as needed.

Setting this declaration to **forced-commands** works with an authorized key but forces a specific command after authentication instead of starting an interactive shell. The command is specified by **ForceCommand** (above).

PermitUserEnvironment yes | no

> Permits a user to modify the environment he logs in to on the remote system. Default is **no**. See **environment** on page 688.

Port *num*   Specifies that the **sshd** server listen on port *num*. It might improve security to change *num* to a nonstandard port. Default is 22.

StrictModes yes | no

> Checks modes and ownership of the user's home directory and files. Login fails for users other than the owner if the directories and/or files can be written to by anyone other than the owner. For a more secure system, set this declaration to **yes**. Default is **yes**.

SyslogFacility *val*

> Specifies the facility name (page 620) **sshd** uses when logging messages. Set *val* to **daemon, user, auth, authpriv, local0, local1, local2, local3, local4, local5, local6,** or **local7**. Default is **auth**.

TCPKeepAlive yes | no

> Periodically checks whether a connection is alive when set to **yes**. Checking causes the **ssh** or **scp** connection to be dropped when the client crashes or the connection dies for another reason, even if it is only temporary. Setting this parameter to **no** causes the server not to check whether the connection is alive. Default is **yes**.
>
> This declaration tests the connection at the transport (TCP) layer (page 291). It uses the TCP **keepalive** option, which is not encrypted and is susceptible to *IP spoofing* (page 1256). Refer to **ClientAliveInterval** (page 704) for a nonspoofable alternative.

X11Forwarding yes | no

> Allows X11 forwarding when set to **yes**. For trusted X11 forwarding to work, the ForwardX11 or the ForwardX11Trusted declaration must also be set to **yes** in either the ~/.ssh/config or /etc/ssh/ssh_config client configuration file (page 698). The default is **no**, but Fedora/RHEL sets X11Forwarding to **yes**. For more information refer to "Forwarding X11" on page 707.

# TROUBLESHOOTING

Log files   There are several places to look for clues when you have a problem connecting with **ssh** or **scp**. First look for **sshd** entries in **/var/log/secure** and **/var/log/messages** on the server. Following are messages you might see when you are using an **AllowUsers** declaration but have not included the user who is trying to log in (page 704). The messages that are marked **pam_unix** originate with PAM (page 476).

```
# grep sshd /var/log/secure | tail -6
guava sshd[10244]: Server listening on :: port 22.
guava sshd[10248]: User sam from 172.16.192.150 not allowed because not listed in AllowUsers
guava sshd[10249]: input_userauth_request: invalid user sam
guava sshd[10248]: pam_unix(sshd:auth): authentication failure; logname= uid=0 euid=0 tty=ssh ruser=
rhost=192.168.206.181 user=sam
guava sshd[10248]: Failed password for invalid user sam from 192.168.206.181 port 59088 ssh2
guava sshd[10249]: Connection closed by 192.168.206.181
```

Check the   You can use the **sshd –t** option to check the syntax of the server configuration file.
configuration file

Debug the client   If entries in these files do not help solve the problem, try connecting with the **–v** option (either **ssh** or **scp**—the results should be the same). OpenSSH displays a lot of debugging messages, one of which might help you figure out what the problem is. You can use a maximum of three **–v** options to increase the number of messages that OpenSSH displays.

```
$ ssh -v plum
OpenSSH_6.2p1, OpenSSL 1.0.1e-fips 11 Feb 2013
debug1: Reading configuration data /etc/ssh/ssh_config
debug1: /etc/ssh/ssh_config line 50: Applying options for *
debug1: Connecting to plum [192.168.206.181] port 22.
debug1: Connection established.
debug1: identity file /home/sam/.ssh/id_rsa type 1
debug1: identity file /home/sam/.ssh/id_rsa-cert type -1
...
debug1: Host 'plum' is known and matches the RSA host key.
debug1: Found key in /home/sam/.ssh/known_hosts:1
debug1: ssh_rsa_verify: signature correct
...
debug1: Authentications that can continue: publickey,gssapi-keyex,gssapi-with-mic,password
...
debug1: Next authentication method: publickey
debug1: Offering public key: /home/sam/.ssh/id_rsa
debug1: Authentications that can continue: publickey,gssapi-keyex,gssapi-with-mic,password
debug1: Trying private key: /home/sam/.ssh/id_dsa
debug1: Next authentication method: password
sam@plum's password:
```

Debug the server   You can debug from the server side by giving the command **/usr/sbin/sshd –de** while working with **root** privileges. The server will run in the foreground, and its display might help you solve the problem.

# TUNNELING/PORT FORWARDING     *LPI*

The **ssh** utility can forward a port (*port forwarding;* page 1266) through the encrypted connection it establishes. Because the data sent across the forwarded port uses the encrypted **ssh** connection as its data link layer (page 291), the term *tunneling* (page 1278) is applied to this type of connection: "The connection is tunneled through **ssh**." You can secure protocols—including POP, X, IMAP, VNC, and WWW—by tunneling them through **ssh**.

## FORWARDING X11

The **ssh** utility makes it easy to tunnel the X11 protocol. For X11 tunneling to work, you must enable it on both the server and the client, and the client must be running the X Window System.

### SERVER

On the **ssh** server, enable X11 forwarding by setting the X11Forwarding declaration (page 706) to **yes** (the default) in the **/etc/ssh/sshd_config** file.

### TRUSTED CLIENT

On a client, enable trusted X11 forwarding by setting the ForwardX11 (default is **no**; page 698) *and* ForwardX11Trusted (default is **no**, but set to **yes** as installed;

page 698) declarations to **yes** in the **/etc/ssh/ssh_config** or **~/.ssh/config** file. Alternately, you can specify the **–Y** option (page 695) on the command line to start the client in trusted mode.

When you enable X11 forwarding on a client, the client connects as a trusted client, which means the client trusts the server and is given full access to the X11 display. With full access to the X11 display, in some situations a client might be able to modify other clients of the X11 display. Make a trusted connection only when you trust the remote system. (You do not want someone tampering with your client.) If this concept is confusing, see the tip "The roles of X client and server might be counterintuitive" on page 459.

## Nontrusted Client

On a client, enable nontrusted X11 forwarding by setting the ForwardX11 (default is **no**; page 698) declaration to **yes** *and* the ForwardX11Trusted (default is **no**, but set to **yes** as installed; page 698) declaration to **no** in the **/etc/ssh/ssh_config** or **~/.ssh/config** file. Alternately, you can specify the **–X** option (page 695) on the command line to start the client in nontrusted mode.

A nontrusted client is given limited access to the X11 display and cannot modify other clients of the X11 display. Few clients work properly when they are run in non-trusted mode. If you are running an X11 client in nontrusted mode and encounter problems, try running in trusted mode (assuming you trust the remote system). Fedora/RHEL sets up ssh clients to run in trusted mode.

## Running ssh

With X11 forwarding turned on, ssh tunnels the X11 protocol, setting the **DISPLAY** environment variable on the system it connects to and forwarding the required port. Typically you will be running from a GUI, which usually means that you are using ssh in a terminal emulator window to connect to a remote system. When you give an X11 command from an ssh prompt, OpenSSH creates a new secure channel that carries the X11 data, and the graphical output from the X11 program appears on the screen. Typically you will need to start the client in trusted mode.

```
[sam@guava ~]$ ssh plum
[sam@plum ~]$ echo $DISPLAY
localhost:10.0
```

By default, ssh uses X Window System display numbers 10 and higher (port numbers 6010 and higher) for forwarded X sessions. After you connect to a remote system using **ssh**, you can give a command to run an X application. The application will then run on the remote system with its display appearing on the local system, such that it appears to run locally.

# PORT FORWARDING

You can forward arbitrary ports using the –L and –R options. The –L option forwards a local port to a remote system, so a program that tries to connect to the forwarded port on the local system transparently connects to the remote system. The –R option does the reverse: It forwards remote ports to the local system. The –N option, which prevents ssh from executing remote commands, is generally used with –L and –R. When you specify –N, ssh works only as a private network to forward ports. An ssh command line using the –L or –R option has the following format:

$ ssh –N –L | –R *local-port:remote-host:remote-port target*

where *local-port* is the number of the local port that is being forwarded to or from *remote-host*, *remote-host* is the name or IP address of the system that *local-port* gets forwarded to or from, *remote-port* is the number of the port on *remote-host* that is being forwarded from or to the local system, and *target* is the name or IP address of the system ssh connects to.

As an example, assume there is a POP mail client on the local system and that the POP server is on a remote network, on a system named **pophost**. POP is not a secure protocol; passwords are sent in cleartext each time the client connects to the server. You can make it more secure by tunneling POP through ssh (POP-3 connects on port 110; port 1550 is an arbitrary port on the local system):

```
$ ssh -N -L 1550:pophost:110 pophost
```

After giving the preceding command, you can point the POP client at **localhost:1550**. The connection between the client and the server will then be encrypted. (When you set up an account on the POP client, specify the location of the server as **localhost, port 1550**; details vary with different mail clients.)

## FIREWALLS

In the preceding example, *remote-host* and *target* were the same system. However, the system specified for port forwarding (*remote-host*) does not have to be the same as the destination of the ssh connection (*target*). As an example, assume the POP server is behind a firewall and you cannot connect to it via ssh. If you can connect to the firewall via the Internet using ssh, you can encrypt the part of the connection over the Internet:

```
$ ssh -N -L 1550:pophost:110 firewall
```

Here *remote-host* (the system receiving the port forwarding) is **pophost**, and *target* (the system that ssh connects to) is **firewall**.

You can also use ssh when you are behind a firewall (that is running **sshd**) and want to forward a port into your system without modifying the firewall settings:

```
$ ssh -R 1678:localhost:80 firewall
```

The preceding command forwards connections from the outside to port 1678 on the firewall to the local Web server. Forwarding connections in this manner allows you to use a Web browser to connect to port 1678 on the firewall when you connect to the Web server on the local system. This setup would be useful if you ran a Webmail program (page 758) on the local system because it would allow you to check your mail from anywhere using an Internet connection.

### COMPRESSION

Compression, which is enabled with the –C option, can speed up communication over a low-bandwidth connection. This option is commonly used with port forwarding. Compression can increase latency to an extent that might not be desirable for an X session forwarded over a high-bandwidth connection.

# CHAPTER SUMMARY

OpenSSH is a suite of secure network connectivity tools that encrypts all traffic, including passwords, thereby helping to thwart malicious users who might otherwise eavesdrop, hijack connections, and steal passwords. The **sshd** server daemon accepts connections from clients including ssh (runs a command on or logs in on another system), scp (copies files to and from another system), and sftp (securely replaces ftp). Helper programs including ssh-keygen (creates, manages, and converts authentication keys), ssh-agent (manages keys during a session), and ssh-add (works with ssh-agent) create and manage authentication keys.

To ensure secure communications, when an OpenSSH client opens a connection, it verifies that it is connected to the correct server. Then OpenSSH encrypts communication between the systems. Finally, OpenSSH makes sure the user is authorized to log in on or copy files to and from the server. You can secure many protocols—including POP, X, IMAP, VNC, and WWW—by tunneling them through ssh.

When it is properly set up, OpenSSH also enables secure X11 forwarding. With this feature, you can run securely a graphical program on a remote system and have the display appear on the local system.

# EXERCISES

1. What is the difference between the scp and sftp utilities?

2. How can you use ssh to find out who is logged in on a remote system?

3. How would you use scp to copy your ~/.bashrc file from the system named **plum** to the local system?

4. How would you use ssh to run xterm on **plum** and show the display on the local system?

5. What problem can enabling compression present when you are using ssh to run remote X applications on a local display?

6. When you try to connect to a remote system using an OpenSSH client and you see a message warning you that the remote host identification has changed, what has happened? What should you do?

# ADVANCED EXERCISES

7. Which scp command would you use to copy your home directory from **plum** to the local system?

8. Which single command could you give to log in as **root** on the remote system named **plum,** if **plum** has remote **root** logins disabled?

9. How could you use ssh to compare the contents of the **~/memos** directories on **plum** and the local system?

10. How would you use rsync with OpenSSH authentication to copy the **memos12** file from the working directory on the local system to your home directory on **plum**? How would you copy the **memos** directory from the working directory on the local system to your home directory on **plum** and cause rsync to display each file as it copied the file?

# 19

# FTP: Transferring Files Across a Network

## Objectives

After reading this chapter you should be able to:

▸ Download files from and upload files to an FTP server

▸ Download files from an anonymous FTP server

▸ Automate FTP logins using a **.netrc** file

▸ Explain the difference between binary and ASCII transfers

▸ Install and configure the **vsftpd** server

713

FTP     FTP (File Transfer Protocol) is a method of downloading files from and uploading files to another system using TCP/IP over a network. FTP is the name of a client/server protocol (FTP) and a client utility (ftp) that invokes the protocol. In addition to the original ftp utility, there are many textual and graphical FTP client programs, including most browsers, that run under many different operating systems. There are also many FTP server programs.

# INTRODUCTION TO FTP

This chapter starts with an introduction to FTP that discusses security, describes types of FTP connections, and presents a list of FTP clients. The first JumpStart section covers basic ftp commands and includes a tutorial on using the ftp client. Next is a section that presents more details of ftp. The final section describes how to set up a **vsftpd** FTP server.

History     First implemented under 4.2BSD, FTP has played an essential role in the propagation of Linux; this protocol/program is frequently used to distribute free software.

FTP site     The term *FTP site* refers to an FTP server that is connected to a network, usually the Internet. FTP sites can be public, allowing anonymous users to log in and download software and documentation. In contrast, private FTP sites require you to log in with a username and password. Some sites allow you to upload programs.

ftp and **vsftpd**     Although most FTP clients are similar, the servers differ quite a bit. This chapter describes the ftp client with references to sftp, a secure FTP client. It also covers the **vsftpd** (very secure FTP daemon) server that Fedora/RHEL uses internally and offers as part of its distribution.

ftp utility     The ftp utility is a user interface to FTP, a standard protocol used to transfer files between systems that communicate over a network.

## SECURITY

FTP is not a secure protocol: All usernames and passwords exchanged in setting up an FTP connection are sent in cleartext, data exchanged over an FTP connection is not encrypted, and the connection is subject to hijacking. Given these facts, FTP is best used for downloading public files. In most cases, the OpenSSH clients, ssh (page 693), scp (page 695), and sftp (page 697), offer secure alternatives to FTP.

### Use FTP only to download public information

security     FTP is not secure. The sftp utility provides better security for all FTP functions other than allowing anonymous users to download information. Because sftp uses an encrypted connection, user passwords and data cannot be sniffed when you use this utility. You can replace all instances of ftp in this chapter with sftp because sftp uses the same commands as ftp. See page 697 for more information on sftp.

The **vsftpd** server does *not* make usernames, passwords, data, and connections more secure. However, it is secure in that a malicious user finds it more difficult to compromise directly the system running it, even if **vsftpd** is poorly implemented.

One feature that makes **vsftpd** more secure than **ftpd** is the fact that it does not run with **root** privileges. See also "Security" on page 725.

# FTP CONNECTIONS

FTP uses two connections: one for control (you establish this connection when you log in on an FTP server) and one for data transfer (FTP sets up this connection when you ask it to transfer a file). An FTP server listens for incoming connections on port 21 by default and handles user authentication and file exchange.

Passive versus active connections
A client can ask an FTP server to establish either a PASV (passive—the default) or a PORT (active) connection for data transfer. Some servers are limited to one type of connection. The difference between a passive and an active FTP connection lies in whether the client or the server initiates the data connection. In passive mode, the client initiates the connection to the server (on port 20 by default); in active mode, the server initiates the connection (there is no default port; see "Connection Parameters" on page 734 for the parameters that determine which ports a server uses). Neither approach is inherently more secure than the other. Passive connections are more common because a client using NAT (page 910) can connect to a passive server and it is simpler to program a scalable passive server.

# FTP CLIENTS

ftp
Fedora/RHEL supplies several FTP clients, including ftp (an older version of the BSD ftp utility). This section discusses ftp because it is commonly used and most other FTP clients, including sftp and lftp, provide a superset of ftp commands.

sftp
Part of the OpenSSH suite, sftp (**openssh-clients** package) is a secure and functionally equivalent alternative to ftp. The sftp utility is not a true FTP client—it does not understand the FTP protocol. It maps ftp commands to OpenSSH commands. See page 697 for more information.

lftp
The lftp utility (**lftp** package) provides the same security as sftp but offers more features. See the lftp man page for more information.

gftp
The gftp utility (**gftp** package) is a graphical client that works with FTP, SSH, and HTTP servers. This client has many useful features, including the ability to resume an interrupted file transfer. See www.gftp.org and freshmeat.net/projects/gftp for more information.

ncftp
The ncftp utility (**ncftp** package) is a textual client that offers many more features than ftp, including filename completion and command-line editing. For details see www.ncftp.com and freshmeat.net/projects/ncftp.

# MORE INFORMATION

Local
Type **help** or **?** at an **ftp>** prompt to display a list of commands. Follow the **?** with a SPACE and an **ftp** command to display information about that command.
Files: **/usr/share/doc/vsftpd-**∗
man pages: ftp, sftp, lftp, **netrc, vsftpd.conf**

Web
**vsftpd** home page: security.appspot.com/vsftpd.html

HOWTO
*FTP mini-HOWTO*

## NOTES

A Linux system running ftp can exchange files with any of the many operating systems that support FTP. Many sites offer archives of free information on an FTP server, although for many it is just an alternative to an easier-to-access Web site (see, for example, ftp://ftp.ibiblio.org/pub/Linux and http://www.ibiblio.org/software/linux). Most browsers can connect to and download files from FTP servers.

The ftp utility makes no assumptions about filesystem nomenclature or structure because you can use ftp to exchange files with non-UNIX/Linux systems (which might use different filenaming conventions).

# RUNNING THE ftp AND sftp FTP CLIENTS

This section describes how to use the ftp and sftp FTP clients. The commands covered here work with both utilities.

## PREREQUISITES

Install the following packages:

- **openssh-clients** (installed by default; contains sftp)

- **ftp**

There is no service to start for ftp or sftp clients.

## JUMPSTART I: DOWNLOADING FILES USING ftp

This JumpStart section is broken into two parts: a description of the basic commands and a tutorial session that shows a user working with ftp.

### BASIC COMMANDS

Give the command

```
$ ftp hostname
```

where *hostname* is the name of the FTP server you want to connect to. If you have an account on the server, log in with your username and password. If it is a public system, log in as the user **anonymous** (or **ftp**) and give your email address as your password. Use the **ls** and **cd** ftp commands on the server as you would use the corresponding utilities from a shell. The command **get** *file* copies *file* from the server to the local system, **put** *file* copies *file* from the local system to the server, **status** displays information about the FTP connection, and **help** displays a list of commands.

The preceding commands, except for **status**, are also available in sftp, lftp, and ncftp.

## TUTORIAL SESSION

Following are two ftp sessions wherein Sam transfers files from and to a **vsftpd** server named **plum**. When Sam gives the command **ftp plum**, the local ftp client connects to the server, which asks for a username and password. Because he is logged in on his local system as **sam**, ftp suggests that Sam log in on **plum** as **sam**. To log in as **sam**, he could just press RETURN. Because his username on **plum** is **sls**, however, he types **sls** in response to the **Name (plum:sam):** prompt. After Sam responds to the **Password:** prompt with his normal system password, the **vsftpd** server greets him and informs him that it is **Using binary mode to transfer files.** With ftp in binary mode, Sam can transfer ASCII and binary files (page 720).

Connect and log in
```
$ ftp plum
Connected to plum (192.168.206.181).
220 (vsFTPd 3.0.2)
Name (plum:sam): sls
331 Please specify the password.
Password:
230 Login successful.
Remote system type is UNIX.
Using binary mode to transfer files.
```

After logging in, Sam uses the ftp **ls** command to see what is in his remote working directory, which is his home directory on **plum**. Then he cds to the **memos** directory and displays the files there.

ls and cd
```
ftp> ls
227 Entering Passive Mode (192,168,206,181,246,88).
150 Here comes the directory listing.
drwxr-xr-x    2 1001     1001         4096 Jun 13 17:17 expenses
drwxr-xr-x    2 1001     1001         4096 Jun 13 17:19 memos
drwxr-xr-x    2 1001     1001         4096 Jun 13 17:17 tech
226 Directory send OK.

ftp> cd memos
250 Directory successfully changed.

ftp> ls
227 Entering Passive Mode (192,168,206,181,254,97).
150 Here comes the directory listing.
-rw-r--r--    1 1001     1001        79915 Jun 13 17:19 memo.0514
-rw-r--r--    1 1001     1001        74069 Jun 13 17:19 memo.0628
-rw-r--r--    1 1001     1001        37489 Jun 13 17:19 memo.0905
-rw-r--r--    1 1001     1001        85699 Jun 13 17:18 memo.0921
-rw-r--r--    1 1001     1001        55181 Jun 13 17:18 memo.1102
226 Directory send OK.
```

Next Sam uses the ftp **get** command to copy **memo.1102** from the server to the local system. His use of binary mode ensures that he will get a good copy of the file regardless of whether it is binary or ASCII. The server confirms that the file was copied successfully and reports on its size and the time required to copy it. Sam then copies the local file **memo.1114** to the remote system. This file is copied into his remote working directory, **memos**.

get and put
```
ftp> get memo.1102
local: memo.1102 remote: memo.1102
227 Entering Passive Mode (192,168,206,181,122,35).
150 Opening BINARY mode data connection for memo.1102 (55181 bytes).
226 Transfer complete.
55181 bytes received in 0.000392 secs (140767.86 Kbytes/sec)

ftp> put memo.1114
local: memo.1114 remote: memo.1114
227 Entering Passive Mode (192,168,206,181,71,174).
150 Ok to send data.
226 Transfer complete.
25897 bytes sent in 0.00174 secs (14857.72 Kbytes/sec)
```

Now Sam decides he wants to copy all the files in the **memo** directory on **plum** to a new directory on his local system. He gives an **ls** command to make sure he will copy the right files, but ftp has timed out. Instead of exiting from ftp and giving another ftp command from the shell, he gives ftp an **open plum** command to reconnect to the server. After logging in, he uses the ftp **cd** command to change directories to **memos** on the server.

Timeout and **open**
```
ftp> ls
No control connection for command: Success
Passive mode refused.
ftp> open plum
Connected to plum (192.168.206.181).
220 (vsFTPd 3.0.2)
Name (plum:sam): sls
...
ftp> cd memos
250 Directory successfully changed.
```

Local cd (**lcd**)   At this point, Sam realizes he has not created the new directory to hold the files he wants to download. Giving an ftp **mkdir** command would create a new directory on the server, but Sam wants a new directory on the local system. He uses an exclamation point (!) followed by a **mkdir memos.hold** command to invoke a shell and run mkdir on the local system, thereby creating a directory named **memos.hold** in his working directory on the local system. (You can display the name of the working directory on the local system using **!pwd**.) Next, because Sam wants to copy files from the server to the **memos.hold** directory on his local system, he has to change his working directory on the local system. Giving the command **!cd memos.hold** will not accomplish what Sam wants to do because the exclamation point will spawn a new shell on the local system and the **cd** command would be effective only in the new shell, which is not the shell that ftp is running under. For this situation, ftp provides the **lcd** (local cd) command, which changes the working directory for ftp and reports on the new local working directory:

```
ftp> !mkdir memos.hold

ftp> lcd memos.hold
Local directory now /home/sam/memos.hold
```

Sam uses the ftp **mget** (multiple get) command followed by the asterisk (**\***) wildcard to copy all files from the remote **memos** directory to the **memos.hold** directory on the local system. When ftp prompts him for the first file, Sam realizes that he forgot to turn off the prompts, so he responds with **n** and presses CONTROL-C to stop copying files in response to the second prompt. The server checks whether he wants to continue with his **mget** command.

Next Sam gives the ftp **prompt** command, which toggles the prompt action (turns it off if it is on and turns it on if it is off). Now when he gives a **mget \*** command, ftp copies the files without prompting him. After getting the desired files, Sam gives a **quit** command to close the connection with the server, exit from ftp, and return to the local shell prompt.

**mget** and **prompt**
```
ftp> mget *
mget memo.0514? n
mget memo.0628? CONTROL-C
Continue with mget? n

ftp> prompt
Interactive mode off.

ftp> mget *
local: memo.0514 remote: memo.0514
227 Entering Passive Mode (192,168,206,181,216,120).
150 Opening BINARY mode data connection for memo.0514 (79915 bytes).
226 Transfer complete.
79915 bytes received in 0.00188 secs (42485.38 Kbytes/sec)
local: memo.0628 remote: memo.0628
227 Entering Passive Mode (192,168,206,181,24,77).
150 Opening BINARY mode data connection for memo.0628 (74069 bytes).
226 Transfer complete.
74069 bytes received in 0.0114 secs (6518.44 Kbytes/sec)
...
150 Opening BINARY mode data connection for memo.1114 (25897 bytes).
226 Transfer complete.
25897 bytes received in 0.00107 secs (24293.62 Kbytes/sec)
ftp> quit
221 Goodbye.
```

# ANONYMOUS FTP

Many systems—most notably those from which you can download free software—allow you to log in as **anonymous**. Most systems that support anonymous logins accept the name **ftp** as an easier-to-spell and quicker-to-enter synonym for **anonymous**. An anonymous user is usually restricted to a portion of a filesystem set aside to hold files that are to be shared with remote users. When you log in as an anonymous user, the server prompts you to enter a password. Although the system accepts any password, by convention you are expected to supply your email address. Do not use an important address if you are logging into a public site because that address could receive spam based on this login.

Many systems that permit anonymous access store interesting files in the **pub** directory. Most browsers, such as Firefox, log in on an anonymous FTP site and transfer a file when you click on the filename.

## AUTOMATIC LOGIN

.netrc  You can store server-specific FTP username and password information so you do not have to enter it each time you visit an FTP site. Each line of ~/.netrc identifies a server. When you connect to an FTP server, ftp reads the ~/.netrc file to determine whether you have an automatic login set up for that server. The format of a line in ~/.netrc is

>   machine **server** login **username** password **passwd**

where **server** is the name of the server, **username** is your username, and **passwd** is your password on **server**. Replace **machine** with **default** on the last line of the file to specify a username and password for systems not listed in ~/.netrc. The **default** line is useful for logging in on anonymous servers. A sample ~/.netrc file follows:

```
$ cat ~/.netrc
machine plum login sls password mypassword
default login anonymous password sam@example.com
```

To protect the account information in **.netrc**, make it readable only by the user whose home directory it appears in. Refer to the **netrc** man page for more information.

## BINARY VERSUS ASCII TRANSFER MODE

The **vsftpd** FTP server can—but does not always—provide two modes to transfer files. Binary mode transfers always copy an exact, byte-for-byte image of a file and never change line endings. Transfer all binary files using binary mode. Unless you need to convert line endings, use binary mode to transfer ASCII files as well.

These descriptions do not apply to files created by word processors such as Word or LibreOffice because those programs generate binary files. The **vsftpd** server can map Linux line endings to Windows line endings as you upload files and Windows line endings to Linux line endings as you download files.

To use ASCII mode on an FTP server that allows it, give an **ascii** command (page 722) after you log in and set **cr** to ON (the default; page 723). If the server does not allow you to change line endings as you transfer a file, you can use the unix2dos (page 260) utility before or after you transfer a file in binary mode.

Security  To enhance security, by default **vsftpd** transfers every file in binary mode, even when it appears to be using ASCII mode. On the server side, you can enable *real* ASCII mode transfers by setting the **ascii_upload_enable** and **ascii_download_enable** parameters (page 732) to YES. With the server set to allow ASCII transfers, the client controls whether line endings are mapped by using the **ascii**, **binary**, and **cr** commands (page 722).

# ftp SPECIFICS

This section covers the details of using ftp.

## FORMAT

An ftp command line has the following format:

*ftp* [*options*] [*ftp-server*]

where *options* is one or more options from the list in the next section and *ftp-server* is the name or IP address of the FTP server you want to exchange files with. If you do not specify an *ftp-server*, you will need to use the ftp **open** command to connect to a server once ftp is running.

## COMMAND-LINE OPTIONS

–g  **(globbing)** Turns off globbing. See **glob** (page 723).

–i  **(interactive)** Turns off prompts during file transfers with **mget** (page 722) and **mput** (page 722). See also **prompt** (page 723).

–n  **(no automatic login)** Disables automatic logins (page 720).

–v  **(verbose)** Tells you more about how ftp is working. Displays responses from the server and reports information on how quickly files are transferred. See also **verbose** (page 724).

## ftp COMMANDS

The ftp utility is interactive: After you start ftp, it prompts you to enter commands to set parameters or transfer files. You can abbreviate commands as long as the abbreviations are unique. Program help is available with the **help** command (page 724).

### SHELL COMMAND

![command]  Without *command*, escapes to (spawns) a shell on the local system. Use CONTROL-D or **exit** to return to ftp when you are finished using the local shell. Follow the exclamation point with *command* to execute that command only; ftp will display an **ftp>** prompt when execution of the command finishes. Because the shell that ftp spawns with this command is a child of the shell that is running ftp, no changes you make in this shell are preserved when you return to ftp. Specifically, when you want to copy files to a local directory other than the directory that you started ftp from, you need to use the ftp **lcd** command to change the local working directory: Issuing a **cd** command in the spawned shell will not make the change you desire. See "Local cd (**lcd**)" on page 718 for an example.

## TRANSFER FILES

In the following descriptions, *remote-file* and *local-file* can be pathnames.

**append** *local-file* [*remote-file*]

Appends *local-file* to the file with the same name on the remote system or to *remote-file* if specified.

**get** *remote-file* [*local-file*]

Copies *remote-file* to the local system under the name *local-file*. Without *local-file*, ftp uses *remote-file* as the filename on the local system.

**mget** *remote-file-list*

(**multiple get**) Copies several files to the local system, with each file maintaining its original filename. You can name the remote files literally or use wildcards (see **glob**). Use **prompt** (page 723) to turn off the prompts during transfers.

**mput** *local-file-list*

(**multiple put**) Copies several files to the server, with each file maintaining its original filename. You can name the local files literally or use wildcards (see **glob**). Use **prompt** (page 723) to turn off the prompts during transfers.

**newer** *remote-file* [*local-file*]

If the modification time of *remote-file* is more recent than that of *local-file* or if *local-file* does not exist, copies *remote-file* to the local system under the name *local-file*. Without *local-file*, ftp uses *remote-file* as the filename on the local system. This command is similar to **get** but will not overwrite a newer file with an older one.

**put** *local-file* [*remote-file*]

Copies *local-file* to the remote system under the name *remote-file*. Without *remote-file*, ftp uses *local-file* as the filename on the remote system.

**reget** *remote-file* [*local-file*]

If *local-file* exists and is smaller than *remote-file*, assumes that a previous **get** of *local-file* was interrupted and continues from where the previous **get** left off. Without *local-file*, ftp uses *remote-file* as the filename on the local system. This command can save time when a **get** of a large file fails partway through the transfer.

## STATUS

ascii   Sets the file transfer type to ASCII. The **cr** command must be ON for **ascii** to work (page 720).

binary   Sets the file transfer type to binary (page 720).

bye   Closes the connection to the server and terminates ftp. Same as **quit**.

case   Toggles and displays the case mapping status. The default is OFF. When it is ON, for **get** and **mget** commands, this command maps filenames that are all uppercase on the server to all lowercase on the local system.

close   Closes the connection to the server without exiting from ftp.

cr   (**carriage** RETURN) Toggles and displays the (carriage) RETURN stripping status. Effective only when the file transfer type is **ascii**. Set **cr** to ON (default) to remove RETURN characters from RETURN/LINEFEED line termination sequences used by Windows, yielding the standard Linux line termination of LINEFEED. Set **cr** to OFF to leave line endings unmapped (page 720).

debug [*n*]   Toggles/sets and displays the debugging status/level, where *n* is the debugging level. OFF or 0 (zero) is the default. When *n* > 0, ftp displays each command it sends to the server.

glob   Toggles and displays the filename expansion (page 165) status for **mdelete** (page 724), **mget** (page 722), and **mput** (page 722) commands.

hash   Toggles and displays the hashmark (#) display status. When it is ON, ftp displays one hashmark for each 1024-byte data block it transfers.

open [*hostname*]
Specifies *hostname* as the name of the server to connect to. Without *hostname*, prompts for the name of the server. This command is useful when a connection times out or otherwise fails. See page 718 for an example.

passive   Toggles between passive (PASV—the default) and active (PORT) transfer modes and displays the transfer mode. For more information refer to "Passive versus active connections" on page 715.

prompt   Toggles and displays the prompt status. When it is ON (default), **mdelete** (page 724), **mget** (page 722), and **mput** (page 722) ask for verification before transferring each file. Set **prompt** to OFF to turn off these prompts.

quit   Closes the connection to the server and terminates ftp. Same as **bye**.

umask [*nnn*]   Changes the umask (page 469) applied to files created on the server to *nnn*. Without *nnn*, displays the umask.

user [*username*] [*password*]
Prompts for or accepts the *username* and *password* that enable you to log in on the server. When you call it with the **–n** option, ftp prompts you for a username and password automatically. For more information refer to "Automatic Login" on page 720.

### DIRECTORIES

cd *remote-directory*
Changes the working directory on the server to *remote-directory*.

cdup   Changes the working directory on the server to the parent of the working directory.

lcd [*local_directory*]
(**local change directory**) Changes the working directory on the local system to *local_directory*. Without an argument, this command changes the working directory on the local system to your home directory (just as the **cd** shell builtin does without an argument). See "Local cd (**lcd**)" on page 718 for an example.

### FILES

chmod *mode remote-file*

> Changes the access permissions of *remote-file* on the server to *mode*. See chmod on page 193 for more information on how to specify the *mode*.

delete *remote-file*

> Removes *remote-file* from the server.

mdelete *remote-file-list*

> (**multiple delete**) Deletes the files specified by *remote-file-list* from the server.

### DISPLAY INFORMATION

? (**question mark**) Same as **help**.

dir [*remote-directory*] [*file*]

> Displays a listing of *remote-directory* from the server. When you do not specify *remote-directory*, displays the working directory. When you specify *file*, the listing is saved on the local system in a file named *file*.

help [*command*]   Displays information about *command*. Without *command*, displays a list of local ftp commands. Also **?**.

ls [*remote-directory*] [*file*]

> Similar to **dir** but produces a more concise listing from some servers. When you specify *file*, the listing is saved on the local system in a file named *file*.

pwd   Displays the pathname of the working directory on the server. Use **!pwd** to display the pathname of the local working directory.

rstatus   Displays ftp connection and status information for the local system (client).

status   Displays ftp connection and status information for the remote system (server).

verbose   Toggles and displays verbose mode, which displays responses from the server and reports how quickly files are transferred. The effect of this command is the same as specifying the **–v** option on the command line.

# SETTING UP AN FTP SERVER (vsftpd)

This section explains how to set up an FTP server implemented by the **vsftpd** daemon as supplied by Fedora/RHEL.

## PREREQUISITES

Install the following package:

- **vsftpd**

Enable and start **vsftpd**   Run systemctl to cause the **vsftpd** service (**vsftpd** daemon) to start each time the system enters multiuser mode and then start the **vsftpd** service. Use the systemctl **status** command to make sure the service is running.

```
$ sudo -c 'systemctl enable vsftpd.service'
$ sudo -c 'systemctl start vsftpd.service'
```

After modifying **vsftpd** configuration files, give the second command again, replacing **start** with **restart** to cause **vsftpd** to reread those files.

# NOTES

Security  The safest policy is not to allow users to authenticate against FTP: Instead, use FTP for anonymous access only. If you do allow local users to authenticate and upload files to the server, be sure to put local users in a chroot jail (page 729). Because FTP sends usernames and passwords in cleartext, a malicious user can easily *sniff* (page 1273) them. Armed with a username and password, the same user can impersonate a local user, upload a *Trojan horse* (page 1278), and compromise the system.

Firewall  An FTP server normally uses TCP port 21. If the server is running a firewall or is behind a firewall, you need to open this port. Give the following commands to open this port each time the system boots (permanently) and on the running system; see page 906 for information on firewall-cmd.

```
$ sudo -c 'firewall-cmd --add-port=21/tcp'
$ sudo -c 'firewall-cmd --permanent --add-port=21/tcp'
```

SELinux  When SELinux is set to use a targeted policy, FTP is protected by SELinux. For more information refer to "Setting the Targeted Policy with system-config-selinux" on page 475.

# JUMPSTART II: STARTING A vsftpd FTP SERVER

By default, under Fedora/RHEL **vsftpd** allows local and anonymous users only to log in on the server; it does not set up a guest account. When someone logs in as an anonymous user, that person works in the **/var/ftp** directory and can download but not upload files. You do not have to configure anything.

# TROUBLESHOOTING

First make sure the firewall and SELinux (both above) are set up to allow a user to log in and copy files using ftp. Also ensure that either **listen** or **listen_ipv6**, but not both, is set to YES (page 727). Next, make sure **vsftpd** is working by logging in from the server system. You can refer to the server as **localhost** or by using its hostname on the command line. Log in as a user and provide that user's password:

```
$ ftp localhost
Trying ::1...
Connected to localhost (::1).
220 (vsFTPd 3.0.2)
Name (localhost:sam): sls
331 Please specify the password.
Password:
230 Login successful.
...
```

If you are not able to connect to the server, first make sure the server is running:

```
# systemctl status vsftpd.service
vsftpd.service - Vsftpd ftp daemon
   Loaded: loaded (/usr/lib/systemd/system/vsftpd.service; disabled)
   Active: active (running) since Tue 2013-09-10 13:02:09 PDT; 58min ago
  Process: 9351 ExecStart=/usr/sbin/vsftpd /etc/vsftpd/vsftpd.conf (code=exited, status=0/SUCCESS)
 Main PID: 9352 (vsftpd)
   CGroup: name=systemd:/system/vsftpd.service
           ??9352 /usr/sbin/vsftpd /etc/vsftpd/vsftpd.conf

Sep 10 13:02:09 guava.example.com systemd[1]: Started Vsftpd ftp daemon.
```

If you want to allow users to log in as **anonymous** or **ftp**, **anonymous_enable** must be set to YES in **/etc/vsftpd/vsftpd.conf** (it is by default; page 728). Restart the **vsftpd** daemon (page 724) if you change **vsftpd.conf**. Any password is acceptable with these login names.

```
$ ftp localhost
Trying ::1...
Connected to localhost (::1).
220 (vsFTPd 3.0.2)
Name (localhost:sam): anonymous
331 Please specify the password.
Password:
230 Login successful.
...
```

Next check that permissions on **/var/ftp**, or the home directory of ftp as specified in **/etc/passwd**, are set to 755 and that the directory is not owned by **ftp**. If the **ftp** user can write to **/var/ftp**, connections will fail.

```
$ ls -ld /var/ftp
drwxr-xr-x. 3 root root 4096 06-13 10:09 /var/ftp
```

Once you are able to log in from the local system, log in from another system—either one on the LAN or another system with access to the server. On the command line, use the hostname from within the LAN or the *FQDN* (page 1250) from outside the LAN. The dialog should appear the same as in the previous example. If you cannot log in from a system that is not on the LAN, use ping (page 305) to test the connection and then make sure the firewall is set up to allow FTP access. See "FTP Connections" on page 715 for a discussion of active and passive modes and the ports that each mode uses.

# Configuring a vsftpd Server

The configuration file for **vsftpd**, **/etc/vsftpd/vsftpd.conf**, lists Boolean, numeric, and string name-value pairs of configuration parameters, called directives. Each name-value pair is joined by an equal sign with no SPACEs on either side. Fedora/RHEL provides a well-commented **vsftpd.conf** file that changes many of the compiled-in defaults. This section covers many of the parameters, noting their default values and their values as specified in the **vsftpd.conf** file supplied with Fedora/RHEL.

Set Boolean parameters to YES or NO and numeric parameters to a nonnegative integer. Octal numbers, which are useful for setting umask parameters, must have a leading 0 (zero). Numbers without a leading zero are treated as base 10 numbers. Following are examples of setting each type of parameter:

```
anonymous_enable=YES
local_umask=022
xferlog_file=/var/log/vsftpd.log
```

Descriptions of the directives are broken into the following groups:

- Server setup (next)
- Logging in (next page)
- Working directory and the chroot jail (page 729)
- Downloading and uploading files (page 730)
- Messages (page 732)
- Display (page 733)
- Logs (page 734)
- Connection parameters (page 734)
- Miscellaneous (page 736)
- Other configuration files (page 737)

## SERVER SETUP

**listen** YES accepts connections from IPv4 clients only. Either this parameter or **listen_ipv6**, but not both, must be set to YES.

Default: NO
Fedora/RHEL: NO

**listen_ipv6** YES accepts connections from IPv6 clients. With **listen_address** unset or set to :: ("any" address), **vsftpd** accepts connections from both IPv4 and IPv6 clients. Either this parameter or **listen**, but not both, must be set to YES.

Default: NO
Fedora/RHEL: YES

**listen_address** Specifies the IP address of the local interface that **vsftpd** listens on for incoming connections. When this parameter is not set, **vsftpd** uses the default network interface.

Default: none

**listen_port** Specifies the port that **vsftpd** listens on for incoming connections.

Default: 21

**max_clients** Specifies the maximum number of clients. Zero (0) indicates unlimited clients.

Default: 0

max_per_ip   Specifies the maximum number of clients from the same IP address. Zero (0) indicates unlimited clients from the same IP address.

Default: 0

## LOGGING IN

Three classes of users can log in on a **vsftpd** server: anonymous, local, and guest. The guest user is rarely used and is not covered in this chapter. A local user logs in using his system username and password. An anonymous user logs in using **anonymous** or **ftp** and his email address as a password. You can control whether each of these classes of users can log in on the server and what they can do once they log in. You can also specify what a local user can do on a per-user basis; for more information refer to **user_config_dir** on page 736.

### LOCAL USERS

userlist_enable   The **/etc/vsftpd/user_list** file (page 737), or another file specified by **userlist_file**, contains a list of zero or more users. YES consults this list and takes action based on **userlist_deny**, either granting or denying users in the list permission to log in on the server. To prevent the transmission of cleartext passwords, access is denied immediately after the user enters her username. NO does not consult the list. Set to NO for a more secure system.

Default: NO
Fedora/RHEL: YES

userlist_deny   YES prevents users listed in **/etc/vsftpd/user_list** (page 737) from logging in on the server. NO allows *only* users listed in **/etc/vsftpd/user_list** to log in on the server. Use **userlist_file** to change the name of the file that this parameter consults. This parameter is checked only when **userlist_enable** is set to YES.

Default: YES

userlist_file   The name of the file consulted when **userlist_enable** is set to YES.

Default: /etc/vsftpd/user_list

local_enable   YES permits local users (users listed in **/etc/passwd**) to log in on the server.

Default: NO
Fedora/RHEL: YES

### ANONYMOUS USERS

anonymous_enable

YES allows anonymous logins. NO disables anonymous logins.

Default: YES

no_anon_password

YES skips asking anonymous users for passwords.

Default: NO

**deny_email_enable**

YES checks whether the password (email address) that an anonymous user enters is listed in **/etc/vsftpd.banned_emails** or another file specified by **banned_email_file**. If it is, the user is not allowed to log in on the system. NO does not perform this check. Using firewall-cmd (page 906) to block specific hosts is generally more productive than using this parameter.

Default: NO

**banned_email_file**

The name of the file consulted when **deny_email_enable** is set to YES.

Default: **/etc/vsftpd/banned_emails**

## THE WORKING DIRECTORY AND THE chroot JAIL

When a user logs in on a **vsftpd** server, standard filesystem access permissions control which directories and files the user can access and how the user can access them. Three basic parameters control a user who is logged in on a **vsftpd** server:

- The user ID (UID)
- The initial working directory
- The root directory

By default, the **vsftpd** server sets the UID of a local user to that user's UID and sets the UID of an anonymous user to that of the user named **ftp**. A local user starts in her home directory and an anonymous user starts in **/var/ftp**.

By default, anonymous users are placed in a chroot jail for security; local users are not. For example, when an anonymous user logs in on a **vsftpd** server, his home directory is **/var/ftp**. All that user sees, however, is that his home directory is **/**. The user sees the directory at **/var/ftp/upload** as **/upload**. The user cannot see or work with, for example, the **/home**, **/usr/local**, or **/tmp** directory because the user is in a chroot jail. For more information refer to "Setting Up a chroot Jail" on page 487.

You can use the **chroot_local_user** parameter to put each local user in a chroot jail whose root is the user's home directory. You can use **chroot_list_enable** to put selected local users in chroot jails.

**chroot_list_enable**

Upon login, YES checks whether a local user is listed in **/etc/vsftpd/chroot_list** (page 737) or another file specified by **chroot_list_file**.

When a user is in the list and **chroot_local_user** is set to NO, the user is put in a chroot jail in his home directory. Only users listed in **/etc/vsftpd/chroot_list** are put in chroot jails.

When a user is in the list and **chroot_local_user** is set to YES, that user is not put in a chroot jail. Users not listed in **/etc/vsftpd/chroot_list** are put in chroot jails.

Default: NO

chroot_local_user

> See **chroot_list_enable**. Set to NO for a more open system but remember to add new users to the **chroot_list_file** as needed when you add users to the system. Set to YES for a more secure system. New users are automatically restricted unless you add them to **chroot_list_file**.
>
> Default: NO

chroot_list_file   The name of the file consulted when **chroot_list_enable** is set to YES.

> Default: **/etc/vsftpd/chroot_list**

passwd_chroot_enable

> YES enables you to change the location of the chroot jail that the **chroot_list_enable** and **chroot_local_user** settings impose on a local user.
>
> The location of the chroot jail can be moved up the directory structure by including a **/./** within the home directory string for that user in **/etc/passwd**. This change has no effect on the standard system login, just as a **cd .** command has no effect on the working directory.
>
> For example, changing the home directory field in **/etc/passwd** (page 508) for Sam from **/home/sam** to **/home/./sam** allows Sam to cd to **/home** after logging in using **vsftpd**. Given the proper permissions, Sam can now view files and collaborate with another user.
>
> Default: NO

secure_chroot_dir   The name of an empty directory that is not writable by the user **ftp**. The **vsftpd** server uses this directory as a secure chroot jail when the user does not need access to the filesystem.

> Default: **/usr/share/empty**

local_root   After a local user logs in on the server, this directory becomes the user's working directory. No error results if the specified directory does not exist.

> Default: none

## DOWNLOADING AND UPLOADING FILES

By default, any user—whether local or anonymous—can download files from the **vsftpd** server, assuming proper filesystem access and permissions. The **write_enable** parameter must be set to YES (Fedora/RHEL sets it this way) to permit local users to upload files. The **local_umask** parameter defaults to 077, although Fedora/RHEL sets it to 022, giving uploaded files 644 permissions (page 191). These permissions allow users to download other users' files. Change **local_umask** to 077 to allow only the user who created a file to download and overwrite it.

Security   Refer to "Security" on page 725 for information on the security hole that is created when you allow local users to upload files.

The following actions set up **vsftpd** to allow anonymous users to upload files:

1. Set **write_enable** (below) to YES. (Fedora/RHEL sets this parameter to YES.)

2. Create a directory under **/var/ftp** that an anonymous user can write to but not read from (mode 333). You do not want a malicious user to be able to see, download, modify, and upload a file that another user originally uploaded. The following commands create a **/var/ftp/uploads** directory that anyone can write to but no one can read from:

```
# mkdir /var/ftp/uploads
# chmod 333 /var/ftp/uploads
```

Because of the security risk, **vsftpd** prevents anonymous connections when an anonymous user (**ftp**) can write to **/var/ftp**.

3. Set **anon_upload_enable** (page 732) to YES.

4. See the other parameters in this section.

### DOWNLOAD/UPLOAD FOR LOCAL USERS

**local_umask**   The umask (page 469) setting for local users.

Default: 077
Fedora/RHEL: 022

**file_open_mode**   Uploaded file permissions for local users. The umask (page 469) is applied to this value. Change to 0777 to make uploaded files executable.

Default: 0666

**write_enable**   YES permits users to create and delete files and directories (assuming appropriate file-system permissions). NO prevents users from making changes to the filesystem.

Default: NO
Fedora/RHEL: YES

### ANONYMOUS USERS

**anon_mkdir_write_enable**

YES permits an anonymous user to create new directories when **write_enable** is set to YES and the anonymous user has permission to write to the working directory.

Default: NO

**anon_other_write_enable**

YES grants an anonymous user write permission in addition to the permissions granted by **anon_mkdir_write_enable** and **anon_upload_enable**. For example, YES allows an anonymous user to delete and rename files, assuming she has permission to write to the working directory. For a more secure site, do not set this parameter to YES.

Default: NO

**anon_root**   After an anonymous user logs in on the server, this directory becomes the user's working directory. No error results if the specified directory does not exist.

Default: none

anon_umask    The umask (page 469) setting for anonymous users. The default setting gives only anonymous users access to files uploaded by anonymous users; set this parameter to 022 to give everyone read access to these files.

Default: 077

anon_upload_enable

YES allows anonymous users to upload files when **write_enable**=YES and the anonymous user has permission to write to the directory.

Default: NO

anon_world_readable_only

YES limits the files that a user can download to those that are readable by the owner of the file, members of the group the file is associated with, and others. It might not be desirable to allow one anonymous user to download a file that another anonymous user uploaded. Setting this parameter to YES can avoid this scenario.

Default: YES

ascii_download_enable

YES allows a user to download files using ASCII mode (page 720). Setting this parameter to YES can create a security risk (page 720).

Default: NO

ascii_upload_enable

YES allows a user to upload files using ASCII mode (page 720).

Default: NO

chown_uploads    YES causes files uploaded by anonymous users to be owned by **root** (or another user specified by **chown_username**). To improve security, change **chown_username** to a name other than **root** if you set this parameter to YES.

Default: NO

chown_username    See **chown_uploads**.

Default: **root**

ftp_username    The username of anonymous users.

Default: **ftp**

nopriv_user    The name of the user with minimal privileges, as used by **vsftpd**. Because other programs use **nobody**, to enhance security you can replace **nobody** with the name of a dedicated user such as **ftp**.

Default: **nobody**

## MESSAGES

You can replace the standard greeting banner that **vsftpd** displays when a user logs in on the system (**banner_file** and **ftpd_banner**). You can also display a message each time a user enters a directory (**dirmessage_enable** and **message_file**). When you set dirmessage_enable=YES, each time a user enters a directory using cd, **vsftpd** displays the contents of the file in that directory named **.message** (or another file specified by **message_file**).

**dirmessage_enable**

YES displays **.message** or another file specified by **message_file** as an ftp user enters a new directory by giving a **cd** command.

Default: NO
Fedora/RHEL: YES

**message_file** See **dirmessage_enable**.

Default: **.message**

**banner_file** The absolute pathname of the file that is displayed when a user connects to the server. Overrides **ftpd_banner**.

Default: none

**ftpd_banner** Overrides the standard **vsftpd** greeting banner displayed when a user connects to the server.

Default: none; uses standard **vsftpd** banner

## DISPLAY

This section describes parameters that can improve security and performance by controlling how **vsftpd** displays information.

**hide_ids** YES lists all users and groups in directory listings as **ftp**. NO lists the real owners.

Default: NO

**setproctitle_enable**

NO causes ps to display the process running **vsftpd** as **vsftpd**. YES causes ps to display what **vsftpd** is currently doing (uploading and so on). Set to NO for a more secure system.

Default: NO

**text_userdb_names**

NO improves performance by displaying numeric UIDs and GIDs in directory listings. YES displays names.

Default: NO

**use_localtime** NO causes the **ls**, **mls**, and **modtime** FTP commands to display *UTC* (page 1279). YES causes these commands to display the local time.

Default: NO

**ls_recurse_enable** YES permits users to give **ls –R** commands. Setting this parameter to YES might pose a security risk because giving an **ls –R** command at the top of a large directory hierarchy can consume a lot of system resources.

Default: NO

## Logs

By default, logging is turned off. However, the **vsftpd.conf** file distributed with Fedora/RHEL turns it on. This section describes parameters that control the details and locations of logs.

A **vsftpd** server can generate logs in two formats: **vsftpd** and **xferlog**. The default **vsftpd** log format is more readable than **xferlog** format but cannot be processed by programs that generate statistical summaries of **xferlog** files. Search for **xferlog** on the Internet to obtain more information on this command.

log_ftp_protocol  YES logs FTP requests and responses in the default **vsftpd** log format, provided that **xferlog_std_format** is set to NO.

Default: NO

xferlog_enable  YES maintains a transfer log in **/var/log/vsftpd.log** (or another file specified by **xferlog_file**). NO does not create a log.

Default: NO
Fedora/RHEL: YES

xferlog_std_format

YES causes a transfer log (not covering connections) to be written in standard **xferlog** format, as used by wu-ftpd, as long as **xferlog_file** is explicitly set. If **xferlog_std_format** is set to YES and **xferlog_file** is not explicitly set, logging is turned off. Setting this parameter to NO causes **vsftpd** to generate logs in **vsftpd** log format, provided **log_ftp_protocol** is set to YES.

Default: NO
Fedora/RHEL: YES

xferlog_file  See **xferlog_enable** and **xferlog_std_format**.

Default: **/var/log/xferlog**

## Connection Parameters

You can allow clients to establish passive and/or active connections (page 715). Setting timeouts and maximum transfer rates can improve server security and performance. This section describes parameters that control the types of connections that a client can establish, the length of time **vsftpd** will wait while establishing a connection, and the speeds of connections for different types of users.

### Passive (PASV) Connections

pasv_enable  NO prevents the use of PASV connections.

Default: YES

pasv_promiscuous

NO causes PASV to perform a security check that ensures that the data and control connections originate from a single IP address. YES disables this check. Set to NO for a more secure system.

Default: NO

pasv_max_port  The highest port number **vsftpd** will allocate for a PASV data connection; useful in setting up a firewall.

Default: 0 (use any port)

pasv_min_port  The lowest port number **vsftpd** will allocate for a PASV data connection; useful in setting up a firewall.

Default: 0 (use any port)

pasv_address  Specifies an IP address other than the one used by the client to contact the server.

Default: none; the address is the one used by the client

### ACTIVE (PORT) CONNECTIONS

port_enable  NO prevents the use of PORT connections.

Default: YES

port_promiscuous

NO causes PORT to perform a security check that ensures that outgoing data connections connect only to the client. YES disables this check. Set to NO for a more secure system.

Default: NO

connect_from_port_20

YES specifies port 20 (**ftp-data**, a privileged port) on the server for PORT connections, as required by some clients. NO allows **vsftpd** to run with fewer privileges (on a nonprivileged port).

Default: NO
Fedora/RHEL: YES

ftp_data_port  With **connect_from_port_20** set to NO, specifies the port that **vsftpd** uses for PORT connections.

Default: 20

### TIMEOUTS

accept_timeout  The number of seconds the server waits for a client to establish a PASV data connection.

Default: 60

connect_timeout  The number of seconds the server waits for a client to respond to a PORT data connection.

Default: 60

data_connection_timeout

The number of seconds the server waits for a stalled data transfer to resume before disconnecting.

Default: 300

**idle_session_timeout**

> The number of seconds the server waits between FTP commands before disconnecting.
>
> Default: 300

**local_max_rate**   For local users, the maximum data transfer rate in bytes per second. Zero (0) indicates no limit.

> Default: 0

**anon_max_rate**   For anonymous users, the maximum data transfer rate in bytes per second. Zero (0) indicates no limit.

> Default: 0

**one_process_model**

> YES establishes one process per connection, which improves performance but degrades security. NO allows multiple processes per connection. Set to NO for a more secure system.
>
> Default: NO

## MISCELLANEOUS

This section describes parameters not discussed elsewhere.

**pam_service_name**

> The name of the PAM service used by **vsftpd**.
>
> Default: **ftp**
> Fedora/RHEL: **vsftpd**

**rsa_cert_file**   Specifies where the RSA certificate for SSL-encrypted connections is kept.

> Default: **/usr/share/ssl/certs/vsftpd.pem**

**rsa_private_key_file**

> Specifies where the RSA key for SSL-encrypted connections is kept.
>
> Default: none

**tcp_wrappers**   YES causes incoming connections to use **tcp_wrappers** (page 485) if **vsftpd** was compiled with **tcp_wrappers** support. When **tcp_wrappers** sets the environment variable **VSFTPD_LOAD_CONF**, **vsftpd** loads the configuration file specified by this variable, allowing per-IP configuration.

> Default: NO
> Fedora/RHEL: YES

**user_config_dir**   Specifies a directory that contains files named for local users. Each of these files, which mimic **vsftpd.conf**, contains parameters that override, on a per-user basis, default parameters and parameters specified in **vsftpd.conf**. For example, assume **user_config_dir** is set to **/etc/vsftpd/user_conf**. Further suppose the default configuration file, **/etc/vsftpd/vsftpd.conf**, sets **idlesession_timeout=300** and Sam's individual configuration file, **/etc/vsftpd/user_conf/sam**, sets **idlesession_timeout=1200**. Then all users' sessions except for Sam's will time out after 300 seconds of inactivity. Sam's sessions will time out after 1,200 seconds.

Default: none

## OTHER CONFIGURATION FILES

In addition to **/etc/vsftpd/vsftpd.conf**, the following files control the functioning of **vsftpd**. The directory hierarchy that **user_config_dir** points to is not included in this list because it has no default name.

/etc/vsftpd/ftpusers
> Lists users, one per line, who are never allowed to log in on the FTP server, regardless of how **userlist_enable** (page 728) is set and regardless of the users listed in the **user_list** file. The default file lists **root, bin, daemon**, and others.

/etc/vsftpd/user_list
> Lists either the only users who can log in on the server or the only users who are not allowed to log in on the server. The **userlist_enable** (page 728) parameter must be set to YES for **vsftpd** to examine the list of users in this file. Setting **userlist_enable** to YES and **userlist_deny** (page 728) to YES (or not setting it) prevents listed users from logging in on the server. Setting **userlist_enable** to YES and **userlist_deny** to NO permits only the listed users to log in on the server.

/etc/vsftpd/chroot_list
> Depending on the **chroot_list_enable** (page 729) and **chroot_local_user** (page 730) settings, lists either users who are forced into a chroot jail in their home directories or users who are not placed in a chroot jail.

/var/log/xferlog
> Log file. For more information refer to "Logs" on page 734.

# CHAPTER SUMMARY

File Transfer Protocol is a protocol for downloading files from and uploading files to another system over a network. FTP is the name of both a client/server protocol (FTP) and a client utility (ftp) that invokes this protocol. Because FTP is not a secure protocol, it should be used only to download public information. You can run the **vsftpd** FTP server in the restricted environment of a chroot jail to make it significantly less likely that a malicious user can compromise the system.

Many servers and clients implement the FTP protocol. The ftp utility is the original client implementation; sftp and lftp are secure implementations that use OpenSSH facilities to encrypt the connection. Although they do not understand the FTP protocol, they map ftp commands to OpenSSH commands. The **vsftpd** daemon is a secure FTP server; it better protects the server from malicious users than do other FTP servers.

Public FTP servers allow you to log in as **anonymous** or **ftp**. By convention, you supply your email address as a password when you log in as an anonymous user. Public servers frequently have interesting files in the **pub** directory.

FTP provides two modes of transferring files: binary and ASCII. It is safe to use binary mode to transfer all types of files, including ASCII files. If you transfer a binary file using ASCII mode, the transfer will fail.

# Exercises

1. What changes does FTP make to an ASCII file when you download it in ASCII mode to a Windows machine from a Linux server? What changes are made when you download the file to a Mac?

2. What happens if you transfer an executable program file in ASCII mode?

3. When would ftp be a better choice than sftp?

4. How would you prevent a local user from logging in on a **vsftpd** server using her system username and password?

5. What advantage does sftp have over ftp?

6. What is the difference between cd and lcd in ftp?

# Advanced Exercises

7. Why might you have problems connecting to an FTP server in PORT mode?

8. Why is it advantageous to run **vsftpd** in a chroot jail?

9. After downloading a file, you find that it does not match the MD5 checksum provided. Downloading the file again gives the same incorrect checksum. What have you done wrong and how would you fix it?

# sendmail: SETTING UP MAIL SERVERS, CLIENTS, AND MORE

## OBJECTIVES

After reading this chapter you should be able to:

▶ Explain what **sendmail** is

▶ Explain the purpose and give examples of an MUA, an MTA, and an MDA

▶ Describe the role of SMTP, IMAP, and POP

▶ Configure the local SMTP service to use a smarthost for outgoing mail

▶ Configure the local SMTP server to accept incoming mail, relay outgoing mail for specific hosts, and deliver mail directly to the remote systems

▶ Configure mail aliases and mail forwarding

▶ Install and configure SpamAssassin on a mail client and a mail server

▶ Install and configure a Webmail service (SquirrelMail)

▶ Setup a mailing list (Mailman)

▶ Install and configure an IMAP server (Dovecot)

▶ Describe the process and purpose of authenticated relaying

Sending and receiving email require three pieces of software. At each end, there is a client, called an MUA (mail user agent), which is a bridge between a user and the mail system. Common MUAs are Evolution, KMail, Thunderbird, mutt, and Outlook. When you send an email, the MUA hands it to an MTA (mail transfer agent, such as **exim4** or **sendmail**), which transfers it to the destination server. At the destination, an MDA (mail delivery agent, such as **procmail**) puts the mail in the recipient's mailbox file. On Linux systems, the MUA on the receiving system either reads the mailbox file or retrieves mail from a remote MUA or MTA, such as an ISP's SMTP (Simple Mail Transfer Protocol) server, using POP (Post Office Protocol) or IMAP (Internet Message Access Protocol).

SMTP   Most Linux MUAs expect a local MTA such as **sendmail** to deliver outgoing email. On some systems, including those with a dial-up connection to the Internet, the MTA sends email to an ISP's mail server. Because most MTAs use SMTP (Simple Mail Transfer Protocol) to deliver email, they are often referred to as SMTP servers.

### You do not need to set up **sendmail** to send and receive email

tip   Most MUAs can use POP or IMAP to receive email from an ISP's server. These protocols do not require an MTA such as **sendmail**. As a consequence, you do not need to install or configure **sendmail** (or another MTA) to receive email. Although you still need SMTP to send email, the SMTP server can be at a remote location, such as your ISP. Thus you might not need to concern yourself with it either.

In the default Fedora setup, the **sendmail** MTA uses **procmail** as the local MDA. In turn, **procmail** writes email to the end of the recipient's mailbox file. You can also use **procmail** to sort email according to a set of rules, either on a per-user basis or globally. The global filtering function is useful for systemwide filtering to detect spam and for other tasks, but the per-user feature is largely superfluous on a modern system. Traditional UNIX MUAs were simple programs that could not filter mail and thus delegated this function to MDAs such as **procmail**. Modern MUAs, by contrast, incorporate this functionality. Although by default RHEL uses **postfix** as the MTA, this chapter explains how to set up **sendmail** as the MTA.

# _LPI_   INTRODUCTION TO sendmail

When the network that was to evolve into the Internet was first set up, it connected a few computers, each serving a large number of users and running several services. Each computer was capable of sending and receiving email and had a unique hostname, which was used as a destination for email.

Today the Internet has a large number of transient clients. Because these clients do not have fixed IP addresses or hostnames, they cannot receive email directly. Users on these systems usually maintain an account on an email server run by their employer or an ISP, and they collect email from this account using POP or IMAP. Unless you own a domain where you want to receive email, you will not need to set up **sendmail** to receive mail from nonlocal systems.

# OUTBOUND EMAIL

When used as a server, **sendmail** accepts outbound email and directs it to the system it is addressed to (the destination system). This section describes the different ways you can set up **sendmail** to perform this task.

## ACCEPTING EMAIL FOR DELIVERY

You can set up a **sendmail** server so it accepts outbound email from the local system only, from specified systems (such as a LAN), or from all systems. Accepting email from unknown systems makes it likely the server will propagate spam.

## DELIVERING EMAIL

Direct connection  You can set up a **sendmail** server so it connects directly to the SMTP server on nonlocal destination systems. This SMTP server then delivers the email. Typically, **sendmail** delivers local email directly.

Smarthost  Alternately, you can set up a **sendmail** server so it sends email bound for nonlocal systems to an SMTP server that relays the mail to its destination. This type of server is called a *smarthost* or *SMTP relay*.

Port 25  By default, SMTP uses port 25. Some Windows viruses use a simple, self-contained SMTP server to propagate themselves. As a partial defense against these types of viruses, some ISPs and larger organizations block all outgoing connections that originate or terminate on port 25, with the exception of connections to their own SMTP server (smarthost). Blocking this port prevents local systems from making a direct connection to send email. These organizations require you to use a smarthost for email bound for nonlocal systems.

# INBOUND EMAIL

Although not typical, you can set up **sendmail** to accept email for a registered domain name as specified in the domain's DNS MX record (page 859). However, most mail clients (MUAs) do not interact directly with **sendmail** to receive email. Instead, they use POP or IMAP—protocols that include features for managing mail folders, leaving messages on the server, and reading only the subject of an email without downloading the entire message. If you want to collect email from a system other than the one running the incoming mail server, you might need to set up a POP or IMAP server, as discussed on page 763.

# *LPI* ALTERNATIVES TO sendmail

Over the years, **sendmail** has grown to be enormously complex. Its complexity makes it challenging to configure if you want to set up something more than a simple mail server. Its size and complexity also add to its vulnerability. For optimal security, make sure you run the latest version of **sendmail** and always keep **sendmail** up-to-date. Or you might want to consider using one of the following alternatives.

**LPI** **exim4**    The default MTA under Ubuntu, **exim4** (www.exim.org; **exim** package), was introduced in 1995 by the University of Cambridge. It can be configured in several different ways and includes many features other MTAs lack.

**LE+** Postfix    Postfix (www.postfix.org; **postfix** package) is an alternative MTA. Postfix is fast and easy to administer but is compatible enough with **sendmail** to not upset **sendmail** users. Postfix has a good reputation for ease of use and security and is a drop-in replacement for **sendmail**.

**LPI** Qmail    Qmail (www.qmail.org) is a direct competitor of Postfix and has the same objectives. By default, Qmail stores email using the **maildir** format as opposed to the **mbox** format that other MTAs use (page 745).

## MORE INFORMATION

Web    **sendmail**: www.sendmail.org
**exim4**: www.exim.org, wiki.debian.org/PkgExim4
**procmail**: www.procmail.org
IMAP and POP3: www.dovecot.org, cyrusimap.org
SpamAssassin: spamassassin.apache.org, wiki.apache.org/spamassassin
Spam database: razor.sourceforge.net
Mailman: www.list.org
SquirrelMail: www.squirrelmail.org
Dovecot: www.dovecot.org
Postfix: www.postfix.org
Qmail: www.qmail.org

Local    Dovecot: **/usr/share/doc/dovecot***
man pages: **sendmail**, aliases, makemap, spamassassin spamc **spamd**
SpamAssassin: **/usr/share/doc/spamassassin***, give the following command:

```
$ perldoc Mail::SpamAssassin::Conf
```

## **LPI** SETTING UP A sendmail MAIL SERVER

This section explains how to set up a **sendmail** mail server.

## PREREQUISITES

Install the following packages:

• **sendmail**

• **sendmail-cf** (required to configure **sendmail**)

Restart **sendmail**    As installed, **sendmail** is active and enabled so it will run when the system is booted. After changing its configuration files, give the following command to restart **sendmail**, causing it to reread its configuration files:

```
# systemctl restart sendmail.service
```

# Notes

Firewall    An SMTP server normally uses TCP port 25. If an SMTP server system that receives nonlocal mail is running a firewall, you need to open this port. Give the following commands to open the port each time the system boots (permanently) and on the running system; see page 906 for information on firewall-cmd.

```
$ sudo -c 'firewall-cmd --add-port=25/tcp'
$ sudo -c 'firewall-cmd --permanent --add-port=25/tcp'
```

cyrus    This chapter covers the IMAP and POP3 servers included in the **dovecot** package. Fedora/RHEL also provides IMAP and POP3 servers in the **cyrus-imapd** package.

FQDN    If the local system does not have an *FQDN* (page 1250), **sendmail** will start very slowly. As a consequence, the system might boot slowly. See **/etc/hostname** on page 507 for instructions on how to determine if the system has an FQDN and how to give the local system an FQDN.

## LPI    JumpStart I: Configuring sendmail on a Client

### You might not need to configure sendmail to send email

tip    With **sendmail** running, give the command described under "Test" on page 744. As long as **sendmail** can connect to port 25 outbound, you should not need to set up **sendmail** to use an SMTP relay as described in this section. If you receive the mail sent by the test, you can skip this section. However, see "FQDN," above.

This JumpStart configures an outbound **sendmail** server. This server

- Uses a remote SMTP server—typically an ISP—to relay outbound email to its destination (a smarthost or SMTP relay).

- Sends to the SMTP server email originating from the local system only. It does not forward email originating from other systems.

- Does not handle inbound email. As is frequently the case, you need to use POP or IMAP to receive email.

Change    To set up this server, you must edit **/etc/mail/sendmail.mc** and restart **sendmail**
sendmail.mc    (page 742).

The **dnl** (page 749) at the start of the following line in **sendmail.mc** indicates that this line is a comment:

```
dnl define(`SMART_HOST', `smtp.your.provider')dnl
```

You can ignore the **dnl** at the end of the line. To specify a remote SMTP server, you must open **sendmail.mc** in an editor and change the preceding line, deleting **dnl** from the beginning of the line and replacing **smtp.your.provider** with the FQDN of your

ISP's SMTP server (obtain this name from your ISP). Be careful not to alter the back ticks ( ` ) and the single quotation marks (') in this line. If your ISP's SMTP server is at **smtp.myisp.com,** you would change the line to

```
define('SMART_HOST', 'smtp.myisp.com')dnl
```

### Do not alter the back ticks ( ` ) or the single quotation marks (')

tip Be careful not to alter the back ticks ( ` ) or the single quotation marks (') in any line in **sendmail.mc.** These symbols control the way the m4 preprocessor converts **sendmail.mc** to **sendmail.cf**; **sendmail** will not work properly if you do not preserve these symbols.

Restart **sendmail** so that it regenerates the **sendmail.cf** file from the **sendmail.mc** file you edited (page 742).

Test Test **sendmail** with the following command:

```
$ echo "my sendmail test" | /usr/sbin/sendmail user@remote.host
```

Replace *user@remote.host* with an email address on *another system* where you receive email. You need to send email to a remote system to make sure that **sendmail** is relaying your email.

## *LPI* JUMPSTART II: CONFIGURING sendmail ON A SERVER

If you want to receive inbound email sent to a registered domain that you own, you need to set up **sendmail** as an incoming mail server. This JumpStart describes how to set up such a server. This server

- Accepts outbound email from the local system only.
- Delivers outbound email directly to the recipient's system, without using an SMTP relay (smarthost).
- Accepts inbound email from any system.

This server does not relay outbound email originating on other systems. Refer to "access: Sets Up a Relay Host" on page 752 if you want the local system to act as a relay. For this configuration to work, you must be able to make outbound connections from and receive inbound connections to port 25.

The line in **sendmail.mc** that limits **sendmail** to accepting inbound email from the local system only is

```
DAEMON_OPTIONS('Port=smtp,Addr=127.0.0.1, Name=MTA')dnl
```

To allow **sendmail** to accept inbound email from other systems, remove the parameter **Addr=127.0.0.1,** from the preceding line:

```
DAEMON_OPTIONS('Port=smtp, Name=MTA')dnl
```

By default, **sendmail** does not use a remote SMTP server to relay email, so there is nothing to change to cause **sendmail** to send email directly to recipients' systems. (JumpStart I set up a SMART_HOST to relay email.)

Once you have restarted **sendmail** (page 742), it will accept mail addressed to the local system, as long as a DNS MX record (page 859) points at the local system. If you are not running a DNS server, you must ask your ISP to set up an MX record.

## *LPI* WORKING WITH sendmail MESSAGES

Outbound email   When you send email, the MUA passes the email to **sendmail**, which creates in the **/var/spool/mqueue** (mail queue) directory two files that hold the message while **sendmail** processes it. To create a unique filename for a particular piece of email, **sendmail** generates a random string and uses that string in filenames pertaining to the email. The **sendmail** daemon stores the body of the message in a file named **df** (data file) followed by the generated string. It stores the headers and envelope information in a file named **qf** (queue file) followed by the generated string.

If a delivery error occurs, **sendmail** creates a temporary copy of the message that it stores in a file whose name starts with **tf** (temporary file) and logs errors in a file whose name starts **xf**. Once an email has been sent successfully, **sendmail** removes all files pertaining to that email from the **mqueue** directory.

Mail addressed to   By default, **sendmail** delivers email addressed to the local system to users' files in the
the local system   mail spool directory, **/var/spool/mail**, in **mbox** format. Within this directory, each user has a mail file named with the user's username. Mail remains in these files until it is collected, typically by an MUA. Once an MUA collects the mail from the mail spool, the MUA stores the mail as directed by the user, usually in the user's home directory.

Mail addressed to   The scheme that **sendmail** uses to process email addressed to a nonlocal system
nonlocal systems   depends on how it is configured: It can send the email to a smarthost, it can send the email to the system pointed to by the DNS MX record of the domain the email is addressed to, or it can refuse to send the email.

**mbox** versus   The **mbox** format holds all messages for a user in a single file. To prevent corrup-
**maildir**   tion, a process must lock this file while it is adding messages to or deleting messages from the file; thus the MUA cannot delete a message at the same time the MTA is adding messages. A competing format, **maildir**, holds each message in a separate file. This format does not use locks, allowing an MUA to delete messages from a user at the same time as mail is delivered to the same user. In addition, the **maildir** format is better able to handle larger mailboxes. The downside is that the **maildir** format adds overhead when you are using a protocol such as IMAP to check messages. The **dovecot** package supports both **mbox** and **maildir** formats. Qmail (page 742), an alternative to **sendmail**, supports the **maildir** format only.

# MAIL LOGS

The **sendmail** daemon stores log messages in **/var/log/maillog**. Other mail servers, such as Dovecot, might also log information to this file. Following is a sample log entry:

**/var/log/maillog**
```
# cat /var/log/maillog
...
Jun 18 11:55:46 guava sendmail[2159]: r5IItjl5002157: to=<mgs@sobell.com>,
ctladdr=<sam@guava.example.com> (1000/1400), delay=00:00:01, xdelay=00:00:01,
mailer=esmtp, pri=120315, relay=gmail-smtp-in.l.google.com. [74.125.129.27],
dsn=2.0.0, stat=Sent (OK 1371581746 o4si8984494pac.163 - gsmtp)
```

Each log entry starts with a timestamp, the name of the system sending the email, the name of the mail server (**sendmail**), and a unique identification number. The address of the recipient follows the **to=** label and the address of the sender follows **ctladdr=**. Additional fields provide the name of the mailer and the time it took to send the message. If a message is sent correctly, the **stat=** label is followed by **Sent**.

A message is marked **Sent** when **sendmail** sends it; **Sent** does not indicate the message has been delivered. If a message is not delivered because an error occurred farther down the line, the sender usually receives an email saying that it was not delivered and giving a reason why.

See the **sendmail** documentation for more information on log files. If you send and receive a lot of email, the **maillog** file can grow quite large. The logrotate (page 618) **syslog** entry archives and rotates these files regularly.

# ALIASES AND FORWARDING

You can use the **aliases, ~/.forward** (page 747), and **virtusertable** (page 753) files to forward email. Table 20-1 on page 753 compares the three files.

**LPI** **/etc/aliases** Most of the time when you send email, it goes to a specific person; the recipient, **user@system**, maps to a real user on the specified system. Sometimes, however, you might want email to go to a class of users and not to a specific recipient. Examples of classes of users include **postmaster, webmaster, root,** and **tech_support**. Different users might receive this email at different times or the email might go to a group of users. You can use the **/etc/aliases** file to map local addresses and classes to local users, files, commands, and local as well as nonlocal addresses.

Each line in **/etc/aliases** contains the name of a local (pseudo)user, followed by a colon, whitespace, and a comma-separated list of destinations. The default installation includes a number of aliases that redirect messages for certain pseudousers to **root**. These have the form

```
adm:        root
```

Sending messages to the **root** account is a good way to make them easy to review. However, because **root**'s email is rarely checked, you might want to send copies to a real user. You can set up an alias to forward email to more than one user. The following line forwards mail sent to **abuse** on the local system to **sam** and **max** in addition to **root**:

```
abuse:      root, sam, max
```

It is common to forward mail sent to many special accounts to **root**. If Zach is to read mail sent and forwarded to **root**, you could fix each alias individually. Alternately, you can simply add the following line *to the end* of the **aliases** file (order does matter in this case). This line forwards to Zach all mail sent and forwarded to **root**:

```
...
root:       zach
```

You can create simple mailing lists with this type of alias. For example, the following alias sends copies of all email sent to **admin** on the local system to several users, including Zach, who is on a different system:

```
admin:      sam, helen, max, zach@example.com
```

You can direct email to a file by specifying an absolute pathname in place of a destination address. The following alias, which is quite popular among less conscientious system administrators, redirects email sent to **complaints** to **/dev/null** (page 503), where it disappears:

```
complaints:    /dev/null
```

You can also send email to standard input of a command by preceding the command with the pipeline character (|). This technique is commonly used by mailing list software such as Mailman (page 762). For each list it maintains, Mailman has entries, such as the following one for **painting_class**, in the **aliases** file:

```
painting_class:    "|/var/lib/mailman/mail/mailman post painting_class"
```

**newaliases**    After you edit **/etc/aliases**, you must either run newaliases while you are working with **root** privileges or restart **sendmail** to re-create the **/etc/aliases.db** file that **sendmail** reads.

**praliases**    You can use praliases to list aliases currently loaded by **sendmail**:

```
# praliases | head -5
@:@
abuse:root
adm:root
amanda:root
daemon:root
```

**~/.forward**    Systemwide aliases are useful in many cases, but nonroot users cannot make or change them. Sometimes you might want to forward your own mail: Maybe you want mail from several systems to go to one address, or perhaps you want to forward your mail while you are working at another office. The **~/.forward** file allows ordinary users to forward their email.

Lines in a **.forward** file are the same as the right column of the **aliases** file explained earlier in this section: Destinations are listed one per line and can be a local user, a remote email address, a filename, or a command preceded by the pipeline character (|).

Mail that you forward does not go to your local mailbox. If you want to forward mail and keep a copy in your local mailbox, you must specify your local username preceded by a backslash to prevent an infinite loop. The following example sends Sam's email to himself on the local system and on the system at **example.com:**

```
$cat ~sam/.forward
sams@example.com
\sam
```

## RELATED PROGRAMS

sendmail   The **sendmail** packages include several programs. The primary program, **sendmail**, reads from standard input and sends an email to the recipient specified by its argument. You can use **sendmail** from the command line to check that the mail delivery system is working and to email the output of scripts. See page 744 for an example. The command **apropos sendmail** displays a list of **sendmail**-related files and utilities.

*LPI*   mailq   The mailq utility displays the status of the outgoing mail queue. When there are no messages in the queue, it reports the queue is empty. Unless they are transient, messages in the queue usually indicate a problem with the local or remote MTA configuration or a network problem.

```
# mailq
/var/spool/mqueue is empty
                Total requests: 0
```

mailstats   The mailstats utility reports on the number and sizes of messages **sendmail** has sent and received since the date it displays on the first line:

```
# mailstats
Statistics from Fri Dec 27 16:02:34 2013
M   msgsfr  bytes_from   msgsto     bytes_to  msgsrej msgsdis msgsqur  Mailer
0        0          0K    17181      103904K        0       0       0  prog
4   368386    4216614K   136456     1568314K    20616       0       0  esmtp
9   226151   26101362K   479025    12776528K     4590       0       0  local
=============================================================================
T   594537   30317976K   632662    14448746K    25206       0       0
C   694638               499700                146185
```

In the preceding output, each mailer is identified by the first column, which displays the mailer number, and by the last column, which displays the name of the mailer. The second through fifth columns display the number and total sizes of messages sent and received by the mailer. The sixth, seventh, and eighth columns display the number of messages rejected, discarded, and quarantined, respectively. The row that starts with **T** lists the column totals, and the row that starts with **C** lists the number of TCP connections.

## *LPI*  CONFIGURING sendmail

The **sendmail** configuration files reside in **/etc/mail**, where the primary configuration file is **sendmail.cf**. This directory contains other text configuration files, such as **access, mailertable,** and **virtusertable**. The **sendmail** daemon does not read these files but instead reads the corresponding **\*.db** files in the same directory.

makemap  You can use makemap or give the command **make** from the **/etc/mail** directory to generate the **\*.db** files, although this step is not usually necessary: When you restart **sendmail** (page 742), it automatically generates these files.

# THE sendmail.mc AND sendmail.cf FILES

The **sendmail.cf** file is not intended to be edited and contains a large warning to this effect:

```
$ cat /etc/mail/sendmail.cf
...
######################################################################
#####
#####    DO NOT EDIT THIS FILE!  Only edit the source .mc file.
#####
######################################################################
...
```

## EDITING sendmail.mc AND GENERATING sendmail.cf

The **sendmail.cf** file is generated from **sendmail.mc** using the m4 macro processor. It can be helpful to use a text editor that supports syntax highlighting, such as vim, to edit **sendmail.mc**.

dnl  Many of the lines in **sendmail.mc** start with **dnl**, which stands for **delete to new line**; this token causes m4 to delete from the **dnl** to the end of the line (the next NEWLINE character). Because m4 ignores anything on a line after a **dnl** instruction, you can use **dnl** to introduce comments; it works the same way as # does in a shell script.

Many of the lines in **sendmail.mc** *end* with **dnl**. Because NEWLINEs immediately follow these **dnls**, these **dnls** are superfluous; you can remove them if you like.

After you edit **sendmail.mc**, you need to regenerate **sendmail.cf** to make your changes take effect. Restarting the **sendmail** service regenerates **sendmail.cf**.

## ABOUT sendmail.mc

Lines near the beginning of **sendmail.mc** provide basic configuration information:

```
include('/usr/share/sendmail-cf/m4/cf.m4')dnl
VERSIONID('setup for linux')dnl
OSTYPE('linux')dnl
```

The **include** statement tells m4 where to find the macro definition file it will use to process the rest of this file; it points to the file named **cf.m4**. The **cf.m4** file contains other **include** statements that include parts of the **sendmail** configuration rule sets.

The **VERSIONID** statement defines a string that indicates the version of this configuration. You can change this string to include a brief comment about changes you have made to this file or other information. The value of this string is not significant to **sendmail**.

Do not change the **OSTYPE** statement unless you are migrating a **sendmail.mc** file from another operating system.

Other statements you might want to change are explained in the following sections and in the **sendmail** documentation.

### Quoting m4 strings

## MASQUERADING

Typically you want your email to appear to come from the user and the domain where you receive email; sometimes the outbound server is in a different domain than the inbound server. You can cause **sendmail** to alter outbound messages so that they appear to come from a user and/or domain other than the one they are sent from: In other words, you *masquerade* (page 1260) the message.

Several lines in **sendmail.mc** pertain to this type of masquerading. Each is commented out in the file distributed by Fedora/RHEL:

```
dnl MASQUERADE_AS(`mydomain.com')dnl
dnl MASQUERADE_DOMAIN(localhost)dnl
dnl FEATURE(masquerade_entire_domain)dnl
```

The MASQUERADE_AS statement causes email you send from the local system to appear to come from the specified domain (**mydomain.com** in the commented-out line). Remove the leading **dnl** and change **mydomain.com** to the domain name you want mail to appear to come from.

The MASQUERADE_DOMAIN statement causes email from the specified system or domain to be masqueraded, just as local email is. That is, email from the system specified in this statement is treated as though it came from the local system: It is changed so that it appears to come from the domain specified in the MASQUERADE_AS statement. Remove the leading **dnl** and change **localhost** to the name of the system or domain that sends the email you want to masquerade. If the name you specify has a leading period, it specifies a domain. If there is no leading period, the name specifies a system or host. The **sendmail.mc** file can include as many MASQUERADE_DOMAIN statements as necessary.

The **masquerade_entire_domain** feature statement causes **sendmail** also to masquerade subdomains of the domain specified in the MASQUERADE_DOMAIN statement. Remove the leading **dnl** to masquerade entire domains.

## ACCEPTING EMAIL FROM UNKNOWN HOSTS

As configured by Fedora/RHEL, **sendmail** accepts email from domains it cannot resolve (and that might not exist). To turn this feature off and cut down the amount of spam you receive, add **dnl** to the beginning of the following line:

```
FEATURE(`accept_unresolvable_domains')dnl
```

When this feature is off, **sendmail** uses DNS to look up the domains of all email it receives. If it cannot resolve the domain, it rejects the email.

### SETTING UP A BACKUP SERVER

You can set up a backup mail server to hold email when the primary mail server experiences problems. For maximum coverage, the backup server should be on a different connection to the Internet from the primary server.

Setting up a backup server is easy. Just remove the leading **dnl** from the following line in the *backup* mail server's **sendmail.mc** file:

```
dnl FEATURE('relay_based_on_MX')dnl
```

DNS MX records (page 859) specify where email for a domain should be sent. You can have multiple MX records for a domain, each pointing to a different mail server. When a domain has multiple MX records, each record usually has a different priority; the priority is specified by a two-digit number, where lower numbers specify higher priorities.

When attempting to deliver email, an MTA first tries to deliver email to the highest-priority server. If that delivery attempt fails, it tries to deliver to a lower-priority server. If you activate the **relay_based_on_MX** feature and point a low-priority MX record at a secondary mail server, the mail server will accept email for the domain. The mail server will then forward email to the server identified by the highest-priority MX record for the domain when that server becomes available.

## OTHER FILES IN /etc/mail

The **/etc/mail** directory holds most of the files that control **sendmail**. This section discusses three of those files: **mailertable**, **access**, and **virtusertable**.

### mailertable: FORWARDS EMAIL FROM ONE DOMAIN TO ANOTHER

When you run a mail server, you might want to send mail destined for one domain to a different location. The **sendmail** daemon uses the **/etc/mail/mailertable** file for this purpose. Each line in **mailertable** holds the name of a domain and a destination mailer separated by whitespace; when **sendmail** receives email for the specified domain, it forwards it to the mailer specified on the same line. Fedora/RHEL enables this feature by default: Put an entry in the **mailertable** file and restart **sendmail** to use it.

The following line in **mailertable** forwards email sent to **tcorp.com** to the mailer at **plum.com**:

```
$ cat /etc/mail/mailertable
tcorp.com          smtp:[plum.com]
```

The square brackets in the example instruct **sendmail** not to use MX records but rather to send email directly to the SMTP server. Without the brackets, email could enter an infinite loop.

A period in front of a domain name acts as a wildcard and causes the name to match any domain that ends in the specified name. For example, **.tcorp.com** matches **sales.tcorp.com**, **mktg.tcrop.com**, and so on.

Restarting the **sendmail** service regenerates **mailertable.db** from **mailertable**.

## access: SETS UP A RELAY HOST

On a LAN, you might want to set up a single server to process outbound mail, keeping local mail inside the network. A system that processes outbound mail for other systems is called a *relay host*. The **/etc/mail/access** file specifies which systems the local server relays email for. As configured by Fedora/RHEL, this file lists only the local system:

```
$ cat /etc/mail/access
...
# by default we allow relaying from localhost...
Connect:localhost.localdomain          RELAY
Connect:localhost                      RELAY
Connect:127.0.0.1                      RELAY
```

You can add systems to the list in **access** by adding an IP address followed by whitespace and the word **RELAY**. The following line adds the 192.168. subnet to the list of hosts the local system relays mail for:

```
Connect:192.168.                       RELAY
```

Restarting the **sendmail** service regenerates **access.db** from **access**.

## virtusertable: SERVES EMAIL TO MULTIPLE DOMAINS

You can set up DNS MX records (page 859) so a single system serves email to multiple domains. On a system that serves mail to many domains, you need a way to sort the incoming mail so it goes to the correct places. The **/etc/mail/virtusertable** file can forward inbound email addressed to different domains (**aliases** cannot do this).

As **sendmail** is configured by Fedora/RHEL, **virtusertable** is enabled. You need to put forwarding instructions in the **virtusertable** file and restart **sendmail** to serve the specified domains. The **virtusertable** file is similar to the **aliases** file (page 746), except the left column contains full email addresses, not just local ones. Each line in **virtusertable** starts with the address the email was sent to, followed by whitespace and the address **sendmail** will forward the email to. As with **aliases**, the destination can be a local user, an email address, a file, or a pipeline symbol (l), followed by a command.

The following line from **virtusertable** forwards mail addressed to **zach@tcorp.com** to **zcs**, a local user:

```
zach@tcorp.com        zcs
```

You can also forward email for a user to a remote email address:

```
sams@plum.com         sams@tcorp.com
```

You can forward all email destined for a domain to another domain without specifying each user individually. To forward email for every user at **plum.com** to **tcorp.com**, specify **@plum.com** as the first address on the line. When **sendmail** forwards email, it replaces the **%1** in the destination address with the name of the recipient. The next line forwards all email addressed to **plum.com** to **tcorp.com**, keeping the original recipients' names:

```
@plum.com       %1@tcorp.com
```

Finally you can specify that email intended for a specific user should be rejected by using the **error** namespace in the destination. The next example bounces email addressed to **spam@tcorp.com** with the message **5.7.0:550 Invalid address**:

```
spam@tcorp.com          error:5.7.0:550 Invalid address
```

.forward, aliases, and virtusertable

The .forward (page 747), **aliases** (page 746), and **virtusertable** files all do the same thing: They forward email addressed to one user to another user. They can also redirect email to a file or to serve as input to a program. The difference between them is scope and ownership; see Table 20-1.

**Table 20-1**  Comparison of forwarding techniques

|  | .forward | aliases | virtusertable |
|---|---|---|---|
| **Controlled by** | non**root** user | **root** | **root** |
| **Forwards email addressed to** | non**root** user | Any real or virtual user on the local system | Any real or virtual user on any domain recognized by **sendmail** |
| **Order of precedence** | Third | Second | First |

# SpamAssassin

Spam—or more correctly UCE (unsolicited commercial email)—accounts for more than three-fourths of all email. SpamAssassin evaluates each piece of incoming email and assigns it a number that indicates the likelihood that the email is spam. The higher the number, the more likely the email is spam. You can filter email based on its rating. SpamAssassin is effective as installed, but you can modify its configuration files to make it better fit your needs. See page 742 for sources of more information on SpamAssassin.

## How SpamAssassin Works

spamc and **spamd**

SpamAssassin comprises the **spamd** daemon and the spamc client. Although it includes the spamassassin utility, the SpamAssassin documentation suggests using spamc and not spamassassin to filter mail because spamc is much quicker to load than spamassassin. While spamassassin works alone, spamc calls **spamd**. The **spamd** daemon spawns children; when **spamd** is running, ps displays several **spamd child** processes in addition to the parent **spamd** process:

```
$ ps -ef | grep spam
root      2235     1  2 12:43 ?        00:00:01 /usr/bin/spamd --pidfile ...
root      2236  2235  0 12:43 ?        00:00:00 spamd child
root      2237  2235  0 12:43 ?        00:00:00 spamd child
sam       2241  1816  0 12:44 pts/1    00:00:00 grep --color=auto spam
```

The **spamc** utility is a filter: It reads each piece of email from standard input, sends the email to **spamd** for processing, and writes the modified email to standard output. The **spamd** daemon uses several techniques to identify spam:

- **Header analysis**—Checks for tricks people who send spam use to make you think email is legitimate.

- **Text analysis**—Checks the body of an email for characteristics of spam.

- **Blacklists**—Checks lists to see whether the sender is known for sending spam email.

- **Database**—Checks the signature of the message against Vipul's Razor (razor.sourceforge.net), a spam-tracking database.

You can set up SpamAssassin on a mail server so it processes all email being delivered to local systems before it is sent to users (page 756). Alternately, individual users can run it from their mail clients (page 757). Either way, the local system must run **spamd** and each email message must be filtered through this daemon using spamc.

## Prerequisites

Install the following packages:

- **spamassassin**

- **procmail** (runs SpamAssassin on a mail server; page 756)

Enable and start
spamassassin

Run systemctl to cause the **spamassassin** service (**spamd** daemon) to start when the system enters multiuser mode and then start **spamassassin**. Use the systemctl **status** command to make sure the service is running.

```
# systemctl enable spamassassin.service
# systemctl start spamassassin.service
```

## Testing SpamAssassin

With **spamd** running, you can see how spamc works by sending it a string:

```
$ echo "hi there" | spamc
X-Spam-Checker-Version: SpamAssassin 3.3.2 (2011-06-06) on guava.example.com
X-Spam-Flag: YES
X-Spam-Level: ******
X-Spam-Status: Yes, score=6.9 required=5.0 tests=EMPTY_MESSAGE,MISSING_DATE,
    MISSING_HEADERS,MISSING_MID,MISSING_SUBJECT,NO_HEADERS_MESSAGE,NO_RECEIVED,
    NO_RELAYS autolearn=no version=3.3.2
```

```
X-Spam-Report:
    *  -0.0 NO_RELAYS Informational: message was not relayed via SMTP
    *   1.2 MISSING_HEADERS Missing To: header
    *   0.1 MISSING_MID Missing Message-Id: header
    *   1.8 MISSING_SUBJECT Missing Subject: header
    *   2.3 EMPTY_MESSAGE Message appears to have no textual parts and no
    *       Subject: text
    *  -0.0 NO_RECEIVED Informational: message has no Received headers
    *   1.4 MISSING_DATE Missing Date: header
    *   0.0 NO_HEADERS_MESSAGE Message appears to be missing most RFC-822
    *       headers
hi there
Subject: [SPAM]
X-Spam-Prev-Subject: (nonexistent)
```

Of course, SpamAssassin complains because the string you gave it did not contain standard email headers. The logical line that starts with **X-Spam-Status** contains the heart of the report on the string **hi there**. First it says **Yes** (it considers the message to be spam). SpamAssassin uses a rating system that assigns a number of hits to a piece of email. If the email receives more than the required number of hits (5.0 by default), SpamAssassin marks it as spam. The string failed for many reasons that are enumerated on this status line. The reasons are detailed in the section labeled X-Spam-Report.

The following listing is from a real piece of spam processed by SpamAssassin. It received 24.5 hits, indicating that it is almost certainly spam.

```
X-Spam-Status: Yes, hits=24.5 required=5.0
    tests=DATE_IN_FUTURE_06_12,INVALID_DATE_TZ_ABSURD,
        MSGID_OE_SPAM_4ZERO,MSGID_OUTLOOK_TIME,
        MSGID_SPAMSIGN_ZEROES,RCVD_IN_DSBL,RCVD_IN_NJABL,
        RCVD_IN_UNCONFIRMED_DSBL,REMOVE_PAGE,VACATION_SCAM,
        X_NJABL_OPEN_PROXY
    version=2.55

X-Spam-Level: *************************
X-Spam-Checker-Version: SpamAssassin 2.55 (1.174.2.19-2003-05-19-exp)
X-Spam-Report:   This mail is probably spam.  The original message has been attached
    along with this report, so you can recognize or block similar unwanted
    mail in future.  See http://spamassassin.org/tag/ for more details.
    Content preview:  Paradise SEX Island Awaits! Tropical 1 week vacations
    where anything goes! We have lots of WOMEN, SEX, ALCOHOL, ETC! Every
    man's dream awaits on this island of pleasure. [...]
    Content analysis details:   (24.50 points, 5 required)
    MSGID_SPAMSIGN_ZEROES (4.3 points)  Message-Id generated by spam tool (zeroes variant)
    INVALID_DATE_TZ_ABSURD (4.3 points)  Invalid Date: header (timezone does not exist)
    MSGID_OE_SPAM_4ZERO (3.5 points)  Message-Id generated by spam tool (4-zeroes variant)
    VACATION_SCAM      (1.9 points)  BODY: Vacation Offers
    REMOVE_PAGE        (0.3 points)  URI: URL of page called "remove"
    MSGID_OUTLOOK_TIME (4.4 points)  Message-Id is fake (in Outlook Express format)
    DATE_IN_FUTURE_06_12 (1.3 points)  Date: is 6 to 12 hours after Received: date
    RCVD_IN_NJABL      (0.9 points)  RBL: Received via a relay in dnsbl.njabl.org
    [RBL check: found 94.99.190.200.dnsbl.njabl.org.]
    RCVD_IN_UNCONFIRMED_DSBL (0.5 points)  RBL: Received via a relay in unconfirmed.dsbl.org
    [RBL check: found 94.99.190.200.unconfirmed.dsbl.org.]
    X_NJABL_OPEN_PROXY (0.5 points)  RBL: NJABL: sender is proxy/relay/formmail/spam-source
    RCVD_IN_DSBL       (2.6 points)  RBL: Received via a relay in list.dsbl.org
    [RBL check: found 211.157.63.200.list.dsbl.org.]
X-Spam-Flag: YES
Subject: [SPAM] re: statement
```

# CONFIGURING SPAMASSASSIN

SpamAssassin looks in many locations for configuration files; for details, refer to the spamassassin man page. The easiest configuration file to work with is **/etc/mail/spamassassin/local.cf**. You can edit this file to configure SpamAssassin globally. Users can override these global options and add their own options in the **~/.spamassassin/user_prefs** file. You can put the options discussed in this section in either of these files.

For example, you can configure SpamAssassin to rewrite the Subject line of email it rates as spam. The **rewrite_header** keyword in the configuration files controls this behavior. The word **Subject** following this keyword tells SpamAssassin to rewrite Subject lines. Remove the **#** from the following line to turn on this behavior:

```
# rewrite_header Subject *****SPAM*****
```

The **required_score** keyword specifies the minimum score a piece of email must receive before SpamAssassin considers it to be spam. The default is 5.00. Set the value of this keyword to a higher number to cause SpamAssassin to mark fewer pieces of email as spam.

```
required_score 5.00
```

Sometimes mail from addresses that should be marked as spam is not, or mail from addresses that should not be marked as spam is. Use the **whitelist_from** keyword to specify addresses that should never be marked as spam and **blacklist_from** to specify addresses that should always be marked as spam:

```
whitelist_from sams@example.com
blacklist_from *@spammer.net
```

You can specify multiple addresses, separated by SPACEs, on the **whitelist_from** and **blacklist_from** lines. Each address can include wildcards. To whitelist everyone sending email from the example.com domain, use **whitelist_from *@example.com**. You can use multiple **whitelist_from** and **blacklist_from** lines.

## RUNNING SPAMASSASSIN ON A MAIL SERVER

This section explains how to set up SpamAssassin on a mail server so it processes all email being delivered to local systems before it is sent to users. It shows how to use **procmail** as the MDA and have **procmail** send email through spamc.

First, make sure the MTA (**sendmail**) uses **procmail** as the MDA. The first two of the following lines in **sendmail.mc** specify the **procmail** path, command, and flags. The MAILER line defines **procmail** as the mailer. You should not have to make changes to these lines.

```
define(`PROCMAIL_MAILER_PATH', `/usr/bin/procmail')dnl
FEATURE(local_procmail, `', `procmail -t -Y -a $h -d $u')dnl
MAILER(procmail)dnl
```

Also make sure the **procmail** package is installed on the server system. Next, if the **/etc/procmailrc** configuration file does not exist, create it so it is owned by **root** and has 644 permissions and the following contents. If it does exist, append the last two lines from the following file to it:

```
$ cat /etc/procmailrc
DROPPRIVS=yes
:0 fw
| /usr/bin/spamc
```

The first line of this file ensures that **procmail** runs with the least possible privileges. The next two lines implement a rule that uses a pipeline to send each user's incoming email through spamc. The **:0** tells **procmail** that a rule follows. The **f** flag indicates a filter; the **w** flag causes **procmail** to wait for the filter to complete and check the exit code. The last line specifies the **/usr/bin/spamc** utility as the filter.

With this file in place, all email the server receives for local delivery passes through SpamAssassin, which rates it according to the options in the global configuration file. Users with accounts on the server system can override the global SpamAssassin configuration settings in their **~/.spamassassin/user_prefs** files.

When you run SpamAssassin on a server, you typically want to rate the email conservatively so fewer pieces of good email are marked as spam. Setting **required_hits** in the range of 6–10 is generally appropriate. Also, you do not want to remove any email automatically because you could prevent a user from getting a piece of non-spam email. When the server marks email as possibly being spam, users can manually or automatically filter the spam and decide what to do with it.

## USING SPAMASSASSIN WITH A MAIL CLIENT

Alternately, individual users can run it from their mail clients.

With the SpamAssassin (**spamd**) daemon running and the configuration files set up, you are ready to have SpamAssassin filter your email. To do so, you need to set up two rules in your mail client: The first passes each piece of email through SpamAssassin using spamc (page 753), and the second filters email based on whether the X-Spam-Flag line has a YES or NO on it.

This section explains how to set up Evolution to work with SpamAssassin. You can set up other mail clients similarly. Evolution is set up to work with SpamAssassin only when you use an IMAP server. With this setup, you must specify you want to use SpamAssassin in two places: Mail Preferences and Mail Accounts. If you have multiple accounts, you must specify each account you want to check for spam.

**Figure 20-1** Evolution Preferences window

Open the Evolution Preferences window by selecting **Evolution menubar: Edit⇨Preferences**. Click the Mail Preferences icon and then the Junk tab. See Figure 20-1. Put a tick in the check box labeled **Check custom headers for junk**. Two custom header tests that work with SpamAssassin are installed by default. The first checks if **X-Spam-Flag** is set to **YES**; the second checks if **X-Spam-Level** is set to **\*\*\*\*\***. One of these tests will return a true value if SpamAssassin has rated a piece of email as spam.

Next, display the Account Editor window by clicking the Mail Accounts icon in the Evolution Preferences window, highlighting the account you want to work with, and clicking **Edit**. In the Receiving Email tab the Server Type must be IMAP for these instructions to work. Click the Receiving Options tab (Figure 20-2). Under Options, put a tick in the check box labeled **Apply filters to new messages in Inbox on this server**. Click **OK** to close the Account Editor window. Click **Close** to close the Evolution Preferences window.

SELinux   When SELinux is set to use a targeted policy, the SpamAssassin daemon, **spamd**, is protected by SELinux. You can disable this protection if necessary. For more information refer to "Setting the Targeted Policy with system-config-selinux" on page 475.

# Additional Email Tools

This section covers Webmail and mailing lists. In addition, it discusses how to set up IMAP and POP3 servers.

## Webmail

Traditionally you read email using a dedicated email client such as mail or Evolution. Recently it has become more common to use a Web application to read email. If you

**Figure 20-2** Account Editor window, Receiving Options tab

have an email account with a commercial provider such as Gmail, HotMail, or Yahoo! Mail, you use a Web browser to read email. Email read in this manner is called *Webmail*. Unlike email you read on a dedicated client, you can read Webmail from anywhere you can open a browser on the Internet: You can check your email from an Internet cafe or a friend's computer, for example.

SquirrelMail SquirrelMail provides Webmail services. It is written in PHP and supports the IMAP and SMTP protocols. For maximum compatibility across browsers, SquirrelMail renders pages in HTML 4.0 without the use of JavaScript.

SquirrelMail is modular, meaning you can easily add functionality using plugins. Plugins can allow you to share a calendar, for example, or give you the ability to change passwords using the Webmail interface. See the plugins section of the SquirrelMail Web site (www.squirrelmail.org) for more information.

To use SquirrelMail, you must run IMAP (page 763) because SquirrelMail uses IMAP to receive and authenticate email. You must also run Apache (Chapter 26) so a user can use a browser to connect to SquirrelMail.

Prerequisites Install the following packages:

- **squirrelmail**

- **httpd** (page 935)

- **sendmail** (page 740)

- **dovecot** (page 763) or another IMAP server

**Figure 20-3** SquirrelMail running a configuration test

Startup   You do not need to start SquirrelMail, nor do you have to open any ports for it. However, you need to configure, start, and open ports (if the server is running on a system with a firewall) for **sendmail** (page 743), IMAP (page 763), and Apache (page 936).

Configuration   The SquirrelMail files reside in **/usr/share/squirrelmail**. Create the following link to make SquirrelMail accessible from the Web:

```
# ln -s /usr/share/squirrelmail /var/www/html/mail
```

Give the following commands to configure SquirrelMail:

```
# cd /usr/share/squirrelmail/config
# ./conf.pl
SquirrelMail Configuration : Read: config_default.php (1.4.0)
---------------------------------------------------------
Main Menu --
1.  Organization Preferences
2.  Server Settings
3.  Folder Defaults
4.  General Options
5.  Themes
6.  Address Books
7.  Message of the Day (MOTD)
8.  Plugins
9.  Database
10. Languages

D.  Set pre-defined settings for specific IMAP servers

C   Turn color on
S   Save data
Q   Quit

Command >>
```

This menu has multiple levels. When you select a setting (and not a submenu), conf.pl displays information that can help you decide how to answer the question it

**Figure 20-4**  SquirrelMail login page

poses. Set the server's domain name (number **1** on the Server Settings page) and the name of the IMAP server you are using (**D** on the main menu). SquirrelMail provides several themes; if you do not like the way SquirrelMail looks, choose another theme from Themes (number **5**). When you are finished making changes, exit from conf.pl. Run conf.pl whenever you want to change the configuration of SquirrelMail.

SquirrelMail provides a Web page that tests its configuration. Point a browser on the server at **localhost/mail/src/configtest.php**. Replace **localhost** with the IP address or FQDN of the server to view the page from another system. SquirrelMail checks its configuration and displays the results on this page. Figure 20-3 shows that SquirrelMail cannot connect to the IMAP server on the local system, probably because IMAP has not been installed.

Logging in   Point a Web browser at **localhost/mail** or **localhost/mail/src/login.php** to display the SquirrelMail login page (Figure 20-4). Replace **localhost** with the IP address or FQDN of the server to view the page from another system. Enter the username and password of a user who has an account on the server system.

## MAILING LISTS

A mailing list can be an asset if you regularly send email to the same large group of people. It offers several advantages over listing numerous recipients in the To or Cc field of an email or sending the same email individually to many people:

- **Anonymity**—None of the recipients of the email can see the addresses of the other recipients.

- **Archiving**—Email sent to the list is stored in a central location where list members or the public, as specified by the list administrator, can browse through it.

- **Access control**—You can specify who can send email to the list.

- **Consistency**—When you send mail to a group of people using To or Cc, it is easy to forget people who want to be on the list and to erroneously include people who want to be off the list.

- **Efficiency**—A mailing list application spreads email transmissions over time so it does not overload the mail server.

Mailman
: Mailman, the GNU list manager, is written mostly in Python and manages email discussions and email newsletter lists. Because it is integrated with the Web, Mailman makes it easy for users to manage their accounts and for administrators to manage lists. For more information, see the Mailman home page (www.list.org) and, once you have installed Mailman, the files in the **/usr/share/doc/mailman✳** directory.

Prerequisites
: Install the **mailman** package and an MTA such as **sendmail** (page 742). To use the Web interface you must install Apache (page 935).

Mailman site list
: Give the following newlist command to create a site list, substituting the name of your mailing site for **painting_class**. You must also create a site list named **mailman** (substitute **mailman** for **painting_class**); otherwise Mailman will not start.

```
# /usr/lib/mailman/bin/newlist
Enter the name of the list: painting_class
Enter the email of the person running the list: helen@example.com
Initial painting_class password:
To finish creating your mailing list, you must edit your /etc/aliases (or equivalent) file
by adding the following lines, and possibly running the 'newaliases' program:

## painting_class mailing list
painting_class:              "|/usr/lib/mailman/mail/mailman post painting_class"
painting_class-admin:        "|/usr/lib/mailman/mail/mailman admin painting_class"
painting_class-bounces:      "|/usr/lib/mailman/mail/mailman bounces painting_class"
painting_class-confirm:      "|/usr/lib/mailman/mail/mailman confirm painting_class"
painting_class-join:         "|/usr/lib/mailman/mail/mailman join painting_class"
painting_class-leave:        "|/usr/lib/mailman/mail/mailman leave painting_class"
painting_class-owner:        "|/usr/lib/mailman/mail/mailman owner painting_class"
painting_class-request:      "|/usr/lib/mailman/mail/mailman request painting_class"
painting_class-subscribe:    "|/usr/lib/mailman/mail/mailman subscribe painting_class"
painting_class-unsubscribe:  "|/usr/lib/mailman/mail/mailman unsubscribe painting_class"

Hit enter to notify painting_class owner...
```

Before users on the list can receive email, you need to copy the lines generated by newlist (the ones that start with the name of the new mailing site) to the end of **/etc/aliases** (page 746) and run newaliases (page 747).

### You must create a site list named **mailman**

tip
: You must use the newlist utility to create a site list named **mailman** in addition to the site lists you want to set up. If you do not create this site list, you will not be able to start Mailman.

mm_cfg.py
: The main Mailman configuration file is **/etc/mailman/mm_cfg.py**. When you install Mailman, it assigns the value of **fqdn** to **DEFAULT_EMAIL_HOST** (the default

domain for mailing lists) and **DEFAULT_URL_HOST** (the default Web server for Mailman) in this file. Change the values assigned to these variables as needed, making sure to enclose the values within single quotation marks, and start or restart Mailman. The following example uses www.example.com as the default Web server and mail.example.com as the default mail server:

```
# grep '^DEFAULT' /etc/mailman/mm_cfg.py
DEFAULT_URL_HOST   = 'www.example.com'
DEFAULT_EMAIL_HOST = 'mail.example.com'
```

**mailman configuration file**    You can configure many aspects of Mailman mailing lists by modifying the file named **/etc/mailman/sitelist.cfg**. See the comments in this file for more information.

**Enable and start mailman**    After setting up the **mailman** site list and a site list of your choice, Run systemctl to start the **mailman** service when the system enters multiuser mode and then start the **mailman** service. Use the systemctl **status** command to make sure the service is running.

```
# systemctl enable mailman.service
# systemctl start mailman.service
```

After modifying any Mailman configuration files or adding a new site list, give the second command again, replacing **start** with **restart** to cause Mailman to reread its configuration files. Remember also to start **sendmail** and Apache as needed.

**Web interface**    You must modify the last line of the **/etc/httpd/conf.d/mailman.conf** file before the Mailman Web interface will work. Remove the leading hashmark (#) and change the domain name to that of the host for the Web interface as previously established in **mm_cfg.py**:

```
# tail -1 /etc/httpd/conf.d/mailman.conf
RedirectMatch ^/mailman[/]*$ http://www.example.com/mailman/listinfo
```

Restart Apache. Assuming the host for the Web interface is **example.com**, anyone can point a browser at **example.com/mailman** to display a list of available mailing lists. Click the name of a mailing list to display a page that allows you to view the list's archives, send a message, or subscribe to the list. At the bottom of the page is a link to the administrative interface for the list.

If Mailman says **there are no publicly-advertised Mailman mailing lists**, add the following line to **mm_cfg.py** and restart Mailman.

```
VIRTUAL_HOST_OVERVIEW = Off
```

# SETTING UP AN IMAP OR POP3 MAIL SERVER

**Dovecot**    IMAP (Internet Message Access Protocol) and POP (Post Office Protocol) allow users to retrieve and manipulate email remotely. This section explains how to set up servers for these protocols. Dovecot (www.dovecot.org and wiki.dovecot.org) implements these protocols. After you install Dovecot, see **/usr/share/doc/dovecot\*** for more information.

**Prerequisites** Install the **dovecot** package. The rpm installation script creates the self-signed certificates **dovecot** requires in the files named **/etc/pki/dovecot/certs/dovecot.pem** and **/etc/pki/dovecot/private/dovecot.pem**. Typically, you do not need to modify the **dovecot** configuration file (**/etc/dovecot/dovecot.conf**).

**Enable and start** Run systemctl to cause **dovecot** to start when the system enters multiuser mode and
**dovecot** then start **dovecot**. Use the systemctl **status** command to make sure the service is running.

```
# systemctl enable dovecot.service
# systemctl start dovecot.service
```

After modifying a **dovecot** configuration file, give the same command, replacing **start** with **restart**, to cause **dovecot** to reread its configuration files.

# AUTHENTICATED RELAYING

If you travel with a portable computer such as a laptop, you might connect to the Internet through a different connection at each location where you work. Perhaps you travel for work, or maybe you just bring your laptop home at night.

This section does not apply if you always dial in to the network through your ISP. In that case, you are always connected to your ISP's network and it is as though you never moved your computer.

On a laptop you do not use a local instance of **sendmail** to send email. Instead, you use SMTP to connect to an ISP or to a company's SMTP server (a smarthost), which then relays your outgoing mail. To avoid relaying email for anyone, including malicious users who would send spam, SMTP servers restrict who they relay email for, based on IP address. By implementing authenticated relaying, you can cause the SMTP server to authenticate, based on user identification. In addition, SMTP can encrypt communication when you send mail from your email client and use an SMTP server.

An authenticated relay provides several advantages over a plain connection:

- You can send email from any Internet connection.
- The secure connection makes it more difficult to intercept email as it traverses the Internet.
- The outgoing mail server requires authentication, preventing it from being used for spam.

You set up authenticated relaying by creating an SSL certificate or using an existing one, enabling SSL in **sendmail**, and telling your email client to connect to the SMTP server using SSL. If you have an SSL certificate from a company such as VeriSign, you can skip the next section in which you create a self-signed certificate.

## CREATING A SELF-SIGNED CERTIFICATE FOR sendmail

The default location for SSL certificates is **/etc/pki/tls/certs** (PKI stands for public key infrastructure). Working with **root** privileges, give the command **make sendmail.pem** in this directory to generate the required certificates. Apache uses a similar procedure for creating a certificate (page 970).

```
# cd /etc/pki/tls/certs
# make sendmail.pem
...
Generating a 2048 bit RSA private key
...................................+++
...........................................................+++
writing new private key to '/tmp/openssl.snxDr0'
-----
You are about to be asked to enter information that will be incorporated
into your certificate request.
What you are about to enter is what is called a Distinguished Name or a DN.
There are quite a few fields but you can leave some blank
For some fields there will be a default value,
If you enter '.', the field will be left blank.
-----
Country Name (2 letter code) [XX]:US
State or Province Name (full name) []:California
Locality Name (eg, city) [Default City]:San Francisco
Organization Name (eg, company) [Default Company Ltd]:Sobell Associates Inc.
Organizational Unit Name (eg, section) []:
Common Name (eg, your name or your server's hostname) []:sobell.com
Email Address []:mgs@sobell.com
```

```
..............++++++
```

You can enter any information you wish in the certificate.

## ENABLING SSL IN sendmail

Once you have a certificate, instruct **sendmail** to use it by uncommenting (removing the leading **dnl** from) the following lines in **sendmail.mc**:

```
TRUST_AUTH_MECH(`EXTERNAL DIGEST-MD5 CRAM-MD5 LOGIN PLAIN')dnl
define(`confAUTH_MECHANISMS', `EXTERNAL GSSAPI DIGEST-MD5 CRAM-MD5 LOGIN PLAIN')dnl
```

These lines specify the authentication mechanisms.

Next, uncomment the following lines in **sendmail.mc** to tell **sendmail** where the certificate is:

```
define(`confCACERT_PATH', `/etc/pki/tls/certs')dnl
define(`confCACERT', `/etc/pki/tls/certs/ca-bundle.crt')dnl
define(`confSERVER_CERT', `/etc/pki/tls/certs/sendmail.pem')dnl
define(`confSERVER_KEY', `/etc/pki/tls/certs/sendmail.pem')dnl
```

Encrypted connections are made in one of two ways: SSL (simpler) or TLS. SSL requires a dedicated port and has the client and the server negotiate a secure connection and continue the transaction as if the connection were not encrypted. TLS has the client connect to the server using an insecure connection and then issue a STARTTLS command to negotiate a secure connection. TLS runs over the same port as an unencrypted connection. Because many clients support only SSL, it is a good idea to instruct **sendmail** to listen on the SMTPS port. The final line you must uncomment in **sendmail.mc** instructs **sendmail** to listen on the SMTPS (SMTP secure) port:

```
DAEMON_OPTIONS(`Port=smtps, Name=TLSMTA, M=s')dnl
```

### ENABLING SSL IN THE MAIL CLIENT

Enabling SSL in a mail client is usually quite simple. For example, Evolution provides the **Edit⇨Preferences⇨Mail Accounts⇨Edit⇨Receiving Email⇨Security⇨ Encryption Method** combo box that allows you to choose the type of encryption you want to use: **No encryption, STARTTLS encryption,** or **SSL on a dedicated port.** There is a similar combo box under the **Sending Email** tab. Alternately, you can specify the type of encryption you want to use when you set up Evolution.

## CHAPTER SUMMARY

The **sendmail** daemon is an MTA (mail transfer agent). When you send a message, **sendmail** works with other software to get the email to the proper recipients. You can set up **sendmail** to send email to an SMTP server that then relays the email to its destination or you can have **sendmail** send email directly to the SMTP servers for the domains receiving the email. By default, **sendmail** stores incoming messages in the mail spool directory, **/var/spool/mail.**

The **sendmail.cf** file controls many aspects of how **sendmail** works. If you edit this file, restart the **sendmail** service to regenerate **sendmail.cf.** The system administrator can use the **/etc/aliases** file and ordinary users can use **~/.forward** files to reroute email to one or more local or remote addresses, to files, or as input to programs.

You can use a program such as SpamAssassin to grade and mark email as to the likelihood of it being spam. You can then decide what to do with the marked email: You can look at each piece of potential spam and decide where to put it, or you can have your MUA automatically put potential spam in a special mailbox for spam.

Other programs that can help with email include SquirrelMail, which provides Webmail services, and Mailman, which provides mailing list support. IMAP (Internet Message Access Protocol) and POP (Post Office Protocol) allow users to retrieve and manipulate email remotely. The Dovecot system provides IMAP and POP servers.

## EXERCISES

1. By default, email addressed to **system** goes to **root.** How would you also save a copy in **/var/logs/systemmail?**

2. How would Max store a copy of his email in **~/mbox** and send a copy to **max@example.com**?

3. If your firewall allowed only the machine with the IP address 192.168.1.1 to send email outside the network, how would you instruct the local copy of **sendmail** to use this server as a relay?

4. What does **dnl** stand for in the m4 macro language? What are **dnl** commands used for?

5. SpamAssassin is installed on your mail server, with the threshold set to an unusually low value of 3, resulting in a lot of false positives. What rule could you give to your mail client to allow it to identify spam with a score of 5 or higher?

6. Describe the software and protocols used when Max sends an email to Sam on a remote Linux system.

# ADVANCED EXERCISES

7. Your company's current mail server runs on a commercial UNIX server, and you are planning to migrate it to Linux. After copying the configuration files across to the Linux system, you find that it does not work. What might you have forgotten to change?

8. Assume a script stores certain information in a variable named **RESULT**. What line could you put in the script that would send the contents of **RESULT** to the email address specified by the first argument on the command line?

9. Give a simple way of reading your email that does not involve the use of an MUA.

10. If you accidentally delete the **/etc/aliases** file, how could you easily re-create it (assuming that you had not restarted **sendmail**)?

# 21

# NIS AND LDAP

## OBJECTIVES

After reading this chapter you should be able to:

▸ Describe the architecture and use of NIS

▸ List advantages and disadvantages of NIS

▸ Install an NIS server using static port assignments

▸ Port existing local users to an NIS server

▸ Configure a client to use the NIS server for authentication

▸ Describe the architecture and use of LDAP

▸ List advantages and disadvantages of LDAP

▸ Install and configure an OpenLDAP server to hold contact information

▸ Determine required and optional attributes from a published schema

▸ Create an LDIF file to add, modify, or delete an entry

▸ Query an LDAP server with multiple clients

NIS (Network Information Service) simplifies the maintenance of common administrative files by keeping them in a central database and having clients contact the database server to retrieve information from the database. Developed by Sun Microsystems, NIS is an example of the client/server paradigm.

Just as DNS addresses the problem of keeping multiple copies of **/etc/hosts** files up-to-date, so NIS deals with the issue of keeping system-independent configuration files (such as **/etc/passwd**) current. Most networks today are *heterogeneous* (page 1253); even though they run different varieties of UNIX or Linux, they have certain common attributes, such as a **passwd** file.

An LDAP (Lightweight Directory Access Protocol) directory can hold many types of information, including names and addresses, lists of network services, and authentication data. Another example of the client/server paradigm, LDAP is appropriate for any type of relatively static, structured information where fast lookups are required. Many types of clients are set up to communicate with LDAP servers, including email clients, browsers, and authentication servers.

# INTRODUCTION TO NIS

A primary goal of a LAN administrator is to make the network transparent to users. One aspect of this transparency is presenting users with similar environments, including usernames and passwords, when they log in on different machines. From the administrator's perspective, the information that supports a user's environment should not be replicated but rather should be kept in a central location and distributed as required. NIS simplifies this task.

As with DNS, users need not be aware that NIS is managing system configuration files. Setting up and maintaining NIS databases are tasks for the system administrator; individual users and users on single-user Linux systems rarely need to work directly with NIS.

Yellow Pages   NIS used to be called the *Yellow Pages,* and some people still refer to it by this name. Sun renamed the service because another corporation holds the trademark to the Yellow Pages name. The names of NIS utilities and files, however, are reminiscent of the old name: ypcat displays and ypmatch searches an NIS file, and the server daemon is named **ypserv**.

# HOW NIS WORKS

No encryption   NIS does not encrypt data it transfers over the network—it transfers data as plaintext.

NIS domain   NIS makes a common set of information available to systems on a network. The network, referred to as an *NIS domain,* is characterized by each system having the same *NIS domain name* (different than a DNS *domain name* [page 1247]). Technically an NIS domain is a set of NIS maps (database files).

Master and slave servers
Each NIS domain must have exactly one master server; larger networks might have slave servers. Each slave server holds a copy of the NIS database from the master server. The need for slave servers is based on the size of the NIS domain and the reliability of the systems and network. A system can belong to only one NIS domain at a time.

When a client determines that a server is down or is not responding fast enough, it selects another server, as specified in the configuration file. If it cannot reach a server, the **ypbind** NIS client daemon terminates with an error.

nsswitch.conf
Whether a system uses NIS, DNS, local files, or a combination of these as the source of certain information, and in which order, is determined by the **/etc/nsswitch.conf** file (page 495). When it needs information from the NIS database, a client requests the information from the NIS server. For example, when a user attempts to log in, the client system might authenticate the user with username and password information from the NIS server.

You can configure **nsswitch.conf** to cause **/etc/passwd** to override NIS password information for the local system. When you do not export the **root** account to NIS (and you should not), this setup allows you to have a unique **root** password for each system.

Source files
Under Fedora/RHEL, NIS derives the information it offers—such as usernames, passwords, and local system names and IP addresses—from local ASCII configuration files such as **/etc/passwd** and **/etc/hosts**. These files are called *source files* or *master files*. (Some administrators avoid confusion by using different files to hold local configuration information and NIS source information.) An NIS server can include information from one or more of the following source files:

| | |
|---|---|
| **/etc/group** | Defines groups and their members |
| **/etc/gshadow** | Provides shadow passwords for groups |
| **/etc/hosts** | Maps local systems and IP addresses |
| **/etc/passwd** | Lists user information |
| **/etc/printcap** | Lists printer information |
| **/etc/rpc** | Maps RPC program names and numbers |
| **/etc/services** | Maps system service names and port numbers |
| **/etc/shadow** | Provides shadow passwords for users |

The information that NIS offers is based on files that change from time to time. NIS is responsible for making the updated information available in a timely manner to all systems in the NIS domain.

NIS maps
Before NIS can store the information contained in a source file, it must be converted to a *dbm* (page 1246) format file called a *map*. Each map is indexed on one field (column). Records (rows) from a map can be retrieved by specifying a value from the indexed field. Some files generate two maps, each indexed on a different field. For example, the **/etc/passwd** file generates two maps: one indexed by username, the other indexed by UID. These maps are named **passwd.byname** and **passwd.byuid**, respectively.

**optional**   NIS maps correspond to C library functions. The **getpwnam**() and **getpwuid**() functions obtain username and UID information, respectively, from **/etc/passwd** on non-NIS systems. On NIS systems, these functions place RPC calls to the NIS server in a process that is transparent to the application calling the function.

Map names   The names of the maps NIS uses correspond to the files in the **/var/yp/***nisdomainname* directory on the master server, where *nisdomainname* is the name of the NIS domain. The examples in this chapter use the NIS domain named **mgs**:

```
$ ls /var/yp/mgs
group.bygid    mail.aliases    protocols.byname    services.byname
group.byname   netid.byname    protocols.bynumber  services.byservicename
hosts.byaddr   passwd.byname   rpc.byname          ypservers
hosts.byname   passwd.byuid    rpc.bynumber
```

Map nicknames   To make it easier to refer to NIS maps, you can assign nicknames to them. The **/var/yp/nicknames** file on clients holds a list of commonly used nicknames:

```
$ cat /var/yp/nicknames
passwd      passwd.byname
group       group.byname
networks    networks.byaddr
hosts       hosts.byname
protocols   protocols.bynumber
services    services.byname
aliases     mail.aliases
ethers      ethers.byname
```

You can also use the command **ypcat −x** to display the list of nicknames. Each line in **nicknames** contains a nickname followed by whitespace and the name of the map corresponding to the nickname. You can add, remove, or modify nicknames by changing the **nicknames** file.

Displaying maps   The ypcat and ypmatch utilities display information from the NIS maps on the server. Using the nickname **passwd**, the following command, which you can run on any NIS client in the local domain, displays the information contained in the **passwd.byname** map:

```
$ ypcat passwd
sam:$6$ ... pjqI.:1000:1400:Sam the Great:/home/sam:/bin/bash
sls:$6$ ... whe00:1001:1001:Sam sls:/home/sls:/bin/bash
...
```

By default, NIS stores passwords only for users with UIDs greater than or equal to 500 (see MINUID on page 783). Thus ypcat does not display lines for **root, bin,** and other system entries. You can display password information for a single user with ypmatch:

```
$ ypmatch sam passwd
sam:$6$ ... pjqI.:1000:1400:Sam the Great:/home/sam:/bin/bash
```

You can retrieve the same information by filtering the output of ypcat through grep, but ypmatch is more efficient because it searches the map directly, using a single process. The ypmatch utility works on the key for the map only. To match members of the group or other fields not in a map, such as the *GECOS* (page 1251) field in **passwd**, you need to use ypcat and grep:

```
$ ypcat passwd | grep Great
sam:$6$ ... pjqI.:1000:1400:Sam the Great:/home/sam:/bin/bash
```

Terminology   This chapter uses the following definitions:

- **NIS source files**—The ASCII files that NIS obtains information from
- **NIS maps**—The dbm-format files created from NIS source files
- **NIS database**—The collection of NIS maps

## MORE INFORMATION

Local   man pages: domainname, makedbm, **netgroup**, revnetgroup, **ypbind**, ypcat, ypinit, ypmatch, yppasswd, yppoll, yppush, ypset, **ypserv, ypserv.conf**, ypwhich, ypxfr, **ypxfrd** (Some of these are available only on a server or client.)

Web   www.linux-nis.org
*NIS-HOWTO*

# RUNNING AN NIS CLIENT

This section explains how to set up an NIS client on the local system.

## PREREQUISITES

Install the following packages:

- **ypbind**
- **yp-tools** (installed automatically with **ypbind**)
- **rpcbind** (installed automatically with the system)

No server   If there is no NIS server for the NIS client to bind to when you start an NIS client or boot the system, the client spends several minutes trying to find a server and then fails.

Check **rpcbind** is running   A new Fedora/RHEL system boots with **rpcbind** installed and running. Use the systemctl **status** command to make sure the service is running.

```
# systemctl status rpcbind.service
```

Enable and start **ypbind**   After you have configured **ypbind**, run systemctl to cause the **ypbind** service to start each time the system enters multiuser mode and then start the **ypbind** service. This service will fail to start (sometimes after a long wait) if it cannot connect to an NIS server. Use the systemctl **status** command to make sure the service is running or to display error messages if it fails to start.

```
# systemctl enable ypbind.service
# systemctl start ypbind.service
```

## NOTES

If there is no NIS server for the local system's NIS domain, you need to set one up (page 779). If there is an NIS server, you need to know the name of the NIS domain the system belongs to and the name or IP address of one or more NIS servers for the NIS domain.

An NIS client can run on the same system as an NIS server.

SELinux   When SELinux is set to use a targeted policy, NIS is protected by SELinux. You can disable this protection if necessary. For more information refer to "Setting the Targeted Policy with system-config-selinux" on page 475.

## CONFIGURING AN NIS CLIENT

This section explains how to set up and start an NIS client.

### /etc/sysconfig/network: SPECIFIES THE NIS DOMAIN NAME

#### A DNS domain name is different from an NIS domain name

tip   The DNS domain name is used throughout the Internet to refer to a group of systems. DNS maps these names to IP addresses to enable systems to communicate with one another.

The NIS domain name is used strictly to identify systems that share an NIS server and is normally not seen or used by users and other programs. Although some administrators use one name as both a DNS domain name and an NIS domain name, this practice can degrade security.

Add the following line to the **/etc/sysconfig/network** file to specify the NIS domain name of the local system:

*NISDOMAIN=nisdomainname*

The *nisdomainname* is the name of the NIS domain the local system belongs to. The **ypbind** and **ypserv** services execute the **network** file and set the name of the system's NIS domain. You can use the nisdomainname utility to set or view the NIS domain name, but setting it in this manner does not maintain the name when the system is rebooted:

```
# nisdomainname
nisdomainname: Local domain name not set
# nisdomainname mgs
# nisdomainname
mgs
```

### To avoid confusion, use **nisdomainname**, not **domainname**

tip The domainname and nisdomainname utilities do the same thing: They display or set the system's NIS domain name. Use nisdomainname to avoid confusion when you are also working with DNS domain names.

### You must set the local system's NIS domain name

tip If you do not set the local system's NIS domain name, when you start **ypbind**, it logs an error and quits.

## /etc/yp.conf: SPECIFIES AN NIS SERVER

Edit **/etc/yp.conf** to specify one or more NIS servers (masters and/or slaves). As explained by comments in the file, you can use one of three formats to specify each server:

domain **nisdomain** server **server_name**

domain **nisdomain** broadcast (**do not use**)

ypserver **server_name**

where **nisdomain** is the name of the NIS domain that the local (client) system belongs to and **server_name** is the hostname of the NIS server that the local system queries. It is best to specify **server_name** as an IP address or a hostname from **/etc/hosts**. If you specify a hostname that requires a DNS lookup and DNS is down, NIS will not find the server. The second format puts **ypbind** in broadcast mode and is less secure than the first and third formats because it exposes the system to rogue servers by broadcasting a request for a server to identify itself.

Following is a simple **yp.conf** file for a client in the **mgs** domain with a server at 192.168.206.181:

```
$ cat /etc/yp.conf
domain mgs server 192.168.206.181
```

You can use multiple lines to specify multiple servers for one or more domains. Specifying multiple servers for a single domain allows the system to change to another server when its current server is slow or down.

When you specify more than one NIS domain, you must set the system's NIS domain name before starting **ypbind** so the client queries the proper server. Specifying the NIS domain name in **/etc/sysconfig/network** before starting the **ypbind** service takes care of this issue (page 774).

## START ypbind

The **ypbind** daemon is **ypbind-mt** renamed—that is, a newer, multithreaded version of the older **ypbind** daemon. Enable and start **ypbind** as explained on page 773.

# TROUBLESHOOTING THE CLIENT

After starting **ypbind**, use nisdomainname to make sure the correct NIS domain name is set. Refer to page 774 if you need to set the NIS domain name. Next use ypwhich to check whether the system is set up to connect to the proper server; the name of this server is set in **/etc/yp.conf** (page 775):

```
$ ypwhich
plum
```

Use rpcinfo to make sure the NIS server is up and running (replace **plum** with the name of the server that ypwhich returned):

```
$ rpcinfo -u plum ypserv
program 100004 version 1 ready and waiting
program 100004 version 2 ready and waiting
```

After starting **ypbind**, check that it is registered with **rpcbind**:

```
$ rpcinfo -u localhost ypbind
program 100007 version 1 ready and waiting
program 100007 version 2 ready and waiting
```

If rpcinfo does not report that **ypbind** is **ready and waiting,** check that **ypbind** is running (message is from a Fedora system, REHL provides a different message):

```
$ systemctl status ypbind.service
ypbind.service - NIS/YP (Network Information Service) Clients to NIS Domain Binder
   Loaded: loaded (/usr/lib/systemd/system/ypbind.service; enabled)
   Active: active (running) since Tue 2013-06-25 11:14:33 PDT; 3min 3s ago
  Process: 33952 ExecStartPost=/usr/libexec/ypbind-post-waitbind (code=exited, status=0/SUCCESS)
  Process: 33943 ExecStartPre=/usr/sbin/setsebool allow_ypbind=1 (code=exited, status=0/SUCCESS)
  Process: 33940 ExecStartPre=/usr/libexec/ypbind-pre-setdomain (code=exited, status=0/SUCCESS)
 Main PID: 33947 (ypbind)
   Status: "Processing requests..."
   CGroup: name=systemd:/system/ypbind.service
           +-33947 /usr/sbin/ypbind -n

Jun 25 11:14:32 guava systemd[1]: Starting NIS/YP Clients to NIS Domain Binder...
Jun 25 11:14:33 guava ypbind[33953]: Binding NIS service
Jun 25 11:14:33 guava ypbind[33957]: Binding took 0 seconds
Jun 25 11:14:33 guava ypbind[33961]: NIS domain: mgs, NIS server: plum
Jun 25 11:14:33 guava systemd[1]: Started NIS/YP Clients to NIS Domain Binder.
```

If NIS still does not work properly, use service to stop the **ypbind** daemon and then start it manually with debugging turned on:

```
# systemctl stop ypbind

# ypbind -debug
34003: parsing config file
34003: Trying entry: domain mgs server 192.168.206.181
34003: parsed domain 'mgs' server '192.168.206.181'
34003: add_server() domain: mgs, host: 192.168.206.181, slot: 0
34003: [Welcome to ypbind-mt, version 1.37.1]

34003: ping interval is 20 seconds

34003: rebind interval is 900 seconds

34005: NetworkManager is running.
```

```
34005: Network is available.
34005: Switch to online mode
34005: Going online, reloading config file.
34005: parsing config file
34005: Trying entry: domain mgs server 192.168.206.181
34005: parsed domain 'mgs' server '192.168.206.181'
34005: add_server() domain: mgs, host: 192.168.206.181, slot: 0
34005: ping host '192.168.206.181', domain 'mgs'
34005: Answer for domain 'mgs' from server '192.168.206.181'
34005: interface: org.freedesktop.DBus, object path: /org/freedesktop/DBus,
          method: NameAcquired
34006: ping host '192.168.206.181', domain 'mgs'
34006: Entry for mgs unchanged, skipping writeout
34006: Answer for domain 'mgs' from server '192.168.206.181'
34006: Pinging all active servers.
34006: Pinging all active servers.
...
```

The **–debug** option keeps **ypbind** in the foreground and causes it to send error messages and debugging output to standard error. Use CONTROL-C to stop **ypbind** when it is running in the foreground.

# yppasswd: CHANGES NIS PASSWORDS

The yppasswd utility—not to be confused with the **yppasswdd** daemon (two **d**'s; page 785) that runs on the NIS server—replaces the functionality of passwd on clients when you use NIS for passwords. Where passwd changes password information in the **/etc/shadow** file on the local system, yppasswd changes password information in the **/etc/shadow** file on the NIS master server *and* in the NIS **shadow.byname** map. Optionally, yppasswd can also change user information in the **/etc/passwd** file and the **passwd.byname** map.

The yppasswd utility changes the way you log in on all systems in the NIS domain that use NIS to authenticate passwords. It cannot change **root** and system passwords; by default, NIS does not store passwords of users with UIDs less than 500. You have to use passwd to change these users' passwords locally.

To use yppasswd, the **yppasswdd** daemon must be running on the NIS master server.

## passwd VERSUS yppasswd

When a user who is authenticated using NIS passwords runs passwd to change her password, all appears to work properly, yet the user's password is not changed: The user needs to use yppasswd. The **root** and system accounts, in contrast, must use passwd to change their passwords. A common solution to this problem is first to rename passwd—for example, to rootpasswd—and then to change its permissions so only a user working with **root** privileges can execute it.[1] Second, create a link to yppasswd named passwd. You must work with **root** privileges when you make these changes.

---

1. The passwd utility has setuid permission with read and execute permissions for all users and read, write, and execute permissions for **root**. If, after changing its name and permissions, you want to restore its original name and permissions, first change its name and then give the command **chmod 4755 /usr/bin/passwd**. You must work with **root** privileges to make these changes.

```
# ls -l /usr/bin/passwd
-rwsr-xr-x. 1 root root 27856 06-21 17:51 /usr/bin/passwd
# mv /usr/bin/passwd /usr/bin/rootpasswd
# chmod 700 /usr/bin/rootpasswd
# ln -s /usr/bin/yppasswd /usr/bin/passwd
# ls -l /usr/bin/{yppasswd,passwd,rootpasswd}
lrwxrwxrwx. 1 root root     17 06-24 19:38 /usr/bin/passwd -> /usr/bin/yppasswd
-rwx------. 1 root root 27856 06-21 17:51 /usr/bin/rootpasswd
-rwxr-xr-x. 3 root root 24336 05-07 05:57 /usr/bin/yppasswd
```

With this setup, a nonroot user changing his password using passwd will run
yppasswd, which is appropriate. If root or a system account user runs passwd (really
yppasswd), yppasswd displays an error that reminds the administrator to run
rootpasswd.

## MODIFYING USER INFORMATION

As long as the **yppasswdd** daemon is running on the NIS master server, a user can use
the yppasswd utility from an NIS client to change her NIS password while a user running with **root** privileges can change any user's password (except that of **root** or a
system account). A user can also use yppasswd to change his login shell and *GECOS*
(page 1251) information if the **yppasswdd** daemon is set up to permit these changes.
Refer to "**yppasswdd**: The NIS Password Update Daemon" on page 785 for information on how to configure **yppasswdd** to permit users to change these values. Use
the –p option with yppasswd to change the password, –f to change GECOS information, and –l to change the login shell:

```
$ yppasswd -f
Changing NIS account information for sam on plum.
Please enter password:

Changing full name for sam on plum.
To accept the default, simply press return. To enter an empty
field, type the word "none".
Name [Sam the Great]: Sam-in-Fact
Location []:
Office Phone []:
Home Phone []:

The GECOS information has been changed on plum.

$ ypmatch sam passwd
sam:$6$ ... pjqI.:1000:1400:Sam-in-Fact:/home/sam:/bin/bash
```

If yppasswd does not work and the server system is running a firewall, refer to "Firewall" on page 780.

## ADDING AND REMOVING USERS

There are several ways to add and remove users from the NIS **passwd** map. The simplest approach is to keep the **/etc/passwd** file on the NIS master server synchronized
with the **passwd** map. You can keep these files synchronized by first making changes

to the **passwd** file using standard tools such as useradd and userdel, or their graphical counterparts, and then running ypinit (page 784) to update the map.

# SETTING UP AN NIS SERVER

This section explains how to install and configure an NIS server.

## PREREQUISITES

Decide on an NIS domain name (page 774) and install the following packages:

- **ypserv**
- **rpcbind** (installed by default)

Check **rpcbind** is running    A new Fedora/RHEL system boots with **rpcbind** installed and running. Use the systemctl **status** command to make sure the service is running.

```
# systemctl status rpcbind.service
```

After modifying **rpcbind** configuration files, give the second command again, replacing **status** with **restart** to cause **rpcbind** to reread those files.

Enable and start **ypserv**    Run systemctl to cause the **ypserv** service to start each time the system enters multiuser mode and then start the **ypserv** service. Use the systemctl **status** command to make sure the service is running.

```
# systemctl enable ypserv.service
# systemctl start ypserv.service
```

After modifying **ypserv** configuration files, give the second command again, replacing **start** with **restart** to cause **ypserv** to reread those files.

Enable and start **ypxfrd**    The **ypxfrd** map server service speeds up the process of copying large NIS databases from the master server to slaves. It allows slaves to copy the maps, thereby avoiding the need for each slave to copy the raw data and then compile the maps. When an NIS slave receives a message from the server saying there is a new map, it starts ypxfr, which reads the map from the server.

On the master server only, run systemctl to cause the **ypxfrd** service to start each time the system enters multiuser mode and then start the **ypxfrd** service. Use the systemctl **status** command to make sure the service is running.

```
# systemctl enable ypxfrd.service
# systemctl start ypxfrd.service
```

After modifying **ypxfrd** configuration files, give the second command again, replacing **start** with **restart** to cause **ypxfrd** to reread those files.

Enable and start **yppasswdd**    In addition, on the master server only, run systemctl to cause the NIS password update service, **yppasswdd** (page 785), to start each time the system enters multiuser mode and then start the **yppasswdd** service. This service will not start if the NIS domain name has not been set (page 774). Use the systemctl **status** command to make sure the service is running.

```
# systemctl enable yppasswdd.service
# systemctl start yppasswdd.service
```

After modifying **yppasswdd** configuration files, give the second command again, replacing **start** with **restart** to cause **yppasswdd** to reread those files. A message saying **can not bind UDP** usually indicates SELinux is blocking the attempt to bind.

## NOTES

An NIS client can run on the same system as an NIS server.

There must be only one master server for each domain.

You can run multiple NIS domain servers (for different domains) on a single system.

An NIS server serves the NIS domains listed in **/var/yp**. For a more secure system, remove the **maps** directories from **/var/yp** when disabling an NIS server.

SELinux    When SELinux is set to use a targeted policy, NIS is protected by SELinux. You can disable this protection if necessary. For more information refer to "Setting the Targeted Policy with system-config-selinux" on page 475.

Firewall    The NIS server (**ypserv**), the map server daemon (**ypxfrd**), and the NIS password daemon (**yppasswdd**) use **rpcbind** (page 483) to choose which ports they accept queries on. The **rpcbind** server uses port 111 and hands out a random unused port below 1024 when a service, such as **ypserv**, requests a port. Having **ypserv**, **ypxfrd**, and **yppasswdd** use random port numbers makes it difficult to set up a firewall on an NIS server. You can specify ports by editing the **/etc/sysconfig/network** file and adding the lines shown following (choose any unused ports less than 1024; see page 786 for instructions on specifying a port for **yppasswdd**):

```
# cat /etc/sysconfig/network
...
YPSERV_ARGS='--port 114'
YPXFRD_ARGS='--port 116'
```

If an NIS server system is running a firewall or is behind a firewall, you need to open these ports. Follow the instructions on page 908 to use firewall-cmd to open the ports you specified (both TCP and UDP) in the Ports tab. You must also open TCP and UDP ports 111 for **rpcbind**. Be sure to change both the Runtime and Permanent Configurations.

## CONFIGURING THE SERVER

This section explains how to configure an NIS server.

### SPECIFY THE SYSTEM'S NIS DOMAIN NAME

Specify the system's NIS domain name as explained on page 774.

## /etc/ypserv.conf: CONFIGURES THE NIS SERVER

The **/etc/ypserv.sconf** file, which holds NIS server configuration information, specifies options and access rules. Options specify server options and have the following format:

> *option: value*

### OPTIONS

Following is a list of *option*s and their default *value*s:

**files**    Specifies the maximum number of map files that **ypserv** caches. Set to 0 to turn off caching. The default is 30.

**trusted_master**    On a slave server, the name/IP address of the master server from which the slave accepts new maps. The default is no master server, meaning no new maps are accepted.

**xfer_check_port**    YES (default) requires the master server to run on a *privileged port* (page 1267). NO allows the master server to run on any port.

### ACCESS RULES

Access rules, which specify which hosts and domains can access which maps, have the following format:

> *host:domain:map:security*

where *host* and *domain* specify the IP address and NIS domain this rule applies to; *map* is the name of the map this rule applies to; and *security* is either **none** (always allow access), **port** (allow access from a privileged port), or **deny** (never allow access).

The following lines appear in the **ypserv.conf** file supplied with Fedora/RHEL:

```
$ cat /etc/ypserv.conf
...
# Not everybody should see the shadow passwords, not secure, since
# under MSDOG everbody is root and can access ports < 1024 !!!
*                          : *      : shadow.byname    : port
*                          : *      : passwd.adjunct.byname : port
...
# *                        : *      : *                        : none
```

These lines restrict the **shadow.byname** and **passwd.adjunct.byname** (the **passwd** map with shadow [asterisk] entries) maps to access from ports numbered less than 1024. However, anyone using a DOS or early Windows system on the network can read the maps because they can access ports numbered less than 1024. If you uncomment it, the last line allows access to the other maps from any port on any host.

The following example describes a LAN with some addresses you want to grant NIS access from and some that you do not; perhaps you have a wireless segment or some public network connections you do not want to expose to NIS. You can list the systems or an IP subnet that you want to grant access to in **ypserv.conf**. Anyone logging in on another IP address will then be denied NIS services. The following line from **ypserv.conf** grants access to anyone logging in from an IP address in the range of 192.168.0.1 to 192.168.0.255 (specified as 192.168.0.1 with a network mask [page 483] of /24):

```
$ cat /etc/ypserv.conf
...
    192.168.0.1/24 : * : * : none
```

## /var/yp/securenets: ENHANCES SECURITY

To enhance system security, you can create the **/var/yp/securenets** file, which prevents unauthorized systems from sending RPC requests to the NIS server and retrieving NIS maps. Notably **securenets** prevents unauthorized users from retrieving the **shadow** map, which contains encrypted passwords. When **securenets** does not exist or is empty, an NIS server accepts requests from any system.

Each line of **securenets** lists a netmask and an IP address. NIS accepts requests from systems whose IP addresses are specified in **securenets**; it ignores and logs requests from other addresses. You must include the (local) server system as **localhost** (127.0.0.1) in **securenets**. A simple **securenets** file follows:

```
$ cat /var/yp/securenets
# you must accept requests from localhost
255.255.255.255        127.0.0.1
#
# accept requests from IP addresses 192.168.0.1 - 192.168.0.62
255.255.255.192        192.168.0.0
#
# accept requests from IP addresses starting with 192.168.14
255.255.255.0          192.168.14.0
```

## /var/yp/Makefile: CREATES MAPS

The make utility, which is controlled by **/var/yp/Makefile**, uses makedbm to create the NIS maps that hold the information distributed by NIS. When you run ypinit (page 784) on the master server, ypinit calls make: You do not need to run make manually.

Edit **/var/yp/Makefile** to set options and specify which maps to create. The following sections discuss **/var/yp/Makefile** in more detail.

### VARIABLES

Following is a list of variables you can set in **/var/yp/Makefile**. The values following Fedora/RHEL are the values set in the file distributed by Fedora/RHEL.

**B**   Do not change.

Fedora/RHEL: not set

**NOPUSH**   Specifies that **ypserv** is not to copy (push) maps to slave servers. Set to TRUE if you do not have any slave NIS servers; set to FALSE to cause NIS to copy maps to slave servers.

Fedora/RHEL: TRUE

YPPUSH_ARGS    Specifies arguments to yppush to use when it copies maps to slave servers.

MINUID,
MINGID    Specify the lowest UID and GID numbers, respectively, to include in NIS maps. In the /etc/passwd and /etc/group files, lower ID numbers belong to **root** and system accounts and groups. To enhance security, NIS does not distribute password and group information about these users and groups. Set **MINUID** to the lowest UID number you want to include in the NIS maps and set **MINGID** to the lowest GID number you want to include.

Fedora/RHEL: 500/500

NFSNOBODYUID,
NFSNOBODYGID
Specify the UID and GID, respectively, of the user named **nfsnobody**. NIS does not export values for this user. Set to 0 to export maps for **nfsnobody**.

Fedora/RHEL: 65534/65534

MERGE_PASSWD,
MERGE_GROUP
When set to TRUE, merge the /etc/shadow and /etc/passwd files in the **passwd** map and the /etc/gshadow and /etc/group files in the **group** map, enabling shadow user passwords and group passwords.

Fedora/RHEL: TRUE/TRUE

### FILE LOCATIONS
The next sections of /var/yp/Makefile specify standard file locations; you do not normally need to change these entries. This part of the makefile is broken into the following groups:

**Commands**—Locates gawk and make and sets a value for umask (page 469)
**Source directories**—Locates directories that contain NIS source files
**NIS source files**—Locates NIS source files used to build the NIS database
**Servers**—Locates the file that lists NIS servers

### THE all: TARGET
The **all:** target in /var/yp/Makefile specifies the maps that make is to build for NIS:

```
all:  passwd group hosts rpc services netid protocols mail \
      # netgrp shadow publickey networks ethers bootparams printcap \
      # amd.home auto.master auto.home auto.local passwd.adjunct \
      # timezone locale netmasks
```

The first line of the **all:** target lists the maps that make builds by default. This line starts with the word **all**, followed by a colon (:) and a TAB. Because each of the first three lines of the **all:** target ends with a backslash, each of the four physical lines in the **all:** target is part of one long logical line. The last three physical lines are commented out. Uncomment lines and delete or move map names until the list matches your needs.

As your needs change, you can edit the **all:** target in **Makefile** and run make in the /var/yp directory to modify the list of maps distributed by NIS.

## START THE SERVERS

Start or restart the master server (**ypserv**) and then the slave servers after completing the preceding steps. See page 779 for details.

## ypinit: BUILDS OR IMPORTS THE MAPS

The ypinit utility builds or imports and then installs the NIS database. On the master server, ypinit gathers information from the **passwd**, **group**, **hosts**, **networks**, **services**, **protocols**, **netgroup**, and **rpc** files in **/etc** and builds the database. On a slave server, ypinit copies the database from the master server.

You must run ypinit by giving its absolute pathname (**/usr/lib64/yp/ypinit** or **/usr/lib/yp/ypinit**). Use the **–m** option to create the domain subdirectory under **/var/yp** and build the maps that go in it on the master server; use the **–s** *master* option on slave servers to import maps from the master server named *master*. In the following example, ypinit asks for the name of each of the slave servers; it already has the name of the master server because this command is run on the system running the master server (**plum** in the example). Terminate the list with CONTROL-D on a line by itself. After you respond to the query about the list of servers being correct, ypinit builds the **ypservers** map and calls make with **/var/yp/Makefile**, which builds the maps specified in **Makefile**. On 32-bit systems use **/usr/lib/yp/ypinit –m** in place of the command in the example.

```
# /usr/lib64/yp/ypinit -m

At this point, we have to construct a list of the hosts which will run NIS
servers.  plum is in the list of NIS server hosts.  Please continue to add
the names for the other hosts, one per line.  When you are done with the
list, type a <control D>.
        next host to add:  plum
        next host to add:  CONTROL-D
        The current list of NIS servers looks like this:
plum

Is this correct?  [y/n: y]  y
We need a few minutes to build the databases...
Building /var/yp/mgs/ypservers...
Running /var/yp/Makefile...
gmake[1]: Entering directory `/var/yp/mgs'
Updating passwd.byname...
Updating passwd.byuid...
Updating group.byname...
Updating group.bygid...
Updating hosts.byname...
Updating hosts.byaddr...
Updating rpc.byname...
Updating rpc.bynumber...
Updating services.byname...
Updating services.byservicename...
Updating netid.byname...
Updating protocols.bynumber...
Updating protocols.byname...
Updating mail.aliases...
```

```
gmake[1]: Leaving directory '/var/yp/mgs'
```

plum has been set up as a NIS master server.

Now you can run ypinit -s plum on all slave server.

After running ypinit, you must restart the server (page 779).

## TROUBLESHOOTING THE SERVER

This section suggests some ways to troubleshoot an NIS server. See "Troubleshooting the Client" on page 776 for techniques you can use to troubleshoot an NIS client.

From the server, check that **ypserv** is connected to **rpcbind**:

```
$ rpcinfo -p | grep ypserv
   100004    2   udp    114   ypserv
   100004    1   udp    114   ypserv
   100004    2   tcp    114   ypserv
   100004    1   tcp    114   ypserv
```

Again from the server system, make sure the NIS server is up and running:

```
$ rpcinfo -u localhost ypserv
program 100004 version 1 ready and waiting
program 100004 version 2 ready and waiting
```

If the server is not working properly, use systemctl to stop the NIS server. Then start **ypserv** manually in the foreground with debugging turned on:

```
# systemctl stop ypserv.service
# ypserv --debug
[ypserv (ypserv) 2.31]

WARNING: no securenets file found!
ypserv.conf: files: 30
ypserv.conf: xfr_check_port: 1
ypserv.conf: 0.0.0.0/0.0.0.0:*:shadow.byname:2
ypserv.conf: 0.0.0.0/0.0.0.0:*:passwd.adjunct.byname:2
...
```

The **--debug** option keeps **ypserv** in the foreground and causes it to send error messages and debugging output to standard error. Press CONTROL-C to stop **ypserv** when it is running in the foreground.

## yppasswdd: THE NIS PASSWORD UPDATE DAEMON

The NIS password update daemon, **yppasswdd**, runs on the master server only; it is not necessary to run it on slave servers. If the master server is down and you try to change your password from a client, yppasswd displays an error message. When a user runs yppasswd (page 777) on a client, this utility exchanges information with the **yppasswdd** daemon to update the user's password (and optionally other) information in the NIS **shadow** (and optionally **passwd**) map and in the **/etc/shadow** (and optionally **/etc/passwd**) file on the NIS master server. Password change requests are sent to **syslogd** (page 620).

If the server system is running a firewall, open a port for **yppasswdd**. Refer to "Firewall" on page 780.

## START yppasswdd

Start **yppasswdd** as explained on page 779.

## ALLOW GECOS AND LOGIN SHELL MODIFICATION

As shipped, **yppasswdd** does not allow users to change their login shell or *GECOS* (page 1251) information. You can change these settings with options on the command line when you start **yppasswdd** or, more conveniently, by modifying the **/etc/sysconfig/yppasswdd** configuration file. The **–e chfn** option to **yppasswdd** allows users to change their GECOS information; **–e chsh** allows users to change their login shell. When you set the options in **/etc/sysconfig/yppasswdd**, these values are set automatically each time **yppasswdd** is run. The following example causes **yppasswdd** to accept calls on port 112 and allows users to change both their GECOS information and their login shell:

```
# cat /etc/sysconfig/yppasswdd
...
YPPASSWDD_ARGS='--port 112 -e chfn -e chsh'
```

# LDAP

*LE*

LDAP (Lightweight Directory Access Protocol) is an alternative to the older X.500 DAP (Directory Access Protocol). It runs over TCP/IP and is network aware, standards-based, and available on many platforms. A client queries an LDAP server, specifying the data it wants. For example, a query could ask for the first names and email addresses of all people with a last name of Smith who live in San Francisco.

Directory  Because LDAP is designed to work with data that does not change frequently, the server holds a search and read optimized database, called a *directory*. LDAP clients query and update this directory.

In addition to name and address information, an LDAP directory can hold lists of network services. Or, other services can use it for authentication. LDAP is appropriate for any kind of relatively static structured information where fast lookups are required. Many types of clients are set up to communicate with LDAP servers, including LDAP-specific clients (page 795), email clients, and authentication servers.

OpenLDAP  Fedora/RHEL provides the OpenLDAP (www.openldap.org) implementation of LDAP. OpenLDAP uses the Sleepycat Berkeley Database (Berkeley DB, or BDB, now owned by Oracle), which meets the needs of an LDAP database. It supports distributed architecture, replication, and encryption. BDB differs from a relational database (RDBMS) in that instead of holding information in rows and columns, BDB implements an LDAP directory as a hierarchical data structure that groups information with similar attributes. This chapter describes OpenLDAP.

In addition to BDB, Fedora/RHEL supplies HDB (Hash Database), which is based on BDB but which organizes data in a true hierarchical fashion. HDB provides faster writes than does BDB. It also supports subtree renaming, which allows subtrees to be moved efficiently within a database.

**Dynamic configuration** Before the release of version 2.3, OpenLDAP had to be statically configured. This setup was problematic for users with large databases: Each time the configuration was modified, the LDAP daemon had to be restarted, which took a long time. OpenLDAP version 2.3 introduced run-time (dynamic or online) configuration. This setup allows the configuration to be modified without restarting the LDAP daemon. Although the current release (2.4) still allows static configuration, the future points toward dynamic configuration, which is what this chapter describes.

**Fedora/RHEL Directory Servers** In addition to OpenLDAP, Fedora provides the 389 Directory Server (**389-ds** package) and RHEL provides the Red Hat Directory Server, both of which are LDAP servers. For more information see the references on the next page.

**Entries and attributes** An *entry* (a node in the LDAP directory hierarchy, or a container) is the basic unit of information in an LDAP directory. Each entry holds one or more *attributes*. Each attribute has a name (an attribute type or description) and one or more values. Attribute names come from a standard schema that is held in files in the **/etc/openldap/schema** directory. This schema is standard across many implementations of LDAP, enabling LDAP clients to obtain data from many LDAP servers. Although it is not usually necessary or advisable, you can augment or modify the standard schema.

**DN and RDN** A DN (Distinguished Name) uniquely identifies each entry in an LDAP directory. A DN comprises an RDN (Relative Distinguished Name), which is constructed from one or more attributes in the entry, followed by the DN of the parent entry. Because a DN can change (e.g., a woman might change her last name), and because a consistent, unique identifier is sometimes required, the server assigns a *UUID* (page 1280) to each entry.

**DSE and DC** The DSE (DSA-Specific Entry) is the root (also called the base, suffix, or top-level) entry in an LDAP directory. (DSA stands for Directory System Agent.) The DSE is defined in the file named **olcDatabase={3}hdb.ldif**. Frequently, the DSE and the domain name are the same. LDAP defines a domain name in terms of its component parts. The following line defines the DSE comprising the DC **brillserve** and the DC **com**:

```
# grep brillserve /etc/openldap/slapd.d/cn=config/olcDatabase={3}hdb.ldif
olcSuffix: dc=brillserve,dc=com
...
```

**LDIF and CN** The LDAP directory specified by the example DSE could contain the following entry, which is specified in LDIF (LDAP Data Interchange Format; see the **ldif** man page for more information):

```
dn: cn=Sam the Great,dc=brillserve,dc=com
cn: Sam the Great
cn: the great
objectClass: inetOrgPerson
mail: sam@brillserve.com
givenName: Sam
sn: the Great
displayName: Sam the Great
telephoneNumber: 888 888 8888
homePhone: 111 111 1111
initials: SLS
```

Each line except the first specifies an attribute. The word on each line preceding the colon is the attribute name. Following the colon and a SPACE is the attribute value. The first line in this example specifies the DN of the entry. The attribute value used in the RDN is a CN (Common Name) from the entry: **Sam the Great**. This second-level entry is a child of the top-level entry; thus the DN of the parent entry is the DN of the top-level entry (**dc=brillserve,dc=com**). You can uniquely identify this entry by its DN: **cn=Sam the Great,dc=brillserve,dc=com**.

Because this entry defines two CNs, a search for **Sam the Great** or **the Great** will return this entry. This entry also defines a given name, a surname (**sn**), an email address (**mail**), and other attributes.

**objectClass attribute**   Entries inherit object class attributes from their parents. In addition, each entry must have at least one **objectClass** attribute. Each **objectClass** value must be a class defined in the schema. The schema specifies both mandatory and optional (allowed) attributes for an object class. For example, the following entry in the schema defines the object class named **person**. The MUST and MAY lines specify which attributes the **person** object class requires (**sn** [surname] and **cn**; attribute names are separated by a dollar sign) and which attributes are optional (**userPassword, telephoneNumber, seeAlso,** and **description**).

```
$ cat /etc/openldap/schema/core.schema
...
objectclass ( 2.5.6.6 NAME 'person'
        DESC 'RFC2256: a person'
        SUP top STRUCTURAL
        MUST ( sn $ cn )
        MAY ( userPassword $ telephoneNumber $ seeAlso $ description ) )
...
```

**Abbreviations**   The following list summarizes the abbreviations covered in this section.

| | |
|---|---|
| CN | Common Name |
| DC | Domain Component |
| DN | Distinguished Name |
| DSE | DSA-Specific Entry |
| LDIF | LDAP Data Interchange Format |
| RDN | Relative Distinguished Name |

## MORE INFORMATION

**Local**   man pages: **ldap.conf**, ldapmodify, ldapsearch, **ldif, slapd, slapd.conf**, slappasswd

**Web**   LDAP home page: www.openldap.org
Administrator's Guide: www.openldap.org/doc/admin24
389 Directory Server home page: directory.fedoraproject.org
Red Hat Directory Server manuals: access.redhat.com/site/documentation/
   Red_Hat_Directory_Server (these manuals apply to both the Fedora and Red Hat
   Directory Servers)
OpenLDAP Faq-O-Matic: www.openldap.org/faq
book: www.zytrax.com/books/ldap
gq: sourceforge.net/projects/gqclient

**HOWTO**   *LDAP Linux HOWTO*

# SETTING UP AN LDAP SERVER

This section explains how to set up an LDAP server.

## PREREQUISITES

Install the following packages:

- **openldap-clients**
- **openldap-servers**

Enable and start **slapd**

Run systemctl to cause the LDAP daemon, **slapd** (stand-alone LDAP daemon—the abbreviation does not quite work), to start each time the system enters multiuser mode and then start the **slapd** service. Use the systemctl **status** command to make sure the service is running. Do not confuse **ldap** and **slapd** in the names of utilities, services, and scripts.

```
# systemctl enable slapd.service
# systemctl start slapd.service
```

After modifying **slapd** configuration files, give the second command again, replacing **start** with **restart** to cause **slapd** to reread those files.

Loading the internal schema

Fedora/RHEL does not load the internal LDAP schema when you install the **openldap-servers** package. You must perform this task manually before you can create a database. Working with **root** privileges, give the following command to load the schema. This command uses ldapadd to process each file in the **/etc/openldap/schema** directory that has a filename extension of **.ldif**. It uses an interactive **for...in** control structure (page 995).

```
# for file in /etc/openldap/schema/*.ldif
> do
> ldapadd -Y EXTERNAL -H ldapi:/// -f $file
> done
SASL/EXTERNAL authentication started
SASL username: gidNumber=0+uidNumber=0,cn=peercred,cn=external,cn=auth
SASL SSF: 0
adding new entry "cn=collective,cn=schema,cn=config"

SASL/EXTERNAL authentication started
SASL username: gidNumber=0+uidNumber=0,cn=peercred,cn=external,cn=auth
SASL SSF: 0
adding new entry "cn=corba,cn=schema,cn=config"
...
```

## NOTES

Downloading example files

You can download the files necessary to set up and run the LDAP server described in this section from www.sobell.com/RH7/code/chapter_21.

Firewall

A **slapd** LDAP server normally uses TCP port 389, which is not encrypted. If you are using LDAP for authentication, use LDAP over SSL on port 636. If the server is running a firewall or is behind a firewall, you need to open one of these ports. Give the following commands to open port 389 each time the system boots (permanently) and on the running system; see page 906 for information on firewall-cmd. Replace 389 with 636 to open port 636 instead of 389.

```
$ su -c 'firewall-cmd --add-port=389/tcp'
$ su -c 'firewall-cmd --permanent --add-port=389/tcp'
```

# STEP-BY-STEP SETUP

This section lists the steps involved in setting up an LDAP server at the brillserve.com domain. When you set up an LDAP server, substitute the domain name of the server you are setting up for **brillserve.com** in the examples. The example in this section is quite simple; you will probably need different entries in the directory you set up.

To experiment with and learn about LDAP, set up and run locally the example server described in this section. Although the example uses brillserve.com, when working from the server system you can refer to the LDAP server as **localhost**.

## CONFIGURE THE SERVER

Load the internal LDAP schema as described on the previous page.

Next, set up an LDAP database, the **brillserve** DC, and the **lpadmin** CN. You can download the **db.ldif** file as explained under "Downloading example files" (previous page).

```
$ cat db.ldif
dn: olcDatabase=hdb,cn=config
objectClass: olcDatabaseConfig
objectClass: olcHdbConfig
olcDatabase: hdb
olcDbDirectory: /var/lib/ldap
olcAccess: {0}to attrs=userPassword,shadowLastChange by self write by anonymous
     auth by dn="cn=ldapadmin,dc=brillserve,dc=com" write by * none
olcAccess: {1}to dn.base="" by * read
olcAccess: {2}to * by self write by dn="cn=ldapadmin,dc=brillserve,dc=com" write
     by * read olcLastMod: TRUE
olcDbCheckpoint: 512 30
olcDbConfig: {0}set_cachesize 0 2097152 0
olcDbConfig: {1}set_lk_max_objects 1500
olcDbConfig: {2}set_lk_max_locks 1500
olcDbConfig: {3}set_lk_max_lockers 1500
olcDbIndex: objectClass eq
#
# Set up brillserve admin with password
olcSuffix: dc=brillserve,dc=com
olcRootDN: cn=ldapadmin,dc=brillserve,dc=com
olcRootPW: porcupine
```

The first part of the **db.ldif** file sets up the LDAP database. The **olcSuffix** line (third from last in **db.ldif**) defines the DSE (page 787). The **olcRootDN** line establishes the user (the LDAP administrator) who can read any information from and write any information to the LDAP directory. The value on this line is the DN for this user. The RDN is the name of the LDAP administrator; the DN includes the DN of the parent node (the DSE as specified on the **olcSuffix** line). In this example, the name of this user is **ldapadmin** (specified on the next to last line of **db.ldif**). This user is an LDAP user and does not need to exist as a user on the system (i.e., the user does not need to be listed in **/etc/passwd**). The **olcRootPW** (last) line sets up a password for the LDAP administrator. This example sets up **porcupine** as a cleartext password; in a real-world setup it is more secure to use an encrypted password (explained shortly).

The following command, run with **root** privileges, uses ldapadd to add the entries in
**db.ldif** to the database.

```
$ su -c 'ldapadd -Y EXTERNAL -H ldapi:/// -f db.ldif'
Password:
SASL/EXTERNAL authentication started
SASL username: gidNumber=0+uidNumber=0,cn=peercred,cn=external,cn=auth
SASL SSF: 0
adding new entry "olcDatabase=hdb,cn=config"
```

If you will be administrating LDAP over a network, use an encrypted password. First
use slappasswd to encrypt a password:

```
# slappasswd
New password:
Re-enter new password:
{SSHA}7h060/qgeUrX1/Tsqy8O1TbGYBOXdc/+
```

Then copy the output of slappasswd to a new **olcRootPW** line in **db.ldif**:

```
olcRootPW: {SSHA}7h060/qgeUrX1/Tsqy8O1TbGYBOXdc/+
```

## START AND TEST THE SERVER

Start the **slapd** daemon as explained on page 789. Then test the server with the following query:

```
$ ldapsearch -x -s base namingContexts
# extended LDIF
#
# LDAPv3
# base <> (default) with scope baseObject
# filter: (objectclass=*)
# requesting: namingContexts
#

#
dn:
namingContexts: dc=my-domain,dc=com
namingContexts: dc=brillserve,dc=com

# search result
search: 2
result: 0 Success

# numResponses: 2
# numEntries: 1
```

The **–x** on the command line specifies simple authentication, **–s base** specifies the scope
of the search as the base object, and **namingContexts** is the attribute you are searching
for. The output of this command should look similar to that shown in the preceding
example. The **namingContexts** returned by the search should be the same as the DSE you
specified when you configured the server. The **dc=my-domain,dc=com** entry is a DSE
that the server package sets up.

## Add Entries to the Directory

You can use many tools, both graphical and textual, to add information to and query an LDAP directory. This section explains how to use the ldapmodify command-line utility to set up an employee LDAP directory. See page 795 for descriptions of other tools.

When you specify the following file on an ldapmodify command line, ldapmodify adds a second-level entry (one below the DSE entry) to the directory:

```
$ cat AA.ldif
dn: dc=brillserve,dc=com
changetype: add
objectClass: dcObject
objectClass: organization
dc: brillserve
organizationName: ZBrill Associates Inc.
description: root
```

The first line of **AA.ldif** specifies the root DN for the entry you are adding. The **changetype** instruction tells ldapmodify to add the entry to the directory. You can omit this instruction if you use the **–a** option on the ldapmodify command line or if you use the ldapadd utility in place of ldapmodify. The **objectClass** lines specify the object classes this entry belongs to. The line that starts with **dc** specifies the DC (domain component). The **organizationName** specifies the name of the organization this entry is part of while the **description** describes the entry. You can put as many entries in a file as you like, but each must be separated from the next by a blank line. For clarity, the examples in this section show one entry per file.

The following command modifies the LDAP directory based on the **AA.ldif** file. The **ldif** filename extension is commonly used but is not required for files holding LDIF entries.

```
$ ldapmodify -xD "cn=ldapadmin,dc=brillserve,dc=com" -w porcupine -f AA.ldif
adding new entry "dc=brillserve,dc=com"
```

The **–x** option causes the server to use simple authentication. The argument following **–D** specifies the DN of the LDAP administrator of the directory the command is to work with (specified in **db.com** on page 790). By specifying this user, this argument also specifies the DSE of the LDAP directory. (The DN of the parent of the LDAP administrator's entry specifies the DSE.) The argument following **–w** is the password for the LDAP administrator. For better security, use **–W** to cause ldapmodify to prompt for this password. The name of the input file follows the **–f** option. The ldapmodify utility reports the DN of the new entry.

The ldapsearch utility displays all entries in the LDAP directory in LDIF format. The **–LLL** option causes ldapsearch to display a minimal amount of information; use fewer Ls to display more information. After executing the preceding command, there is one entry:

```
$ ldapsearch -x -LLL -b dc=brillserve,dc=com
dn: dc=brillserve,dc=com
objectClass: dcObject
objectClass: organization
```

```
dc: brillserve
o: ZBrill Associates Inc.
description: root
```

The **o** attribute name is an abbreviation for **organizationName**.

The next file adds to the LDAP directory the object class **organizationalUnit** named **employees (ou=employees)**. The DN is **ou=employees** followed by the DSE:

```
$ cat BB.ldif
dn: ou=employees,dc=brillserve,dc=com
changetype: add
objectClass: organizationalUnit
ou: employees

$ ldapmodify -xD "cn=ldapadmin,dc=brillserve,dc=com" -w porcupine -f BB.ldif
adding new entry "ou=employees,dc=brillserve,dc=com"
```

With this object class in place, you can add employees to the LDAP directory. The following file adds an employee:

```
$ cat CC.ldif
dn: cn=Zach Brill,ou=employees,dc=brillserve,dc=com
changetype: add
cn: Zach Brill
cn: brillserve
objectClass: inetOrgPerson
mail: zbrill@brillserve.com
givenName: Zach
surname: Brill
displayName: Zach Brill
telephoneNumber: 999 999 9999
homePhone: 000 000 0000
initials: ZCB

$ ldapmodify -xD "cn=ldapadmin,dc=brillserve,dc=com" -w porcupine -f CC.ldif
adding new entry "cn=Zach Brill,ou=employees,dc=brillserve,dc=com"
```

Now ldapsearch shows the employee you just added:

```
$ ldapsearch -x -LLL -b dc=brillserve,dc=com
dn: dc=brillserve,dc=com
objectClass: dcObject
...
dn: cn=Zach Brill,ou=employees,dc=brillserve,dc=com
cn: Zach Brill
cn: brillserve
objectClass: inetOrgPerson
mail: zbrill@brillserve.com
givenName: Zach
sn: Brill
displayName: Zach Brill
telephoneNumber: 999 999 9999
homePhone: 000 000 0000
initials: ZCB
```

The DN shows that the new employee is at the third level of the directory structure: The first level is **dc=brillserve,dc=com**; **ou=employees,dc=brillserve,dc=com** is at the second level; and **cn=Zach Brill,ou=employees,dc=brillserve,dc=com**, the employee, is at the third level.

The following example adds another employee at the third level:

```
$ cat DD.ldif
dn: cn=Sam the Great,ou=employees,dc=brillserve,dc=com
changetype: add
cn: Sam the Great
cn: the great
objectClass: inetOrgPerson
mail: sam@brillserve.com
givenName: Sam
surname: the Great
displayName: Sam the Great
telephoneNumber: 888 888 8888
homePhone: 111 111 1111
initials: SLS

$ ldapmodify -xD "cn=ldapadmin,dc=brillserve,dc=com" -w porcupine -f DD.ldif
adding new entry "cn=Sam the Great,ou=employees,dc=brillserve,dc=com"
```

The next example uses the ldapmodify **modify** instruction to replace the **mail** attribute value and add a **title** attribute for the employee named Sam the Great. The hyphen on a line by itself separates multiple modifications in a single file. Because the file specifies Sam's DN, the server knows which entry to modify.

```
$ cat EE.ldif
dn: cn=Sam the Great,ou=employees,dc=brillserve,dc=com
changetype: modify
replace: mail
mail: sls@brillserve.com
-
add: title
title: CTO

$ ldapmodify -xD "cn=ldapadmin,dc=brillserve,dc=com" -w porcupine -f EE.ldif
modifying entry "cn=Sam the Great,ou=employees,dc=brillserve,dc=com"
```

You can use ldapsearch to verify the change. The final example deletes Sam from the LDAP directory:

```
$ cat FF.ldif
dn: cn=Sam the Great,ou=employees,dc=brillserve,dc=com
changetype: delete

$ ldapmodify -xD "cn=ldapadmin,dc=brillserve,dc=com" -w porcupine -f FF.ldif
deleting entry "cn=Sam the Great,ou=employees,dc=brillserve,dc=com"
```

# TOOLS FOR WORKING WITH LDAP

You can use a variety of tools to work with LDAP. For example, most email clients are able to retrieve data from an LDAP database.

## EVOLUTION MAIL

This section explains how to use Evolution (Mail) to retrieve data from the example LDAP database created earlier. Evolution must be configured on the local system before you can follow the example in this section. If you just want to experiment with Evolution, you can set it up with an email address such as **user@localhost**. If you are running KDE, you can use KAddressBook, which is integrated into many KDE tools, including Kontact.

Open the Mail-Evolution window by giving the command **evolution** from a terminal emulator or an Enter a Command window (ALT-F2). To query an LDAP database, select **menubar: File⇨New⇨Address Book**. Evolution displays a small New Address Book window. Select **On LDAP Servers** from the drop-down list labeled **Type**. Evolution displays the Connecting to LDAP tab of the New Address Book window (Figure 21-1).

**Figure 21-1**   The New Address Book window, Connecting to LDAP tab

**Figure 21-2**   The New Address Book window, Using LDAP tab

Connecting to
LDAP tab

**On LDAP Servers** appears in the drop-down list labeled **Type**. Enter the name Evolution Mail will use to refer to this LDAP directory in the text box labeled **Name**; the example uses **employees**. Enter the FQDN of the LDAP server in the text box labeled **Server**. If you are experimenting on the local system, enter **localhost** in this box. If appropriate, change the value in the text box labeled **Port**. To follow the example in this chapter, select **None** from the drop-down list labeled **Encryption**.

In the section labeled **Authentication**, select **Using distinguished name (DN)** from the drop-down list labeled **Method**. Enter the DN of the LDAP administrator in the text box labeled **Username** (the example uses **cn=ldapadmin,dc=brillserve,dc=com**).

Using LDAP tab

Next, click the tab labeled **Using LDAP** (Figure 21-2). Click **Find Possible Search Bases**. If all is working properly, Evolution will display an entry in the drop-down list labeled **Search Base**. Select the DN of the directory you want to use (the example uses **dc=brillserve,dc=com**). Select **Subtree** from the drop-down list labeled **Search Scope** to enable searches at all levels of the directory. Click **OK**.

Next click the **Contacts** button at the lower-left corner of the Mail-Evolution window. **On LDAP Servers** appears at the left side of the window. If the name of the address book you specified (**employees** in the example) does not appear below **On LDAP servers**, click the triangle to the left of this label. Then click the name of the address book you want to work with. Evolution prompts for the LDAP administrator password. Enter the password (**porcupine** in the example) and click **OK**. Evolution highlights the name of the address book; you can now search the LDAP database.

**Figure 21-3**   Contacts, Evolution window

Enter the name of an entry in the text box labeled **Search** at the upper-right corner of the window and press RETURN. Evolution displays the entry. Figure 21-3 shows the result of following the example in this chapter and entering **Zach** in the **Search** text box.

## gq: AN LDAP CLIENT (FEDORA)

The gq utility (sourceforge.net/projects/gqclient; **gq** package) is a graphical (GTK+-based) LDAP client you can use to display and modify entries. Open the GQ window by giving the command **gq** from a terminal emulator or an Enter a Command window (ALT-F2). Before you can work with gq, you must specify the DN for the administrator. Select **menubar: File⇨Preferences**, click the Servers tab, highlight the server (**localhost** in the example), click **Edit**, click the **Connections** tab, and enter the DN for the administrator (**cn=ldapadmin,dc=brillserve,dc=com** in the example) in the text box labeled **Bind DN**. Click **Close** twice.

Click the Browse tab and click the plus signs (+) to the left of entries to display successive levels. Click a CN entry to display information about that CN. Figure 21-4 (next page) shows gq displaying an entry from the example LDAP directory.

You can also use gq for browsing the schema: Click the Schema tab and select the server from the left side of the window (**localhost** in Figure 21-5, next page). Click the plus sign (+) to the left of **objectClasses** and then click an object class to view information about that object class, including a list of required and optional attributes.

**Figure 21-4** Using gq to browse an LDAP directory

# CHAPTER SUMMARY

NIS (Network Information Service) simplifies the management of common administrative files by maintaining them in a central database and having clients contact the database server to retrieve information from the database. The network that NIS serves is called an NIS domain. Each NIS domain has one master server; larger networks might have slave servers.

NIS derives the information it offers from local configuration files, such as **/etc/passwd** and **/etc/hosts**. These files are called source files or master files. Before NIS can store the information contained in a source file, it must be converted to dbm-format files, called maps. The ypcat and ypmatch utilities display information from NIS maps.

**Figure 21-5** The gq Schema tab

The yppasswd utility replaces the functionality of passwd on clients when you use NIS to authenticate passwords. The **/etc/ypserv.conf** file, which holds NIS server configuration information, specifies options and access rules for the NIS server. To enhance system security, you can create a **/var/yp/securenets** file, which prevents unauthorized systems from retrieving NIS maps.

An LDAP (Lightweight Directory Access Protocol) server holds a search- and read-optimized database, called a directory. LDAP clients, such as email clients, query and update this directory. In addition, authentication servers can use an LDAP directory to authenticate users.

Fedora/RHEL provides the OpenLDAP implementation of LDAP. OpenLDAP uses the Sleepycat Berkeley Database, which supports distributed architecture, replication, and encryption.

# EXERCISES

1. What is the difference between the passwd and yppasswd utilities?

2. How would you prevent NIS from exporting the **root** user and other system users to clients?

3. How would you make NIS user information override local user information on client systems?

4. Why does the **/etc/passwd** file need two NIS maps?

5. How does an LDAP directory differ from a relational database system?

6. What is the basic unit of information in an LDAP directory? What is the structure of an attribute?

# ADVANCED EXERCISES

7. How can you use NIS to mirror the functionality of a private DNS server for a small network? Why should NIS not be used this way on a large network?

8. How can you determine whether the working directory is the home directory of an NIS user?

9. a. What advantage does NIS provide when you use it with NFS?

   b. Suggest a way to implement NIS maps so they can be indexed on more than one field.

10. Where is the LDAP **device** object class defined? Which of its attributes are mandatory and which are optional?

11. How would you determine the longer name for the l (lowercase "el") LDAP object class?

# 22

# NFS: Sharing Directory Hierarchies

## Objectives

After reading this chapter you should be able to:

▶ Describe the use, history, and architecture of NFS

▶ Mount remote NFS shares

▶ Configure an NFS server to share directories with specific clients

▶ Troubleshoot mount failures

▶ Set up automount to mount directories on demand

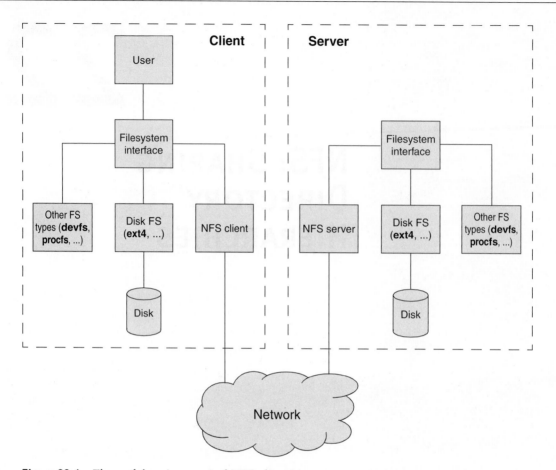

**Figure 22-1**  Flow of data in a typical NFS client/server setup

The NFS (Network Filesystem) protocol, a UNIX de facto standard developed by Sun Microsystems, allows a server to share selected local directory hierarchies with client systems on a heterogeneous network. NFS runs on UNIX, DOS, Windows, VMS, Linux, and more. Files on the remote computer (the server) appear as if they are present on the local system (the client). Most of the time, the physical location of a file is irrelevant to an NFS user; all standard Linux utilities work with NFS remote files the same way as they operate with local files.

NFS reduces storage needs and system administration workload. As an example, each system in a company traditionally holds its own copy of an application program. To upgrade the program, the administrator needs to upgrade it on each system. NFS allows you to store a copy of a program on a single system and give other users access to it over the network. This scenario minimizes storage requirements by reducing the number of locations that need to maintain the same data. In addition to boosting efficiency, NFS gives users on the network access to the same data (not just application programs), thereby improving data consistency and reliability. By consolidating data, it reduces administrative overhead and provides a convenience to users.

NFS has been pejoratively referred to as the *Nightmare Filesystem*, but NFSv4 has fixed many of the shortcomings of NFSv3. NFSv4

- Performs well over high-latency, low-bandwidth Internet connections.
- Because it uses a single port, NFSv4 is much easier to set up with firewalls and NAT than NFSv3 was.
- Has strong, built-in security.
- Has lock and mount protocols integrated into the NFS protocol.
- Handles client and server crashes better than NFSv3 because it provides stateful operations.
- Improves performance by making extensive use of caching on the client.
- Supports ACLs (Access Control Lists).

AUTH_SYS authentication   NFSv4 supports AUTH_SYS authentication, the standard method of authentication under NFSv3. Because AUTH_SYS uses UIDs and GIDs to authenticate users, it is easy to crack. NFSv4 uses AUTH_SYS security by default. See the **sec** option (page 816) for more information.

RPCSEC_GSS authentication   NFSv4 also supports the newer RPCSEC_GSS (see the **rpc.gssd** man page and www.citi.umich.edu/projects/nfsv4/gssd), which provides secure authentication as well as verification and encryption. RPCSEC_GSS is based on GSS-API (Generic Security Services Application Programming Interface; www.faqs.org/faqs/kerberos-faq/general/section-84.html) and can use Kerberos 5 (best for enterprise or LAN use) and LIBKEY (based on SPKM-3; best for Internet use) among other authentication protocols.

This chapter describes setting up an NFSv4 client and server using AUTH_SYS authentication, the Fedora/RHEL default mode.

# INTRODUCTION TO NFS

Figure 22-1 shows the flow of data in a typical NFS client/server setup. An NFS directory hierarchy appears to users and application programs as just another directory hierarchy. By looking at it, you cannot tell a given directory holds a remotely mounted NFS directory hierarchy and not a local filesystem. The NFS server translates commands from the client into operations on the server's filesystem.

Diskless systems   In many computer facilities, user files are stored on a central fileserver equipped with many large-capacity disk drives and devices that quickly and easily make backup copies of the data. A *diskless* system boots from a fileserver (netboots—discussed next), a DVD, or a USB flash drive and loads system software from a fileserver. The Linux Terminal Server Project (LTSP.org) Web site says it all: "Linux makes a great platform for deploying diskless workstations that boot from a network server. The LTSP is all about running thin client computers in a Linux environment." Because a diskless workstation does not require a lot of computing power, you can give older, retired computers a second life by using them as diskless systems.

Netboot/PXE — You can *netboot* (page 1262) systems that are appropriately set up. Fedora/RHEL includes TFTP (Trivial File Transfer Protocol; **tftp-server** package) that you can use to set up a PXE (Preboot Execution Environment) boot server for Intel systems. Non-Intel architectures have historically included netboot capabilities, which Fedora/RHEL also supports. In addition, you can build the Linux kernel so it mounts **root** (**/**) using NFS. Given the many ways to set up a system, the one you choose depends on what you want to do. See the *Remote-Boot mini-HOWTO* for more information.

Dataless systems — Another type of Linux system is a *dataless* system, in which the client has a disk but stores no user data (only Linux and the applications are kept on the disk). Setting up this type of system is a matter of choosing which directory hierarchies are mounted remotely.

**LPI** df: shows where directory hierarchies are mounted — The df utility displays a list of the directory hierarchies available on the system, along with the amount of disk space, free and used, on each. The **–h** (human) option makes the output more intelligible. Device names in the left column that are prepended with *hostname:* specify directory hierarchies that are available through NFS.

```
[zach@guava ~]$ cd; pwd

[zach@guava ~]$ df -h
Filesystem                  Size  Used Avail Use% Mounted on
/dev/mapper/fedora-root      37G  3.8G   32G  11% /
...
/dev/sda1                   477M   99M  354M  22% /boot
plum:/home/zach              37G  3.8G   32G  11% /home/zach
```

When Zach logs in on **guava**, his home directory, **/home/zach**, is on the remote system **plum**. Using NFS, the **/home/zach** directory hierarchy on **plum** is mounted on **guava** as **/home/zach**. Any files in the **zach** directory on **guava** are hidden while the **zach** directory from **plum** is mounted; they reappear when the directory is unmounted. The **/** filesystem is local to **guava**.

The df **–T** option adds a Type column to the display. The following output shows the directory mounted at **/home/zach** is an **nfs4** directory hierarchy; **/** and **/boot** are local **ext4** filesystems.

```
$ df -hT
Filesystem                  Type   Size  Used Avail Use% Mounted on
/dev/mapper/fedora-root     ext4    37G  3.8G   32G  11% /
...
/dev/sda1                   ext4   477M   99M  354M  22% /boot
plum:/home/zach             nfs4    37G  3.8G   32G  11% /home/zach
```

The df **–t** option displays a single filesystem type. With an argument of **nfs4** it displays NFS directory hierarchies:

```
$ df -ht nfs4
Filesystem        Size  Used Avail Use% Mounted on
plum:/home/zach   37G   3.8G   32G  11% /home/zach
```

Security    By default, an NFS server uses AUTH_SYS (page 803) authentication, which is based on the trusted-host paradigm (page 302) and has all the security shortcomings that plague other services based on this paradigm. In addition, in this mode NFS file transfers are not encrypted. Because of these issues, you should implement NFS on a single LAN segment only, where you can be (reasonably) sure systems on the LAN segment are what they claim to be. Make sure a firewall blocks NFS traffic from outside the LAN and never use NFS over the Internet. To improve security, make sure UIDs and GIDs are the same on the server and clients (page 817).

Alternately, you can use RPCSEC_GSS (page 803) authentication, one of the new security features available under NFSv4. RPCSEC_GSS provides authentication, verification, and encryption. This chapter does not cover setting up an NFS server that uses RPCSEC_GSS authentication.

## MORE INFORMATION

Web    NFSv4 secure installation tutorial:
       nfsv4.bullopensource.org/doc/kerberosnfs/krbnfs_howto_v3.pdf
     NFS: nfs.sourceforge.net, www.citi.umich.edu/projects/nfsv4, wiki.linux-nfs.org
     GSS-API: www.faqs.org/faqs/kerberos-faq/general/section-84.html
     PXE boot server tutorial (TFTP): alteeve.ca/w/Setting_Up_a_PXE_Server_in_Fedora

Local    man pages: **autofs** (sections 5 and 8), **automount, auto.master,** exportfs, **exports,** mountstats, **nfs** (especially see SECURITY CONSIDERATIONS), **rpc.idmapd, rpc.gssd, rpc.mountd, rpc.nfsd,** and showmount

HOWTO    NFS-HOWTO: nfs.sourceforge.net/nfs-howto

Book    *NFS Illustrated* by Callaghan, Addison-Wesley (January 2000)

## RUNNING AN NFS CLIENT

This section describes how to set up an NFS client, mount remote directory hierarchies, and improve NFS performance. See page 819 for a list of error messages and troubleshooting tips.

## PREREQUISITES

Install the following packages:

- **nfs-utils** (installed by default)
- **rpcbind** (installed by default; not needed with NFSv4)

Check **rpcbind** is running  A new Fedora/RHEL system boots with **rpcbind** installed and running; For NFSv3 only (not NFSv4) **rpcbind** must be running before you can start the **nfs** service. Use the systemctl **status** command to make sure **rpcbind** is running.

```
# systemctl status rpcbind.service
```

# JumpStart I: Mounting a Remote Directory Hierarchy

To set up an NFS client, mount the remote directory hierarchy the same way you mount a local directory hierarchy (page 520).

The following examples show two ways to mount a remote directory hierarchy, assuming **dog** is on the same network as the local system and is sharing **/home** and **/export** with the local system. The **/export** directory on **dog** holds two directory hierarchies you want to mount: **/export/progs** and **/export/oracle**. The example mounts **dog**'s **/home** directory on **/dog.home** on the local system, **/export/progs** on **/apps**, and **/export/oracle** on **/oracle**.

First run mkdir on the local (client) system to create the directories that are the mount points for the remote directory hierarchies:

```
# mkdir /dog.home /apps /oracle
```

You can mount any directory hierarchy from an exported directory hierarchy. In this example, **dog** exports **/export** and the local system mounts **/export/progs** and **/export/oracle**. The following commands manually mount the directory hierarchies one time:

```
# mount dog:/home /dog.home
# mount -o ro,nosuid dog:/export/progs /apps
# mount -o ro dog:/export/oracle /oracle
```

By default, directory hierarchies are mounted read-write, assuming the NFS server is exporting them with read-write permissions. The first of the preceding commands mounts the **/home** directory hierarchy from **dog** on the local directory **/dog.home**. The second and third commands use the **–o ro** option to force a readonly mount. The second command adds the **nosuid** option, which forces setuid (page 196) executables in the mounted directory hierarchy to run with regular permissions on the local system.

**nosuid** option  If a user has the ability to run a setuid program, that user has the power of a user with **root** privileges. This ability should be limited. Unless you know a user will need to run a program with setuid permissions from a mounted directory hierarchy, always mount a directory hierarchy with the **nosuid** option. For example, you would need to mount a directory hierarchy with setuid privileges when the root partition of a diskless workstation is mounted using NFS.

**nodev** option  Mounting a device file creates another potential security hole. Although the best policy is not to mount untrustworthy directory hierarchies, it is not always possible to implement this policy. Unless a user needs to use a device on a mounted directory hierarchy, mount directory hierarchies with the **nodev** option, which prevents character and block special files (page 518) on the mounted directory hierarchy from being used as devices.

*LPI* fstab file  If you mount directory hierarchies frequently, you can add entries for the directory hierarchies to the **/etc/fstab** file (page 811). (Alternately, you can use **automount**; see page 821.) The following **/etc/fstab** entries mount the same directory hierarchies as in the previous example at the same time that the system mounts the local filesystems:

```
$ cat /etc/fstab
...
dog:/home          /dog.home    nfs4   rw         0  0
dog:/export/progs  /apps        nfs4   ro,nosuid  0  0
dog:/export/oracle /oracle      nfs4   ro         0  0
```

A file mounted using NFS is always of type **nfs4** on the local system, regardless of what type it is on the remote system. Typically you do not run fsck on or back up an NFS directory hierarchy. The entries in the third, fifth, and sixth columns of **fstab** are usually **nfs** (filesystem type), **0** (do not back up this directory hierarchy with dump [page 606]), and **0** (do not run fsck [page 525] on this directory hierarchy). The options for mounting an NFS directory hierarchy differ from those for mounting an **ext4** or other type of filesystem. See the section on mount (next) for details.

Unmounting directory hierarchies  Use umount to unmount a remote directory hierarchy the same way you unmount a local filesystem (page 523).

## *LPI* mount: MOUNTS A DIRECTORY HIERARCHY

The mount utility (page 520) associates a directory hierarchy with a mount point (a directory). You can use mount to mount an NFS (remote) directory hierarchy. This section describes some mount options. It lists default options first, followed by non-default options (enclosed in parentheses). You can use these options on the command line or set them in **/etc/fstab** (page 811). For a complete list of options, refer to the mount and nfs man pages.

Following are two examples of mounting a remote directory hierarchy. Both mount the **/home/public** directory from the system **plum** on the **/plum.public** mount point on the local system. When called without arguments, mount displays a list of mounted filesystems, including the options the filesystem is mounted with.

The first mount command mounts the remote directory without specifying options. The output from the second mount command, which lists the mounted filesystems, is sent through a pipeline to grep, which displays the single (very long) logical line that provides information about the remotely mounted directory. All the options, starting with **rw** (read-write) are defaults or are specified by mount.

```
# mount plum:/home/public /plum.public
# mount | grep plum
plum:/home/public on /plum.public type nfs4
(rw,relatime,vers=4.0,rsize=131072,wsize=131072,namlen=255,hard,proto=tcp,port=0,timeo=60
0,retrans=2,sec=sys,clientaddr=192.168.206.180,local_lock=none,addr=192.168.206.181)
# umount /plum.public
```

The next mount command mounts the remote directory specifying the **noac** option (**–o noac**; next). The output from the second mount command shows the addition of the **noac** option. When you specify **noac**, mount adds the **acregmin**, **acregmax**, **acdirmin**, and **acdirmax** options (all next) and sets them to 0.

```
# mount -o noac plum:/home/public /plum.public
# mount | grep plum
plum:/home/public on /plum.public type nfs4
(rw,relatime,sync,vers=4.0,rsize=131072,wsize=131072,namlen=255,acregmin=0,acregmax=0,acd
irmin=0,acdirmax=0,hard,noac,proto=tcp,port=0,timeo=600,retrans=2,sec=sys,clientaddr=192.
168.206.180,local_lock=none,addr=192.168.206.181)
```

## ATTRIBUTE CACHING

A file's inode (page 515) stores file attributes that provide information about a file, such as file modification time, size, links, and owner. File attributes do not include the data stored in a file. Typically file attributes do not change very often for an ordinary file; they change even less often for a directory file. Even the size attribute does not change with every write instruction: When a client is writing to an NFS-mounted file, several write instructions might be given before the data is transferred to the server. In addition, many file accesses, such as that performed by ls, are readonly operations and, therefore, do not change the file's attributes or its contents. Thus a client can cache attributes and avoid costly network reads.

The kernel uses the modification time of the file to determine when its cache is out-of-date. If the time the attribute cache was saved is later than the modification time of the file itself, the data in the cache is current. The server must periodically refresh the attribute cache of an NFS-mounted file to determine whether another process has modified the file. This period is specified as a minimum and maximum number of seconds for ordinary and directory files. Following is a list of options that affect attribute caching:

ac (noac)    (**attribute cache**) Permits attribute caching. The **noac** option disables attribute caching. Although **noac** slows the server, it avoids stale attributes when two NFS clients actively write to a common directory hierarchy. See the example in the preceding section that shows that when you specify **noac**, mount sets each of the following four options to 0, which in effect specifies that attributes will not be cached. Default is **ac**.

acdirmax=$n$    (**attribute cache directory file maximum**) The $n$ is the number of seconds, at a maximum, that NFS waits before refreshing directory file attributes. Default is **60** seconds.

acdirmin=$n$    (**attribute cache directory file minimum**) The $n$ is the number of seconds, at a minimum, that NFS waits before refreshing directory file attributes. Default is **30** seconds.

acregmax=*n* (**attribute cache regular file maximum**) The *n* is the number of seconds, at a maximum, that NFS waits before refreshing regular file attributes. Default is **60** seconds.

acregmin=*n* (**attribute cache regular file minimum**) The *n* is the number of seconds, at a minimum, that NFS waits before refreshing regular file attributes. Default is **3** seconds.

actimeo=*n* (**attribute cache timeout**) Sets **acregmin**, **acregmax**, **acdirmin**, and **acdirmax** to *n* seconds. Without this option, each individual option takes on its assigned or default value.

## Error Handling

The following options control what NFS does when the server does not respond or when an I/O error occurs. To allow for a mount point located on a mounted device, a missing mount point is treated as a timeout.

fg (bg) (**foreground**) Exits with an error status if a foreground NFS mount fails. The **bg** (**background**) option retries failed NFS mount attempts in the background. Default is **fg**.

hard (soft) With the **hard** option, NFS retries indefinitely when an NFS request times out. With the **soft** option, NFS retries the connection **retrans** times and then reports an I/O error to the calling program. In general, it is not advisable to use **soft**. As the mount man page says of **soft**, "Usually it just causes lots of trouble." For more information refer to "Improving Performance" on page 810. Default is **hard**.

retrans=*n* (**retransmission value**) NFS generates a **server not responding** message after *n* timeouts. NFS continues trying after *n* timeouts if **hard** is set and fails if **soft** is set. Default is **3**.

retry=*n* (**retry value**) The number of minutes that NFS retries a mount operation before giving up. Set to **0** to cause mount to exit immediately if it fails. Default is **2** minutes for foreground mounts (**fg**) and **10,000** minutes for background mounts (**bg**).

timeo=*n* (**timeout value**) The *n* is the number of tenths of a second NFS waits for a response before retransmitting. For NFS over TCP, the default is **600** (60 seconds). See the **nfs** man page for information about the defaults used by NFS over UDP. On a busy network, in case of a slow server, or when the request passes through multiple routers, increasing this value might improve performance. See "Timeouts" on the next page for more information.

## Miscellaneous Options

Following are additional useful options:

lock (nolock) Permits NFS locking. The **nolock** option disables NFS locking and is useful with older servers that do not support NFS locking. Default is **lock**.

nfsvers=*n* The *n* specifies the NFS version number used to contact the NFS server (**2**, **3**, or **4**). The mount fails if the server does not support the specified version. By default, the client negotiates the version number, starting with **4**, followed by **3** and then **2**.

port=*n*  The *n* specifies the number of the port used to connect to the NFS server. A 0 causes NFS to query rpcbind on the server to determine the port number. When this option is not specified, NFS uses port 2049.

rsize=*n*  (**read block size**) The *n* specifies the maximum number of bytes read at one time from an NFS server. Refer to "Improving Performance." Default is negotiated by the client and server and is the largest both can support.

wsize=*n*  (**write block size**) The *n* specifies the maximum number of bytes written at one time to an NFS server. Refer to "Improving Performance." Default is negotiated by the client and server and is the largest both can support.

udp  Uses UDP for an NFS mount. Default is **tcp**.

tcp  Uses TCP for an NFS mount. Default is **tcp**.

# IMPROVING PERFORMANCE

hard/soft  Several parameters can affect the performance of NFS, especially over slow connections such as a line with a lot of traffic or a line controlled by a modem. If you have a slow connection, make sure **hard** (default; page 809) is set so timeouts do not abort program execution.

Block size  One of the easiest ways to improve NFS performance is to increase the block size—that is, the number of bytes NFS transfers at a time. Try not specifying **rsize** and **wsize** (previous) so the client and server set these options to their maximum values. Experiment until you find the optimal block size. Unmount and mount the directory hierarchy each time you change an option. See the *Linux NFS-HOWTO* at nfs.sourceforge.net/nfs-howto for more information on testing different block sizes.

Timeouts  NFS waits the amount of time specified by the **timeo** (timeout; page 809) option for a response to a transmission. If it does not receive a response in this amount of time, NFS sends another transmission. The second transmission uses bandwidth that, over a slow connection, might slow things down even more. You might be able to increase performance by increasing **timeo**.

You can test the speed of a connection with the size of packets you are sending (**rsize** and **wsize**; both above) by using ping with the **–s** (size) option. The **–c** (count) option specifies the number of transmissions ping sends.

```
$ ping -s 4096 -c 4 plum
PING plum (192.168.206.181) 4096(4124) bytes of data.
4104 bytes from plum (192.168.206.181): icmp_seq=1 ttl=64 time=0.460 ms
4104 bytes from plum (192.168.206.181): icmp_seq=2 ttl=64 time=0.319 ms
4104 bytes from plum (192.168.206.181): icmp_seq=3 ttl=64 time=0.372 ms
4104 bytes from plum (192.168.206.181): icmp_seq=4 ttl=64 time=0.347 ms

--- plum ping statistics ---
4 packets transmitted, 4 received, 0% packet loss, time 3000ms
rtt min/avg/max/mdev = 0.319/0.374/0.460/0.056 ms
```

The preceding example uses a packet size of 4096 bytes and shows a fast average packet round-trip time of about one-half of a millisecond. Over a modem line, you can expect times of several seconds. If the connection is dealing with other traffic, the time will be even longer. Run the test during a period of heavy traffic. Try increasing **timeo** to three or four times the average round-trip time (to allow for unusually bad network conditions, such as when the connection is made) and see whether performance improves. Remember that the **timeo** value is given in tenths of a second (100 milliseconds = one-tenth of a second).

## **LPI** /etc/fstab: **MOUNTS DIRECTORY HIERARCHIES AUTOMATICALLY**

The **/etc/fstab** file (page 524) lists directory hierarchies that the system might mount automatically as it comes up. You can use the options discussed in the preceding sections on the command line or in the **fstab** file.

The following line from the **fstab** file on **guava** mounts the **/home/public** directory from **plum** on the **/plum.public** mount point on **guava**:

```
plum:/home/public /plum.public   nfs4    rsize=8192,wsize=8192 0 0
```

A mount point should be an empty, local directory. (Files in a mount point are hidden when a directory hierarchy is mounted on it.) The type of a filesystem mounted using NFS is always **nfs4**, regardless of its type on its local system. You can increase the **rsize** and **wsize** options to improve performance. Refer to "Improving Performance" on page 810.

The next example from **fstab** mounts a filesystem from **dog**:

```
dog:/export       /dog.export    nfs4    timeo=50,hard         0 0
```

Because the local system connects to **dog** over a slow connection, **timeo** is increased to 5 seconds (50-tenths of a second). Refer to "Timeouts" on page 810. In addition, **hard** is set to make sure NFS keeps trying to communicate with the server after a major timeout. Refer to **hard/soft** on page 810.

The final example from **fstab** shows a remote-mounted home directory. Because **dog** is a local server and is connected via a reliable, high-speed connection, **timeo** is decreased and **rsize** and **wsize** are increased substantially:

```
dog:/home         /dog.home      nfs4 timeo=4,rsize=16384,wsize=16384 0 0
```

# SETTING UP AN NFS SERVER

## PREREQUISITES

Install the following packages:

- **nfs-utils** (installed by default)
- **rpcbind** (installed by default; not needed for NFSv4)
- **system-config-nfs** (Fedora; optional)

Check **rpcbind** is running   A new Fedora/RHEL system boots with **rpcbind** installed and running; For NFSv3 only (not NFSv4) **rpcbind** must be running before you can start the **nfs** service. Use the systemctl **status** command to make sure **rpcbind** is running.

```
# systemctl status rpcbind.service
```

Enable and start **nfs**   Run systemctl to cause the **nfs** service to start each time the system enters multiuser mode and then start the **nfs** service. Use the systemctl **status** command to make sure the service is running.

```
# systemctl enable nfs.service
# systemctl start nfs.service
```

After modifying **nfs** configuration files, give the second command again, replacing **start** with **restart** to cause **nfs** to reread those files.

## NOTES

Troubleshooting   See page 819 for a list of error messages and troubleshooting tips.

SELinux   When SELinux is set to use a targeted policy, NFS is protected by SELinux. You can disable this protection if necessary. For more information refer to "Setting the Targeted Policy with system-config-selinux" on page 475.

Firewall   When NFSv4 is using AUTH_SYS authentication, as it does by default, it uses port 2049. When NFS is using rpcbind to assign a port, which NFSv4 does not do by default, it uses port 111. If the NFS server system is running a firewall or is behind a firewall, you must open one or both of these ports. Give the following commands to open the ports each time the system boots (permanently) and on the running system; see page 906 for information on firewall-cmd.

```
# firewall-cmd --add-port=2049/tcp
# firewall-cmd --permanent --add-port=2049/tcp
# firewall-cmd --add-port=2049/udp
# firewall-cmd --permanent --add-port=2049/udp
# firewall-cmd --add-port=111/tcp # not usually needed
# firewall-cmd --permanent --add-port=111/tcp # not usually needed
# firewall-cmd --add-port=111/udp # not usually needed
# firewall-cmd --permanent --add-port=111/udp # not usually needed
```

Security   NFSv3 (and not NFSv4) uses TCP wrappers to control client access to the server. As explained on page 485, you can set up **/etc/hosts.allow** and **/etc/hosts.deny** files to specify which clients can contact **rpc.mountd** on the server and thereby use NFSv3. The name of the daemon to use in these files is **mountd**.

## JUMPSTART II: CONFIGURING AN NFS SERVER USING system-config-nfs (FEDORA)

Open the NFS Server Configuration window (Figure 22-2) by giving the command **system-config-nfs** from an Enter a Command window (ALT-F2) or a terminal emulator. From this window you can generate an **/etc/exports** file, which is almost all there is to setting up an NFS server. If the system is running a firewall, see "Firewall" in the

**Figure 22-2** NFS Server Configuration window

preceding section. The system-config-nfs utility allows you to specify which directory hierarchies you want to share and how they are shared using NFS. Each exported hierarchy is called a *share*.

To add a share, click **Add** on the toolbar. To modify a share, highlight the share and click **Properties** on the toolbar. Clicking **Add** displays the Add NFS Share window; clicking **Properties** displays the Edit NFS Share window. These windows are identical except for their titles.

The Add/Edit NFS Share window has three tabs: Basic, General Options, and User Access. On the Basic tab (Figure 22-3) you can specify the pathname of the root of the shared directory hierarchy, the names or IP addresses of the systems (clients) the hierarchy will be shared with, and whether users from the specified systems will be able to write to the shared files.

**Figure 22-3** Edit NFS Share window

The selections in the other two tabs correspond to options you can specify in the
**/etc/exports** file. Following is a list of the check box descriptions in these tabs and
the option each corresponds to:

General Options tab   Allow connections from ports 1024 and higher: **insecure** (page 816)
Allow insecure file locking: **no_auth_nlm** or **insecure_locks** (page 815)
Disable subtree checking: **no_subtree_check** (page 816)
Sync write operations on request: **sync** (page 816)
Force sync of write operations immediately: **no_wdelay** (page 816)
Hide filesystems beneath: **nohide** (page 816)
Export only if mounted: **mountpoint** (page 816)

User Access tab   Treat remote root user as local root: **no_root_squash** (page 817)
Treat all client users as anonymous users: **all_squash** (page 817)
Local user ID for anonymous users: **anonuid** (page 818)
Local group ID for anonymous users: **anongid** (page 818)

After making the changes you want, click **OK** to close the Add/Edit NFS Share
window and click **OK** again to close the NFS Server Configuration window. There
is no need to restart any daemons.

# MANUALLY EXPORTING A DIRECTORY HIERARCHY

Exporting a directory hierarchy makes the directory hierarchy *available* for mounting
by designated systems via a network. "Exported" does not mean "mounted": When a
directory hierarchy is exported, it is placed in the list of directory hierarchies that can
be mounted by other systems. An exported directory hierarchy might be mounted (or
not) at any given time.

### Exporting symbolic links and device files

tip   When you export a directory hierarchy that contains a symbolic link, make sure the object of the
link is available on the client (remote) system. If the object of the link does not exist on a client
system, you must export and mount it along with the exported link. Otherwise, the link will not
point to the same file it points to on the server.

A device file refers to a Linux kernel interface. When you export a device file, you export that
interface. If the client system does not have the same type of device available, the exported
device will not work. To improve security on a client, you can use mount's **nodev** option
(page 806) to prevent device files on mounted directory hierarchies from being used as devices.

Exported partition   A mounted directory hierarchy whose mount point is within an exported partition
holding a mount   is not exported with the exported partition. You need to explicitly export each
point   mounted directory hierarchy you want exported, even if it resides within an already
exported directory hierarchy. For example, assume two directory hierarchies,
**/opt/apps** and **/opt/apps/oracle**, reside on two partitions. You must export each
directory hierarchy explicitly, even though **oracle** is a subdirectory of **apps**. Most
other subdirectories and files are exported automatically. See also **mountpoint** and
**nohide,** both on page 816.

## /etc/exports: HOLDS A LIST OF EXPORTED DIRECTORY HIERARCHIES

The **/etc/exports** file is the ACL (access control list) for exported directory hierarchies that NFS clients can mount; it is the only file you need to edit to set up an NFS server. The exportfs utility (page 818) reads this file when it updates the files in **/var/lib/nfs** (page 818), which the kernel uses to keep its mount table current. The **exports** file controls the following NFS characteristics:

- Which clients can access the server (see also "Security" on page 805)
- Which directory hierarchies on the server each client can access
- How each client can access each directory hierarchy
- How client usernames are mapped to server usernames
- Various NFS parameters

Each line in the **exports** file has the following format:

*export-point client1(option-list) [client2(option-list) ... ]*

where *export-point* is the absolute pathname of the root directory of the directory hierarchy to be exported. The *client1-n* are the names or IP addresses of one or more clients, separated by SPACEs, that are allowed to mount the *export-point*. The *option-list* is a comma-separated list of options (next) that applies to the preceding *client;* it must not contain any SPACEs. There must not be any SPACE between each client name and the open parenthesis that starts the *option-list*.

You can either use system-config-nfs (page 812) to make changes to **exports** or edit this file manually. The following **exports** file gives the system at 192.168.206.180 read-write access to **/home/public** and **/home/zach**:

```
$ cat /etc/exports
/home/public    192.168.206.180(rw,sync)
/home/zach      192.168.206.180(rw,sync)
```

The specified directories are on the local server. In each case, access is implicitly granted for the directory hierarchy rooted at the exported directory. You can specify IP addresses or hostnames and you can specify more than one client system on a line. By default, directory hierarchies are exported in readonly mode.

### GENERAL OPTIONS

The left column of this section lists default options, followed by nondefault options enclosed in parentheses. Refer to the **exports** man page for more information.

auth_nlm (no_auth_nlm) or secure_locks (insecure_locks)
Setting the **auth_nlm** or **secure_locks** option (these two options are the same) causes the server to require authentication of lock requests. Use **no_auth_nlm** for older clients when you find that only files that anyone can read can be locked. Default is **auth_nlm**.

mountpoint[=*path*]

> Allows a directory to be exported only if it has been mounted. This option prevents a mount point that does not have a directory hierarchy mounted on it from being exported and prevents the underlying mount point from being exported. Also **mp**.

nohide (hide)

> When a server exports two directory hierarchies, one of which is mounted on the other, the **hide** option requires a client to mount both directory hierarchies explicitly to access both. When the second (child) directory hierarchy is not explicitly mounted, its mount point appears as an empty directory and the directory hierarchy is hidden. The **nohide** option causes the underlying second directory hierarchy to appear when it is not explicitly mounted, but this option does not work in all cases. See "Exported partition holding a mount point" on page 814. Default is **nohide**.

ro (rw)

> (**readonly**) The **ro** option permits only read requests on an NFS directory hierarchy. Use **rw** to permit read and write requests. Default is **ro**.

secure (insecure)

> The **secure** option requires NFS requests to originate on a *privileged port* (page 1267) so a program running without **root** privileges cannot mount a directory hierarchy. This option does not guarantee a secure connection. Default is **secure**.

no_subtree_check (subtree_check)

> The **subtree_check** option checks subtrees for valid files. Assume you have an exported directory hierarchy that has its root below the root of the filesystem that holds it (that is, an exported subdirectory of a filesystem). When the NFS server receives a request for a file in that directory hierarchy, it performs a subtree check to confirm the file is in the exported directory hierarchy.
>
> Subtree checking can cause problems with files that are renamed while opened and, when **no_root_squash** is used, files that only a process running with **root** privileges can access. The **no_subtree_check** option disables subtree checking and can improve reliability in some cases.
>
> For example, you might need to disable subtree checking for home directories. Home directories are frequently subtrees (of **/home**), are written to often, and can have files within them frequently renamed. You would probably not need to disable subtree checking for directory hierarchies that contain files that are mostly read, such as **/usr**. Default is **no_subtree_check**.

sec=*mode*

> The *mode* is the type of RPCGSS security to use to access files on this mount point and can be **sys** (AUTH_SYS), **krb5**, **krb5i**, **krb5p**, **lkey**, **lkeyi**, **lkeyp**, **spkm**, **spkmi**, or **spkmp**. Refer to SECURITY CONSIDERATIONS in the **nfs** man page for more information. Default is **sys**.

sync (async)

> (**synchronize**) The **sync** option specifies that the server should reply to requests only after disk changes made by the request are written to disk. The **async** option specifies that the server does not have to wait for information to be written to disk and can improve performance, albeit at the cost of possible data corruption if the server crashes or the connection is interrupted. Default is **sync**.

wdelay (no_wdelay)

> (**write delay**) The **wdelay** option causes the server to delay committing write requests when it anticipates that another, related request will follow, thereby

improving performance by committing multiple write requests within a single operation. The **no_wdelay** option does not delay committing write requests and can improve performance when the server receives multiple, small, unrelated requests. Default is **wdelay**.

### USER ID MAPPING OPTIONS

Each user has a UID number and a primary GID number on the server. The **/etc/passwd** and **/etc/group** files on the server might map these numbers to names. When a user on a client makes a request of an NFS server, the server uses these numbers to identify the user on the client, raising several issues:

- The user might not have the same ID numbers on both systems. As a consequence, the user might have owner access to files of another user and not have owner access to his own files (see "NIS and NFS" [below] for a solution).

- You might not want a user with **root** privileges on the client system to have owner access to **root**-owned files on the server.

- You might not want a remote user to have owner access to some important system files that are not owned by **root** (such as those owned by **bin**).

*Owner access* to a file means the remote user can execute or—worse—modify the file. NFS gives you two ways to deal with these cases:

- You can use the **root_squash** option to map the ID number of the **root** account on a client to the **nfsnobody** user (UID 65534) on the server.

- You can use the **all_squash** option to map all NFS users on the client to **nfsnobody** (UID 65534) on the server.

The **/etc/passwd** file shows that **nfsnobody** has a UID and GID of 65534. Use the **anonuid** and **anongid** options to override these values.

NIS and NFS    When you use NIS (page 769) for user authorization, users automatically have the same UIDs on both systems. If you are using NFS on a large network, it is a good idea to use a directory service such as NIS or LDAP (page 786) for authorization. Without such a service, you must synchronize the **passwd** files on all systems manually.

root_squash (no_root_squash)

The **root_squash** option maps requests from **root** on a client so they appear to come from the UID for **nfsnobody** (UID 65534), a nonprivileged user on the server, or as specified by **anonuid**. This option does not affect other sensitive UIDs such as **bin**. The **no_root_squash** option turns off this mapping so requests from **root** appear to come from **root**. Default is **root_squash**.

no_all_squash (all_squash)

The **no_all_squash** option does not change the mapping of users on clients making requests of the NFS server. The **all_squash** option maps requests from all users—not just **root**—on client systems to appear to come from the UID for **nfsnobody** (UID 65534), a nonprivileged user on the server, or as specified by **anonuid**. This option is useful for controlling access to exported public FTP, news, and other directories. Default is **no_all_squash**.

### Critical files in NFS-mounted directories should be owned by **root**

**security**   Despite the mapping done by the **root_squash** option, a user with **root** privileges on a client system can use su**do** or **su** to assume the identity of any user on the system and then access that user's files on the server. Thus, without resorting to **all_squash**, you can protect only files owned by **root** on an NFS server. Make sure that **root**—and not **bin** or another user—owns and is the only user who can modify or delete critical files within any NFS-mounted directory hierarchy.

Taking this precaution does not completely protect the system against an attacker with **root** privileges, but it can help thwart an attack from a less experienced malicious user.

**anonuid=*un* and**   Set the UID or the GID of the anonymous account to *un* or *gn*, respectively. NFS uses
**anongid=*gn***   these accounts when it does not recognize an incoming UID or GID and when it is instructed to do so by **root_squash** or **all_squash**. Both options default to **nfsnobody** (UID 65534).

## WHERE THE SYSTEM KEEPS NFS MOUNT INFORMATION

A server holds several lists of directory hierarchies it can export. The list that you as a system administrator work with is **/etc/exports**. This section describes the important files and pseudofiles that NFS works with. The following discussion assumes that the server, **plum**, is exporting the **/home/public** and **/home/zach** directory hierarchies.

**/var/lib/nfs/etab**   (export table) On the server, **/var/lib/nfs/etab** holds a list of the directory hierarchies that are exported (can be mounted but are not necessarily mounted at the moment) and the options they are exported with:

```
$ cat /var/lib/nfs/etab
/home/zach 192.168.206.180(rw,sync,wdelay,hide,nocrossmnt,secure,root_s
quash,no_all_squash,no_subtree_check,secure_locks,acl,anonuid=65534,ano
ngid=65534,sec=sys,rw,root_squash,no_all_squash)

/home/public 192.168.206.180(rw,sync,wdelay,hide,nocrossmnt,secure,root
_squash,no_all_squash,no_subtree_check,secure_locks,acl,anonuid=65534,a
nongid=65534,sec=sys,rw,root_squash,no_all_squash)
```

The preceding output shows that 192.168.206.180 can mount **/home/zach** and **/home/public**. The **etab** file is initialized from **/etc/exports** when the system is brought up, read by **mountd** when a client asks to mount a directory hierarchy, and modified by exportfs (page 818) as the list of exported directory hierarchies changes. The **/proc/fs/nfsd/exports** pseudofile holds similar information.

## exportfs: MAINTAINS THE LIST OF EXPORTED DIRECTORY HIERARCHIES

The exportfs utility maintains the **/var/lib/nfs/etab** file (above). When **mountd** is called, it checks this file to see if it is allowed to mount the requested directory hierarchy. Typically exportfs is called with simple options and modifies the **etab** file based on changes in **/etc/exports**. When called with client and directory arguments, it can add to or remove the directory hierarchies specified by those arguments from the list kept in **etab**, without reference to the **exports** file. An exportfs command has the following format:

*exportfs [options] [client:dir ...]*

where **options** is one or more options (next), **client** is the name of the system that **dir** is exported to, and **dir** is the absolute pathname of the directory at the root of the directory hierarchy being exported. Without any arguments, exportfs reports which directory hierarchies are exported to which systems:

```
# exportfs
/home/public   192.168.206.180
/home/zach     192.168.206.180
```

The system executes the following command when it starts the **nfsd** daemon. This command reexports the entries in **/etc/exports** and removes invalid entries from **/var/lib/nfs/etab** so etab is synchronized with **/etc/exports**:

```
# exportfs -r
```

## OPTIONS

–a  (**all**) Exports directory hierarchies specified in **/etc/exports**. This option does not *unexport* entries you have removed from **exports** (that is, it does not remove invalid entries from **/var/lib/nfs/etab**); use **–r** to perform this task.

–f  (**flush**) Removes everything from the kernel's export table.

–i  (**ignore**) Ignores **/etc/exports**; uses what is specified on the command line only.

–o  (**options**) Specifies options. You can specify options following **–o** the same way you do in the **exports** file. For example, exportfs **–i –o ro dog:/home/sam** exports **/home/sam** on the local system to **dog** for readonly access.

–r  (**reexport**) Synchronizes **/var/lib/nfs/etab** with **/etc/exports**, removing invalid entries from **/var/lib/nfs/etab**.

–u  (**unexport**) Makes an exported directory hierarchy no longer exported. If a directory hierarchy is mounted when you unexport it, users see the message **Stale NFS file handle** when they try to access the directory hierarchy from a remote system.

–v  (**verbose**) Provides more information. Displays export options when you use exportfs to display export information.

# TROUBLESHOOTING

This section describes NFS error messages and what you can do to fix the problems they report on. It also suggests some ways to test an NFS server.

## ERROR MESSAGES

Sometimes a client might lose access to files on an NFS server. For example, a network problem or a remote system crash might make these files temporarily unavailable. If you try to access a remote file in these circumstances, you will get an error message, such as **NFS server *xxx* not responding**. When the local system can contact the server again, NFS will display another message, such as **NFS server *xxx* OK**. A stable network and server (or not using NFS) is the best defense against this problem.

The **mount: RPC: Program not registered** message might mean NFS is not running on the server. Start the **nfsd** and **rpcbind** daemons on the server.

The **Stale NFS filehandle** message appears when a file that is opened on a client is removed, renamed, or replaced. Try remounting the directory hierarchy.

## TESTING THE SERVER

From the server, run systemctl. If all is well, the system displays something similar to the following:

```
# systemctl status nfs.service
nfs-server.service - NFS Server
   Loaded: loaded (/usr/lib/systemd/system/nfs-server.service; disabled)
   Active: active (exited) since Tue 2013-06-25 19:22:31 PDT; 26s ago
  Process: 1972 ExecStartPost=/usr/lib/nfs-utils/scripts/nfs-server.postconfig (code=exited,
       status=0/SUCCESS)
  Process: 1955 ExecStart=/usr/sbin/rpc.nfsd $RPCNFSDARGS $RPCNFSDCOUNT (code=exited, status=0/SUCCESS)
  Process: 1947 ExecStartPre=/usr/sbin/exportfs -r (code=exited, status=0/SUCCESS)
  Process: 1940 ExecStartPre=/usr/lib/nfs-utils/scripts/nfs-server.preconfig (code=exited,
       status=0/SUCCESS)

Jun 25 19:22:31 plum systemd[1]: Starting NFS Server...
Jun 25 19:22:31 plum systemd[1]: Started NFS Server.
```

Also check that **mountd** is running:

```
$ ps -ef | grep mountd
root      2110      1  0 18:31 ?        00:00:00 /usr/sbin/rpc.mountd
```

Next, from the server, use rpcinfo to make sure NFS is registered with rpcbind:

```
$ rpcinfo -p localhost | grep nfs
    100003    2   tcp   2049  nfs
    100003    3   tcp   2049  nfs
    100003    4   tcp   2049  nfs
    100227    2   tcp   2049  nfs_acl
    100227    3   tcp   2049  nfs_acl
    100003    2   udp   2049  nfs
    100003    3   udp   2049  nfs
    100003    4   udp   2049  nfs
    100227    2   udp   2049  nfs_acl
    100227    3   udp   2049  nfs_acl
```

Repeat the preceding command from the client, replacing **localhost** with the name of the server. The results should be the same.

If you get a permission denied message, check that

- You have not specified **rw** access in **/etc/exports** when the client has only read permission to the directory hierarchy.

- You have specified the directory hierarchy and client correctly in **/etc/exports**.

- You have not edited **/etc/exports** since you last ran **exportfs –r**.

- You are not trying to export a directory hierarchy and a subdirectory of that hierarchy. From the client you can mount a directory hierarchy and a subdirectory of that hierarchy separately, but you cannot export both from the server. Export the higher-level directory only.

Finally, try mounting directory hierarchies from remote systems and verify access.

# automount: **MOUNTS DIRECTORY HIERARCHIES ON DEMAND**

In a distributed computing environment, when you log in on any system on the network, all your files—including startup scripts—are available. All systems are also commonly able to mount all directory hierarchies on all servers: Whichever system you log in on, your home directory is waiting for you.

As an example, assume **/home/zach** is a remote directory hierarchy that is mounted on demand. When Zach logs in or when you issue the command **ls /home/zach**, autofs goes to work: It looks in the **/etc/auto.misc** map, finds **/home/zach** is a key that says to mount **plum:/home/zach**, and mounts the remote directory hierarchy. Once the directory hierarchy is mounted, ls displays the list of files in that directory.

NIS and LDAP   The automount maps can be stored on NIS and LDAP servers in addition to the local filesystem. Unless you change the **automount** entry in the **/etc/nsswitch.conf** file (page 495), the **automount** daemon will look for maps as files on the local system.

## PREREQUISITES

Install the following package:

- **autofs**

Enable and start   Run systemctl to cause the **autofs** service (**automount** daemon) to start each time the
**autofs**   system enters multiuser mode and then start the **autofs** service. Use the systemctl **status** command to make sure the service is running.

```
# systemctl enable autofs.service
# systemctl start autofs.service
```

After modifying **autofs** configuration files, give the second command again, replacing **start** with **restart** to cause **autofs** to reread those files.

# autofs: AUTOMATICALLY MOUNTED DIRECTORY HIERARCHIES

An **autofs** directory hierarchy is like any other directory hierarchy but remains unmounted until it is needed, at which time the system mounts it automatically (*demand mounting*). The system unmounts an **autofs** directory hierarchy when it is no longer needed—by default, after five minutes of inactivity. Automatically mounted directory hierarchies are an important part of managing a large collection of systems in a consistent way. The **automount** daemon is particularly useful when an installation includes a large number of servers or a large number of directory hierarchies. It also helps to remove server-server dependencies (next).

Server-server dependency    When you boot a system that uses traditional **fstab**-based mounts and an NFS server is down, the system can take a long time to come up as it waits for the server to time out. Similarly, when you have two servers, each mounting directory hierarchies from the other, and both systems are down, both might hang as they are brought up while each tries to mount a directory hierarchy from the other. This situation is called a *server–server dependency*. The **automount** facility gets around these issues by mounting a directory hierarchy from another system only when a process tries to access it.

When a process attempts to access one of the files within an unmounted **autofs** directory hierarchy, the kernel notifies the **automount** daemon, which mounts the directory hierarchy. You must give a command, such as **cd /home/zach**, that accesses the **autofs** mount point (in this case **/home/zach**) to create the demand that causes **automount** to mount the **autofs** directory hierarchy; only then can the system display or use the **autofs** directory hierarchy. Before you issue this cd command, **zach** does not appear in **/home**.

The main file that controls the behavior of **automount** is **/etc/auto.master**. Each line in this file describes a mount point and refers to an **autofs** map that specifies the directory that is to be mounted on the mount point. A simple example follows:

```
$ cat /etc/auto.master
/-      /etc/auto.misc --timeout=60
/plum   /etc/auto.plum
```

Mount point    The **auto.master** file has three columns. The first column names the parent of the **autofs** *mount point*—the location where the **autofs** directory hierarchy is to be mounted. A **/–** in the first column means the mount point is the root directory.

Map files    The second column names the file, called a *map file*, that stores supplemental configuration information. The optional third column holds **autofs** options for the map entry. In the preceding example, the first line sets the timeout (the length of time a directory stays mounted when it is not in use) to 60 seconds; the default timeout is 300 seconds. You can change **autofs** default values in **/etc/sysconfig/autofs**.

Although the map files can have any names, one is traditionally named **auto.misc**. Following are the two map files specified in the preceding **auto.master** file:

```
$ cat /etc/auto.misc
/music          -fstype=ext4        :/dev/mapper/fedora-music
/home/zach      -fstype=nfs4        plum:/home/zach

$ cat /etc/auto.plum
public          -fstype=nfs4 plum:/home/public
```

Relative mount point
: The first column of a map file holds the absolute or relative **autofs** mount point. A pathname other than **/–** appearing in the first column of **auto.master** specifies a relative **autofs** mount point. A relative mount point is appended to the corresponding **autofs** mount point from column 1 of the **auto.master**. In this example, **public** (from **auto.plum**) is appended to **/plum** (from **auto.master**) to form **/plum/public**.

Absolute mount point
: A **/–** appearing in the first column of **auto.master** specifies an absolute **autofs** mount point. In this example, **auto.master** specifies **/–** as the mount point for the **auto.misc** map file, so the mount points specified in this map file are absolute and are specified entirely in an **auto.misc** map file. The **auto.misc** file specifies the **autofs** mount points **/music** and **/home/zach**.

The second column holds **autofs** options, and the third column shows the server and directory hierarchy to be mounted.

The **auto.misc** file specifies a local filesystem (**/dev/mapper/vg_guava-music**; an LV (page 44) and a remote NFS directory (**plum:/home/zach**). You can identify a local directory hierarchy by the absence of a system name before the colon and usually the **ext4** filesystem type. A system name appears before the colon of a remote directory hierarchy filesystem and the filesystem type is always **nfs4**.

Before the new setup can work, you must restart the **autofs** service (page 821). This process creates the directories that hold the mount points if necessary.

The following example starts with the **automount** daemon (**autofs** service) not running. The first **ls** command shows that the **/music** and **/plum** directories are empty. The next command, run with **root** privileges, starts the **autofs** service. Now when you list **/music**, **autofs** mounts it and **ls** displays its contents. The **/plum** listing shows nothing: It is not an **autofs** mount point.

```
$ ls /music /plum
/music:

/plum:

$ su -c 'systemctl start autofs.service'

$ ls /music /plum
/music:
lost+found  mp3  ogg

/plum:
```

When you give an **ls** command and specify the mount point (**/plum/public**), **automount** mounts it and **ls** displays its contents. Once **public** is mounted on **/plum**, **ls /plum** shows the **public** directory is in place.

```
$ ls /plum/public
memos   personal
$ ls /plum
public
```

A df command shows the remotely mounted directory hierarchy and the locally mounted filesystem:

```
$ df -h
Filesystem                    Size  Used Avail Use% Mounted on
...
plum:/home/public             37G   3.8G   32G  11% /plum/public
/dev/mapper/fedora-music       7G   2.4G    4G  34% /music
```

# CHAPTER SUMMARY

NFS allows a server to share selected local directory hierarchies with client systems on a heterogeneous network, thereby reducing storage needs and administrative overhead. NFS defines a client/server relationship in which a server provides directory hierarchies that clients can mount.

On the server, the **/etc/exports** file lists the directory hierarchies that the system exports. Each line in **exports** specifies a directory hierarchy and the client systems that are allowed to mount it, including options for each client (readonly, read-write, and so on). An **exportfs –r** command causes NFS to reread this file.

From a client, a **mount** command mounts an exported NFS directory hierarchy. Alternately, you can put an entry in **/etc/fstab** to have the system automatically mount the directory hierarchy when it mounts the local filesystems.

Automatically mounted directory hierarchies help manage large groups of systems containing many servers and directory hierarchies in a consistent way and can help remove server–server dependencies. The **automount** daemon automatically mounts **autofs** directory hierarchies when they are needed and unmounts them when they are no longer needed.

# EXERCISES

1. What are three reasons to use NFS?

2. Which command would you give to mount on the local system the **/home** directory hierarchy that resides on the file server named **plum**? Assume the mounted directory hierarchy will appear as **/plum.home** on the local system. How would you mount the same directory hierarchy if it resided on the fileserver at 192.168.1.1? How would you unmount **/home**?

3. How would you list the mount points on the remote server named **plum** that the local client named **guava** can mount?

4. Which command line lists the currently mounted NFS directory hierarchies?

5. What does the **/etc/fstab** file do?

6. From a server, how would you allow readonly access to **/opt** for any system in **example.com**?

# ADVANCED EXERCISES

7. When is it a good idea to disable attribute caching?

8. Describe the difference between the **root_squash** and **all_squash** options in **/etc/exports**.

9. Why does the **secure** option in **/etc/exports** not really provide any security?

10. Some diskless workstations use NFS as swap space. Why is this approach useful? What is the downside?

11. NFS maps users on the client to users on the server. Explain why this mapping is a security risk.

12. What does the mount **nosuid** option do? Why would you want to use this option?

# 23

# SAMBA: LINUX AND WINDOWS FILE AND PRINTER SHARING

## OBJECTIVES

After reading this chapter you should be able to:

▶ Describe the use, history, and components of Samba

▶ List capabilities of the Samba server

▶ Use a variety of Samba client tools

▶ Describe Samba authentication methods

▶ Configure a Samba share for local accounts

▶ Troubleshoot Samba connections

827

Samba is a suite of programs that enables UNIX-like operating systems, including Linux, Solaris, FreeBSD, and Mac OS X, to share files and printers with other operating systems, such as OS/2 and Windows, as both a server and a client.

As a server, Samba shares Linux files and printers with Windows systems. As a client, Samba gives Linux users access to files and printers on Windows systems. Its ability to share files across operating systems makes Samba an ideal tool in a heterogeneous computing environment.

Refer to pages 574 and 576 for information about printing to and from a Windows machine using CUPS and Samba.

# INTRODUCTION TO SAMBA

This chapter starts by providing a list of Samba tools followed by some basic information about Samba. The section on Samba clients explains how to use Samba to work with files and printers on a remote system. The next section describes three ways to configure a Samba server. First, a JumpStart section explains how to use the system-config-samba GUI (Fedora only) to set up a Samba server. The next sections cover using a text editor to edit Samba configuration files. The final section, "Troubleshooting" on page 846, offers tips on what to do when Samba does not work properly.

Table 23-1 lists some of the utilities and daemons that make up the Samba suite of programs. See the **samba** man page for a complete list.

**Table 23-1**   Samba utilities and daemons

| Utility or daemon | Function |
|---|---|
| net | This utility has the same syntax as the DOS **net** command and, over time, will eventually replace other Samba utilities such as smbpasswd. |
| **nmbd** | The *NetBIOS* (page 1262) nameserver program, run as a daemon by default. Provides NetBIOS over IP naming services for Samba clients. Also provides browsing support for Samba shares on remote systems. |
| nmblookup | Queries the *NetBIOS* (page 1262) name; see page 847. |
| pdbedit | Maintains the Samba user database (page 831). |
| smbclient | Displays shares on a Samba server such as a Windows machine; uses ftp-like commands (page 833). |
| **smbd** | The Samba program, run as a daemon by default. Provides file and print services for Samba and Windows clients. |
| smbpasswd | Changes Windows NT password hashes on Samba and Windows NT servers (page 831). |
| smbstatus | Displays information about current **smbd** connections. |

**Table 23-1**    Samba utilities and daemons (continued)

| Utility or daemon | Function |
| --- | --- |
| smbtar | Backs up and restores data from Samba servers; similar to tar. |
| smbtree | Displays a hierarchical diagram of available shares (page 832). |
| testparm | Checks the syntax of the **smb.conf** file (page 846). |

## MORE INFORMATION

Web    Samba: www.samba.org (mailing lists, documentation, downloads, and more)

HOWTO    *Unofficial Samba HOWTO*: www.oregontechsupport.com/samba.

## NOTES

Client firewall    The Samba *clients* normally use UDP ports 137 and 138. If the client is running a firewall or is behind a firewall, you need to open these ports. Give the following commands to open the ports each time the system boots (permanently) and on the running system; see page 906 for information on firewall-cmd.

```
# firewall-cmd --add-port=137/udp
# firewall-cmd --permanent --add-port=137/udp
# firewall-cmd --add-port=138/udp
# firewall-cmd --permanent --add-port=138/udp
```

Share    Under Samba and Windows, an exported directory hierarchy is called a *share*.

Mapping a share    The Samba/Windows term *mapping a share* is equivalent to the Linux term *mounting a directory hierarchy*.

Samba    The name *Samba* is derived from *SMB* (page 1273), the protocol that is the native method of file and printer sharing for Windows. Also CIFS (next).

CIFS    *CIFS* (page 1242) is an Internet filesystem protocol based on SMB (previous). The terms SMB and CIFS are used interchangeably.

Printing    Using CUPS to print on a printer connected to a Linux system is easier and can be made more secure than using Samba to print from Windows. For more information refer to "Printing from Windows" on page 574.

Troubleshooting    If the server does not work properly, see "Troubleshooting" on page 846.

## SAMBA USERS, USER MAPS, AND PASSWORDS

Authentication    For a Windows user to access Samba services on a Linux system, the user must provide a Windows username and a Samba password. In some cases, Windows supplies the username and password for you. Alternately, you can log in as the user named **guest** (the Anonymous user; next page). It is also possible to authenticate using other methods. For example, Samba can use *LDAP* (page 1257) or PAM (page 476) instead of the default password file. Refer to the Samba documentation for more information on authentication methods.

**Windows users**   The username supplied by Windows must be the same as a Linux username or must map to a Linux username (see "User maps," below).

**Samba users**   A Samba user must have the same name as a Linux user (the username must appear in **/etc/passwd**). You can use pdbedit (page 831) to display Samba users.

**Samba passwords**   By default, under Fedora/RHEL Samba uses Samba passwords to authenticate users. As installed, no Samba passwords exist. You can use smbpasswd (page 831) to work with Samba passwords. Each Samba user, except for **nobody**, must have a Samba password. See the next page for more information.

**Linux passwords**   By default, Linux passwords are different from Samba passwords.

**No password**   By default, a Windows user logging in without a password logs in as the Samba/Linux user **nobody** (the Anonymous user); you do not have to add this user as a Samba user. You need to add users and passwords for all other users who want to access shares on the Samba server

**The user named guest**   When the **guest ok** (page 845) parameter in the **smb.conf** configuration file (page 839) is set to YES and **guest account** (page 842) is set to **nobody** (default), Samba gives a Windows user logging in as **guest** the privileges of the Linux user named **nobody**. This user does not need to supply a password. The Samba user named **nobody** does not need to exist, but the user named **nobody** must appear in the **/etc/passwd** file. This user is referred to as the Anonymous user.

**User maps**   You can create a file, called a *user map*, that maps Windows usernames to Linux usernames. The **username map** (page 843) parameter in the **smb.conf** configuration file (page 839) specifies the location of this file. The default Samba configuration does not specify a user map. See page 838 for a sample **username map** parameter.

A user map can map Windows usernames to Linux usernames and/or map multiple Windows usernames to a single Linux username to facilitate file sharing. Each line in a user map file starts with a server (Linux) username, followed by a SPACE, an equal sign, another SPACE, and one or more SPACE-separated client (Windows) usernames. An asterisk (*) on the client side matches any client username. Following is an example file:

```
$ cat /etc/samba/smbusers
# Unix_name = SMB_name1 SMB_name2 ...
root = administrator admin
nobody = guest pcguest smbguest
```

The first entry maps the two Windows usernames (**administrator** and **admin**) to the Linux username **root**. The second entry maps three Windows usernames to the Linux username **nobody**.

Add the following line to the file the **username map** parameter points to, creating the file if necessary, to map the Windows username **sam** to the Linux username **sls**:

```
sls = sam
```

After you add a user to this file, you must give the user a password using smbpasswd (next). When Sam logs in as **sam**, Samba now maps **sam** to **sls** and looks up **sls** in the Samba password database. Assuming Sam provides the correct password, he logs in on the Samba server as **sls**.

# smbpasswd AND pdbedit: WORK WITH SAMBA USERS AND PASSWORDS

Samba passwords   Samba can use Linux passwords or Samba passwords to authenticate users. The **passdb backend** (page 842) parameter in the **smb.conf** (page 839) configuration file controls which type of passwords Samba uses. Setting **passdb backend** to **tdbsam** (default) causes Samba to use Samba passwords. Samba stores the passwords in a Trivial Database (tdb.sourceforge.net). Setting **passdb backend** to **smbpasswd** causes Samba to use Linux passwords that are stored in the text file named **/etc/samba/smbpasswd**. This section discusses how to use smbpasswd to work with Samba passwords and how to use pdbedit to display Samba users.

pdbedit   With the –L option, pdbedit displays a list of Samba users; when you install Samba, no Samba users are defined:

```
# pdbedit -L
#
```

The Samba user named **nobody** does not have to exist for the Windows user named **guest** to log in as the Anonymous user. See "The user named **guest**" in the preceding section for more information.

Adding a Samba user and password   As installed, no users have Samba passwords (there are no Samba users). You can add Samba users and optionally passwords only for users listed in **/etc/passwd**. Working with **root** privileges, use smbpasswd with the –a option to add a Samba user and password for a Linux user (a user listed in **/etc/passwd**):

```
# smbpasswd -a sam
New SMB password:
Retype new SMB password:
Added user sam.
```

The pdbedit utility shows the Samba user you just added, although it does not display password information:

```
# pdbedit -L
sam:1000:Sam the Great
```

Changing your own Samba password   Once a user has a Samba password, he can use smbpasswd without any arguments to change his password. The smbpasswd utility will display a nondescriptive error message if the new password is too simple or if the two passwords you enter do not match.

```
$ smbpasswd
Old SMB password:
New SMB password:
Retype new SMB password:
Password changed for user sam
```

If a user has different usernames on the Linux and Windows systems, you must map the Windows username to a Linux username (see "User maps" on page 830). Except for the Windows user specified by the **guest** account (page 842), make sure all Linux users who will log in using Samba have Samba passwords.

# RUNNING SAMBA CLIENTS

To run a Samba client under Linux you need to install a package and open a couple of ports on the client firewall. No Samba daemon runs on a client. Samba clients run on Linux and Windows. Under Linux you can use smbtree (page 832) to display shares, smbclient (page 833) to connect to shares in a manner similar to ftp, browse shares using Nautilus (page 833), and mount shares (page 834). Under Windows you can browse (page 835) and map (mount; page 835) shares.

## PREREQUISITES

Install the following packages:

- **samba-client** (installed by default)
- **samba-common** (installed by default)

The **samba-client** package has no daemon, and therefore you do not have to run chkconfig or service when you install it.

Firewall    Open the client firewall as explained on page 829.

Usernames and    You might have to set up a user and password on the server. For more information
passwords    refer to "Samba Users, User Maps, and Passwords" on page 829.

## WORKING WITH SHARES FROM LINUX

Samba enables you to view and work with files on a server system from a Linux system (client). This section discusses several ways of accessing Windows files from Linux.

### smbtree: DISPLAYS SHARES

The smbtree utility displays a hierarchical diagram of available shares. Unless you use the –N option, smbtree prompts you for a password; use the –N option or do not enter a password (just press RETURN) if you want to browse shares that are visible to the Anonymous user (browseable). The password allows you to view restricted shares, such as a user's home directory in the [homes] share. Following is sample output from smbtree:

```
$ smbtree -N
MGS
    \\PLUM              Samba Server Version 4.0.6
      \\PLUM\HL-2140-series  Brother HL-2140 series
      \\PLUM\tmp              Temporary directory
      \\PLUM\IPC$             IPC Service (Samba Server Version 4.0.6)
```

In the preceding output, **MGS** is the name of the workgroup and **PLUM** is the name of the Samba server. Workgroup and machine names are always shown in uppercase letters. If smbtree does not display output, set the **workgroup** (page 841) and **wins server** (page 845) parameters in **smb.conf**. Refer to the smbtree man page for more information.

## smbclient: CONNECTS TO SHARES

The smbclient utility functions similarly to ftp (page 713) and connects to a share. However, smbclient uses Linux-style forward slashes (/) as path separators rather than Windows-style backslashes (\). As with smbtree, entering a password allows you to view restricted shares. The **–N** option prevents smbclient from requesting a password. The next example connects to a restricted share on **PLUM**:

```
$ smbclient //plum/sam
Enter sam's password: password RETURN
Domain=[MGS] OS=[Unix] Server=[Samba 4.0.6]
smb: \> ls
  .                        D        0  Thu Jun 27 15:19:19 2013
  ..                       D        0  Fri Jun 21 05:52:24 2013
  .bashrc                  H      124  Mon Mar 11 12:53:01 2013
  .config                 DH        0  Mon Jun 17 13:24:13 2013
  .bash_profile            H      193  Mon Mar 11 12:53:01 2013
...
  .local                  DH        0  Tue Jun 11 19:30:00 2013
  .mozilla                DH        0  Tue Jun  4 19:28:00 2013

        37645 blocks of size 1048576. 31993 blocks available
smb: \>
```

You can use most ftp commands from smbclient. Refer to "Tutorial Session" on page 717 for examples of ftp commands. Alternately, give the command **help** to display a list of commands or **help** followed by a command for information on a specific command:

```
smb: \> help history
HELP history:
        displays the command history
```

## BROWSING SHARES

Browsing shares using smbtree and smbclient is quite awkward compared with the ease of browsing a network from Windows; GNOME provides a more user-friendly alternative. Display a Nautilus File Browser window by entering **nautilus** from a terminal emulator or an Enter a Command window (ALT-F2). Select **Connect to Server** (on the left) to display a Connect to Server window. Enter **smb://** followed by the name or IP address of the server in the text box labeled **Server Address** and click **Connect** to display Windows shares on the server. Or, follow the server name with the name of a user (e.g., **smb://plum/sam**) and click **Connect**. Nautilus displays a window that allows you to enter a domain (workgroup) and password for the user. Enter that information and click **Connect** to display that user's directory.

Nautilus uses virtual filesystem add-ons, which are part of the desktop environment and not part of the native Linux system. As a consequence, only native GNOME applications can open files on remote shares; normal Linux programs cannot. For example, gedit can open files on remote shares; LibreOffice, mplayer, and xedit cannot.

## *LPI*  Mounting Shares

The mount utility (page 520) with a **–t cifs** option mounts a share as if it were a Linux directory hierarchy. See page 1242 for more information on the CIFS protocol. When you mount a share, you can write to the files on the share; you cannot write to files on a share using smbclient.

A mount command that mounts a share has the following syntax (you must run this command with **root** privileges):

>   mount -t cifs *//host/share dir*

where *host* is the name of the system the share is on, *share* is the name of the share you want to mount, and *dir* is the absolute pathname of the Linux directory you are mounting the share on (the mount point).

The following command, when run with **root** privileges, mounts on the **/plum.sam** directory the **sam** share on **plum**:

```
# mount -t cifs //plum/sam /plum.sam -o username=sam
Password for sam@//plum/sam:  ****** RETURN
# ls /plum.sam
Desktop  Documents  Downloads  Music  Pictures  Public ...
```

Omit the **username** argument and provide a blank password to mount shares that are visible to an anonymous user.

Use the **uid, file_mode,** and **dir_mode** mount options with type **cifs** filesystems to establish ownership and permissions of mounted files:

```
# mount -t cifs //plum/sam /plum.sam -o username=sam,uid=sam,file_mode=0644,dir_mode=0755
```

Permissions must be expressed as octal numbers preceded by a zero. For more information refer to the mount.cifs man page.

Credentials file   You can also store the username, password, and optionally the workgroup (domain) in a credentials file. To prevent another user from mounting this share, a credentials file should be owned by **root** and readable and writable only by a user working with **root** privileges (600 permissions). When you specify the credentials file in **fstab** (page 524), the share can be mounted automatically when the system is booted. Following is the credentials file for the share in the preceding example:

```
# cat /etc/plum.sam.credentials
username=sam
password=password
domain=MGS

# ls -l /etc/plum.sam.credentials
-rw-------. 1 root root 40 06-27 17:38 /etc/plum.sam.credentials
```

The following command mounts this share using the credentials file:

```
# mount -t cifs //plum/sam /plum.sam -o credentials=/etc/plum.sam.credentials
```

The following line in **/etc/fstab** would cause the share to be mounted when the system boots:

```
//plum/sam      /plum.sam       cifs    defaults,credentials=/etc/plum.sam.credentials
```

Each share must have its own credentials file unless it uses the same login information as another share, in which case the files can use the same credentials file.

# WORKING WITH SHARES FROM WINDOWS

This section describes how to access Linux (or Windows) directories from a Windows machine. You do not need to set up a Linux client to browse or map Linux shares from a Windows machine.

## BROWSING SHARES

To access a share on a Samba server from Windows, open My Computer or Explorer on the Windows system, and in the text box labeled **Address**, enter \\ followed by the NetBIOS name (or just the hostname if you have not assigned a different NetBIOS name) of the Samba server. Windows then displays the share names of the directories the remote system is sharing. To view the shares on the Linux system named **plum**, for example, enter **\\plum**. From this window, you can view and, if permitted, browse the shares available on the remote system. If you set a share on the server so it is not browseable, you need to enter the path of the share using the format \\*servername*\*sharename* to display the share.

## MAPPING A SHARE

Another way to access a share on a Samba server from a Windows machine is by mapping (mounting) a share. Open My Computer or Explorer on the Windows system and click **Map network drive** at the top of the window or from one of the drop-down lists on the menubar (found on the **Tools** menu on many Windows machines). Windows displays the Map Network Drive window. Select an unused Windows drive letter from the list box labeled **Drive** and enter the Windows path to the share you want to map in the text box labeled **Folder**. (When you use system-config-samba [Fedora only] to create a share, the share has the same name as the name of the directory you are sharing.) The format of the windows path is \\*hostname*\*sharename*. For example, to map **/tmp** on **plum** to Windows drive J, assuming the share is named **tmp**, select **J** in the list box labeled **Drive**, enter **\\plum\tmp** in the text box labeled **Folder**, and click **Finish**. After supplying a username and password, you should be able to access the **/tmp** directory from **plum** as J (**tmp**) on the Windows machine. If you cannot map the drive, refer to "Troubleshooting" on page 846.

# SETTING UP A SAMBA SERVER

This section describes how to install and configure a Samba server using the system-config-samba GUI (Fedora only) and an editor to edit the configuration files.

## PREREQUISITES

Install the following packages:

- **samba**
- **system-config-samba** (optional; Fedora only)
- **samba-common** (installed with **samba**)

Enable and start
smb

Run systemctl to cause the **smb** service (**smbd** daemon) to start each time the system enters multiuser mode and then start the **xxxxxxxx** service. Use the systemctl **status** command to make sure the service is running.

```
# systemctl enable smb.service
# systemctl start smb.service
```

Although it is not usually necessary, after modifying **smb** configuration files, you can give the second command again, replacing **start** with **reload** to cause **smb** to reread those files.

Enable and start
nmb

Run systemctl to cause the **nmb** service (**nmbd** daemon) to start each time the system enters multiuser mode and then start the **nmb** service. Use the systemctl **status** command to make sure the service is running.

```
# systemctl enable nmb.service
# systemctl start nmb.service
```

Although it is not usually necessary, after modifying **nmb** configuration files, you can give the second command again, replacing **start** with **reload** to cause **nmb** to reread those files.

Server firewall

The Samba *server* uses UDP ports 137 and 138 and TCP ports 139 and 445. If the server is running a firewall or is behind a firewall, you need to open these ports. Give the following commands to open the ports each time the system boots (permanently) and on the running system; see page 906 for information on firewall-cmd.

```
# firewall-cmd --add-port=137/udp
# firewall-cmd --permanent --add-port=137/udp
# firewall-cmd --add-port=138/udp
# firewall-cmd --permanent --add-port=138/udp
# firewall-cmd --add-port=139/tcp
# firewall-cmd --permanent --add-port=139/tcp
# firewall-cmd --add-port=445/tcp
# firewall-cmd --permanent --add-port=445/tcp
```

SELinux

When SELinux is set to use a targeted policy, Samba is protected by SELinux. You can use system-config-selinux (page 475) to disable this protection if necessary. If you want to allow users to share their home directories, see "SELinux" on page 840. The **smb.conf** file has extensive notes on setting up SELinux for Samba.

Printers

The default **smb.conf** configuration file shares printers on the Samba server; no configuration is necessary.

**Figure 23-1** Samba Server Configuration window

Home directories  The default **smb.conf** configuration file shares home directories of users on the Samba server; no configuration is necessary.

Configuration  The **/etc/sysconfig/samba** file causes **smbd** and **nmbd** each to start with the **–D** option, causing the **smbd** and **nmbd** processes to run as daemons.

# JumpStart: Configuring a Samba Server Using system-config-samba (Fedora)

The system-config-samba utility, which is not available under RHEL, can set up only basic features of a Samba server. It is, however, the best tool to use if you are not familiar with Samba and you want to set up a simple Samba server quickly. The system-config-samba utility performs three basic functions: configuring the server, configuring users, and setting up shares (directory hierarchies) that are exported to Windows machines.

To display the Samba Server Configuration window (Figure 23-1), enter **system-config-samba** from a terminal emulator or an Enter a Command window (ALT-F2).

Configure the server  Select **menubar: Preferences⇨Server Settings** to display the Server Settings window Basic tab (Figure 23-2). Change the workgroup to the one in use on the Windows

**Figure 23-2** Server Settings window, Basic tab

**Figure 23-3**   Samba Users window

machines. Change the description of the server if you like. Click the **Security** tab and make sure Authentication Mode is set to **User**; you do not need to specify an Authentication Server or a Kerberos Realm. If you are using Windows 98 or later, set Encrypt Passwords to **Yes**. When you specify a username in the Guest Account, anyone logging in on the Samba server as **guest** maps to that user's ID. Click **OK**.

Add or modify
Samba users

Select **menubar: Preferences⇨Samba Users** to display the Samba Users window (Figure 23-3). If the user you want to log in as is not listed in this window, click **Add User**. When you have the proper permissions, the Create New Samba User window displays a combo box labeled **Unix Username** that allows you to select a Linux user; otherwise, your username is displayed as the Unix Username. The Windows Username is the Windows username that you want to map to the specified Linux (UNIX) username. The Samba Password is the password this user or Windows enters to gain access to the Samba server.

If Sam's username is **sam** on both the Linux and Windows systems, you would select **sam** from the Unix Username combo box and enter **sam** in the Windows Username text box. If his username were **sls** under Linux and **sam** under Windows, you would select **sls** from the Unix Username combo box and enter **sam** in the Windows Username text box. Finally you would enter Sam's Windows password in the two Samba Password text boxes. Click **OK** to close the Create New Samba User window, then click **OK** to close the Samba Users window.

User map

If you are mapping a Windows username to a *different* Linux username, you must add the following **username map** (page 843) parameter to the [**global**] section of **/etc/samba/smb.conf** (page 839):

```
username map = /etc/samba/smbusers
```

Without this line in **smb.conf**, Samba will not consult the user map file.

Linux shares

Next you need to add a *share*, which is the directory hierarchy you export from the server (Linux) system to the client (Windows) system. Click the plus sign (**+**) on the toolbar to display the Basic tab of the Create Samba Share window (Figure 23-4). In

**Figure 23-4**   Create Samba Share window, Basic tab

the text box labeled **Folder,** enter the absolute pathname of the directory you want to share (**/tmp** is an easy directory to practice with). Enter a description if you like. It can be useful to enter the Linux hostname and the pathname of the directory you are sharing here. Put a tick in the check box labeled **Writable** if you want to be able to write to the directory from the client machine; putting a tick in the check box labeled **Visible** allows the share to be seen (browsed) from the client machine. Click the Access tab and specify whether you want to limit access to specified users or whether you want to allow anyone to access this share. Click **OK**. Close the Samba Server Configuration window.

You should now be able to access the share from a Windows machine (page 835). There is no need to start or restart the Samba server.

Troubleshooting   If the server does not work properly, see "Troubleshooting" on page 846.

### You do not need to restart Samba when you change **smb.conf**

tip   Samba rereads its configuration files each time a client connects. Unless you change the **security** parameter (page 843), you do not need to restart Samba when you change **smb.conf**.

# smb.conf: MANUALLY CONFIGURING A SAMBA SERVER

The **/etc/samba/smb.conf** file controls most aspects of how Samba works and is divided into sections. Each section begins with a line that holds some text between brackets (**[...]**). The text within the brackets identifies the section. Typical sections are

| | |
|---|---|
| **[global]** | Defines global parameters |
| **[printers]** | Defines printers |
| **[homes]** | Defines shares in user home directories |
| **[*share name*]** | Defines a share (you can have more than one of these sections) |

smb.conf   As installed under Fedora/RHEL, the **smb.conf** sample configuration file contains
comments   extensive comments and commented-out examples. Comment lines start with either a hashmark (**#**) or a semicolon (**;**). The sample file uses hashmarks to begin lines that

are intended to remain as comments. Semicolons begin lines you might want to mimic or use as is by removing the semicolons.

Basic **smb.conf** file   Following is a basic **smb.conf** file. It depends on default values for many parameters. To make the code clearer, important default values are written as comments beginning with a semicolon as they are in the default **smb.conf** file. To make the system more secure, change the default **server string** to eliminate the Samba version number; this value might aid hackers in penetrating the system. The **hosts allow** and **hosts deny** parameters are not required. When included, they prevent systems other than those listed from contacting the Samba server. If you uncomment these lines, replace 192.168.206.180 with the IP address of the system you want to allow to connect to the Samba server. You must open the firewall (page 836) and start the **smb** and **nmb** services (page 836) before a client can contact the server.

```
$ cat /etc/samba/smb.conf
[global]
        workgroup = MGS
        server string = Samba Server Version %v
        log file = /var/log/samba/log.%m
        max log size = 50
;       hosts allow = 127.0.0.1, 192.168.206.180
;       hosts deny = ALL
;       security = user
;       encrypt passwords = YES
;       guest ok = NO
;       guest account = nobody

[homes]
        comment = Home Directories
        read only = NO
        browseable = NO

[tmp]
        comment = Temporary Directory
        path = /tmp
        read only = NO
        guest ok = YES
;       available = YES
;       browseable = YES
```

The **[homes]** share   The sample **smb.conf** file includes the **[homes]** share, which allows users to share their Linux home directories with a Windows machine. The default **smb.conf** file includes the same share. This share causes each user's home directory to be shared with the specified parameters. The pathname of the share is */username*; Sam's share on **plum** would be **/plum/sam**. The default settings, which are used in the file shown above, prevent users other than the owners from browsing or accessing home directories while allowing logged-in owners full access.

SELinux   If the system is running SELinux with a targeted policy and you want to allow users to share their home directories as explained in this section, you must modify the SELinux policy to allow this access. You can use system-config-selinux (page 475) to allow this access: In the Boolean tab, **samba** module, put a tick mark adjacent to **Allow samba to share users home directories.**

Defining a share   The **tmp** share in the preceding **smb.conf** file enables a user on a Windows system to be able to read from and write to the **/tmp** directory on the server. The name of the share under Windows is **tmp;** the path under Linux is **/tmp.** Any Windows user who can log in on Samba, including **guest,** can read from and write to this directory, assuming the user's Linux permissions allow it. To allow a user to log in on Samba, you must run smbpasswd (page 831). The **browseable** parameter, which defaults to **YES,** causes the share to appear as a share on the server. The Linux permissions that apply to a Windows user using Samba are the same permissions that apply to the Linux user that the Windows user logs in as or maps to.

Troubleshooting   Follow the steps in "Prerequisites" on page 836 and add users and passwords as necessary (page 831). From a Windows machine, you should now be able to access the share you just created (page 835). If the server does not work properly, see "Troubleshooting" on page 846.

## PARAMETERS IN THE smbd.conf FILE

The **smb.conf** man page lists all the parameters you can set in **smb.conf.** The following sections identify some of the parameters you might need to change.

### GLOBAL PARAMETERS

interfaces   A SPACE-separated list of networks Samba listens on. Specify as interface names (such as **lo** and **eth0**) or as IP address/net mask pairs (page 483).

Default: all active interfaces except 127.0.0.1

server string   The string the client (Windows) machine displays in various places. Within the string, Samba replaces **%v** with the Samba version number and **%h** with the hostname of the server. To make the system more secure, eliminate the Samba version number; this value might aid hackers in penetrating the system.

Default: Samba %v
Fedora/RHEL: Samba Server Version %v

workgroup   The workgroup the server belongs to. Set to the same workgroup as the Windows clients that use the server. This parameter controls the domain name that Samba uses when **security** (page 843) is set to DOMAIN.

Default: WORKGROUP
Fedora/RHEL: MYGROUP

### SECURITY PARAMETERS

encrypt passwords   YES accepts only encrypted passwords from clients. Windows 98 and Windows NT 4.0 Service Pack 3 and later use encrypted passwords by default. This parameter uses smbpasswd to authenticate passwords unless you set **security** to SERVER or DOMAIN, in which case Samba authenticates using another server.

Default: YES

**guest account**  The username that is assigned to users logging in as **guest** or mapped to **guest**; applicable only when **guest ok** (page 845) is set to YES. This username should be present in **/etc/passwd** but should not be able to log in on the system. Typically **guest account** is assigned a value of **nobody** because the user **nobody** can access only files that any user can access. If you are using the **nobody** account for other purposes on the server system, set this parameter to a name other than **nobody**. See page 830 for more information.

Default: **nobody**

**hosts allow**  Analogous to the **/etc/hosts.allow** file (page 485); specifies hosts that are allowed to connect to the server. Overrides hosts specified in **hosts deny**. A good strategy is to specify ALL in **hosts deny** and to specify the hosts you want to grant access to in this file. Specify hosts in the same manner as in the **hosts.allow** file.

Default: none (all hosts permitted access)

**hosts deny**  Analogous to the **/etc/hosts.deny** file (page 485); specifies hosts that are not allowed to connect to the server. Overridden by hosts specified in **hosts allow**. If you specify ALL in this parameter, remember to include the local system (127.0.0.1) in **hosts allow**. Specify hosts in the same manner as in the **hosts.deny** file.

Default: none (no hosts excluded)

**invalid users**  Lists users who are not allowed to log in using Samba.

Default: none (all users are permitted to log in)

**map to guest**  Defines when a failed login is mapped to the **guest account**. Useful only when security (next page) is not set to SHARE or SERVER.

**Never:** Allows **guest** to log in only when the user explicitly provides **guest** as the username and a blank password.

**Bad User:** Treats any attempt to log in as a user who does not exist as a **guest** login. This parameter is a security risk because it allows a malicious user to retrieve a list of users on the system quickly.

**Bad Password:** Silently logs in as **guest** any user who incorrectly enters her password. This parameter might confuse a user when she mistypes her password and is unknowingly logged in as **guest** because she will suddenly see fewer shares than she is used to seeing.

Default: never

**passdb backend**  Specifies how Samba stores passwords. Set to **ldapsam** for LDAP, **smbpasswd** for Samba, or **tdbsam** for TDB (Trivial Database) password storage. See page 831 for instructions on using smbpasswd to change or add Samba passwords.

Default: **tdbsam**

**passwd chat**  The chat script Samba uses to converse with the program defined by **passwd program** (next). If this script is not followed, Samba does not change the password. Used only when **unix password sync** (page 843) is set to YES.

Default: *new*password* %n\n*new*password* %n\n *changed*

**passwd program**    The program Samba uses to set *Linux* passwords. Samba replaces **%u** with the user's username.

Default: none

**security**    Specifies if and how clients transfer user and password information to the server. Choose one of the following:

**USER:** Causes Samba to require a username and password from Windows users when logging in on the Samba server. With this setting you can use

- **username map** (below) to map Samba usernames to Linux usernames
- **encrypt passwords** (page 841) to encrypt passwords (recommended)
- **guest account** (previous page) to map users to the **guest** account

**SHARE:** Causes Samba not to authenticate clients on a per-user basis. Instead, Samba uses the Windows 9*x* setup, in which each share can have an individual password for either read or full access. This option is not compatible with recent versions of Windows.

**SERVER:** Causes Samba to use another SMB server to validate usernames and passwords. If the remote validation fails, the local Samba server tries to validate usernames and passwords as though **security** were set to USER.

**DOMAIN:** Samba passes an encrypted password to a Windows NT domain controller for validation. The **workgroup** parameter (page 841) must be properly set in **smb.conf** for DOMAIN to work.

**ADS:** Instructs Samba to use an Active Directory server for authentication, allowing a Samba server to participate as a native Active Directory member. (Active Directory is the centralized information system that Windows 2000 and later use. It replaces Windows Domains, which was used by Windows NT and earlier.)

Default: USER

**unix password sync**    YES causes Samba to change a user's Linux password when the associated user changes the encrypted Samba password.

Default: NO

**username map**    Points to a user map file that maps Windows usernames to Linux usernames. See "User maps" on page 830 for more information.

Default: no map

### Logging Parameters

**log file**    The name of the Samba log file. Samba replaces **%m** with the name of the client system, allowing you to generate a separate log file for each client.

Default: none
Fedora/RHEL: **/var/log/samba/log.%m**

**log level**    Sets the log level, with 0 (zero) being off and higher numbers being more verbose.

Default: 0 (off)

max log size   An integer specifying the maximum size of the log file in kilobytes. A 0 (zero) specifies no limit. When a file reaches this size, Samba appends **.old** to the filename and starts a new log, deleting any old log file.

Default: 5000
Fedora/RHEL: 50

### BROWSER PARAMETERS

The *domain master browser* is the system responsible for maintaining the list of machines on a network used when browsing. *SMB* (page 1273) uses weighted elections every 11–15 minutes to determine which machine is the domain master browser.

Whether a Samba server wins this election depends on two parameters:

* Setting **domain master** to YES instructs the Samba server to enter the election.

* The **os level** determines how much weight the Samba server's vote receives. The maximum setting for **os level** is 255, although setting it to 65 should ensure that the Samba server wins. NT Server series domain controllers—including Windows 2000, XP, and 2003—use an **os level** of 32.

domain master   YES causes **nmbd** to attempt to be the domain master browser. If a domain master browser exists, then local master browsers will forward copies of their browse lists to it. If there is no domain master browser, then browse queries might not be able to cross subnet boundaries. A Windows PDC (primary domain controller) will always try to become the domain master and might behave in unexpected ways if it fails. Refer to the preceding discussion for more information.

Default: AUTO

local master   YES causes **nmbd** to enter elections for the local master browser on a subnet. A local master browser stores a cache of the *NetBIOS* (page 1262) names of entities on the local subnet, allowing browsing. Windows machines automatically enter elections; for browsing to work, the network must have at least one Windows machine or one Samba server with **local master** set to YES. It is poor practice to set **local master** to NO. If you do not want a computer to act as a local master, set its **os level** to a lower number, allowing it to be used as the local master if all else fails.

Default: YES

os level   An integer that controls how much Samba advertises itself for browser elections and how likely **nmbd** is to become the local master browser for its workgroup. A higher number increases the chances of the local server becoming the local master browser. Refer to the discussion at the beginning of this section for more information.

Default: 20

preferred master   YES forces **nmbd** to hold an election for local master and enters the local system with a slight advantage. With **domain master** set to YES, this parameter helps ensure the local Samba server becomes the domain master. Setting this parameter to YES on more than one server causes the servers to compete to become master, generating a lot of network traffic and sometimes leading to unpredictable results. A Windows PDC automatically acts as if this parameter is set to YES.

Default: AUTO

### COMMUNICATION PARAMETERS

**dns proxy**   When acting as a *WINS server* (page 1281), YES causes **nmbd** to use DNS if *NetBIOS* (page 1262) resolution fails.

Default: YES

**socket options**   Tunes the network parameters used when exchanging data with a client.

Default: TCP_NODELAY

**wins server**   The IP address of the WINS server **nmbd** should register with.

Default: not enabled

**wins support**   YES specifies **nmbd** is to act as a WINS server.

Default: NO

### SHARE PARAMETERS

Each of the following parameters can appear many times in **smb.conf**, once in each share definition.

**available**   YES specifies the share as active. Set this parameter to NO to disable the share but continue logging requests for it.

Default: YES

**browseable**   Determines whether the share can be browsed, for example, in Windows My Network Places.

Default: YES
Fedora/RHEL: varies

**comment**   A description of the share, shown when browsing the network from Windows.

Default: none
Fedora/RHEL: varies

**guest ok**   Allows a user who logs in as **guest** to access this share.

Default: NO
Fedora/RHEL: varies

**path**   The path of the directory being shared.

Default: none
Fedora/RHEL: various

**read only**   Does not allow write access. Use **writable** to allow read-write access.

Default: YES
Fedora/RHEL: various

# TROUBLESHOOTING

Samba and Windows provide tools that can help troubleshoot a connection. This section discusses these tools and suggests other techniques that can help narrow down the problem when you cannot get Samba to work.

1. Restart the Samba daemons. Normally you do not need to restart these daemons after changing the **smb.conf** file. Make sure **smbd** and **nmbd** are running.

   ```
   # systemctl reload smb
   # systemctl reload nmb
   # systemctl status smb
   ...
   # systemctl status nmb
   ...
   ```

testparm    2. Run testparm to confirm that the **smb.conf** file is syntactically correct:

   ```
   $ testparm
   Load smb config files from /etc/samba/smb.conf
   Processing section "[homes]"
   Processing section "[printers]"
   Processing section "[tmp]"
   Loaded services file OK.
   Server role: ROLE_STANDALONE
   Press enter to see a dump of your service definitions
   ...
   ```

   You can ignore an error message about **rlimit_max**. If you misspell a keyword in **smb.conf**, you get an error such as the following:

   ```
   $ testparm
   Load smb config files from /etc/samba/smb.conf
   Unknown parameter encountered: "workgruop"
   Ignoring unknown parameter "workgruop"
   ...
   ```

Log files    3. Check the log files in **/var/log/samba** (page 843).

ping    4. Use ping (page 305) from both sides of the connection to make sure the network is up.

Firewall    5. Confirm the firewall on the server is not blocking the Samba connection on either the server or the client (page 836). The command **firewall-cmd --list-ports** displays the open ports on the local system.

User    6. Make sure the user who is trying to log in exists as a Samba user. See pdbedit on page 831.

Password    7. Make sure you have set up a password for the Samba user who is trying to log in. See smbpasswd on page 831.

SELinux    8. You might need to modify the SELinux policy. See pages 836 and 840.

hosts allow    9. If you specify a value for **hosts deny,** be sure to specify values for **hosts allow,** including 127.0.0.1 so you can access Samba from the local system. See page 842 for more information.

**net view** 10. From a Windows command prompt, use net view to display a list of shares available from the server (**plum** in this example):

```
C:>net view \\plum
Shared resources at \\plum

Samba Server Version 4.0.6

Share name   Type   Used as   Comment

-----------------------------------------------------------------
sam          Disk             Home Directories
tmp          Disk             Temporary Directory
The command completed successfully.
```

**net use** 11. Try to map (mount) the drive from a Windows command prompt. The following command attempts to mount the share named **sam** on **plum** as drive X:

```
C:>net use x: \\plum\sam
Enter the user name for 'plum': sam
Enter the password for plum:
The command completed successfully.
```

**nmblookup** 12. From the Samba server, use nmblookup (**samba-client** package) to query the **nmbd** server, using the special name **__SAMBA__** for the server's NetBIOS name. The **–d 2** option turns the debugger on at level 2, which generates a moderate amount of output. The **–B** option specifies the server you are querying.

```
$ nmblookup -d 2 -B 127.0.0.1 __SAMBA__
...
querying __SAMBA__ on 127.0.0.1
Got a positive name query response from 127.0.0.1 ( 192.168.206.181 )
192.168.206.181 __SAMBA__<00>
```

The next example uses nmblookup, without setting the debug level, to query the local system for all NetBIOS names.

```
$ nmblookup -B 127.0.0.1 \*
querying * on 127.0.0.1
192.168.206.181 *<00>
```

To query for the master browser from the local server, run nmblookup with the **–A** option followed **localhost** or the name of the server:

```
$ nmblookup -A 127.0.0.1
Looking up status of 127.0.0.1
        PLUM            <00> -          B <ACTIVE>
        PLUM            <03> -          B <ACTIVE>
        PLUM            <20> -          B <ACTIVE>
        MGS             <00> - <GROUP>  B <ACTIVE>
        MGS             <1e> - <GROUP>  B <ACTIVE>

        MAC Address = 00-00-00-00-00-00
```

smbclient  13. From the Samba server, use smbclient (**samba-client** package) with the **–L** option followed by the name of the server to generate a list of shares offered by the server. When you do not enter a password, smbclient displays shares available to the Anonymous user. When you enter a password, it also displays restricted shares including the [**homes**] share for the user.

```
$ smbclient -L localhost
Enter sam's password: RETURN  (do not enter a password)
Anonymous login successful
Domain=[MGS] OS=[Unix] Server=[Samba 4.0.6]

        Sharename       Type       Comment
        ---------       ----       -------
        tmp             Disk       Temporary Directory
        IPC$            IPC        IPC Service (Samba Server Version 4.0.6)
Anonymous login successful
Domain=[MGS] OS=[Unix] Server=[Samba 4.0.6]

        Server                  Comment
        ---------               -------
        PEACH
        PLUM                    Samba Server Version 4.0.6

        Workgroup               Master
        ---------               -------
        MGS                     PEACH
```

# Chapter Summary

Samba is a suite of programs that enables a server to share directory hierarchies and printers with a client. Typically the server is a Linux system and the client is a Windows machine. A directory hierarchy or printer that Samba shares between server and client systems is called a *share*. To access a share on a Linux system, a Windows user must supply a username and password. Usernames must correspond to Linux usernames either directly or as mapped by the file that is pointed to by the **username map** parameter in **smb.conf**, often **/etc/samba/smbusers**. Samba passwords are generated by smbpasswd and kept in a Trivial Database named **tdbsam**. The main Samba configuration file is **/etc/samba/smb.conf**, which you can edit using system-config-samba (Fedora only) or a text editor.

From a Windows machine, you can access a share on a Samba server by opening a directory or Explorer window and, in the location text box near the top of the window, entering \\ followed by the name of the server. In response, Windows displays the shares on the server. You can work with these shares as though they were Windows files.

From a Linux system, you can use any of several Samba tools to access shares. These tools include smbtree (displays shares), smbclient (similar to ftp), and mount with the **–t cifs** option (mounts shares). In addition, you can enter **nautilus** from a terminal emulator or an Enter a Command window (ALT-F2) to browse shares.

# EXERCISES

1. Which two daemons are part of the Samba suite? What does each do?

2. What steps are required for mapping a Windows user to a Linux user?

3. How can a system administrator add a Samba password for a new user?

4. What is the purpose of the [homes] share? Should this share be browseable? Why?

# ADVANCED EXERCISES

5. Describe how Samba's handling of users differs from that of NFS.

6. Which configuration changes would you need to apply to routers if you wanted to allow SMB/CIFS browsing across multiple subnets without configuring master browsers?

7. WINS resolution allows hosts to define their own names. Suggest a way to use Samba to assign names from a centralized list.

# DNS/BIND: TRACKING DOMAIN NAMES AND ADDRESSES

## OBJECTIVES

After reading this chapter you should be able to:

▶ Explain what DNS does, how it is structured, and why it is necessary

▶ Describe the purpose of a resolver, forward and reverse name resolution, and an FQDN

▶ Describe the differences between an iterative query and a recursive query

▶ Use dig to determine the IP address and mail server address for a domain

▶ Describe each of the three types of DNS servers

▶ List the components of the **named.conf** configuration files and explain their purpose

▶ Describe the use and required components of a zone file

▶ Explain the use of several types of resource records

▶ Configure a DNS cache server

▶ Discuss security options within DNS including **allow-transfer** directives, views, chroot jails, and dnssec keys

DNS (Domain Name System) maps domain names to IP addresses, and vice versa. It reduces the need for humans to work with IP addresses, which, with the introduction of IPv6, are complex. The DNS specification defines a secure, general-purpose database that holds Internet host information. It also specifies a protocol that is used to exchange this information. Further, DNS defines library routines that implement the protocol. Finally, DNS provides a means for routing email. Under DNS, *nameservers* work with clients, called *resolvers,* to distribute host information in the form of *resource records* in a timely manner as needed.

This chapter describes BIND (Berkeley Internet Name Domain) version 9, a popular open-source implementation of DNS. Part of Fedora/RHEL, BIND includes the DNS server daemon (**named**), a DNS resolver library, and tools for working with DNS. Although DNS can be used for private networks, this chapter covers DNS as used by the Internet.

# INTRODUCTION TO DNS

You typically use DNS when you display a Web page. For example, to display Red Hat's home page, you enter its name, www.redhat.com, in a browser; the browser then displays the page you want. You never enter or see the IP address for the displayed page. However, without the IP address, the browser could not display the page. DNS works behind the scenes to find the IP address when you enter the name in the browser. The DNS database is

- **Hierarchical,** so it provides quick responses to queries. DNS has a root, branches, and nodes.

- **Distributed,** so it offers fast access to servers. The DNS database is spread across thousands of systems worldwide; each system is referred to as a *DNS server* (or a *domain server* or *nameserver*).

- **Replicated,** to enhance reliability. Because many systems hold the same information, when some systems fail, DNS does not stop functioning.

As implemented, DNS is

- **Secure,** so your browser or email is directed to the correct location.

- **Flexible,** so it can adapt to new names, deleted names, and names whose information changes.

- **Fast,** so Internet connections are not delayed by slow DNS lookups.

History   The mapping that DNS does was originally handled statically in a **/etc/hosts** file (page 507) on each system on a network. Small LANs still make use of this file. As networks—specifically the Internet—grew, a dynamic mapping system was required. DNS was specified in 1983 and BIND became part of BSD in 1985. Today BIND is by far the most popular implementation of DNS.

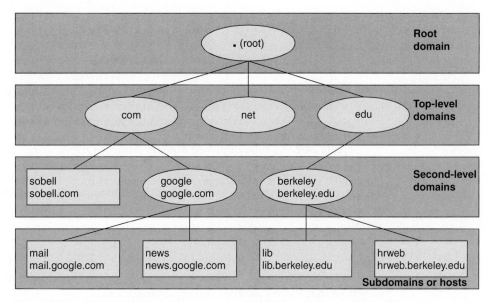

**Figure 24-1**   The DNS domain structure (FQDNs are shown below hostnames.)

Security   Historically BIND has not been very secure. Recently, however, developers have focused on improving the security of BIND. You might want to run BIND inside a chroot jail (page 883) or under SELinux (page 472) and use transaction signatures (TSIG, page 881) to improve security.

host and dig   The host and dig utilities (page 307) query DNS servers. When called without any options, the host utility is simpler, is easier to use, and returns less information than dig. The −v option causes host to display full RFC-format output. This chapter uses both tools to explore DNS.

## NODES, DOMAINS, AND SUBDOMAINS

Node   Each node in the hierarchical DNS database is called a *domain* and is labeled with a (domain) name. As with the Linux file structure, the node at the top of the DNS hierarchy is called the *root node* or *root domain*. While the Linux file structure separates the nodes (directory and ordinary files) with slashes (/) and labels the root node (directory) with a slash, the DNS structure uses periods in place of the file structure's slashes (Figure 24-1).

You read an absolute pathname in a Linux filesystem from left to right: It starts with the root directory (represented by /) at the left and, as you read to the right, describes the path to the file being identified (for example, **/var/spool/cups**). Unlike a Linux pathname, you read a DNS domain name from right to left: It starts with the root domain at the right (represented by a period [.]) and, as you read to the left, works its way down through the top-level and second-level domains to a subdomain or host. Frequently the name of the root domain (the period at the right) is omitted from a domain name.

**Figure 24-2**   A fully qualified domain name (FQDN)

Domain   The term *domain* refers both to a single node in the DNS domain structure and to a catenated, period-separated list (path) of domain names that describes the location of a domain.

FQDN   A fully qualified domain name (FQDN) is the DNS equivalent of a filesystem's absolute pathname: It is a pointer that positively locates a domain on the Internet. Just as you (and Linux) can identify an absolute pathname by its leading slash (/) that represents the root directory, so an FQDN can be identified by its trailing period (.) that names the root domain (Figure 24-2).

*LPI*  Resolver   The resolver comprises the routines that turn an unqualified domain name into an FQDN that is passed to DNS to be mapped to an IP address. The resolver can append several domains, one at a time, to an unqualified domain name, producing several FQDNs that it then passes, one at a time, to DNS. For each FQDN, DNS reports success (it found the FQDN and is returning the corresponding IP address) or failure (the FQDN does not exist).

The resolver always appends the root domain (.) to an unqualified domain name first, thereby allowing you to type **www.sobell.com** instead of **www.sobell.com.** (including the trailing period) in a browser. You can specify other domains for the resolver to try if the root domain fails. Put the domain names, in the order you want them tried, after the **search** keyword in **/etc/resolv.conf** (page 510). For example, if your search domains include **sobell.com.**, then the domains **wiki** and **wiki.sobell.com.** will resolve to the same address.

Subdomains   Each node in the domain hierarchy is a domain. Each domain that has a parent (that is, every domain except the root domain) is also a subdomain, regardless of whether it has children. All subdomains *can* resolve to hosts—even those with children. For example, the **sobell.com.** domain resolves to the host that serves the Sobell Web site, without preventing its children—domains such as **wiki.sobell.com**—from resolving. The leftmost part of an FQDN is often called the *hostname*.

Hostnames   In the past, hostnames could contain only characters from the set a–z, A–Z, 0–9, and –. As of March 2004, however, hostnames can include various accents, umlauts, and so on (www.switch.ch/id/idn). DNS considers uppercase and lowercase letters to be the same (it is not case sensitive), so www.sobell.com is the same as WWW.sObEll.coM.

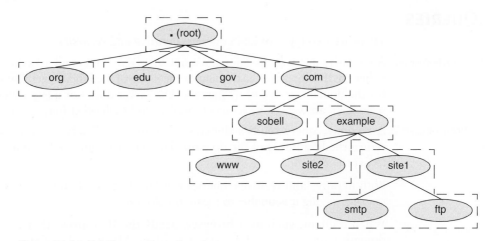

**Figure 24-3** DNS structure showing zones

# ZONES

For administrative purposes, domains are grouped into zones that extend downward from a domain (Figure 24-3). A single DNS server is responsible for (holds the information required to resolve) all domains within a zone. The DNS server for a zone also holds pointers to DNS servers that are responsible for the zones immediately below the zone it is responsible for. Information about zones originates in zone files, one zone per file.

Root domain   The highest zone—the one containing the root domain—does not contain any hosts. Instead, this domain delegates to the DNS servers for the top-level domains (Figure 24-1, page 853).

Authority   Each zone has at least one authoritative DNS server. This server holds all information about the zone. A DNS query returns information about a domain and specifies which DNS server is authoritative for that domain.

DNS employs a hierarchical structure to keep track of names and authority. At the top or root of the structure is the root domain, which employs 13 authoritative nameservers. These are the only servers that are authoritative for the root and top-level domains.

Delegation of   When referring to DNS, the term *delegation* means *delegation of authority*. ICANN
authority   (Internet Corporation for Assigned Names and Numbers, www.icann.org) delegates authority to the root and top-level domains. In other words, ICANN says which servers are authoritative for these domains. Authority is delegated to each domain below the top-level domains by the authoritative server at the next-higher-level domain. ICANN is not authoritative for most second-level domains. For example, Sobell Associates is authoritative for the sobell.com domain. This scheme of delegating authority allows for local control over segments of the DNS database while making all segments available to the public.

# QUERIES

There are two types of DNS queries: *iterative* and *recursive*.[1]

Iterative queries   An iterative query sends a domain name to a DNS server and asks the server to return either the IP address of the domain or the name of the DNS server that is authoritative for the domain or one of its parents: The server does not query other servers when seeking an answer. Nameservers typically send each other iterative queries.

Recursive queries   A recursive query sends a domain name to a DNS server and asks the server to return the IP address of the domain. The server might need to query other servers to get the answer.

Both iterative and recursive queries can fail. In case of failure, the server returns a message saying it is unable to locate the domain.

When a client, such as a browser, needs the IP address that corresponds to a domain name, the client queries a resolver. Most resolvers are quite simple and require a DNS server to do most of the work—that is, they send recursive queries. The resolver communicates with a single DNS server, which can perform multiple iterative queries in response to the resolver's recursive query.

All DNS servers must answer iterative queries. DNS servers can also be set up to answer recursive queries. A DNS server that is not set up to answer recursive queries treats a recursive query as though it is an iterative query.

In Figure 24-4, the resolver on a client system is trying to discover the IP address of the server ftp.site1.example.com. on the network with the DNS layout shown in Figure 24-3 on page 855. The resolver on the client sends a recursive query to its primary DNS server. This server interrogates the root server and one additional server for each zone until it receives an answer, which it returns to the resolver on the client. In practice, the query would not start with the root server because most servers have the location of the authoritative nameserver for the **com.** domain stored in cache (memory).

# SERVERS

There are three main types of DNS servers: primary (master), secondary (slave), and caching-only.

- A *primary master server,* also called a *primary server* or *master server,* is the authoritative server that holds the master copy of zone data. It copies information from the *zone* or *master file,* a local file that the server administrator maintains. For security and efficiency, a primary master server should provide iterative answers only. A primary master server

---

1. A third type of query is not covered in this book: *inverse.* An inverse query provides a domain name given a resource record. Reverse name resolution (page 862), not an inverse query, is used to query for a domain name given an IP address.

**Figure 24-4**   A recursive query that starts several iterative queries to find the answer

that provides recursive answers is more easily subverted by a *DoS attack* (page 1248) than one that provides iterative answers only.

- *Slave servers*, also called *secondary servers*, are authoritative and copy zone information from the primary master server or another slave server. On some systems, when information on the primary master server changes, the primary master server notifies the slave servers. When a slave receives such a message, it uses a process called *zone transfer* to copy the new zone information from the master server to itself.

- *DNS caches*, also called *caching-only servers*, are not authoritative. These servers store answers to previous queries in cache (memory). When a DNS cache receives a query, it answers it from cache if it can. If the DNS cache does not have the answer in cache, it forwards the query to an authoritative server.

### Do not make a primary server also function as a DNS cache

security   It is possible—but for security reasons not recommended—for the same server to be the primary master server (authoritative) for some zones and a DNS cache for others. When the same server acts as both a DNS cache and a master server, if a malicious local user or malfunctioning resolver on the local network floods the DNS cache with more traffic than it can handle (a DoS attack), users might be prevented from accessing the public servers handled by the primary master server. Conversely, if the authoritative server is compromised, the attacker can subvert all traffic leaving the network.

# RESOURCE RECORDS

Resource records store information about nodes (domains) in the DNS database and are kept in zone files (page 874). The zone that a resource record pertains to is defined by the zone file that contains the resource record. The zone is named in the **named.conf** file (page 872) that references the zone file.

A resource record has the following fields:

- **Name**—The domain name or IP address
- **TTL**—Time to live (not in all resource records; see page 1278)
- **Class**—Always IN for Internet (the only class supported by DNS)
- **Type**—Record type (discussed in the next section)
- **Data**—Varies with record type

If the Name field is missing, the resource record inherits the name from the previous resource record in the same file. If the Name field ends in a period (.), it specifies an FQDN; otherwise it is relative to the zone named in **named.conf**.

Cached resource records become out-of-date when the information in the record changes on the authoritative server. The TTL field indicates the maximum amount of time a server might keep a record in cache before checking whether a newer one is available. Typically the TTL is on the order of days. A TTL of 0 (zero) means that the resource record should not be cached.

More than 30 types of resource records exist, ranging from common types, such as address records that store the address of a host, to those that contain geographical information. The following paragraphs describe the types of resource records you are most likely to encounter.

**A**   **IPv4 Address** Maps a domain name to the IPv4 address of a host. There must be at least one address record for each domain; multiple address records can point to the same IP address. The Name field holds the domain name, which is assumed to be in the same zone as the domain. The Data field holds the IP address associated with the name. The following address resource record maps the **ns** domain in the zone to 192.168.0.1:

```
ns      IN      A       192.168.0.1
```

**AAAA**   **IPv6 Address** Maps a domain name to the IPv6 address of a host. The following address resource record maps the **ns** domain in the zone to an IPv6 address:

```
ns      IN      AAAA    2001:630:d0:131:a00:20ff:feb5:ef1e
```

**CNAME**   **Canonical Name** Maps an alias or nickname to a domain name. The Name field holds the alias or nickname; the Data field holds the official or canonical name. CNAME is useful for specifying an easy-to-remember name or multiple names for the same domain. It is also useful when a system changes names or IP addresses. In this case the alias can point to the real name that must resolve to an IP address.

When a query returns a CNAME, a client or DNS tool performs a DNS lookup on the domain name returned with the CNAME. It is acceptable to provide multiple CNAME records all pointing to the name that has the A record. The following resource record maps **ftp** in the zone to www.sam.net.:

```
ftp     IN      CNAME   www.sam.net.
```

MX **Mail Exchange** Specifies a destination for mail addressed to the domain. MX records must always point to A (or AAAA) records. The Name field holds the domain name, which is assumed to be in the zone; the Data field holds the name of a mail server preceded by its priority. Unlike A records, MX records contain a priority number that allows mail delivery agents to fall back to a backup server if the primary server is down. Several mail servers can be ranked in priority order, where the lowest number has the highest priority. DNS selects randomly from among mail servers with the same priority. The following resource records forward mail sent to **speedy** in the zone first to **mail** in the zone and then, if that attempt fails, to **mail.sam.net.**. The value of **speedy** in the Name field on the second line is implicit.

```
speedy IN     MX      10 mail
       IN     MX      20 mail.sam.net.
```

NS **Nameserver** Specifies the name of the system that provides domain service (DNS records) for the domain. The Name field holds the domain name; the Data field holds the name of the DNS server. Each domain must have at least one NS record. DNS servers do not need to reside in the domain, and in fact, it is better if at least one does not. The system name **ns** is frequently used to specify a nameserver, but this name is not required and does not have any significance beyond assisting humans in identifying a nameserver. The following resource record specifies **ns.max.net.** as a nameserver for **peach** in the zone:

```
peach  IN     NS      ns.max.net.
```

PTR **Pointer** Maps an IP address to a domain name and is used for reverse name resolution. The Name field holds the IP address; the Data field holds the domain name. Do not use PTR resource records with aliases. The following resource record maps 3 in a reverse zone (for example, 3 in the 0.168.192.in-addr.arpa zone is 192.168.0.3) to **peach** in the zone:

```
3      IN     PTR     peach
```

For more information refer to "Reverse Name Resolution" on page 862.

SOA **Start of Authority** Designates the start of a zone. Each zone must have exactly one SOA record. An authoritative server maintains the SOA record for the zone it is authoritative for.

All zone files must have one SOA resource record, which must be the first resource record in the file. The Name field holds the name of the domain at the start of the zone. The Data field holds the name of the host the data was created on, the email address of the person responsible for the zone, and the following information, which must be enclosed within parentheses if the record does not fit on one line. If this information is enclosed within parentheses (and it usually is), the opening parenthesis must appear on the first physical line of the SOA record:

**serial** A value in the range 1 to 2,147,483,647. A change in this number indicates the zone data has changed. By convention, this field is set to the string **yyyymmddnn** (year, month, day, change number). Along with the date, the final two digits—that is, the change number—should be incremented each time you change the SOA record.

**refresh** The elapsed time after which the primary master server notifies slave (secondary) servers to refresh the record; the amount of time between updates.

**retry** The time to wait after a refresh fails before trying to refresh again.

**expiry** The elapsed time after which the zone is no longer authoritative and the root servers must be queried. The expiry applies to slave servers only.

**minimum** The *negative caching* (page 1262) TTL, which is the amount of time that a nonexistent domain error (NXDOMAIN) can be held in a slave server's cache. A negative caching TTL is the same as a normal TTL except that it applies to domains that do not exist rather than to domains that do exist.

The $TTL directive (page 875) specifies the default zone TTL (the maximum amount of time data stays in a slave server's cache). Jointly, the default zone TTL and the negative caching TTL encompass all types of replies the server can generate. If you will be adding subdomains or modifying existing domains frequently, set the negative caching TTL to a low number. A short TTL increases traffic to DNS for clients requesting domains that do not exist, but allows new domains to propagate quickly, albeit at the expense of increased traffic.

The following two SOA resource records are equivalent (the parentheses in the first record are optional because the record fits on one physical line):

```
@ IN SOA ns.zach.net. mgs@sobell.com. ( 2013111247 8H 2H 4W 1D )
```

```
@       IN      SOA      ns.zach.net. mgs@sobell.com. (
                                2013111247      ; serial
                                8H              ; refresh
                                2H              ; retry
                                4W              ; expire
                                1D )            ; minimum
```

The second format is more readable because of its layout and the comments. The at symbol (**@**) at the start of the SOA resource record stands for the zone name (also called the *origin*) as specified in the **named.conf** file. Because the **named.conf** file specifies the zone name to be **zach.net**, you could rewrite the first line as follows:

```
zach.net.   IN  SOA      ns.zach.net. mgs@sobell.com. (
```

The **host** utility returns something closer to the first format with each of the times specified in seconds:

```
$ host -t soa zach.net
zach.net. SOA ns.zach.net. mgs\@sobell.com. 03111 28800 7200 2419200 86400
```

**TXT  Text** Associates a character string with a domain. The Name field holds the domain name. The Data field can contain up to 256 characters and must be enclosed within quotation marks. TXT records can contain any arbitrary text value. As well as general information, they can be used for things such as public key distribution. Following is a TXT resource record that specifies a company name:

```
zach.net.   IN  TXT      "Sobell Associates Inc."
```

# DNS Queries and Responses

Queries    A DNS query has three parts:

1. Name—Domain name, FQDN, or, for reverse name resolution, IP address

2. Type—Type of record requested (page 857)

3. Class—Always IN for Internet class

Cache    Most DNS servers store in cache memory the query responses from other DNS servers. When a DNS server receives a query, it first tries to resolve the query from its cache. If that attempt fails, the server might query other servers to get an answer. Because DNS uses cache, when you make a change to a DNS record, the change takes time—sometimes a matter of days—to propagate throughout the DNS hierarchy.

Responses    A DNS message sent in response to a query can hold the following records:

- Header record—Information about this message

- Query record—Repeats the query

- Answer records—Resource records that answer the query

- Authority records—Resource records for servers that have authority for the answers

- Additional records—Additional resource records, such as NS records

**LE+**  dig    The dig and host utilities do not consult **/etc/nsswitch.conf** (page 495) to determine which server to query. The following example uses dig to query a DNS server. The **+all** option causes dig to query for all records.

```
$ dig +all google.com
...
;; QUESTION SECTION:
;google.com.                         IN      A

;; ANSWER SECTION:
google.com.             5            IN      A       74.125.19.147
google.com.             5            IN      A       74.125.19.99
google.com.             5            IN      A       74.125.19.103
google.com.             5            IN      A       74.125.19.104

;; AUTHORITY SECTION:
google.com.             5            IN      NS      ns3.google.com.
google.com.             5            IN      NS      ns4.google.com.
google.com.             5            IN      NS      ns1.google.com.
google.com.             5            IN      NS      ns2.google.com.

;; ADDITIONAL SECTION:
ns1.google.com.         5            IN      A       216.239.32.10
ns2.google.com.         5            IN      A       216.239.34.10
...
```

# REVERSE NAME RESOLUTION

In addition to normal or forward name resolution, DNS provides *reverse name resolution* (also referred to as *inverse mapping* or *reverse mapping*) so you can look up domain names given an IP address. Because resource records in the forward DNS database are indexed hierarchically by domain name, DNS cannot perform an efficient search by IP address on this database.

DNS implements reverse name resolution by means of special domains named **in-addr.arpa** (IPv4) and **ip6.int** (IPv6). Resource records in these domains have Name fields that hold IP addresses; the records are indexed hierarchically by IP address. The Data fields hold the FQDNs that correspond to these IP addresses.

Reverse name resolution can verify that someone is who he says he is or at least is from the domain he says he is from. In general, it allows a server to retrieve and record the domain names of the clients it provides services to. For example, legitimate mail contains the domain of the sender and the IP address of the sending machine. A mail server can verify the stated domain of a sender by checking the domain associated with the IP address. Reverse name resolution can also be used by anonymous FTP servers to verify that a domain specified in an email address used as a password is legitimate.

For example, to determine the domain name that corresponds to the IP address 209.132.183.42 in Figure 24-5, a resolver would query DNS for information about the domain named 42.183.132.209.in-addr.arpa.

**LE+**   dig   The following example uses dig to query DNS for the IP address that corresponds to www.sobell.com, which is 209.157.128.22. The second command line uses the dig utility to query the same IP address, reversed and appended with **.in-addr.arpa** (22.128.157.209.in-addr.arpa) to display a PTR resource record (page 859). The data portion of the resultant resource record is the domain name from the original query: www.sobell.com.

```
$ dig www.sobell.com
...
;; QUESTION SECTION:
;www.sobell.com.                    IN      A

;; ANSWER SECTION:
www.sobell.com.         2274    IN      A       209.157.128.22
...

$ dig 22.128.157.209.in-addr.arpa PTR
...
;; QUESTION SECTION:
;22.128.157.209.in-addr.arpa.    IN      PTR

;; ANSWER SECTION:
22.128.157.209.in-addr.arpa. 2244 IN     PTR     www.sobell.com.
...
```

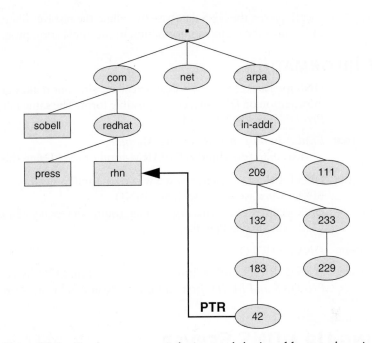

**Figure 24-5**   Reverse name resolution and the **in-addr.arpa** domain

Instead of reformatting the IP address as in the preceding example, you can use the **–x** option to dig to perform a reverse query:

```
$ dig -x 209.157.128.22
...
;; QUESTION SECTION:
;22.128.157.209.in-addr.arpa.    IN      PTR

;; ANSWER SECTION:
22.128.157.209.in-addr.arpa. 2204 IN    PTR     www.sobell.com.
...
```

Alternately, you can just use host:

```
$ host 209.157.128.22
22.128.157.209.in-addr.arpa domain name pointer www.sobell.com.
```

## How DNS Works

Application programs do not issue DNS queries directly but rather use the **gethostbyname()** system call. How the system comes up with the corresponding IP address is transparent to the calling program. The **gethostbyname()** call examines the **hosts** line in **/etc/nsswitch.conf** (page 495) to determine which files it should examine and/or which services it should query and in what order to obtain the IP address corresponding to a domain name. When it needs to query DNS, the local system (i.e., the DNS client) queries the DNS database by calling the resolver library on the local system. This call returns the required information to the application program.

## MORE INFORMATION

DNS for Rocket Scientists is an excellent site that makes good use of links to present information on DNS in a very digestible form. The same information is available in the *Pro DNS and BIND* book.

Local *Bind Administrator Reference Manual:*
**/usr/share/doc/bind∗/Bv9ARM.html** or see "Using this JumpStart" on page 868.

Web DNS for Rocket Scientists: www.zytrax.com/books/dns
BIND: www.isc.org/downloads/BIND
DNS security: www.sans.org/reading_room/whitepapers/dns/security-issues-dns_1069
(downloadable PDF file)

HOWTO *DNS HOWTO*

Book *DNS & BIND*, fifth edition, by Albitz & Liu, O'Reilly & Associates (June 2006)
*Pro DNS and BIND*, first edition, by Ron Aitchison, Apress (August 2005)

# SETTING UP A DNS SERVER

This section explains how to set up the simplest type of DNS server, a DNS cache. See page 885 for information on setting up other types of DNS servers.

## PREREQUISITES

Install the following packages:

- **bind**
- **bind-utils** (installed by default)
- **system-config-bind** (Fedora), optional, page 867)
- **named-chroot** (optional, used to set up BIND to run in a chroot jail, page 883)

### Before you set up a BIND server

tip Before you configure a BIND server, set up a static IP address for the server system. See "Configuring a Static IP Address for a Wired NIC" on page 641 for instructions.

Enable and start Run systemctl to cause the **named** service (**named** daemon) to start each time the sys-
named tem enters multiuser mode and then start the **named** service. Use the systemctl **status** command to make sure the service is running.

```
# systemctl enable named.service
# systemctl start named.service
```

After changing the BIND configuration on an active server, you can use **reload** in place of **start** to reload **named** configuration files without disturbing clients connected to the server. Although it will interrupt clients, **restart** generates better error messages than reload: After giving the command **systemctl restart named**, look in **/var/log/messages** for information about loading zone files, updated serial numbers, and so on.

Enable and start
**named-chroot**

If you want to run **named** in a chroot jail as explained on page 883, run systemctl to cause the **named-chroot** service to start each time the system enters multiuser mode and then start the **named-chroot** service. Use the systemctl **status** command to make sure the service is running.

```
# systemctl enable named-chroot.service
# systemctl start named-chroot.service
```

# NOTES

Terms:
DNS and **named**

The name of the DNS server is **named**. This chapter uses "DNS" and "named" interchangeably.

Firewall

A **named** server normally accepts queries on TCP and UDP port 53. If the server is running a firewall or is behind a firewall, you need to open these ports. Give the following commands to open the ports each time the system boots (permanently) and on the running system; see page 906 for information on firewall-cmd.

```
# firewall-cmd --add-port=53/tcp
# firewall-cmd --permanent --add-port=53/tcp
# firewall-cmd --add-port=53/udp
# firewall-cmd --permanent --add-port=53/udp
```

SELinux

According to the Fedora/RHEL **named** man page, the default Fedora/RHEL SELinux policy for **named** is very secure and prevents known BIND security vulnerabilities from being exploited. This setup has some limitations, however. Refer to the **named** man page for more information.

If the system is running SELinux with a targeted policy and you want to modify the SELinux **named** settings, you must turn on one or more of the SELinux settings under the **Name Service** clause as displayed by system-config-selinux (page 475).

chroot jail

The **named-chroot** package sets up **named** to run in a chroot jail. With this package installed, all files that control BIND are located within this jail.

**named** options

See the comments in the **/etc/sysconfig/named** file for information about **named** options that you can set there. One of the most important of these options sets the value of the **ROOTDIR** variable that controls the location of the chroot jail (page 883) that BIND runs in.

**named.conf**

The Fedora/RHEL **named** daemon obtains configuration information from the file named **/etc/named.conf** (page 875).

Error messages

In some situations **named** generates error messages regarding files it cannot find. These messages generally appear in **/var/log/messages**. To eliminate these messages, you can try creating an empty file with the name specified in the log. For example, if **named** generates the message

```
managed-keys.bind failed: file not found
```

give these commands to create the file and make **named** the owner of the file:

```
# touch /var/named/managed-keys.bind
# chown named:named /var/named/managed-keys.bind
```

Restart **named** and see if it still generates the error. You can safely ignore the **working directory is not writable** error message.

## *LPI*  JUMPSTART I: SETTING UP A DNS CACHE

As explained earlier, a DNS cache is a bridge between a resolver and authoritative DNS servers: It is not authoritative but simply stores the results of its queries in memory. Most ISPs provide a DNS cache for the use of their customers. Setting up a local cache can reduce the traffic between the LAN and the outside world, thereby improving response times. While it is possible to set up a DNS cache on each system on a LAN, setting up a single DNS cache on a LAN prevents multiple systems on the LAN from having to query a remote server for the same information.

After installing BIND (the **bind** package), you have most of a caching-only nameserver ready to run. Refer to "Setting Up a DNS Cache" on page 875 for an explanation of which files this nameserver uses and how it works.

**ifcfg-eth0 and resolv.conf**   Before you start the DNS cache, set up a static IP address for the server system; see page 641 for instructions.

Next, modifty the **/etc/sysconfig/network-scripts/ifcfg-eth0** file, or whichever **ifcfg-\*** file the server uses, to make **localhost** (127.0.0.1) the primary nameserver. To do so, change the current primary nameserver to be the secondary nameserver. This change makes room for the local DNS cache to be the primary nameserver. To make this change, change the **1** to a **2** in the existing line that starts with **DNS1** in the **ifcfg-\*** file. If the file specifies additional nameservers, demote each (change **DNS2** to **DNS3**, etc.) For example, if the **ifcfg-eth0** file has the line **DNS1=192.0.32.10**, change it to **DNS2=192.0.32.10**. Then add the following line to the same file:

```
DNS1=127.0.0.1
```

This line tells the resolver to use the local system (**localhost** or 127.0.0.1) as the primary nameserver. To experiment with using the local system as the only nameserver, comment out other DNS lines in the **ifcfg-\*** file by preceding each with a hashmark (#).

In some cases you might need to comment out the three lines that start with **dnssec** (put a hash mark [#] at the left end of the line) and add a **forwarders** line (page 873) that points to a remote DNS server in the options clause.

The last step is to start or restart the **named** service using systemctl (page 864). Restarting this service overwrites the **/etc/resolv.conf** file (page 510) with the new nameserver information.

Once you have started or restarted **named**, you can see the effect of the local cache by using dig to look up the IP address of a remote system:

```
$ dig www.sobell.com
...
;; QUESTION SECTION:
;www.sobell.com.                        IN      A

;; ANSWER SECTION:
www.sobell.com.          14400   IN      CNAME   sobell.com.
sobell.com.              14400   IN      A       216.38.53.176
...
;; Query time: 84 msec
;; SERVER: 216.38.53.176#53(216.38.53.176)
;; WHEN: Fri Oct 18 13:36:21 2013
;; MSG SIZE  rcvd: 141
```

**Figure 24-6**   The BIND Configuration GUI window

The fourth line from the bottom of the preceding example shows this query took 84 milliseconds (a little less than one-tenth of a second). The third line from the bottom of the same example shows the IP address of the DNS server that dig queried. When you run the same query again, it runs more quickly because the DNS cache has saved the information locally in memory. This time dig shows the time of the query as 1 millisecond and the DNS server as 127.0.0.1:

```
$ dig www.sobell.com
...
;; Query time: 1 msec
;; SERVER: 127.0.0.1#53(127.0.0.1)
;; WHEN: Fri Oct 18 13:36:23 2013
...
```

### If the DNS cache does not improve the query time

tip   If the DNS cache does not improve the query time, you might already be using a DNS cache provided by your ISP. Try specifying a different secondary nameserver in **ifcfg-***. Alternately, you can try using a public DNS server; see the lists of servers at code.google.com/speed/public-dns, www.tech-faq.com/public-dns-servers.html, and www.opennicproject.org/publictier2servers.

## JumpStart II: Setting Up a Domain Using system-config-bind (Fedora)

The BIND Configuration GUI window (Figure 24-6) enables you to set up a DNS server. To display this window, give the command **system-config-bind** from a terminal emulator or an Enter a Command window (ALT-F2).

If **/etc/named.conf** does not exist, system-config-bind displays a dialog box that informs you it is installing a default configuration. Click **OK**.

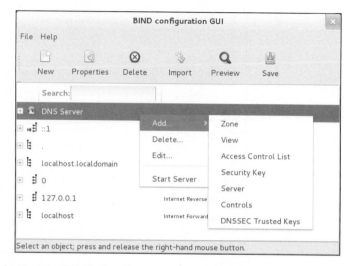

**Figure 24-7**   The BIND Configuration GUI window with a right-click menu

### Using this JumpStart

tip   The system-config-bind utility is a complex tool you might find helpful for setting up BIND. Run this utility and click **Help⇨Manual** on the menubar to display the Fedora/RHEL manual for this utility. Click **Help⇨ISC ARM** to display the BIND 9 Administrator Reference Manual. You might want to experiment with this utility after you have set up one of the servers described at the end of this chapter, as its configuration information might make more sense after you go through the process of manually configuring BIND.

This section explains how to use system-config-bind but does not go into detail about what each of the files and settings does; that information is covered elsewhere in this chapter.

## NOTES

Each zone file that system-config-bind creates has a filename extension of **.db**.

Because the windows displayed by system-config-bind contain a lot of information, you might find it helpful to expand or maximize these windows so that you can view the information more easily.

## USING THE BIND CONFIGURATION GUI WINDOW

Right-click an object (line) in the BIND Configuration GUI window to display a pop-up context menu. This menu always has an Edit selection, which displays a window in which you can edit information pertaining to the object you clicked. You can display the same window by double-clicking the object or by highlighting the object and clicking **Properties** on the toolbar. This pop-up menu also always has an Add selection that displays a submenu with choices appropriate to the object you are working with. Figure 24-7 shows the pop-up menu for the DNS Server object along with the Add submenu.

**Figure 24-8**   The first New Zone window

In the BIND Configuration GUI window, a plus sign (**+**) at the left end of a line indicates that the object holds other objects. Click a plus sign so that it turns into a minus sign (**–**) to expand an entry. Click a minus sign to collapse an entry.

## SETTING UP A DOMAIN SERVER

Highlight DNS Server in the BIND Configuration GUI window and click **New**⇨**Zone** on the toolbar (or right-click and select **Add**⇨**Zone**) to add a new zone (page 855) and its associated nameserver. In response, system-config-bind displays the first New Zone window (Figure 24-8), which allows you to specify information about the zone you are setting up. With the Class combo box displaying **IN Internet**, click **OK** under this box.

Next select the origin type from the combo box under Origin Type. The most common choices are Forward or IPV4 Reverse. Click **OK** under this box. Assuming you selected a forward zone, the Forward Zone Origin text box replaces the origin type information. Enter the domain name of the zone, including a trailing period, in the text box.

Finally select the type of zone you want to set up by clicking the combo box in the Zone Type frame. You can select from master, slave, forward, hint, and other types of zones. Refer to "Servers" on page 856 and **type** on page 874 for information on types of zones.

After you make your selections and click **OK**, system-config-bind displays the second New Zone window (Figure 24-9 on the next page). This window enables you to set up SOA information for the zone. Refer to "SOA" on page 859 for information about the fields in the SOA record, including the serial number and the various times (refresh intervals). In this window, the authoritative (primary) nameserver (page 856) defaults to the local system and the email address of the person responsible for the zone defaults to **root** on the local system. If you enter names that do not end with a period in these text boxes, system-config-bind appends the domain name of the zone to the name you have entered. Change the values in this window as necessary. All zone files that system-config-bind creates have a filename extension of **.db** by default. The default filename for the zone file is the name of the domain you are setting up with an extension of **.db**. Click **OK** to close the window when you are done making changes.

**Figure 24-9**   The second New Zone window

After you add a new zone, the information about this zone appears in the BIND Configuration GUI window (Figure 24-6, page 867). Click **Save** on the toolbar to save the changes you made before you close the window.

To view information about the new zone, you can expand the object that holds the name of the new zone. You can further expand the Zone Authority Information and Name Server objects that appear when you expand the new zone object. Right-click any object to add to or modify the information in the object or to delete the object.

## ADDING RESOURCE RECORDS

You can add any of an extensive list of resource records to a domain. Right-click the object representing the domain you just added to display a pop-up menu. Slide the

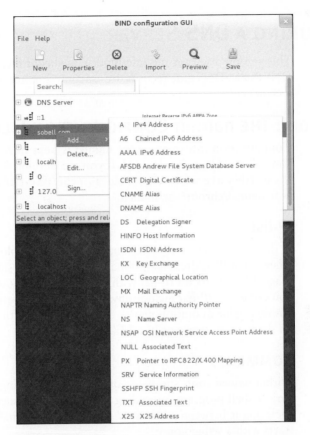

**Figure 24-10**   The domain Add drop-down menu

mouse pointer over **Add** to display the domain Add menu (Figure 24-10). The upper-case letters at the left end of each selection specify the type of resource record (page 857) the selection adds to the domain. Following are some of the choices available on this menu:

- **A**        IPv4 Address record (page 858)
- **CNAME**    Alias record (page 858)
- **MX**       Mail Exchange record (page 859)
- **NS**       Nameserver record (page 859)
- **TXT**      Text record (page 860)

To add a reverse zone (a PTR record [page 859]), add a new zone as before, but this time select **IPv4** (or **IPv6**) **Reverse** as the origin type. For more information refer to "Reverse Name Resolution" on page 862.

Click **Save** when you are done, close the BIND Configuration GUI window, and start or restart the **named** daemon as explained on page 864.

# CONFIGURING A DNS SERVER

This section discusses the **/etc/bind/named.conf** file, zone files, implementation of a DNS cache, DNS glue records, transaction signatures (TSIGs), and running BIND in a chroot jail.

## named.conf: THE named CONFIGURATION FILE

Configuration information for **named** is kept in **/etc/named.conf**. By default, the zone files reside in **/var/named**. If you are running **named** in a chroot jail (page 883), these files are also available as **/var/named/chroot/etc/named.conf** and **/var/named/chroot/var/named**.

### IP-list

In the descriptions in this section, *IP-list* is a semicolon-separated list of IP addresses, where each IP address is optionally followed by a slash and a network mask length (page 483). Prefix an *IP-list* with an exclamation point (!) to negate it. Builtin names you can use in *IP-list* include **any**, **none**, and **localhost**; these names must be enclosed within double quotation marks. The **localhost** builtin name refers to all IP addresses on the local system, not just 127.0.0.1.

### COMMENTS

Within **named.conf**, specify a comment by preceding it with a hashmark (#) as in a Perl or shell program, preceding it with a double slash (//) as in a C++ program, or enclosing it between /* and */ as in a C program. Within a zone file, a comment starts with a semicolon (;).

### INCLUDED FILES

An **include** statement within the **named.conf** file includes the file named as its argument as though its contents appeared inline in the **named.conf** file. The default **named.conf** file includes the **/etc/named.rfc1912.zones** and **/etc/named.root.key** files.

### OPTIONS CLAUSE

Option statements can appear in two sections of **named.conf**: Options and Zone. Option statements within the Options clause apply globally. When an option statement appears in a Zone clause, the option applies to the zone and, within that zone, overrides a corresponding global option.

An Options clause starts with the keyword **options** and continues with a pair of braces surrounding one or more statements. Following is a list of some option statements. Statements that can appear only in an Options clause and statements that cannot appear in a View clause (page 890) are so noted.

**allow-query** {*IP-list*}

Allows queries from *IP-list* only. Without this option, the server responds to all queries.

**allow-recursion** {*IP-list*}

Specifies systems for which this server will perform recursive queries (page 856). For systems not in *IP-list,* the server performs iterative queries only. Without this option, the server performs recursive queries for any system. This statement might be overridden by the **recursion** statement.

**allow-transfer** {*IP-list*}

Specifies systems that are allowed to perform zone transfers from this server. Specify an *IP-list* of "**none**" (include the quotation marks) to prevent zone transfers. For a more secure network, include only trusted systems in *IP-list* because systems on the list can obtain a list of all systems on the network.

**directory** *path*   Specifies the absolute pathname of the directory containing the zone files. Under Fedora/RHEL, this directory is initially **/var/named**. Relative pathnames specified in **named.conf** are relative to this directory. Options clause only; not in View clause.

**forward ONLY|FIRST**

**ONLY** forwards all queries and fails if it does not receive an answer. **FIRST** forwards all queries and, if a query does not receive an answer, attempts to find an answer using additional queries. Valid with the **forwarders** statement only.

**forwarders** {*IP* [*port*] [; ...]}

Specifies IP addresses and optionally port numbers that queries are forwarded to. See the **forward** statement.

**notify YES|NO**   **YES** sends a message to slave servers for the zone when zone information changes. Master servers only. See page 890.

**recursion YES|NO**

**YES** (default) provides recursive queries (page 856) if the client requests. **NO** provides iterative queries only (page 856). An answer is always returned if it appears in the server's cache. This statement overrides **allow-recursion** statements. Options clause only.

## ZONE CLAUSE

A Zone clause defines a zone and can include any of the statements listed for the Options clause except as noted. A Zone clause is introduced by the keyword **zone**, the name of the zone enclosed within double quotation marks, and the class (always IN). The body of the Zone clause consists of a pair of braces surrounding one or more Zone statements. See the listing of **named.rfc1912.zones** on page 877 for examples of Zone clauses. Following is a list of some Zone statements.

allow-update {*IP-list*}

> Specifies systems that are allowed to update this zone dynamically. This statement might be useful when hosting a master DNS server for a domain owned by someone other than the local administrator because it allows a remote user to update the DNS entry without granting the user access to the server.

file *filename*

> Specifies the *zone file*—the file that specifies the characteristics of the zone. The *filename* is relative to the directory specified by the **directory** statement in the Options clause. The **file** statement is mandatory for master and hint zones. Including it for slave zones is a good idea (see **type**).

masters (*IP-list*)

> Specifies systems that a slave zone can use to update zone files. Slave zones only.

type *ztype*

> Specifies the type of zone defined by this clause. Choose *ztype* from the following list:

> - **forward**—Specifies a forward zone, which forwards queries directed to this zone. See the **forward** and/or **forwarders** statements in the Options clause.

> - **hint**—Specifies a hint zone. A hint zone lists root servers that the local server queries when it starts and when it cannot find an answer in its cache.

> - **master**—Specifies the local system as a primary master server (page 856) for this zone.

> - **slave**—Specifies the local system as a slave server (page 856) for this zone.

# ZONE FILES

Zone files define zone characteristics. The name of the zone is typically specified in **named.conf**. In contrast to **named.conf**, zone files use periods at the ends of domain names. See page 878 for example zone files. To improve security, master and hint zone files should be kept in **/var/named**, which is owned by **root** and is not writable by processes running with a UID of **named**. Slave zone files should be kept in **/var/named/slaves**, which is owned by **named** and is writable by processes running with a UID of **named**. This configuration enables SELinux to offer better security. When you set up a chroot jail, the slaves directory is not put in the jail. Both of these setups ensure that master and hint zone files cannot be updated by dynamic DNS updates or by zone transfers. See the **named** man page for more information.

## TIME FORMATS

All times in BIND files are given in seconds, unless they are followed by one of these letters (uppercase or lowercase): S (seconds), M (minutes), H (hours), D (days), or W (weeks). You can combine formats. For example, the time 2h25m30s means 2 hours, 25 minutes, and 30 seconds and is the same as 8,730 seconds.

## DOMAIN QUALIFICATION

An unqualified domain in a zone file is assumed to be in the current zone (the zone defined by the zone file and named by the **named.conf** file that refers to the zone file). The name **zach** in the zone file for **myzone.com**, for example, would be expanded to the FQDN **zach.myzone.com.**. Use an FQDN (include the trailing period) to specify a domain that is not in the current zone. Any name that does not end with a period is regarded as a subdomain of the current zone.

## ZONE NAME

Within a zone file, an at sign (@) is replaced with the zone name specified by the $ORIGIN directive (next). If there is no $ORIGIN directive in the zone file, an at sign is replaced with the zone name specified by the Zone clause in the **named.conf** file that refers to the zone file. For documentation and clarity, it is common practice to put an $ORIGIN directive near the top of all zone files, even if the $ORIGIN matches the zone name in **named.conf**. The zone name is also referred to as the *origin*.

## ZONE FILE DIRECTIVES

The following directives can appear within a zone file. Each directive is identified by a leading dollar sign. The $TTL directive is mandatory and must be the first entry in a zone file.

$TTL    Defines the default time to live for all resource records in the zone. This directive must appear in a zone file before any resource records it applies to. Any resource record can include a TTL value that overrides this value, except for the resource record in the root zone (.).

$ORIGIN    Changes the zone name from that specified in the **named.conf** file. This name, or the zone name if this directive does not appear in the zone file, replaces an @ sign in the Name field of a resource record.

$INCLUDE    Includes a file as though it were part of the zone file. The scope of an $ORIGIN directive within an included file is the included file. That is, an $ORIGIN directive within an included file does not affect the file that holds the $INCLUDE directive.

# SETTING UP A DNS CACHE

You install a DNS cache (also called a resolving, caching nameserver) when you install the **bind** package. The section "JumpStart I: Setting Up a DNS Cache" (page 866) explains how to run this server. This section describes how the files provided by Fedora/RHEL implement this server.

## named.conf: THE named CONFIGURATION FILE

The default **/etc/named.conf** file follows.

```
# cat /etc/named.conf//
// named.conf
//
// Provided by Red Hat bind package to configure the ISC BIND named(8) DNS
// server as a caching only nameserver (as a localhost DNS resolver only).
//
// See /usr/share/doc/bind*/sample/ for example named configuration files.
//

options {
        listen-on port 53 { 127.0.0.1; };
        listen-on-v6 port 53 { ::1; };
        directory       "/var/named";
        dump-file       "/var/named/data/cache_dump.db";
        statistics-file "/var/named/data/named_stats.txt";
        memstatistics-file "/var/named/data/named_mem_stats.txt";
        allow-query     { localhost; };
        recursion yes;

        dnssec-enable yes;
        dnssec-validation yes;
        dnssec-lookaside auto;

        /* Path to ISC DLV key */
        bindkeys-file "/etc/named.iscdlv.key";

        managed-keys-directory "/var/named/dynamic";
};

logging {
        channel default_debug {
                file "data/named.run";
                severity dynamic;
        };
};

zone "." IN {
        type hint;
        file "named.ca";
};

include "/etc/named.rfc1912.zones";
include "/etc/named.root.key";
```

Options clause  The first two lines of the Options clause instruct **named** to listen on port 53 (the default **named** port) on the local system for incoming queries. The **directory** statement specifies the directory that all relative pathnames in this file are relative to. Specifically, the files named in the Zone clauses (of the included **named.rfc1912.zones** file) are in the **/var/named** directory. If you are running **named** in a chroot jail, this directory is located under **/var/named/chroot** (page 883). The file also specifies the locations of the **dump-file** (cache dump), **statistics-file** (statistics file), and **memstatistics-file** (memory statistics file). The **allow-query** statement specifies the IP addresses that are allowed to query the server. This file specifies that only **localhost** can query the server. The **recursion** statement specifies that this server perform recursive queries. The **dnssec** statements implement DNSSEC (DNS Security Extensions), which adds security to DNS.

Logging section  The Logging section causes debugging messages to be sent to **data/named.run**. For more information refer to "Logging" on page 887.

Zone clause   The Zone clause specifies the hint zone, whose name is a period. This zone specifies that when the server starts or when it does not know which server to query, it should look in the **/var/named/named.ca** (**ca** stands for *cache*) file to find the addresses of authoritative servers for the root domain.

Include statement   The **include** statements incorporate **/etc/named.rfc1912.zones** (specifies additional zones; next section) and **/etc/named.root.key** (provides the DNS key for the root zone) as though they were present in this file.

## named.rfc1912.zones: THE ZONE CONFIGURATION FILE

The **/etc/named.rfc1912.zones** file, which the **named.conf** file incorporates with an **include** statement, holds five Zone clauses. The comments in this file are out-of-date.

```
# cat /etc/named.rfc1912.zones
// named.rfc1912.zones:
//
// Provided by Red Hat caching-nameserver package
//
// ISC BIND named zone configuration for zones recommended by
// RFC 1912 section 4.1 : localhost TLDs and address zones
// and http://www.ietf.org/internet-drafts/draft-ietf-dnsop-default-local-zones-02.txt
// (c)2007 R W Franks
//
// See /usr/share/doc/bind*/sample/ for example named configuration files.
//

zone "localhost.localdomain" IN {
        type master;
        file "named.localhost";
        allow-update { none; };
};

zone "localhost" IN {
        type master;
        file "named.localhost";
        allow-update { none; };
};

zone "1.0.0.0.0.0.0.0.0.0.0.0.0.0.0.0.0.0.0.0.0.0.0.0.0.0.0.0.0.0.0.0.ip6.arpa" IN {
        type master;
        file "named.loopback";
        allow-update { none; };
};

zone "1.0.0.127.in-addr.arpa" IN {
        type master;
        file "named.loopback";
        allow-update { none; };
};

zone "0.in-addr.arpa" IN {
        type master;
        file "named.empty";
        allow-update { none; };
};
```

Zone clauses  Each of the five Zone clauses has an **allow-update** statement that specifies dynamic updates of the zone are not allowed. All filenames in the **named.rfc1912.zones** file are relative to **/var/named**, the directory specified by the **directory** statement in the Options section of **named.conf**.

- **localhost.localdomain**—Specifies that **localhost.localdomain** points to 127.0.0.1, preventing the local server from looking upstream for this information.
- **localhost**—Sets up the normal server on the local system.
- **1.0 ... 0.0.ip6.arpa**—Sets up IPv6 reverse name resolution.
- **1.0.0.127.in-addr.arpa**—Sets up IPv4 reverse name resolution.
- **0.in-addr.arpa**—Specifies that IP addresses that start with 0 have their reverse lookup handled by the local server, preventing the local server from looking upstream for this information.

## ZONE FILES

There are four zone files in **/var/named**:

The root zone: **named.ca**  The hint zone file, **named.ca** (**named** cache), is an edited copy of the output of a query of the root domain (**dig +bufsize=1200 +norec @a.root-servers.net**). This information does not change frequently. See ftp://ftp.internic.net/domain/named.cache for more information. The **named.ca** file specifies authoritative servers for the root domain. The DNS server initializes its cache from this file and can determine an authoritative server for any domain from this information.

The root zone is required only for servers that answer recursive queries: If a server responds to recursive queries, it needs to perform a series of iterative queries starting at the root domain. Without the root domain hint file, it would not know where to find the root domain servers.

```
# cat /var/named/named.ca
; <<>> DiG 9.9.2-P1-RedHat-9.9.2-6.P1.fc18 <<>> +bufsize=1200 +norec
@a.root-servers.net
; (2 servers found)
;; global options: +cmd
;; Got answer:
;; ->>HEADER<<- opcode: QUERY, status: NOERROR, id: 25828
;; flags: qr aa; QUERY: 1, ANSWER: 13, AUTHORITY: 0, ADDITIONAL: 23

;; OPT PSEUDOSECTION:
; EDNS: version: 0, flags:; udp: 512
;; QUESTION SECTION:
;.                               IN      NS

;; ANSWER SECTION:
.                       518400  IN      NS      a.root-servers.net.
.                       518400  IN      NS      b.root-servers.net.
.                       518400  IN      NS      d.root-servers.net.
...
```

```
;; ADDITIONAL SECTION:
a.root-servers.net.        3600000 IN    A       198.41.0.4
a.root-servers.net.        3600000 IN    AAAA    2001:503:ba3e::2:30
b.root-servers.net.        3600000 IN    A       192.228.79.201
c.root-servers.net.        3600000 IN    A       192.33.4.12
d.root-servers.net.        3600000 IN    A       199.7.91.13
...
;; Query time: 78 msec
;; SERVER: 198.41.0.4#53(198.41.0.4)
;; WHEN: Mon Jan 28 15:33:31 2013
;; MSG SIZE  rcvd: 699
```

**named.empty**
```
# cat /var/named/named.empty
$TTL 3H
@   IN    SOA     @ rname.invalid. (
                            0          ; serial
                            1D         ; refresh
                            1H         ; retry
                            1W         ; expire
                            3H )       ; minimum

      NS      @
      A       127.0.0.1
      AAAA    ::1
```

**named.localhost** The **named.localhost** zone file defines the **localhost** zone, the normal server on the local system. It starts with a $TTL directive and holds four resource records: SOA, NS, A, and AAAA. The $TTL directive in the following file specifies that the default time to live for the resource records specified in this file is one day (1D):

```
# cat /var/named/named.localhost
$TTL 1D
@   IN    SOA     @ rname.invalid. (
                            0          ; serial
                            1D         ; refresh
                            1H         ; retry
                            1W         ; expire
                            3H )       ; minimum

      NS      @
      A       127.0.0.1
      AAAA    ::1
```

As explained earlier, the @ stands for the origin (the name of the zone), which is **localhost**, as specified in **named.rfc1912.zones**. The last three lines are the NS resource record that specifies the nameserver for the zone as **localhost** (@), the A resource record that specifies the IPv4 address of the host as 127.0.0.1, and the AAAA resource record that specifies the IPv6 address of the host as ::1. Because these three records have blank Name fields, each inherits this value from the preceding resource record—in this case, @.

**named.loopback** The **named.loopback** zone file provides information about the 1.0.0.127.in-addr.arpa reverse lookup zone and the equivalent IPv6 zone. It follows the same pattern as the

**localhost** zone file, with one exception: In addition to the A resource record, this file has a PTR record that provides the name the zone associates with the IP address (**localhost**):

```
# cat /var/named/named.loopback
$TTL    1D
@       IN      SOA     @ rname.invalid. (
                                0               ; serial
                                1D              ; refresh
                                1H              ; retry
                                1W              ; expire
                                3H )            ; minimum
        NS      @
        A       127.0.0.1
        AAAA    ::1
        PTR     localhost.
```

Once **named** is started (page 864), you can use the tests described under "Troubleshooting" on page 884 to make sure the server is working.

# DNS GLUE RECORDS

It is common practice to put the nameserver for a zone inside the zone it serves. For example, you might put the nameserver for the zone starting at site1.example.com (Figure 24-3, page 855) in ns.site1.example.com. When a DNS cache tries to resolve www.site1.example.com, the authoritative server for example.com gives it the NS record pointing to ns.site1.example.com. In an attempt to resolve ns.site1.example.com, the DNS cache again queries the authoritative server for example.com, which points back to ns.site1.example.com. This loop does not allow ns.site1.example.com to be resolved.

The simplest solution to this problem is to prohibit any nameserver from residing inside the zone it points to. Because every zone is a child of the root zone, this solution means every domain would be served by the root server and would not scale at all.

A better solution is to use *glue* records. A glue record is an A record for a nameserver that is returned in addition to the NS record when an NS query is performed. Because the A record provides an IP address for the nameserver, it does not need to be resolved and does not create the problematic loop.

The nameserver setup for google.com illustrates the use of glue records. When you query for NS records for google.com, DNS returns four NS records. In addition, it returns four A records that provide the IP addresses for hosts that the NS records point to:

```
$ dig -t NS google.com
...
;; QUESTION SECTION:
;google.com.                    IN      NS

;; ANSWER SECTION:
```

```
google.com.              5     IN    NS    ns4.google.com.
google.com.              5     IN    NS    ns1.google.com.
google.com.              5     IN    NS    ns2.google.com.
google.com.              5     IN    NS    ns3.google.com.

;; ADDITIONAL SECTION:
ns4.google.com.          5     IN    A     216.239.38.10
ns1.google.com.          5     IN    A     216.239.32.10
ns2.google.com.          5     IN    A     216.239.34.10
ns3.google.com.          5     IN    A     216.239.36.10
...
```

You can create a glue record by providing an A record for the nameserver inside the delegating domain's zone file:

```
site1.example.com                 IN    NS    ns.site1.example.com
ns.site1.example.com              IN    A     1.2.3.4
```

# TSIGs: TRANSACTION SIGNATURES

Interaction between DNS components is based on the query–response model: One part queries another and receives a reply. Traditionally a server determines whether and how to reply to a query based on the client's IP address. *IP spoofing* (page 1256) is relatively easy to carry out, making this situation less than ideal. Recent versions of BIND support transaction signatures (TSIGs), which allow two systems to establish a trust relationship by using a shared secret key.

TSIGs provide an additional layer of authentication between master and slave servers for a zone. When a slave server is located at a different site than the master server (as it should be), a malicious person operating a router between the sites can spoof the IP address of the master server and change the DNS data on the slave (a man-in-the-middle scenario). With TSIGs, this person would need to know the secret key to change the DNS data on the slave.

## CREATING A SECRET KEY

### If dnssec-keygen **hangs**

tip   Running dnssec-keygen can cause the system to hang for a long time if there is not enough entropy. This problem is common on virtual systems. You can create entropy and free the system by moving the mouse, typing on the keyboard, or copying files. Alternately, you can read from **/dev/urandom** (page 504):

```
$ dnssec-keygen -r /dev/urandom -a hmac-md5 -b 512 -n HOST keyname
```

A secret key is an encoded string of up to 512 bits. The dnssec-keygen utility, which is included with BIND, generates this key. The following command, which might take a while to run, generates a 512-bit random key using MD5, a *one-way hash function* (page 1264):

```
$ dnssec-keygen -a hmac-md5 -b 512 -n HOST keyname
Kkeyname.+157+47586
```

In the preceding command, replace *keyname* with a string that is unique yet meaningful. This command creates a key in a file whose name is similar to the string **K***keyname***.+157+47586.private**, where *keyname* is replaced by the name of the key, **+157** indicates the algorithm used, and **+47586** is a hash of the key. If you run the same command again, the hash part will be different.

The key file is not used directly. Use **cat** with an argument of the private filename to display the algorithm and key information you will need in the next step:

```
$ cat Kkeyname.+157+47586.private
Private-key-format: v1.3
Algorithm: 157 (HMAC_MD5)
Key: uNPDouqVwR7fvo/zFyjkqKbQhcTd6Prm...
...
```

## USING THE SHARED SECRET

The next step is to tell the nameservers about the shared secret by inserting the following code in the **/etc/named.conf** file on both servers. This code is a top-level clause in **named.conf**; insert it following the Options clause:

```
key keyname {
    algorithm "hmac-md5";
    secret "uNPDouqVwR7fvo/zFyjkqKbQhcTd6Prm...";
};
```

The *keyname* is the name of the key you created. The **algorithm** is the string that appears within parentheses in the output of **cat**, above. The **secret** is the string that follows **Key:** in the output of **cat**. You must enclose each string within double quotation marks. Be careful when you copy the key; although it is long, you must not break it into multiple lines.

Because key names are unique, you can insert any number of Key clauses into **named.conf**. To keep the key a secret, make sure users other than **root** cannot read it: Either give **named.conf** permissions such that no one except **root** has access to it or put the key in a file that only **root** can read and incorporate it in **named.conf** using an **include** statement.

Once both servers know about the key, use a **server** statement in **named.conf** to tell them when to use it:

```
server 1.2.3.4 {
# 1.2.3.4 is the IP address of the other server using this key
    keys {
        "keyname";
    };
};
```

Each server must have a Server clause, each containing the IP address of the other server. The servers will now communicate with each other only if they first authenticate each other using the secret key.

## Running BIND in a chroot Jail

To increase security, you can run BIND in a chroot jail. See page 487 for information about the security advantages of, and ways to set up, a chroot jail. See also the note about SELinux on page 865 and the **named** man page for information about BIND, SELinux, and chroot jails. When you start the **named-chroot** service (page 865; part of the **named-chroot** package), it sets up BIND to run in a chroot jail, creating a directory named **/var/named/chroot** that takes the place of the root directory (/) for all BIND files.

While **named-chroot** and **named** are running, all files that control BIND are mounted (available) in two places. For example, the **/var/named** directory is also mounted at **/var/named/chroot/var/named**:

```
# ls -li /var/named /var/named/chroot/var/named
2102980 drwxr-x---. 7 root  named 4096 06-28 16:08 chroot
2102072 drwxrwx---. 2 named named 4096 06-28 16:17 data
2102968 drwxrwx---. 2 named named 4096 06-28 16:22 dynamic
2102971 -rw-r-----. 1 root  named 2076 01-28 06:38 named.ca
2102972 -rw-r-----. 1 root  named  152 2009-12-15 named.empty
2102973 -rw-r-----. 1 root  named  152 2007-06-21 named.localhost
2102974 -rw-r-----. 1 root  named  168 2009-12-15 named.loopback
2102975 drwxrwx---. 2 named named 4096 06-05 01:31 slaves

/var/named/chroot/var/named:
2102980 drwxr-x---. 7 root  named 4096 06-28 16:08 chroot
2102072 drwxrwx---. 2 named named 4096 06-28 16:17 data
2102968 drwxrwx---. 2 named named 4096 06-28 16:22 dynamic
2102971 -rw-r-----. 1 root  named 2076 01-28 06:38 named.ca
2102972 -rw-r-----. 1 root  named  152 2009-12-15 named.empty
2102973 -rw-r-----. 1 root  named  152 2007-06-21 named.localhost
2102974 -rw-r-----. 1 root  named  168 2009-12-15 named.loopback
2102975 drwxrwx---. 2 named named 4096 06-05 01:31 slaves
```

Similarly, **/etc/named.conf** is also mounted at **/var/named/chroot/etc/named.conf**:

```
# ls -li /etc/named.conf /var/named/chroot/etc/named.conf
1969014 -rw-r-----. 1 root named 1540 05-03 03:26 /etc/named.conf
1969014 -rw-r-----. 1 root named 1540 05-03 03:26 /var/named/chroot/etc/named.conf
```

When you stop the **named-chroot** service, it unmounts the second copy of the files:

```
# systemctl stop named-chroot.service
# ls -li /etc/named.conf /var/named/chroot/etc/named.conf
ls: cannot access /var/named/chroot/etc/named.conf: No such file or directory
1969014 -rw-r-----. 1 root named 1540 05-03 03:26 /etc/named.conf
```

**optional**  The **named-chroot** service uses the mount **--bind** option to remount part of a directory hierarchy (which can be a single file) in another location. This option allows you to do what you cannot do with hard links: access a directory hierarchy from another location in a filesystem. It also bypasses some of the limitations of symbolic links, including permissions issues. However, it does not create another link to a file—see the preceding listing for **named.conf**: The links count (page 192) to each file is 1. See the mount man page for more information.

# TROUBLESHOOTING

When you start a DNS cache, the **/var/log/messages** file contains lines similar to the following:

```
# cat /var/log/messages
...
17:00:51 guava systemd[1]: Starting Berkeley Internet Name Domain (DNS)...
17:00:52 guava named-checkconf[2003]: zone localhost.localdomain/IN: loaded serial 0
17:00:52 guava named-checkconf[2003]: zone localhost/IN: loaded serial 0
17:00:52 guava named-checkconf[2003]: zone 1.0.0.127.in-addr.arpa/IN: loaded serial 0
17:00:52 guava named-checkconf[2003]: zone 0.in-addr.arpa/IN: loaded serial 0
17:00:52 guava named[2008]: starting BIND 9.9.3-rl.156.01-P1-RedHat-...P1.fc19 -u named
17:00:52 guava named[2008]: adjusted limit on open files from 4096 to 1048576
17:00:52 guava named[2008]: found 1 CPU, using 1 worker thread
17:00:52 guava named[2008]: using 1 UDP listener per interface
17:00:52 guava named[2008]: using up to 4096 sockets
17:00:52 guava named[2008]: loading configuration from '/etc/named.conf'
17:00:52 guava named[2008]: reading built-in trusted keys from '/etc/named.iscdlv.key'
17:00:52 guava named[2008]: using default UDP/IPv4 port range: [1024, 65535]
17:00:52 guava named[2008]: using default UDP/IPv6 port range: [1024, 65535]
17:00:52 guava named[2008]: listening on IPv4 interface lo, 127.0.0.1#53
17:00:52 guava named[2008]: listening on IPv6 interface lo, ::1#53
17:00:52 guava named[2008]: generating session key for dynamic DNS
17:00:52 guava named[2008]: sizing zone task pool based on 6 zones
17:00:52 guava named[2008]: using built-in DLV key for view _default
17:00:52 guava named[2008]: automatic empty zone: 125.100.IN-ADDR.ARPA
17:00:52 guava named[2008]: automatic empty zone: 126.100.IN-ADDR.ARPA
17:00:52 guava named[2008]: automatic empty zone: 255.255.255.255.IN-ADDR.ARPA
17:00:52 guava named[2008]: automatic empty zone: D.F.IP6.ARPA
17:00:52 guava named[2008]: automatic empty zone: 8.E.F.IP6.ARPA
17:00:52 guava named[2008]: automatic empty zone: 9.E.F.IP6.ARPA
17:00:52 guava named[2008]: automatic empty zone: A.E.F.IP6.ARPA
17:00:52 guava named[2008]: automatic empty zone: B.E.F.IP6.ARPA
17:00:52 guava named[2008]: automatic empty zone: 8.B.D.0.1.0.0.2.IP6.ARPA
17:00:52 guava named[2008]: command channel listening on 127.0.0.1#953
17:00:52 guava named[2008]: command channel listening on ::1#953
17:00:52 guava named[2008]: managed-keys-zone: journal is out of date: removing journal
17:00:52 guava named[2008]: managed-keys-zone: loaded serial 3
17:00:52 guava named[2008]: zone 0.in-addr.arpa/IN: loaded serial 0
17:00:52 guava named[2008]: zone 1.0.0.127.in-addr.arpa/IN: loaded serial 0
17:00:52 guava named[2008]: zone localhost.localdomain/IN: loaded serial 0
```

```
17:00:52 guava named[2008]: zone localhost/IN: loaded serial 0
17:00:52 guava named[2008]: all zones loaded
17:00:52 guava systemd[1]: Started Berkeley Internet Name Domain (DNS).
17:00:52 guava named[2008]: running
```

When you create or update DNS information, you can use dig or host to test whether the server works as planned. The most useful part of the output from dig is usually the answer section, which gives the nameserver's reply to your query:

```
$ dig example.com
...
;; ANSWER SECTION:
example.com.              172800  IN      A       192.0.32.10
...
```

The preceding output shows that the **example.com** domain has a single A record that points to 192.0.32.10. The TTL of this record, which tells you how long the record can be held in cache, is 172,800 seconds (two days). You can also use dig to query other record types by using the –t option followed by the type of record you want to query for (–t works with host, too):

```
$ dig -t MX tldp.com
...
;; ANSWER SECTION:
tldp.com.   5       IN      MX      0 mx1.sub5.homie.mail.dreamhost.com.
tldp.com.   5       IN      MX      0 mx2.sub5.homie.mail.dreamhost.com.
...
```

If you query for a domain that does not exist, dig returns the SOA record for the authority section of the highest-level domain in your query that does exist:

```
$ dig domaindoesnotexist.info
...
;; AUTHORITY SECTION:
info.    900  IN  SOA  a0.info.afilias-nst.info. noc.afilias-nst.info. ...
...
```

Because it tells you the last zone that was queried correctly, this information can be useful in tracing faults.

TSIGs  If two servers using TSIGs (page 881) fail to communicate, confirm the system clock is set to the same time on both servers. The TSIG authentication mechanism is dependent on the current time. If the clocks on the two servers are not synchronized, TSIG will fail. Consider setting up *NTP* (page 1264) on the servers to prevent this problem.

# SETTING UP DIFFERENT TYPES OF DNS SERVERS

This section describes how to set up a full-functioned nameserver, a slave server, and a split-horizon server.

# A FULL-FUNCTIONED NAMESERVER

Because the IP addresses used in this example are part of the *private address space* (page 1267), you can copy the example and run the server without affecting global DNS. Also, to prevent contamination of the global DNS, each zone has the **notify** option set to NO. When you build a nameserver that is integrated with the Internet, you will want to use IP addresses that are unique to your installation. You might want to change the settings of the **notify** statements.

**named.conf**  The **named.conf** file in this example limits the IP addresses that **named** answers queries from and sets up logging.

```
$ cat /etc/named.conf
options {
    directory "/var/named";
    allow-query {127.0.0.1; 192.168.0.0/24;};};

zone "." IN {
    type    hint;
    file    "named.ca";};

zone "0.168.192.in-addr.arpa" IN {
    type    master;
    file    "named.local";
    notify  NO;
};

zone "sam.net" IN {
    type    master;
    file    "sam.net";
    notify  NO;
};

logging{
    channel "misc" {
        file "/var/log/bind/misc.log" versions 4 size 4m;
        print-time YES;
        print-severity YES;
        print-category YES;
    };
    channel "query" {
        file "/var/log/bind/query.log" versions 4 size 4m;
        print-time YES;
        print-severity NO;
        print-category NO;
    };
    category default {
        "misc";
    };
    category queries {
        "query";
    };
};
```

The **allow-query** statement in the Options clause specifies the IP addresses of systems the server answers queries from. You must include the local system as 127.0.0.1 if it will be querying the server. The server is authoritative for the zone **sam.net**; the zone file for **sam.net** is **/var/named/sam.net**.

Logging Logging is turned on by the Logging clause. Logging is separate from **named** messages, which go to **syslogd**. The Logging clause in the preceding example opens two logging channels: one that logs information to **/var/log/bind/misc.log** and one that logs information to **/var/log/bind/query.log**. When either of these logs grows to 4 megabytes (**size 4m** in the file statement), it is renamed by appending **.1** to its filename and a new log is started. The numbers at the ends of other, similarly named logs are incremented. Any log that would have a larger number than that specified by the **versions** keyword (**4** in the example) is removed. See logrotate (page 618) for another way to maintain log files.

The print statements determine whether the time, severity, and category of the information are sent to the log; specify each as YES or NO. The category determines what information is logged to the channel. In the previous example, default information is sent to the **misc** channel and queries are sent to the **query** channel. Refer to the **named.conf** man page for more choices.

named.local The origin for the reverse zone file (**named.local**) is 0.168.192.in-addr.arpa (as specified in the Zone clause that refers to this file in **named.**). Following the SOA and NS resource records, the first three PTR resource records equate address 1 in the subnet 0.168.192.in-addr.arpa (192.168.0.1) with the names **gw.sam.net.**, **www.sam.net.**, and **ftp.sam.net.**, respectively. The next three PTR records equate 192.168.0.3 with **mark.sam.net.**, 192.168.0.4 with **mail.sam.net.**, and 192.168.0.6 with **ns.sam.net.**.

```
$ cat named.local
; zone "0.168.192.in-addr.arpa"
;
$TTL    3D
@       IN      SOA     ns.sam.net. mgs@sobell.com. (
                                2005110501      ; serial
                                8H              ; refresh
                                2H              ; retry
                                4W              ; expire
                                1D)             ; minimum
        IN      NS      ns.sam.net.
1       IN      PTR     gw.sam.net.
3       IN      PTR     mark.sam.net.
4       IN      PTR     mail.sam.net.
6       IN      PTR     ns.sam.net.
```

sam.net The zone file for **sam.net** takes advantage of many BIND features and includes TXT (page 860), CNAME (page 858), and MX (page 859) resource records. When you query for resource records, **named** returns the TXT resource record along with the records you requested. The first of the two NS records specifies an unqualified name (**ns**) to which BIND appends the zone name (**sam.net**), yielding an FQDN of

**ns.sam.net**. The second nameserver is specified with an FQDN name that BIND does not alter. The MX records specify mail servers in a similar manner and include a priority number at the start of the Data field, where lower numbers indicate preferred servers.

```
$ cat sam.net
; zone "sam.net"
;
$TTL    3D
@       IN      SOA     ns.sam.net. mgs@sobell.com. (
                                2013110501      ; serial
                                8H              ; refresh
                                2H              ; retry
                                4W              ; expire
                                1D  )           ; minimum

                TXT     "Sobell Associates Inc."
                NS      ns          ; Nameserver address (unqualified)
                NS      ns.max.net.; Nameserver address (qualified)
                MX      10 mail     ; Mail exchange (primary/unqualified)
                MX      20 mail.max.net.; Mail exchange (2nd/qualified)

localhost IN    A       127.0.0.1

www     IN      CNAME   ns
ftp     IN      CNAME   ns

gw      IN      A       192.168.0.1
                TXT     "Router"

ns      IN      A       192.168.0.6
                MX      10 mail
                MX      20 mail.max.net.

mark    IN      A       192.168.0.3
                MX      10 mail
                MX      20 mail.max.net.
                TXT     "MGS"

mail    IN      A       192.168.0.4
                MX      10 mail
                MX      20 mail.max.net.
```

Some resource records have a value in the Name field; those without a name inherit the name from the previous resource record. In a similar manner, the previous resource record might have an inherited name value, and so on. The five resource records following the SOA resource record inherit the @, or zone name, from the SOA resource record. These resource records pertain to the zone as a whole. In the preceding example, the first TXT resource record inherits its name from the SOA resource record; it is the TXT resource record for the **sam.net** zone (give the command **host –t TXT sam.net** to display the TXT resource record).

Following these five resource records are resource records that pertain to a domain within the zone. For example, the MX resource records that follow the A resource record with the Name field set to **mark** are resource records for the **mark.sam.net.** domain.

The A resource record for **localhost** is followed by two CNAME resource records that specify www(.sam.net.) and ftp(.sam.net.) as aliases for the nameserver **ns.sam.net.**. For example, a user connecting to ftp.sam.net will connect to 192.168.0.6. The resource records named **gw**, **ns**, **mark**, and **mail** are resource records for domains within the **sam.net** zone.

Log files    Before restarting **named,** create the directory for the log files and give it permissions and ownership as shown below. If you are running **named** in a chroot jail, create the **bind** directory in **/var/named/chroot/var/log**.

```
# mkdir /var/log/bind
# chmod 744 /var/log/bind
# chown named /var/log/bind
# ls -ld /var/log/bind
drwxr--r--. 2 named root 4096 10-19 14:43 /var/log/bind
```

With the log directory in place, **named.conf** in **/etc** (or in **/var/named/chroot/etc** if you are running **named** in a chroot jail), **named.ca**, **named.local**, and **sam.net** zone files in **/var/named** (or in **/var/named/chroot/var/named** if you are running **named** in a chroot jail), restart **named** and check the log files. The file **/var/log/messages** should show something like the following:

```
# cat /var/log/messages
...
15:11:40 guava named[9824]: starting BIND 9.9.3-rl.156.01-P1-RedHat-...P1.fc19 -u named
...
15:11:40 guava named[9824]: loading configuration from '/etc/named.conf'
15:11:40 guava named[9824]: using default UDP/IPv4 port range: [1024, 65535]
15:11:40 guava named[9824]: using default UDP/IPv6 port range: [1024, 65535]
15:11:40 guava named[9824]: listening on IPv4 interface lo, 127.0.0.1#53
...
15:11:40 guava named[9824]: command channel listening on 127.0.0.1#953
15:11:40 guava named[9824]: command channel listening on ::1#953
15:11:40 guava named[9824]: the working directory is not writable
```

You can safely ignore the **working directory is not writable** error message. The **misc.log** file might show errors that do not appear in the **messages** file:

```
# cat /var/log/bind/misc.log
15:11:40.594 general: info: zone 0.168.192.in-addr.arpa/IN: loaded serial 2013110501
15:11:40.596 general: info: zone sam.net/IN: loaded serial 2013110501
15:11:40.596 general: info: managed-keys-zone ./IN: loaded serial 0
15:11:40.600 general: notice: running
```

See "Error messages" on page 865 if **named** generates an error message.

# A SLAVE SERVER

To set up a slave server, copy the **/etc/named.conf** file from the master server to the slave server, replacing the **type master** statement with **type slave** and adding a **masters { *1.2.3.4;* };** directive. Remove any zones the slave server will not be acting as a slave for, including the root (.) zone, if the slave server will not respond to recursive queries. If necessary, create the **/var/log/bind** directory for log files as explained at the end of the previous section.

**notify** statement     Slave servers copy zone information from the primary master server or another slave server. The **notify** statement specifies whether you want a master server to notify slave servers when information on the master server changes. Set the (global) value of **notify** in the Options clause or set it within a Zone clause, which overrides a global setting for a given zone. The format is

> *notify YES | NO | EXPLICIT*

*YES* causes the master server to notify all slaves listed in NS resource records for the zone as well as servers at IP addresses listed in an **also-notify** statement. When you set **notify** to *EXPLICIT*, the server notifies servers listed in the **also-notify** statement only. *NO* turns off notification.

When you start **named**, it copies the zone files to **/var/named**. If you specify **notify YES** on the master server, the zone files on the slave server will be updated each time you change the serial field of the SOA resource record in a zone. You must manually distribute changes to **/etc/named.conf** and included files.

# A SPLIT HORIZON (DMZ) SERVER

Assume you want to set up a LAN that provides all of its systems and services to local users on internal systems, which might be behind a firewall, but only certain public services—such as Web, FTP, and mail—to Internet (public) users. A *split horizon* (also called *DMZ*) DNS server takes care of this situation by treating queries from internal systems differently from queries from public systems (systems on the Internet).

View clauses     BIND 9 introduced View clauses in **named.conf**. View clauses facilitate the implementation of a split DNS server. Each view provides a different perspective of the DNS namespace to a group of clients. When there is no View clause, all zones specified in **named.conf** are part of the implicit default view.

Assume an office has several systems on a LAN and public Web, FTP, DNS, and mail servers. The single connection to the Internet is NATed (page 1262), so it is shared by the local systems and the servers. The system connected directly to the Internet is a router, firewall, and server. This scenario takes advantage of the View clauses in **named.conf** and supports separate secondary nameservers for local and public users. Although public users need access to the DNS server as the authority on the domain that supports the servers, they do not require the DNS server to support recursive queries. Not supporting recursion for public users limits the load on

**Figure 24-11**   A split horizon DNS server

the DNS server and the Internet connection. For security reasons, public users must not have access to information about local systems other than the servers. Local users should have access to information about local systems and should be able to use the DNS server recursively.

Figure 24-11 shows that the server responds differently to queries from the LAN and from the Internet.

The firewall-config (page 900) or firewall-cmd utility (page 906) controls which ports on which systems users on internal and external systems can access. DNS controls which systems are advertised to which users.

The **named.conf** file has four clauses: an Options clause, two View clauses, and a Logging clause. The Options clause specifies that the zone files be located in the **/var/named** directory. The View clauses specify the characteristics and zones that a resolver is given access to, which depend on the resolver's address. One zone is for use by the LAN/local users; the other is used by Internet/public users. The Logging clause sets up the **misc2.log** file for default messages; you must create a **/var/log/bind** directory as explained under "Log files" (page 889).

There are several ways to specify which clients see a view. The following **named.conf** file uses **match-clients** statements:

```
$ cat /etc/named.conf
options {
    directory "/var/named";
}; //end options


view "local" IN {                        // start local view
match-clients { 127.0.0.1; 192.168.0.0/24;};
recursion YES;


zone"zach.net" IN {
    type    master;
    file    "local.net";
    notify YES;
};
```

```
    zone "0.168.192.in-addr.arpa" IN {
        type    master;
        file    "named.local";
        notify  YES;
    };

    zone "." IN {
        type    hint;
        file    "named.ca";
    };

    };                                          // end local view

    view "public" IN {                          // start public view
    match-clients { "any";};
    recursion NO;

    zone"zach.net" IN {
        type    master;
        file    "public.net";
        notify  YES;
    };

    zone "0.168.192.in-addr.arpa" IN {
        type    master;
        file    "named.public";
        notify  YES;
    };

    zone "." IN {
        type    hint;
        file    "named.ca";
    };

    };                                          // end public view

    logging{
        channel "misc" {
            file "/var/log/bind/misc2.log" versions 2 size 1m;
            print-time YES;
            print-severity YES;
            print-category YES;
        };
        category default {
            "misc";
        };
    };                                          //end logging
```

The ordering of View clauses within **named.conf** is critical because the view that is presented to a client is the first view that the client matches. The preceding **named.conf** file holds two View clauses: one for local users and one for public users, in that order. Local users are defined to be those on the 192.168.0.0/24 subnet or **localhost** (127.0.0.1); public users are defined to be any users. If you reversed the order of the View clauses, all users—including local users—would get the view intended for the public and no users would see the local view.

Many statements from the Options clause can be used within View clauses, where they override statements in the (global) Options clause. The **recursion** statement, which can appear within an Options clause, appears in each View clause. This **named.conf** file sets up a server that provides recursive answers to queries that originate locally and iterative answers to queries from the public. This setup provides quick, complete answers to local users, limiting the network and processor bandwidth that is devoted to other users while continuing to provide authoritative name service for the local servers.

To make **named.conf** easier to understand and maintain, zones in different View clauses can have the same name but different zone files. Both the local and public View clauses in the example have zones named **zach.net**: The public **zach.net** zone file is named **public.net** and the local one is named **local.net**.

The Logging clause is described on page 887.

The zone files defining **zach.net** are similar to the ones in the previous examples; the public file is a subset of the local one. Following the SOA resource record in both files is a TXT, two NS, and two MX resource records. Next are three CNAME resource records that direct queries addressed to www.zach.net, ftp.zach.net, and mail.zach.net to the system named **ns.zach.net**. The next four resource records specify two nameserver addresses and two mail servers for the ns.zach.net domain.

The final four resource records appear in the local **zach.net** zone file and not in the public zone file; they are address (A) resource records for local systems. Instead of keeping this information in **/etc/hosts** files on each system, you can keep it on the DNS server, where it can be updated easily. When you use DNS instead of **/etc/hosts**, you must change the **hosts** line in **/etc/nsswitch.conf** (page 495) accordingly.

```
$ cat local.net
; zach.net local zone file
;
$TTL    3D
@       IN      SOA     ns.zach.net. mgs@sobell.com. (
                                201311118       ; serial
                                8H              ; refresh
                                2H              ; retry
                                4W              ; expire
                                1D )            ; minimum

        IN      TXT     "Sobell Associates Inc."
        IN      NS      ns              ; Nameserver address (unqualified)
        IN      NS      ns.speedy.net.; Nameserver address (qualified)
        IN      MX      10 mail         ; Mail exchange (primary/unqualified)
        IN      MX      20 mail.max.net.; Mail exchange (2nd/qualified)
```

```
ns      IN      A       192.168.0.1
mail    IN      A       192.168.0.2

www     IN      CNAME   mail
ftp     IN      CNAME   mail
gw      IN      CNAME   ns

speedy  IN      A       192.168.0.5
grape   IN      A       192.168.0.3
potato  IN      A       192.168.0.4
peach   IN      A       192.168.0.6
```

The public version of the **zach.net** zone file follows:

```
$ cat public.net
; zach.net public zone file
;
$TTL    3D
@       IN      SOA     ns.zach.net. mgs@sobell.com. (
                            201311118       ; serial
                            8H              ; refresh
                            2H              ; retry
                            4W              ; expire
                            1D )            ; minimum

        IN      TXT     "Sobell Associates Inc."
        IN      NS      ns          ; Nameserver address (unqualified)
        IN      NS      ns.speedy.net.; Nameserver address (qualified)

        IN      MX      10 mail ; Mail exchange (primary/unqualified)
        IN      MX      20 mail.max.net.; Mail exchange (2nd/qualified)

www     IN      CNAME   mail
ftp     IN      CNAME   mail
gw      IN      CNAME   ns

ns      IN      A       192.168.0.1
mail    IN      A       192.168.0.2
```

Here there are two reverse zone files, each of which starts with SOA and NS resource records, followed by PTR resource records for each of the names of the servers. The local version of this file also lists the names of the local systems:

```
$ cat named.local
;"0.168.192.in-addr.arpa" reverse zone file
;
$TTL    3D
@       IN      SOA     ns.zach.net. mgs@sobell.com. (
                            2013110501      ; serial
                            8H              ; refresh
                            2H              ; retry
                            4W              ; expire
                            1D)             ; minimum
```

```
                    IN      NS       ns.zach.net.
                    IN      NS       ns.speedy.net.
          1         IN      PTR      ns.zach.net.
          2         IN      PTR      mail.zach.net.
          3         IN      PTR      grape.zach.net.
          4         IN      PTR      potato.zach.net.
          5         IN      PTR      speedy.zach.net.
          6         IN      PTR      peach.zach.net.

          $ cat named.public
          ;"0.168.192.in-addr.arpa" reverse zone file
          ;
          $TTL    3D
          @         IN      SOA      ns.zach.net. mgs@sobell.com. (
                                        2013110501      ; serial
                                        8H              ; refresh
                                        2H              ; retry
                                        4W              ; expire
                                        1D)             ; minimum
                    IN      NS       ns.zach.net.
                    IN      NS       ns.speedy.net.
          1         IN      PTR      ns.zach.net.
          2         IN      PTR      mail.zach.net.
```

# CHAPTER SUMMARY

DNS maps domain names to IP addresses, and vice versa. It is implemented as a hierarchical, distributed, and replicated database on the Internet. You can improve the security of BIND, which implements DNS, by running it inside a chroot jail and using transaction signatures (TSIGs) and SELinux.

When a program on the local system needs to look up an IP address that corresponds to a domain name, it calls the resolver. The resolver queries the local DNS cache, if available, and then queries DNS servers on the LAN or Internet. There are two types of queries: iterative and recursive. When a server responds to an iterative query, it returns whatever information it has at hand; it does not query other servers. Recursive queries cause a server to query other servers if necessary to respond with an answer.

There are three types of servers. Master servers, which hold the master copy of zone data, are authoritative for a zone. Slave servers are also authoritative and copy their data from a master server or other slave servers. DNS caches are not authoritative and either answer queries from cache or forward queries to another server.

The DNS database holds resource records for domains. Many types of resource records exist, including A (address), MX (mail exchange), NS (nameserver), PTR (pointer for performing reverse name resolution), and SOA (start of authority, which describes the zone).

# EXERCISES

1. What kind of server responds to recursive queries? How does this server work?

2. What kind of DNS record is likely to be returned when a Web browser tries to resolve the domain part of a URI?

3. What are MX resource records for?

4. How would you find the IP address of example.com from the command line?

5. How would you instruct a Linux system to use the local network's DNS cache, located at 192.168.1.254, or the ISP's DNS cache, located at 1.2.3.4, if the LAN nameserver is unavailable?

6. How would you instruct a DNS server to respond only to queries from the **137.44.** IP range?

7. How might a resolver attempt to find the IP address of the **example** domain?

# ADVANCED EXERCISES

8. How would you set up a private domain name hierarchy that does not include any of the official InterNIC-assigned domain names?

9. Which part of DNS is most vulnerable to an attack from a malicious user and why?

10. It is often irritating to have to wait for DNS records to update around the world when you change DNS entries. You could prevent this delay by setting the TTL to a small number. Why is setting the TTL to a small number a bad idea?

11. Outline a method by which DNS could be used to support encryption.

# 25

# firewalld AND iptables: SETTING UP A FIREWALL

## OBJECTIVES

After reading this chapter you should be able to:

▶ Explain how the **firewalld** and **iptables** services differ

▶ Configure a basic firewall using firewall-config

▶ Configure a basic firewall using firewall-cmd

▶ Describe the purpose of **firewalld** zones

▶ Explain the difference between the runtime and permanent configurations

▶ Configure NAT so several clients on a LAN can use a single Internet connection

# THE firewalld SERVICE

iptables    The **firewalld** service (which uses the **firewalld** daemon) is replacing the **iptables** service. As contrasted with the **iptables** service, the **firewalld** service does not need to be reloaded with every change; it accepts changes to the firewall while it is running. Reloading the **iptables** service frequently breaks established connections. Nowhere is this problem more evident than with virtualization because the firewall changes each time a VM is brought up or down. The **libvirt** library (page 662) now uses **firewalld** to adjust the firewall as needed.

A firewall set up under **firewalld** must be managed directly by the **firewalld** daemon so that the state in the daemon and the state in the kernel remain in sync. Thus you cannot use iptables commands to add rules to a firewall controlled by **firewalld**.

The **firewalld** daemon introduces a level of abstraction that makes setting up a firewall simpler and more intuitive. Instead of writing firewall rules as iptables requires, with **firewalld** you use firewall-config (GUI) or firewall-cmd (CLI) to set up a firewall.

The **firewalld** daemon is managed by systemd (page 438) using the **firewalld.service** unit. It is started before networking so that it can immediately protect the network when the network is brought up.

netfilter    Running in *kernelspace* (page 1257), **netfilter** is a set of tables that hold rules the kernel uses to control network packet filtering. To be useful, **netfilter** requires a front end. The **firewalld** front end runs in *userspace* (page 1279) and enables an administrator to set up a firewall (just as **iptables** does).

*LE+*  D-BUS    D-BUS (www.freedesktop.org/wiki/Software/dbus) is an IPC (interprocess communication system), also called a message bus system, that allows applications and processes to talk with one another and request services over a bus. The **dbus** service (which runs **dbus-daemon**) notifies processes of events (e.g., when a new device is added or when a user logs in).

The **firewalld** daemon has a D-BUS interface that allows it to communicate with processes. Applications, daemons, and administrators can enable/disable a **firewalld** feature using D-BUS. These features can include opening ports, forwarding ports or packets, and performing more advanced tasks.

## firewalld CONFIGURATION

This section describes some aspects of the **firewalld** configuration.

### RUNTIME VERSUS PERMANENT CONFIGURATION

When you set up or change a firewall feature, you can do so in the runtime configuration, which causes the change to be made immediately on the running system. Or you can make the change in the permanent (persistent) configuration, which takes effect when the firewall is reloaded or when the system is rebooted.

## ZONES

A (network) zone defines a level of trust for a network connection. For example, you might have one zone for a LAN and one for the Internet. On a laptop the zone might change depending on whether the computer is using a public Wi-Fi network or a wired connection at work. Table 25-1 lists the default set of zones.

**public** zone    The default zone is **public** and is the only zone this chapter discusses.

**Table 25-1**    The **firewalld** zones

| Zone | Function |
|------|----------|
| **drop** | Drop incoming packets with no reply; allow outgoing connections |
| **block** | Reject incoming connections with icmp-host-prohibited (ipv4) or icmp6-adm-prohibited (ipv6); allow outgoing connections; see page 1254 for a definition of ICMP |
| **public** | Do not trust other systems not to harm the local system; accept the **ssh**, **mdns**, and **dhcpv6-client** services (the default zone) |
| **external** | Do not trust other systems not to harm the local system; for use on external networks with masquerading enabled (especially for routers); accept selected incoming connections |
| **dmz** | For use on publicly accessible computers in the local DMZ (page 890) that have limited access to the local network; accept selected incoming connections |
| **work** | Mostly trust other systems not to harm the local system; accept selected incoming connections |
| **home** | Mostly trust other systems not to harm the local system; accept selected incoming connections |
| **internal** | Mostly trust other systems not to harm the local system; accept selected incoming connections |
| **trusted** | Completely trust other systems not to harm the local system; accept all connections |

## SERVICES

A service is a combination of one or more ports and protocols (TCP or UDP). For example, the SSH service uses TCP port 22. Optionally, a service can include a destination address.

## LOCKDOWN WHITELIST

The primary authentication mechanism that **firewalld** uses is called polkit (www.freedesktop.org/wiki/Software/polkit). By default, the **firewalld** lockdown whitelist is off and does not affect what or who can modify the firewall. When it is on, **firewalld** uses this whitelist in addition to polkit and only applications running with a (SELinux) context specified in the lockdown whitelist, and commands and users specified in this list, are permitted to modify the firewall. As initially set up, only NetworkManager (page 637), **libvirt** (page 662), and a user/process running with **root** privileges are on this whitelist.

## USER INTERFACES

You can use one of two interfaces to set up **firewalld**: the firewall-config GUI (next) or the firewall-cmd CLI (page 906). Other processes communicate with **firewalld** using D-BUS. Some desktops also display the firewall-applet (**firewall-applet** package) that you can use to work with **firewalld**. As of this writing, GNOME 3 does not display this applet properly so you cannot use firewall-applet with GNOME 3.

# PREREQUISITES

Install the following packages (both are installed by default):

- **firewalld**
- **firewall-config**

Check **firewalld** is running    A new Fedora/RHEL system boots with **firewalld** installed and running. Use the **systemctl status** command to make sure the service is running. The following output shows **firewalld** running normally. If **firewalld** is not running, the Active line will show **inactive (dead)**.

```
$ systemctl status firewalld.service
firewalld.service - firewalld - dynamic firewall daemon
   Loaded: loaded (/usr/lib/systemd/system/firewalld.service; enabled)
   Active: active (running) since Thu 2013-08-15 14:33:00 PDT; 6 days ago
 Main PID: 374 (firewalld)
   CGroup: name=systemd:/system/firewalld.service
           +-374 /usr/bin/python /usr/sbin/firewalld --nofork --nopid

Aug 15 14:33 guava.example.com systemd[1]: Started firewalld - dynamic firewall daemon
```

Reloading and stopping **firewalld**    While working with **root** privileges, you can give the preceding command, replacing **status** with **reload** to cause **firewalld** to reread its configuration files, with **stop** to stop **firewalld,** or with **start** to start it when it is stopped.

Panic mode    If the system is under attack, give the following command to shut down the network immediately. See the caution tip on page 902.

```
$ su -c "firewall-cmd --panic-on"
```

Use the **--panic-off** option to restore the firewall to its previous state.

# JumpStart: Building a Firewall Using firewall-config

This section explains how to trust a service (open a port) using the graphical firewall-config utility. Follow these instructions to open the port in both the running system

**Figure 25-1**  Firewall Configuration window

(runtime configuration) and in the system after it is rebooted (permanent configuration). See "firewall-config: The Firewall Configuration Window" on the next page for more information. For more complex firewalls see firewall-cmd (page 906) or iptables (page 908).

### The firewall is enabled by default

**tip**  When you install Fedora/RHEL, **firewalld** is installed on the system. The firewall is running and blocks most inbound traffic. However, **firewalld** accepts inbound traffic on TCP port 22, allowing remote systems to connect to the **sshd** daemon on the local system. See page 700 for information on setting up an OpenSSH server. In addition, **firewalld** accepts mDNS (multicast DNS; www.multicastdns.org; Fedora only) and dhcpv6 client traffic.

The Firewall Configuration window (Figure 25-1) allows you to build a simple firewall or, in an emergency, put the firewall in panic mode, which cuts off all network communication. Open this window by giving the command **firewall-config** from an Enter a Command window (ALT-F2) or a terminal emulator. If you do not run firewall-config with **root** privileges, it displays an authentication window; enter the requested password and click **Authenticate**.

## PUTTING firewalld IN PANIC MODE

In an emergency, such as when the system is being attacked, you can block all network communication by putting **firewalld** in panic mode. In panic mode, **firewalld** drops all incoming and outgoing packets and allows active connections to expire. Panic mode affects the **firewalld** runtime configuration only: The firewall will revert to its permanent configuration when the system reboots.

Put **firewalld** in panic mode by selecting **Firewall Configuration menubar: Options⇨ Panic Mode**. A tick appears next to the selection. Repeat the selection to remove the tick and revert to the runtime configuration.

### Panic mode can disconnect you from the system

**caution**   Putting the firewall in panic mode cuts off all network communication. If you are logged in remotely (e.g., using ssh), when you put the system in panic mode you will be disconnected. Put the system in panic mode only when you are working from the console.

## TRUSTING A SERVICE (OPENING A PORT) IN THE RUNTIME AND PERMANENT CONFIGURATIONS

In its simplest form, a **firewalld** service is defined by a port and protocol (e.g., the HTTP service uses TCP port 80). More complex services can include multiple or ranges of ports, **netfilter** helper modules, and destination addresses. You can set up **firewalld** to trust a service in the runtime configuration, the permanent configuration, or both. A trusted service is accessible from all hosts and networks that can reach the local system using any active network connection or interface (called the *active zone*; the **public** zone is the active zone by default).

Assume the local system is running Apache and you want to open the firewall to allow HTTP traffic. If the **public** zone is active, which it is by default, follow these steps to set up this zone to allow HTTP traffic.

1. Select **Permanent** in the drop-down list labeled **Configuration**.
2. Select **Zones** from the main tabs.
3. Select **public** from the list on the left labeled **Zone**.
4. Select **Services** from the secondary tabs.
5. Put a tick in the check box adjacent to the service you want to trust (**http** in this case).
6. Select **Runtime** in the drop-down list labeled **Configuration**.
7. Repeat steps 2–5; you are done.

After following these steps the HTTP service will be trusted immediately and will be trusted when the system boots.

## firewall-config: THE FIREWALL CONFIGURATION WINDOW

The Firewall Configuration window (Figure 25-1, page 901) includes many instructions and descriptions. This section continues from the preceding section and describes a few of the changes you can make using this window. After experimenting with the examples in this section, try working with other parts of this window. You can always return an entry in the list on the left to its default value: With the Configuration set to Permanent, highlight the entry and click the rightmost button (the one with the yellow arrow) below the list. This action returns the highlighted zone to its default setup.

### Routers have firewalls, too

tip    Many systems are already protected by a firewall located in a router. If you use a router that has a firewall, you might need to open ports on the router firewall in addition to opening ports on any firewall you set up on the local system.

If several systems are connected to the router, you might want to set up different, more restrictive rules on the systems than you set up on the router.

# WINDOW FEATURES

Open the Firewall Configuration window by giving the command **firewall-config** from an Enter a Command window (ALT-F2) or a terminal emulator. Authenticate as necessary. The Firewall Configuration window displays the Zones/Services tabs of the **public** (default) zone for the runtime configuration.

Configuration    At the top of the Firewall Configuration window is a drop-down list labeled **Configuration**. This list allows you to select Runtime or Permanent (page 898). All the work you do in the window applies to the selected configuration.

The main tabs    Immediately below the word **Configuration** is a set of tabs that this chapter refers to as *the main tabs*. Selecting one of these tabs changes what appears in the rest of the window. Each tab allows you to work with a different aspect of the firewall. For example, if you select the Zones tab, the information in the window pertains to zones. See "The Main Tabs," below.

The explanation of the selected main tab appears immediately below the set of main tabs. For example, with the Zones tab selected, the definition explains what a zone is and which aspects of the firewall it encompasses.

The secondary tabs    Below the explanation, a list appears on the left and *the secondary tabs* appear on the right. The list has a label that is similar to the selected tab in the main tabs: With the Zones tab selected the list is labeled **Zone**, and the list holds the names of each of the zones.

The secondary tabs hold items that pertain to the list on the left. See "The Secondary Tabs for Zones" and "The Secondary Tabs for Services" (both on the next page).

## THE MAIN TABS

The two tabs listed on the next page appear near the top of the Firewall Configuration window.

- **Zones**—Define levels of trust for connections and interfaces (page 899)

- **Services**—Define combinations of ports and protocols (page 899)

When highlighted, each of the main tabs presents a different set of secondary tabs.

## THE SECONDARY TABS FOR ZONES

Figure 25-1 on page 901 shows six tabs in the secondary tabs. Click the arrow at the right end of the tabs to select the next tab to the right and, when the last tab is highlighted, to scroll the tabs and display additional tabs. Click the arrow at the left end to work in the other direction. With Zones selected in the main tabs, the secondary tabs define the highlighted zone. The secondary tabs comprise

- **Services**—Selects trusted services.

- **Ports**—Selects trusted ports and protocols.

- **Masquerading**—Maps the local, private network to a public IP address; the local network is not visible from outside the network. Masquerading is a form of *NAT* (page 1262). For more information refer to "Connecting Several Clients to a Single Internet Connection" on page 926.

- **Port Forwarding**—Maps a port to another port on the local system or a remote system.

- **ICMP Filter**—By default the firewall allows inbound *ICMP* (page 1254) packets, such as those sent by ping (page 305), through. You can use the selections in this tab to block these packets. Put ticks in the check boxes adjacent to the types of packets you want the firewall to block. To block ping packets, put a tick in the check box labeled **Echo Request**.

- **Rich Rules**—Specifies complex firewall rules using an abstract representation of iptables rules; see the **firewalld.richlanguage** man page for more information.

- **Interfaces**—Specifies an interface to bind to the selected zone.

- **Sources**—Specifies a source address to bind to the selected zone.

## THE SECONDARY TABS FOR SERVICES

The secondary tabs for Services allow you to define or modify services that you can trust when you select Services in the main tabs. The secondary tabs for Services comprise

- **Ports and Protocols**—Specifies ports and a protocol (TCP or UDP) for a service (see "Modifying an Existing Service" on the next page)

**Figure 25-2**   The Base Service Settings window

- **Modules**—Specifies **netfilter** helper modules
- **Destination**—Specifies an address that limits the service to packets bound for that address

## DEFINING A NEW SERVICE

If no predefined service meets your needs, you can modify an existing service or define a new one in the Firewall Configuration window (Figure 25-1, page 901). After you define a new service, you set up the service by modifying it (next).

Define a new service by selecting Permanent from the drop-down list labeled **Configuration**. You cannot define a new service or modify an existing service in the running configuration. Select Services from the main tabs. Click the plus sign (**+**) at the bottom of the list labeled **Service** at the left of the window; firewall-config displays the Base Service Settings window (Figure 25-2). Fill in the text box labeled **Name** with an appropriate name; all other information is optional. Click **OK** and continue with the next section.

## MODIFYING AN EXISTING SERVICE

Modify an existing service, including one you just defined, by selecting Permanent from the drop-down list labeled **Configuration** in the Firewall Configuration window (Figure 25-1, page 901). Select Services from the main tabs. In the list on the left labeled **Service**, highlight the service you want to modify. Select Ports and Protocols from the secondary tabs. Three buttons at the bottom right of the window allow you to work with the highlighted service. Highlight a port and protocol to edit (click **Edit**) or remove

**Figure 25-3** The Port and/or Protocol window

(click **Remove**) it. Click **Add** to add a port and protocol. These actions open the Port and/or Protocol window (Figure 25-3).

In the Port and/or Protocol window enter or change a port number or a range of port numbers (two numbers separated by a hyphen) in the text box labeled **Port/Port Range** and select **tcp** or **udp** from the drop-down list labeled **Protocol**. Entering information in the text box labeled **Other Protocol** is usually not necessary. Click **OK**.

After creating or modifying a service, you can add the service so it is trusted in a zone (page 902).

# firewall-cmd: CONTROLLING firewalld FROM THE COMMAND LINE

The firewall-cmd utility is the command-line interface to the **firewalld** daemon. You can use it to set up and modify firewalls. Using direct options it can invoke iptables commands (page 908). This section describes just a few firewall-cmd options; see the firewall-cmd man page for a complete list.

## STATUS COMMANDS

The firewall-cmd --**state** option tells you whether **firewalld** is running:

```
$ firewall-cmd --state
running
```

This chapter assumes the zone named **public** is the default zone (it is by default) and that **public** is the active zone:

```
$ firewall-cmd --get-default-zone
public
$ firewall-cmd --get-active-zones
public
  interfaces: ens33
```

You must work with **root** privileges to make all but the most basic queries of and changes to the firewall. The first of the following commands uses the **--list-services** option to list the services that the running system trusts (has ports open for). The second command adds the **--permanent** option to **--list-services** to list the services that the permanent configuration trusts. In this case the lists are the same.

```
# firewall-cmd --list-services
mdns dhcpv6-client ssh

# firewall-cmd --permanent --list-services
ssh mdns dhcpv6-client
```

## TRUSTING A SERVICE

The following example shows how to turn on the HTTP and HTTPS services in the running and permanent configurations. First, use the **--add-service** option to turn on the services in the running configuration:

```
# firewall-cmd --add-service=http
success
# firewall-cmd --add-service=https
success
```

The following commands show HTTP and HTTPS are trusted in the running configuration, but not in the permanent configuration:

```
# firewall-cmd --list-services
mdns http dhcpv6-client https ssh

# firewall-cmd --permanent --list-services
mdns dhcpv6-client ssh
```

Next, use the **--permanent** and **--add-service** options to turn on the services in the permanent configuration. The **--list-services** option shows that HTTP and HTTPS are now trusted in the permanent configuration.

```
# firewall-cmd --permanent --add-service=http
success
# firewall-cmd --permanent --add-service=https
success

# firewall-cmd --permanent --list-services
mdns http dhcpv6-client https ssh
```

You can use the **--remove-service** option to remove a service from the list of trusted services:

```
# firewall-cmd --permanent --remove-service=http
success
# firewall-cmd --permanent --remove-service=https
success
# firewall-cmd --permanent --list-services
mdns dhcpv6-client ssh
```

## OPENING A PORT

Use the **--add-port** and **--remove-port** options to work with port numbers and protocols in place of services. The following example shows how to open TCP port 80 (HTTP) and TCP port 443 (HTTPS) in both configurations.

```
# firewall-cmd --add-port=80/tcp
success
# firewall-cmd --permanent --add-port=80/tcp
success
# firewall-cmd --add-port=443/tcp
success
# firewall-cmd --permanent --add-port=443/tcp
success
# firewall-cmd --permanent --list-ports
443/tcp 80/tcp

# firewall-cmd --list-ports
443/tcp 80/tcp
```

The **firewalld** daemon keeps track of ports and services separately so **--list-ports** does not show trusted services and **--list-services** does not show open ports.

## DIRECT OPTIONS

The direct options allow you to give firewall-cmd commands that are similar to iptables commands. This chapter covers iptables starting below. When you use the **--direct** and **--passthrough** options together, you can use exact iptables syntax in a firewall-cmd command. The format of this type of command is

*firewall-cmd --direct --passthrough ipv4\ipv6* ***iptables-command***

where *ipv4* or *ipv6* specifies that an iptables or ip6tables command follows and ***iptables-command*** is an iptables command without the **iptables** at the beginning. For example, the following iptables command opens port 22:

```
# iptables -I INPUT -p tcp -m state --state NEW -m tcp --dport 22 -j ACCEPT
```

Using the **--direct** and **--passthrough** options, you can wrap the iptables command and give it as a firewall-cmd command:

```
# firewall-cmd --direct --passthrough ipv4 -I INPUT -p tcp -m state --state NEW -m tcp --dport 22 -j ACCEPT
```

### The system is running iptables *or* firewalld

caution    When the system is running **firewalld**, as it is by default, you can give only firewall-cmd commands, not iptables commands. Similarly, when it is running iptables, you can give only iptables commands. The firewall-cmd **--direct** option wraps iptables commands so you can give them to a system running **firewalld**.

# INTRODUCTION TO iptables

The iptables utility is flexible and extensible, allowing you to set up both simple and complex network packet filtering solutions. It builds and manipulates network *packet filtering* (page 1265) rules in the Linux kernel.

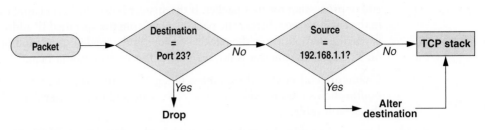

**Figure 25-4**    Example of how rules in a chain work

The iptables utility also provides connection tracking (stateful packet filtering), allowing you to handle *packets* (page 1265) based on the state of their connection. For example, you can set up rules that reject inbound packets trying to open a new connection and accept inbound packets that are responses to a locally initiated connection. Many features not included in the base **iptables** package are available as patches via the patch-o-matic program.

The system-config-firewall utility (**system-config-firewall** package) is a user-friendly, graphical front end for iptables and ip6tables (both referred to in this chapter as iptables). You can use system-config-firewall or iptables directly to create a firewall that protects a system from malicious users and to set up *NAT* (Network Address Translation, page 1262), which can allow several systems to share a single Internet connection.

Some of the concepts required to fully understand iptables are beyond the scope of this book. You can use iptables at different levels; this chapter presents the fundamentals. Some sections of this chapter, however, delve into areas that might require additional understanding or explanation. If a concept is not clear, refer to one of the resources in "More Information" on page 911.

**netfilter** and **iptables**    The functionality referred to as iptables and ip6tables is composed of two components: **netfilter** and iptables. Running in *kernelspace* (page 1257), the **netfilter** component is a set of tables that hold rules the kernel uses to control network packet filtering. Running in *userspace* (page 1279), the iptables utility sets up, maintains, and displays the rules stored by **netfilter**.

Rules, matches, targets, and chains    A *rule* comprises one or more criteria (*matches* or *classifiers*) and a single action (a *target*). If, when a rule is applied to a network packet, the packet matches all the criteria, the action is applied to the packet. Rules are stored in *chains*. Each rule in a chain is applied, in order, to a packet until a match is found. If there is no match, the chain's *policy*, or default action, is applied to the packet (page 917).

History    In the kernel, iptables replaces the earlier ipchains as a method of filtering network packets. It provides multiple chains for increased filtration flexibility. The iptables utility also provides stateful packet inspection (page 911).

Example rules    As an example of how rules work, assume a chain has two rules (Figure 25-4). The first rule tests whether a packet's destination is port 23 (TELNET) and drops the packet if it is. The second rule tests whether a packet was received from the IP address 192.168.1.1 and alters the packet's destination if it was. When a packet is processed by the example chain, the kernel applies the first rule in the chain to see whether the packet arrived on port 23. If the answer is yes, the packet is dropped and that is the end of processing for that packet. If the answer is no, the kernel applies the second rule in the chain to see whether the packet came from the specified IP address. If the answer is yes, the destination in the packet's header is changed and the modified packet is sent on its way. If the answer is no, the packet is sent on without being changed.

Chains are collected in three tables: Filter, NAT, and Mangle. Each of these tables has builtin chains (described next). You can create additional, user-defined chains in Filter, the default table.

Filter table    The default table. This table is mostly used to DROP, ACCEPT, or REJECT packets based on their content; it does not alter packets. Builtin chains are INPUT, FORWARD, and OUTPUT.

NAT table    The Network Address Translation table. Packets that create new connections are routed through this table, which is used exclusively to translate the source or destination fields of packets. Builtin chains are PREROUTING, OUTPUT, and POSTROUTING. Use this table with DNAT, SNAT, and MASQUERADE targets only.

- **DNAT** (destination NAT) alters the destination IP address of the first inbound packet in a connection so it is rerouted to another host. Subsequent packets in the connection are automatically DNATed. DNAT is useful for redirecting packets from the Internet that are bound for a firewall or a NATed server (page 928).

- **SNAT** (source NAT) alters the source IP address of the first outbound packet in a connection so it appears to come from a fixed IP address—for example, a firewall or router. Subsequent packets in the connection are automatically SNATed. Replies to SNATed packets are automatically de-SNATed so they go back to the original sender. SNAT is useful for hiding LAN addresses from systems outside the LAN and using a single IP address to serve multiple local hosts.

- **MASQUERADE** differs from SNAT only in that it checks for an IP address to apply to each outbound packet, making it suitable for use with dynamic IP addresses such as those provided by DHCP (page 491). MASQUERADE is slightly slower than SNAT.

Mangle table    Used exclusively to alter the TOS (type of service), TTL (time to live), and MARK fields in a packet. Builtin chains are PREROUTING and OUTPUT.

Network packets    When a packet from the network enters the kernel's network protocol stack, it is given some basic sanity tests, including checksum verification. After passing these tests, the packet goes through the PREROUTING chain, where its destination address can be changed (Figure 25-5).

Next the packet is routed based on its destination address. If it is bound for the local system, it first goes through the INPUT chain, where it can be filtered (accepted, dropped, or sent to another chain) or altered. If the packet is not addressed to the local system (the local system is forwarding the packet), it goes through the FORWARD and POSTROUTING chains, where it can again be filtered or altered.

Packets created locally pass through the OUTPUT and POSTROUTING chains, where they can be filtered or altered before being sent to the network.

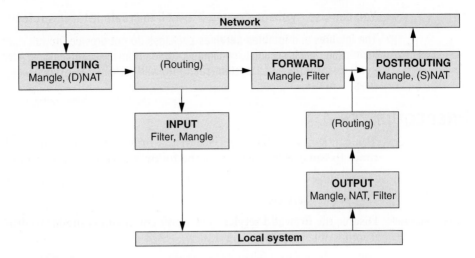

**Figure 25-5**   Filtering a packet in the kernel

State   The connection tracking machine (also called the state machine) provides information on the state of a packet, allowing you to define rules that match criteria based on the state of the connection the packet is part of. For example, when a connection is opened, the first packet is part of a NEW connection, whereas subsequent packets are part of an ESTABLISHED connection. Connection tracking is handled by the **conntrack** module.

The OUTPUT chain handles connection tracking for locally generated packets. The PREROUTING chain handles connection tracking for all other packets. For more information refer to "State" on page 920.

Before the advent of connection tracking, it was sometimes necessary to open many or all nonprivileged ports to make sure that the system accepted all RETURN and RELATED traffic. Because connection tracking allows you to identify these kinds of traffic, you can keep many more ports closed to general traffic, thereby increasing system security.

Jumps and targets   A *jump* or *target* (page 921) specifies the action the kernel takes if a network packet matches all the match criteria (page 915) for the rule being processed.

# MORE INFORMATION

Web   Documentation, HOWTOs, FAQs, patch-o-matic, security information:
     www.netfilter.org
     Tutorial: www.faqs.org/docs/iptables
     Scripts and more: www.yourwebexperts.com/viewforum.php?f=35

HOWTO   *KernelAnalysis-HOWTO*
     *IP-Masquerade-HOWTO* (contains useful scripts)
     *Netfilter Extensions HOWTO*: www.netfilter.org
     *Netfilter Hacking-HOWTO*: www.netfilter.org

Book   *TCP/IP Illustrated* by W. Richard Stevens, Addison-Wesley, January 2002

## **You can use** system-config-firewall **to create** iptables **rules**

tip The **iptables** and **iptables-services** packages do not provide firewall rules. You can use the instructions in this section to configure iptables from the command line. Alternately, you can use system-config-firewall (**system-config-firewall** package), a GUI configuration tool for iptables rules.

# PREREQUISITES

You can run the **iptables** service or the **firewalld** service, but not both at the same time. To run iptables, make sure the following packages are installed:

- iptables
- iptables-services

Disable **firewalld**  Disable the **firewalld** service. The **mask** command is similar to **disable**, but it makes it impossible to start the service.

```
# systemctl mask firewalld.service
ln -s '/dev/null' '/etc/systemd/system/firewalld.service'
```

Enable **iptables** and  Run systemctl to cause the **iptables** and **ip6tables** services to start each time the system
**ip6tables**  enters multiuser mode:

```
# systemctl enable iptables.service
# systemctl enable ip6tables.service
```

The systemctl utility will not start the **iptables.service** unit unless there is a set of rules for it to load from the **/etc/sysconfig/iptables** file. See "system-config-firewall: Generates a Set of Rules" on page 923 for more information about this file. The following file sets up a basic firewall that allows outbound traffic and rejects all incoming traffic except that which is in response to outbound traffic. Copy this sample file to the file named **iptables** to get started.

```
# cat /etc/sysconfig/iptables
*filter
:INPUT ACCEPT [0:0]
:FORWARD ACCEPT [0:0]
:OUTPUT ACCEPT [0:0]
-A INPUT -m state --state ESTABLISHED,RELATED -j ACCEPT
-A INPUT -p icmp -j ACCEPT
-A INPUT -i lo -j ACCEPT
-A INPUT -j REJECT --reject-with icmp-host-prohibited
-A FORWARD -j REJECT --reject-with icmp-host-prohibited
COMMIT
```

You can save and reload iptables rules as explained in "Saving rules" on page 914.

Stop **firewalld**  Stop the **firewalld** service.

```
# systemctl stop firewalld.service
```

Start **iptables** and  Next, run systemctl to start the **iptables** and **ip6tables** services.
**ip6tables**

```
# systemctl start iptables.service
# systemctl start ip6tables.service
```

After starting these services, use the systemctl **status** command to make sure the services are running. If you do not create the **iptables** file shown on the previous page, or if the service did not start for another reason, the output of this command will include the line **Active: inactive (dead)**.

With the **iptables** file shown above installed and the **iptables.service** unit started, the iptables –L option produces the following output:

```
# iptables -L
Chain INPUT (policy ACCEPT)
target     prot opt source               destination
ACCEPT     all  --  anywhere             anywhere             state RELATED,ESTABLISHED
ACCEPT     icmp --  anywhere             anywhere
ACCEPT     all  --  anywhere             anywhere
REJECT     all  --  anywhere             anywhere             reject-with icmp-host-prohibited

Chain FORWARD (policy ACCEPT)
target     prot opt source               destination
REJECT     all  --  anywhere             anywhere             reject-with icmp-host-prohibited

Chain OUTPUT (policy ACCEPT)
target     prot opt source               destination
```

You can use systemctl to turn off the iptables service:

```
# systemctl stop iptables.service
```

With the iptables service turned off, the –L option shows that no rules are in effect (and the system accepts all traffic):

```
# iptables -L
Chain INPUT (policy ACCEPT)
target     prot opt source               destination

Chain FORWARD (policy ACCEPT)
target     prot opt source               destination

Chain OUTPUT (policy ACCEPT)
target     prot opt source               destination
```

Give the command **service iptables save** to save the rules iptables is running. See the next section for more information.

**Emergency disconnect** An argument of **panic** severs all connections with the network. This command unloads all iptables modules from the kernel and sets a policy of DROP for all tables. It locks down the local system so no traffic can get in or out of it. Use this command if the system is under attack and you want to stop all network traffic in and out of the system immediately. Make sure you have backed up firewall rules you want to save before giving this command. See the caution tip on page 902.

```
# /usr/libexec/iptables/iptables.init panic
iptables: Flushing firewall rules:                          [  OK  ]
iptables: Setting chains to policy DROP: filter             [  OK  ]
```

# NOTES

**Startup** The iptables utility is a tool that manipulates rules in the kernel. It differs from daemons (servers) in its setup and use. Whereas Linux daemons such as Apache, **vsftpd**, and **sshd** read the data that controls their operation from a configuration file, you must provide iptables with a series of commands that build a set of packet filtering rules that are kept in the kernel.

Displaying rules   Give the command **iptables –L** or **service iptables status** to display the rules iptables is running.

Saving rules   There are two ways to set up the same set of rules each time you bring the system up. First, you can put iptables commands in a script and run that script each time the system boots. You can call this script from **/etc/rc.d/rc.local**.

Second, you can put the arguments to the iptables commands you want to execute in **/etc/sysconfig/iptables**. The system-config-firewall utility (page 923) and the Anaconda installer (page 62) both use this technique, building sets of rules and storing the corresponding iptables command arguments in **/etc/sysconfig/iptables**. These rules are read into the kernel when the system boots. If you use the **/etc/sysconfig/iptables** file in this manner, be aware that system-config-firewall overwrites this file.

See page 922 for information on copying packet filtering rules to and from the kernel.

iptables-config   The **iptables** service executes the **/etc/sysconfig/iptables-config** file. Refer to the comments in this file for options you can set.

Resetting iptables   If you encounter problems related to the firewall rules, you can return the packet processing rules in the kernel to their default state without rebooting by giving the following commands:

```
# iptables --flush
# iptables --delete-chain
```

These commands delete all rules from all chains and delete any user-defined chains; they do not change policy. Therefore, if the policy is ACCEPT (**–P ACCEPT**), flushing opens the firewall so that it accepts all packets; if the policy is DROP (**–P DROP**), flushing causes the firewall to drop all packets.

See "Emergency disconnect" on page 913 if you need to lock down the system quickly.

# ANATOMY OF AN iptables COMMAND

Command line   This section describes the components of an iptables command line that follow the name of the utility, iptables. Except as noted, the iptables utility is not sensitive to the positions of arguments on the command line. The examples in this chapter reflect a generally accepted syntax that allows commands to be easily read, understood, and maintained. Not all commands have all components.

Many tokens on an iptables command line have two forms: a short form, consisting of a single letter preceded by a single hyphen, and a long form, consisting of a word preceded by two hyphens. Most scripts use the short forms for brevity; lines using the long forms can get unwieldy. The following iptables command lines are equivalent and are used as examples in this section:

```
# iptables --append FORWARD --in-interface eth1 --out-interface eth0 --jump ACCEPT
# iptables -A FORWARD -i eth1 -o eth0 -j ACCEPT
```

Table  The table specifies the name of the table the command operates on: Filter, NAT, or Mangle. You can specify a table name in any iptables command. When you do not specify a table name, the command operates on the Filter table. Most examples in this chapter do not specify table names and, therefore, work on the Filter table. Specify a table as –t *tablename* or **––table** *tablename*.

Command  The command tells iptables what to do with the rest of the command line—for example, add or delete a rule, display rules, or add a chain. The example commands, **–A** and **––append**, append the rule specified by the command line to the specified table (defaults to Filter table) and chain. See page 916 for information on commands.

Chain  The chain specifies the name of the chain that this rule belongs to or that this command works on. The chain is INPUT, OUTPUT, FORWARD, PREROUTING, POSTROUTING, or the name of a user-defined chain. Specify a chain by putting the name of the chain on the command line without any preceding hyphens. The examples at the beginning of this section work with the FORWARD chain.

Match criteria  There are two kinds of match criteria: *packet match* criteria, which match a network packet, and *rule match* criteria, which match an existing rule.

Packet match criteria/rule specifications  Packet match criteria identify network packets and implement rules that take action on packets that match the criteria. The combination of packet match criteria and an action is called a *rule specification*. Rule specifications form the basis for packet filtering. The first example at the beginning of this section uses the **––in-interface eth1 ––out-interface eth0** rule match criteria. The second example uses the short form of the same criteria: **–i eth1 –o eth0**. Both of these rules forward packets that come in on device **eth1** and go out on device **eth0**.

Rule match criteria  Rule match criteria identify existing rules. An iptables command can modify, remove, or position a new rule adjacent to a rule specified by a rule match criterion. There are two ways to identify an existing rule: You can use the same rule specification that was used to create the rule or you can use the rule's ordinal number, called a *rule number*. Rule numbers begin with 1, signifying the first rule in a chain, and can be displayed using **iptables –L ––line-numbers**. The first command below deletes the rule listed at the beginning of this section; the second command replaces (**–R**) INPUT chain rule number 3 with a rule that rejects all packets from IP address 192.168.0.10:

```
# iptables --delete -A FORWARD -i eth1 -o eth0 -j ACCEPT
# iptables -R INPUT 3 --source 192.168.0.10 --jump REJECT
```

A jump or target specifies what action the kernel takes on packets that match all match criteria for a rule. Specify a jump or target as **–j** *target* or **––jump** *target*. The examples at the beginning of this section specify the ACCEPT target using the following commands: **––jump ACCEPT** and **–j ACCEPT**.

Jumps  A jump transfers control to a different chain within the same table. The following command adds (**––append**) a rule to the INPUT chain that transfers packets that use the TCP protocol (**––protocol tcp**) to a user-defined chain named **tcp_rules** (**––jump tcp_rules**):

```
# iptables --append INPUT --protocol tcp --jump tcp_rules
```

When the packet finishes traversing the **tcp_rules** chain, assuming it has not been dropped or rejected, it continues traversing the INPUT chain from the rule following the one it jumped from.

Targets   A target specifies an action the kernel takes on the packet; the simplest actions are ACCEPT, DROP, and REJECT. The following command adds a rule to the FORWARD chain that rejects TCP packets coming from the FTP port (**/etc/services**, the file iptables consults to determine which port to use, shows that FTP uses port 21):

```
# iptables --append FORWARD -p tcp --sport ftp --jump REJECT
```

Some targets, such as LOG, are *nonterminating:* Control passes to the next rule after the target is executed. See page 921 for information on how to use targets.

# BUILDING A SET OF RULES USING iptables

This section describes the specifics that compose an iptables rule. It starts with iptables commands; continues with packet match criteria, display criteria, and match extensions; and concludes with targets.

To specify a table, it is common practice to put the table declaration on the command line immediately following **iptables**. For example, the following command flushes (deletes all the rules from) the NAT table:

```
# iptables -t NAT -F
```

## COMMANDS

Following is a list of iptables commands:

--append   **–A**   Adds rule(s) specified by *rule-specifications* to the end of *chain*. When a packet matches all of the *rule-specifications*, *target* processes it.

*iptables –A chain rule-specifications --jump target*

--delete   **–D**   Removes one or more rules from *chain*, as specified by the *rule-numbers* or *rule-specifications*.

*iptables –D chain rule-numbers | rule-specifications*

--insert   **–I**   Adds rule(s) specified by *rule-specifications* and *target* to the location in *chain* specified by *rule-number*. If you do not specify *rule-number*, it defaults to 1, the head of the chain.

*iptables –I chain rule-number | rule-specifications --jump target*

--replace   **–R**   Replaces rule number *rule-number* in *chain* with *rule-specification* and *target*. The command fails if *rule-number* or *rule-specification* resolves to more than one address.

*iptables –R chain rule-number | rule-specification --jump target*

**--list** **–L** Displays the rules in *chain*. Omit *chain* to display the rules for all chains. Use **--line-numbers** to display rule numbers or select other display criteria from the list on the next page.

> *iptables –L [chain] display-criteria*

**--flush** **–F** Deletes all rules from *chain*. Omit *chain* to delete all rules from all chains. This command does not change policy; see "Resetting iptables" on page 914 for more information.

> *iptables –F [chain]*

**--zero** **–Z** Changes to zero the value of all packet and byte counters in *chain* or in all chains when you do not specify *chain*. Use with –L to display the counters before clearing them.

> *iptables –Z [–L] [chain]*

**--delete-chain** **–X** Removes the user-defined chain named *chain*. If you do not specify *chain*, removes all user-defined chains. You cannot delete a chain that a target points to.

> *iptables –X chain*

**--policy** **–P** Sets the default target or policy *builtin-target* for the builtin chain *builtin-chain*. This policy is applied to packets that do not match any rule in the chain. If a chain does not have a policy, unmatched packets are ACCEPTed.

> *iptables –P builtin-chain builtin-target*

**--rename-chain** **–E** Changes the name of the chain *old* to *new*.

> *iptables –E old new*

**--help** **–h** Displays a summary of the iptables command syntax.

> *iptables –h*

Follow a match extension protocol with –h to display options you can use with that protocol. For more information refer to "Help with extensions" on the next page.

## PACKET MATCH CRITERIA

The following criteria match network packets. When you precede a criterion with an exclamation point (!), the rule matches packets that do not match the criterion.

**[!] --protocol *proto***

**–p** Matches if the packet uses the *proto* protocol. This criterion is a match extension (next page).

**[!] --source *address[/mask]***

**–s** or **--src** Matches if the packet came from *address*. The *address* should be an IP address and not a name because, when the system boots, iptables starts before the network and will not be able to resolve a name. See page 483 for formats of the optional *mask* (only with an IP address).

[!] −−destination *address*[*/mask*]

> −d or −−dst   Matches if the packet is going to **address**. The **address** should be an IP address and not a name because, when the system boots, iptables starts before the network and will not be able to resolve a name. See page 483 for formats of the optional **mask** (only with an IP address).

[!] −−in-interface *iface*[+]

> −i   For the INPUT, FORWARD, and PREROUTING chains, matches if **iface** is the name of the interface the packet was received from. Append a plus sign (+) to **iface** to match any interface whose name begins with **iface**. When you do not specify **in-interface**, the rule matches packets coming from any interface.

[!] −−out-interface *iface*[+]

> −o   For the OUTPUT, FORWARD, and POSTROUTING chains, matches if **iface** is the interface the packet will be sent to. Append a plus sign (+) to **iface** to match any interface whose name begins with **iface**. When you do not specify **out-interface**, the rule matches packets going to any interface.

[!] −fragment   −f   Matches the second and subsequent fragments of fragmented packets. Because these packets do not contain source or destination information, they do not match any other rules.

## DISPLAY CRITERIA

The following criteria display information. All packets match these criteria.

−−verbose   −v   Displays additional output.

−−numeric   −n   Displays IP addresses and port numbers as numbers, not names.

−−exact   −x   When used with −L, displays exact packet and byte counts instead of rounded values.

−−line-numbers   Displays line numbers when listing rules. These line numbers are also the rule numbers that you can use in rule match criteria (page 915).

## MATCH EXTENSIONS

Rule specification (packet match criteria) extensions, called *match extensions*, add matches based on protocols and state to the matches described previously. Each of the protocol extensions is kept in a module that must be loaded before that match extension can be used. The command that loads the module must appear in the same rule specification as, and to the left of, the command that uses the module. There are two types of match extensions: implicit and explicit.

### IMPLICIT MATCH EXTENSIONS

Help with extensions   Implicit extensions are loaded (somewhat) automatically when you use a −−protocol command (described on the next page). Each protocol has its own extensions. Follow the protocol with −h to display extensions you can use with that protocol. For example, the following command displays TCP extensions *at the end* of the Help output:

```
$ iptables -p tcp -h
...
tcp match options:
 --tcp-flags [!] mask comp      match when TCP flags & mask == comp
                                (Flags: SYN ACK FIN RST URG PSH ALL NONE)
 [!] --syn                      match when only SYN flag set
                                (equivalent to --tcp-flags SYN,RST,ACK SYN)
 --source-port [!] port[:port]
 --sport ...
                                match source port(s)
 --destination-port [!] port[:port]
 --dport ...
                                match destination port(s)
 --tcp-option [!] number        match if TCP option set
```

This section does not describe all extensions. Use **–h**, as in the preceding example, to display a complete list.

**--protocol [!]** *proto*

**–p**   Loads the *proto* module and matches if the packet uses the *proto* protocol. The *proto* can be a name or number from **/etc/protocols**, including **tcp**, **udp**, and **icmp** (page 1254). Specifying **all** or **0** (zero) matches all protocols and is the same as not including this match in a rule.

The following criteria load the TCP module and match TCP protocol packets coming from port 22 (ssh packets):

```
--protocol tcp --source-port 22
```

The following command expands the preceding match to cause the kernel to drop all incoming ssh packets. This command uses **ssh**, which iptables looks up in **/etc/services**, in place of **22**:

```
# iptables -A --protocol tcp --source-port ssh --jump DROP
```

## TCP

The extensions in this section are loaded when you specify **--protocol tcp**.

**--destination-port [!]** [*port*[:*port*]] | port: | :port

**--dport**   Matches a destination port number or service name (see **/etc/services**). You can also specify a range of port numbers. Specifically, *:port* specifies ports 0 through *port*, and *port:* specifies ports *port* through 65535.

**--source-port [!]** [*port*[:*port*]] | port: | :port

**--sport**   Matches a source port number or service name (see **/etc/services**). You can also specify a range of port numbers. Specifically, *:port* specifies ports 0 through *port*, and *port:* specifies ports *port* through 65535.

**[!] --syn**   Matches packets with the SYN bit set and the ACK and FIN bits cleared. This match extension is shorthand for **--tcp-flags SYN,RST,ACK SYN**.

**--tcp-flags [!]** *mask comp*

Defines which TCP flag settings constitute a match. Valid flags are SYN, ACK, FIN, RST, URG, PSH, ALL, and NONE. The *mask* is a comma-separated list of flags to be examined; *comp* is a comma-separated subset of *mask* that specifies the flags that must be set for a match to occur. Flags not specified in *mask* must be unset.

**--tcp-option [!]** *n* Matches a TCP option with a decimal value of *n*.

### UDP

When you specify **--protocol udp,** you can specify a source and/or destination port in the same manner as described under "TCP" on the preceding page.

### ICMP

The extension in this section is loaded when you specify **--protocol icmp.** *ICMP* (page 1254) packets carry messages only.

**--icmp-type [!]** *name*

Matches when the packet is an ICMP packet of type *name*. The *name* can be a numeric ICMP type or one of the names returned by

```
$ iptables -p icmp -h
```

## EXPLICIT MATCH EXTENSIONS

Explicit match extensions differ from implicit match extensions in that you must use a **-m** or **--match** option to specify a module before you can use the extension. Many explicit match extension modules are available; this section covers **state,** one of the most important.

### STATE

The **state** extension matches criteria based on the state of the connection the packet is part of (page 911).

**--state** *state*  Matches a packet whose state is defined by *state*, a comma-separated list of states from the following list:

- **ESTABLISHED**—Any packet, within a specific connection, following the exchange of packets in both directions for that connection.

- **INVALID**—A stateless or unidentifiable packet.

- **NEW**—The first packet within a specific connection, typically a SYN packet.

- **RELATED**—Any packets exchanged in a connection spawned from an ESTABLISHED connection. For example, an FTP data connection might be related to the FTP control connection. (The **ip_conntrack_ftp** module is required for FTP connection tracking.)

The following command loads the **state** extension and establishes a rule that matches and drops both invalid packets and packets from new connections:

```
# iptables --match state --state INVALID,NEW --jump DROP
```

# TARGETS

All targets are built in; there are no user-defined targets. This section lists some of the targets available with iptables. Applicable target options are listed following each target.

**ACCEPT** Causes the packet to leave the chain. The packet can then be processed by another chain or be up the TCP stack.

**DNAT** **Destination Network Address Translation**   Rewrites the destination address of the packet (page 910).

**--to-destination** *ip[-ip][:port-port]*

Same as SNAT (next page) with **to-source**, except it changes the destination addresses of packets to the specified addresses and ports and is valid only in the PREROUTING or OUTPUT chains of the NAT table and any user-defined chains called from those chains. The following command adds to the PREROUTING chain of the NAT table a rule that changes the destination in the headers of TCP packets with a destination of 66.187.232.50 to 192.168.0.10:

```
# iptables -t NAT -A PREROUTING -p tcp -d 66.187.232.50 -j DNAT --to-destination 192.168.0.10
```

**DROP** Ends the packet's life without notice.

**LOG** Turns on logging for the packet being processed. The kernel uses **syslogd** (page 620) to process output generated by this target. LOG is a nonterminating target, so processing continues with the next rule. Use two rules to LOG packets that you REJECT or DROP, one each with the targets LOG and REJECT or DROP, with the same matching criteria.

**--log-level** *n*   Specifies logging level *n* as per **syslog.conf** (page 620).

**--log-prefix** *string*

Prefixes log entries with *string*, which can be a maximum of 14 characters long.

**--log-tcp-options** Logs options from the TCP packet header.

**--log-ip-options** Logs options from the IP packet header.

**MASQUERADE** Similar to SNAT (next page) with **--to-source**, except that it grabs the IP information from the interface on the specified port. For use on systems with dynamically assigned IP addresses, such as those using DHCP, including most dial-up lines. Valid only in rules in the POSTROUTING chain of the NAT table.

**--to-ports** *port[-port]*

Specifies the port for the interface you want to masquerade. Forgets connections when the interface goes down, as is appropriate for dial-up lines. You must specify the TCP or UDP protocol (**--protocol tcp** or **udp**) with this target.

**REJECT** Similar to DROP, except it notifies the sending system that the packet was blocked.

**--reject-with** *type* Returns the error *type* to the originating system. The *type* can be any of the following, all of which return the appropriate *ICMP* (page 1254) error: **icmp-net-unreachable**, **icmp-host-unreachable**, **icmp-port-unreachable**, **icmp-proto-unreachable**, **icmp-net-prohibited**, or **icmp-host-prohibited**. You can specify *type* as **echo-reply** from rules that require an ICMP ping (page 305) packet to return a ping reply. You can specify **tcp-reset** from rules in or called from the INPUT chain to return a TCP RST packet. This parameter is valid in the INPUT, FORWARD, and OUTPUT chains and user-defined chains called from these chains.

RETURN   Stops traversing this chain and returns the packet to the calling chain.

SNAT   **Source Network Address Translation**   Rewrites the source address of the packet. Appropriate for hosts on a LAN that share an Internet connection.

--to-source *ip[-ip][:port-port]*

Alters the source IP address of an outbound packet, and the source IP addresses of all future packets in this connection, to *ip*. Skips additional rules, if any exist. Returning packets are automatically de-SNATed so they return to the originating host. Valid only in the POSTROUTING chain of the NAT table.

When you specify a range of IP addresses (*ip-ip*) or use multiple **to-source** targets, iptables assigns the addresses in a round-robin fashion, cycling through the addresses, one for each new connection.

When the rule specifies the TCP or UDP protocol (**–p tcp** or **–p udp**), you can specify a range of ports. When you do not specify a range of ports, the rule matches all ports. Every connection on a NATed subnet must have a unique IP address and port combination. If two systems on a NATed subnet try to use the same port, the kernel maps one of the ports to another (unused) port. Ports less than 512 are mapped to other ports less than 512, ports from 512 to 1024 are mapped to other ports from 512 to 1024, and ports above 1024 are mapped to other ports above 1024.

# COPYING RULES TO AND FROM THE KERNEL

The iptables-save utility copies packet filtering rules from the kernel to standard output; you can redirect the output to a file. The iptables-restore utility copies rules from standard input, as written by iptables-save, to the kernel. Following is the output from iptables-save as the system is installed (system-config-firewall has not been run):

```
# iptables-save
# Generated by iptables-save v1.4.9 on Tue Nov  5 14:57:10 2013
*filter
:INPUT ACCEPT [0:0]
:FORWARD ACCEPT [0:0]
:OUTPUT ACCEPT [78:7254]
-A INPUT -m state --state RELATED,ESTABLISHED -j ACCEPT
-A INPUT -p icmp -j ACCEPT
-A INPUT -i lo -j ACCEPT
-A INPUT -d 224.0.0.251/32 -p udp -m state --state NEW -m udp --dport 5353 -j ACCEPT
-A INPUT -j REJECT --reject-with icmp-host-prohibited
-A FORWARD -j REJECT --reject-with icmp-host-prohibited
COMMIT
# Completed on Tue Nov  5 14:57:10 2013
```

Most lines that iptables-save writes are iptables command lines without the **iptables** at the beginning. Lines that begin with a hashmark (#) are comments. Lines that begin with an asterisk (✳) are names of tables that the following commands work on; the commands in the preceding example work on the Filter table. The COMMIT line must appear at the end of all commands for a table; it executes the preceding commands. Lines that begin with colons specify chains in the following format:

> *:chain policy [packets:bytes]*

where *chain* is the name of the chain, *policy* is the policy (default target) for the chain, and *packets* and *bytes* are the packet and byte counters, respectively. The square brackets must appear in the line; they do not indicate optional parameters.

Refer to the next section and visit www.faqs.org/docs/iptables/iptables-save.html for more information.

# system-config-firewall: GENERATES A SET OF RULES

This section describes the set of rules generated by system-config-firewall (page 900) when you ask it to create a firewall with only ssh (TCP port 22) running as a trusted service and no other ports specified. The system-config-firewall utility writes the rules in the format used by iptables-save (see the preceding section) to the **/etc/sysconfig/iptables** file, which is read by the **iptables** service so that the firewall is implemented each time the system boots.

In the following listing, ✳**filter** indicates that the commands appearing after it work on the Filter table. The first line that begins with a colon specifies that the policy for the INPUT chain in the Filter table is ACCEPT. FORWARD and OUTPUT chains are specified similarly. Because the counters for all the chains are zero, the counters will be reset to zero each time the system boots and initializes iptables from this file. The system-config-firewall utility works mostly with the INPUT chain.

```
# cat /etc/sysconfig/iptables
# Firewall configuration written by system-config-firewall
# Manual customization of this file is not recommended.
*filter
:INPUT ACCEPT [0:0]
:FORWARD ACCEPT [0:0]
:OUTPUT ACCEPT [0:0]
-A INPUT -m state --state ESTABLISHED,RELATED -j ACCEPT
-A INPUT -p icmp -j ACCEPT
-A INPUT -i lo -j ACCEPT
-A INPUT -m state --state NEW -m tcp -p tcp --dport 22 -j ACCEPT
-A INPUT -j REJECT --reject-with icmp-host-prohibited
-A FORWARD -j REJECT --reject-with icmp-host-prohibited
COMMIT
```

Most of the lines append rules to the INPUT chain. Following is a description of what these lines do.

The first line that works with the INPUT chain uses **–m** to specify the **state** module and accepts ESTABLISHED and RELATED packets:

```
-A INPUT -m state --state ESTABLISHED,RELATED -j ACCEPT
```

The next line accepts all ICMP packets:

```
-A INPUT -p icmp -j ACCEPT
```

This line accepts packets from the local interface:

```
-A INPUT -i lo -j ACCEPT
```

This line allows new TCP connections on port 22 (ssh):

```
-A INPUT -m state --state NEW -m tcp -p tcp --dport 22 -j ACCEPT
```

These lines reject all packets that have not been accepted and return ICMP error **icmp-host-prohibited** to the system that sent the packet:

```
-A INPUT -j REJECT --reject-with icmp-host-prohibited
-A FORWARD -j REJECT --reject-with icmp-host-prohibited
```

mDNS  Running **system-config-firewall** (see the previous section), added the rule that accepts TCP packets on port 22 and removed the default rule that accepts multicast DNS (mDNS; www.multicastdns.org) packets:

```
-A INPUT -d 224.0.0.251/32 -p udp -m state --state NEW -m udp --dport 5353 -j ACCEPT
```

COMMIT executes the preceding commands. With the preceding rules loaded, you can use iptables to list the rules and see the defaults that iptables puts in place:

```
# iptables -L
Chain INPUT (policy ACCEPT)
target     prot opt source               destination
ACCEPT     all  --  anywhere             anywhere             state RELATED,ESTABLISHED
ACCEPT     icmp --  anywhere             anywhere
ACCEPT     all  --  anywhere             anywhere
ACCEPT     tcp  --  anywhere             anywhere             state NEW tcp dpt:ssh
REJECT     all  --  anywhere             anywhere             reject-with icmp-host-prohibited

Chain FORWARD (policy ACCEPT)
target     prot opt source               destination
REJECT     all  --  anywhere             anywhere             reject-with icmp-host-prohibited

Chain OUTPUT (policy ACCEPT)
target     prot opt source               destination
```

# SHARING AN INTERNET CONNECTION USING NAT

Many scripts that set up Internet connection sharing using iptables are available on the Internet. Each of these scripts boils down to the same few basic iptables commands, albeit with minor differences. This section discusses those few statements to explain how a connection can be shared. You can use the statements presented in this section or refer to the *Linux IP Masquerade HOWTO* for complete scripts. The tldp.org/HOWTO/IP-Masquerade-HOWTO/firewall-examples.html Web page holds the simplest of these scripts.

There are two ways you can share a single connection to the Internet (one IP address), both of which involve setting up NAT to alter addresses in packets and then forward them. The first allows clients (browsers, mail readers, and so on) on several systems on a LAN to share a single IP address to connect to servers on the Internet. The second allows servers (mail, Web, FTP, and so on) on different systems on a LAN to provide their services over a single connection to the Internet. You can use iptables to set up one or both of these configurations. In both cases, you need to set up a system that is a router: It must have two network connections—one connected to the Internet and the other to the LAN.

For optimal security, use a dedicated system as a router. Because data transmission over a connection to the Internet—even over a broadband connection—is relatively slow, using a slower, older system as a router does not generally slow down a LAN. This setup also offers some defense against intrusion from the Internet. A workstation on the LAN can function as a router as well, but this setup means that you maintain data on a system that is directly connected to the Internet. The following sections discuss the security of each setup.

The examples in this section assume the device named **eth0** connects to the Internet on 10.255.255.255 and that **eth1** connects to the LAN on 192.168.0.1. Substitute the devices and IP addresses that the local systems use. If you use a modem to connect to the Internet, you need to substitute **ppp0** (or another device) for **eth0** in the examples.

For the examples in this section to work, you must turn on IP forwarding. First give the following command and make sure everything is working:

```
# sysctl -w net.ipv4.ip_forward=1
net.ipv4.ip_forward = 1
```

If you want to forward IPv6 packets, give this command instead:

```
# sysctl -w net.ipv6.conf.all.forwarding=1
net.ipv6.conf.all.forwarding = 1
```

Once you know that iptables is working correctly, change the 0 to a **1** in the following line in **/etc/sysctl.conf** to make the kernel always perform IP forwarding:

```
net.ipv4.ip_forward = 0
```

After making this change, give the command **/sbin/sysctl –e –p** to apply the change and to make sure that there are no typographical errors in the configuration file.

# CONNECTING SEVERAL CLIENTS TO A SINGLE INTERNET CONNECTION

Configuring the kernel of the router system to allow clients on multiple local systems on the LAN to connect to the Internet requires you to set up *IP masquerading,* or *SNAT* (source NAT). IP masquerading translates the source and destination addresses in the headers of network packets that originate on local systems and the packets that remote servers send in response to those packets. These packets are part of connections that originate on a local system. The example in this section does nothing to packets that are part of connections that originate on the remote systems (on the Internet): These packets cannot get past the router system, which provides some degree of security.

The point of rewriting the packet headers is to allow systems with different local IP addresses to share a single IP address on the Internet. The router system translates the source or origin address of packets from the local systems to that of the Internet connection, so all packets passing from the router to the Internet appear to come from a single system—10.255.255.255 in the example. All packets sent in response by remote systems on the Internet to the router system have the address of the Internet connection—10.255.255.255 in the example—as their destination address. The router system remembers each connection and alters the destination address of each response packet to that of the local, originating system.

The router system is established by four iptables commands, one of which sets up a log of masqueraded connections. The first command puts the first rule in the FORWARD chain of the Filter (default) table (**–A FORWARD**):

```
# iptables -A FORWARD -i eth0 -o eth1 -m state --state ESTABLISHED,RELATED -j ACCEPT
```

To match this rule, a packet must be

1. Received on **eth0** (coming in from the Internet): **–i eth0**

2. Going to be sent out on **eth1** (going out to the LAN): **–o eth1**

3. Part of an established connection or a connection that is related to an established connection: **––state ESTABLISHED,RELATED**

The kernel accepts (**–j ACCEPT**) packets that meet these three criteria. Accepted packets pass to the next appropriate chain or table. Packets from the Internet that attempt to create a new connection are not matched and, therefore, are not accepted by this rule. Packets that are not accepted pass to the next rule in the FORWARD chain.

The second command puts the second rule in the FORWARD chain of the Filter table:

```
# iptables -A FORWARD -i eth1 -o eth0 -j ACCEPT
```

To match this rule, a packet must be

1. Received on **eth1** (coming in from the LAN): **–i eth1**

2. Going to be sent out on **eth0** (going out to the Internet): **–o eth0**

The kernel accepts packets that meet these two criteria, which means all packets that originate locally and are going to the Internet are accepted. Accepted packets pass to the next appropriate chain/table; packets that are not accepted pass to the next rule in the FORWARD chain.

The third command puts the third rule in the FORWARD chain of the Filter table:

```
# iptables -A FORWARD -j LOG
```

Because this rule has no match criteria, it acts on all packets it processes. This rule's action is to log packets—that is, it logs packets from the Internet that attempt to create a new connection.

Packets that reach the end of the FORWARD chain of the Filter table are done with the rules set up by iptables and are handled by the local TCP stack. Packets from the Internet that attempt to create a new connection on the router system are accepted or returned, depending on whether the service they are trying to connect to is available on the router system.

The fourth command puts the first rule in the POSTROUTING chain of the NAT table. Only packets that are establishing a new connection are passed to the NAT table. Once a connection has been set up for SNAT or MASQUERADE, the headers on all subsequent ESTABLISHED and RELATED packets are altered the same way as the header of the first packet. Packets sent in response to these packets automatically have their headers adjusted so they return to the originating local system.

```
# iptables -t NAT -A POSTROUTING -o eth0 -j MASQUERADE
```

To match this rule, a packet must be

1. Establishing a new connection (otherwise it would not have come to the NAT table)
2. Going to be sent out on **eth0** (going out to the Internet): **–o eth0**

The kernel MASQUERADEs all packets that meet these criteria. In other words, all locally originating packets that are establishing new connections have their source address changed to the address that is associated with **eth0** (10.255.255.255 in the example). If the local system has a static IP address, substitute SNAT for MASQUERADE.

The following example shows all four commands together:

```
# iptables -A FORWARD -i eth0 -o eth1 -m state --state ESTABLISHED,RELATED -j ACCEPT
# iptables -A FORWARD -i eth1 -o eth0 -j ACCEPT
# iptables -A FORWARD -j LOG
# iptables -t NAT -A POSTROUTING -o eth0 -j MASQUERADE
```

See page 914 for instructions on how to save these rules so the firewall comes up each time the system boots. To limit the local systems that can connect to the Internet, you can add a **–s** (source) match criterion to the last command:

```
# iptables -t NAT -A POSTROUTING -o eth0 -s 192.168.0.0-192.168.0.32 -j MASQUERADE
```

In the preceding command, **–s 192.168.0.0-192.168.0.32** causes only packets from an IP address in the specified range to be MASQUERADEd.

# CONNECTING SEVERAL SERVERS TO A SINGLE INTERNET CONNECTION

DNAT (destination NAT) can set up rules that allow clients from the Internet to send packets to servers on the LAN. This example sets up an SMTP mail server on 192.168.1.33 and an HTTP (Web) server on 192.168.1.34. Both protocols use TCP. SMTP uses port 25 and HTTP uses port 80, so the rules match TCP packets with destination ports of 25 and 80. The example assumes the mail server does not make outgoing connections and uses another server on the LAN for DNS and mail relaying. Both commands put rules in the PREROUTING chain of the NAT table (**–A PREROUTING –t NAT**):

```
# iptables -A PREROUTING -t NAT -p tcp --dport 25 -j DNAT --to-destination 192.168.0.33:25
# iptables -A PREROUTING -t NAT -p tcp --dport 80 -j DNAT --to-destination 192.168.0.34:80
```

To match these rules, the packet must use the TCP protocol (**–p tcp**) and have a destination port of either 25 (first rule, **––dport 25**) or 80 (second rule, **––dport 80**).

The **––to-destination** is a target specific to the PREROUTING and OUTPUT chains of the NAT table; it alters the destination address and port of matched packets as specified. As with MASQUERADE and SNAT, subsequent packets in the same and related connections are altered the same way.

The fact that the servers cannot originate connections means that neither server can be exploited to participate in a *DDoS attack* (page 1246) on systems on the Internet, nor can they send private data from the local system back to a malicious user's system.

# CHAPTER SUMMARY

A firewall, as implemented by **firewalld**, is designed to prevent unauthorized access to a system or network. Such a firewall can protect just the single system it runs on or can protect the system it runs on plus other systems on a LAN that connect to the Internet through the system running the firewall. The **firewalld** service is replacing the older **iptables** service. The **firewalld** daemon accepts changes to the firewall while it is running. The **firewalld** daemon (which runs in userspace) works with **netfilter** (which runs in kernelspace) to filter network packets. A **firewalld** firewall allows you to configure the runtime configuration and the permanent configuration.

The **firewalld** daemon has a D-BUS interface that allows it to communicate with processes, including allowing authenticated processes to reconfigure the firewall as they run. It also has a GUI (firewall-config) and a CLI (firewall-cmd). The firewall-cmd utility has direct commands that allow you to give iptables commands to **firewalld**. In an emergency you can put the firewall in panic mode, in which it drops all packets.

An iptables command sets up or maintains in the kernel rules that control the flow of network packets; rules are stored in chains. Each rule includes a criteria part and an action part, called a target. When the criteria part matches a network packet, the kernel applies the action from the rule to the packet.

Chains are collected in three tables: Filter, NAT, and Mangle. Filter (the default table) DROPs or ACCEPTs packets based on their content. NAT (the Network Address Translation table) translates the source or destination field in packet headers. Mangle is used exclusively to alter the TOS (type of service), TTL (time to live), and MARK fields in a packet. The connection tracking machine, which is handled by the **conntrack** module, defines rules that match criteria based on the state of the connection a packet is part of.

# EXERCISES

1. How would you put a **firewalld** firewall in panic mode from firewall-config? From firewall-cmd?

2. How can you tell whether **firewalld** is running?

3. Which firewall-cmd command would you use to cause the runtime configuration of the firewall to trust the FTP service? Which command would cause the permanent configuration to trust the FTP service?

4. Which firewall-cmd command would verify that the FTP service was trusted in the runtime configuration? In the permanent configuration?

5. How would you use firewall-cmd to open ports for SMTP packets (TCP and UDP port 25) in the permanent configuration? Verify that these ports are open.

# ADVANCED EXERCISES

6. Define an iptables rule that will reject incoming connections on the TELNET port.

7. Which iptables command would list all rules including line numbers that specify each rule's position in the chain?

8. Write an iptables (IPv4) rule that silently blocks incoming SMTP connections from **10.10.0.10**.

9. Run the rule from exercise 8 using the direct option of firewall-cmd.

# 26

# APACHE (httpd): SETTING UP A WEB SERVER

## OBJECTIVES

After reading this chapter you should be able to:

▶ Explain the purpose of Apache and describe the use of several available modules

▶ Configure an Apache server to listen on the network and provide simple content

▶ Customize names, addresses, ports, and the location of content, logs, and scripts of an Apache server

▶ Allow users to publish content from their home directories

▶ Configure virtual hosts to display different content

▶ Configure password-protected directory hierarchies, host-based access control, directory options, and SELinux Booleans to secure access to Web content

The World Wide Web (WWW or Web for short), is a collection of servers that hold material, called *content,* that (Web) browsers can display. Each of the servers on the Web is connected to the Internet, a network of networks (an *internetwork*). Much of the content on the Web is coded in HTML (Hypertext Markup Language, page 1254). *Hypertext,* the links you click on a Web page, allows browsers to display and react to links that point to other Web pages on the Internet.

Apache is the most popular Web server on the Internet. It is both robust and extensible. The ease with which you can install, configure, and run it in the Linux environment makes it an obvious choice for publishing content on the World Wide Web. The Apache server and related projects are developed and maintained by the Apache Software Foundation (ASF), a not-for-profit corporation formed in June 1999. The ASF grew out of the Apache Group, which was established in 1995 to develop the Apache server.

This chapter starts by providing introductory information about Apache. Following this information is the JumpStart section, which describes the minimal steps needed to get Apache up and running. Next is "Filesystem Layout," which details where the various Apache files are located.

Configuration directives are a key part of Apache and are discussed starting on page 939. This section includes coverage of contexts and containers, two features/ concepts that are critical to understanding Apache. The next section, which starts on page 962, covers advanced Apache configuration: redirects, content negotiation, directory indexing, virtual hosts, troubleshooting, and modules you can use with Apache, including CGI and SSL.

# INTRODUCTION

Apache is a server that responds to requests from Web browsers, or *clients,* such as Firefox, Netscape, lynx, elinks, and Internet Explorer. When you enter the address of a Web page (a *URI,* page 1279) in a Web browser's location bar, the browser sends a request over the Internet to the (Apache) server at that address. In response, the server sends (serves) the requested content back to the browser. The browser then displays or plays the content, which might be a textual document, song, picture, video clip, or other information.

Content    Aside from add-on modules that can interact with the content, Apache looks only at the type of data it is sending so that it can specify the correct *MIME* (page 1261) type; otherwise it remains oblivious to the content itself. Server administration and content creation are two different aspects of bringing up a Web site. This chapter concentrates on setting up and running an Apache server; it spends little time discussing content creation.

Modules    Apache, like the Linux kernel, uses external modules to increase load-time flexibility and to allow parts of its code to be recompiled without recompiling the whole program. Rather than being part of the Apache binary, modules are stored as separate files that can be loaded when Apache is started.

Apache uses external modules, called dynamic shared objects (DSOs), for basic and advanced functions; there is not much to Apache without these modules. Apache also uses modules to extend its functionality. For example, modules can process scripts written in Perl, PHP, Python, and other languages; use several different methods to authenticate users; facilitate publishing content; and process nontextual content, such as audio. The list of modules written by the ASF and third-party developers is constantly growing. For more information refer to "Modules" on page 968.

Graphical configuration You can use the HTTP Server Configuration window (**system-config-httpd** package) to configure Apache graphically. Open this window by giving the command **system-config-httpd** from an Enter a Command window (ALT-F2) or a terminal emulator. Click **Help** in this window for more information.

# MORE INFORMATION

Local Apache documentation: With Apache running and the **httpd-manual** package installed, point a browser at *server*/**manual**. On the server system, substitute **localhost** for *server;* from a remote system, substitute the name or IP address of the Apache server for *server*. If Apache is not running, point a browser on the server system only at **/usr/share/httpd/manual/index.html**.

apachectl and httpd man pages
Apache directives: *server*/**manual/mod/directives.html**
SSI directives: *server*/**manual/howto/ssi.html**

Web Apache documentation: httpd.apache.org/docs/2.4
Apache directives: httpd.apache.org/docs/2.4/mod/directives.html
Apache Software Foundation (newsletters, mailing lists, projects, module registry, and more): www.apache.org
webalizer: www.webalizer.org
awstats: awstats.sourceforge.net
**mod_perl**: perl.apache.org
**mod_php**: www.php.net
**mod_python**: www.modpython.org; see **mod_wsgi**
**mod_ssl**: www.modssl.org
**mod_wsgi**: wsgi.readthedocs.org/en/latest, code.google.com/p/modwsgi
MRTG: oss.oetiker.ch/mrtg
SNMP: net-snmp.sourceforge.net
SSI directives: httpd.apache.org/docs/2.4/howto/ssi.html

# NOTES

Terms: Apache and **httpd** *Apache* is the name of a server that serves HTTP and other content. The Apache daemon is named **httpd** because it is an HTTP server daemon. This chapter uses the terms *Apache* and *httpd* interchangeably.

Terms: server and process An Apache *server* is the same thing as an Apache *process*. An Apache child process exists to handle incoming client requests; hence it is referred to as a server.

Firewall   An Apache server normally uses TCP port 80; a secure server uses TCP port 443. If the server is running a firewall or is behind a firewall, you need to open one or both of these ports. Give the following commands to open the ports each time the system boots (permanently) and on the running system; see page 906 for information on firewall-cmd.

```
# firewall-cmd --add-port=80/tcp
# firewall-cmd --permanent --add-port=80/tcp
# firewall-cmd --add-port=443/tcp
# firewall-cmd --permanent --add-port=443/tcp
```

SELinux   When SELinux is set to use a targeted policy, **httpd** is protected by SELinux. You can disable this protection if necessary. For more information refer to "Setting the Targeted Policy with system-config-selinux" on page 475.

Running with **root** privileges   Because Apache serves content on privileged ports, you must start it running with **root** privileges. For security reasons, Fedora/RHEL sets up Apache to spawn processes that run as the user and group **apache**.

Locale   The **httpd** daemon starts using the C locale by default. You can modify this behavior—for example, to use the configured system locale—by setting the **HTTPD_LANG** variable in the **/etc/sysconfig/httpd** file.

Document root   The root of the directory hierarchy that Apache serves content from is called the *document root* and is controlled by the DocumentRoot directive (page 942). This directive defines a directory on the server that maps to **/**. This directory appears to users who are browsing a Web site as the root directory. As distributed by Fedora/RHEL, the document root is **/var/www/html**.

Modifying content   With the default Fedora/RHEL configuration of Apache, only a user working with **root** privileges can add or modify content in **/var/www/html**. To avoid having people work with **root** privileges when they are manipulating content, create a group (**webwork**, for example), put people who need to work with Web content in this group, and make the directory hierarchy starting at **/var/www/html** (or another document root) writable by that group. In addition, if you give the directory hierarchy setgid permission, all new files created within this hierarchy will belong to the group, which facilitates sharing files. The first three commands below add the new group, change the mode of the document root to setgid, and change the group that the document root belongs to. The last command adds *username* to the **webwork** group; you must repeat this command for each user you want to add to the group.

```
# groupadd webwork
# chmod g+rws /var/www/html
# chown :webwork /var/www/html

# usermod -aG webwork username
```

See page 600 for more information about working with groups.

Version   Fedora/RHEL runs Apache version 2.4.

# RUNNING AN APACHE WEB SERVER

This section explains how to install, test, and configure a basic Web server.

## PREREQUISITES

Group installation Give the following command to install the Web Server group of packages. In addition to **httpd**, this command installs support for PHP, Perl, and Python; Apache documentation; encrypted content using HTTPS protocol; and database-driven Web sites.

```
# yum groupinstall "Web Server"
```

Minimal installation Install the following packages:

- **httpd**
- **apr** (Apache portable runtime; installed with **httpd**)
- **apr-util** (installed with **httpd**)

### Before you set up an Apache server

tip Before you configure an Apache server, set up a static IP address for the server system. See "Configuring a Static IP Address for a Wired NIC" on page 641 for instructions.

Enable and start Run systemctl to cause the **httpd** service to start each time the system enters multiuser
httpd mode and then start the **httpd** service. Use the systemctl **status** command to make sure the service is running.

```
# systemctl enable httpd.service
# systemctl start httpd.service
```

After modifying Apache configuration files, give the second command again, replacing **start** with **reload** to cause Apache to reread those files.

Optional packages You might want to install the following optional packages:

- **httpd-manual**—The Apache manual; see "Local" on page 933 for more information
- **webalizer**—Web server log analyzer (page 975)
- **awstats**—Web server log analyzer
- **mod_perl**—Embedded Perl scripting language
- **mod_wsgi**—Embedded Python scripting language
- **mod_ssl**—Secure Sockets Layer extension (page 970)
- **php**—Includes embedded PHP scripting language, with IMAP and LDAP support
- **mrtg**—MRTG traffic monitor (page 975)
- **net-snmp** and **net-snmp-utils**—SNMP, required for MRTG (page 975)

# JUMPSTART: GETTING APACHE UP AND RUNNING

To get Apache up and running, modify the **/etc/httpd/conf/httpd.conf** configuration file as described in this section. "Directives You Might Want to Modify as You Get Started" on page 940 explains more about this file and explores other changes you might want to make to it.

## MODIFYING THE httpd.conf CONFIGURATION FILE

Apache runs as installed, but it is a good idea to add/modify the three lines of the **/etc/httpd/conf/httpd.conf** configuration file described in this section before starting Apache. If you do not add/modify these lines, Apache will assign values that might not work on the server.

ServerName   The ServerName line establishes a name for the server. Add one of the following lines to **httpd.conf** to set the name of the server to the domain name of the server or, if you do not have a domain name, to the IP address of the server. Add the line just below the commented-out ServerName line in the **httpd.conf** file. The commented-out line specifies port 80 (:80 at the end of the line); port 80 is the default so you do not need to specify it.

> *ServerName* **example.com**

*or*

> *ServerName* **IP_address**

where **example.com** is the domain name of the server and **IP_address** is the IP address of the server. If you are not connected to a network, you can use the **localhost** address, 127.0.0.1, so you can start the server and experiment with it using a browser on the server system. See page 942 for more information on the ServerName directive.

ServerAdmin and   When a client has trouble getting information from a server, the server typically dis-
ServerSignature   plays an error page that identifies the problem. For example, when Apache cannot find a requested page, it displays an error page that says **Error 404: Not Found**. The ServerSignature directive (page 956) enables you to add a signature line to server-generated pages, including error pages. You can turn the signature line on or off using this directive. You can also specify that the signature line include a **mailto:** link that the user can click to send mail to the server's administrator. This link appears as the domain name the user called in the browser. The ServerAdmin (page 941) directive specifies the email address that the server sends mail to when a user clicks the link on an error page. Change the first of these two lines and add the second in **httpd.conf**.

> *ServerAdmin* **email_address**

> *ServerSignature EMail*

where *email_address* is the email address of the person who needs to know when people are having trouble using the server. Make sure that someone checks this email account frequently. But also see the tip "ServerAdmin attracts spam" on page 942.

It can make system administration much easier if you use a role alias (e.g., **webmaster@example.com**) instead of a specific username (e.g., **max@example.com**) as an *email_address*. See the discussion of email aliases on page 746.

After making changes to **httpd.conf**, start or restart **httpd** as explained on page 935.

## Testing Apache

Once you start the **httpd** daemon, you can confirm that Apache is working correctly by pointing a browser on the local (server) system to **http://localhost/**. From a remote system, point a browser to **http://** followed by the ServerName you specified in the previous section. If you are displaying a page from a system other than the server, the local system must know how to resolve a domain name you enter (e.g., by using DNS or the **/etc/hosts** file). For example, you might use either of these URI formats: **http://192.168.0.16** or **http://example.org**.

The browser should display the Fedora/RHEL test page, which is actually an error page that says there is no content (next). If the server is behind a firewall, open TCP port 80 (page 934). If Apache is not working, see "Troubleshooting" on page 967.

Fedora/RHEL test page · When you install Apache, there is no **index.html** file in **/var/www/html**; when you point a browser at the local Web server, Apache generates Error 403 (Forbidden), which returns the Fedora/RHEL test page. The mechanism by which this page is returned is convoluted: The Fedora/RHEL **httpd.conf** file holds an Include directive that includes all files with a filename extension of **.conf** that reside in the **conf.d** directory, that is in the ServerRoot directory (**/etc/httpd**; page 955). The **/etc/httpd/conf.d/welcome.conf** file contains an ErrorDocument 403 directive (page 953) that redirects users to **/usr/share/httpd/noindex/index.html**. This file is the Fedora/RHEL test page that confirms the server is working but there is no content to display. Apache will no longer display this page when you put an **index.html** file in **/var/www/html**.

## Putting Content in Place

Place the content you want Apache to serve in **/var/www/html**. Apache automatically displays the file named **index.html** in this directory. Working with **root** privileges (or as a member of the group you set up for this purpose [e.g., **webwork**]), create such a page:

```
# cat /var/www/html/index.html
<html><body><p>This is <i>my</i> test page.</p></body></html>
```

After you create this file, either refresh the page on the browser or restart the browser and point it at the server. The browser should display the page you created.

# FILESYSTEM LAYOUT

This section lists the locations and uses of files you can work with to configure Apache and serve Web pages.

*Binaries, scripts, and modules*
The Apache server and related binary files are kept in several directories:

**/usr/sbin/httpd**—The Apache server (daemon).

**/usr/sbin/apachectl**—Starts and stops Apache.

**/usr/bin/htpasswd**—Creates and maintains the password files used by the Apache authentication module (page 972).

**/usr/sbin/rotatelogs**—Rotates Apache log files so that these files do not get too large. See logrotate (page 618) for more information.

**/etc/httpd/modules**—Holds module binaries. Two of the most frequently used module binary files are **mod_perl.so** (**mod_perl** package) and **mod_wsgi.so** (**mod_wsgi** package). This directory is a symbolic link to **/usr/lib64/httpd/modules** (page 968).

*Configuration files*
By default, **/etc/httpd** is the ServerRoot (page 955); all Apache configuration files are kept in this directory hierarchy, specifically in the **/etc/httpd/conf** and **/etc/httpd/conf.d** directories:

**/etc/httpd/conf/httpd.conf**—Holds configuration directives. This file is the main Apache configuration file. The discussion of configuration directives starts on the next page.

**/etc/httpd/conf/magic**—Provides *MIME* (page 1261) file type identification (the MIME hints file). It is not normally changed. See *magic number* (page 1259) for more information.

**/etc/httpd/conf.d**—Holds configuration files.

**/etc/pki/tls/certs**—Holds files and directories used by **mod_ssl** (page 970).

*Logs*
Log files are kept in **/var/log/httpd** (there is a symbolic link at **/etc/httpd/logs**):

**/var/log/httpd/access_log**—Logs requests made to the server.

**/var/log/httpd/error_log**—Logs request and runtime server errors.

**/var/log/httpd/ssl_*_log**—Holds **mod_ssl** logs.

*Web documents*
Web documents (including the Web pages displayed by client browsers), custom error messages, and CGI scripts are kept in **/var/www** by default:

**/usr/share/httpd/error**—Holds error documents in several languages. By default, Fedora/RHEL displays hardcoded error messages. See ErrorDocument (page 953).

**/usr/share/httpd/icons**—Holds icons used to display directory entries. This directory is aliased to **/icons/** in the **autoindex.conf** file.

/usr/share/httpd/manual—Holds the Apache Server Manual. Present only if the **httpd-manual** package is installed. This directory is aliased to **/manual/**.

/var/www/cgi-bin—Holds CGI scripts (page 969).

Document root By default, the document root (page 934) is **/var/www/html**. You can change this location using the DocumentRoot directive (page 942).

.htaccess files A **.htaccess** file contains configuration directives and can appear in any directory in the document root hierarchy. The location of a **.htaccess** file is critical: The directives in a **.htaccess** file apply to all files in the hierarchy rooted at the directory that holds the **.htaccess** file. You must use an AllowOverride directive to cause Apache to examine **.htaccess** files and process directives in those files. This protection is duplicated and enhanced in the **httpd.conf** file distributed by Fedora/RHEL, where a directive instructs Apache not to serve files whose names start with **.ht**. Because of this directive, Apache does not serve **.htaccess** files (nor does it serve **.htpassword** files).

# CONFIGURATION DIRECTIVES

*Configuration directives*, or simply *directives*, are lines in a configuration file that control some aspect of how Apache functions. A configuration directive is composed of a keyword followed by one or more arguments separated by SPACEs. For example, the following configuration directive sets **Timeout** to 300 (seconds):

```
Timeout 300
```

You must enclose arguments that contain SPACEs within double quotation marks. Keywords are not case sensitive, but arguments (pathnames, filenames, and so on) often are.

httpd.conf The main file that holds Apache configuration directives is, by default, **/etc/httpd/conf/httpd.conf**. This file holds global directives that affect all content served by Apache. An Include directive (page 957) within **httpd.conf** can incorporate the contents of another file as though it were part of **httpd.conf**.

.htaccess Local directives can appear in **.htaccess** files. A **.htaccess** file can appear in any directory within the document root hierarchy; it affects files in the directory hierarchy rooted at the directory it appears in.

Pathnames When you specify an absolute pathname in a configuration directive, the directive uses that pathname without modifying it. When you specify a relative pathname, such as a simple filename or the name of a directory, Apache prepends to that name the value specified by the ServerRoot (page 955) directive (**/etc/httpd** by default).

Prefork MPM The **/etc/httpd/conf.modules.d/00-mpm.conf** file loads the **prefork** multiprocessing module (MPM, page 974). You can edit this file to load the **worker** or **event** module instead. (The **worker** module does not work with PHP.) This chapter assumes you have loaded the **prefork** module.

# DIRECTIVES YOU MIGHT WANT TO MODIFY AS YOU GET STARTED

When it starts, Apache reads the **/etc/httpd/conf/httpd.conf** configuration file (by default) for instructions governing every aspect of how Apache runs and serves content. The **httpd.conf** file shipped with Fedora/RHEL is more than 350 lines long.

This section details some directives you might want to change as you start using Apache. You can add/modify each of the following directives in **httpd.conf**. The **Context** line in each explanation tells you which locations the directives can appear in; contexts are explained on page 945. The section titled "Advanced Configuration Directives" on page 949 describes more directives.

**Listen**    *Specifies the IP address and port that Apache listens for requests on.*

*Listen [IP-address:]portnumber*

where **IP-address** is the IP address that Apache listens on and **portnumber** is the number of the port that Apache listens on for the given **IP-address**. When **IP-address** is absent or is set to 0.0.0.0, Apache listens on all network interfaces. At least one Listen directive must appear in the configuration files or Apache will not work.

The following minimal directive from the **httpd.conf** file listens for requests on all network interfaces on port 80:

```
Listen 80
```

The next directive changes the port from the default value of 80 to 8080:

```
Listen 8080
```

When you specify a port other than 80, each request to the server must include a port number (as in **www.example.org:8080**) or the kernel will return a **Connection Refused** message. Use multiple Listen directives to have Apache listen on multiple IP addresses and ports. For example:

```
Listen 80
Listen 192.168.1.1:8080
Listen 192.168.1.2:443
```

accepts connections on all network interfaces on port 80, on 192.168.1.1 on port 8080, and on 192.168.1.2 on port 443.

Context: **server config**
Default: none (Apache will not start without this directive.)
Fedora/RHEL: Listen 80

**Redirect**    *Tells the client to fetch a requested resource from a different, specified location.*

*Redirect [status] requested-path [new-URI]*

where **status** is the status that Apache returns along with the redirect. If you omit **status**, Apache assumes **temp**. The **status** can be an Apache error code in the range 300–399 or one of the following:

| | |
|---|---|
| **permanent** | Returns status 301 (the resource has moved permanently) |
| **temp** | Returns status 302 (the resource has moved temporarily) |
| **seeother** | Returns status 303 (the resource has been replaced) |
| **gone** | Returns status 410 (the resource has been removed—does not take a *new-URI* argument) |

The *requested-path* is the absolute pathname of the ordinary file or directory that Apache is to redirect requests for. Apache redirects all requests that start with the absolute pathname specified by *requested-path* (see the example below). Use RedirectMatch (discussed next) if you want to use a regular expression in this argument.

The *new-URI* is the URI that Apache redirects requests to. If the *new-URI* starts with a slash (/) and not **http://**, **ftp://**, or a similar prefix, Apache uses the same prefix it was called with. Most Redirect directives require a *new-URI* argument.

A request must match all segments of the *requested-path* argument. Assume the following directive:

```
Redirect /www.example.com/pictures http://pictures.example.com/
```

Apache will redirect a request for **http://www.example.com/pictures/mom.jpg** to **http://pictures.example.com/mom.jpg** but, because the final segment does not match, it will not redirect a request for **http://www.example.com/pictures_mom.jpg**.

Contexts: **server config, virtual host, directory, .htaccess**
Default: none
Fedora/RHEL: none

**RedirectMatch** *Tells the client to fetch a requested resource from a different location specified by a regular expression.*

*RedirectMatch [status] requested-path-re [new-URI]*

This directive is the same as Redirect (discussed on the previous page), except you can use a regular expression (Appendix A) in *requested-path-re*.

Contexts: **server config, virtual host, directory, .htaccess**
Default: none
Fedora/RHEL: none

**ServerAdmin** *Sets the email address used in **mailto** links on error pages.*

*ServerAdmin email-address*

where *email-address* is the email address of the person who is responsible for managing the Web content. Apache includes this address as a link on Apache-generated error pages. However, Fedora/RHEL sets ServerSignature (page 956) to **On**, which causes Apache to display information about the server—rather than a link to an email address—on error pages. If you want Apache to display the link on error pages, set ServerSignature (page 956) to **EMail**. Make sure *email-address* points to an email account that someone checks frequently. Users can use this address to get help with the Web site or to inform the administrator of problems. There is no default value for ServerAdmin; if you do not use this directive, and ServerSignature is set to **EMail**, the **mailto:** link on error pages displays [**no address given**].

### ServerAdmin attracts spam

**security**   The email address you put in ServerAdmin often attracts spam. Use a spam-guarded address such as **"mgs at sobell dot com"** (you must use the quotation marks) or use a custom error page to point to a Web page with a form for sending mail to the right person.

You can use a role alias such as **webmaster** at your domain and use a mail alias to forward mail that is sent to **webmaster** to the person who is responsible for maintaining the Web site. See the discussion of mail aliases on page 746.

Contexts: **server config, virtual host**
Default: none
Fedora/RHEL: **root@localhost**

**ServerName**   *Specifies the server's name and the port it listens on.*

*ServerName FQDN [:port]*

where *FQDN* is the fully qualified domain name or IP address of the server and *port* is the optional port number Apache listens on. The domain name of the server must be able to be resolved (by DNS or **/etc/hosts**) and might differ from the hostname of the system running the server. If you do not specify a ServerName, Apache performs a DNS reverse name resolution (page 862) on the system's IP address and assigns that value to ServerName. If the reverse lookup fails, Apache assigns the system's IP address to ServerName.

Fedora/RHEL provides the following ServerName template in the **httpd.conf** file:

```
#ServerName www.example.com:80
```

Copy this line, remove the **#**, and substitute the FQDN or IP address of the server for **www.example.com**. You can omit the **:80** because it specifies the default port. Change the 80 to the port number Apache listens on if it does not listen on port 80.

The ports specified by ServerName and Listen (page 940) must be the same if you want the FQDN specified by ServerName to be tied to the IP address specified by the Listen directive.

Apache uses ServerName to construct a URI when it redirects a client (page 962). See also UseCanonicalName (page 951).

Contexts: **server config, virtual host**
Default: none
Fedora/RHEL: none

**DocumentRoot**   *Points to the root of the directory hierarchy that holds the server's content.*

*DocumentRoot dirname*

where *dirname* is the absolute pathname of the directory at the root of the directory hierarchy that holds the content Apache serves. Do not use a trailing slash. The FHS (page 189) specifies **/srv** as the top-level directory for this purpose. You can put the document root wherever you like, as long as the user **apache** has read access to the ordinary files and execute access to the directory files in the directory hierarchy. Access control includes both discretionary access controls (chmod, including ACLs for the user **apache**) and mandatory access controls (selinux for **httpd**). The following directive puts the document root at **/srv/www**:

```
DocumentRoot /srv/www
```

Contexts: **server config, virtual host**
Default: **/usr/local/apache/htdocs**
Fedora/RHEL: **/var/www/html**

### You might want to change the location of the document root

tip   By design, the **/var** directory hierarchy (page 41) is designed to hold data that changes frequently, which is not usually the case with static Web site data. Data in such a partition is more likely to become corrupted than data in a partition that holds static data. Thus you might want to place Web site data in a different partition. Good candidates for the document root include **/usr/local** (holds site-specific data), **/home/www** (the home directory is frequently backed up while other directories might not be), and **/srv/www** (specified by FHS).

UserDir   *Allows users to publish content from their home directories.*

*UserDir **dirname** | disabled | enabled **user-list***

where *dirname* is the name of a directory that, if it appears in a local user's home directory, Apache publishes to the Web. When you do not specify a *dirname*, Apache publishes content in ~**/public_html**. The *disabled* keyword prevents content from being published from users' home directories; *enabled* causes content to be published from the home directories of users specified in the SPACE-separated *user-list*.

Apache can combine the effects of multiple UserDir directives. For example, assume you use the following directives:

```
UserDir disabled
UserDir enabled user1 user2 user3
UserDir web
```

The first directive turns off user publishing for all users. The second directive enables user publishing for three users. The third directive makes **web** the name of the directory that, if it appears in one of the specified users' home directories, Apache publishes to the Web.

To cause a browser to display the content published by a user, specify in the location bar the name of the Web site followed by a **/~** and the user's username. For example, if Sam published content in the **public_html** directory in his home directory and the URI of the Web site was **www.example.com,** you would enter **http://www.example.com/~sam** to display Sam's Web page. To display a user's Web page, Apache must have execute permission (as user **apache**) for the user's home directory and the directory holding the content, and read permission for the content files.

Fedora/RHEL provides the following ServerName directive and template in the **/etc/httpd/conf.d/userdir.conf** file. Because the statements are in an IfModule container (page 947), they are executed only if the **mod_userdir** module is loaded, which it is by default. These directives are surrounded by many comments.

```
<IfModule mod_userdir.c>
    UserDir disabled
    #UserDir public_html
</IfModule>
```

Put a hashmark (#) in front of the first line and remove the hashmark from the second line to allow users to publish content from directories named **public_html** in their home directories.

Contexts: **server config, virtual host**
Default: none
Fedora/RHEL: disabled

**DirectoryIndex**   *Specifies which file Apache serves when a user requests a directory.*

*DirectoryIndex **filename** [**filename** ...]*

where ***filename*** is the name of the file that Apache serves.

This directive specifies a list of filenames. When a client requests a directory, Apache attempts to find a file in the specified directory whose name matches a file in the list. When Apache finds a match, it returns that file. When this directive is absent or when none of the files specified by this directive exists in the specified directory, Apache displays a directory listing as specified by the IndexOptions directive (page 954).

Fedora/RHEL provides the following DirectoryIndex directive in the **httpd.conf** file:

```
DirectoryIndex index.html
```

This directive causes Apache to search the specified directory and return the file named **index.html**, which is the name of the standard, default HTML document. If you supply CGI documents, you might want to add the **index.cgi** value to this directive. The name **index** is standard but arbitrary.

A **.var** filename extension denotes a content-negotiated document that allows Apache to serve documents in one of several languages as specified by the client. If you are providing content in different languages, you can add this filename extension to the DirectoryIndex directive. For more information refer to "Type Maps" on page 963.

Contexts: **server config, virtual host**
Default: **index.html**
Fedora/RHEL: **index.html**

# CONTEXTS AND CONTAINERS

To make it flexible and easy to customize, Apache uses configuration directives, contexts, and containers. Some configuration directives are covered in the previous section. This section discusses contexts and containers, which are critical to managing an Apache server.

## CONTEXTS

Four locations, called *contexts*, define where configuration directives can appear. This chapter marks each configuration directive to indicate which context(s) it can appear in. Table 26-1 describes each of these contexts.

**Table 26-1**    Contexts

| Context | Location(s) directives can appear |
|---------|-----------------------------------|
| **server config** | In the **httpd.conf** file or included files only, but not inside <VirtualHost> or <Directory> containers (next section) unless so marked |
| **virtual host** | Inside <VirtualHost> containers in the **httpd.conf** file or included files only |
| **directory** | Inside <Directory>, <Location>, and <Files> containers in the **httpd.conf** file or included files only |
| **.htaccess** | In **.htaccess** files (page 939) only |

Directives in files incorporated by means of an Include directive (page 957) are part of the context they are included in and must be allowed in that context.

Putting a directive in the wrong context generates a configuration error and can cause Apache not to serve content correctly or not to start.

## CONTAINERS

*Containers*, or *special directives*, are directives that group other directives. Containers are delimited by XML-style tags. Three examples are shown here:

```
<Directory> ... </Directory>
<Location> ... </Location>
<VirtualHost> ... </VirtualHost>
```

Look in **httpd.conf** for examples of containers. Like other directives, containers are limited to use within specified contexts. This section describes some of the more frequently used containers.

<Directory>  *Applies directives to all directories within the specified directory hierarchy.*

*<Directory **directory**> ... </Directory>*

where **directory** is an absolute pathname specifying the root of the directory hierarchy that holds the directories the directives in the container apply to. The **directory** can include wildcards; a ✻ does not match a /.

A <Directory> container provides the same functionality as a **.htaccess** file (page 939). While an administrator can use a <Directory> container in Apache configuration files, regular users cannot. Regular users must use **.htaccess** files to control access to their own directories.

The directives in the <Directory> container shown in the following example apply to the **/var/www/html/corp** directory hierarchy. The Deny directive denies access to all clients, the Allow directive grants clients from the 192.168.10. subnet access, and the AllowOverride directive (page 960) enables Apache to process directives in **.htaccess** files in the hierarchy:

```
<Directory /var/www/html/corp>
    Deny from all
    Allow from 192.168.10.
    AllowOverride All
</Directory>
```

The following <Directory> container appears in the **httpd.conf** file and sets up a restrictive environment for the entire server filesystem (specified by **/**):

```
<Directory />
    AllowOverride None
    Require all denied
</Directory>
```

The AllowOverride directive causes Apache not to process directives in **.htaccess** files. The Require directive (page 961) denies all users access to the entire server filesystem directory. You must explicitly enable less restrictive options if you want them, but doing so can expose the server filesystem and compromise system security. This restrictive <Directory> container is followed immediately in **httpd.conf** by one that sets up less restrictive options for **/var/www**.

```
<Directory "/var/www">
    AllowOverride None
    Require all granted
</Directory>
```

The previous <Directory> container is followed by one that sets up options for the DocumentRoot (**/var/www/html**); this container affects all content. The code in **httpd.conf** is interspersed with many comments. Without the comments it looks like this:

```
<Directory "/var/www/html">
    Options Indexes FollowSymLinks
    AllowOverride None
    Require all granted
</Directory>
```

The Indexes option in the Options directive allows Apache to display directory listings and the FollowSymLinks option causes Apache to follow symbolic links. This container is less restrictive than the preceding one, although it still does not allow Apache to follow directives in **.htaccess** files.

Contexts: **server config, virtual host**

**<Files>**  *Applies directives to specified ordinary files.*

*<Files **directory**> ... </Files>*

where ***directory*** is an absolute pathname specifying the root of the directory hierarchy that holds the ordinary files the directives in the container apply to. The ***directory*** can include wildcards; a ✳ does not match a **/**. This container is similar to <Directory> but applies to ordinary files rather than to directories.

The following directive, from the Fedora/RHEL **httpd.conf** file, denies access to all files whose filenames start with **.ht**, meaning that Apache will not serve the **.htaccess** and **.htpasswd** files.

```
<Files ".ht*">
    Require all denied
</Files>
```

Contexts: **server config, virtual host, directory, .htaccess**

**<IfModule>**  *Applies directives if a specified module is loaded.*

*<IfModule [!]**module-name**> ... </IfModule>*

where ***module-name*** is the name of the module (page 968) Apache tests for. Apache executes the directives in this container if ***module-name*** is loaded or with **!** if ***module-name*** is not loaded.

Apache will not start if you specify a configuration directive that is specific to a module that is not loaded.

The following <IfModule> container, which is located in the Fedora/RHEL **httpd.conf** file, depends on the **mime_magic_module** module being loaded. If this module is loaded, Apache runs the MIMEMagicFile directive, which tells the **mime_magic_module** where its hints file is located.

```
<IfModule mime_magic_module>
    MIMEMagicFile conf/magic
</IfModule>
```

Contexts: **server config, virtual host, directory, .htaccess**

**<Limit>**  *Limits access-control directives to specified HTTP methods.*

*<Limit **method** [**method**] ... > ... </Limit>*

where ***method*** is an HTTP method. An HTTP method specifies which action is to be performed on a URI. The most frequently used methods are GET, PUT, POST, and OPTIONS; method names are case sensitive. GET (the default method) sends any data indicated by the URI. PUT stores data from the body section of the communication at the specified URI. POST creates a new document containing the body of the request at the specified URI. OPTIONS requests information about the capabilities of the server.

The <Limit> container binds a group of access-control directives to specified HTTP methods: Only methods named by this container are affected by this group of directives.

The following example disables HTTP uploads (PUTs) from systems that are not in a subdomain of **example.com**:

```
<Limit PUT>
    order deny,allow
    deny from all
    allow from .example.com
</Limit>
```

Contexts: **server config, virtual host, directory, .htaccess**

### Use <LimitExcept> instead of <Limit>

caution   It is safer to use the <LimitExcept> container than to use the <Limit> container, as the former protects against arbitrary methods. When you use <Limit>, you must be careful to name explicitly all possible methods that the group of directives could affect.

**<LimitExcept>**   *Limits access-control directives to all except specified HTTP methods.*

*<LimitExcept **method** [**method**] ... > ... </LimitExcept>*

where ***method*** is an HTTP method. See <Limit> for a discussion of methods.

This container causes a group of access-control directives *not* to be bound to specified HTTP methods. Thus methods *not* named in <LimitExcept> are affected by this group of directives.

The access-control directives within the following <LimitExcept> container affect HTTP methods other than GET, POST, and OPTIONS. You could put this container in a <Directory> container to limit its scope:

```
<LimitExcept GET POST OPTIONS>
    Order deny,allow
    Deny from all
</LimitExcept>
```

Contexts: **server config, virtual host, directory, .htaccess**

**<Location>**   *Applies directives to specified URIs.*

*<Location **URI**> ... </Location>*

where ***URI*** points to content; it specifies a file or the root of the directory hierarchy that the directives in the container apply to. While the <Directory> container points within the local filesystem, <Location> points outside the local filesystem. The ***URI*** can include wildcards; a * does not match a /.

The following <Location> container limits access to **http://*server*/pop** to clients from the **example.net** domain, where ***server*** is the FQDN of the server:

```
<Location /pop>
    Order deny,allow
    Deny from all
    Allow from .example.net
</Location>
```

Contexts: **server config, virtual host**

### Use <Location> with care

**caution**  Use this powerful container with care. Do not use it to replace the <Directory> container: When several URIs point to the same location in a filesystem, a client might be able to circumvent the desired access control by using a URI not specified by this container.

**<LocationMatch>** *Applies directives to URIs specified by a regular expression.*

*<LocationMatch **regexp**> ... </LocationMatch>*

where **regexp** is a regular expression that matches one or more URIs. This container works the same way as <Location>, except that it applies to any URIs that **regexp** matches.

Contexts: **server config, virtual host**

**<VirtualHost>** *Applies directives to a specified virtual host.*

*<VirtualHost **addr[:port]** [**addr[:port]**] ... > ... </VirtualHost>*

where **addr** is the IP address (or FQDN, although it is not recommended) of the virtual host (or * to represent all addresses) and **port** is the port that Apache listens on for the virtual host. This directive does not control which addresses and ports Apache listens on; use a Listen directive (page 940) for that purpose. This container holds commands that Apache applies to a virtual host. For more information refer to "Virtual Hosts" on page 965.

Context: **server config**

# ADVANCED CONFIGURATION DIRECTIVES

This section discusses configuration directives that you might add to **httpd.conf** after you gain some experience using Apache. The Fedora/RHEL configuration files include the directives in this section that specify a value for Fedora/RHEL in addition to a default value.

## DIRECTIVES THAT CONTROL PROCESSES

**MaxRequestWorkers (was MaxClients)**

*Specifies the maximum number of child processes.*

*MaxRequestWorkers **num***

where **num** is the maximum number of child processes (servers) Apache runs at one time, including idle processes and processes serving requests. When Apache is running **num** processes and there are no idle processes, Apache issues **Server too busy** errors to new connections; it does not start new child processes.

Context: **server config**
Default: 256

**MaxConnectionsPerChild (was MaxRequestsPerChild)**

> *Specifies the maximum number of requests a child process can serve.*
>
> *MaxConnectionsPerChild **num***
>
> where **num** is the maximum number of requests a child process (server) can serve during its lifetime. After a child process serves **num** requests, it does not process any more requests but dies after it finishes processing its current requests. Apache can start another child process to replace the one that dies. Additional requests are processed by other processes from the server pool.
>
> Set **num** to 0 to not set a limit on the number of requests a child can process, except for the effects of MinSpareServers. By limiting the lives of processes, this directive can prevent memory leaks from consuming too much system memory. However, setting MaxConnectionsPerChild to a too-small value can hurt performance by causing Apache to create new child servers constantly.
>
> Context: **server config**
> Default: 0

**MaxSpareServers**   *Specifies the maximum number of idle processes.*

> *MaxSpareServers **num***
>
> where **num** is the maximum number of idle processes (servers) Apache keeps running to serve requests as they come in. Do not set this number too high, as each process consumes system resources.
>
> Context: **server config**
> Default: 10

**MinSpareServers**   *Specifies the minimum number of idle processes.*

> *MinSpareServers **num***
>
> where **num** is the minimum number of idle processes (servers) Apache keeps running to serve requests as they come in. More idle processes occupy more computer resources; increase this value for busy sites only.
>
> Context: **server config**
> Default: 5

**StartServers**   *Specifies the number of child processes that Apache starts with.*

> *StartServers **num***
>
> where **num** is the number of child processes (servers) that Apache starts when it is brought up. This value is significant only when Apache starts; MinSpareServers and MaxSpareServers control the number of idle processes once Apache is up and running. Starting Apache with multiple servers ensures that a pool of servers is waiting to serve requests immediately.
>
> Context: **server config**
> Default: dynamically controlled based on load

## NETWORKING DIRECTIVES

**HostnameLookups**

*Specifies whether Apache puts a client's hostname or its IP address in the logs.*

*HostnameLookups On | Off | Double*

***On:*** Performs DNS reverse name resolution (page 862) to determine the hostname of each client for logging purposes.

***Off:*** Logs each client's IP address.

***Double:*** To provide greater security, performs DNS reverse name resolution (page 862) to determine the hostname of each client, performs a forward DNS lookup to verify the original IP address, and logs the hostname. Denies access if it cannot verify the original IP address.

Contexts: **server config, virtual host, directory**
Default: Off

### Lookups can consume a lot of system resources

tip Use the **On** and **Double** options with caution: They can consume a lot of resources on a busy system. You can use a program such as logresolve to perform reverse name resolution offline for statistical purposes.

If you perform hostname resolution offline, you run the risk that the name might have changed; you usually want the name that was current at the time of the request. To minimize this problem, perform the hostname resolution as soon as possible after Apache writes the log.

**Timeout** *Specifies the amount of time Apache waits for network operations to complete.*

*Timeout num*

where ***num*** is the number of seconds that Apache waits for network operations to finish.

Context: **server config**
Default: 60

**UseCanonicalName**

*Specifies the method the server uses to identify itself.*

*UseCanonicalName On | Off | DNS*

***On:*** Apache uses the value of the ServerName directive (page 942) as its identity.

***Off:*** Apache uses the name and port from the incoming request as its identity.

***DNS:*** Apache performs a DNS reverse name resolution (page 862) on the IP address from the incoming request and uses the result as its identity. Rarely used.

This directive is important when a server has more than one name and needs to perform a redirect. Fedora/RHEL does not set this directive because it does not set the ServerName directive (page 942). Once you set ServerName, change UseCanonicalName to **On**. See page 962 for a discussion of redirects and this directive.

Contexts: **server config, virtual host, directory**
Default: Off

## LOGGING DIRECTIVES

**ErrorLog** *Specifies where Apache sends error messages.*

*ErrorLog **filename** | syslog[:**facility**]*

where ***filename*** specifies the name of the file, relative to ServerRoot (page 955), that Apache sends error messages to. The *syslog* keyword specifies that Apache send errors to **syslogd** (page 620); ***facility*** specifies which **syslogd** facility to use. The default facility is **local7**.

Contexts: **server config, virtual host**
Default: **logs/error_log**
Fedora/RHEL: **logs/error_log**

**LogLevel** *Specifies the level of error messages that Apache logs.*

*LogLevel **level***

where ***level*** specifies that Apache log errors of that level and higher (more urgent). Choose ***level*** from the following list, which is presented here in order of decreasing urgency and increasing verbosity:

**emerg**   System unusable messages
**alert**   Need for immediate action messages
**crit**    Critical condition messages
**error**   Error condition messages
**warn**    Nonfatal warning messages
**notice**  Normal but significant messages
**info**    Operational messages and recommendations
**debug**   Messages for finding and solving problems

Contexts: **server config, virtual host**
Default: warn
Fedora/RHEL: warn

## DIRECTIVES THAT CONTROL CONTENT

**AddHandler** *Creates a mapping between filename extensions and a builtin Apache handler.*

*AddHandler **handler extension** [**extension**] ...*

where ***handler*** is the name of a builtin handler and ***extension*** is a filename extension that maps to the ***handler***. Handlers are actions that are built into Apache and are directly related to loaded modules. Apache uses a handler when a client requests a file with a specified filename extension.

For example, the following AddHandler directive causes Apache to process files that have a filename extension of **.cgi** with the **cgi-script** handler:

```
AddHandler cgi-script .cgi
```

See "Type Maps" on page 963 for another example of an AddHandler directive.

Contexts: **server config, virtual host, directory, .htaccess**
Default: none

**Alias**  *Maps a URI to a directory or file.*

*Alias **alias pathname***

where ***alias*** must match part of the URI that the client requested in order to invoke the alias. The ***pathname*** is the absolute pathname of the target of the alias, usually a directory.

For example, the following alias causes Apache to serve **/usr/local/pix/milk.jpg** when a client requests **http://www.example.com/pix/milk.jpg**:

```
Alias /pix /usr/local/pix
```

In some cases, you need to use a <Directory> container (page 945) to grant access to aliased content.

Contexts: **server config, virtual host**
Default: none
Fedora/RHEL: **/icons/ /usr/share/httpd/icons/** (in **autoindex.conf**)

**ErrorDocument**  *Specifies the action Apache takes when the specified error occurs.*

*ErrorDocument **code action***

where ***code*** is the error code (page 975) this directive defines a response for and ***action*** is one of the following:

**string**—Defines the message that Apache returns to the client.

**absolute pathname**—Points to a local script or other content that Apache redirects the client to.

**URI**—Points to an external script or other content that Apache redirects the client to.

When you do not specify this directive for a given error code, Apache returns a hardcoded error message when that error occurs. See page 937 for an explanation of how an ErrorDocument directive returns the Fedora/RHEL test page when Apache is installed (before you add content).

Some examples of ErrorDocument directives follow:

```
ErrorDocument 403 "Sorry, access is forbidden."
ErrorDocument 403 /cgi-bin/uh-uh.pl
ErrorDocument 403 http://errors.example.com/not_allowed.html
```

Contexts: **server config, virtual host, directory, .htaccess**
Default: none; Apache returns hardcoded error messages
Fedora/RHEL: none; Apache returns hardcoded error messages, but refer to "Fedora/RHEL test page" on page 937

**IndexOptions**    *Specifies how Apache displays directory listings.*

*IndexOptions [±]option [[±]option] ...*

where **option** can be any combination of the following:

**DescriptionWidth=*n***—Sets the width of the description column to *n* characters. Use ✽ in place of *n* to accommodate the widest description.

**FancyIndexing**—In directory listings, displays column headers that are links. When you click one of these links, Apache sorts the display based on the content of the column. Clicking the link a second time reverses the order.

**FoldersFirst**—Sorts the listing so that directories come before plain files. Use only with FancyIndexing.

**HTMLTable**—Displays a directory listing in a table.

**IconsAreLinks**—Makes the icons clickable. Use only with FancyIndexing.

**IconHeight=*n***—Sets the height of icons to *n* pixels. Use only with IconWidth.

**IconWidth=*n***—Sets the width of icons to *n* pixels. Use only with IconHeight.

**IgnoreCase**—Ignores case when sorting names.

**IgnoreClient**—Ignores options the client supplied in the URI.

**NameWidth=*n***—Sets the width of the filename column to *n* characters. Use ✽ in place of *n* to accommodate the widest filename.

**ScanHTMLTitles**—Extracts and displays titles from HTML documents. Use only with FancyIndexing. Not normally used because it is CPU and disk intensive.

**SuppressColumnSorting**—Suppresses clickable column headings that can be used for sorting columns. Use only with FancyIndexing.

**SuppressDescription**—Suppresses file descriptions. Use only with FancyIndexing.

**SuppressHTMLPreamble**—Suppresses the contents of the file specified by the HeaderName directive, even if that file exists.

**SuppressIcon**—Suppresses icons. Use only with FancyIndexing.

**SuppressLastModified**—Suppresses the modification date. Use only with FancyIndexing.

**SuppressRules**—Suppresses horizontal lines. Use only with FancyIndexing.

**SuppressSize**—Suppresses file sizes. Use only with FancyIndexing.

**VersionSort**—Sorts version numbers (in filenames) in a natural way; character strings, except for substrings of digits, are not affected.

As an example of the use of IndexOptions, suppose a client requests a URI that points to a directory (such as **http://www.example.com/support/**) and none of the files specified by the DirectoryIndex directive (page 944) is present in that directory. If the directory hierarchy is controlled by a Directory container or **.htaccess** file, and AllowOverride (page 960) has been set to allow indexes, Apache displays a directory listing according to the options specified by this directive.

When an IndexOptions directive appears more than once within a directory, Apache merges the options from the directives. Use **+** and **–** to merge IndexOptions options with options from higher-level directories. (Unless you use **+** or **–** with all options, Apache discards any options set in higher-level directories.) For example, the following directives and containers set the options for **/custsup/download** to VersionSort; Apache discards FancyIndexing and IgnoreCase in the **download** directory because there is no **+** or **–** before VersionSort in the second <Directory> container:

```
<Directory /custsup>
    IndexOptions FancyIndexing
    IndexOptions IgnoreCase
</Directory>

<Directory /custsup/download>
    IndexOptions VersionSort
</Directory>
```

Because **+** appears before VersionSort, the following directives and containers set the options for **/custsup/download** to FancyIndexing, IgnoreCase, and VersionSort:

```
<Directory /custsup>
    IndexOptions FancyIndexing
    IndexOptions IgnoreCase
</Directory>

<Directory /custsup/download>
    IndexOptions +VersionSort
</Directory>
```

Contexts: **server config, virtual host, directory, .htaccess**
Default: none; lists only filenames
Fedora/RHEL: FancyIndexing HTMLTable VersionSort (in **autoindex.conf**)

**ServerRoot**   *Specifies the root directory for server files (not content).*

*ServerRoot* **directory**

where **directory** specifies the pathname of the root directory for the files that make up the server. Apache prepends **directory** to relative pathnames in **httpd.conf**. This directive does not specify the location of the content that Apache serves; the DocumentRoot directive (page 942) performs that function. Do not change this value unless you move the server files.

Context: **server config**
Default: **/usr/local/apache**
Fedora/RHEL: **/etc/httpd**

ServerTokens   *Specifies the server information that Apache returns to a client.*

*ServerTokens Prod | Major | Minor | Min | OS | Full*

**Prod:** Returns the product name: **Apache**; also *ProductOnly*.

**Major:** Returns the major release number of the server: **Apache/2**.

**Minor:** Returns the major and minor release numbers of the server: **Apache/2.4**.

**Min:** Returns the complete version: **Apache/2.4.4**; also *Minimal*.

**OS:** Returns the name of the operating system and the complete version: **Apache/2.4.4 (Fedora)**. Provides less information that might help a malicious user than *Full* does.

**Full:** Same as **OS**, except that *Full* also sends the names and versions of non-ASF modules: **Apache/2.4.4 (Fedora) PHP/5.5.0**.

Unless you want clients to know the details of the software you are running, set ServerTokens to reveal as little as possible.

Context: **server config**
Default: Full

ServerSignature   *Adds a line to server-generated pages.*

*ServerSignature On | Off | EMail*

**On:** Turns the signature line on. The signature line contains the server version as specified by the ServerTokens directive (above) and the name specified by the <VirtualHost> container (page 949).

**Off:** Turns the signature line off.

**EMail:** To the signature line, adds a **mailto:** link to the server email address. This option produces output that can attract spam. See ServerAdmin (page 941) for information on specifying an email address.

Contexts: **server config, virtual host, directory, .htaccess**
Default: Off

## CONFIGURATION DIRECTIVES

Group   *Sets the GID of the processes that run the servers.*

*Group #groupid | groupname*

where *groupid* is a GID value, preceded by **#**, and *groupname* is the name of a group. The processes (servers) that Apache spawns are run as the group specified by this directive. See the User directive (page 959) for more information.

Context: **server config**
Default: #–1
Fedora/RHEL: apache

**Include**
**IncludeOptional**

*Loads directives from files.*

*Include | IncludeOptional **filename** | **directory***

where ***filename*** is the relative pathname of a file that contains directives. Apache prepends ServerRoot (page 955) to ***filename***. The directives in ***filename*** are included in the file holding this directive at the location of the directive. Because ***filename*** can include wildcards, it can specify more than one file.

The ***directory*** is the relative pathname that specifies the root of a directory hierarchy that holds files containing directives. Apache prepends ServerRoot to ***directory***. The directives in ordinary files in this hierarchy are included in the file holding this directive at the location of the directive. The ***directory*** can include wildcards.

Whereas Include displays an error when wildcards do not match a file or directory, IncludeOptional does not display an error when there is no match for a wildcard.

The Apache installer puts configuration files for modules, which have a filename extension of **conf**, in the **conf.d** and **conf.modules.d** directories within the ServerRoot directory. The Include directives in the Fedora/RHEL **httpd.conf** file incorporate module configuration files for whichever modules are installed.

Contexts: **server config, virtual host, directory**
Default: none
Fedora/RHEL: **conf.d/*.conf conf.modules.d/*.conf**

**LoadModule**

*Loads a module.*

*LoadModule **module filename***

where ***module*** is the name of an external DSO module and ***filename*** is the relative pathname of the named module. Apache prepends ServerRoot (page 955) to ***filename*** and loads the external module specified by this directive. For more information refer to "Modules" on page 968.

Context: **server config**
Default: none; nothing is loaded by default if this directive is omitted
Fedora/RHEL: loads many modules; refer to the configuration files

**Options**

*Controls server features by directory.*

*Options [±]**option** [[±]**option** ...]*

This directive controls which server features are enabled for a directory hierarchy. The directory hierarchy is specified by the container this directive appears in. A **+** or the absence of a **–** turns an option on, and a **–** turns it off.

The ***option*** might be one of the following:

**None**—None of the features this directive can control are enabled.

**All**—All of the features this directive can control are enabled, except for MultiViews, which you must explicitly enable.

**ExecCGI**—Apache can execute CGI scripts (page 969).

**FollowSymLinks**—Apache follows symbolic links.

**Includes**—Permits SSIs (server-side includes). SSIs are containers embedded in HTML pages that are evaluated on the server before the content is passed to the client.

**IncludesNOEXEC**—The same as Includes but disables the **#exec** and **#exec cgi** commands that are part of SSIs. Does *not* prevent the **#include** command from referencing CGI scripts.

**Indexes**—Generates a directory listing if DirectoryIndex (page 944) is not set.

**MultiViews**—Allows MultiViews (page 963).

**SymLinksIfOwnerMatch**—The same as FollowSymLinks but follows the link only if the file or directory being pointed to has the same owner as the link.

The following Options directive from the Fedora/RHEL **httpd.conf** file sets the Indexes and FollowSymLinks options and, because the <Directory> container specifies the **/var/www/html** directory hierarchy (the document root), affects all content. The AllowOverride None directive causes Apache to ignore directives in **.htaccess** files (page 960).

```
<Directory "/var/www/html">
    Options Indexes FollowSymLinks
    AllowOverride None
</Directory>
```

Context: **directory**
Default: All
Fedora/RHEL: Indexes, FollowSymLinks

ScriptAlias  *Maps a URI to a directory or file and declares the target to be a server (CGI) script.*

*ScriptAlias **alias pathname***

where *alias* must match part of the URI the client requested to invoke the ScriptAlias. The *pathname* is the absolute pathname of the target of the alias, usually a directory. Similar to the Alias directive, this directive specifies that the target is a CGI script (page 969).

The following ScriptAlias directive from the Fedora/RHEL **httpd.conf** file maps client requests that include **/cgi-bin/** to the **/var/www/cgi-bin** directory (and indicates that these requests will be treated as CGI requests):

```
ScriptAlias /cgi-bin/ "/var/www/cgi-bin/"
```

Contexts: **server config, virtual host**
Default: none
Fedora/RHEL: /cgi-bin/ "/var/www/cgi-bin"

**User** *Sets the UID of the processes that run the servers.*

*User #userid* | *username*

where ***userid*** is a UID value, preceded by #, and ***username*** is the name of a local user. The processes that Apache spawns are run as the user specified by this directive.

Apache must start with **root** privileges to listen on a privileged port. For reasons of security, Apache's child processes (servers) run as nonprivileged users. The default UID of –1 does not map to a user under Fedora/RHEL. Instead, the Fedora/RHEL **httpd** package creates a user named **apache** during installation and sets User to that user.

Context: **server config**
Default: #–1
Fedora/RHEL: **apache**

### Do not set User to **root** or **0**

security For a more secure system, do not set User to **root** or **0** (zero) and do not allow the **apache** user to have write access to the DocumentRoot directory hierarchy (except as needed for storing data), especially not to configuration files.

## SECURITY DIRECTIVES

**Allow** *Specifies which clients can access specified content.*

*Allow from All* | ***host*** *[**host** ...]* | *env=var [env=var ...]*

This directive, which must be written as **Allow from**, grants access to a directory hierarchy to the specified clients. The directory hierarchy is specified by the container or **.htaccess** file this directive appears in. See the Order directive (page 961) for an example.

**All**—Serves content to any client.

***host:*** Serves content to the client(s) specified by ***host***, which can take several forms: an FQDN, a partial domain name (such as **example.com**), an IP address, a partial IP address, or a network/netmask pair.

***var:*** Serves content when the environment variable named ***var*** is set. You can set a variable with the SetEnvIf directive.

Contexts: **directory, .htaccess**
Default: none; default behavior depends on the Order directive
Fedora/RHEL: none

**AllowOverride** *Specifies whether Apache examines .htaccess files and which classes of directives in those files it processes.*

*AllowOverride All | None | **directive-class** [**directive-class** ...]*

This directive specifies whether Apache examines **.htaccess** files in the directory hierarchy specified by its container. If Apache does examine **.htaccess** files, this directive specifies which classes of directives within **.htaccess** files Apache processes. See the tip on page 973 for performance considerations.

**All**—Processes all classes of directives in **.htaccess** files.

**None**—Ignores directives in **.htaccess** files. However, Apache will still serve the content of **.htaccess** files, possibly exposing sensitive information. This choice does not affect **.htpasswd** files. The example in the description of the <Files> container (page 947) shows how to prevent Apache from serving the content of files whose names begin with **.ht**.

The *directive-class* is one of the following directive class identifiers:

**AuthConfig**—Class of directives that control authorization (AuthName, AuthType, Require, and so on). This class is used mostly in **.htaccess** files to require a username and password to access the content. For more information refer to "Authentication Modules and **.htaccess** Files" on page 972.

**FileInfo**—Class of directives that controls document types (DefaultType, ErrorDocument, SetHandler, and so on).

**Indexes**—Class of directives relating to directory indexing (DirectoryIndex, FancyIndexing, IndexOptions, and so on).

**Limit**—Class of client-access directives (Allow, Deny, and Order).

**Options**—Class of directives controlling directory features.

Context: **directory**
Default: All
Fedora/RHEL: None

**Deny** *Specifies which clients are not allowed to access specified content.*

*Deny from All | **host** [**host** ...] | env=**var** [env=**var** ...]*

This directive, which must be written as **Deny from**, denies access to a directory hierarchy to the specified clients. The directory hierarchy is specified by the container or **.htaccess** file this directive appears in. See the Order directive (next) for an example.

**All**—Denies content to all clients.

*host:* Denies content to the client(s) specified by *host*, which can take several forms: an FQDN, a partial domain name (such as **example.com**), an IP address, a partial IP address, or a network/netmask pair.

*var:* Denies content when the environment variable named *var* is set. You can set a variable using the SetEnvIf directive.

Contexts: **directory, .htaccess**
Default: none
Fedora/RHEL: none

Order     *Specifies the default access and the order in which Allow and Deny directives are evaluated.*

*Order Deny,Allow | Allow,Deny*

**Deny,Allow**—Allows access by default; denies access only to clients specified in Deny directives (first evaluates Deny directives and then evaluates Allow directives).

**Allow,Deny**—Denies access by default; allows access only to clients specified in Allow directives (first evaluates Allow directives and then evaluates Deny directives).

There must not be SPACES on either side of the comma. Access defaults to the second entry in the pair (Deny,Allow defaults to Allow) if there is no Allow from or Deny from directive that matches the client. If a single Allow from or Deny from directive matches the client, that directive overrides the default. If multiple Allow from and Deny from directives match the client, Apache evaluates the directives in the order specified by the Order directive; the last match takes precedence.

Access granted or denied by this directive applies to the directory hierarchy specified by the container or **.htaccess** file this directive appears in. In the next directive, **Allow from all** grants access to all clients:

```
Order allow,deny
Allow from all
```

You can restrict access by specifying Deny,Allow to deny all access and then specifying only those clients you want to grant access to in an Allow directive. The following directives grant access to clients from the **example.net** domain only and would typically appear within a <Directory> container (page 945):

```
Order deny,allow
Deny from all
Allow from .example.net
```

Contexts: **directory, .htaccess**
Default: Deny,Allow

Require     *Tests/specifies whether a user is authorized to access a directory hierarchy.*

*Require all granted | all denied | ip **addr***

where ***addr*** is one or more SPACE-separated IP addresses of systems that are allowed to access the directory hierarchy.

***all granted:*** Any user can access the directory hierarchy.

***all denied:*** No user can access the directory hierarchy.

The **httpd.conf** file contains several Require directives. The first, because it is in a <Directory> container that specifies the root directory, denies access to the entire filesystem:

```
<Directory />
    AllowOverride none
    Require all denied
</Directory>
```

However, that restriction is immediately relaxed for the **www** child directory.

```
<Directory "/var/www">
    AllowOverride None
    Require all granted
</Directory>
```

Context: **directory, .htaccess**
Default: none

# ADVANCED CONFIGURATION

This section describes how to configure some advanced features of Apache.

## REDIRECTS

Apache can respond to a request for a URI by asking the client to request a different URI. This response is called a *redirect*. A redirect works because redirection is part of the HTTP implementation: Apache sends the appropriate response code and the new URI, and a compliant browser requests the new location.

The Redirect directive can establish an explicit redirect that sends a client to a different page when a Web site is moved. Or, when a user enters the URI of a directory in a browser but leaves off the trailing slash, Apache can automatically redirect the client to the same URI terminated with a slash.

UseCanonicalName  The ServerName directive (page 942), which establishes the name of the server, and the UseCanonicalName directive (page 951) are both important when a server has more than one name and needs to perform an automatic redirect. For example, assume the server with the name **zach.example.com** and the alias **www.example.com** has Server-Name set to **www.example.com**. When a client specifies a URI of a directory but leaves off the trailing slash (**zach.example.com/dir**), Apache has to perform a redirect to determine the URI of the requested directory. When UseCanonicalName is set to On, Apache uses the value of ServerName and returns **www.example.com/dir/**. With UseCanonicalName set to Off, Apache uses the name from the incoming request and returns **zach.example.com/dir/**.

## CONTENT NEGOTIATION

Apache can serve multiple versions of the same page, using a client's preference to determine which version to send. The process Apache uses to determine which version of a page (file) to send is called *content negotiation*. Apache supports two methods of content negotiation: type maps and MultiViews search, which can work together.

## TYPE MAPS

The following AddHandler directive from **httpd.conf** would tell Apache to use any filename ending in **.var** as a type map (if it were not commented out):

```
# AddHandler type-map var
```

To see how type maps work, create the following files in **/var/www/html**:

```
$ cat /var/www/html/index.html.en
<html><body><h1>Hello</h1></body></html>

$ cat /var/www/html/index.html.fr
<html><body><h1>Bonjour</h1><body></html>

$ cat /var/www/html/index.html.var
URI: index.html.en
Content-Language: en
Content-type: text/html; charset=ISO-8859-1

URI: index.html.fr
Content-Language: fr
Content-type: text/html; charset=ISO-8859-1
```

If your browser's preferred language is set to English (**en**), it will display the **Hello** page when you browse to **http://localhost/index.html.var**. If your browser's preferred language is set to French (**fr**), it will display the **Bonjour** page. (With the MultiViews option turned on, as it is by default, the browser displays the correct page when you browse to **http://localhost**. See the next section.) You can change the default language in Firefox by selecting **Edit⇨Preferences** from the menubar, clicking the Content icon, and finally clicking **Choose** from the Languages frame. Select a language from the **Select a language to add** combo box, if necessary, and then move the preferred language to the top of the list. In the example, the **charset** assignments are not necessary. However, they would be helpful if you were sending pages using different encodings such as English, Russian, and Korean.

Type maps are used for more than selecting among different languages. Instead of matching **Content-Language** as in the preceding example, the map could match **Content-type** and send **jpeg** or **png** images depending on how the browser's preferences are set.

## MULTIVIEWS

When you set the MultiViews option on a directory, Apache attempts to deliver the correct page when a requested resource does not exist. In **httpd.conf**, add **MultiViews** to the Options line in the <Directory> container as follows:

```
<Directory "/var/www/html">
...
    Options Indexes FollowSymLinks MultiViews
...
```

**Figure 26-1**  A server-generated directory listing

To see how MultiViews work, remove the **/var/www/html/index.html.var** type map file you created in the preceding section. Now browse to **http://localhost**. The proper language page is displayed, but why?

When a browser sends Apache a request for a directory, Apache looks for a file named **index.html** in that directory. In the example, Apache does not find the file. If MultiViews is enabled, Apache looks for files named **index.html.✳**. In the example it finds **index.html.en** and **index.html.fr**. Apache effectively creates a type map on the fly, mapping the **index.html.✳** files to various languages, and sends its best guess as to the page you want.

### Which to use: MultiViews or type maps?

caution   MultiViews provides an easy way to serve multiple versions of the same file without having to cre-ate a type map. However, MultiViews is slower than type maps. Also, if you require finer-grained control over which version of a resource should be sent, type maps are a better solution.

## SERVER-GENERATED DIRECTORY LISTINGS (INDEXING)

When a client requests a directory, the Apache configuration determines what is returned to the client. Apache can return a file as specified by the DirectoryIndex directive (page 944), a directory listing if no file matches DirectoryIndex and the Options Indexes directive (page 957) is set, or an error message if no file matches DirectoryIndex and Options Indexes is not set. Figure 26-1 shows a server-generated directory listing.

# VIRTUAL HOSTS

Apache supports *virtual hosts,* which means that one instance of Apache can respond to requests directed to multiple IP addresses or hostnames as though it were multiple servers. Each IP address or hostname can then provide different content and be configured differently.

There are two types of virtual hosts: *host-by-name* (also called *host-based*) and *host-by-IP*. Host-by-name relies on the FQDN the client uses in its request to Apache—for example, **www.example.com** versus **www2.example.com**. Host-by-IP examines the IP address the host resolves as and responds according to that match.

Host-by-name is handy if there is only one IP address, but Apache must support multiple FQDNs. Although you can use host-by-IP if a given Web server has aliases, Apache should serve the same content regardless of which name is used.

The NameVirtualHost directive specifies which IP address supports host-by-name virtual hosting; the ServerName (or ServerAlias) directive must match the client request to match that virtual host. Without a NameVirtualHost directive, the virtual host is a host-by-IP virtual host; the ServerName directive specifies the name the server uses to identify itself.

You can specify many virtual hosts for a single instance of Apache.

## EXAMPLES

The following examples of host-by-name virtual hosting use wildcards (*) to remain as flexible as possible. You might want to replace the wildcards with the IP address of the server for more precise control when Apache is serving multiple virtual hosts.

The first <VirtualHost> container sets up host-by-name for the site named **example.com**. This virtual host handles requests that are directed to **example.com**. The ServerAlias directive allows it to also process requests directed to **www.example.com**.

```
<VirtualHost *>
    ServerName      example.com
    ServerAlias     www.example.com
    ServerAdmin     webmaster@example.com
    DocumentRoot    /var/www/html/example.com
    CustomLog       /var/log/httpd/example.com.log combined
    ErrorLog        /var/log/httpd/example.com.err
</VirtualHost>
```

The next example is similar to the previous one. It adds a Directory directive that prevents remote users (users not coming from the 192.168. subnet) from accessing the Web site.

```
<VirtualHost *>
    ServerName      intranet.example.com
    ServerAdmin     webmaster@example.com
    DocumentRoot    /var/www/html
    ErrorLog        /var/log/httpd/intra.error_log
    CustomLog       /var/log/httpd/example.com.log combined
    <Directory      /var/www/html>
        Order deny,allow
        Deny from all
        Allow from 192.168.   # allow from private subnet only
    </Directory>
</VirtualHost>
```

The next example sets up two virtual hosts. The VirtualHost containers accept all traffic directed to the server by specifying *. The ServerName directives accept traffic for **sam.example.com** (or the alias **www.example.com/sam**) and **mail.example.com**. The first virtual host serves documents from Sam's **public_html** directory; the second is a Webmail server with its content at **/var/www/html/squirrelmail**. This example works because all three addresses resolve to the IP address of the server.

```
NameVirtualHost *:
<VirtualHost *>
    ServerName      sam.example.com
    ServerAlias     www.example.com/sam
    ServerAdmin     webmaster@example.com
    DocumentRoot    /home/sam/public_html
</VirtualHost>

<VirtualHost *:>
    ServerName      mail.example.com
    ServerAdmin     webmaster2@example.com
    DocumentRoot    /var/www/html/squirrelmail
</VirtualHost>
```

If the user specifies an IP address and not a URI, that address might match more than one of the virtual hosts, as in the example. In this case, Apache serves the virtual host that best matches. If none of the virtual host addresses matches the IP address better than another, Apache serves the first virtual host. In the preceding example, both virtual hosts match an IP address the same way; neither is a better match, so Apache serves the first virtual host (**sam.example.com**). If **mail.example.com** was defined as <VirtualHost 192.168.1.102> and a user specified that IP address, Apache would serve **mail.example.com** because it is a better match for the IP address than the wildcard that the other virtual host specifies.

The next example shows VirtualHost containers for a host-by-IP server. The example assumes that 111.111.0.0 and 111.111.0.1 point to the local server. Here each virtual host has its own IP/port combination. The third virtual host is distinguished from the first by the port that a request comes in on.

```
<VirtualHost 111.111.0.0:80>
    DocumentRoot /var/www/html/www0
</VirtualHost>
```

```
<VirtualHost 111.111.0.1:80>
    DocumentRoot /var/www/html/www1
</VirtualHost>

<VirtualHost 111.111.0.0:8080>
    DocumentRoot /var/www/html/www2
    Listen 8080
</VirtualHost>
```

The final example sets up a virtual server for Webmail that can be accessed only over SSL. To use this example you must create an SSL certificate (page 970).

```
<VirtualHost mail.example.com:80>
    Redirect permanent / https://mail.example.com/
</VirtualHost>
<VirtualHost mail.example.com:443>
    ServerName      mail.example.com
    ServerAdmin     postmaster@example.com
    DocumentRoot    /var/www/html/mail.example.com
    ErrorLog        /var/log/httpd/mail.example.com.err
    CustomLog       /var/log/httpd/mail.example.com.log combined
    SSLEngine On
    SSLCertificateFile /etc/pki/tls/certs/apache.pem
</VirtualHost>
```

# TROUBLESHOOTING

If the browser does not display the information you expect, make sure it is not displaying a cached version of the page. Try clearing the browser's cache and reloading the page. Also make sure that Apache has permission to read the files it is serving and the scripts it is running.

The **httpd** service checks the syntax of the Apache configuration files and logs an error if there is a problem. You can also call apachectl directly to check the syntax:

```
$ apachectl configtest
Syntax OK
```

Once you start the **httpd** daemon, you can confirm Apache is working correctly by pointing a browser on the local system at **http://localhost/**. From a remote system, use **http://**server**/**, substituting the hostname or IP address of the server for *server*. In response, Apache displays the Fedora/RHEL test page (page 937) unless you have added an index file or changed the default virtual host.

If the browser does not display the test page, it will display one of two errors: **Connection refused** or an error page. If it displays **Connection refused**, make sure port 80 is not blocked by a firewall (page 934), check that SELinux (page 934) is set up properly, and check that the server is running:

```
# systemctl status httpd.service
httpd.service - The Apache HTTP Server
    Loaded: loaded (/usr/lib/systemd/system/httpd.service; enabled)
    Active: active (running) since ...
```

If the server is running, confirm that you did not specify a port other than 80 in a Listen directive. If you did, the URI you specify in the browser must reflect this port number (**http://localhost:*port*** specifies port *port*). Otherwise, check the error log (**/var/log/httpd/error_log**) for information about what is not working.

To verify the browser is not at fault, use telnet to connect to port 80 of the server:

```
$ telnet www.example.com 80
Trying 192.0.34.166...
Connected to www.example.com.
Escape character is '^]'.
CONTROL-]
telnet> quit
Connection closed.
```

If telnet displays **Connection refused**, it means the local system cannot connect to the server.

# MODULES

Apache is a skeletal program that relies on external modules, called DSOs (dynamic shared objects), to provide most of its functionality. In addition to the modules included with Fedora/RHEL, many other modules are available. For more information see httpd.apache.org/modules and httpd.apache.org/docs/2.4/mod.

Following is a list of some of the modules that are available under Apache.

**actions** (mod_actions.so) Allows execution of CGI scripts based on the request method.
**alias** (mod_alias.so) Allows outside directories to be mapped to DocumentRoot.
**asis** (mod_asis.so) Allows sending files that contain their own headers.
**auth_basic** (mod_auth_basic.so) Provides user authentication via **.htaccess**.
**auth_digest** (mod_auth_digest.so) Uses MD5 digest for authentication.
**authn_anon** (mod_authn_anon.so) Provides anonymous user access to restricted areas.
**authn_dbd** (mod_authn_dbd.so) Uses SQL files for authentication.
**autoindex** (mod_autoindex.so) Allows directory indexes to be generated.
**cgi** (mod_cgi.so) Allows the execution of CGI scripts.
**dav** (mod_dav.so) Allows Distributed Authoring and Versioning.
**dav_fs** (mod_dav_fs.so) Provides a filesystem for mod_dav.
**dir** (mod_dir.so) Allows directory redirects and listings as index files.
**env** (mod_env.so) Allows CGI scripts to access environment variables.
**expires** (mod_expires.so) Allows generation of Expires HTTP headers.
**headers** (mod_headers.so) Allows customization of request and response headers.
**include** (mod_include.so) Provides server-side includes (SSIs).
**info** (mod_info.so) Allows the server configuration to be viewed.
**log_config** (mod_log_config.so) Allows logging of requests made to the server.
**mime** (mod_mime.so) Allows association of file extensions with content.
**mime_magic** (mod_mime_magic.so) Determines MIME types of files.

negotiation (mod_negotiation.so) Allows content negotiation.

proxy (mod_proxy.so) Allows Apache to act as a proxy server.

proxy_connect (mod_proxy_connect.so) Allows connect request handling.

proxy_ftp (mod_proxy_ftp.so) Provides an FTP extension proxy.

proxy_http (mod_proxy_http.so) Provides an HTTP extension proxy.

rewrite (mod_rewrite.so) Allows on-the-fly URI rewriting based on rules.

setenvif (mod_setenvif.so) Sets environment variables based on a request.

speling (mod_speling.so) Auto-corrects spelling if the requested URI has incorrect capitalization and one spelling mistake.

status (mod_status.so) Allows the server status to be queried and viewed.

unique_id (mod_unique_id.so) Generates a unique ID for each request.

userdir (mod_userdir.so) Allows users to have content directories (public_html).

usertrack (mod_usertrack.so) Allows tracking of user activity on a site.

vhost_alias (mod_vhost_alias.so) Allows the configuration of virtual hosting.

# mod_cgi AND CGI SCRIPTS

The CGI (Common Gateway Interface) allows external application programs to interface with Web servers. Any program can be a CGI program if it runs in real time (at the time of the request) and relays its output to the requesting client. Various kinds of scripts, including shell, Perl, Python, and PHP, are the most commonly encountered CGI programs because a script can call a program and reformat its output in HTML for a client.

Apache can handle requests for CGI programs in several different ways. The most common method is to put a CGI program in the **cgi-bin** directory and then enable its execution from that directory only. The location of the **cgi-bin** directory, as specified by the ScriptAlias directive (page 958), is **/var/www/cgi-bin**. Alternately, an AddHandler directive (page 952) can identify the filename extensions of scripts, such as **.cgi** or **.pl**, within the regular content (e.g., **AddHandler cgi-script .cgi**). If you use AddHandler, you must also specify the ExecCGI option in an Options directive within the appropriate <Directory> container. The **mod_cgi** module must be loaded to access and execute CGI scripts.

The following Perl CGI script displays the Apache environment. This script should be used for debugging only because it presents a security risk if remote clients can access it:

```perl
#!/usr/bin/perl
##
##  printenv -- demo CGI program that prints its environment
##

print "Content-type: text/plain\n\n";
foreach $var (sort(keys(%ENV))) {
    $val = $ENV{$var};
    $val =~ s|\n|\\n|g;
    $val =~ s|"|\\"|g;
    print "${var}=\"${val}\"\n";
}
```

# mod_ssl

SSL (Secure Sockets Layer), which is implemented by the **mod_ssl** module, has two functions: It allows a client to verify the identity of a server and it enables secure two-way communication between a client and a server. SSL is used on Web pages in conjunction with forms that require passwords, credit card numbers, or other sensitive data.

Apache uses the HTTPS protocol—not HTTP—for SSL communication. When Apache uses SSL, it listens on a second port (443 by default) for a connection and performs a handshaking sequence before sending the requested content to the client.

Server verification is critical for financial transactions: You do not want to give your credit card number to a fraudulent Web site posing as a known company. SSL uses a certificate to positively identify a server. Over a public network such as the Internet, the identification is reliable only if the certificate contains a digital signature from an authoritative source such as VeriSign or Thawte. SSL Web pages are denoted by a URI beginning with **https://**.

Data encryption prevents malicious users from eavesdropping on Internet connections and copying personal information. To encrypt communication, SSL sits between the network and an application and encrypts communication between the server and the client.

## SETTING UP mod_ssl

You must install the **mod_ssl** package to run SSL. The **/etc/httpd/conf.d/ssl.conf** file configures and loads **mod_ssl**. The first few directives in this file instruct Apache to listen on port 443, and set various parameters for SSL operation. About a third of the way through the file is a section labeled **SSL Virtual Host Context** that sets up virtual hosts (page 965).

As with any virtual host, a virtual host for SSL holds directives such as ServerName and ServerAdmin that need to be configured. In addition, it holds some SSL-related directives. See the example on page 967.

## USING A SELF-SIGNED CERTIFICATE FOR ENCRYPTION

If you require SSL for encryption and not verification—that is, if the client already trusts the server—you can generate and use a self-signed certificate, bypassing the time and expense involved in obtaining a digitally signed certificate. Self-signed certificates generate a warning when you connect to the server: Most browsers display a dialog box that allows you to examine and accept the certificate. The **sendmail** daemon also uses certificates (page 765).

The self-signed certificate depends on two files: a private key and the certificate. The location of each file is specified in **/etc/httpd/conf.d/ssl.conf**:

```
# grep '^SSLCertificate' /etc/httpd/conf.d/ssl.conf
SSLCertificateFile /etc/pki/tls/certs/localhost.crt
SSLCertificateKeyFile /etc/pki/tls/private/localhost.key
```

The following example creates a self-signed certificate. To generate the private key that the encryption relies on, cd to **/etc/pki/tls/certs** and enter a make command:

```
# cd /etc/pki/tls/certs
# make localhost.key
umask 77 ; \
/usr/bin/openssl genrsa -aes128 2048 > localhost.key
Generating RSA private key, 2048 bit long modulus
.+++
..................+++
e is 65537 (0x10001)
Enter pass phrase:
Verifying - Enter pass phrase:
```

The preceding command generates a file named **localhost.key** that is protected by the passphrase you entered: *You will need this passphrase to start the server.* Keep the **localhost.key** file secret.

The next command generates the certificate. This process uses the private key you just created. You need to supply the same passphrase you entered when you created the private key.

```
# make localhost.crt
umask 77 ; \
/usr/bin/openssl req -utf8 -new -key localhost.key -x509 -days 365 -out
localhost.crt -set_serial 0
Enter pass phrase for localhost.key:
You are about to be asked to enter information that will be incorporated
into your certificate request.
What you are about to enter is what is called a Distinguished Name or a DN.
There are quite a few fields but you can leave some blank
For some fields there will be a default value,
If you enter '.', the field will be left blank.
-----
Country Name (2 letter code) [GB]:US
State or Province Name (full name) [Berkshire]:California
Locality Name (eg, city) [Newbury]:San Francisco
Organization Name (eg, company) [My Company Ltd]:Sobell Associates Inc.
Organizational Unit Name (eg, section) []:
Common Name (eg, your name or your server's hostname) []:www.sobell.com
Email Address []:mgs@sobell.com
```

The answers to the first five questions are arbitrary: They can help clients identify a site when they examine the certificate. The answer to the sixth question (**Common Name**) is critical. Because certificates are tied to the name of the server, you must enter the server's FQDN accurately. If you mistype this information, the server name and that of the certificate will not match. The browser will then generate a warning message each time a connection is made.

As specified by **ssl.conf**, Apache looks for the files in the directory that you created them in. Do not move these files. After you restart Apache, the new certificate will be in use.

## NOTES ON CERTIFICATES

- As long as the server is identified by the name for which the certificate was issued, you can use the certificate on another server or IP address.

- A root certificate is the certificate that identifies the root certificate authority (root CA). Every browser contains a database of the public keys for the root certificates of the major signing authorities, including VeriSign and Thawte.

- It is possible to generate a root certificate and sign all your server certificates with this root CA. Regular clients can import the public key of the root CA so that they recognize every certificate signed by that root CA. This setup is convenient for a server with multiple SSL-enabled virtual hosts and no commercial certificates. For more information see www.modssl.org/docs/2.8/ssl_faq.html#ToC29.

- A self-signed certificate does not enable clients to verify the identity of the server.

# AUTHENTICATION MODULES AND .htaccess FILES

To restrict access to a Web page, Apache and third parties provide authentication modules and methods that can verify a user's credentials, such as a username and password. Some modules support authentication against various databases including NIS (page 770) and LDAP (page 786).

User authentication directives are commonly placed in a **.htaccess** file. A basic **.htaccess** file that uses the Apache default authentication module (**mod_auth**) follows. When placed in **/var/www/html**, this file causes Apache to request a password before a browser can access content in the **/var/www/html** directory hierarchy. Substitute appropriate values for the local server.

```
# cat .htaccess
AuthUserFile /var/www/html/.htpasswd
AuthGroupFile /dev/null
AuthName "Browser dialog box query"
AuthType Basic
require valid-user
```

The **/var/www/html/.htpasswd** is a typical absolute pathname of a **.htpasswd** file and **Browser dialog box query** is the string that the user will see as part of the dialog box that requests a username and password.

The second line of the preceding **.htaccess** file turns off the group function. The fourth line specifies the user authentication type **Basic**, which is implemented by the default **mod_auth** module. The last line tells Apache which users can access the protected directory. The entry **valid-user** grants access to the directory to any user whose username appears in the Apache password file and who enters the correct password.

You can put the Apache password file anywhere on the system, as long as Apache can read it. It is safe to put this file in the same directory as the **.htaccess** file because, by default, Apache will not answer any requests for files whose names start with **.ht**. However, be sure you have not changed the **httpd.conf** configuration file to allow Apache to answer requests for files whose names begin with **.ht**. See page 939 for more information on **.htaccess** files.

The following command creates (–c) a **.htpasswd** file with an entry for Sam in the working directory. Omit the –c option to add a user or to change a password in an existing **.htpasswd** file.

```
$ htpasswd -c .htpasswd sam
New password:
Re-type new password:
Adding password for user sam
```

The **default httpd.conf** file includes an **AllowOverride None** directive (page 960) for **/var/www/html**. You must change this directive to at least **AllowOverride AuthConfig** or remove it to enable Apache to process user authentication directives (such as reading an **.htaccess** file).

### .htaccess files can degrade performance

tip  With Apache configured to process **.htaccess** files, when it receives a request for a file, it has to traverse the directory hierarchy from the requested file upward, toward the root, looking for a **.htacess** file to determine whether it can serve the requested file. This search can affect performance. Typically performance degradation is not severe, but this issue can become important if performance is critical.

## SCRIPTING MODULES

Apache can process content before serving it to a client. In earlier versions of Apache, only CGI scripts could process content. In the current version, *scripting modules* can work with scripts embedded in HTML documents. The downside is that major bugs in scripting modules can affect the stability of Apache processes.

Scripting modules manipulate content before Apache serves it to a client. Because they are built into Apache, scripting modules are fast. Scripting modules are especially efficient at working with external data sources such as relational databases. Clients can pass data to a scripting module that modifies the information that Apache serves.

Scripting modules stand in contrast to CGI scripts that are run externally to Apache. In particular, CGI scripts do not allow client interaction and are slow because they must make external calls.

You can embed Perl (**mod_perl**), Python, and PHP code in HTML content. Perl and Python are general-purpose scripting languages and are implemented in the **mod_perl** and **mod_wsgi** modules.

PHP, which was developed for manipulating Web content, outputs HTML by default. It is encapsulated for use directly in Apache, is easy to set up, has a syntax similar to that of Perl and C, and comes with a large number of Web-related functions.

# MULTIPROCESSING MODULES (MPMs)

If Apache were to execute in only one process, then each time a client requested a page, Apache would have to ignore other requests while it read that page from disk (or waited for a CGI script to generate it). After it read the page, it could send the page to the client and respond to the next request. With this setup, Apache could serve only one client at a time.

prefork MPM   Apache 1.3 and earlier forked servers to respond to multiple clients. Apache 2 moved the forking behavior to the **prefork** MPM (multiprocessing module). MPMs introduced the ability to switch between various multiprocessing techniques.

The **prefork** MPM uses the **fork**() system call to create an exact copy of the running Apache process to serve each request. The MaxServers, MaxRequestWorkers, and similar directives control how many copies of Apache run at the same time. Because the operating system has to spend time context switching between Apache processes, and because each process has its own memory, the **prefork** MPM generates considerable overhead on a busy server. Fedora/RHEL runs the **prefork** MPM by default.

worker MPM   The **worker** MPM reduces this overhead by using **threads**. A thread is similar to a process in that it can execute independently of other threads or processes. Waiting for a read to complete in one thread does not stop (block) other threads from executing. The difference between threads and processes is that all the threads running under one process share the same memory, and the program—rather than the operating system—is responsible for managing the threads. The **worker** MPM maintains a pool of threads it can use to serve each request. Instead of the parent Apache process forking a child to serve each request for content as in **prefork**, the **worker** MPM uses threads to serve requests for content.

Threads   Because all these threads run under the same process, they share the same memory. Code that is not *thread safe* (see *reentrant* on page 1269) can return inconsistent results. For example, some PHP library functions use the **strtok**() C function to convert a string to tokens. This function maintains internal variables. If it is called by multiple threads sharing the same memory, **strtok**()'s internal variables are put in an inconsistent state.

PHP   If you want to use PHP, either you must use the **prefork** MPM or, if you want to use the **worker** MPM and PHP, you must remove **mod_php** and run PHP as a CGI script (page 969).

To run the **worker** MPM, in **/etc/httpd/conf.modules.d/00-mpm.conf**, move the hash sign from the **worker module** line to the **prefork module** line as follows:

```
#LoadModule mpm_prefork_module modules/mod_mpm_prefork.so
LoadModule mpm_worker_module modules/mod_mpm_worker.so
```

After making this change, restart the **httpd** daemon (page 935).

# webalizer: ANALYZES WEB TRAFFIC

The **webalizer** package creates a directory at **/var/www/usage**, a cron file (page 607) at **/etc/cron.daily/00webalizer**, a webalizer configuration file at **/etc/webalizer.conf**, and an Apache configuration file at **/etc/httpd/conf.d/webalizer.conf**. After installing the package, restart the **httpd** daemon (page 935). Once a day, the cron file generates usage data and puts it in the **usage** directory; you can view this data by pointing a browser at **http://***server***/usage/**, where *server* is the name or IP address of the server. However, the cron script must have run at least once so there is data in the **usage** directory before Apache will display results and not display an error.

The **/etc/webalizer.conf** file controls the behavior of the webalizer utility. If you want information on virtual hosts (which by definition change the location of the Document-Root and often change the location of log files), you must modify the **/etc/webalizer.conf** file. The **/etc/httpd/conf.d/webalizer.conf** file includes a Require local directive. If you want to view statistics from a remote browser, you must add an appropriate Require directive (page 961) to this file. For more information on webalizer, refer to the webalizer man page and the sites listed under "More Information" on page 933.

# MRTG: MONITORS TRAFFIC LOADS

Multi Router Traffic Grapher (MRTG; **mrtg** package) is an open-source application that graphs statistics available through SNMP (Simple Network Management Protocol). SNMP information is available on all high-end routers and switches as well as on some other networked equipment, such as printers and wireless access points. You can use the **net-snmp** and **net-snmp-utils** packages supplied by Fedora/RHEL to install SNMP on a system. You also need to install the **mrtg** package. The **/etc/httpd/conf.d/mrtg.conf** file includes Require local directive. If you want to view statistics from a remote browser, you must add an appropriate Require directive (page 961) to this file.

Once MRTG and SNMP are installed and running, you can view the reports at **http://***server***/mrtg**, where *server* is the hostname of the server. For more information see the mrtg man page and the sites listed under "More Information" on page 933. See also "Introduction to Cacti" on page 645 for information on capturing and displaying SNMP information.

# ERROR CODES

Following is a list of Apache error codes:

| | |
|---|---|
| 100 Continue | 201 Created |
| 101 Switching Protocols | 202 Accepted |
| 200 OK | 203 Non-Authoritative Info... |

| | |
|---|---|
| 204 No Content | 407 Proxy Authentication Required |
| 205 Reset Content | 408 Request Timed Out |
| 206 Partial Content | 409 Conflict |
| 300 Multiple Choices | 410 Gone |
| 301 Moved Permanently | 411 Length Required |
| 302 Moved Temporarily | 412 Precondition Failed |
| 303 See Other | 413 Request Entity Too Large |
| 304 Not Modified | 414 Request-URI Too Large |
| 305 Use Proxy | 415 Unsupported Media Type |
| 400 Bad Request | 500 Internal Server Error |
| 401 Unauthorized | 501 Not Implemented |
| 402 Payment Required | 502 Bad Gateway |
| 403 Forbidden | 503 Service Unavailable |
| 404 Not Found | 504 Gateway Time-out |
| 405 Method Not Allowed | 505 HTTP Version Not Supported |
| 406 Not Acceptable | |

# CHAPTER SUMMARY

Apache is the most popular Web server on the Internet. It is both robust and extensible. The **/etc/httpd/conf/httpd.conf** configuration file controls many aspects of how Apache runs. The Fedora/RHEL **httpd.conf** file, which is based on the **httpd.conf** file distributed by Apache, is heavily commented.

Content to be served is typically placed in **/var/www/html**, called the *document root*. Apache automatically displays the file named **index.html** in this directory.

Configuration directives, or simply directives, are lines in a configuration file that control some aspect of how Apache functions. Four locations, called *contexts,* define where a configuration directive can appear: **server config, virtual host, directory,** and **.htaccess.** Containers, or special directives, are directives that group other directives.

To restrict access to a Web page, Apache and third parties provide authentication modules and methods that can verify a user's credentials, such as a username and password. Some modules enable authentication against various databases, including LDAP and NIS.

Apache can respond to a request for a URI by asking the client to request a different URI. This response is called a *redirect.* Apache can also process content before serving it to a client using scripting modules that work with scripts embedded in HTML documents.

Apache supports virtual hosts, which means that one instance of Apache can respond to requests directed to multiple IP addresses or hostnames as though it were multiple servers. Each IP address or hostname can provide different content and be configured differently.

The CGI (Common Gateway Interface) allows external application programs to interface with Web servers. Any program can be a CGI program if it runs in real time and relays its output to the requesting client.

SSL (Secure Sockets Layer) has two functions: It allows a client to verify the identity of a server and it enables secure two-way communication between a client and server.

# EXERCISES

1. What is Apache? Very basically, how does it work (i.e., what happens when you point a browser at a Web page)?

2. What is the function of the document root? Where is it located by default? How would you change the location of the document root?

3. How would you tell Apache that the content is in **/usr/local/www**?

4. How would you instruct an Apache server to listen on port 81 instead of port 80?

5. How would you enable Sam to publish Web pages from his **~/website** directory but not allow anyone else to publish to the Web?

6. Apache must be started with **root** privileges. Why? Why does this action not present a security risk?

7. What is the relationship between Apache and **httpd**?

8. What does the ServerName directive do? Which value can you use as a ServerName if you want to experiment with an Apache server locally (on the server system)?

# ADVANCED EXERCISES

9. If you are running Apache on a firewall system, perhaps to display a Web front end for firewall configuration, how would you make sure that it is accessible only from inside the local network?

10. Why is it more efficient to run scripts using **mod_perl** than to run them through CGI?

11. What two things does SSL provide, and how does this situation differ if the certificate is self-signed?

12. Some Web sites generate content by retrieving data from a database and inserting it into a template using PHP or CGI each time the site is accessed. Why is this practice often a poor idea?

13. Assume you want to provide Webmail access for employees on the same server that hosts the corporate Web site. The Web site address is example.com, you want to use mail.example.com for Webmail, and the Webmail application is located in **/var/www/webmail**. Describe two ways you can set up this configuration.

14. Part of a Web site is a private intranet. Describe how you would prevent people outside the company's internal 192.168.0.0/16 network from accessing this site. The site is defined as follows:

```
<VirtualHost *>
ServerName example.com
DocumentRoot /var/www
<Directory /var/www/intranet>
  AllowOverride AuthConfig
</Directory>
</VirtualHost>
```

15. What is a container? Give an example of container syntax.

16. What does CGI do? What are the characteristics of a CGI program?

17. What are the functions of SSL?

# PART V
## PROGRAMMING TOOLS

# 27

# PROGRAMMING THE BOURNE AGAIN SHELL (bash)

## OBJECTIVES

After reading this chapter you should be able to:

▶ Use control structures to implement decision making and repetition in shell scripts

▶ Handle input to and output from scripts

▶ Use shell variables (local) and environment variables (global)

▶ Evaluate the value of numeric variables

▶ Use bash builtin commands to call other scripts inline, trap signals, and kill processes

▶ Use arithmetic and logical expressions

▶ List standard programming practices that result in well-written scripts

Chapter 5 introduced the shells and Chapter 9 went into detail about the Bourne Again Shell. This chapter introduces additional Bourne Again Shell commands, builtins, and concepts that carry shell programming to a point where it can be useful. Although you might make use of shell programming as a system administrator, you do not have to read this chapter to perform system administration tasks. Feel free to skip this chapter and come back to it if and when you like.

The first part of this chapter covers programming control structures, also called control flow constructs. These structures allow you to write scripts that can loop over command-line arguments, make decisions based on the value of a variable, set up menus, and more. The Bourne Again Shell uses the same constructs found in programming languages such as C.

The next part of this chapter discusses parameters and variables, going into detail about array variables, shell versus environment variables, special parameters, and positional parameters. The exploration of builtin commands covers type, which displays information about a command, and read, which allows a shell script to accept user input. The section on the exec builtin demonstrates how to use exec to execute a command efficiently by replacing a process and explains how to use exec to redirect input and output from within a script.

The next section covers the trap builtin, which provides a way to detect and respond to operating system signals (such as the signal generated when you press CONTROL-C). The discussion of builtins concludes with a discussion of kill, which can abort a process, and getopts, which makes it easy to parse options for a shell script. Table 27-6 on page 1055 lists some of the more commonly used builtins.

Next the chapter examines arithmetic and logical expressions as well as the operators that work with them. The final section walks through the design and implementation of two major shell scripts.

This chapter contains many examples of shell programs. Although they illustrate certain concepts, most use information from earlier examples as well. This overlap not only reinforces your overall knowledge of shell programming but also demonstrates how you can combine commands to solve complex tasks. Running, modifying, and experimenting with the examples in this book is a good way to become comfortable with the underlying concepts.

### Do not name a shell script test

tip  You can unwittingly create a problem if you name a shell script **test** because a bash builtin has the same name. Depending on how you call your script, you might run either your script or the builtin, leading to confusing results.

## LPI  CONTROL STRUCTURES

The *control flow* commands alter the order of execution of commands within a shell script. Control structures include the **if...then, for...in, while, until,** and **case**

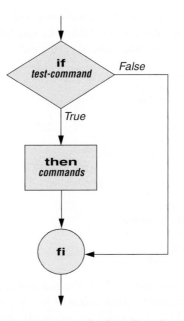

**Figure 27-1** An **if...then** flowchart

statements. In addition, the **break** and **continue** statements work in conjunction with the control structures to alter the order of execution of commands within a script.

Getting help with control structures — You can use the bash **help** command to display information about bash control structures. See page 134 for more information.

## LE+ if...then

The **if...then** control structure has the following syntax:

> *if* ***test-command***
>> *then*
>>> ***commands***
> *fi*

The ***bold*** words in the syntax description are the items you supply to cause the structure to have the desired effect. The *nonbold* words are the keywords the shell uses to identify the control structure.

LE+ test builtin — Figure 27-1 shows that the **if** statement tests the status returned by the ***test-command*** and transfers control based on this status. The end of the **if** structure is marked by a **fi** statement (*if* spelled backward). The following script prompts for two words, reads them, and then uses an **if** structure to execute commands based on the result returned by the test builtin when it compares the two words. (See the test info page for information on the test utility, which is similar to the test builtin.) The test builtin returns a status of *true* if the two words are the same and *false* if they are not. Double quotation marks around **$word1** and **$word2** make sure test works properly if you enter a string that contains a SPACE or other special character.

```
$ cat if1
read -p "word 1: " word1
read -p "word 2: " word2

if test "$word1" = "$word2"
    then
          echo "Match"
fi
echo "End of program."

$ ./if1
word 1: peach
word 2: peach
Match
End of program.
```

In the preceding example the ***test-command*** is **test "$word1" = "$word2"**. The test builtin returns a *true* status if its first and third arguments have the relationship specified by its second argument. If this command returns a *true* status (= 0), the shell executes the commands between the **then** and **fi** statements. If the command returns a *false* status (not = 0), the shell passes control to the statement following **fi** without executing the statements between **then** and **fi**. The effect of this **if** statement is to display **Match** if the two words are the same. The script always displays **End of program.**

Builtins In the Bourne Again Shell, test is a builtin—part of the shell. It is also a stand-alone utility kept in **/usr/bin/test**. This chapter discusses and demonstrates many Bourne Again Shell builtins. The shell will use the builtin version if it is available and the utility if it is not. Each version of a command might vary slightly from one shell to the next and from the utility to any of the shell builtins. See page 1040 for more information on shell builtins.

Checking arguments The next program uses an **if** structure at the beginning of a script to confirm that you have supplied at least one argument on the command line. The test –**eq** criterion compares two integers; the shell expands the **$#** special parameter (page 1027) to the number of command-line arguments. This structure displays a message and exits from the script with an exit status of 1 if you do not supply at least one argument.

```
$ cat chkargs
if test $# -eq 0
    then
          echo "You must supply at least one argument."
          exit 1
fi
echo "Program running."
```

```
$ ./chkargs
You must supply at least one argument.
$ ./chkargs abc
Program running.
```

A test like the one shown in **chkargs** is a key component of any script that requires arguments. To prevent the user from receiving meaningless or confusing information from the script, the script needs to check whether the user has supplied the appropriate arguments. Some scripts simply test whether arguments exist (as in **chkargs**); other scripts test for a specific number or specific kinds of arguments.

You can use test to verify the status of a file argument or the relationship between two file arguments. After verifying that at least one argument has been given on the command line, the following script tests whether the argument is the name of an ordinary file (not a directory or other type of file). The test builtin with the –f criterion and the first command-line argument (**$1**) checks the file.

```
$ cat is_ordfile
if test $# -eq 0
    then
        echo "You must supply at least one argument."
        exit 1
fi
if test -f "$1"
    then
        echo "$1 is an ordinary file."
    else
        echo "$1 is NOT an ordinary file."
fi
```

You can test many other characteristics of a file using test criteria; see Table 27-1.

**Table 27-1**    test builtin criteria

| Criterion | Tests file to see if it |
| --- | --- |
| **–d** | Exists and is a directory file |
| **–e** | Exists |
| **–f** | Exists and is an ordinary file (not a directory) |
| **–r** | Exists and is readable |
| **–s** | Exists and has a size greater than 0 bytes |
| **–w** | Exists and is writable |
| **–x** | Exists and is executable |

Other test criteria provide ways to test relationships between two files, such as whether one file is newer than another. Refer to examples later in this chapter for more information.

## Always test the arguments

tip  To keep the examples in this book short and focused on specific concepts, the code to verify arguments is often omitted or abbreviated. It is good practice to test arguments in shell programs that other people will use. Doing so results in scripts that are easier to debug, run, and maintain.

**LE:** [ ] is a synonym for test  The following example—another version of **chkargs**—checks for arguments in a way that is more traditional for Linux shell scripts. This example uses the bracket ([]) synonym for test. Rather than using the word test in scripts, you can surround the arguments to test with brackets. The brackets must be surrounded by whitespace (SPACEs or TABs).

```
$ cat chkargs2
if [ $# -eq 0 ]
    then
        echo "Usage: chkargs2 argument..." 1>&2
        exit 1
fi
echo "Program running."
exit 0

$ ./chkargs2
Usage: chkargs2 argument...
$ ./chkargs2 abc
Program running.
```

Usage messages  The error message that **chkargs2** displays is called a *usage message* and uses the **1>&2** notation to redirect its output to standard error (page 335). After issuing the usage message, **chkargs2** exits with an exit status of 1, indicating an error has occurred. The **exit 0** command at the end of the script causes **chkargs2** to exit with a 0 status after the program runs without an error. The Bourne Again Shell returns the exit status of the last command the script ran if you omit the status code.

The usage message is commonly used to specify the type and number of arguments the script requires. Many Linux utilities provide usage messages similar to the one in **chkargs2**. If you call a utility or other program with the wrong number or wrong kind of arguments, it will often display a usage message. Following is the usage message that cp displays when you call it with only one argument:

```
$ cp a
cp: missing destination file operand after 'a'
Try 'cp --help' for more information.
```

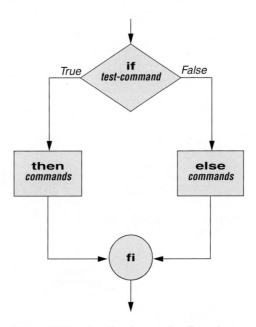

**Figure 27-2**   An **if...then...else** flowchart

## if...then...else

The introduction of an **else** statement turns the **if** structure into the two-way branch shown in Figure 27-2. The **if...then...else** control structure has the following syntax:

> *if* **test-command**
>         *then*
>                 ***commands***
>         *else*
>                 ***commands***
> *fi*

Because a semicolon (;) ends a command just as a NEWLINE does, you can place **then** on the same line as **if** by preceding it with a semicolon. (Because **if** and **then** are separate builtins, they require a control operator between them; a semicolon and NEWLINE work equally well [page 341].) Some people prefer this notation for aesthetic reasons; others like it because it saves space.

> *if* **test-command**; *then*
>                 ***commands***
>         *else*
>                 ***commands***
> *fi*

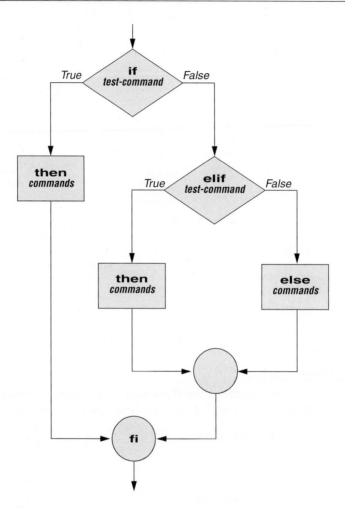

**Figure 27-3**   An if...then...elif flowchart

If the *test-command* returns a *true* status, the **if** structure executes the commands between the **then** and **else** statements and then diverts control to the statement following **fi**. If the *test-command* returns a *false* status, the **if** structure executes the commands following the **else** statement.

When you run the **out** script with arguments that are filenames, it displays the files on the terminal. If the first argument is **–v** (called an option in this case), **out** uses less (page 220) to display the files one screen at a time. After determining that it was called with at least one argument, **out** tests its first argument to see whether it is **–v**. If the result of the test is *true* (the first argument is **–v**), **out** uses the shift builtin (page 1025) to shift the arguments to get rid of the **–v** and displays the files using less. If the result of the test is *false* (the first argument is *not* **–v**), the script uses cat to display the files.

```
$ cat out
if [ $# -eq 0 ]
    then
        echo "Usage: $0 [-v] filenames..." 1>&2
        exit 1
fi

if [ "$1" = "-v" ]
    then
        shift
        less -- "$@"
    else
        cat -- "$@"
fi
```

**optional**  In *out*, the –– argument to cat and less tells these utilities that no more options follow on the command line and not to consider leading hyphens (–) in the following list as indicating options. Thus –– allows you to view a file whose name starts with a hyphen (page 146). Although not common, filenames beginning with a hyphen do occasionally occur. (You can create such a file by using the command **cat > –fname**.) The –– argument works with all Linux utilities that use the getopts builtin (page 1052) to parse their options; it does not work with more and a few other utilities. This argument is particularly useful when used in conjunction with rm to remove a file whose name starts with a hyphen (**rm –– –fname**), including any you create while experimenting with the –– argument.

*LE+*  # if...then...elif

The **if...then...elif** control structure (Figure 27-3) has the following syntax:

> *if test-command*
>> *then*
>>> *commands*
>> *elif test-command*
>>> *then*
>>>> *commands*
> . . .
>> *else*
>>> *commands*
> *fi*

The **elif** statement combines the **else** statement and the **if** statement and enables you to construct a nested set of **if...then...else** structures (Figure 27-3). The difference between the **else** statement and the **elif** statement is that each **else** statement must be paired with a **fi** statement, whereas multiple nested **elif** statements require only a single closing **fi** statement.

The following example shows an **if...then...elif** control structure. This shell script compares three words the user enters. The first **if** statement uses the Boolean AND operator (**–a**) as an argument to test. The test builtin returns a *true* status if the first and second logical comparisons are *true* (that is, **word1** matches **word2** and **word2** matches **word3**). If test returns a *true* status, the script executes the command following the next **then** statement, passes control to the statement following **fi**, and terminates.

```
$ cat if3
read -p "word 1: " word1
read -p "word 2: " word2
read -p "word 3: " word3
if [ "$word1" = "$word2" -a "$word2" = "$word3" ]
    then
        echo "Match: words 1, 2, & 3"
    elif [ "$word1" = "$word2" ]
    then
        echo "Match: words 1 & 2"
    elif [ "$word1" = "$word3" ]
    then
        echo "Match: words 1 & 3"
    elif [ "$word2" = "$word3" ]
    then
        echo "Match: words 2 & 3"
    else
        echo "No match"
fi


$ ./if3
word 1: apple
word 2: orange
word 3: pear
No match
$ ./if3
word 1: apple
word 2: orange
word 3: apple
Match: words 1 & 3
$ ./if3
word 1: apple
word 2: apple
word 3: apple
Match: words 1, 2, & 3
```

If the three words are not the same, the structure passes control to the first **elif**, which begins a series of tests to see if any pair of words is the same. As the nesting continues, if any one of the **elif** statements is satisfied, the structure passes control to the next **then** statement and subsequently to the statement following **fi**. Each time an **elif** statement is not satisfied, the structure passes control to the next **elif** statement. The double quotation marks around the arguments to echo that contain ampersands (**&**) prevent the shell from interpreting the ampersands as special characters.

## optional THE lnks SCRIPT

The following script, named **lnks**, demonstrates the **if...then** and **if...then...elif** control structures. This script finds hard links to its first argument, a filename. If you provide the name of a directory as the second argument, **lnks** searches for links in the directory hierarchy rooted at that directory. If you do not specify a directory, **lnks** searches the working directory and its subdirectories. This script does not locate symbolic links.

```bash
$ cat lnks
#!/bin/bash
# Identify links to a file
# Usage: lnks file [directory]

if [ $# -eq 0 -o $# -gt 2 ]; then
    echo "Usage: lnks file [directory]" 1>&2
    exit 1
fi
if [ -d "$1" ]; then
    echo "First argument cannot be a directory." 1>&2
    echo "Usage: lnks file [directory]" 1>&2
    exit 1
else
    file="$1"
fi
if [ $# -eq 1 ]; then
        directory="."
    elif [ -d "$2" ]; then
        directory="$2"
    else
        echo "Optional second argument must be a directory." 1>&2
        echo "Usage: lnks file [directory]" 1>&2
        exit 1
fi

# Check that file exists and is an ordinary file
if [ ! -f "$file" ]; then
    echo "lnks: $file not found or is a special file" 1>&2
    exit 1
fi
# Check link count on file
set -- $(ls -l "$file")

linkcnt=$2
if [ "$linkcnt" -eq 1 ]; then
    echo "lnks: no other hard links to $file" 1>&2
    exit 0
fi

# Get the inode of the given file
set $(ls -i "$file")

inode=$1

# Find and print the files with that inode number
echo "lnks: using find to search for links..." 1>&2
find "$directory" -xdev -inum $inode -print
```

Max has a file named **letter** in his home directory. He wants to find links to this file in his and other users' home directory file hierarchies. In the following example, Max calls **lnks** from his home directory to perform the search. The second argument to **lnks**, **/home**, is the pathname of the directory where Max wants to start the search. The **lnks** script reports that **/home/max/letter** and **/home/zach/draft** are links to the same file:

```
$ ./lnks letter /home
lnks: using find to search for links...
/home/max/letter
/home/zach/draft
```

In addition to the **if...then...elif** control structure, **lnks** introduces other features that are commonly used in shell programs. The following discussion describes **lnks** section by section.

Specify the shell    The first line of the **lnks** script uses **#!** (page 338) to specify the shell that will execute the script:

```
#!/bin/bash
```

In this chapter, the **#!** notation appears only in more complex examples. It ensures that the proper shell executes the script, even when the user is running a different shell or the script is called from a script running a different shell.

Comments    The second and third lines of **lnks** are comments; the shell ignores text that follows a hashmark (**#**) up to the next NEWLINE character. These comments in **lnks** briefly identify what the file does and explain how to use it:

```
# Identify links to a file
# Usage: lnks file [directory]
```

Usage messages    The first **if** statement tests whether **lnks** was called with zero arguments or more than two arguments:

```
if [ $# -eq 0 -o $# -gt 2 ]; then
    echo "Usage: lnks file [directory]" 1>&2
    exit 1
fi
```

If either of these conditions is *true*, **lnks** sends a usage message to standard error and exits with a status of 1. The double quotation marks around the usage message prevent the shell from interpreting the brackets as special characters. The brackets in the usage message indicate that the **directory** argument is optional.

The second **if** statement tests whether the first command-line argument (**$1**) is a directory (the **–d** argument to **test** returns *true* if the file exists and is a directory):

```
if [ -d "$1" ]; then
    echo "First argument cannot be a directory." 1>&2
    echo "Usage: lnks file [directory]" 1>&2
    exit 1
else
    file="$1"
fi
```

If the first argument is a directory, **lnks** displays a usage message and exits. If it is not a directory, **lnks** saves the value of **$1** in the **file** variable because later in the script set resets the command-line arguments. If the value of **$1** is not saved before the **set** command is issued, its value is lost.

Test the arguments The next section of **lnks** is an **if...then...elif** statement:

```
if [ $# -eq 1 ]; then
        directory="."
    elif [ -d "$2" ]; then
        directory="$2"
    else
        echo "Optional second argument must be a directory." 1>&2
        echo "Usage: lnks file [directory]" 1>&2
        exit 1
fi
```

The first *test-command* determines whether the user specified a single argument on the command line. If the *test-command* returns 0 (*true*), the **directory** variable is assigned the value of the working directory (.). If the *test-command* returns a nonzero value (*false*), the **elif** statement tests whether the second argument is a directory. If it is a directory, the **directory** variable is set equal to the second command-line argument, **$2**. If **$2** is not a directory, **lnks** sends a usage message to standard error and exits with a status of 1.

The next **if** statement in **lnks** tests whether **$file** does not exist. This test keeps **lnks** from wasting time looking for links to a nonexistent file. The **test** builtin, when called with the three arguments **!**, **–f**, and **$file**, evaluates to *true* if the file **$file** does *not* exist:

```
[ ! -f "$file" ]
```

The **!** operator preceding the **–f** argument to **test** negates its result, yielding *false* if the file **$file** *does* exist and is an ordinary file.

Next **lnks** uses **set** and **ls –l** to check the number of links **$file** has:

```
# Check link count on file
set -- $(ls -l "$file")

linkcnt=$2
if [ "$linkcnt" -eq 1 ]; then
    echo "lnks: no other hard links to $file" 1>&2
    exit 0
fi
```

The **set** builtin uses command substitution (page 410) to set the positional parameters to the output of **ls –l**. The second field in this output is the link count, so the user-created variable **linkcnt** is set equal to **$2**. The **--** used with **set** prevents **set** from interpreting as an option the first argument produced by **ls –l** (the first argument is the access permissions for the file and typically begins with –). The **if** statement checks whether **$linkcnt** is equal to 1; if it is, **lnks** displays a message and exits. Although this message is not truly an error message, it is redirected to standard error. The way **lnks** has been written, all informational messages are sent to standard error. Only the final product of **lnks**—the pathnames of links to the specified file—is sent to standard output, so you can redirect the output.

If the link count is greater than 1, **lnks** goes on to identify the *inode* (page 1254) for **$file**. As explained on page 206, comparing the inodes associated with filenames is a good way to determine whether the filenames are links to the same file. The **lnks** script uses **set** to set the positional parameters to the output of **ls –i**. The first argument to **set** is the inode number for the file, so the user-created variable named **inode** is assigned the value of **$1**:

```
# Get the inode of the given file
set $(ls -i "$file")

inode=$1
```

Finally **lnks** uses the **find** utility to search for files having inode numbers that match **$inode**:

```
# Find and print the files with that inode number
echo "lnks: using find to search for links..." 1>&2
find "$directory" -xdev -inum $inode -print
```

The **find** utility searches the directory hierarchy rooted at the directory specified by its first argument (**$directory**) for files that meet the criteria specified by the remaining arguments. In this example, the remaining arguments send the names of files having inode numbers matching **$inode** to standard output. Because files in different filesystems can have the same inode number yet not be linked, **find** must search only directories in the same filesystem as **$directory**. The **–xdev** (cross-device) argument prevents **find** from searching directories on other filesystems. Refer to page 203 for more information about filesystems and links.

The **echo** command preceding the **find** command in **lnks**, which tells the user that **find** is running, is included because **find** can take a long time to run. Because **lnks** does not include a final **exit** statement, the exit status of **lnks** is that of the last command it runs, **find**.

## DEBUGGING SHELL SCRIPTS

When you are writing a script such as **lnks**, it is easy to make mistakes. You can use the shell's **–x** option to help debug a script. This option causes the shell to display each command after it expands it but before it runs the command. Tracing a script's execution in this way can give you information about where a problem lies.

You can run **lnks** (above) and cause the shell to display each command before it is executed. Either set the **–x** option for the current shell (**set –x**) so all scripts display commands as they are run or use the **–x** option to affect only the shell running the script called by the command line.

```
$ bash -x lnks letter /home
+ '[' 2 -eq 0 -o 2 -gt 2 ']'
+ '[' -d letter ']'
+ file=letter
+ '[' 2 -eq 1 ']'
+ '[' -d /home ']'
+ directory=/home
+ '[' '!' -f letter ']'
...
```

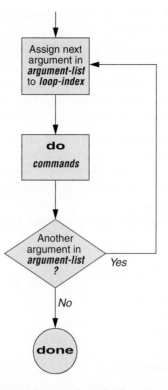

**Figure 27-4** A **for...in** flowchart

PS4    Each command the script executes is preceded by the value of the **PS4** variable—a plus sign (**+**) by default—so you can distinguish debugging output from output produced by the script. You must export **PS4** if you set it in the shell that calls the script. The next command sets **PS4** to **>>>>** followed by a SPACE and exports it:

```
$ export PS4='>>>> '
```

You can also set the **–x** option of the shell running the script by putting the following set command near the beginning of the script:

```
set -x
```

You can put **set –x** anywhere in the script to turn debugging on starting at that location. Turn debugging off using **set +x**. The **set –o xtrace** and **set +o xtrace** commands do the same things as **set –x** and **set +x,** respectively.

## LE+  for...in

The **for...in** control structure has the following syntax:

> *for loop-index in argument-list*
> *do*
> > **commands**
> *done*

The **for...in** structure (Figure 27-4) assigns the value of the first argument in the ***argument-list*** to the ***loop-index*** and executes the ***commands*** between the **do** and

**done** statements. The **do** and **done** statements mark the beginning and end of the **for** loop, respectively.

After it passes control to the **done** statement, the structure assigns the value of the second argument in the *argument-list* to the *loop-index* and repeats the *commands*. It repeats the *commands* between the **do** and **done** statements one time for each argument in the *argument-list*. When the structure exhausts the *argument-list*, it passes control to the statement following **done**.

The following **for...in** structure assigns **apples** to the user-created variable **fruit** and then displays the value of **fruit**, which is **apples**. Next the structure assigns **oranges** to **fruit** and repeats the process. When it exhausts the argument list, the structure transfers control to the statement following **done**, which displays a message.

```
$ cat fruit
for fruit in apples oranges pears bananas
do
    echo "$fruit"
done
echo "Task complete."

$ ./fruit
apples
oranges
pears
bananas
Task complete.
```

The next script lists the names of the directory files in the working directory by looping through the files in the working directory and using test to determine which are directory files:

```
$ cat dirfiles
for i in *
do
    if [ -d "$i" ]
        then
            echo "$i"
    fi
done
```

The ambiguous file reference character * matches the names of all files (except hidden files) in the working directory. Prior to executing the **for** loop, the shell expands the * and uses the resulting list to assign successive values to the index variable **i**.

**optional** STEP VALUES

As an alternative to explicitly specifying values for *argument-list*, you can specify step values. A **for...in** loop that uses step values assigns an initial value to or increments the *loop-index*, executes the statements within the loop, and tests a termination condition at the end of the loop.

The following example uses brace expansion with a sequence expression (page 406) to generate the *argument-list*. This syntax works on bash version 4.0 and above; give the command **echo $BASH_VERSION** to see which version you are using. The first time through the loop, bash assigns a value of 0 to **count** (the *loop-index*) and executes the statement between **do** and **done**. At the bottom of the loop, bash tests whether the termination condition has been met (is **count>10?**). If it has, bash passes control to the statement following **done**; if not, bash increments **count** by the increment value (**2**) and makes another pass through the loop. It repeats this process until the termination condition is met.

```
$ cat step1
for count in {0..10..2}
do
    echo -n "$count "
done
echo

$ ./step1
0 2 4 6 8 10
```

Older versions of bash do not support sequence expressions; you can use the seq utility to perform the same function:

```
$ for count in $(seq 0 2 10); do echo -n "$count "; done; echo
0 2 4 6 8 10
```

The next example uses bash's C-like syntax to specify step values. This syntax gives you more flexibility in specifying the termination condition and the increment value. Using this syntax, the first parameter initializes the *loop-index*, the second parameter specifies the condition to be tested, and the third parameter specifies the increment.

```
$ cat rand
# $RANDOM evaluates to a random value 0 < x < 32,767
# This program simulates 10 rolls of a pair of dice
for ((x=1; x<=10; x++))
do
    echo -n "Roll #$x: "
    echo -n    $(( $RANDOM % 6 + 1 ))
    echo "    " $(( $RANDOM % 6 + 1 ))
done
```

**LE+** # for

The **for** control structure has the following syntax:

*for loop-index*
*do*
      *commands*
*done*

In the **for** structure, the *loop-index* takes on the value of each of the command-line arguments, one at a time. The **for** structure is the same as the **for...in** structure (Figure 27-4, page 995) except in terms of where it gets values for the *loop-index*. The **for** structure performs a sequence of commands, usually involving each argument in turn.

The following shell script shows a **for** structure displaying each command-line argument. The first line of the script, **for arg**, implies **for arg in "$@"**, where the shell expands **"$@"** into a list of quoted command-line arguments (i.e., **"$1"** **"$2"** **"$3"** ...). The balance of the script corresponds to the **for...in** structure.

```
$ cat for_test
for arg
do
    echo "$arg"
done

$ for_test candy gum chocolate
candy
gum
chocolate
```

The next example uses a different syntax. In it, the *loop-index* is named **count** and is set to an initial value of 0. The condition to be tested is **count<=10**: bash continues executing the loop as long as this condition is *true* (as long as **count** is less than or equal to 10; see Table 27-8 on page 1059 for a list of operators). Each pass through the loop, bash adds 2 to the value of count (**count+=2**).

```
$ cat step2
for (( count=0; count<=10; count+=2 ))
do
    echo -n "$count "
done
echo

$ ./step2
0 2 4 6 8 10
```

**optional  THE whos SCRIPT**

The following script, named **whos**, demonstrates the usefulness of the implied "**$@**" in the **for** structure. You give **whos** one or more users' full names or usernames as arguments, and **whos** displays information about the users. The **whos** script gets the information it displays from the first and fifth fields in the **/etc/passwd** file. The first field contains a username, and the fifth field typically contains the user's full name. You can provide a username as an argument to **whos** to display the user's name or provide a name as an argument to display the username. The **whos** script is similar to the finger utility, although **whos** delivers less information.

```
$ cat whos
#!/bin/bash

if [ $# -eq 0 ]
    then
        echo "Usage: whos id..." 1>&2
        exit 1
fi
```

```
        for id
        do
            gawk -F: '{print $1, $5}' /etc/passwd |
            grep -i "$id"
        done
```

In the next example, **whos** identifies the user whose username is **chas** and the user whose name is **Marilou Smith**:

```
$ ./whos chas "Marilou Smith"
chas Charles Casey
msmith Marilou Smith
```

Use of **"$@"**   The **whos** script uses a **for** statement to loop through the command-line arguments. In this script the implied use of **"$@"** in the **for** loop is particularly beneficial because it causes the **for** loop to treat an argument that contains a SPACE as a single argument. This example encloses **Marilou Smith** in quotation marks, which causes the shell to pass it to the script as a single argument. Then the implied **"$@"** in the **for** statement causes the shell to regenerate the quoted argument **Marilou Smith** so that it is again treated as a single argument. The double quotation marks in the grep statement perform the same function.

gawk   For each command-line argument, **whos** searches the **/etc/passwd** file. Inside the **for** loop, the gawk utility extracts the first (**$1**) and fifth (**$5**) fields from each line in **/etc/passwd**. The **–F:** option causes gawk to use a colon (:) as a field separator when it reads **/etc/passwd**, allowing it to break each line into fields. The gawk command sets and uses the **$1** and **$5** arguments; they are included within single quotation marks and are not interpreted by the shell. Do not confuse these arguments with positional parameters, which correspond to command-line arguments. The first and fifth fields are sent to grep (page 232) via a pipeline. The grep utility searches for **$id** (to which the shell has assigned the value of a command-line argument) in its input. The **–i** option causes grep to ignore case as it searches; grep displays each line in its input that contains **$id**.

A pipeline symbol (|)   Under bash, a control operator such as a pipeline symbol (|) implies continuation:
at the end of a line   bash "knows" another command must follow it. Therefore, in **whos**, the NEWLINE following the pipeline symbol at the end of the line with the gawk command does not have to be quoted. For more information refer to "Implicit Command-Line Continuation" on page 1063.

## *LPI*   while

The **while** control structure has the following syntax:

> *while test-command*
> *do*
>     *commands*
> *done*

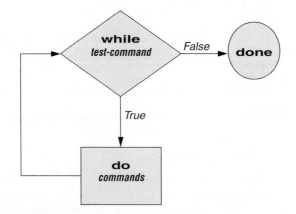

**Figure 27-5**   A **while** flowchart

As long as the *test-command* (Figure 27-5) returns a *true* exit status, the **while** structure continues to execute the series of *commands* delimited by the **do** and **done** statements. Before each loop through the *commands,* the structure executes the *test-command.* When the exit status of the *test-command* is *false,* the structure passes control to the statement after the **done** statement.

**LE+** **test builtin**   The following shell script first initializes the **number** variable to zero. The test builtin then determines whether **number** is less than 10. The script uses test with the –lt argument to perform a numerical test. For numerical comparisons, you must use **–ne** (not equal), **–eq** (equal), **–gt** (greater than), **–ge** (greater than or equal to), **–lt** (less than), or **–le** (less than or equal to). For string comparisons, use = (equal) or != (not equal) when you are working with test. In this example, test has an exit status of 0 (*true*) as long as **number** is less than 10. As long as test returns *true,* the structure executes the commands between the **do** and **done** statements. See page 983 for information on the test builtin.

```
$ cat count
#!/bin/bash
number=0
while [ "$number" -lt 10 ]
    do
        echo -n "$number"
        ((number +=1))
    done
echo
$ ./count
0123456789
$
```

The echo command following **do** displays **number.** The –n prevents echo from issuing a NEWLINE following its output. The next command uses arithmetic evaluation [((...)); page 1056] to increment the value of **number** by 1. The **done** statement terminates the loop and returns control to the **while** statement to start the loop over again. The final echo causes **count** to send a NEWLINE character to standard output, so the next prompt is displayed at the left edge of the display rather than immediately following the 9.

## optional THE spell_check SCRIPT

The aspell utility (**aspell** package) checks the words in a file against a dictionary of correctly spelled words. With the **list** command, aspell runs in list mode: Input comes from standard input and aspell sends each potentially misspelled word to standard output. The following command produces a list of possible misspellings in the file **letter.txt**:

```
$ aspell list < letter.txt
quikly
portible
frendly
```

The next shell script, named **spell_check**, shows another use of a **while** structure. To find the incorrect spellings in a file, **spell_check** calls aspell to check a file against a system dictionary. But it goes a step further: It enables you to specify a list of correctly spelled words and removes these words from the output of aspell. This script is useful for removing words you use frequently, such as names and technical terms, that do not appear in a standard dictionary. Although you can duplicate the functionality of **spell_check** by using additional aspell dictionaries, the script is included here for its instructive value.

The **spell_check** script requires two filename arguments: the file containing the list of correctly spelled words and the file you want to check. The first **if** statement verifies that the user specified two arguments. The next two **if** statements verify that both arguments are readable files. (The exclamation point negates the sense of the following operator; the **–r** operator causes test to determine whether a file is readable. The result is a test that determines whether a file is *not readable*.)

```
$ cat spell_check
#!/bin/bash
# remove correct spellings from aspell output

if [ $# -ne 2 ]
    then
        echo "Usage: spell_check dictionary filename" 1>&2
        echo "dictionary: list of correct spellings" 1>&2
        echo "filename: file to be checked" 1>&2
        exit 1
fi

if [ ! -r "$1" ]
    then
        echo "spell_check: $1 is not readable" 1>&2
        exit 1
fi
if [ ! -r "$2" ]
    then
        echo "spell_check: $2 is not readable" 1>&2
        exit 1
fi
```

```
        aspell list < "$2" |
        while read line
        do
            if ! grep "^$line$" "$1" > /dev/null
                then
                    echo $line
            fi
        done
```

The **spell_check** script sends the output from aspell (with the **list** argument, so it produces a list of misspelled words on standard output) through a pipeline to standard input of a **while** structure, which reads one line at a time (each line has one word on it) from standard input. The *test-command* (that is, **read line**) returns a *true* exit status as long as it receives a line from standard input.

Inside the **while** loop, an **if** statement monitors the return value of grep, which determines whether the line that was read is in the user's list of correctly spelled words. The pattern grep searches for (the value of **$line**) is preceded and followed by special characters that specify the beginning and end of a line (**^** and **$**, respectively). These special characters ensure that grep finds a match only if the **$line** variable matches an entire line in the file of correctly spelled words. (Otherwise, grep would match a string, such as **paul**, in the output of aspell if the file of correctly spelled words contained the word **paulson**.) These special characters, together with the value of the **$line** variable, form a regular expression (Appendix A).

The output of grep is redirected to **/dev/null** (page 158) because the output is not needed; only the exit code is important. The **if** statement checks the negated exit status of grep (the leading exclamation point negates or changes the sense of the exit status—*true* becomes *false*, and vice versa), which is 0 or *true* (*false* when negated) when a matching line is found. If the exit status is *not* 0 or *false* (*true* when negated), the word was *not* in the file of correctly spelled words. The echo builtin sends a list of words that are not in the file of correctly spelled words to standard output.

Once it detects the EOF (end of file), the read builtin returns a *false* exit status, control passes out of the **while** structure, and the script terminates.

Before you use **spell_check**, create a file of correct spellings containing words that you use frequently but that are not in a standard dictionary. For example, if you work for a company named **Blinkenship and Klimowski, Attorneys**, you would put **Blinkenship** and **Klimowski** in the file. The following example shows how **spell_check** checks the spelling in a file named **memo** and removes **Blinkenship** and **Klimowski** from the output list of incorrectly spelled words:

```
$ aspell list < memo
Blinkenship
Klimowski
targat
hte
$ cat word_list
Blinkenship
Klimowski
$ ./spell_check word_list memo
targat
hte
```

Refer to **/usr/share/doc/aspell** or aspell.net for more information.

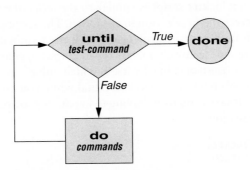

**Figure 27-6** An **until** flowchart

# until

The **until** and **while** structures are similar, differing only in the sense of the test performed at the top of the loop. Figure 27-6 shows that **until** continues to loop *until* the *test-command* returns a *true* exit status. The **while** structure loops *while* the *test-command* continues to return a *true* or nonerror condition. The **until** control structure has the following syntax:

*until **test-command***
*do*
        *commands*
*done*

The following script demonstrates an **until** structure that includes read (page 1041). When the user enters the correct string of characters, the *test-command* is satisfied and the structure passes control out of the loop.

```
$ cat until1
secretname=zach
name=noname
echo "Try to guess the secret name!"
echo
until [ "$name" = "$secretname" ]
do
     read -p "Your guess: " name
done
echo "Very good."

$ ./until1
Try to guess the secret name!

Your guess: helen
Your guess: barbara
Your guess: rachael
Your guess: zach
Very good
```

The following **locktty** script is similar to the lock command on Berkeley UNIX and the **Lock Screen** menu selection in GNOME. The script prompts for a key (password) and uses an **until** control structure to lock the terminal. The **until** statement causes the system to ignore any characters typed at the keyboard until the user types the key followed by a RETURN on a line by itself, which unlocks the terminal. The **locktty** script can keep people from using your terminal while you are away from it for short periods of time. It saves you from having to log out if you are concerned about other users using your session.

```
$ cat locktty
#! /bin/bash

trap '' 1 2 3 18
stty -echo
read -p "Key: " key_1
echo
read -p "Again: " key_2
echo
key_3=
if [ "$key_1" = "$key_2" ]
    then
        tput clear
        until [ "$key_3" = "$key_2" ]
        do
            read key_3
        done
    else
        echo "locktty: keys do not match" 1>&2
fi
stty echo
```

### Forget your password for locktty?

tip    If you forget your key (password), you will need to log in from another (virtual) terminal and give a command to kill the process running **locktty** (e.g., **killall –9 locktty**).

trap builtin    The trap builtin (page 1047) at the beginning of the **locktty** script stops a user from being able to terminate the script by sending it a signal (for example, by pressing the interrupt key). Trapping signal 20 means that no one can use CONTROL-Z (job control, a stop from a tty) to defeat the lock. Table 27-5 on page 1047 provides a list of signals. The **stty –echo** command turns on keyboard echo (causes the terminal not to display characters typed at the keyboard), preventing the key the user enters from appearing on the screen. After turning off keyboard echo, the script prompts the user for a key, reads it into the user-created variable **key_1**, prompts the user to enter the same key again, and saves it in **key_2**. The statement **key_3=** creates a variable with a NULL value. If **key_1** and **key_2** match, **locktty** clears the screen (with the tput command) and starts an **until** loop. The **until** loop keeps reading from the terminal and assigning the input to the **key_3** variable. Once the user types a string that matches one of the original keys (**key_2**), the **until** loop terminates and keyboard echo is turned on again.

# break **AND** continue

You can interrupt a **for, while,** or **until** loop by using a **break** or **continue** statement. The **break** statement transfers control to the statement following the **done** statement, thereby terminating execution of the loop. The **continue** command transfers control to the **done** statement, continuing execution of the loop.

The following script demonstrates the use of these two statements. The **for...in** structure loops through the values 1–10. The first **if** statement executes its commands when the value of the index is less than or equal to 3 (**$index –le 3**). The second **if** statement executes its commands when the value of the index is greater than or equal to 8 (**$index –ge 8**). In between the two **if**s, echo displays the value of the index. For all values up to and including 3, the first **if** statement displays **continue**, executes a **continue** statement that skips **echo $index** and the second **if** statement, and continues with the next **for** statement. For the value of 8, the second **if** statement displays the word **break** and executes a **break** statement that exits from the **for** loop.

```
$ cat brk
for index in 1 2 3 4 5 6 7 8 9 10
    do
        if [ $index -le 3 ] ; then
            echo "continue"
            continue
        fi
#
    echo $index
#
    if [ $index -ge 8 ] ; then
        echo "break"
        break
    fi
done

$ ./brk
continue
continue
continue
4
5
6
7
8
break
$
```

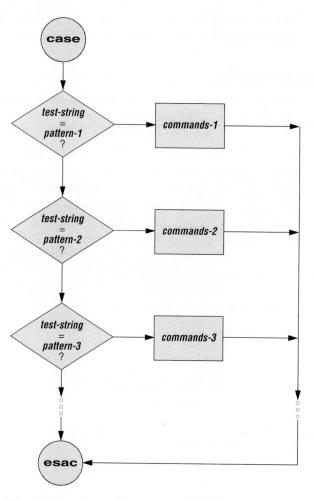

**Figure 27-7**    A **case** flowchart

## case

The **case** structure (Figure 27-7) is a multiple-branch decision mechanism. The path taken through the structure depends on a match or lack of a match between the *test-string* and one of the *patterns*. When the *test-string* matches one of the *patterns*, the shell transfers control to the *commands* following the *pattern*. The *commands* are terminated by a double semicolon (;;) control operator. When control reaches this control operator, the shell transfers control to the command following the **esac** statement. The **case** control structure has the following syntax:

```
case test-string in
    pattern-1)
        commands-1
        ;;
```

```
    pattern-2)
        commands-2
        ;;
    pattern-3)
        commands-3
        ;;
    . . .
esac
```

The following **case** structure uses the character the user enters as the *test-string*. This value is held in the variable **letter**. If the *test-string* has a value of **A**, the structure executes the command following the *pattern* **A**. The right parenthesis is part of the **case** control structure, not part of the *pattern*. If the *test-string* has a value of **B** or **C**, the structure executes the command following the matching *pattern*. The asterisk (✳) indicates *any string of characters* and serves as a catchall in case there is no match. If no *pattern* matches the *test-string* and if there is no catchall (✳) *pattern*, control passes to the command following the **esac** statement, without the **case** structure taking any action.

```
$ cat case1
read -p "Enter A, B, or C: " letter
case "$letter" in
    A)
        echo "You entered A"
        ;;
    B)
        echo "You entered B"
        ;;
    C)
        echo "You entered C"
        ;;
    *)
        echo "You did not enter A, B, or C"
        ;;
esac

$ ./case1
Enter A, B, or C: B
You entered B
```

The next execution of **case1** shows the user entering a lowercase **b**. Because the *test-string* **b** does not match the uppercase **B** *pattern* (or any other *pattern* in the **case** statement), the program executes the commands following the catchall *pattern* and displays a message:

```
$ ./case1
Enter A, B, or C: b
You did not enter A, B, or C
```

The *pattern* in the **case** structure is a glob (it is analogous to an ambiguous file reference). It can include any special characters and strings shown in Table 27-2.

**Table 27-2**   Patterns

| Pattern | Function |
|---------|----------|
| * | Matches any string of characters. Use for the default case. |
| ? | Matches any single character. |
| [...] | Defines a character class. Any characters enclosed within brackets are tried, one at a time, in an attempt to match a single character. A hyphen between two characters specifies a range of characters. |
| \| | Separates alternative choices that satisfy a particular branch of the **case** structure. |

The next script accepts both uppercase and lowercase letters:

```
$ cat case2
read -p "Enter A, B, or C: " letter
case "$letter" in
    a|A)
        echo "You entered A"
        ;;
    b|B)
        echo "You entered B"
        ;;
    c|C)
        echo "You entered C"
        ;;
    *)
        echo "You did not enter A, B, or C"
        ;;
esac

$ ./case2
Enter A, B, or C: b
You entered B
```

**optional**  The following example shows how to use the **case** structure to create a simple menu. The **command_menu** script uses echo to present menu items and prompt the user for a selection. (The **select** control structure [page 1012] is a much easier way of coding a menu.) The **case** structure then executes the appropriate utility depending on the user's selection.

```
$ cat command_menu
#!/bin/bash
# menu interface to simple commands

echo -e "\n      COMMAND MENU\n"
echo "  a.  Current date and time"
echo "  b.  Users currently logged in"
```

```
echo "  c.  Name of the working directory"
echo -e "  d.  Contents of the working directory\n"
read -p "Enter a, b, c, or d: " answer
echo
#
case "$answer" in
    a)
        date
        ;;
    b)
        who
        ;;
    c)
        pwd
        ;;
    d)
        ls
        ;;
    *)
        echo "There is no selection: $answer"
        ;;
esac
```

**$ ./command_menu**

```
            COMMAND MENU

    a.  Current date and time
    b.  Users currently logged in
    c.  Name of the working directory
    d.  Contents of the working directory

Enter a, b, c, or d: a

Sun Jan  6 12:31:12 PST 2013
```

**LE+** **echo –e**   The –e option causes echo to interpret \n as a NEWLINE character. If you do not include this option, echo does not output the extra blank lines that make the menu easy to read but instead outputs the (literal) two-character sequence \n. The –e option causes echo to interpret several other backslash-quoted characters (Table 27-3). Remember to quote (i.e., place double quotation marks around the string) the backslash-quoted character so the shell does not interpret it but rather passes the backslash and the character to echo. See **xpg_echo** (page 403) for a way to avoid using the –e option.

**Table 27-3**   Special characters in echo (must use **–e**)

| Quoted character | echo **displays** |
| --- | --- |
| \a | Alert (bell) |
| \b | BACKSPACE |
| \c | Suppress trailing NEWLINE |

**Table 27-3** Special characters in echo (must use **–e**) (continued)

| Quoted character | echo displays |
|---|---|
| \f | FORMFEED |
| \n | NEWLINE |
| \r | RETURN |
| \t | Horizontal TAB |
| \v | Vertical TAB |
| \\ | Backslash |
| \nnn | The character with the ASCII octal code *nnn;* if *nnn* is not valid, echo displays the string literally |

You can also use the **case** control structure to take various actions in a script, depending on how many arguments the script is called with. The following script, named **safedit**, uses a **case** structure that branches based on the number of command-line arguments ($#). It calls vim and saves a backup copy of a file you are editing.

```
$ cat safedit
#!/bin/bash

PATH=/bin:/usr/bin
script=$(basename $0)
case $# in

    0)
        vim
        exit 0
        ;;

    1)
        if [ ! -f "$1" ]
            then
                vim "$1"
                exit 0
            fi
        if [ ! -r "$1" -o ! -w "$1" ]
            then
                echo "$script: check permissions on $1" 1>&2
                exit 1
            else
                editfile=$1
            fi
        if [ ! -w "." ]
            then
                echo "$script: backup cannot be " \
                    "created in the working directory" 1>&2
                exit 1
            fi
        ;;
```

```
                    *)
                        echo "Usage: $script [file-to-edit]" 1>&2
                        exit 1
                        ;;
                esac
                tempfile=/tmp/$$.$script
                cp $editfile $tempfile
                if vim $editfile
                    then
                        mv $tempfile bak.$(basename $editfile)
                        echo "$script: backup file created"
                    else
                        mv $tempfile editerr
                        echo "$script: edit error--copy of " \
                            "original file is in editerr" 1>&2
            fi
```

If you call **safedit** without any arguments, the **case** structure executes its first branch and calls vim without a filename argument. Because an existing file is not being edited, **safedit** does not create a backup file. If you call **safedit** with one argument, it runs the commands in the second branch of the **case** structure and verifies that the file specified by **$1** does not yet exist or is the name of a file for which the user has read and write permission. The **safedit** script also verifies that the user has write permission for the working directory. If the user calls **safedit** with more than one argument, the third branch of the **case** structure presents a usage message and exits with a status of 1.

Set **PATH**  At the beginning of the script, the **PATH** variable is set to search **/bin** and **/usr/bin**. Setting **PATH** in this way ensures that the commands executed by the script are standard utilities, which are kept in those directories. By setting this variable inside a script, you can avoid the problems that might occur if users have set **PATH** to search their own directories first and have scripts or programs with the same names as the utilities the script calls. You can also include absolute pathnames within a script to achieve this end, although this practice can make a script less portable.

Name of the  The next line declares a variable named **script** and initializes it with the simple filename
program  of the script:

```
    script=$(basename $0)
```

The basename utility sends the simple filename component of its argument to standard output, which is assigned to the **script** variable, using command substitution. The **$0** holds the command the script was called with (page 1022). No matter which of the following commands the user calls the script with, the output of basename is the simple filename **safedit**:

```
    $ /home/max/bin/safedit memo
    $ ./safedit memo
    $ safedit memo
```

After the **script** variable is set, it replaces the filename of the script in usage and error messages. By using a variable that is derived from the command that invoked the script rather than a filename that is hardcoded into the script, you can create links to the script or rename it, and the usage and error messages will still provide accurate information.

**Naming temporary files**   Another feature of **safedit** relates to the use of the **$$** parameter in the name of a temporary file. The statement following the **esac** statement creates and assigns a value to the **tempfile** variable. This variable contains the name of a temporary file that is stored in the **/tmp** directory, as are many temporary files. The temporary filename begins with the PID number of the shell and ends with the name of the script. Using the PID number ensures that the filename is unique. Thus **safedit** will not attempt to overwrite an existing file, as might happen if two people were using **safedit** at the same time. The name of the script is appended so that, should the file be left in **/tmp** for some reason, you can figure out where it came from.

The PID number is used in front of—rather than after—**$script** in the filename because of the 14-character limit placed on filenames by some older versions of UNIX. Linux systems do not have this limitation. Because the PID number ensures the uniqueness of the filename, it is placed first so that it cannot be truncated. (If the **$script** component is truncated, the filename is still unique.) For the same reason, when a backup file is created inside the **if** control structure a few lines down in the script, the filename consists of the string **bak.** followed by the name of the file being edited. On an older system, if **bak** were used as a suffix rather than a prefix and the original filename were 14 characters long, **.bak** might be lost and the original file would be overwritten. The basename utility extracts the simple filename of **$editfile** before it is prefixed with **bak.**.

The **safedit** script uses an unusual *test-command* in the **if** structure: **vim $editfile**. The *test-command* calls vim to edit **$editfile**. When you finish editing the file and exit from vim, vim returns an exit code. The **if** control structure uses that exit code to determine which branch to take. If the editing session completed successfully, vim returns 0 and the statements following the **then** statement are executed. If vim does not terminate normally (as would occur if the user killed [page 465] the vim process), vim returns a nonzero exit status and the script executes the statements following **else**.

# select

The **select** control structure is based on the one found in the Korn Shell. It displays a menu, assigns a value to a variable based on the user's choice of items, and executes a series of commands. The **select** control structure has the following syntax:

> select *varname [in arg . . . ]*
> do
>       *commands*
> done

The **select** structure displays a menu of the *arg* items. If you omit the keyword **in** and the list of arguments, **select** uses the positional parameters in place of the *arg* items. The menu is formatted with numbers before each item. For example, a **select** structure that begins with

```
select fruit in apple banana blueberry kiwi orange watermelon STOP
```

displays the following menu:

```
1) apple     3) blueberry   5) orange      7) STOP
2) banana    4) kiwi        6) watermelon
```

The **select** structure uses the values of the **LINES** (default is 24) and **COLUMNS** (default is 80) variables to specify the size of the display. With **COLUMNS** set to 20, the menu looks like this:

```
1) apple
2) banana
3) blueberry
4) kiwi
5) orange
6) watermelon
7) STOP
```

**PS3**   After displaying the menu, **select** displays the value of **PS3**, the **select** prompt. The default value of **PS3** is ?#, but it is typically set to a more meaningful value. When you enter a valid number (one in the menu range) in response to the **PS3** prompt, **select** sets *varname* to the argument corresponding to the number you entered. An invalid entry causes the shell to set *varname* to null. Either way, **select** stores your response in the keyword variable **REPLY** and then executes the *commands* between **do** and **done**. If you press RETURN without entering a choice, the shell redisplays the menu and the **PS3** prompt.

The **select** structure continues to issue the **PS3** prompt and execute the *commands* until something causes it to exit—typically a **break** or an **exit** statement. A **break** statement exits from the loop and an **exit** statement exits from the script.

The following script illustrates the use of **select**:

```
$ cat fruit2
#!/bin/bash
PS3="Choose your favorite fruit from these possibilities: "
select FRUIT in apple banana blueberry kiwi orange watermelon STOP
do
    if [ "$FRUIT" == "" ]; then
        echo -e "Invalid entry.\n"
        continue
    elif [ $FRUIT = STOP ]; then
        echo "Thanks for playing!"
        break
    fi
echo "You chose $FRUIT as your favorite."
echo -e "That is choice number $REPLY.\n"
done
```

```
$ ./fruit2
1) apple      3) blueberry  5) orange      7) STOP
2) banana     4) kiwi       6) watermelon
Choose your favorite fruit from these possibilities: 3
You chose blueberry as your favorite.
That is choice number 3.

Choose your favorite fruit from these possibilities: 99
Invalid entry.

Choose your favorite fruit from these possibilities: 7
Thanks for playing!
```

After setting the **PS3** prompt and establishing the menu with the **select** statement, **fruit2** executes the *commands* between **do** and **done**. If the user submits an invalid entry, the shell sets *varname* (**$FRUIT**) to a null value. If **$FRUIT** is null, echo displays an error message; **continue** then causes the shell to redisplay the **PS3** prompt. If the entry is valid, the script tests whether the user wants to stop. If so, echo displays an appropriate message and **break** exits from the **select** structure (and from the script). If the user enters a valid response and does not want to stop, the script displays the name and number of the user's response. (See page 1009 for information about the echo –e option.)

# HERE DOCUMENT

A Here document allows you to redirect input to a shell script from within the shell script itself. A Here document is so named because it is *here*—immediately accessible in the shell script—instead of *there*, perhaps in another file.

The following script, named **birthday**, contains a Here document. The two less than symbols (**<<**) in the first line indicate a Here document follows. One or more characters that delimit the Here document follow the less than symbols—this example uses a plus sign. Whereas the opening delimiter must appear adjacent to the less than symbols, the closing delimiter must be on a line by itself. The shell sends everything between the two delimiters to the process as standard input. In the example it is as though you have redirected standard input to grep from a file, except that the file is embedded in the shell script:

```
$ cat birthday
grep -i "$1" <<+
Max      June 22
Barbara  February 3
Darlene  May 8
Helen    March 13
Zach     January 23
Nancy    June 26
+
$ ./birthday Zach
Zach     January 23
```

```
$ ./birthday june
Max     June 22
Nancy   June 26
```

When you run **birthday**, it lists all the Here document lines that contain the argument you called it with. In this case the first time **birthday** is run, it displays Zach's birthday because it is called with an argument of **Zach**. The second run displays all the birthdays in June. The –**i** argument causes grep's search not to be case sensitive.

**optional**   The next script, named **bundle**,[1] includes a clever use of a Here document. The **bundle** script is an elegant example of a script that creates a shell archive (**shar**) file. The script creates a file that is itself a shell script containing several other files as well as the code needed to re-create the original files:

```
$ cat bundle
#!/bin/bash
# bundle:  group files into distribution package

echo "# To unbundle, bash this file"
for i
do
    echo "echo $i 1>&2"
    echo "cat >$i <<'End of $i'"
    cat $i
    echo "End of $i"
done
```

Just as the shell does not treat special characters that occur in standard input of a shell script as special, so the shell does not treat the special characters that occur between the delimiters in a Here document as special.

As the following example shows, the output of **bundle** is a shell script, which is redirected to a file named **bothfiles**. It contains the contents of each file given as an argument to **bundle** (**file1** and **file2** in this case) inside a Here document. To extract the original files from **bothfiles**, you simply give it as an argument to a bash command. Before each Here document is a cat command that causes the Here document to be written to a new file when **bothfiles** is run:

```
$ cat file1
This is a file.
It contains two lines.
$ cat file2
This is another file.
It contains
three lines.
```

---

1. Thanks to Brian W. Kernighan and Rob Pike, *The Unix Programming Environment* (Englewood Cliffs, N.J.: Prentice-Hall, 1984), 98. Reprinted with permission.

```
$ ./bundle file1 file2 > bothfiles
$ cat bothfiles
# To unbundle, bash this file
echo file1 1>&2
cat >file1 <<'End of file1'
This is a file.
It contains two lines.
End of file1
echo file2 1>&2
cat >file2 <<'End of file2'
This is another file.
It contains
three lines.
End of file2
```

In the next example, **file1** and **file2** are removed before **bothfiles** is run. The **bothfiles** script echoes the names of the files it creates as it creates them. The **ls** command then shows that **bothfiles** has re-created **file1** and **file2**:

```
$ rm file1 file2
$ bash bothfiles
file1
file2
$ ls
bothfiles
file1
file2
```

# FILE DESCRIPTORS

As discussed on page 334, before a process can read from or write to a file, it must open that file. When a process opens a file, Linux associates a number (called a *file descriptor*) with the file. A file descriptor is an index into the process's table of open files. Each process has its own set of open files and its own file descriptors. After opening a file, a process reads from and writes to that file by referring to its file descriptor. When it no longer needs the file, the process closes the file, freeing the file descriptor.

A typical Linux process starts with three open files: standard input (file descriptor 0), standard output (file descriptor 1), and standard error (file descriptor 2). Often these are the only files the process needs. Recall that you redirect standard output with the symbol > or the symbol **1>** and that you redirect standard error with the symbol **2>**. Although you can redirect other file descriptors, because file descriptors other than 0, 1, and 2 do not have any special conventional meaning, it is rarely useful to do so. The exception is in programs that you write yourself, in which case you control the meaning of the file descriptors and can take advantage of redirection.

## *LPI* OPENING A FILE DESCRIPTOR

The Bourne Again Shell opens files using the exec builtin with the following syntax:

*exec n> outfile*
*exec m< infile*

The first line opens **outfile** for output and holds it open, associating it with file descriptor **n**. The second line opens **infile** for input and holds it open, associating it with file descriptor **m**.

## *LPI* DUPLICATING A FILE DESCRIPTOR

The <& token duplicates an input file descriptor; >& duplicates an output file descriptor. You can duplicate a file descriptor by making it refer to the same file as another open file descriptor, such as standard input or output. Use the following syntax to open or redirect file descriptor **n** as a duplicate of file descriptor **m:**

*exec n<&m*

Once you have opened a file, you can use it for input and output in two ways. First, you can use I/O redirection on any command line, redirecting standard output to a file descriptor with >&*n* or redirecting standard input from a file descriptor with <&*n*. Second, you can use the read (page 1041) and echo builtins. If you invoke other commands, including functions (page 396), they inherit these open files and file descriptors. When you have finished using a file, you can close it using the following syntax:

*exec n<&–*

## FILE DESCRIPTOR EXAMPLES

When you call the following **mycp** function with two arguments, it copies the file named by the first argument to the file named by the second argument. If you supply only one argument, the script copies the file named by the argument to standard output. If you invoke **mycp** with no arguments, it copies standard input to standard output.

### A function is not a shell script

tip  The **mycp** example is a shell function; it will not work as you expect if you execute it as a shell script. (It *will* work: The function will be created in a very short-lived subshell, which is of little use.) You can enter this function from the keyboard. If you put the function in a file, you can run it as an argument to the . (dot) builtin (page 332). You can also put the function in a startup file if you want it to be always available (page 397).

```
function mycp () {
case $# in
    0)
            # Zero arguments
            # File descriptor 3 duplicates standard input
            # File descriptor 4 duplicates standard output
            exec 3<&0 4<&1
            ;;
    1)
            # One argument
            # Open the file named by the argument for input
            # and associate it with file descriptor 3
            # File descriptor 4 duplicates standard output
            exec 3< $1 4<&1
            ;;
    2)
            # Two arguments
            # Open the file named by the first argument for input
            # and associate it with file descriptor 3
            # Open the file named by the second argument for output
            # and associate it with file descriptor 4
            exec 3< $1 4> $2
            ;;
    *)
            echo "Usage: mycp [source [dest]]"
            return 1
            ;;
esac

# Call cat with input coming from file descriptor 3
# and output going to file descriptor 4
cat <&3 >&4

# Close file descriptors 3 and 4
exec 3<&- 4<&-
}
```

The real work of this function is done in the line that begins with cat. The rest of the script arranges for file descriptors 3 and 4, which are the input and output of the cat command, respectively, to be associated with the appropriate files.

**optional**   The next program takes two filenames on the command line, sorts both, and sends the output to temporary files. The program then merges the sorted files to standard output, preceding each line by a number that indicates which file it came from.

```
$ cat sortmerg
#!/bin/bash
usage () {
if [ $# -ne 2 ]; then
    echo "Usage: $0 file1 file2" 2>&1
    exit 1
    fi
}

# Default temporary directory
: ${TEMPDIR:=/tmp}
```

```
# Check argument count
usage "$@"

# Set up temporary files for sorting
file1=$TEMPDIR/$$.file1
file2=$TEMPDIR/$$.file2

# Sort
sort $1 > $file1
sort $2 > $file2

# Open $file1 and $file2 for reading. Use file descriptors 3 and 4.
exec 3<$file1
exec 4<$file2

# Read the first line from each file to figure out how to start.
read Line1 <&3
status1=$?
read Line2 <&4
status2=$?
# Strategy: while there is still input left in both files:
#    Output the line that should come first.
#    Read a new line from the file that line came from.
while [ $status1 -eq 0 -a $status2 -eq 0 ]
    do
        if [[ "$Line2" > "$Line1" ]]; then
            echo -e "1.\t$Line1"
            read -u3 Line1
            status1=$?
        else
            echo -e "2.\t$Line2"
            read -u4 Line2
            status2=$?
        fi
    done

# Now one of the files is at end of file.
# Read from each file until the end.
# First file1:
while [ $status1 -eq 0 ]
    do
        echo -e "1.\t$Line1"
        read Line1 <&3
        status1=$?
    done
# Next file2:
while [[ $status2 -eq 0 ]]
    do
        echo -e "2.\t$Line2"
        read Line2 <&4
        status2=$?
    done

# Close and remove both input files
exec 3<&- 4<&-
rm -f $file1 $file2
exit 0
```

# DETERMINING WHETHER A FILE DESCRIPTOR IS ASSOCIATED WITH THE TERMINAL

The test –t criterion takes an argument of a file descriptor and causes test to return a value of 0 (*true*) or not 0 (*false*) based on whether the specified file descriptor is associated with the terminal (screen or keyboard). It is typically used to determine whether standard input, standard output, and/or standard error is coming from/going to the terminal.

In the following example, the **is.term** script uses the test –t criterion ([ ] is a synonym for test; page 1000) to see if file descriptor 1 (initially standard output) of the process running the shell script is associated with the screen. The message the script displays is based on whether test returns *true* (file descriptor 1 is associated with the screen) or *false* (file descriptor 1 is *not* associated with the screen).

```
$ cat is.term
if [ -t 1 ] ; then
        echo "FD 1 (stdout) IS going to the screen"
    else
        echo "FD 1 (stdout) is NOT going to the screen"
 fi
```

When you run **is.term** without redirecting standard output, the script displays **FD 1 (stdout) IS going to the screen** because standard output of the **is.term** script has not been redirected:

```
$ ./is.term
FD 1 (stdout) IS going to the screen
```

When you redirect standard output of a program using **>** on the command line, bash closes file descriptor 1 and then reopens it, associating it with the file specified following the redirect symbol.

The next example redirects standard output of the **is.term** script: The newly opened file descriptor 1 associates standard output with the file named **hold**. Now the test command ([ –t 1 ]) fails, returning a value of 1 (*false*), because standard output is not associated with a terminal. The script writes **FD 1 (stdout) is NOT going to the screen** to hold:

```
$ ./is.term > hold
$ cat hold
FD 1 (stdout) is NOT going to the screen
```

If you redirect standard error from **is.term**, the script will report **FD 1 (stdout) IS going to the screen** and will write nothing to the file receiving the redirection; standard output has not been redirected. You can use [ –t 2 ] to test if standard error is going to the screen:

```
$ ./is.term 2> hold
FD 1 (stdout) IS going to the screen
```

In a similar manner, if you send standard output of **is.term** through a pipeline, test reports standard output is not associated with a terminal. In this example, cat copies standard input to standard output:

```
$ ./is.term | cat
FD 1 (stdout) is NOT going to the screen
```

**optional**   You can also experiment with test on the command line. This technique allows you to make changes to your experimental code quickly by taking advantage of command history and editing (page 378). To better understand the following examples, first verify that test (called as [ ]) returns a value of 0 (*true*) when file descriptor 1 is associated with the screen and a value other than 0 (*false*) when file descriptor 1 is not associated with the screen. The **$?** special parameter (page 1029) holds the exit status of the previous command.

```
$ [ -t 1 ]
$ echo $?
0

$ [ -t 1 ] > hold
$ echo $?
1
```

As explained on page 343, the **&&** (AND) control operator first executes the command preceding it. Only if that command returns a value of 0 (*true*) does **&&** execute the command following it. In the following example, if [ –t 1 ] returns 0, **&&** executes echo "FD 1 to screen". Although the parentheses (page 344) are not required in this example, they are needed in the next one.

```
$ ( [ -t 1 ] && echo "FD 1 to screen" )
FD 1 to screen
```

Next, the output from the same command line is sent through a pipeline to cat, so test returns 1 (*false*) and **&&** does not execute echo.

```
$ ( [ -t 1 ] && echo "FD 1 to screen" ) | cat
$
```

The following example is the same as the previous one, except test checks whether file descriptor 2 is associated with the screen. Because the pipeline redirects only standard output, test returns 0 (*true*) and **&&** executes echo.

```
$ ( [ -t 2 ] && echo "FD 2 to screen" ) | cat
FD 2 to screen
```

In this example, test checks whether file descriptor 2 is associated with the screen (it is) and echo sends its output to file descriptor 1 (which goes through the pipeline to cat).

# PARAMETERS

Shell parameters were introduced on page 352. This section goes into more detail about positional parameters and special parameters.

## POSITIONAL PARAMETERS

Positional parameters comprise the command name and command-line arguments. These parameters are called *positional* because you refer to them by their position on the command line. You cannot use an assignment statement to change the value of a positional parameter. However, the set builtin (page 1024) enables you to change the value of any positional parameter except the name of the calling program (the command name).

### $0: NAME OF THE CALLING PROGRAM

The shell expands $0 to the name of the calling program (the command you used to call the program—usually the name of the program you are running). This parameter is numbered zero because it appears before the first argument on the command line:

```
$ cat abc
echo "This script was called by typing $0"
$ ./abc
This script was called by typing ./abc
$ /home/sam/abc
This script was called by typing /home/sam/abc
```

The preceding shell script uses echo to verify the way the script you are executing was called. You can use the basename utility and command substitution to extract the simple filename of the script:

```
$ cat abc2
echo "This script was called by typing $(basename $0)"
$ /home/sam/abc2
This script was called by typing abc2
```

When you call a script through a link, the shell expands $0 to the value of the link.

```
$ ln -s abc2 mylink
$ /home/sam/mylink
This script was called by typing mylink
```

When you display the value of $0 from an interactive shell, the shell displays its name because that is the name of the calling program (the program you are running).

```
$ echo $0
bash
```

### bash versus –bash

tip On some systems, **echo $0** displays **–bash** while on others it displays **bash**. The former indicates a login shell (page 330); the latter indicates a shell that is not a login shell. In a GUI environment, some terminal emulators launch login shells while others do not.

## $1 – $n: POSITIONAL PARAMETERS

The shell expands **$1** to the first argument on the command line, **$2** to the second argument, and so on up to **$n**. These parameters are short for **${1}**, **${2}**, **${3}**, and so on. For values of *n* less than or equal to 9, the braces are optional. For values of *n* greater than 9, the number must be enclosed within braces. For example, the twelfth positional parameter is represented by **${12}**. The following script displays positional parameters that hold command-line arguments:

```
$ cat display_5args
echo First 5 arguments are $1 $2 $3 $4 $5

$ ./display_5args zach max helen
First 5 arguments are zach max helen
```

The **display_5args** script displays the first five command-line arguments. The shell expands each parameter that represents an argument that is not present on the command line to a null string. Thus the **$4** and **$5** parameters have null values in this example.

### Always quote positional parameters

caution You can "lose" positional parameters if you do not quote them. See the following text for an example.

Enclose references to positional parameters between double quotation marks. The quotation marks are particularly important when you are using positional parameters as arguments to commands. Without double quotation marks, a positional parameter that is not set or that has a null value disappears:

```
$ cat showargs
echo "$0 was called with $# arguments, the first is :$1:."

$ ./showargs a b c
./showargs was called with 3 arguments, the first is :a:.

$ echo $xx

$ ./showargs $xx a b c
./showargs was called with 3 arguments, the first is :a:.
$ ./showargs "$xx" a b c
./showargs was called with 4 arguments, the first is ::.
```

The **showargs** script displays the number of arguments it was called with (**$#**) followed by the value of the first argument between colons. In the preceding example, **showargs** is initially called with three arguments. Next the echo command shows that the $xx variable, which is not set, has a null value. The $xx variable is the first argument to the second and third showargs commands; it is not quoted in the second command and quoted using double quotation marks in the third command. In the second showargs command, the shell expands the arguments to a b c and passes showargs three arguments. In the third showargs command, the shell expands the arguments to " " a b c, which results in calling showargs with four arguments. The difference in the two calls to showargs illustrates a subtle potential problem when using positional parameters that might not be set or that might have a null value.

### LPI  set: INITIALIZES POSITIONAL PARAMETERS

When you call the set builtin with one or more arguments, it assigns the values of the arguments to the positional parameters, starting with $1. The following script uses set to assign values to the positional parameters $1, $2, and $3:

```
$ cat set_it
set this is it
echo $3 $2 $1
$ ./set_it
it is this
```

**optional**  A single hyphen (–) on a set command line marks the end of options and the start of values the shell assigns to positional parameters. A – also turns off the **xtrace** (–x) and **verbose** (–v) options (Table 9-13 on page 401). The following set command turns on **posix** mode and sets the first two positional parameters as shown by the echo command:

```
$ set -o posix - first.param second.param
$ echo $*
first.param second.param
```

A double hyphen (––) on a set command line without any following arguments unsets the positional parameters; when followed by arguments, –– sets the positional parameters, including those that begin with a hyphen (–).

```
$ set --
$ echo $*

$
```

Combining command substitution (page 410) with the set builtin is a convenient way to alter standard output of a command to a form that can be easily manipulated in a shell script. The following script shows how to use date and set to provide the date in a useful format. The first command shows the output of date. Then cat displays the contents of the **dateset** script. The first command in this script uses command substitution to set the positional parameters to the output of the date utility. The next command, echo $*, displays all positional parameters resulting from the previous set. Subsequent commands display the values of $1, $2, $3, and $6. The final command displays the date in a format you can use in a letter or report.

```
$ date
Wed Aug 15 17:35:29 PDT 2012
$ cat dateset
set $(date)
echo $*
echo
echo "Argument 1: $1"
echo "Argument 2: $2"
echo "Argument 3: $3"
echo "Argument 6: $6"
echo
echo "$2 $3, $6"

$ ./dateset
Wed Aug 15 17:35:34 PDT 2012

Argument 1: Wed
Argument 2: Aug
Argument 3: 15
Argument 6: 2012

Aug 15, 2012
```

You can also use the +*format* argument to date to specify the content and format of its output.

set displays shell
variables

When called without arguments, set displays a list of the shell variables that are set, including user-created variables and keyword variables. Under bash, this list is the same as that displayed by declare (page 357) when it is called without any arguments.

```
$ set
BASH_VERSION='4.2.24(1)-release'
COLORS=/etc/DIR_COLORS
COLUMNS=89
LESSOPEN='|||/usr/bin/lesspipe.sh %s'
LINES=53
LOGNAME=sam
MAIL=/var/spool/mail/sam
MAILCHECK=60
...
```

The set builtin can also perform other tasks. For more information refer to "set: Works with Shell Features, Positional Parameters, and Variables" on page 1036.

## shift: PROMOTES POSITIONAL PARAMETERS

The shift builtin promotes each positional parameter. The first argument (which was represented by $1) is discarded. The second argument (which was represented by $2) becomes the first argument (now $1), the third argument becomes the second, and so on. Because no "unshift" command exists, you cannot bring back arguments that have been discarded. An optional argument to shift specifies the number of positions to shift (and the number of arguments to discard); the default is 1.

The following **demo_shift** script is called with three arguments. Double quotation marks around the arguments to echo preserve the spacing of the output but allow the shell to expand variables. The program displays the arguments and shifts them repeatedly until no arguments are left to shift.

```
$ cat demo_shift
echo "arg1= $1     arg2= $2     arg3= $3"
shift
echo "arg1= $1     arg2= $2     arg3= $3"
shift
echo "arg1= $1     arg2= $2     arg3= $3"
shift
echo "arg1= $1     arg2= $2     arg3= $3"
shift

$ ./demo_shift alice helen zach
arg1= alice    arg2= helen    arg3= zach
arg1= helen    arg2= zach     arg3=
arg1= zach     arg2=          arg3=
arg1=          arg2=          arg3=
```

Repeatedly using shift is a convenient way to loop over all command-line arguments in shell scripts that expect an arbitrary number of arguments. See page 989 for a shell script that uses shift.

## $* AND $@: EXPAND TO ALL POSITIONAL PARAMETERS

The shell expands the **$\*** parameter to all positional parameters, as the **display_all** program demonstrates:

```
$ cat display_all
echo All arguments are $*

$ ./display_all a b c d e f g h i j k l m n o p
All arguments are a b c d e f g h i j k l m n o p
```

### "$\*" VERSUS "$@"

The **$\*** and **$@** parameters work the same way except when they are enclosed within double quotation marks. Using "**$\***" yields a single argument with the first character in **IFS** (page 363; normally a SPACE) between the positional parameters. Using "**$@**" produces a list wherein each positional parameter is a separate argument. This difference typically makes "**$@**" more useful than "**$\***" in shell scripts.

The following scripts help explain the difference between these two parameters. In the second line of both scripts, the single quotation marks keep the shell from interpreting the enclosed special characters, allowing the shell to pass them to echo so echo can display them. The **bb1** script shows that **set** "**$\***" assigns multiple arguments to the first command-line parameter.

```
$ cat bb1
set "$*"
echo $# parameters with '"$*"'
echo 1: $1
echo 2: $2
echo 3: $3

$ ./bb1 a b c
1 parameters with "$*"
1: a b c
2:
3:
```

The **bb2** script shows that **set "$@"** assigns each argument to a different command-line parameter.

```
$ cat bb2
set "$@"
echo $# parameters with '"$@"'
echo 1: $1
echo 2: $2
echo 3: $3

$ ./bb2 a b c
3 parameters with "$@"
1: a
2: b
3: c
```

# SPECIAL PARAMETERS

Special parameters enable you to access useful values pertaining to positional parameters and the execution of shell commands. As with positional parameters, the shell expands a special parameter when it is preceded by a **$**. Also as with positional parameters, you cannot modify the value of a special parameter using an assignment statement.

## $#: NUMBER OF POSITIONAL PARAMETERS

The shell expands **$#** to the decimal number of arguments on the command line (positional parameters), not counting the name of the calling program:

```
$ cat num_args
echo "This script was called with $# arguments."
$ ./num_args sam max zach
This script was called with 3 arguments.
```

The next example shows set initializing four positional parameters and echo displaying the number of parameters set initialized:

```
$ set a b c d; echo $#
4
```

## $$: PID NUMBER

The shell expands the **$$** parameter to the PID number of the process that is executing it. In the following interaction, echo displays the value of this parameter and the ps utility confirms its value. Both commands show the shell has a PID number of 5209:

```
$ echo $$
5209
$ ps
  PID TTY          TIME CMD
 5209 pts/1    00:00:00 bash
 6015 pts/1    00:00:00 ps
```

Because echo is built into the shell, the shell does not create another process when you give an echo command. However, the results are the same whether echo is a builtin or not, because the shell expands **$$** *before* it forks a new process to run a command. Try giving this command using the echo utility (**/bin/echo**), which is run by another process, and see what happens.

Naming temporary files  In the following example, the shell substitutes the value of **$$** and passes that value to cp as a prefix for a filename:

```
$ echo $$
8232
$ cp memo $$.memo
$ ls
8232.memo  memo
```

Incorporating a PID number in a filename is useful for creating unique filenames when the meanings of the names do not matter; this technique is often used in shell scripts for creating names of temporary files. When two people are running the same shell script, having unique filenames keeps the users from inadvertently sharing the same temporary file.

The following example demonstrates that the shell creates a new shell process when it runs a shell script. The **id2** script displays the PID number of the process running it (not the process that called it—the substitution for **$$** is performed by the shell that is forked to run **id2**):

```
$ cat id2
echo "$0 PID= $$"
$ echo $$
8232
$ ./id2
./id2 PID= 8362
$ echo $$
8232
```

The first echo displays the PID number of the interactive shell. Then **id2** displays its name (**$0**) and the PID number of the subshell it is running in. The last echo shows that the PID number of the interactive shell has not changed.

## $!: PID NUMBER OF MOST RECENT BACKGROUND PROCESS

The shell expands **$!** to the value of the PID number of the most recent process that ran in the background. The following example executes sleep as a background task and uses echo to display the value of **$!**:

```
$ sleep 60 &
[1] 8376
$ echo $!
8376
```

## _LE_  $?: EXIT STATUS

When a process stops executing for any reason, it returns an *exit status* to its parent process. The exit status is also referred to as a *condition code* or a *return code*. The shell expands the **$?** parameter to the exit status of the most recently executed command.

By convention, a nonzero exit status is interpreted as *false* and means the command failed; a zero is interpreted as *true* and indicates the command executed successfully. In the following example, the first ls command succeeds and the second fails; the exit status displayed by echo reflects these outcomes:

```
$ ls es
es
$ echo $?
0
$ ls xxx
ls: xxx: No such file or directory
$ echo $?
1
```

You can specify the exit status a shell script returns by using the exit builtin, followed by a number, to terminate the script. If you do not use exit with a number to terminate a script, the exit status of the script is that of the last command the script ran.

```
$ cat es
echo This program returns an exit status of 7.
exit 7
$ es
This program returns an exit status of 7.
$ echo $?
7
$ echo $?
0
```

The es shell script displays a message and terminates execution with an exit command that returns an exit status of 7, the user-defined exit status in this script. The first echo then displays the exit status of es. The second echo displays the exit status of the first echo: This value is 0, indicating the first echo executed successfully.

## $-: Flags of Options That Are Set

The shell expands the $– parameter to a string of one-character bash option flags. These flags are set by the set or shopt builtins, when bash is invoked, or by bash itself (e.g., –i). For more information refer to "Controlling bash: Features and Options" on page 398. The following command displays typical bash option flags for an interactive shell:

```
$ echo $-
himBH
```

Table 9-13 on page 401 lists each of these flags (except i) as options to set in the **Alternative syntax** column. When you start an interactive shell, bash sets the i (interactive) option flag. You can use this flag to determine if a shell is being run interactively. In the following example, **display_flags** displays the bash option flags. When run as a script in a subshell, it shows the i option flag is not set; when run using source (page 332), which runs a script in the current shell, it shows the i option flag is set.

```
$ cat display_flags
echo $-

$ ./display_flags
hB

$ source ./display_flags
himBH
```

## $_: Last Argument of Previously Executed Command

When bash starts, as when you run a shell script, it expands the $_ parameter to the pathname of the file it is running. After running a command, it expands this parameter to the last argument of the previously executed command.

```
$ cat last_arg
echo $_
echo here I am
echo $_

$ ./last_arg
./last_arg
here I am
am
```

In the next example, the shell never executes the echo command; it expands $_ to the last argument of the ls command (which it executed, albeit unsuccessfully).

```
$ ls xx && echo hi
ls: cannot access xx: No such file or directory
$ echo $_
xx
```

## *LE+*  VARIABLES

Variables, introduced on page 352, are shell parameters denoted by a name. Variables can have zero or more attributes (page 356; e.g., export, readonly). You, or a shell program, can create and delete variables, and can assign values and attributes to variables. This section adds to the previous coverage with a discussion of the shell variables, environment variables, inheritance, expanding null and unset variables, array variables, and variables in functions.

## SHELL VARIABLES

By default, when you create a variable it is available only in the shell you created it in; it is not available in subshells. This type of variable is called a *shell variable*. In the following example, the first command displays the PID number of the interactive shell the user is working in (2802) and the second command initializes the variable x to 5. Then a bash command spawns a new shell (PID 29572). This new shell is a child of the shell the user was working in (a subprocess; page 373). The ps –l command shows the PID and PPID (parent PID) numbers of each shell: PID 29572 is a child of PID 2802. The final echo command shows the variable x is not set in the spawned (child) shell: It is a shell variable and is local to the shell it was created in.

```
$ echo $$
2802

$ x=5
$ echo $x
5

$ bash
$ echo $$
29572

$ ps -l
F S   UID    PID  PPID  C PRI  NI ADDR SZ WCHAN  TTY          TIME CMD
0 S  1000   2802  2786  0  80   0 -  5374 wait   pts/2    00:00:00 bash
0 S  1000  29572  2802  0  80   0 -  5373 wait   pts/2    00:00:00 bash
0 R  1000  29648 29572  0  80   0 -  1707 -      pts/2    00:00:00 ps
$ echo $x

$
```

# ENVIRONMENT, ENVIRONMENT VARIABLES, AND INHERITANCE

This section explains the concepts of the command execution environment and inheritance.

## ENVIRONMENT

When the Linux kernel invokes a program, the kernel passes to the program a list comprising an array of strings. This list, called the *command execution environment* or simply the *environment*, holds a series of name-value pairs in the form *name=value*.

## *LPI* ENVIRONMENT VARIABLES

When bash is invoked, it scans its environment and creates parameters for each name-value pair, assigning the corresponding *value* to each *name*. Each of these parameters is an *environment variable*; these variables are in the shell's environment. Environment variables are sometimes referred to as *global variables* or *exported variables*.

Inheritance   A child process (a subprocess; see page 373 for more information about the process structure) inherits its environment from its parent. An inherited variable is an environment variable for the child, so its children also inherit the variable: All children and grandchildren, to any level, inherit environment variables from their ancestor. A process can create, remove, and change the value of environment variables, so a child process might not inherit the same environment its parent inherited.

Because of process locality (next), a parent cannot see changes a child makes to an environment variable and a child cannot see changes a parent makes to an environment variable once the child has been spawned (created). Nor can unrelated processes see changes to variables that have the same name in each process, such as commonly inherited environment variables (e.g., **PATH**).

## PROCESS LOCALITY: SHELL VARIABLES

Variables are *local,* which means they are specific to a process: *Local* means *local to a process.* For example, when you log in on a terminal or open a terminal emulator, you start a process that runs a shell. Assume in that shell the **LANG** environment variable (page 368) is set to **en_US.UTF-8**.

If you then log in on a different terminal or open a second terminal emulator, you start another process that runs a different shell. Assume in that shell the **LANG** environment variable is also set to **en_US.UTF-8**. When you change the value of **LANG** on the second terminal to **de_DE.UTF-8**, the value of **LANG** on the first terminal does not change. It does not change because variables (both names and values) are local to a process and each terminal is running a separate process (even though both processes are running shells).

## *LPI* export: PUTS VARIABLES IN THE ENVIRONMENT

When you run an **export** command (a synonym for **declare –x**; page 357) with variable names as arguments, the shell places the names (and values, if present) of those variables in the environment. Without arguments, export lists environment (exported) variables.

The following **extest1** shell script assigns the value of **american** to the variable named **cheese** and then displays its name (the shell expands $0 to the name of the calling program) and the value of **cheese**. The **extest1** script then calls **subtest**, which attempts to display the same information, declares a **cheese** variable by initializing it, displays the value of the variable, and returns control to the parent process, which is executing **extest1**. Finally, **extest1** again displays the value of the original **cheese** variable.

```
$ cat extest1
cheese=american
echo "$0 1: $cheese"
./subtest
echo "$0 2: $cheese"

$ cat subtest
echo "$0 1: $cheese"
cheese=swiss
echo "$0 2: $cheese"

$ ./extest1
./extest1 1: american
./subtest 1:
./subtest 2: swiss
./extest1 2: american
```

The **subtest** script never receives the value of **cheese** from **extest1** (and **extest1** never loses the value): **cheese** is a shell variable, not an environment variable (it is not in the environment of the parent process and therefore is not available in the child process). When a process attempts to display the value of a variable that has not been declared and is not in the environment, as is the case with **subtest**, the process displays nothing; the value of an undeclared variable is that of the null string. The final echo shows the value of **cheese** in **extest1** has not changed: In bash—unlike in the real world—a child can never affect its parent's attributes.

The **extest2** script is the same as **extest1** except it uses export to put **cheese** in the environment of the current process. The result is that **cheese** appears in the environment of the child process running the **subtest** script.

```
$ cat extest2
export cheese=american
echo "$0 1: $cheese"
./subtest
echo "$0 2: $cheese"

$ ./extest2
./extest2 1: american
./subtest 1: american
./subtest 2: swiss
./extest2 2: american
```

Here the child process inherits the value of **cheese** as **american** and, after displaying this value, changes *its copy* to **swiss**. When control is returned to the parent, the parent's copy of **cheese** retains its original value: **american**.

Alternately, as the next program shows, you can put a variable in the environment of a child shell without declaring it in the parent shell. See page 148 for more information on this command-line syntax.

```
$ cheese=cheddar ./subtest
./subtest 1: cheddar
./subtest 2: swiss
$ echo $cheese

$
```

You can export a variable without/before assigning a value to it. Also, you do not need to export an already-exported variable after you change its value. For example, you do not usually need to export **PATH** when you assign a value to it in **~/.bash_profile** because it is typically exported in a global startup file.

You can place several **export** declarations (initializations) on a single line:

```
$ export cheese=swiss coffee=colombian avocados=us
```

Unexport   An **export –n** or **declare +x** command removes the export attribute from the named environment variable (unexports the variable), demoting it to become a shell variable while preserving its value.

Export a function   An **export –f** command places the named function (page 396) in the environment so it is available to child processes.

## printenv: DISPLAYS ENVIRONMENT VARIABLE NAMES AND VALUES

The printenv utility displays environment variable names and values. When called without an argument, it displays all environment variables. When called with the name of an environment variable, it displays the value of that variable. When called with the name of a variable that is not in the environment or has not been declared, it displays nothing. You can also use export (page 1032) and env (next page) to display a list of environment variables.

```
$ x=5                    # not in the environment
$ export y=10            # in the environment
$ printenv x
$ printenv y
10
$ printenv
...
SHELL=/bin/bash
TERM=xterm
USER=sam
PWD=/home/sam
y=10
...
```

## *LPI* env: RUNS A PROGRAM IN A MODIFIED ENVIRONMENT

The env utility runs a program as a child of the current shell, allowing you to modify the environment the current shell exports to the newly created process. See page 148 for an easier way to place a variable in the environment of a child process. The env utility has the following syntax:

*env [options] [-] [name=value] ... [command-line]*

where *options* is one of the following options:

**--ignore-environment**
**-i or –**
Causes *command-line* to run in a clean environment; no environment variables are available to the newly created process.

**--unset=*name*  -u *name***
Unsets the environment variable named *name* so it is not available to the newly created process.

Just as on a bash command line (page 148), zero or more *name=value* pairs may be used to set or modify environment variables in the newly created process, except you cannot specify a *name* without a *value*. The env utility evaluates the *name=value* pairs from left to right, so if *name* appears more than once in this list, the rightmost *value* takes precedence.

The *command-line* is the command (including any options and arguments) that env executes. The env utility takes its first argument that does not contain an equal sign as the beginning of the command line and, if you specify a command that does not include a slash (i.e., if you specify a simple filename), uses the value of **PATH** (page 359) to locate the command. It does not work with builtin commands.

In the following example, env runs **display_xx**, a script that displays the value of the **xx** variable. On the command line, env initializes the variable **xx** in the environment of the script it calls and echo in the script displays the value of **xx**.

```
$ cat display_xx
echo "Running $0"
echo $xx

$ env xx=remember ./display_xx
Running ./display_xx
remember
```

If you want to declare only environment variables for a program, it is simpler to use the following bash syntax (page 148):

```
$ xx=remember ./display_xx
Running ./display_xx
remember
```

When called without a *command-line*, env displays a list of environment variables (it behaves similarly to printenv [page 1034]):

```
$ env
...
SHELL=/bin/bash
TERM=xterm
USER=sam
PWD=/home/sam
y=10
...
```

## set: WORKS WITH SHELL FEATURES, POSITIONAL PARAMETERS, AND VARIABLES

The set builtin can perform the following tasks:

- Set or unset shell features (also called attributes; page 400).

- Assign values to positional parameters (page 1024).

- Display variables that are available to the current shell. These variables comprise shell variables (variables not in the environment) and environment variables. The set builtin displays variables in a format you can use in a shell script or as input to set to declare and initialize variables. Output is sorted based on the current locale (page 368). You cannot reset readonly variables.

```
$ set
...
BASH=/bin/bash
COLUMNS=70
PWD=/home/sam
SHELL=/bin/bash
x=5
y=10
...
```

## EXPANDING NULL AND UNSET VARIABLES

The expression ${name} (or just $name if it is not ambiguous) expands to the value of the **name** variable. If **name** is null or not set, bash expands ${name} to a null string. The Bourne Again Shell provides the following alternatives to accepting the null string as the value of the variable:

- Use a default value for the variable.

- Use a default value and assign that value to the variable.

- Display an error.

You can choose one of these alternatives by using a modifier with the variable name. In addition, you can use **set –o nounset** (page 402) to cause bash to display an error message and exit from a script whenever the script references an unset variable.

## :− USES A DEFAULT VALUE

The **:−** modifier uses a default value in place of a null or unset variable while allowing a nonnull variable to represent itself:

> *${name:−default}*

The shell interprets **:−** as "If *name* is null or unset, expand *default* and use the expanded value in place of *name;* else use *name.*"

The following command lists the contents of the directory named by the **LIT** variable. If **LIT** is null or unset, it lists the contents of **/home/max/literature:**

```
$ ls ${LIT:-/home/max/literature}
```

The shell expands variables in *default:*

```
$ ls ${LIT:-$HOME/literature}
```

## := ASSIGNS A DEFAULT VALUE

The **:−** modifier does not change the value of a variable. However, you can change the value of a null or unset variable to the expanded value of *default* by using the **:=** modifier:

> *${name:=default}*

The shell expands the expression *${name:=default}* in the same manner as it expands *${name:−default}*, but also sets the value of *name* to the expanded value of *default.*

If a script contains a line such as the following and **LIT** is unset or null at the time this line is executed, the shell assigns **LIT** the value **/home/max/literature:**

```
$ ls ${LIT:=/home/max/literature}
```

**: (null) builtin**  Some shell scripts include lines that start with the **:** (null) builtin followed on the same line by the **:=** expansion modifier. This syntax sets variables that are null or unset. The **:** builtin evaluates each token in the remainder of the command line but does not execute any commands.

Use the following syntax to set a default for a null or unset variable in a shell script (a SPACE follows the first colon). Without the leading colon (**:**), the shell would evaluate and attempt to execute the "command" that results from the evaluation.

> **:**  *${name:=default}*

When a script needs a directory for temporary files and uses the value of **TEMPDIR** for the name of this directory, the following line assigns to **TEMPDIR** the value **/tmp** if **TEMPDIR** is null:

```
: ${TEMPDIR:=/tmp}
```

### :? SENDS AN ERROR MESSAGE TO STANDARD ERROR

Sometimes a script needs the value of a variable, but you cannot supply a reasonable default at the time you write the script. In this case you want the script to exit if the variable is not set. If the variable is null or unset, the :? modifier causes the script to send an error message to standard error and terminate with an exit status of 1. Interactive shells do not exit when you use :?.

*${name:?message}*

If you omit **message**, the shell displays **parameter null or not set**. In the following command, **TESTDIR** is not set, so the shell sends to standard error the expanded value of the string following **:?**. In this case the string includes command substitution for date with the **%T** syntax, followed by the string **error, variable not set**.

```
cd ${TESTDIR:?$(date +%T) error, variable not set.}
bash: TESTDIR: 16:16:14 error, variable not set.
```

## ARRAY VARIABLES

The Bourne Again Shell supports one-dimensional array variables. The subscripts are integers with zero-based indexing (i.e., the first element of the array has the subscript 0). The following syntax declares and assigns values to an array:

*name=(element1 element2 ...)*

The following example assigns four values to the array **NAMES**:

```
$ NAMES=(max helen sam zach)
```

You reference a single element of an array as follows; the braces are not optional.

```
$ echo ${NAMES[2]}
sam
```

The subscripts [*] and [@] both extract the entire array but work differently when used within double quotation marks. An @ produces an array that is a duplicate of the original array; an * produces a single element of an array (or a plain variable) that holds all the elements of the array separated by the first character in **IFS** (normally a SPACE; page 363). In the following example, the array **A** is filled with the elements of the **NAMES** variable using an *, and **B** is filled using an @. The declare builtin (page 357) with the **–a** option displays the values of the arrays (and reminds you that bash uses zero-based indexing for arrays):

```
$ A=("${NAMES[*]}")
$ B=("${NAMES[@]}")

$ declare -a
declare -a A='([0]="max helen sam zach")'
declare -a B='([0]="max" [1]="helen" [2]="sam" [3]="zach")'
...
declare -a NAMES='([0]="max" [1]="helen" [2]="sam" [3]="zach")'
```

The output of declare shows that **NAMES** and **B** have multiple elements. In contrast, **A**, which was assigned its value with an ✶ within double quotation marks, has only one element: **A** has all its elements enclosed between double quotation marks.

In the next example, echo attempts to display element 1 of array **A**. Nothing is displayed because **A** has only one element and that element has an index of 0. Element 0 of array **A** holds all four names. Element 1 of **B** holds the second item in the array and element 0 holds the first item.

```
$ echo ${A[1]}

$ echo ${A[0]}
max helen sam zach
$ echo ${B[1]}
helen
$ echo ${B[0]}
max
```

The ${#*name*[✶]} operator returns the number of elements in an array:

```
$ echo ${#NAMES[✶]}
4
```

The same operator, when given the index of an element of an array in place of ✶, returns the length of the element:

```
$ echo ${#NAMES[1]}
5
```

You can use subscripts on the left side of an assignment statement to replace selected elements of an array:

```
$ NAMES[1]=max
$ echo ${NAMES[✶]}
max max sam zach
```

## LPI VARIABLES IN FUNCTIONS

Because functions run in the same environment as the shell that calls them, variables are implicitly shared by a shell and a function it calls.

```
$ nam () {
> echo $myname
> myname=zach
> }

$ myname=sam
$ nam
sam
$ echo $myname
zach
```

In the preceding example, the **myname** variable is set to **sam** in the interactive shell. The **nam** function then displays the value of **myname** (**sam**) and sets **myname** to **zach**. The final echo shows that, in the interactive shell, the value of **myname** has been changed to **zach**.

Function local
variables

Local variables are helpful in a function written for general use. Because the function is called by many scripts that might be written by different programmers, you need to make sure the names of the variables used within the function do not conflict with (i.e., duplicate) the names of the variables in the programs that call the function. Local variables eliminate this problem. When used within a function, the local builtin declares a variable to be local to the function it is defined in.

The next example shows the use of a local variable in a function. It features two variables named **count**. The first is declared and initialized to 10 in the interactive shell. Its value never changes, as echo verifies after **count_down** is run. The other **count** is declared, using local, to be local to the **count_down** function. Its value, which is unknown outside the function, ranges from 4 to 1, as the echo command within the function confirms.

The following example shows the function being entered from the keyboard; it is not a shell script. See the tip "A function is not a shell script" on page 1017.

```
$ count_down () {
> local count
> count=$1
> while [ $count -gt 0 ]
> do
> echo "$count..."
> ((count=count-1))
> sleep 1
> done
> echo "Blast Off."
> }

$ count=10
$ count_down 4
4...
3...
2...
1...
Blast Off.
$ echo $count
10
```

The **count=count–1** assignment is enclosed between double parentheses, which cause the shell to perform an arithmetic evaluation (page 1056). Within the double parentheses you can reference shell variables without the leading dollar sign ($). See page 397 for another example of function local variables.

# BUILTIN COMMANDS

Builtin commands, which were introduced in Chapter 5, do not fork a new process when you execute them. This section discusses the type, read, exec, trap, kill, and getopts builtins. Table 27-6 on page 1055 lists many bash builtin commands.

**LPI**   type: DISPLAYS INFORMATION ABOUT A COMMAND

The type builtin provides information about a command:

```
$ type cat echo who if lt
cat is hashed (/bin/cat)
echo is a shell builtin
who is /usr/bin/who
if is a shell keyword
lt is aliased to 'ls -ltrh | tail'
```

The preceding output shows the files that would be executed if you gave **cat** or **who** as a command. Because cat has already been called from the current shell, it is in the hash table (page 376) and type reports that **cat is hashed**. The output also shows that a call to **echo** runs the echo builtin, **if** is a keyword, and **lt** is an alias.

**LE+**   read: ACCEPTS USER INPUT

A common use for user-created variables is storing information that a user enters in response to a prompt. Using read, scripts can accept input from the user and store that input in variables. The read builtin reads one line from standard input and assigns the words on the line to one or more variables:

```
$ cat read1
echo -n "Go ahead: "
read firstline
echo "You entered: $firstline"

$ ./read1
Go ahead: This is a line.
You entered: This is a line.
```

The first line of the **read1** script uses echo to prompt for a line of text. The –n option suppresses the following NEWLINE, allowing you to enter a line of text on the same line as the prompt. The second line reads the text into the variable **firstline**. The third line verifies the action of read by displaying the value of **firstline**.

The –p (prompt) option causes read to send to standard error the argument that follows it; read does not terminate this prompt with a NEWLINE. This feature allows you to both prompt for and read the input from the user on one line:

```
$ cat read1a
read -p "Go ahead: " firstline
echo "You entered: $firstline"

$ ./read1a
Go ahead: My line.
You entered: My line.
```

The variable in the preceding examples is quoted (along with the text string) because you, as the script writer, cannot anticipate which characters the user might enter in response to the prompt. Consider what would happen if the variable were not quoted and the user entered ✻ in response to the prompt:

```
$ cat read1_no_quote
read -p "Go ahead: " firstline
echo You entered: $firstline

$ ./read1_no_quote
Go ahead: *
You entered: read1 read1_no_quote script.1
$ ls
read1    read1_no_quote      script.1
```

The ls command lists the same words as the script, demonstrating that the shell expands the asterisk into a list of files in the working directory. When the variable **$firstline** is surrounded by double quotation marks, the shell does not expand the asterisk. Thus the **read1** script behaves correctly:

```
$ ./read1
Go ahead: *
You entered: *
```

REPLY   When you do not specify a variable to receive read's input, bash puts the input into the variable named **REPLY**. The following **read1b** script performs the same task as **read1**:

```
$ cat read1b
read -p "Go ahead: "
echo "You entered: $REPLY"
```

The **read2** script prompts for a command line, reads the user's response, and assigns it to the variable **cmd**. The script then attempts to execute the command line that results from the expansion of the **cmd** variable:

```
$ cat read2
read -p "Enter a command: " cmd
$cmd
echo "Thanks"
```

In the following example, **read2** reads a command line that calls the echo builtin. The shell executes the command and then displays **Thanks**. Next **read2** reads a command line that executes the who utility:

```
$ ./read2
Enter a command: echo Please display this message.
Please display this message.
Thanks
$ ./read2
Enter a command: who
max      pts/4        2013-06-17 07:50   (:0.0)
sam      pts/12       2013-06-17 11:54   (guava)
Thanks
```

If **cmd** does not expand into a valid command line, the shell issues an error message:

```
$ ./read2
Enter a command: xxx
./read2: line 2: xxx: command not found
Thanks
```

The **read3** script reads values into three variables. The read builtin assigns one word (a sequence of nonblank characters) to each variable:

```
$ cat read3
read -p "Enter something: " word1 word2 word3
echo "Word 1 is: $word1"
echo "Word 2 is: $word2"
echo "Word 3 is: $word3"
$ ./read3
Enter something: this is something
Word 1 is: this
Word 2 is: is
Word 3 is: something
```

When you enter more words than read has variables, read assigns one word to each variable, assigning all leftover words to the last variable. Both **read1** and **read2** assigned the first word and all leftover words to the one variable the scripts each had to work with. In the following example, read assigns five words to three variables: It assigns the first word to the first variable, the second word to the second variable, and the third through fifth words to the third variable.

```
$ ./read3
Enter something: this is something else, really.
Word 1 is:  this
Word 2 is:  is
Word 3 is:  something else, really.
```

Table 27-4 lists some of the options supported by the read builtin.

**Table 27-4**   read options

| Option | Function |
| --- | --- |
| **–a** *aname* | (array) Assigns each word of input to an element of array ***aname***. |
| **–d** *delim* | (delimiter) Uses ***delim*** to terminate the input instead of NEWLINE. |
| **–e** | (Readline) If input is coming from a keyboard, uses the Readline Library (page 386) to get input. |
| **–n** *num* | (number of characters) Reads ***num*** characters and returns. As soon as the user types ***num*** characters, read returns; there is no need to press RETURN. |
| **–p** *prompt* | (prompt) Displays ***prompt*** on standard error without a terminating NEWLINE before reading input. Displays ***prompt*** only when input comes from the keyboard. |
| **–s** | (silent) Does not echo characters. |
| **–u***n* | (file descriptor) Uses the integer ***n*** as the file descriptor that read takes its input from. Thus<br><br>    `read –u4 arg1 arg2`<br><br>is equivalent to<br><br>    `read arg1 arg2 <&4`<br><br>See "File Descriptors" (page 1016) for a discussion of redirection and file descriptors. |

The read builtin returns an exit status of 0 if it successfully reads any data. It has a nonzero exit status when it reaches the EOF (end of file).

The following example runs a **while** loop from the command line. It takes its input from the **names** file and terminates after reading the last line from **names**.

```
$ cat names
Alice Jones
Robert Smith
Alice Paulson
John Q. Public
$ while read first rest
> do
> echo $rest, $first
> done < names
Jones, Alice
Smith, Robert
Paulson, Alice
Q. Public, John
$
```

The placement of the redirection symbol (<) for the **while** structure is critical. It is important that you place the redirection symbol at the **done** statement and not at the call to read.

**optional**   Each time you redirect input, the shell opens the input file and repositions the read pointer at the start of the file:

```
$ read line1 < names; echo $line1; read line2 < names; echo $line2
Alice Jones
Alice Jones
```

Here each read opens **names** and starts at the beginning of the **names** file. In the following example, **names** is opened once, as standard input of the subshell created by the parentheses. Each read then reads successive lines of standard input:

```
$ (read line1; echo $line1; read line2; echo $line2) < names
Alice Jones
Robert Smith
```

Another way to get the same effect is to open the input file with **exec** and hold it open (refer to "File Descriptors" on page 1016):

```
$ exec 3< names
$ read -u3 line1; echo $line1; read -u3 line2; echo $line2
Alice Jones
Robert Smith
$ exec 3<&-
```

whiptail   When run in a graphical environment, whiptail can display a dialog box from a shell script. The following command displays **What is your name?** in a dialog box. When the user types an answer and presses RETURN, whiptail sends the response to standard error, which the command line redirects to the file named **answer**. See the whiptail man page for more information.

```
$ whiptail --inputbox "What is your name?" 10 30 2> answer
$ cat answer
Sam the Great$
```

# **LPI** exec: EXECUTES A COMMAND OR REDIRECTS FILE DESCRIPTORS

The exec builtin has two primary purposes: to run a command without creating a new process and to redirect a file descriptor—including standard input, output, or error—of a shell script from within the script (page 1016). When the shell executes a command that is not built into the shell, it typically creates a new process. The new process inherits environment (exported) variables from its parent but does not inherit variables that are not exported by the parent (page 1032). In contrast, exec executes a command in place of (overlays) the current process.

### exec: EXECUTES A COMMAND

The exec builtin used for running a command has the following syntax:

*exec command arguments*

**LPI** exec versus . (dot)    Insofar as exec runs a command in the environment of the original process, it is similar to the . (dot) command (page 332). However, unlike the . command, which can run only shell scripts, exec can run both scripts and compiled programs. Also, whereas the . command returns control to the original script when it finishes running, exec does not. Finally the . command gives the new program access to local variables, whereas exec does not.

exec does not return control    Because the shell does not create a new process when you use exec, the command runs more quickly. However, because exec does not return control to the original program, it can be used only as the last command in a script. The following script shows that control is not returned to the script:

```
$ cat exec_demo
who
exec date
echo "This line is never displayed."

$ ./exec_demo
zach      pts/7    May 20  7:05 (guava)
hls       pts/1    May 20  6:59 (:0.0)
Fri May 24 11:42:56 PDT 2013
```

The next example, a modified version of the **out** script (page 989), uses exec to execute the final command the script runs. Because **out** runs either cat or less and then terminates, the new version, named **out2**, uses exec with both cat and less:

```
$ cat out2
if [ $# -eq 0 ]
    then
        echo "Usage: out2 [-v] filenames" 1>&2
        exit 1
fi
if [ "$1" = "-v" ]
    then
        shift
        exec less "$@"
    else
        exec cat -- "$@"
fi
```

### exec: REDIRECTS INPUT AND OUTPUT

The second major use of exec is to redirect a file descriptor—including standard input, output, or error—from within a script. The next command causes all subsequent input to a script that would have come from standard input to come from the file named **infile**:

```
exec < infile
```

Similarly the following command redirects standard output and standard error to **outfile** and **errfile**, respectively:

```
exec > outfile 2> errfile
```

When you use exec in this manner, the current process is not replaced with a new process and exec can be followed by other commands in the script.

**/dev/tty**   When you redirect the output from a script to a file, you must make sure the user sees any prompts the script displays. The **/dev/tty** device is a pseudonym for the screen the user is working on; you can use this device to refer to the user's screen without knowing which device it is. (The tty utility displays the name of the device you are using.) By redirecting the output from a script to **/dev/tty**, you ensure that prompts and messages go to the user's terminal, regardless of which terminal the user is logged in on. Messages sent to **/dev/tty** are also not diverted if standard output and standard error from the script are redirected.

The **to_screen1** script sends output to three places: standard output, standard error, and the user's screen. When run with standard output and standard error redirected, **to_screen1** still displays the message sent to **/dev/tty** on the user's screen. The **out** and **err** files hold the output sent to standard output and standard error, respectively.

```
$ cat to_screen1
echo "message to standard output"
echo "message to standard error" 1>&2
echo "message to screen" > /dev/tty

$ ./to_screen1 > out 2> err
message to screen
$ cat out
message to standard output
$ cat err
message to standard error
```

The following command redirects standard output from a script to the user's screen:

```
exec > /dev/tty
```

Putting this command at the beginning of the previous script changes where the output goes. In **to_screen2**, exec redirects standard output to the user's screen so the **> /dev/tty** is superfluous. Following the exec command, all output sent to standard output goes to **/dev/tty** (the screen). Output to standard error is not affected.

```
$ cat to_screen2
exec > /dev/tty
echo "message to standard output"
echo "message to standard error" 1>&2
echo "message to screen" > /dev/tty

$ ./to_screen2 > out 2> err
message to standard output
message to screen
```

One disadvantage of using **exec** to redirect the output to **/dev/tty** is that all subsequent output is redirected unless you use **exec** again in the script.

You can also redirect the input to **read** (standard input) so that it comes from **/dev/tty** (the keyboard):

```
read name < /dev/tty
```

*or*

```
exec < /dev/tty
```

# trap: Catches a Signal

A *signal* is a report to a process about a condition. Linux uses signals to report interrupts generated by the user (for example, pressing the interrupt key) as well as bad system calls, broken pipelines, illegal instructions, and other conditions. The **trap** builtin catches (traps) one or more signals, allowing you to direct the actions a script takes when it receives a specified signal.

This discussion covers six signals that are significant when you work with shell scripts. Table 27-5 lists these signals, the signal numbers that systems often ascribe to them, and the conditions that usually generate each signal. Give the command **kill –l** (lowercase "el"), **trap –l** (lowercase "el"), or **man 7 signal** to display a list of all signal names.

**Table 27-5** *LPI* Signals

| Type | Name | Number | Generating condition |
|------|------|--------|----------------------|
| Not a real signal | EXIT | 0 | Exit because of **exit** command or reaching the end of the program (not an actual signal but useful in **trap**) |
| Hang up | SIGHUP or HUP | 1 | Disconnect the line |
| Terminal interrupt | SIGINT or INT | 2 | Press the interrupt key (usually CONTROL-C) |

**Table 27-5**   *LPI*   Signals (continued)

| Type | Name | Number | Generating condition |
|---|---|---|---|
| Quit | SIGQUIT or QUIT | 3 | Press the quit key (usually CONTROL-SHIFT-\| or CONTROL-SHIFT-\) |
| Kill | SIGKILL or KILL | 9 | The **kill** builtin with the **–9** option (cannot be trapped; use only as a last resort) |
| Software termination | SIGTERM or TERM | 15 | Default of the **kill** command |
| Stop | SIGTSTP or TSTP | 20 | Press the suspend key (usually CONTROL-Z) |
| Debug | DEBUG | | Execute ***commands*** specified in the **trap** statement after each command (not an actual signal but useful in **trap**) |
| Error | ERR | | Execute ***commands*** specified in the **trap** statement after each command that returns a nonzero exit status (not an actual signal but useful in **trap**) |

When it traps a signal, a script takes whatever action you specify: It can remove files or finish other processing as needed, display a message, terminate execution immediately, or ignore the signal. If you do not use **trap** in a script, any of the six actual signals listed in Table 27-5 (not EXIT, DEBUG, or ERR) will terminate the script. Because a process cannot trap a KILL signal, you can use **kill –KILL** (or **kill –9**) as a last resort to terminate a script or other process. (See page 1050 for more information on **kill**.)

The **trap** command has the following syntax:

> *trap* [*'commands'*] [*signal*]

The optional ***commands*** specifies the commands the shell executes when it catches one of the signals specified by ***signal***. The ***signal*** can be a signal name or number—for example, INT or 2. If ***commands*** is not present, **trap** resets the trap to its initial condition, which is usually to exit from the script.

Quotation marks   The **trap** builtin does not require single quotation marks around ***commands*** as shown in the preceding syntax but it is a good practice to use them. The single quotation marks cause shell variables within the ***commands*** to be expanded when the signal occurs, rather than when the shell evaluates the arguments to **trap**. Even if you do not use any shell variables in the ***commands,*** you need to enclose any command that takes arguments within either single or double quotation marks. Quoting *commands* causes the shell to pass to trap the entire command as a single argument.

After executing the ***commands***, the shell resumes executing the script where it left off. If you want trap to prevent a script from exiting when it receives a signal but not to run any commands explicitly, you can specify a null (empty) ***commands*** string, as shown in the **locktty** script (page 1004). The following command traps signal number 15, after which the script continues:

```
trap '' 15
```

The following script demonstrates how the trap builtin can catch the terminal interrupt signal (2). You can use SIGINT, INT, or 2 to specify this signal. The script returns an exit status of 1:

```
$ cat inter
#!/bin/bash
trap 'echo PROGRAM INTERRUPTED; exit 1' INT
while true
do
    echo "Program running."
    sleep 1
done
$ ./inter
Program running.
Program running.
Program running.
CONTROL-C
PROGRAM INTERRUPTED
$
```

: (null) builtin   The second line of **inter** sets up a trap for the terminal interrupt signal using INT. When trap catches the signal, the shell executes the two commands between the single quotation marks in the trap command. The echo builtin displays the message **PROGRAM INTERRUPTED**, exit terminates the shell running the script, and the parent shell displays a prompt. If exit were not there, the shell would return control to the **while** loop after displaying the message. The **while** loop repeats continuously until the script receives a signal because the true utility always returns a *true* exit status. In place of true you can use the : (null) builtin, which is written as a colon and always returns a 0 (*true*) status.

The trap builtin frequently removes temporary files when a script is terminated prematurely, thereby ensuring the files are not left to clutter the filesystem. The following shell script, named **addbanner**, uses two traps to remove a temporary file when the script terminates normally or because of a hangup, software interrupt, quit, or software termination signal:

```
$ cat addbanner
#!/bin/bash
script=$(basename $0)

if [ ! -r "$HOME/banner" ]
    then
        echo "$script: need readable $HOME/banner file" 1>&2
        exit 1
fi

trap 'exit 1' 1 2 3 15
trap 'rm /tmp/$$.$script 2> /dev/null' EXIT

for file
do
    if [ -r "$file" -a -w "$file" ]
        then
            cat $HOME/banner $file > /tmp/$$.$script
            cp /tmp/$$.$script $file
            echo "$script: banner added to $file" 1>&2
        else
            echo "$script: need read and write permission for $file" 1>&2
        fi
done
```

When called with one or more filename arguments, **addbanner** loops through the files, adding a header to the top of each. This script is useful when you use a standard format at the top of your documents, such as a standard layout for memos, or when you want to add a standard header to shell scripts. The header is kept in a file named **~/banner**. Because **addbanner** uses the **HOME** variable, which contains the pathname of the user's home directory, the script can be used by several users without modification. If Max had written the script with **/home/max** in place of **$HOME** and then given the script to Zach, either Zach would have had to change it or **addbanner** would have used Max's **banner** file when Zach ran it (assuming Zach had read permission for the file).

The first trap in **addbanner** causes it to exit with a status of 1 when it receives a hangup, software interrupt (terminal interrupt or quit signal), or software termination signal. The second trap uses **EXIT** in place of **signal-number**, which causes trap to execute its command argument *whenever* the script exits because it receives an exit command or reaches its end. Together these traps remove a temporary file whether the script terminates normally or prematurely. Standard error of the second trap is sent to **/dev/null** whenever trap attempts to remove a nonexistent temporary file. In those cases rm sends an error message to standard error; because standard error is redirected, the user does not see the message.

See page 1004 for another example that uses trap.

## *LPI*   kill: ABORTS A PROCESS

The kill builtin sends a signal to a process or job. The kill command has the following syntax:

*kill [–signal] PID*

where *signal* is the signal name or number (for example, INT or 2) and *PID* is the process identification number of the process that is to receive the signal. You can specify a job number (page 163) as **%n** in place of *PID*. If you omit *signal*, kill sends a TERM (software termination, number 15) signal. For more information on signal names and numbers, see Table 27-5 on page 1047.

The following command sends the TERM signal to job number 1, regardless of whether it is running or stopped in the background:

```
$ kill -TERM %1
```

Because TERM is the default signal for kill, you can also give this command as **kill %1**. Give the command **kill –l** (lowercase "el") to display a list of signal names.

A program that is interrupted can leave matters in an unpredictable state: Temporary files might be left behind (when they are normally removed), and permissions might be changed. A well-written application traps signals and cleans up before exiting. Most carefully written applications trap the INT, QUIT, and TERM signals.

To terminate a program, first try INT (press CONTROL-C, if the job running is in the foreground). Because an application can be written to ignore this signal, you might need to use the KILL signal, which cannot be trapped or ignored; it is a "sure kill." For more information refer to "kill: Sends a Signal to a Process" on page 465.

# eval: SCANS, EVALUATES, AND EXECUTES A COMMAND LINE

The eval builtin scans the command that follows it on the command line. In doing so, eval processes the command line in the same way bash does when it executes a command line (e.g., it expands variables, replacing the name of a variable with its value). For more information refer to "Processing the Command Line" on page 403. After scanning (and expanding) the command line, it passes the resulting command line to bash to execute.

The following example first assigns the value **frog** to the variable **name**. Next eval scans the command **$name=88** and expands the variable **$name** to **frog**, yielding the command **frog=88**, which it passes to bash to execute. The last command displays the value of **frog**.

```
$ name=frog
$ eval $name=88
$ echo $frog
88
```

Brace expansion with a sequence expression The next example uses eval to cause brace expansion with a sequence expression (page 406) to accept variables, which it does not normally do. The following command demonstrates brace expansion with a sequence expression:

```
$ echo {2..5}
2 3 4 5
```

One of the first things bash does when it processes a command line is to perform brace expansion; later it expands variables (page 403). When you provide an invalid argument in brace expansion, bash does not perform brace expansion; instead, it passes the string to the program being called. In the next example, bash cannot expand {$m..$n} during the brace expansion phase because it contains variables, so it continues processing the command line. When it gets to the variable expansion phase, it expands $m and $n and then passes the string {2..5} to echo.

```
$ m=2 n=5
$ echo {$m..$n}
{2..5}
```

When eval scans the same command line, it expands the variables as explained previously and yields the command echo {2..5}. It then passes that command to bash, which can now perform brace expansion:

```
$ eval echo {$m..$n}
2 3 4 5
```

# getopts: PARSES OPTIONS

The getopts builtin parses command-line arguments, making it easier to write programs that follow the Linux argument conventions. The syntax for getopts is

> getopts *optstring varname* [arg ...]

where *optstring* is a list of the valid option letters, **varname** is the variable that receives the options one at a time, and *arg* is the optional list of parameters to be processed. If *arg* is not present, getopts processes the command-line arguments. If *optstring* starts with a colon (:), the script must take care of generating error messages; otherwise, getopts generates error messages.

The getopts builtin uses the **OPTIND** (option index) and **OPTARG** (option argument) variables to track and store option-related values. When a shell script starts, the value of **OPTIND** is 1. Each time getopts is called and locates an argument, it increments **OPTIND** to the index of the next option to be processed. If the option takes an argument, bash assigns the value of the argument to **OPTARG**.

To indicate that an option takes an argument, follow the corresponding letter in *optstring* with a colon (:). For example, the *optstring* dxo:lt:r instructs getopts to search for the −d, −x, −o, −l, −t, and −r options and tells it the −o and −t options take arguments.

Using getopts as the *test-command* in a **while** control structure allows you to loop over the options one at a time. The getopts builtin checks the option list for options that are in *optstring*. Each time through the loop, getopts stores the option letter it finds in *varname*.

As an example, assume you want to write a program that can take three options:

1. A **–b** option indicates that the program should ignore whitespace at the start of input lines.

2. A **–t** option followed by the name of a directory indicates that the program should store temporary files in that directory. Otherwise, it should use **/tmp**.

3. A **–u** option indicates that the program should translate all output to uppercase.

In addition, the program should ignore all other options and end option processing when it encounters two hyphens (––).

The problem is to write the portion of the program that determines which options the user has supplied. The following solution does not use getopts:

```
SKIPBLANKS=
TMPDIR=/tmp
CASE=lower
while [[ "$1" = -* ]] # [[ = ]] does pattern match
do
    case $1 in
        -b)     SKIPBLANKS=TRUE ;;
        -t)     if [ -d "$2" ]
                then
                    TMPDIR=$2
                    shift
                else
                    echo "$0: -t takes a directory argument." >&2
                    exit 1
                fi ;;
        -u)     CASE=upper ;;
        --)     break   ;;      # Stop processing options
        *)      echo "$0: Invalid option $1 ignored." >&2 ;;
    esac
    shift
done
```

This program fragment uses a loop to check and shift arguments while the argument is not ––. As long as the argument is not two hyphens, the program continues to loop through a **case** statement that checks for possible options. The –– **case** label breaks out of the **while** loop. The * **case** label recognizes any option; it appears as the last **case** label to catch any unknown options, displays an error message, and allows processing to continue. On each pass through the loop, the program uses shift so it accesses the next argument on the next pass through the loop. If an option takes an argument, the program uses an extra shift to get past that argument.

The following program fragment processes the same options using getopts:

```
SKIPBLANKS=
TMPDIR=/tmp
CASE=lower

while getopts :bt:u arg
do
    case $arg in
        b)      SKIPBLANKS=TRUE ;;
        t)      if [ -d "$OPTARG" ]
                    then
                        TMPDIR=$OPTARG
                else
                    echo "$0: $OPTARG is not a directory." >&2
                    exit 1
                fi ;;
        u)      CASE=upper ;;
        :)      echo "$0: Must supply an argument to -$OPTARG." >&2
                exit 1 ;;
        \?)     echo "Invalid option -$OPTARG ignored." >&2 ;;
    esac
done
```

In this version of the code, the **while** structure evaluates the getopts builtin each time control transfers to the top of the loop. The getopts builtin uses the **OPTIND** variable to keep track of the index of the argument it is to process the next time it is called. There is no need to call shift in this example.

In the getopts version of the script, the **case** patterns do not start with a hyphen because the value of **arg** is just the option letter (getopts strips off the hyphen). Also, getopts recognizes -- as the end of the options, so you do not have to specify it explicitly, as in the **case** statement in the first example.

Because you tell getopts which options are valid and which require arguments, it can detect errors in the command line and handle them in two ways. This example uses a leading colon in *optstring* to specify that you check for and handle errors in your code; when getopts finds an invalid option, it sets *varname* to ? and **OPTARG** to the option letter. When it finds an option that is missing an argument, getopts sets *varname* to : and **OPTARG** to the option lacking an argument.

The **\?** case pattern specifies the action to take when getopts detects an invalid option. The : case pattern specifies the action to take when getopts detects a missing option argument. In both cases getopts does not write any error message but rather leaves that task to you.

If you omit the leading colon from *optstring*, both an invalid option and a missing option argument cause *varname* to be assigned the string ?. **OPTARG** is not set and getopts writes its own diagnostic message to standard error. Generally this method is less desirable because you have less control over what the user sees when an error occurs.

Using getopts will not necessarily make your programs shorter. Its principal advantages are that it provides a uniform programming interface and that it enforces standard option handling.

# A PARTIAL LIST OF BUILTINS

Table 27-6 lists some of the bash builtins. You can use type (page 1041) to see if a command runs a builtin. See "Listing bash builtins" on page 170 for instructions on how to display complete lists of builtins.

Table 27-6   bash builtins

| Builtin | Function |
| --- | --- |
| : | Returns 0 or *true* (the null builtin; pages 1037 and 1049) |
| . (dot) | Executes a shell script as part of the current process (page 332) |
| bg | Puts a suspended job in the background (page 348) |
| **break** | Exits from a looping control structure (page 1005) |
| cd | Changes to another working directory (page 185) |
| **continue** | Starts with the next iteration of a looping control structure (page 1005) |
| echo | Displays its arguments (page 219) |
| eval | Scans and evaluates the command line (page 1051) |
| exec | Executes a shell script or program in place of the current process (page 1045) |
| exit | Exits from the current shell (usually the same as CONTROL-D from an interactive shell; page 1029) |
| export | Makes the variable an environment variable (page 1032) |
| fg | Brings a job from the background to the foreground (page 347) |
| getopts | Parses arguments to a shell script (page 1052) |
| jobs | Displays a list of background jobs (page 346) |
| kill | Sends a signal to a process or job (page 465) |
| pwd | Displays the name of the working directory (page 143) |
| read | Reads a line from standard input (page 1041) |
| readonly | Declares a variable to be readonly (page 356) |
| set | Sets shell flags or positional parameters; with no argument, lists all variables (pages 400 and 1024) |
| shift | Promotes each positional parameter (page 1025) |
| test | Compares arguments (page 983) |
| times | Displays total times for the current shell and its children |
| trap | Traps a signal (page 1047) |

**Table 27-6**   bash builtins (continued)

| Builtin | Function |
| --- | --- |
| type | Displays how each argument would be interpreted as a command (page 1041) |
| umask | Sets and displays the file-creation mask (page 469) |
| unset | Removes a variable or function (page 356) |
| wait | Waits for a background process to terminate |

# EXPRESSIONS

An expression comprises constants, variables, and operators that the shell can process to return a value. This section covers arithmetic, logical, and conditional expressions as well as operators. Table 27-8 on page 1059 lists the bash operators.

## ARITHMETIC EVALUATION

The Bourne Again Shell can perform arithmetic assignments and evaluate many different types of arithmetic expressions, all using integers. The shell performs arithmetic assignments in a number of ways. One is with arguments to the let builtin:

```
$ let "VALUE=VALUE * 10 + NEW"
```

In the preceding example, the variables **VALUE** and **NEW** hold integer values. Within a let statement you do not need to use dollar signs ($) in front of variable names. Double quotation marks must enclose a single argument, or expression, that contains SPACEs. Because most expressions contain SPACEs and need to be quoted, bash accepts *((expression))* as a synonym for let *"expression"*, obviating the need for both quotation marks and dollar signs:

```
$ ((VALUE=VALUE * 10 + NEW))
```

You can use either form wherever a command is allowed and can remove the SPACEs. In these examples, the asterisk (*) does not need to be quoted because the shell does not perform pathname expansion on the right side of an assignment (page 354):

```
$ let VALUE=VALUE*10+NEW
```

Because each argument to let is evaluated as a separate expression, you can assign values to more than one variable on a single line:

```
$ let "COUNT = COUNT + 1" VALUE=VALUE*10+NEW
```

You must use commas to separate multiple assignments within a set of double parentheses:

```
$ ((COUNT = COUNT + 1, VALUE=VALUE*10+NEW))
```

### Arithmetic evaluation versus arithmetic expansion

tip Arithmetic evaluation differs from arithmetic expansion. As explained on page 408, arithmetic expansion uses the syntax *$((expression))*, evaluates *expression*, and replaces *$((expression))* with the result. You can use arithmetic expansion to display the value of an expression or to assign that value to a variable.

Arithmetic evaluation uses the *let expression* or *((expression))* syntax, evaluates *expression*, and returns a status code. You can use arithmetic evaluation to perform a logical comparison or an assignment.

Logical expressions   You can use the *((expression))* syntax for logical expressions, although that task is frequently left to *[[expression]]* (next). The next example expands the **age_check** script (page 408) to include logical arithmetic evaluation in addition to arithmetic expansion:

```
$ cat age2
#!/bin/bash
read -p "How old are you? " age
if ((30 < age && age < 60)); then
        echo "Wow, in $((60-age)) years, you'll be 60!"
    else
        echo "You are too young or too old to play."
fi

$ ./age2
How old are you? 25
You are too young or too old to play.
```

The *test-statement* for the **if** structure evaluates two logical comparisons joined by a Boolean AND and returns 0 (*true*) if they are both *true* or 1 (*false*) otherwise.

# LOGICAL EVALUATION (CONDITIONAL EXPRESSIONS)

The syntax of a conditional expression is

>  *[[ expression ]]*

where *expression* is a Boolean (logical) expression. You must precede a variable name with a dollar sign ($) within *expression*. The result of executing this builtin, as with the test builtin, is a return status. The *conditions* allowed within the brackets are almost a superset of those accepted by test (page 983). Where the test builtin uses –a as a Boolean AND operator, *[[ expression ]]* uses &&. Similarly, where test uses –o as a Boolean OR operator, *[[ expression ]]* uses ||.

To see how conditional expressions work, replace the line that tests **age** in the **age2** script with the following conditional expression. You must surround the [[ and ]] tokens with whitespace or a command terminator, and place dollar signs before the variables:

```
if [[ 30 < $age && $age < 60 ]]; then
```

You can also use test's relational operators –gt, –ge, –lt, –le, –eq, and –ne:

```
if [[ 30 -lt $age && $age -lt 60 ]]; then
```

String comparisons The test builtin tests whether strings are equal. The *[[ expression ]]* syntax adds comparison tests for strings. The > and < operators compare strings for order (for example, "aa" < "bbb"). The = operator tests for pattern match, not just equality: *[[ string = pattern ]]* is *true* if **string** matches **pattern**. This operator is not symmetrical; the **pattern** must appear on the right side of the equal sign. For example, [[ artist = a* ]] is *true* (= 0), whereas [[ a* = artist ]] is *false* (= 1):

```
$ [[ artist = a* ]]
$ echo $?
0
$ [[ a* = artist ]]
$ echo $?
1
```

The next example uses a command list that starts with a compound condition. The condition tests whether the directory **bin** and the file **src/myscript.bash** exist. If the result is *true,* cp copies **src/myscript.bash** to **bin/myscript**. If the copy succeeds, chmod makes **myscript** executable. If any of these steps fails, echo displays a message. Implicit command-line continuation (page 1063) obviates the need for backslashes at the ends of lines.

```
$ [[ -d bin && -f src/myscript.bash ]] &&
cp src/myscript.bash bin/myscript &&
chmod +x bin/myscript ||
echo "Cannot make executable version of myscript"
```

# STRING PATTERN MATCHING

The Bourne Again Shell provides string pattern-matching operators that can manipulate pathnames and other strings. These operators can delete from strings prefixes or suffixes that match patterns. Table 27-7 lists the four operators.

**Table 27-7**   String operators

| Operator | Function |
| --- | --- |
| # | Removes minimal matching prefixes |
| ## | Removes maximal matching prefixes |
| % | Removes minimal matching suffixes |
| %% | Removes maximal matching suffixes |

The syntax for these operators is

*${varname op pattern}*

where *op* is one of the operators listed in Table 27-7 and **pattern** is a match pattern similar to that used for filename generation. These operators are commonly used to manipulate pathnames to extract or remove components or to change suffixes:

```
$ SOURCEFILE=/usr/local/src/prog.c
$ echo ${SOURCEFILE#/*/}
local/src/prog.c
$ echo ${SOURCEFILE##/*/}
prog.c
$ echo ${SOURCEFILE%/*}
/usr/local/src
$ echo ${SOURCEFILE%%/*}

$ echo ${SOURCEFILE%.c}
/usr/local/src/prog
$ CHOPFIRST=${SOURCEFILE#/*/}
$ echo $CHOPFIRST
local/src/prog.c
$ NEXT=${CHOPFIRST%%/*}
$ echo $NEXT
local
```

**String length**  The shell expands ${#*name*} to the number of characters in **name**:

```
$ echo $SOURCEFILE
/usr/local/src/prog.c
$ echo ${#SOURCEFILE}
21
```

# ARITHMETIC OPERATORS

Arithmetic expansion and arithmetic evaluation in bash use the same syntax, precedence, and associativity of expressions as the C language. Table 27-8 lists arithmetic operators in order of decreasing precedence (priority of evaluation); each group of operators has equal precedence. Within an expression you can use parentheses to change the order of evaluation.

**Table 27-8**  Arithmetic operators

| Type of operator/operator | Function |
|---|---|
| **Post** | |
| *var*++ Postincrement | |
| *var*-- Postdecrement | |
| **Pre** | |
| ++*var* Preincrement | |
| --*var* Predecrement | |
| **Unary** | |
| − Unary minus | |
| + Unary plus | |

**Table 27-8**   Arithmetic operators (continued)

| Type of operator/operator | Function |
| --- | --- |
| **Negation** | |
| ! | Boolean NOT (logical negation) |
| ~ | Complement (bitwise negation) |
| **Exponentiation** | |
| ** | Exponent |
| **Multiplication, division, remainder** | |
| * | Multiplication |
| / | Division |
| % | Remainder |
| **Addition, subtraction** | |
| + | Addition |
| − | Subtraction |
| **Bitwise shifts** | |
| << | Left bitwise shift |
| >> | Right bitwise shift |
| **Comparison** | |
| <= | Less than or equal |
| >= | Greater than or equal |
| < | Less than |
| > | Greater than |
| **Equality, inequality** | |
| == | Equality |
| != | Inequality |
| **Bitwise** | |
| & | Bitwise AND |
| ^ | Bitwise XOR (exclusive OR) |
| \| | Bitwise OR |

**Table 27-8** Arithmetic operators (continued)

| Type of operator/operator | Function |
| --- | --- |
| **Boolean (logical)** | |
| && | Boolean AND |
| \|\| | Boolean OR |
| **Conditional evaluation** | |
| ? : | Ternary operator |
| **Assignment** | |
| =, *=, /=, %=, +=, −=, <<=, >>=, &=, ^=, \|= | Assignment |
| **Comma** | |
| , | Comma |

Pipeline symbol   The | control operator has higher precedence than arithmetic operators. For example, the command line

```
$ cmd1 | cmd2 || cmd3 | cmd4 && cmd5 | cmd6
```

is interpreted as if you had typed

```
$ ((cmd1 | cmd2) || (cmd3 | cmd4)) && (cmd5 | cmd6)
```

### Do not rely on rules of precedence: use parentheses

tip   Do not rely on the precedence rules when you use command lists (page 162). Instead, use parentheses to explicitly specify the order in which you want the shell to interpret the commands.

Increment and decrement   The postincrement, postdecrement, preincrement, and predecrement operators work with variables. The pre- operators, which appear in front of the variable name (as in **++COUNT** and **−−VALUE**), first change the value of the variable (**++** adds 1; **−−** subtracts 1) and then provide the result for use in the expression. The post- operators appear after the variable name (as in **COUNT++** and **VALUE−−**); they first provide the unchanged value of the variable for use in the expression and then change the value of the variable.

```
$ N=10
$ echo $N
10
$ echo $((--N+3))
12
$ echo $N
9
$ echo $((N++ - 3))
6
$ echo $N
10
```

Remainder   The remainder operator (%) yields the remainder when its first operand is divided by its second. For example, the expression $((15\%7))$ has the value 1.

Ternary   The ternary operator, ? :, decides which of two expressions should be evaluated, based on the value returned by a third expression. The syntax is

*expression1 ? expression2 : expression3*

If *expression1* produces a *false* (0) value, *expression3* is evaluated; otherwise, *expression2* is evaluated. The value of the entire expression is the value of *expression2* or *expression3*, depending on which is evaluated. If *expression1* is *true*, *expression3* is not evaluated. If *expression1* is *false*, *expression2* is not evaluated.

```
$ ((N=10,Z=0,COUNT=1))
$ ((T=N>COUNT?++Z:--Z))
$ echo $T
1
$ echo $Z
1
```

Assignment   The assignment operators, such as +=, are shorthand notations. For example, N+=3 is the same as ((N=N+3)).

Other bases   The following commands use the syntax *base#n* to assign base 2 (binary) values. First v1 is assigned a value of 0101 (5 decimal) and then v2 is assigned a value of 0110 (6 decimal). The echo utility verifies the decimal values.

```
$ ((v1=2#0101))
$ ((v2=2#0110))
$ echo "$v1 and $v2"
5 and 6
```

Next the bitwise AND operator (&) selects the bits that are on in both 5 (0101 binary) and 6 (0110 binary). The result is binary 0100, which is 4 decimal.

```
$ echo $(( v1 & v2 ))
4
```

The Boolean AND operator (&&) produces a result of 1 if both of its operands are nonzero and a result of 0 otherwise. The bitwise inclusive OR operator (|) selects the bits that are on in either 0101 or 0110, resulting in 0111, which is 7 decimal. The Boolean OR operator (||) produces a result of 1 if either of its operands is nonzero and a result of 0 otherwise.

```
$ echo $(( v1 && v2 ))
1
$ echo $(( v1 | v2 ))
7
$ echo $(( v1 || v2 ))
1
```

Next the bitwise exclusive OR operator (^) selects the bits that are on in either, but not both, of the operands 0101 and 0110, yielding 0011, which is 3 decimal. The Boolean NOT operator (!) produces a result of 1 if its operand is 0 and a result of 0 otherwise. Because the exclamation point in $(( ! v1 )) is enclosed within double parentheses, it does not need to be escaped to prevent the shell from interpreting the exclamation point as a history event. The comparison operators produce a result of 1 if the comparison is *true* and a result of 0 otherwise.

```
$ echo $(( v1 ^ v2 ))
3
$ echo $(( ! v1 ))
0
$ echo $(( v1 < v2 ))
1
$ echo $(( v1 > v2 ))
0
```

# IMPLICIT COMMAND-LINE CONTINUATION

Each of the following control operators (page 341) implies continuation:

```
; ;; | & && |& ||
```

For example, there is no difference between this set of commands:

```
cd mydir && rm *.o
```

and this set:

```
cd mydir &&
rm *.o
```

Both sets of commands remove all files with a filename extension of **.o** only if the **cd mydir** command is successful. If you give the second set of commands in an interactive shell, the shell issues a secondary prompt (>; page 362) after you enter the first line and waits for you to complete the command line.

The following commands create the directory named **mydir** if **mydir** does not exist. You can put the commands on one line or two.

```
[ -d mydir ] ||
mkdir mydir
```

Pipeline symbol (|) implies continuation   Similarly the pipeline symbol implies continuation:

```
sort names            |
grep -i '^[a-m]'      |
sed 's/Street/St/'    |
pr --header="Names from A-M"  |
lpr
```

When a command line ends with a pipeline symbol, you do *not* need backslashes to indicate continuation.

```
sort names                     | \
grep -i '^[a-m]'               | \
sed 's/Street/St/'             | \
pr --header="Names from A-M"   | \
lpr
```

Although it will work, the following example is also a poor way to write code because it is hard to read and understand:

```
sort names \
| grep -i '^[a-m]' \
| sed 's/Street/St/' \
| pr --header="Names from A-M" \
| lpr
```

Another way to improve the readability of code you write is to take advantage of implicit command-line continuation to break lines without using backslashes. These commands are easier to read and understand:

```
$ [ -e /home/sam/memos/helen.personnel/november ] &&
~sam/report_a november alphaphonics totals
```

than these commands:

```
$ [ -e /home/sam/memos/helen.personnel/november ] && ~sam/report_a \
november alphaphonics totals
```

# SHELL PROGRAMS

The Bourne Again Shell has many features that make it a good programming language. The structures that bash provides are not a random assortment, but rather have been chosen to provide most of the structural features found in other procedural languages, such as C and Perl. A procedural language provides the following abilities:

- Declare, assign, and manipulate variables and constant data. The Bourne Again Shell provides both string variables, together with powerful string operators, and integer variables, along with a complete set of arithmetic operators.

- Break large problems into small ones by creating subprograms. The Bourne Again Shell allows you to create functions and call scripts from other scripts. Shell functions can be called recursively; that is, a Bourne Again Shell function can call itself. You might not need to use recursion often, but it might allow you to solve some apparently difficult problems with ease.

- Execute statements conditionally using statements such as **if**.

- Execute statements iteratively using statements such as **while** and **for**.
- Transfer data to and from the program, communicating with both data files and users.

Programming languages implement these capabilities in different ways but with the same ideas in mind. When you want to solve a problem by writing a program, you must first figure out a procedure that leads you to a solution—that is, an *algorithm*. Typically you can implement the same algorithm in roughly the same way in different programming languages, using the same kinds of constructs in each language.

Chapter 9 and this chapter have introduced numerous bash features, many of which are useful for both interactive use and shell programming. This section develops two complete shell programs, demonstrating how to combine some of these features effectively. The programs are presented as problems for you to solve, with sample solutions provided.

# A Recursive Shell Script

A recursive construct is one that is defined in terms of itself. Alternately, you might say that a recursive program is one that can call itself. This concept might seem circular, but it need not be. To avoid circularity, a recursive definition must have a special case that is not self-referential. Recursive ideas occur in everyday life. For example, you can define an ancestor as your mother, your father, or one of their ancestors. This definition is not circular; it specifies unambiguously who your ancestors are: your mother or your father, or your mother's mother or father or your father's mother or father, and so on.

A number of Linux system utilities can operate recursively. See the **–R** option to the chmod, chown, and cp utilities for examples.

**Solve the following problem by using a recursive shell function:**

Write a shell function named **makepath** that, given a pathname, creates all components in that pathname as directories. For example, the command **makepath a/b/c/d** should create directories **a**, **a/b**, **a/b/c**, and **a/b/c/d**. (The mkdir –p option creates directories in this manner. Solve the problem without using **mkdir –p**.)

One algorithm for a recursive solution follows:

1. Examine the path argument. If it is a null string or if it names an existing directory, do nothing and return.

2. If the path argument is a simple path component, create it (using mkdir) and return.

3. Otherwise, call **makepath** using the path prefix of the original argument. This step eventually creates all the directories up to the last component, which you can then create using mkdir.

In general, a recursive function must invoke itself with a simpler version of the problem than it was given until it is finally called with a simple case that does not need to call itself. Following is one possible solution based on this algorithm:

**makepath**

```
# This is a function
# Enter it at the keyboard; do not run it as a shell script
#
function makepath()
{
    if [[ ${#1} -eq 0 || -d "$1" ]]
        then
            return 0          # Do nothing
    fi
    if [[ "${1%/*}" = "$1" ]]
        then
            mkdir $1
            return $?
    fi
    makepath ${1%/*} || return 1
    mkdir $1
    return $?
}
```

In the test for a simple component (the **if** statement in the middle of the function), the left expression is the argument after the shortest suffix that starts with a / character has been stripped away (page 1058). If there is no such character (for example, if **$1** is **max**), nothing is stripped off and the two sides are equal. If the argument is a simple filename preceded by a slash, such as **/usr**, the expression **${1%/*}** evaluates to a null string. To make the function work in this case, you must take two precautions: Put the left expression within quotation marks and ensure that the recursive function behaves sensibly when it is passed a null string as an argument. In general, good programs are robust: They should be prepared for borderline, invalid, or meaningless input and behave appropriately in such cases.

By giving the following command from the shell you are working in, you turn on debugging tracing so that you can watch the recursion work:

```
$ set -o xtrace
```

(Give the same command but replace the hyphen with a plus sign [+] to turn debugging off.) With debugging turned on, the shell displays each line in its expanded form as it executes the line. A + precedes each line of debugging output.

In the following example, the first line that starts with + shows the shell calling **makepath**. The **makepath** function is initially called from the command line with arguments of **a/b/c**. It then calls itself with arguments of **a/b** and finally **a**. All the work is done (using mkdir) as each call to **makepath** returns.

```
$ ./makepath a/b/c
+ makepath a/b/c
+ [[ 5 -eq 0 ]]
+ [[ -d a/b/c ]]
+ [[ a/b = \a\/\b\/\c ]]
```

```
+ makepath a/b
+ [[ 3 -eq 0 ]]
+ [[ -d a/b ]]
+ [[ a = \a\/\b ]]
+ makepath a
+ [[ 1 -eq 0 ]]
+ [[ -d a ]]
+ [[ a = \a ]]
+ mkdir a
+ return 0
+ mkdir a/b
+ return 0
+ mkdir a/b/c
+ return 0
```

The function works its way down the recursive path and back up again.

It is instructive to invoke **makepath** with an invalid path and see what happens. The following example, which is run with debugging turned on, tries to create the path **/a/b**. Creating this path requires that you create directory **a** in the root directory. Unless you have permission to write to the root directory, you are not permitted to create this directory.

```
$ ./makepath /a/b
+ makepath /a/b
+ [[ 4 -eq 0 ]]
+ [[ -d /a/b ]]
+ [[ /a = \/\a\/\b ]]
+ makepath /a
+ [[ 2 -eq 0 ]]
+ [[ -d /a ]]
+ [[ '' = \/\a ]]
+ makepath
+ [[ 0 -eq 0 ]]
+ return 0
+ mkdir /a
mkdir: cannot create directory '/a': Permission denied
+ return 1
+ return 1
```

The recursion stops when **makepath** is denied permission to create the **/a** directory. The error returned is passed all the way back, so the original **makepath** exits with nonzero status.

### Use local variables with recursive functions

tip  The preceding example glossed over a potential problem that you might encounter when you use a recursive function. During the execution of a recursive function, many separate instances of that function might be active simultaneously. All but one of them are waiting for their child invocation to complete.

Because functions run in the same environment as the shell that calls them, variables are implicitly shared by a shell and a function it calls. As a consequence, all instances of the function share a single copy of each variable. Sharing variables can give rise to side effects that are rarely what you want. As a rule, you should use local to make all variables of a recursive function local. See page 1040 for more information.

# THE quiz SHELL SCRIPT

Solve the following problem using a bash script:

Write a generic multiple-choice quiz program. The program should get its questions from data files, present them to the user, and keep track of the number of correct and incorrect answers. The user must be able to exit from the program at any time and receive a summary of results to that point.

The detailed design of this program and even the detailed description of the problem depend on a number of choices: How will the program know which subjects are available for quizzes? How will the user choose a subject? How will the program know when the quiz is over? Should the program present the same questions (for a given subject) in the same order each time, or should it scramble them?

Of course, you can make many perfectly good choices that implement the specification of the problem. The following details narrow the problem specification:

- Each subject will correspond to a subdirectory of a master quiz directory. This directory will be named in the environment variable **QUIZDIR**, whose default will be **~/quiz**. For example, you could have the following directories correspond to the subjects engineering, art, and politics: **~/quiz/engineering**, **~/quiz/art**, and **~/quiz/politics**. Put the **quiz** directory in **/usr/games** if you want all users to have access to it (requires **root** privileges).

- Each subject can have several questions. Each question is represented by a file in its subject's directory.

- The first line of each file that represents a question holds the text of the question. If it takes more than one line, you must escape the NEWLINE with a backslash. (This setup makes it easy to read a single question with the read builtin.) The second line of the file is an integer that specifies the number of choices. The next lines are the choices themselves. The last line is the correct answer. Following is a sample question file:

      Who discovered the principle of the lever?
      4
      Euclid
      Archimedes
      Thomas Edison
      The Lever Brothers
      Archimedes

- The program presents all the questions in a subject directory. At any point the user can interrupt the quiz using CONTROL-C, whereupon the program will summarize the results up to that point and exit. If the user does not interrupt the program, the program summarizes the results and exits when it has asked all questions for the chosen subject.

- The program scrambles the questions related to a subject before presenting them.

Following is a top-level design for this program:

1. Initialize. This involves a number of steps, such as setting the counts of the number of questions asked so far and the number of correct and wrong answers to zero. It also sets up the program to trap CONTROL-C.

2. Present the user with a choice of subjects and get the user's response.

3. Change to the corresponding subject directory.

4. Determine the questions to be asked (that is, the filenames in that directory). Arrange them in random order.

5. Repeatedly present questions and ask for answers until the quiz is over or is interrupted by the user.

6. Present the results and exit.

Clearly some of these steps (such as step 3) are simple, whereas others (such as step 4) are complex and worthy of analysis on their own. Use shell functions for any complex step, and use the trap builtin to handle a user interrupt.

Here is a skeleton version of the program with empty shell functions:

```
function initialize
{
# Initializes variables.
}

function choose_subj
{
# Writes choice to standard output.
}

function scramble
{
# Stores names of question files, scrambled,
# in an array variable named questions.
}

function ask
{
# Reads a question file, asks the question, and checks the
# answer. Returns 1 if the answer was correct, 0 otherwise. If it
# encounters an invalid question file, exits with status 2.
}

function summarize
{
# Presents the user's score.
}

# Main program
initialize                              # Step 1 in top-level design

subject=$(choose_subj)                  # Step 2
[[ $? -eq 0 ]] || exit 2                # If no valid choice, exit
```

```
cd $subject || exit 2                    # Step 3
echo                                     # Skip a line
scramble                                 # Step 4

for ques in ${questions[*]}; do          # Step 5
    ask $ques
    result=$?
    (( num_ques=num_ques+1 ))
    if [[ $result == 1 ]]; then
        (( num_correct += 1 ))
    fi
    echo                                 # Skip a line between questions
    sleep ${QUIZDELAY:=1}
done

summarize                                # Step 6
exit 0
```

To make reading the results a bit easier for the user, a sleep call appears inside the question loop. It delays **$QUIZDELAY** seconds (default = 1) between questions.

Now the task is to fill in the missing pieces of the program. In a sense this program is being written backward. The details (the shell functions) come first in the file but come last in the development process. This common programming practice is called top-down design. In top-down design you fill in the broad outline of the program first and supply the details later. In this way you break the problem up into smaller problems, each of which you can work on independently. Shell functions are a great help in using the top-down approach.

One way to write the **initialize** function follows. The cd command causes **QUIZDIR** to be the working directory for the rest of the script and defaults to **~/quiz** if **QUIZDIR** is not set.

```
function initialize ()
{
trap 'summarize ; exit 0' INT       # Handle user interrupts
num_ques=0                          # Number of questions asked so far
num_correct=0                       # Number answered correctly so far
first_time=true                     # true until first question is asked
cd ${QUIZDIR:=~/quiz} || exit 2
}
```

Be prepared for the cd command to fail. The directory might not be searchable or conceivably another user might have removed it. The preceding function exits with a status code of 2 if cd fails.

The next function, **choose_subj**, is a bit more complicated. It displays a menu using a **select** statement:

```
function choose_subj ()
{
subjects=($(ls))
PS3="Choose a subject for the quiz from the preceding list: "
select Subject in ${subjects[*]}; do
    if [[ -z "$Subject" ]]; then
        echo "No subject chosen.  Bye." >&2
        exit 1
    fi
    echo $Subject
    return 0
done
}
```

The function first uses an **ls** command and command substitution to put a list of subject directories in the **subjects** array. Next the **select** structure (page 1012) presents the user with a list of subjects (the directories found by **ls**) and assigns the chosen directory name to the **Subject** variable. Finally the function writes the name of the subject directory to standard output. The main program uses command substitution to assign this value to the **subject** variable [**subject=$(choose_subj)**].

The **scramble** function presents a number of difficulties. In this solution it uses an array variable (**questions**) to hold the names of the questions. It scrambles the entries in an array using the **RANDOM** variable (each time you reference **RANDOM**, it has the value of a [random] integer between 0 and 32767):

```
function scramble ()
{
declare -i index quescount
questions=($(ls))
quescount=${#questions[*]}              # Number of elements
((index=quescount-1))
while [[ $index > 0 ]]; do
    ((target=RANDOM % index))
    exchange $target $index
    ((index -= 1))
done
}
```

This function initializes the array variable **questions** to the list of filenames (questions) in the working directory. The variable **quescount** is set to the number of such files. Then the following algorithm is used: Let the variable index count down from **quescount – 1** (the index of the last entry in the array variable). For each value of **index**, the function chooses a random value target between 0 and **index**, inclusive. The command

```
((target=RANDOM % index))
```

produces a random value between 0 and **index – 1** by taking the remainder (the **%** operator) when **$RANDOM** is divided by **index**. The function then exchanges the elements of **questions** at positions **target** and **index**. It is convenient to take care of this step in another function named **exchange**:

```
function exchange ()
{
temp_value=${questions[$1]}
questions[$1]=${questions[$2]}
questions[$2]=$temp_value
}
```

The **ask** function also uses the **select** structure. It reads the question file named in its argument and uses the contents of that file to present the question, accept the answer, and determine whether the answer is correct. (See the code that follows.)

The **ask** function uses file descriptor 3 to read successive lines from the question file, whose name was passed as an argument and is represented by **$1** in the function. It reads the question into the **ques** variable and the number of questions into **num_opts**. The function constructs the variable **choices** by initializing it to a null string and successively appending the next choice. Then it sets **PS3** to the value of **ques** and uses a **select** structure to prompt the user with **ques**. The **select** structure places the user's answer in **answer**, and the function then checks that response against the correct answer from the file.

The construction of the **choices** variable is done with an eye toward avoiding a potential problem. Suppose that one answer has some whitespace in it—then it might appear as two or more arguments in **choices**. To avoid this problem, make sure that **choices** is an array variable. The **select** statement does the rest of the work:

quiz

```
$ cat quiz
#!/bin/bash

# remove the # on the following line to turn on debugging
# set -o xtrace

#==================
function initialize ()
{
trap 'summarize ; exit 0' INT      # Handle user interrupts
num_ques=0                         # Number of questions asked so far
num_correct=0                      # Number answered correctly so far
first_time=true                    # true until first question is asked
cd ${QUIZDIR:=~/quiz} || exit 2
}


#==================
function choose_subj ()
{
subjects=($(ls))
PS3="Choose a subject for the quiz from the preceding list: "
select Subject in ${subjects[*]}; do
    if [[ -z "$Subject" ]]; then
        echo "No subject chosen.  Bye." >&2
        exit 1
    fi
    echo $Subject
    return 0
done
}
```

```
#==================
function exchange ()
{
temp_value=${questions[$1]}
questions[$1]=${questions[$2]}
questions[$2]=$temp_value
}

#==================
function scramble ()
{
declare -i index quescount
questions=($(ls))
quescount=${#questions[*]}              # Number of elements
((index=quescount-1))
while [[ $index > 0 ]]; do
    ((target=RANDOM % index))
    exchange $target $index
    ((index -= 1))
done
}

#==================
function ask ()
{
exec 3<$1
read -u3 ques || exit 2
read -u3 num_opts || exit 2

index=0
choices=()
while (( index < num_opts )) ; do
    read -u3 next_choice || exit 2
    choices=("${choices[@]}" "$next_choice")
    ((index += 1))
done
read -u3 correct_answer || exit 2
exec 3<&-

if [[ $first_time = true ]]; then
    first_time=false
    echo -e "You may press the interrupt key at any time to quit.\n"
fi

PS3=$ques"  "                          # Make $ques the prompt for select
                                       # and add some spaces for legibility
select answer in "${choices[@]}"; do
    if [[ -z "$answer" ]]; then
            echo  Not a valid choice. Please choose again.
        elif [[ "$answer" = "$correct_answer" ]]; then
            echo "Correct!"
            return 1
        else
            echo "No, the answer is $correct_answer."
            return 0
    fi
done
}
```

```
#==================
function summarize ()
{
echo                               # Skip a line
if (( num_ques == 0 )); then
    echo "You did not answer any questions"
    exit 0
fi

(( percent=num_correct*100/num_ques ))
echo "You answered $num_correct questions correctly, out of \
$num_ques total questions."
echo "Your score is $percent percent."
}

#==================
# Main program
initialize                          # Step 1 in top-level design

subject=$(choose_subj)              # Step 2
[[ $? -eq 0 ]] || exit 2            # If no valid choice, exit

cd $subject || exit 2               # Step 3
echo                                # Skip a line
scramble                            # Step 4

for ques in ${questions[*]}; do     # Step 5
    ask $ques
    result=$?
    (( num_ques=num_ques+1 ))
    if [[ $result == 1 ]]; then
        (( num_correct += 1 ))
    fi
    echo                            # Skip a line between questions
    sleep ${QUIZDELAY:=1}
done

summarize                           # Step 6
exit 0
```

# CHAPTER SUMMARY

The shell is a programming language. Programs written in this language are called shell scripts, or simply scripts. Shell scripts provide the decision and looping control structures present in high-level programming languages while allowing easy access to system utilities and user programs. Shell scripts can use functions to modularize and simplify complex tasks.

Control structures   The control structures that use decisions to select alternatives are **if...then**, **if...then...else**, and **if...then...elif**. The **case** control structure provides a multiway branch and can be used when you want to express alternatives using a simple pattern-matching syntax.

The looping control structures are **for...in**, **for**, **until**, and **while**. These structures perform one or more tasks repetitively.

The **break** and **continue** control structures alter control within loops: **break** transfers control out of a loop, and **continue** transfers control immediately to the top of a loop.

The Here document allows input to a command in a shell script to come from within the script itself.

File descriptors   The Bourne Again Shell provides the ability to manipulate file descriptors. Coupled with the read and echo builtins, file descriptors allow shell scripts to have as much control over input and output as do programs written in lower-level languages.

Variables   By default, variables are local to the process they are declared in; these variables are called *shell variables*. You can use export to cause variables to be *environment variables*, which are available to children of the process they are declared in.

The declare builtin assigns attributes, such as readonly, to bash variables. The Bourne Again Shell provides operators to perform pattern matching on variables, provide default values for variables, and evaluate the length of variables. This shell also supports array variables and local variables for functions and provides built-in integer arithmetic, using the let builtin and an expression syntax similar to that found in the C programming language.

Builtins   Bourne Again Shell builtins include type, read, exec, trap, kill, and getopts. The type builtin displays information about a command, including its location; read allows a script to accept user input.

The exec builtin executes a command without creating a new process. The new command overlays the current process, assuming the same environment and PID number of that process. This builtin executes user programs and other Linux commands when it is *not* necessary to return control to the calling process.

The trap builtin catches a signal sent to the process running the script and allows you to specify actions to be taken upon receipt of one or more signals. You can use this builtin to cause a script to ignore the signal that is sent when the user presses the interrupt key.

The kill builtin terminates a running program. The getopts builtin parses command-line arguments, making it easier to write programs that follow standard Linux conventions for command-line arguments and options.

Utilities in scripts   In addition to using control structures, builtins, and functions, shell scripts generally call Linux utilities. The find utility, for instance, is commonplace in shell scripts that search for files in the system hierarchy and can perform a wide range of tasks.

Expressions   There are two basic types of expressions: arithmetic and logical. Arithmetic expressions allow you to do arithmetic on constants and variables, yielding a numeric result. Logical (Boolean) expressions compare expressions or strings, or test conditions, to yield a *true* or *false* result. As with all decisions within shell scripts, a *true* status is represented by the value 0; *false,* by any nonzero value.

Good programming practices  A well-written shell script adheres to standard programming practices, such as specifying the shell to execute the script on the first line of the script, verifying the number and type of arguments that the script is called with, displaying a standard usage message to report command-line errors, and redirecting all informational messages to standard error.

# EXERCISES

1. Rewrite the **journal** script of Chapter 9 (exercise 5, page 416) by adding commands to verify that the user has write permission for a file named **journal-file** in the user's home directory, if such a file exists. The script should take appropriate actions if **journal-file** exists and the user does not have write permission to the file. Verify that the modified script works.

2. The special parameter "**$@**" is referenced twice in the **out** script (page 989). Explain what would be different if the parameter "**$∗**" were used in its place.

3. Write a filter that takes a list of files as input and outputs the basename (page 1011) of each file in the list.

4. Write a function that takes a single filename as an argument and adds execute permission to the file for the user.

   a. When might such a function be useful?

   b. Revise the script so it takes one or more filenames as arguments and adds execute permission for the user for each file argument.

   c. What can you do to make the function available every time you log in?

   d. Suppose that, in addition to having the function available on subsequent login sessions, you want to make the function available in your current shell. How would you do so?

5. When might it be necessary or advisable to write a shell script instead of a shell function? Give as many reasons as you can think of.

6. Write a shell script that displays the names of all directory files, but no other types of files, in the working directory.

7. Write a script to display the time every 15 seconds. Read the date man page and display the time, using the %r field descriptor. Clear the window (using the clear command) each time before you display the time.

8. Enter the following script named **savefiles**, and give yourself execute permission to the file:

```
$ cat savefiles
#! /bin/bash
echo "Saving files in working directory to the file savethem."
exec > savethem
for i in *
        do
        echo
"================================================="
        echo "File: $i"
        echo
"================================================="
        cat "$i"
        done
```

a. Which error message do you receive when you execute this script? Rewrite the script so that the error does not occur, making sure the output still goes to **savethem**.

b. What might be a problem with running this script twice in the same directory? Discuss a solution to this problem.

9. Read the bash man or info page, try some experiments, and answer the following questions:

   a. How do you export a function?

   b. What does the hash builtin do?

   c. What happens if the argument to exec is not executable?

10. Using the find utility, perform the following tasks:

   a. List all files in the working directory and all subdirectories that have been modified within the last day.

   b. List all files you have read access to on the system that are larger than 1 megabyte.

   c. Remove all files named **core** from the directory structure rooted at your home directory.

   d. List the inode numbers of all files in the working directory whose filenames end in .c.

   e. List all files you have read access to on the root filesystem that have been modified in the last 30 days.

11. Write a short script that tells you whether the permissions for two files, whose names are given as arguments to the script, are identical. If the permissions for the two files are identical, output the common permission field. Otherwise, output each filename followed by its permission field. (*Hint:* Try using the cut utility.)

12. Write a script that takes the name of a directory as an argument and searches the file hierarchy rooted at that directory for zero-length files. Write the names of all zero-length files to standard output. If there is no option on the command line, have the script delete the file after displaying its name, asking the user for confirmation, and receiving positive confirmation. A **–f** (force) option on the command line indicates that the script should display the filename but not ask for confirmation before deleting the file.

# ADVANCED EXERCISES

13. Write a script that takes a colon-separated list of items and outputs the items, one per line, to standard output (without the colons).

14. Generalize the script written in exercise 13 so the character separating the list items is given as an argument to the function. If this argument is absent, the separator should default to a colon.

15. Write a function named **funload** that takes as its single argument the name of a file containing other functions. The purpose of **funload** is to make all functions in the named file available in the current shell; that is, **funload** loads the functions from the named file. To locate the file, **funload** searches the colon-separated list of directories given by the environment variable **FUNPATH**. Assume the format of **FUNPATH** is the same as **PATH** and the search of **FUNPATH** is similar to the shell's search of the **PATH** variable.

16. Rewrite **bundle** (page 1015) so the script it creates takes an optional list of filenames as arguments. If one or more filenames are given on the command line, only those files should be re-created; otherwise, all files in the shell archive should be re-created. For example, suppose all files with the filename extension **.c** are bundled into an archive named **srcshell**, and you want to unbundle just the files **test1.c** and **test2.c**. The following command will unbundle just these two files:

    $ **bash srcshell test1.c test2.c**

17. Which kind of links will the **lnks** script (page 991) not find? Why?

18. In principle, recursion is never necessary. It can always be replaced by an iterative construct, such as **while** or **until**. Rewrite **makepath** (page 1066) as a nonrecursive function. Which version do you prefer? Why?

19. Lists are commonly stored in environment variables by putting a colon (:) between each of the list elements. (The value of the **PATH** variable is an example.) You can add an element to such a list by catenating the new element to the front of the list, as in

    PATH=/opt/bin:$PATH

If the element you add is already in the list, you now have two copies of it in the list. Write a shell function named **addenv** that takes two arguments: (1) the name of a shell variable and (2) a string to prepend to the list that is the value of the shell variable only if that string is not already an element of the list. For example, the call

```
addenv PATH /opt/bin
```

would add **/opt/bin** to **PATH** only if that pathname is not already in **PATH**. Be sure your solution works even if the shell variable starts out empty. Also make sure you check the list elements carefully. If **/usr/opt/bin** is in **PATH** but **/opt/bin** is not, the example just given should still add **/opt/bin** to **PATH**. (*Hint:* You might find this exercise easier to complete if you first write a function **locate_field** that tells you whether a string is an element in the value of a variable.)

20. Write a function that takes a directory name as an argument and writes to standard output the maximum of the lengths of all filenames in that directory. If the function's argument is not a directory name, write an error message to standard output and exit with nonzero status.

21. Modify the function you wrote for exercise 20 to descend all subdirectories of the named directory recursively and to find the maximum length of any filename in that hierarchy.

22. Write a function that lists the number of ordinary files, directories, block special files, character special files, FIFOs, and symbolic links in the working directory. Do this in two different ways:

    a. Use the first letter of the output of **ls –l** to determine a file's type.

    b. Use the file type condition tests of the *[[ expression ]]* syntax to determine a file's type.

23. Modify the **quiz** program (page 1072) so that the choices for a question are randomly arranged.

# 28

# THE PYTHON PROGRAMMING LANGUAGE

## OBJECTIVES

After reading this chapter you should be able to:

▶ Give commands using the Python interactive shell

▶ Write and run a Python program stored in a file

▶ Demonstrate how to instantiate a list and how to remove elements from and add elements to a list

▶ Describe a dictionary and give examples of how it can be used

▶ Describe three Python control structures

▶ Write a Python program that iterates through a list or dictionary

▶ Read from and write to a file

▶ Demonstrate exception processing

▶ Preserve an object using **pickle**()

▶ Write a Python program that uses regular expressions

▶ Define a function and use it in a program

# INTRODUCTION

Python is a friendly and flexible programming language in widespread use everywhere from Fortune 500 companies to large-scale open-source projects. Python is an interpreted language: It translates code into *bytecode* (page 1241) at runtime and executes the bytecode within the Python virtual machine. Contrast Python with the C language, which is a compiled language. C differs from Python in that the C compiler *compiles* C source code into architecture-specific machine code. Python programs are not compiled; you run a Python program the same way you run a bash or Perl script. Because Python programs are not compiled, they are portable between operating systems and architectures. In other words, the same Python program will run on any system to which the Python virtual machine has been ported.

Object oriented   While not required to use the language, Python supports the object-oriented (OO) paradigm. It is possible to use Python with little or no understanding of object-oriented concepts and this chapter covers OO programming minimally while still explaining Python's important features.

Libraries   Python comes with hundreds of prewritten tools that are organized into logical libraries. These libraries are accessible to Python programs, but not loaded into memory at runtime because doing so would significantly increase startup times for Python programs. Entire libraries (or just individual modules) are instead loaded into memory when the program requests them.

Version   Python is available in two main development branches: Python 2.x and Python 3.x. This chapter focuses on Python 2.x because the bulk of Python written today uses 2.x. The following commands show that two versions of Python are installed and that the **python** command runs Python 2.7.5:

```
$ whereis python
python: /usr/bin/python3.3m /usr/bin/python2.7 /usr/bin/python ...
$ ls -l $(which python)
lrwxrwxrwx. 1 root root 7 07-02 12:53 /usr/bin/python -> python2
$ python -V
Python 2.7.5
```

# INVOKING PYTHON

This section discusses the methods you can use to run a Python program.

Interactive shell   Most of the examples in this chapter use the Python interactive shell because you can use it to debug and execute code one line at a time and see the results immediately. Although this shell is handy for testing, it is not a good choice for running longer, more complex programs. You start a Python interactive shell by calling the **python** utility (just as you would start a bash shell by calling bash). The primary Python prompt is **>>>**. When Python requires more input to complete a command, it displays its secondary prompt (**...**).

```
$ python
Python 2.7.5 (default, May 16 2013, 13:44:12)
[GCC 4.8.0 20130412 (Red Hat 4.8.0-2)] on linux2
Type "help", "copyright", "credits" or "license" for more information.
>>>
```

While you are using the Python interactive shell, you can give Python a command by entering the command and pressing RETURN.

```
>>> print 'Good morning!'
Good morning!
```

## Implied display

tip   Within the Python interactive shell, Python displays output from any command line that does not have an action. The output is similar to what **print** would display, although it might not be exactly the same. The following examples show explicit **print** and implicit display actions:

```
>>> print 'Good morning!'
Good morning!
>>> 'Good morning!'
'Good morning!'

>>> print 2 + 2
4
>>> 2 + 2
4
```

Implied display allows you to display the value of a variable by typing its name:

```
>>> x = 'Hello'
>>> x
'Hello'
```

Implied display does not work unless you are running the Python interactive shell (i.e., Python does not invoke an implicit display action when it is run from a file).

Program file   Most of the time a Python program is stored in a text file. Although not required, the file typically has a filename extension of **.py.** Use chmod (page 193) to make the file executable. As explained on page 338, the **#!** at the start of the first line of the file instructs the shell to pass the rest of the file to **/usr/bin/python** for execution.

```
$ chmod 755 gm.py
$ cat gm.py
#!/usr/bin/python
print 'Good morning!'

$ ./gm.py
Good morning!
```

You can also run a Python program by specifying the name of the program file as an argument or as standard input to python.

```
$ python gm.py
Good morning!

$ python < gm.py
Good morning!

$ cat gm.py | python
Good morning!

$ echo "print 'Good morning! '" | python
Good morning!
```

Because the shell interprets an exclamation point immediately followed by a character other than a SPACE as an event number (page 381), the final command includes a SPACE after the exclamation point.

Command line  Using the python –c option, you can run a program from the shell command line. In the preceding and following commands, the double quotation marks keep the shell from removing the single quotation marks from the command line before passing it to Python.

```
$ python -c "print 'Good morning! '"
Good morning!
```

### Single and double quotation marks are functionally equivalent

tip  You can use single quotation marks and double quotation marks interchangeably in a Python program and you can use one to quote the other. When Python displays quotation marks around a string it uses single quotation marks.

```
>>> a = "hi"
>>> a
'hi'
>>> print "'hi'"
'hi'
>>> print '"hi"'
"hi"
```

## MORE INFORMATION

Local  python man page, pydoc program

Python interactive shell  From the Python interactive shell give the command **help()** to use the Python **help** feature. When you call it, this utility displays information to help you get started using it. Alternately, you can give the command **help('*object*')** where *object* is the name of an object you have instantiated or the name of a data structure or module such as **list** or **pickle**.

Web  Python home page: www.python.org
Documentation: docs.python.org
Index of Python Enhancement Proposals (PEPs): www.python.org/dev/peps
PEP 8 Style Guide for Python Code: www.python.org/dev/peps/pep-0008
PyPI (Python Package Index): pypi.python.org

# WRITING TO STANDARD OUTPUT AND READING FROM STANDARD INPUT

**raw_input()**  Python makes it easy to write to standard output and read from standard input, both of which the shell (e.g., bash) connects to the terminal by default. The **raw_input()** function writes to standard output and reads from standard input. It returns the value of the string it reads after stripping the trailing control characters (RETURN-NEWLINE or NEWLINE).

In the following example, **raw_input()** displays its argument (**Enter your name:**) and waits for the user. When the user types something and presses RETURN, Python assigns the value returned by **raw_input()**, which is the string the user entered, to the variable **my_in**.

**print**  Within a **print** statement, a plus sign (**+**) catenates the strings on either side of it. The **print** statement in the example displays **Hello**, the value of **my_in**, and an exclamation point.

```
>>> my_in = raw_input ('Enter your name: ')
Enter your name: Neo
>>> print 'Hello, ' + my_in + '!'
Hello, Neo!
```

# FUNCTIONS AND METHODS

Functions  Functions in Python, as in most programming languages, are key to improving code readability, efficiency, and maintenance. Python has a number of builtin functions and functions you can immediately import into a Python program. These functions are available when you install Python. For example, the **int()** function returns the integer (truncated) part of a floating-point number:

```
>>> int(8.999)
8
```

Additional downloadable libraries hold more functions. For more information refer to "Using Libraries" on page 1103. Table 28-1 lists a few of the most commonly used functions.

**Table 28-1**  Commonly used functions

| Function | What it does |
| --- | --- |
| **exit()** | Exits from a program |
| **float()** | Returns its argument as a floating-point number |
| **help()** | Displays help on the object specified by its argument; without an argument opens interactive help (Python interactive shell only; page 1084) |
| **int()** | Returns the integer (truncated) portion of its argument |
| **len()** | Returns the number of elements in a list or dictionary (page 1089) |
| **map()** | Returns the list that results from applying its first argument (a function) to its remaining arguments (page 1107) |

**Table 28-1**   Commonly used functions (continued)

| Function | What it does |
| --- | --- |
| max() | Returns the maximum value from its argument, which can be a list or other iterable (page 1090) data structure (page 1107) |
| open() | Opens the file in the mode specified by its arguments (page 1097) |
| range() | Returns a list of integers between the two values specified by its arguments (page 1096) |
| raw_input() | Prompts with its argument and returns the string the user enters (page 1085) |
| sorted() | Takes a list (or other iterable data structure) as an argument and returns the same type of data structure with its elements in order |
| type() | Returns the type of its argument (e.g., int, file, method, function) |
| xrange() | Returns a list of integers between the two values specified by its arguments [more efficient than **range()**; page 1096] |

Methods   Functions and methods are very similar. The difference is that functions stand on their own while methods work on and are specific to objects. You will see the **range()** function used by itself [range(*args*)] and the **readall()** method used as an object method [**f.readall**(*args*), where **f** is the object (a file) **readall()** is reading from]. Table 28-2 on page 1089 and Table 28-4 on page 1097 list some methods.

# SCALAR VARIABLES, LISTS, AND DICTIONARIES

This section discusses some of the Python builtin data types. Scalar data types include number and string types. Compound data types include dictionary and list types.

## SCALAR VARIABLES

As in most programming languages, you declare and initialize a variable using an equal sign. Python does not require the SPACEs around the equal sign, nor does it require you to identify a scalar variable with a prefix (Perl and bash require a leading dollar sign). As explained in the tip on page 1083, you can use the **print** function to display the value of a variable or you can just specify the variable name as a command:

```
>>> lunch = 'Lunch time!'
>>> print lunch
Lunch time!
>>> lunch
'Lunch time!'
```

Python performs arithmetic as you might expect:

```
>>> n1 = 5
>>> n2 = 8
>>> n1 + n2
13
```

**Floating-point numbers**  Whether Python performs floating-point or integer arithmetic depends on the values it is given. If all of the numbers involved in a calculation are integers—that is, if none of the numbers includes a decimal point—Python performs integer arithmetic and will truncate answers that include a fractional part. If at least one of the numbers involved in a calculation is a floating-point number (includes a decimal point), Python performs floating-point arithmetic. Be careful when performing division: If the answer could include a fraction, be sure to include a decimal point in one of the numbers or explicitly specify one of the numbers as a floating-point number:

```
>>> 3/2
1
>>> 3/2.0
1.5
>>> float(3)/2
1.5
```

# Lists

A Python list is an object that comprises one or more elements; it is similar to an array in C or Java. Lists are ordered and use zero-based indexing (i.e., the first element of a list is numbered zero). A list is called *iterable* because it can provide successive elements on each iteration through a looping control structure such as **for**; see page 1090 for a discussion.

This section shows one way to instantiate (create) a list. The following commands instantiate and display a list named **a** that holds four values:

```
>>> a = ['bb', 'dd', 'zz', 'rr']
>>> a
['bb', 'dd', 'zz', 'rr']
```

**Indexes**  You can access an element of a list by specifying its index (remember—the first element of a list is numbered zero). The first of the following commands displays the value of the third element of **a**; the next assigns the value of the first element of **a** to **x** and displays the value of **x**.

```
>>> a[2]
'zz'

>>> x = a[0]
>>> x
'bb'
```

When you specify a negative index, Python counts from the end of the array.

```
>>> a[-1]
'rr'

>>> a[-2]
'zz'
```

Replacing an element  You can replace an element of a list by assigning a value to it.

```
>>> a[1] = 'qqqq'
>>> a
['bb', 'qqqq', 'zz', 'rr']
```

Slicing  The next examples show how to access a slice or portion of a list. The first example displays elements 0 up to 2 of the list (elements 0 and 1):

```
>>> a[0:2]
['bb', 'dd']
```

If you omit the number that follows the colon, Python displays from the element with the index specified before the colon through the end of the list. If you omit the number before the colon, Python displays from the beginning of the list up to the element with the number specified after the colon.

```
>>> a[2:]
['zz', 'rr']
>>> a[:2]
['bb', 'dd']
```

You can use negative numbers when slicing a list. The first of the following commands displays element 1 up to the last element of the list (element $-1$); the second displays from the next-to-last element of the list (element $-2$) through the end of the list.

```
>>> a[1:-1]
['dd', 'zz']
>>> a[-2:]
['zz', 'rr']
```

remove()  Following Python's object-oriented paradigm, the list data type includes builtin methods. The **remove(x)** method removes the first element of a list whose value is *x*, and decreases the length of the list by 1. The following command removes the first element of list **a** whose value is **bb**.

```
>>> a.remove('bb')
>>> a
['dd', 'zz', 'rr']
```

append()  The **append(x)** method appends an element whose value is *x* to the list, and increases the length of the list by 1.

```
>>> a.append('mm')
>>> a
['dd', 'zz', 'rr', 'mm']
```

reverse()  The **reverse()** method does not take an argument. It is an efficient method that reverses elements of a list in place, overwriting elements of the list with new values.

```
>>> a.reverse()
>>> a
['mm', 'rr', 'zz', 'dd']
```

sort()  The **sort()** method does not take an argument. It sorts the elements in a list in place, overwriting elements of the list with new values.

```
>>> a.sort()
>>> a
['dd', 'mm', 'rr', 'zz']
```

**sorted()**   If you do not want to alter the contents of the list (or other iterable data structure) you are sorting, use the **sorted()** function. This function returns the sorted list and does not change the original list.

```
>>> b = sorted(a)
>>> a
['mm', 'rr', 'zz', 'dd']
>>> b
['dd', 'mm', 'rr', 'zz']
```

**len()**   The **len()** function returns the number of elements in a list or other iterable data structure.

```
>>> len(a)
4
```

Table 28-2 lists some of the methods that work on lists. The command **help(list)** displays a complete list of methods you can use with a list.

**Table 28-2**    List methods

| Method | What it does |
| --- | --- |
| **append(*x*)** | Appends the value *x* to the list (previous page) |
| **count(*x*)** | Returns the number of times the value *x* occurs in the list |
| **index(*x*)** | Returns the index of the first occurrence of *x* in the list |
| **remove(*x*)** | Removes the first element of a list whose value is *x* (previous page) |
| **reverse()** | Reverses the order of elements in the list (previous page) |
| **sort()** | Sorts the list in place (previous page) |

## WORKING WITH LISTS

Passing a list by reference   Python passes all objects, including lists, by reference. That is, it passes an object by passing a pointer to the object. When you assign one object to another, you are simply creating another name for the object—you are not creating a new object. When you change the object using either name, you can view the change using either name. In the following example, **names** is instantiated as a list that holds the values **sam**, **max**, and **zach**; **copy** is set equal to **names**, setting up another name for (reference to) the same list. When the value of the first element of **copy** is changed, displaying **names** shows that its first element has also changed.

```
>>> names = ['sam', 'max', 'zach']
>>> copy = names
>>> names
['sam', 'max', 'zach']
>>> copy[0] = 'helen'
>>> names
['helen', 'max', 'zach']
```

Copying a list   When you use the syntax $b = a[:]$ to copy a list, each list remains independent of the other. The next example is the same as the previous one, except **copy2** points to a different location than **names** because the list was copied, not passed by reference: Look at the difference in the values of the first element (zero index) of both lists.

```
>>> names = ['sam', 'max', 'zach']
>>> copy2 = names[:]
>>> copy2[0] = 'helen'
>>> names
['sam', 'max', 'zach']
>>> copy2
['helen', 'max', 'zach']
```

## LISTS ARE ITERABLE

An important feature of lists is that they are *iterable,* meaning a control structure such as **for** (page 1095) can loop (iterate) through each item in a list. In the following example, the **for** control structure iterates over the list **a**, assigning one element of **a** to **item** each time through the loop. The loop terminates after it has assigned each of the elements of **a** to **item**. The comma at the end of the **print** statement replaces the NEWLINE **print** normally outputs with a SPACE. You must indent lines within a control structure (called a logical block; page 1092).

```
>>> a
['bb', 'dd', 'zz', 'rr']
>>> for item in a:
...      print item,
...
bb dd zz rr
```

The next example returns the largest element in a list. In this example, the list is embedded in the code; see page 1106 for a similar program that uses random numbers. The program initializes **my_rand_list** as a list holding ten numbers and **largest** as a scalar with a value of –1. The **for** structure retrieves the elements of **my_rand_list** in order, one each time through the loop. It assigns the value it retrieves to **item**. Within the **for** structure, an **if** statement tests to see if **item** is larger than **largest**. If it is, the program assigns the value of **item** to **largest** and displays the new value (so you can see how the program is progressing). When control exits from the **for** structure, the program displays a message and the largest number. Be careful when a logical block (a subblock) appears within another logical block: You must indent the subblock one level more than its superior logical block.

```
$ cat my_max.py
#!/usr/bin/python

my_rand_list = [5, 6, 4, 1, 7, 3, 2, 0, 9, 8]
largest = -1
for item in my_rand_list:
    if (item > largest):
        largest = item
        print largest,
print
print 'largest number is ', largest
```

```
$ ./my_max.py
5 6 7 9
largest number is  9
```

See page 1107 for an easier way to find the maximum value in a list.

# DICTIONARIES

A Python dictionary holds unordered key–value pairs in which the keys must be unique. Other languages refer to this type of data structure as an associative array, hash, or hashmap. Like lists, dictionaries are iterable. A dictionary provides fast lookups. The class name for dictionary is **dict**; thus you must type **help(dict)** to display the help page for dictionaries. Use the following syntax to instantiate a dictionary:

*dict = { key1 : value1, key2 : value2, key3 : value3 ... }*

## WORKING WITH DICTIONARIES

The following example instantiates and displays a telephone extension dictionary named **ext**. Because dictionaries are unordered, Python does not display a dictionary in a specific order and usually does not display it in the order it was created.

```
>>> ext = {'sam': 44, 'max': 88, 'zach': 22}
>>> ext
{'max': 88, 'zach': 22, 'sam': 44}
```

**keys() and values()** You can use the **keys()** and **values()** methods to display all keys or values held in a dictionary:

```
>>> ext.keys()
['max', 'zach', 'sam']
>>> ext.values()
[88, 22, 44]
```

You can add a key–value pair:

```
>>> ext['helen'] = 92
>>> ext
{'max': 88, 'zach': 22, 'sam': 44, 'helen': 92}
```

If you assign a value to a key that is already in the dictionary, Python replaces the value (keys must be unique):

```
>>> ext['max'] = 150
>>> ext
{'max': 150, 'zach': 22, 'sam': 44, 'helen': 92}
```

The following example shows how to remove a key–value pair from a dictionary:

```
>>> del ext['max']
>>> ext
{'zach': 22, 'sam': 44, 'helen': 92}
```

You can also query the dictionary. Python returns the value when you supply the key:

```
>>> ext['zach']
22
```

**items()**   The **items()** method returns key–value pairs as a list of tuples (pairs of values). Because a dictionary is unordered, the order of the tuples returned by **items()** can vary from run to run.

```
>>> ext.items()
[('zach', 22), ('sam', 44), ('helen', 92)]
```

Because dictionaries are iterable, you can loop through them using **for**.

```
>>> ext = {'sam': 44, 'max': 88, 'zach': 22}
>>> for i in ext:
...     print i
...
max
zach
sam
```

Using this syntax, the dictionary returns just keys; it is as though you wrote **for i in ext.keys()**. If you want to loop through values, use **for i in ext.values()**.

Keys and values can be of different types within a dictionary:

```
>>> dic = {500: 2, 'bbbb': 'BBBB', 1000: 'big'}
>>> dic
{1000: 'big', 'bbbb': 'BBBB', 500: 2}
```

# CONTROL STRUCTURES

Control flow statements alter the order of execution of statements within a program. Starting on page 982, Chapter 27 discusses bash control structures in detail and includes flow diagrams of their operation. Python control structures perform the same functions as their bash counterparts, although the two languages use different syntaxes. The description of each control structure in this section references the discussion of the same control structure under bash.

In this section, the **bold italic** words in the syntax description are the items you supply to cause the structure to have the desired effect; the *nonbold italic* words are the keywords Python uses to identify the control structure. Many of these structures use an expression, denoted as *expr,* to control their execution. The examples in this chapter delimit *expr* using parentheses for clarity and consistency; the parentheses are not always required.

Indenting logical   In most programming languages, control structures are delimited by pairs of parentheses, blocks   brackets, or braces; bash uses keywords (e.g., **if...fi, do...done**). Python uses a colon (:) as the opening token for a control structure. While including SPACEs (or TABs) at the beginning of lines in a control structure is good practice in other languages, Python requires these elements; they indicate a *logical block,* or section of code, that is part of a control structure. The last indented line marks the end of the control structure; the change in indent level is the closing token that matches the opening colon.

# if

Similar to the bash **if...then** control structure (page 983), the Python **if** control structure has the following syntax:

*if expr:*

*...*

As with all Python control structures, the control block, denoted by **...**, must be indented.

In the following example, **my_in != ''** (if **my_in** is not an empty string) evaluates to *true* if the user entered something before pressing RETURN. If *expr* evaluates to *true*, Python executes the following indented **print** statement. Python executes any number of indented statements that follow an **if** statement as part of the control structure. If *expr* evaluates to *false*, Python skips any number of indented statements following the **if** statement.

```
$ cat if1.py
#!/usr/bin/python
my_in = raw_input('Enter your name: ')
if (my_in != ''):
    print 'Thank you, ' + my_in
print 'Program running, with or without your input.'

$ ./if1.py
Enter your name: Neo
Thank you, Neo.
Program running, with or without your input.
```

# if...else

Similar to the bash **if...then...else** control structure (page 987), the **if...else** control structure implements a two-way branch using the following syntax:

*if expr:*

*...*

*else:*

*...*

If *expr* evaluates to *true*, Python executes the statements in the **if** control block. Otherwise, it executes the statements in the **else** control block. The following example builds on the previous one, displaying an error message and exiting from the program if the user does not enter something.

```
$ cat if2.py
#!/usr/bin/python
my_in = raw_input('Enter your name: ')
if (my_in != ''):
    print 'Thank you, ' + my_in
else:
    print 'Program requires input to continue.'
    exit()
print 'Program running with your input.'
```

```
$ ./if2.py
Enter your name: Neo
Thank you, Neo
Program running with your input.

$ ./if2.py
Enter your name:
Program requires input to continue.
```

# if...elif...else

Similar to the bash **if...then...elif** control structure (page 989), the Python **if...elif...else** control structure implements a nested set of **if...else** structures using the following syntax:

*if (expr):*

   ...

*elif (expr):*

   ...

*else:*

   ...

This control structure can include as many **elif** control blocks as necessary. In the following example, the **if** statement evaluates the Boolean expression following it within parentheses and enters the indented logical block below the statement if the expression evaluates to *true*. The **if, elif,** and **else** statements are part of one control structure and Python will execute statements in only one of the indented logical blocks.

The **if** and **elif** statements are each followed by a Boolean expression. Python executes each of their corresponding logical blocks only if their expression evaluates to *true*. If none of the expressions evaluates to *true*, control falls through to the **else** logical block.

```
$ cat bignum.py
#!/usr/bin/python
input = raw_input('Please enter a number: ')
if (input == '1'):
    print 'You entered one.'
elif (input == '2'):
    print 'You entered two.'
elif (input == '3'):
    print 'You entered three.'
else:
    print 'You entered a big number...'
print 'End of program.'
```

In the preceding program, even though the user enters an integer/scalar value, Python stores it as a string. Thus each of the comparisons checks whether this value is equal to a string. You can use **int()** to convert a string to an integer. If you do so, you must remove the quotation marks from around the values:

```
...
input = int(raw_input('Please enter a number: '))
if (input == 1):
    print 'You entered one.'
...
```

# while

The **while** control structure (page 999) evaluates a Boolean expression and continues execution while the expression evaluates to *true*. The following program, run using the Python interactive shell, displays 0 through 9. As you enter the command, Python displays its secondary prompt (**...**) when it requires more input to complete a statement; you must still enter SPACE or TAB characters to indent the logical block.

First, the program initializes **count** to 0. The first time through the loop, the **while** expression evaluates to *true* and Python executes the indented statements that make up the **while** control structure logical block. The comma at the end of the **print** statement causes **print** to output a SPACE instead of a NEWLINE after each string, and the **count += 1** statement increments **count** each time through the loop. When control reaches the bottom of the loop, Python returns control to the **while** statement, where **count** is now 1. The loop continues while **count** is less than or equal to 10. When **count** equals 11, the **while** statement evaluates to *false* and control passes to the first statement after the logical block (the first statement that is not indented; there is none in this example).

```
>>> count = 0
>>> while (count <= 10):
...     print count,
...     count += 1
...
0 1 2 3 4 5 6 7 8 9 10
```

### Be careful not to create an infinite loop

tip  It is easy to accidentally create an infinite loop using a **while** statement. Ensure there is a reachable exit condition (e.g., a counter is compared to a finite value *and* the counter is incremented each time through the loop).

# for

The **for** control structure (page 997) assigns values from a list, string, or other iterable data structure (page 1090) to a loop index variable each time through the loop.

Lists are iterable  In the following example, **lis** is a list that holds the names of four types of animals. The **for** statement iterates through the elements of **lis** in order, starting with **turkey**, and assigning a value to **nam** each time it is called. The **print** statement in the logical block displays the value of **nam** each time through the loop. Python exits from the logical block when it runs out of elements in **lis**.

```
>>> lis = ['turkey', 'pony', 'dog', 'fox']
>>> for nam in lis:
...     print nam
...
turkey
pony
dog
fox
```

Strings are iterable  The next example demonstrates that strings are iterable. The string named **string** holds **My name is Sam.** and the **for** statement iterates through **string**, assigning one character to **char** each time through the loop. The **print** statement displays each character; the comma causes **print** to put a SPACE after each character instead of a NEWLINE.

```
>>> string = 'My name is Sam.'
>>> for char in string:
...     print char,
...
M y   n a m e   i s   S a m .
```

range()  The **range()** function returns a list that holds the integers between the two values specified as its arguments, including the first but excluding the last. An optional third parameter defines a step value.

```
>>> range(1,6)
[1, 2, 3, 4, 5]
>>> range(0,10,3)
[0, 3, 6, 9]
```

The next example shows how to use **range()** in a **for** loop. In this example, **range()** returns a list comprising 0, 3, 6, and 9. The **for** control structure loops over these values, executing the indented statement each time through the loop.

```
>>> for cnt in range(0,10,3):
...     print cnt
...
0
3
6
9
```

**optional**

xrange()  The **range()** function is useful for generating short lists but, because it stores the list it returns in memory, it takes up a lot of system resources when it generates longer lists. In contrast, **xrange()** has a fixed memory footprint that is independent of the length of the list it returns; as a consequence, it uses fewer system resources than **range()** when working with long lists.

The two functions work differently. Whereas **range()** fills a list with values and stores that list in memory, **xrange()** works only when you iterate through the values it returns: The entire list is never stored in memory.

```
>>> range(1,11)
[1, 2, 3, 4, 5, 6, 7, 8, 9, 10]
>>> xrange(1,11)
xrange(1, 11)

>>> for cnt in xrange(1,11):
...     print cnt,
...
1 2 3 4 5 6 7 8 9 10
```

# READING FROM AND WRITING TO FILES

Python allows you to work with files in many ways. This section explains how to read from and write to text files and how to preserve an object in a file using **pickle**.

## FILE INPUT AND OUTPUT

**open()**   The **open()** function opens a file and returns a file object called a *file handle*; it can open a file in one of several modes (Table 28-3). Opening a file in **w** (write) mode truncates the file; use **a** (append) mode if you want to add to a file. The following statement opens the file in Max's home directory named **test_file** in read mode; the file handle is named **f**.

```
f = open('/home/max/test_file', 'r')
```

**Table 28-3**   File modes

| Mode | What it does |
|---|---|
| r | **Read only**   Error if file does not exist. |
| w | **Write only**   File is created if it does not exist. File is truncated if it exists. |
| r+ | **Read and write**   File is created if it does not exist. |
| a | **Append**   File is created if it does not exist. |
| a+ | **Append and read**   File is created if it does not exist. |
| b | **Binary**   Append to **r** or **w** to work with binary files. |

Once the file is opened, you direct input and output using the file handle with one of the methods listed in Table 28-4. When you are finished working with a file, use **close()** to close it and free the resources the open file is using.

**Table 28-4**   File object methods

| Method | Arguments | Returns or action |
|---|---|---|
| **close()** | None | Closes the file |
| **isatty()** | None | Returns *true* if the file is connected to a terminal; *false* otherwise |
| **read()** | Maximum number of bytes to read (optional) | Reads until EOF or specified maximum number of bytes; returns file as a string |
| **readline()** | Maximum number of bytes to read (optional) | Reads until NEWLINE or specified maximum number of bytes; returns line as a string |
| **readlines()** | Maximum number of bytes to read (optional) | Calls **readline()** repeatedly and returns a list of lines (iterable) |
| **write(str)** | String to be written | Writes to the file |
| **writelines(strs)** | List of strings | Calls **write()** repeatedly, once with each item in the list |

The following example reads from **/home/max/test_file**, which holds three lines. It opens this file in read mode and assigns the file handle **f** to the open file. It uses the **readlines()** method, which reads the entire file into a list and returns that list. Because the list is iterable, Python passes to the **for** control structure one line from **test_file** each time through the loop. The **for** structure assigns the string value of this line to **ln**, which **print** then displays. The **strip()** method removes whitespace and/or a NEWLINE from the end of a line. Without **strip()**, **print** would output two NEWLINES: the one that terminates the line from the file and the one it automatically appends to each line it outputs. After reading and displaying all lines from the file, the example closes the file.

```
>>> f = open('/home/max/test_file', 'r')
>>> for ln in f.readlines():
...     print ln.strip()
...
This is the first line
and here is the second line
of this file.
>>> f.close()
```

The next example opens the same file in append mode and writes a line to it using **write()**. The **write()** method does not append a NEWLINE to the line it outputs, so you must terminate the string you write to the file with a **\n**.

```
>>> f = open('/home/max/test_file','a')
>>> f.write('Extra line!\n')
>>> f.close()
```

**optional**   In the example that uses **for**, Python does not call the **readlines()** method each time through the **for** loop. Instead, it reads the file into a list the first time **readlines()** is called and then iterates over the list, setting **ln** to the value of the next line in the list each time it is called subsequently. It is the same as if you had written

```
>>> f = open('/home/max/test_file', 'r')
>>> lines = f.readlines()
>>> for ln in lines:
...     print ln.strip()
```

It is more efficient to iterate over the file handle directly because this technique does not store the file in memory.

```
>>> f = open('/home/max/test_file', 'r')
>>> for ln in f:
...     print ln.strip()
```

## EXCEPTION HANDLING

An *exception* is an error condition that changes the normal flow of control in a program. Although you can try to account for every problem your code will need to deal with, it is not always possible to do so: Unknown circumstances might arise. What if the file the previous programs opened does not exist? Python raises an IOError (input/output error) number 2 and displays the message **No such file or directory**.

```
>>> f = open('/home/max/test_file', 'r')
Traceback (most recent call last):
  File "<stdin>", line 1, in <module>
IOError: [Errno 2] No such file or directory: '/home/max/test_file'
```

Instead of allowing Python to display what might be an incomprehensible error message and quit, a well-written program handles exceptions like this one gracefully. Good exception handling can help you debug a program and can also provide a nontechnical user with clear information about why the program failed.

The next example wraps the **open** statement that failed with an exception handler in the form of a **try...except** control structure. This structure attempts to execute the **try** block. If execution of the **try** block fails (has an exception), it executes the code in the **except** block. If execution of the **try** block succeeds, it skips the **except** block. Depending on the severity of the error, the **except** block should warn the user that something might not be right or should display an error message and exit from the program.

```
>>> try:
...     f = open('/home/max/test_file', 'r')
... except:
...     print "Error on opening the file."
...
Error on opening the file.
```

You can refine the type of error an **except** block handles. Previously, the **open** statement returned an IOError. The following program tests for an IOError when it attempts to open a file, displays an error message, and exits. If it does not encounter an IOError, it continues normally.

```
$ cat except1.py
#!/usr/bin/python
try:
    f = open('/home/max/test_file', 'r')
except IOError:
    print "Cannot open file."
    exit()
print "Processing file."

$ ./except1.py
Cannot open file.
$
$ touch test_file
$ ./except1.py
Processing file.
```

# PICKLE

The **pickle** module allows you to store an object in a file in a standard format for later use by the same or a different program. The object you store can be any type of object as long as it does not require an operating system resource such as a file handle or network socket. The standard **pickle** filename extension is **.p**. For more information visit wiki.python.org/moin/UsingPickle.

## Never unpickle data received from an untrusted source

security   The **pickle** module is not secure against maliciously constructed data. When you unpickle an object, you are trusting the person who created it. Do not unpickle an object if you do not know or trust its source.

This section discusses two **pickle** methods: **dump**(), which writes an object to disk, and **load**(), which reads an object from disk. The syntax for these methods is

> *pickle.dump(**objectname**, open(**filename**, 'wb'))*

> *pickle.load(**objectname**, open(**filename**, 'rb'))*

It is critical that you open the file in binary mode (**wb** and **rb**). The **load**() method returns the object; you can assign the object the same name as or a different name from the original object. Before you can use **pickle**, you must import it (page 1105).

In the following example, after importing **pickle**, **pickle.dump**() creates a file named **pres.p** in **wb** (write binary) mode with a dump of the **preserves** list, and **exit**() leaves the Python interactive shell:

```
>>> import pickle

>>> preserves = ['apple', 'cherry', 'blackberry', 'apricot']
>>> preserves
['apple', 'cherry', 'blackberry', 'apricot']
>>> pickle.dump(preserves, open('pres.p', 'wb'))
exit()
```

The next example calls the Python interactive shell and **pickle.load**() reads the **pres.p** file in **rb** (read binary) mode. This method returns the object you originally saved using **dump**(). You can give the object any name you like.

```
$ python
...
>>> import pickle

>>> jams = pickle.load(open('pres.p', 'rb'))
>>> jams
['apple', 'cherry', 'blackberry', 'apricot']
```

# REGULAR EXPRESSIONS

The Python **re** (regular expression) module handles regular expressions. Python regular expressions follow the rules covered in Appendix A. This section discusses a few of the tools in the Python **re** library. You must give the command **import re** before you can use the **re** methods. To display Python help on the re module, give the command **help()** from the Python interactive shell and then type **re**.

**findall()**   One of the simplest **re** methods is **findall()**, which returns a list that holds matches using the following syntax:

> *re.findall(**regex**, **string**)*

where **regex** is the regular expression and **string** is the string you are looking for a match in.

The **regex** in the following example (**hi**) matches the three occurrences of **hi** in the **string** (hi hi hi hello).

```
>>> import re
>>> a = re.findall('hi', 'hi hi hi hello')
>>> print a
['hi', 'hi', 'hi']
```

Because **findall()** returns a list (it is iterable), you can use it in a **for** statement. The following example uses the period (.) special character, which, in a regular expression, matches any character. The **regex** (**hi.**) matches the three occurrences of **hi** followed by any character in the **string**.

```
>>> for mat in re.findall('hi.', 'hit him hid hex'):
...     print mat,
...
hit him hid
```

**search()**   The **search()** re method uses the same syntax as **findall()** and looks through **string** for a match to **regex**. Instead of returning a list if it finds a match, however, it returns a MatchObject. Many **re** methods return a MatchObject (and not a list) when they find a match for the **regex** in the **string**.

```
>>> a = re.search('hi.', 'bye hit him hex')
>>> print a
<_sre.SRE_Match object at 0xb7663a30>
```

**bool()**   The **bool()** function returns *true* or *false* based on its argument. Because you can test the MatchObject directly, **bool()** is not used often in Python programming, but is included here for its instructional value. A MatchObject evaluates to *true* because it indicates a match. [Although **findall()** does not return a MatchObject, it does evaluate to *true* when it finds a match.]

```
>>> bool(a)
True
```

**group()**   The **group()** method allows you to access the match a MatchObject holds.

```
>>> a.group(0)
'hit'
```

**type()**   When no match exists, **search()** returns a NoneType object [as shown by the **type()** function], which evaluates to **None** or in a Boolean expression evaluates to *false*.

```
>>> a = re.search('xx.', 'bye hit him hex')
>>> type(a)
<type 'NoneType'>
>>> print a
None
>>> bool(a)
False
```

Because a **re** method in a Boolean context evaluates to *true* or *false*, you can use a **re** method as the expression an **if** statement evaluates. The next example uses **search()** as the expression in an **if** statement; because there is a match, **search()** evaluates as *true*, and Python executes the **print** statement.

```
>>> name = 'sam'
>>> if(re.search(name,'zach max sam helen')):
...     print 'The list includes ' + name
...
The list includes sam
```

**match()**   The **match()** method of the re object uses the same syntax as **search()**, but looks only at the beginning of *string* for a match to *regex*.

```
>>> name = 'zach'
>>> if(re.match(name,'zach max sam helen')):
...     print 'The list includes ' + name
...
The list includes zach
```

# Defining a Function

A Python function definition must be evaluated before the function is called, so it generally appears in the code before the call to the function. The contents of the function, as with other Python logical blocks, must be indented. The syntax of a function definition is

> *def my_function(args):*
>
> ...

Python passes lists and other data structures to a function by reference (page 1089), meaning that when a function modifies a data structure that was passed to it as an argument, it modifies the original data structure. The following example demonstrates this fact:

```
>>> def add_ab(my_list):
...     my_list.append('a')
...     my_list.append('b')
...
>>> a = [1,2,3]
>>> add_ab(a)
>>> a
[1, 2, 3, 'a', 'b']
```

You can pass arguments to a function in three ways. Assume the function **place_stuff** is defined as follows. The values assigned to the arguments in the function definition are defaults.

```
>>> def place_stuff(x = 10, y = 20, z = 30):
...     return x, y, z
...
```

If you call the function and specify arguments, the function uses those arguments:

```
>>> place_stuff(1,2,3)
(1, 2, 3)
```

If you do not specify arguments, the function uses the defaults:

```
>>> place_stuff()
(10, 20, 30)
```

Alternately, you can specify values for some or all of the arguments:

```
>>> place_stuff(z=100)
(10, 20, 100)
```

# Using Libraries

This section discusses the Python standard library, nonstandard libraries, and Python namespace, as well as how to import and use a function.

## Standard Library

The Python standard library, which is usually included in packages installed with Python, provides a wide range of facilities, including functions, constants, string services, data types, file and directory access, cryptographic services, and file formats. Visit docs.python.org/library/index.html for a list of the contents of the standard library.

## Nonstandard Libraries

In some cases a module you want might be part of a library that is not included with Python. You can usually find what you need in the Python Package Index (PyPI; pypi.python.org), a repository of more than 22,000 Python packages.

You can find lists of modules for the distribution you are using by searching the Web for *distro* **package database**, where *distro* is the name of the Linux distribution you are using, and then searching one of the databases for **python**.

## SciPy and NumPy Libraries

Two popular libraries are SciPy and NumPy. The SciPy ("Sigh Pie"; scipy.org) library holds Python modules for mathematics, science, and engineering. It depends on NumPy (numpy.scipy.org), a library of Python modules for scientific computing.

You must download and install the package that holds NumPy before you can use any of its modules. Under Debian/Ubuntu/Mint and openSuSE, the package is named **python-numpy**; under Fedora/RHEL, it is named **numpy**. See page 534 for instructions on downloading and installing packages. Alternately, you can obtain the libraries from scipy.org or pypi.python.org. Once you import SciPy (**import scipy**), **help(scipy)** will list the functions you can import individually.

## Namespace

A *namespace* comprises a set of names (identifiers) in which all names are unique. For example, the namespace for a program might include an object named **planets**. You might instantiate **planets** as an integer:

```
>>> planets = 5
>>> type(planets)
<type 'int'>
```

Although it is not good programming practice, later on in the program you could assign **planets** a string value. It would then be an object of type string.

```
>>> planets = 'solar system'
>>> type(planets)
<type 'str'>
```

You could make **planets** a function, a list, or another type of object. Regardless, there would always be only one object named **planets** (identifiers in a namespace must be unique).

When you import a module (including a function), Python can merge the namespace of the module with the namespace of your program, creating a conflict. For example, if you import the function named **sample** from the library named **random** and then define a function with the same name, you will no longer be able to access the original function:

```
>>> from random import sample
>>> sample(range(10), 10)
[6, 9, 0, 7, 3, 5, 2, 4, 1, 8]
>>> def sample(a, b):
...     print 'Problem?'
...
```

```
>>> sample(range(10), 10)
Problem?
```

The next section discusses different ways you can import objects from a library and steps you can take to avoid the preceding problem.

## IMPORTING A MODULE

You can import a module in one of several ways. How you import the module determines whether Python merges the namespace of the module with that of your program.

The simplest thing to do is to import the whole module. In this case Python does not merge the namespaces but allows you to refer to an object from the module by prefixing its name with the name of the module. The following code imports the **random** module. Using this syntax, the function named **sample** is not defined: You must call it as **random.sample**.

```
>>> import random
>>> sample(range(10), 10)
Traceback (most recent call last):
  File "<stdin>", line 1, in <module>
NameError: name 'sample' is not defined

>>> random.sample(range(10), 10)
[1, 0, 6, 9, 8, 3, 2, 7, 5, 4]
```

This setup allows you to define your own function named **sample**. Because Python has not merged the namespaces from your program and the module named **random**, the two functions can coexist.

```
>>> def sample(a, b):
...     print 'Not a problem.'
...
>>> sample(1, 2)
Not a problem.
>>> random.sample(range(10), 10)
[2, 9, 6, 5, 1, 3, 4, 0, 7, 8]
```

*Importing part of a module*   Another way to import a module is to specify the module and the object.

```
>>> from random import sample
```

When you import an object using this syntax, you import only the function named **sample**; no other objects from that module will be available. This technique is very efficient. However, Python merges the namespaces from your program and from the object, which can give rise to the type of problem illustrated in the previous section.

You can also use **from** *module* **import** *. This syntax imports all names from *module* into the namespace of your program; it is generally not a good idea to use this technique.

# EXAMPLE OF IMPORTING A FUNCTION

The **my_max.py** program on page 1090 finds the largest element in a predefined list. The following program works the same way, except at runtime it fills a list with random numbers.

The following command imports the **sample()** function from the standard library module named **random**. You can install an object from a nonstandard library, such as NumPy, the same way.

```
from random import sample
```

After importing this function, the command **help(sample)** displays information about **sample()**. The **sample()** function has the following syntax:

*sample(list, number)*

where *list* is a list holding the population, or values **sample()** can return, and *number* is the number of random numbers in the list **sample()** returns.

```
>>> sample([0, 1, 2, 3, 4, 5, 6, 7, 8, 9], 4)
[7, 1, 2, 5]
>>> sample([0, 1, 2, 3, 4, 5, 6, 7, 8, 9], 6)
[0, 5, 4, 1, 3, 7]
```

The following program uses the **range()** function (page 1096), which returns a list holding the numbers from 0 through 1 less than its argument:

```
>>> range(8)
[0, 1, 2, 3, 4, 5, 6, 7]
>>> range(16)
[0, 1, 2, 3, 4, 5, 6, 7, 8, 9, 10, 11, 12, 13, 14, 15]
```

When you combine the two functions, **range()** provides a list of values and **sample()** selects values randomly from that list.

```
>>> sample(range(100),10)
[5, 32, 70, 93, 74, 29, 90, 7, 30, 11]
```

In the following program, **sample** generates a list of random numbers and **for** iterates through them.

```
$ cat my_max2.py
#!/usr/bin/python

from random import sample
my_rand_list = sample(range(100), 10)
print 'Random list of numbers:', my_rand_list
largest = -1
for item in my_rand_list:
        if (item > largest):
                largest = item
                print largest,
print
print 'largest number is ', largest
```

```
$ ./my_max2.py
random list of numbers: [67, 40, 1, 29, 9, 49, 99, 95, 77, 51]
67 99
largest number is  99
$ ./my_max2.py
random list of numbers: [53, 33, 76, 35, 71, 13, 75, 58, 74, 50]
53 76
largest number is  76
```

**max()**  The algorithm used in this example is not the most efficient way of finding the maximum value in a list. It is more efficient to use the **max()** builtin function.

```
>>> from random import sample
>>> max(sample(range(100), 10))
96
```

optional

# LAMBDA FUNCTIONS

Python supports *Lambda* functions—functions that might not be bound to a name. You might also see them referred to as *anonymous* functions. Lambda functions are more restrictive than other functions because they can hold only a single expression. In its most basic form, Lambda is another syntax for defining a function. In the following example, the object named **a** is a Lambda function and performs the same task as the function named **add_one**:

```
>>> def add_one(x):
...       return x + 1
...
>>> type (add_one)
<type 'function'>

>>> add_one(2)
3

>>> a = lambda x: x + 1
>>> type(a)
<type 'function'>

>>> a(2)
3
```

**map()**  You can use the Lambda syntax to define a function inline as an argument to a function such as **map()** that expects another function as an argument. The syntax of the **map()** function is

*map(func, seq1[, seq2, ...])*

where *func* is a function that is applied to the sequence of arguments represented by *seq1* (and *seq2* ...). Typically the sequences that are arguments to **map()** and the object returned by **map**() are lists. The next example first defines a function named **times_two**():

```
>>> def times_two(x):
...     return x * 2
...
>>> times_two(8)
16
```

Next, the **map**() function applies **times_two**() to a list:

```
>>> map(times_two, [1, 2, 3, 4])
[2, 4, 6, 8]
```

You can define an inline Lambda function as an argument to **map**(). In this example the Lambda function is not bound to a name.

```
>>> map(lambda x: x * 2, [1, 2, 3, 4])
[2, 4, 6, 8]
```

# LIST COMPREHENSIONS

List comprehensions apply functions to lists. For example, the following code, which does not use a list comprehension, uses **for** to iterate over items in a list:

```
>>> my_list = []
>>> for x in range(10):
...     my_list.append(x + 10)
...
>>> my_list
[10, 11, 12, 13, 14, 15, 16, 17, 18, 19]
```

You can use a list comprehension to perform the same task neatly and efficiently. The syntax is similar, but a list comprehension is enclosed within square brackets and the operation (**x + 10**) precedes the iteration [**for x in range**(10)].

```
>>> my_list = [x + 10 for x in range(10)]
>>> my_list
[10, 11, 12, 13, 14, 15, 16, 17, 18, 19]
```

The results when using a **for** structure and a list comprehension are the same. The next example uses a list comprehension to fill a list with powers of 2:

```
>>> potwo = [2**x for x in range(1, 13)]
>>> print potwo
[2, 4, 8, 16, 32, 64, 128, 256, 512, 1024, 2048, 4096]
```

The next list comprehension fills a list with even numbers. The **if** clause returns values only if the remainder after dividing a number by 2 is 0 (if **x % 2 == 0**).

```
>>> [x for x in range(1,11) if x % 2 == 0]
[2, 4, 6, 8, 10]
```

The final example shows nested list comprehensions. It nests **for** loops and uses **x + y** to catenate the elements of both lists in all combinations.

```
>>> A = ['a', 'b', 'c']
>>> B = ['1', '2', '3']
>>> all = [x + y for x in A for y in B]
>>> print all
['a1', 'a2', 'a3', 'b1', 'b2', 'b3', 'c1', 'c2', 'c3']
```

# CHAPTER SUMMARY

Python is an interpreted language: It translates code into bytecode at runtime and executes the bytecode within the Python virtual machine. You can run a Python program from the Python interactive shell or from a file. The Python interactive shell is handy for development because you can use it to debug and execute code one line at a time and see the results immediately. Within the Python interactive shell, Python displays output from any command line that does not have an action. From this shell you can give the command **help**() to use the Python **help** feature or you can give the command **help**('*object*') to display help on *object*.

Functions help improve code readability, efficiency, and expandability. Many functions are available when you first call Python (builtin functions) and many more are found in libraries that you can download and/or import. Methods are similar to functions except they work on objects whereas functions stand on their own. Python allows you to define both normal functions and nameless functions called Lambda functions.

Python enables you to read from and write to files in many ways. The **open**() function opens a file and returns a file object called a file handle. Once the file is opened, you direct input and output using the file handle. When you are finished working with a file, it is good practice to close it. The **pickle** module allows you to store an object in a file in a standard format for later use by the same or a different program.

A Python list is an object that comprises one or more elements; it is similar to an array in C or Java. An important feature of lists is that they are *iterable*, meaning a control structure such as **for** can loop (iterate) through each item in a list. A Python dictionary holds unordered key–value pairs in which the keys are unique. Like lists, dictionaries are iterable.

Python implements many control structures, including **if...else, if...elif...else, while,** and **for.** Unlike most languages, Python requires SPACEs (or TABs) at the beginning of lines in a control structure. The indented code marks a *logical block*, or section of code, that is part of the control structure.

Python regular expressions are implemented by the Python **re** (regular expression) module. You must give the command **import re** before you can use the **re** methods.

# EXERCISES

1. What is meant by implied display? Is it available in the Python interactive shell or from a program file? Provide a simple example of implied display.

2. Write and run a Python program that you store in a file. The program should demonstrate how to prompt the user for input and display the string the user entered.

3. Using the Python interactive shell, instantiate a list that holds three-letter abbreviations for the first six months of the year and display the list.

4. Using the Python interactive shell, use a **for** control structure to iterate through the elements of the list you instantiated in exercise 3 and display each abbreviated name followed by a period on a line by itself. (*Hint:* The period is a string.)

5. Using the Python interactive shell, put the elements of the list you instantiated in exercise 3 in alphabetical order.

6. Instantiate a dictionary in which the keys are the months in the third quarter of the year and the values are the number of days in the corresponding month. Display the dictionary, the keys, and the values. Add the tenth month of the year to the dictionary and display the value of that month only.

7. What does *iterable* mean? Name two builtin objects that are iterable. Which control structure can you use to loop through an iterable object?

8. Write and demonstrate a Lambda function named **stg**() that appends .txt to its argument. What happens when you call the function with an integer?

# ADVANCED EXERCISES

9. Define a function named **cents** that returns its argument divided by 100 and truncated to an integer. For example:

```
>>> cents(12345)
123
```

10. Define a function named **cents2** that returns its argument divided by 100 exactly (and includes decimal places if necessary). Make sure your function does not truncate the answer. For example:

```
>>> cents2(12345)
123.45
```

11. Create a list that has four elements. Make a copy of the list and change one of the elements in the copy. Show that the same element in the original list did not change.

12. Why does the following assignment statement generate an error?

```
>>> x.y = 5
Traceback (most recent call last):
    File "<stdin>", line 1, in <module>
NameError: name 'x' is not defined
```

13. Call **map()** with two arguments:
    1. A Lambda function that returns the square of the number it was called with
    2. A list holding the even numbers between 4 and 15; generate the list inline using **range()**

14. Use a list comprehension to display the numbers from 1 through 30 inclusive that are divisible by 3.

15. Write a function that takes an integer, **val**, as an argument. The function asks the user to enter a number. If the number is greater than **val**, the function displays **Too high.** and returns 1; if the number is less than **val**, the function displays **Too low.** and returns −1; if the number equals **val**, the function displays **Got it!** and returns 0. Call the function repeatedly until the user enters the right number.

16. Rewrite exercise 15 to call the function with a random number between 0 and 10 inclusive. (*Hint:* The **randint** function in the **random** library returns a random number between its two arguments inclusive.)

17. Write a function that counts the characters in a string the user inputs. Then write a routine that calls the function and displays the following output.

```
$ ./count_letters.py
Enter some words: The rain in Spain
The string "The rain in Spain" has  17 characters in it.
```

18. Write a function that counts the vowels (**aeiou**) in a string the user inputs. Make sure it counts upper- and lowercase vowels. Then write a routine that calls the function and displays the following output.

```
$ ./count_vowels.py
Enter some words: Go East young man!
The string "Go East young man!" has  6 vowels in it.
```

19. Write a function that counts all the characters and the vowels in a string the user inputs. Then write a routine that calls the function and displays the following output.

```
$ ./count_all.py
Enter some words: The sun rises in the East and sets in the West.
13 letters in 47 are vowels.
```

# 29

# THE MARIADB SQL
# DATABASE
# MANAGEMENT SYSTEM

## OBJECTIVES

After reading this chapter you should be able to:

▶ Explain what SQL is and how it relates to MariaDB

▶ Explain what a database, table, row, and column are and the relationship between them

▶ Install a MariaDB server and client on the local system

▶ Set up MariaDB, including a ~/.my.cnf file for a user

▶ Create a database and add a user

▶ Add data to and retrieve data from the database

▶ Modify data in the database

▶ Add a second table and write joins to retrieve data from both tables

1113

# HISTORY

MySQL    MySQL (My Structured Query Language) is an implementation of SQL. It is the world's most popular open-source RDBMS (relational database management system). It is extremely fast and is used by some of the most frequently visited Web sites on the Internet, including Google, Facebook, Twitter, Yahoo, YouTube, and Wikipedia. Recently, however, some of these companies have moved to MariaDB, which is explained next. Fedora/RHEL has replaced MySQL in its repositories with MariaDB, and Wikipedia has also converted.

Michael "Monty" Widenius and David Axmark started development of MySQL in 1994. In 2008 Sun Microsystems bought MySQL.

MariaDB    In 2009, not happy with the development process of MySQL under Sun Microsystems, Mr. Widenius left Sun and founded a company named The Monty Program to work on a fork of MySQL named MariaDB. In 2010, when Oracle Corporation acquired Sun Microsystems, most of the MySQL developers left Sun to join the MySQL forks MariaDB and Drizzle (www.drizzle.org).

Compatibility    Today, MariaDB is a community-developed fork of MySQL that is dedicated to FOSS software (page 7) released under the GNU GPL (page 5). Currently, MariaDB is a drop-in replacement for MySQL and uses the same commands as MySQL; only the package names differ (but see mariadb.com/kb/en/mariadb-vs-mysql-compatibility). However, MariaDB is planning to introduce significant changes in the next version; at that time there might no longer be compatibility at the feature level. However, one would expect MariaDB to maintain protocol compatibility with MySQL into the future. Visit mariadb.com/blog/explanation-mariadb-100 for more information.

## MariaDB or MySQL?

tip    Because MariaDB is a fork of MySQL, almost all of the code is the same. The places where the code differs do not affect the examples or descriptions in this chapter. The examples in this chapter were tested against MariaDB. If you want to work with MySQL, install the **community-mysql** package. Unless you explicitly install the **community-mysql** package, Fedora installs MariaDB. For more information visit fedoraproject.org/wiki/Features/ReplaceMySQLwithMariaDB.

Interfaces    Many programming languages provide interfaces and bindings to MariaDB, including C, Python, PHP, and Perl. In addition, you can access a MariaDB database using the industry-standard ODBC (Open Database Connectivity) API. You can also call MariaDB from a shell script or the command line. MariaDB is a core component of the popular LAMP (Linux, Apache, MariaDB, PHP/Perl/Python) open-source enterprise software stack.

# LPI NOTES

MariaDB has a separate set of users from Linux: Users who have MariaDB accounts might not have Linux accounts, and vice versa. As installed, the name of the MariaDB administrator is **root**. Because the MariaDB **root** user is not the same as the Linux **root** user, it can (and should) have a different password.

**Figure 29-1**   A few rows from the **people** table in the **maxdb** database

MariaDB does not automatically create a database when you create a MariaDB user; users and databases are not rigidly bound.

SQL is free form with respect to whitespace and NEWLINEs.

## TERMINOLOGY

This section briefly describes some basic terms used when working with a relational database. See Figure 29-1.

**Database**—A structured set of persistent data comprising one or more tables.

**Row**—An ordered set of columns in a table. Also *record* or *tuple*.

**Column**—A set of one type of values, one per row in a table. Certain columns might be designated as keys. Keys are indexed to speed up access to specific values in the column. Also *field* or *attribute*.

**Join**—Two (or more) rows, each from a different table, that are tied together by means of the relationships between values in two (or more) columns. For example, two rows, each from a different table, can be joined based on equal values in two columns.

**RDBMS**—Relational database management system. A database based on the relational model developed by E. F. Codd comprising tables of data. Codd used the term *relations* for what SQL calls tables, thus the name of the database.

**SQL**— Structured Query Language. An industry-standard language for creating, updating, and querying relational databases. SQL is not part of the relational model but is often associated with it.

**MariaDB/MySQL**—Software brands or implementations of SQL.

**Table**—A collection of rows in a relational database. Also *relation*.

### MariaDB/MySQL is an implementation of SQL

**tip**   This chapter is about SQL and MariaDB. It explains how to set up a MariaDB server and client. It also shows examples of how to run SQL queries under MariaDB.

# SYNTAX AND CONVENTIONS

An SQL program comprises one or more statements, each terminated by a semicolon (;) or \g. Although keywords in statements are not case sensitive, this book shows keywords in uppercase letters for clarity. Database and table names are case sensitive; column names are not.

The following example shows a multiline SQL statement (query) that includes both the primary interpreter prompt (**MariaDB [maxdb]>;** **maxdb** is the name of the selected database) and the secondary interpreter prompt (**–>**). SELECT, FROM, and WHERE are keywords. This statement displays the value of the **name** column from the table named **people** in rows where the value in the **store** column is **4**.

```
MariaDB [maxdb]> SELECT      name
        ->              FROM   people
        ->              WHERE  store = 4;
```

## COMMENTS

You can specify a comment in one of three ways in an SQL program. These techniques work in SQL command files and when you are working with MariaDB interactively.

1. A hash sign (#) marks the beginning of a comment that continues to the end of the line (the NEWLINE character).

   ```
   # The following line holds an SQL statement and a comment
   USE maxdb;    # Use the maxdb database
   ```

2. A double hyphen (––) marks the beginning of a comment that continues to the end of the line (the NEWLINE character). The double hyphen must be followed by whitespace (one or more SPACEs and/or TABs).

   ```
   -- The following line holds an SQL statement and a comment
   USE maxdb;    -- Use the maxdb database
   ```

3. As in the C programming language, you can surround a (multiline) comment with /* and */.

   ```
   /* The line following this multiline
   comment holds an SQL statement
   and a comment */
   USE maxdb;    /* Use the maxdb database */
   ```

## DATA TYPES

When you create a table, you specify the name and data type of each column in the table. Each data type is designed to hold a certain kind of data. For example, data type CHAR holds strings of characters while DATE holds dates. The examples in this section use the following data types, a small sampling of those available under MariaDB.

- **CHAR($n$)**—Stores a string of up to $n$ characters where $0 <= n <= 255$. You must enclose strings within single or double quotation marks. When you store a string in a type CHAR column, MariaDB right-pads the string with SPACES to make an *n*-character string. When you retrieve a type CHAR string, MariaDB strips the trailing SPACES. Occupies *n* bytes (CHAR has a fixed length).

- **VARCHAR(*n*)**—Stores a string of up to *n* characters where $0 <= n <= 65,535$. You must enclose strings within single or double quotation marks. MariaDB does not pad strings stored in type VARCHAR columns. With a string length of *L*, occupies $L + 1$ bytes if $0 <= L <= 255$ and $L + 2$ bytes if $L > 255$. (VARCHAR has a variable length.) See page 1130 for an example.

### VARCHARs might slow large queries

tip  MariaDB converts VARCHAR columns to CHAR for operations that generate temporary tables (e.g., sorting, including ORDER BY and GROUP BY). Thus declaring large VARCHAR values [e.g., VARCHAR(255)] for columns that require frequent sorting will result in very large temporary tables that tend to slow queries.

- **INTEGER**—Stores a 4-byte integer.
- **DATE**—Stores a date. MariaDB sets a DATE variable to 0 if you specify an illegal value. Occupies 3 bytes.
- **BOOL**—A synonym for TINYINT. A value of 0 evaluates as *false* and 1–255 evaluate as *true*. Occupies 1 byte. When you specify data type BOOL, MariaDB changes it to a TINYINT.

## MORE INFORMATION

Home pages: mariadb.org, www.mysql.com
Documentation: mariadb.com/kb/en/MariaDB, dev.mysql.com/doc
Introduction: mariadb.com/kb/en/getting-started,
   dev.mysql.com/tech-resources/articles/mysql_intro.html
Fedora moves to MariaDB:
   fedoraproject.org/wiki/Features/ReplaceMySQLwithMariaDB
MariaDB/MySQL compatibility:
   mariadb.com/kb/en/mariadb-vs-mysql-compatibility
MariaDB next version: mariadb.com/blog/explanation-mariadb-100
Command syntax: dev.mysql.com/doc/refman/5.6/en/sql-syntax.html
Data types: dev.mysql.com/doc/refman/5.6/en/data-types.html
Joins: www.codinghorror.com/blog/2007/10/a-visual-explanation-of-sql-joins.html,
   mysqljoin.com
ODBC: dev.mysql.com/downloads/connector/odbc
Security: blog.mariadb.org/tag/security, www.kitebird.com/articles/ins-sec.html
   (dated)
Backing up databases: webcheatsheet.com/SQL/mysql_backup_restore.php,
   www.thegeekstuff.com/2008/09/backup-and-restore-mysql-database-using-
   mysqldump

# INSTALLING A MARIADB SERVER AND CLIENT

This section briefly covers installing the MariaDB client and server packages and starting the server running.

### You must remove anonymous MariaDB users

tip   When you install the MariaDB server, the MariaDB database is set up to allow anonymous users to log in and use MariaDB. The examples in this chapter will not work unless you remove these users from the MariaDB database. See "Removing Anonymous Users" on page 1119.

Install the following packages:

- mariadb
- mariadb-server

Working as a privileged user under Fedora, give the following commands to always start the **mariadb** service when the system enters multiuser mode and to start the **mariadb** service immediately:

```
# systemctl enable mariadb.service
# systemctl start mariadb.service
```

# CLIENT OPTIONS

This section describes some of the options you can use on the MariaDB client command line. The options preceded by a single hyphen and those preceded by a double hyphen are equivalent.

--disable-reconnect

Does not attempt to connect to the server again if the connection is dropped. See **--reconnect**.

--host=*hostname*
　　**–h** *hostname*

Specifies the address of the MariaDB server as *hostname*. Without this option MariaDB connects to a local unix socket (/var/lib/mysql/mysql.sock).

--password[=*passwd*]
　　**–p**[*passwd*]

Specifies the MariaDB password as *passwd*. For improved security, do not specify the password on the command line. With this option and no password, MariaDB prompts for a password. By default MariaDB does not use a password. The short form of this option does not accept a SPACE between the **–p** and *passwd*.

--reconnect     Attempts to connect to the server again if the connection is dropped (default). Disable this behavior using **--disable-reconnect**.

--skip-column-names
                Does not display column names in results.

--user=*usr*  -u *usr*
                Specifies the MariaDB user as **usr**. Without this option, **usr** defaults to the username of the user running the MariaDB command.

--verbose   -v  Increases the amount of information MariaDB displays. Use this option multiple times to increase verbosity. This option displays MariaDB statements as they are executed when running from a command file.

# SETTING UP MARIADB

You must remove the anonymous users from the MariaDB database before MariaDB will allow you to run commands working as yourself (or as Max if you follow the examples in this section). You can work as the MariaDB user named **root** without removing the anonymous users. To run commands as the MariaDB user named **root** in cases where this user does not have a password, you can either not specify a password or else press RETURN when prompted for a password. In a production environment, you can improve security of a MariaDB database by giving a password to the MariaDB user named **root**.

Of the following three steps, only the second, "Removing Anonymous Users," is required. The first step, "Assigning a Password to the MariaDB User Named **root**," makes a database more secure and is a good idea in a production environment.

You can use the third step, "Running the Secure Installation Script," in place of the first two steps. This script removes anonymous users, assigns a password to the MariaDB user named **root**, and takes other actions to make MariaDB more secure.

## ASSIGNING A PASSWORD TO THE MARIADB USER NAMED root

The following command, run as a nonprivileged user, assigns *mysql-password* as the password for the MariaDB user named **root**.

```
$ mysqladmin -u root password 'mysql-password'
```

## REMOVING ANONYMOUS USERS

The following commands, which you can run as a nonprivileged user, remove the anonymous users from the MariaDB database, yielding a more secure system. The **–u** option causes MariaDB to run as the MariaDB user named **root**. The **–p** option causes MariaDB to prompt for the password (for the MariaDB user named **root**).

In response to the prompt, enter the password you assigned to the MariaDB user named **root**.

```
$ mysql -u root -p
Enter password:
...
MariaDB [(none)]> DELETE FROM       mysql.user
    ->                  WHERE    user='';
Query OK, 2 rows affected (0.00 sec)

MariaDB [(none)]> FLUSH PRIVILEGES;
Query OK, 0 rows affected (0.00 sec)

MariaDB [(none)]> quit
Bye
```

## RUNNING THE SECURE INSTALLATION SCRIPT

In place of the two preceding steps, you can run the following command, which allows you to assign a password to the MariaDB user named **root**, removes anonymous users, disallows remote MariaDB **root** logins, and removes the test database that ships with MariaDB.

```
$ mysql_secure_installation
```

## ~/.my.cnf: CONFIGURES A MARIADB CLIENT

You can use the **~/.my.cnf** file to set MariaDB client options. The following example shows Max's **.my.cnf** file. The **[mysql]** specifies the MariaDB group. The **user** line is useful if your Linux and MariaDB usernames are different. Setting **user** to **max** when Max's Linux username is **max** is not necessary. The **password** line sets Max's MariaDB password to **mpasswd**. With this setup, Max does not have to use **–p** on the command line; MariaDB logs him in automatically. The **database** line specifies the name of the MariaDB database you want to work with so you do not need a USE statement at the beginning of a MariaDB program or session. Do not add the **database** line to this file until *after* you create the database (next) or you will not be able to use MariaDB.

```
$ cat /home/max/.my.cnf
[mysql]
user="max"
password="mpasswd"
database="maxdb"
```

Because this file can hold a password and other sensitive information, setting permissions on this file so the user in whose home directory the file resides owns the file and only the owner can read the file makes the MariaDB data more secure.

## ~/.mysql_history: STORES YOUR MARIADB HISTORY

MariaDB writes each of the statements it executes to a file named **~/.mysql_history**. Because MariaDB can write passwords to this file, setting permissions on this file so the user in whose home directory the file resides owns the file and only the owner can read the file makes the MariaDB data more secure. If you do not want to store your MariaDB history, delete this file and re-create it as a symbolic link to **/dev/null**.

```
$ rm ~/.mysql_history
$ ln -s /dev/null ~/.mysql_history
```

# CREATING A DATABASE

If the MariaDB username you add is the same as your Linux username, you will not have to specify a username on the MariaDB command line. In the following example, Max works as the MariaDB user named **root** (**–u root**). The **–p** option causes MariaDB to prompt for the password. In response to the **Enter password** prompt, Max supplies the password for the MariaDB user named **root**. If the MariaDB user named **root** does not have a password, press RETURN in response to the prompt.

CREATE DATABASE, SHOW DATABASES
Max uses a CREATE DATABASE statement to create a database named **maxdb** and a SHOW DATABASES statement to display the names of all databases. This command shows the name of the **maxdb** database and several system databases.

```
$ mysql -u root -p
Enter password:
Welcome to the MariaDB monitor.  Commands end with ; or \g.
Your MariaDB connection id is 5
Server version: 5.5.31-MariaDB MariaDB Server
...
Type 'help;' or '\h' for help. Type '\c' to clear the current input
statement.

MariaDB [(none)]> CREATE DATABASE maxdb;
Query OK, 1 row affected (0.00 sec)

MariaDB [(none)]> SHOW DATABASES;
+--------------------+
| Database           |
+--------------------+
| information_schema |
| maxdb              |
| mysql              |
| performance_schema |
| test               |
+--------------------+
5 rows in set (0.00 sec)
```

If you try to create a database that already exists, MariaDB displays an error message.

```
MariaDB [(none)]> CREATE DATABASE maxdb;
ERROR 1007 (HY000): Can't create database 'maxdb'; database exists
```

USE
You must tell MariaDB the name of the database you want to work with. If you do not give MariaDB this information, you must prefix the names of tables with the name of the database. For example, you would need to specify the **people** table in the **maxdb** database as **maxdb.people**. When you specify the **maxdb** database in the

~/.my.cnf file (page 1120) or with a USE statement, you can refer to the same table as **people**. In the following example, Max uses a USE statement to specify **maxdb** as the database he is working with. Once you specify a database, MariaDB includes its name in the prompt.

```
$ mysql
MariaDB [(none)]> USE maxdb;
Database changed
MariaDB [maxdb]>
```

## ADDING A USER

Before starting to work with the database, create a user so you do not have to work as the MariaDB user named **root**. You must work as the MariaDB user named **root** to create a MariaDB user.

Continuing with his previous MariaDB session, Max adds the MariaDB user named **max** with a password of **mpasswd**. The GRANT statement gives Max the permissions he needs to work (as the user named **max**) with the **maxdb** database. When using the MariaDB interpreter, **Query OK** indicates that the preceding statement was syntactically correct. Within an SQL statement, you must surround all character and date strings with quotation marks.

```
MariaDB [(none)]> GRANT           ALL PRIVILEGES
    ->                  ON        maxdb.* to 'max'
    ->                  IDENTIFIED BY 'mpasswd'
    ->                  WITH GRANT OPTION;
Query OK, 0 rows affected (0.00 sec)

MariaDB [(none)]> SELECT          user, password
    ->                  FROM      mysql.user;
+------+------------------------------------------+
| user | password                                 |
+------+------------------------------------------+
| root | *96D4C5B9348F896B0B593EA4DC1B653156799FDD |
...
| max  | *34432555DD6C778E7CB4A0EE4551425CE3AC0E16 |
+------+------------------------------------------+
5 rows in set (0.00 sec)

MariaDB [(none)]> quit
Bye
```

In the preceding example, after setting up the new user, Max uses a SELECT statement to query the **user** table of the **mysql** database and display the **user** and **password** columns. The **password** column displays encrypted passwords. Two users now exist: **root** and **max**. Max gives the command **quit** to exit from the MariaDB interpreter.

Working as the MariaDB user **max**, Max can now set up a simple database to keep track of people. He does not need to use the **–u** option on the command line because his Linux username and his MariaDB username are the same.

## LPI   EXAMPLES

This section follows Max as he works with MariaDB. You must follow the steps described under "Setting Up MariaDB" on page 1119 to remove anonymous users and under "Adding a User" on page 1122 to create the **maxdb** database and add the MariaDB user named **max**. If you do not follow these steps, you will not be able to use MariaDB as described in this section.

## LOGGING IN

You must log in to MariaDB before you can use it interactively.

You can specify a MariaDB username in the **~/.my.cnf** file (page 1120) or by using the **--user** (**-u**) option on the command line. If you do not specify a user in one of these ways, MariaDB assumes your MariaDB username is the same as your Linux username. The examples in this section assume Max is logging in to MariaDB as **max** (and has not specified a username in the **~/.my.cnf** file).

If a MariaDB account has a password, you must specify that password to log in. You can specify a password in the **~/.my.cnf** file or by using the **--password** (**-p**) option on the command line. Without specifying his password in his **~/.my.cnf** file, Max would log in on the MariaDB interactive interpreter using the following command:

```
$ mysql -p
Enter password: mpasswd
...
```

With his password specified in the **~/.my.cnf** file as shown on page 1120, Max can log in without the **-p** option:

```
$ mysql
...
```

## CREATING A TABLE

This section assumes Max has specified his password in his **~/.my.cnf** file.

CREATE TABLE    Before you can work with a database, you must create a table to hold data. To get started, Max uses the following CREATE TABLE statement to create a table named **people** in the **maxdb** database. This table has four columns. The USE statement specifies the name of the database.

```
$ mysql
MariaDB [(none)]> USE maxdb;
Database changed

MariaDB [maxdb]> CREATE TABLE     people (
    ->                   name    CHAR(10),
    ->                   hired   DATE,
    ->                   store   INTEGER,
    ->                   hourly  BOOL
    ->                   );
Query OK, 0 rows affected (0.01 sec)
```

SQL is free form with respect to whitespace and NEWLINEs. Max could have written the preceding statement as follows:

```
MariaDB [maxdb]> CREATE TABLE people (name CHAR(10),
    ->                  hired DATE, store INTEGER, hourly BOOL);
```

SHOW TABLES    After creating the table, Max uses a SHOW TABLES statement to display a list of tables in the **maxdb** database.

```
MariaDB [maxdb]> SHOW TABLES;
+-----------------+
| Tables_in_maxdb |
+-----------------+
| people          |
+-----------------+
1 row in set (0.00 sec)
```

DESCRIBE    Next, Max uses a DESCRIBE statement to display a description of the table named **people**.

```
MariaDB [maxdb]> DESCRIBE people;
+--------+------------+------+-----+---------+-------+
| Field  | Type       | Null | Key | Default | Extra |
+--------+------------+------+-----+---------+-------+
| name   | char(10)   | YES  |     | NULL    |       |
| hired  | date       | YES  |     | NULL    |       |
| store  | int(11)    | YES  |     | NULL    |       |
| hourly | tinyint(1) | YES  |     | NULL    |       |
+--------+------------+------+-----+---------+-------+
4 rows in set (0.00 sec)
```

Figure 29-1 on page 1115 shows part of the **people** table after data has been entered in it.

ALTER TABLE    Max decides that the **hourly** column should default to *true*. He uses an ALTER TABLE statement to modify the table so he does not have to delete the table and create it again. He then checks his work using a DESCRIBE statement; the **hourly** column now defaults to **1**, which evaluates as *true*.

```
MariaDB [maxdb]> ALTER TABLE      people
    ->                    MODIFY  hourly BOOL DEFAULT TRUE;
Query OK, 0 rows affected (0.00 sec)
Records: 0  Duplicates: 0  Warnings: 0

MariaDB [maxdb]> DESCRIBE people;
+--------+------------+------+-----+---------+-------+
| Field  | Type       | Null | Key | Default | Extra |
+--------+------------+------+-----+---------+-------+
| name   | char(10)   | YES  |     | NULL    |       |
| hired  | date       | YES  |     | NULL    |       |
| store  | int(11)    | YES  |     | NULL    |       |
| hourly | tinyint(1) | YES  |     | 1       |       |
+--------+------------+------+-----+---------+-------+
4 rows in set (0.00 sec)
```

# ADDING DATA

This section describes several ways to enter information into a database.

**LPI**  INSERT INTO  Next, Max uses an INSERT INTO statement to try to add a row of data to the **people** table. Following the first command, MariaDB displays an error saying it does not know about a column named **topsy**; Max forgot to put quotation marks around the string **topsy** so MariaDB parsed **topsy** as the name of a column. Max includes the quotation marks in the second command.

```
MariaDB [maxdb]> INSERT INTO     people
    ->                    VALUES ( topsy, '2012/11/01', 4, FALSE);
ERROR 1054 (42S22): Unknown column 'topsy' in 'field list'

MariaDB [maxdb]> INSERT INTO     people
    ->                    VALUES ( 'topsy', '2012/11/01', 4, FALSE);
Query OK, 1 row affected (0.00 sec)
```

The preceding INSERT INTO statement did not specify which columns the values were to be inserted into; it specified values for all four columns. The next INSERT INTO statement specifies values to be added to the **name** and **store** columns; MariaDB sets the other columns in the new rows to their default values.

```
MariaDB [maxdb]> INSERT INTO     people (name, store)
    ->                    VALUES ( 'percy', 2 ),
    ->                           ( 'bailey', 2 );
Query OK, 2 rows affected (0.00 sec)
Records: 2  Duplicates: 0  Warnings: 0

MariaDB [maxdb]> QUIT
Bye
```

LOAD DATA  The preceding examples showed how to work with MariaDB interactively. The next
LOCAL INFILE  example shows how to run MariaDB with statements in a command file. At the beginning of the preceding interactive session, Max gave the command USE **maxdb** so MariaDB knew which database the following commands worked with. When you specify commands in a file, you must tell MariaDB which database the commands work with; each file of commands must start with a USE statement or MariaDB will return an error. Alternately, you can specify the name of the database in your ~/.my.cnf file (page 1120).

The following example adds three rows to the **people** table from a text file named **addfile**. In **addfile**, each line holds data for a single row, with a single TAB separating each column from the next. The **\N** specifies a null value. The file is not terminated with a NEWLINE; if it were, MariaDB would insert a row of NULLs. Unlike interactive mode, when you run MariaDB from a command file, it does not display a message if everything worked properly. You can use the –v (verbose) option to cause MariaDB to display information about the commands it is executing. Multiple –v options display more information.

To run SQL commands from a file, enter the command **mysql** and redirect input to come from the command file. The following **mysql** command uses two **–v** options so MariaDB displays statements as it executes them and displays the results of statements after it executes them; input is redirected to come from **load**.

```
$ cat load
USE maxdb;

LOAD DATA LOCAL INFILE '/home/max/addfile'
        INTO TABLE people;

$ cat addfile
max     \N      4       0
zach    09-03-24        6       0
sam     2008-01-28      6       1

$ mysql -vv < load
--------------
LOAD DATA LOCAL INFILE '/home/max/addfile'
        INTO TABLE people
--------------

Query OK, 3 rows affected
Records: 3  Deleted: 0  Skipped: 0  Warnings: 0

Bye
```

## *LPI* RETRIEVING DATA

SELECT  The SELECT statement queries the database and displays the data the query returns. Within a SELECT statement, SQL interprets an asterisk (*) to mean all columns in a table. The following interactive query displays all columns of all rows of the **people** table in the **maxdb** database.

```
$ mysql
MariaDB [(none)]> USE maxdb;
MariaDB [maxdb]> SELECT          *
    ->                  FROM    people;
+--------+------------+-------+--------+
| name   | hired      | store | hourly |
+--------+------------+-------+--------+
| topsy  | 2012-11-01 |     4 |      0 |
| percy  | NULL       |     2 |      1 |
| bailey | NULL       |     2 |      1 |
| max    | NULL       |     4 |      0 |
| zach   | 2009-03-24 |     6 |      0 |
| sam    | 2008-01-28 |     6 |      1 |
+--------+------------+-------+--------+
6 rows in set (0.00 sec)
```

*LPI* ORDER BY  When you run queries from a command file, MariaDB does not line up in columns the data it outputs, but rather simply separates each column from the next using a TAB. This minimal formatting allows you to redirect and format the output as you please. Typically, if you want to redirect the data, you will not specify any **–v** options so MariaDB does not display any messages. The next command includes an ORDER BY clause in the SELECT statement to sort the output. It uses the **sel2** command file and sends the output through tail to strip the header.

```
$ cat sel2
use maxdb;
SELECT              *
        FROM    people
        ORDER BY name;

$ mysql < sel2 | tail -n +2
bailey  NULL    2        1
max     NULL    4        0
percy   NULL    2        1
sam     2008-01-28    6    1
topsy   2012-11-01    4    0
zach    2009-03-24    6    0
```

**_LPI_** WHERE  The next example shows a SELECT statement with a WHERE clause. A WHERE clause causes SELECT to return only those rows that match specified criteria. In this example, the WHERE clause causes SELECT to return only rows in which the value in the **store** column is 4. In addition, this SELECT statement returns a single column (**name**). The result is a list of the names of the people who work in store number 4.

```
MariaDB [maxdb]> SELECT          name
    ->                   FROM    people
    ->                   WHERE   store = 4;
+-------+
| name  |
+-------+
| topsy |
| max   |
+-------+
2 rows in set (0.00 sec)
```

The next example shows the use of a relational operator in a WHERE clause. Here the SELECT statement returns the names of people who work in stores with numbers greater than 2.

```
MariaDB [maxdb]> SELECT          name
    ->                   FROM    people
    ->                   WHERE   store > 2;
+-------+
| name  |
+-------+
| topsy |
| max   |
| zach  |
| sam   |
+-------+
4 rows in set (0.00 sec)
```

LIKE    You can also use the LIKE operator in a WHERE clause. LIKE causes SELECT to return rows in which a column contains a specified string. Within the string that follows LIKE, a percent sign (%) matches any string of zero or more characters while an underscore (_) matches any single character. The following query returns rows in which the **name** column contains an **m**.

```
MariaDB [maxdb]> SELECT          name,
             ->                  store
             ->              FROM people
             ->              WHERE name LIKE '%m%';
+------+-------+
| name | store |
+------+-------+
| max  |     4 |
| sam  |     6 |
+------+-------+
2 rows in set (0.00 sec)
```

# BACKING UP A DATABASE

mysqldump   The mysqldump utility can back up and restore a database. Backing up a database generates a file of SQL statements that create the tables and load the data. You can use this file to restore the database from scratch. The next example shows how Max can back up the **maxdb** database to a file named **maxdb.bkup.sql**.

```
$ mysqldump -u max -p maxdb > maxdb.bkup.sql
Enter password:
```

Be careful: The following restore procedure will overwrite an existing database. Before you can restore a database, you must create the database as explained on page 1121. After creating the **maxdb** database, Max runs MariaDB with input coming from the file that mysqldump created. After giving the following command, the **maxdb** database is in the same state it was in when Max backed it up.

```
$ mysql -u max -p maxdb < maxdb.bkup.sql
Enter password:
```

# MODIFYING DATA

*LPI*   DELETE FROM   The DELETE FROM statement removes one or more rows from a table. The next example deletes the rows from the **people** table where the **name** column holds **bailey** or **percy**.

```
MariaDB [maxdb]> DELETE FROM    people
             ->              WHERE name='bailey'
             ->              OR name='percy';
Query OK, 2 rows affected (0.00 sec)
```

*LPI*   UPDATE   The UPDATE statement changes data in a table. The following example sets the **hourly** column to TRUE (1) in the rows where the **name** column contains **sam** or **topsy**. The MariaDB messages show the query matched two rows (**sam** and **topsy**) but changed only one row. It changed **hourly** in the row with **topsy**; in the row with **sam**, **hourly** was already set to TRUE.

```
MariaDB [maxdb]> UPDATE          people
    ->                  SET      hourly = TRUE
    ->                  WHERE    name = 'sam' OR
    ->                           name = 'topsy';
Query OK, 1 row affected (0.00 sec)
Rows matched: 2  Changed: 1  Warnings: 0
```

CURDATE()  The CURDATE() function returns today's date. The next example sets the **hired** column to today's date in the row where **name** contains **max**.

```
MariaDB [maxdb]> UPDATE          people
    ->                  SET      hired = CURDATE()
    ->                  WHERE    name = 'max';
Query OK, 1 row affected (0.00 sec)
Rows matched: 1  Changed: 1  Warnings: 0
```

The next query shows the results of the preceding DELETE FROM and UPDATE statements.

```
MariaDB [maxdb]> select * from people;
+-------+------------+-------+--------+
| name  | hired      | store | hourly |
+-------+------------+-------+--------+
| topsy | 2012-11-01 |     4 |      1 |
| max   | 2012-02-12 |     4 |      0 |
| zach  | 2009-03-24 |     6 |      0 |
| sam   | 2008-01-28 |     6 |      1 |
+-------+------------+-------+--------+
4 rows in set (0.00 sec)
```

## CREATING A SECOND TABLE

Next, the **setup.stores** SQL command file creates, populates, and displays the **stores** table in the **maxdb** database.

```
$ mysql -vv < setup.stores
--------------
CREATE TABLE    stores (
                name VARCHAR(20),
                number INTEGER,
                city VARCHAR(20)
                )
--------------

Query OK, 0 rows affected


--------------
INSERT INTO     stores
        VALUES  ( 'headquarters', 4, 'new york' ),
                ( 'midwest', 5, 'chicago' ),
                ( 'west coast', 6, 'san francisco' )
--------------

Query OK, 3 rows affected
Records: 3  Duplicates: 0  Warnings: 0


--------------
```

```
SELECT        *
        FROM    stores
--------------

name    number  city
headquarters    4       new york
midwest 5       chicago
west coast      6       san francisco
3 rows in set
```

VARCHAR   The **stores** table has columns named **name, number,** and **city**. The data type for the **name** and **city** columns is VARCHAR. A VARCHAR column stores a variable-length string without the padding required by a CHAR column. In this example, the **name** and **city** columns can store up to 20 characters each.

The size of a VARCHAR is the sum of the length prefix plus the number of characters in the string being stored. The length prefix for a column declared to hold fewer than 255 characters is 1 byte; larger columns have a 2-byte length prefix. In contrast, a CHAR column always occupies the number of characters it was declared to be.

The number in parentheses in a VARCHAR declaration specifies the maximum number of characters any row in the column can hold. In the example, the **city** column is declared to be VARCHAR(20) so a row in that column cannot hold more than 20 characters. The row with **new york** in the **city** column takes up 9 bytes of storage (8 + 1). If the column had been declared to be CHAR(20), each row would occupy 20 bytes, regardless of the length of the string it held.

# *LPI* JOINS

A join operation combines rows from/across two or more related tables in a database according to some relationship between these tables. Take the **maxdb** database, for example: The **people** table has columns that hold information about employee name, hire date, the store where the employee works, and whether the employee is hourly (as opposed to salaried); the **stores** table has columns that hold information about the store name, number, and city it is located in. With this setup, you cannot determine which city an employee works in by querying either the **people** or **stores** table alone; you must join the tables to get this information.

You join tables using a SELECT statement that specifies a column in each of the tables and the relationship between those columns. The query that would satisfy the example specifies the **store** column in the **people** table and the **number** column in the **stores** table; the relationship between those columns is equality because both of those columns hold the store number. When you equate like values in these columns, you can display **stores** information for each **name** in the **people** table (or **people** information for each [store] **number** in the **stores** table).

The following query selects rows from the **people** and **stores** tables and joins the rows where the value of **store** in the **people** table equals the value of **number** in the **stores** table (**store = number**). This query uses an implicit join; it does not use the JOIN keyword. The examples following this one use JOIN. Using this keyword makes no difference in the results of the query, but you must use JOIN in certain types of queries.

```
MariaDB [maxdb]> SELECT          *
    ->              FROM     people, stores
    ->              WHERE    store = number;
+-------+------------+-------+--------+--------------+--------+---------------+
| name  | hired      | store | hourly | name         | number | city          |
+-------+------------+-------+--------+--------------+--------+---------------+
| topsy | 2012-11-01 |     4 |      1 | headquarters |      4 | new york      |
| max   | 2012-02-12 |     4 |      0 | headquarters |      4 | new york      |
| zach  | 2009-03-24 |     6 |      0 | west coast   |      6 | san francisco |
| sam   | 2008-01-28 |     6 |      1 | west coast   |      6 | san francisco |
+-------+------------+-------+--------+--------------+--------+---------------+
4 rows in set (0.00 sec)
```

Inner join    The preceding query demonstrates an *inner join*. If you like, you can use the keywords INNER JOIN in place of JOIN in this type of query. In each returned row, the value in **people.store** equals the value in **stores.number**. However, the **stores** table has a row with the value of 5 in the **number** column but no row exists in the **people** table with this value in the **store** column. As a result, these queries do not return a row with **people.store** and **stores.number** equal to 5.

Table names    When working with a relational database, you can refer to a column in a specific table as **table_name.column_name** (e.g., **stores.name** in the example database). While you are working with a single table, a column name is sufficient to uniquely identify the data you want to work with. When you work with several tables, you might need to specify both a table name and a column name to uniquely identify certain data. Specifically, if two columns have the same name in two tables that are being joined, you must specify both the table and the column to disambiguate the columns. The following query demonstrates the problem.

```
MariaDB [maxdb]> SELECT          *
    ->              FROM     people, stores
    ->              WHERE    store = number and
    ->                       name = 'max';
ERROR 1052 (23000): Column 'name' in where clause is ambiguous
```

In the preceding query, the column **name** is ambiguous: A column named **name** exists in both the **people** and **stores** tables. MariaDB cannot determine which table to use in the WHERE clause. The next query solves this problem. It uses **people.name** in the WHERE clause to specify that MariaDB is to use the **name** column from the **people** table.

```
MariaDB [maxdb]> SELECT          *
    ->              FROM     people, stores
    ->              WHERE    store = number and
    ->                       people.name = 'max';
+-------+------------+-------+--------+--------------+--------+----------+
| name  | hired      | store | hourly | name         | number | city     |
+-------+------------+-------+--------+--------------+--------+----------+
| max   | 2012-05-01 |     4 |      0 | headquarters |      4 | new york |
+-------+------------+-------+--------+--------------+--------+----------+
1 row in set (0.01 sec)
```

Even though it might not be necessary, it can make code and comments clearer to specify both a table and a column as in the following examples.

Table aliases  An alias for a table is another, usually shorter, name for the table. Aliases can make a SELECT statement easier to read. You declare table aliases in the FROM clause of a query. For example, the following clause declares **p** to be an alias for the **people** table and **s** to be an alias for the **stores** table.

```
FROM    people p JOIN stores s
```

With these aliases in place, you can refer to the **people** table as **p** and the **stores** table as **s** in the rest of the query.

The next example rewrites an earlier query using aliases and the JOIN keyword. In place of a comma between the table (and alias) names, this syntax uses the keyword JOIN. In place of WHERE it uses ON. Specifying **p.store** and **s.number** makes it clear that the **store** column of the **people** table (**p.store**) is being joined with the **number** column of the **stores** table (**s.number**). This query returns the same results as the preceding one.

```
SELECT          *
        FROM    people p JOIN stores s
        ON      p.store = s.number;
```

Outer join  An *outer join* can return rows in which the common column has a value that does not exist in both tables. You can specify a LEFT OUTER JOIN (or just LEFT JOIN) or a RIGHT OUTER JOIN (or just RIGHT JOIN). Left and right refer to the tables specified on the left and right of the keyword JOIN, respectively.

The next example demonstrates a right outer join. The outer table is **stores**, which has a value in the **number** column that does not have a match in the **store** column of the **people** table. SQL inserts null values in the columns from **people** in the joined row that does not have a match (**stores.number = 5**).

```
MariaDB [maxdb]> SELECT          *
    ->                  FROM    people p RIGHT JOIN stores s
    ->                  ON      p.store = s.number;
+-------+------------+-------+--------+--------------+--------+---------------+
| name  | hired      | store | hourly | name         | number | city          |
+-------+------------+-------+--------+--------------+--------+---------------+
| topsy | 2012-11-01 |     4 |      1 | headquarters |      4 | new york      |
| max   | 2012-02-12 |     4 |      0 | headquarters |      4 | new york      |
| zach  | 2009-03-24 |     6 |      0 | west coast   |      6 | san francisco |
| sam   | 2008-01-28 |     6 |      1 | west coast   |      6 | san francisco |
| NULL  | NULL       |  NULL |   NULL | midwest      |      5 | chicago       |
+-------+------------+-------+--------+--------------+--------+---------------+
5 rows in set (0.00 sec)
```

The following query performs an inner join to list the city that each person works in. A right outer join would show the cities that have no one working in them. A left outer join would show people who are not assigned to a store.

```
MariaDB [maxdb]> SELECT          p.name,
    ->                          city
    ->                  FROM     people p JOIN stores s
    ->                  ON       p.store = s.number;
+-------+---------------+
| name  | city          |
+-------+---------------+
| topsy | new york      |
| max   | new york      |
| zach  | san francisco |
| sam   | san francisco |
+-------+---------------+
4 rows in set (0.00 sec)
```

**Subqueries** A subquery is a SELECT statement within the WHERE clause of another SELECT statement. The subquery returns a value or values that restrict the main query.

In the next example, the subquery returns the value of the **number** column from the **stores** table where the **city** column has a value of **new york**. The main query returns the value(s) from the **name** column of the **people** table where the value of the **store** column is equal to the value returned by the subquery. The result is a query that returns the names of people who work in New York.

```
$ cat sel4
use maxdb;

SELECT          name
        FROM    people
        WHERE   store =
        (SELECT         number
        FROM    stores
        WHERE   city = 'new york'
        );

$ mysql < sel4
name
topsy
max
```

The final example is a bash script that queries the MariaDB database created in this chapter. If you have not run the example commands it will not work. First the script checks that the user knows the database password. Then it displays a list of employees and asks which employee the user is interested in. It queries the database for information about that employee and displays the name of the store the employee works in and the city the store is located in.

```
$ cat employee_info
#! /bin/bash


#
# Script to display employee information
#

# Make sure user is authorized: Get database password
#
echo -n "Enter password for maxdb database: "
stty -echo
read pw
stty echo
echo
echo

# Check for valid password
#
mysql -u max -p$pw maxdb > /dev/null 2>&1 < /dev/null
if [ $? -ne 0 ]
    then
        echo "Bad password."
        exit 1
fi

# Display list of employees for user to select from
#
echo "The following people are employed by the company:"
mysql -u max -p$pw --skip-column-names maxdb <<+
SELECT name FROM people ORDER BY name;
+
echo
echo -n "Which employee would you like information about? "
read emp

# Query for store name
#
storename=$(mysql -u max -p$pw --skip-column-names maxdb <<+
SELECT stores.name FROM people, stores WHERE store = number AND people.name = "$emp";
+
)

# if null then user entered bad employee name
#
if [ "$storename" = "" ]
    then
        echo "Not a valid name."
        exit 1
fi

# Query for city name
#
storecity=$(mysql -u max -p$pw --skip-column-names maxdb <<+
SELECT city FROM people, stores WHERE store = number AND people.name = "$emp";
+
)

# Display report
#
echo
echo $emp works at the $storename store in $storecity
```

# CHAPTER SUMMARY

System administrators are frequently called upon to set up and run MariaDB databases. MariaDB/MySQL is the world's most popular open-source RDBMS (relational database management system). It is extremely fast and is used by some of the most frequently visited Web sites on the Internet. Many programming languages provide interfaces and bindings to MariaDB, including C, PHP, Python, and Perl. You can also call MariaDB directly from a shell script or use it in a pipeline on the command line. MariaDB is a core component of the popular LAMP (Linux, Apache, MariaDB, PHP/Perl/Python) open-source enterprise software stack.

# EXERCISES

1. List two ways you can specify the MariaDB password for a user to access MariaDB.

2. Using MariaDB interactively, create a database named **dbsam** that the user named **sam** can modify and grant privileges on. Set up Sam's password to be **porcupine**. The MariaDB user named **root** has the password **five22four**.

3. What is a table? A row? A column?

4. Which commands would you use to set up a table in **dbsam** (created in exercise 2) named **shoplist** with the following columns of the specified types: **day** [DATE], **store** [CHAR(20)], **lettuce** [SMALLINT], **soupkind** [CHAR(20)], **soupnum** [INTEGER], and **misc** [VARCHAR(40)]?

5. Where can you find a list of MariaDB commands you have previously run?

# ADVANCED EXERCISES

6. List two ways you can specify the name of a specific MariaDB database to work with.

7. What does a join do? When is a join useful?

8. Assume you are working with the **people** table in the **maxdb** database described in this chapter. Write a query that lists the names of all the people and their hire dates sorted by their names.

9. Assume you are working with the **people** and **stores** tables in the **maxdb** database described in this chapter. Write a query that sets up the aliases **q** and **n** for the **people** and **stores** tables, respectively. Have the query join the tables using the **store** column in the **people** table with the **number** column in the **stores** table. From left to right, have the query display the name of the city the person works in, the name of the person, and the person's hire date. Sort the output by city name.

# PART VI

# APPENDIXES

# A

# REGULAR EXPRESSIONS

A *regular expression* defines a set of one or more strings of characters. A simple string of characters is a regular expression that defines one string of characters: itself. A more complex regular expression uses letters, numbers, and special characters to define many different strings of characters. A regular expression is said to *match* any string it defines.

This appendix describes the regular expressions used by ed, vim, emacs, grep, mawk/gawk, sed, Perl, and many other utilities. The regular expressions used in shell ambiguous file references are different and are described in "Filename Generation/Pathname Expansion" on page 165.

# CHARACTERS

As used in this appendix, a *character* is any character *except* a NEWLINE. Most characters represent themselves within a regular expression. A *special character,* also called a *metacharacter,* is one that does not represent itself. If you need to use a special character to represent itself, you must quote it as explained on page 1143.

# DELIMITERS

A character called a *delimiter* usually marks the beginning and end of a regular expression. The delimiter is always a special character for the regular expression it delimits (that is, it does not represent itself but marks the beginning and end of the expression). Although vim permits the use of other characters as delimiters and grep does not use delimiters at all, the regular expressions in this appendix use a forward slash (/) as a delimiter. In some unambiguous cases, the second delimiter is not required. For example, you can sometimes omit the second delimiter when it would be followed immediately by RETURN.

# SIMPLE STRINGS

The most basic regular expression is a simple string that contains no special characters except the delimiters. A simple string matches only itself (Table A-1). In the examples in this appendix, the strings that are matched are underlined and look like this.

Table A-1    Simple strings

| Regular expression | Matches | Examples |
|---|---|---|
| /ring/ | ring | ring, spring, ringing, stringing |
| /Thursday/ | Thursday | Thursday, Thursday's |
| /or not/ | or not | or not, poor nothing |

# SPECIAL CHARACTERS

You can use special characters within a regular expression to cause the regular expression to match more than one string. A regular expression that includes a special character always matches the longest possible string, starting as far toward the beginning (left) of the line as possible.

# PERIODS

A period (.) matches any character (Table A-2).

**Table A-2**   Periods

| Regular expression | Matches | Examples |
|---|---|---|
| / .alk/ | All strings consisting of a SPACE followed by any character followed by alk | will talk, might balk |
| /.ing/ | All strings consisting of any character preceding ing | sing song, ping, before inglenook |

# BRACKETS

Brackets ([]) define a *character class*[1] that matches any single character within the brackets (Table A-3). If the first character following the left bracket is a caret (^), the brackets define a character class that matches any single character not within the brackets. You can use a hyphen to indicate a range of characters. Within a character-class definition, backslashes and asterisks (described in the following sections) lose their special meanings. A right bracket (appearing as a member of the character class) can appear only as the first character following the left bracket. A caret is special only if it is the first character following the left bracket. A dollar sign is special only if it is followed immediately by the right bracket.

**Table A-3**   Brackets

| Regular expression | Matches | Examples |
|---|---|---|
| /[bB]ill/ | Member of the character class b and B followed by ill | bill, Bill, billed |
| /t[aeiou].k/ | t followed by a lowercase vowel, any character, and a k | talkative, stink, teak, tanker |
| /# [6–9]/ | # followed by a SPACE and a member of the character class 6 through 9 | # 60, # 8:, get # 9 |
| /[^a–zA–Z]/ | Any character that is not a letter (ASCII character set only) | 1, 7, @, ., }, Stop! |

---

1. GNU documentation and POSIX call these List Operators and define Character Class operators as expressions that match a predefined group of characters, such as all numbers (page 1242).

# ASTERISKS

An asterisk can follow a regular expression that represents a single character (Table A-4). The asterisk represents *zero* or more occurrences of a match of the regular expression. An asterisk following a period matches any string of characters. (A period matches any character, and an asterisk matches zero or more occurrences of the preceding regular expression.) A character-class definition followed by an asterisk matches any string of characters that are members of the character class.

**Table A-4**    Asterisks

| Regular expression | Matches | Examples |
|---|---|---|
| /ab*c/ | <u>a</u> followed by zero or more <u>b</u>'s followed by a <u>c</u> | <u>ac</u>, <u>abc</u>, <u>abbc</u>, debbca<u>abbbc</u> |
| /ab.*c/ | <u>ab</u> followed by zero or more characters followed by <u>c</u> | <u>abc</u>, <u>abxc</u>, <u>ab45c</u>, x<u>ab 756.345 x c</u>at |
| /t.*ing/ | <u>t</u> followed by zero or more characters followed by <u>ing</u> | <u>thing</u>, <u>ting</u>, I <u>thought of going</u> |
| /[a–zA–Z ]*/ | A string composed only of letters and SPACES | 1.<u> any string without numbers or punctuation</u>! |
| /(.*)/ | As long a string as possible between ( and ) | Get <u>(this) and (that)</u>; |
| /([^)]*)/ | The shortest string possible that starts with ( and ends with ) | <u>(this)</u>, Get <u>(this and that)</u> |

# CARETS AND DOLLAR SIGNS

A regular expression that begins with a caret (^) can match a string only at the beginning of a line. In a similar manner, a dollar sign ($) at the end of a regular expression matches the end of a line. The caret and dollar sign are called anchors because they force (anchor) a match to the beginning or end of a line (Table A-5).

**Table A-5**    Carets and dollar signs

| Regular expression | Matches | Examples |
|---|---|---|
| /^T/ | A <u>T</u> at the beginning of a line | <u>T</u>his line..., <u>T</u>hat Time..., In Time |
| /^+[0–9]/ | A plus sign followed by a digit at the beginning of a line | <u>+5</u> +45.72, <u>+7</u>59    Keep this... |
| /:$/ | A colon that ends a line | ...below<u>:</u> |

# QUOTING SPECIAL CHARACTERS

You can quote any special character (but not parentheses [except in Perl] or a digit) by preceding it with a backslash (Table A-6). Quoting a special character makes it represent itself.

**Table A-6**  Quoted special characters

| Regular expression | Matches | Examples |
|---|---|---|
| /end\./ | All strings that contain <u>end</u> followed by a period | The <u>end.</u>, s<u>end.</u>, pret<u>end.</u>mail |
| / \\/ | A single backslash | <u>\</u> |
| / \*/ | An asterisk | <u>*</u>.c, an asterisk (<u>*</u>) |
| / \[5\]/ | <u>[5]</u> | it was five <u>[5]</u> |
| /and\/or/ | <u>and/or</u> | <u>and/or</u> |

# RULES

The following rules govern the application of regular expressions.

## LONGEST MATCH POSSIBLE

A regular expression always matches the longest possible string, starting as far toward the beginning (left end) of the line as possible. Perl calls this type of match a *greedy match*. For example, given the string

```
This (rug) is not what it once was (a long time ago), is it?
```

the expression **/Th.\*is/** matches

```
This (rug) is not what it once was (a long time ago), is
```

and **/(.\*)/** matches

```
(rug) is not what it once was (a long time ago)
```

However, **/([^)]\*)/** matches

```
(rug)
```

Given the string

```
singing songs, singing more and more
```

the expression **/s.\*ing/** matches

```
singing songs, singing
```

and **/s.\*ing song/** matches

```
singing song
```

# EMPTY REGULAR EXPRESSIONS

Within some utilities, such as vim and less (but not grep), an empty regular expression represents the last regular expression you used. For example, suppose you give vim the following Substitute command:

```
:s/mike/robert/
```

If you then want to make the same substitution again, you can use the following command:

```
:s//robert/
```

Alternatively, you can use the following commands to search for the string **mike** and then make the substitution

```
/mike/
:s//robert/
```

The empty regular expression (**//**) represents the last regular expression you used (**/mike/**).

# BRACKETING EXPRESSIONS

You can use quoted parentheses, \( and \), to *bracket* a regular expression. (However, Perl uses unquoted parentheses to bracket regular expressions.) The string the bracketed regular expression matches can be recalled, as explained in "Quoted Digit" on the next page. A regular expression does not attempt to match quoted parentheses. Thus a regular expression enclosed within quoted parentheses matches what the same regular expression without the parentheses would match. The expression **/\(rexp\)/** matches what **/rexp/** would match; **/a\(b✽\)c/** matches what **/ab✽c/** would match.

You can nest quoted parentheses. The bracketed expressions are identified only by the opening \(, so no ambiguity arises in identifying them. The expression **/\([a–z]\([A–Z]✽\)x\)/** consists of two bracketed expressions, one nested within the other. In the string **3 t dMNORx7 l u**, the preceding regular expression matches **dMNORx**, with the first bracketed expression matching **dMNORx** and the second matching **MNOR**.

# THE REPLACEMENT STRING

The vim and sed editors use regular expressions as search strings within Substitute commands. You can use the ampersand (**&**) and quoted digits (**\n**) special characters to represent the matched strings within the corresponding replacement string.

# AMPERSAND

Within a replacement string, an ampersand (&) takes on the value of the string that the search string (regular expression) matched. For example, the following vim Substitute command surrounds a string of one or more digits with **NN**. The ampersand in the replacement string matches whatever string of digits the regular expression (search string) matched:

> `:s/[0-9][0-9]*/NN&NN/`

Two character-class definitions are required because the regular expression [0–9]* matches *zero* or more occurrences of a digit, and *any* character string constitutes zero or more occurrences of a digit.

# QUOTED DIGIT

Within the search string, a bracketed regular expression, \(**xxx**\) [(**xxx**) in Perl], matches what the regular expression would have matched without the quoted parentheses, **xxx**. Within the replacement string, a quoted digit, \\*n*, represents the string that the bracketed regular expression (portion of the search string) beginning with the *n*th \( matched. Perl accepts a quoted digit for this purpose, but the preferred style is to precede the digit with a dollar sign (**$*n***). For example, you can take a list of people in the form

> `last-name, first-name initial`

and put it in the form

> `first-name initial last-name`

with the following vim command:

> `:1,$s/\([^,]*\), \(.*\)/\2 \1/`

This command addresses all the lines in the file (**1,$**). The Substitute command (**s**) uses a search string and a replacement string delimited by forward slashes. The first bracketed regular expression within the search string, \([^,]*\), matches what the same unbracketed regular expression, [^,]*, would match: zero or more characters not containing a comma (the **last-name**). Following the first bracketed regular expression are a comma and a SPACE that match themselves. The second bracketed expression, \(.*\), matches any string of characters (the **first-name** and **initial**).

The replacement string consists of what the second bracketed regular expression matched (\2), followed by a SPACE and what the first bracketed regular expression matched (\1).

# EXTENDED REGULAR EXPRESSIONS

This section covers patterns that use an extended set of special characters. These patterns are called *full regular expressions* or *extended regular expressions*. In addition to ordinary regular expressions, Perl and vim provide extended regular expressions. The three utilities egrep, grep when run with the –E option (similar to egrep), and mawk/gawk provide all the special characters included in ordinary regular expressions, except for \( and \), as well those included in extended regular expressions.

Two of the additional special characters are the plus sign (+) and the question mark (?). They are similar to *, which matches *zero* or more occurrences of the previous character. The plus sign matches *one* or more occurrences of the previous character, whereas the question mark matches *zero* or *one* occurrence. You can use any one of the special characters *, +, and ? following parentheses, causing the special character to apply to the string surrounded by the parentheses. Unlike the parentheses in bracketed regular expressions, these parentheses are not quoted (Table A-7).

**Table A-7**　Extended regular expressions

| Regular expression | Matches | Examples |
| --- | --- | --- |
| /ab+c/ | <u>a</u> followed by one or more <u>b</u>'s followed by a <u>c</u> | y<u>abc</u>w, <u>abbc</u>57 |
| /ab?c/ | <u>a</u> followed by zero or one <u>b</u> followed by <u>c</u> | b<u>ac</u>k, <u>abc</u>def |
| /(ab)+c/ | One or more occurrences of the string <u>ab</u> followed by <u>c</u> | z<u>abc</u>d, <u>ababc</u>! |
| /(ab)?c/ | Zero or one occurrence of the string <u>ab</u> followed by <u>c</u> | x<u>c</u>, <u>abc</u>c |

In full regular expressions, the vertical bar (|) special character is a Boolean OR operator. Within vim, you must quote the vertical bar by preceding it with a backslash to make it special (\|). A vertical bar between two regular expressions causes a match with strings that match the first expression, the second expression, or both. You can use the vertical bar with parentheses to separate from the rest of the regular expression the two expressions that are being ORed (Table A-8).

**Table A-8**　Full regular expressions

| Regular expression | Matches | Examples |
| --- | --- | --- |
| /ab\|ac/ | Either <u>ab</u> or <u>ac</u> | <u>ab</u>, <u>ac</u>, <u>abac</u> (***abac*** *is two matches of the regular expression*) |
| /^Exit\|^Quit/ | Lines that begin with <u>Exit</u> or <u>Quit</u> | <u>Exit</u>, <u>Quit</u>, No Exit |
| /(D\|N)\. Jones/ | <u>D. Jones</u> or <u>N. Jones</u> | P.<u>D. Jones</u>, <u>N. Jones</u> |

# APPENDIX SUMMARY

A regular expression defines a set of one or more strings of characters. A regular expression is said to match any string it defines.

In a regular expression, a special character is one that does not represent itself. Table A-9 lists special characters.

**Table A-9** Special characters

| Character | Meaning |
|---|---|
| . | Matches any single character |
| * | Matches zero or more occurrences of a match of the preceding character |
| ^ | Forces a match to the beginning of a line |
| $ | A match to the end of a line |
| \ | Quotes special characters |
| \< | Forces a match to the beginning of a word |
| \> | Forces a match to the end of a word |

Table A-10 lists ways of representing character classes and bracketed regular expressions.

**Table A-10** Character classes and bracketed regular expressions

| Class | Meaning |
|---|---|
| [*xyz*] | Defines a character class that matches *x*, *y*, or *z* |
| [^ *xyz*] | Defines a character class that matches any character except *x*, *y*, or *z* |
| [*x–z*] | Defines a character class that matches any character *x* through *z* inclusive |
| \( *xyz*\) | Matches what *xyz* matches (a bracketed regular expression; not Perl) |
| ( *xyz* ) | Matches what *xyz* matches (a bracketed regular expression; Perl only) |

In addition to the preceding special characters and strings (excluding quoted parentheses, except in vim), the characters in Table A-11 are special within full, or extended, regular expressions.

**Table A-11** Extended regular expressions

| Expression | Matches |
|---|---|
| + | One or more occurrences of the preceding character |
| ? | Zero or one occurrence of the preceding character |

**Table A-11**   Extended regular expressions (continued)

| Expression | Matches |
| --- | --- |
| (*xyz*)+ | One or more occurrences of what *xyz* matches |
| (*xyz*)? | Zero or one occurrence of what *xyz* matches |
| (*xyz*)✻ | Zero or more occurrences of what *xyz* matches |
| *xyz*\|*abc* | Either what *xyz* or what *abc* matches (use \\| in vim) |
| (*xy*\|*ab*)*c* | Either what *xyc* or what *abc* matches (use \\| in vim) |

Table A-12 lists characters that are special within a replacement string in sed and vim.

**Table A-12**   Replacement strings

| String | Represents |
| --- | --- |
| & | What the regular expression (search string) matched |
| \\*n* | A quoted number, *n*, represents what the *n*th bracketed regular expression in the search string matched |
| $*n* | A number preceded by a dollar sign, *n*, represents what the *n*th bracketed regular expression in the search string matched (Perl only) |

# B

# HELP

You need not be a user or system administrator in isolation. A large community of Linux experts is willing to assist you in learning about, helping you solve problems with, and getting the most out of a Linux system. Before you ask for help, however, make sure you have done everything you can to solve the problem yourself. No doubt, someone has experienced the same problem before you and the answer to your question exists somewhere on the Internet. Your job is to find it. This appendix lists resources and describes methods that can help you in that task.

# SOLVING A PROBLEM

Following is a list of steps that can help you solve a problem without asking someone for help. Depending on your understanding of and experience with the hardware and software involved, these steps might lead to a solution.

1. Fedora/RHEL comes with extensive documentation. Read the documentation on the specific hardware or software you are having a problem with. If it is a GNU product, use info; otherwise, use man to find local information. Also look in **/usr/share/doc** for documentation on specific tools. For more information see "Getting Help" on page 113 and "Getting Help from the Command Line" on page 128.

2. When the problem involves some type of error or other message, use a search engine, such as Google (www.google.com) or Google Groups (groups.google.com), to look up the message on the Internet. If the message is long, pick a unique part of the message to search for; 10 to 20 characters should be enough. Enclose the search string within double quotation marks. See "Using the Internet to Get Help" on page 113 for an example of this kind of search.

3. Check whether the Linux Documentation Project (www.tldp.org) has a HOWTO or mini-HOWTO on the subject in question. Search its site for keywords that relate directly to the product and problem. Read the FAQs.

4. GNU manuals are available at www.gnu.org/manual. In addition, you can visit the GNU home page (www.gnu.org) to obtain other documentation and GNU resources. Many of the GNU pages and resources are available in a variety of languages.

5. Use Google or Google Groups to search on keywords that relate directly to the product and problem.

6. When all else fails (or perhaps before you try anything else), examine the system logs in **/var/log**. First look at the end of the **messages** file using the following command:

```
# tail -20 /var/log/messages
```

If **messages** contains nothing useful, run the following command. It displays the names of the log files in chronological order, with the most recently modified files appearing at the bottom of the list.

```
$ ls -ltr /var/log
```

Look at the files at the bottom of the list first. If the problem involves a network connection, review the **secure** file on the local and remote systems. Also look at **messages** on the remote system.

7. The **/var/spool** directory contains subdirectories with useful information: **cups** holds the print queues; **postfix, mail,** or **exim4** holds the user's mail files; and so on.

If you are unable to solve a problem yourself, a thoughtful question to an appropriate newsgroup (next page) or mailing list (page 1153) can elicit useful information. When you send or post a question, make sure you describe the problem and identify the local system carefully. Include the version numbers of Fedora/RHEL and any software packages that relate to the problem. Describe the hardware, if appropriate. There is an etiquette to posting questions—see www.catb.org/~esr/faqs/smart-questions.html for a good paper by Eric S. Raymond and Rick Moen titled "How To Ask Questions the Smart Way." For a fee, Red Hat provides many types of support.

The author's home page (www.sobell.com) contains corrections to this book, answers to selected chapter exercises, and pointers to other Linux sites.

# FINDING LINUX-RELATED INFORMATION

Fedora/RHEL comes with reference pages stored online. You can read these documents by using the man (page 128) or info (page 131) utility. You can read man and info pages to get more information about specific topics while reading this book or to determine which features are available with Linux. To search for topics, use apropos (see page 130 or give the command **man apropos**).

## DESKTOP APPLICATIONS

Many graphical applications are available for Linux; Table B-1 lists a few of them.

**Table B-1**    Desktop applications

| Site | About the site | URL |
|------|----------------|-----|
| openoffice.org | The openoffice.org suite includes word processing, spreadsheet, presentation, graphics, and database applications. | openoffice.org |
| LibreOffice | The LibreOffice suite includes word processing, spreadsheet, presentation, graphics, and database applications. | libreoffice.org |
| Thunderbird | Thunderbird is a cross-platform email, news, and chat client. | mozilla.org/thunderbird |
| Firefox | Firefox is a Web browser. | mozilla.org/firefox |
| blender | Blender is a suite for modelling, animation, rendering, post-production, interactive creation, and playback (games). | blender.org |

**Table B-1**   Desktop applications (continued)

| Site | About the site | URL |
| --- | --- | --- |
| gimp | GIMP (GNU Image Manipulation Program) is software for such tasks as photo retouching, image composition, and image authoring. | gimp.org |
| audacity | Audacity is a multi-track audio editor and recorder. | audacity.sourceforge.net |
| ImageMagick | ImageMagick is a software suite to create, edit, compose, or convert bitmap images. | imagemagick.org |
| pico | Pico is a text editor originally used with the **pine** mail system. | accc.uic.edu/service/shell-accounts/pico |

# PROGRAMMING LANGUAGES

Running Linux gives you access to a wide range of programming languages; Table B-2 lists a few of them.

**Table B-2**   Programming languages

| Site | About the site | URL |
| --- | --- | --- |
| PostgreSQL | PostgreSQL is a powerful object-relational database system; **postgresql-server** package. | postgresql.org |
| C | C is a general-purpose programming language; **gcc** package. | wikipedia.org/wiki/C_(programming_language) gcc.gnu.org |
| Perl | The Perl language is a general-purpose programming language; **perl** package. | perl.org |
| PHP | PHP is a general-purpose scripting language that is suited for Web development and can be embedded into HTML; **php** package. | php.net |

# LINUX NEWSGROUPS

One of the best ways of getting specific information is through a newsgroup. You can often find the answer to a question by reading postings to the newsgroup. Try using Google Groups (groups.google.com) to search through newsgroups to see whether your question has already been asked and answered. Alternately, open a newsreader program and subscribe to appropriate newsgroups. If necessary, you can post a question for someone to answer. Before you do so, make sure you are posting to the correct group and that your question has not already been answered.

The **comp.os.linux.answers** newsgroup provides postings of solutions to common problems and periodic postings of the most up-to-date versions of FAQ and HOWTO documents. The **comp.os.linux.misc** newsgroup has answers to miscellaneous Linux-related questions.

## MAILING LISTS

Subscribing to a mailing list (page 761) allows you to participate in an electronic discussion. With most lists, you can send and receive email dedicated to a specific topic to and from a group of users. Moderated lists do not tend to stray as much as unmoderated lists, assuming the list has a good moderator. The disadvantage of a moderated list is that some discussions might be cut off when they get interesting if the moderator deems that the discussion has gone on for too long. Mailing lists described as bulletins are strictly unidirectional: You cannot post information to these lists but can only receive periodic bulletins. If you have the subscription address for a mailing list but are not sure how to subscribe, put the word **help** in the body and/or header of email you send to the address. You will usually receive instructions via return email. Red Hat hosts several mailing lists; visit www.redhat.com/mailman/listinfo for more information. You can also use a search engine to search for **mailing list linux**.

## SPECIFYING A TERMINAL

Because vim, emacs, and other textual and pseudographical programs take advantage of features specific to various kinds of terminals and terminal emulators, you must tell these programs the name of the terminal you are using or the terminal your terminal emulator is emulating. Most of the time the terminal name is set for you. If the terminal name is not specified or is not specified correctly, the characters on the screen will be garbled or, when you start a program, the program will ask which type of terminal you are using.

Terminal names describe the functional characteristics of a terminal or terminal emulator to programs that require this information. Although terminal names are referred to as either Terminfo or Termcap names, the difference relates to the method each system uses to store the terminal characteristics internally—not to the manner in which you specify the name of a terminal. Terminal names that are often used with Linux terminal emulators and with graphical monitors while they are run in textual mode include **ansi**, **linux**, **vt100**, **vt102**, **vt220**, and **xterm**.

When you are running a terminal emulator, you can specify the type of terminal you want to emulate. Set the emulator to either **vt100** or **vt220**, and set **TERM** to the same value.

When you log in, you might be prompted to identify the type of terminal you are using:

```
TERM = (vt100)
```

You can respond to this prompt in one of two ways. First you can press RETURN to set your terminal type to the name in parentheses. If that name does not describe the terminal you are using, you can enter the correct name and then press RETURN.

```
TERM = (vt100) ansi
```

You might also receive the following prompt:

```
TERM = (unknown)
```

This prompt indicates that the system does not know which type of terminal you are using. If you plan to run programs that require this information, enter the name of the terminal or terminal emulator you are using before you press RETURN.

**TERM**  If you do not receive a prompt, you can give the following command to display the value of the **TERM** variable and check whether the terminal type has been set:

```
$ echo $TERM
```

If the system responds with the wrong name, a blank line, or an error message, set or change the terminal name. From bash (the Bourne Again Shell), enter a command similar to the following to set the **TERM** variable so the system knows which type of terminal you are using:

*export TERM=name*

Replace *name* with the terminal name for the terminal you are using, making sure you do not put a SPACE before or after the equal sign. If you always use the same type of terminal, you can place this command in your **~/.bashrc** file (page 329), causing the shell to set the terminal type each time you log in. For example, give the following command to set your terminal name to **vt100**:

```
$ export TERM=vt100
```

**LANG**  For some programs to display information correctly, you might need to set the **LANG** variable (page 368). Frequently you can set this variable to C. Under bash use the command

```
$ export LANG=C
```

# C

# SECURITY
# INCLUDING GPG

Security is a major part of the foundation of any system that is not totally cut off from other machines and users. Some aspects of security have a place even on isolated machines. Examples of these measures include periodic system backups, BIOS or power-on passwords, and self-locking screensavers.

A system that is connected to the outside world requires other mechanisms to secure it: tools to check files (tripwire), audit tools (tiger/cops), secure access methods (kerberos/ssh), services that monitor logs and machine states (swatch/watcher), packet-filtering and routing tools (ipfwadm/iptables), and more.

System security has many dimensions. The security of a system as a whole depends on the security of individual components, such as email, files, network, login, and remote access policies, as well as the physical security of the host itself. These dimensions frequently overlap, and their borders are not always static or clear. For instance, email security is affected by the security of both files and the network. If the medium (the network) over which you send and receive your email is not secure, then you must take extra steps to ensure the security of your messages. If you save your secure email in a file on the local system, then you rely on the filesystem and host access policies for file security. A failure in any one of these areas can start a domino effect, diminishing reliability and integrity in other areas and potentially compromising system security as a whole.

This short appendix cannot cover all facets of system security in depth, but it does provide an overview of the complexity of setting up and maintaining a secure system. This appendix offers some specifics, concepts, guidelines to consider, and many pointers to security resources (Table C-1 on page 1180).

### Other sources of system security information

security    Depending on how important system security is to you, you might want to purchase one or more books dedicated to system security, visit some of the Internet sites that are dedicated to security, or hire someone who is an expert in the field.

*Do not rely on this appendix as your sole source of information on system security.*

# ENCRYPTION

One of the building blocks of security is *encryption*, which provides a means of scrambling data for secure transmission to other parties. In cryptographic terms, the data or message to be encrypted is referred to as *plaintext*, and the resulting encrypted block of text as *ciphertext*. Processes exist for converting plaintext into ciphertext through the use of *keys*, which are essentially random numbers of a specified length used to *lock* and *unlock* data. This conversion is achieved by applying the keys to the plaintext according to a set of mathematical instructions, referred to as the *encryption algorithm*.

Developing and analyzing strong encryption software is extremely difficult. Many nuances exist, many standards govern encryption algorithms, and a background in mathematics is requisite. Also, unless an algorithm has undergone public scrutiny for a significant period of time, it is generally not considered secure; it is often impossible to know an algorithm is completely secure but possible to know that it is not secure. Ultimately time is the best test of any algorithm. Also, a solid algorithm does not guarantee an effective encryption mechanism because the fallibility of an encryption scheme frequently arises from problems with its implementation and distribution.

An encryption algorithm uses a key that is a certain number of bits long. Each bit added to the length of a key effectively doubles the *key space* (the number of combinations allowed by the number of bits in the key—2 to the power of the length of the key in bits[1]) and means it will take twice as long for an attacker to decrypt a message (assuming the scheme lacks any inherent weaknesses or vulnerabilities to exploit). However, it is a mistake to compare algorithms based only on the number of bits used. In some cases an algorithm that uses a 64-bit key can be more secure than an algorithm that uses a 128-bit key.

---

1. A 2-bit key would have a key space of 4 ($2^2$), a 3-bit key would have a key space of 8 ($2^3$), and so on.

The two primary classifications of encryption schemes are *public key encryption* and *symmetric key encryption*. Public key encryption, also called *asymmetric encryption*, uses two keys: a public key and a private key. These keys are uniquely associated with a specific user. Public key encryption schemes are used mostly to exchange keys and signatures. Symmetric key encryption, also called *symmetric encryption* or *secret key encryption*, uses one key that you and the person you are communicating with (hereafter referred to as your *friend*) share as a secret. Symmetric key encryption is typically used to encrypt large amounts of data because it is fast. Public key algorithm keys typically have a length of 512 bits to 2,048 bits, whereas symmetric key algorithms use keys in the range of 64 bits to 512 bits.

Asymmetric and symmetric algorithms complement each other. Asymmetric algorithms are good at providing digital signatures and authentication, but are slower. Symmetric algorithms are good at encrypting large blocks of data using a shared key and are faster. The algorithms are often combined to provide the best of both worlds: Text can first be processed using symmetric encryption and a random key. Then the random key can be encrypted using your friend's public key (so your friend can read it) and signed with your private key (to prove it came from you). The next sections cover these concepts in detail.

When you are choosing an encryption scheme, realize that security comes at a price. There is usually a tradeoff between resilience of the cryptosystem and ease of administration.

The practicality of a security solution is a far greater factor in encryption, and in security in general, than most people realize. With enough time and effort, nearly every algorithm can be broken. In fact, you can often unearth the mathematical instructions for a widely used algorithm by flipping through a cryptography book, reviewing a vendor's product specifications, or performing a quick search on the Internet. The challenge is to ensure the effort required to follow the twists and turns taken by an encryption algorithm and its resulting encryption solution outweighs the worth of the information it is protecting.

### How much time and money should you spend on encryption?

**tip**  When the cost of obtaining the information exceeds the value realized by its possession, the solution is an effective one.

## PUBLIC KEY (ASYMMETRIC) ENCRYPTION

To use public key encryption, you must generate two keys: a public key and a private key. You keep the private key for yourself and give the public key to the world. In a similar manner, each of your friends will generate a pair of keys and give you their public keys. Public key encryption is marked by two distinct features:

1. When you encrypt data with someone's public key, only that person's private key can decrypt it.

2. When you encrypt data with your private key, anyone can decrypt it with your public key.

You might wonder why the second point is useful: Why would you want everyone else to be able to decrypt something you just encrypted? The answer lies in the purpose of the encryption. Although encryption changes the original message into unreadable ciphertext, its purpose is to provide a *digital signature*. If the message can be properly decrypted with your public key, *only you* could have encrypted it with your private key, proving the message is authentic. Combining these two modes of operation yields privacy and authenticity. You can sign a message with your private key so it can be verified as authentic, and then you can encrypt it with your friend's public key so that only your friend can decrypt it.

Public key encryption has three major shortcomings:

1. Public key encryption algorithms are generally much slower than symmetric key algorithms and usually require a much larger key size and a way to generate large prime numbers[2] to use as components of the key, making them more resource intensive.

2. The private key must be stored securely and its integrity safeguarded. If a person's private key is obtained by another party, that party can encrypt, decrypt, and sign messages while impersonating the original owner of the key. If the private key is lost or becomes corrupted, any messages previously encrypted with it are also lost, and a new key pair must be generated.

3. It is difficult to authenticate the origin of a key—that is, to prove whom it originally came from. This so-called key-distribution problem is the raison d'être for such companies as VeriSign (www.verisign.com).

Algorithms such as RSA, Diffie-Hellman, and ElGamal implement public key encryption methodology. Today a 512-bit key is considered barely adequate for RSA encryption and offers marginal protection; 1,024-bit keys are expected to hold off determined attackers for several more years. Keys that are 2,048 bits long are now becoming commonplace and are rated as *espionage strength*. A mathematical paper published in late 2001 and reexamined in spring 2002 describes how a machine can be built—for a very large sum of money—that could break 1,024-bit RSA encryption in seconds to minutes (this point is debated in an article at www.schneier.com/crypto-gram-0203.html#6). Although the cost of such a machine exceeds the resources available to most individuals and smaller corporations, it is well within the reach of large corporations and governments. Since the publication of that paper, subsequent algorithmic and hardware improvements have led to designs of machines that can be built for around $10,000.

---

2. In particular, RSA public key encryption is based on the property that if you take two large prime numbers and multiply them together you get a much larger number. Identifying the factors of this number is a very difficult computational problem. When you keep one prime number and give away the other, the numbers act like a private key and public key.

# SYMMETRIC KEY ENCRYPTION

Symmetric key encryption is generally fast and simple to deploy. First you and your friend agree on which algorithm to use and a key you will share. Then either of you can decrypt or encrypt a file with the chosen key. Behind the scenes, symmetric key encryption algorithms are most often implemented as a network of black boxes, which can involve hardware components, software, or a combination of the two. Each box imposes a reversible transformation on the plaintext and passes it to the next box, where another reversible transformation further alters the data. The security of a symmetric key algorithm relies on the difficulty of determining which boxes were used and the number of times the data was fed through the set of boxes. A good algorithm will cycle the plaintext through a given set of boxes many times before yielding the result, and there will be no obvious mapping from plaintext to ciphertext.

The disadvantage of symmetric key encryption is that it depends heavily on the availability of a secure channel through which to send the key to your friend. For example, you would not use email to send your key; if your email is intercepted, a third party is in possession of your secret key, and your encryption is useless. You could relay the key over the phone, but your call could be intercepted if your phone were tapped or someone overheard your conversation.

Common implementations of symmetric key algorithms include DES (Data Encryption Standard), 3-DES (triple DES), IDEA, RC5, Blowfish, and AES (Advanced Encryption Standard). AES is the new (FIPS-197) Federal Information Processing Standard algorithm endorsed for governmental use and has been selected to replace DES as the de facto encryption algorithm. AES uses the Rijndael algorithm, chosen after a thorough evaluation of 15 candidate algorithms by the cryptographic research community.

None of the aforementioned algorithms has undergone more scrutiny than DES, which has been in use since the late 1970s. However, the use of DES has drawbacks and is no longer considered secure because the weakness of its 56-bit key makes it unreasonably easy to break. Given the advances in computing power and speed since DES was developed, the small size of this algorithm's key renders it inadequate for operations requiring more than basic security for a relatively short period of time. For a few thousand dollars, you can link off-the-shelf computer systems so they can crack DES keys in a few hours.

The 3-DES application of DES is intended to combat its degenerating resilience by running the encryption three times; it is projected to be secure for years to come. DES is probably sufficient for such tasks as sending email to a friend when you need it to be confidential or secure for only a few days (e.g., to send a notice of a meeting that will take place in a few hours). It is unlikely anyone is sufficiently interested in your email to invest the time and money to decrypt it. Because of 3-DES's wide availability and ease of use, it is advisable to use it instead of DES.

# ENCRYPTION IMPLEMENTATION

Most of today's commercial software packages use both public and symmetric key encryption algorithms, taking advantage of the strengths of each and avoiding their weaknesses. The public key algorithm is used first, as a means of negotiating a randomly generated secret key and providing for message authenticity. Then a secret key algorithm, such as 3-DES, IDEA, AES, or Blowfish, encrypts and decrypts the data on both ends for speed. Finally a hash algorithm, such as DSA (Digital Signature Algorithm), generates a message digest that provides a signature that can alert you to tampering. The digest is digitally signed with the sender's private key.

# GnuPG/PGP

The most popular personal encryption packages available today are GPG (GNU Privacy Guard, also called GnuPG; www.gnupg.org) and PGP (Pretty Good Privacy; www.symantec.com/business/theme.jsp?themeid=pgp). GPG was designed as a free replacement for PGP, a security tool that made its debut during the early 1990s. Phil Zimmerman developed PGP as a PKI (Public Key Infrastructure), featuring a convenient interface, ease of use and management, and the security of digital certificates. One critical characteristic set PGP apart from the majority of cryptosystems then available: PGP functions entirely without CAs (certification authorities). Until the introduction of PGP, PKI implementations were built around the concept of CAs and centralized key management controls. See page 1169 for a tutorial on using PGP.

Both PGP and GPG rely on the notion of a web of trust:[3] If you trust someone and that person trusts someone else, the person you trust can provide an introduction to the third party. When you trust someone, you perform an operation called *key signing*. By signing someone else's key, you verify that the person's public key is authentic and safe for you to use to send email. When you sign a key, you are asked whether you trust this person to introduce other keys to you. It is common practice to assign this trust based on several criteria, including your knowledge of a person's character or a lasting professional relationship with the person. The best practice is to sign someone's key only after you have met face to face to avert any chance of a man-in-the-middle scenario (see the adjacent tip). The disadvantage of this scheme is the lack of a central registry for associating with people you do not already know.

### MTM (man-in-the-middle) attack

security If Max and Zach try to carry on a secure email exchange over a network, Max first sends Zach his public key. However, suppose Mr. X sits between Max and Zach on the network and intercepts Max's public key. Mr. X then sends *his* public key to Zach. Zach then sends his public key to Max, but once again Mr. X intercepts it and substitutes *his* public key and sends that to Max. Without some kind of active protection (a piece of shared information), Mr. X, the *man in the middle*, can decrypt all traffic between Max and Zach, reencrypt it, and send it on to the other party. This type of deception is called a MTM attack.

---

3. For more information see www.gnupg.org/gph/en/manual/x334.html.

Symantec owns PGP. Although it is available without cost for personal use, its deployment in a commercial environment requires the purchase of a license. GnuPG is a free and compatible implementation of PGP.

GnuPG supports most features and implementations made available by PGP and complies with the OpenPGP Message Format standard. Because GnuPG does not use the patented IDEA algorithm but rather relies on BUGS (Big and Useful Great Security; www.gnu.org/directory/bugs.html), you can use it almost without restriction: It is released under the GNU GPL (refer to "The Code Is Free" on page 5). PGP and GnuPG are considered to be interchangeable and interoperable. The command sequences for and internal workings of these two tools are very similar.

### The GnuPG system includes the gpg program

tip  GnuPG is frequently referred to as gpg, but gpg is the name of the main program for the GnuPG system.

# FILE SECURITY

From an end user's perspective, file security is one of the most critical areas of security. Some file security is built into Linux: chmod (page 193) gives you basic security control. ACLs (Access Control Lists) allow more fine-grained control of file access permissions. ACLs are part of Solaris, Windows NT/2000/XP, VAX/VMS, and mainframe operating systems. Fedora/RHEL supports ACLs (page 198). Even these tools are insufficient, however, when your account is compromised (e.g., by someone watching your fingers on the keyboard as you type your password). To provide maximum file security, you must encrypt your files. Then even someone who knows your login password cannot read your files. Of course, if someone knows your key, that person can decrypt your files if she can get to them.

# EMAIL SECURITY

Email security overlaps file security and, as discussed later, network security. GnuPG is the tool most frequently used for email security, although you can also use PGP.

## MTAs (MAIL TRANSFER AGENTS)

An increasingly common protocol option is STARTTLS (Start Transport Layer Security; www.sendmail.org/~ca/email/starttls.html). TLS itself usually refers to SSL (Secure Sockets Layer) and has become the de facto method for encrypting TCP/IP traffic on the Internet. The **sendmail** (Chapter 20) and **exim4** daemons fully support STARTTLS, and much documentation exists on how to configure them. STARTTLS enhancements are also available for Qmail (page 742) and Postfix (page 742) and other popular MTAs (mail transfer agents). This capability provides encryption between two mail servers but not necessarily between the local system and the mail server. Also, the advantages of using TLS are negated if the email must pass through a relay that does not support TLS.

# MUAs (Mail User Agents)

Many popular mail user agents, such as mutt, elm, Thunderbird, and emacs, include the ability to use PGP or GnuPG for encryption. Evolution, the default Fedora/RHEL MUA (mail user agent), has built-in GnuPG support. This approach has become the default way to exchange email securely.

# Network Security

Network security is a vital component for ensuring the security of a computing site. However, without the right infrastructure, providing network security is difficult, if not impossible. For example, if you run a shared network topology,[4] such as wireless, without the latest security implementation to prevent snooping, how can you prevent someone from plugging in a machine and capturing all the *packets* (page 1265) that traverse the network?[5] You cannot—so you have a potential security hole. Another common security hole relates to the use of telnet for logins. Because telnet sends and receives cleartext, anyone "listening in" on the line can easily capture usernames and passwords, compromising security. Fortunately, this problem is serious only for legacy devices that support only telnet.

Do not allow any unauthenticated PC (any PC that does not require users to supply a local name and password) on a network. On UNIX/Linux, only a user working with **root** privileges can put the network interface in promiscuous mode and collect packets. On UNIX/Linux, ports numbered less than 1,024[6] are privileged—that is, normal user protocols cannot bind to these ports. This is an important but regrettable means of security for some protocols, such as NIS, NFS, RSH, and LPD. Normally a data switch on a LAN automatically protects machines from people snooping on the network for data. In high-load situations, switches have been known to behave unpredictably, directing packets to the wrong ports. Certain programs can overload the switch tables that hold information about which machine is on which port. When these tables are overloaded, the switch becomes a repeater and broadcasts all packets to all ports. An attacker on the same switch as you can potentially see the traffic the local system sends and receives.

## Network Security Solutions

One solution to shared-network problems is to encrypt messages that travel between machines. IPSec (Internet Protocol Security) provides an appropriate technology. IPSec is

---

4. Shared network topology: A network in which each packet might be seen by machines other than its destination. "Shared" means that the network bandwidth is shared by all users.
5. Do not make the mistake of assuming the local network is secure just because you have a switch. Switches are designed to allocate bandwidth, not to guarantee security.
6. The term *port* has many meanings; here it is a number assigned to a program. This number links incoming data with a specific service. For example, port 21 is used by FTP traffic, and port 23 is used by TELNET.

commonly used to establish a secure point-to-point virtual network (*VPN*, page 1280) that allows two hosts to communicate securely over an unsecure channel, such as the Internet. This protocol provides integrity, confidentiality, authenticity, and flexibility of implementation that supports multiple vendors.

IPSec is an amalgamation of protocols (IPSec = AH + ESP + IPComp + IKE):

- **AH (Authentication Header)**—A cryptographically secure, irreversible *checksum* (page 1242) for an entire packet. AH guarantees that the packet is authentic.

- **ESP (Encapsulating Security Payload)**—Encrypts a packet to make the data unreadable.

- **IPComp (IP Payload Compression)**—Compresses a packet. Encryption can increase the size of a packet, and IPComp counteracts this increase in size.

- **IKE (Internet Key Exchange)**—Provides a way for the endpoints to negotiate a common key securely. For AH to work, both ends of the exchange must use the same key to prevent a "man in the middle" (see the tip on page 1160) from spoofing the connection.

While IPSec is an optional part of IPv4, IPv6 (page 293) mandates its use.

## NETWORK SECURITY GUIDELINES

The following list of general guidelines for establishing and maintaining a secure system is not a complete list, but rather is meant as a guide.

- Fiberoptic cable is more secure than copper cable. Copper is subject to both active and passive eavesdropping. With access to copper cable, all a data thief needs to monitor your network traffic is a passive device for measuring magnetic fields. In contrast, it is much more difficult to tap a fiberoptic cable without interrupting the signal. Sites requiring top security keep fiberoptic cable in pressurized conduits, where a change in pressure signals that the physical security of the cable has been breached.

- Avoid leaving unused ports available in public areas. If a malicious user can plug a laptop into the network without being detected, you are at risk of a serious security problem. Network drops that will remain unused for extended periods should be disabled at the switch, preventing them from accepting or passing network traffic.

- Use the latest in wireless encryption. At the time of this writing, WEP is totally broken and WPA with TKIP is seriously flawed. WPA2 with AES is generally believed to be relatively secure.

- Many network switches have provisions for binding a hardware address to a port for enhanced security. If someone unplugs one machine and plugs in another machine to capture traffic, chances are that the second machine will have a different hardware address. When it detects a device with a different hardware address, the switch can disable the port. Even this solution is no guarantee, however, as some programs enable you to change or mask the hardware address of a network interface. This setup can be inconvenient when you need to swap out a machine for repair.

## Install a small kernel and run only the programs you need

security    Linux systems contain a huge number of programs that, although useful, significantly reduce the security of the host. Install the smallest operating system kernel that meets your needs. For servers, install only the needed components and do not install a graphical interface. Fewer packages mean fewer urgent security patches. Users might require additional packages.

- Do not allow NFSv3 or NIS access outside the local network. Otherwise, it is a simple matter for a malicious user to steal the password map. Default NFSv3 security is marginal to nonexistent (a common joke is that NFS stands for No File Security or Nightmare File System) so such access should not be allowed outside your network to machines you do not trust. Versions of NFS for Linux that support much better authentication algorithms are available. Use IPSec, NFSv4 (which includes improved authentication), or firewalls to provide access outside of the local domain. Kerberos, when combined with NFSv4 or NFSv3 provides very good security, but configuring Kerberos requires a book unto itself.

- Support for VPN configuration is often built into new firewalls or provided as a separate product, enabling your system to join securely with the systems of your customers or partners. If you must allow business partners, contractors, or other outside parties to access local files, consider using a secure filesystem, such as NFS with *Kerberos* (page 1257), secure NFS (encrypts authentication, not traffic), NFS over a VPN such as IPSec, or **cfs** (cryptographic filesystem).

- Specify **/usr** as readonly (**ro**) in **/etc/fstab**. Following is an example of such a configuration:

```
/dev/sda6      /usr      ext2      ro      0    0
```

This approach is not suitable for all operating systems, or even all Linux distributions. Some applications put changeable files in **/usr**. Also, this setup entrenches security flaws and makes the system difficult to update.

- Mount filesystems other than **/** and **/usr nosuid** to prevent setuid programs from executing on this filesystem. For example:

```
/dev/sda4      /var          ext4      nosuid    0    0
/dev/sda5      /usr/local    ext4      nosuid    0    0
```

- Use a barrier or firewall product between the local network and the Internet. Several valuable mailing lists cover firewalls, including the free firewalls Web site (www.freefire.org). Fedora/RHEL includes firewall-config (page 900) and iptables (page 908), which allow you to set up a firewall.

- Use a program that checks file integrity. Some examples are tripwire, samhain, and AIDE. These tools include a database of checksums of files you want to monitor and alert you when any of the monitored files change.

# HOST SECURITY

Your host must be secure. Simple security steps include preventing remote logins and leaving the **/etc/hosts.equiv** and individual users' **~/.rhosts** files empty (or not having them at all). Complex security steps include installing IPSec for VPNs between hosts. Many other security measures, some of which are discussed in this section, fall somewhere between these extremes. See Table C-1 on page 1180 for relevant URLs.

- Although potentially tricky to implement and manage, IDSs (intrusion detection systems) are an excellent way to keep an eye on the integrity of a device. An IDS can warn of possible attempts to subvert security on the host on which it runs. The great-granddaddy of intrusion detection systems is tripwire. This host-based system checks modification times and integrity of files by using strong algorithms (cryptographic checksums or signatures) that can detect even the most minor modifications. A commercial version of tripwire is also available. Another commercial IDS is DragonSquire. Other free, popular, and flexible IDSs include samhain and AIDE. The last two IDSs offer even more features and means of remaining invisible to users than tripwire does. Commercial IDSs that are popular in enterprise environments include Cisco Secure IDS (formerly NetRanger), Enterasys Dragon, and ISS RealSecure.

- Keep Fedora systems up-to-date by downloading and installing the latest updates. Use yum to update the system regularly (page 534) or allow the system to update itself every night automatically.

- Complementing host-based IDSs are network-based IDSs. The latter programs monitor the network and nodes on the network and report suspicious occurrences (attack signatures) via user-defined alerts. These signatures can be matched based on known worms, overflow attacks against programs, or unauthorized scans of network ports. Such programs as snort, klaxon, and NFR are used in this capacity. Commercial programs, such as DragonSentry, also fill this role.

- Provided with Fedora/RHEL is PAM, which allows you to set up different methods and levels of authentication in many ways (page 476).

- Process accounting—a good supplement to system security—can provide a continuous record of user actions on your system. See the accton man page (part of the **acct** package) for more information.

- Emerging standards for things such as RBAC (Role-Based Access Control) allow tighter delegation of privileges along defined organizational boundaries. You can delegate roles to each user as appropriate to the access required.

- General mailing lists and archives are useful repositories of security information, statistics, and papers. The most useful are the BugTraq mailing list and CERT.[7] The BugTraq site and email service offer immediate notifications about specific vulnerabilities, whereas CERT provides notice of widespread vulnerabilities and useful techniques to fix them, plus links to vendor patches.

- The syslog facility can direct messages from system daemons to specific files such as those in **/var/log**. On larger groups of systems, you can send all important syslog information to a secure host, where that host's only function is to store syslog data so it cannot be tampered with. See page 316 and the **syslogd** man page for more information.

# LOGIN SECURITY

Without a secure host, good login security cannot add much protection. Table C-1 on page 1180 lists some of the best login security tools, including replacement daemons for **telnetd**, **rlogind**, and **rshd**. Many sites use **ssh**, which comes as both freeware and a commercially supported package that works on UNIX/Linux, Windows, and Macintosh platforms.

The PAM facility (page 476) allows you to set up multiple authentication methods for users in series or in parallel. In-series PAM requires multiple methods of authentication for a user. In-parallel PAM uses any one of a number of methods for authentication.

Although not the most popular choice, you can configure a system to take advantage of one-time passwords. S/Key is the original implementation of one-time passwords by Bellcore. OPIE (one-time passwords in everything), which was developed by the U.S. Naval Research Labs, is an improvement over the original Bellcore system. In one permutation of one-time passwords, the user gets a piece of paper listing a set of one-time passwords. Each time a user logs in, she enters a password from the piece of paper. Once used, a password becomes obsolete, and the next password in the list is the only one that will work. Even if a malicious user compromises the network and sees your password, this information will be of no use because the password can be used only once. This setup makes it very difficult for someone to log in as you but does nothing to protect the data you type at the keyboard. One-time passwords is a good solution if you are at a site where no encrypted login is available. A truly secure (or paranoid) site will combine one-time passwords and encrypted logins.

Another type of secure login that is becoming more common is facilitated by a token or a *smartcard*. Smartcards are credit-card-like devices that use a challenge–response method of authentication. Smartcard and token authentication rely on something you have (the card) and something you know (a passphrase, user ID, or PIN). For example, you might enter your username in response to the login prompt and get a

---

7. CERT is slow but useful as a medium for coordination between sites. It acts as a tracking agency to document the spread of security problems.

password prompt. You would then enter your PIN and the number displayed on the access token. The token has a unique serial number that is stored in a database on the authentication server. The token and the authentication server use this serial number as a means of computing a challenge every 30 to 60 seconds. If the PIN and token number you enter match what they should be as computed by the access server, you are granted access to the system.

# REMOTE ACCESS SECURITY

Issues and solutions surrounding remote access security overlap with those pertaining to login and host security. Local logins might be secure with simply a username and password, whereas remote logins (and all remote access) should be made more secure. Many break-ins can be traced back to reusable passwords. It is a good idea to use an encrypted authentication client, such as ssh or kerberos. You can also use smartcards for remote access authentication.

Modem pools can also be an entry point into a system. Most people are aware of how easy it is to monitor a network line, but they might take for granted the security of the PSTN (public switched telephone network, also known as POTS—plain old telephone service). You might want to set up an encrypted channel after dialing in to a modem pool. One way to do so is by running ssh over PPP (page 292).

There are ways to implement stringent modem authentication policies so unauthorized users cannot use local modems. The most common techniques are PAP (Password Authentication Protocol), CHAP (Challenge Handshake Authentication Protocol), and Radius. PAP and CHAP are relatively weak compared to Radius, so the latter has rapidly gained in popularity. Cisco also provides a method of authentication called TACACS/TACACS+ (Terminal Access Controller Access Control System).

One or more of these authentication techniques are available in a RAS (remote access server—in a network, a computer that provides network access to remote users via modem).

Two other techniques for remote access security can be built into a modem (or RAS if it has integrated modems). One is callback: After you dial in, you get a password prompt. Once you type your password, the modem hangs up and calls you back at a phone number it has stored internally. Unfortunately this technique is not foolproof. Some modems have a built-in callback table that holds about ten entries, so this strategy works for small sites with only a few modems. If you use more modems, the RAS software must provide the callback.

The second technique is to use CLID (caller line ID) or ANI (automatic number identification) to decide whether to answer the call. Depending on your wiring and the local phone company, you might not be able to use ANI. ANI information is provided before the call, whereas CLID information is provided in tandem with the call.

# VIRUSES AND WORMS

Viruses spread through systems by infecting executable files. Examples of UNIX/Linux viruses include the Bliss virus/worm released in 1997 and the RST.b virus discovered in December 2001. Both are discussed in detail in articles on the Web. In the cases of Bliss and RST.b, the Linux native executable format, ELF, was used as a propagation vector.

Just after 5 PM on November 2, 1988, Robert T. Morris, Jr., a graduate student at Cornell University, released the first big virus onto the Internet. Called an Internet worm, this virus was designed to propagate copies of itself over many machines on the Internet. The worm was a piece of code that exploited four vulnerabilities, including one in finger, to force a buffer to overflow on a system. Once the buffer overflowed, the code was able to get a shell and then recompile itself on the remote machine. The worm spread around the Internet very quickly and was not disabled, despite many people's efforts, for 36 hours.

The chief characteristic of any worm is propagation over a public network, such as the Internet. A virus propagates by infecting executables on the machine, whereas a worm tends to prefer exploiting known security holes in network servers to gain **root** access and then tries to infect other machines in the same way.

UNIX/Linux file permissions help to inoculate systems against many viruses. Windows NT is resistant for similar reasons. You can easily protect the local system against many viruses and worms by keeping its system patches up-to-date, not executing untrusted binaries from the Internet, limiting **PATH** (page 359) to include only necessary system directories, and doing as little as possible while working with **root** privileges. You can prevent a disaster in case a virus strikes by frequently backing up the local system.

# PHYSICAL SECURITY

Often overlooked as a defense against intrusion, physical security covers access to the computer itself and to the console or terminal attached to the machine. If the machine is unprotected in an unlocked room, there is very little hope for physical security. (A simple example of physical vulnerability is someone walking into the room where the computer is, removing the hard drive from the computer, taking it home, and analyzing it.) You can take certain steps to improve the physical security of a computer.

- Keep servers in a locked room with limited access. A key, a combination, or a swipe card should be required to gain access. Protect windows as well as doors. Maintain a single point of entry. (Safety codes might require multiple exits, but only one must be an entry.)

- For public machines, use a security system, such as a fiberoptic security system, that can secure a lab full of machines. With such a system, you run a fiberoptic cable through each machine such that the machine cannot be removed (or opened) without cutting the cable. When the cable is cut, an alarm goes off. Some machines—for example, PCs with plastic cases—are much more difficult to secure than others. Although it is not a perfect solution, a fiberoptic security system might improve local security enough to persuade a would-be thief to go somewhere else.

- Most modern PCs have a BIOS password. You can set the order in which a PC searches for a boot device, preventing the PC from being booted from a CD/DVD or USB flash drive. Some BIOSs can prevent the machine from booting altogether without a proper password. The password protects the BIOS from unauthorized modification. Beware, however: Many BIOSs have well-known *back doors* (page 1238). In addition, you can blank the BIOS password by setting the clear-CMOS jumper on a PC motherboard; if you are relying on a BIOS password, lock the case.

- Run only fiberoptic cable between buildings. This strategy is not only more secure but also safer in the event of lightning strikes and is required by many commercial building codes.

- Maintain logs of who goes in and out of secure areas. Sign-in/out sheets are useful only if everyone uses them. Sometimes a guard is warranted. Often a simple proximity badge or smartcard can tell when anyone has entered or left an area and keep logs of these events.

- Anyone who has access to the physical hardware has the keys to the palace. Someone with direct access to a computer system can do such things as swap components and insert an installation medium, all of which are security threats.

- Avoid having activated, unused network jacks in public places. Such jacks provide unnecessary risk.

- Many modern switches can lock a particular switch port so it accepts only traffic from an NIC (network interface card) with a particular hardware address and shuts down the port if another address is seen. However, commonly available programs can enable someone to reset this address.

- Make periodic security sweeps. Check doors for proper locking. If you must have windows, make sure they are locked or are permanently sealed.

- Waste receptacles are often a source of information for intruders. Have policies for containment and disposal of sensitive documents.

- Use a UPS (uninterruptable power supply). Without a clean source of power, your system is vulnerable to corruption.

## LPI TUTORIAL: USING GPG TO SECURE A FILE

GPG (GNU Privacy Guard, also GnuPG; www.gnupg.org) enables you to encrypt a document so that only the person you specify when you encrypt the document can decrypt and read it. It also enables you to sign a document digitally so anyone can be sure it came from you and was not altered. See page 1160 for a discussion of how GPG works.

GPG uses public key encryption (page 1157) wherein you create a key pair: one private or secret key you keep to yourself and one public key you share with your correspondents or the world. The important part of this two-key system is that neither key can be calculated by having the other. They are each an independent and necessary part of the system and are based upon solid mathematical foundations. This setup allows you to

- Use your private key to sign a document to provide identification and message integrity to a recipient who has your public key.

    ◆ *Identification* means the recipient can be certain the document came from you.

    ◆ *Message integrity* means the recipient knows the message has not been altered.

    You can provide these features because only you have your private key.

- Use the recipient's public key to encrypt a document and provide secrecy.

    ◆ *Secrecy* means that only the recipient (who has the corresponding private key) can decrypt the document.

- Combine these steps to provide identification, message integrity, and secrecy (i.e., only the recipient can decrypt the document, the recipient knows the document came from you, and the recipient knows the document was not altered).

# CREATING A KEY PAIR

**LPI** ~/.gnupg    To start working with GPG you need to create a key pair for yourself. Use gpg with the **--gen-key** option to create a key pair. With this option, gpg creates and populates the ~/.**gnupg** directory if it does not exist. The **secring.gpg** file is the keyring that holds your secret keys; the **pubring.gpg** file is the keyring that holds your holds public keys. The following steps show Sam creating a key pair for himself.

```
$ gpg --gen-key
gpg (GnuPG) 1.4.14; Copyright (C) 2013 Free Software Foundation, Inc.
This is free software: you are free to change and redistribute it.
There is NO WARRANTY, to the extent permitted by law.

gpg: directory '/home/sam/.gnupg' created
gpg: new configuration file '/home/sam/.gnupg/gpg.conf' created
gpg: WARNING: options in '/home/sam/.gnupg/gpg.conf' are not yet active during this run
gpg: keyring '/home/sam/.gnupg/secring.gpg' created
gpg: keyring '/home/sam/.gnupg/pubring.gpg' created
```

The first question is about which kind of encryption ("what kind of key") you want to use. The default, RSA and RSA, is a good choice.

```
Please select what kind of key you want:
   (1) RSA and RSA (default)
   (2) DSA and Elgamal
```

```
  (3) DSA (sign only)
  (4) RSA (sign only)
Your selection? 1
```

The next question concerns the size of the key. Larger keys are more secure but take longer to process. A key that is 2,048 bits long is a good compromise.

```
RSA keys may be between 1024 and 4096 bits long.
What keysize do you want? (2048) 2048
Requested keysize is 2048 bits
```

Your answer to the next question determines when or if the key will expire. For most uses, a key that does not expire is a good choice. You must confirm this choice by typing **y**.

```
Please specify how long the key should be valid.
         0 = key does not expire
      <n>  = key expires in n days
      <n>w = key expires in n weeks
      <n>m = key expires in n months
      <n>y = key expires in n years
Key is valid for? (0)
Key does not expire at all
Is this correct? (y/N) y
```

Next you specify your real name (you can specify a nickname or handle in the comment section), your email address (the one most people associate with you), and an optional comment. After you specify these traits, a prompt allows you to edit them, quit, or continue (Okay).

```
You need a user ID to identify your key; the software constructs the user ID
from the Real Name, Comment and Email Address in this form:
    "Heinrich Heine (Der Dichter) <heinrichh@duesseldorf.de>"

Real name: Sam Smith
Email address: sam@example.com
Comment: Sam the Great
You selected this USER-ID:
    "Sam Smith (Sam the Great) <sam@example.com>"

Change (N)ame, (C)omment, (E)mail or (O)kay/(Q)uit? o
```

The last step in generating a key pair is specifying a passphrase that will keep your secret key secure. The passphrase should have the same characteristics as a password except it should be longer. Protect the passphrase as you would a password. For more information refer to "Password Security" on page 136.

```
You need a Passphrase to protect your secret key.

Enter passphrase:
Repeat passphrase:
```

After you enter a passphrase, gpg generates your keys. Generating truly random keys requires many random bytes, and generating random bytes requires entropy. As the instructions suggest, type on the keyboard, move the mouse, and use the disk (e.g., copy several large files) to gain entropy.

```
We need to generate a lot of random bytes. It is a good idea to perform
some other action (type on the keyboard, move the mouse, utilize the
disks) during the prime generation; this gives the random number
generator a better chance to gain enough entropy.

Not enough random bytes available.  Please do some other work to give
the OS a chance to collect more entropy! (Need 284 more bytes)
..+++++
.............+++++
gpg: /home/sam/.gnupg/trustdb.gpg: trustdb created
gpg: key D26C84B3 marked as ultimately trusted
public and secret key created and signed.

gpg: checking the trustdb
gpg: 3 marginal(s) needed, 1 complete(s) needed, PGP trust model
gpg: depth: 0  valid:   1  signed:   0  trust: 0-, 0q, 0n, 0m, 0f, 1u
pub 2048R/D26C84B3 2013-10-03
      Key fingerprint = 036A DE6E D653 3769 B243  A9EE 286A C3E0 D26C 84B3
uid                   Sam Smith (Sam the Great) <sam@example.com>
sub 2048R/569BA710 2013-10-03
```

When gpg finishes, you have generated your key pair. The gpg utility stores all information in the ~/.gpg directory. Your keys, and public keys you import using gpg, are stored on your keyring. The output shows two items you will use while working with gpg: the key ID (569BA710 in the example) and the key fingerprint.

fingerprint  After you have generated your key pair, you can display information about the pair using the gpg --list-keys and --fingerprint options. A *fingerprint* is a shorthand for the public portion of a key; you can use it for manual identification of the key.

```
$ gpg --list-keys
/home/sam/.gnupg/pubring.gpg
---------------------------
pub    2048R/D26C84B3 2013-10-03
uid                   Sam Smith (Sam the Great) <sam@example.com>
sub    2048R/569BA710 2013-10-03

$ gpg --fingerprint
/home/sam/.gnupg/pubring.gpg
---------------------------
pub    2048R/D26C84B3 2013-10-03
      Key fingerprint = 036A DE6E D653 3769 B243  A9EE 286A C3E0 D26C 84B3
uid                   Sam Smith (Sam the Great) <sam@example.com>
sub    2048R/569BA710 2013-10-03
```

## EXPORTING AND IMPORTING PUBLIC KEYS

You need to give your public key to people you want to share information with securely. The best way to share public keys is on a public keyserver (e.g., pgp.mit.edu). Public keyservers propagate keys to other keyservers so over time your keys will appear in many places. In addition, you can put your public key fingerprint on your business card. The more places your public key appears, the better. For more information refer to "Using a Keyserver" on page 1178.

Alternately, you can manually exchange public keys. It is poor practice to use email to give someone your public key because such an exchange can give rise to a man-in-the-middle attack (see the tip on page 1160). A better practice is to use a removable medium (e.g., a USB flash drive) to exchange keys. The following paragraphs explain how to manually exchange keys.

The following command exports public keys (**--export**) in ASCII format (**--armor**; or **–a**) to a file named **sam_pgp.asc** (**--output**; or **–o** followed by the name of the file you want to write to). If you specify a user, the command exports the public key for that user, otherwise it exports the public keys for all users on the public keyring. Following, Sam writes his public key to **sam_pgp.asc** and then displays that file. Then he saves it on a USB flash drive and gives the drive to Max.

```
$ gpg --export --armor --output sam_pgp.asc sam@example.com

$ cat sam_pgp.asc
-----BEGIN PGP PUBLIC KEY BLOCK-----
Version: GnuPG v1.4.14 (GNU/Linux)

mQENBFJNuu0BCADPBC2CrmGrkpluYVGH1U1zUKhAabHAeav1MGguv16js6wNdDt7
VUiuXu3DOqep9tejO0FZT0NzEboWEoYI1ukm0PRUNEeSIUdZqUdo2dZFPOas4xBa

...
KU2H61X8Kktn2Ct1kDy7ka2gjy24KiukkpuXsrBhNZFn751k3BTJYK/PemSGFhkY
tnaZZykjQO4d5Sh73jxRMpfaTxEZ32C5bXnxJ8ebz90SctFsChkBZX52
=I1kW
-----END PGP PUBLIC KEY BLOCK-----
```

Without the **--armor** or **–a** option gpg writes a binary file.

After Max copies Sam's public key from the flash drive, he adds it to his keyring using the following command

```
[max@guava ~]$ gpg --import sam_pgp.asc
gpg: key D26C84B3: public key "Sam Smith (Sam the Great) <sam@example.com>" imported
gpg: Total number processed: 1
gpg:               imported: 1  (RSA: 1)
```

Next, Sam follows the same procedure to add Max's public key to his keyring. The following examples assume Sam and Max have each other's public keys on their keyrings.

## Signing and Verifying a File

Next, Sam wants to send Max a text file named **memoA**.

```
$ cat memoA
This is memoA.
This is memoA.
This is memoA.
This is memoA.
```

Sam wants to make sure Max knows the messages is from him and that it has not been tampered with but does not care if anyone else can read it; he signs the file but does not encrypt it.

You can use one of two options to sign a file: **--clearsign** or **--detach-sign** (**-b**). The **--clearsign** option creates a clear-text signature that gpg appends to the file. This option is good for text files but does not work with binary files. The **--detach-sign** (**-b**) option creates a separate file that holds the signature and works with binary files. This section discusses both options.

Signing a file with either of these options does two things. It provides a digital signature that can prove who signed the file. It also generates a hash of the original file. When the recipient verifies the file, gpg confirms who signed the file *and* confirms that the file has not been tampered with.

## USING THE --clearsign OPTION

Sam signs the file using the **--clearsign** option, which generates a single, readable text file. The gpg utility requires Sam to enter his passphrase to unlock his secret key that gpg uses to sign the file.

```
$ gpg --clearsign memoA

You need a passphrase to unlock the secret key for
user: "Sam Smith (Sam the Great) <sam@example.com>"
2048-bit RSA key, ID D26C84B3, created 2013-10-03

Enter passphrase:
```

The preceding command generates the following file:

```
$ cat memoA.asc
-----BEGIN PGP SIGNED MESSAGE-----
Hash: SHA1

This is memoA.
This is memoA.
This is memoA.
This is memoA.
-----BEGIN PGP SIGNATURE-----
Version: GnuPG v1.4.14 (GNU/Linux)

iQEcBAEBAgAGBQJSTcEvAAoJEChqw+DSbISzWNMH/0mfj5DENMPCJyAk2JqPADc3

...
wvCffxSdTEAnp7u+juIfVGkZy4l3rwF8Vi4Imbvh9UFIXwgFrz3O+tVgDVhyPzo=
=Xmqk
-----END PGP SIGNATURE-----
```

*Sam* can verify the identity of the file (it was properly signed by himself) and message integrity (it was not tampered with) using the gpg **--verify** option. However, the message is not secret.

```
$ gpg --verify memoA.asc
gpg: Signature made Thu 03 Oct 2013 12:10:39 PM PDT using RSA key ID D26C84B3
gpg: Good signature from "Sam Smith (Sam the Great) <sam@example.com>"
```

If the file had been altered, gpg would display the following message:

```
$ gpg --verify memoA.asc
gpg: Signature made Thu 03 Oct 2013 12:10:39 PM PDT using RSA key ID D26C84B3
gpg: BAD signature from "Sam Smith (Sam the Great) <sam@example.com>"
```

When Sam sends the file to Max and *Max* verifies the file (using Sam's public key, which is on his keyring) gpg displays the following message

```
[max@guava ~]$ gpg --verify memoA.asc
gpg: Signature made Thu 03 Oct 2013 12:10:39 PM PDT using RSA key ID D26C84B3
gpg: Good signature from "Sam Smith (Sam the Great) <sam@example.com>"
gpg: WARNING: This key is not certified with a trusted signature!
gpg:          There is no indication that the signature belongs to the owner.
Primary key fingerprint: 036A DE6E D653 3769 B243  A9EE 286A C3E0 D26C 84B3
```

This message says that the signature and file are good based on the copy of Sam's public key on Max's keyring, but that the signature cannot be trusted. Someone (a man in the middle; page 1160) could have generated a key pair with Sam's name on it, sent the public key to Max, and signed the document using the bogus private key. To be trusted, a public key must be signed; see "Signing a Public Key" on page 1177.

## USING THE --detach-sign OPTION

The **--clearsign** option does not work with binary files: Appending an ASCII signature to a binary file would render the file useless. Instead, the **--detach-sign** (**-b**) option creates a separate signature file that gpg can use to verify the source of the file and also verify that the file has not been tampered with.

Max wants to send Sam **binfile**. He wants to ensure that Sam knows the file is from him and that it has not been altered, but does not care if someone else can use the file. When Max uses the **--detach-sign** option, gpg prompts Max to enter his passphrase and creates a **binfile.sig** file that holds the signature. Max must send both the **binfile** and **binfile.sig** files to Sam for Sam to verify the signature (and use the file).

```
[max@guava ~]$ gpg --detach-sign binfile

You need a passphrase to unlock the secret key for
user: "Max Wild <max@example.com>"
2048-bit RSA key, ID 643E62B8, created 2013-10-03

Enter passphrase:

[max@guava ~]$ ls -l binfile*
-rwxr-xr-x. 1 max pubs 982296 10-03 12:28 binfile
-rw-r--r--. 1 max pubs    287 10-03 12:30 binfile.sig
```

Assuming Max's public key is on Sam's keyring, when Sam specifies the name of the signature file as an argument to gpg, gpg verifies the file and signature.

```
$ gpg binfile.sig
gpg: Signature made Thu 03 Oct 2013 12:30:02 PM PDT using RSA key ID 643E62B8
gpg: Good signature from "Max Wild <max@example.com>"
gpg: WARNING: This key is not certified with a trusted signature!
gpg:          There is no indication that the signature belongs to the owner.
Primary key fingerprint: 92CB 83B7 8439 C740 8B80  6C75 72E3 1884 643E 62B8
```

Again, Max's public key must be signed to be trusted.

## Encrypting and Decrypting a File

When you encrypt a file using a public key, only the corresponding private key can decrypt the file. If you want to send a file to someone such that only that person can read (or run) that file, you can encrypt the file using the recipient's public key. Then the recipient can decrypt the file using her private key; no one else can read the file.

Following, Max encrypts the **memoB** file using Sam's public key, yielding an unreadable file named **memoB.gpg**.

```
[max@guava ~]$ gpg --recipient sam@example.com --encrypt memoB
[max@guava ~]$ ls -l memoB*
-rw-r--r--. 1 max pubs  60 10-03 12:45 memoB
-rw-r--r--. 1 max pubs 349 10-03 12:45 memoB.gpg
```

When Sam receives the file, he decrypts it using his secret key:

```
$ gpg --output memoB --decrypt memoB.gpg

You need a passphrase to unlock the secret key for
user: "Sam Smith (Sam the Great) <sam@example.com>"
2048-bit RSA key, ID 569BA710, created 2013-10-03 (main key ID D26C84B3)

gpg: encrypted with 2048-bit RSA key, ID 569BA710, created 2013-10-03
       "Sam Smith (Sam the Great) <sam@example.com>"
```

```
$ cat memoB
This is memoB.
This is memoB.
This is memoB.
This is memoB.
```

## Signing and Encrypting a File

If you want to keep a file from prying eyes and ensure that it comes from the person it says it comes from and that it has not be altered, you can sign the file using your private key and encrypt it using the recipient's public key. The recipient can then decrypt it using his public key and verify the signature using the sender's public key.

In the next example, Max encrypts **memoC** using Sam's public key and signs the file using his private key. The resulting file is named **memoC.gpg**. Because Max is using his private key, he must supply his passphrase.

```
$ gpg --recipient sam@example.com --encrypt --sign memoC

You need a passphrase to unlock the secret key for
user: "Max Wild <max@example.com>"
```

```
2048-bit RSA key, ID 643E62B8, created 2013-10-03

Enter passphrase:
...
```

When Sam gets the file he decrypts it, sending the output (the decrypted file) to **memoC**. Because the file was encrypted using Sam's public key, Sam must provide his private key to decrypt it. At the bottom of the output, gpg confirms that Max's signature is good.

```
$ gpg --output memoC memoC.gpg

You need a passphrase to unlock the secret key for
user: "Sam Smith (Sam the Great) <sam@example.com>"
2048-bit RSA key, ID 569BA710, created 2013-10-03 (main key ID D26C84B3)
Enter passphrase:

gpg: encrypted with 2048-bit RSA key, ID 569BA710, created 2013-10-03
      "Sam Smith (Sam the Great) <sam@example.com>"
gpg: Signature made Thu 03 Oct 2013 12:50:51 PM PDT using RSA key ID 643E62B8
gpg: Good signature from "Max Wild <max@example.com>"
```

## SIGNING A PUBLIC KEY

If you trust that a public key belongs to the person it says it belongs to, you can sign that key to make it more trustworthy. The more people who sign a key, the more trustworthy it becomes.

A key ID identifies a key. You can use the gpg **--list-key** option to list the IDs of all the keys on your keyring. The following output shows that Sam's key is 2,048 bits long, uses RSA encryption (R), and has a key ID of D26C84B3.

```
$ gpg --list-key
/home/max/.gnupg/pubring.gpg
-------------------------
...
pub   2048R/D26C84B3 2013-10-03
uid                 Sam Smith (Sam the Great) <sam@example.com>
sub   2048R/569BA710 2013-10-03
```

Before you sign a key, make sure it belongs to the person it says it belongs to. Download the key from several sources (e.g., keyservers). Each key has a unique fingerprint that you can use to identify that key. Use the gpg **--fingerprint** option followed by the key ID to display the fingerprint of a key and compare the fingerprints.

```
[max@guava ~]$ gpg --fingerprint D26C84B3
pub   2048R/D26C84B3 2013-10-03
      Key fingerprint = 036A DE6E D653 3769 B243  A9EE 286A C3E0 D26C 84B3
uid                 Sam Smith (Sam the Great) <sam@example.com>
sub   2048R/569BA710 2013-10-03
```

Check that the fingerprint is correct by comparing it to one supplied by the person who owns it. Use a keyserver, the phone, or a printout, not email, to verify the fingerprint. Once you are sure you have a valid key you can sign it using the gpg **--sign-key** option followed by the key ID you have just verified. Following, Max signs the copy of Sam's public key that is on Max's keyring.

```
[max@guava ~]$ gpg --sign-key D26C84B3

pub  2048R/D26C84B3  created: 2013-10-03  expires: never     usage: SC
                     trust: unknown      validity: unknown
sub  2048R/569BA710  created: 2013-10-03  expires: never     usage: E
[ unknown] (1). Sam Smith (Sam the Great) <sam@example.com>

pub  2048R/D26C84B3  created: 2013-10-03  expires: never     usage: SC
                     trust: unknown      validity: unknown
 Primary key fingerprint: 036A DE6E D653 3769 B243  A9EE 286A C3E0 D26C 84B3

     Sam Smith (Sam the Great) <sam@example.com>

Are you sure that you want to sign this key with your
key "Max Wild <max@example.com>" (643E62B8)

Really sign? (y/N) y

You need a passphrase to unlock the secret key for
user: "Max Wild <max@example.com>"
2048-bit RSA key, ID 643E62B8, created 2013-10-03

Enter passphrase:
```

You use your secret key to sign a document, proving you signed the document. To gain access to your secret key, gpg requires you to enter your passphrase.

Now when Max verifies Sam's document gpg checks the trust database, displays some information about Sam's public key, and declares that Sam's signature is good.

```
$ gpg --verify memoA.asc
gpg: Signature made Thu 03 Oct 2013 12:10:39 PM PDT using RSA key ID D26C84B3
gpg: checking the trustdb
gpg: 3 marginal(s) needed, 1 complete(s) needed, PGP trust model
gpg: depth: 0  valid:   1  signed:   1  trust: 0-, 0q, 0n, 0m, 0f, 1u
gpg: depth: 1  valid:   1  signed:   0  trust: 1-, 0q, 0n, 0m, 0f, 0u
gpg: Good signature from "Sam Smith (Sam the Great) <sam@example.com>"
```

# Using a Keyserver

If you want to share your public key with the world, you can upload it to a keyserver. Having your key on a keyserver makes it easier for several people to sign it. It also makes it easier for people to find and use to encrypt documents they send to you. Once it is uploaded, it will be distributed to all keyservers; there is no need to upload it to more than one. The keys.gnupg.net URL uses a round-robin DNS that points to a different keyserver each time you reference it.

The following example sends the public key with the key ID 99ZZ99ZZ from the user's keyring to the keyserver that keys.gnupg.net points to. The gpg utility uses keys.gnupg.net by default; you can specify a different keyserver by using the --keyserver option. The argument following the --send-keys option specifies the key ID of the public key gpg is to send from the user's keyring to the keyserver.

```
$ gpg  --send-keys 99ZZ99ZZ
gpg: sending key 99ZZ99ZZ to hkp server keys.gnupg.net
```

If you want to sign a key that is stored on a keyserver, first determine the key ID of the key (get it from your friend or look it up on a keyserver [e.g., pgp.mit.edu]). Then download the key. Again, gpg defaults to keys.gnupg.net. The **--recv-keys** option specifies the key ID of the key you want to download. The gpg utility stores the key on your keyring.

```
$ gpg --recv-keys 99ZZ99ZZ
gpg: requesting key 99ZZ99ZZ from hkp server keys.gnupg.net
gpg: key 99ZZ99ZZ: public key "Zach Brill <zach@example.com>" imported
gpg: Total number processed: 1
gpg:                 imported: 1
```

Next use the **--fingerprint** option followed by the key ID of the key you just downloaded to display the fingerprint of the key.

```
$ gpg --fingerprint 99ZZ99ZZ
pub   1024D/99ZZ99ZZ 1998-10-23
      Key fingerprint = 5E1C  544D 83BF D3D0 6ED9  61EA C1B2 A984 68DB 67AE
uid                      Zach Brill <zach@example.com>
sub   2048g/C548F7C0 1998-10-23
```

Always make sure the key you are signing belongs to the person it says it belongs to and that that person is a real person. Obtain the fingerprint of the key from a source other than a keyserver and verify the fingerprint before signing a key. In the following example, the argument following the **--sign-key** option specifies the key ID of the key the user will sign on the keyserver. Because this command signs the key on the keyserver, there is no need to upload the key from your keyring.

```
$ gpg --keyserver keys.gnupg.net --sign-key 99ZZ99ZZ

pub  1024D/99ZZ99ZZ  created: 1998-10-23  expires: never       usage: SCA
                     trust: unknown       validity: unknown
sub  2048g/C548F7C0  created: 1998-10-23  expires: never       usage: E
[ unknown] (1). Zach Brill <zach@example.com>


pub  1024D/99ZZ99ZZ  created: 1998-10-23  expires: never       usage: SCA
                     trust: unknown       validity: unknown
 Primary key fingerprint: 9Z9Z 999Z 99ZZ 9Z9Z 999Z  9Z9Z 999Z 9Z9Z 999Z 99ZZ

     Zach Brill <zach@example.com>

Are you sure that you want to sign this key with your
key "Max Wild <max@example.com>" (643E62B8)

Really sign? (y/N) y

You need a passphrase to unlock the secret key for
user: "Max Wild <max@example.com>"
2048-bit RSA key, ID 643E62B8, created 2013-10-03

Enter passphrase:
```

# SECURITY RESOURCES

Many free and commercial programs can enhance system security. Some of these are listed in Table C-1. Many of these sites have links to other, interesting sites that are worth looking at.

Table C-1   Security resources

| Tool | What it does | Where to get it |
|------|--------------|-----------------|
| AIDE | Advanced Intrusion Detection Environment. Similar to **tripwire** with extensible verification algorithms. | sourceforge.net/projects/aide |
| BugTraq | A moderated mailing list for the announcement and detailed discussion of all aspects of computer security vulnerabilities. | www.securityfocus.com/archive/1 |
| CERT | Computer Emergency Response Team. A repository of papers and data about major security events and a list of security tools. | www.cert.org |
| dsniff | Sniffing and network audit tool suite. Free. | monkey.org/~dugsong/dsniff |
| GIAC | A security certification and training Web site. | www.giac.org |
| hping | Multipurpose network auditing and packet analysis tool. | www.hping.org |
| ISC$^2$ | Educates and certifies industry professionals and practitioners under an international standard. | www.isc2.org |
| John | John the Ripper: a fast, flexible, weak password detector. | www.openwall.com/john |
| Kerberos | Complete, secure network authentication system. | web.mit.edu/kerberos/www |
| LinuxSecurity.com | A solid news site dedicated to Linux security issues. | www.linuxsecurity.com |
| LWN.net | Security alert database for all major Linux distributions. | lwn.net/Alerts |

**Table C-1**  Security resources (continued)

| Tool | What it does | Where to get it |
|------|-------------|----------------|
| Microsoft Security | Microsoft security information. | www.microsoft.com/security |
| nessus | A plugin-based remote security scanner that can perform more than 370 security checks. Free. | www.nessus.org |
| nmap | Scans hosts to see which ports are available. It can perform stealth scans, determine operating system type, find open ports, and more. | nmap.org |
| RBAC | Role-Based Access Control. Assigns roles and privileges associated with the roles. | csrc.nist.gov/groups/SNS/rbac |
| Red Hat Security | Red Hat security information. | www.redhat.com/security |
| Rootkit Hunter (RKH) | Checks system for rootkits and other unwanted tools. | rkhunter.sourceforge.net |
| SAINT | Security Administrator's Integrated Network Tool. Assesses and analyzes network vulnerabilities. | www.saintcorporation.com |
| samhain | A file integrity checker. Has a GUI configurator, client/server capability, and real-time reporting capability. | www.la-samhna.de |
| SANS | Security training and certification. | www.sans.org |
| SARA | The Security Auditor's Research Assistant security analysis tool. | www-arc.com/sara |
| Schneier, Bruce | Security visionary. | www.schneier.com |
| Secunia | Monitors a broad spectrum of vulnerabilities. | secunia.com |
| SecurityFocus | Home for security tools, mail lists, libraries, and cogent analysis. | www.securityfocus.com |
| snort | A flexible IDS. | www.snort.org |

**Table C-1**   Security resources (continued)

| Tool | What it does | Where to get it |
|------|--------------|-----------------|
| ssh | A secure rsh, ftp, and rlogin replacement with encrypted sessions and other options. Supplied with Fedora/RHEL. | openssh.org |
| swatch | A Perl-based log parser and analyzer. | sourceforge.net/projects/swatch |
| Treachery | A collection of tools for security and auditing. | www.treachery.net/tools |
| tripwire | Checks for possible signs of intruder activity. Supplied with Fedora/RHEL. | www.tripwire.com |
| wireshark | Network protocol analyzer. Free. | www.wireshark.org |

# APPENDIX SUMMARY

Security is inversely proportional to usability. There must be a balance between users' requirements to get their work done and the amount of security that is implemented. It is often unnecessary to provide top security for a small business with only a few employees. By contrast, if you work for a government military contractor, you are bound to have extreme security constraints and an official audit policy to determine whether security policies are being implemented correctly.

Review your own security requirements periodically. Several of the tools mentioned in this appendix can help you monitor a system's security measures. Tools such as nessus, samhain, and SAINT, for example, provide auditing mechanisms.

Some companies specialize in security and auditing. Hiring one of them to examine your site can be costly but might yield specific recommendations for areas you might have overlooked in your initial setup. When you hire someone to audit your security, recognize that you might be providing both physical and **root** access to local systems. Make sure the company that you hire has a good history, has been in business for several years, and has impeccable references. Check up on the company periodically: Things change over time. Avoid the temptation to hire former system crackers as consultants. Security consultants should have an irreproachable ethical background or you will always have doubts about their intentions.

Your total security package is based on your risk assessment of local vulnerabilities. Strengthen those areas that are most important for your business. For example, many sites rely on a firewall to protect them from the Internet, whereas internal hosts might receive little or no security attention. Crackers refer to this setup as "the crunchy outside surrounding the soft chewy middle." Yet this setup is entirely sufficient to protect some sites. Perform your own risk assessment and address your needs accordingly. If need be, hire a full-time security administrator whose job it is to design and audit local security policies.

# D

# KEEPING THE SYSTEM UP-TO-DATE USING apt-get

The apt-get utility fills the same role as yum, described in Chapter 12: They install and update software packages. Both utilities compare the files in a repository (generally on the Internet) with those on the local system and update the files on the local system according to your instructions. Both utilities automatically install and update any additional files that a package depends on (dependencies). Most Linux distributions come with apt-get or yum. Debian-based systems such as Ubuntu and Mint are set up to use apt-get, which works with **deb** packages. RHEL (Red Hat Enerprise Linux) and Fedora use yum, which works with **rpm** packages. There are also versions of apt-get that work with **rpm** packages.

To facilitate the update process, apt-get and yum keep locally a list of packages that are held in each of the repositories they use. Any software you want to install or update must reside in a repository.

When you give apt-get or yum a command to install a package, they look for the package in a local package list. If the package appears in the list, apt-get or yum fetches both that package and any packages the package you are installing depends on and installs the packages.

The apt-get examples in this section are from an Ubuntu system. Although the files, input, and output on the local system might look different, how you use the tools—and the results—will be the same.

*LPI* apt-get and **dpkg**
APT (Advanced Package Tool) is a collection of utilities that download, install, remove, upgrade, and report on software packages. APT utilities download packages and call **dpkg** utilities to manipulate the packages once they are on the local system. For more information refer to help.ubuntu.com/community/AptGet/Howto.

Updating the package list
The primary APT command is apt-get; its arguments determine what the command does. Working with **root** privileges, give the command **apt-get update** to update the local package list:

```
# apt-get update
Get:1 http://extras.ubuntu.com precise Release.gpg [72 B]
Get:2 http://security.ubuntu.com precise-security Release.gpg [198 B]
Hit http://extras.ubuntu.com precise Release
Get:3 http://security.ubuntu.com precise-security Release [49.6 kB]
Hit http://extras.ubuntu.com precise/main Sources
Get:4 http://us.archive.ubuntu.com precise Release.gpg [198 B]
Hit http://extras.ubuntu.com precise/main i386 Packages
Get:5 http://us.archive.ubuntu.com precise-updates Release.gpg [198 B]
Get:6 http://us.archive.ubuntu.com precise-backports Release.gpg [198 B]
Get:7 http://us.archive.ubuntu.com precise Release [49.6 kB]
Get:8 http://security.ubuntu.com precise-security/main Sources [22.5 kB]
Get:9 http://security.ubuntu.com precise-security/restricted Sources [14 B]
...
Fetched 13.4 MB in 2min 20s (95.4 kB/s)
Reading package lists... Done
```

Check the dependency tree
The apt-get utility does not tolerate a broken dependency tree. To check the status of the local dependency tree, give the command **apt-get check**:

```
# apt-get check
Reading package lists... Done
Building dependency tree
Reading state information... Done
```

The easiest way to fix errors that apt-get reveals is to remove the offending packages and then reinstall them using apt-get.

# *LPI* Using apt-get to Install, Remove, and Update Packages

Installing packages
The following command uses apt-get to install the **zsh** package:

```
# apt-get install zsh
Reading package lists... Done
Building dependency tree
Reading state information... Done
Suggested packages:
```

```
          zsh-doc
The following NEW packages will be installed:
    zsh
0 upgraded, 1 newly installed, 0 to remove and 2 not upgraded.
Need to get 0 B/4,667 kB of archives.
After this operation, 11.5 MB of additional disk space will be used.
Selecting previously unselected package zsh.
(Reading database ... 166307 files and directories currently installed.)
Unpacking zsh (from .../zsh_4.3.17-1ubuntu1_i386.deb) ...
Processing triggers for man-db ...
Setting up zsh (4.3.17-1ubuntu1) ...
update-alternatives: using /bin/zsh4 to provide /bin/zsh (zsh) in auto mode.
update-alternatives: using /bin/zsh4 to provide /bin/rzsh (rzsh) in auto mode.
update-alternatives: using /bin/zsh4 to provide /bin/ksh (ksh) in auto mode.
```

Removing packages
Remove a package the same way you install a package, substituting **remove** for **install**:

```
# apt-get remove zsh
Reading package lists... Done
Building dependency tree
Reading state information... Done
The following packages will be REMOVED:
    zsh
0 upgraded, 0 newly installed, 1 to remove and 2 not upgraded.
After this operation, 11.5 MB disk space will be freed.
Do you want to continue [Y/n]? y
(Reading database ... 167467 files and directories currently installed.)
Removing zsh ...
Processing triggers for man-db ...
```

To ensure you can later reinstall a package with the same configuration, the apt-get **remove** command does not remove configuration files from the **/etc** directory hierarchy. Although it is not recommended, you can use the **purge** command instead of **remove** to remove all the package files, including configuration files. Alternately, you can move these files to an archive so you can restore them later if necessary.

## *LPI*  USING apt-get TO UPGRADE THE SYSTEM

Two arguments cause apt-get to upgrade all packages on the system: **upgrade** upgrades all packages on the system that do not require new packages to be installed and **dist-upgrade** upgrades all packages on the system, installing new packages as needed; this argument will install a new version of the operating system if one is available.

The following command updates all packages on the system that depend only on installed packages:

```
# apt-get upgrade
Reading package lists... Done
Building dependency tree
Reading state information... Done
The following packages will be upgraded:
  eog libtiff4
2 upgraded, 0 newly installed, 0 to remove and 0 not upgraded.
Need to get 906 kB of archives.
After this operation, 20.5 kB disk space will be freed.
Do you want to continue [Y/n]? y
```

```
Get:1 http://us.archive.ubuntu.com/ubuntu/ precise-updates/main libtiff4 i386 3.9.5-2ubuntu1.1 [142 kB]
Get:2 http://us.archive.ubuntu.com/ubuntu/ precise-updates/main eog i386 3.4.2-0ubuntu1 [763 kB]
Fetched 906 kB in 2s (378 kB/s)
(Reading database ... 167468 files and directories currently installed.)
Preparing to replace libtiff4 3.9.5-2ubuntu1 (using .../libtiff4_3.9.5-2ubuntu1.1_i386.deb) ...
Unpacking replacement libtiff4 ...
Preparing to replace eog 3.4.1-0ubuntu1 (using .../eog_3.4.2-0ubuntu1_i386.deb) ...
Unpacking replacement eog ...
Processing triggers for libglib2.0-0 ...
Processing triggers for man-db ...
Processing triggers for gconf2 ...
Processing triggers for hicolor-icon-theme ...
Processing triggers for bamfdaemon ...
Rebuilding /usr/share/applications/bamf.index...
Processing triggers for desktop-file-utils ...
Processing triggers for gnome-menus ...
Setting up libtiff4 (3.9.5-2ubuntu1.1) ...
Setting up eog (3.4.2-0ubuntu1) ...
Processing triggers for libc-bin ...
ldconfig deferred processing now taking place
```

When apt-get asks whether you want to continue, enter **Y** to upgrade the listed packages; otherwise, enter **N**. Packages that are not upgraded because they depend on packages that are not already installed are listed as **kept back**.

Use **dist-upgrade** to upgrade all packages, including packages that depend on packages that are not installed. This command also installs dependencies.

## *LPI*  OTHER apt-get COMMANDS

| | |
|---|---|
| autoclean | Removes old archive files. |
| check | Checks for broken dependencies. |
| clean | Removes archive files. |
| dist-upgrade | Upgrades packages on the system, installing new packages as needed. If a new version of the operating system is available, this option upgrades to the new version. |
| purge | Removes a package and all its configuration files. |
| source | Downloads source files. |
| update | Retrieves new lists of packages. |
| upgrade | Upgrades all packages on the system that do not require new packages to be installed. |

## REPOSITORIES

*Repositories* hold collections of software packages and related information, including headers that describe each package and provide information on other packages the package depends on. Typically, a Linux distribution maintains repositories for each of its releases.

Software package categories    Software packages are frequently divided into several categories. Ubuntu uses the following categories:

- **main**—Ubuntu-supported open-source software
- **universe**—Community-maintained open-source software
- **multiverse**—Software restricted by copyright or legal issues
- **restricted**—Proprietary device drivers
- **backports**—Packages from later releases of Ubuntu that are not available for an earlier release

The apt-get utility selects packages from repositories it searches based on the categories specified in the **sources.list** file.

# *LPI*    sources.list: **SPECIFIES REPOSITORIES FOR** apt-get **TO SEARCH**

The **/etc/apt/sources.list** file specifies the repositories apt-get searches when you ask it to find or install a package. You must modify the **sources.list** file to enable apt-get to download software from nondefault repositories. Typically, you do not need to configure apt-get to install supported software.

Each line in **sources.list** describes one repository and has the following syntax:

*type URI repository category-list*

where *type* is **deb** for packages of executable files and **deb-src** for packages of source files; *URI* is the location of the repository, usually **cdrom** or an Internet address that starts with **http://**; *repository* is the name of the repository apt-get is to search; and *category-list* is a SPACE-separated list of categories apt-get selects packages from. Comments begin with a pound sign (#) anywhere on a line and end at the end of the line.

The following line from **sources.list** on an Ubuntu system causes apt-get to search the Precise archive located at us.archive.ubuntu.com/ubuntu for **deb** packages that contain executable files. It accepts packages that are categorized as **main, restricted,** and **multiverse:**

```
deb http://us.archive.ubuntu.com/ubuntu/ precise main restricted multiverse
```

Replace **deb** with **deb-src** to search for packages of source files in the same manner. Use the apt-get **source** command to download source packages.

Default repositories    The default **sources.list** file on an Ubuntu system includes repositories such as **precise** (Precise as originally released), **precise-updates** (major bug fixes after the release of Precise), **precise-security** (critical security-related updates), and **precise-backports** (newer, less-tested software that is not reviewed by the Ubuntu security team). Some repositories in **sources.list** might be commented out. Remove the leading pound sign (#) on the lines of the repositories you want to enable. After you modify **sources.list**, give the command **apt-get update** (page 1184) to update the local package indexes.

The next line, which was added to **sources.list,** enables apt-get to search a third-party repository (but see the following security tip):

```
deb http://download.skype.com/linux/repos/debian/ stable non-free
```

In this case, the repository is named **stable** and the category is **non-free.** Although the code is compiled for Debian, it runs on Ubuntu, as is frequently the case.

### Use repositories you trust

security There are many repositories of software packages. Be selective regarding which repositories you add to **sources.list:** When you add a repository, you are trusting the person who runs the repository not to put malicious software in packages you might download. In addition, unsupported packages might conflict with other packages or cause upgrades to fail.

# LPI AND CompTIA CERTIFICATION

This book is used as the adopted text in many college classes. Because students who take these classes often seek LPI or CompTIA certification, instructors have asked for a mapping of certification objectives to the material covered in this book. This book fully covers LPI's Linux Essentials certification learning goals and provides extensive coverage of CompTIA's Linux+ exam objectives. This appendix maps these learning goals and exam objectives to pages in this book. The following icons are used throughout the book to mark the places where learning goals and exam objectives are discussed.

**LE** This icon indicates coverage of a topic in the LPI's Linux Essentials certification learning goals.

**LPI** This icon indicates coverage of a topic in the CompTIA's Linux+ exam objectives.

**LE+** This icon indicates coverage of a topic in the CompTIA's Linux+ exam objectives and a topic in the LPI's Linux Essentials certification learning goals.

## MORE INFORMATION

LPI Linux Essentials: www.lpi.org/linux-certifications/introductory-programs/linux-essentials
LPI Certification Exams: www.lpi.org/linux-certifications/programs/lpic-1
CompTIA Exams: certification.comptia.org/getCertified/certifications/linux.aspx
CompTIA and LPI partnership: www.lpi.org/linux-certifications/partnership-programs/comptia

## LINUX ESSENTIALS

## TOPIC 1: THE LINUX COMMUNITY AND A CAREER IN OPEN SOURCE

### 1.1 LINUX EVOLUTION AND POPULAR OPERATING SYSTEMS

DESCRIPTION: KNOWLEDGE OF LINUX DEVELOPMENT AND MAJOR DISTRIBUTIONS

**Key Knowledge Areas**
Open Source Philosophy
  ▸ Open-Source Software and Licensing page 6
Distributions
  ▸ Distribution page 6
Embedded Systems
  ▸ Embedded and moble Linux page 6

**Partial List of Used Files, Terms, and Utilities**
Android
  ▸ Embedded and moble Linux page 6
Debian
  ▸ Distribution page 6
CentOS
  ▸ CentOS page 33

### 1.2 MAJOR OPEN SOURCE APPLICATIONS

DESCRIPTION: AWARENESS OF MAJOR APPLICATIONS AND THEIR USES

**Key Knowledge Areas**
Desktop Applications
  ▸ Desktop applications page 1151
Server Applications
  ▸ DHCP: Configures Network Interfaces page 491
  ▸ Chapter 13: Printing with CUPS page 555
  ▸ Chapter 18: OpenSSH: Secure Network Communication page 685
  ▸ Chapter 19: FTP: Transferring Files Across a Network page 713
  ▸ Chapter 20: sendmail: Setting Up Mail Servers, Clients, and More page 739
  ▸ Chapter 21: NIS and LDAP page 769
  ▸ Chapter 22: NFS: Sharing Directory Hierarchies page 801

Mobile Applications

Development Languages

Package Management Tools and repositories

**Partial List of Used Files, Terms, and Utilities**
OpenOffice.org, LibreOffice, Thunderbird, Firefox, Blender, Gimp, Audacity, ImageMagick

Apache, MySQL, PostgreSQL

NFS, Samba, OpenLDAP, Postfix, DNS, DHCP

C, Perl, shell, Python, PHP

## 1.3 UNDERSTANDING OPEN SOURCE SOFTWARE AND LICENSING
**DESCRIPTION: OPEN COMMUNITIES AND LICENSING OPEN SOURCE SOFTWARE FOR BUSINESS**

**Key Knowledge Areas**
Licensing

Free Software Foundation (FSF), Open Source Initiative (OSI)

**Partial List of Used Files, Terms, and Utilities**

GPL, BSD, Creative Commons

▸ GPL page 5

▸ Berkeley UNIX (BSD) page 3

▸ Creative Commons page 1245 (Glossary)

Free Software, Open Source Software, FOSS, FLOSS

▸ FOSS/FLOSS page 7

Open Source business models

▸ Making money page 7

## 1.4 ICT Skills and Working in Linux

**Description: Basic Information and Communication Technology (ICT) skills and working in Linux**

**Key Knowledge Areas**

Desktop Skills

▸ Chapter 4: Introduction to Fedora and Red Hat Enterprise Linux page 89

Getting to the Command Line

▸ Working from the Command Line page 119

▸ Chapter 7: The Linux Utilities page 215

Industry uses of Linux, Cloud Computing, and Virtualization

▸ Chapter 17: Setting Up Virtual Machines Locally and in the Cloud page 659

**Partial List of Used Files, Terms, and Utilities**

Using a browser, privacy concerns, configuration options, searching the Web, and saving content

▸ Firefox: www.mozilla.org/en-US/firefox/central

▸ Chrome: www.google.com/intl/en/chrome/browser/features.html

▸ Opera: www.opera.com

Terminal and Console

▸ Using a Virtual Console page 121

Password issues

▸ Users: Changing Your Account Type and Password (GUI) page 112

▸ Password Security page 136

▸ passwd: Changing Your Password (CLI) page 137

▸ Passwords page 625

Privacy issues and tools

▸ Search the Web for **browser privacy**

▸ Mozilla: support.mozilla.org/en-US/kb/private-browsing-browse-web-without-saving-info

▸ lifehacker.com/the-best-browser-extensions-that-protect-your-privacy-479408034

Use of common open-source applications in presentations and projects

▸ Desktop Applications page 1151

# TOPIC 2: FINDING YOUR WAY ON A LINUX SYSTEM

## 2.1 COMMAND LINE BASICS

### DESCRIPTION: BASICS OF USING THE LINUX COMMAND LINE

**Key Knowledge Areas**

Basic shell

Formatting commands

Working with Options

Variables

Globbing

Quoting

**Partial List of Used Files, Terms, and Utilities**

echo

history

**PATH** env variable

which

**Nice to Know**

Substitutions

||, &&, and ; control operators

## 2.2 USING THE COMMAND LINE TO GET HELP

**DESCRIPTION: RUNNING HELP COMMANDS AND NAVIGATION OF THE VARIOUS HELP SYSTEMS**

### Key Knowledge Areas

man
  ▶ man: Displays the System Manual page 128

info
  ▶ info: Displays Information About Utilities page 131

### Partial List of Used Files, Terms, and Utilities

man
  ▶ man: Displays the System Manual page 128

info
  ▶ info: Displays Information About Utilities page 131

man pages
  ▶ man: Displays the System Manual page 128

**/usr/share/doc**
  ▶ **/usr/share/doc** page 134

locate
  ▶ locate: Searches for a File page 256

### Nice to Know

apropos, whatis, whereis
  ▶ apropos: Searches for a Keyword page 130
  ▶ whatis page 130
  ▶ whereis page 255

## 2.3 USING DIRECTORIES AND LISTING FILES

**DESCRIPTION: NAVIGATION OF HOME AND SYSTEM DIRECTORIES AND LISTING FILES IN VARIOUS LOCATIONS**

### Key Knowledge Areas

Files, directories
  ▶ Ordinary Files and Directory Files page 177

Hidden files and directories
  ▶ Hidden Filenames page 180

Home
  ▶ Your Home Directory page 143

Absolute and relative paths
  ▶ Absolute Pathnames page 181
  ▶ Relative Pathnames page 182

### Partial List of Used Files, Terms, and Utilities

Common options for ls
  ▶ Options page 221

## 2.4 Creating, Moving, and Deleting Files

**Description: Create, move, and delete files and directories under the home directory**

**Key Knowledge Areas**

Files and directories

Case sensitivity

Simple globbing and quoting

**Partial List of Used Files, Terms, and Utilities**

mv, cp, rm, touch

mkdir, rmdir

# TOPIC 3: THE POWER OF THE COMMAND LINE

## 3.1 ARCHIVING FILES ON THE COMMAND LINE

### DESCRIPTION: ARCHIVING FILES IN THE USER HOME DIRECTORY

**Key Knowledge Areas**

Files, directories

▶ Ordinary Files and Directory Files page 177

Archives, compression

▶ Compressing and Archiving Files page 245

**Partial List of Used Files, Terms, and Utilities**

tar

▶ tar: Stores or Extracts Files to/from an Archive File page 249

▶ tar: Archives Files page 603

Common tar options

▶ Options page 249

▶ Modifiers page 251

gzip, bzip2

▶ xz, bzip2, and gzip: Compress and Decompress Files page 245

zip, unzip

▶ zip page 249

▶ unzip page 249

**Nice to Know**

Extracting individual files from archives

▶ Extract page 250

## 3.2 SEARCHING AND EXTRACTING DATA FROM FILES

### DESCRIPTION: SEARCH AND EXTRACT DATA FROM FILES IN THE HOME DIRECTORY

**Key Knowledge Areas**

Command line pipes

▶ Pipelines page 158

I/O redirection

▶ Redirection page 153

Partial POSIX Regular Expressions (., [ ], *, ?)

▶ Appendix A: Regular Expressions page 1139

**Partial List of Used Files, Terms, and Utilities**

find

▶ find: Finds Files Based on Criteria page 229

grep

▶ grep: Searches for a Pattern in Files page 232

less

▶ less Is more: Display a Text File One Screen at a Time page 220

head, tail
sort
cut
wc

**Nice to Know**
Partial POSIX Basic Regular Expressions ([^ ], ^, $)
Partial POSIX Extended Regular Expressions (+, ( ), |)
xargs

## 3.3 TURNING COMMANDS INTO A SCRIPT
### DESCRIPTION: TURNING REPETITIVE COMMANDS INTO SIMPLE SCRIPTS

**Key Knowledge Areas**
Basic text editing
Basic shell scripting

**Partial List of Used Files, Terms, and Utilities**
**/bin/sh**
Variables
Arguments
**for** loops
echo
Exit status

**Nice to Know**
pico, nano, vi (only basics for creating scripts)

bash

**if, while, case** statements

read and test, and [ commands

# TOPIC 4: THE LINUX OPERATING SYSTEM

## 4.1 CHOOSING AN OPERATING SYSTEM

**DESCRIPTION: KNOWLEDGE OF MAJOR OPERATING SYSTEMS AND LINUX DISTRIBUTIONS**

**Key Knowledge Areas**
Windows, Mac, Linux differences

Distribution life cycle management

**Partial List of Used Files, Terms, and Utilities**
GUI versus command line, desktop configuration

Maintenance cycles, Beta and Stable

## 4.2 UNDERSTANDING COMPUTER HARDWARE

**DESCRIPTION: FAMILIARITY WITH THE COMPONENTS THAT GO INTO BUILDING DESKTOP AND SERVER COMPUTERS**

**Key Knowledge Areas**
Hardware

**Partial List of Used Files, Terms, and Utilities**

Hard drives and partitions, motherboards, processors, power supplies, optical drives, peripherals

▸ Setting Up the Hard Disk page 36

▸ motherboard page 1261 (Glossary)

▸ Processor Architecture page 31

▸ power supply page 1267 (Glossary)

▸ optical drive page 1264 (Glossary)

▸ Peripheral, see device page 1246 (Glossary)

Display types

▸ Interfaces: Installer and Installed System page 32

▸ Working from the Command Line page 119

▸ ASCII terminal page 1237 (Glossary)

▸ graphical display page 1251 (Glossary)

Drivers

▸ Device files page 515

▸ Block and Character Devices page 518

▸ device driver page 1246 (Glossary)

## 4.3 WHERE DATA IS STORED

**DESCRIPTION: WHERE VARIOUS TYPES OF INFORMATION ARE STORED ON A LINUX SYSTEM**

**Key Knowledge Areas**

Kernel

▸ Chapter 14: Building a Linux Kernel page 579

▸ kernel page 1257 (Glossary)

Processes

▸ Process page 150

▸ Processes page 373

▸ ps page 466

▸ process page 1267 (Glossary)

syslog, klog, dmesg

▸ **rsyslogd**: Logs System Messages page 620

▸ **klogd**: deprecated; www.linuxjournal.com/article/4058

▸ **dmesg**: Displays Kernel Messages page 595

/lib, /usr/lib, /etc, /var/log

▸ **/lib** page 190

▸ **/lib64** page 190

▸ **/usr/lib** page 190

▸ **/usr/lib64** page 191

▸ **/etc** page 190

▸ **/etc** page 506

▸ **/var/log** page 191

▸ **/var/log** page 514

▸ Log Files and Mail for **root** page 626

## Partial List of Used Files, Terms, and Utilities
Programs, libraries, packages and package databases, system configuration
- ▸ /lib page 190
- ▸ /lib64 page 190
- ▸ /usr/lib page 190
- ▸ /usr/lib64 page 191
- ▸ /usr/bin page 190
- ▸ /usr/sbin page 190
- ▸ /etc page 190
- ▸ /etc page 506
- ▸ library page 1258 (Glossary)
- ▸ Software package page 532
- ▸ PMS page 532
- ▸ Software package formats page 532
- ▸ Repositories page 533

Processes and process tables, memory addresses, system messaging, and logging
- ▸ Process page 150
- ▸ Processes page 373
- ▸ ps page 466
- ▸ dmesg: Displays Kernel Messages page 595
- ▸ rsyslogd: Logs System Messages page 620
- ▸ D-BUS page 898
- ▸ process page 1267 (Glossary)

ps, top, free
- ▸ Process Identification page 374
- ▸ ps page 466
- ▸ top: Lists Processes Using the Most Resources page 612
- ▸ free: Displays Memory Usage Information page 253

## 4.4 Your Computer on the Network
### Description: Querying vital networking settings and determining the basic requirements for a computer on a Local Area Network (LAN)

**Key Knowledge Areas**
Internet, network, routers
- ▸ Internet page 280
- ▸ Introduction to Networking page 280
- ▸ Internetworking Through Gateways and Routers page 287

Domain Name Service
- ▸ Chapter 24: DNS/BIND: Tracking Domain Names and Addresses page 851

Network configuration
- ▸ Chapter 16: Configuring and Monitoring a LAN page 631

**Partial List of Used Files, Terms, and Utilities**
route
- ▸ deprecated (route man page): see ip man page, **route** object instead

resolv.conf
  ▶ /etc/resolv.conf page 510

IPv4, IPv6
  ▶ IPv4 page 292
  ▶ IPv6 page 293

ifconfig
  ▶ deprecated: (ifconfig man page): see ip man page, **addr** and **link** objects instead

netstat
  ▶ netstat: see the netstat man page and wikipedia.org/wiki/netstat

ping
  ▶ ping: Tests a Network Connection page 305

**Nice to Know**
ssh
  ▶ ssh: Logs in or Executes Commands on a Remote System page 693

dig
  ▶ host and dig: Query Internet Nameservers page 307
  ▶ dig page 861
  ▶ dig page 862

# TOPIC 5: SECURITY AND FILE PERMISSIONS
## 5.1 BASIC SECURITY AND IDENTIFYING USER TYPES
### DESCRIPTION: VARIOUS TYPES OF USERS ON A LINUX SYSTEM

**Key Knowledge Areas**
Root and Standard Users
  ▶ Running Commands with **root** Privileges page 422
  ▶ The Special Powers of a Privileged User page 422
  ▶ Gaining **root** Privileges page 423
  ▶ Real UID Versus Effective UID page 425

System users
  ▶ /etc/passwd page 508

**Partial List of Used Files, Terms, and Utilities**
/etc/passwd, /etc/group
  ▶ /etc/passwd page 508
  ▶ /etc/group page 506

id, who, w
  ▶ id page 426
  ▶ who: Lists Users on the System page 254
  ▶ who, whoami page 426
  ▶ w: Lists Users on the System page 254

sudo
  ▶ Using sudo to Gain **root** Privileges page 428

**Nice to Know**

su

  ▶ Using su to Gain **root** Privileges page 425

## 5.2 CREATING USERS AND GROUPS

**DESCRIPTION: CREATING USERS AND GROUPS ON A LINUX SYSTEM**

**Key Knowledge Areas**

User and group commands

  ▶ useradd: Adds a User Account page 600
  ▶ groupadd: Adds a Group page 601
  ▶ usermod: Modifies a User Account page 601
  ▶ userdel: Removes a User Account page 600
  ▶ groupdel and groupmod: Remove and Modify a Group page 601

User IDs

  ▶ Real UID Versus Effective UID page 425
  ▶ /etc/passwd page 508
  ▶ user ID page 1279 (Glossary)

**Partial List of Used Files, Terms, and Utilities**

/etc/passwd, /etc/shadow, /etc/group

  ▶ /etc/passwd page 508
  ▶ /etc/shadow page 511
  ▶ /etc/group page 506

id, last

  ▶ id page 426
  ▶ last: see the last man page

useradd, groupadd

  ▶ useradd: Adds a User Account page 600
  ▶ groupadd: Adds a Group page 601

passwd

  ▶ Users: Changing Your Account Type and Password (GUI) page 112
  ▶ passwd: Changing Your Password (CLI) page 137

**Nice to Know**

usermod, userdel

  ▶ usermod: Modifies a User Account page 601
  ▶ userdel: Removes a User Account page 600

groupmod, groupdel

  ▶ groupdel and groupmod: Remove and Modify a Group page 601

## 5.3 MANAGING FILE PERMISSIONS AND OWNERSHIP

**DESCRIPTION: UNDERSTANDING AND MANIPULATING FILE PERMISSIONS AND OWNERSHIP SETTINGS**

**Key Knowledge Areas**

File/directory permissions and owners

  ▶ Access Permissions page 191

**Partial List of Used Files, Terms, and Utilities**
ls –l
▸ ls –l: Displays Permissions page 191

chmod, chown
▸ chmod: Changes File Access Permissions page 193
▸ chmod: Makes a File Executable page 337
▸ chown: Changes File Ownership page 195

**Nice to Know**
chgrp
▸ chgrp: Changes File Group Association page 195

## 5.4 SPECIAL DIRECTORIES AND FILES
**DESCRIPTION: SPECIAL DIRECTORIES AND FILES ON A LINUX SYSTEM INCLUDING SPECIAL PERMISSIONS**

**Key Knowledge Areas**
System files, libraries
▸ Important Standard Directories and Files page 189
▸ library page 1258 (Glossary)

Symbolic links
▸ Symbolic Links page 206
▸ Symbolic links page 515
▸ symbolic link page 1276 (Glossary)

**Partial List of Used Files, Terms, and Utilities**
/etc, /var
▸ /etc page 190
▸ /etc page 506
▸ /var page 41
▸ /var page 191

/tmp, /var/tmp and Sticky Bit
▸ /tmp page 190
▸ /var page 191
▸ Sticky bit page 196
▸ sticky bit page 1275 (Glossary)

ls –d
▸ Directory page 221

ln –s
▸ Size page 222

**Nice to Know**
Hard links
▸ Hard Links page 204

Setuid/Setgid
▸ Setuid and Setgid Permissions page 196
▸ Setuid file page 424

▶ Setuid files page 626
▶ setuid page 1272 (Glossary)
▶ setgid page 1272 (Glossary)

# CERTIFICATION EXAM 1 OBJECTIVES: LX0-101

## 101 SYSTEM ARCHITECTURE

### 101.1 DETERMINE AND CONFIGURE HARDWARE SETTINGS

Enable and disable integrated peripherals

Configure systems with or without external peripherals such as keyboards

Differentiate between the various types of mass storage devices
▶ /dev page 503

Set the correct hardware ID for different devices, especially the boot device

Know the differences between coldplug and hotplug devices
▶ Hotplug page 516

Determine hardware resources for devices

Tools and utilities to list various hardware information (e.g., lsusb, lspci, etc.)
▶ dmesg: Displays Kernel Messages page 595
▶ lspci: Lists PCI Information page 635
▶ lsblk: Lists Block Device Information page 635
▶ lshw: Lists Hardware Information page 636
▶ lsusb: Lists USB Devices page 636

Tools and utilities to manipulate USB devices
▶ Writing to a USB Flash Drive page 50

Conceptual understanding of sysfs, udev, hald, dbus
▶ udev page 516
▶ D-BUS page 898

**Partial List of Used Files, Terms, and Utilities**
/sys
▶ /sys page 190
▶ /sys page 514
▶ /sys page 516
/proc
▶ /proc page 190
▶ /proc page 512
▶ proc page 520
/dev
▶ Device file page 152
▶ /dev page 190

## 101.2 BOOT THE SYSTEM

## 101.3 CHANGE RUNLEVELS AND SHUTDOWN OR REBOOT SYSTEM

Set the default runlevel

Change between runlevels including single-user mode

Shutdown and reboot from the command line

Alert users before switching runlevels or other major system events

Properly terminate processes

**Partial List of Used Files, Terms, and Utilities**
**/etc/inittab**

shutdown

init

**/etc/init.d**

telinit

# 102 LINUX INSTALLATION AND PACKAGE MANAGEMENT

## 102.1 DESIGN HARD DISK LAYOUT

Allocate filesystems and swap space to separate partitions or disks

Tailor the design to the intended use of the system
  ▶ Planning the Installation page 29

Ensure the **/boot** partition conforms to the hardware architecture requirements for booting
  ▶ Where to put the **/boot** partition page 41
  ▶ LBA addressing mode and the **/boot** partition page 590

**Partial List of Used Files, Terms, and Utilities**
**/** (root) filesystem
  ▶ **/** (root) page 40
  ▶ **/** (root) page 181
  ▶ **/** page 189
  ▶ root filesystem page 1271 (Glossary)

**/var** filesystem
  ▶ **/var** page 41
  ▶ **/var** page 191

**/home** filesystem
  ▶ **/home** page 41
  ▶ **/home** page 190

swap space
  ▶ (swap) page 40
  ▶ swap page 513
  ▶ swap space page 1276 (Glossary)

mount points
  ▶ Mount Points page 38
  ▶ Mount point page 521

partitions
  ▶ Partitions page 36
  ▶ Partition table page 36
  ▶ Primary, Extended, and Logical Partitions page 37
  ▶ Default Partitioning page 39
  ▶ Manual Partitioning: Planning Partitions page 39
  ▶ Example minimum partition sizes page 42
  ▶ Manual/Custom Partitioning page 74
  ▶ partition page 1265 (Glossary)

## 102.2 INSTALL A BOOT MANAGER

Providing alternative boot locations and backup boot options

Install and configure a boot loader such as GRUB
  ▶ GRUB: The Linux Boot Loader page 590

Interact with the boot loader
  ▶ Booting the System to Single-User/Rescue Mode page 450

**Partial List of Used Files, Terms, and Utilities**
**/boot/grub/menu.lst**
  ▶ Configuring GRUB page 591

grub-install
- ▸ grub2-install: Installs the MBR and GRUB Files page 594

MBR
- ▸ Reinstalling the MBR page 456
- ▸ MBR page 590
- ▸ grub2-install: Installs the MBR and GRUB Files page 594

superblock
- ▸ superblock page 1276 (Glossary)

/etc/lilo.conf

lilo

## 102.3 Manage Shared Libraries

Identify shared libraries
- ▸ ldd page 487

Identify the typical locations of system libraries

Load shared libraries

**Partial List of Used Files, Terms, and Utilities**

ldd
- ▸ ldd & **libwrap** page 486
- ▸ ldd page 487

ldconfig

/etc/ld.so.conf

**LD_LIBRARY_PATH**

## 102.4 Use Debian Package Management

Install, upgrade, and uninstall Debian binary packages
- ▸ Using apt-get to Install, Remove, and Update Packages page 1184

Find packages containing specific files or libraries which may or may not be installed

Obtain package information like version, content, dependencies, package integrity, and installation status (whether or not the package is installed)

**Partial List of Used Files, Terms, and Utilities**

**/etc/apt/sources.list**
- ▸ **sources.list:** Specifies Repositories for apt-get to Search page 1187

dpkg
- ▸ apt-get and dpkg page 1184

dpkg-reconfigure

apt-get
- ▸ Using apt-get to Install, Remove, and Update Packages page 1184
- ▸ Using apt-get to Upgrade the System page 1185
- ▸ Other apt-get Commands page 1186

apt-cache

aptitude

## 102.5 USE RPM AND YUM PACKAGE MANAGEMENT

Install, re-install, upgrade, and remove packages using RPM and YUM

Obtain information on RPM packages such as version, status, dependencies, integrity, and signatures

Determine what files a package provides, as well as find which package a specific file comes from

**Partial List of Used Files, Terms, and Utilities**

rpm

rpm2cpio

**/etc/yum.conf**

**/etc/yum.repos.d/**

yum

yumdownloader

## 103 GNU AND UNIX COMMANDS

### 103.1 WORK ON THE COMMAND LINE

Use single shell commands and one line command sequences to perform basic tasks on the command line

▸ Chapter 5: The Shell page 141
▸ Chapter 7: The Linux Utilities page 215
▸ Chapter 9: The Bourne Again Shell (bash) page 327

Use and modify the shell environment including defining, referencing, and exporting environment variables

▸ Parameters and Variables page 352
▸ Variables page 1031

Use and edit command history

▸ History page 376

Invoke commands inside and outside the defined path

▸ Absolute versus relative pathnames page 149
▸ **PATH:** Where the Shell Looks for Programs page 359

**Partial List of Used Files, Terms, and Utilities**

. (dot)

▸ . (Dot) or source: Runs a Startup File in the Current Shell page 332
▸ exec versus . (dot) page 1045

bash

▸ Chapter 5: The Shell page 141
▸ Chapter 9: The Bourne Again Shell (bash) page 327
▸ Chapter 27: Programming the Bourne Again Shell (bash) page 981

echo

▸ echo: Displays Arguments page 219
▸ **echo –e** page 1009

env

▸ env: Runs a Program in a Modified Environment page 1035

exec

▸ Opening a File Descriptor page 1017
▸ Duplicating a File Descriptor page 1017
▸ exec: Executes a Command or Redirects File Descriptors page 1045

export

▸ declare: Lists and Assigns Attributes to Variables page 357
▸ readonly and export page 357
▸ export: Puts Variables in the Environment page 1032

pwd

▸ pwd page 143

set

▸ **set ±o:** Turns Shell Features On and Off page 400
▸ set: Initializes Positional Parameters page 1024

unset

▸ unset: Removes a Variable page 356

man
  ▶ man: Displays the System Manual page 128

uname
  ▶ uname: Displays System Information page 470

history
  ▶ History page 376

# 103.2 PROCESS TEXT STREAMS USING FILTERS

Send text files and output streams through text utility filters to modify the output using standard UNIX commands found in the GNU **textutils** package
  ▶ Redirection page 153
  ▶ Pipelines page 158
  ▶ Filters page 161

**Partial List of Used Files, Terms, and Utilities**

cat
  ▶ cat: Joins and Displays Files page 216
  ▶ cat page 152
  ▶ Redirection page 153

cut
  ▶ cut: Selects Characters or Fields from Input Lines page 225

expand

fmt

head
  ▶ head: Displays the Beginning of a File page 235

od

join

nl

paste

pr

sed

sort
  ▶ sort: Sorts and/or Merges Files page 239

split

tail
  ▶ tail: Displays the Last Part of a File page 241

tr
  ▶ tr page 159
  ▶ tr page 260

unexpand

uniq

wc

▶ wc: Displays the Number of Lines, Words, and Bytes in Files page 244

## 103.3 Perform Basic File Management

Copy, move, and remove files and directories individually

▶ rmdir: Deletes a Directory page 186

▶ mv, cp: Move or Copy Files page 187

▶ mv: Moves a Directory page 188

▶ rm: Removes a Link page 208

▶ rm: Removes a File (Deletes a Link) page 222

▶ cp: Copies Files page 224

▶ mv: Renames or Moves a File page 237

Copy multiple files and directories recursively

▶ cp: Copies Files page 224

Remove files and directories recursively

▶ rm: Removes a File (Deletes a Link) page 222

Use simple and advanced wildcard specifications in commands

▶ Filename Generation/Pathname Expansion page 165

▶ Pathname Expansion page 412

Using find to locate and act on files based on type, size, or time

▶ find: Finds Files Based on Criteria page 229

Usage of tar, cpio, and dd

▶ tar: Stores or Extracts Files to/from an Archive File page 249

▶ tar: Archives Files page 603

▶ cpio: Archives Files page 605

**Partial List of Used Files, Terms, and Utilities**

cp

▶ mv, cp: Move or Copy Files page 187

▶ cp: Copies Files page 224

find

▶ find: Finds Files Based on Criteria page 229

mkdir

▶ mkdir: Creates a Directory page 184

mv

▶ mv: Moves a Directory page 188

▶ mv: Renames or Moves a File page 237

▶ mv, cp: Move or Copy Files page 187

ls

▶ ls –l: Displays Permissions page 191

▶ ls: Displays Information About Files page 221

rm
  ▸ rm: Removes a Link page 208
  ▸ rm: Removes a File (Deletes a Link) page 222

rmdir
  ▸ rmdir: Deletes a Directory page 186

touch
  ▸ touch: Changes File Modification and Access Times page 243

tar
  ▸ tar: Stores or Extracts Files to/from an Archive File page 249
  ▸ tar: Archives Files page 603

cpio
  ▸ cpio: Archives Files page 605

dd

file
  ▸ file: Displays the Classification of a File page 229

gzip
  ▸ xz, bzip2, and gzip: Compress and Decompress Files page 245

gunzip
  ▸ unxz bunzip2 gunzip page 248

bzip2
  ▸ xz, bzip2, and gzip: Compress and Decompress Files page 245

file globbing
  ▸ Filename Generation/Pathname Expansion page 165
  ▸ Pathname Expansion page 412

## 103.4 USE STREAMS, PIPES, AND REDIRECTS

Redirecting standard input, standard output, and standard error
  ▸ Redirecting Standard Output page 154
  ▸ Redirecting Standard Input page 155
  ▸ Redirecting Standard Error page 333
  ▸ redirection page 1269 (Glossary)
  ▸ standard input page 1274 (Glossary)
  ▸ standard output page 1275 (Glossary)
  ▸ standard error page 1274 (Glossary)

Pipe the output of one command to the input of another command
  ▸ Pipelines page 158
  ▸ Filters page 161
  ▸ filter page 1250 (Glossary)
  ▸ pipeline page 1266 (Glossary)

Use the output of one command as arguments to another command
  ▸ xargs: Converts Standard Input to Command Lines page 260

Send output to both stdout and a file
  ▸ tee page 162

**Partial List of Used Files, Terms, and Utilities**

tee

▸ tee page 162

xargs

▸ xargs: Converts Standard Input to Command Lines page 260

## 103.5 CREATE, MONITOR, AND KILL PROCESSES

Run jobs in the foreground and background

▸ Running a Command in the Background page 163

▸ Moving a Job from the Foreground to the Background page 164

▸ Background process page 375

▸ background process page 1238 (Glossary)

▸ foreground process page 1250 (Glossary)

Signal a program to continue running after logout

Monitor active processes

▸ Process Identification page 374

▸ ps page 374

▸ ps page 466

Select and sort processes for display

▸ Process Identification page 374

▸ ps page 466

▸ top: Lists Processes Using the Most Resources page 612

Send signals to processes

▸ Aborting Execution page 123

▸ kill: Aborting a Background Job page 164

▸ kill: Sends a Signal to a Process page 465

▸ killall: Kills a Command page 467

▸ pkill: Kills a Command page 468

▸ Signals page 1047

**Partial List of Used Files, Terms, and Utilities**

&

▸ Running a Command in the Background page 163

▸ Background process page 375

▸ background process page 1238 (Glossary)

▸ foreground process page 1250 (Glossary)

bg

▸ Moving a Job from the Foreground to the Background page 164

▸ bg: Sends a Job to the Background page 348

▸ background process page 1238 (Glossary)

fg

▸ Foreground page 163

▸ Moving a Job from the Foreground to the Background page 164

▸ fg: Brings a Job to the Foreground page 347

▸ foreground process page 1250 (Glossary)

## 103.6 MODIFY PROCESS EXECUTION PRIORITIES

Know the default priority of a job that is created

Run a program with higher or lower priority than the default

Change the priority of a running process

**Partial List of Used Files, Terms, and Utilities**

## 103.7 SEARCH TEXT FILES USING REGULAR EXPRESSIONS

*See Appendix A: Regular Expressions page 1139*

Create simple regular expressions containing several notational elements

Use regular expression tools to perform searches through a filesystem or file content
  ▸ *See preceding entry.*

**Partial List of Used Files, Terms, and Utilities**

grep

egrep

fgrep

sed

regex(7)

## 103.8 PERFORM BASIC FILE EDITING OPERATIONS USING VI

*A Practical Guide to Fedora and Red Hat Enterprise Linux, Seventh Edition covers the vim editor. All commands discussed here are compatible between vi and vim.*

Navigate a document using vi

Use basic vi modes

Insert, edit, delete, copy, and find text

**Partial List of Used Files, Terms, and Utilities**

vi

/, ?

h, j, k, l

i, o, a

c, d, p, y, dd, yy

ZZ, :w!, :q!, :e!

## 104 DEVICES, LINUX FILESYSTEMS, FILESYSTEM HIERARCHY STANDARD

## 104.1 CREATE PARTITIONS AND FILESYSTEMS

Use various mkfs commands to set up partitions and create various filesystems such as:

ext2

**ext3**

**xfs**

**reiserfs v3**

**vfat**

**Partial List of Used Files, Terms, and Utilities**

fdisk

mkfs

mkswap

## 104.2 MAINTAIN THE INTEGRITY OF FILESYSTEMS

Verify the integrity of filesystems

Monitor free space and inodes

Repair simple filesystem problems

**Partial List of Used Files, Terms, and Utilities**

du

df

fsck

e2fsck

mke2fs

debugfs

dumpe2fs

tune2fs

xfs tools (such as xfs_metadump and xfs_info)

## 104.3 Control Mounting and Unmounting of Filesystems

Manually mount and unmount filesystems

Configure filesystem mounting on bootup

Configure user mountable removable filesystems

**Partial List of Used Files, Terms, and Utilities**
/etc/fstab

/media

mount

umount

## 104.4 Manage Disk Quotas

Set up a disk quota for a filesystem

Edit, check, and generate user quota reports

**Partial List of Used Files, Terms, and Utilities**
quota

edquota

repquota

quotaon

## 104.5 Manage File Permissions and Ownership

Manage access permissions on regular and special files as well as directories

# 104.6 CREATE AND CHANGE HARD AND SYMBOLIC LINKS

## 104.7 Find System Files and Place Files in the Correct Location

Understand the correct locations of files under the FHS
- ▶ Important Standard Directories and Files page 189
- ▶ Important Files and Directories page 502

Find files and commands on a Linux system
- ▶ whereis page 255
- ▶ locate: Searches for a File page 256

Know the location and purpose of important files and directories as defined in the FHS
- ▶ Important Standard Directories and Files page 189
- ▶ Important Files and Directories page 502

**Partial List of Used Files, Terms, and Utilities**

find
- ▶ find: Finds Files Based on Criteria page 229

locate
- ▶ locate: Searches for a File page 256

updatedb
- ▶ updatedb page 256

whereis
- ▶ whereis page 255

which
- ▶ which page 255

type
- ▶ type: Displays Information About a Command page 1041

/etc/updatedb.conf

# Certification Exam 2 Objectives: LX0-102

## 105 Shells, Scripting, and Data Management

### 105.1 Customize and Use the Shell Environment

*See Chapter 9: The Bourne Again Shell (bash) page 327*

Set environment variables (e.g., **PATH**) at login or when spawning a new shell
- ▶ Startup Files page 329
- ▶ Set **PATH** in .bash_profile page 331
- ▶ Keyword variables page 353
- ▶ Keyword Variables page 358

Write bash functions for frequently used sequences of commands
- ▶ Functions page 396
- ▶ Variables in Functions page 1039

Maintain skeleton directories for new user accounts

Set command search path with the proper directory

**Partial List of Used Files, Terms, and Utilities**
/etc/profile

env

export

set

unset

~/.bash_profile

~/.bash_login

~/.profile

~/.bashrc

~/.bash_logout

functions

alias

lists

# 105.2 CUSTOMIZE OR WRITE SIMPLE SCRIPTS

*See Chapter 9: The Bourne Again Shell (bash) page 327*

*See Chapter 27: Programming the Bourne Again Shell (bash) page 981*

Use standard sh syntax (loops, tests)
- ▶ Control Structures page 982

Use command substitution
- ▶ Command Substitution page 410

Test return values for success or failure or other information provided by a command
- ▶ test builtin page 983
- ▶ [] is a synonym for test page 986
- ▶ test builtin page 1000

Perform conditional mailing to the superuser

Correctly select the script interpreter through the shebang (#!) line
- ▶ #! Specifies a Shell page 338

Manage the location, ownership, execution, and suid-rights of scripts
- ▶ Listing setuid files page 458

**Partial List of Used Files, Terms, and Utilities**
for
- ▶ **for...in** page 995
- ▶ **for** page 997

while
- ▶ **while** page 999

test
- ▶ test builtin page 983
- ▶ [] is a synonym for test page 986
- ▶ test builtin page 1000

if
- ▶ **if...then** page 983
- ▶ **if...then...else** page 987
- ▶ **if...then...elif** page 989

read
- ▶ read: Accepts User Input page 1041

seq
- ▶ seq page 407

# 105.3 SQL Data Management

*See Chapter 29: The MariaDB SQL Database Management System page 1113*

Use of basic SQL commands
- ▶ Notes page 1114

Perform basic data manipulation
- ▶ Examples page 1123

**Partial List of Used Files, Terms, and Utilities**
insert
- ▶ INSERT INTO page 1125

# 106 USER INTERFACES AND DESKTOPS

## 106.1 INSTALL AND CONFIGURE X11

*See X Window System page 459*

Verify that the video card and monitor are supported by an X server

Awareness of the X font server

Basic understanding and knowledge of the X Window configuration file

**Partial List of Used Files, Terms, and Utilities**

**/etc/X11/xorg.conf**

xhost

**DISPLAY**

xwininfo

xdpyinfo

X

## 106.2 SET UP A DISPLAY MANAGER

Turn the display manager on or off

Change the display manager greeting

Change default color depth for the display manager

Configure display managers for use by X-stations

**Partial List of Used Files, Terms, and Utilities**
**/etc/inittab**
  ▶ **/etc/inittab** page 508

**xdm** configuration files

**kdm** configuration files

**gdm** configuration files
  ▶ Graphical login page 453
  ▶ The **Xorg –nolisten tcp** Option page 460

## 106.3 ACCESSIBILITY

Keyboard Accessibility Settings (AccessX?)

Visual Settings and Themes

Assistive Technology (ATs)

**Partial List of Used Files, Terms, and Utilities**
Sticky/Repeat Keys

Slow/Bounce/Toggle Keys

Mouse Keys

High Contrast/Large Print Desktop Themes

Screen Reader

Braille Display

Screen Magnifier

On-Screen Keyboard

Gestures (used at login, for example gdm)

Orca

GOK

emacspeak

# 107 ADMINISTRATIVE TASKS

## 107.1 MANAGE USER AND GROUP ACCOUNTS AND RELATED SYSTEM FILES

Add, modify, and remove users and groups
  ▶ system-config-users: Manages User Accounts page 598
  ▶ Managing User Accounts from the Command Line page 600

Manage user/group info in password/group databases
  ▶ Modifying a User page 600
  ▶ Working with Groups page 600

Create and manage special purpose and limited accounts

**Partial List of Used Files, Terms, and Utilities**
**/etc/passwd**

**/etc/shadow**

**/etc/group**

**/etc/skel**

chage

groupadd

groupdel

groupmod

passwd

useradd

userdel

usermod

# 107.2 AUTOMATE SYSTEM ADMINISTRATION TASKS BY SCHEDULING JOBS

Manage **cron** and at jobs

Configure user access to **cron** and at services

**Partial List of Used Files, Terms, and Utilities**
**/etc/cron.{d,daily,hourly,monthly,weekly}**

**/etc/at.deny**

## 107.3 LOCALIZATION AND INTERNATIONALIZATION

# 108 Essential System Services

## 108.1 Maintain System Time

## 108.2 System Logging

syslog
▶ **rsyslogd:** Logs System Messages page 620

standard facilities, priorities, and actions
▶ Selectors page 620
▶ Facilities page 620
▶ Priorities page 620
▶ Actions page 621

**Partial List of Used Files, Terms, and Utilities**
**syslog.conf**
▶ **rsyslog.conf** page 620

**syslogd**
▶ **rsyslogd:** Logs System Messages page 620

**klogd**

logger

# 108.3 Mail Transfer Agent (MTA) Basics

*See Chapter 20: sendmail: Setting Up Mail Servers, Clients, and More page 739*

Create e-mail aliases
▶ **/etc/aliases** page 746

Configure e-mail forwarding
▶ **~/.forward** page 747

Knowledge of commonly available MTA programs (Postfix, **sendmail,** Qmail, **exim**) (no configuration)
▶ Alternatives to sendmail page 741

**Partial List of Used Files, Terms, and Utilities**
**~/.forward**
▶ **~/.forward** page 747

**sendmail** emulation layer commands

newaliases
▶ newaliases page 747

mail

mailq
▶ mailq page 748

Postfix
▶ Postfix page 742

**sendmail**
▶ Introduction to **sendmail** page 740
▶ Setting Up a **sendmail** Mail Server page 742
▶ JumpStart I: Configuring **sendmail** on a Client page 743
▶ JumpStart II: Configuring **sendmail** on a Server page 744
▶ Working with **sendmail** Messages page 745
▶ Configuring **sendmail** page 748

exim
> **exim4** page 742

qmail
> Qmail page 742

## 108.4 MANAGE PRINTERS AND PRINTING

*See Chapter 13: Printing with CUPS page 555*

Basic CUPS configuration (for local and remote printers)
> The System Configures a Local Printer Automatically page 558
> JumpStart I: Configuring a Printer Using system-config-printer page 558
> JumpStart II: Setting Up a Local or Remote Printer page 560
> Working with the CUPS Web Interface page 565
> Configuring Printers page 566

Manage user print queues
> Managing Print Queues page 572

Troubleshoot general printing problems

Add and remove jobs from configured printer queues
> BSD and System V command-line print utilities page 574

**Partial List of Used Files, Terms, and Utilities**
CUPS configuration files, tools, and utilities
> JumpStart I: Configuring a Printer Using system-config-printer page 558
> Working with the CUPS Web Interface page 565
> Sharing CUPS Printers page 572

/etc/cups
> Example lpadmin Commands page 570

**lpd** legacy interface (lpr, lprm, lpq)
> Traditional UNIX Printing page 573

## 109 NETWORKING FUNDAMENTALS

*See Chapter 8: Networking and the Internet page 279*

## 109.1 FUNDAMENTALS OF INTERNET PROTOCOLS

*See Network Protocols page 290*

Demonstrate an understanding of network masks
> Subnet mask page 298
> network mask page 1263 (Glossary)

Knowledge of the differences between private and public "dotted quad" IP Addresses
> Private address space page 637
> private address space page 1267 (Glossary)

Setting a default route

Knowledge about common TCP and UDP ports (20, 21, 22, 23, 25, 53, 80, 110, 119, 139, 143, 161, 443, 465, 993, 995)

▸ Each chapter covering a server discusses which ports that server uses.
▸ Ports page 312
▸ port page 1266 (Glossary)

Knowledge about the differences and major features of UDP, TCP, and ICMP

▸ UDP page 290
▸ UDP: User Datagram Protocol page 292
▸ TCP page 290
▸ TCP: Transmission Control Protocol page 291
▸ ping: Tests a Network Connection page 305
▸ UDP page 1278 (Glossary)
▸ TCP page 1276 (Glossary)
▸ ICMP page 1254 (Glossary)

Knowledge of the major differences between IPv4 and IPv6

▸ IPv4 page 292
▸ IPv6 page 293

**Partial List of Used Files, Terms, and Utilities**

/etc/services

▸ Network Services page 313
▸ **/etc/services** page 511

ftp

▸ Chapter 19: FTP: Transferring Files Across a Network page 713

telnet

▸ telnet: Logs In on a Remote System page 303

host

▸ host and dig: Query Internet Nameservers page 307

ping

▸ ping: Tests a Network Connection page 305

dig

▸ host and dig: Query Internet Nameservers page 307
▸ dig page 861
▸ dig page 862

traceroute

▸ traceroute: Traces a Route over the Internet page 306

tracepath

## 109.2 BASIC NETWORK CONFIGURATION

Manually and automatically configure network interfaces

▸ Configuring the Systems page 636
▸ NetworkManager: Configures Network Connections page 637

Basic TCP/IP host configuration

**Partial List of Used Files, Terms, and Utilities**
**/etc/hostname**
**/etc/hosts**
**/etc/resolv.conf**
**/etc/nsswitch.conf**
ifconfig

ifup

ifdown

route

ping

# 109.3 BASIC NETWORK TROUBLESHOOTING

Manually and automatically configure network interfaces and routing tables to include adding, starting, stopping, restarting, deleting, or reconfiguring network interfaces

Change, view, or configure the routing table and correct an improperly set default route manually

Debug problems associated with the network configuration

**Partial List of Used Files, Terms, and Utilities**
ifconfig

ifup

ifdown

route

host
hostname
dig
netstat

ping

traceroute
‣ traceroute: Traces a Route over the Internet page 306

## 109.4 CONFIGURE CLIENT SIDE DNS

*See Chapter 24: DNS/BIND: Tracking Domain Names and Addresses page 851*

Demonstrate the use of DNS on the local system
‣ JumpStart I: Setting Up a DNS Cache page 866

Modify the order in which name resolution is done
‣ Resolver page 854

**Partial List of Used Files, Terms, and Utilities**
/etc/hosts
‣ Hostnames page 300
‣ /etc/hosts page 507

/etc/resolv.conf
‣ /etc/resolv.conf page 510

/etc/nsswitch.conf
‣ nsswitch.conf: Which Service to Look at First page 495

# 110 SECURITY

## 110.1 PERFORM SECURITY ADMINISTRATION TASKS

Audit a system to find files with the suid/sgid bit set
‣ Listing setuid files page 458
‣ Listing setgid files page 459

Set or change user passwords and password aging information
‣ Users: Changing Your Account Type and Password (GUI) page 112
‣ passwd: Changing Your Password (CLI) page 137
‣ Modifying a User page 600
‣ chage page 601

Being able to use nmap and netstat to discover open ports on a system

Set up limits on user logins, processes, and memory usage

Basic sudo configuration and usage
‣ Using sudo to Gain **root** Privileges page 428

**Partial List of Used Files, Terms, and Utilities**
find
‣ find: Finds Files Based on Criteria page 229

passwd
‣ Users: Changing Your Account Type and Password (GUI) page 112
‣ passwd: Changing Your Password (CLI) page 137

lsof
‣ lsof: Finds Open Files page 624

## 110.2 SET UP HOST SECURITY

/etc/hosts.deny
> hosts.allow and hosts.deny page 486

## 110.3 Securing Data with Encryption

Perform basic OpenSSH 2 client configuration and usage
> Configuring OpenSSH Clients page 690
> Running the ssh, scp, and sftp OpenSSH Clients page 689

Understand the role of OpenSSH 2 server host keys
> How OpenSSH Works page 687
> Authorized Keys: Automatic Login page 700

Perform basic GnuPG configuration and usage
> Tutorial: Using GPG to Secure a File page 1169

Understand SSH port tunnels (including X11 tunnels)
> Tunneling/Port Forwarding page 707

**Partial List of Used Files, Terms, and Utilities**

ssh
> ssh: Logs in or Executes Commands on a Remote System page 693

ssh-keygen
> ssh-keygen page 701

ssh-agent
> ssh-agent: Holds Your Private Keys page 703

ssh-add
> ssh-add page 703

~/.ssh/id_rsa and id_rsa.pub
> id_rsa id_rsa.pub page 689
> id_rsa and id_rsa.pub page 701

~/.ssh/id_dsa and id_dsa.pub
> id_dsa id_dsa.pub page 689

/etc/ssh/ssh_host_rsa_key and ssh_host_rsa_key.pub
> ssh_host_rsa_key, ssh_host_rsa_key.pub page 688

/etc/ssh/ssh_host_dsa_key and ssh_host_dsa_key.pub
> ssh_host_dsa_key, ssh_host_dsa_key.pub page 688

~/.ssh/authorized_keys
> authorized_keys page 688

/etc/ssh_known_hosts
> ssh_known_hosts page 692

gpg
> GnuPG/PGP page 1160
> Tutorial: Using GPG to Secure a File page 1169

~/.gnupg/*
> ~/.gnupg page 1170

# GLOSSARY

All entries marked with <sup>FOLDOC</sup> are based on definitions in the Free On-Line Dictionary of Computing (foldoc.org), Denis Howe, editor. Used with permission.

**10.0.0.0**    See *private address space* on page 1267.

**172.16.0.0**    See *private address space* on page 1267.

**192.168.0.0**    See *private address space* on page 1267.

**802.11**    A family of specifications developed by IEEE for wireless LAN technology, including 802.11 (1–2 megabits per second), 802.11a (54 megabits per second), 802.11b (11 megabits per second), and 802.11g (54 megabits per second).

**absolute pathname**    A pathname that starts with the root directory (represented by /). An absolute pathname locates a file without regard to the working directory.

**access**    In computer jargon, a verb meaning to use, read from, or write to. To access a file means to read from or write to the file.

**Access Control List**    See *ACL*.

**access permissions**    Permission to read from, write to, or execute a file. If you have write access permission to a file (usually just called *write permission*), you can write to the file. Also *access privilege*.

**ACL**    Access Control List. A system that performs a function similar to file permissions but with much finer-grain control.

**active window**    On a desktop, the window that receives the characters you type on the keyboard. Same as *focus, desktop* (page 1250).

**address mask**    See *network mask* on page 1263.

**alias**    A mechanism of a shell that enables you to define new commands.

**alphanumeric character**    One of the characters, either uppercase or lowercase, from A to Z and 0 to 9, inclusive.

**ambiguous file reference**    A reference to a file that does not necessarily specify any one file but can be used to specify a group of files. The shell expands an ambiguous file reference into a list of filenames. Special characters represent single characters (?), strings of zero or more characters (*), and character classes ([]) within ambiguous file references. An ambiguous file reference is a type of *regular expression* (page 1269).

**angle bracket**    A left angle bracket (<) and a right angle bracket (>). The shell uses < to redirect a command's standard input to come from a file and > to redirect the standard output. The shell uses the characters << to signify the start of a Here document and >> to append output to a file.

**animate**    When referring to a window action, means that the action is slowed down so the user can view it. For example, when you minimize a window, it can disappear all at once (not animated) or it can slowly telescope into the panel so you can get a visual feel for what is happening (animated).

**anti-aliasing**    Adding gray pixels at the edge of a diagonal line to get rid of the jagged appearance and thereby make the line look smoother. Anti-aliasing sometimes makes type on a screen look better and sometimes worse; it works best on small and large fonts and is less effective on fonts from 8 to 15 points. See also *subpixel hinting* (page 1275).

**API**
Application program interface. The interface (calling conventions) by which an application program accesses an operating system and other services. An API is defined at the source code level and provides a level of abstraction between the application and the kernel (or other privileged utilities) to ensure the portability of the code.[FOLDOC]

**append**
To add something to the end of something else. To append text to a file means to add the text to the end of the file. The shell uses >> to append a command's output to a file.

**applet**
A small program that runs within a larger program. Examples are Java applets that run in a browser and panel applets that run from a desktop panel.

**archive**
A file that contains a group of smaller, typically related, files. Also, to create such a file. The tar and cpio utilities can create and read archives.

**argument**
A number, letter, filename, or another string that gives some information to a command and is passed to the command when it is called. A command-line argument is anything on a command line following the command name that is passed to the command. An option is a kind of argument.

**arithmetic expression**
A group of numbers, operators, and parentheses that can be evaluated. When you evaluate an arithmetic expression, you end up with a number. The Bourne Again Shell uses the expr command to evaluate arithmetic expressions; the TC Shell uses @, and the Z Shell uses let.

**ARP**
Address Resolution Protocol. A method for finding a host's *MAC address* (page 1259; also Ethernet address) from its IP address. ARP allows the IP address to be independent of the MAC address. See page 297 for more information.[FOLDOC]

**array**
An arrangement of elements (numbers or strings of characters) in one or more dimensions. The Bourne Again, TC, and Z Shells and awk/mawk/gawk can store and process arrays.

**ASCII**
American Standard Code for Information Interchange. A code that uses seven bits to represent both graphic (letters, numbers, and punctuation) and CONTROL characters. You can represent textual information, including program source code and English text, in ASCII code. Because ASCII is a standard, it is frequently used when exchanging information between computers. See the file **/usr/pub/ascii** or give the command **man ascii** to see a list of ASCII codes.

Extensions of the ASCII character set use eight bits. The seven-bit set is common; the eight-bit extensions are still coming into popular use. The eighth bit is sometimes referred to as the *metabit*.

**ASCII terminal**
A textual terminal. Contrast with *graphical display* (page 1251).

**ASP**
Application service provider. A company that provides applications over the Internet.

**asynchronous event**
An event that does not occur regularly or synchronously with another event. Linux system signals are asynchronous; they can occur at any time because they can be initiated by any number of nonregular events.

**attachment**
A file that is attached to, but is not part of, a piece of email. Attachments are frequently opened by programs (including your Internet browser) that are called by your mail program so you might not be aware that they are not an integral part of an email message.

**authentication**    The verification of the identity of a person or process. In a communication system, authentication verifies that a message really comes from its stated source, like the signature on a (paper) letter. The most common form of authentication is typing a user name (which might be widely known or easily guessable) and a corresponding password that is presumed to be known only to the individual being authenticated. Other methods of authentication on a Linux system include the **/etc/passwd** and **/etc/shadow** files, LDAP, biometrics, Kerberos 5, and SMB.ᶠᴼᴸᴰᴼᶜ

**automatic mounting**    A way of demand mounting directories from remote hosts without having them hard configured into **/etc/fstab**. Also called *automounting*.

**avoided**    An object, such as a panel, that should not normally be covered by another object, such as a window.

**back door**    A security hole deliberately left in place by the designers or maintainers of a system. The motivation for creating such holes is not always sinister; some operating systems, for example, come out of the box with privileged accounts intended for use by field service technicians or the vendor's maintenance programmers.

Ken Thompson's 1983 Turing Award lecture to the ACM revealed the existence, in early UNIX versions, of a back door that might be the most fiendishly clever security hack of all time. The C compiler contained code that would recognize when the **login** command was being recompiled and would insert some code recognizing a password chosen by Thompson, giving him entry to the system whether or not an account had been created for him.

Normally such a back door could be removed by removing it from the source code for the compiler and recompiling the compiler. But to recompile the compiler, you have to *use* the compiler, so Thompson arranged that the compiler would *recognize when it was compiling a version of itself*. It would insert into the recompiled compiler the code to insert into the recompiled **login** the code to allow Thompson entry, and, of course, the code to recognize itself and do the whole thing again the next time around. Having done this once, he was then able to recompile the compiler from the original sources; the hack perpetuated itself invisibly, leaving the back door in place and active but with no trace in the sources.

Sometimes called a wormhole. Also *trap door*.ᶠᴼᴸᴰᴼᶜ

**background process**    A process that is not run in the foreground. Also called a *detached process,* a background process is initiated by a command line that ends with an ampersand (**&**) control operator. You do not have to wait for a background process to run to completion before giving the shell additional commands. If you have job control, you can move background processes to the foreground, and vice versa.

**basename**    The name of a file that, in contrast with a pathname, does not mention any of the directories containing the file (and therefore does not contain any slashes [/]). For example, **hosts** is the basename of **/etc/hosts**.ᶠᴼᴸᴰᴼᶜ

**baud**    The maximum information-carrying capacity of a communication channel in symbols (state transitions or level transitions) per second. It coincides with bits per second only for two-level modulation with no framing or stop bits. A symbol is a unique state of the communication channel, distinguishable by the receiver from all other possible states. For example, it might be one of two voltage levels on a wire for a direct digital connection, or it might be the phase or frequency of a carrier.<sup>FOLDOC</sup>

Baud is often mistakenly used as a synonym for bits per second.

**baud rate**  Transmission speed. Usually used to measure terminal or modem speed. Common baud rates range from 110 to 38,400 baud. See *baud*.

**Berkeley UNIX**  One of the two major versions of the UNIX operating system. Berkeley UNIX was developed at the University of California at Berkeley by the Computer Systems Research Group and is often referred to as *BSD* (Berkeley Software Distribution).

**beta release**  Evaluation, pre-release software that is potentially unreliable. Beta software is made available to selected users (beta testers) before it is released to the general public. Beta testing aims to discover bugs that only occur in certain environments or under certain patterns of use, while reducing the volume of feedback to a manageable level. The testers benefit by having earlier access to new products, features, and fixes. The term derives from early 1960s terminology for product cycle checkpoints, first used at IBM but later made standard throughout the industry. Contrast with *stable release* (page 1274).<sup>FOLDOC</sup>

**BIND**  Berkeley Internet Name Domain. An implementation of a *DNS* (page 1247) server developed and distributed by the University of California at Berkeley.

**BIOS**  Basic Input/Output System. On PCs, *EEPROM*-based (page 1248) system software that provides the lowest-level interface to peripheral devices and controls the first stage of the *bootstrap* (page 1240) process, which loads the operating system. The BIOS can be stored in different types of memory. The memory must be nonvolatile so that it remembers the system settings even when the system is turned off. Also BIOS ROM.

**bit**  The smallest piece of information a computer can handle. A *bit* is a binary digit: either 1 or 0 (*on* or *off*).

**bit depth**  Same as *color depth* (page 1243).

**bit-mapped display**  A graphical display device in which each pixel on the screen is controlled by an underlying representation of zeros and ones.

**blank character**  Either a SPACE or a TAB character, also called *whitespace* (page 1280). In some contexts, NEWLINEs are considered blank characters.

**block**  A section of a disk or tape (usually 1,024 bytes long but shorter or longer on some systems) that is written at one time.

**block device**  A disk or tape drive. A block device stores information in blocks of characters and is represented by a block device (block special) file. Contrast with *character device* (page 1242).

**block number**  Disk and tape *blocks* are numbered so that Linux can keep track of the data on the device.

**blocking factor**  The number of logical blocks that make up a physical block on a tape or disk. When you write 1K logical blocks to a tape with a physical block size of 30K, the blocking factor is 30.

**Boolean**    The type of an expression with two possible values: *true* and *false*. Also, a variable of Boolean type or a function with Boolean arguments or result. The most common Boolean functions are AND, OR, and NOT.<sup>FOLDOC</sup>

**boot**    See *bootstrap*.

**boot loader**    A very small program that takes its place in the *bootstrap* process that brings a computer from off or reset to a fully functional state. See "GRUB: The Linux Boot Loader" on page 590.

**bootstrap**    Derived from "Pull oneself up by one's own bootstraps," the incremental process of loading an operating system kernel into memory and starting it running without any outside assistance. Frequently shortened to *boot*.

**Bourne Again Shell**    bash. GNU's command interpreter for UNIX, bash is a POSIX-compliant shell with full Bourne Shell syntax and some C Shell commands built in. The Bourne Again Shell supports emacs-style command-line editing, job control, functions, and online help.<sup>FOLDOC</sup>

**Bourne Shell**    sh. This UNIX command processor was developed by Steve Bourne at AT&T Bell Laboratories.

**brace**    A left brace ({) and a right brace (}). Braces have special meanings to the shell.

**bracket**    A *square bracket* (page 1274) or an *angle bracket* (page 1236).

**branch**    In a tree structure, a branch connects nodes, leaves, and the root. The Linux filesystem hierarchy is often conceptualized as an upside-down tree. The branches connect files and directories. In a source code control system, such as SCCS or RCS, a branch occurs when a revision is made to a file and is not included in subsequent revisions to the file.

**bridge**    Typically a two-port device originally used for extending networks at layer 2 (data link) of the Internet Protocol model.

**broadcast**    A transmission to multiple, unspecified recipients. On Ethernet, a broadcast packet is a special type of *multicast* (page 1262) packet; it has a special address indicating that all devices that receive it should process it. Broadcast traffic exists at several layers of the network stack, including Ethernet and IP. Broadcast traffic has one source but indeterminate destinations (all hosts on the local network).

**broadcast address**    The last address on a subnet (usually 255), reserved as shorthand to mean all hosts.

**broadcast network**    A type of network, such as Ethernet, in which any system can transmit information at any time, and all systems receive every message.

**BSD**    See *Berkeley UNIX* on page 1239.

**buffer**    An area of memory that stores data until it can be used. When you write information to a file on a disk, Linux stores the information in a disk buffer until there is enough to write to the disk or until the disk is ready to receive the information.

**bug**    An unwanted and unintended program property, especially one that causes the program to malfunction.<sup>FOLDOC</sup>

| | |
|---|---|
| **builtin (command)** | A command that is built into a shell. Each of the three major shells—the Bourne Again, TC, and Z Shells—has its own set of builtins. |
| **byte** | A component in the machine data hierarchy, usually larger than a bit and smaller than a word; now most often eight bits and the smallest addressable unit of storage. A byte typically holds one character.ᶠᴼᴸᴰᴼᶜ |
| **bytecode** | A binary file containing an executable program consisting of a sequence of (op code, data) pairs. A bytecode program is interpreted by a bytecode interpreter; Python uses the Python virtual machine. The advantage of bytecode is that it can be run on any processor for which there is a bytecode interpreter. Compiled code (machine code) can run only on the processor for which it was compiled.ᶠᴼᴸᴰᴼᶜ |
| **C programming language** | A modern systems language that has high-level features for efficient, modular programming as well as lower-level features that make it suitable for use as a systems programming language. It is machine independent so that carefully written C programs can be easily transported to run on different machines. Most of the Linux operating system is written in C, and Linux provides an ideal environment for programming in C. |
| **C Shell** | csh. The C Shell command processor was developed by Bill Joy for BSD UNIX. It was named for the C programming language because its programming constructs are similar to those of C. See *shell* on page 1272. |
| **cable modem** | A type of modem that allows you to access the Internet by using your cable television connection. |
| **cache** | Holding recently accessed data, a small, fast memory designed to speed up subsequent access to the same data. Most often applied to processor-memory access but also used for a local copy of data accessible over a network, from a hard disk, and so on.ᶠᴼᴸᴰᴼᶜ |
| **calling environment** | A list of variables and their values that is made available to a called program. Refer to "Executing a Command" on page 375. |
| **cascading stylesheet** | See *CSS* on page 1245. |
| **cascading windows** | An arrangement of windows such that they overlap, generally with at least part of the title bar visible. Opposite of *tiled windows* (page 1277). |
| **case sensitive** | Able to distinguish between uppercase and lowercase characters. Unless you set the **ignorecase** parameter, vim performs case-sensitive searches. The grep utility performs case-sensitive searches unless you use the –i option. |
| **catenate** | To join sequentially, or end to end. The Linux cat utility catenates files: It displays them one after the other. Also *concatenate*. |
| **chain loading** | The technique used by a boot loader to load unsupported operating systems. Used for loading such operating systems as DOS or Windows, it works by loading another boot loader. |
| **character-based** | A program, utility, or interface that works only with *ASCII* (page 1237) characters. This set of characters includes some simple graphics, such as lines and corners, and can display colored characters. It cannot display true graphics. Contrast with *GUI* (page 1252). |

**character-based terminal**   A terminal that displays only characters and very limited graphics. See *character-based* (previous page).

**character class**   In a regular expression, a group of characters that defines which characters can occupy a single character position. A character-class definition is usually surrounded by square brackets. The character class defined by [**abcr**] represents a character position that can be occupied by **a**, **b**, **c**, or **r**. Also *list operator*.

In GNU documentation and POSIX, used to refer to sets of characters with a common characteristic, denoted by the notation [:*class*:]; for example, [:upper:] denotes the set of uppercase letters.

This book uses the term character class as explained under "Brackets" on page 1141.

**character device**   A terminal, printer, or modem. A character device stores or displays characters one at a time. A character device is represented by a character device (character special) file. Contrast with *block device* (page 1239).

**check box**   A GUI widget, usually the outline of a square box with an adjacent caption, that a user can click to display or remove a *tick* (page 1277). When the box holds a tick, the option described by the caption is on or *true*. Also *tick box*.

**checksum**   A computed value that depends on the contents of a block of data and is transmitted or stored along with the data to detect corruption of the data. The receiving system recomputes the checksum based on the received data and compares this value with the one sent with the data. If the two values are the same, the receiver has some confidence that the data was received correctly.

The checksum might be 8, 16, or 32 bits, or some other size. It is computed by summing the bytes or words of the data block, ignoring overflow. The checksum might be negated so that the total of the data words plus the checksum is zero.

Internet packets use a 32-bit checksum.FOLDOC

**child process**   A process that is created by another process, the parent process. Every process is a child process except for the first process, which is started when Linux begins execution. When you run a command from the shell, the shell spawns a child process to run the command. See *process* on page 1267.

**CIDR**   Classless Inter-Domain Routing. A scheme that allocates blocks of Internet addresses in a way that allows summarization into a smaller number of routing table entries. A CIDR block is a block of Internet addresses assigned to an ISP by the InterNIC. Refer to "CIDR: Classless Inter-Domain Routing" on page 300.FOLDOC

**CIFS**   Common Internet File System. An Internet filesystem protocol based on *SMB* (page 1273). CIFS runs on top of TCP/IP, uses DNS, and is optimized to support slower dial-up Internet connections. SMB and CIFS are used interchangeably.FOLDOC

**CIPE**   Crypto IP *Encapsulation* (page 1249). This *protocol* (page 1267) *tunnels* (page 1278) IP packets within encrypted *UDP* (page 1278) packets, is lightweight and simple, and works over dynamic addresses, *NAT* (page 1262), and *SOCKS* (page 1273) *proxies* (page 1268).

**cipher (cypher)**   A cryptographic system that uses a key to transpose/substitute characters within a message, the key itself, or the message.

| | |
|---|---|
| ciphertext | Text that is encrypted. Contrast with *plaintext* (page 1266). See also "Encryption" on page 1156. |
| Classless Inter-Domain Routing | See *CIDR*. |
| cleartext | Text that is not encrypted. Also *plaintext*. Contrast with *ciphertext*. |
| CLI | Command-line interface. See also *character-based* (page 1241). Also *textual interface*. |
| client | A computer or program that requests one or more services from a server. |
| cloud | A system that provides access via a network (typically the Internet) to hardware and/or software computing resources, often via a Web browser. |
| CODEC | Coder/decoder or compressor/decompressor. A hardware and/or software technology that codes and decodes data. MPEG is a popular CODEC for computer video. |
| color depth | The number of bits used to generate a pixel—usually 8, 16, 24, or 32. The color depth is directly related to the number of colors that can be generated. The number of colors that can be generated is 2 raised to the color-depth power. Thus a 24-bit video adapter can generate about 16.7 million colors. |
| color quality | See *color depth*. |
| combo box | A combination of a *drop-down list* (page 1248) and *text box* (page 1277). You can enter text in a combo box. Or, you can click a combo box to cause it to expand and display a static list of selections for you to choose from. |
| command | What you give the shell in response to a prompt. When you give the shell a command, it executes a utility, another program, a builtin command, or a shell script. Utilities are often referred to as commands. When you are using an interactive utility, such as vim or mail, you use commands that are appropriate to that utility. |
| command line | A line containing instructions and arguments that executes a command. This term usually refers to a line you enter in response to a shell prompt on a character-based terminal or terminal emulator. |
| command substitution | Replacing a command with its output. The shells perform command substitution when you enclose a command between $( and ) or between a pair of back ticks ( ` ` ), also called grave accent marks. |
| component architecture | A notion in object-oriented programming where "components" of a program are completely generic. Instead of having a specialized set of methods and fields, they have generic methods through which the component can advertise the functionality it supports to the system into which it is loaded. This strategy enables completely dynamic loading of objects. JavaBeans is an example of a component architecture.<sup>FOLDOC</sup> |
| concatenate | See *catenate* on page 1241. |
| condition code | See *exit status* on page 1249. |

| | |
|---|---|
| connection-oriented protocol | A type of transport layer data communication service that allows a host to send data in a continuous stream to another host. The transport service guarantees that all data will be delivered to the other end in the same order as sent and without duplication. Communication proceeds through three well-defined phases: connection establishment, data transfer, and connection release. The most common example is *TCP* (page 1276). |
| | Also called connection-based protocol and stream-oriented protocol. Contrast with *connectionless protocol* and *datagram* (page 1246).ᶠᴼᴸᴰᴼᶜ |
| connectionless protocol | The data communication method in which communication occurs between hosts with no previous setup. Packets sent between two hosts might take different routes. There is no guarantee that packets will arrive as transmitted or even that they will arrive at the destination at all. *UDP* (page 1278) is a connectionless protocol. Also called packet switching. Contrast with circuit switching and *connection-oriented protocol*.ᶠᴼᴸᴰᴼᶜ |
| console | The main system terminal, usually directly connected to the computer and the one that receives system error messages. Also *system console* and *console terminal*. |
| console terminal | See *console*. |
| control character | A character that is not a graphic character, such as a letter, number, or punctuation mark. Such characters are called control characters because they frequently act to control a peripheral device. RETURN and FORMFEED are control characters that control a terminal or printer. |
| | The word CONTROL is shown in this book in THIS FONT because it is a key that appears on most terminal keyboards. Control characters are represented by ASCII codes less than 32 (decimal). See also *nonprinting character* on page 1264. |
| control operator | A token that performs a control function. The Bourne Again Shell uses the following symbols as control operators: ‖, &, &&, ;, ;;, (, ), |, |&, and RETURN. |
| control structure | A statement used to change the order of execution of commands in a shell script or other program. Each shell provides control structures (for example, **if** and **while**) as well as other commands that alter the order of execution (for example, **exec**). Also *control flow commands*. |
| cookie | Data stored on a client system by a server. The client system browser sends the cookie back to the server each time it accesses that server. For example, a catalog shopping service might store a cookie on your system when you place your first order. When you return to the site, it knows who you are and can supply your name and address for subsequent orders. You might consider cookies to be an invasion of privacy. |
| CPU | Central processing unit. The part of a computer that controls all the other parts. The CPU includes the control unit and the arithmetic and logic unit (ALU). The control unit fetches instructions from memory and decodes them to produce signals that control the other parts of the computer. These signals can cause data to be transferred between memory and ALU or peripherals to perform input or output. A CPU that is housed on a single chip is called a microprocessor. Also *processor* and *central processor*. |

| | |
|---|---|
| cracker | An individual who attempts to gain unauthorized access to a computer system. These individuals are often malicious and have many means at their disposal for breaking into a system. Contrast with *hacker* (page 1252).ᶠᴼᴸᴰᴼᶜ |
| crash | The system suddenly and unexpectedly stops or fails. Derived from the action of the hard disk heads on the surface of the disk when the air gap between the two collapses. |
| Creative Commons | (creativecommons.org) Creative Commons is a nonprofit organization that provides copyright licenses that enable you to share and use creativity and knowledge. The licenses give the public permission to share and use your creative work while reserving some rights. |
| cryptography | The practice and study of encryption and decryption—encoding data so that only a specific individual or machine can decode it. A system for encrypting and decrypting data is a cryptosystem. Such systems usually rely on an algorithm for combining the original data (plaintext) with one or more keys—numbers or strings of characters known only to the sender and/or recipient. The resulting output is called *ciphertext* (page 1243). |
| | The security of a cryptosystem usually depends on the secrecy of keys rather than on the supposed secrecy of an algorithm. Because a strong cryptosystem has a large range of keys, it is not possible to try all of them. Ciphertext appears random to standard statistical tests and resists known methods for breaking codes.ᶠᴼᴸᴰᴼᶜ |
| .cshrc file | In your home directory, a file that the TC Shell executes each time you invoke a new TC Shell. You can use this file to establish variables and aliases. |
| CSS | Cascading stylesheet. Describes how documents are presented on screen and in print. Attaching a stylesheet to a structured document can affect the way it looks without adding new HTML (or other) tags and without giving up device independence. Also *stylesheet.* |
| current (process, line, character, directory, event, etc.) | The item that is immediately available, working, or being used. The current process is the program you are running, the current line or character is the one the cursor is on, and the current directory is the working directory. |
| cursor | A small lighted rectangle, underscore, or vertical bar that appears on a terminal screen and indicates where the next character will appear. Differs from the *mouse pointer* (page 1261). |
| daemon | A program that is not invoked explicitly but lies dormant, waiting for some condition(s) to occur. The perpetrator of the condition need not be aware that a daemon is lurking (although often a program will commit an action only because it knows that it will implicitly invoke a daemon). From the mythological meaning, later rationalized as the acronym Disk And Execution MONitor.ᶠᴼᴸᴰᴼᶜ |
| data structure | A particular format for storing, organizing, working with, and retrieving data. Frequently, data structures are designed to work with specific algorithms that facilitate these tasks. Common data structures include trees, files, records, tables, arrays, etc. |

| | |
|---|---|
| datagram | A self-contained, independent entity of data carrying sufficient information to be routed from the source to the destination computer without reliance on earlier exchanges between this source and destination computer and the transporting network. *UDP* (page 1278) uses datagrams; *IP* (page 1255) uses *packets* (page 1265). Packets are indivisible at the network layer; datagrams are not.ᶠᴼᴸᴰᴼᶜ See also *frame* (page 1251). |
| dataless | A computer, usually a workstation, that uses a local disk to boot a copy of the operating system and access system files but does not use a local disk to store user files. |
| dbm | A standard, simple database manager. Implemented as **gdbm** (GNU database manager), it uses hashes to speed searching. The most common versions of the **dbm** database are **dbm**, **ndbm**, and **gdbm**. |
| DDoS attack | Distributed denial of service attack. A *DoS attack* (page 1248) from many systems that do not belong to the perpetrator of the attack. |
| debug | To correct a program by removing its bugs (that is, errors). |
| default | Something that is selected without being explicitly specified. For example, when used without an argument, ls displays a list of the files in the working directory by default. |
| delta | A set of changes made to a file that has been encoded by the Source Code Control System (SCCS). |
| denial of service | *See DoS attack* on page 1248. |
| dereference | To access the thing to which a pointer points, that is, to follow the pointer. At first sight the word *dereference* might be thought to mean "to cause to stop referring," but its meaning is well established in jargon.ᶠᴼᴸᴰᴼᶜ

When speaking of symbolic links, dereference means to follow the link rather than working with the reference to the link. For example, the **–L** or **––dereference** option causes ls to list the entry that a symbolic link points to rather than the symbolic link (the reference) itself. |
| desktop | A collection of windows, toolbars, icons, and buttons, some or all of which appear on your display. A desktop comprises one or more *workspaces* (page 1281). |
| desktop manager | An icon- and menu-based user interface to system services that allows you to run applications and use the filesystem without using the system's command-line interface. |
| detached process | *See background process* on page 1238. |
| device | A disk drive, printer, terminal, plotter, or other input/output unit that can be attached to the computer. Short for *peripheral device*. |
| device driver | Part of the Linux kernel that controls a device, such as a terminal, disk drive, or printer. |
| device file | A file that represents a device. Also *special file*. |

| | |
|---|---|
| device filename | The pathname of a device file. All Linux systems have two kinds of device files: block and character device files. Linux also has FIFOs (named pipes) and sockets. Device files are traditionally located in the **/dev** directory. |
| device number | See *major device number* (page 1259) and *minor device number* (page 1261). |
| DHCP | Dynamic Host Configuration Protocol. A protocol that dynamically allocates IP addresses to computers on a LAN.<sup>FOLDOC</sup> |
| dialog box | In a GUI, a special window, usually without a titlebar, that displays information. Some dialog boxes accept a response from the user. |
| directory | Short for *directory file*. A file that contains a list of other files. |
| directory hierarchy | A directory, called the root of the directory hierarchy, and all the directory and ordinary files below it (its children). |
| directory service | A structured repository of information on people and resources within an organization, facilitating management and communication.<sup>FOLDOC</sup> |
| disk partition | See *partition* on page 1265. |
| diskless | A computer, usually a workstation, that has no disk and must contact another computer (a server) to boot a copy of the operating system and access the necessary system files. |
| distributed computing | A style of computing in which tasks or services are performed by a network of cooperating systems, some of which might be specialized. |
| DMZ | Demilitarized zone. A host or small network that is a neutral zone between a LAN and the Internet. It can serve Web pages and other data to the Internet and allow local systems access to the Internet while preventing LAN access to unauthorized Internet users. Even if a DMZ is compromised, it holds no data that is private and none that cannot be easily reproduced. |
| DNS | Domain Name Service. A distributed service that manages the correspondence of full hostnames (those that include a domain name) to IP addresses and other system characteristics. |
| DNS domain name | See *domain name*. |
| document object model | See *DOM*. |
| DOM | Document Object Model. A platform-/language-independent interface that enables a program to update the content, structure, and style of a document dynamically. The changes can then be made part of the displayed document. Go to www.w3.org/DOM for more information. |
| domain name | A name associated with an organization, or part of an organization, to help identify systems uniquely. Technically, the part of the *FQDN* (page 1250) to the right of the leftmost period. Domain names are assigned hierarchically. The domain berkeley.edu refers to the University of California at Berkeley, for example; it is part of the top-level edu (education) domain. Also *DNS domain name*. Different than *NIS domain name* (page 1263). |

**Domain Name Service**  See *DNS*.

**door**  An evolving filesystem-based *RPC* (page 1271) mechanism.

**DoS attack**  Denial of service attack. An attack that attempts to make the target host or network unusable by flooding it with spurious traffic.

**DPMS**  Display Power Management Signaling. A standard that can extend the life of CRT monitors and conserve energy. DPMS supports four modes for a monitor: Normal, Standby (power supply on, monitor ready to come to display images almost instantly), Suspend (power supply off, monitor takes up to ten seconds to display an image), and Off.

**drag**  The motion part of *drag-and-drop*.

**drag-and-drop**  To move an object from one position or application to another within a GUI. To drag an object, the user clicks a mouse button (typically the left one) while the mouse pointer *hovers* (page 1253) over the object. Then, without releasing the mouse button, the user drags the object, which stays attached to the mouse pointer, to a different location. The user can then drop the object at the new location by releasing the mouse button.

**drop-down list**  A *widget* (page 1281) that displays a static list for a user to choose from. When the list is not active, it appears as text in a box, displaying the single selected entry. When a user clicks the box, a list appears; the user can move the mouse cursor to select an entry from the list. Different from a *list box* (page 1258).

**druid**  In role-playing games, a character that represents a magical user. Fedora/RHEL uses the term *druid* at the ends of names of programs that guide you through a task-driven chain of steps. Other operating systems call these types of programs *wizards*.

**DSA**  Digital Signature Algorithm. A public key cipher used to generate digital signatures.

**DSL**  Digital Subscriber Line/Loop. Provides high-speed digital communication over a specialized, conditioned telephone line. See also *xDSL* (page 1282).

**Dynamic Host Configuration Protocol**  See *DHCP* on page 1247.

**editor**  A utility, such as vim or emacs, that creates and modifies text files.

**EEPROM**  Electrically erasable, programmable, readonly memory. A *PROM* (page 1267) that can be written to.

**effective UID**  The UID (user ID) that a process appears to have; usually the same as the *real UID* (page 1269). For example, while you are running a setuid program, the effective UID of the process running the program is that of the owner of the program, frequently **root**, while the real UID remains your UID.

**element**  One thing; usually a basic part of a group of things. An element of a numeric array is one of the numbers stored in the array.

**emoticon**  See *smiley* on page 1273.

| | |
|---|---|
| encapsulation | See *tunneling* on page 1278. |
| environment | See *calling environment* on page 1241. |
| environment variable (shell) | A variable that was in the environment the shell was called with or a variable that has been marked for export via the environment. An environment variable is available to children of the shell; also called a global variable. As explained on page 357, you can use the export builtin, or the **–x** option to the declare builtin, to mark a variable for export via the environment. |
| EOF | End of file. |
| EPROM | Erasable programmable readonly memory. A *PROM* (page 1267) that can be written to by applying a higher than normal voltage. |
| escape | See *quote* on page 1268. |
| Ethernet | A type of *LAN* (page 1257) capable of transfer rates as high as 1,000 megabits per second. Refer to "Ethernet" on page 284. |
| Ethernet address | See *MAC address* on page 1259. |
| event | An occurrence, or happening, of significance to a task or program—for example, the completion of an asynchronous input/output operation, such as a keypress or mouse click.FOLDOC |
| exabyte | $2^{60}$ bytes or about $10^{18}$ bytes. See also *large number* (page 1257). |
| exit status | The status returned by a process; either successful (usually 0) or unsuccessful (usually 1). |
| exploit | A security hole or an instance of taking advantage of a security hole.FOLDOC |
| expression | See *logical expression* (page 1259) and *arithmetic expression* (page 1237). |
| extranet | A network extension for a subset of users (such as students at a particular school or engineers working for the same company). An extranet limits access to private information even though it travels on the public Internet. |
| failsafe session | A session that allows you to log in on a minimal desktop in case your standard login does not work well enough to allow you to log in to fix a login problem. |
| FDDI | Fiber Distributed Data Interface. A type of *LAN* (page 1257) designed to transport data at the rate of 100 million bits per second over fiberoptic cable. |
| file | A collection of related information referred to with a *filename* and frequently stored on a disk. Text files typically contain memos, reports, messages, program source code, lists, or manuscripts. Binary or executable files contain utilities or programs that you can run. Refer to "Ordinary Files and Directory Files" on page 177. |
| filename | The name of a file. A filename refers to a file. |
| filename completion | Automatic completion of a filename after you specify a unique prefix. |
| filename extension | The part of a filename following a period. |

| | |
|---|---|
| **filename generation** | What occurs when the shell expands ambiguous file references. See *ambiguous file reference* on page 1236. |
| **filesystem** | A *data structure* (page 1245) that usually resides on part of a disk. All Linux systems have a root filesystem, and many have other filesystems. Each filesystem is composed of some number of blocks, depending on the size of the disk partition that has been assigned to the filesystem. Each filesystem has a control block, named the superblock, that contains information about the filesystem. The other blocks in a filesystem are inodes, which contain control information about individual files, and data blocks, which contain the information in the files. |
| **filling** | A variant of maximizing in which window edges are pushed out as far as they can go without overlapping another window. |
| **filter** | A command that can take its input from standard input and send its output to standard output. A filter transforms the input stream of data and sends it to standard output. A pipeline symbol (|) usually connects a filter's input to standard output of one command, and a second pipeline symbol connects the filter's output to standard input of another command. The grep and sort utilities are commonly used as filters. |
| **firewall** | A device for policy-based traffic management used to keep a network secure. A firewall can be implemented in a single router that filters out unwanted packets, or it can rely on a combination of routers, proxy servers, and other devices. Firewalls are widely used to give users access to the Internet in a secure fashion and to separate a company's public WWW server from its internal network. They are also employed to keep internal network segments more secure. |
| | Recently the term has come to be defined more loosely to include a simple packet filter running on an endpoint machine. |
| | See also *proxy server* on page 1268. |
| **firmware** | Software built into a computer, often in *ROM* (page 1270). Might be used as part of the *bootstrap* (page 1240) procedure. |
| **focus, desktop** | On a desktop, the window that is active. The window with the desktop focus receives the characters you type on the keyboard. Same as *active window* (page 1236). |
| **footer** | The part of a format that goes at the bottom (or foot) of a page. Contrast with *header* (page 1252). |
| **foreground process** | When you run a command in the foreground, the shell waits for the command to finish before giving you another prompt. You must wait for a foreground process to run to completion before you can give the shell another command. If you have job control, you can move background processes to the foreground, and vice versa. See *job control* on page 1256. Contrast with *background process* (page 1238). |
| **fork** | To create a process. When one process creates another process, it forks a process. Also *spawn*. |
| **FQDN** | Fully qualified domain name. The full name of a system, consisting of its hostname and its domain name, including the top-level domain. Technically the name that **gethostbyname**(2) returns for the host named by **gethostname**(2). For example, |

**speedy** is a hostname and **speedy.example.com** is an FQDN. An FQDN is sufficient to determine a unique Internet address for a machine on the Internet.<sup>FOLDOC</sup>

frame
A data link layer packet that contains, in addition to data, the header and trailer information required by the physical medium. Network layer packets are encapsulated to become frames.<sup>FOLDOC</sup> See also *datagram* (page 1246) and *packet* (page 1265).

free list
In a filesystem, the list of blocks that are available for use. Information about the free list is kept in the superblock of the filesystem.

free space
The portion of a hard disk that is not within a partition. A new hard disk has no partitions and contains all free space.

full duplex
The ability to receive and transmit data simultaneously. A *network switch* (page 1263) is typically a full-duplex device. Contrast with *half-duplex* (page 1252).

fully qualified domain name
See *FQDN*.

function
See *shell function* on page 1272.

gateway
A generic term for a computer or a special device connected to more than one dissimilar type of network to pass data between them. Unlike a router, a gateway often must convert the information into a different format before passing it on. The historical usage of gateway to designate a router is deprecated.

GCOS
See *GECOS*.

GECOS
General Electric Comprehensive Operating System. For historical reasons, the user information field in the **/etc/passwd** file is called the GECOS field. Also *GCOS*.

gibibyte
Giga binary byte. A unit of storage equal to $2^{30}$ bytes = 1,073,741,824 bytes = 1024 *mebibytes* (page 1260). Abbreviated as GiB. Contrast with *gigabyte*.

gigabyte
A unit of storage equal to $10^9$ bytes. Sometimes used in place of *gibibyte*. Abbreviated as GB. See also *large number* on page 1257.

global variable (shell)
See *environment variable (shell)* on page 1249.

glyph
A symbol that communicates a specific piece of information nonverbally. A *smiley* (page 1273) is a glyph.

GMT
Greenwich Mean Time. See *UTC* on page 1279.

graphical display
A bitmapped monitor that can display graphical images. Contrast with *ASCII terminal* (page 1237).

graphical user interface
See *GUI*.

group (of users)
A collection of users. Groups are used as a basis for determining file access permissions. If you are not the owner of a file and you belong to the group the file is assigned to, you are subject to the group access permissions for the file. A user can simultaneously belong to several groups.

| | |
|---|---|
| **group (of windows)** | A way to identify similar windows so they can be displayed and acted on similarly. Typically windows started by a given application belong to the same group. |
| **group ID** | A unique number that identifies a set of users. It is stored in the password and group databases (**/etc/passwd** and **/etc/group** files or their NIS equivalents). The group database associates group IDs with group names. Also *GID*. |
| **GUI** | Graphical user interface. A GUI provides a way to interact with a computer system by choosing items from menus or manipulating pictures drawn on a display screen instead of by typing command lines. Under Linux, the X Window System provides a graphical display and mouse/keyboard input. GNOME and KDE are two popular desktop managers that run under X. Contrast with *character-based* (page 1241). |
| **hacker** | A person who enjoys exploring the details of programmable systems and learning how to stretch their capabilities, as opposed to users, who prefer to learn only the minimum necessary. One who programs enthusiastically (even obsessively) or who enjoys programming rather than just theorizing about programming.<sup>FOLDOC</sup> Contrast with *cracker* (page 1245). |
| **half-duplex** | A half-duplex device can only receive or transmit at a given moment; it cannot do both. A *hub* (page 1254) is typically a half-duplex device. Contrast with *full duplex* (page 1251). |
| **hard link** | A directory entry that contains the filename and inode number for a file. The inode number identifies the location of control information for the file on the disk, which in turn identifies the location of the file's contents on the disk. Every file has at least one hard link, which locates the file in a directory. When you remove the last hard link to a file, you can no longer access the file. See *link* (page 1258) and *symbolic link* (page 1276). |
| **hash** | A string that is generated from another string. See *one-way hash function* on page 1264. When used for security, a hash can prove, almost to a certainty, that a message has not been tampered with during transmission: The sender generates a hash of a message, encrypts the message and hash, and sends the encrypted message and hash to the recipient. The recipient decrypts the message and hash, generates a second hash from the message, and compares the hash that the sender generated to the new hash. When they are the same, the message has probably not been tampered with. Hashed versions of passwords can be used to authenticate users. A hash can also be used to create an index called a *hash table*. Also *hash value*. |
| **hash table** | An index created from hashes of the items to be indexed. The hash function makes it highly unlikely that two items will create the same hash. To look up an item in the index, create a hash of the item and search for the hash. Because the hash is typically shorter than the item, the search is more efficient. |
| **header** | When you are formatting a document, the header goes at the top, or head, of a page. In electronic mail the header identifies who sent the message, when it was sent, what the subject of the message is, and so forth. |
| **Here document** | A shell script that takes its input from the file that contains the script. |
| **hesiod** | The nameserver of project Athena. Hesiod is a name service library that is derived from *BIND* (page 1239) and leverages a DNS infrastructure. |

**heterogeneous**   Consisting of different parts. A heterogeneous network includes systems produced by different manufacturers and/or running different operating systems.

**hexadecimal number**   A base 16 number. Hexadecimal (or *hex*) numbers are composed of the hexadecimal digits 0–9 and A–F. Computers use *bits* (page 1239) to represent data. A group of 4 bits represents 16 possible values, 0 through F. A hexadecimal digit provides a convenient way to represent a group of 4 bits. See Table G-1.

**Table G-1**   Decimal, octal, and hexadecimal numbers

| Decimal | Octal | Hex | Decimal | Octal | Hex |
|---------|-------|-----|---------|-------|-----|
| 1 | 1 | 1 | 17 | 21 | 11 |
| 2 | 2 | 2 | 18 | 22 | 12 |
| 3 | 3 | 3 | 19 | 23 | 13 |
| 4 | 4 | 4 | 20 | 24 | 14 |
| 5 | 5 | 5 | 21 | 25 | 15 |
| 6 | 6 | 6 | 31 | 37 | 1F |
| 7 | 7 | 7 | 32 | 40 | 20 |
| 8 | 10 | 8 | 33 | 41 | 21 |
| 9 | 11 | 9 | 64 | 100 | 40 |
| 10 | 12 | A | 96 | 140 | 60 |
| 11 | 13 | B | 100 | 144 | 64 |
| 12 | 14 | C | 128 | 200 | 80 |
| 13 | 15 | D | 254 | 376 | FE |
| 14 | 16 | E | 255 | 377 | FF |
| 15 | 17 | F | 256 | 400 | 100 |
| 16 | 20 | 10 | 257 | 401 | 101 |

**hidden filename**   A filename that starts with a period. These filenames are called hidden because the ls utility does not normally list them. Use the –a option of ls to list all files, including those with hidden filenames. The shell does not expand a leading asterisk (*) in an ambiguous file reference to match files with hidden filenames. Also *hidden file, invisible file.*

**hierarchy**   An organization with a few things, or thing—one at the top—and with several things below each other thing. An inverted tree structure. Examples in computing include a file tree where each directory might contain files or other directories, a hierarchical network, and a class hierarchy in object-oriented programming.ᶠᴼᴸᴰᴼᶜ Refer to "The Hierarchical Filesystem" on page 176.

**history**   A shell mechanism that enables you to modify and reexecute recent commands.

**home directory**   The directory that is the working directory when you first log in. The pathname of this directory is stored in the **HOME** shell variable.

**hover**   To leave the mouse pointer stationary for a moment over an object. In many cases hovering displays a *tooltip* (page 1278).

| | |
|---|---|
| **HTML** | Hypertext Markup Language. A *hypertext* document format used on the World Wide Web. Tags, which are embedded in the text, consist of a less than sign (<), a directive, zero or more parameters, and a greater than sign (>). Matched pairs of directives, such as <TITLE> and </TITLE>, delimit text that is to appear in a special place or style. For more information on HTML, visit www.htmlhelp.com/faq/html/all.html.<sup>FOLDOC</sup> |
| **HTTP** | Hypertext Transfer Protocol. The client/server TCP/IP protocol used on the World Wide Web for the exchange of *HTML* documents. |
| **hub** | A multiport repeater. A hub rebroadcasts all packets it receives on all ports. This term is frequently used to refer to small hubs and switches, regardless of the device's intelligence. It is a generic term for a layer 2 shared-media networking device. Today the term *hub* is sometimes used to refer to small intelligent devices, although that was not its original meaning. Contrast with *network switch* (page 1263). |
| **hypertext** | A collection of documents/nodes containing (usually highlighted or underlined) cross-references or links, which, with the aid of an interactive browser program, allow the reader to move easily from one document to another.<sup>FOLDOC</sup> |
| **Hypertext Markup Language** | See *HTML*. |
| **Hypertext Transfer Protocol** | See *HTTP*. |
| **i18n** | Internationalization. An abbreviation of the word *internationalization*: the letter *i* followed by 18 letters (*nternationalizatio*) followed by the letter *n*. |
| **i/o device** | Input/output device. See *device* on page 1246. |
| **IANA** | Internet Assigned Numbers Authority. A group that maintains a database of all permanent, registered system services (www.iana.org). |
| **ICMP** | Internet Control Message Protocol. A type of network packet that carries only messages, no data. The most common ICMP packet is the echo request that is sent by the ping utility. |
| **icon** | In a GUI, a small picture representing a file, directory, action, program, and so on. When you click an icon, an action, such as opening a window and starting a program or displaying a directory or Web site, takes place. From miniature religious statues.<sup>FOLDOC</sup> |
| **iconify** | To change a window into an *icon*. Contrast with *restore* (page 1270). |
| **ignored window** | A state in which a window has no decoration and therefore no buttons or titlebar to control it with. |
| **indentation** | See *indention*. |
| **indention** | The blank space between the margin and the beginning of a line that is set in from the margin. |
| **inode** | A *data structure* (page 1245) that contains information about a file. An inode for a file contains the file's length, the times the file was last accessed and modified, the |

time the inode was last modified, owner and group IDs, access privileges, number of links, and pointers to the data blocks that contain the file itself. Each directory entry associates a filename with an inode. Although a single file might have several filenames (one for each link), it has only one inode.

**input**  Information that is fed to a program from a terminal or other file. See *standard input* on page 1274.

**installation**  A computer at a specific location. Some aspects of the Linux system are installation dependent. Also *site*.

**interactive**  A program that allows ongoing dialog with the user. When you give commands in response to shell prompts, you are using the shell interactively. Also, when you give commands to utilities, such as vim and mail, you are using the utilities interactively.

**interface**  The meeting point of two subsystems. When two programs work together, their interface includes every aspect of either program that the other deals with. The *user interface* (page 1279) of a program includes every program aspect the user comes into contact with: the syntax and semantics involved in invoking the program, the input and output of the program, and its error and informational messages. The shell and each of the utilities and built-in commands have a user interface.

**International Organization for Standardization**  See *ISO* on the next page.

**internet**  A large network that encompasses other, smaller networks.

**Internet**  The largest internet in the world. The Internet (uppercase "I") is a multilevel hierarchy composed of backbone networks (ARPANET, NSFNET, MILNET, and others), midlevel networks, and stub networks. These include commercial (**.com** or **.co**), university (**.ac** or **.edu**), research (**.org** or **.net**), and military (**.mil**) networks and span many different physical networks around the world with various protocols, including the Internet Protocol (IP). Outside the United States, country code domains are popular (**.us, .es, .mx, .de**, and so forth), although you will see them used within the United States as well.

**Internet Protocol**  See *IP*.

**Internet service provider**  See *ISP* on the next page.

**intranet**  An inhouse network designed to serve a group of people such as a corporation or school. The general public on the Internet does not have access to an intranet. See page 281.

**invisible file**  See *hidden filename* on page 1253.

**IP**  Internet Protocol. The network layer for TCP/IP. IP is a best-effort, packet-switching, *connectionless protocol* (page 1244) that provides packet routing, fragmentation, and reassembly through the data link layer. *IPv4* is slowly giving way to *IPv6*.[FOLDOC]

**IP address**     Internet Protocol address. A four-part address associated with a particular network connection for a system using the Internet Protocol (IP). A system that is attached to multiple networks that use the IP will have a different IP address for each network interface.

**IP multicast**     See *multicast* on page 1262.

**IP spoofing**     A technique used to gain unauthorized access to a computer. The would-be intruder sends messages to the target machine. These messages contain an IP address indicating that the messages are coming from a trusted host. The target machine responds to the messages, giving the intruder (privileged) access to the target.

**IPC**     Interprocess communication. A method to communicate specific information between programs.

**IPv4**     *IP* version 4. See *IP* and *IPv6*.

**IPv6**     *IP* version 6. The next generation of Internet Protocol, which provides a much larger address space ($2^{128}$ bits versus $2^{32}$ bits for IPv4) that is designed to accommodate the rapidly growing number of Internet addressable devices. IPv6 also has built-in autoconfiguration, enhanced security, better multicast support, and many other features.

**iSCSI**     Internet Small Computer System Interface. A network storage protocol that encapsulates SCSI data into TCP packets. You can use this protocol to connect a system to a storage array using an Ethernet connection.

**ISDN**     Integrated Services Digital Network. A set of communications standards that allows a single pair of digital or standard telephone wires to carry voice, data, and video at a rate of 64 kilobits per second.

**ISO**     International Organization for Standardization. A voluntary, nontreaty organization founded in 1946. It is responsible for creating international standards in many areas, including computers and communications. Its members are the national standards organizations of 89 countries, including the American National Standards Institute.[FOLDOC]

**ISO9660**     The *ISO* standard defining a filesystem for CD-ROMs.

**ISP**     Internet service provider. Provides Internet access to its customers.

**job control**     A facility that enables you to move commands from the foreground to the background, and vice versa. Job control enables you to stop commands temporarily.

**journaling filesystem**     A filesystem that maintains a noncached log file, or journal, which records all transactions involving the filesystem. When a transaction is complete, it is marked as complete in the log file.

     The log file results in greatly reduced time spent recovering a filesystem after a crash, making it particularly valuable in systems where high availability is an issue.

**JPEG**     Joint Photographic Experts Group. This committee designed the standard image-compression algorithm. JPEG is intended for compressing either full-color or gray-scale digital images of natural, real-world scenes and does not work as well on nonrealistic images, such as cartoons or line drawings. Filename extensions: **.jpg**, **.jpeg**.[FOLDOC]

**justify**  To expand a line of type in the process of formatting text. A justified line has even margins. A line is justified by increasing the space between words and sometimes between letters on the line.

**Kerberos**  An MIT-developed security system that authenticates users and machines. It does not provide authorization to services or databases; it establishes identity at logon, which is used throughout the session. Once you are authenticated, you can open as many terminals, windows, services, or other network accesses as you like until your session expires.

**kernel**  The part of the operating system that allocates machine resources, including memory, disk space, and *CPU* (page 1244) cycles, to all other programs that run on a computer. The kernel includes the low-level hardware interfaces (drivers) and manages *processes* (page 1267), the means by which Linux executes programs. The kernel is the part of the Linux system that Linus Torvalds originally wrote (see the beginning of Chapter 1).

**kernelspace**  The part of memory (RAM) where the kernel resides. Code running in kernelspace has full access to hardware and all other processes in memory. See the *KernelAnalysis-HOWTO*.

**key binding**  A *keyboard* key is said to be bound to the action that results from pressing it. Typically keys are bound to the letters that appear on the keycaps: When you press **A**, an **A** appears on the screen. Key binding usually refers to what happens when you press a combination of keys, one of which is CONTROL, ALT, META, or SHIFT, or when you press a series of keys, the first of which is typically ESCAPE.

**keyboard**  A hardware input device consisting of a number of mechanical buttons (keys) that the user presses to input characters to a computer. By default a keyboard is connected to standard input of a shell.ᶠᴼᴸᴰᴼᶜ

**kilo-**  In the binary system, the prefix *kilo-* multiplies by $2^{10}$ (i.e., 1,024). Kilobit and kilobyte are common uses of this prefix. Abbreviated as *k*.

**Korn Shell**  ksh. A command processor, developed by David Korn at AT&T Bell Laboratories, that is compatible with the Bourne Shell but includes many extensions. See also *shell* on page 1272.

**l10n**  Localization. An abbreviation of the word *localization*: the letter *l* followed by 10 letters (*ocalizatio*) followed by the letter *n*.

**LAN**  Local area network. A network that connects computers within a localized area (such as a single site, building, or department).

**large number**  Visit mathworld.wolfram.com/LargeNumber.html for a comprehensive list.

**LDAP**  Lightweight Directory Access Protocol. A simple protocol for accessing online directory services. LDAP is a lightweight alternative to the X.500 Directory Access Protocol (DAP). It can be used to access information about people, system users, network devices, email directories, and systems. In some cases, it can be used as an alternative for services such as NIS. Given a name, many mail clients can use LDAP to discover the corresponding email address. See *directory service* on page 1247.

**leaf**  In a tree structure, the end of a branch that cannot support other branches. When the Linux filesystem hierarchy is conceptualized as a tree, files that are not directories are leaves. See *node* on page 1264.

| | |
|---|---|
| least privilege, concept of | Mistakes made by a user working with **root** privileges can be much more devastating than those made by an ordinary user. When you are working on the computer, especially when you are working as the system administrator, always perform any task using the least privilege possible. If you can perform a task logged in as an ordinary user, do so. If you must work with **root** privileges, do as much as you can as an ordinary user, log in as **root** or give an su or sudo command so you are working with **root** privileges, do as much of the task that has to be done with **root** privileges, and revert to being an ordinary user as soon as you can.

Because you are more likely to make a mistake when you are rushing, this concept becomes more important when you have less time to apply it. |
| library | Software library. A collection of subroutines and functions stored in one or more files, usually in compiled form, for linking with other programs. Libraries are often supplied by the operating system or software development environment developer to be used in many different programs. Libraries are linked with a user's program to form an executable.FOLDOC |
| Lightweight Directory Access Protocol | See *LDAP* on the previous page. |
| link | A pointer to a file. Two kinds of links exist: *hard links* (page 1252) and *symbolic links* (page 1276) also called *soft links*. A hard link associates a filename with a place on the disk where the content of the file is located. A symbolic link associates a filename with the pathname of a hard link to a file. |
| Linux-PAM | See *PAM* on page 1265. |
| Linux-Pluggable Authentication Modules | See *PAM* on page 1265. |
| list box | A *widget* (page 1281) that displays a static list for a user to choose from. The list appears as multiple lines with a *scrollbar* (page 1272) if needed. The user can scroll the list and select an entry. Different from a *drop-down list* (page 1248). |
| loadable kernel module | See *loadable module*. |
| loadable module | A portion of the operating system that controls a special device and that can be loaded automatically into a running kernel as needed to access that device. |
| local area network | See *LAN* on the previous page. |
| locale | The language; date, time, and currency formats; character sets; and so forth that pertain to a geopolitical place or area. For example, en_US specifies English as spoken in the United States and dollars; en_UK specifies English as spoken in the United Kingdom and pounds. See the locale man page in Section 5 of the system manual for more information. Also the locale utility. |

| | |
|---|---|
| log in | To gain access to a computer system by responding correctly to the **login:** and **Password:** prompts. Also *log on, login*. |
| log out | To end your session by exiting from your login shell. Also *log off*. |
| logical expression | A collection of strings separated by logical operators (>, >=, =, !=, <=, and <) that can be evaluated as *true* or *false*. Also *Boolean* (page 1240) *expression*. |
| .login file | A file in a user's home directory that the TC Shell executes when you log in. You can use this file to set environment variables and to run commands that you want executed at the beginning of each session. |
| login name | See *username* on page 1279. |
| login shell | The shell you are using when you log in. The login shell can fork other processes that can run other shells, utilities, and programs. See page 330. |
| .logout file | A file in a user's home directory that the TC Shell executes when you log out, assuming that the TC Shell is your login shell. You can put in the **.logout** file commands that you want run each time you log out. |
| MAC address | Media Access Control address. The unique hardware address of a device connected to a shared network medium. Each network adapter has a globally unique MAC address that it stores in ROM. MAC addresses are 6 bytes long, enabling $256^6$ (about 300 trillion) possible addresses or 65,536 addresses for each possible IPv4 address.<br><br>A MAC address performs the same role for Ethernet that an IP address performs for TCP/IP: It provides a unique way to identify a host. Also called an Ethernet address. |
| machine collating sequence | The sequence in which the computer orders characters. The machine collating sequence affects the outcome of sorts and other procedures that put lists in alphabetical order. Many computers use ASCII codes so their machine collating sequences correspond to the ordering of the ASCII codes for characters. |
| macro | A single instruction that a program replaces by several (usually more complex) instructions. The C compiler recognizes macros, which are defined using a #define instruction to the preprocessor. |
| magic number | A magic number, which occurs in the first 512 bytes of a binary file, is a 1-, 2-, or 4-byte numeric value or character string that uniquely identifies the type of file (much like a DOS 3-character filename extension). See **/usr/share/magic** and the **magic** man page for more information. |
| main memory | Random access memory (RAM), an integral part of the computer. Although disk storage is sometimes referred to as memory, it is never referred to as main memory. |
| major device number | A number assigned to a class of devices, such as terminals, printers, or disk drives. Using the **ls** utility with the **–l** option to list the contents of the **/dev** directory displays the major and minor device numbers of many devices (as major, minor). |
| MAN | Metropolitan area network. A network that connects computers and *LANs* (page 1257) at multiple sites in a small regional area, such as a city. |
| man-in-the-middle attack | A security attack wherein the attacker interposes himself between two subjects. For example, if Max and Zach try to carry on a secure email exchange over a network, |

Max first sends Zach his public key. However, suppose Mr. X sits between Max and Zach on the network and intercepts Max's public key. Mr. X then sends *his* public key to Zach. Zach then sends his public key to Max, but once again Mr. X intercepts it and substitutes *his* public key and sends that to Max. Without some kind of active protection (a piece of shared information), Mr. X, the *man in the middle,* can decrypt all traffic between Max and Zach, reencrypt it, and send it on to the other party. Also MTM attack.

**masquerade**  To appear to come from one domain or IP address when actually coming from another. Said of a packet (iptables) or message (**sendmail/exim4**). See also *NAT* on page 1262.

**MD5**  Message Digest 5. A *one-way hash function* (page 1264). The *SHA1* (page 1272) algorithm has supplanted MD5 in many applications.

**MDA**  Mail delivery agent. One of the three components of a mail system; the other two are the *MTA* (page 1261) and *MUA* (page 1261). An MDA accepts inbound mail from an MTA and delivers it to a local user.

**mebibyte**  Mega binary byte. A unit of storage equal to $2^{20}$ bytes = 1,048,576 bytes = 1,024 kibibytes. Abbreviated as MiB. Contrast with *megabyte*.

**megabyte**  A unit of storage equal to $10^6$ bytes. Sometimes used in place of *mebibyte*. Abbreviated as MB.

**memory**  See *RAM* on page 1268.

**menu**  A list from which the user might select an operation to be performed. This selection is often made with a mouse or other pointing device under a GUI but might also be controlled from the keyboard. Very convenient for beginners, menus show which commands are available and facilitate experimenting with a new program, often reducing the need for user documentation. Experienced users usually prefer keyboard commands, especially for frequently used operations, because they are faster to use.FOLDOC

**merge**  To combine two ordered lists so that the resulting list is still in order. The sort utility can merge files.

**META key**  On the keyboard, a key that is labeled META or ALT. Use this key as you would the SHIFT key. While holding it down, press another key. The emacs editor makes extensive use of the META key.

**metacharacter**  A character that has a special meaning to the shell or another program in a particular context. Metacharacters are used in the ambiguous file references recognized by the shell and in the regular expressions recognized by several utilities. You must quote a metacharacter if you want to use it without invoking its special meaning. See *regular character* (page 1269) and *special character* (page 1274).

**metadata**  Data about data. In data processing, metadata is definitional data that provides information about, or documentation of, other data managed within an application or environment.

For example, metadata can document data about data elements or attributes (name, size, data type, and so on), records or *data structures* (page 1245) (length, fields, columns, and so on), and data itself (where it is located, how it is associated, who owns it, and so on). Metadata can include descriptive information about the context, quality and condition, or characteristics of the data.[FOLDOC]

**metropolitan area network**  See *MAN* on page 1259.

**MIME**  Multipurpose Internet Mail Extension. Originally used to describe how specific types of files that were attached to email were to be handled. Today MIME types describe how a file is to be opened or worked with, based on its contents, determined by its *magic number* (page 1259), and filename extension. An example of a MIME *type* is **image/jpeg**: The MIME *group* is **image** and the MIME *subtype* is **jpeg**. Many MIME groups exist, including application, audio, image, inode, message, text, and video.

**minimize**  See *iconify* on page 1254.

**minor device number**  A number assigned to a specific device within a class of devices. See *major device number* on page 1259.

**modem**  Modulator/demodulator. A peripheral device that modulates digital data into analog data for transmission over a voice-grade telephone line. Another modem demodulates the data at the other end.

**module**  See *loadable module* on page 1258.

**motherboard**  The main printed circuit board in a personal computer. It contains the bus, the microprocessor, and integrated circuits used for controlling any built-in peripherals such as the keyboard, display, serial and parallel ports, joystick, and mouse interfaces. Most motherboards contain sockets that accept additional boards. Also mobo.[FOLDOC]

**mount**  To make a filesystem accessible to system users. When a filesystem is not mounted, you cannot read from or write to files it contains.

**mount point**  A directory that you mount a local or remote filesystem on. See page 38.

**mouse**  A device you use to point to a particular location on a display screen, typically so you can choose a menu item, draw a line, or highlight some text. You control a pointer on the screen by sliding a mouse around on a flat surface; the position of the pointer moves relative to the movement of the mouse. You select items by pressing one or more buttons on the mouse.

**mouse pointer**  In a GUI, a marker that moves in correspondence with the mouse. It is usually a small black **x** with a white border or an arrow. Differs from the *cursor* (page 1245).

**mouseover**  The action of passing the mouse pointer over an object on the screen.

**MTA**  Mail transfer agent. One of the three components of a mail system; the other two are the *MDA* and *MUA*. An MTA accepts mail from users and MTAs.

**MTM attack**  See *man-in-the-middle attack* on page 1259.

**MUA**  Mail user agent. One of the three components of a mail system; the other two are the *MDA* and *MTA*. An MUA is an end-user mail program such as KMail, mutt, or Outlook.

**multiboot specification**  Specifies an interface between a boot loader and an operating system. With compliant boot loaders and operating systems, any boot loader should be able to load any operating system. The object of this specification is to ensure that different operating systems will work on a single machine. For more information, go to odin-os.sourceforge.net/guides/multiboot.html.

**multicast**  A multicast packet has one source and multiple destinations. In multicast, source hosts register at a special address to transmit data. Destination hosts register at the same address to receive data. In contrast to *broadcast* (page 1240), which is LAN-based, multicast traffic is designed to work across routed networks on a subscription basis. Multicast reduces network traffic by transmitting a packet one time, with the router at the end of the path breaking it apart as needed for multiple recipients.

**multitasking**  A computer system that allows a user to run more than one job at a time. A multitasking system, such as Linux, allows you to run a job in the background while running a job in the foreground.

**multiuser system**  A computer system that can be used by more than one person at a time. Linux is a multiuser operating system. Contrast with *single-user system* (page 1273).

**namespace**  A set of names (identifiers) in which all names are unique.FOLDOC

**NAS**  Network Attached Storage. A system of fixed disks, *RAID* (page 1268) arrays, and magnetic tape drives connected directly to a *SAN* (page 1271) or other direct network connection. Contrast with a file server where the peripherals are connected to the network via a computer (the server).FOLDOC

**NAT**  Network Address Translation. A scheme that enables a LAN to use one set of IP addresses internally and a different set externally. The internal set is for LAN (private) use. The external set is typically used on the Internet and is Internet unique. NAT provides some privacy by hiding internal IP addresses and allows multiple internal addresses to connect to the Internet through a single external IP address. See also *masquerade* on page 1260.

**NBT**  NetBIOS over TCP/IP. A protocol that supports NetBIOS services in a TCP/IP environment. Also NetBT.

**negative caching**  Storing the knowledge that something does not exist. A cache normally stores information about something that exists. A negative cache stores the information that something, such as a record, does not exist.

**NetBIOS**  Network Basic Input/Output System. An *API* (page 1237) for writing network-aware applications.

**netboot**  To boot a computer over the network (as opposed to booting from a local disk).

**netiquette**  The conventions of etiquette—that is, polite behavior—recognized on Usenet and in mailing lists, such as not (cross-)posting to inappropriate groups and refraining from commercial advertising outside the business groups.

The most important rule of netiquette is "Think before you post." If what you intend to post will not make a positive contribution to the newsgroup and be of interest to several readers, do not post it. Personal messages to one or two individuals should not be posted to newsgroups; use private email instead.FOLDOC

| | |
|---|---|
| **network address** | The network portion (**netid**) of an IP address. For a class A network, it is the first byte, or segment, of the IP address; for a class B network, it is the first two bytes; and for a class C network, it is the first three bytes. In each case the balance of the IP address is the host address (**hostid**). Assigned network addresses are globally unique within the Internet. Also *network number*. |
| **Network Filesystem** | See *NFS*. |
| **Network Information Service** | See *NIS*. |
| **network mask** | A bit mask used to identify which bits in an IP address correspond to the network address and subnet portions of the address. Called a network mask because the network portion of the address is determined by the number of bits that are set in the mask. The network mask has ones in positions corresponding to the network and subnet numbers and zeros in the host number positions. Also *subnet mask* or *mask*. |
| **network number** | See *network address*. |
| **network segment** | A part of an Ethernet or other network on which all message traffic is common to all nodes; that is, it is broadcast from one node on the segment and received by all others. This commonality normally occurs because the segment is a single continuous conductor. Communication between nodes on different segments is via one or more routers.ᶠᴼᴸᴰᴼᶜ |
| **network switch** | A connecting device in networks. Switches are increasingly replacing shared media hubs in an effort to increase bandwidth. For example, a 16-port 10BaseT hub shares the total 10 megabits per second bandwidth with all 16 attached nodes. By replacing the hub with a switch, both sender and receiver can take advantage of the full 10 megabits per second capacity. Each port on the switch can give full bandwidth to a single server or client station or to a hub with several stations. Network switch refers to a device with intelligence. Contrast with *hub* (page 1254). |
| **Network Time Protocol** | See *NTP* on page 1264. |
| **NFS** | Network Filesystem. A remote filesystem designed by Sun Microsystems, available on computers from most UNIX system vendors. |
| **NIC** | Network interface card (or controller). An adapter circuit board installed in a computer to provide a physical connection to a network. Each NIC has a unique *MAC address* (page 1259).ᶠᴼᴸᴰᴼᶜ |
| **NIS** | Network Information Service. A distributed service built on a shared database to manage system-independent information (such as usernames and passwords). |
| **NIS domain name** | A name that describes a group of systems that share a set of NIS files. Different from *domain name* (page 1247). |
| **NNTP** | Network News Transfer Protocol. |

| | |
|---|---|
| node | In a tree structure, the end of a branch that can support other branches. When the Linux filesystem hierarchy is conceptualized as a tree, directories are nodes. See *leaf* on page 1257. |
| nonprinting character | See *control character* on page 1244. Also *nonprintable character*. |
| nonvolatile storage | A storage device whose content is preserved when its power is off. Also NVS and persistent storage. Some examples are CD-ROM, USB flash drive, paper punch tape, hard disk, *ROM* (page 1270), *PROM* (page 1267), *EPROM* (page 1249), and *EEPROM* (page 1248). Contrast with *RAM* (page 1268). |
| NTP | Network Time Protocol. Built on top of TCP/IP, NTP maintains accurate local time by referring to known accurate clocks on the Internet. |
| null string | A string that could contain characters but does not. A string of zero length. |
| octal number | A base 8 number. Octal numbers are composed of the digits 0–7, inclusive. Refer to Table G-1 on page 1253. |
| one-way hash function | A one-way function that takes a variable-length message and produces a fixed-length hash. Given the hash, it is computationally infeasible to find a message with that hash; in fact, you cannot determine any usable information about a message with that hash. Also *message digest function*. See also *hash* (page 1252). |
| open source | A method and philosophy for software licensing and distribution designed to encourage use and improvement of software written by volunteers by ensuring that anyone can copy the source code and modify it freely. |
| | The term *open source* is now more widely used than the earlier term *free software* (promoted by the Free Software Foundation; www.fsf.org) but has broadly the same meaning—free of distribution restrictions, not necessarily free of charge. |
| OpenSSH | A free version of the SSH (secure shell) protocol suite that replaces TELNET, rlogin, and more with secure programs that encrypt all communication—even passwords—over a network. Refer to "OpenSSH: Secure Network Communication" on page 685. |
| operating system | A control program for a computer that allocates computer resources, schedules tasks, and provides the user with a way to access resources. |
| optical drive | A disk drive that uses light to read data from and write data to optical media. CD-ROMs and DVDs are types of optical media. See also *ISO9660* (page 1256). |
| option | A command-line argument that modifies the effects of a command. Options are usually preceded by hyphens on the command line and traditionally have single-character names (such as **–h** or **–n**). Some commands allow you to group options following a single hyphen (for example, **–hn**). GNU utilities frequently have two arguments that do the same thing: a single-character argument and a longer, more descriptive argument that is preceded by two hyphens (such as **––show-all** and **––invert-match**). |
| ordinary file | A file that is used to store a program, text, or other user data. See *directory* (page 1247) and *device file* (page 1246). |
| output | Information that a program sends to the terminal or another file. See *standard output* on page 1275. |

**P2P**  Peer-to-Peer. A network that does not divide nodes into clients and servers. Each computer on a P2P network can fulfill the roles of client and server. In the context of a file-sharing network, this ability means that once a node has downloaded (part of) a file, it can act as a server. BitTorrent implements a P2P network.

**packet**  A unit of data sent across a network. *Packet* is a generic term used to describe a unit of data at any layer of the OSI protocol stack, but it is most correctly used to describe network or application layer data units ("application protocol data unit," APDU).FOLDOC See also *frame* (page 1251) and *datagram* (page 1246).

**packet filtering**  A technique used to block network traffic based on specified criteria, such as the origin, destination, or type of each packet. See also *firewall* (page 1250).

**packet sniffer**  A program or device that monitors packets on a network. See *sniff* on page 1273.

**pager**  A utility that allows you to view a file one screen at a time (for example, less and more).

**paging**  The process by which virtual memory is maintained by the operating system. The content of process memory is moved (paged out) to the *swap space* (page 1276) as needed to make room for other processes.

**PAM**  Linux-PAM or Linux-Pluggable Authentication Modules. These modules allow a system administrator to determine how various applications authenticate users.

**parent process**  A process that forks other processes. See *process* (page 1267) and *child process* (page 1242).

**partition**  A section of a (hard) disk that has a name so you can address it separately from other sections. A disk partition can hold a filesystem or another structure, such as the swap area. Under DOS and Windows, partitions (and sometimes whole disks) are labeled **C:**, **D:**, and so on. Also *disk partition* and *slice*.

**passive FTP**  Allows FTP to work through a firewall by allowing the flow of data to be initiated and controlled by the client FTP program instead of the server. Also called PASV FTP because it uses the FTP PASV command.

**passphrase**  A string of words and characters that you type in to authenticate yourself. A passphrase differs from a *password* only in length. A password is usually short—6 to 10 characters. A passphrase is usually much longer—up to 100 characters or more. The greater length makes a passphrase harder to guess or reproduce than a password and therefore more secure.FOLDOC

**password**  To prevent unauthorized access to a user's account, an arbitrary string of characters chosen by the user or system administrator and used to authenticate the user when attempting to log in.FOLDOC See also *passphrase*.

**PASV FTP**  See *passive FTP*.

**pathname**  A list of directories separated by slashes (**/**) and ending with the name of a file, which can be a directory. A pathname is used to trace a path through the file structure to locate or identify a file.

**pathname, last element of a**  The part of a pathname following the final **/**, or the whole filename if there is no **/**. A simple filename. Same as *basename* (page 1238).

**pathname element**    One of the filenames that forms a pathname.

**peripheral device**    See *device* on page 1246.

**persistent**    Data that is stored on nonvolatile media, such as a hard disk.

**phish**    An attempt to trick users into revealing or sharing private information, especially passwords or financial information. The most common form is email purporting to be from a bank or vendor that requests that a user fill out a form to "update" an account on a phoney Web site disguised to appear legitimate. Generally sent as *spam* (page 1274).

**physical device**    A tangible device, such as a disk drive, that is physically separate from other, similar devices.

**PID**    Process identification, usually followed by the word *number*. Linux assigns a unique PID number as each process is initiated.

**pipeline**    One or more simple commands. If a pipeline comprises two or more commands, the commands are connected such that standard output of one command is connected by a pipeline symbol (|; a control operator) to standard input of the next.

**pixel**    The smallest element of a picture, typically a single dot on a display screen.

**plaintext**    Text that is not encrypted. Also *cleartext*. Contrast with *ciphertext* (page 1243).

**Pluggable Authentication Modules**    See *PAM* on page 1265.

**point-to-point link**    A connection limited to two endpoints, such as the connection between a pair of modems.

**port**    A logical channel or channel endpoint in a communications system. The *TCP* (page 1276) and *UDP* (page 1278) transport layer protocols used on Ethernet use port numbers to distinguish between different logical channels on the same network interface on the same computer.

The **/etc/services** file (see the beginning of this file for more information) or the *NIS* (page 1263) **services** database specifies a unique port number for each application program. The number links incoming data to the correct service (program). Standard, well-known ports are used by everyone: Port 80 is used for HTTP (Web) traffic. Some protocols, such as TELNET and HTTP (which is a special form of TELNET), have default ports specified as mentioned earlier but can use other ports as well.[FOLDOC]

**port forwarding**    The process by which a network *port* on one computer is transparently connected to a port on another computer. If port X is forwarded from system A to system B, any data sent to port X on system A is sent to system B automatically. The connection can be between different ports on the two systems. See also *tunneling* (page 1278).

**portmapper**    A server that converts TCP/IP port numbers into *RPC* (page 1271) program numbers. See "RPC Network Services" on page 317.

**power supply**    An electronic module that converts high-voltage (110 or 240 VAC) alternating current mains electricity into smoothed direct current at the various different voltages required by the motherboard, internal peripheral devices, and external connections such as USB.ᶠᴼᴸᴰᴼᶜ

**printable character**    One of the graphic characters: a letter, number, or punctuation mark. Contrast with a nonprintable, or CONTROL, character. Also *printing character*.

**private address space**    *IANA* (page 1254) has reserved three blocks of IP addresses for private internets or LANs:

```
10.0.0.0   - 10.255.255.255
172.16.0.0 - 172.31.255.255
192.168.0.0 - 192.168.255.255
```

You can use these addresses without coordinating with anyone outside of your LAN (you do not have to register the system name or address). Systems using these IP addresses cannot communicate directly with hosts using the global address space but must go through a gateway. Because private addresses have no global meaning, routing information is not stored by DNSs and most ISPs reject privately addressed packets. Make sure that your router is set up not to forward these packets onto the Internet.

**privileged port**    A *port* (page 1266) with a number less than 1024. On Linux and other UNIX-like systems, only a process running with **root** privileges can bind to a privileged port. Any user on Windows 98 and earlier Windows systems can bind to any port. Also *reserved port*.

**procedure**    A sequence of instructions for performing a particular task. Most programming languages, including machine languages, enable a programmer to define procedures that allow the procedure code to be called from multiple places. Also *subroutine*.ᶠᴼᴸᴰᴼᶜ

**process**    The execution of a command by Linux. See "Processes" on page 373.

**.profile file**    A startup file in a user's home directory that the Bourne Again or Z Shell executes when you log in. The TC Shell executes **.login** instead. You can use the **.profile** file to run commands, set variables, and define functions.

**program**    A sequence of executable computer instructions contained in a file. Linux utilities, applications, and shell scripts are all programs. Whenever you run a command that is not built into a shell, you are executing a program.

**PROM**    Programmable readonly memory. A kind of nonvolatile storage. *ROM* (page 1270) that can be written to using a PROM programmer.

**prompt**    A cue from a program, usually displayed on the screen, indicating that it is waiting for input. The shell displays a prompt, as do some of the interactive utilities, such as mail. By default the Bourne Again and Z Shells use a dollar sign ($) as a prompt, and the TC Shell uses a percent sign (%).

**protocol**    A set of formal rules describing how to transmit data, especially across a network. Low-level protocols define the electrical and physical standards, bit and byte ordering, and transmission, error detection, and correction of the bit stream. High-level protocols deal with data formatting, including message syntax, terminal-to-computer dialog, character sets, and sequencing of messages.ᶠᴼᴸᴰᴼᶜ

**proxy**     A service that is authorized to act for a system while not being part of that system. See also *proxy gateway* and *proxy server*.

**proxy gateway**     A computer that separates clients (such as browsers) from the Internet, working as a trusted agent that accesses the Internet on their behalf. A proxy gateway passes a request for data from an Internet service, such as HTTP from a browser/client, to a remote server. The data that the server returns goes back through the proxy gateway to the requesting service. A proxy gateway should be transparent to the user.

A proxy gateway often runs on a *firewall* (page 1250) system and acts as a barrier to malicious users. It hides the IP addresses of the local computers inside the firewall from Internet users outside the firewall.

You can configure browsers, such as Mozilla/Firefox and Netscape, to use a different proxy gateway or to use no proxy for each URL access method including FTP, netnews, SNMP, HTTPS, and HTTP. See also *proxy*.

**proxy server**     A *proxy gateway* that usually includes a *cache* (page 1241) that holds frequently used Web pages so that the next request for that page is available locally (and therefore more quickly). The terms proxy server and proxy gateway are frequently interchanged so that the use of cache does not rest exclusively with the proxy server. See also *proxy*.

**Python**     A simple, high-level, interpreted, object-oriented, interactive language that bridges the gap between C and shell programming. Suitable for rapid prototyping or as an extension language for C applications, Python supports packages, modules, classes, user-defined exceptions, a good C interface, and dynamic loading of C modules. It has no arbitrary restrictions. See Chapter 28.<sub>FOLDOC</sub>

**quote**     When you quote a character, you take away any special meaning that it has in the current context. You can quote a character by preceding it with a backslash. When you are interacting with the shell, you can also quote a character by surrounding it with single quotation marks. For example, the command **echo \\*** or **echo '*'** displays *. The command **echo *** displays a list of the files in the working directory. See *ambiguous file reference* (page 1236), *metacharacter* (page 1260), *regular character* (page 1269), *regular expression* (page 1269), and *special character* (page 1274). See also *escape* on page 1249.

**radio button**     In a GUI, one of a group of buttons similar to those used to select the station on a car radio. Radio buttons within a group are mutually exclusive; only one button can be selected at a time.

**RAID**     Redundant array of inexpensive/independent disks. Two or more (hard) disk drives used in combination to improve fault tolerance and performance. RAID can be implemented in hardware or software.

**RAM**     Random access memory. A kind of volatile storage. A data storage device for which the order of access to different locations does not affect the speed of access. Contrast with a hard disk or tape drive, which provides quicker access to sequential data because accessing a nonsequential location requires physical movement of the storage medium and/or read/write head rather than just electronic switching. Contrast with *nonvolatile storage* (page 1264). Also *memory*.<sub>FOLDOC</sub>

**RAM disk**    *RAM* that is made to look like a floppy diskette or hard disk. A RAM disk is frequently used as part of the *boot* (page 1240) process.

**RAS**    Remote access server. In a network, a computer that provides access to remote users via analog modem or ISDN connections. RAS includes the dial-up protocols and access control (authentication). It might be a regular fileserver with remote access software or a proprietary system, such as Shiva's LANRover. The modems might be internal or external to the device.

**RDF**    Resource Description Framework. Being developed by W3C (the main standards body for the World Wide Web), a standard that specifies a mechanism for encoding and transferring *metadata* (page 1260). RDF does not specify what the metadata should or can be. It can integrate many kinds of applications and data, using XML as an interchange syntax. Examples of the data that can be integrated include library catalogs and worldwide directories; syndication and aggregation of news, software, and content; and collections of music and photographs. Visit www.w3.org/RDF for more information.

**real UID**    The UID (user ID) that a user logs in with as defined in **/etc/passwd**. Differentiated from *effective UID* (page 1248). See also *UID* on page 1278.

**redirection**    The process of directing standard input for a program to come from a file rather than from the keyboard. Also, directing standard output or standard error to go to a file rather than to the screen.

**reentrant**    Code that can have multiple simultaneous, interleaved, or nested invocations that do not interfere with one another. Noninterference is important for parallel processing, recursive programming, and interrupt handling.

It is usually easy to arrange for multiple invocations (that is, calls to a subroutine) to share one copy of the code and any readonly data. For the code to be reentrant, however, each invocation must use its own copy of any modifiable data (or synchronized access to shared data). This goal is most often achieved by using a stack and allocating local variables in a new stack frame for each invocation. Alternately, the caller might pass in a pointer to a block of memory that that invocation can use (usually for output), or the code might allocate some memory on a heap, especially if the data must survive after the routine returns.

Reentrant code is often found in system software, such as operating systems and teleprocessing monitors. It is also a crucial component of multithreaded programs, where the term *thread-safe* is often used instead of reentrant.ᶠᴼᴸᴰᴼᶜ

**regular character**    A character that always represents itself in an ambiguous file reference or another type of regular expression. Contrast with *special character*.

**regular expression**    A string—composed of letters, numbers, and special symbols—that defines one or more strings. See Appendix A.

**relative pathname**    A pathname that starts from the working directory. Contrast with *absolute pathname* (page 1236).

**remote access server**    See *RAS*.

| | |
|---|---|
| remote filesystem | A filesystem on a remote computer that has been set up so that you can access (usually over a network) its files as though they were stored on your local computer's disks. An example of a remote filesystem is NFS. |
| remote procedure call | See *RPC* on page 1271. |
| resolver | The TCP/IP library software that formats requests to be sent to the *DNS* (page 1247) for hostname-to-Internet address conversion.ᶠᴼᴸᴰᴼᶜ |
| Resource Description Framework | See *RDF* on page 1269. |
| restore | The process of turning an icon into a window. Contrast with *iconify* (page 1254). |
| return code | See *exit status* on page 1249. |
| RFC | Request for comments. Begun in 1969, one of a series of numbered Internet informational documents and standards widely followed by commercial software and freeware in the Internet and UNIX/Linux communities. Few RFCs are standards, but all Internet standards are recorded in RFCs. Perhaps the single most influential RFC has been RFC 822, the Internet electronic mail format standard. |
| | The RFCs are unusual in that they are floated by technical experts acting on their own initiative and reviewed by the Internet at large rather than being formally promulgated through an institution such as ANSI. For this reason they remain known as RFCs, even after they are adopted as standards. The RFC tradition of pragmatic, experience-driven, after-the-fact standard writing done by individuals or small working groups has important advantages over the more formal, committee-driven process typical of ANSI or ISO. For a complete list of RFCs, visit www.rfc-editor.org.ᶠᴼᴸᴰᴼᶜ |
| roam | To move a computer between *wireless access points* (page 1281) on a wireless network without the user or applications being aware of the transition. Moving between access points typically results in some packet loss, although this loss is transparent to programs that use TCP. |
| ROM | Readonly memory. A kind of nonvolatile storage. A data storage device that is manufactured with fixed contents. In general, ROM describes any storage system whose contents cannot be altered, such as a phonograph record or printed book. When used in reference to electronics and computers, ROM describes semiconductor integrated circuit memories, of which several types exist, and CD-ROM. |
| | ROM is nonvolatile storage—it retains its contents even after power has been removed. ROM is often used to hold programs for embedded systems, as these usually have a fixed purpose. ROM is also used for storage of the *BIOS* (page 1239) in a computer. Contrast with *RAM* (page 1268).ᶠᴼᴸᴰᴼᶜ |
| root directory | The ancestor of all directories and the start of all absolute pathnames. The root directory has no name and is represented by / standing alone or at the left end of a pathname. |

**root filesystem**     The filesystem that is available when the system is brought up in single-user mode. This filesystem is always represented by /. You cannot unmount or mount the root filesystem. You can remount root to change its mount options.

**root login**     Usually the username of *Superuser* (page 1276).

**root (user)**     Another name for *Superuser* (page 1276).

**root window**     Any place on the desktop not covered by a window, object, or panel.

**rootkit**     Software that provides a user with **root** privileges while hiding its presence.

**rotate**     When a file, such as a log file, gets indefinitely larger, you must keep it from taking up too much space on the disk. Because you might need to refer to the information in the log files in the near future, it is generally not a good idea to delete the contents of the file until it has aged. Instead you can periodically save the current log file under a new name and create a new, empty file as the current log file. You can keep a series of these files, renaming each as a new one is saved. You will then *rotate* the files. For example, you might remove **xyzlog.4, xyzlog.3**⇨**xyzlog.4, xyzlog.2**⇨**xyzlog.3, xyzlog.1**⇨ **xyzlog.2, xyzlog**⇨**xyzlog.1**, and create a new **xyzlog** file. By the time you remove **xyzlog.4**, it will not contain any information more recent than you want to remove.

**router**     A device (often a computer) that is connected to more than one similar type of network to pass data between them. See *gateway* on page 1251.

**RPC**     Remote procedure call. A call to a *procedure* (page 1267) that acts transparently across a network. The procedure itself is responsible for accessing and using the network. The RPC libraries make sure that network access is transparent to the application. RPC runs on top of TCP/IP or UDP/IP.

**RSA**     A public key encryption (page 1157) technology that is based on the lack of an efficient way to factor very large numbers. Because of this lack, it takes an extraordinary amount of computer processing time and power to deduce an RSA key. The RSA algorithm is the de facto standard for data sent over the Internet.

**run**     To execute a program.

**runlevel**     Before the introduction of the systemd **init** daemon, runlevels specified the state of the system, including single-user and multiuser. See Table 10-1 on page 449.

**Samba**     A free suite of programs that implement the Server Message Block (SMB) protocol. See *SMB* (page 1273).

**SAN**     Storage Area Network. A high-speed subnetwork of shared storage devices wherein all storage devices are available to all servers on a LAN or WAN. This setup offloads disk I/O overhead from the servers, allowing them to give more resources to the applications they are running. It also allows disk space to be added without altering individual machines.

**schema**     Within a GUI, a pattern that helps you see and interpret the information that is presented in a window, making it easier to understand new information that is presented using the same schema.

**scroll**     To move lines on a terminal or window up and down or left and right.

**scrollbar**   A *widget* (page 1281) found in graphical user interfaces that controls (scrolls) which part of a document is visible in the window. A window can have a horizontal scrollbar, a vertical scrollbar (more common), or both.ꜰᴏʟᴅᴏᴄ

**server**   A powerful centralized computer (or program) designed to provide information to clients (smaller computers or programs) on request.

**session**   The lifetime of a process. For a desktop, it is the desktop session manager. For a character-based terminal, it is the user's login shell process. In KDE, it is launched by kdeinit. A session might also be the sequence of events between when you start using a program, such as an editor, and when you finish.

**setgid**   When you execute a file that has setgid (set group ID) permission, the process executing the file takes on the privileges of the group the file belongs to. The ls utility shows setgid permission as an **s** in the group's executable position. See also *setuid*.

**setuid**   When you execute a file that has setuid (set user ID) permission, the process executing the file takes on the privileges of the owner of the file. As an example, if you run a setuid program that removes all the files in a directory, you can remove files in any of the file owner's directories, even if you do not normally have permission to do so. When the program is owned by **root**, you can remove files in any directory that a user working with **root** privileges can remove files from. The ls utility shows setuid permission as an **s** in the owner's executable position. See also *setgid*.

**sexillion**   In the British system, $10^{36}$. In the American system, this number is named *undecillion*. See also *large number* (page 1257).

**SHA1**   Secure Hash Algorithm 1. The SHA family is a set of cryptographic *hash* (page 1252) algorithms that were designed by the National Security Agency (NSA). The second member of this family is SHA1, a successor to *MD5* (page 1260). See also *cryptography* on page 1245.

**SHA2**   Secure Hash Algorithm 2. The third member of the SHA family (see *SHA1*), SHA2 is a set of four cryptographic hash functions named SHA-224, SHA-256, SHA-384, SHA-512 with digests that are 224, 256, 384, and 512 bits, respectively.

**share**   A filesystem hierarchy that is shared with another system using *SMB* (page 1273). Also *Windows share* (page 1281).

**shared network topology**   A network, such as Ethernet, in which each packet might be seen by systems other than its destination system. *Shared* means that the network bandwidth is shared by all users.

**shell**   A Linux system command processor. The three major shells are the *Bourne Again Shell* (page 1240), the *TC Shell* (page 1276), and the *Z Shell* (page 1282).

**shell function**   A series of commands that the shell stores for execution at a later time. Shell functions are like shell scripts but run more quickly because they are stored in the computer's main memory rather than in files. Also, a shell function is run in the shell that calls it (unlike a shell script, which is typically run in a subshell).

**shell script**   An ASCII file containing shell commands. Also shell program.

| | |
|---|---|
| signal | A very brief message that the UNIX system can send to a process, apart from the process's standard input. Refer to "trap: Catches a Signal" on page 1047. |
| simple filename | A single filename containing no slashes (/). A simple filename is the simplest form of pathname. Also the last element of a pathname. Also *basename* (page 1238). |
| single-user system | A computer system that only one person can use at a time. Contrast with *multiuser system* (page 1262). |
| slider | A *widget* (page 1281) that allows a user to set a value by dragging an indicator along a line. Many sliders allow the user also to click on the line to move the indicator. Differs from a *scrollbar* (page 1272) in that moving the indicator does not change other parts of the display. |
| SMB | Server Message Block. Developed in the early 1980s by Intel, Microsoft, and IBM, SMB is a client/server protocol that is the native method of file and printer sharing for Windows. In addition, SMB can share serial ports and communications abstractions, such as named pipes and mail slots. SMB is similar to a remote procedure call (*RPC*, page 1271) that has been customized for filesystem access. Also *Microsoft Networking* or *CIFS* (page 1242).<sub>FOLDOC</sub> |
| SMP | Symmetric multiprocessing. Two or more similar processors connected via a high-bandwidth link and managed by one operating system, where each processor has equal access to I/O devices. The processors are treated more or less equally, with application programs able to run on any or all processors interchangeably, at the discretion of the operating system.<sub>FOLDOC</sub> |
| smiley | A character-based *glyph* (page 1251), typically used in email, that conveys an emotion. The characters :-) in a message portray a smiley face (look at it sideways). Because it can be difficult to tell when the writer of an electronic message is saying something in jest or in seriousness, email users often use :-) to indicate humor. The two original smileys, designed by Scott Fahlman, were :-) and :-(. Also *emoticon, smileys,* and *smilies.* For more information search for **smiley** on the Internet. |
| smilies | See *smiley.* |
| SMTP | Simple Mail Transfer Protocol. A protocol used to transfer electronic mail between computers. It is a server-to-server protocol, so other protocols are used to access the messages. The SMTP dialog usually happens in the background under the control of a message transport system such as **sendmail/exim4.**<sub>FOLDOC</sub> |
| snap (windows) | As you drag a window toward another window or edge of the workspace, it can move suddenly so that it is adjacent to the other window/edge. Thus the window *snaps* into position. |
| sneakernet | Using hand-carried magnetic media to transfer files between machines. |
| sniff | To monitor packets on a network. A system administrator can legitimately sniff packets and a malicious user can sniff packets to obtain information such as usernames and passwords. See also *packet sniffer* (page 1265). |
| SOCKS | A networking proxy protocol embodied in a SOCKS server, which performs the same functions as a *proxy gateway* (page 1268) or *proxy server* (page 1268). SOCKS works |

at the application level, requiring that an application be modified to work with the SOCKS protocol, whereas a *proxy* (page 1268) makes no demands on the application.

SOCKSv4 does not support authentication or UDP proxy. SOCKSv5 supports a variety of authentication methods and UDP proxy.

**sort**  To put in a specified order, usually alphabetic or numeric.

**SPACE character**  A character that appears as the absence of a visible character. Even though you cannot see it, a SPACE is a printable character. It is represented by the ASCII code 32 (decimal). A SPACE character is considered a *blank* or *whitespace* (page 1280).

**spam**  Posting irrelevant or inappropriate messages to one or more Usenet newsgroups or mailing lists in deliberate or accidental violation of *netiquette* (page 1262). Also, sending large amounts of unsolicited email indiscriminately. This email usually promotes a product or service. Another common purpose of spam is to *phish* (page 1266). Spam is the electronic equivalent of junk mail. From the Monty Python "Spam" song.<sup>FOLDOC</sup>

**sparse file**  A file that is large but takes up little disk space. The data in a sparse file is not dense (thus its name). Examples of sparse files are core files and dbm files.

**spawn**  See *fork* on page 1250.

**special character**  A character that has a special meaning when it occurs in an ambiguous file reference or another type of regular expression, unless it is quoted. The special characters most commonly used with the shell are * and ?. Also *metacharacter* (page 1260) and *wildcard*.

**special file**  See *device file* on page 1246.

**spin box**  In a GUI, a type of *text box* (page 1277) that holds a number you can change by typing over it or using the up and down arrows at the end of the box. Also *spinner*.

**spinner**  See *spin box*.

**spoofing**  See *IP spoofing* on page 1256.

**spool**  To place items in a queue, each waiting its turn for some action. Often used when speaking about printers. Also used to describe the queue.

**SQL**  Structured Query Language. A language that provides a user interface to relational database management systems (RDBMS). SQL, the de facto standard, is also an ISO and ANSI standard and is often embedded in other programming languages.<sup>FOLDOC</sup>

**square bracket**  A left square bracket ([) or a right square bracket (]). These special characters define character classes in ambiguous file references and other regular expressions.

**stable release**  A fully tested, reliable software release that is typically available to the general public. Contrast with *beta release* (page 1239).

**standard error**  A file to which a program can send output. Usually only error messages are sent to this file. Unless you instruct the shell otherwise, it directs this output to the screen (that is, to the device file that represents the screen).

**standard input**  A file from which a program can receive input. Unless you instruct the shell otherwise, it directs this input so that it comes from the keyboard (that is, from the device file that represents the keyboard).

| | |
|---|---|
| standard output | A file to which a program can send output. Unless you instruct the shell otherwise, it directs this output to the screen (that is, to the device file that represents the screen). |
| startup file | A file that the login shell runs when you log in. The Bourne Again and Z Shells run **.profile**, and the TC Shell runs **.login**. The TC Shell also runs **.cshrc** whenever a new TC Shell or a subshell is invoked. The Z Shell runs an analogous file whose name is identified by the **ENV** variable. |
| status line | The bottom (usually the twenty-fourth) line of the terminal. The vim editor uses the status line to display information about what is happening during an editing session. |
| sticky bit | Originally, an access permission bit that caused an executable program to remain on the swap area of the disk. Today, Linux kernels do not use the sticky bit for this purpose but rather use it to control who can remove files from a directory. In this new capacity, the sticky bit is called the *restricted deletion flag*. If this bit is set on a directory, a file in the directory can be removed or renamed only by a user who is working with **root** privileges or by a user who has write permission for the directory *and* who owns the file or the directory. |
| streaming tape | A tape that moves at a constant speed past the read/write heads rather than speeding up and slowing down, which can slow the process of writing to or reading from the tape. A proper blocking factor helps ensure that the tape device will be kept streaming. |
| streams | See *connection-oriented protocol* on page 1244. |
| string | A sequence of characters. |
| stylesheet | See *CSS* on page 1245. |
| subdirectory | A directory that is located within another directory. Every directory except the root directory is a subdirectory. |
| subnet | Subnetwork. A portion of a network, which might be a physically independent network segment, that shares a network address with other portions of the network and is distinguished by a subnet number. A subnet is to a network as a network is to an internet.<sup>FOLDOC</sup> |
| subnet address | The subnet portion of an IP address. In a subnetted network, the host portion of an IP address is split into a subnet portion and a host portion using a network mask (also subnet mask). See also *subnet number*. |
| subnet mask | See *network mask* on page 1263. |
| subnet number | The subnet portion of an IP address. In a subnetted network, the host portion of an IP address is split into a subnet portion and a host portion using a *network mask*. Also *subnet mask*. See also *subnet address*. |
| subpixel hinting | Similar to *anti-aliasing* (page 1236) but takes advantage of colors to do the anti-aliasing. Particularly useful on LCD screens. |
| subroutine | See *procedure* on page 1267. |
| subshell | A shell that is forked as a duplicate of its parent shell. When you run an executable file that contains a shell script by using its filename on the command line, the shell forks a subshell to run the script. Also, commands surrounded with parentheses are run in a subshell. |

**superblock**   A block that contains control information for a filesystem. The superblock contains housekeeping information, such as the number of inodes in the filesystem and free list information.

**superserver**   The extended Internet services daemon.

**Superuser**   A user working with **root** privileges. This user has access to anything any other system user has access to and more. The system administrator must be able to become Superuser (work with **root** privileges) to establish new accounts, change passwords, and perform other administrative tasks. The username of Superuser is usually **root**. Also *root* or *root user*.

**swap**   The operating system moving a process from main memory to a disk, or vice versa. Swapping a process to the disk allows another process to begin or continue execution.

**swap space**   An area of a disk (that is, a swap file) used to store the portion of a process's memory that has been paged out. Under a virtual memory system, the amount of swap space—rather than the amount of physical memory—determines the maximum size of a single process and the maximum total size of all active processes. Also *swap area* or *swapping area*.FOLDOC

**switch**   1. A GUI *widget* (page 1281) that allows a user to select one of two options, typically On and Off.

2. See *network switch* on page 1263.

**symbolic link**   A directory entry that points to the pathname of another file. In most cases a symbolic link to a file can be used in the same ways a hard link can be used. Unlike a hard link, a symbolic link can span filesystems and can connect to a directory.

**system administrator**   The person responsible for the upkeep of the system. The system administrator has the ability to log in as **root** or use sudo to work with **root** privileges. See also *Superuser*.

**system console**   See *console* on page 1244.

**system mode**   The designation for the state of the system while it is doing system work. Some examples are making system calls, running NFS and autofs, processing network traffic, and performing kernel operations on behalf of the system. Contrast with *user mode* (page 1279).

**System V**   One of the two major versions of the UNIX system.

**TC Shell**   tcsh. An enhanced but completely compatible version of the BSD UNIX C shell, csh.

**TCP**   Transmission Control Protocol. The most common transport layer protocol used on the Internet. This connection-oriented protocol is built on top of *IP* (page 1255) and is nearly always seen in the combination TCP/IP (TCP over *IP*). TCP adds reliable communication, sequencing, and flow control and provides full-duplex, process-to-process connections. *UDP* (page 1278), although connectionless, is the other protocol that runs on top of *IP*.FOLDOC

**tera-**   In the binary system, the prefix *tera-* multiplies by $2^{40}$ (1,099,511,627,776). Terabyte is a common use of this prefix. Abbreviated as *T*. See also *large number* on page 1257.

**termcap**   Terminal capability. On older systems, the **/etc/termcap** file contained a list of various types of terminals and their characteristics. *System V* replaced the function of this file with the *terminfo* system.

**terminal**   Differentiated from a *workstation* (page 1281) by its lack of intelligence, a terminal connects to a computer that runs Linux. A workstation runs Linux on itself.

**terminfo**   Terminal information. The **/usr/lib/terminfo** directory contains many subdirectories, each containing several files. Each of those files is named for and holds a summary of the functional characteristics of a particular terminal. Visually oriented textual programs, such as vim, use these files. An alternative to the **termcap** file.

**text box**   A GUI *widget* (page 1281) that allows a user to enter text.

**theme**   Defined as an implicit or recurrent idea, *theme* is used in a GUI to describe a look that is consistent for all elements of a desktop. Go to themes.freshmeat.net for examples.

**thicknet**   A type of coaxial cable (thick) used for an Ethernet network. Devices are attached to thicknet by tapping the cable at fixed points.

**thinnet**   A type of coaxial cable (thin) used for an Ethernet network. Thinnet cable is smaller in diameter and more flexible than *thicknet* cable. Each device is typically attached to two separate cable segments by using a T-shaped connector; one segment leads to the device ahead of it on the network and one to the device that follows it.

**thread-safe**   See *reentrant* on page 1269.

**thumb**   The movable button in the *scrollbar* (page 1272) that positions the image in the window. The size of the thumb reflects the amount of information in the buffer. Also *bubble*.

**tick**   A mark, usually in a *check box* (page 1242), that indicates a positive response. The mark can be a check mark (✔) or an **x**. Also *check mark* or *check*.

**TIFF**   Tagged Image File Format. A file format used for still-image bitmaps, stored in tagged fields. Application programs can use the tags to accept or ignore fields, depending on their capabilities.ᶠᵒˡᵈᵒᶜ

**tiled windows**   An arrangement of windows such that no window overlaps another. The opposite of *cascading windows* (page 1241).

**time to live**   See *TTL* on the next page.

**toggle**   To switch between one of two positions. For example, the ftp **glob** command toggles the **glob** feature: Give the command once, and it turns the feature on or off; give the command again, and it sets the feature back to its original state.

**token**   A basic, grammatically indivisible unit of a language, such as a keyword, operator, or identifier.ᶠᵒˡᵈᵒᶜ

**token ring**   A type of *LAN* (page 1257) in which computers are attached to a ring of cable. A token packet circulates continuously around the ring. A computer can transmit information only when it holds the token.

**tooltip**  A minicontext help system that a user activates by allowing the mouse pointer to *hover* (page 1253) over an object (such as those on a panel).

**transient window**  A dialog or other window that is displayed for only a short time.

**Transmission Control Protocol**  See *TCP* on page 1276.

**Trojan horse**  A program that does something destructive or disruptive to your system. Its action is not documented, and the system administrator would not approve of it if she were aware of it. See "Avoiding a Trojan Horse" on page 458.

The term *Trojan horse* was coined by MIT-hacker-turned-NSA-spook Dan Edwards. It refers to a malicious security-breaking program that is disguised as something benign, such as a directory lister, archive utility, game, or (in one notorious 1990 case on the Mac) a program to find and destroy viruses. Similar to *back door* (page 1238).FOLDOC

**TTL**  Time to live.

1. All DNS records specify how long they are good for—usually up to a week at most. This time is called the record's *time to live*. When a DNS server or an application stores this record in *cache* (page 1241), it decrements the TTL value and removes the record from cache when the value reaches zero. A DNS server passes a cached record to another server with the current (decremented) TTL guaranteeing the proper TTL, no matter how many servers the record passes through.

2. In the IP header, a field that indicates how many more hops the packet should be allowed to make before being discarded or returned.

**TTY**  Teletypewriter. The terminal device that UNIX was first run from. Today TTY refers to the screen (or window, in the case of a terminal emulator), keyboard, and mouse that are connected to a computer. This term appears in UNIX, and Linux has kept the term for the sake of consistency and tradition.

**tunneling**  Encapsulation of protocol A within packets carried by protocol B, such that A treats B as though it were a data link layer. Tunneling is used to transfer data between administrative domains that use a protocol not supported by the internet connecting those domains. It can also be used to encrypt data sent over a public internet, as when you use ssh to tunnel a protocol over the Internet.FOLDOC See also *VPN* (page 1280) and *port forwarding* (page 1266).

**UDP**  User Datagram Protocol. The Internet standard transport layer protocol that provides simple but unreliable datagram services. UDP is a *connectionless protocol* (page 1244) that, like *TCP* (page 1276), is layered on top of *IP* (page 1255).

Unlike *TCP*, UDP neither guarantees delivery nor requires a connection. As a result it is lightweight and efficient, but the application program must handle all error processing and retransmission. UDP is often used for sending time-sensitive data that is not particularly sensitive to minor loss, such as audio and video data.FOLDOC

**UID**  User ID. A number that the **passwd** database associates with a username. See also *effective UID* (page 1248) and *real UID* (page 1269).

**undecillion**  In the American system, $10^{36}$. In the British system, this number is named *sexillion*. See also *large number* (page 1257).

**unicast**  A packet sent from one host to another host. Unicast means one source and one destination.

**Unicode**  A character encoding standard that was designed to cover all major modern written languages with each character having exactly one encoding and being represented by a fixed number of bits.

**unmanaged window**  See *ignored window* on page 1254.

**URI**  Universal Resource Identifier. The generic set of all names and addresses that are short strings referring to objects (typically on the Internet). The most common kinds of URIs are *URLs*.FOLDOC

**URL**  Uniform (was Universal) Resource Locator. A standard way of specifying the location of an object, typically a Web page, on the Internet. URLs are a subset of *URIs*.

**usage message**  A message displayed by a command when you call the command using incorrect command-line arguments.

**User Datagram Protocol**  *See UDP.*

**user ID**  *See UID.*

**user interface**  See *interface* on page 1255.

**user mode**  The designation for the state of the system while it is doing user work, such as running a user program (but not the system calls made by the program). Contrast with *system mode* (page 1276).

**username**  The name you enter in response to the **login:** prompt. Other users use your username when they send you mail or write to you. Each username has a corresponding UID, which is the numeric identifier for the user. Both the username and the UID are stored in the **passwd** database (**/etc/passwd** or the NIS equivalent). Also *login name*.

**userspace**  The part of memory (RAM) where applications reside. Code running in userspace cannot access hardware directly and cannot access memory allocated to other applications. Also *userland*. See the *KernelAnalysis-HOWTO*.

**UTC**  Coordinated Universal Time. UTC is the equivalent to the mean solar time at the prime meridian (0 degrees longitude). Also called Zulu time (Z stands for longitude zero) and GMT (Greenwich Mean Time).

**UTF-8**  An encoding that allows *Unicode* (above) characters to be represented using sequences of 8-bit bytes.

**utility**  A program included as a standard part of Linux. You typically invoke a utility either by giving a command in response to a shell prompt or by calling it from within a shell script. Utilities are often referred to as commands. Contrast with *builtin (command)* (page 1241).

UUID   Universally Unique Identifier. A 128-bit number that uniquely identifies an object on the Internet. Frequently used on Linux systems to identify an **ext2**, **ext3**, or **ext4** disk partition.

variable   A name and an associated value. The shell allows you to create variables and use them in the interactive shell and in shell scripts. Also, the shell inherits variables when it is invoked (environment variables; page 1032). Some shell variables establish characteristics of the shell; others have values that reflect different aspects of your ongoing interaction with the shell.

viewport   Same as *workspace*.

virtual console   Additional consoles, or displays, that you can view on the system, or physical, console.

virtual machine   *See VM.*

virus   A *cracker* (page 1245) program that searches out other programs and "infects" them by embedding a copy of itself in them, so that they become *Trojan horses* (page 1278). When these programs are executed, the embedded virus is executed as well, propagating the "infection," usually without the user's knowledge. By analogy with biological viruses.FOLDOC

VLAN   Virtual LAN. A logical grouping of two or more nodes that are not necessarily on the same physical network segment but that share the same network number. A VLAN is often associated with switched Ethernet.FOLDOC

VM   Virtual machine. A software/hardware emulation of a physical computing environment (i.e., a computer). A virtual machine executes programs just as a physical machine would.

VPN   Virtual private network. A private network that exists on a public network, such as the Internet. A VPN is a less expensive substitute for company-owned/leased lines and uses encryption to ensure privacy. A nice side effect is that you can send non-Internet protocols, such as AppleTalk, IPX, or *NetBIOS* (page 1262), over the VPN connection by *tunneling* (page 1278) them through the VPN IP stream.

W2K   Windows 2000 Professional or Server.

W3C   World Wide Web Consortium (www.w3.org).

WAN   Wide area network. A network that interconnects *LANs* (page 1257) and *MANs* (page 1259), spanning a large geographic area (typically states or countries).

WAP   Wireless access point. A bridge or router between wired and wireless networks. WAPs typically support some form of access control to prevent unauthorized clients from connecting to the network.

Web ring   A collection of Web sites that provide information on a single topic or group of related topics. Each home page that is part of the Web ring has a series of links that let you go from site to site.

whitespace   A collective name for SPACEs and/or TABs and occasionally NEWLINEs. Also *white space*.

wide area network   See *WAN*.

| | |
|---|---|
| **widget** | The basic objects of a graphical user interface. A button, *combo box* (page 1243), *switch* (page 1276), and *scrollbar* (page 1272) are examples of widgets. |
| **wildcard** | See *metacharacter* on page 1260. |
| **Wi-Fi** | Wireless Fidelity. A generic term that refers to any type of *802.11* (page 1236) wireless network. |
| **window** | On a display screen, a region that runs or is controlled by a particular program. |
| **window manager** | A program that controls how windows appear on a display screen and how you manipulate them. |
| **Windows share** | See *share* on page 1272. |
| **WINS** | Windows Internet Naming Service. The service responsible for mapping NetBIOS names to IP addresses. WINS has the same relationship to NetBIOS names that DNS has to Internet domain names. |
| **WINS server** | The program responsible for handling WINS requests. This program caches name information about hosts on a local network and resolves them to IP addresses. |
| **wireless access point** | See *WAP*. |
| **word** | A sequence of one or more nonblank characters separated from other words by TABs, SPACEs, or NEWLINEs. Used to refer to individual command-line arguments. In vim, a word is similar to a word in the English language—a string of one or more characters bounded by a punctuation mark, a numeral, a TAB, a SPACE, or a NEWLINE. |
| **Work buffer** | A location where vim stores text while it is being edited. The information in the Work buffer is not written to the file on the disk until you give the editor a command to write it. |
| **working directory** | The directory that you are associated with at any given time. The relative pathnames you use are *relative to* the working directory. Also *current directory*. |
| **workspace** | A subdivision of a *desktop* (page 1246) that occupies the entire display. |
| **workstation** | A small computer, typically designed to fit in an office and be used by one person and usually equipped with a bit-mapped graphical display, keyboard, and mouse. Differentiated from a *terminal* (page 1277) by its intelligence. A workstation runs Linux on itself while a terminal connects to a computer that runs Linux. |
| **worm** | A program that propagates itself over a network, reproducing itself as it goes. Today the term has negative connotations, as it is assumed that only *crackers* (page 1245) write worms. Compare to *virus* (page 1280) and *Trojan horse* (page 1278). From **Tapeworm** in John Brunner's novel, *The Shockwave Rider*, Ballantine Books, 1990 (via XEROX PARC).<sup>FOLDOC</sup> |
| **WYSIWYG** | What You See Is What You Get. A graphical application, such as a word processor, whose display is similar to its printed output. |
| **X server** | The X server is the part of the *X Window System* that runs the mouse, keyboard, and display. (The application program is the client.) |

**X terminal**    A graphics terminal designed to run the X Window System.

**X Window**    A design and set of tools for writing flexible, portable windowing applications,
**System**    created jointly by researchers at MIT and several leading computer manufacturers.

**XDMCP**    X Display Manager Control Protocol. XDMCP allows the login server to accept
requests from network displays. XDMCP is built into many X terminals.

*x***DSL**    Different types of *DSL* (page 1248) are identified by a prefix, for example, ADSL,
HDSL, SDSL, and VDSL.

**Xinerama**    An extension to X.org. Xinerama allows window managers and applications to use
the two or more physical displays as one large virtual display. Refer to the Xinerama-
HOWTO.

**XML**    Extensible Markup Language. A universal format for structured documents and data
on the Web. Developed by *W3C* (page 1280), XML is a pared-down version of
SGML. See www.w3.org/XML and www.w3.org/XML/1999/XML-in-10-points.

**XSM**    X Session Manager. This program allows you to create a session that includes certain
applications. While the session is running, you can perform a *checkpoint* (saves the
application state) or a *shutdown* (saves the state and exits from the session). When
you log back in, you can load your session so that everything in your session is running
just as it was when you logged off.

**Z Shell**    zsh. A *shell* (page 1272) that incorporates many of the features of the *Bourne Again
Shell* (page 1240), *Korn Shell* (page 1257), and *TC Shell* (page 1276), as well as many
original features.

**Zulu time**    See *UTC* on page 1279.

# JumpStart Index

# FILE TREE INDEX

A light page number such as 456 indicates a brief mention.

/bin 189, 190
  echo 1028
  false 509
/boot 40, 190, 589, 590, 616
  grub
    menu.lst 591
  grub2
    grub.cfg 593
/dev 152, 190, 503–505, 515
  disk
    by-path 503
    by-uuid 503
  null 158, 503, 628, 1002
  pts 504
  random 504
  sd*n* 503
  shm 505
  sr0 503
  tty 1046
  urandom 504
  zero 505
/etc 190, 506
  aliases 624, 746
  aliases.db 747
  alternatives 506
  anacrontab 314, 610

/etc, *continued*
  apt
    sources.list 1187
  at.allow 506
  at.deny 506
  auto.master 822
  bashrc 331
  bind
    named.conf 872, 886, 891
  cron.allow 506
  cron.d 314, 607
    0hourly 609
    cacti 649
  cron.daily 610
  cron.deny 506
  cron.hourly
    0anacron 609
  cron.monthly 610
  cron.weekly 610
  crontab 314, 608
  cups
    cupsd.conf 572
    ppd 570
  default 506
    grub 591–593
    snmpd 653
    useradd 600

# UTILITY INDEX

A light page number such as 456 indicates a brief mention. Page numbers followed by the letter t refer to tables.

# MAIN INDEX

An italic page number such as *123* indicates a definition. A light page number such as 456 indicates a brief mention. Page numbers followed by the letter t refer to tables. Only variables that must always appear with a leading dollar sign are indexed with a leading dollar sign. Other variables are indexed without a leading dollar sign.

## SYMBOLS

–– argument 147, 989

^ in regular expressions 1142

^ quick substitution character 384

, (comma) operator 1061

; control operator 162, 341, 1063

;; control operator 1006, 1063

: (null) builtin 1037, 1049

:– substitutes default values for a variable 1037

::1 (IP address) 507

:? sends to standard error an error message for a variable 1038

:= assigns default values for a variable 1037

! (NOT) Boolean operator 1063

! event reference 381

!! reexecutes the previous event 382

? in extended regular expressions 1146

? special character 165

. (dot) builtin 332, 1045

. directory 186, 515

. in regular expressions 1141

./ executes a file in the working directory 338, 360

.. directory 186, 515

.jpg filename extension *1256*

` ... ` *see* command, substitution

( ) control operator 344

((...)) *see* arithmetic, evaluation

[] character class (regular expressions) 1141, *1242*

[] special characters 168

[...] *see* test utility

[[...]] builtin 1058

{} around positional parameters 1023

{} around variable names 355

{} expansion 405, 996, 1051

{} in array variables 1038

{} in functions 396

@ (origin, DNS) 875

@ in a network address 301

* in regular expressions 1142

* special character 166

/ (root) directory 38, 40, *177*, 181, 189, 487, *1270*

/ trailing within pathnames 38

/ within pathnames 38

\ escape character 142, 345, 354

\( in regular expressions 1144

\) in regular expressions 1144

& (AND) bitwise operator 1062

& control operator 162, 163, 342, 375, 1063

& in replacement strings (regular expressions) 1145

&& (AND) Boolean operator 552, 1057, 1062

&& control operator 162, 343, 1021, 1063

&> redirects standard output and standard error 163, 335

# comment 340, 992

# prompt 423

#! specifies a script shell 338, 992

+ in extended regular expressions 1146

< redirects standard input 155–156

<< Here document 1014–1016

> redirects standard output 154–155

>& duplicates output file descriptor 335, 986

>&2 duplicates file descriptor 335, 986

>> redirects and appends standard output 157

>| redirects output without **clobber** 157

>1 redirects standard output 334

| (OR) bitwise operator 1062

| (OR) Boolean operator (extended regular expression) 1146

| control operator 159, 342, 999, 1061, 1063

| *see* pipeline

|& control operator 159, 335, 1063

|& shorthand for 2>&1 335

|| (OR) Boolean operator 1057, 1062

|| control operator 162, 343, 1063

~– synonym for **OLDPWD** 408

1295

Your purchase of **A Practical Guide to Fedora™ and Red Hat® Enterprise Linux®, Seventh Edition,** includes access to a free online edition for 45 days through the **Safari Books Online** subscription service. Nearly every Prentice Hall book is available online through **Safari Books Online**, along with thousands of books and videos from publishers such as Addison-Wesley Professional, Cisco Press, Exam Cram, IBM Press, O'Reilly Media, Que, Sams, and VMware Press.

**Safari Books Online** is a digital library providing searchable, on-demand access to thousands of technology, digital media, and professional development books and videos from leading publishers. With one monthly or yearly subscription price, you get unlimited access to learning tools and information on topics including mobile app and software development, tips and tricks on using your favorite gadgets, networking, project management, graphic design, and much more.

## Activate your FREE Online Edition at
## informit.com/safarifree

**STEP 1:** Enter the coupon code: ARZHEBI.

**STEP 2:** New Safari users, complete the brief registration form.
Safari subscribers, just log in.

If you have difficulty registering on Safari or accessing the online edition,
please e-mail customer-service@safaribooksonline.com